Winston S. Churchill

VOLUME III

The Challenge of War

1914–1916

Also by Martin Gilbert

THE APPEASERS (*with Richard Gott*)
THE EUROPEAN POWERS 1900–1945
THE ROOTS OF APPEASEMENT
RECENT HISTORY ATLAS
BRITISH HISTORY ATLAS
AMERICAN HISTORY ATLAS
JEWISH HISTORY ATLAS
FIRST WORLD WAR ATLAS

Editions of documents

BRITAIN AND GERMANY BETWEEN THE WARS
PLOUGH MY OWN FURROW, THE LIFE OF
LORD ALLEN OF HURTWOOD
SERVANT OF INDIA: DIARIES OF THE VICEROY'S
PRIVATE SECRETARY 1905–1910
CHURCHILL (*Spectrum Books*)
LLOYD GEORGE (*Spectrum Books*)

For young readers

WINSTON CHURCHILL (*Clarendon Biography*)
WINSTON CHURCHILL (*Jackdaw*)
THE SECOND WORLD WAR

Editor

A CENTURY OF CONFLICT: ESSAYS FOR
A. J. P. TAYLOR

Churchill in April 1916, when Lieutenant-Colonel, commanding the 6th
Battalion, Royal Scots Fusiliers. Part of a battalion group photograph,
taken near Ploegsteert, Belgium

MARTIN GILBERT

Winston S. Churchill

VOLUME III · 1914–1916

The Challenge of War

ILLUSTRATED WITH PHOTOGRAPHS
AND MAPS

HOUGHTON MIFFLIN COMPANY BOSTON

1971

Dedicated to the Memory of
Randolph Churchill

Acknowledgements

I AM grateful to Her Majesty the Queen, who graciously gave permission for me to have access to the Royal Archives; for help in selection of this material, I should like to thank Mr Robin Mackworth Young, Librarian, Miss Jane Langton, Registrar, and Miss Frances Dimond, Assistant Registrar. I wish to thank Bodley's Librarian, Dr Robert Shackleton, and the Curators of the Bodleian Library, Oxford, who greatly facilitated the research by their generous offer to house the Churchill papers in the Bodleian for the duration of my work on them. I am grateful to members of the Churchill family who helped me obtain material for this volume: Mr Winston S. Churchill put his grandfather's press cutting books and photograph albums at my disposal; the Hon Mrs Christopher Soames gave me access to those of her father's and mother's letters in her possession; Mr Peregrine S. Churchill gave me access to the letters which his father John Churchill, who served first on the western front, and then on Sir Ian Hamilton's staff at the Dardanelles, received from Churchill throughout this period.

While doing the research for the Dardanelles chapters I made two journeys to Turkey, visiting the Gallipoli Peninsula, Istanbul and Ankara. These visits would not have been possible without the encouragement of His Excellency U. Halük Bayülken, formerly Turkish Ambassador in London, and the help which I received from the Turkish Government, and from His Excellency Zeki Kuneralp, Secretary-General of the Turkish Foreign Office and subsequently Turkish Ambassador to London. At the Gallipoli Peninsula I was helped by the Kaymakam of Eceabat, Mr Vedat Okay, who provided me with transport and accompanied me to the remoter areas. On both visits I was made welcome by Mr Norman Pemberton, representative of the Commonwealth War Graves Commission at Chanak, who did everything possible to make my work go smoothly.

Many people have helped me in the search for material, and given me access to material in their possession. I should like to thank: Mr Guy Acloque, the Grosvenor Estates, London; Captain G. R. G. Allen, RN; Mr G. E. V. Awdry, Librarian of the National Liberal Club; Mr

John Barnes; the 6th Marquess of Bath; Kapitän zur See Bildingmaier, Militärgeschichtliches Forschungsamt, Freiburg im Briesgau; the 2nd Earl Beatty; Lieutenant-Commander G. P. Berengan, Assistant Naval Attaché, Italian Embassy, London; Mr Coss Billson, Secretary of the National Liberal Club; the 2nd Earl of Birkenhead; the University of Birmingham Library; the Hon Mark Bonham Carter; the Curators of the British Museum; Miss Rosemary Brooks, the Beaverbrook Library, London; Mr H. A. Cahn; Mr I. K. Comacho, the German Institute, London; the Cambridge University Library; Lord Coleraine; Mr Charles Clore; Mr David Coombs; Miss D. Cummins, Office services, Ministry of Defence; Mr A. G. Davey, Army Records Centre; Signor Filippo Donini, Director of the Italian Institute, London; Lieutenant-General Baron M. Donnet, Military, Naval and Air Attaché, Belgian Embassy, London; Dr Christopher Dowling, Imperial War Museum, London; M. Albert Duchesne, Conservateur, Musée Royal de l'Armée et D'Histoire Militaire, Brussels; Sir John Elliot; Mrs Sheila Elton, former Secretary to the Beaverbrook Foundation; the 3rd Viscount Esher; the 3rd Baron Fisher; Colonel Peter Fleming; Capitaine de Frégate de la Forcade, Assistant Naval Attaché, French Embassy, London; Dr Noble Frankland, Director of the Imperial War Museum, London; the late Lieutenant-Colonel the Hon Gerald French; Mrs Milton Gendel; Mr John Gordon, Editor in Chief, *Sunday Express*; Lieutenant-Colonel R. J. Griffith of the Foreign and Commonwealth Office, London; Mr John Grigg; Dr J. Grützner, Cultural Attaché, German Embassy, London; Mr Kamil Günel, Cultural Attaché, Turkish Embassy, London; Commander Richard Hall, RN; Miss Grace Hamblin, Administrator of Chartwell; the 14th Duke of Hamilton; the 2nd Baron Hankey; the 2nd Viscount Harcourt; Mr S. Hayashida, Director of the Japan Information Centre, London; Mrs Mary M. Hirth, Librarian of the Academic Center, University of Texas; Miss Ann Hoffman; Vice-Admiral Sir Ian Hogg; the 6th Viscount Hood; Mr G. Ronald Howe, National Council of YMCAs; Lieutenant-Colonel H. N. Ingles, acting Librarian, Longleat; Mr Stephen Inwood; Mr T. W. M. Jaine, Assistant Registrar, National Register of Archives, London; Mr R. L. James, former Head Master of Harrow School; Mr Robert Rhodes James; the 2nd Earl Jellicoe, former First Lord of the Admiralty; Dr J. T. Killen, former Librarian of Churchill College, Cambridge; Miss T. Kozutsumi, Japan Information Centre, London; the 8th Marquess of Lansdowne; M. Jean Lequiller, Conseiller Culturel, French Embassy, London; the 3rd Earl Lloyd-George of Dwyfor; the late Mr Donald McLachlan; Mr Angus I.

Macnaghten; Sir Philip Magnus, Bt; Professor Arthur J. Marder; Sir Charles Markham, Bt; Admiral of the Fleet Earl Mountbatten of Burma; Mr I. Mumford, The Survey Production Centre, R.E., Sussex; The National Maritime Museum, Greenwich; Major John North; Vice-Admiral R. D. Oliver; Lady Paynter; J. Gordon Phillips, Archivist, *The Times*; the 6th Earl of Rosebery; Sir Leslie Rowan; Dr H. Pogge von Strandman; The Public Record Office, London; Brigadier B. B. Rackham, President of the Royal Naval Division Association; Miss Felicity Ranger, the Historical Manuscripts Commission, London; Mr David Robinson; Mr Kenneth Rose; Captain Stephen Roskill; Mr David Satinoff; Herr Karsten Schröder; the Scottish Record Office; the 10th Earl of Selkirk; Mrs George Shield, General Sir Ian Hamilton's Literary Executor; Mr and Mrs Arthur Simon; the 3rd Baron Southborough; Mr A. J. P. Taylor; Mr George Thomson, former Chancellor of the Duchy of Lancaster; Contrammiraglio Vittorio E. Tognelli, Ministry of Marine, Rome; Mrs M. Travis, Archivist, Broadlands; Dr J. Van Roey, Antwerp City Archivist; Dr Edwin Welch, Archivist of Churchill College, Cambridge; Le Colonel Wemaire, Musée de l'Armée, Paris; Major Cyril Wilson; Mr Frederick Woods; Mr S. S. Wilson, former Keeper of the Public Records.

The following have given me permission to quote from documents and letters for which they hold the copyright: Her Majesty the Queen (the papers of King George V and of Lord Stamfordham), Sir Derrick Bailey, Bt (Sir Abe Bailey, Bt), the 4th Earl of Balfour (1st Earl of Balfour), the 2nd Earl Beatty (1st Earl Beatty), the First Beaverbrook Foundation (Baron Beaverbrook; Andrew Bonar Law; 1st Earl Lloyd-George of Dwyfor; Frances, Countess Lloyd-George of Dwyfor), the 2nd Earl of Birkenhead (1st Earl of Birkenhead), the Birmingham University Library (Austen Chamberlain), the Hon Mark Bonham Carter (1st Earl of Oxford and Asquith; Countess of Oxford and Asquith; Baroness Asquith of Yarnbury), Mr Peregrine S. Churchill (Lady Gwendeline Churchill; John Churchill), Churchill College, Cambridge, Library (Reginald McKenna), C & T Publications Ltd (Lady Randolph Churchill; Sir Winston Churchill), Mrs C. Dawnay and the Imperial War Museum (General Guy Dawnay), the 18th Earl of Derby (17th Earl of Derby), the 7th Baron de Robeck (Admiral Sir John de Robeck), the 4th Viscount Esher (2nd Viscount Esher; the Hon Maurice Brett), Colonel Peter Fleming (Valentine Fleming), Mrs Milton Gendel (Edwin Montagu), Mr Nigel M. Dewar Gibb (Andrew Dewar Gibb), the 2nd Baron Gretton (1st Baron Gretton), Mr John Grigg (Baron Altrincham), the Hon Raymond R. Guest (Frederick

Guest), the 2nd Earl Haig (1st Earl Haig), Dr A. R. B. Haldane (1st
Viscount Haldane), Commander Richard Hall (Admiral Sir Reginald
Hall), the 14th Duke of Hamilton and Brandon (1st Baron Fisher), the
2nd Baron Hankey (1st Baron Hankey), the 2nd Viscount Harcourt
(1st Viscount Harcourt), Her Majesty's Stationery Office (State papers;
Hansard), Vice-Admiral Sir Ian Hogg (H. A. Gwynne), the 2nd Earl
Jellicoe (1st Earl Jellicoe), the 2nd Baron Keyes (1st Baron Keyes),
Lady Patricia Kingsbury (1st Earl of Ypres), the Hon Margaret
Lambert (1st Viscount Lambert), Mrs Allen Leeper and Mrs Mary
Shield (General Sir Ian Hamilton), 4th Viscount Long (1st Viscount
Long), Mr John H. MacCallum Scott (Alexander MacCallum Scott),
Sir Charles Markham, Bt (Sir Henry Markham, Bt), the 10th Duke of
Marlborough (9th Duke of Marlborough), the 4th Baron Mottistone
(1st Baron Mottistone), Admiral of the Fleet Earl Mountbatten of
Burma (1st Marquess of Milford Haven), Mrs Avis Napier-Clavering
(Major F. N. Napier-Clavering), the Trustees of the National Maritime
Museum (Admiral Sir Herbert Richmond), Mr Philip Noel-Baker
(Viscount Cecil of Chelwood), the 2nd Baron Noel-Buxton (1st Baron
Noel-Buxton), the Hon Joseph Pease (1st Baron Gainford), the Public
Record Office of Northern Ireland (Sir Edward Carson), Stella,
Marchioness of Reading (1st Marquis of Reading), the 2nd Viscount
Rothermere (1st Viscount Rothermere), the 5th Marquess of Salisbury
(Viscount Quickswood), the 2nd Viscount Scarsdale (Marquess of
Curzon), Mr Laurence P. Scott (C. P. Scott), the 4th Baron Shuttle-
worth (1st Baron Shuttleworth), Mrs Brian Simon (Baron Emmott),
the Hon Mrs Christopher Soames (Lady Spencer-Churchill; William
Hozier), the 3rd Baron Southborough (1st Baron Southborough),
Mr Christopher Sykes (Sir Mark Sykes), Marigold, Viscountess
Thurso (1st Viscount Thurso), Brigadier Dame Mary Tyrwhitt
(Admiral of the Fleet Sir Reginald Tyrwhitt, Bt), the 3rd Baron Wedg-
wood (1st Baron Wedgwood), Major Cyril Wilson (Field-Marshal
Sir Henry Wilson), and the 3rd Viscount Wimborne (1st Viscount
Wimborne).
    The following have given me permission to quote from their own
letters and recollections: Mr J. H. Bentham, Lieutenant-Colonel Ralph
Bingham, Mr J. R. Colville, Air Vice-Marshal Sir John W. Cordingley,
Mr Robert Fox, Mr Robert Fulton, Major-General Sir Edmund
Hakewill Smith, Sir Ralph Hawtrey, Mr Reginald Hurt, Mr Jock
McDavid, Mr C. J. F. Mitchell, Major-General Sir Edward Louis
Spears, Mr Henry Stevens and General Sir Ivo Vesey.
    I hope that those copyright holders whom I have been unable to

trace will accept my apologies. I am grateful to the publishers or other copyright holders of all printed books for permission to quote extracts from them. I have received photographs for inclusion in this volume from both private and public sources. I should like to thank Argus Press Ltd, Bassano & Vandyk Ltd, the First Beaverbrook Foundation, Mlle Antoinette Chaignon, Mr Winston S. Churchill MP, Mr James Dawson, Lord James Douglas-Hamilton, Elliott and Fry Ltd, European Picture Service, Major-General Sir Edmund Hakewill Smith, Hutchinson & Co, the Imperial War Museum, Lady Patricia Kingsbury, the Dowager Countess Lloyd-George of Dwyfor, Mr Jock McDavid, the London News Agency Ltd, Mirrorpic, Admiral of the Fleet Earl Mountbatten of Burma, the late Major F. D. Napier-Clavering, the Press Association Ltd, the Radio Times Hulton Picture Library, M. Robert Ryckaert, Mr Harry Skinner, the *Tatler*, *The Times*, Mr E. S. Turner, Art Editor of the *Daily Telegraph*, and the YMCA, for letting me use photographs in their possession, or of which they hold the copyright.

The following newspapers have given me permission to reprint extracts from their leading articles: *Advertiser* (Dundee), *Daily Express*, *Daily Mail*, *Daily Telegraph* (also for *Morning Post*), *Observer*, *Star*, and *The Times*.

While compiling the footnotes for this volume, I received information which I had not been able to find elsewhere from the following individuals and institutions: Mr J. Ardley, Privy Council Office, London; Dr Arenz, Militärgeschtliches Forschungsamt, Freiburg; Associazione della Stampa Romana; Mr F. Birrer, Cultural Attaché, Swiss Embassy, London; Captain Eric Bush RN; Mr B. Cheeseman, Library and Records Department, Foreign and Commonwealth Office, London; Mr E. H. Cornelius, Librarian, Royal College of Surgeons of England, London; Mr Norman Craig; Cox and Kings, London; Mrs Winifred Fernée; Dr Fleischer, Bundesarchiv Militärarchiv, Freiburg; Vice-Admiral C. R. Fliche, Chef du Service Historique de la Marine, Ministère d'Etat Chargé de la Défense National, Paris; Mr A. J. Francis, Ministry of Defence (Office Services); Mr Harry Franks, Deal and Walmer Local History Society, Deal; Mr R. Gordon, Clerk to the Trustees, Loretto School Trustees, Edinburgh; Mr G. A. Grahame, General Manager, Ritz Hotel, London; Mr Thomas Greig, William Kemp & Co, Glasgow; Mrs Alice Gwynn; Mrs I. Medora Harrison; Sir Rupert Hart-Davis; Miss Hawkins, Army Records Centre, Ministry of Defence; The Librarian, Institut Français du Royaume-Uni, London; Lloyds Bank Ltd, London; Lloyd's Register of Shipping,

London; Mr Ruddock Mackay; Macmillan & Co, Publishers; Monsieur le Maire, Ville de Calais; Miss Cynthia Metcalfe; Lady Audrey Morris; Mr N. A. Nagler, the Treasury; Mr William Park, Keeper of Manuscripts, National Library of Scotland, Edinburgh; Dr Pette, Bundesarchiv Zentralnachweisstelle, Koblenz; Mr J. Innes Pritchard, MacKay, Mackintosh & Co, Glasgow; Miss Minna Ray, Ministry of Defence (Naval Secretary), London; Mrs Eva Reichmann; M. René Robinet, Conservateur en Chef, Directeur des Services d'Archives du Nord, Lille; the RSPCA; le Comte Benoit Le Gouz de Saint Seine; the Savile Club, London; Mr Robert Montgomery Scott, Embassy of the United States of America, London; Dr Harry Shukman; Vice-Admiral Giovanni Sleiter, Ministero della Difessa, Rome; Mr Patrick Strong, Keeper of College Library and Collections, Eton College, Windsor; Dr D. M. Torbet, City Librarian, Dundee; Mr T. P. Tracey, Ministry of Defence (RAF); and Mr R. M. Ward.

I should like to express my thanks to the Directors of C & T Publications Limited, Lord Hartwell, Mr Christopher Clarke and Mr John McCracken, who asked me to continue with this biography after Randolph Churchill's death, and who have given me every assistance in my work and been most considerate of my needs. I am also grateful to the Warden and Fellows of Merton College, Oxford, for extending my Fellowship in order that I could remain at Merton while writing the biography, and to the Master and Fellows of Churchill College, Cambridge, for granting me membership of their Senior Common Room.

While working on this volume I have drawn personal encouragement from the interest and enthusiasm of Mrs R. A. Bevan, Mr Paul Brooks, the late Dr Philip Conwell-Evans, the late Mr Joseph Robinson, Lord Salter, Mr Nigel Viney, Sir John Wheeler-Bennett and the late Mr Guy Wint. I am extremely grateful to those who have read the book in typescript or proof, and whose suggestions have been of great value; Mr Mark Cousins, Mr John Darling, Mr Richard Gott, Mr Robert Rhodes James, Mr Andrew Kerr, Mr Ivor Samuels and Mrs George Shield.

I have been greatly helped in my work by Dr Cameron Hazlehurst, who has discussed with me the many historical problems raised in this volume, has given me the advantage of his own wide researches, and has read all my chapters both in draft and proof.

I should like to thank Mrs Elizabeth Hennessy, who worked at the British Museum Library at Colindale, inspecting national and local press comment on Churchill's activities; Miss Diana Colvin, who examined the photographic archives of several newspapers and agencies; and the Oxford cartographer, Mr Peter Atwell, who drew the maps with patience and care. Mr Jerry Moeran of Studio Edmark, Oxford, prepared prints of the photographs and facsimiles used in this volume; many of these were copied from faded or damaged originals, and owe their excellence to his skill. My thanks are also due to his assistant, Jean Hunt.

I have been particularly helped by Dr Sidney Aster, who undertook the task of scrutinizing the Admiralty, Foreign Office, and War Office papers, and gave up his teaching post at Glasgow University in order to help with this important aspect of the research—his patience and thoroughness led to the successful conclusion of many difficult searches. Jane K. Cousins assisted me with many of the interviews, helped me with the research both at Ploegsteert and on the Gallipoli Peninsula, examined a number of archives, and subjected the typescript to a thorough scrutiny. Sarah Graham joined me when I began writing in November 1968, typed the first draft of over half a million words and then retyped it. By her perseverance she ensured that the book was legible when it went to the printers. Kate Fleming helped me to trace many obscure footnotes, to check the narrative, and to complete the list of documents. Susie Sacher assisted me in the compilation of the index: her help in the final stages of the work was invaluable.

Contents

ACKNOWLEDGEMENTS   vii

PREFACE   xxiii

SOURCES   xxvii

1	'A REALLY HAPPY MAN'	1
2	THE FIRST MONTH OF WAR	32
3	'THE ADMIRALTY IS NOW ON ITS TRIAL'	65
4	THE DEFENCE OF ANTWERP	96
5	THE RETURN OF LORD FISHER	135
6	THE TURKISH PUZZLE	188
7	'OUR TROOPS ARE ROTTING'	224
8	BY SHIPS ALONE	248
9	THE SEARCH FOR MEN	276
10	THE ASSUMPTION OF VICTORY	312
11	18 MARCH 1915: THE NAVAL ATTACK	351
12	25 APRIL 1915: THE GALLIPOLI LANDINGS	381
13	CRISIS	411
14	'I THOUGHT HE WOULD DIE OF GRIEF'	448
15	LOYALTIES	474
16	THE DUCHY OF LANCASTER	482
17	UNHEEDED COUNSEL	518
18	'THE ESCAPED SCAPEGOAT'	572

19 THE SEVEN-DAY GENERAL   596

20 IN TRAINING   628

21 PLOEGSTEERT   648

22 'YOU CAN BE PRIME MINISTER'   679

23 HUMILIATION   716

24 'MY TRUE WAR STATION'   738

25 'I AM LEARNING TO HATE'   761

26 CAST ASIDE   789

FACSIMILES   827

INDEX OF DOCUMENTS QUOTED   843

GENERAL INDEX   885

Illustrations

Frontispiece
Lieutenant-Colonel Churchill: near Ploegsteert, April 1916
[*Major-General Sir Edmund Hakewill Smith*]

Section 1 (between pages 156 and 157)

1. Churchill as First Lord of the Admiralty, inset Clementine Churchill, 1914
[*'Tatler': 12 August 1914*]

2. 'Full Steam Ahead': cartoon of Churchill by Poy, 4 August 1914
[*Argus Press Ltd*]

3. H. H. Asquith, at the end of 1915
[*Radio Times Hulton Picture Library*]

4. Field-Marshal Earl Kitchener of Khartoum in 1914
[*Mansell Collection*]

5. Churchill and Field-Marshal Sir John French, summer 1914
[*Lady Patricia Kingsbury*]

6. Prince Louis of Battenberg, January 1914
[*Admiral of the Fleet Earl Mountbatten of Burma*]

7. Churchill and Sir Edward Grey, 1914
[*The Press Association Ltd*]

8. British armoured train in action at Antwerp, October 1914
[*The Times History of the War 1914*]

9. A London bus used by the Royal Naval Division, and captured by the Germans at Antwerp, October 1914
[*The Times History of the War 1914*]

10. Colonel J. E. B. Seely and Churchill at Antwerp, October 1914
[*'Great Deeds of the War': 12 December 1914*]

11. Churchill at Antwerp, October 1914
[*Mirrorpic*]

12. Churchill, Lord Kitchener, and David Lloyd George: cartoon by
Poy on Churchill's birthday, 30 November 1914
[*Argus Press Ltd*]

13. Churchill Family Portrait, late 1914
[*Mr Peregrine S. Churchill*]

Section 2 (between pages 348 and 349)

14. Admiral of the Fleet Lord Fisher, 1915
[*Lord James Douglas-Hamilton*]

15. Admiral Sir John Jellicoe, 1914
[*Bassano & Vandyk Ltd*]

16. Vice-Admiral Carden, 1914
[*The Times History of the War*]

17. General Sir Ian Hamilton and Vice-Admiral de Robeck at the
Dardanelles, 1915
[*Imperial War Museum*]

18. Talaat Bey, Turkish Minister of the Interior
[*Radio Times Hulton Picture Library*]

19. Enver Pasha, Turkish Minister of War
[*Radio Times Hulton Picture Library*]

20. Djavid Bey, Turkish Minister of Finance
[*The Times History of the War*]

21. King George V and Churchill arriving at Blandford to inspect the
Royal Naval Division before its departure to the Dardanelles,
25 February 1915
[*Mr Harry Skinner*]

22. H.M.S. *Irresistible* foundering at the Dardanelles, 18 March 1915
[*The Times History of the War*]

23. Jack Churchill, while a Major on Sir Ian Hamilton's staff at
Mudros, 1915
[*Imperial War Museum*]

24. Lieutenant-Commander Wedgwood, MP, 17 September 1914
[*Hutchinson & Co*]

25. Major-General Braithwaite and General Sir Ian Hamilton going
ashore, the Gallipoli Peninsula, 1915
[*Imperial War Museum*]

26. British Armoured Motor Cars at Helles, Gallipoli Peninsula, 1915
[*Imperial War Museum*]

27. Churchill, February 1915
[*The Press Association Ltd*]

Section 3 (between pages 604 and 605)

28. Churchill as Chancellor of the Duchy of Lancaster
[*'Bystander': 2 June*]

29. Churchill, Lord Lansdowne and Lord Curzon, 1915
[*London News Agency Ltd*]

30. Churchill and A. J. Balfour, 1915
[*Daily Mail*]

31. Sir Edward Carson and F. E. Smith, before 1914
[*2nd Earl of Birkenhead*]

32. Andrew Bonar Law
[*Elliott and Fry Ltd*]

33. Sir Max Aitken, 1916
[*The Press Association Ltd*]

34. Churchill and his wife arriving at Enfield, 18 September 1915
[*YM The British Empire YMCA Weekly: 24 September 1915*]

35. Churchill addressing munitions workers at Enfield, 18 September 1915: a sequence of five photographs
[*The Press Association Ltd*]

36. A Sopwith biplane which Churchill had just piloted, 1913: biplanes of this type were used on the western front and at the Dardanelles, 1914–16
[*Mr James Dawson*]

37. Wing-Commander Samson, 1915
[*Radio Times Hulton Picture Library*]

38. Churchill and Lloyd George at Wormwood Scrubs, 28 June 1915
[*Imperial War Museum*]

39. Evacuation of a gun and men from the Gallipoli Peninsula, December 1915
[*Imperial War Museum*]

40. Churchill and Lloyd George, autumn, 1915
[*Radio Times Hulton Picture Library*]

Section 4 (between pages 796 and 797)

41. Churchill leaving for the Front, early 1916
[*European Picture Service*]

42. Churchill and Sir Archibald Sinclair, Armentières, 11 February 1916
[*The late Hon Randolph S. Churchill*]

43. Captain Gibb, Adjutant, 6th Royal Scots Fusiliers, April 1916
[*Major-General Sir Edmund Hakewill Smith*]

44. Lieutenant Napier-Clavering, Royal Engineers, 1916
[*Mrs Avis Napier-Clavering*]

45. 2nd Lieutenant Hakewill Smith, 6th Royal Scots Fusiliers, April 1916
[*Major-General Sir Edmund Hakewill Smith*]

46. 2nd Lieutenant McDavid, 6th Royal Scots Fusiliers, 1916
[*Mr Jock McDavid*]

47. Churchill with General Fayolle, Captain Spiers and others, 29 December 1915
[*Imperial War Museum*]

48. Violet Bonham Carter, Clementine Churchill and David Lloyd George, Ponders End, 3 February 1916
[*YM The British Empire YMCA Weekly: 11 February 1916*]

49. German shell exploding above Ploegsteert Wood, early 1916
[*Imperial War Museum*]

50. Ploegsteert Church, spring 1916
[*M R. Ryckaert*]

51. British trench in the Ploegsteert sector, after a snowfall, January 1916
[*Mlle A. Chaignon*]

52. Churchill, 1916
[*The London Magazine: October 1916*]

53. Clementine Churchill, 1915
[*YM The British Empire YMCA Weekly: 3 September 1915*]

54. Churchill, summer 1916
[*The Press Association Ltd*]

55. David Lloyd George, 1916
[*Frances, Countess Lloyd-George of Dwyfor*]

Maps

1. Possible British bases intended for offensive operations against Germany, 1913–14   19

2. Route of *Goeben* and *Breslau* from Messina (2 August 1914) to the Algerian coast (4 August 1914) and thence to Constantinople (11 August 1914)   29

3. Churchill's plan for Russian attacks on Germany, 19 August 1914   53

4. The German advance by 22 August 1914   54

5. Towns visited by units of Churchill's 'Dunkirk Circus', September and October 1914   75

6. Towns bombed by the Royal Naval Air Service, September–December 1914   88

7. The isolation of Antwerp by 3 October 1914   99

8. Air raid on Friedrichshafen, 21 November 1914   173

9. Lord Fisher's eight-point plan of attack, 3 January 1915   235

10. The Anglo-French Naval attack at the Dardanelles, 18 March 1915   353

11. The Advances on the Gallipoli Peninsula, 25 April 1915   403

12. The Military Landings on the Gallipoli Peninsula, 6–10 August 1915   519

13. Churchill's four-point plan of attack against Bulgaria, 5 October 1915   545

14. The Ostend to Arras sector of the western front, November and December 1915   575

15. British and German trenches, Neuve Chapelle, November and December 1915   577

16. The Wytschaete to Armentières sector of the western front, January 1916   631

17. The Ploegsteert sector of the western front, January–May 1916   649

The following maps have been placed at the end of the book, pages 838–842, for general reference:

18. The Turkish Empire, August 1914   838
19. The Gallipoli Peninsula and the Sea of Marmara, August
    1914   840
20. The alternate war zones discussed in January 1915   842

Preface

THIS volume spans two and a half years of Winston Churchill's life, from July 1914 to December 1916. As First Lord of the Admiralty during the first nine months of the war he was responsible for one of the two fighting services of the Government. As a member of the War Council from its inception in November 1914, he was at the centre of British war policy. During those nine months he had greater responsibilities than at any time until he became Prime Minister in 1940. The Royal Navy depended upon him for its orders and its morale. He was in charge of the air defence of Britain, and launched a series of air attacks on Germany. He established the Royal Naval Division, a military force under direct Admiralty control, which fought at the siege of Antwerp in October 1914. At Antwerp he himself supervised the British military effort, and for three days took command of the city's defences. In January 1915 he embarked upon the plans which were to lead to the naval attack on Turkey at the Dardanelles. His authority was wide, extending over every aspect of naval planning and action. These responsibilities exhilarated him. He was only thirty-nine at the outbreak of war; his youth, energy and zeal made possible continuous exertions, plans and stratagems, not all limited to naval affairs.

When Asquith formed his Coalition Government in May 1915 Churchill was excluded from the centre of power and given the sinecure of Chancellor of the Duchy of Lancaster. Six months later he resigned from the Cabinet and served on the western front as a Lieutenant-Colonel in command of an infantry Battalion. In May 1916 he returned to the House of Commons, where he found himself a lonely opposition figure in a hostile parliament.

Between May and November 1915 a succession of humiliating setbacks shattered Churchill's career and deeply affected his character. His enthusiasm, first for the naval, and then for the military, attacks at the Dardanelles and on the Gallipoli Peninsula, convinced many of his contemporaries that he was a man of blood, lacking sound judgement, and unfit for high office. The ebullient politician of August 1914, confident of his powers, exuberant in manner, certain of a distinguished future, optimistic in his assessment of men and events, was gone by the summer of 1916; men saw instead a broken figure, unsure of his career, pessimistic about the outcome of the war, lacking faith in the country's leaders, consumed by brooding and bitterness.

When Churchill was forced to leave the Admiralty in May 1915, with his work incomplete, the Dardanelles remained the subject to which he returned again and again, both in Cabinet and in his speeches. 'What about the Dardanelles?' became the cry which he was insistently called upon to answer. He devoted much energy and time to preparing his defence for the Dardanelles Commission of Inquiry during the summer of 1916. In 1923 he published his defence in the first two volumes of his book, *The World Crisis*. The story he told was based upon the documents which he had kept in his private archive, and upon his own recollections. But his collection of documents was incomplete and his memory imperfect. In writing about the Dardanelles, Churchill could not make use of the full official records of the Cabinet Office, the Admiralty, the War Office and the Foreign Office. Yet without these records the daily workings of Government and the complex evolution of policy cannot be traced. Nor could Churchill know what his colleagues in the Cabinet, his critics in political circles, and his subordinates at the Admiralty were writing about him in their private correspondence and diaries. Without a combination of these official and private materials a balanced account is impossible.

By using these materials to reconstruct, where necessary day by day, or even hour by hour, the sequence of the events with which Churchill was involved, it has become possible to understand the pressures that affected his actions, and the diplomatic, military and political considerations beyond his control which shaped Government policy. Churchill was not the first to push for an attack on Turkey at the Dardanelles; initially he preferred, and pressed continually for, an assault upon the north German coast. Nor did he choose as the ideal operation at the Dardanelles a purely naval attack, as was launched with his ultimate approval in March 1915; he argued repeatedly at the War Council that troops must assist the navy, and protested when they were not made available. Nor did Churchill either plan or supervise the military landings on the Gallipoli Peninsula of April and August 1915; but once those landings had been made, he pressed Kitchener to reinforce them, and wanted a military victory even if the cost were high. As 1915 progressed he became convinced that the defeat of Turkey would shorten the war in Europe and lead to an Allied victory over Germany and Austria-Hungary; by the end of 1915 his mind was dominated by this conviction.

While serving on the western front during the early months of 1916 Churchill was tormented by news of the evacuation of the Gallipoli Peninsula, and brooded upon the series of naval and military failures which had made the evacuation inevitable. On his return to Parliament later that year he sought to justify the expedition, and to castigate those who had abandoned it. Because he was widely accused of having been responsible for the deaths at Gallipoli, he began to defend even those aspects of the attack which he had neither planned nor supported. His colleagues saw this obsession. They saw him bind the whole disaster to his back. For them, this complete identification with failure marred his credibility. Many, while recognizing his outstanding abilities, believed that these possessed some tragic flaw which would always keep him from his goal, and that whatever he touched would come to grief, as the Dardanelles had done. During the summer of 1916, Churchill believed that his knowledge of war policy and his experience of trench warfare could enable him to contribute to shortening the war and reducing the scale of the slaughter which he abhorred. But his advice was ignored and he was cut off from all influence on war policy. When Lloyd George became Prime Minister in December 1916, Churchill was not asked to serve.

While he was at the Admiralty, in charge of the naval policies which were to shatter his career, Churchill did not and could not act alone. Asquith, as Prime Minister, was the final arbiter of all war policy. When he gave Churchill's plans his support, Churchill could usually go ahead with them; when he opposed these plans, Churchill could not continue with them. On occasions Kitchener and Grey both persuaded Asquith to accept policies which Churchill strenuously opposed. These three ministers were not the only people to whom Churchill had at times to defer; his professional advisers in the Admiralty could also turn decisively against the policies he proposed, and did so in March 1915 to prevent a second naval attack at the Dardanelles. Churchill could not overrule the collective opinion either of the War Council or of the supreme naval authority, the Admiralty War Group. However impressive his reasoning, however strong his arguments, however intense his convictions, however dominating his personality, he had no independent power to control war policy. It was this very lack of power that frustrated and depressed him most during the two and a half years covered by this volume.

MARTIN GILBERT

Merton College
Oxford
20 May 1971

Sources

I HAVE tried wherever possible to find the original text of every document quoted in this volume, because in many instances I have discovered large discrepancies between the original document and later published versions. This is particularly true of official documents and telegrams printed for the Cabinet or published subsequently in Government collections of documents; in these, sentences thought to be damaging to security or embarrassing to the Government were often omitted or altered. Many published diaries and private letters also differ considerably from their original versions, authors and editors at times omitting material without any indication being given that they have done so, and on occasions contemporary judgements being deliberately altered to accord with hindsight.

Many of the official documents used by Churchill in *The World Crisis* were the altered or paraphrased versions, for he himself did not have access to all the originals: there are therefore frequent textual differences between important documents which have already been published, either by Churchill or others, and the original versions quoted here.

In transcribing documents and letters, I have thought it important to keep to the style of the originals, retaining the contemporary spellings, grammatical peculiarities, and all abbreviations. As it has proved technically impossible to use underlinings, I have followed the convention whereby single-underlined words are printed in ordinary italics, double-underlined words in small capitals, and triple-underlined words in large italicized capitals. I have also followed the convention of italicizing the names of ships, newspapers and books in the text; but where these names appear in documents I have retained the style of the original.

Beginning on p. 843, I have set out a source list which gives, in chronological order, the date of every document quoted in the narrative, the names of the sender and recipient, the page on which the document appears in this volume, and the archive from which it comes. The source list also indicates whenever I have used a copy of a document rather than the document actually sent; often it has been impossible to find the originals, which in several cases are known to have been destroyed.

I have consulted all the principal published works covering this period. I have only quoted from these where they provide one of either of two kinds of evidence: first, extracts from contemporary letters, diaries and official documents (if I have been unable to find the original versions); second, recollections of conversations, moods and events written later (where I have been unable to find a contemporary record). All Parliamentary quotations are taken from Hansard. Speeches made by Churchill elsewhere are quoted from contemporary press reports.

On the first occasion when a person is mentioned in this volume, I have included a short footnote giving brief biographical details.

In order to establish the historical narrative and to begin the exploration of Churchill's character, I have consulted seventy-three collections of papers. If a collection is publicly available, I have indicated its location. If no indication is given, it was at the time of writing in private possession. The principal collection on which I have drawn is the *Churchill papers*. These contain many official documents as well as private material. Churchill kept most of the political, departmental and personal letters which he received between July 1914 and December 1916, and copies of up to a half of the letters which he wrote, or which his Private Secretaries, Edward Marsh and James Masterton-Smith, took down at his dictation or drafted for him. These papers contain, for the nine wartime months during which Churchill was First Lord of the Admiralty, several thousand official letters, telegrams, memoranda and notes, both to and from Churchill himself, and also covering aspects of Government, Admiralty and War Council transactions. There are copies of many Foreign Office telegrams and War Office despatches; copies of memoranda circulated inside the Admiralty; and printed sets of selected secret telegrams circulated during the war to senior Ministers. The papers also contain many of Churchill's unpublished notes, some intended for his memoirs, others for newspaper and magazine articles which he wrote during and immediately after the war. There are also many drafts of speeches, some never used, some incorporated in other speeches. Churchill also kept a large number of letters to colleagues which, on reflection, he had decided not to send; I have always indicated when a letter quoted was not sent. There is much personal material in these papers. During his lifetime Churchill acquired his mother's collection of letters, including many of his own letters to her of which he had kept no copy. Also acquired were his brother Jack's diary written while he was at the Dardanelles, and some papers belonging to his insurance broker, W. H. Bernau, which include material relating to the Dardanelles. The largest personal section of the Churchill papers contains fifty-nine letters from Clementine Churchill to her husband while he was on the western front, written between December 1915 and April 1916.

The letters which Clementine Churchill wrote to her husband between July and December 1914, and a further fourteen letters which she wrote to him in November and December 1915, form part of a separate collection, the *Baroness Spencer-Churchill papers*. These also include, for the period covered by this volume, all Churchill's letters to his wife, the letters which Clementine Churchill received from her husband's colleagues, and several letters sent to Churchill while he was on the western front, which his wife kept for him.

An important source for Churchill's personal feelings are the letters which he wrote throughout this period to his brother, which form part of the *John Churchill papers*. His letters to his friend Jack Seely, later Lord Mottistone, who was serving in Flanders, are in the *Mottistone papers* at Nuffield College, Oxford. His letters to F. E. Smith, later Earl of Birkenhead, to whom he often turned for guidance, are in the *Birkenhead papers*, but not all of these letters appear to have survived. Churchill's letter to his son from the western front is in the *Randolph Churchill papers*; his letter to his aunt Leonie Leslie on the death of her son Norman is in the *Leslie papers*, which also contain Churchill's letter to his mother of 29 January 1916 which Lady Randolph had presumably shown to her sister.

The letters, both personal and political, which Churchill wrote to David Lloyd George, are in the *Lloyd George papers*, the bulk of which are at the Beaverbrook Library, London. These papers contain much political material for this period. There are further letters from Churchill to Lloyd George in the *Lloyd George papers* still in private possession. The diary of Frances Stevenson, which gives several indications of Lloyd George's sometimes extremely critical attitude towards Churchill, is part of the *Countess Lloyd-George of Dwyfor papers*, also at the Beaverbrook Library.

H. H. Asquith expressed his opinions of Churchill in many of his numerous letters to the Hon Venetia Stanley, later the Hon Mrs Edwin Montagu. These letters are in that part of the *Montagu papers* which remains in private possession. These letters contain frequent, and at times daily, accounts of political developments from July 1914 to May 1915, and describe proceedings at Cabinet, in the War Council, and at the centre of Government policy-making. A few of these letters were quoted by Asquith himself in his memoirs as 'contemporary notes'; but even the extracts which he had used in this disguised form were not always accurately transcribed. Further comments by Asquith, made to his wife Margot, as well as her own opinions, and reports of her conversations with Churchill, Lloyd George and Lord Fisher, are in her diary, part of the *Countess Oxford and Asquith papers*: I have seen this diary for the period October 1914 to May 1915. I have used a letter from Margot Asquith which is in the *Balfour papers* at the British Museum.

Some of the letters which Asquith received from his colleagues, and several letters from Churchill of which Churchill kept no copies, are in the *Asquith papers* at the Bodleian Library, Oxford. Asquith's letters to King George V describing Cabinet proceedings are in the *George V papers*, in the Royal Archives at Windsor. From these papers I have also quoted references to Churchill in George V's diary, and in a letter he wrote to Queen Mary. The *Stamfordham papers*, also in the Royal Archives, contain detailed accounts of the replacement of Prince Louis of Battenberg as First Sea Lord by Lord Fisher, of the political crisis of May 1915, and several letters about Churchill from the Civil Lord of Admiralty, Sir Francis Hopwood, later Lord Southborough, whose own correspondence, including a letter from Stamfordham at the time of the siege of Antwerp, is in the *Southborough papers*. Another source of royal and court opinion is the *Esher papers* at Churchill College, Cambridge, which contain Lord Esher's original diary; this is much fuller than, and differs markedly at several points from, the published version. These papers also contain the letters to Esher quoted in this volume from Lord Stamfordham, J. A. Spender, his sons Maurice and Oliver Brett, and from the Secretary to the War Council, Lieutenant-Colonel M. P. A. Hankey. Hankey's original diary, and much correspondence, are in the *Hankey papers*, also at Churchill College, which contain many references to Churchill, as well as the letters from Lord Fisher, Lord Esher and Margot Asquith quoted in this volume.

Government policy can be followed in part through the official papers which Churchill, Lloyd George, Asquith and Hankey kept in their private archives, as well as through the official material in the *Harcourt papers*, which contain several memoranda by Churchill and other Cabinet Ministers of which no copies survive among their own papers. But the most comprehensive sets of official papers are those in the Public Record Office. These have several gaps, but no single private archive can approach them in comprehensiveness. There are five sets of official papers used here. The *Cabinet papers* contain the minutes of the meetings of the War Council and its successor the

Dardanelles Committee, as well as a file of papers kept by James Masterton-Smith, Churchill's Naval Secretary at the Admiralty. The Masterton-Smith file includes Asquith's letter to Lord Fisher ordering him to return to his post in May 1915. The *Air Ministry papers* contain material relating to early aerial policy, defensive and offensive, for which Churchill was responsible while First Lord. The *War Office papers* contain correspondence between the Admiralty and the War Office, and between Churchill and Earl Kitchener of Khartoum, as well as Sir Ian Hamilton's despatches from Gallipoli, and the war diaries of the 2nd Battalion of the Grenadier Guards, and the 6th Battalion of the Royal Scots Fusiliers for the period when Churchill was serving with them on the western front. Churchill's attempts to influence foreign policy can be followed in the *Foreign Office papers*, which have a special section, FO 800/35–113, containing the correspondence of Sir Edward Grey, including many letters from Churchill of which he kept no copy. Another section, the private correspondence of Grey's Private Secretary, William Tyrrell, FO 800/220, contains a letter from Lord Fisher. The principal official set of documents used in this volume is the *Admiralty papers*, from which it is possible to reconstruct, on a daily basis, the development of naval policy. These papers are much fuller than Churchill's own papers, on which he drew for his published account of his work as First Lord. They can nevertheless be supplemented by further archival material neither in the official collections, nor in the Churchill papers: Churchill's letters to Lord Fisher, Fisher's other correspondence, and several naval memoranda not available elsewhere, are in the *Fisher papers*; Fisher's letters to Sir John Jellicoe are in the *Jellicoe papers* at the British Museum, his letters to Pamela and Reginald McKenna in the *McKenna papers* at Churchill College; Sir David Beatty's letters to his wife are in the *Beatty papers*; Commodore Keyes' letters to his wife are in the *Keyes papers* at Churchill College. Sir Berkeley Milne's material on the escape of the two German cruisers to Turkey, and the Admiralty telegrams which he received on the outbreak of war, are in the *Milne papers* at the National Maritime Museum, Greenwich. Admiral Oliver's material on Antwerp and the Dardanelles, together with several pages of recollections, are in the *Oliver papers* at the National Maritime Museum, Greenwich. There is material on the Dardanelles in the *de Robeck papers* at Churchill College; the memorandum by Sir Francis Hopwood on the crisis of May 1915 and on Churchill's speech demanding Fisher's return is in the *Milford Haven papers*, which also contain material relating to the resignation of Prince Louis of Battenberg, later Marquess of Milford Haven; the

Hall papers contain the draft memoirs of the Director of Naval Intelligence, whose recollections in March and May 1915 are quoted in this volume; the *Richmond papers* at the National Maritime Museum, Greenwich, include the diary and correspondence of the Assistant Director of Naval Operations, Captain Richmond, one of Churchill's severest critics at the Admiralty. Churchill's instructions to Admiral Hood for the bombardment of the Belgian coast are in the *Hood papers* at Churchill College, Cambridge. There is material on Fisher's resignation collected by his naval assistant, Captain Crease, in the *Crease papers*. Churchill's letters to Kitchener, of many of which he kept no copy, are in the *Kitchener papers* at the Public Record Office.

There is material on military aspects of Gallipoli in the *Dawnay papers* at the Imperial War Museum, London, and in the *Hamilton papers* at King's College, London. Hamilton kept no diary while at Gallipoli. In June 1916, more than seven months after his recall, and over a year after he had gone to Gallipoli, he began to dictate the 'Private Diary of General Sir Ian Hamilton' to his secretary. He was aided in reconstructing past events by a brief factual account kept by his personal clerk, Sergeant-Major H. G. Stuart, and by official telegrams and letters in his possession. Hamilton dictated quickly, in order that his recollections could be ready for Churchill, who was then preparing his evidence for the Dardanelles Commission. Hamilton later elaborated on the details and in places altered the content of these recollections, which were published in 1920 with the title 'Gallipoli Diary', a title which has misled several commentators into believing that it was a document written during the campaign. I have quoted throughout from the original dictated typescript of June 1916.

There are letters from Churchill of which he kept no copy in the papers of several of his colleagues. Those used in this volume are from the *Crewe papers* at the Cambridge University Library, the *Haldane papers* at the National Library of Scotland, the *Runciman papers* at the University of Newcastle upon Tyne Library, and the *Steel-Maitland papers* at the Scottish Record Office. Two Liberal Ministers, Lord Emmott and J. A. Pease, later Lord Gainford, kept diaries which contain references to Cabinet discussions otherwise unrecorded; I have quoted these from the *Emmott papers* and the *Gainford papers*, both at Nuffield College, Oxford.

Churchill's relations with the Press can be followed both in the *C. P. Scott papers* in the British Museum, which contain notes of conversations with Churchill, Lloyd George and other political figures, and in the *Garvin papers* at the Texas University Library. There are some Churchill letters in the *Northcliffe papers*. There is much material in the

H. A. Gwynne papers, including several letters from Major-General Callwell, the Director of Operations and Intelligence at the War Office. There are criticisms of Churchill by Liberal politicians in the *Buxton papers* and the *Burns papers* at the British Museum. Conservative hostility to Churchill can be studied in the *Bonar Law papers* at the Beaverbrook Library, in the *Austen Chamberlain papers* at Birmingham University Library, and in the *Milner papers* at the Bodleian Library. These three sets of papers contain substantial material on the political background.

There is material for Churchill's period on the western front in the *Altrincham papers*, which contain the correspondence of Edward Grigg, later Lord Altrincham, who was serving with the 2nd Battalion of the Grenadier Guards in November 1915; and in the *Spears papers*, which contain many diary references to Churchill at St Omer in December 1915. The *Hakewill Smith papers* contain letters from a subaltern serving with the 6th Royal Scots Fusiliers from January to June 1916. The *Tudor papers* contain the diary of the 9th Division's Royal Artillery Commander, Hugh Tudor, with several references to Churchill. There are two letters from Churchill to Curzon in early 1916, of which Churchill kept no copy, in the *Curzon papers* at the India Office Library, and a letter from Churchill to Lansdowne in the *Lansdowne papers*. While he was in Flanders Churchill wrote several times to Edward Marsh; these letters are in the *Marsh papers*. The *Henry Wilson papers* contain General Wilson's diary, with references to Churchill both during his service on the western front, and at other periods covered by this volume. The *Bentham papers* contain an able-seaman's letter to his father from Antwerp, and several press cuttings about the siege. Churchill's annotations to Lord Beaverbrook's historical writings, made in 1928 and 1931, and bearing on 1914 to 1916, are in the *Beaverbrook papers* at the Beaverbrook Library. The Beaverbrook papers also contain Churchill's telegram to Asquith from Antwerp of 5 October 1914, offering to give up his Cabinet office and take command in the field, and Churchill's letter to Bonar Law of 21 May 1915, seeking the Conservative leader's support during the political crisis. Beaverbrook obtained the telegram from Venetia Stanley, to whom Asquith had sent it; and the letter direct from Bonar Law.

I have also obtained documentary material used in this volume from the *Conan Doyle papers*, the *Dawson papers* at Printing House Square, the *Haig papers* at the National Library of Scotland, the *National Liberal Club papers* at the National Liberal Club, London, the *Rawlinson papers* at Churchill College, Cambridge, and the *Robertson papers* at King's College, London. For further background material on the Dardanelles,

I have consulted the *Roch papers* at Ampleforth Abbey, York, and the *Williamson papers* at Churchill College, Cambridge.

I have been unable to use several sets of papers which might have contained material of importance. The papers of Baroness Asquith of Yarnbury and of 1st Viscount Wimborne were both closed. The papers of 1st Viscount Thurso and 1st Viscount Rothermere are both believed to have been destroyed. The papers of the 9th Duke of Marlborough could not be found. Almost none of Venetia Stanley's letters to Asquith survive.

I have supplemented the archival material as much as possible by conversation and correspondence with those who knew Churchill during this period, or who were associated in some way in the enterprises with which he was involved. By this means I have been able to include reminiscences of Churchill's moods, and of the atmosphere of events not always obvious from the documents, and have been able to describe several incidents not recorded in any contemporary source.

Lady Spencer-Churchill answered many queries and gave me a most valuable insight into her husband's life and into his relationships with his colleagues. I have shown her each section of the book, and I have been greatly encouraged by her interest and enthusiasm.

For an understanding of Churchill's character between 1914 and 1916 I have benefited from the personal reminiscences of the late Baroness Asquith of Yarnbury, whose father was Prime Minister throughout the period covered by this volume; the late Lord Beaverbrook, whose close friendship with Churchill began in 1916 when Churchill was in the trenches; Sir Herbert Creedy, Kitchener's Military Secretary, 1914–16; Sir Ralph Hawtrey, one of Lloyd George's Private Secretaries at the Treasury; the Hon Sylvia Henley, Clementine Churchill's cousin; Sir Shane Leslie, Bt, Churchill's cousin; Frances, Countess Lloyd-George of Dwyfor, Lloyd George's Private Secretary during these years; and the 10th Duke of Marlborough, Churchill's cousin. The late Field-Marshal Earl Alexander of Tunis recalled a conversation with Churchill about military command in the First World War; Mr John Colville described Churchill's reflections on 1916.

My knowledge of what happened during the siege of Antwerp in October 1914 was increased by discussion and correspondence with members of the Royal Naval Division: Mr Jack Bentham, Major-General A. R. Chater, Mr Robert Hall, Mr C. J. F. Mitchell, Mr Stewart Owler, Mr William Rice and Mr Henry M. Stevens, all of whom were present during the siege. Air Vice-Marshal Sir John Cor-

dingley gave me a young officer's impressions of the formation of the
Royal Naval Division. The late Vice-Admiral Richard Bell Davies,
one of Churchill's flying instructors, who subsequently fought at
Antwerp and the Dardanelles, gave me information about Churchill's
interest in the development of aerial warfare.

In November 1915 Churchill was introduced to trench warfare by
the 2nd Battalion of the Grenadier Guards. Mr Ralph Bingham, then
a machine-gun officer, and Viscount Chandos, then, as Oliver Lyttelton,
Adjutant of another Grenadier Battalion, gave me their reminiscences
of this period.

In December 1915, while waiting at Sir John French's headquarters
uncertain of both his military and political future, Churchill befriended
a young cavalry captain in whom he confided. I received much important information from that captain, now Major-General Sir Edward
Louis Spears, Bt, who talked to me about those weeks, allowed me to
see his diary, and answered my detailed queries.

From January to May 1916 Churchill commanded the 6th Battalion
of the Royal Scots Fusiliers in the trenches of Flanders. I have obtained
much information about this period from several of those who served
under his command. Major-General Sir Edmund Hakewill Smith, and
Mr Jock McDavid, both subalterns at the time, gave me detailed
accounts of life at Churchill's headquarters, and added to my account
of Moolenacker and Ploegsteert. The late Major F. D. Napier-Clavering, a sapper who lived for some weeks at Churchill's headquarters,
gave me many recollections of Churchill's interest in trench engineering
and fortifications. Mr Ralph Fox, a Lewis gunner in the 6th Royal
Scots Fusiliers, Mr Reginald Hurt, then serving as a private in the
Battalion, and the late M. André Maurois, then liaison officer with the
9th Division, answered my queries in correspondence and gave me information about Churchill in the trenches. I have talked with profit to
Lord Casey, then a captain attached to the 6th Royal Scots Fusiliers,
and to the painter Paul Maze, then serving with the British Army, both
of whom saw something of Churchill during his period in the trenches. I
have benefited from the reminiscences of General Sir Ivo Vesey and
Major Sir Desmond Morton, then both serving on the staff of Sir
Douglas Haig at St Omer.

During the course of my researches into Churchill's three months as
a battalion commander I visited the areas of the western front where
he served. Mme Planche of Meteren gave me a vivid account of life in
1916 in Churchill's reserve area, Moolenacker, where she helped in her
mother's estaminet, favourite café of the 6th Royal Scots Fusiliers. I

benefited from a visit to the two Belgian parishes of Warneton, through which his trenches ran, and Ploegsteert, in which he had his various headquarters, receiving help from M. Jean Petillon, M. Robert Ryckaert and M. Joël Wgeuw, the present occupants of 'Soyer Farm', the 'Hospice' and 'Burnt Out Farm' respectively. M. Omer Parmentier, Mlle Antoinette Chaignon and Mme Elise Devroedt gave me their reminiscences of Ploegsteert both before and at the beginning of the First World War.

In Ankara I gained much from talking to Ismet Inönü, former President of Turkey, who served on the Gallipoli Peninsula, and gave me an insight into the effect of the attack on Turkish morale. At the Maritime Museum in Istanbul I was able to examine Mustafa Kemal's campaign maps. The following soldiers who served at Gallipoli gave me reminiscences of great interest: Mr S. E. Carter, Mr F. W. Crompton, the late Mr T. Macmillan, Sir Clifford Norton, Sir Geoffrey Shakespeare, Bt, Mr Harry Skinner. I am grateful to those who gave me their recollections of particular events between 1914 and 1916: Mr A. J. P. Andrews, former motor-cycle despatch rider with the 9th Division, the late Mr H. E. Ardiss, formerly of RN Transport, Dover, Mr Frank Ashton-Gwatkin, formerly in the British Embassy, Tokyo, Mr W. J. Baldwin, formerly a sapper with the 64th Field Company, Royal Engineers, Mr T. E. Cresswell, formerly of the RND, Mr Thomas Hope Floyd, Mr Robert Fulton, former bandsman, 9th Division, Mr T. B. Johnson, formerly lieutenant in the RNAS Armoured Cars, Mr Hermon Marsden, a former infantry captain, Mr Andy O'Brien, formerly a corporal in the Highland Light Infantry, who fought at Loos, and served in the trenches near Ploegsteert, Mr F. C. Shuter, formerly of the 10th Royal Fusiliers, and Mr J. G. Tomlin, also of the 10th Royal Fusiliers.

I have been doing research into this period of Churchill's life for nearly nine years. But no research can be exhaustive. The location of historical material is arbitrary and its discovery often accidental. I learned of the existence of several archives cited in this source list purely by chance, and a number of documents quoted in this book might easily have remained unknown. There may well be several collections of papers, some containing letters relevant to this volume, of which I know nothing. I have made strong efforts to seek out the principal evidence; but there is no moment in the writing of biography—any more than in the writing of political, diplomatic or military history—at which it can be said that no more research need be done.

1

'A Really Happy Man'

CHURCHILL's instinct was not for war with Germany. During the Agadir crisis in 1911, when Germany had seemed to be willing to hustle France into war for the sake of a small port on the Atlantic coast of Morocco, Churchill had been attracted, not to war but to the idea of an alliance which might deter the Germans from aggression. In search of a deterrent, he had, while Home Secretary, proposed a triple alliance between Britain, France and Russia, hoping thereby to safeguard the independence of Belgium, Holland and Denmark without hostilities. From the moment of the Agadir crisis, he focused his mind increasingly upon world affairs. He believed that international chaos could come as easily to Europe as to Africa or Asia. This new concern of Churchill's had influenced the Prime Minister, H. H. Asquith,[1] in sending him to the Admiralty in October 1911. The principal task with which Asquith entrusted him was to ensure that the Royal Navy did not find itself in a position where Germany could gain sudden advantage over it.

While Churchill was at the Admiralty he pressed for agreement with Germany, and hoped for a relaxation of the naval arms race. On 20 May 1914 he wrote to Asquith and to the Foreign Secretary, Sir Edward Grey,[2] asking whether they would agree to his meeting Admiral Tirpitz,[3] in order to discuss four specific proposals for improved

[1] Herbert Henry Asquith, 1852–1928. Liberal MP, 1886–1918; 1920–4. Home Secretary, 1892–5. Chancellor of the Exchequer, 1905–8. Prime Minister, 1908–16. Secretary of State for War, 30 March–5 August 1914; acting Secretary of State for War, 5–30 November 1915 and 6 June–5 July 1916. Created Earl of Oxford and Asquith, 1925.

[2] Edward Grey, 1862–1933. 3rd Baronet, 1882. Liberal MP, 1885–1916. Foreign Secretary, 1905–16. Created Viscount Grey of Fallodon, 1916. Ambassador on a special Mission to the USA, 1919.

[3] Alfred von Tirpitz, 1849–1930. Secretary of State for the German Navy, 1897–1916. Grand-Admiral, 1911. A believer in Anglo-German co-operation, he favoured a fixed ratio of shipbuilding which would leave Britain with permanent superiority. In May 1914 he wished Germany to take all possible steps to avoid war with Britain, but he had no political influence.

Anglo-German naval relations. Churchill wanted to reduce what he described to them as 'the unwholesome concentration of fleets in home waters', proposing that Britain and Germany agree to send their ships to African and Far Eastern stations. He advised 'the abandonment of secrecy' over a wide spectrum of naval information about all British and German ships, whether already launched or still under construction. He suggested that British and German Naval Attachés should be given 'equal and reciprocal facilities to visit the dockyards and see what was going on'. Such an exchange, he wrote, 'would go a long way to stopping the espionage on both sides which is a continued cause of suspicion and ill feeling'. Churchill wanted these discussions to take place in the last week of June 1914. But Grey deprecated the plan, writing to both Churchill and Asquith on May 25 that a meeting with Tirpitz would make 'a terrible splash in the European press', and that as a result of it 'the wildest reports will be circulated and we shall be involved in constant explanations to Ambassadors at the Foreign Office and denials in the press of the things that will be attributed to us'. Grey argued from a position of seniority and long experience of European affairs; the plan to meet Tirpitz was abandoned. Still hoping to ease Anglo-German naval tensions, in the middle of June Churchill sent a British naval squadron to the Kiel regatta. 'Officers and men,' he later wrote in *The World Crisis*, 'strolled arm in arm through the hospitable town, or dined with all goodwill in mess and wardroom. Together they stood bareheaded at the funeral of a German officer killed in flying an English seaplane.'

On June 28, while the Kiel regatta was still in progress, the Austrian Archduke Franz Ferdinand[1] was assassinated at Sarajevo. Churchill did not see this as the prelude to any conflict involving Britain. He had confidence in the power of diplomacy to resolve a crisis, should one develop. He did not believe that Germany would dare to challenge British naval power which he had so augmented since becoming First Lord. Underlying his Admiralty policies was his calculation, made in 1912, that by 1920 the balance of naval forces would be such that no European state would risk a war which might bring in Britain as an enemy.

During the three weeks following Franz Ferdinand's assassination, Austria and Russia became increasingly belligerent. Germany pressed Austria in its quarrel with Serbia. It seemed inevitable that France would join its ally Russia in any Russo-German war. Britain stood aside,

---

[1] Franz Ferdinand, 1863-1914. A nephew of the Emperor Franz Josef, and heir to the throne of Austria-Hungary from 1889. He advocated a pro-British policy for Austria. He and his wife were shot dead by a Bosnian of Serb nationality.

little perturbed by the sight of Europe in disarray. The Cabinet's concern was over the mounting violence in Ireland, where daily increasing turmoil seemed about to pitch the Catholic Irish and the Ulster Protestants into civil war. On July 22 Churchill wrote to Grey about a possible solution to the Irish question. By way of analogy, he referred to the European crisis; if the problem were to uphold British interests in Europe, he explained to the Foreign Secretary, 'you wd proceed by two stages. First you wd labour to stop Austria & Russia going to war: second, if that failed, you wd try to prevent England, France, Germany & Italy being drawn in.' Churchill took for granted the need for conciliation in Europe as in Ireland. The Chancellor of the Exchequer, David Lloyd George[1] took a similar view, assuring the House of Commons on the following day that 'civilization' would have no difficulty in regulating disputes which arose between nations, by means 'of some sane and well-ordered arbitrament'.

During July Churchill had ordered a test mobilization of the Third Fleet to take place in the English Channel. This mobilization had been decided upon earlier in the year as part of the naval economy insisted upon by the Cabinet; manoeuvres, with whole Fleets deployed over vast areas of ocean, had been considered too expensive. The mobilization had nothing to do with the European crisis. On July 19, when it was satisfactorily ended, the ships of every Fleet, including seventy battleships, had passed in front of the Royal Yacht at Spithead while King George V[2] had taken the salute. No sense of crisis had interfered with the pageantry of the occasion. On July 23 the ships were ready to disperse; their captains made plans to return to their respective ports. Churchill saw no reason to halt this process of dispersal and demobilization. That evening he returned from Spithead to London to prepare for the Cabinet meeting to be held on the following day, Friday July 24. Ireland dominated the agenda. Home Rule was now a certainty. But the Protestants of Ulster insisted upon secession. The Cabinet spent much time in arguing about the precise boundaries that should be drawn between a self-governing Ulster and the autonomous South.[3] Churchill recalled in *The World Crisis* how, 'turning this way and

[1] David Lloyd George, 1863–1945. Liberal MP, 1890–1931. Chancellor of the Exchequer, 1908–15. Minister of Munitions, May 1915–July 1916. Secretary of State for War, July–December 1916. Prime Minister, December 1916–October 1922. Independent Liberal MP, 1931–45. Created Earl Lloyd-George of Dwyfor, 1945.

[2] George Frederick Ernest Albert, 1865–1936. Succeeded his father as King George V, 1910.

[3] No Cabinet records were kept before 1918. Asquith sent George V accounts of Cabinet meetings, but these were brief, and normally recorded only the conclusions, not the arguments used.

that in search of an exit from the deadlock', he and his colleagues, 'toiled around the muddy byways of Fermanagh and Tyrone', but without result:

The discussion had reached its inconclusive end, and the Cabinet was about to separate, when the quiet grave tones of Sir Edward Grey's voice were heard reading a document which had just been brought to him from the Foreign Office. It was the Austrian note to Serbia.[1] He had been reading or speaking for several minutes before I could disengage my mind from the tedious and bewildering debate which had just closed. We were all very tired, but gradually as the phrases and sentences followed one another, impressions of a wholly different character began to form in my mind. This note was clearly an ultimatum; but it was an ultimatum such as had never been penned in modern times. As the reading proceeded it seemed absolutely impossible that any State in the world could accept it, or that any acceptance, however abject, would satisfy the aggressor. The parishes of Fermanagh and Tyrone faded back into the mists and squalls of Ireland, and a strange light began immediately, but by perceptible gradations, to fall and grow upon the map of Europe.

The Cabinet broke up late that afternoon. On the following day Asquith informed George V about the European crisis. 'Happily,' he wrote, 'there seems to be no reason why we should be anything more than spectators.' Churchill shared Asquith's view that Britain could keep out of the European war, and on the evening of July 24 had postponed an Admiralty conference which had been fixed for the following morning. He decided to spend part of the weekend with his wife Clementine[2] and their two children, Diana[3] and Randolph,[4] who were staying at Cromer on the Norfolk coast. Clementine Churchill was expecting their third child in October. Writing that evening, Churchill gave her an outline of the day's events:

My darling one,
    I have managed to put off my naval conference and am coming to you & the kittens tomorrow by the 1 o'clock train.

[1] The Austrian ultimatum to Serbia was delivered in Belgrade at 6 pm on July 23. Accusing Serbian officials of planning the murder of Franz Ferdinand, it demanded the end to all anti-Austrian propaganda in Serbia, the arrest of officials allegedly guilty of conspiring against Austria, and direct Austrian participation in the suppression of all anti-Austrian activity.
[2] Clementine Ogilvy Hozier, 1885–   . Daughter of Lady Blanche and Sir Henry Hozier. She married Churchill in 1908. Created Baroness Spencer-Churchill, 1965.
[3] Diana Churchill, 1909–63. Churchill's eldest child.
[4] Randolph Frederick Edward Spencer Churchill, 1911–68. Churchill's only son. His godfathers were F. E. Smith and Sir Edward Grey. Conservative MP, 1940–5. Major, British mission to Yugoslav Army of National Liberation, 1943–4. Journalist and historian; author of the first two volumes of this biography.

I will tell you all the news then. Europe is trembling on the verge of a general war. The Austrian ultimatum to Servia being the most insolent document of its kind ever devised. Side by side with this the Provincial Govt in Ulster wh is now imminent appears comparatively a humdrum affair.

We are to go ahead with the Amending Bill, abolishing the time limit & letting any Ulster county vote itself out if it chooses. The Irish acquiesced in this reluctantly.

We must judge further events in Ulster when they occur. No one seems much alarmed.

Tender & fondest love
W

In a postscript Churchill told his wife that he was dining that night with Sir Ernest Cassel[1] to meet the German shipowner Albert Ballin.[2] After the dinner he sat next to Ballin, who expressed the fear, Churchill recalled in *The World Crisis*, that an Austrian attack on Serbia would lead to a general European war. 'If Russia marches against Austria, we must march,' Ballin told Churchill; 'and if we march France must march, and what would England do?' Churchill replied that he could not know what Britain's decision would be if Germany and France were at war. The Cabinet would have to decide. But, he added, it would be a mistake for Germany to assume that England would do nothing in such an eventuality. The British Government, he said, 'would judge events as they arose'. In his biography of *Albert Ballin*, published in 1922, Bernhard Huldermann[3] wrote of how, when Churchill took leave of Ballin, he 'implored him, almost with tears in his eyes, not to go to war'.

On the morning of Saturday July 25 Churchill discussed the crisis at length with the First Sea Lord, Prince Louis of Battenberg.[4] The reservists who had taken part in the test mobilization of the Fleet were

---

[1] Ernest Joseph Cassel, 1852–1921. Of German birth and Jewish descent. Naturalized as a British subject, 1878. Financier and philanthropist. Instrumental in acquiring for Vickers the Barrow Naval and Shipbuilding Construction Company, and the Maxim Gun Company. Knighted, 1899. In 1909 the National Bank of Turkey was created under his auspices. Churchill's financial adviser, 1900–17.

[2] Albert Ballin, 1857–1918. German shipping magnate. Owner of the Hamburg-Amerika Line. Confidant of the Kaiser. Before 1914 he played a leading role in the development of the German merchant marine. He committed suicide two days before the Armistice.

[3] Bernhard Huldermann. A Director of the Hamburg-Amerika Line. He wrote in the preface to his book: 'I am carrying out the behest of the deceased who asked me to collect his papers and to make whatever use I thought fit of them.'

[4] Prince Louis Alexander of Battenberg, 1854–1921. Cousin of George V. Naturalized as a British subject in 1868, when he entered the Royal Navy. First Sea Lord, 1912–14. At the King's request he discontinued the title of Prince and assumed the surname of Mountbatten, 1917. Created Marquess of Milford Haven, 1917. Admiral of the Fleet, 1921.

already on their way home. The Fleets which were then at Portland were to remain there until early on Monday morning, when they too would be dispersed. That afternoon, convinced that war might be avoided, Churchill left London to join his family at Cromer.

At nine o'clock on Sunday morning, July 26, Churchill telephoned Prince Louis from Cromer and learned that Austria was apparently dissatisfied with Serbia's conciliatory reply to its ultimatum. He went to the beach, and for three hours played with his children, returning to the town at noon to speak to Prince Louis again. This time he learned more disturbing news: the Austrian Government had entirely rejected Serbia's answer. Churchill and Prince Louis discussed what action ought to be taken. It proved difficult to conduct Admiralty business on the telephone. Churchill believed, as he wrote to Prince Louis a year later, on 12 August 1915, that he had specifically asked Prince Louis 'not to let the Fleet disperse'. Prince Louis recalled the conversation differently. In a letter to Churchill on 13 August 1915 he denied that Churchill had given him specific instructions to halt the dispersal of the Fleet, but had instead, he recalled, 'begged me to take whatever steps I might consider advisable without waiting to consult you over the telephone. . . . I had great difficulty in hearing you . . . I certainly never heard any reference to keeping the Fleet together.' According to his own recollection, Prince Louis had gone at once to the Foreign Office, looked at all the European telegrams, re-read the Admiralty orders under which the Fleet was to be dispersed, and then, at five minutes past four, had, entirely on his own initiative, telegraphed to the Commander of the Home Fleets, Sir George Callaghan,[1] ordering him not to disperse the Fleet. Prince Louis' telegram, which was unsigned, read: 'Admiralty to C in C Home Fleets. Decypher. No ships of First Fleet or Flotillas are to leave Portland until further orders. Acknowledge.'

Churchill reached London at ten that evening. He went at once to see Grey, who was already discussing the crisis with his Private Secretary, Sir William Tyrrell.[2] Grey told Churchill that although he did not think that a really dangerous moment had yet been reached, the situation was grave. Austria clearly intended to force her quarrel with Serbia to the point of war. Churchill asked whether it would be helpful

[1] George Astley Callaghan, 1852–1920. Entered Navy, 1866. Rear-Admiral, 1905. Knighted, 1909. Admiral commanding the First and Second Fleets, 1911–14. Commander-in-Chief, the Nore, 1915–18. Admiral of the Fleet, 1917.

[2] William George Tyrrell, 1866–1947. Entered the Foreign Service, 1889. Private Secretary to Sir Edward Grey, 1907–15. Knighted, 1913. Assistant Under-Secretary of State at the Foreign Office, 1919–25; Permanent Under-Secretary, 1925–8. Ambassador in Paris, 1928–34. Created Baron, 1929. President of the British Board of Film Censors, 1935–47.

if the Admiralty were to issue a public statement announcing that the dispersal of the Fleet had been halted. Grey and Tyrrell both urged him to make the announcement at the earliest possible moment, telling him that it would serve as a salutary warning to both Germany and Austria. Churchill returned to the Admiralty, and together with Prince Louis drafted an official communiqué: 'Orders have been given to the First Fleet, which is concentrated at Portland, not to disperse for manoeuvre leave for the present. All vessels of the Second Fleet are remaining at their home ports in proximity to their balance crews.'

This communiqué appeared as a small item of information in the newspapers on the following morning. 'It looked innocent enough,' Churchill wrote after the war in an unpublished note, 'but we hoped the German Emperor [1] at any rate would understand.' *The Times* approved the announcement as 'a welcome earnest of our intention to be ready for any course'. During the morning Churchill telephoned his wife, anxious to hear her reaction. He was upset when she told him that she had not seen the announcement in the papers. Later that day she wrote to him: 'I scampered home "with back & tail outstretched" & devoured the Times from cover to cover including advertisements & agony column but it wasn't there! The edition of the Times delivered in this distant spot, I suspect of being printed overnight!'

The first Cabinet specifically devoted to the European crisis met on the morning of Monday July 27. Neither Churchill nor his colleagues could tell in which direction events might move once Austria invaded Serbia. Russia might come to Serbia's immediate aid. Germany, adhering to her alliance with Austria, might attack Russia. France, bound by her alliance, might come to Russia's aid by attacking Germany. Germany might seek to anticipate an attack by France, and press for a decisive victory in the west before serious fighting could begin in the east. If Germany did strike at France, what would Britain do? No formal alliance committed Britain to defend France against a German attack. Britain's only relevant treaty obligation in Europe was to uphold Belgian neutrality. [2] Churchill was convinced that Asquith meant to challenge German aggression, whether it was against Belgium or France. But at the Cabinet that Monday a majority of the Ministers were not prepared to go to war with Germany on account of a German attack on France. They argued that Britain had no treaty obligations to

[1] Wilhelm, 1859–1941. First cousin of George V. Succeeded his father as German Emperor, 1888. Abdicated, November 1918. In exile in Holland from 1918 until his death.

[2] The Anglo-Portuguese Alliance, signed at Windsor on 9 May 1386, was still technically in force in 1914. But it signified little; in the summer of 1914 Grey had approved secret Anglo-German talks about the eventual partition of Portugal's African Empire.

France, and that the Entente Cordiale of 1904 was not a binding alliance but a sentimental liaison. 'The Cabinet,' Churchill later wrote in an unpublished note, 'was absolutely against war and would never have agreed to being committed to war at this moment.'

As First Lord of the Admiralty, Churchill's duty was to do all in his power to ensure that, if war came, the Navy was prepared. That afternoon he went to 10 Downing Street and obtained Asquith's approval for the setting up of special guards on all ammunition supplies and oil tanks. Orders were also sent out from the Admiralty for armed guards to man all coastal lights and guns. Aircraft were collected around the Thames Estuary to guard against Zeppelin attack. At a conference held under the joint auspices of the Admiralty and the War Office, the Press agreed to accept voluntary censorship, and to publish no further facts about ship or troop movements which the Government considered detrimental to national security. That night Churchill telegraphed to the Naval Commanders of all British Fleets and Squadrons scattered about the oceans: 'European political situation makes war between triple alliance and triple entente Powers by no means impossible. This is not the warning telegram but be prepared to shadow possible hostile men-of-war. . . . Measure is purely precautionary. The utmost secrecy is to be observed and no unnecessary person is to be informed.'

On Tuesday July 28 Churchill continued with the many necessary preparations. He ordered minesweepers to be collected; he took steps to reinforce the small British squadron in the Far East to prevent it being outmatched by superior German forces in the event of war; he appealed for close co-operation between the Naval and Military authorities to establish an effective aerial gun defence at the mouth of the Thames against Zeppelin attack; and he instructed the Director of the Intelligence Division at the Admiralty, Rear-Admiral Oliver,[1] to prepare the most recent statistics on relative British and German battleship strength. Since the previous Sunday the Fleet had been held together off the Isle of Wight. Although in such a position it constituted an imposing fighting force, its proper war station was not in the English Channel but in the North Sea. Churchill and Prince Louis

---

[1] Henry Francis Oliver, 1865–1965. Entered Navy, 1878. Naval Assistant to Sir John Fisher, 1908–10. Rear-Admiral, 1913. Director of the Intelligence Division at the Admiralty, 1913–14. Churchill's Naval Secretary, October 1914. Acting Vice-Admiral and Chief of the Admiralty War Staff, November 1914 to 1917. Knighted, 1916. Commanded 1st Battle Cruiser Squadron, 1918. Commanded the Home Fleet, 1919; the Reserve Fleet, 1919–20. Second Sea Lord, 1920–4. Admiral, 1923. Commander-in-Chief, Atlantic Fleet, 1924–7. Admiral of the Fleet, 1928.

decided that they must send the First Fleet into the North Sea as soon as possible. Churchill hoped that this would have a double effect: deterring the Germans from any sudden attack upon Britain itself and serving as clear evidence that Britain was prepared, if necessary, to enter the European conflict. 'I feared to bring this matter before the Cabinet,' Churchill later wrote in *The World Crisis*, 'lest it should mistakenly be considered a provocative action likely to damage the chances of peace.' He went instead to 10 Downing Street, where he explained his intention to Asquith. 'He looked at me with a hard stare,' Churchill later recorded in *Great Contemporaries*, 'and gave a sort of grunt. I did not require anything else.' Following Asquith's approval, Churchill at once telegraphed to Sir George Callaghan, ordering the First Fleet to leave Portland on the following day, Wednesday July 29, for Scapa Flow: 'Destination is to be kept secret except to flag and commanding officers . . . Course from Portland is to be shaped to southward, then a middle Channel course to the Straits of Dover. The Squadrons are to pass through the Straits without lights during the night and to pass outside the shoals on their way north. . . .'

On July 29 the First Fleet sailed eastwards according to plan through the Dover Strait into the North Sea. As a result of this secret move, Britain was secure against invasion; the nightmares of an alarmist decade were over.

As the European crisis intensified, many Liberals denied that a German attack on France would be cause for war. Some did not even feel that Britain need necessarily be bound by her pledge to uphold Belgian neutrality. The problem of German intentions towards Belgium was paramount. When Churchill lunched with Lord Kitchener[1] on July 28 they discussed Belgium at length. The Field-Marshal was on one of his rare visits to England, having received an earldom on the previous day. He needed to know Churchill's opinions of the crisis; as British Agent and Consul-General in Egypt he would be concerned, in the event of war, with the transportation of troops from India to Europe, and with the security of the Suez Canal. Churchill, who was

[1] Horatio Herbert Kitchener, 1850–1916. Entered Army, 1868. 2nd Lieutenant, Royal Engineers, 1871. Attached to the Palestine Exploration Fund, 1874–8. Surveyed Cyprus, 1878–82; the Sinai Peninsula, 1883. Governor-General, Eastern Sudan, 1886–8. Commander-in-Chief of the Egyptian Army, 1892–8. Knighted, 1894. Defeated the Dervishes at Omdurman, 1898. Created Baron Kitchener of Khartoum, 1898. Commander-in-Chief, South Africa, 1900–2. Created Viscount, 1902. Commander-in-Chief, India, 1902–9. Field-Marshal, 1909. A Member of the Committee of Imperial Defence, 1910. British Agent and Consul-General in Egypt, 1911–14. Created Earl, 27 July 1914. Secretary of State for War, 5 August 1914 until drowned at sea, 5 June 1916.

responsible for the naval aspects of both these problems, kept a private note of their discussion. Both men thought that there might already exist a secret agreement between Germany and Belgium which would allow German troops to cross Belgium on their way to France. They both agreed that in such an event it would be difficult for Britain to claim the 'invasion' of Belgium as sufficient cause for war. Churchill himself had no particular pro-Belgian feelings, nor, as he later recorded in an unpublished note, did he foresee the heroism with which the Belgians would, only a week later, resist the German onslaught. His attitude was also influenced by his long-felt distrust of Belgian policy in the Congo. He believed that the final decision for war would turn upon a German invasion of France, not of Belgium. If France were invaded, he told Kitchener, it would either split the Cabinet, or move the majority in favour of war.

Returning to the Admiralty on the evening of July 28, Churchill continued to supervise the general alert. But, he informed the King later that evening, none of these measures meant that war was inevitable, or that England was committed to joining. His own instinct remained conciliatory. At midnight he wrote to his wife: 'I wondered whether those stupid Kings & Emperors cd not assemble together & revivify kingship by saving the nations from hell but we all drift on in a kind of dull cataleptic trance. As if it was somebody else's operation!' When the Cabinet met on the morning of Wednesday July 29 Churchill repeated this suggestion, urging Asquith to propose a conference of European kings to try to settle the crisis without war. No official record was kept of Cabinet proceedings, but the President of the Board of Education, J. A. Pease,[1] recorded Churchill's remarks in his diary:

> Churchill said we were now in a better than average condition, & the fleet was at war strength—24 to 16 battleships in the N Sea, & 3 to 1 in the Mediterranean—the 2nd fleet could be ready in a few days, our magazines were now being protected—& flotillas placed on the North Sea—coal & oil supplies were ready. . . . Churchill, however, added: it was an appalling calamity for civilised nations to contemplate & thought possibly sovereigns could be brought together for sake of Peace.

Churchill's hopes for a royal conference led to nothing. The Cabinet decided that the time had come to send warning telegrams to all

---

[1] Joseph Albert Pease, 1860–1943. Liberal MP, 1892–1917. Chancellor of the Duchy of Lancaster, 1910–11. President of the Board of Education, 1911–15. Postmaster-General, 1916. Created Baron Gainford, 1917. Chairman of the British Broadcasting Company, 1922–6. President of the Federation of British Industries, 1927–8.

British Military, Colonial and Naval Stations, instituting a precautionary period of general alert. At two o'clock that afternoon the 'War
Book' was opened by the Secretary to the Committee of Imperial
Defence, Captain Hankey.[1] The Committee of Imperial Defence, of
which Churchill had been a member since 1907, had worked out the
specific steps which each Government Department would have to
take in time of grave emergency. A series of precautionary measures
were at once put into operation: naval harbours were cleared of all
civilian vessels, armed guards were sent to bridges and viaducts,
steamers were boarded and examined, watchers lined the coasts to spot
a hostile ship, or an invading armada. These measures were kept
entirely secret. On July 29 the Liberal MP, the Baron de Forest,[2] was
summoned by telegram to Dover, as his yacht had been ordered out of
the Harbour. Two days later Churchill wrote to his wife of how, on his
way to Dover, de Forest, had 'found every bridge & tunnel guarded &
became increasingly terrified. He telegraphed frantically clamouring
for debates & questions in Parliament. But not a man moved—not a
question nor so far any mention in the papers.'

Churchill had to prepare for naval, military and aerial action. If the
British Expeditionary Force were to go to France, the Admiralty would
have to get it there; the Royal Naval Air Service had to be adapted
to the needs of war; the Royal Marines might have to be used in
land operations. On July 29 Churchill saw Kitchener again, to discuss the military aspects of the crisis. 'He spoke of high explosive shells,'
Churchill recorded after the war in an unpublished note. 'He said that
the Germans were preparing to use these in great quantities instead of
shrapnels as these shells would not only kill the French gunners but
would blow to pieces the guns, carriages and limbers themselves. This
was the first time I had heard any British soldier raise this disagreeable
possibility.'

At their previous meeting Kitchener had impressed upon Churchill

[1] Maurice Pascal Alers Hankey, 1877–1963. Entered Royal Marine Artillery, 1895.
Captain, 1899. Retired, 1912. Secretary to the Committee of Imperial Defence, 1912–38.
Lieutenant-Colonel, Royal Marines, October 1914. Secretary to the War Council, November
1914–May 1915; to the Dardanelles Committee, May–November 1915; to the Cabinet War
Committee, December 1915–December 1916. Knighted, February 1916. Secretary to the
War Cabinet, 1916–18; to the Cabinet, 1919–38. Created Baron, 1939. Minister without
Portfolio, September 1939–May 1940. Chancellor of the Duchy of Lancaster, 1940–1.
Paymaster-General, 1941–2.

[2] Maurice Arnold de Forest, 1879–1968. An Austrian subject; hereditary Baron of the
Austrian Empire. Educated at Eton and Christchurch. Received Royal authority to use title
of Baron in the United Kingdom, 1900. Liberal MP, 1911–18. Lieutenant-Commander,
Royal Naval Volunteer Reserve, 1914, in charge of a detachment of armoured cars. Lived in
France and Liechtenstein, 1918–68.

his urgent desire to return to Egypt at once. But after telling the Field-Marshal that he had made arrangements to escort his ship from Dover, Churchill told him emphatically: 'If war comes, you will not go back to Egypt.' Both at Army manoeuvres in 1910 and at the Malta Conference of 1912, Churchill had been impressed by Kitchener. The old hostilities which there had been between them when Churchill, a subaltern, had publicly attacked Kitchener, his commander-in-chief, for his conduct of the Sudan campaign of 1898, were already assuaged by 1914. As a result of their two long conversations on July 28 and 29, Churchill had formed an even more favourable impression. He felt certain that if war came, Kitchener's presence in the Government would be a necessary strength. Asquith, he believed, could not continue to hold, as he did at that moment, the offices both of Prime Minister and of Secretary of State for War.

During the course of the Cabinet discussion on July 29, Churchill feared that the different opinions in the Cabinet, particularly over Britain's obligations to France, would prove irreconcilable and lead to the break-up of the Government. He had no desire to see a Conservative Government come to power; yet this might well be the result of a Liberal split. He therefore favoured, as he had done during the political crisis of 1910, the idea of a Coalition Government, which would demonstrate national unity, and serve as a strong governing instrument in time of crisis. It would also be a Coalition, led by Asquith, of those who were prepared to contemplate war on behalf, not only of Belgium but also of France. Lloyd George did not support Churchill entirely in his view of Britain's obligation to France. But he had looked favourably, during the political crisis of 1910, towards Coalition. Churchill was encouraged by the support of his intimate friend, the Conservative MP, F. E. Smith,[1] who was eager to see Churchill and Lloyd George working with the Conservatives as members of a national, all-Party administration. On Wednesday morning Churchill passed Lloyd George a note across the Cabinet table: 'Keep Friday night clear, FE is inquiring.' Two days later F. E. Smith approached Bonar Law,[2] Sir Edward

---

[1] Frederick Edwin Smith, 1872–1930. Known as 'F.E.'. Conservative MP, 1906–19. Head of the Press Bureau, August 1914; resigned, October 1914. Lieutenant-Colonel, attached to the Indian Corps in France, 1914–15. Solicitor-General, May 1915. Knighted, 1915. Attorney-General, November 1915–19. Created Baron Birkenhead, 1919. Lord Chancellor, 1920–2. Created Viscount, 1921. Created Earl, 1922. Secretary of State for India, 1924–8.

[2] Andrew Bonar Law, 1858–1923. Conservative MP, 1900–10; 1911–23. Parliamentary Secretary at the Board of Trade, 1902–5. Leader of the Conservatives in the House of Commons, 1911. Secretary of State for the Colonies, May 1915–December 1916. Chancellor of the Exchequer, 1916–19. Lord Privy Seal, 1919–21. Prime Minister, 1922–3.

Carson[1] and Sir Max Aitken,[2] and asked each of them whether they would be willing to join a reconstituted all-Party Government. Bonar Law, the Party Leader, rejected this suggestion.

While Churchill and his Sea Lords were at their daily Staff Meeting on the morning of Thursday July 30, a signal reached them from the *Iron Duke* to say that the First Fleet had reached the safety of the North Sea. Churchill was filled with a sense of relief. 'Always in my mind in the years of preparation,' he recorded after the war in an unpublished note, 'had been the episode of the Russian Fleet surprised by a torpedo attack at anchor off Port Arthur. Hostilities before or simultaneous with the declaration of war had been one of our many nightmares.'

Later that morning a former First Sea Lord, Admiral of the Fleet Lord Fisher,[3] arrived at the Admiralty, hoping to discover what was afoot. Fisher's achievements as First Sea Lord, and the trust which Churchill had reposed in him for over three years, meant that this old but still vigorous sailor was among the best informed of all naval officers. Fisher had made many enemies in the Service, but Churchill had a high regard for his judgement and style. In recognition of his abilities, Churchill had, in 1912, made him Chairman of the Royal Commission on Fuel and Engines, which had helped determine the change from coal-burning to oil-burning ships. In July 1914 Fisher was seventy-three years old. But the frequent letters which he sent Churchill revealed no apparent failing of his volcanic qualities. On learning that Fisher was in the Admiralty building, Churchill invited him into his room and told him that the Fleet had reached the North Sea. In *The World Crisis* Churchill later wrote: 'His delight was wonderful to see.'

[1] Edward Henry Carson, 1854–1935. Conservative MP, 1892–1921. Knighted, 1900. Solicitor-General, 1900–6. Leader of the Ulster Unionists in the House of Commons, 1910–21. Attorney-General, May–October 1915. First Lord of the Admiralty, December 1916–July 1917. Minister without Portfolio in the War Cabinet, July 1917–January 1918. Created Baron, 1921.

[2] William Maxwell Aitken, 1879–1964. A Canadian financier. Conservative MP, 1910–16. Knighted, 1911. Canadian Eye-Witness in France, May–August 1915. Canadian Representative at the Front, September 1915–16. Newspaper proprietor: bought the *Daily Express*, his largest circulation newspaper, in December 1916. Created Baron Beaverbrook, 1917. Chancellor of the Duchy of Lancaster and Minister of Information, 1918. Minister for Aircraft Production, 1940–1. Minister of State, 1941. Minister of Supply, 1941–2. Lord Privy Seal, 1943–5.

[3] John Arbuthnot Fisher, 1841–1920. Known both as 'Jackie' and, because of his somewhat oriental appearance, 'the old Malay'. Entered Navy, 1854. First Sea Lord, 1904–10. Admiral of the Fleet, 1905. Created Baron, 1909. Retired, 1911. Head of the Royal Commission on Fuel and Engines, 1912–14. Re-appointed First Sea Lord, October 1914; resigned, May 1915. Chairman of the Admiralty Inventions Board, 1915–16.

The Fleet was secure at its war station; but Churchill had to make one further decision before all was ready. Since 1911 the First Fleet had been commanded by Sir George Callaghan. In 1913 Churchill had, against tradition, extended Callaghan's command for a further year. By July 1914 this extra year had only three more months to run. As war became imminent, Churchill judged it necessary to replace Callaghan immediately, and had therefore requested him to stay behind at Portland when the Fleet sailed through the Dover Strait. Vice-Admiral Sir John Jellicoe[1] had already been selected as Callaghan's eventual successor. Churchill did not wish this long-planned change to take place during the course of war itself. No one could be certain at what moment the British and German Fleets might clash, and it would be most disruptive if such an important change in command had to take place on the eve of a major naval action. For three years Fisher had been telling Churchill that Jellicoe was the only possible Commander-in-Chief in time of war. On July 30, after discussion with Prince Louis, Churchill decided to give Jellicoe sealed instructions by which, on the outbreak of war, he would be appointed Commander-in-Chief. Later, when this decision became known in naval circles, there was momentary pandemonium. Jellicoe himself sent Churchill six telegrams in rapid succession urging Callaghan's retention: '. . . step contemplated is most dangerous,' he telegraphed on August 3. 'Quite impossible to be ready at such notice,' he reiterated on August 4; 'I feel it my duty to warn you emphatically you court disaster if you carry out intention of changing before I have thorough grip of fleet and situation.' Churchill's former Naval Secretary, Rear-Admiral Sir David Beatty,[2] also telegraphed to Churchill, insisting that the change 'would cause unprecedented disaster. . . . Moral effect upon Fleet at such a moment would be worse than a defeat at sea.'

Churchill believed that it was his duty to give Jellicoe immediate command. 'I have reached with regret the conclusion that Sir George Callaghan is not equal to the strains wh it wd entail upon the C-in-C,' he wrote to the King on July 31: 'These are not times when personal feelings can be considered unduly. We must have a younger man. Your

[1] John Rushworth Jellicoe, 1859–1935. Entered Navy, 1872. Captain, 1897. Knighted, 1907. Vice-Admiral, 1910. Second Sea Lord, 1912–14. Commander-in-Chief of the Grand Fleet, 1914–16. Admiral, 1915. First Sea Lord, 1916–17. Chief of the Naval Staff, 1917. Created Viscount, 1918. Admiral of the Fleet, 1919. Governor-General of New Zealand, 1920–4. Created Earl, 1925.

[2] David Beatty, 1871–1936. Entered Navy, 1884. Rear-Admiral, 1910. Churchill's Naval Secretary, 1912. Commander of the 1st Battle Cruiser Squadron, 1913–16. Knighted, 1914. Vice-Admiral, 1915. Commander-in-Chief of the Grand Fleet, 1916–18. First Sea Lord, 1919–27. Created Earl, 1919. Admiral of the Fleet, 1919.

Majesty knows well the purely physical exertion wh the command of a gt fleet demands.'

Clementine Churchill, who was concerned about the aftermath of the change, wrote to her husband on August 4:

Burn this
My Darling,

I have been cogitating for an hour or two over the 'Callico Jellatine' crisis, which, Thank God, is over as far as essentials are concerned.

There only remains the deep wound in an old man's heart.

If you put the wrong sort of poultice on, it will fester—(Do not be vexed, when you are so occupied with vital things my writing to you about this, which, in its way, is important too.) An interview with the Sovereign and a decoration to my mind is the wrong practice—To a proud sensitive man, at this moment a decoration must be an insult.

Please see him yourself & take him by the hand and (additional) offer him a seat on the Board, or if this is impossible give him *some* advisory position at the Admiralty. It does not matter if he 'cannot say Boo to a Goose'—His lips will then be sealed and his wife's too—don't think this is a trivial matter. At this moment you want everyone's heart & soul—you don't want even a small clique of retired people to feel bitter & to cackle. If you give him a position of honour and confidence, the whole service will feel that he has been as well treated as possible under the circumstances, & that he has not been humiliated.

This will prevent people now at the top of the Tree feeling 'In a few years *I* shall be cast off like an old shoe'—Jellicoe & Beatty & Warrender[1] & Bailey[2] now the flower of the service are only a few years younger than Callaghan.

Then, don't underrate the power of women to do mischief. I don't want Lady Callaghan[3] & Lady Bridgeman[4] to form a league of retired Officers' Cats, to abuse you. Poor old Lady Callaghan's grief will be intense but if you are good to him now it will be softened; if he is still employed she is bound to be comparatively silent.

Anyhow I beg of you to see him——

If I were doing it—If he refused the appointment I would earnestly urge

[1] George John Scott Warrender, 1860–1917. Entered Navy, 1873. 7th Baronet, 1901. Rear-Admiral, 1908. Knighted, 1911. Commanded the 2nd Battle Squadron, 1912–15. Vice-Admiral, 1913. Removed from his command on Jellicoe's advice as a result of increasing deafness and absent-mindedness, December 1915.

[2] Lewis Bayly, 1857–1938. Entered Navy, 1870. Vice-Admiral commanding the 3rd Battle Squadron, 1913–14. Knighted, 1914. Commanded the 1st Battle Squadron, 1914–15. Commander-in-Chief of the Western Approaches, 1915–19. Admiral, 1917.

[3] Edith Saumarez Grosvenor, *c.* 1856–1939. Daughter of the Rev Frederick Grosvenor, rector of Dunkerton, Bath. Married (Sir) George Callaghan, 1876.

[4] Emily Charlotte Shiffner, 1842–1922. Married, 1889, (Sir) Francis Charles Bridgeman-Bridgeman (1848–1929). He was First Sea Lord, 1911; Churchill replaced him by Prince Louis in 1912.

him again & again (thro' Prince Louis or Graham Greene[1]) to accept it, saying you need his services—then he will believe it & come round & there will not be any disagreeableness left from this difficult business. . . .

There was no place for Callaghan on the Board of Admiralty, but Churchill did offer him an advisory post at the Admiralty. On 1 January 1915 he was appointed Commander-in-Chief of the Nore, and held this command until 1918. In 1917 he was promoted Admiral of the Fleet.

On leaving the Admiralty building on July 30 Fisher had met the former Conservative Prime Minister, A. J. Balfour,[2] and explained to him the gravity of the situation. He also passed on the news of Callaghan's impending dismissal. On the following day Fisher followed up their conversation with a letter:

Dear Mr Balfour,
With our conversation of yesterday fresh in my mind as to Winston scrapping Admirals 'with a courageous stroke of the pen'! I want to mention to you that since being a Midshipman I have adored the English principle of having *civilian* First Lords of Admiralty, because I read how Lord Spencer, then First Lord, on his own initiative and against the Navy traditions sent Nelson to the Mediterranean over the head of Sir John Orde and others (who had their Flags flying), and *hence we got the Battle of the Nile!* The finest of all sea fights since the world began! . . . So *NOW* we get Jellicoe as Admiralissimo, and there will be a hell of a row among the Admirals! (If there is, I've promised Winston to go on the stump!)
Yours truly
Fisher

In his postscript Fisher wrote: 'I know you won't breathe a word of all I said yesterday, but the "*completeness*" of everything is lovely!' He also found time that day to give Churchill some advice on another naval matter:

My dear Winston,
I have just received a most patriotic letter from Deterding[3] to say he means you shant want for oil or tankers in case of war. GOOD OLD DETERDING!

[1] William Graham Greene, 1857–1950. Entered Admiralty, 1881. Private Secretary to successive First Lords of the Admiralty, 1887–1902. Principal Clerk, Admiralty, 1902–7. Assistant Secretary, Admiralty, 1907–11. Knighted, 1911. Permanent Secretary, Admiralty, 1911–17. Secretary, Ministry of Munitions, 1917–20.
[2] Arthur James Balfour, 1848–1930. Conservative MP, 1874–85; 1885–1906; 1906–22. Prime Minister, 1902–5. First Lord of the Admiralty, 1915–16. Foreign Secretary, 1916–19. Lord President to the Council, 1919–22; 1925–9. Created Earl, 1922.
[3] Henri Wilhelm August Deterding, 1866–1939. Director-General of the Royal Dutch Petroleum Company; a Director of the Shell Transport and Trading Company Limited. A Dutch citizen, he received an honorary knighthood in 1921.

How these Dutchmen do hate the Germans! Knight him when you get the chance . . .

I enjoyed seeing you immensely & those devilled whitebait were delicious!

Yours till a cinder!

Fisher

In his postscript, Fisher gave Churchill a breezy description of his encounter with Balfour: 'Arthur Balfour rushed into my arms as I walked out of the Admiralty and he thanked God that you were First Lord! *This was absolutely spontaneous on his part!* Dont you think it was nice of him? He was going to Gastein in Austria to-morrow, but had just cancelled going!'

It was over four years since Fisher had reached the end of his Naval career. He believed that his own energies and abilities were greater than those of Prince Louis, whose calm behaviour contrasted in every way to his own exuberance. Churchill wanted Fisher's energies at his side and in his service. But the old Admiral remained a spectator, lurking about the streets of Whitehall, penetrating at times into the corridors of the Admiralty, writing each day to a large circle of intimates of all professions and Parties, and eagerly circulating stories about his own activities. More than a week after his visit to Churchill he was still excited by it, writing to Hankey on August 8: 'I got so hot talking that I got a bad chill coming down late and got a severe attack of pleurisy.' The attack soon passed.

On July 30 the Admiralty learned that one of the most powerful ships in the German Navy, the battle-cruiser *Goeben*, mounting ten 11-inch guns, was about to leave the Austrian port of Pola in the Adriatic, and sail into the Mediterranean. In the event of war between France and Germany, the *Goeben* would have an easy task sinking French troopships as they transported soldiers from Algeria to France. France would need these soldiers desperately, yet only the British Navy had sufficient fire-power to prevent the *Goeben* from carrying out such attacks. Churchill could not know either whether Germany would attack France, or whether Britain would come to France's aid. But he saw it as his duty to take steps to cover such an eventuality. He therefore signalled to the commander of the Second Battle Cruiser Squadron, Admiral Sir Berkeley Milne:[1]

Should war break out and England and France engage in it . . . your first task should be to aid the French in the transportation of their African army by covering and if possible bringing to action individual fast German ships, particularly Goeben, which may interfere with that transportation. You will be notified by telegraph when you may consult with the French Admiral.[2] Do not at this stage be brought to action against superior forces except in combination with the French as part of a general battle. The speed of your Squadrons is sufficient to enable you to choose your moment. . . .

That Thursday night Churchill dined with Asquith: 'serene as ever', Churchill wrote next morning to his wife, 'but he backs me well in all the necessary measures'. He also described some of the Admiralty preparations, unable to curb his pride that all was proceeding smoothly. 'I am deeply interested by all you tell me in your letter,' she replied on August 3; 'I much wish I were with you during these anxious thrilling days & know how you are feeling—tingling with life to the tips of your fingers.' She also sent him the family news:

The babies are well and blooming. They were utterly disappointed when they saw Jack[3] coming down the cliff towards the Beach & found it was *not* their Papa but John George's.[4]

Randolph asked persevering questions for 5 minutes about your absence. He is now resigned, but not convinced of its necessity! I tried to telephone to you 3 times today (to the office) but each time the line was engaged.

On the afternoon of July 30 the French Naval Attaché, the Comte de Saint-Seine,[5] called at the Admiralty to propose on behalf of the French Admiralty, as Prince Louis recorded in an official note of the conversation: 'That the signal-books which have been prepared for use between the two fleets in the event of an active Alliance between the two Countries being concluded, and which are now in the hands of the principal Flag Officers of both fleets, in sealed packets ready for distri-

[1] Archibald Berkeley Milne, 1855–1938. Entered Navy, 1869. Rear-Admiral, 1903. Knighted, 1904. Admiral, 1911. Commander-in-Chief of the Mediterranean Fleet, 1912–14.
[2] Auguste Emmanuel Hubert Gaston Marie Boué de Lapeyrère, 1852–1924. Minister of Marine, 1909–11. Vice-Admiral Commanding the French naval forces, Mediterranean, 1914–15.
[3] John Strange Spencer Churchill, 1880–1947. Churchill's younger brother, known as Jack. A stockbroker. Major, Queen's Own Oxfordshire Hussars, 1914–18. Served at Dunkirk, 1914; on Sir John French's staff, 1914–15; on Sir Ian Hamilton's staff, 1915; on General Birdwood's staff, 1916–18.
[4] John George Spencer Churchill, 1909–   . Churchill's nephew. Artist.
[5] Jean Charles Just Benigne de Saint-Seine, 1865–1954. French Naval Attaché in London, 1911–16. Commanded the battleship *Démocratie* in the eastern Mediterranean, 1916.

bution—should be distributed amongst the individual ships forthwith.'
Churchill acted with restraint. This was a matter not for the two
Admiralties, he replied, but for the two Cabinets. In forwarding the
proposal to Grey, Churchill advised that 'such action was premature',
and that 'our strength & preparedness enable us to wait'.

Churchill believed that in the event of war it would not be enough for
the Fleet to remain inactive at Scapa Flow or patrolling the open waters
of the North Sea, even if by such a relatively static policy the Germans
would be prevented from launching an invasion of Britain or winning
a decisive naval victory. In January 1913 he had instructed Rear-
Admiral Sir Lewis Bayly to study the possibility of some offensive action
such as a British force seizing a base on the Dutch, German, Danish or
Scandinavian coasts on the outbreak of war with Germany. Rear-

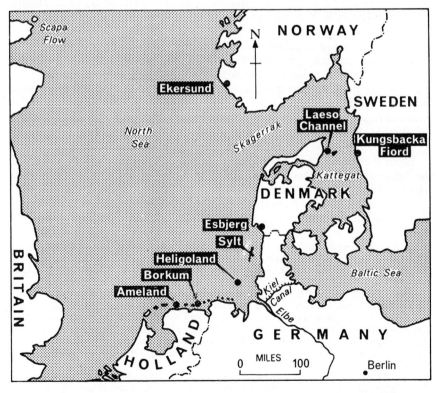

POSSIBLE BRITISH BASES INTENDED FOR OFFENSIVE
OPERATIONS AGAINST GERMANY, 1913–14

Admiral Leveson,[1] and a Royal Marine Officer, Sir George Aston,[2] had worked with Bayly. Within six months they had submitted to Churchill a series of reports on the capture of the German islands of Borkum, Sylt and Heligoland, and the Danish town of Esbjerg. They also examined a plan for seizing the western end of the Kiel Canal, to be followed by a raid up the Elbe by six destroyers, each equipped with torpedoes and explosives. 'Keep the people across the North Sea quiet till July,' Bayly had written to Churchill on 22 February 1914, 'then, as soon as you like.'

On July 31 Churchill sent copies of the Admiralty reports to Asquith. His covering letter was marked 'Most Secret':

Prime Minister,

Last year by my directions Admiral Bayly, Colonel Aston & Admiral Leveson made a prolonged examination of all points on the German, Dutch, Danish, Swedish & Norwegian coasts, suitable for oversea bases for offensive action against Germany.

Their reports are attached with charts etc.

It is now necessary that the War Office shd study these plans so that military and naval action can be coordinated & concerted in harmony.

Two officers of highest attainments shd therefore be detailed in strictest secrecy for this duty. Reports shd deal with each project separately, and without regard either to (a) questions of violation of neutrality (b) questions of whether the troops could be better employed elsewhere. These are matters of policy wh must be decided later by higher authorities.

From the Admiralty Colonel Aston, & Major Ollivant[3] will be detailed: & Admiral Leveson will be available if naval questions require further elucidation.

No time shd be lost. Reports shd be furnished one by one. I do not now discuss the questions of policy.

[1] Arthur Cavenagh Leveson, 1868–1929. Midshipman, 1883. Rear-Admiral, 1913. Director of Operations Division, Admiralty, 1914–15. Served at the Battle of Jutland, 1916. Knighted, 1919. Commanded the Second Battle Squadron, 1919–20. Commander-in-Chief, China Station, 1922–4.

[2] George Grey Aston, 1861–1938. Entered Royal Marine Artillery, 1879. Naval Intelligence Department, Admiralty, 1887–90. Professor of Fortification, Royal Naval College, Greenwich, 1896–9. Brigadier-General, General Staff, South Africa, 1908–12. Attached to the Admiralty War Staff for special services, 1913–14. Knighted, 1913. Commanded the Marine expeditions to Ostend and Dunkirk, 1914. Retired from active service through ill-health, 1914. Employed in the War Cabinet Secretariat 1918–19. Military historian and biographer.

[3] Alfred Henry Ollivant, 1871–1919. Entered Royal Artillery, 1891. Major, 1911. General Staff Officer attached to the Colonial Office, 1909–11, and to the Admiralty, 1913–14. Lieutenant-Colonel, September 1914. Attached to the Royal Naval Division at Antwerp, October 1914; the Dardanelles, 1915; France, 1916–17.

The following shd be the order in wh the work shd be undertaken.

1. Ameland or Born Deep [the channel on the western side of Ameland]
2. Ekersund
3. Laeso Channel
4. Kungsbacka Fiord
5. Esbjerg
6. Sylt ⎫ These last 4 are less urgent on account of the forces
7. Borkum ⎬ required being probably not available.
8. Heligoland ⎭

WSC

Asquith agreed that these studies should proceed, and instructed a General Staff Officer from the War Office, Major Hereward Wake,[1] to co-operate with the Admiralty.

None of these plans implied that Britain would necessarily go to war; Churchill was himself uncertain. 'There is still hope,' he wrote to his wife on July 31, 'although the clouds are blacker & blacker. Germany is realising I think how great are the forces against her & is trying tardily to restrain her idiot ally. We are working to soothe Russia.' On July 31 Arthur Ponsonby,[2] a leading Liberal non-interventionist, wrote to Churchill of 'the very strong feeling' in the Liberal Party that Britain should avoid being drawn into war, and concluded: 'You are probably living at the moment in an atmosphere of expert strategists and of naval and military men some of whom may hold the view that "this is our moment to strike". It is important therefore that you should know how very widespread the opposite view is so that you may use all your influence towards moderation.' Churchill replied that same day: 'So long as no treaty obligation or true British interest is involved I am of your opinion that we shd remain neutral. Balkan quarrels are no vital concern of ours.' But at lunch that day at Admiralty House, Kitchener told Churchill that a German attack on France was the real danger. Asquith, who was also present at the lunch, reported to Venetia Stanley,[3] in whom at this time he increasingly confided, that Kitchener

---

[1] Hereward Wake, 1876–1963. Entered Army, 1897. Major at the War Office, 1914. 13th Baronet, 1916. Brigadier-General, General Staff, 1917. Commanded the 4th Battalion in India, 1920–3. Major-General, 1932.

[2] Arthur Augustus William Harry Ponsonby, 1871–1949. Liberal MP, 1908–18. Labour MP, 1922–30. Under-Secretary of State for Foreign Affairs, 1924; Parliamentary Secretary Ministry of Transport, 1929–31. Created Baron Ponsonby of Shulbrede, 1930. Chancellor of the Duchy of Lancaster, 1931. Leader of the Opposition in the House of Lords, 1931–5.

[3] Beatrice Venetia Stanley, 1887–1948. Clementine Churchill's cousin. On 26 July 1915 she married Edwin Montagu. Of some of Asquith's letters, Churchill wrote in *Great Contemporaries*: 'They were addressed to brighter eyes than peer through politicians' spectacles'; hers were the eyes to which he was referring.

believed 'that if we don't back up France when she is in real danger, we shall never be regarded or exercise real power again'.

Churchill's friend and best man, Lord Hugh Cecil,[1] was one of the few Conservatives who advocated a neutral policy for Britain. He wrote to Churchill, expressing his fears that Britain would go to war without sufficient cause. 'My dear Linky,' Churchill replied on July 31. 'Divergent views are certainly to be expected in the gt issues now afoot. But you will be wrong if you suppose that this country will be committed to any war in wh its profound national interests—among wh I include its honour—are not clearly engaged.' Lord Robert Cecil[2] was aware of his brother Hugh's dissent, writing to Churchill on August 1 in more pugnacious mood, pledging his fellow Conservatives to an interventionist policy. 'I think it well to inform you,' Cecil wrote, 'that I am confident that if the Govt decide to take action whether by the despatch of an expeditionary force or otherwise they may count on the support of the whole Unionist party. I gather from Linkey that he has had some correspondence with you which may have produced a false impression on this point on your mind. Whatever his personal views may be I am sure that he would take no public action inconsistent with this view.' F. E. Smith wrote to Churchill in similar vein about the Conservative attitude to war on July 31. He had failed to interest Bonar Law and his senior Party colleagues in the idea of a Coalition, but gave Churchill an assurance that 'on the facts as we understand them—& more particularly on the assumption (which we understand to be certain) that Germany contemplates a violation of Belgian neutrality—the Government can rely upon the support of the Unionist party'. Churchill replied on August 1:

My dear FE,
    Very grateful for your letter with its generous and patriotic offer. I read it to the Cabinet, where it produced a profound impression. I cannot think war will be averted now. Germany *must* march through Belgium, and I believe that the bulk of both parties will stand firm against that. I really think you and BL ought to be in London on Sunday. It would give me great

---

[1] Lord Hugh Richard Heathcote Gascoyne Cecil, 1869–1956. Known as 'Linky'. Fifth son of the 3rd Marquess of Salisbury. Conservative MP, 1895–1906; 1910–37. Provost of Eton, 1936–44. Created Baron Quickswood, 1941.

[2] Lord Edgar Algernon Robert Cecil, 1864–1958. Third son of the 3rd Marquess of Salisbury. Independent Conservative MP, 1911–23. Under-Secretary of State for Foreign Affairs, 1915–16. Minister of Blockade, 1916–18. Created Viscount Cecil of Chelwood, 1923. Lord Privy Seal, 1923–4. President of the League of Nations Union, 1923–45. Chancellor of the Duchy of Lancaster, 1924–7. Nobel Peace Prize, 1937.

pleasure if you would both come and lunch or dine with me here. I could put you thoroughly au fait.

Yours always
W

By the morning of August 1 Churchill felt certain that Germany intended to attack France and to violate Belgian neutrality. He also felt confident, as a result of the letters from Lord Robert Cecil and F. E. Smith, that the Conservative Party would support the Government if it decided to go to France's aid. He therefore asked the Cabinet that morning to authorize full naval mobilization. But the Cabinet was still divided. Lloyd George remained reluctant to commit Britain in support of France. The Governor of the Bank of England, Walter Cunliffe,[1] had called at the Treasury that morning to tell Lloyd George that bankers and businessmen in the City of London were, as Lloyd George recalled in his *War Memoirs*, 'totally opposed to our intervening in the war'. Asquith characterized the deepening conflict in a letter to Venetia Stanley: 'Lloyd George, all for peace, is more sensible and statesman-like for keeping the position open . . . Winston very bellicose and demanding immediate mobilization.' Asquith did not inform her that he himself had approved Churchill's original naval initiative in sending the Fleet into the North Sea, or that he, like Churchill, was in favour of coming to France's aid. 'The people have not the smallest enthusiasm for war,' Hankey wrote to his wife on August 1.

Lloyd George was probably the only Cabinet Minister with the ability to lead neutralist opinion. Had he declared himself forcefully against British intervention in Europe, a majority of the Cabinet, and even of the Liberal Party in the House of Commons, might have followed his lead.

Churchill made every effort to persuade Lloyd George of the need to support France from the outset of the conflict. In a series of notes which passed between them across the Cabinet Table he used strong appeals, to patriotism, to ambition and to personal friendship, in order to influence the Chancellor of the Exchequer. He also asked Major Ollivant, whom the War Office had sent in 1913 as its liaison officer with the Admiralty War Staff, to try to influence Lloyd George. The Director of Military Operations at the War Office, General Wilson,[2] noted in his

---

[1] Walter Cunliffe, 1855–1920. Governor of the Bank of England, 1913–18. Created Baron, December 1914. Employed on a Special Mission to the United States, 1917.

[2] Henry Hughes Wilson, 1864–1922. Entered Army, 1884. Director of Military Operations, War Office, 1910–14. Lieutenant-General, 1914. Chief liaison officer with the French Army, January 1915. Knighted, April 1915. Commanded the 4th Corps, 1916. Chief of the Imperial General Staff, 1918–22. Shot dead by Sinn Feiners on the steps of his London house.

diary on August 1: 'Ollivant to see me at 4.00 pm and report that Winston wanted him to lecture Lloyd George on European military situation!' That afternoon Ollivant sent Lloyd George a memorandum setting out the strategic arguments for immediate British participation. 'Germany's chief object, as far as this country is concerned,' he declared, 'lies in preventing the arrival of the British expeditionary army. Its absence from the battlefield will exercise an influence out of all proportion to its numerical strength. . . . There is reason to suppose that the presence or absence of the British army will determine the action of the Belgian army. It will very probably decide the fate of France.' Lloyd George did not brush aside this argument in favour of British intervention in Europe. Two days later Asquith wrote to Venetia Stanley that it was not Grey or Churchill who had appealed to the remaining neutralists in the Cabinet not to resign, but Lloyd George. But on August 1 a majority of the Cabinet were unwilling to follow the arguments which Grey and Churchill put forward. When Grey asked for a decision about whether Britain would eventually send an expeditionary force to France, the Cabinet decided firmly against it. Grey had on several occasions hinted to Paul Cambon,[1] the French Ambassador in London, that if Germany was the aggressor, Britain would stand by France. But France had nothing in writing to that effect. If Britain went to war to help France, it would have to be on a point of honour, not of obligation.

When news of these Cabinet hesitations reached Printing House Square, Geoffrey Robinson,[2] the editor of *The Times*, wrote to his aunts: 'Saturday was a black day for everyone who knew what was going on—more than half the Cabinet rotten and every prospect of a complete schism or a disastrous and dishonouring refusal to help France. . . . Winston has really done more than anyone else to save the situation.'

On the night of August 1 Churchill dined alone at the Admiralty. In Europe the diplomatic crisis continued upon its apparently uncertain course. 'The news tonight opens again hope,' he wrote to Lord Robert Cecil after dinner; and as he read the telegrams coming in from the European capitals throughout the evening he felt that peace might be preserved. No armies were yet in conflict; no frontiers had yet been crossed. At about half past nine F. E. Smith and Sir Max Aitken called to see him. He told them of his impression that there was still a chance

---

[1] Paul Cambon, 1843–1924. French Ambassador in London, 1898–1920. Honorary knighthood, 1903. One of the most active promoters of the Anglo-French Entente of 1904.

[2] Geoffrey Robinson, 1874–1944. Private Secretary to Lord Milner, South Africa, 1901–5. Editor of *The Times*, 1912–19 and 1925–41. He assumed the surname of Dawson in 1917. His aunts were Katherine Elizabeth Perfect and Margaret Jane Perfect (who changed her name to Dawson in 1900).

of peace, or at least of war being staved off for a while. 'The suspense was becoming intolerable,' he later wrote in an unpublished note. 'I was to see the Prime Minister at 11 that night. Meanwhile there was nothing to be done. We sat down at a card table and began a game of bridge. The cards had just been dealt when another red Foreign Office box came in. I opened it and read "War declared by Germany on Russia".'

Churchill knew that a German attack on Russia would probably set off a chain of consequences that would destroy all chance of Britain remaining neutral. Leaving his two friends, he crossed the Horse Guards' Parade to 10 Downing Street to inform Asquith that, despite the Cabinet's earlier refusal, he wished to issue an immediate order for full naval mobilization. Grey, Lord Haldane[1] and Lord Crewe[2] were already with the Prime Minister. Churchill told them all that he would answer for this decision at the Cabinet on the following morning. In 1928 he recounted Asquith's reaction to his request in a letter to Max Aitken, then Lord Beaverbrook:

... The Prime Minister simply sat and looked at me and said no word. No doubt he felt himself bound by the morning's decision of the Cabinet. I certainly however sustained the impression that he would not put out a finger to stop me. I then walked back to the Admiralty across the Parade Ground and gave the order. Legal authority was not obtained until the Sunday. ... However all the Reserves came up immediately with hardly one hundred exceptions, in spite of there being no Royal Proclamation. ... The actual fact which is of interest for the future is that the mobilization was actually ordered against Cabinet decision and without legal authority.

It was shortly after midnight when Churchill returned to the Admiralty. 'I cannot think the rupture with Germany can be long delayed,' he wrote to Lord Robert Cecil. Then he wrote to his wife, who had written to him on the previous day that 'it would be a wicked war':

Cat—dear,
    It is all up. Germany has quenched the last hopes of peace by declaring war on Russia, & the declaration against France is momentarily expected.

[1] Richard Burdon Haldane, 1856–1928. Liberal MP, 1885–1911. Secretary of State for War, 1905–12. Created Viscount, 1911. Lord Chancellor, first under Asquith, 1912–15; then under Ramsay MacDonald, 1924.
[2] Robert Offley Ashburton Crewe-Milnes, 1858–1945. Lord-Lieutenant of Ireland, 1892–5. Secretary of State for India, 1910–15. Created Marquess of Crewe, 1911. Lord President of the Council, 1915–16. President of the Board of Education, 1916. Ambassador to Paris, 1922–8. Secretary of State for War, 1931.

I profoundly understand your view. But the world is gone mad—& we must look after ourselves—& our friends. . . .

Sweet Kat—my tender love—

Your devoted
W

Kiss the kittens.

On the morning of Sunday August 2 the Cabinet ratified Churchill's initiative.

On August 1 the German battle-cruiser *Goeben* put in at the Italian port of Brindisi to coal, but was refused permission to do so. On August 2 she was refused coal at Taranto. She then sailed westwards, in the hope of coaling at Messina. News of these movements reached the Admiralty on August 2. Churchill and Prince Louis telegraphed at once to Sir Berkeley Milne: '"Goeben" must be shadowed by two battle-cruisers. Approach [to] Adriatic must be watched by cruisers and destroyers. Remain near Malta yourself. It is believed that Italy will remain neutral but you cannot yet count absolutely on this knowledge.'

The movements of the *Goeben* were a constant anxiety to Churchill during the first four days of August. He bore a heavy responsibility for any possible moves by the potential enemy, and had to make plans for action before it could be known when, or in what circumstances, war would begin.

When the Cabinet met on the evening of August 2, Ministers learned that Germany had invaded Luxembourg. This was evidence of the German intention to invade Belgium. It was clear at last that whether or not the Cabinet decided to honour its unwritten obligation to France, Britain could be drawn into war on account of its written pledge to Belgium. After consulting with Grey and Haldane, Asquith gave immediate written authority for the mobilization of the Army. With Cabinet approval, Churchill returned to the Admiralty and telegraphed to all Commanders-in-Chief instructing them to make direct contact with their French opposite numbers: 'Situation very critical. Be prepared to meet surprise attacks. You can enter into communication with the French Senior Officer on your station for combined action in case Great Britain should decide to become ally of France against Germany.' Churchill then telegraphed to Jellicoe, informing him that despite all his protests, he had become Commander-in-Chief of the First Fleet.

On the morning of Monday August 3 the Cabinet learned of the German ultimatum to Belgium. Almost all the Ministers accepted that Britain must intervene on Belgium's behalf. Lloyd George took the lead in arguing against Lord Morley[1] and Sir John Simon,[2] who were still opposed to any British involvement in the war. Churchill tried to influence Morley against resignation, but in vain. Morley resigned; Simon agreed to remain. That afternoon Grey spoke to the House of Commons. He gave the House its first official account of the main development of the crisis, and warned of the possibility of a German attack through Belgium which might force Britain to go to war. As soon as Grey's speech was over, he left the Commons, and Churchill went out with him. In *The World Crisis* Churchill recalled their conversation. 'What happens now?' he asked. 'Now,' replied Grey, 'we shall send them an ultimatum to stop the invasion of Belgium within twenty-four hours.' As Churchill left the Commons, Lord Hugh Cecil rushed up. Seizing Churchill violently, he accused him of being responsible for all that had happened. Churchill could not calm his friend. Immediately on reaching his room at the Admiralty, Churchill wrote to Asquith and Grey:

In consequence of declarations in the House this afternoon, I must request authorisation immediately to put into force the combined Anglo-French dispositions for the defence of the channel. The French have already taken station & this partial disposition does not ensure security.

My naval colleagues & advisers desire me to press for this; & unless I am forbidden I shall act accordingly.

This of course implies no offensive action & no warlike action unless we are attacked.

Both Asquith and Grey gave their approval to full Anglo-French naval collaboration. The Cabinet were not consulted. On the authority of the Prime Minister and two of his colleagues, the Entente Cordiale of 1904 was thereby turned into a working alliance. No formal treaty marked this transformation. The House of Commons, which had never approved of anything more than a sentimental Entente with France, was never

[1] John Morley, 1838–1923. Liberal MP, 1883–1908. Secretary of State for India, 1905–10. Created Viscount Morley of Blackburn, 1908. Lord President of the Council, 1910–14. Resigned from the Government in protest against the coming war, August 1914. Biographer.

[2] John Allsebrook Simon, 1873–1954. Liberal MP, 1906–18; 1922–31. Solicitor-General, 1910–13. Knighted, 1911. Attorney-General, with a seat in the Cabinet, 1913–15. Home Secretary, May 1915–January 1916, when he resigned in opposition to conscription. Major, Royal Air Force, serving in France, 1917–18. Liberal National MP, 1931–40. Secretary of State for Foreign Affairs, 1931–5. Home Secretary, 1935–7. Chancellor of the Exchequer, 1937–40. Created Viscount, 1940. Lord Chancellor, 1940–5.

asked to debate or vote upon the greater responsibilities and binding features of what was now decided. Under the immediate pressures of an unexpected crisis, Asquith, Grey and Churchill finally ended the policy of British isolation from Europe which had for so long been the policy of successive Conservative and Liberal Administrations.

Throughout Tuesday August 4 the Cabinet waited to learn whether German troops would indeed cross the Belgian frontier. Churchill had no doubt that this was the German intention. He had been present at a meeting of the Committee of Imperial Defence in 1911 when General Wilson had demonstrated, on a large wall map, the strategic reasons why a German attack on France would begin by a thrust through Belgium. Churchill, after initial disagreement, had accepted the soundness of Wilson's views; now he could only wait for them to be put to the test.

That morning Kitchener left London to return to Egypt. At noon he was on his way to Dover by train, intending to embark that afternoon on a fast destroyer. During the morning Churchill went to see Asquith at 10 Downing Street. He left an account of their meeting in an unpublished note among his papers:

I pointed out to the Prime Minister the impossibility of his continuing to hold the seals of the Secretary of State for War as well as those of his own supreme office. I pointed to the continuous flow of inter-departmental work which must proceed between the War Office and the Admiralty which must be transacted between Ministers and with which the Prime Minister could not possibly be burdened. I asked him whether he would consider the appointment of Lord Kitchener.

I could see by Mr Asquith's reception of my remarks that his mind was moving, or had already moved, along the same path. Action was taken the same day: the Field-Marshal was intercepted at Dover and invited to take office.

Churchill had become increasingly worried about the situation in the Mediterranean. He was afraid that the *Goeben* would begin its attacks on French troopships unimpeded, despite the presence in the Mediterranean of powerful British squadrons. On August 2 he had ordered Milne to send his two battle-cruisers, the *Indomitable* and the *Indefatigable*, to find the *Goeben* and 'follow her and shadow her wherever she goes and be ready to act on declaration of war which appears probable and imminent'. He was also instructed to keep close watch on a German light cruiser, the *Breslau*, which was with her. On the morning of August 4 he learned that both the *Goeben* and the *Breslau* had at last been sighted. Having left Messina and sailed westward, they were being

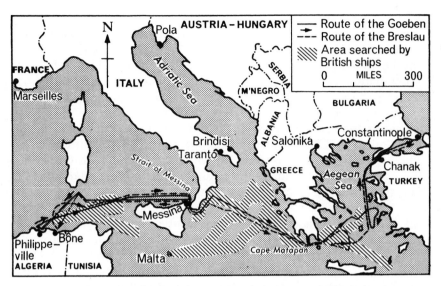

ROUTE OF 'GOEBEN' AND 'BRESLAU' FROM MESSINA (2 AUGUST 1914) TO THE ALGERIAN COAST (4 AUGUST 1914) AND THENCE TO CONSTANTINOPLE (11 AUGUST 1914)

closely followed by the two British ships. During August 4 the *Goeben* began to bombard the French North African port of Philippeville. Because Britain was not yet at war with Germany, it was impossible for the British ships following her to take action. At the same time, the *Breslau* bombarded Bône, likewise without interruption. Churchill was determined to prevent these two ships from doing further damage to French ports and fortifications. He pressed Asquith and Grey to approve the action which he had already ordered, giving them his reasons: 'It would be a great misfortune to lose these vessels as is possible in the dark hours. She is evidently going to interfere with the French transports which are crossing today. The following telegram has been sent: "Good. Hold her. War imminent." We wish to add this: "If Goeben attacks French transports you should at once engage her." An immediate decision is required.'

Anticipating a favourable reply from Asquith to this request, Churchill telegraphed to Sir Berkeley Milne shortly after midday: 'If Goeben attacks French transports you should at once engage her. You should give him fair warning of this beforehand.'

The Cabinet met immediately after Churchill had sent this telegram.

'Winston,' Asquith wrote to Venetia Stanley, 'who has got on all his war paint, is longing for a sea fight in the early hours of the morning to result in the sinking of the Goeben.' Churchill explained to his colleagues why he wanted them to agree to immediate action. They refused to contemplate naval support for France before Britain's formal declaration of war, and would not sanction the action which Churchill had already ordered. No act of war could be allowed before the British ultimatum expired. Immediately on his return to the Admiralty, at two that afternoon, Churchill telegraphed a caution to all British ships: 'The British ultimatum to Germany will expire at midnight GMT[1] 4th August. No acts of war should be committed before that hour, at which time the telegram to commence hostilities against Germany will be despatched from Admiralty.' A special addition to this signal had to be sent to Milne: 'This cancels the authorisation to "Indomitable" and "Indefatigable" to engage "Goeben" if she attacks French transports.' Milne was also warned not to follow the *Goeben* or the *Breslau* too closely to the Italian shore: 'The Italian government have declared neutrality. You are to respect this neutrality rigidly and should not allow any of HM Ships to come within six miles of the Italian coasts.' Later that afternoon Prince Louis remonstrated with Churchill; only if immediate action were taken would there still be time to sink the *Goeben* before sunset; once it was dark, she could disappear in any direction. But, as a result of the Cabinet decision, Churchill was powerless to act.

The Germans never replied to Britain's demand to respect Belgian neutrality. As the evening of August 4 progressed, the Liberal Ministers realized that their ultimatum was leading inexorably to war. Churchill returned to the Admiralty and at ten to six, greatly afraid that the Germans might attempt some surprise attack, telegraphed to every ship's captain in the Royal Navy: 'The war telegram will be issued at midnight authorizing you commence hostilities against Germany. But in view of terms our ultimatum they may decide open fire at any moment. You must be ready for this.'

On the evening of August 4 Churchill dined at Admiralty House with his mother, Lady Randolph Churchill,[2] his brother Jack, and Geoffrey

---

[1] This was a mistake on Churchill's part. The British ultimatum was due to expire at midnight German time, 11.00 pm GMT.

[2] Jennie Jerome, 1854–1921. Daughter of Leonard Jerome of New York. Married Lord Randolph Churchill, 1874. Mother of Winston and Jack Churchill. Editor of the *Anglo-Saxon Review*, 1899–1901. Married George Cornwallis-West, 1900; marriage dissolved, 1913. Married Montagu Porch, 1918.

Robinson, who had singled out Churchill in *The Times* that morning as the one Minister 'whose grasp of the situation and whose efforts to meet it have been above all praise'. After dinner Churchill held a conference with a number of senior French Admirals, who were anxious to share a British naval base in the Mediterranean from which they could protect their civil trade and military transports against German attack. Churchill responded with alacrity, informing the French Admirals that they could use the naval facilities of Malta as if it were Toulon. A few days later he gave them similar facilities at Gibraltar.

The Germans ignored the British ultimatum. They were determined to march through Belgium, wanting first to defeat the French Army before turning eastwards against Russia. The British ultimatum expired at eleven o'clock British time, midnight German time. At eleven o'clock, from the Admiralty building, Churchill authorized the signal to all ships: 'Commence hostilities at once with Germany. . . .' Then, at a quarter past eleven, he hurried to 10 Downing Street to inform the Prime Minister that the war signal had been sent.

In May 1915 Lloyd George gave Margot Asquith[1] his recollections of what had happened in the Cabinet room that night, and in her diary she recorded Lloyd George's words: 'Winston dashed into the room, radiant, his face bright, his manner keen, one word pouring out on another how he was going to send telegrams to the Mediterranean, the North Sea, and God knows where. You could see he was a really happy man.' Churchill had relished the activity of the crisis and been stimulated by the increasing pressures. The Fleet seemed ready for every strain and challenge. The ships needed to protect Britain's commercial arteries were all in their places, alert and armed. The French Navy was working in harness with its British counterpart. The North Sea had not been left defenceless. The German Fleet could no longer land an invasion force on the east coast without being intercepted. When war came, Churchill was exhilarated, both because Britain's naval preparations were complete, and because he believed that he now had the power to control events at the storm centre. On July 28 he had described his feelings in a letter to his wife: 'I am interested, geared up & happy. Is it not horrible to be built like that? The preparations have a hideous fascination for me. I pray to God to forgive me for such fearful moods of levity.'

[1] Emma Alice Margaret Tennant, 1864–1945. Known as Margot. Asquith's second wife; they were married in 1894.

2

The First Month of War

CHURCHILL believed that he could be an effective wartime Minister. But he feared that the hostility of his former Conservative critics would make his work more difficult. Since he had joined the Liberals in 1904, most Conservatives had regarded him with open suspicion. They had felt threatened by his vitriolic attacks on the House of Lords. They had been horrified by his passionate demands for Irish Home Rule, and his refusal to accept the arguments of Protestant Ulster against it. In March 1914 he had ordered units of the Mediterranean Fleet to the Irish Sea to deter Ulster from rebellion. Speaking in the House of Commons in May 1914, he had accused Ulster's champion, Sir Edward Carson, of 'a treasonable conspiracy' against Home Rule. In August 1914 the Conservatives agreed on a Party truce for the duration of the war. Four letters which Churchill received at the outbreak of war seemed proof that this truce would apply even to him. On August 4 Walter Long,[1] one of the unsuccessful candidates for the Leadership of the Conservative Party in 1911, wrote: 'Let me say that I feel you have placed us all under a debt which we cannot easily repay. This is no time for sentiment but it is right you should know that we realise and appreciate the work you have done in this supreme crisis.' On August 5 Carson himself wrote:

Dear Churchill,
    I know too well what a strain you are going through & at such a moment a friendly line from an opponent may be a little help. Whatever bitterness has existed in the past believe me I desire to shew to you my appreciation of the

[1] Walter Hume Long, 1854–1924. Conservative MP, 1880–1921. President of the Local Government Board, 1900–5. Chief Secretary, Ireland, 1905. Created the Union Defence League, the leading anti-Home Rule organization, 1907–14. President of the Local Government Board, May 1915–December 1916. Under-Secretary of State for the Colonies, 1916–19. First Lord of the Admiralty, 1919–21. Created Viscount, 1921.

patriotic & courageous way you have acted in the present grave crisis for our country's best interests & the honour of the Empire. Whatever be the result you may rest assured that for whatever it is worth my present admiration of what you have done will not be transitory & I wish you every comfort & assurance in yr present anxieties that yr most devoted friends cd desire for you & I remain

Yrs sincerely
Edward Carson

Two days later Churchill received a letter from John Gretton,[1] one of the brewers whom he had attacked as a group during the 1906 election:

Dear Churchill,

I have often as one of the Opposition written you controversial letters. I would like, at this time, to write you something to give you pleasure. It is known that you have done well for the Admiralty and when the troops and Reservists marched down through Belfast to embark two nights ago your name was cheered enthusiastically. This comes from a reliable source, a strong Orangeman and relation of mine who is delighted differences are sunk to defend the country.

Yours sincerely
John Gretton

Another consistent Conservative critic who wrote to Churchill appreciatively after the outbreak of war was H. A. Gwynne,[2] the editor of the *Morning Post*, in whose columns Churchill had been frequently denounced. On August 28 Gwynne sent Churchill a scheme for exploding Zeppelins by sending up bombs on balloons to strike them. 'Though we have been bitter political opponents for many years,' Gwynne wrote, 'I hope you will accept from me my tribute of appreciation for what you have done for the nation in this grave crisis.' Churchill sent these letters to his wife. 'It is a great triumph,' she replied.

On the afternoon of August 5 Asquith held a Council of War in the Cabinet room at 10 Downing Street. Kitchener took his place as Secretary of State for War. Churchill gave the Council an account of the naval preparations, and informed them that the Dover Strait was

---

[1] John Gretton, 1867–1949. Director and Chairman of Bass, Ratcliffe and Gretton Limited, brewers. Conservative MP, 1895–1943. Created Baron, 1944.

[2] Howell Arthur Gwynne, 1865–1950. Reuter's chief war correspondent in South Africa, 1899–1902. Editor of the *Standard*, 1904–11. Editor of the *Morning Post*, 1911–37.

completely sealed against any German intervention. From the naval aspect, all was therefore ready to transport the British Expeditionary Force to France. On the following day Kitchener called on Churchill at Admiralty House to discuss the details of the transportation. Churchill later recalled their conversation in an unpublished note:

I explained to him the naval dispositions, particularly the system of patrol flotillas and the Dover cordon on which we relied both to prevent invasion and to protect the passage of the Army across the Channel. I explained the role of the Fleet in both these operations. He asked what would happen if the Germans made a dash into the Channel with their fast ships to attack our transports. I replied that we should know of their movement at latest as they passed the Straits in time to suspend the transportation till we could deal with them.

He then asked what danger the troopships would run from submarines. I replied that this was a serious risk but that it must be accepted. The great bulk of the Army would get across, and we would have a multitude of small craft at hand to save life in cases where ships were torpedoed.

Churchill went on to say that the danger would be less in darkness than in daylight. Without further discussion, Kitchener turned to the Chief of the Imperial General Staff, General Douglas,[1] and gave him a direct order to suspend all day crossings at once. 'All of us were astonished,' Churchill recorded, 'at the precipitation and overwhelming authority with which this far-reaching decision was given, but no one said a word.' Churchill's note continued:

I did not myself know what reactions limiting the transportation to the hours of darkness would have upon the concentration dates of the Army in France, but seeing how elaborate were the railway timetables I was sure it would be considerable. The Admirals were relieved at the diminution of the risks. The conference then terminated and the Secretary of State departed, followed by his Chief of the Staff and several other officers.

Within an hour, Churchill found that Kitchener's order to limit the British Expeditionary Force to night-time crossings was full of difficulty. 'I find on enquiry from our Transport Department,' he wrote at once to the War Office, 'That if the ships go only by night, the passage may take nearly twice as long. In these circumstances, after consultation with the First Sea Lord, I think the risk from submarines must be faced.

[1] Charles Wittingham Horsley Douglas, 1850–1914. Entered Army, 1869. Major-General, 1900. Knighted, 1907. General, commanding Southern Command, 1909–11. Inspector-General, Home Forces, 1911–14. Chief of the Imperial General Staff, 4 August 1913. He died on 25 October 1914.

Otherwise it will throw out all your railway arrangements as well as those for embarkation and transport, and cause a delay which I expect you would regard as fatal.' Kitchener immediately cancelled his veto on day-time crossings. In his unpublished note, Churchill reflected on this incident. It was, he wrote, 'a revelation of the War Minister's personal authority, of his readiness to accept unlimited responsibility, and to take the gravest decisions by word of mouth as if he were a commander issuing orders on the field of battle, and also of the inevitable but very serious limitations of his knowledge of the business in hand at the moment of taking up his new duties'.

On August 6 'The Other Club', an all-Party dining club which Churchill and F. E. Smith had founded in 1911, held its first meeting of the war. Kitchener was in the chair. Among the other members present were Lord Stamfordham,[1] Bonar Law, Lloyd George, F. E. Smith, Admiral of the Fleet Lord Charles Beresford,[2] and Jack Seely.[3] Sir George Riddell,[4] who was present, recorded in his *War Diary* how, at the end of the dinner, 'Winston rose and said he proposed to disregard the rules of the club, which forbade any toast but that of the King, by proposing "Success to the British Arms". The toast was drunk in silence.' On the following morning Kitchener held out the hand of friendship to his former subaltern critic: 'My dear Churchill, . . . Please do not address me as Lord as I am only yours Kitchener.'

Early in September Churchill turned to Kitchener for help in a family matter. For over two years he had been estranged from his cousin the Duke of Marlborough,[5] who had been provoked to anger when he

[1] Arthur John Bigge, 1849–1931. Entered Army, 1869. Entered the Royal Household, 1880. Private Secretary to Queen Victoria, 1895–1901. Private Secretary to George V, 1910–31. Created Baron Stamfordham, 1911. His only son was killed in action on 15th May, 1915.

[2] Charles William de la Poer Beresford, 1846–1919. Entered Navy, 1859. Conservative MP, 1874–80; 1885–9; 1897–1900; 1902; 1910–16. Knighted, 1903. Commanded the Mediterranean Fleet, 1905–7; the Channel Fleet, 1907–9. Retired from the Navy, 1911. Created Baron, 1916.

[3] John Edward Bernard Seely, 1868–1947. Liberal MP, 1900–22; 1923–4. Under-Secretary of State for the Colonies, 1908–11. Under-Secretary of State for War, 1912–14. Resigned in March 1914, following the Curragh incident. Commanded the Canadian Cavalry Brigade, 1914–18. Gassed, 1918, and retired from Army with rank of Major-General. Under-Secretary of State to Churchill, Ministry of Munitions and Deputy Minister of Munitions, 1918. Under-Secretary of State for Air, 1919. Created Baron Mottistone, 1933.

[4] George Allardice Riddell, 1865–1934. Newspaper proprietor. Chairman of the *News of World*, 1903. Knighted, 1909. Member of the Admiralty, War Office and Press Committee, 1914. Liaison officer between the Government and the Press, 1914–18. Baronet, 1918. Created Baron, 1920.

[5] Charles Richard John Spencer-Churchill, 1871–1934. 9th Duke of Marlborough, 1892. Paymaster General of the Forces, 1899–1902. Staff captain and ADC. to General Hamilton during the South African War, 1900. Under-Secretary of State for the Colonies, 1903–5.

found Clementine Churchill writing to Lloyd George, the architect of the People's Budget, on Blenheim Palace notepaper. Despite the Duke's attempts to apologize, Clementine Churchill had not been mollified, and the Churchills had subsequently refused to spend their usual Christmas at Blenheim. While Churchill was waiting anxiously to learn of the fate of the *Goeben*, the Duke of Marlborough, intent on settling the family quarrel, arrived at the Admiralty with his two sons, the Marquess of Blandford[1] and Lord Ivor Spencer-Churchill.[2] Fifty-six years later the former recalled to the author Churchill's keen enthusiasm as he showed his visitors the plans that had been made to track down the *Goeben*. The Duke asked Churchill to find some position in which he could help the war effort. As a Conservative, he could have no political appointment; not being a professional soldier, he was too old to serve at the front. Churchill approached Kitchener, who at once agreed to attach the Duke to the War Office as a Special Messenger. Churchill was delighted, writing on September 13: 'I am touched by the promptness with wh you have looked after Marlborough. It is a gt pleasure to work with you, & the two Departments pull well together. As you say— they are only one Department really.'

On August 8 the newly constituted Channel Fleet, containing nineteen battleships, was fully mobilized and cruising at the western end of the Channel. The Dover Strait was guarded by squadrons from Harwich and the Thames, by the British and French destroyer flotillas of the Dover cordon, and by the submarine flotilla commanded by Commodore Keyes.[3] Protected by this powerful screen, and escorted

---

Lieutenant-Colonel, Queen's Own Oxfordshire Hussars, 1910. Employed at the War Office as a Special Messenger, 1914–15. Joint Parliamentary Secretary, Board of Agriculture and Fisheries, 1917–18.

[1] John Albert Edward William Spencer-Churchill, 1897–   . Marquess of Blandford. Captain, 1st Life Guards, 1916. 10th Duke of Marlborough, 1934. Mayor of Woodstock, 1937–8; 1938–9. Lieutenant-Colonel, Liaison officer with the United States Forces, 1942–5.

[2] Ivor Charles Spencer-Churchill, 1898–1956. At Eton College, 1912–16. Lieutenant, Royal Army Service Corps, 1917–18.

[3] Roger John Brownlow Keyes, 1872–1945. Entered Navy, 1885. Naval Attaché, Athens and Constantinople, 1905–7. Commodore in charge of submarines, North Sea and adjacent waters, August 1914–February 1915. Chief of Staff, Eastern Mediterranean Squadron, 1915. Director of Plans, Admiralty, 1917. Vice-Admiral in command of the Dover Patrol, 1918. Knighted, 1918. Created Baronet, 1919. Deputy Chief of the Naval Staff, 1921–5. Commander-in-Chief, Mediterranean, 1925–8; Portsmouth, 1929–31. Admiral of the Fleet, 1930. National Conservative MP, 1934–43. Director of Combined Operations, 1940–1. Created Baron, 1943.

by the 12th cruiser squadron commanded by Rear-Admiral Wemyss,[1] the British Expeditionary Force began its transit to France. Between August 12 and August 22, a hundred and twenty thousand men were transported across the Channel without the loss of a single life or ship. The secrecy of the operation was so well kept that on August 21, after ten days of continual troop movements, the German Supreme Command still doubted whether any significant landing of British troops had yet taken place. The Admiralty had two similar successes in the following months. By the end of September all fifty thousand troops of the Indian Corps had been transported safely from Bombay and Karachi to Marseilles, and by the middle of October nearly twenty-five thousand Canadian Army volunteers, who had embarked in a convoy of thirty-one ships in the St Lawrence river, together with men from Newfoundland and Bermuda, crossed the Atlantic without loss. No German battleship or submarine was able to disrupt these decisive movements. 'We remember nothing like this feat,' wrote the *Manchester Guardian*, 'in the whole of naval history.' Nevertheless, Churchill wrote in an unpublished note:

This was a period of great anxiety to us. All the most fateful possibilities were open. We were bound to expect a military descent upon our coasts with the intention of arresting or recalling our Army, or a naval raid into the Channel to cut down the transports, or a concentrated submarine attack upon these vessels crammed with men. The great naval battle might begin at any moment independently or in connection with any of these operations. It was a period of extreme psychological tension.

The tensions and challenges of five days of war stimulated Churchill to look again at schemes for the offensive. On August 9 he sent Prince Louis a four-page handwritten survey of possible action against Germany. 'It is necessary,' he began, 'to sustain and relieve our general strategic defensive by active minor operations. The objective sh'd be to establish for a time a close observation and control of the Southern approaches to the Elbe.' To this end Churchill proposed a naval assault on Ameland, one of the East Frisian islands, which could be fortified,

[1] Rosslyn Erskine Wemyss, 1864–1933. Entered Navy, 1877. Commodore, Royal Naval Barracks Devonport, 1909–11. Rear-Admiral in command of the 12th Cruiser Squadron, August 1914, charged with escorting the British Expeditionary Force to France. Convoyed the first Canadian troops to France, September 1914. Governor of Mudros, February–April 1915. Commanded the naval squadron at Cape Helles, April 1915. Acting Vice-Admiral at the Dardanelles, November–December 1915; directed the naval aspects of the evacuation of the Gallipoli Peninsula. Knighted, 1916. Second Sea Lord, 1917. First Sea Lord, 1917–19. Created Baron Wester Wemyss, 1919. Admiral of the Fleet, 1919.

and used to hem in the German Fleet, and to serve as a base from which aeroplanes and seaplanes 'can report all movement in the Heligoland Bight, & later attack with explosives the locks of the Kiel canal or vessels in the canal'. Above all, such action would, he wrote, 'maintain in lively vigour the spirit of enterprise & attack wh when excluded from warlike operations, means that you are only waiting wondering where you will be hit'.

Even before the British ultimatum to Germany had expired, the *Königen Luise*, a German minelayer, had sailed from Borkum with a load of mines. At 11 am on August 5 the British light cruiser *Amphion* sighted the minelayer, and by noon had sunk her and taken the survivors on board. Returning to base on August 6, the triumphant *Amphion* struck one of the mines laid by her victim and sank immediately. One British officer and a hundred and fifty men, and nearly all the German prisoners, were drowned.

The sinking of the *Amphion* was the first British disaster of the war. Churchill decided that the best policy was to give the House of Commons full details of what had happened. 'We much admired Mr Churchill's frankness in giving the account of the loss of the Amphion at once to the public,' wrote the *Manchester Guardian*. 'There is nothing that impairs confidence so easily as the suspicion that news of losses is being kept back. Let the Admiralty trust the people and the trust will be returned.'

The *Manchester Guardian* had supported Churchill since, in 1904, he had turned to Manchester as a renegade Tory in search of a Liberal seat. The weekly *Observer* had been his critic for just as long. Its editor, J. L. Garvin,[1] had for many years asserted that Churchill was a troublemaker, and irresponsible. But on the first Sunday of the war the *Observer* struck a new tone:

We close the differences we have had with Mr Churchill. When the records of this crisis can be written he will be proved, we think, to have exerted from beginning to end the qualities of a great executive Minister; never deceived as to the nature of the coming ordeal, and never in doubt as to the 'swift competence in emergency' by which it ought to be met as he has met it. In mobilising the fleet at the first instant of danger and making Sir John

[1] James Louis Garvin, 1868–1947. Editor, the *Observer*, 1908–42. Editor, *Pall Mall Gazette*, 1912–15. Editor-in-Chief, *Encylopædia Britannica*, 1926–9.

Jellicoe its fighting head he showed himself to be a statesman who well understands the nature of war, and has the nerve to face its immense responsibilities.

During the first two weeks of the war Clementine Churchill remained at Cromer with her two children. On August 9 her husband sent her an official War Office summary of what was known of the German military advance through Belgium, and wrote in his covering letter:

My darling one,
    The enclosed will tell you what is known officially. It is a good summary. You must *not* fail to burn it at once.
    I am over head & ears in work & am much behindhand.
    It makes me a little anxious that you shd be on the coast. It is 100 to 1 agst a raid—but still there is the chance: & Cromer has a good landing place near.
    I wish you wd get the motor repaired & keep it so that you can whisk away, at the first sign of trouble. I am really in doubt whether I ought not to recall you at once à la Callaghan—'Strike your flag & come ashore'.
    Kiss the Kittens for me.
    Tender love to you all.
                                        Your fondest & devoted
                                                W

Clementine Churchill was eager to know about the Expeditionary Force. 'Do I guess right that some have gone already?' she asked on August 9. 'Be a good one and write again & feed me with tit-bits. I am being so wise & good & sitting on the Beach & playing with my kittens, & doing my little housekeeping, but how I long to dash up & be near you and the pulse of things.' Two days later Churchill was able to satisfy her curiosity:

My dear one,
    This is only a line from a vy tired Winston. The Expedy Force about wh you are so inquisitive is on its road & will be all on the spot in time. I wish I cd whisk down to you & dig a little on the beach. My work here is vy heavy & so interesting that I cannot leave it.
    Now I am really going to knock off.
                                        Your ever loving
                                                W

Sensing a 'note of fatigue' in her husband's letter, Clementine Churchill replied urging him to take three particular points seriously in order to

avoid becoming too tired: '1) Never missing your morning ride.
2) Going to bed well *before* midnight & sleeping well & *not* allowing
yourself to be woken up every time a Belgian kills a German. (You *must*
have 8 hours sleep every night to be your best self.) 3) Not smoking too
much & not having indigestion.'

In mid-August Robert Houston,[1] a wealthy shipowner and Conservative MP, sent Clementine Churchill a letter of praise for her
husband, and a present of a valuable emerald and diamond ring. She
wrote at once to her husband, amazed, as was her sister-in-law Gwendeline,[2] by the beauty of the ring, but realizing that she must not keep it.
She wrote of what an illogical world it was where, because her husband
was a prominent statesmen, she was given an expensive ring, whereas
if he had been less famous, and she in need of consolation, she would
have been given nothing. She sent back the ring at once. 'My dear one,'
Churchill replied on August 13, 'How right you were not to hesitate to
send back the ring, & what a good thing it is to have high & inflexible
principles! You are a dear & splendid Kat. I am very proud of you.
What you have done for me no one can measure.'

On August 10, while the Expeditionary Force was still in transit, and
its safe arrival uncertain, the *Goeben* and the *Breslau*, having finally
escaped the massive search operation mounted by the Admiralty, passed
through the Dardanelles and anchored off Constantinople. Their
arrival at the Turkish capital was hailed by the Turks as a triumph for
German skill. The Kaiser at once offered the ships to the Turkish Navy.
Their escape was a sharp rebuff to Admiralty vigilance. On August 5
the *Goeben* was reported having sailed eastward, back to the Italian
port of Messina. Respect for Italian neutrality prevented the British
ships from attacking. No attempt was made by Admiral Milne to act in
concert with his French counterpart. Rear-Admiral Troubridge,[3]
who commanded the British armoured cruiser squadron, having
sighted the *Goeben* in open water, decided that it would be too great a
risk to his sixteen cruisers and destroyers to challenge the two German
ships. On August 7 the captains of the *Dublin* and the *Gloucester*, the

[1] Robert Paterson Houston, 1853–1926. Principal owner of the Houston line of steamers.
Conservative MP, 1892–1924. Created Baronet, 1922.

[2] Lady Gwendeline Bertie, 1885–1941. Known as 'Goonie'. Daughter of the 7th Earl of
Abingdon. She married Churchill's brother Jack in 1908.

[3] Ernest Charles Thomas Troubridge, 1860–1926. Entered Navy, 1875. Naval Attaché,
Tokyo, 1901–4. Chief of the Admiralty War Staff, 1912. Vice-Admiral commanding
the Mediterranean Cruiser Squadron, 1912–14. Admiral commanding on the Danube,
1918. President, International Danube Commission, 1919–24. Knighted, 1919. Admiral,
1919.

brothers John[1] and William[2] Kelly, attempted in vain, against heavy odds, to thwart the *Goeben*'s escape. Then the mistake of a clerk at the Admiralty in sending Milne the quite erroneous news that Britain and Austria were at war led him to call off the chase in order to carry out automatic instructions pursuant upon the outbreak of an Austro-British war. By the time this mistake was corrected, twenty-four hours had been lost and the *Goeben* had passed Cape Matapan. Troubridge thereupon decided that as the *Goeben* had reached the Aegean Sea, he should call off the pursuit. Later that month an Admiralty court of enquiry examined Milne's report, and approved of his actions. They informed Churchill that in their opinion the failure to sink the *Goeben* and *Breslau* was 'primarily due to the failure of Rear-Admiral Troubridge to carry out your instructions'. Troubridge was then court-martialled. In his defence he pleaded that the *Goeben* constituted a superior force and that the Admiralty signal of July 30 had specifically instructed him not to engage the enemy under such conditions. He was acquitted. Captain Kelly of the *Gloucester*, who had engaged a superior force contrary to orders, was awarded the Companionship of the Bath for his conduct. Churchill himself wrote Kelly's official commendation:

The Goeben could have caught and sunk the Gloucester at any time. . . . She was apparently deterred by the latter's boldness which gave the impression of support close at hand. The combination of audacity with restraint, unswerving attention to the principal military object, viz, holding on to the Goeben, and strict conformity to orders constitute a naval episode which may justly be regarded as a model.

Prince Louis sent Churchill a summary of the documents relating to the *Goeben*'s escape, together with Milne's report. Churchill minuted on August 27: 'The explanation is satisfactory; the result unsatisfactory.'

[1] John Donald Kelly, 1871–1936. Entered Navy, 1884. Captain, 1911. Commanded HMS *Dublin*, Adriatic and Dardanelles, 1914–15. Rear-Admiral, 1922. Fourth Sea Lord, 1924–7. Knighted, 1929. Vice-Admiral, Commander-in-Chief Portsmouth, 1934–6. Admiral of the Fleet, 1936.

[2] William Archibald Howard Kelly, 1873–1952. Entered Navy, 1886. Captain, 1911. Naval Attaché, Paris, 1911–14. Commanded HMS *Gloucester*, 1914–16. Commodore, Commanding the 8th Light Cruiser Squadron, 1917; the British Adriatic Force, 1918–19. Head of the British Naval Mission to Greece, with rank of Vice-Admiral in the Greek Navy, 1919–21. Rear-Admiral, Commanding 2nd Cruiser Squadron, 1925–7. Knighted, 1931. Vice-Admiral, Commanding the China Station, 1931–3. British Naval Representative, Turkey, 1940–4.

Churchill believed that the real failure arose because Italian neutrality had been respected. In an unpublished note written after the war he attacked Milne for what he believed was the most serious failure of the chase:

It must be admitted that the orders to respect rigidly Italian neutrality & to keep six miles from the Italian coasts, issued without any idea of the Goeben being at Messina, seriously complicated the task of the British forces. Had this point been referred to the Admiralty by Sir Berkeley Milne the prohibition wld at once have been cancelled. The prize was worth the risk. In fact permission to chase through the Straits was given unasked by the Admiralty as soon as it was realised that the Goeben was escaping unblocked to the Southward.

He could at any moment after he first suspected that the Goeben was at Messina have telegraphed to the Admiralty in the following sense:—'I believe Goeben is at Messina. Submit since she has entered Italian territorial waters I may follow her, observing that otherwise I shall be much hampered in my operations.' It would not have been unreasonable to expect a Commander-in-Chief to ask the Admiralty a simple vital question like this. One would have expected him to do so, if only for his own protection. He said nothing.

Britain had, since 1902, secured naval predominance in the Far East by an alliance with Japan. Early in August the Japanese Government informed Grey that they were prepared to declare war on Germany; but they did not wish to limit their naval action in the Far East merely to supporting Britain. They wanted to attack the Germans wherever possible throughout the Pacific, hoping thereby to gain some portion of Germany's large island Empire for themselves. Grey doubted whether Britain's special interests in the Far East were seriously enough menaced to accept Japanese demands on so wide a scale. Churchill saw grave danger in any hesitation. He feared a naval setback in the Pacific if Britain were not generous to Japan. When Grey sent a telegram to Sir Conyngham Greene,[1] the British Ambassador in Tokyo, on August 11 stating that if the Japanese declared war on Germany they should not extend their military action 'beyond Asiatic waters westward of the China Sea, or to any foreign territory except territory in German occupation on the continent in Eastern Asia', Churchill was alarmed,

[1] Conyngham Greene, 1854–1934. Entered Foreign Office, 1877. Knighted, 1900. Ambassador to Japan, 1912–19.

writing to Grey immediately he saw a copy of the telegram that same day:

My dear Grey,
   . . . I must say I think you are chilling indeed to these people. I can't see any half way house myself between having them in and keeping them out. If they are to come in, they may as well be welcomed as comrades. This last telegram is almost hostile. I am afraid I do not understand what is in yr mind on this aspect—tho' I followed it so clearly till today.
   . . . This telegram gives me a shiver. We are all in this together & I only wish to give the fullest effect & support to your main policy. But I am altogether perplexed by the line opened up by these Japanese interchanges.
   You may easily give mortal offence—wh will not be forgotten—we are not safe yet—by a long chalk. The storm has yet to burst. . . .

Yours ever
W

Grey was surprised by the intensity of Churchill's rebuke. He modified his telegram, writing to Churchill later that day: 'I think it is all right now with Japan.' In order to show the Japanese that they would be welcomed as an ally, Churchill sent his own telegram to the Japanese Minister of Marine, Admiral Yashiro,[1] on August 13: 'On behalf of the Board of Admiralty I express the warm feeling of comradeship & pleasure with which the officers & men of the British Navy will find themselves allied in a common cause & against a common foe with the gallant & seamanlike Navy of Japan.'

No record exists of the Cabinet's discussion about the inducements which Japan could be offered to persuade them to join the Allies. Churchill was a leading advocate of encouraging their participation. A young diplomat in the Tokyo Embassy, Frank Ashton-Gwatkin,[2] later told the author that he heard, shortly afterwards, the story that when someone had asked in Cabinet, 'what should we do to bring the Japanese into the war?', Churchill had allegedly replied: 'They can have China.'

On August 23 Japan declared war on Germany. Later that month

---

[1] Rokurō Yashiro, 1861–1930. A 2nd Lieutenant in the Imperial Japanese Navy during the Sino-Japanese war, 1894–5. Captain, commanding the *Asama* during the Russo-Japanese war, 1904–5. Minister of the Navy with the rank of Admiral, 1914–16. He won fame by exposing a bribery scandal in the Imperial Navy early in 1914.

[2] Frank Trelawny Arthur Ashton-Gwatkin, 1889–   . Entered Consular Service, Far East, 1913. Member of the British Delegation at the Washington Disarmament Conference, 1921–2; the Imperial Economic Conference at Ottawa, 1932; the World Monetary and Economic Conference, London, 1933; the Munich Conference, 1938. Policy Adviser, Ministry of Economic Warfare, 1939–40. Novelist, under the *nom de plume* John Paris.

Churchill saw a chance to turn the Anglo-Japanese alliance of 1902 to immediate advantage. On August 29 he wrote to Grey:

Now that Austria has declared war on Japan, and in view of the general situation, including the attitude of Turkey, it would seem only fitting that the Japanese Government should be sounded as to their readiness to send a battle squadron to co-operate with the Allied Powers in the Mediterranean or elsewhere. The influence and value of this powerful aid could not be overrated. It would steady and encourage Italy, and would bring nearer the situation, so greatly desired, of our being able to obtain command of the Baltic. There is reason to believe that the Japanese would take such an invitation as a compliment.

No such battle squadron was forthcoming.[1]

Grey resented Churchill's keenness to involve Japan. These were not plans that he intended to spend time on. But Churchill's persistence did not disrupt their friendship. Each realized that the strains of working out war policies could lead to frayed tempers and sharp words. Earlier, on August 11, it was Grey who felt he had caused offence in sending Churchill a particularly curt note. That same day he wrote again to apologize: 'I am so very sorry I sent you that hasty reply this afternoon —I was being awfully knotted at the time & felt I must swear. Do forgive me.' On September 24 it was Churchill who felt moved to begin a letter, about Turkey: 'You are always kind in letting me express my opinion without being vexed.'

Clementine Churchill continued to keep her husband informed of her adventures. Foreign-looking men, suspected of being German spies, provided an almost daily diet of excitement on the Norfolk coast. Her sister-in-law Gwendeline, she reported, had seen two soldiers catch up with a suspect and 'give him a small prod with his bayonette!' The result, she reported, 'tho' very exhilarating to the pursuers had the effect of making the "spy" run so fast that Goonie fears he got away'. During August there were rumours that carrier pigeons released by

---

[1] It was not until February 1915 that, at Churchill's request, Japanese warships assisted the British Navy—together with the French and Russian marines—in the suppression of a mutiny among the Indian soldiers of the Singapore garrison. In 1917 a Japanese naval squadron under Vice-Admiral Kozo Sato undertook convoy duties in the Mediterranean, escorting in two years nearly 800 allied troopships and merchantmen. In 1917 the Japanese also undertook all allied convoy duties in the Indian Ocean.

another spy had carried the information of Clementine Churchill's whereabouts across the North Sea. She wrote to her husband with details of one of the rumours: the Germans were to send an aeroplane to Cromer to kidnap her, and would then demand, as the price of her return, several of the Navy's best ships. She had no intention of allowing such villainy to succeed, begging her husband 'not to sacrifice the smallest or cheapest submarine or even the oldest ship'. If he were to pay the ransom, she wrote, she would be unable to bear the subsequent unpopularity; if she died unransomed, she would be a heroine, and he be hailed as a spartan.

On August 12 Britain declared war on Austria–Hungary. The two countries had no long-standing quarrel. The alliance system, not conflicting interests, brought the two nations to war. Churchill had many Austrian friends, with whom he had often stayed, and who were frequent guests at his home. He had known the Baron de Forest since his youth, hunted on his Austrian estates, and travelled on his yacht. The Austrian diplomat Count Kinsky[1] had been a close friend of Churchill's mother. Since the battle of Omdurman, Churchill had known the distinguished Austrian soldier, Sir Rudolph Slatin,[2] and was a friend of Count Albert Mensdorff,[3] who had been Austro-Hungarian Ambassador in London since 1904. He learned of Britain's declaration of war with sadness. The official reason for war was the appearance of Austrian military units, in small numbers, among the German forces invading France. To Churchill fell the task of arranging the Ambassador's departure. He wrote to him on August 13:

My dear Mensdorff,
    My naval sec Adl Hood,[4] who brings this letter, is instructed to put himself at yr disposal in arranging for the comfort & contrivance of yr journey by sea.

[1] Charles Kinsky, 1858–1919. Served in the Austro-Hungarian diplomatic service. Lady Randolph Churchill had hoped to marry him after Lord Randolph's death.
[2] Rudolf Carl Slatin, 1857–1932. An Austrian by birth. Appointed by General Gordon to be Governor of Darfor, 1879. A prisoner of the Mahdi, 1884–91. Knighted, 1898. Appointed by Kitchener Inspector-General of the Sudan, 1900–14. Honorary Major-General in the British Army, 1900. Created Baron of the Austrian Empire, 1906. Head of the Austrian Red Cross Aid for Prisoners of War, 1914–18.
[3] Albert Mensdorff-Pouilly-Dietrichstein, 1861–1945. Austro-Hungarian Ambassador to London, 1904–14.
[4] Horace Lambert Alexander Hood, 1870–1916. Entered Navy, 1883. Rear-Admiral, 1913. Churchill's Naval Secretary, 1914. Accompanied Churchill to Antwerp, October 1914. Commanded the Dover Patrol, 1914–15. Commanded the 3rd Battle Cruiser Squadron, 1915–16. Knighted, 1916. Killed at the Battle of Jutland.

If there is any way in wh I can be of service to you at this time you will not
I hope fail to command me.

Altho' the terrible march of events has swept aside the ancient friendship
between our countries, the respect & regard wh springs from so many years
of personal association cannot pass from the hearts of yr English friends.

Yours vy sincerely
WSC

Churchill arranged for over two hundred Austrian subjects, who
might otherwise have been interned, to leave on the same boat with
the Ambassador. Mensdorff replied to Churchill from the Austro-
Hungarian Embassy in Belgrave Square that same day:

My dear Churchill,

Please accept my sincerest thanks for the great courtesy with which you
placed a boat at our disposal to get home and for all the trouble the Admiralty
is taking about the arrangements. I have just seen Admiral Hood.

I shall never forget the happy years I spent in this country and all the
kindness shown to me by my English friends.

Hoping that in future happier quieter days we may meet again.

Yrs very sincerely
Mensdorff

Personal sympathies for Austria, childhood memories, friendships
built up over past years, his belief that Balkan quarrels were no vital
concern of Britain's; none of these was allowed to stand in the way of
'the terrible march of events'. On August 12, the day before Mensdorff
left England, Churchill decided, with Cabinet approval, to set up an
Admiralty Committee to supervise the blockade of all German and
Austrian ports. The aim of the blockade, Churchill wrote in a minute to
Prince Louis, and to the Chief of the Admiralty War Staff, Sir Frederick
Sturdee,[1] was to find out by what methods, commercial, diplomatic
and military, German and Austrian trade 'may be hampered, restricted, and if possible stopped'. An Adriatic blockade was set up under
French control. The British supervised the North Sea blockade. In a
note of 5 March 1915 Churchill was able to report to his Cabinet
colleagues: 'No instance is known to the British Admiralty of any vessel,

---

[1] Frederick Charles Doveton Sturdee, 1859–1925. Entered Navy, 1871. Assistant Director
of Naval Intelligence, 1900–2. Rear-Admiral, Home Fleet, 1909–10. Knighted, 1913. Chief
of the Admiralty War Staff, 1914. Commander-in-Chief at the Battle of the Falkland Islands,
December 1914. Commander of the Fourth Battle Squadron, 1915–18. Created Baronet,
1916. Admiral, 1917. Commander-in-Chief, the Nore, 1918–21.

the stopping of which has been authorized by the Foreign Office, passing them unchallenged. It is not a case of a paper blockade, but of a blockade as real and as efficient as any that has ever been established. . . .'

For two weeks the German armies marched westwards across Belgium. But no decisive battle was fought and the military outcome was unclear. On August 14 the Commander-in-Chief of the British Expeditionary Force, Sir John French,[1] reached Amiens, where five British Divisions were assembling, ready to march to the front. Churchill had always listened attentively to French's military opinions, and although he had not supported the pre-war campaign for conscription, he doubted whether either side could win the war until far greater numbers of men were committed to the conflict. By 1917 almost every able-bodied man was to be drawn greedily into the military machine; but in 1914 there were few places for those who wished to serve. Churchill decided to build upon the naval manpower at his disposal in order to establish a new fighting force, to be called the Royal Naval Division. On August 16 he outlined his plan to Prince Louis and to the Second Sea Lord, Sir Frederick Hamilton:[2]

In order to make the best possible use of the surplus naval reservists of different classes, it is proposed to constitute permanent cadres of one marine and two naval brigades. The marine brigade has already been partially formed in four battalions, aggregating 1,880 active service men. To this will be added an approximately equal number of reservists, making the total strength of the brigade 3,900, organized in four battalions of four double companies of approximately 250 men. The two naval brigades will also consist of four battalions, each, if possible, of 880 men, organized in sixteen double companies of 220. . . .

The formation of these brigades should be completed so far as resources allow in the present week. The officers commanding the companies and

---

[1] John Denton Pinkstone French, 1852–1925. Entered Navy, 1866. Transferred to Army, 1874. Lieutenant-General, commanding the Cavalry in South Africa, 1899–1902. Knighted, 1900. Chief of the Imperial General Staff, 1912–14. Field-Marshal, 1913. Commander-in-Chief of the British Expeditionary Force in France, August 1914–December 1915. Commander-in-Chief, Home Forces, 1915–18. Created Viscount, 1916. Lord Lieutenant of Ireland, 1918–21. Created Earl of Ypres, 1922.

[2] Frederick Tower Hamilton, 1856–1917. Entered Navy, 1869. Vice-Admiral commanding the Second and Third Fleets, 1911–13. Knighted, 1913. Second Sea Lord, 1914–16. Commander-in-Chief, Rosyth, 1916–17.

battalions must be appointed forthwith. The first essential is to get the men drilling together in brigades; and the deficiencies of various ranks in the battalions can be filled up later. It may ultimately be found possible in the course of the war to build up all battalions of the marine and naval brigades to the army strength of 1,070, and the organization will readily adapt itself to this. All the men, whether sailors or marines, while training in the three brigades will be available if required for service afloat, and it must be distinctly understood that this is the paramount claim upon them; but in the meanwhile they will be left to be organized for land service.

The Royal Naval Division was set up that same day. Its men regarded Churchill as their patron. Later, in action, when things went well they called themselves 'Churchill's Pets'. When things went badly they were known as 'Churchill's Innocent Victims'.

Many requests for a place in the Division came direct to Churchill. He was quick to respond. When Bonar Law wrote on September 12 on behalf of his two nephews, John Robley[1] and Christopher Robley,[2] Churchill replied at once by telegram: 'Please send names and addresses of your nephews they shall be considered at once.' Another request came from Sir Max Aitken, who asked Churchill to help secure a commission for his brother Allan.[3] Churchill did so, and Aitken replied on September 10:

Dear Mr Churchill,
The Commission you have given my brother I regard as a personal kindness to me.
The debt of gratitude that I owe you in common with every other British subject far outstrips any liability the Empire has ever contracted.
I am proud of my slight connection with you in the days before the War.
I said to you then that I hoped sincerely to follow you & my friends in a reorganized party.
Now I am determined that it is my duty to support you in any party & under any circumstances.
Please don't answer.

Yours faithfully
W. M. Aitken

[1] John Pitcairn Robley, 1895–1915. Entered the Royal Naval Division as a Sub-Lieutenant, 18 October 1914. Killed in action at the Dardanelles, 8 June 1915.
[2] Christopher Harrington Robley, 1895–   . Entered the Royal Naval Division as a Sub-Lieutenant, 18 October 1914. Left the Division on account of ill-health, February 1915.
[3] Allan Anderson Aitken, 1887–1959. Sub-Lieutenant, Royal Naval Division, 24 September 1914. Served at Antwerp, October 1914. Wounded at Gallipoli, 26 May 1915. Lieutenant, June 1915. Captain, Headquarters Staff Canadian Expeditionary Force, October 1915; Brigade Major, 1918. Member of the Montreal Stock Exchange, 1923–8. Managed Lord Beaverbrook's Canadian interests. Vice-President, Federal Aircraft Company, 1940–6.

J. L. Garvin also turned to Churchill, hoping for a commission for his son Roland.[1] Again Churchill responded, and on September 23 Garvin wrote to thank him:

My dear Churchill,
    My son is gazetted and though I should never have taxed your good offices could the trouble have been foreseen, I shall never forget your friendship. Your proofs have been so strong that every boy almost is your friend now, in a sense, but whether it is all fair weather or there comes a bit of the foul, you will find me to be always

Yours faithfully
J. L. Garvin

Two members of Churchill's family were also drawn into the Royal Naval Division. His cousin, the 4th Earl Howe,[2] commanded the 6th, and his former stepfather, George Cornwallis-West,[3] the 8th Battalion. Some of the recruiting for the Division was done personally by Churchill's Private Secretary, Edward Marsh.[4] Many of the young men in Marsh's wide circle of friends were anxious to go to the war, but unable to find any means of doing so. Lord Fisher was also involved in the enterprise, writing to his son Cecil[5] on September 6:

Winston Churchill got me on the telephone this morning and wants me to be the head of something—some sort of Naval Brigade, I think . . . but the telephone not very clear. He said he had written, but I had never got the letter. Probably some German spy postman has sent it to Berlin! I've promised to have a tête-à-tête lunch with him at the Admiralty on Tuesday to see plans, etc. . . .
    Of course, I told Winston Churchill I am ready to do any mortal thing, *even to co-operating with Beresford!* if any good for the War.

[1] Roland Gerard Garvin, 1896–1916. J. L. Garvin's only son. Killed in action during the battle of the Somme.

[2] Richard George Penn Curzon, 1861–1929. Conservative MP, 1885–1900. 4th Earl Howe, 1900. Lord Chamberlain to Queen Alexandra, 1903–25. His first wife, Lady Georgiana Elizabeth Spencer-Churchill, who died in 1906, was Churchill's aunt.

[3] George Frederick Myddelton Cornwallis-West, 1874–1951. Lieutenant, Scots Guards, 1895–1900. Married Lady Randolph Churchill, 1900; the marriage was dissolved, 1913. Married the actress Mrs Patrick Campbell, April 1914. Lieutenant-Colonel, commanding a battalion of the Royal Naval Division at Antwerp, October 1914. Married Georgette, widow of Adolph Hirsch, 1940.

[4] Edward Howard Marsh, 1872–1953. Known as 'Eddie'. Entered Colonial Office as a 2nd Class Clerk, 1896. Private Secretary to Churchill, December 1905–November 1915. Assistant Private Secretary to Asquith, November 1915–December 1916. Private Secretary to Churchill, 1917–22; 1924–9. Private Secretary to successive Secretaries of State for the Colonies, 1929–36. Knighted, 1937.

[5] Cecil Fisher, 1868–1955. Indian Civil Service, 1890–1906; retired on medical grounds. 2nd Baron, 1920.

Churchill took a close interest in the Royal Naval Division's affairs.[1] On August 17 he gave instructions for its entertainment. 'A Band must be provided,' he minuted. 'The quality is not important. There must be sufficient pupils under instruction at the Naval School of Music to provide for this. The Band is to join on Saturday next.' The outlet provided by the Royal Naval Division for men anxious to serve prompted *The Times* to praise Churchill's 'characteristic genius and energy'. But the setting up of a new fighting force was for others a provocative step, suggesting that Churchill, not content with the naval forces under his command, wanted to control land operations as well. His own insistence that the Division was primarily for service afloat, not ashore, did not satisfy those who suspected him of wanting to edge over into Kitchener's domain. Many of the men themselves were puzzled by the switch from sea to land. One young officer, John Cordingley,[2] later explained, in a letter to the author:

In those days we of the pre-war RNVR regarded Mr Churchill almost as 'Public Enemy No 1' for the simple reason that we had spent our time and energies, at some financial expense to ourselves, in training for service at sea in the event of war and, when war happened, we were turned into soldiers without the option although, as you know, we retained naval terminology and many customs and practices but the fact remains that we were a land force.

The Assistant Director of Operations at the Admiralty, Captain Richmond,[3] revealed the extent to which Churchill's action in setting

---

[1] In his introduction to Douglas Jerrold, *The Royal Naval Division* (Hutchinson, 1923), Churchill wrote: 'Again and again shot to pieces, always rising anew unconquerable, never failing, never faltering, until in the end their story stands out as an epic ineffaceable in national gratitude and long fortified against the ravages of time.'

[2] John Walter Cordingley, 1890–   . Enlisted in Royal Naval Volunteer Reserve, 1905. Assistant Chief Writer, August 1914; commissioned, October 1914. Major, Royal Air Force, 1918. Officer-in-Charge, Records, Royal Air Force, 1922–39. Director-General of Manning, Air Ministry, 1939–46. Knighted, 1946. Air Vice-Marshal, 1947. Controller, Royal Air Force Benevolent Fund, 1947–62.

[3] Herbert William Richmond, 1871–1946. Entered Navy, 1885. Captain, 1908. Commanded HMS *Dreadnought*, 1909–11, Assistant Director of Operations, Admiralty, 1913–15. British Liaison officer, Italian Fleet, 1915. Commanded HMS *Commonwealth*, 1915–16; HMS *Conqueror*, 1917; HMS *Erin*, 1918. Commander-in-Chief, East Indies, 1923–5. Knighted, 1926. Commandant, Imperial Defence College, 1926–8. Admiral, 1929. Professor of Naval and Imperial History, Cambridge, 1934–6. Master of Downing College, Cambridge, 1936–46. Naval historian.

up the Division could anger someone under his authority when he
wrote in his diary on August 20:

> I really believe Churchill is not sane. His entire energies have since last
> Monday been devoted to forming a naval battalion for shore service, con-
> sisting of the RNVR not embarked, the stokers, etc of the RNR & some odds
> & ends of marines & marine artillerymen. For cavalry, I am told (but this
> can hardly be true), the yeomanry. Jack Fisher to be Colonel-in-Chief,
> Beresford some other high rank of an honorary nature. . . .
>
> What this force is to do, Heaven only knows. They are to have light guns
> of some kind & be put now into camps & drilled by Heavy-weather Wilfred.[1]
> A special uniform has been designed by Winston of khaki colour & seaman-
> like shape. It was brought here yesterday & the Lords of the Admiralty
> called in to look at it, Winston as pleased as Punch! This is the beginning of a
> great war in which our whole future rests upon the proper use of the Navy!!
> It is astounding.
>
> These men who are thus to be employed in soldiering know nothing about
> the business. They are all amateurs of the most marked kind. They are
> mostly undisciplined. Such use as they could be in the stokeholds of the ships
> is left out of account. Yet I can foresee that before many months have gone
> by, the strain on the men in the North Sea will have made us cry out for
> every man who has even a tincture of training to keep up our complements.
> Even now we should be wise to begin making provision for sending reliefs to
> Foreign Stations, for the ordinary wastage in peace is going on; & to it is to
> be added the extra wastage of war. The whole thing is so wicked that
> Churchill ought to be hanged before he should be allowed to do such a thing.
> The Cabinet appear to have opposed it, but it is said (rumour of course,
> only) that he said he'd resign if his scheme wasn't approved. I can hardly
> believe that to be true. But how the Board can permit him to indulge in such
> foolery, without a word of serious protest, I don't know.

In late September Kitchener informed Churchill that he wanted the
Royal Naval Division to form a part of one of his new armies, which
would be ready for military action in May 1915. Churchill accepted
that the Royal Naval Division would then pass out of Admiralty control.
'In the interval,' he wrote to Kitchener on October 1, 'brigades from
the division may be used in emergencies and wd play a part in Home
defence of Naval ports.' He had already been acting upon this assumption. When, at the beginning of September, fearing a German attack on

---

[1] Wilfred Henderson, 1873–1930. Entered Navy, 1888. Commander, Admiralty, under
Sir John Fisher, 1905–9. Commanded Destroyer Flotillas, 1909–13. Naval Attaché, Berlin,
1913–14. Commodore, commanding the 1st Naval Brigade, 1914. Interned in Holland after
the siege of Antwerp. Rear-Admiral, 1920. Vice-Admiral, 1925.

Calais, the Governor of the city[1] had asked Churchill to send units of the new Division to help its defence, he had refused. He did not believe there was any immediate danger to Calais, and he did not wish to send the Division before it was ready. 'It is of great importance,' he wrote on September 4 to Prince Louis and Sir Frederick Sturdee, 'not to interrupt the training and formation of the Marine Brigade, which will now have to absorb a larger proportion of the recruits who have poured into Lord Kitchener's Army. In an emergency, if no other means were available, we no doubt should have to help the Governor, but I propose for the present to refuse his request.'

One idea which attracted Churchill was that of joint naval and military action in the Baltic. He believed that it was possible, while keeping the German High Sea Fleet penned in at the mouth of the Elbe, to send a British Fleet through the Skagerrak and Kattegat into the Baltic Sea. The British ships would then be at Russia's disposal for immediate action. On August 19 Churchill explained what he had in mind in a telegram to the Supreme Commander of the Russian Armies, the Grand Duke Nicholas:[2]

... It would be possible if we had the command of the Baltic to land a Russian army in order:—
1) to turn the flank & rear of German armies holding the Danzig–Thorn line, or which were elsewhere resisting the main Russian attack;
2) to attack Berlin from the North—only 90 miles in the direct line;
3) to attack Kiel & the Canal in force and to drive the German fleet to sea. ...

Churchill offered to supply 'at any time' the troop transports needed for the Russian force. The Grand Duke telegraphed his reply on August 24:

We appreciate in the highest degree the First Lord's offer to co-operate with us in the execution by our land forces of a landing operation on the North German Coast, should the British Fleet gain command of the Baltic Sea. The attainment of the aforesaid command would, in our opinion, in itself prove a most valuable and desirable factor towards the development of our offensive operations against Germany. We consider that the suggested landing operation, under favourable circumstances, would be quite feasible

[1] Edouard Berard, died 1918. Général de Brigade. Governor of Calais, April–November 1914.
[2] Nicholas Nicolaevitch, 1856–1929. Uncle of Tsar Nicholas II. Supreme Commander of the Russian Armies, 1914–15. Viceroy of the Caucasus, 1916–17. He died in exile in Paris.

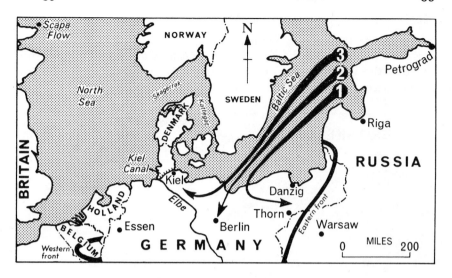

CHURCHILL'S PLAN FOR RUSSIAN ATTACKS ON GERMANY
19 AUGUST 1914

and fully expedient. We therefore gratefully accept in principle the First Lord's offer, but we add that we could avail ourselves thereof only should the general military situation lend itself to its application.

Nothing came of Churchill's scheme. The Russian military situation was never good enough to enable them to contemplate a sea invasion of Germany. But within a month, on September 17, Churchill decided, with Jellicoe's approval, to send several submarines to assist the Russians in the Baltic. On October 17 the first British submarine entered the Baltic, followed by two more within a week.

By nightfall on August 22 the German First and Second Armies were assembled across the centre of Belgium. Facing them were the troops of three nations: Belgians defending the great fortress of Namur, the French Fifth Army south of Charleroi and the British Expeditionary Force between Mons and the French border. Throughout August 23 the British troops were engaged in fierce fighting. It was the first occasion in the memory of anyone alive that British and German troops had fought each other on the field of battle. Late that evening Churchill asked Kitchener his opinion of the outcome, and learned that, although the Secretary of State for War had as yet received no news from the front, he was not entirely without hope. Kitchener told Churchill that it was still possible for the French, using Namur as their base, to thrust through the German lines, cutting off the German armies from their supply bases in Germany, and attacking them from behind.

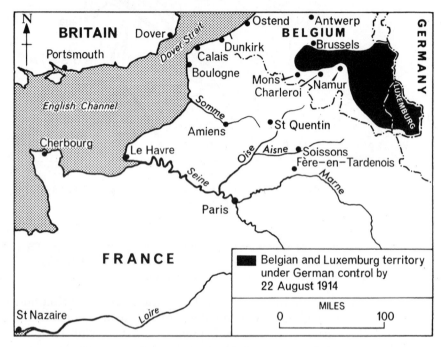

THE GERMAN ADVANCE BY 22 AUGUST 1914

On the following morning Churchill was at work at Admiralty House before seven o'clock. While he was studying the telegrams which had arrived during the night the door of his bedroom opened and Kitchener stood in the doorway. Churchill realized at once that something was wrong: 'Though his manner was quite calm, his face was different,' he recalled in *The World Crisis*. 'I had the subconscious feeling that it was distorted and discoloured as if it had been punched with a fist. His eyes rolled more than ever.' Kitchener read Churchill a telegram which he had just received from Sir John French. Namur had fallen. The British Expeditionary Force had been forced to retreat. Sir John French asked that 'immediate attention should be directed to the defence of Havre'. The German capture of Namur was ominous news, the need to defend

Le Havre sombre counsel. Churchill conferred at once with Prince Louis and the other members of the Board of Admiralty. All were deeply perturbed by the news of the British retreat. Instead of taking up Sir John French's proposal to reinforce Le Havre, the Admirals told Churchill that precautions must be taken even further west, at Cherbourg and St Nazaire. The fall of Namur seemed the prelude to disaster. Churchill telegraphed the news to Jellicoe at Scapa Flow, adding stern assurances:

News from France is disappointing & serious results of battle cannot yet be measured as it still continues over enormous front.

I have had the telegrams about it repeated to you.

We have not entered this business without resolve to see it through and you may rest assured that our action will be proportioned to the gravity of the need.

I have absolute confidence in final result.

No special action is required from you at present but you should address your mind to a naval situation which may arise where Germans control Calais and French coasts, and what ought to be the position of Grand Fleet in that event.

Churchill was able to stiffen Jellicoe's morale, but his own confidence was shaken. He needed reassurance, and the support of someone in whom he could confide. Crossing the Horse Guards' Parade, he sought out Lloyd George at the Treasury. 'I felt intensely the need of contact with him,' he wrote in *The World Crisis*, 'and I wanted to know how it would strike him and how he would face it.' Lloyd George was in conference when Churchill arrived, but seeing his friend beckoning him from the doorway, he went out immediately. It was their first private conversation since the outbreak of war three weeks earlier. Lloyd George gave Churchill the strength he sought.

The British retreat continued throughout August 24. All day Churchill worked at the Admiralty on the complex problem of transferring the British Army base from Le Havre to St Nazaire. That evening he wrote to his brother Jack: 'The news from Belgium is disappointing & may be serious. Our men seem to have stood up well to them & no doubt exacted a heavy forfeit. No one can tell how far this great adventure may carry us all. Unless we win, I do not want to live any more. But win we will.'

The retreat continued throughout August 25. That morning Churchill sent Jellicoe more hopeful news: 'British retirement on French frontier successfully and skilfully effected,' he telegraphed. 'Army now in strong position, well supported. Our casualties reported not severe considering continued engagement with two German corps and two cavalry divisions. Enemy was well punished and lost heavily. Main battle has still to be fought. General impression better this morning. Hope all is well with you.'

Churchill decided that one way in which he could influence the crisis was by sending the Marine Brigade to Ostend. They were to distract the German attention, and give the impression that a large British reinforcement was about to land. Kitchener approved of Churchill's initiative. The Marines were immediately alerted for action. That evening Churchill sent instructions to their commander, Sir George Aston:

1. At daylight to-morrow, if circumstances allow, you will disembark such portions of your brigade as have arrived at Ostend and occupy the town. You will push out reconnaissances of cyclists to Bruges, Thourout, and Dixmude. You will establish yourself at Ostend, forming an entrenched picket line around the town in such a way as to enable you to cover the debarkation of a Division of the Army. A squadron of aeroplanes will reach you before noon, having previously made an aerial reconnaissance of the country within 30 miles of Ostend. The aeroplanes will be placed under your orders.

2. The object of this movement is to create a diversion, favourable to the Belgians, who are advancing from Antwerp, and to threaten the western flank of the German southward advance. It should therefore be ostentatious. You should not advance inland from Ostend without further orders, but some enterprise may be permitted to the patrols. Information about the enemy will be supplied you personally at the Admiralty.

The object in view would be fully attained if a considerable force of the enemy were attracted to the coast. You will be re-embarked as soon as this is accomplished.

On August 26 the Cabinet approved the expedition to Ostend as an operation, Asquith reported to George V, 'involving little loss and calculated to give both material and moral support to Belgium'. That day three thousand Marines landed at Ostend. No German submarines interfered with their crossing, nor were any men lost while the Brigade was in Belgium. As Churchill had hoped, the German High Command was disturbed by rumours of large numbers of British troops landing on the Belgian coast. These rumours grew, transforming the force into eighty thousand Russians. After a week in Belgium, the Marines returned to Britain.

Churchill believed that the time would soon come when the British

Expeditionary Force would need continual reinforcements. Two days of retreat, and the prospect of many more, had momentarily convinced him that conscription, which he had always opposed, was now essential if defeat were to be avoided. On August 26 he raised the question in Cabinet, but without success. Lord Emmott,[1] the most recent member of the Cabinet, wrote in his diary: 'Winston wasted our time most atrociously today in pressing on our notice a premature scheme of conscription. He was both stupid and boring. Asquith contemptuous at first, but did not bear him down.' J. A. Pease was likewise unimpressed by Churchill's appeal, writing in his diary:

Churchill harangued us for half an hour on the necessity of compulsory service. Pointing out the importance of young unmarried men going to the front rather than the Territorial, a married man who had trained with a limited obligation, & now his patriotism was exploited by being pressed into going abroad & almost compelled to agree to do so, whilst others were loafing & cheering & doing nothing for their country etc etc etc.

We all sat and listened, much bored. The PM took it with impatience— the matter he said was not urgent. George said we need not be in a panic— the people would not listen to such proposals. The PM asked how many of our own men in the H of C would not assent, such a proposal would divide the country from one end to the other. . . .

K said it might come to this later on. He made no appeal for compulsion yet, he had got his 120,000 men & recruiting was still going on although he had only asked for 100,000—he could not arm more before April.

Despite this rebuff, Churchill never abandoned his belief that every possible source of manpower would have to be brought into action in order to check and ultimately to defeat the German advance; but as the immediate crisis passed he returned to his earlier faith in the voluntary system.

Meanwhile the situation in France was worsening. Sir John French was, however, encouraged on August 28 when he learned from London that a further Division, the 6th, was on its way to reinforce him. Its departure from England stripped the country of its professional soldiers. Churchill had given Kitchener the assurance which made this move possible. 'The Admiralty are confident of their ability to secure this country against invasion,' he had written on August 22. 'If you wish to send the 6th Division abroad at once, we should not raise any objection

[1] Alfred Emmott, 1858–1926. Defeated Churchill at the Oldham by-election, 1899. Liberal MP, 1899–1911. Created Baron, 1911. Under-Secretary of State for the Colonies, 1911–14. First Commissioner of Works, 1914–15. Director of the War Trade Department, 1915–19.

from the naval standpoint. . . . if you want to send the last Regular Division, the First Sea Lord and I are quite ready to agree, and so far as possible to accept responsibility.'

With Russian troops already on his mind, Churchill pondered upon another scheme that had been put to him: the transfer of Russian troops from Siberia to the western front. On August 28 he sent a message to Kitchener:

Here is an idea which deserves examination. The Siberian troops wd, if used against Germany & Austria, have to come South at an awkward moment & derange the communications (so I am told). On the other hand, it wd probably be easy to send them to Archangel, & it is (roughly) only 6 days from Archangel to Ostend.

If a couple of Russian Corps d'Armee were transported round this route, it wd be possible to strike at the German Communications in a very effective manner.

It is an interesting idea, though I dare say it would not greatly commend itself to the Russians. Don't trouble to answer.

Nothing came of this plan. But Churchill was determined to examine every possible solution. After the war F. E. Smith, then Lord Birkenhead, wrote in *Contemporary Personalities*: 'No one Department, hardly one war, was enough for him.' His brother's imminent departure for France with the Oxfordshire Hussars stimulated Churchill's thoughts to military action. 'I think a great deal of you all,' he wrote to his brother on August 26. 'As soon as the decisive battle has been fought at sea—I shall try to come out too, if there is any use for me.'

On August 28 the Admiralty was able to strike a note of optimism. In a naval action in the Heligoland Bight, three German cruisers were destroyed and three others damaged. No British ships were sunk. 'It was a fine feat of arms,' Churchill minuted on the report of the action, 'vindicated by success.' Churchill was elated by this first naval success of the war. On the evening of August 28, before the full details were known, his wife, who had just returned to Admiralty House with her two children, sent Kitchener the following note:

Dear Lord Kitchener,

Winston apologises for not writing himself but he is hastily dressing for dinner.

He asks me to tell you that the bag to-day consists of 2 enemy's Destroyers sunk & many injured, 2 Cruisers sunk & one on fire & apparently sinking which disappeared into mist.

None of our ships sunk, some of them damaged, but it is hoped not badly— Winston thinks this is rather a 'Coup'——

Yours v sincerely
Clementine S. Churchill

As soon as the full details of the victory were known, Churchill telegraphed the news to Haldane, who replied at once: 'Your telegram has just come & I have read it to Grey. Warmest congratulations on this splendid piece of work done by the fleet. It is worthy of the inspiring spirit of their First Lord. The British public & our allies will grow a cubit in confidence when they read the news tomorrow.' There was general euphoria. Commodore Tyrwhitt,[1] who brought the damaged light cruiser *Arethusa* into Sheerness under tow, wrote to his wife: 'We had a great response on the way from the Nore to Chatham. Every ship and everybody cheered like mad. Winston met us at Sheerness and came up to Chatham with us and fairly slobbered over me. Offered me any ship I liked and all the rest of it. . . . Everybody quite mad with delight at the success of our first naval venture.' Clementine Churchill welcomed another hero of the action, who during the battle had rescued 220 of the men from the German cruiser *Mainz*.

Dear Commodore Keyes,

I hear you are in London, just back from your splendid Heligoland achievement.

Will you give us the pleasure of lunching with us to-day at 1.45? It would be a great pleasure to see you.

Yours v sincerely
Clementine S. Churchill

Within a month of the outbreak of war Lord Kitchener and Sir John French had begun to quarrel. Churchill admired them both, and had been accepted by both as a friend. On August 31 the dispute reached a climax when Sir John French telegraphed that he was unwilling to co-operate any longer with the French Army, and that he intended to fall back behind Paris. The Cabinet were alarmed by his decision, and

---

[1] Reginald Yorke Tyrwhitt, 1870–1951. Entered Navy, 1883. Commodore, commanding the Destroyer Flotilla of the Frist Fleet, 1913–16. Knighted, 1917. Created Baronet, 1919. Commanded the Third Light Squadron, Mediterranean, 1921–2. Commanding officer, coast of Scotland, 1923–5. Commander-in-Chief, China Station, 1927–9. Admiral, 1929. Commander-in-Chief, the Nore, 1930–3. Admiral of the Fleet, 1934. He married, 1930, Angela Corbally.

feared the complete breakdown of Anglo-French co-operation. With the approval of his colleagues, Kitchener replied that the Cabinet expected 'that you will, as far as possible, conform to the plans of General Joffre[1] for the conduct of the campaign'. But Sir John French telegraphed again. Many of his troops, he declared, were 'shattered'. All of them needed 'to rest and refit'. He was willing to 'advance into the front line to-morrow and do our utmost if you choose to order it', but he was sure 'that the result of this would be grave disaster to the French troops'. This telegram reached London just before midnight on August 31. Asquith called an emergency conference of Ministers at 10 Downing Street. Kitchener, Churchill, Lloyd George and McKenna[2] were present. 'We came to the decided conclusion,' Asquith informed Venetia Stanley, 'that the only thing to be done was for Kitchener to go there without delay, & unravel the situation, & if necessary put the fear of God into them all. He is a real sportsman when an emergency appears, & went straight home to change his clothes & collect his kit, & started by special train from Charing Cross about 1.30 am this morning. Winston provided him with a fast cruiser at Dover . . .'

Kitchener and French met at the British Embassy in Paris on September 1. It was a strained meeting, not the least because Kitchener appeared in the uniform of a Field-Marshal, which French considered an insult to his own Field-Marshal's status in France. Encouraged by Asquith, Churchill tried to mediate between the two Field-Marshals. Writing to Sir John French on September 2, he tried to soothe his friend:

I have wanted so much to write to you and yet not to bother you with reading letters. Still, I suppose there are moments when you can find the leisure to read a few lines from a friend. The Cabinet was bewildered by your telegram proposing to retire from the line, coming on the top of a casualty list of 6,000 and your reports as to the good spirit of the troops. We feared that you and Joffre might have quarrelled, or that something had happened to the Army of which we had not been informed. In these circumstances telegraphing was useless, and a personal consultation was indispensable if further misunderstandings were to be avoided.

[1] Joseph Jacques Césaire Joffre, 1852–1931. As a 2nd Lieutenant, he took part in the defence of Paris in 1870. Appointed Commander-in-Chief of the French Army, 5 August 1914. In December 1916 he was deprived of all real authority. The British Government awarded him an honorary GCB in 1914 and an honorary OM in 1919.

[2] Reginald McKenna, 1863–1943. Liberal MP, 1895–1918. President of the Board of Education, 1907–8. First Lord of the Admiralty, 1908–11. Home Secretary, 1911–15. Chancellor of the Exchequer, May 1915–December 1916. Chairman, Midland Bank, 1919–43.

I am sure it would be wise to have some good officer on your staff . . . who could without troubling you unduly, give us a clear and complete impression of what is taking place day by day. Our only wish is to sustain and support you. We are at a point where losses will only rouse still further the spirit of the nation, provided they are incurred, as yours have been, in brilliant and successful action. But we ought to be kept in a position to form a true and connected impression of the course of events.

For my own part, I am only anxious that you shall be sustained and re-inforced in every way, and I look forward confidently to seeing you ere long at the head of a quarter of a million men, and in the spring, of half a million. . . .

In case any further difficulties arise, and you think I can be of any use, you have only to send for me, and subject to the naval situation I could reach you very quickly by motor-car or aeroplane.

It is hard sitting here day after day with so many friends engaged. The resolution of the nation is splendid. It is a different country to the one you left. . . .

God guard you and prosper our arms.

Sir John French replied on September 3:

My dear Churchill,

Thank you very much for your kind & encouraging letter. It was a keen pleasure to hear from you & to read your words.

I have had a terribly anxious time & the troops have suffered severely but they are simply *glorious*! I have $2\frac{1}{2}$ Army Corps here now & a Cavalry Division; multiply the former by 6 & the latter by 4, and I would get to Berlin in 6 weeks without any French help at all. . . .

There has been some outstanding misunderstanding at home as to my relations with Gen Joffre, the French C in C. We have been on the very best terms all thro' & he has spoken most kindly of the help he has received from us. I can't understand what brought Kitchener to Paris. I am writing to you as one of my greatest friends & I'm sure you'll let me write freely & privately.

K's visit was really most unfortunate—He took me away from the front to visit him in Paris on a very critical day when I should have been directing the operations most carefully and I tell you between ourselves *strictly* that when I returned to my Head Quarters I found a very critical situation existing (8 pm! !) and authoritative orders & directions badly needed. It was the day that the Guards & Cavalry Brigades were so heavily engaged.

I do beg of you, my dear Friend, to add one more to all the many & great kindnesses you have done me & *stop this interference* with field operations. Kitchener *knows nothing* about European warfare. Of course he's a fine organiser but he never was & never will be a Commander in the field. . . .

You say in your postscript 'You ought to tell more'—I assure you Kitchener has been told *almost everything*. In spite of sleepless nights I have written him long private accounts of the whole affair and my telegrams have been very full—*as to casualties,* in the continual fighting we have had it has been absolutely impossible to get at them a moment sooner.

My warmest thanks for your kindness & friendship which I value immensely. I am hoping to see you with us. Come whenever you can & everything shall be arranged for your comfort & safety.

Yrs alys, my dear Churchill
JDP French

To this letter Sir John French added a postscript at six the following morning:

On reading over what I wrote at 12 last night I think it may be rather strong—for I have to remember you are a Cabinet Minister as well as a Great Friend of mine. If I have erred in any way forgive me please!

I have opened my heart to you! What I feel is that I have been quite enough tried now between South Africa & this Campaign & I have not given the Gov any reason to distrust me.

To send another FM out here to lecture me (he came in FM's uniform!) seems to me a sign of distrust & it *hurts* me. Remember this if you think I should not have written like this & burn this letter PLEASE.

The pressure of the German military advance was severe. Despite brave rearguard actions, the British Expeditionary Force was being pushed almost to the suburbs of Paris. In thirteen days it retreated nearly a hundred and fifty miles. Over fifteen hundred men were killed, wounded or taken prisoner. The newspapers listed the dead; and the daily appearance of familiar names made a deep impact.

The victory in the Heligoland Bight had focused public hopes on the Admiralty. On September 4 the two Party leaders, Asquith and Bonar Law, were the main speakers at a Guildhall Banquet. Churchill was present, but not billed to speak. Balfour, in whose constituency the meeting was held, was also on the platform. Asquith made a stirring speech which *The Times* considered 'of the noblest order, solemn and impressive'. He declared that Britain would not sheathe the sword until Belgium's wrongs were righted. Bonar Law spoke next, more briefly but with 'force and fervour'. Then, while Balfour was about to speak, there came a chant of mounting intensity from the City audience: 'Churchill! Churchill! Churchill! We want Churchill! We want Churchill!' Churchill told the audience briefly that they could trust the Royal Navy, and concluded amid their cheers: 'Sure I am of this, that you have only to endure to conquer. You have only to persevere to save yourselves, and to save all those who rely upon you. You have only to go right on, and at the end of the road, be it short or long, victory and honour will be found!' The impact of his few remarks was considerable. 'My dear Winston,' Lord Esher[1] reported on the following day, 'I met Bonar Law yesterday who told me that you had by far the greatest reception at the Guildhall. He said that this in the City of London with AJB present was a most remarkable tribute.'

Churchill had reason for his assertive self-confidence and optimism. During the Agadir crisis of 1911, after examining the naval, diplomatic and military problems of war with Germany, he had written a memorandum entitled 'Military Aspects of the Continental Problem'. Basing his arguments upon the premise that Britain, France and Russia were in alliance, at war simultaneously with Germany and Austria, he had envisaged the decisive military operations being between France and Germany. He forecast that the initial German advance would have sufficient power to drive the French back, in twenty days, on Paris and the south. 'All plans based upon the opposite assumption,' he wrote, 'ask too much of fortune.' But he had argued that during each successive day of the German advance the German armies would be weakened by many causes: by the heavier losses always borne by attacking forces, by growing Russian pressure 'from the thirtieth day', by the arrival of the British Expeditionary Force and by the lengthening German lines of communication. His memorandum had continued:

By the fortieth day Germany should be extended at full strain both internally and on her war fronts, and this strain will become daily more severe and ultimately overwhelming, unless it is relieved by decisive victories in France. If the French army has not been squandered by precipitate or desperate action, the balance of forces should be favourable after the fortieth day, and will improve steadily as time passes. For the German armies will be confronted with a situation which combines an ever-growing need for a successful offensive with a battle-front which tends continually towards numerical equality. Opportunities for the decisive trial of strength may then occur.

Such a policy demands heavy and hard sacrifices from France, who must,

[1] Reginald Baliol Brett, 1852–1930. Liberal MP, 1880–5. Secretary to the Office of Works, 1895–1902. 2nd Viscount Esher, 1899. A permanent member of the Committee of Imperial Defence, 1905–18. In 1914 he established himself in Paris as the head of a British Mission, and remained there for the rest of the war.

with great constancy, expose herself to invasion, to having her provinces occupied by the enemy, and to the investment of Paris, and whose armies may be committed to retrograde or defensive operations. Whether her rulers could contemplate or her soldiers endure this trial may depend upon the military support which Great Britain can give.

The first part of Churchill's memorandum was fulfilled in the twenty days he stipulated. By the thirtieth day, with the British and French forces still in retreat, a mood of depression had fallen upon a shocked Britain. On September 2, ten days before 'the fortieth day', Churchill reprinted his forecast, sending copies to many of his colleagues. He wanted them to see, assuming that his forecast was correct, that the period of greatest danger was over, that the impetus of the German attack was likely to weaken, and that the moment for counter-attack would soon arrive. Many of those who read the memorandum were excited and relieved. 'I have tonight read your remarkable military appreciation written in 1911,' Haldane wrote on September 3: 'It is extraordinarily accurate as a forecast of events up to now, & shows great insight—a memorable document in full. Asquith said to me this afternoon that you were the equivalent of a large force in the field & this is true. You inspire us all by your courage & resolution.'

On September 8 Balfour wrote to Edward Marsh: 'It is a triumph of prophecy!' General Sir Ian Hamilton,[1] who was in command of the forces gathered to intercept an invading army, was similarly impressed, writing from the War Office on the same day: 'This is indeed a masterly paper. All the way down you hit the nail bang on the head as if you were a historian recapitulating rather than a statesman risking prophecies!' Fisher was also enthusiastic; he too was given to prophecy, writing on September 9: 'Your memorandum of AUGUST 1911 is both astonishing and exhilarating! *It makes one trust your further forecast!* I also have a minor coincidence! A friend sends me a letter of mine also written in *August 1911* saying that Armageddon would begin in August 1914 and that Jellicoe would be our Admiralissimo! . . .'

---

[1] Ian Standish Monteith Hamilton, 1853–1947. Entered Army, 1872. Major-General, 1900. Knighted, 1900. Chief of Staff to Lord Kitchener, 1901–2. General, 1914. Commander of the Central Force, responsible for the defence of England in the event of invasion, August 1914–March 1915. Commanded the Mediterranean Expeditionary Force, March–October 1915.

3

'The Admiralty is now on its trial'

AT the end of August Churchill had sent Commander Samson[1] to
Dunkirk with instructions to establish an air base from which
Zeppelins could be attacked before they set off on the final stage of
their flight to England. The Royal Naval Air Service pilots took part in
a series of reconnaisance flights. On September 3 Samson reported in
his log: '3 pm. No 42, Lieut Dalrymple Clark[2] (2½ hours' flight) proceeded to Douai and Cambrai and back, and expended one bomb on
about 40 Germans—some evidently hurt.' On the following morning
Samson himself, in a flight lasting one hour and forty minutes, flew from
Dunkirk to Armentières and back. Once again he reported on the
action: 'Expended two large bombs on four motor-cars, about 40 men
round the cars.'

These brief sorties were part of Churchill's plan to put the skills of the
Royal Naval Air Service to military use. As a result of the many hours
which he had spent flying with the young pilots before the war, he knew
what they were capable of doing, and wanted to satisfy their keenness
for action in some positive way. He knew many of the pilots personally.
Several of them had been his flying instructors when, between 1912 and
1914, he had spent many of his weekends at Eastchurch learning to fly.

On September 3 Kitchener asked Churchill to take over from the
War Office full responsibility for the aerial defence of Britain. Churchill
was therefore in charge, not only of the Royal Naval Air Service

[1] Charles Rumney Samson, 1883–1931. Entered Navy, 1898. A pioneer aviator who
carried out some of the earliest experiments with seaplanes and night flights. Commander,
Royal Naval Air Service, 1913–15. Commanded the air forces at the siege of Antwerp,
October 1914; the Dardanelles, 1915. Wing-Captain RNAS, 1918. Group Captain, RAF,
1919. Air Commodore, 1922.
[2] Ian Hew Waldegrave Dalrymple Clark, c. 1888–1916. Sub-Lieutenant, Royal Naval
Reserve, 1913. Flight-Commander, Royal Naval Air Service, 1915. Killed in an aeroplane
accident at Cranwell.

aircraft but of all those aircraft of the Army-controlled Royal Flying Corps which were needed for home defence. His extra tasks included the mounting of searchlights and anti-aircraft barrages around London, and the purchase of sufficient aircraft to ensure that, despite the inevitable loss, there would be enough to meet Zeppelin attacks. Two months later, on October 31, having read a favourable report of the trial flight of the first flying boat in the United States, he minuted: 'Order a dozen as soon as possible.'[1]

On his first day as aerial overlord, Churchill wrote to the Director of the Air Division at the Admiralty, Captain Sueter:[2] 'Let me have a return on one sheet of paper showing all anti-aircraft guns, regular or improvised, available afloat and ashore, at the present time; and what deliveries may be expected in the next two months. Let me have also any suggestions for increasing their number. No one can doubt that aerial attack upon England must be a feature of the near future.' Two days later, on September 5, Churchill asserted, in a departmental memorandum, the principle that the best means of aerial defence was to attack the German aircraft as near as possible to their point of departure, informing the Board of Admiralty:

(a) A strong oversea force of aeroplanes to deny the French and Belgian coasts to the enemy's aircraft, and to attack all Zeppelins and air bases or temporary air bases which it may be sought to establish, and which are in reach.

(b) We must be in constant telegraphic and telephonic communication with the oversea aeroplane squadrons. We must maintain an intercepting force of aeroplanes and airships at some convenient point within range of a line drawn from Dover to London, and local defence flights at Eastchurch and Calshot.

(c) A squadron of aeroplanes will be established at Hendon, also in telephonic communication with the other stations, for the purpose of attacking enemy aircraft which may attempt to molest London. Landing grounds must be prepared in all the parks; railings must be removed, and the area marked out by a large white circle by day and by a good system of lighting at night. It is indispensable that airmen of the Hendon flight should be able to fly by night, and their machines must be fitted with the necessary lights and instruments.

[1] On November 7 the Admiralty ordered four flying boats from the Curtiss Company of New York and Buffalo, eight from the Aircraft Manufacturing Company of New York.

[2] Murray Fraser Sueter, 1872–1960. Entered Navy, 1886. Assistant Director of Naval Ordnance at the Admiralty, 1903–5. Member, Advisory Committee in Aeronautics, 1908–17. Captain, 1909. Director of the Air Department at the Admiralty, 1911–15. Commodore, 1915. Superintendent of Aircraft Construction, 1915–17. Commanded Royal Naval Air Service units, Southern Italy, 1917–18. Rear-Admiral, 1920. Conservative MP, 1921–45. Knighted, 1934.

On that same day Churchill wrote to Prince Louis and Captain Sueter with further plans for the Dunkirk base:

In order to discharge adequately the responsibilities which we have assumed for the aerial defence of England, it is necessary that we should maintain an aerial control over the area approximately 100 miles radius from Dunkirk. To do this, we must support the aeroplanes which are stationed on the French coast with sufficient armed motor cars and personnel to enable advanced subsidiary aeroplane bases to be established 30, 40 and 50 miles inland.

The armoured motor-cars were sent at once to France. They acted in co-ordination with Samson and his pilots, protecting their forward aeroplane bases. The armoured cars had to ensure that all the outlying aeroplane bases were kept clear of raiding parties of Germans. Churchill also sent to Dunkirk two hundred Royal Marines whose task was to follow up the advantages secured by the armoured cars. This Dunkirk enterprise, which Churchill's critics soon nicknamed the 'Dunkirk Circus', was on a small scale. Each of its three squadrons of aeroplanes contained less than twelve machines. The armoured car section consisted of sixty motor-cars, each protected by armour-plating and armed with a single Maxim gun. Samson's orders, dated September 1, laid down that in all sorties from Dunkirk, 'French soldiers if possible should accompany the English, so as to make up a Franco-English expedition'; but in the event, it remained entirely in British hands. A base hospital was set up at Dunkirk, with four motor ambulances. Provisions were sent direct to Dunkirk from the Royal Naval Air Service Station at Sheerness. A small Headquarters' staff of six officers was set up in Dunkirk itself.

The three squadrons of aircraft were commanded by E. L. Gerrard,[1] Spenser Grey[2] and Richard Bell Davies,[3] each of whom had, within the previous year, been among those who had taught Churchill to fly.

[1] Eugene Louis Gerrard, 1881–1963. 2nd Lieutenant, Royal Marine Light Infantry, 1901. Squadron Commander, Royal Flying Corps (Naval Wing), 1912. Commander, December 1914. Group Captain, Royal Air Force, 1919. Air Commodore, commanding the forces in Palestine, 1929.

[2] Spenser Douglas Adair Grey, 1889–1937. Lieutenant, Royal Naval Air Service, 1913. Lieutenant-Commander, August 1914. Lieutenant-Commander, August 1914. Sent on Admiralty mission to United States to purchase six flying boats, December 1914. Commander, flying boat experimental flying tests, Hendon, March 1915.

[3] Richard Bell Davies, 1886–1966. Lieutenant, Royal Naval Air Service, 1913–14. Served at the Dardanelles, 1915, winning the Victoria Cross. In charge of the Air Section of the Naval Staff, 1920–4. Captain, 1st Cruiser Squadron, 1928–30. Commanded Royal Naval Barracks, Devonport, 1936–8. Rear-Admiral, Naval Air Stations, 1939–40.

Another of his former flying instructors, Reginald Marix,[1] was also at Dunkirk. The four armoured car squadrons were each divided into three sections, one of which was commanded by his friend, Baron de Forest. Among the squadron commanders was Josiah Wedgwood,[2] a Liberal MP who during the debate in Parliament on the outbreak of war had been among the few who protested against Britain's involvement.

The first combined aeroplane and armoured car reconnaissance took place on the afternoon of September 4. Samson, who had returned that morning from his successful bombing raid near Armentières, sent an account of the afternoon's activities to the Admiralty:

I have the honour to report that scouting has been carried out by aeroplanes in the region beyond Cassel, and while waiting at this place for the return of a machine I was informed that a German motor-car containing 6 Germans was advancing on Cassel.

As it is essential for the safety of aeroplanes scouting that Germans should not get into Cassel, I determined to prevent them proceeding any further.

The force at my disposal was 3 officers and 5 men in two motor-cars, one fitted with a maxim. To avoid a fight in the streets of Cassel with consequent German reprisals on the Town, I went out to meet them, intending to form an ambush at a suitable place. Unfortunately there was not time to do this, and the German car was met one mile outside the Town.

As soon as they saw us they stopped 400 yards away. Our second car was turned round in case a retreat was necessary and fire was opened with the maxim and rifles. One German was seen to drop. The German car backed 20 yards towards a corner which gave some cover, turned and fled towards Lille. Unfortunately, after firing 80 rounds, the maxim gun was disabled. I did not consider it expedient to give chase owing to the fact that numerous German cars, including some armoured motor-cars, were on the road between Lille and Bailleul. I have ample proof that 2 Germans were rather severely wounded.

The scouting aeroplane No 42, pilot Lieut Dalrymple Clark, saw the German motor-car flying towards Armentières at a great speed. He followed it beyond Bailleul.

[1] Reginald Lennox George Marix, 1889–1966. Lieutenant, Royal Naval Air Service, 1912–15. Served in Belgium, France and the Dardanelles, 1914–16. Lost a leg after a crash while testing an aeroplane near Paris, 1916. Served in Coastal Command and Transport Command, Royal Air Force, 1939–45. Retired as Air Vice-Marshal, 1945.

[2] Josiah Clement Wedgwood, 1872–1943. Liberal MP, 1906–19. Commanded armoured cars in France, Antwerp, Gallipoli and East Africa, 1914–17. Assistant Director, Trench Warfare Department, Ministry of Munitions, 1917. War Office Mission to Siberia, 1918. Labour MP, 1919–42. Vice-chairman of the Labour Party, 1921–4. Chancellor of the Duchy of Lancaster, 1924. Created Baron, 1942.

I wish to bring to your notice the conduct of Lieut F. R. Samson,[1] RNVR, who turned his car round to prepare our retreat and remained seated in his car under fire according to my previous orders; Sub-Lieut Nalder,[2] RNVR, who stood by his car ready to drive it at my orders; Armourer's Mate Harper,[3] RN, who fired the maxim in a very exposed position very calmly and did not fire too rapidly, but paused every 10 rounds to see how his shots were falling. The other officers and men of the party behaved without any flurry or excitement, and fired very steadily and obeyed all orders with promptitude. . . .

There were no injuries of any sort to my party. This slight encounter will, I hope, discourage the Germans, who have up to the present gone about the neighbourhood in motor-cars doing what they liked.

Aerial reconnaissance, armoured car support and bombing raids continued throughout September. There were unexpected dangers. On September 12 a wind of seventy miles an hour caught the aeroplanes of Gerrard's squadron while they were on the ground at their base. All were blown from 100 to 300 yards across the airfield, turning cartwheels as they went. So bad was the damage that most of the machines had to be dismantled, and some of them destroyed.

The 'Dunkirk Circus' did valuable reconnaissance work, and its bombing activities, despite their small scale, provided the offensive action which Churchill believed was important in maintaining public morale. On September 12 Philip Sarell,[4] the British Consul at Dunkirk, wrote to Sir Eyre Crowe[5] at the Foreign Office: 'Samson's raids have been so extraordinarily successful hitherto, and we have evidently disconcerted the Germans so much, that we must manage somehow or other to enable him to carry on what he has so brilliantly and successfully initiated.'

During the British retreat from Mons, a special correspondent of *The Times* who was covering the fortunes of the British Expeditionary

[1] Felix Rumney Samson, 1885–   . Lieutenant, Royal Naval Volunteer Reserve, August 1914. Lieutenant-Commander, 1916. Major, Royal Air Force, 1918.

[2] John Fielding Nalder, 1896–   . Royal Naval Air Service, 1914–16. Flight Sub-Lieutenant, 1917.

[3] *Possibly:* William Harper, 1884–1951. Entered Navy, 1910. Gunner, November 1912. Mate, April 1914. Lieutenant, August 1915. Retired, 1922. Lieutenant-Commander, active list, 1939–45.

[4] Philip Charles Sarell, 1866–1942. Entered Consular Service, 1883. British Consul at Dunkirk, 1908–18. Consul-General, Tunis, 1920–3; Barcelona, 1923–6.

[5] Eyre Crowe, 1864–1925. Entered Foreign Office as a Clerk, 1885; Senior Clerk, 1906. Knighted, 1911. Assistant Under-Secretary of State, Foreign Office, 1912–19; Permanent Under-Secretary of State, 1920–5.

Force, Arthur Moore,[1] sent a despatch from Amiens to Printing House Square in which he wrote of the 'terrible defeat' sustained by the British forces. Anticipating the usual censorship, *The Times* had themselves deleted certain passages before sending the report to F. E. Smith at the Press Bureau. F. E. Smith not only reinstated the deletions but added an extra paragraph of his own at the end of the despatch, calling for more reinforcements to be sent to the front. The despatch had appeared in *The Times* on August 30. It told of 'the broken bits of many regiments', and of British soldiers 'battered with marching'. The morale of the troops was still high, the despatch concluded, but reinforcements were urgently needed. The publication of this report caused consternation throughout Britain. Churchill did not believe that the alarm was justified. On September 5 he wrote to the proprietor of *The Times*, Lord Northcliffe[2]: 'I think you ought to realise the harm that has been done by Sunday's publication in the 'Times'. . . . I never saw such panic-stricken stuff written by any war correspondent before; and this served up on the authority of the 'Times' can be made, and has been made, a weapon against us in every doubtful state. . . .' Northcliffe replied tersely on September 7 that Moore was 'one of the most experienced correspondents in the service of the paper', and that in view of F. E. Smith's additions 'there was no other possible conclusion except that this was the Government's deliberate wish'. To this, Churchill could give no reply.

Asquith asked Churchill to draft a Press communiqué which might allay public fears. The communiqué, which was published anonymously on September 5, gave fuller details about the retreat than had yet appeared in the Press, and reassured the public that all was not lost. 'There is no doubt,' Churchill concluded, 'that our men have established a personal ascendancy over the Germans, and that they are conscious of the fact that with anything like even numbers the result would not be doubtful.' The Press clamoured for more information. 'I

---

[1] Arthur Moore, 1880–1962. Special Correspondent of *The Times*, in Constantinople, during Young Turk rebellion, 1908; Persia, 1909, 1910–12; St Petersburg, 1913; Albania, 1914; France, August 1914. Captured by German cavalry patrol, 2 September 1914, but released. Joined Rifle Brigade, 1915; served at Dardanelles and Salonika. Lieutenant-Colonel, 1917. Entered Royal Flying Corps, 1917. Assistant Editor, Calcutta *Statesman*, 1924–34. Member, Legislative Assembly, Delhi, 1932–3. Managing Editor, Calcutta *Statesman*, 1934–42. Public Relations Adviser to Lord Mountbatten in South-East Asia 1944–5.

[2] Alfred Charles William Harmsworth, 1865–1922. Newspaper proprietor. Bought the *Evening News* (1894), *Daily Mail* (1896), *Daily Mirror* (1903), *The Times* (1908). Created Baronet, 1903. Created Baron Northcliffe, 1905. Chairman, British War Mission to the United States, 1917. Director of Propaganda in Enemy Countries, 1918. Created Viscount, 1918.

am just going to tell Winston to repeat his feat of last Sunday,' Asquith wrote to Venetia Stanley on September 5, 'and to dish up for them with all his best journalistic condiments the military history of the week. K is absolutely no use for this kind of thing, and has an undisguised contempt for the "public" in all its moods & manifestations.' Asquith then wrote to Churchill to explain what he wanted:

Private
My dear Winston,
    The papers are complaining, not without reason, that we keep them on starvation diet.
    I think the time has come for you to repeat last Sunday's feat, & let them have thro' the Bureau an 'appreciation' of the events of the week; with such a seasoning of condiments as your well-skilled hand can supply.
    For all that the public know, they might as well be living in the days of the prophet Isaiah, whose idea of a battle was 'confused noise & garments rolled in blood'.

Yrs always
HHA

In his memorandum of August 1911 Churchill had forecast that by the fortieth day of war the German advance would be halted. This was what occurred. On September 3, thirty-three days after the German attack had begun, the French and British forces began to move forward, across the Marne. After five days of intense and often confused fighting the immediate danger was over. The French armies, supported by the whole of the British Expeditionary Force, drove the Germans away from Paris. During the last phase of the battle, Churchill's cousin Frederick Guest,[1] who was serving on Sir John French's staff, sent him a report from the front. 'The tide of invasion seems to have ebbed,' he wrote on September 8, 'and without a serious conflict. One is inclined to think that they have shot their bolt and spent their strength within sight of their goal. It is clear that they suddenly realised that their great outflanking movement was being itself outflanked and sudden orders were given to turn about and trek NE.' On September 10, when the battle was over, Sir John French himself hastened to inform Churchill of the dramatic upsurge of Allied fortunes:

Since I wrote last to you the whole atmosphere has changed and for 5 solid days we have been pursuing instead of pursued & the Germans have had simple Hell.

[1] Frederick Edward Guest, 1875–1937. Liberal MP, 1910–29. ADC to Sir John French, 1914–16. Secretary of State for Air, 1921–2. Conservative MP, 1931–7. The third son of 1st Baron Wimborne; Churchill's cousin.

This very day we have captured several hundred, cut off a whole lot of Transport and got 10 to 12 guns—and the ground is strewn with dead & wounded Germans. Something like this happened yesterday & the day before. But that is nothing to what they have lost in front of the 5 & 6 French Armies which have been much more strongly opposed. They are indeed fairly on the run & we are following hard. . . .

I was afraid of Joffre's strategy at first & thought he ought to have taken the offensive much sooner—but he was just right.

Each day the German resistance has slackened—I was up with the Cavalry till almost dark last night and noticed a great change. . . .

The Battle of the Marne was decisive, and the Germans began to fall back. But Churchill continued to worry about the small size of the British Army, and the potential weakness of the voluntary system. He wanted to plan for a swift and impressive victory on a large scale. 'Winston was in his most characteristic mood,' Balfour reported to his sister[1] after dining with Asquith on September 8. 'He talks airily of a British Army of a million men, and tells me he is making siege mortars at Woolwich as big, or bigger, than the German ones, in order to crush the Rhine fortresses.'

The German armies were in retreat; but they had no intention of returning to the Rhine. It was still within their power to make a dash for the Channel ports. If they could capture Calais or Dunkirk, it would be possible for them to try to reassert their military superiority. Churchill had sensed the danger to the Channel ports. On September 3, at the opening of the Battle of the Marne, he had expressed his fears in an official minute to Prince Louis. 'The danger from aerial attack must not be underrated,' he wrote. 'The possibility of the Germans taking very heavy guns to Calais after taking the town, and getting submarines down from the Elbe to operate from Calais as a base, should also be considered. We could of course stop any surface craft, but submarines might slip through secretly and be a great nuisance when once established.'

Fearing danger to the Channel ports, and anxious to see if his airmen at Dunkirk could take a useful part in keeping the Germans from the coast, Churchill crossed over to France on September 10. His departure was kept secret, not only from the Press but also from the Cabinet. Asquith, who alone knew of it, told Venetia Stanley: 'Entre nous, the adventurous Winston is just off to Dunkirk to superintend his new flying base: he will be back by lunch time to-morrow. Don't say anything of this, as he doesn't want the colleagues to know.' Churchill did

[1] Alice Blanche Balfour, 1850–1936. Acted as Balfour's housekeeper at Whittingehame.

useful work during his brief visit. He was accompanied by two senior Admiralty officials, Admiral Hood and Admiral Oliver, as well as by Captain Sueter, the Director of the Air Department. They examined the fortifications of Dunkirk and discussed the defence of the port with the French authorities. Churchill promised them the assistance of British warships in the event of a siege, and was much impressed by the measures which they had already taken for the city's defence. His visit was a success. The British Consul at Dunkirk, Philip Sarell, reported to the Foreign Office on September 10 that the Governor had 'been very much encouraged' by Churchill's visit; on September 12 he telegraphed again that the visit had had a 'most wholesome' effect on the city's morale.

Within a few days of Churchill's visit to Dunkirk, Joffre asked Kitchener to send British reinforcements to the Dunkirk garrison. He wanted the British troops for a dual purpose: to defend the city in the event of a German attack, and to give the Germans the impression that a large British force was in the area. Kitchener brought the problem to Churchill, who agreed to send the Marine Brigade on condition that the War Office would contribute a Yeomanry force. Kitchener declared that he would send, not a small force but a whole regiment of Yeomanry. Colonel Ollivant took charge of the administration of the expedition. As Sir George Aston, who had commanded the Marines during their sortie to Ostend, had fallen ill, Major-General Paris[1] was given the command. The Marines moved ostentatiously through Ypres, Lille, Tournai and Douai.

Kitchener had chosen the Oxfordshire Hussars as the territorial force to accompany the Marines. This was the regiment in which Churchill and his brother had served for many years, and of which their cousin the Duke of Marlborough was Colonel-in-Chief. Churchill arranged for the Oxfordshire Hussars to take with them eight 3-ton lorries and several other vehicles from naval stores. 'Probably no regiment ever went to France,' their regimental historian, Adrian Keith-Falconer,[2] recorded, 'accompanied by such a fleet of motor transport solely for its

[1] Archibald Paris, 1861–1937. Entered Royal Marine Artillery, 1879. Commanded a column of troops in South Africa, 1900–2; forced to surrender owing to the flight of most of his troops and promoted Lieutenant-Colonel for distinguished service in the field, 1902. Commanded Royal Marine Brigade, September 1914. Major-General, commanding Royal Naval Division, Antwerp, October 1914; Dardanelles, 1915; France, 1916. Severely wounded, 1916, losing a leg. Knighted, 1916.

[2] Adrian Wentworth Keith-Falconer, 1888–1959. Lieutenant, Queen's Own Oxfordshire Hussars, 1914. Served Dunkirk, September 1914; Antwerp, October 1914. Major, British Armistice Commission, Spa and Cologne, 1919–20. Private Secretary to Lord Curzon, 1921–3. He published *The Oxfordshire Hussars in the Great War* in 1927.

own personal use.' Such special Admiralty patronage did not endear Churchill to the War Office.

On September 14, shortly before the regiment left for France, Churchill wrote to his brother:

My dear,

. . . I am hopeful that this business will not be serious. It is intended only as a demonstration on the enemy's flank: & I expected that the armed motor cars wd do the work: you being merely a support & to enable the infantry to move. But now it seems that German cavalry in gt force has come all over this area. You will be kept in close relation to the perimeter of the fortress wh is extensive & well fortified—as I know from personal inspection. . . .

I hope to come over in a day or two to see that things are well started. You know how much I care about you—but it is a gt honour for the regiment —& I am glad to have you in my hands.

Your ever loving
W

The armoured cars, together with fifty double-decker buses sent over by Ollivant, and the aeroplane detachment, were all under the command of Commander Samson. The drivers who had come with their buses from London were immediately enlisted in the Marine Brigade. When Asquith wrote to Venetia Stanley on September 19 he was critical of the arrangements for which Joffre had asked, and which Churchill had worked out with Kitchener's support:

And what do you think I discovered? That he had (with K's consent, who is heartily glad to get rid of them) despatched the Oxfordshire Yeomanry! his own corps, with brother Jack (who is a Major in it) &c. . . . There are about 450 of them, all told, and if they encounter the Germans in any force, I fear we shall see very few of them back again. I hope, however, that like that other little jaunt to Ostend, of wh I told you some weeks ago, they will follow the example of the 'good old Duke of York' who 'led his men to the top of a hill', and 'led them down again'.

Three days later Asquith showed again his scepticism of the whole enterprise, writing to Venetia Stanley:

I have been talking seriously to Winston to-day about his 'little army': I am not at all comfortable as to its prospects, having little faith in the fighting or staying powers of the Oxfordsh Yeomanry. In addition to his 60 or so of armoured motor cars, he has now chartered & is despatching some 200 or

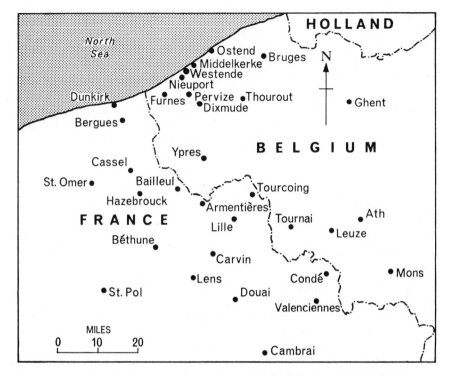

TOWNS VISITED BY UNITS OF CHURCHILL'S 'DUNKIRK
CIRCUS', SEPTEMBER AND OCTOBER 1914

300 motor buses! Their immediate objective is Douai, wh you will see on the map, but as the Germans have now brought some 60,000 men to Brussels & the neighbourhood, who will be on their flank, it is clear that they must be very cautious. Happily we have a large reconnoitring force of the best aeroplanes.

On September 11 Churchill spoke at a 'Call to Arms' meeting at the London Opera House. It was the first joint meeting of senior members of the three political Parties. Churchill spoke for the Liberals, F. E. Smith for the Conservatives, and William Crooks[1] for Labour. Apart from his brief interjection at the Guildhall a week earlier, it was

---

[1] William Crooks, 1852–1921. Elected Mayor of Poplar, 1901, the first Labour Mayor in London. Labour MP, 1906–21. Active on war recruiting platforms throughout the war.

Churchill's first public speech since the outbreak of war. 'Mr Churchill has made a speech of tremendous voltage and carrying power,' the *Manchester Guardian* reported. 'His comparison of the British Navy to a bulldog—"the nose of the bulldog has been turned backwards so that he can breathe without letting go"—will live. At the moment of delivery, with extraordinary appositeness, it was particularly vivid, as the speaker was able by some histrionic gift to suggest quite the bulldog as he spoke.' In his speech, Churchill warned that although the French and British armies had turned back the German assault, facile optimism would be a mistake. 'With battles taking place over a front of 100 or 150 miles,' he said, 'one must be very careful not to build high hopes on results which are achieved even in a great area of the field of war. We are not children looking for light and vain encouragement, but men engaged upon a task which has got to be put through.' After giving details of the battle itself, Churchill introduced his personal attitude towards the war, realistic about its dangers but determined to overcome them:

We did not enter upon this war with the hope of easy victory; we did not enter upon it in any desire to extend our territory, or to advance and increase our position in the world; or in any romantic desire to shed our blood and spend our money in Continental quarrels. We entered upon this war reluctantly after we had made every effort compatible with honour to avoid being drawn in, and we entered upon it with a full realization of the sufferings, losses, disappointments, vexations, and anxieties, and of the appalling and sustained exertions which would be entailed upon us by our action. The war will be long and sombre. It will have many reverses of fortune and many hopes falsified by subsequent events, and we must derive from our cause and from the strength that is in us, and from the traditions and history of our race, and from the support and aid of our Empire all over the world the means to make our British plough go over obstacles of all kinds and continue to the end of the furrow, whatever the toil and suffering may be.

Churchill ended with an appeal for national unity which, after the war, could be geared to constructive action:

I hope, even in this dark hour of strife and struggle, that the unity which has been established in our country under the pressure of war will not cease when the great military effort upon which we are engaged and the great moral causes which we are pursuing have been achieved. I hope, and I do not think my hope is a vain one, that the forces which have come together in our islands and throughout our Empire may continue to work together, not only in a military struggle but to try to make our country more quickly a more happy and more prosperous land, where social justice and free institutions are more firmly established than they have been in the past. If that is so, we shall not have fought in vain at home as well as abroad.

In accord with the non-partisan spirit which had brought him to the Opera House, Churchill agreed to speak again at Birmingham on September 14. Austen Chamberlain[1] was to take the platform with him. Chamberlain had been one of the leading Conservative critics of the Liberal Home Rule policy for Ireland. Before the meeting took place, Asquith put down an amending Bill which would allow the Home Rule Bill of 1914 to be put on the Statute Book immediately, even though Home Rule would not become operative until after the war. To the Conservatives it appeared that Asquith was abusing the promised suspension of the Irish controversy. Protest was immediate. Churchill explained to Lord Robert Cecil why it was necessary to proceed with the Home Rule Bill: 'I do beg you to consider, as a military measure,' he wrote on September 8, 'the importance of giving the Irish their Bill, & so bringing them round in England & America to our side. The denial of this will certainly be repaid with disloyalty & rancour, & an element of weakness & discord introduced into our affairs. It is well worth while giving them their trophy, subject to proper conditions as to postponement of operation, and amendment.' The Conservatives would not accept this argument. 'The Govt propose to cheat us after all,' Lord Hugh Cecil wrote to Churchill on September 11. If they proceeded in their course, he warned, the Conservatives would do their utmost to make their position 'as difficult and painful as it can be made', not only over Ireland but over every issue not directly connected with the war. In an attempt to dissuade the Government from continuing with the amending bill, the Conservatives threatened to cancel Churchill's imminent appearance at Birmingham. They believed that this threat of political controversy would shake the Liberal resolve; but they were wrong. On September 11 Churchill wrote angrily to Austen Chamberlain:

My dear Austen,
   I regret more than I can say the view you take of the arrangement proposed. I should hope that on reflection you will see that the practical differences between what you ask and what we propose are utterly disproportionate

[1] Joseph Austen Chamberlain, 1863–1937. Conservative MP, 1892–1937. Chancellor of the Exchequer, 1903–5. Unsuccessful candidate for the leadership of the Conservative Party, 1911. Secretary of State for India, May 1915. Resigned, July 1917. Minister without Portfolio, 1918–19. Chancellor of the Exchequer, 1919–21. Lord Privy Seal, 1921–2. Foreign Secretary, 1924–9. Knighted, 1925. First Lord of the Admiralty, 1931.

to the advantages of a friendly Ireland, and the disadvantages of a hostile Ireland, at such a time. It will of course be made clear that in no circumstances shall we ever be parties to coercion into Home Rule of Orange Ulster.

I cannot myself see the relevance of this controversy, however it be settled, to the object of our meeting on Monday. But in view of your wishes I am glad to escape from the labour of another speech, and shall be greatly indebted to you if you will take the necessary steps to have it all put off.

Yours sincerely
Winston S. Churchill

In his reply Chamberlain reiterated that it was impossible for him to appear on a public platform with Churchill 'at the very moment which the Prime Minister chooses, in defiance of all he has said, to break the political truce'. Asquith, he wrote, was 'trading on the patriotism of his opponents' in order to accelerate the triumph of Home Rule. Churchill replied on the same day, having obtained Asquith's approval for his letter:

My dear Austen,

The Irish policy to which you and your friends would condemn us means the alienation of Irish Nationalism all over the world, combined with serious disaffection in Liberal and Labour ranks. This would amount to a grave weakening in the forces that can now be gathered together for the prosecution of the war. . . .

Greatly as I should deplore the renewal of party controversy, I am sure that the nation and the Empire will regard you as wanting in judgment and in sense of proportion if on the difference between our policy and yours you either weaken the unity which prevails in Great Britain or seek to force us into a quarrel with the Irish nation.

The Government had a right to claim the absolute support of the Opposition in the measures necessary to carry on the war, and Conservatives throughout the country would not have tolerated any other attitude. Recognizing as we do the advantages which have flowed from that support, and the high motives which evoke it, I am bound to point out in view of your letter that we command, for the purposes of the war and for all measures connected with it, an intact and independent majority of our own of about 100.

In these circumstances I cannot feel that the support which you and your friends were bound in honour to give to the prosecution of the war ought to be made a lever to force us into a breach of faith with our own supporters, or into a fatally unwise policy towards the Irish nation. . . .

Yours very sincerely
Winston S. Churchill

On September 13 Chamberlain replied at length, ending with a bitter reference to Liberal criticism of the Conservative Government during the Boer War, and to Churchill's own former Conservatism: 'You must wish that the party with which you now act could show an equally good record for the last great war in which our country was engaged.' Churchill made one further attempt to prevent a Conservative attack on the Government over its Irish policy:

My dear Austen,

I beseech you to realise what an act of recklessness and unwisdom it wd be for us—either party—to start a quarrel with Irish nationalism here, in the Colonies, and above all in America at this time of crisis. Really we ought not to be forced to choose between a scandalous row here, and open Irish disloyalty. Why should the State be impoverished by either catastrophe? Our plan prevents anything being done—except the sentimental satisfaction of having an inoperative bill on the Statute book—till the war and the election are both over. And even then—how nearly the differences were adjusted —one poor Irish county—At the end of all the delays, that is all that will be left to fight about.

And why shd we want to fight at all? No one can tell how parties will emerge from this war. And once the old party flags of the Victorian era have been hung up, new principles of action must prevail.

I am sure if you think about it all, you will see that the concession to the Irish of the sentimental point, while reserving every safeguard for the subsequent treatment of outstanding differences—is a prudent and necessary measure wh all parties shd take in common. It will rally to the Empire forces wh otherwise are utterly estranged. It will remove from party warfare the principal obstacle to a real unity of political action.

Never can the Ulstermen who have put aside their weapons to aid the Belgians, and have gone to the front to serve the country be the subject of coercion to put them under Home Rule. Never can Englishmen look upon Irishmen as traitors and rebels, if in this struggle they bear a loyal part and shed their blood willingly and generously with our own men.

It will be a new world. Don't bar it out. . . .

Yours very sincerely
WSC

On September 14 Chamberlain wrote yet again with increasing bitterness. The Liberals, he declared, had destroyed the Conservatives' belief 'in the honour of public men', and had 'shattered the hopes that some of us entertained' that the war would bring the two Parties together. Churchill brought the acrimonious correspondence to a close with a final letter. 'Compared to winning the war,' he declared, 'I do not care about Home Rule; but that does not mean apart from this comparison I do not care about it or think it a wise and hopeful policy. . . . Don't bother to answer. With deep regret I must realise that we cannot understand each other's point of view; and it remains for us to confront you with successful results at home as well as abroad.'

Once again the cause of Ireland had poisoned British politics. The Conservatives remained convinced that Liberalism would betray Ulster, despite Churchill's specific pledges, given on Asquith's behalf. Liberals were confirmed in their view that the Conservatives would use the claims of Ulster as an excuse to disrupt any Irish settlement, and as an opportunity to kill Liberalism. For over a week Churchill had found himself held up once more as an enemy of Conservatism; once more he appeared to be the leader of an aggressive Liberal move. As a result of the acrimonious exchanges, the suspicions of the Conservative leaders were strengthened. The effect of his appeal for Party unity at the Opera House was impaired. The inter-Party recruiting rallies went on; but Churchill's hopes for a post-war polity freed from the old divisions and based upon a national reforming programme were undermined.

Churchill could not afford to be distracted by political controversy for long. The needs of the Royal Navy were paramount. On September 15 he summoned an aeroplane conference at the Admiralty in order to accelerate aircraft production. At the conference, Captain Sueter was asked to prepare a table showing the maximum possible deliveries of aircraft week by week over the next six months. Aircraft firms were told to furnish weekly timetables of their forthcoming deliveries. Parts which were proving difficult to manufacture were to be produced 'at one centre and on the largest scale necessary'. Three companies were detailed to concentrate entirely upon seaplane construction. These details put in hand, Churchill left that same day, at Kitchener's specific request and with Asquith's approval, on his second visit to France. Together with the Duke of Westminster,[1] he drove from Calais to Sir John French's Headquarters at La Fère-en-Tardenois. Because information about the position of the German forces was imprecise, Churchill and the Duke had to make a wide detour to avoid being caught up in the German flank. Churchill later recalled his visit in *The World Crisis*:

Sir John had all his arrangements ready for me, and the next day between daylight and dark I was able to traverse the entire British artillery front . . . I

[1] Hugh Richard Arthur Grosvenor, 1879–1953. 2nd Duke of Westminster, 1899. ADC to Lord Roberts, South Africa, 1900–2. Commanded an armoured car detachment, Royal Naval Division, 1914–15. Personal Assistant, Ministry of Munitions, 1917.

met everybody I wanted to meet and saw everything that could be seen without unnecessary danger. . . . I had a long talk with Sir Henry Rawlinson[1] on a haystack from which we could observe the fire of the French artillery near Soissons. I saw for the first time what then seemed the prodigy of a British aeroplane threading its way among the smoke-puffs of searching shells. I saw the big black German shells, 'the coal boxes' and 'Jack Johnsons' as they were then called, bursting in Paissy village or among our patient, impassive batteries on the ridge. . . . When darkness fell I saw the horizon lighted with the quick flashing of the cannonade. Such scenes were afterwards to become commonplace: but their first aspect was thrilling.

That evening Churchill dined with the officers of French's staff. Among those present was his friend Hugh Dawnay,[2] who had served with him both in the Sudan and South Africa. They had been at Omdurman together. This meeting in France was their last; Dawnay was killed in action shortly afterwards.

Kitchener had asked Churchill to explain to Sir John French the advantages of moving the British Army from its existing position on the Aisne to its 'natural station' on the Channel coast, in contact with the Royal Navy. As the German Army could no longer reach or outflank Paris, its next logical move, unless it were to retreat to Germany, was to race to the Channel ports. Churchill convinced French that Kitchener's reasoning was sound. After a brief visit to the Marines and Yeomanry at Dunkirk, he then returned to England. Once more he had acted as an intermediary between Kitchener and French, and had succeeded in averting serious friction over the major question of future strategy.

On September 17, only a few hours after his return from France, Churchill left London by train for Scotland, having arranged to visit the Grand Fleet at Loch Ewe. Leaving the train at Inverness, he motored westwards towards the Loch, where the Grand Fleet was at anchor.

[1] Henry Seymour Rawlinson, 1864–1925. Entered Army, 1884. On Kitchener's staff in the Sudan, 1898. Brigadier-General, 1903. Major-General commanding the 4th Division, September 1914; the 7th Division & 3rd Cavalry Division, October 1914; the IV Corps, December 1914–December 1915. Knighted, 1915. Lieutenant-General commanding the Fourth Army, 1916–18. General, 1917. Created Baron, 1919. Commanded the forces in North Russia, 1919. Commander-in-Chief, India, 1920–5.

[2] Hugh Dawnay, 1875–1914. Second son of the 8th Viscount Downe. Lieutenant, Nile Expedition, 1898. ADC to Lord Roberts, South Africa, 1901. Major, 2nd Life Guards, August 1914. Killed in action, 6 November 1914.

With him were Admiral Hood, Admiral Oliver, and the two heroes of
the Heligoland Bight, Commodore Keyes and Commodore Tyrwhitt.
At Achnasheen, on the way to the Loch, Tyrwhitt drew Churchill's
attention to a searchlight on the roof of a large private house. The
sailors were mystified. Oliver knew of no Admiralty searchlight in the
area, and there seemed no explanation for this one. As they drove on,
each wondered whether it might not be a spy's searchlight, used to
signal to a Zeppelin information about fleet movements, and able to
direct Zeppelins to naval anchorages. On reaching Loch Ewe, they
mentioned their fears to Jellicoe, who added to the alarm by saying that
an aeroplane had been seen in the neighbourhood since the war began,
But had never been traced. Churchill's sense of adventure was aroused;
he was determined to find out for himself what the searchlight was for.
but if it belonged to a German spy, there was danger in a senior
Minister arriving unexpectedly. Churchill decided that he and his
companions would have to go armed, and persuaded Jellicoe to give
them four pistols, and ammunition, from the armoury of the *Iron Duke*.
Returning across the highlands, they stopped outside the house, put
the pistols in their pockets and marched up the drive, prepared for
violence. The butler answered the door, and calmly informed them that
it was the house of a former Conservative MP, Sir Arthur Bignold.[1]
They demanded to see him, and he came at once. To their amazement,
he admitted without demur that he did have a searchlight on the roof.
Oliver then revealed that he was the Director of Naval Intelligence,
and had a right to know what the searchlight was for. Bignold told
them, to their total disbelief, that he used it to catch the gleam in the
eyes of the deer lying on the hillside, so that he would know where to
stalk them the next morning. This story seemed so improbable that
Churchill was by then convinced that he had indeed stumbled upon a
nest of spies. He insisted upon seeing the searchlight. Bignold led them
to the bottom of a narrow, winding staircase. Fearing foul play,
Churchill ordered Hood to guard the bottom of the staircase, while he,
Oliver and Tyrwhitt, taking Bignold as a potential hostage, climbed to
the top, their pistols ready for any emergency. But nothing untoward
happened. They reached the searchlight, and, still sceptical of Bignold's
explanation, took away various essential parts of its mechanism.
Bignold was indignant. But Churchill was still in doubt about the true
story, and on September 19, after his return to the Admiralty, he wrote
formally to Oliver:

[1] Arthur Bignold, 1839–1915. Conservative MP, 1900–10. Knighted, 1904. A founder of
the Kennel Club.

I do not understand why the searchlight placed on the roof of Sir Arthur Bignold's house in close proximity to an anchorage of the fleet, has not been made the subject of police report. Let the fullest report be made on the circumstances in which this searchlight came to be placed in position, together with all other facts about Sir Arthur Bignold, his guests, friends and servants. There are repeated rumours of aeroplane activities in the neighbourhood. Are there any suitable landing grounds for aeroplanes in the neighbourhood? It is reported that an aeroplane incident took place here last year.

On close examination, the facts proved unexceptional. The party Bignold was entertaining consisted of quite innocent and respectable people. No Germans could be found in the neighbourhood. No confirmation could be obtained of aeroplanes crashing or flying near the estate. Nor indeed, so the experts reported, was the searchlight itself capable of being used at that particular moment. The adventure had been harmless. But had the house contained German spies instead of patriotic Scotsmen it might have had a less simple ending, and the risk Churchill took in arming himself and his companions might have provoked even greater criticism than his actions at Sidney Street four years before.

On September 20 Churchill found time to write a personal letter to his friend, Jack Seely, the former Secretary of State for War who had resigned after the Curragh Mutiny in May 1914, and had gone to the western front on the outbreak of war in command of the Canadian Cavalry Division. Churchill was in a confident mood:

My dear Jack,
The days pass in an unbroken succession of events & decisions; & I have hardly had time to write the letters of sympathy wh our severe losses among cherished friends demand. . . .
Here the feeling is absolutely united; & running breast high for a prolonged & relentless struggle. There will I think be no difficulty in putting a million men in the field in the spring of 1915. But we must keep the necessary minimum of officers to train them.
I rejoice more than I can say at the splendid deeds of the army and the military repute wh our army has by a few weeks of their achievements altogether revived.
The Navy has been thrilled by all their prowess & valour.
We sit still in the steady cold blooded game & can I think keep it up indefinitely.
Doom has fallen upon Prussian military arrogance. Time & determination are all that is needed.

Yours ever
W

One result of the Heligoland battle at the end of August was that the German High Sea Fleet remained cautiously in its harbours. The Admiralty were not at all pleased that this should be so. Naval thinking and planning before the war had been based on the belief that a decisive naval engagement would be fought in the North Sea within a few weeks of the outbreak of hostilities. Energetic naval officers like Tyrwhitt and Keyes were frustrated at the lack of action. Some officers feared a drop in naval morale should the Fleet not see action. Many of the plans which had been worked out by naval strategists were based upon an early British naval victory. The proposal which Churchill and the Grand Duke Nicholas had discussed for a joint Anglo-Russian landing on the Baltic coast depended for its feasibility on a German naval defeat in the North Sea.

On September 21, after only three days in London, Churchill spoke at an all-Party recruiting rally at Liverpool, giving vent to his, and the Admiralty's, sense of frustration. 'Although we hope the navy will have a chance of settling the question of the German Fleet,' he told an audience of fifteen thousand, 'yet if they do not come out and fight in time of war they will be dug out like rats in a hole.' The audience cheered with delight. But the phrase 'rats in a hole' provoked hostile comment. On October 2 Vice-Admiral Sir Lewis Bayly wrote to the Second Sea Lord, Sir Frederick Hamilton, of 'how very annoyed and angry the senior officers (and possibly juniors) in the First Fleet are'. 'We all pride ourselves,' he continued, 'on keeping from any bombast, and remaining quiet and ready. . . . We feel that we have been dragged down to the level of boasting and breathing bombastic defiance, and we hate it.' The Conservative newspaper, the *Morning Post*, also found cause for complaint: 'It would perhaps have been more in accordance with the amenities,' it declared, 'to have adopted a less homely and more appropriate figure of speech. The German Navy remains in port for strategic reasons, and the Commander-in-Chief will come out to suit his own convenience, and not the convenience of his enemies.' Churchill regretted having used the expression, which was often used against him. But the speech itself was a success. Churchill had judged that the time was right to win public confidence by blunt speaking. The *Manchester Guardian* responded at once, praising his refusal to pander to the prevailing optimism:

We like the strictness with which Mr Churchill in his speeches guards himself against raising our hopes of an easy and quick victory. . . . We all believe firmly that if we maintain whatever efforts we can make, the ultimate victory of the Allies is assured. Believing that, the country as a whole is just as well able as Mr Churchill himself to face any vicissitudes of fortune that may intervene before the end. Mr Churchill recognises the fact, and does not shrink from discussing publicly such possibilities as a reverse on the Aisne and even other reverses after it. It is what one Minister would do privately with another, and that it should be done calmly and frankly at a great public meeting is a credit to the relations between British Ministers and the British people.

During Churchill's visit to the Grand Fleet at Loch Ewe, Commodore Keyes had spoken in his presence of 'the live-bait squadron'. When Churchill asked him what he meant, Keyes explained that the phrase referred to a number of old cruisers of the *Bacchantes* class which were at that time patrolling near the Dogger Bank, and were believed to be vulnerable to German attack. Churchill, appalled that the cruisers had been allowed to take such risks, wrote to Prince Louis on his return to the Admiralty on September 18:

The Bacchantes ought not to continue on this beat. The risk to such ships is not justified by any services they can render. The narrow seas, being the nearest point to the enemy, should be kept by a small number of good modern ships.

The Bacchantes should go to the western entrance of the Channel and set Bethell's[1] battleships—and later Wemyss's cruisers—free for convoy and other duties.

Prince Louis agreed with Churchill's proposal, and the *Bacchantes* squadron was instructed to discontinue the Dogger Bank patrol. But on September 22, before the order had been acted upon, one of the three cruisers, the *Aboukir*, was struck by a German torpedo and capsized. Hundreds of her crew remained in the water clinging to wreckage and swimming about. The other two cruisers, the *Cressy* and the *Hogue* came to the rescue, stopping a few hundred yards from the sinking ship and lowering their boats. Within a few moments of their coming to a halt, first the *Hogue* and then the *Cressy* were torpedoed by the same submarine, and sunk. Eight hundred men were saved, but more than fourteen hundred were drowned.

As soon as the news of the disaster was known, the Admiralty convened a Court of Inquiry. The two Rear-Admirals responsible for the

[1] Alexander Edward Bethell, 1855–1932. Entered Navy, 1869. Director of Naval Intelligence, 1909–12. Knighted, 1912. Vice-Admiral Commanding battleships of Third Fleet, 1914. Commanded Channel Fleet, 1915. Admiral, 1916. Commander-in-Chief Plymouth, 1916–18.

patrol, Christian[1] and Campbell,[2] were both placed on half pay. But before the Admiralty could issue any statement, and before the Court of Inquiry had reached its verdict, Thomas Gibson Bowles,[3] a journalist and pamphleteer, published a venomous brochure with charges against Churchill which were repeated in different forms throughout the Press. 'The loss on September 22 of the *Aboukir*, the *Cressy* and the *Hogue*, with 1,459 officers and men killed, occurred,' wrote Bowles, 'because, despite the warnings of admirals, commodores and captains, Mr Churchill refused, until it was too late, to recall them from a patrol so carried on as to make them certain to fall victims to the torpedoes of an active enemy.' This accusation was widely believed. When the Court of Inquiry produced its report, Churchill wished to circulate it, in order to vindicate himself. But Asquith was unwilling to have any publicity given to a detailed operation of war. The loss of the three cruisers was repeatedly laid to Churchill's charge. In face of Asquith's prohibition, there was no action Churchill could take. After he had left the Admiralty in the summer of 1915, his successor, A. J. Balfour, claimed that it was still not in the public interest to put the documents before Parliament. But he told the House of Commons that if they could be published, they 'would entirely dispose of much erroneous and ill-informed criticism passed upon the late First Lord'.

Churchill's immediate reaction had been to seek means to avert the drowning of men from torpedoed ships in future. Two days after the sinkings, he summoned several rubber manufacturers to the Admiralty, and instructed them to make rubber bladders which could be issued to all sailors, to be hung round their necks to support them in the water.

It was unfortunate that Churchill's pugnacious Liverpool speech of September 21 should have been followed within only a few hours by the sinking of the three cruisers. The juxtaposition of these two events caused discontent. 'His Majesty did not quite like the tone of Winston

[1] Arthur Henry Christian, 1863–1926. Entered Navy, 1879. Rear-Admiral, commanding the 'Southern Force', which included the 7th Cruiser Squadron, August–September 1914. Took part in the Heligoland action, August 28. Neither he nor his flagship *Euryalus* was present with the 7th Cruiser Squadron on September 22, having returned to harbour two days earlier for coaling and repairs. Placed on half pay, December 1914. Commanded the Naval Forces at the Suvla Bay landings, August 1915. Admiral, 1919.

[2] Henry Hervey Campbell, 1865–1933. Entered Navy, 1878. Rear-Admiral, commanding the 7th Cruiser Squadron, 1914. Commanded the supporting cruiser force during the Heligoland action, October 1914. Commanded the Home Fleets, the Nore, 1914–17. Knighted, 1930.

[3] Thomas Gibson Bowles, 1843–1922. Clerk, Inland Revenue Department, 1860–8. Conservative MP, 1892–1906. Liberal MP, 1910. Announced his return to the Conservative Party, 1911, but never re-elected to Parliament. In 1914 he launched a *Candid Quarterly Review* aimed at denouncing 'insincerity, dishonesty, corruption'.

Churchill's speech especially the reference to "Rats in a Hole"!'
Stamfordham wrote from Buckingham Palace to Asquith's Private
Secretary, Maurice Bonham Carter,[1] on September 22; 'Indeed seeing
what alas! happened today when the rats came out of their own accord
and to our cost, the threat was unfortunate and the King feels it was
hardly dignified for a Cabinet Minister.'

Churchill's relations with George V seemed to bear out his family
motto, *Fiel Pero Desdichado*: 'Faithful, though unfortunate.' In 1912 the
King had been angry when Churchill tactlessly pressed him to name
a battleship after Cromwell. At some time before 1914 he became
convinced that Churchill could not be trusted. Lord Esher learned of
what had occurred some years later, while staying at Windsor on 30
June 1915, and explained it in his diary: 'The King had once (believing
W. Churchill was a "gentleman") unguardedly said that although he
respected Asquith, he was always conscious that he was not "quite a
gentleman". "I ought not to have said it," the King told Esher, "and
it was a damned stupid thing to say; but Winston repeated it to
Asquith, which was a monstrous thing to do, and made great mischief." '

The King never abandoned his view of Churchill as irresponsible and
unreliable. Although he had helped him during the Naval Estimates
crisis in January 1914, by supporting the proposed increase in naval
expenditure, he had nevertheless disapproved of Churchill's threat to
resign if the increases were not accepted. A few months later there was
further friction between Churchill and the King over the question of
promoting Admirals to the rank of Admiral of the Fleet, the highest
rank in the service. The King had wanted these appointments to be
made entirely by seniority. Churchill insisted that they should be made
'by selection from among those qualified', and that, provided the
Admiral in question had either served as First Sea Lord or commanded
a principal Fleet for twelve months, or given conspicuous service since
he had reached the rank of captain, he should be able to be selected as
an Admiral of the Fleet whenever a vacancy occurred. The King had
finally approved of these regulations. But when in June 1916 A. J.
Balfour wanted to publish them, the King minuted: 'These regulations
were forced upon me by Churchill after many discussions. I disagree
with them but they were passed by Order in Council in 1914. I suppose
they ought to be published. Of course they could be altered again if
Balfour & the Board wish it.'

[1] Maurice Bonham Carter, 1880–1960. Called to the Bar, 1909. Private Secretary to
H. H. Asquith, 1910–16. Married Asquith's daughter Violet, November 1915. Knighted,
1916. Assistant Secretary, Ministry of Reconstruction, 1917; Air Ministry, 1918.

With the coming of war a series of incidents such as the 'rats in a hole' speech kept the sovereign and Churchill at a distance. After the Heligoland victory Churchill became convinced of the need to reward bravery after each action, as was done in the Army. The King wanted sailors to wait until the war was over. Stamfordham reported on the disagreement in a letter to Lord Esher on September 27:

HM is not at all keen about honours being conferred until after the War. Winston has, however, persuaded HM to promote & decorate officers, Petty Officers & men for e.g. the Heligoland 'affair' and this is to be done shortly. . . .

Winston argues that a man may be killed during the interval between his act of Gallantry & the end of the War: & of course that is true. I expect HM will have to change his views tho' I confess I heartily share them.

Churchill had returned from France on September 17. Five days later, on September 22, he was in France again. At Dunkirk, in a conference with the French, he was, as Commander Samson recorded in his log book, 'very insistent on attacking German Communications'; and this offensive air policy was adopted. Aircraft and armoured cars, based on Douai, harassed the Germans in their advance towards the Channel coast, bombing and seizing German vehicles, troops and stores.

Throughout the second half of September, E. L. Gerrard and his squadron of four aircraft had been at Ostend, making plans for an air

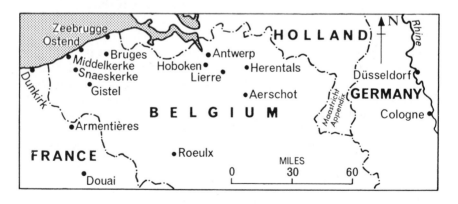

TOWNS BOMBED BY THE ROYAL NAVAL AIR SERVICE,
SEPTEMBER–DECEMBER 1914

attack on the Zeppelin sheds at Düsseldorf and Cologne. Churchill, Prince Louis and Admiral Oliver were all enthusiastic about such an attack. This was an opportunity for the Navy to take the initiative. The raid took place on September 22 from Antwerp, the Allied airfield nearest to Germany. Four aeroplanes took part. Gerrard himself, and Lieutenant Collet,[1] flew to Düsseldorf; Spenser Grey and Marix to Cologne. Only Collet succeeded in locating his objective, and dropped his three bombs from a height of 400 feet. The first fell short of the Zeppelin shed and exploded harmlessly. The other two hit the shed but failed to explode. 'The surprise was complete,' Gerrard reported to the Admiralty, 'and the numerous Germans in the vicinity ran in all directions. . . . The moral effect must have been considerable. A great many people must have been disturbed by the sound of our engines close over their heads.' But Gerrard deprecated similar attacks. His report continued:

Lieut Collet's feat is notable: Gliding down from 6,000 feet, the last 1,500 feet through the mist, and finally coming in sight of the shed at 400 feet only a quarter of a mile from it. It is discouraging when officers take such considerable risks that their weapons should fail them. . . .

The Germans are undoubtedly good soldiers, and I think that another attack on these lines, ie simultaneous approach from a great height and silent glide right down to the shed, is bound to fail. It would be easy to arrange a zone of fire over the sheds such that every attacking machine must pass through it. Something of the sort will probably now be done.

I would submit that further attacks on these sheds should not be attempted until a properly organised flight of very fast machines with practised pilots is ready. . . .

Lieut.-Commander S. Grey reported that a bomb accidentally dropped from his machine—he does not know where. I have reported the matter to the British Minister.[2] All our machines passed over a portion of Holland yesterday—mostly at a great height. Submitted that I may be informed of any international ruling there might be on the subject of the neutrality of the air.

Even the news that all the windows in the Zeppelin shed at Düsseldorf had been smashed could not invest the raid with an air of success.

On September 22, while Churchill was at Dunkirk in conference with the French air authorities, the Cabinet learned that New Zealand was refusing to send its expeditionary force to Europe unless the British

---

[1] Charles Herbert Collett, 1888–1915. Entered Royal Naval Air Service, 1913. Killed at the Dardanelles.

[2] Francis Hyde Villiers, 1852–1925. Entered Foreign Office, 1870. Minister to Portugal, 1906–11. Knighted, 1909. Minister to Belgium, 1911–19. Ambassador to Belgium, 1919–20.

provided a full destroyer escort. Churchill was familiar with all the details of this problem. 'Unfortunately,' Asquith wrote to Venetia Stanley, 'on this day, when of all others he was most needed, Winston is away, on one of his furtive missions—this time to Dunkirk: and is not expected back till evening.'

This criticism of Churchill's absence was not particularly serious. Asquith often expressed his irritations of the moment to Venetia Stanley, and did so about all his colleagues. But Max Aitken, then Lord Beaverbrook, later used this letter in *Politicians and the War* as the basis for the charge that Churchill had caused 'a very serious delay' by being out of England on that occasion. Churchill only learned of Asquith's censure when he read a proof copy of Aitken's book after the war. He noted in the margin: 'Asquith may have written this in his love letters to Viola[1] or Venetia—but it is quite unjustified. The 1st Sea Lord was fully competent to deal with such a matter. How ludicrous to suggest that "a vy serious delay occurred".' In the final version, Aitken still quoted the letter, adding: 'This at any rate was Asquith's opinion. . . . The Premier was obviously irritated by the incident.' This was indeed so, although Churchill did not know it at the time. He failed to see that his travels and stratagems were being interpreted as signs of irresponsibility. He never knew the extent to which his actions were being belittled privately by those whom he thought supported them.

Churchill persisted in his visits. As a result of them Asquith, the Conservatives and the Press found something to criticize. But also as a result of them, he alone of his Cabinet colleagues began to realize from personal experience the extent to which the war differed from its predecessors. He had been made aware of the decisive effect of German artillery superiority, and tried to find some means of challenging it. He was therefore much impressed when, on September 24, Admiral Sir Percy Scott,[2] the senior expert on naval gunnery, sent him a letter proposing the addition to Sir John French's army of twenty naval guns, which, Scott wrote, 'would outrange every gun that the Allies or the Germans have now in the Field'. These guns, Scott believed, would be of greater value than fifty thousand extra infantrymen. Churchill agreed.

[1] Viola Tree, 1884–1938. Daughter of the actor Sir Herbert Beerbohm Tree; herself an actress. Married Alan Parsons, 1912.

[2] Percy Moreton Scott, 1853–1924. Entered Navy, 1866. Captain, 1893. Devised land-mountings and carriages for the heavy naval guns used both in the defence of Ladysmith in South Africa, and in the defeat of the Boxer Rebellion in China, 1900. Knighted, 1906. Admiral, 1913. Retired from the Navy, 1913. Created Baronet, 1913. Appointed to the Admiralty for Special Service, September 1914–May 1918. In charge of gunnery defences of London against aircraft attack, 1915–16.

Immediately on receiving Scott's letter, he sent it to Kitchener, together with a personal appeal:

My dear Kitchener,

This has reached me today, & emphasizes what I said on Thursday night. It will be a great mistake not to supply the Army with heavy guns as soon as possible. The sense of inferiority imposed upon the troops by heavier metal is vy far-reaching. All my friends at the front tell me the same thing. The gun with its range is in spite of its weight the true answer to the heavy Howitzer. Percy Scott is right on gunnery questions, & can do what he says. I do not think the argument about the difficulty of transporting them to the front is conclusive, having regard to the number of roads & railways available.

It is surely wrong that we shd continuously have to oppose flesh and blood to German cannon, when we can so easily match them with naval artillery.

Yours vy sincerely
Winston S. Churchill

No evidence survives to indicate Kitchener's reaction to this proposal. But someone in the War Office minuted in the margin: 'Sir J. French has told us he does not want us to send out any 6-inch guns, which we have already offered.'

On September 25 Churchill approached Grey with the request that he be allowed to instruct his pilots to bomb military objectives in a German town. This had never been done before; the raids on Zeppelin sheds three days earlier had not involved town centres:

My dear Grey,

It is reported that yesterday the German airship dropped two bombs into Ostend, wh is an open town of no military significance. It is most important to teach the Germans the uselessness of such warfare. After discussing the matter with Kitchener, who agrees, I should propose to instruct the Naval airmen at Antwerp to drop an equal number (or shd we observe the ratio of 16 to 10?)[1] into Aix-la-Chapelle, or some other convenient German town. After this had been done, I shd explain the reason & announce that this course will be invariably followed in the future.

This is the only effective way of protecting civilians & non-combatants. Care will of course be taken to aim at barracks & military property, & to avoid ancient monuments.

Yours vy sincerely
W

[1] The ratio of British to German capital ships on which Admiralty shipbuilding policy had been based in 1914.

Grey turned down this proposal. 'They have more aircraft than we have,' he wrote, '& it will only put us on the same plane morally as they are.' Churchill believed that the time would come when it would be necessary to bomb military targets in German towns. But the idea of reprisals was repugnant to Grey, and Churchill did not raise the matter again.

Churchill was distressed that neither his visits to France, nor the lessons which he drew from them, were appreciated by his colleagues. They only served to make him appear volatile and troublesome. Clementine Churchill saw clearly why her husband's repeated visits to France upset his colleagues. In an undated letter before one of these visits—probably the one he proposed to make on September 26—she sent him an anxious warning:

> . . . Now please don't think me tiresome; but I want you to tell the PM of your projected visit to Sir John French. It would be very bad manners if you do not & he will be displeased and hurt.
>
> Of course I know you will consult K. Otherwise the journey will savour of a week-end escapade & not of a mission. You would be surprised & incensed if K slipped off to visit Jellicoe on his own. I wish my darling you didn't crave to go. It makes me grieve to see you gloomy & dissatisfied with the unique position you have reached thro' years of ceaseless industry & foresight. The PM leans on you & listens to you more & more. You are the only young vital person in the Cabinet. It is really wicked of you not to be swelling with pride at being 1st Lord of the Admiralty during the greatest War since the beginning of the World. And there is still much to be done & only *you* can do it. . . .
>
> You know the sailors can't do anything alone & just becos' your preparations are so perfect, that for the moment there seems little to do, this is not the moment to hand over the whole concern to another or to allow the sailors who have been tutored & bent to the yoke for the last 2 years to take charge. Be a good one & rejoice & don't hanker. Great & glorious as have been the achievements of our army, it is only a small one, 1/8 of the allied forces. Whereas you rule this gigantic Navy which will in the end decide the War. . . .

Churchill took his wife's advice, and sent Kitchener a note on September 26 suggesting that he visit Sir John French to discuss the 'general situation' as well as his specific Dunkirk responsibilities. Kitchener replied immediately: 'No objection. I hope you will discountenance any wild talk.' 'How right you were about telling K,' Churchill wrote to his wife from on board the light cruiser *Adventure* carrying him to France.

On September 28 the Royal Marine Brigade moved forward from Dunkirk to Lille, which a small group of German troops had entered a short time before. Churchill himself had drafted the Marines' instructions. 'Select your point and hit hard,' he had directed General Paris on September 24. 'Your object will be either to destroy an important bridge on the enemy's communications or to overwhelm some detached force which is exposed.' For over a week the Marines moved about the countryside, seeking to give the impression of a large and powerful British force. No evidence is known that the Germans were impressed by this subterfuge. But the British forces did play a part in raising the morale of the local inhabitants. Commander Samson reported to Churchill: 'Our presence in the town caused extraordinary delight to the populace and the Prefet[1] informed me that our visit had wholly restored confidence among the townspeople. . . . All the towns en route are now absolutely in a state of restored confidence. The sight of the armed motor cars proceeding in an organized procession, with all military precautions, and full of armed men, along the road between Lille and Cassel, appears to give confidence to the inhabitants. All my men behaved with quietness and sobriety.'

The fear that the Germans might win the naval advantage could not be dispelled. Invasion had to be prevented, merchant ships protected. On September 29 Asquith advised Churchill to lay mines in the neutral waters of the North Sea, a controversial innovation which Churchill had resisted throughout September. But Asquith was insistent. 'I am strongly of opinion,' he wrote, 'that the time has come for you to start mining; and to do it without stinting, and if necessary on a Napoleonic scale. I don't know what supplies you have in hand of the infernal machinery, but I feel sure you can't do better than make the most ample provision, and use it freely & even lavishly.'

Such ruthless measures became a commonplace of war policy. In October Churchill took a similar initiative. On the western front German troops had on several occasions used the white flag of surrender as a subterfuge to trap British troops who, having come forward to take their supposed prisoners, were shot dead while unprepared to resist. As First Lord, Churchill had to draw up the orders which would make sure that no such device was used at sea to trick the coastal defenders during

---

[1] Félix Trépont, 1861–1950. Préfet de Nord, 1911–15. After the German occupation in November 1914 he refused to collaborate with the military authorities. Arrested, February 1915; interned in Magdeburg, 1915–18. His war memoirs, deposited in the Archives du Nord, will be open to the public in 1972.

a German invasion. On October 22 he drafted the rules which he believed were needed to deal with such an emergency:

A precise order shd be given that all transports believed to be conveying German troops to England are to be sunk at once by torpedo or gunfire. No parley with or surrender by a transport on the high seas is possible. Transports enclosed in a bay which surrender wholesale & immediately may be dealt with as mercifully as circumstances allow. British officers will be held responsible that the enemy gains no advantage by any exercise of humanity.

On the other hand when the fighting has altogether stopped men swimming in the water may be made prisoners of war in the regular way provided the fighting efficiency of the ships is not affected.

This was a stern order; yet within two months Churchill had learned that it was not enough, for a similar order had proved of no avail on the western front. There, by showing a white flag and appearing to be in earnest, German troops had still been able to catch British troops unawares and temporarily defenceless. Two days before Christmas, Churchill was forced to add three further paragraphs to his October instructions:

There is no obligation to recognize a white flag, & this signal only acquires validity if recognized. Sir John French has found it necessary to order instant fire to be made on any German white flag, experience having shown that the Germans habitually & systematically abuse that emblem. Consequently any white flag hoisted by a German ship is to be fired on as a matter of principle. This does not mean that no surrender may be accepted from an obviously helpless ship. But officers will be held strictly responsible if mishap or disadvantage to H.M. ships results therefrom.

In all cases of doubt the enemy's ship shd be sunk.

In an action, white flags shd be fired upon with promptitude.

There appears to have been no occasion between 1914 and 1918 on which these orders had to be carried out.

During the first two months of war Churchill was confronted by a heavier and more varied concentration of work than at any previous period of his career. Each day brought new correspondence and new anxieties to his desk. He lived in Admiralty House; his office was his home. Like Kitchener, he put official duties and public affairs at the centre of his being. Like Lloyd George, he probed impatiently the myriad activities of his Department. He felt an urgent, personal need to know what was going on in every branch of naval affairs; on the seas, in the dockyards, at the Naval Air Stations, at the air bases in France, and in the different departments of the Admiralty. Some of his officials resented his probings; some Admirals doubted his grasp of naval realities. But his powers of work and concentration were obvious to all. He was twenty-six years younger than Kitchener, twenty-four years younger than Asquith, twelve years younger than Grey, eleven years younger than Lloyd George. He relished the strains which his own restless and relentless methods brought upon him. Nevertheless, the task at times seemed heavy, and its relief far away. The support which he received from his two principal Secretaries, Edward Marsh and James Masterton-Smith,[1] made the daily pressure of work more bearable. Marsh had been his private secretary since 1905, and had followed him from the Colonial Office, where he was a permanent Civil Servant, first to the Board of Trade, then to the Home Office and in 1911 to the Admiralty. Marsh saw Churchill every day. He dealt with all routine administrative problems. He drafted most of the formal letters. He intercepted unwelcome callers. He ensured that urgent matters were brought promptly to Churchill's attention. When Marsh suggested, as he often did, that a particular letter ought not to be sent, or that a harsh reply needed modification, Churchill almost always followed his advice. His confidence in Marsh was absolute.

Masterton-Smith had only known Churchill since October 1911, when Churchill arrived at the Admiralty. He too had won his confidence, and was able to influence him in many directions. The parts played by these two civil servants is hard to gauge. Their powers of work satisfied Churchill's stringent demands. 'I am writing in the Cabinet room, at the beginning of twilight,' Asquith wrote to Venetia Stanley on December 21 'and thro' the opposite window across the Parade I see the Admiralty flag flying & the lights "beginning to twinkle" from the rooms where Winston and his two familiars (Eddie and Masterton) are beating out their plans.'

---

[1] James Edward Masterton-Smith, 1878–1938. Entered Admiralty, 1901. Private Secretary to five First Lords: McKenna, 1910–11; Churchill, 1911–15; Balfour, 1915–16; Carson, 1916–17; Sir E. Geddes, 1917. Assistant Secretary to Churchill, Ministry of Munitions, 1917–19; War Office, 1919–20. Knighted, 1919. Permanent Under-Secretary of State, Colonial Office, 1921–4.

4

The Defence of Antwerp

IN 1914 Antwerp was Belgium's largest port, and one of Europe's
most powerful fortresses. It depended for its livelihood upon access
to the North Sea through the Dutch territorial waters of the River
Scheldt. No one could be certain that Holland might not decide to join
Germany in the event of war, or insist upon the fullest definition of its
neutrality, thereby cutting Antwerp off from all chance of help from the
sea. Churchill believed that any British pledge to Belgium must, if
possible, include a determination to defend Antwerp, even if Dutch
neutrality made this difficult. On the day after Britain's declaration of
war he sent a memorandum to Grey urging him to find some means of
reducing Belgium's dependence upon Dutch goodwill. 'If Holland,'
wrote Churchill, '(a) condones the violation of her territory by Germany, (b) closes the Scheldt to the supplies for Antwerp, (c) allows
free importation of supplies to Germany through Rotterdam, we shall
be at grave disadvantage if we are forced to respect her neutrality.'
Churchill believed that the Dutch ought to accept a British offer of
alliance. Failing this, he wrote, 'we must insist on absolute equality
with Germany in the use made by either belligerent of Dutch territory
or ports'. Grey saw no means whereby Holland could be persuaded to
join the Allies, or be forced to make special concessions. This was a
problem which before the war had much exercised the Committee of
Imperial Defence, of which both he and Churchill were members.

Churchill was exceedingly angry when he saw a telegram from the
British Minister to Belgium, Sir Francis Villiers, sent on August 19,
reporting that the Dutch were said to be allowing 'large importation of
food-stuffs' for Germany, while refusing to allow the Belgians to take
food down the Scheldt. 'If this were true it would be serious,' he wrote to

Grey on August 20. 'I have always felt that if Holland were to try to strangle her small neighbour who is fighting for her life, she wd commit an offence wh wd deprive her of all claims to our sympathy. The Scheldt *must* be kept open to merchant vessels.' The Admiralty, he concluded, 'are capable of doing this at any time you think it necessary'. But the rumour of Dutch action was not confirmed, nor did Grey want to take any precipitate initiative that might turn Holland from its neutrality.

Antwerp's sea outlet remained secure for the rest of August. But on September 5 the Belgian Government warned the British Foreign Office that the Germans might soon make a serious attempt to besiege Antwerp by land, and asked Britain for as many guns, anti-aircraft guns, and aircraft as possible. On receiving this appeal, Grey immediately sent it to both Kitchener and Churchill. 'Please let me know as soon as possible what answer I can send . . .' he asked them both in his covering note; 'Time presses for the Belgians. I am afraid we can do very little if anything, but if we can do nothing the Belgians may surrender Antwerp very soon.' Kitchener replied on September 7 that he was unable to offer either guns or men. He did not believe that the danger was very pressing. 'I expect they will hang on to Antwerp,' he wrote, and explained that 'the requests they make are only for articles to defend themselves from aircraft—which though annoying will not take Antwerp'. Churchill took the Belgian request more seriously, writing to Grey:

6 naval aeroplanes are now at Antwerp and will be supported so far as is necessary to deal with Zeppelins.
I am awaiting their report.
I will find them a few aerial guns.
I will send you a fuller answer later.
WE MUST HOLD ANTWERP.

During the first week of September, an increasing number of German troops gathered south of Antwerp, Ghent and Bruges. On September 7 Villiers telegraphed to Grey to ask if he should encourage the citizens of these towns to seek refuge in England. Grey consulted Churchill, who replied:

There is a military reason for relieving the fortress of Antwerp of refugees (bouches inutiles) and we ought to help this in every way as part of our policy for the sustained defence of Antwerp. But we ought not to concern ourselves with merely helping Belgians from the unpleasant consequences of residing in Ghent & Bruges under German occupation. They ought to stay there & eat up continental food, & occupy German police attention. There is no reason why the civil population of Belgium, not concerned in the defence of Antwerp, shd come & live in England. The point is important. Everything must be done to help Belgium's military resistance—but this is no time for charity.

Military intelligence reports made it clear that it would not be long before the Germans were ready to launch a sustained attack on Antwerp and its forts. On September 7 the Belgians appealed for thirty thousand British troops to hold open the road between Ostend and Antwerp. Churchill wrote at once to Asquith, Grey and Kitchener, doubting whether it were possible to agree to this appeal, which, he wrote, would be 'a most costly and dangerous operation', which would be powerless against a determined German attack. He was against exposing British troops along so weak a line. He wanted instead an immediate agreement with Holland whereby the Dutch would allow Antwerp to be defended by British troops and supplies coming down through the Dutch territorial waters of the Scheldt. But Grey informed Churchill that he had already put this proposal to the Dutch, who had refused to accept it, insisting that their neutrality made it impossible for any military forces to use the river. Churchill was angered by the Dutch refusal. In his letter of September 7 he advised Asquith, Grey and Kitchener to consider a strong policy:

. . . Tell the Dutch now bluntly that we insist upon the Scheldt being kept open permanently for supplies and reinforcements of all kinds for Antwerp under siege, and that any attempt to close or obstruct those waters must be regarded by us as a disloyal act to a small neighbour and as an unfriendly act to Great Britain; that we propose now and henceforward to send in and bring out all traffic necessary for the support of Antwerp under the white ensign and that if any ship flying that flag miscarries, is fired on, or is mined, we shall immediately take the necessary naval steps to keep the Scheldt open by force, and we shall also make an effective blockade of the Rhine.

The Dutch, who are simply responding to German pressure, and who, if free agents, would be relieved of the odious function of strangling Belgium, will be all the better off for our taking a strong line. Anything short of this is simply chucking up the Belgian sponge and playing the German game.

For the sake of keeping at peace with Holland we are giving up all the advantages of blockading the Rhine; all the facilities of seizing Dutch islands; of controlling the Elbe; and if on the top of this we are to allow Antwerp to

be choked and murdered and fall into German hands, we shall find it difficult
to prove that we have taken the necessary measures to secure the success of
the war. . . .

Churchill's appeal was in vain. Grey did not wish to antagonize the
Dutch, fearing that if they were pressed too hard they would join
Germany. As the Germans advanced further across Belgium, it became

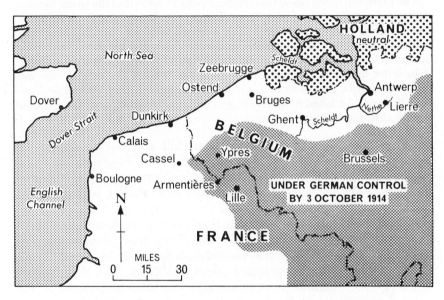

THE ISOLATION OF ANTWERP BY 3 OCTOBER 1914

clear that Antwerp's survival would soon depend upon the very line
Antwerp–Ghent–Ostend which Churchill considered so difficult to
defend. 'You have only to look at a map,' he wrote in his letter of
September 7, 'to see the folly of trying to feed Antwerp by Ostend and
Ghent.' But by mid-September this was the only road open to the
Allies should they decide to make an attempt to defend the city. While
Holland upheld its neutrality, Antwerp could no longer be protected or
reinforced, as Churchill had wished, from the sea, but depended
entirely upon a thin and exposed land corridor more than fifty miles
long.

In response to Grey's request for immediate help to Belgium,
Churchill took positive action. On September 9 he outlined his

proposals to the Additional Civil Lord, Sir Francis Hopwood.[1] He was determined to use the Scheldt, if only once:

I have promised the Belgians, for the defence of Antwerp, six 6″ or 4·7″ guns with six gunners to teach them how to use them; three new 3″ high-angle guns; and six of the 38 converted anti-aircraft pom-poms, together with the necessary ammunition. Ascertain when these guns will be ready for despatch. They are urgently needed at Antwerp.

The President of the Local Government Board[2] states that the Great Eastern Railway boat goes every day from Tilbury to Antwerp to fetch refugees. These sailings began yesterday. The war material for Antwerp should go in one of these boats at the earliest moment. If possible, all should go in one boat so as to give no time for questions to be raised about subsequent voyages.

In order to conform to the conditions of the Scheldt Convention, the war material must be sent as from a private British firm. Either Vickers or Armstrongs should be asked to handle it, and all indents and bills of lading should sustain this impression. . . .

Six days later, on September 15, Churchill sent Grey a list of the Admiralty help which had by then reached the Belgians: '24 naval maxims and 500,000 rounds of ammunition were supplied to them on the 18th of August. 6 4·7″ naval guns and ammunition, with an officer in charge and 6 gunners, were delivered 3 days ago. 3 high-angle 3″ guns and 6 converted anti-aircraft pom-poms have been sent today.' On September 17 Churchill informed Grey that nine aeroplanes could go to Antwerp 'as soon as the Belgians are ready to receive them'. On September 24 he telegraphed direct to Villiers, then at Antwerp: 'Six 6″ guns on central pivot mountings with ammunition are at the immediate disposal of Belgian military authorities. Telegraph when and how they would like delivery made.' He also offered the Belgians two guns for an armoured train. The Belgians accepted, and the Admiralty armoured train expert, Commander Littlejohns,[3] was despatched immediately to Antwerp with the two guns.

[1] Francis John Stephens Hopwood, 1860–1947. Entered Board of Trade as Assistant Solicitor, 1885. Knighted, 1901. Permanent Under-Secretary of State for the Colonies, 1907–11. Additional Civil Lord, Admiralty, 1912–17. Created Baron Southborough, 1917. Honorary Secretary, Irish Convention, 1917–18. President, Commission to India on Reform, 1918–19.

[2] Herbert Louis Samuel, 1870–1963. Liberal MP, 1902–18; 1929–35. Chancellor of the Duchy of Lancaster, 1909–10. Postmaster-General, 1910–14. President of the Local Government Board, 1914–15. Postmaster-General, May 1915–January 1916. Chancellor of the Duchy of Lancaster, November–December 1915. Home Secretary, January–December 1916. High Commissioner for Palestine, 1920–5. Home Secretary, 1931–2. Created Viscount, 1937.

[3] Astle Scott Littlejohns, 1875–1939. Entered Navy, 1886. Commanded the British armoured trains in Flanders, 1914–16. Staff, High Commissioner for Australia, 1918–22. Captain, 1921. Served on the Non-Intervention Committee, Spanish Civil War, 1937.

Kitchener saw a direct danger to Britain if Antwerp were captured by the Germans, and on September 29 asked Churchill to send Admiral Oliver to the city. Oliver later recorded, in notes written in 1959, how Kitchener sent for him and told him that 'a lot of German steamers were at Antwerp which might be used in invade GB & I was to sink them'. Churchill gave Oliver his orders on September 30: he was to report on what should be done with the German ships at anchor in the Scheldt, and 'make such arrangements as will ensure their timely destruction'. In the course of five days, assisted only by a single Belgian officer, four privates and a Belgian boy-scout, Oliver inserted explosive charges in the propelling machinery of thirty-eight merchant ships. As a result of his action, none of the ships was able to go to sea during the subsequent four years of German occupation.

By the end of the month the Germans, having secured their occupation of Brussels, were ready to turn their attention to the capture of Antwerp. They opened fire with 17-inch howitzers against the wide circle of forts upon which the city depended for its defence. On hearing that the siege of Antwerp had begun, Kitchener sent Colonel Dallas[1] to the city to report on the battle and to act as his liaison officer with the Belgian forces. On Dallas' advice, Kitchener decided to send some British heavy artillery and personnel to strengthen the city's defences. Asquith, who was much disturbed by the thought of Antwerp's fall, supported Kitchener's decision for a direct British involvement in the siege. He also agreed with a request from Grey that the French should be asked to do likewise. The Cabinet approved of these special efforts on Antwerp's behalf. 'We had a long Cabinet this morning,' Asquith wrote to Venetia Stanley on September 30. 'The Belgians are rather out of "morale", & are alarmed at the bombardment of Antwerp wh has just begun. They are sending their archives & treasure over here, & talk of moving the seat of Government to Ostend. Kitchener has given them some good advice—namely not to mind the bombardment of their forts, but to entrench themselves with barbed wire &c in the intervening spaces, & challenge the Germans to come on.'

On October 1 Dallas telegraphed to the War Office that the Belgian Prime Minister, de Broqueville,[2] considered that 'the situation was very

[1] Alister Grant Dallas, 1866–1931. Entered Army, 1886. Colonel, 1911. General Staff Officer, War Office, 1911–14. Brigadier-General, General Staff, 1915. Commanded 32nd Brigade, Gallipoli, 1915. Major-General, commanding 53rd Division, Egypt and Palestine, 1916–17.

[2] Charles Marie Pierre Albert de Broqueville, Comte de Broqueville, 1860–1940. Prime Minister of Belgium, 1911–18. Introduced compulsory military service bill, 1913. Responsible for mobilization, 1914. Undertook reorganization of Belgian Army and established munition factories while in charge of Belgian Government in exile at Le Havre, 1915–17. Prime Minister, 1932–4.

grave' and that the only way 'to save Antwerp from falling' was by a diversion from outside. Asquith was perturbed at the development of events. 'The fall of Antwerp would be a great moral blow to the Allies,' he wrote to Venetia Stanley that day, 'for it would leave the whole of Belgium for the moment at the mercy of the Germans.' He added:

The French telegraph that they are willing to send a division (of 15,000 to 20,000) & to put it under a British general—but they do not say what is the quality of the soldiers, who may be very likely are only Territorials. However, we resolved at the Cabinet to-day that, if the French co-operation is satisfactory, we would divert our 7th Division (of the finest troops) wh was just going to join Sir J. French, and not throw it into Antwerp but endeavour to raise the siege & capture the German big guns.

On October 2 Grey telegraphed to the British Ambassador in France, Sir Francis Bertie,[1] to say that, as Britain was sending heavy guns to assist the Belgians, General Joffre 'should make an effort and send French regular troops to region of Dunkirk, from which port they could operate in conjunction with our reinforcements to relieve Antwerp'. Grey's telegram ended with the disturbing news that unless Joffre could send regular troops immediately, 'the loss of Antwerp must be contemplated'. 'The news from Antwerp this morning,' Asquith wrote to Venetia Stanley, 'is far from good & gives me some anxiety. The Germans battered down 2 of the forts, and what is worse got in between them & drove a lot of Belgians out of their entrenchments.' He saw little chance of helping the city:

Meanwhile the only relieving force that the French offer is a mass of Territorials & the like, who would be no use for hard fighting and are quite unfit to co-operate with a trained division of ours like the 7th. On the other hand to send the 7th alone is to court almost certain disaster. It is a very difficult situation—particularly as our officer reports that it is the morale of the Belgian Commanders rather than of the men wh shows signs of collapse. He says (early this morning) that 'any definite statement of assistance that could be given to the Belgian Government would have immediate & excellent effect'. But it is no good to lure them with false hopes.

Having sent this letter, Asquith left London for Cardiff, where he was to make an important recruiting speech. During the course of the after-

[1] Francis Leveson Bertie, 1844–1919. Second son of 6th Earl of Abingdon; uncle of Lady Gwendeline Churchill. Entered the Foreign Office, 1863. Knighted, 1902. British Ambassador, Rome, 1903–5; Paris, 1905–18. Created Baron Bertie of Thame, 1915. Created Viscount, 1918.

noon the Belgians became increasingly uncertain about their ability to prolong the defence of the city. Kitchener asked Sir Percy Girouard[1] to go at once from Ostend to Antwerp to impress upon Colonel Dallas that the Belgians must be made to continue to resist. That evening Kitchener and Grey met at Kitchener's house in Carlton Gardens and had a long discussion about how to bolster Belgian morale and help Antwerp. They both felt the need for a further senior opinion before deciding what emergency action to take. It was too late to bring the Prime Minister back from Cardiff that night; they therefore decided to consult Churchill.

Earlier that evening Churchill had left by train for a further visit to France. The rapid German advance towards the Channel ports had made it necessary for Samson's aeroplanes, the armoured cars and the Royal Marine Brigade to leave their advance base at Cassel and return to Dunkirk. Churchill wished to see for himself the state of their morale, and to discuss their future employment with Sir John French. He was in a special train on the way to Dover when Kitchener and Grey decided that they must consult him. They sent a message halting the train and calling it back to London. On reaching Victoria Station, Churchill was informed that he was wanted immediately at Kitchener's house. When he arrived, he found Kitchener, Grey, Prince Louis and Sir William Tyrrell, in urgent and anxious conclave. Kitchener at once explained that unless immediate and substantial Allied exertions were made, Antwerp would have to surrender. The loss of the city would immediately prejudice the course of the battle elsewhere in France. As soon as Antwerp were occupied, the Germans could advance westward along the North Sea coast from Zeebrugge to Calais. In such an event, Kitchener stressed, the military position of the British Expeditionary Force, and indeed of the Allies, would be in danger. He even feared that once the Germans reached Calais they would be able to launch an invasion of Britain.

As soon as Kitchener had ended his bleak survey, Grey read Churchill a telegram which Villiers had sent from Antwerp that evening, and which the others had already heard. In it, Villiers reported that the Belgian Government had decided to leave Antwerp for Ostend on the following morning, October 3.

[1] Edouard Percy Cranwill Girouard, 1867–1932. Entered Royal Engineers, 1888. Major, responsible for the construction of the Sudan railway during the Nile Expedition, 1896–8. Director of Railways in South Africa through the Boer War. Knighted, 1900. Governor and Commander-in-Chief, East Africa Protectorate, 1909–12. A director of Armstrong, Whitworth & Co, 1912. Director-General of Munitions Supply, 1915–17; resigned to return to Armstrong, Whitworth.

The decision to abandon Belgium's most powerful, and last remaining, fortress had not been made lightly. The Belgian Superior Council of War had recommended it unanimously after long discussion, in the presence of the Belgian King.[1] The Prime Minister, de Broqueville, had explained to Villiers that no other course was possible for the King or the Government; if they stayed in Antwerp any longer they might be captured by the Germans. Grey read to Churchill Villiers' opinion that, although it was being said that the city would hold out for a further five or six days, 'it seems most unlikely that when the Court and Government are gone resistance will be so much prolonged'.

Kitchener had strong reasons for wishing to defend Antwerp for as long as possible. It was behind the German line of advance and was therefore, while in Allied hands, a constant threat to German communications and supplies. Until September it had been unimportant in German plans; but as a result of the battle of the Marne, Antwerp had become all-important. The opposing armies were attempting to turn each other's flanks in their 'race to the sea'. As First Lord, Churchill was also directly involved. One of his main responsibilities was to ensure that the Channel was kept open for men and equipment crossing to France. He also believed that only by Allied control of the Channel ports could the German march across France be halted. Antwerp was the only fortress left in Allied hands between the German Army and the sea.

The Germans were employing only reserve troops in the Antwerp area, but by October 3 there were sixty thousand of them closing in on the city. Churchill and Kitchener both believed that the more pressure Britain could place upon the Germans at this point, the more troops they would be forced to divert to the siege, and the more coastline would remain in Allied hands. Apart from the strategic advantage in defending the city, there was also a moral one, of which Grey was much aware. Belgium was Britain's treaty ally. For two months the British people had been pledged to do all they could to defend her against Germany. But the force Britain had sent to Mons had been driven from Belgian soil in only a few hours. Antwerp was Britain's first real opportunity to honour her obligation. If Belgium fell, unaided, other neutrals would have cause to doubt British protestations of support, and would be even more hesitant to abandon their neutrality for a place among the Allies.

For several hours Kitchener, Grey, Churchill, Tyrrell and Prince Louis discussed the fate of Antwerp, and the probable repercussions of

[1] Albert, 1875–1934. King of the Belgians, 1909–34. Said to have fired the last shot before Antwerp surrendered, October 1914. Order of the Garter, December 1914.

its fall. Kitchener agreed to Churchill's suggestion that the Marine Brigade, then returning from Cassel to Dunkirk, should be sent at once to the city. In the early hours of October 3 Grey telegraphed to Villiers at Antwerp with a message for the Belgian Prime Minister:

We feel that the importance of Antwerp being held till the course of the main battle in France is determined justifies a further effort. We are trying to send you help from the main army, and if this were possible, would add reinforcements from here. Meanwhile a brigade of marines will reach you tomorrow to sustain the defence. We urge you to make one further struggle to hold out. Even a few days may make the difference. We hope Government will find it possible to remain and field army to continue operations.

Ten minutes after Grey had sent this telegram, he received one from Sir Francis Bertie, who reported that the French Government, then in emergency session at Bordeaux, had agreed to send to Antwerp two complete territorial divisions, together with artillery and cavalry, 'with the shortest delay possible'. The French had also decided, as a matter of urgency, to launch a major offensive in the region of Lille which, Bertie reported, was intended to have 'the effect of causing German troops in the neighbourhood of Antwerp to retreat, and so effect its relief'. Bertie had been read a report sent that afternoon from the French military mission in Antwerp. The report declared that 'though the military situation there is not good, it cannot be regarded as really bad. The Germans have suffered severe losses in the attacks which they have made on some of the outer works.'

The situation at Antwerp was obscure, the danger immediate, the outcome uncertain. Churchill suggested that as arrangements had already been made for him to spend October 3 at Dunkirk, he should go instead to Antwerp and send back an immediate report on the situation which would enable Kitchener to decide what further resistance, if any, was possible. As Secretary of State for War, Kitchener had the task of despatching troops, of ensuring that military supplies reached the city as quickly as possible, and of co-ordinating military policy with the French and the Belgians. Churchill would be able to report to him directly on the situation by telegraph and telephone. With Kitchener's support, and a full briefing from Grey, Churchill left Carlton Gardens for Victoria Station, where he was joined by his naval secretary, Admiral Hood. Shortly after midnight the special train took him once more towards Dover. As soon as Churchill had left, Grey telegraphed to Villiers:

First Lord of the Admiralty will be at Antwerp between 9 and 10 to-morrow. He is fully acquainted with our views, and it is hoped he may have the honour of an audience with the King before a final decision as to the departure of the Government is taken. If any military change takes place which renders the Ostend–Antwerp route insecure, please telegraph to Hotel Chapeau Rouge, Dunkirk up to 6 and Town Hall, Bruges, up to 8 am. . . .

On receiving this telegram in the early hours of the morning of October 3, Villiers called on de Broqueville, who told him that plans for the evacuation had already been put into operation. As a result of Villiers' request, de Broqueville agreed to summon an immediate meeting of Ministers to discuss whether to postpone the departure of the Belgian Government from Antwerp until Churchill's arrival. The Ministers met while it was still dark and agreed to postpone the decision to evacuate until they had talked to Churchill. As dawn was breaking, de Broqueville sent out the order to all Belgian forces to remain at their posts.

During the morning of October 3, while Churchill was on his way to Antwerp, Kitchener was at the War Office making further military arrangements for the city's defence. The Royal Marine Brigade was ordered to leave Dunkirk and try to reach Antwerp within twenty-four hours. At 9.40 am Kitchener telegraphed to the French Government at Bordeaux asking for the despatch of the French territorials as soon as possible. Throughout the day telegrams between Bordeaux and the War Office dealt with the detailed composition of the French relieving force. Asquith returned to London that morning. During the day he described the situation in a letter to Venetia Stanley:

I found on my return that strange things had been going on here. The Belgian Government notwithstanding that we were sending them heavy guns, and trying hard to get together troops to raise the siege of Antwerp, resolved yesterday to throw up the sponge & to leave to-day for Ostend, the King with his field army withdrawing in the direction of Ghent—They calculated that after their departure Antwerp might hold out for 5 or 6 days—wh seems very doubtful. This is a *mad* decision, quite unwarranted by the situation, for the German besieging army is only a scratch force, and one way or another a diversion is certain in the course of a few days. So we at once replied urging them to hold out, & promising Winston's marines to-morrow, with the hope of help from the main army & reinforcements from here. I was of course away, but Grey, Kitchener & Winston held a later meeting, and (I fancy with Grey's rather reluctant assent) the intrepid Winston set off at midnight & ought to have reached Antwerp by about 9 this morning. He will go straightway & beard the King & his Ministers, and try to infuse into their backbones the necessary quantity of starch. . . .

I have had a long talk with K this morning, & we are now both rather anxiously awaiting Winston's report. I don't know how fluent he is in French, but if he was able to do himself justice in a foreign tongue, the Belges will have listened to a discourse the like of which they have never heard before. I cannot but think that he will stiffen them up to the sticking point. Don't say anything of Winston's mission, at any rate at present; it is one of the many unconventional incidents of the war.

Churchill and Hood were delayed by the uncertain military situation between Ostend and Antwerp, reaching the city shortly after midday. They were at once joined by Colonel Seely, and by Admiral Oliver. Kitchener's emissary, Colonel Dallas, gave them a confident account of the military situation. The outer ring of forts, he reported, was still resisting the heavy German shellfire. Churchill then drove to the Hôtel de Ville to see de Broqueville and explained to him Kitchener's plan for a joint British and French relief force. De Broqueville assured Churchill that provided the Belgian line of retreat were safeguarded by the arrival of Allied troops, the Belgians themselves would be prepared to continue the resistance of Antwerp. The Belgian Government, he said, was willing to continue to defend Antwerp for at least ten days. But after three days the British must state unequivocally whether or not they were willing to launch a major relief operation. If the British were unable to give sufficient help, the Belgians would reserve the right to abandon the defence of the city on the fourth day. In such an event, they wished the British to help their army escape by sending covering troops along the line of retreat. Churchill assured de Broqueville that in addition to the Marine Brigade it might be possible to call upon further British troops. He had in mind the two Naval Brigades which he had set up in August and which were in training. He believed that they could reach the city within three days. On October 1 he had written to Kitchener that they would be used for home defence; but as no other British troops could possibly be available in time, he decided to ask Kitchener to send them over to Antwerp. Having left de Broqueville, Churchill sent Kitchener and Grey a detailed account of the discussion, and of his offer to send the Naval Brigades. 'If you clinch these propositions,' he telegraphed, 'pray give the following order to the Admiralty: Send at once both naval brigades, minus recruits, via Dunkirk, into Antwerp, without tents or much impedimenta, but with five days' rations and 2,000,000 rounds of ammunition. When can they arrive?' Churchill read this telegram to de Broqueville, who was much moved, believing that the British were in earnest about coming to Antwerp's aid. Not all the Belgian Ministers shared their Prime Minister's new-found confidence. 'I must impress on you,' Churchill stressed in his telegram to Kitchener and Grey, 'the necessity of making these worn and weary men throw their souls into it, or the whole thing will go with a run.'

Two thousand marines would arrive in Antwerp that evening or early the following morning. To ensure their co-operation with the Belgians, Churchill proposed to stay in the city until the following day. Then he would also learn whether Kitchener would approve his request for the immediate despatch of the two Naval Brigades which were still under training, and which he himself had refused to send to Calais a few weeks earlier because they were not yet ready for action.

On the morning of Sunday October 4, while waiting for Kitchener's reply, and the arrival of the Marine Brigade, Churchill visited Antwerp's defences. He was not as optimistic as Dallas had been on the previous afternoon. The Belgian defenders, he telegraphed to Kitchener on his return to the city, were 'weary and disheartened'. Large sections of the perimeter had been flooded in order to keep the Germans at bay. As a result, the ground was so waterlogged that the Belgians were unable to dig trenches to protect themselves from German shellfire. Even where trenches could be dug, they were extremely shallow and, he reported, gave little protection 'to their worn out and in many cases inexperienced troops'. An ordinary seaman of the Royal Naval Volunteer Reserve, Henry Stevens,[1] was in charge of Churchill's transport; later he recalled in a letter to the author:

I was ordered to muster our cars (which had just arrived at Antwerp) and to report to the Hotel de Ville. I collected 5 or 6 of as many different makes, all open tourers, and was told by a British military officer we were to convey Mr Churchill and his party wherever required. A Rolls Royce was selected for him and led the convoy, I riding in the front seat. I had acquired a rifle and bayonet, together with 60 rounds of ammunition, the latter carried down my jumper and secured with a piece of string round my waist.

Mr Churchill wore a dark overcoat and what was then known as a box hat, a fashion then rapidly passing out, and generally worn by elderly gentlemen on semi-formal occasions. With him he had several officers (mostly Guardsmen) and one or two civilians as his Staff.

[1] Henry Marquis Stevens, 1891–   . Ordinary Seaman, London Division, Royal Naval Volunteer Reserve, 7 September 1914. Crossed to Dunkirk, 24 September 1914. Served with the Royal Naval Division Motor Transport at Antwerp, October 1914, in Northern France, 1914–15. Petty Officer, March 1915. Timber buyer and inspector, 1919–39. River Thames Auxiliary Fire Service, 1939–40. Lieutenant, RNVR, 1940–5.

The convoy made a tour of the outer defences of the City—a ring of several forts with trenches in places. Route chiefly to north east, east and south, but some diversions were made. Forts did not appear heavily manned.

Mr Churchill was energetic and imperative. He discussed the situation with his own Staff and some of the Belgian officers, emphasising his points with his walking stick. Being well in the background, I heard little of what was said, but his actions were emphatic. He appeared on occasions to criticise the siting and construction of the trenches which had I believe been constructed by the Belgian Army. Lengthy discussions and arguments took place. General Paris RM and other RND officers took part, and on occasions the Belgian GOC (General de Guise[1]) and his Staff also joined in.

To me it appeared that Mr Churchill dominated the proceedings and the impression formed that he was by no means satisfied with the position generally. He put forward his ideas forcefully, waving his stick and thumping the ground with it. After obviously pungent remarks, he would walk away a few steps and stare towards the enemy's direction. On other occasions he would stride away without another word, get into the car and wait impatiently to go off to the next area.

At one line of trenches he found the line very thinly held and asked where 'the bloody men were'. He certainly was not mollified when he was told that was all that were available at that point.

As part of his tour of the Antwerp defences Churchill inspected the armoured train detachment under Commander Littlejohns, who wrote in his log that 'the trains were visited whilst under fire. . . . The First Lord was greatly interested in the construction of the trains. . . .'

During the morning of October 4 Kitchener sent Churchill details of the arrangements which he had made with the French Government for a strong French territorial division, together with a French marine force, to reach Antwerp as soon as possible. Churchill also learned from Kitchener that the Cabinet had approved of the Naval Brigades being sent to the city immediately. That afternoon Prince Louis arranged for their embarkation from Dover. Antwerp's future seemed less bleak. In a telegram to Kitchener, Colonel Dallas gave it as his opinion that 'one good army corps and a cavalry division to operate against the left flank of German investing army, with some second-line troops to keep open the army corps' communications with the coast, would create sufficient diversion to prevent fall of the fortress'. Kitchener was busy all day at the War Office attempting to obtain both from Sir John

[1] Victor Deguise, 1855–1925. Entered Belgian Army, 1874. Lieutenant-General, July 1914. Appointed Governor of the Fortress of Antwerp, 6 September 1914. Taken prisoner of war by the Germans, 10 October 1914.

French and from Marshal Joffre the necessary troops for diversionary activity on so large a scale.

At Antwerp the arrival of two thousand men of the Marine Brigade filled the citizens with enthusiasm, although these men were intended only as the first token of a massive Allied reinforcement. The effort to help Antwerp seemed rash and wasteful to many of those in Britain who could not know why it was being attempted. At the Admiralty, Captain Richmond, knowing nothing of the political and military background, was furious that the Marine Brigade had been sent to Antwerp. 'The siege of Antwerp looks ugly,' he wrote in his diary on October 4: 'I hope it may hold out. The 1st Lord is sending *his* army there; I don't mind his tuppenny untrained rabble going, but I do strongly object to 2000 invaluable marines being sent to be locked up in the fortress & become prisoners of war if the place is taken. They are our last reserve. No Board of Admiralty with two pennyworth of knowledge & backbone would have allowed marines to be used in such a way. We shall be crying out for men presently & our invaluable marines, & several seamen gunners, will be interned in Holland or locked up in a German fortress. It is a tragedy that the Navy should be in such lunatic hands at this time.'

During October 4, Churchill went to see de Broqueville again, giving him Kitchener's message that further British and French forces were on their way to the city. The Belgian Prime Minister wrote appreciatively as soon as Churchill had left him that the Belgians were 'determined, whatever the cost, to hold Antwerp. It is for us a national duty of the first order.' He was, he added, 'particularly glad at the close relationship which I have established with the eminent statesman sent here by the great nation which Belgium so much appreciates and loves'. All that Sunday, Churchill took direct charge of the search for men, rifles and ammunition. That night he telegraphed to the Admiralty for specific supplies:

Following required at once for attacking enemy's fire control balloons: Two of the latest long 4-inch guns, battleship pattern, with pedestal mounting complete, with 500 rounds of shrapnel and 500 rounds of high-explosive shells. The very longest range time fuses required for shrapnel.

Following required for 4·7 guns: 500 rounds of shrapnel with very long-range time fuses. Present time fuses too short.

Fuse scales.

100 fathoms of 2½ flexible steel wire rope.

150 duffle suits for crews of armoured trains.

Entrenching tools required for marine brigade.

300 Maxim guns on tripod mountings, with establishment of proportionate ammunition.

Sufficient material for twelve field telephone sets.

Shortly after midnight Churchill instructed the British Consul-General at Antwerp, Sir Cecil Hertslet,[1] to telegraph for further stores, including two million rounds of rifle ammunition and fifteen motor-cars.

Churchill woke early on Monday October 5. Admiralty business demanded that he return to London. When he had left the Admiralty in the early hours of October 3 he had arranged for Prince Louis to be in charge. This was the normal procedure in the event of a short absence. But Prince Louis was perturbed at having to bear the full responsibilities of the Admiralty for a second day. Churchill's single day visits to France had begun to annoy those at the Admiralty who disliked the unexpected and spasmodic disruptions in routine which they involved. This longer absence was even less acceptable. But Churchill had come to believe that Antwerp's continued resistance depended to a large extent upon his remaining in the city. He wanted to stay at least until the arrival of the two Naval Brigades, believing that his personal influence would help to compensate for their lack of training, and act as a stimulus to their morale. He had seen the extent to which, as a result of his presence, the Belgian Government had already been encouraged to persevere in prolonging the defence of the city, and he believed that he would be able to supervise the whole siege operation. The atmosphere of crisis and action excited him. The presence of troops, the immediacy of battle, and the importance of the outcome to the whole progress of the German advance, aroused his desire to participate, and to command.[2] That morning he took the extraordinary step of telegraphing to Asquith offering to resign from the Cabinet. His telegram read:

If it is thought by HM Government that I can be of service here, I am willing to resign my office and undertake command of relieving and defensive forces assigned to Antwerp in conjunction with Belgian Army, provided that I am given necessary military rank and authority, and full powers of a commander of a detached force in the field. I feel it my duty to offer my services,

[1] Cecil Hertslet, 1850–1934. Entered Foreign Office, 1868. Consul-General, Le Havre, 1896–1903; Antwerp, 1903–15. Knighted, 1905. Consul-General, Zürich, 1915–17; Antwerp, 1918–19.

[2] In 1968 Field-Marshal Earl Alexander of Tunis recalled, in a conversation with the author, that Churchill said to him during the Second World War: 'I do envy you, you've done what I've always wanted to do—to command great victorious armies in battle. I thought I got very near to it once, in the First World War, when I commanded those forces at Antwerp. I thought it was going to be my great opportunity.'

because I am sure this arrangement will afford the best prospects of a victorious result to an enterprise in which I am deeply involved. I should require complete staff proportionate to the force employed, as I have had to use all the officers now here in positions of urgency. I wait your reply. Runciman[1] would do Admiralty well.

Asquith was amazed by Churchill's request. He took the telegram to the Cabinet that morning, but did not mention it to his colleagues. At the Cabinet, Kitchener and Grey described the steps which had been taken to relieve the siege. A mood of optimism prevailed. Asquith, whose son 'Oc'[2] was on his way to the city with the Naval Brigades, reported to Venetia Stanley:

Winston succeeded in bucking up the Belges, who gave up their panicky idea of retreating to Ostend, and are now going to hold Antwerp for as long as they can, trusting upon our coming to their final deliverance. Winston had already moved up his Marines from Dunkirk, and they are now in the Antwerp trenches, where we hear to-day they are doing well but have already had 70 casualties. He had also sent for the rest of his Naval Brigade from Betteshanger, and I have a telegram from Oc sent off from Dover pier on Sunday evening: 'Embarking to-night: love'. I suppose most of the territorials & recruits would envy him, being sent off *after 3 days* to the front! I am sure he will do well, but it is a hazardous adventure.

We are doing our best for the Belgians, for tho' we are dangerously short of regulars in this country, K is sending off to-day to their help an Expeditionary Force, consisting of the 7th division (18,000 of our best infantry) and a Cavalry Division (also of the best) running to 4,000. These with 8,000 of Winston's to co-operate with them—Mainly Territorials & 'Fusilier Marines' —will amount to 23,500 men & 40 guns; wh gives a total of over 53,500 men, & 127 guns: quite a big army. They ought all to be in Belgium by Wednesday or Thursday at the latest, and it is to be hoped that Antwerp can last as long as that.

In his Cabinet letter to George V, Asquith was less detailed, but equally

[1] Walter Runciman, 1870–1949. Liberal MP, 1899–1900; 1902–18. Shipowner. President of the Board of Education, 1908–11. President of the Board of Agriculture and Fisheries, 1911–14. President of the Board of Trade, 1914–16. Liberal MP, 1924–9; 1929–31. Liberal National MP, 1931–7. President of the Board of Trade, 1931–7. 2nd Baron, 1937. Created Viscount Runciman of Doxford, 1937. Head of Mission to Czechoslovakia, 1938.
[2] Arthur Melland Asquith, 1883–1939. Known as 'Oc'. Sudan Civil Service, 1906–11. In business, 1911–14. Enlisted in the Royal Naval Volunteer Reserve, 1914. Served in the Royal Naval Division at Antwerp, Dardanelles and western front, 1914–16. Four times wounded. Served in the Ministry of Munitions, 1918; in the Ministry of Labour, 1919. Company director.

optimistic. 'Mr Churchill has been in Antwerp since Saturday afternoon,' he wrote, '& has successfully dissuaded the King & his Ministers from retiring to Ostend. He reports that the town can hold out certainly for 3, & perhaps for as long as 10 days, if the resistance is backed up.' At the Cabinet meeting, Kitchener outlined his arrangements for the despatch of a substantial British force, and these were approved. Under Kitchener's plan the 7th Division would eventually replace both the Marines, who were already bearing the brunt of the fighting, and the two Naval Brigades which were at that moment on their way to the city. The Cabinet also agreed to the appointment of General Sir Henry Rawlinson, then at Ostend, as Commander of the Antwerp Expeditionary Force, and he was instructed to make for the city as quickly as possible. During the discussion, several members of the Cabinet pressed Asquith to tell them when Churchill would be returning. It was only then that Asquith informed his colleagues, as he reported to the King, 'that he had this morning received from Mr Churchill a patriotic offer to resign his office & take command of the forces at Antwerp, but that, while expressing warm appreciation of the zeal & skill with which Mr Churchill had conducted his mission, he had felt it right to inform him that his services could not be dispensed with at home'. In his letter to Venetia Stanley Asquith sent a fuller account of Churchill's request to resign:

Then comes in a real bit of tragi-comedy. I found when I arrived here this morning the enclosed telegram from Winston, who, as you will see, proposed to resign his Office, in order to take the command in the field of this great military force! Of course without consulting anybody, I at once telegraphed to him warm appreciation of his mission & his offer, with a *most decided* negative, saying that we could not spare him at the Admiralty &c. I had not meant to read it to the Cabinet, but as everybody, including K, began to ask how soon he was going to return, I was at last obliged to do so, carefully suppressing the last sentence, in wh he nominates *Runciman* as his successor![1]

I regret to say that it was received with a Homeric laugh. W is an ex-Lieutenant of Hussars, and would if his proposal had been accepted, have been in command of 2 distinguished Major Generals, not to mention Brigadiers, Colonels &c: while the Navy were only contributing its little brigades.

Asquith did not inform Venetia Stanley that the Navy's 'little brigades', whose role he minimized, were in fact the only British forces at that

---

[1] Churchill's proposal may have seemed absurd to Asquith in October 1914; but in December 1916 Asquith himself contemplated sending Runciman to the Admiralty in place of Balfour.

moment available for immediate despatch to Antwerp, and that one of them, the Marine Brigade, constituted at the time of his letter the only British force engaged in the city's defence. In describing Churchill as 'an ex-Lieutenant of Hussars', Asquith overlooked the more relevant facts that Churchill, a Major at the outbreak of war, was no stranger to the strategic problems of modern warfare, as his memorandum of 1911 had shown. He had attended territorial manoeuvres almost every year. He was a member of the Committee of Imperial Defence. He had twice been a witness of German army manoeuvres. During the Agadir crisis he had been much concerned with military problems. He had already organized two Marine expeditions, one to Ostend, the other to Dunkirk, and had established a flying base at Antwerp for reconnaissance and attack. Kitchener, determined that Antwerp should resist as long as possible, and aware of Churchill's experience, wrote in the margin of Churchill's telegram that he was quite prepared to commission him as a Lieutenant-General, the necessary rank to supervise the military operations. But Asquith insisted that Churchill must return as soon as possible.

Rawlinson had some difficulty in reaching Antwerp. During October 5 he was at Dunkirk, where he found the military situation confused. 'The naval heavy guns that were to come have not yet arrived and we do not know where the ships have gone,' he wrote in his war journal. 'If there are many mines about and the channels have not been swept we may lose some transport. The situation is complicated—I cannot move forward with my divn for at least 3 or 4 days by which time it is quite possible Antwerp may have fallen.' Rawlinson's inability to reach Antwerp confirmed Churchill in his resolve to remain in the city himself. Shortly after midday, having received Asquith's telegram asking when he was going to return, he telegraphed to Kitchener:

In view of the situation and developing German attack, it is my duty to remain here and continue my direction of affairs unless relieved by some person of consequence.

If we can hold out for next three days, prospects will not be unfavourable. But Belgians require to be braced to their task, and my presence is necessary. Collapse on their part would be fatal. We have a good deal of ground to sell, if it is well disputed, even if Nethe River is forced.

That afternoon the Marine Brigade went into action. Despite heavy German bombardment it held its position on the outskirts of the city and along the Nethe. Later that afternoon Kitchener telegraphed Churchill to impress upon him that 'it is most necessary that Belgians should not give way before the forces now on the sea arrive for their support'. At the same time Kitchener warned that he was unable to accelerate the despatch of the Naval Brigades, 'owing to difficulties of navigation'. Prince Louis, he explained, was doing all that was possible, but the long sea crossing, and the danger of mines, made extreme caution essential. Churchill telegraphed to Kitchener and Grey: 'I am to attend council of Ministers at 9 pm tonight and shall exert myself to prevent an exodus.' That evening Kitchener learned with dismay that the French Marine Fusilier Brigade had been delayed, and telegraphed to the French Government to speed up their arrival at Antwerp. There was now little doubt that the brunt of the German attack would fall on the Belgians, and on the three Brigades of the Royal Naval Division.

During the evening of October 5 Churchill motored to the Marine Brigade headquarters at Lierre. Accompanied by the Marine Commander, General Paris, he visited the front-line trenches and found the men, he reported to Kitchener, 'cheerful and well dug in'. Despite the severity of the German bombardment, General Paris did not think that more than one hundred and fifty men had been killed or wounded. Churchill's visit to Marine headquarters was witnessed by the war correspondent of the *Giornale D'Italia*, Gino Calza Bedolo,[1] who, a few weeks later, described it in a talk at the Lyceum Club in London. His description was to be much repeated, and embellished:

I was in the battle line near Lierre, and in the midst of a group of officers stood a man. He was still young, and was enveloped in a cloak, and on his head wore a yachtman's cap. He was tranquilly smoking a large cigar and looking at the progress of the battle under a rain of shrapnel, which I can only call fearful. It was Mr Churchill, who had come to view the situation himself. It must be confessed that it is not easy to find in the whole of Europe a Minister who would be capable of smoking peacefully under that shellfire. He smiled, and looked quite satisfied.

On returning from the trenches, Churchill received a telegram from the Admiralty to inform him that the two Naval Brigades were now likely to arrive at Antwerp in the early hours of the following morning, but that although Rawlinson was about to leave Dunkirk for the city, he would not be able to get beyond Bruges that night. Many of the men in the Naval Brigades were only partly trained; but they constituted in the circumstances a significant force of over six thousand men. Both

---

[1] Gino Calza Bedolo, 1890–1925. London correspondent, *Il Giornale D'Italia*, 1914. Correspondent on the Belgian Front, October 1914. Reserve Infantry Officer (Lieutenant). After the war, Editor *Il Giornale D'Italia*; Editor-in-Chief, *Epoca*.

Kitchener and Churchill believed that, under the influence of the trained men among them, and conscious of the urgency of the occasion, they would be able to provide the relief needed for the exhausted Belgians, and for the Royal Marine defenders.

At nine o'clock that evening Churchill attended the Belgian Council of War, presided over by King Albert. Shortly after midnight he telegraphed to Kitchener and Grey:

All well. I have met Ministers in Council, who resolved to fight it out here, whatever happens.

All positions are held along the Nethe. I hope you will not decide finally on plan of operations till I can give you my views.

No 9·2's have arrived yet, even at Ostend.

In the early hours of October 6 the Belgians launched a counter-attack against the German forces, and fighting was severe. Early that morning Churchill went to see General Deguise at the Belgian Head-quarters, and learned that the attack had failed. The Belgian troops were very tired, and the situation had worsened. The Marine Brigade had also been heavily engaged. But Rawlinson's forces, the 7th Division and the 3rd Cavalry Division, were still disembarking at Dunkirk and Ostend, and had no chance of reaching the city that day. The only hope of checking the German onslaught lay in the two Naval Brigades which had arrived in the city during the night and early morning. These six thousand men represented at that dangerous moment the only succour of the Belgians. Few of them had seen action before; some had never fired a rifle even in practice. Among their officers were the poet, Rupert Brooke,[1] and Asquith's son, Arthur.

The two Naval Brigades marched towards the front line. Because General Paris was at that moment deeply involved with his Marine Brigade in the front-line action, Churchill took it upon himself to make the decisions about their deployment. He knew that they were needed in the front line, but that the line was breaking, and the tired reinforcements incapable of any prolonged manoeuvre. He therefore decided that they must not be exposed to the full fury of the German attack. Having motored to the Belgian Headquarters and obtained Deguise's approval for his decision, he gave personal orders for the Naval Brigades to take up a more secure, defensive position between the front line and the city. That afternoon he inspected the Marines in their front-line

[1] Rupert Brooke, 1887–1915. Poet. 2nd Lieutenant Royal Naval Division, September 1914. Served at Antwerp. Died of blood poisoning on his way to the Dardanelles, 23 April 1915. Churchill's obituary of Brooke was published in *The Times*, 26 April 1915.

positions; then he visited the Naval Brigades, who were still moving forward according to their original orders. One sailor, John Mitchell,[1] later told the author:

A battalion of Marines—regulars—were already there, right out at the front, taking a considerable brunt of the fighting. We marched out to relieve them. . . . We pulled up at a cross-roads. A car came from the direction of the front lines and drew up—an open tourer. Its windscreen was all smashed, and the Marine who was driving had a bandage round his head. Churchill was in the car, together with Colonel Seely of the WO. They had a lengthy chat with our CO. We then about turned and retired to a second line of trenches, where we stayed the night. Then we moved off to somewhere else. In one place we drew the full artillery fire from the Gerries because, from just behind us, they were being fired on by our six-inch naval guns mounted on railway trucks. . . . We got it fairly heavily. From this point my recollection is hazy. I'd had no sleep for three nights. It was impossible to sleep on the boat on Sunday, or in the train on Monday, or in the trenches on Tuesday.

There was a lull in the fighting during the afternoon. Asquith continued to keep Venetia Stanley informed of developments:

Things are interesting & rather critical. . . . Our immediate pre-occupations however are still with Antwerp, where under Winston's stimulus the Belgians are making a resolute stand. I have just seen a telegram sent off at 2 this afternoon, which shews that this morning both the Belgians & our Marines were pushed back. The inner forts (it says) are being held by our naval brigade—which shows that Oc & his companions in arms have arrived, & are already within range. Gen Rawlinson was 'expected shortly'. Meanwhile the 7th Division & the Cavalry & the French Marines must be well on in their march. It is to be hoped that they will arrive in time, but it is an anxious situation. Winston persists in remaining there, which leaves the Admiralty here without a head, and I have had to tell them (not being, entre nous, very trustful of the capacity of Prince Louis & his Board) to submit all decisions to me. He (ie Prince Louis) is coming here directly (5 pm) to see me. I think that Winston ought to return now that a capable General is arriving. He has done good service in the way of starching & ironing the Belges.

1 Cyril John Francis Mitchell, 1896–   . Apprentice engineer. Ordinary Deckhand, RNVR, 6 August 1914. Left Dover with the RND, 5 October 1914. Given a rifle for the first time in his life on Dunkirk Quay, 6 October 1914. Captured by the Germans, 10 October 1914. Prisoner of war in Germany, 1914–18. Escaped, but recaptured, May 1916. In plastics industry after the war.

Rawlinson reached Antwerp at five o'clock that afternoon and joined Churchill on the Lierre road. The General had come alone: the vast British reinforcement of over forty thousand men which he commanded remained at the Channel coast, still disembarking. Rawlinson at once took command of the eight thousand British troops already engaged in the fighting. At seven o'clock that evening Churchill and Rawlinson went to the Belgian Council of War. They were able to convince the Belgians that the British Government was determined to bring a large force into the city on the following day. But the Belgians no longer believed in the ability of fresh troops, even in large numbers, to save the city. Antwerp had already resisted for three days longer than they had anticipated. But the ground which the Germans had gained during their counter-attack that morning would soon enable them to bombard the city itself with their heavy howitzers. This, coupled with what Churchill described to Kitchener as the 'complete exhaustion and imminent demoralization' of the Belgian Army, led the Belgian Government to decide that although the city might still resist for a few days longer, no further attempt to take the offensive was possible, and plans had to be made for a rapid withdrawal. Churchill sent Kitchener an account of the agreement which he and Rawlinson had reached with the Belgians:

That while the town endures bombardment General Paris with naval division and Belgian support will defend inner line forts to the utmost.

That the rest of the Belgian Field Army shall be immediately withdrawn across the Scheldt to what they call the entrenched camp of the left bank. This area is protected by the Scheldt, various forts and entrenchments, and large inundations, and here they hope to find time to recover and re-form. From this position they will aid to the best of their ability any relieving movement which may be possible from the west.

Rawlinson will organize relieving force at Ghent and Bruges and prepare to move forward as soon as possible.

Churchill and Rawlinson were agreed that even if the regular divisions were unable to reach Antwerp, and it was becoming extremely unlikely that they could do so, it would still be possible for the Royal Marine Brigade and the two Naval Brigades—the whole of the Royal Naval Division—to hold the inner line of defences for several days. That evening Churchill visited each of the three Brigades. A member of one of the Naval Brigades, Jack Bentham,[1] sent his father an account of his first night in action:

We were all put in the trenches and having been there ½ hour were ordered out and then commenced to march nearer the enemy. Met a small party of Marines (regulars) who told us that they had been forced to leave the trenches where we were off to as half their number had been killed, having been so cheered up we went on under a severe shell fire, but which was mainly directed on Antwerp. Their final greeting 'God help you'. Having reached our destination we had to dig trenches and earthworks until dusk and were not allowed to sleep or talk. Severe frost and all shivered all night as half of us only had oilskins which were no protection. We cursed a car containing Churchill who came out to see what was going on & we were glad when he departed. We were standing by to receive a Uhlan charge.

On his return from this visit to the front, Churchill left Antwerp for London.

Speculative accounts of Churchill's absence from the Admiralty had gained wide circulation in London. When Sir Francis Hopwood asked Prince Louis, Lord Crewe and the President of the Local Government Board, Herbert Samuel, for information, they told him a strange story, inaccurate in almost every detail, which Hopwood passed on to Lord Stamfordham on October 5:

My dear Stamfordham,
    With the aid of talks today I know more about the Churchill business— mostly from Crewe and Prince Louis. On Friday evening Churchill started about 10.30 in a car for his usual weekend visit to Dunkirk—ewe lamb hunting as our soldiers describe the useless game. Somewhere on the way he heard that the Belgian Government intended to evacuate Antwerp. He rushed back to London and saw K & E. Grey in the small hours of the morning. Then in spite of their remonstrances he left for Antwerp. He summoned some people including Admiral Oliver over and since then has been telegraphing for

---

[1] John Henry Bentham, 1891–   . Enlisted in the Royal Naval Volunteer Reserve, July 1914. Able Seaman, Antwerp, October 1914. Sub-Lieutenant, Gallipoli, 1915. Served in France, 1916. Transferred to the Royal Naval Air Service, 1917. Flight-Lieutenant, Flying Boats, 1917–18. Subsequently in commerce. Called up, 1939. Wing-Commander, 1940; seconded to Army. Retired, 1946.

supplies of all kinds. Oliver came back today and says that the Germans are well aware that Churchill has bucked up the Belgian Government & is in charge—20,000 marks & the Iron Cross have been put on his head. He would be very wrath at the sum for it buys him at only one year's salary!

The Cabinet gave him peremptory orders to return & H. Samuel & Crewe said he would arrive at Charing X 1.45 this afternoon. Only his messenger turned up! . . .

Ever yrs
Francis S. J. Hopwood

Hopwood could not know that he had been given a grossly inaccurate account. As a result of what he had been told he drew the obvious conclusion that 'I don't think Winston can come away now with credit'. In his reply that same evening, Stamfordham accepted the story, and commented: 'Our friend must be quite off his head!' This was the view of many people who could not know the details; for most it was not to be dispelled.

On the night of October 6 Churchill reached Dover. Because of the mounting German military pressure, Rawlinson also left Antwerp, and set up his Headquarters at Bruges. The Royal Naval Division remained in the front line. When Churchill reached London on the morning of Wednesday October 7 he learned that he had just become a father for the third time. His new daughter, who had been born a few hours before, was christened Sarah Millicent Hermione.[1] Churchill family tradition later asserted that she had been born on the night Antwerp fell, but this was not so, for the city continued to resist.

On the morning of October 7 Churchill reported to the Cabinet on his three days at Antwerp. 'Winston is in great form & I think has thoroughly enjoyed his adventure,' Asquith wrote to Venetia Stanley. 'He is certainly one of the people one would choose to go tiger-hunting with, tho' as you very truly say he ought to have [been] born in the centuries before specialism. He was quite ready to take over in Belgium, and did so in fact for a couple of days, the army the navy & the civil government.'

With first-hand evidence of the weakness of a military position which could not be backed up by rapid and massive reinforcements, Churchill

---

[1] Sarah Millicent Hermione Churchill, 1914–   . Edward Marsh was her godfather. Actress. Author of *The Empty Spaces* (poems) and *A Thread in the Tapestry* (recollections).

was enthusiastic about Kitchener's scheme to raise a million volunteers in eight months to form new armies to hurl into the conflict. Still under the influence of his brief and unexpected military responsibilities, he longed to resign from the Admiralty in order to take up an army command. Asquith reported on Churchill's excited mood to Venetia Stanley in his letter of October 7:

I have had a long call from Winston, who, after dilating in great detail on the actual situation, became suddenly very confidential, and implored me not to take a 'conventional' view of his future. Having, as he says, 'tasted blood' these last few days, he is beginning like a tiger to raven for more, and begs that sooner or later, & the sooner the better, he may be relieved of his present office & put in some kind of military command.

I told him that he could not be spared from the Admiralty, but he scoffs at that, alleging that the naval part of the business is practically over, as our superiority will grow greater & greater every month. His mouth waters at the sight & thought of K's new armies. Are these 'glittering commands' to be entrusted to 'dug-out trash', bred on the obsolete tactics of 25 years ago—'mediocrities, who have led a sheltered life mouldering in military routine'? &c &c. For about ¼ of an hour he poured forth a ceaseless cataract of invective and appeal, & I much regretted that there was no short-hand writer within hearing—as some of his unpremeditated phrases were quite priceless. He was, however, quite three parts serious, and declared that a political career was nothing to him in comparison with military glory.

He has now left to have a talk with Arthur Balfour, but will be back here at dinner. He is a wonderful creature, with a curious dash of schoolboy simplicity (quite unlike Edward Grey's), and what someone said of genius—'a zigzag streak of lightning in the brain'.

'I am sitting next Winston . . .' Grey wrote to Clementine Churchill on October 7, 'having just welcomed his return from Antwerp. And I feel a glow imparted by the thought that I am sitting next a Hero. I cant tell you how much I admire his courage & gallant spirit & genius for war. It inspires us all.' During the Cabinet meeting on October 7 two of Churchill's colleagues passed him encouraging notes across the table. 'A great and heroic episode,' wrote Lord Haldane, 'you are a figure for history.' 'Congratulations on your brilliant effort to rescue Antwerp,' Lloyd George declared, asking: 'What are the prospects?' The prospects were poor. The Germans continued to bombard Antwerp throughout the night. On October 8 the French decided not to send the Marine Fusiliers, who were already at Ghent, to the defence of the city. That day, General Paris reported to Churchill on the 'lamentable state of the Belgian troops', who, he telegraphed, were 'no longer in a state to offer effective resistance'. Because the British 7th Division and 3rd Cavalry Division had not been able to go further than Ostend, General Paris decided to ask for permission to evacuate his trenches. Asquith reported in his letter of October 8 to Venetia Stanley:

Winston was furious (and I quite share his anger) at his General, who is in an almost impregnable entrenched position & ought to hold on even by his eye-brows, until either the situation becomes really desperate, or succour is at hand. Rawlinson with his 7th Division (unsupported by the French) is not quite strong enough to keep the road of retirement open. Winston got on the telephone with Gen Paris & put the fear of God into him, and the reports both as to the effects of the bombardment & as to the German flank movement now seem to have been grossly exaggerated. . . .

Later. Just had conference with K & Winston. The French having failed us, & the Belgian field army being quite untrustworthy, there is alas! nothing to be done but to order our naval men to evacuate the trenches to-night & Rawlinson will meet them & the remains of the Belgians at Ghent, after which point they are safe. Antwerp is I am afraid now in flames, but if the naval men get safely away, Sir J. French's army will be well reinforced, and ought to be able to make what Winston calls a 'punch' of an effective kind on the German right. Poor Winston is very depressed, as he feels that his mission has been in vain.

'The failure of French co-operation,' Asquith informed the King on October 9, 'made it impossible to despatch Gen Rawlinson's division as a relieving force; and as the Belgian army has become tired and dis-pirited,[1] and the German bombardment of the town was being steadily pressed, no useful object would have been served by a continued defence of the entrenchments by our unsupported Naval Division.' The British forces were given the order to withdraw.

While in Antwerp Churchill had discussed with the pilots of the Royal Naval Air Service their plan for a second air raid on Düsseldorf and Cologne, and given his approval. Using Antwerp as their base, they hoped to launch the raid on October 8. In order to avoid damage from German shells falling on the city, their aeroplanes had to be taken out of the shed a day before the raid. The base was situated half-way be-tween Antwerp and the German front line, with the result that shells

---

[1] It was not only the Belgians who were demoralized at the end of the siege. Sub-Lieutenant Owler (1895–   ) later wrote to the author of how, during the withdrawal, Churchill's former stepfather, Cornwallis-West, 'kept shouting to the men he was ashamed of our cowardice but the men were quite out of control and intent only on escape and home to England'.

passed continuously overhead. Throughout October 8 the two aeroplanes detailed for the attack on Germany were drawn up in the middle
of the aerodrome. Bad weather prevented them from taking off. On the
following morning the intensity of the German bombardment increased,
while at the same time mist made it impossible for the raid to begin. The
mist had still not cleared by noon. But as it was obvious to Spenser
Grey, who was to lead the attack, that further delay would mean the
capture of their aerodrome; he decided to start. At 1.20 pm he was
airborne. As he reported to the Admiralty on October 17:

On arriving at Cologne I found a thick mist. I had been given two different
positions for the airship sheds, one to the north-west and one to the south of
the town. I came down to 600 feet, but, after searching for 10 to 12 minutes
under a heavy fire, I failed to locate them. . . . Failing to locate the sheds, I
considered the best point to attack would be the main station in the middle
of the town where I saw many trains drawn up, so let fall my two bombs in
this. I arrived back at Antwerp at 4.45 pm and landed.

The second pilot involved in the attack, Reginald Marix, left Antwerp
ten minutes after Spenser Grey. On arriving at Düsseldorf he successfully located the Zeppelin shed, dropping his bombs at 600 feet. The
shed was hit and completely destroyed; flames rising 500 feet high
seemed evidence that a Zeppelin must have been inside. Spenser
Grey's report of the raid continued:

Lieutenant Marix was under a heavy rifle and shell fire during this period,
and his machine suffered considerable damage. In spite of this he managed
to fly back to within 20 miles of Antwerp, at which point his petrol ran out.
From here he succeeded in returning to Antwerp by a bicycle which he
borrowed from a peasant and a car which he got later. It was hoped to take
out more petrol in an armed car at daylight and recover the machine, but
the order to evacuate prevented this.

The attack was not in vain; not only had a Zeppelin been destroyed
in its shed but a report which reached the Admiralty from Germany
later in the month asserted that 'the occurrence produced great
consternation in Berlin as they did not believe such a raid was possible
for a British aviator'. During the evening of October 9, after Spenser
Grey and Marix had returned to their base, the Germans began deliberately shelling the aerodrome itself. The machines were so badly hit
that they could no longer fly. The pilots were obliged to leave Antwerp

by car. They managed to escape the German cordon, and reached Ostend.

Antwerp surrendered to the Germans on the night of October 10. Churchill and Kitchener believed that their action in organizing the city's resistance was justified by the effect which the fighting had in delaying the German advance to the Channel ports. On October 10 Asquith and Hankey discussed with Churchill the value of Britain's efforts at Antwerp. 'We both agree with Hankey (who is a good opinion),' Asquith wrote to Venetia Stanley, 'that this last week—which has delayed the fall of Antwerp by at least 7 days, and has prevented the Germans from linking up their forces—has not been thrown away, and may with Sir J. French all the time coming round have been even of vital value.' Writing to Venetia Stanley on October 29, Asquith again reported that Hankey, with whom he had lunched that day, thought that 'the week at Antwerp was well spent, & had a real effect on the general campaign'.

Much bitterness was felt in British Government circles towards alleged French intransigence throughout the siege. Kitchener, angry because the French had failed to send a Territorial Division to Antwerp as promised, wrote to Sir John French on October 11 that as a result of this Joffre was 'to a considerable extent responsible for the fall of Antwerp and moreover placed 8000 British marines and Bluejackets who were in Antwerp in considerable peril'. When, on October 11, the French Government complained to Grey that the British had failed to co-ordinate their military action at Antwerp with the French High Command, Grey was much angered, and sent a blunt telegram to Bertie, for communication to the French:

His Majesty's Government must have the right to send troops for separate operations against the Germans under whatever command seems to them most desirable. Developments might occur that would render possible and desirable operations that could not be directly combined with operations of Anglo-French army.

The attempt to relieve Antwerp was initiated by His Majesty's Government as a separate operation, in which British forces took much risk and incurred some losses; and it was impossible to subordinate the separate forces sent from England expressly for this purpose to the operations of Field-Marshal French without sacrificing *ab initio* the object for which the new forces were sent.

Grey ended his telegram by stating that 'the object was not achieved partly because General Joffre did not fulfil the expectation of sending a sufficient French force in time to co-operate with the British force for the relief of Antwerp'.

During a week of intense fighting at Antwerp, seven officers and fifty other ranks of the Royal Naval Division were killed. One hundred and fifty-eight men were wounded. Nine hundred and thirty-six were taken prisoner by the Germans and sent to a prisoner-of-war camp near Berlin. Fifteen hundred men, in the confusion of the retreat, crossed into Holland where they were interned for the remainder of the war. These losses were soon levelled against Churchill personally. The fifty-seven dead were quickly multiplied in the public mind. There were those who doubted whether Churchill's success in persuading the Belgians to fight on, and the support of the Royal Naval Division which enabled them to do so for seven days, really rendered any significant service to the Allied cause. The King of the Belgians had no such doubts. In March 1918 he had a long conversation with General Paris, which he later dictated, in the form of a memorandum.

. . . You are wrong in considering the RND Expedition as a forlorn hope. In my opinion it rendered great service to us and those who deprecate it simply do not understand the history of the War in its early days. Only one man of all your people had the prevision of what the loss of Antwerp would entail and that man was Mr Churchill. . . . Delaying an enemy is often of far greater service than the defeat of the enemy, and in the case of Antwerp the delay the RND caused to the enemy was of inestimable service to us. These 3 days allowed the French and British Armies to move NW. Otherwise our whole army might have been captured and the Northern French Ports secured by the enemy. Moreover, the advent of the RND inspired our troops, and owing to your arrival, and holding out for 3 days, great quantities of supplies were enabled to be destroyed. You kept a large army employed, and I repeat the RND rendered a service we shall never forget.

Churchill had every reason for satisfaction when he returned to England, after only four days' absence, with so much accomplished. But a severe shock awaited him in London. To his surprise he was confronted by widespread criticism and even misrepresentation. The editor of the *Morning Post*, H. A. Gwynne, was the most persistent of the critics; on October 13, in a leading article entitled 'The Antwerp Blunder', he advised the Government 'to keep a tight hand upon their impulsive colleague', and suggested that it was the duty of the Opposition leaders to use their influence 'to see that no more mischief of the sort is done'. Gwynne asserted that 'The attempt to relieve Antwerp by a small force of Marines and Naval Volunteers was a costly blunder, for which Mr W. Churchill must be held responsible', and went on to ask:

Is it not true that the energies of Mr W. Churchill have been directed upon this eccentric expedition, and that he has been using the resources of the Admiralty as if he were personally responsible for the naval operations? It is not right or proper that Mr Churchill should use his position as Civil Lord to press his tactical and strategical fancies upon unwilling experts. . . . We suggest to Mr Churchill's colleagues that they should, quite firmly and definitely, tell the First Lord that on no account are the military and naval operations to be conducted or directed by him.

Before the outbreak of war Churchill had often been attacked, particularly in Conservative newspapers. But such an attack, in time of war, had no precedent. A Cabinet Minister engaged in secret work could not take up cudgels on his own behalf, as would have been possible in peace-time. He could only watch with consternation as the Press attacks continued. On October 14 the editor[1] of the *Daily Mail* reprinted the *Morning Post*'s article and continued the charge in its own leader. 'The public has a right to know,' he declared, 'who is responsible for a gross example of mal-organization which has cost valuable lives and sacrificed the services during the continuance of the war not only of a considerable number of gallant young Englishmen but also of a considerable section of the Belgian Army.' On the same day *The Times*, also owned by Northcliffe, published a letter from Frederick Hulke,[2] protesting against the sending of the two Naval Brigades to Antwerp:

When rumours first got about in this neighbourhood that these raw levies were going to the front, it was scoffed at as incredible. The opinions of many naval and military officers were unanimous that to send the Brigade in their present condition to any fighting line was nothing less than 'deliberate murder'. Individual officers, non-commissioned officers, and men of the force itself laughed at the bare suggestion of being employed as a fighting unit.

[1] Thomas Marlowe, 1868–1935. Editor, *Daily Mail*, 1899–1926. Chairman, Associated Newspapers, 1918–26.
[2] Frederick Backhouse Hulke, 1862–1925. Member, Royal College of Surgeons of England, 1886. Senior Surgeon, Victoria Hospital, Deal, 1897–1925. Freemason. Chairman, Deal, Walmer and District Conservative Association. Captain, East Kent Volunteer Regiment, 1916.

When, shortly after their departure, it was reported on undeniable evidence that these Naval Volunteers and recruits had been actually sent to Antwerp, the general feeling throughout this district was one of intense anger and consternation.

On October 14 the *Pall Mall Gazette*, which, like the *Observer*, was edited by J. L. Garvin, defended Churchill's actions on the grounds that Britain had been morally bound to come to Antwerp's aid. 'That was a v. kind & shrewd column . . .' Churchill wrote to Garvin that night. 'But you must one day let me show you the good military reasons upon wh—apart from sentiment—the action was taken.'

The attacks on Churchill continued. On October 14 the *Morning Post* published a letter from Walter Long, again headed 'The Antwerp Blunder'. 'When the news first became public that the Marines had been sent to Antwerp,' Long wrote, 'there was, to my certain knowledge, a general and profound feeling of consternation.' On October 16 H. A. Gwynne wrote to six Liberal Ministers—Asquith, Lloyd George, Grey, McKenna, Pease and Masterman [1]—declaring that what had happened at Antwerp was proof 'that Mr Churchill is unfitted for the office which he now holds, and I am firmly convinced that the country will be in a state of considerable disquietude, if not panic, unless a change is made at the Admiralty'. Gwynne threatened to publish an article entitled 'true facts of the despatch of British troops to Antwerp and their subsequent retreat'; but he offered 'gladly and willingly' to suppress all further mention of Antwerp if Churchill were removed. He ended his letter: 'I feel I have a duty as Editor of a paper to protest against the continuance in office of a man who has shown most signally his incompetence to hold this office at least in time of war.'

On October 15 an English shipbroker [2] formerly resident in Antwerp sent the *Morning Post* a detailed defence of Churchill's action. But the paper did not print it. On October 16 they defended its exclusion on the grounds that they had received so many letters about 'the Antwerp blunder' that they could not find space for them all, and that 'to publish a selection might be invidious'. 'Moreover,' the paper continued, in time of war, newspaper controversy is as much as possible to be avoided.'

[1] Charles Frederick Gurney Masterman, 1874–1927. Liberal MP, 1906–14. Under-Secretary to Churchill, Home Office, 1909–12. Financial Secretary to the Treasury, 1912–14. Chancellor of the Duchy of Lancaster, 1914–15. Forced to leave the Government after nine months of being unable to find a parliamentary constituency after being defeated at a by-election in February 1914. Liberal MP, 1923–4.

[2] I have been unable to discover the name of the shipbroker, who had wished to remain anonymous.

Such hypocrisy was too much for A. G. Gardiner,[1] editor of the *Daily News*, who published the suppressed letter in full, and for James Douglas,[2] editor of the *Star*, which in its leading article headed 'WHAT WE THINK—A Mean Campaign' defended Churchill's actions and also reprinted the shipbroker's letter, part of which read:

Had Mr Churchill not arrived in Antwerp about 1 pm on Saturday, October 3, it may be proved that the city would that very morning have been surrendered to the enemy. What a splendid haul the enemy would have secured in provisions, grain, stores, and last, but not least, immense quantities of petrol! . . . There is an English saying, 'Give the devil his due.' I used to think Mr Winston Churchill was a devil in the way he behaved over the Ulster question, but not after the signal and incalculable service he, and his advisers, have undoubtedly rendered this country, Belgium, and the Allies. They gave the Allies time to strengthen their left wing by the time Antwerp fell, and moreover gave the Belgians time to destroy everything worth having in Antwerp, and leaving it a skeleton and deserted city for the enemy to enter with their would-be-all-powerful goose-step. Instead, therefore, of criticising Mr Churchill and the British Cabinet in the way you are doing, take a leaf out of the brave Belgians' book, and don't complain about what was done for the best, and don't denounce the man who helped to save a desperate position, and moreover risked his life in doing so.

On Sunday October 18 the *Observer* also came to Churchill's defence, rejecting Gwynne's charge that he was an amateur strategist who took unnecessary, and therefore dangerous risks:

A principle of the first importance is raised by the personal attacks on the First Lord after the fall of Antwerp. Are we to encourage initiative, energy, enterprise on the part of our leaders in war time or are we to paralyse them by clamouring for a victim at every disappointment or mishap? . . .

Mr Churchill did his duty like a strong man and like a representative of the spirit of the British Navy, in advising the fight to the last that delayed the besiegers of Antwerp for a week. . . . When we sent the Marines and the Naval Brigades it was, simply, the best we could do in an emergency. We are engaged in real war. Risks must be taken, whether success always follows or not. If prompt, courageous and determined men are not to receive the benefit of the doubt the wrong spirit will creep into the Services. . . .

[1] Alfred George Gardiner, 1865–1946. Editor, *Daily News*, 1902–19. President of the Institute of Journalists, 1915–16.

[2] James Douglas, 1867–1940. Journalist. Editor of the *Star*, 1908–20. Editor of the *Sunday Express*, 1920–31. Exercised editorial power for only two weeks, being found unsuitable in that time. A director of Express Newspapers, 1920–40.

We have even noticed that the First Lord of the Admiralty is called an amateur. It happens to be just what he is not. He has seen war; he has written about war; he has studied war. If he left office tomorrow he would be very capable of serving with distinction in the field.

The *Morning Post* was unimpressed. On October 19 it returned to the attack, denouncing Churchill's 'impropriety' in undertaking business which 'did not properly belong to his sphere' as First Lord:

What we desire chiefly to enforce upon Mr Churchill is that this severe lesson ought to teach him that he is not, as a matter of fact, a Napoleon; but a Minister of the Crown with no time either to organise or to lead armies in the field. . . . To be photographed and cinematographed under fire at Antwerp is an entirely unnecessary addition to the risks and horrors of war. . . . He should seek rather to earn the nation's gratitude by a steady devotion to his proper duties than to dazzle the world by the gallantry of an ex-captain of dragoons.

The violent attacks of the *Morning Post*, although rebutted by many other papers, formed the basis of continuing public criticism. Because of the highly secret nature of the operation, and the fact that its principal benefits were even at that moment being worked out on the battlefield along the Yser and in the Ypres salient, no official answer was possible. Churchill was upset by the continued attacks of the *Morning Post*. After the publication of its first hostile leader he asked the new head of the Press Bureau, Sir Stanley Buckmaster,[1] to try to stop such crude publications in future. Buckmaster replied: 'I have written to the Editor of the *Morning Post*, pointing out the unfairness of criticism to which in the public interest no answer can be made. To go further would I believe be to court defiance and defeat.'

Faced with the reluctance of the Press Bureau to help him, Churchill could do little to combat the spread of wild charges. When he welcomed the Royal Naval Division back from Antwerp on October 18, he used the opportunity to defend himself as fully as possible. Untrained troops had been chosen, be explained, not by an oversight or any personal quirk of his own, as was being alleged, but 'because the need for them was urgent and bitter'; they were the nearest troops available, and they 'could be embarked the quickest'. Although their training was

[1] Stanley Owen Buckmaster, 1861–1934. Liberal MP, 1906–14. Solicitor-General, 1913–15. Knighted, 1913. Director of the Press Bureau, 1914–15. Lord Chancellor, 1915–16. Created Baron, 1915. Created Viscount, 1933.

incomplete it was, he declared, 'as far advanced as that of a large portion, not only of the forces defending Antwerp, but of the enemy forces attacking'. In his speech Churchill explained that 'The Naval Division was sent to Antwerp, not as an isolated incident, but as part of a large operation for the relief of the city'. Military security prevented him from referring to the Belgian appeal, the French offer of help, Grey's desire to sustain Belgian morale or Kitchener's determination to hold Antwerp for as long as possible.

The principal charge that was emerging against Churchill was the despatch of untrained recruits to Antwerp. On October 5, when Asquith had learned of the despatch of the Naval Brigades, including his 'raw recruit' son, he had written to Venetia Stanley: 'I suppose most of the territorials & recruits would envy him, being sent off *after three days* to the front!' But after hearing his son's first-hand experiences he wrote angrily to Venetia Stanley on October 13:

Strictly between ourselves, I can't tell you what I feel of the *wicked* folly of it all. The Marines of course are splendid troops & can go anywhere & do anything: but nothing can excuse Winston (who knew all the facts) from sending in the two other Naval Brigades. I was assured that all the recruits were being left behind, and that the main body at any rate consisted of seasoned Naval Reserve men. As a matter of fact only about ¼ were Reservists, and the rest were a callow crowd of the rawest tiros, most of whom had never fired off a rifle, while none of them had ever handled an entrenching tool. Oc's battalion was commanded by George [Cornwallis] West—an ex (very-ex) Subaltern in the Guards who was incompetent & overbearing & hated impartially by both officers and men. Among its principal officers were R. Brooke (the poet) Oc himself & one Denis Browne (a pianist),[1] who had respectively served 1 week, 3 days, & 1 day. It was like sending sheep to the shambles. Of course when they got into the trenches they behaved most gallantly—but what could they do? The Belges ran away & had to be forced back at the point of the bayonet into the forts, while the Germans at a safe distance of 5 or 6 miles thundered away with their colossal howitzers. When at last (most unwillingly) our men obeyed the order to retire, they found the bridge across the Scheldt & most of the lighters & boats in flames: they just got across on a pontoon, but Oc says that if the wind had blown the other way they cd never have crossed & would have been left in the burning town. Then for 7 or 8 hours they marched (the one thing sailors can't do) for more than 20

---

[1] William Denis Browne, 1888–1915. Between 1908 and 1914 Organist at Guy's Hospital; Conductor at the Working Man's College; musical critic of the *New Statesman*. Composer of Latin church music, several songs and a short ballet. Sub-Lieutenant, Royal Naval Volunteer Reserve, 15 September 1914. Served at Antwerp, October 1914. Wounded on Gallipoli Peninsula, 8 May 1915; returned to action, and killed, 4 June 1915.

miles over cobbled roads, with a ceaseless stream of Belgian refugees & soldiers blocking the way; and at last, more dead than alive, got into trains at St Gilles, wh gradually took them to Ostend. If the Germans had had any initiative, they might with a couple of squadrons of cavalry have cut them into mincemeat at any stage of their retreat. No doubt it is a wonderful experience to look back upon, but what cruel & terrible risks! Thank God they are all now back in England, except the 1,500 who, when dead beat, crossed the Dutch frontier in despair, & are now interned in Holland.

The popular misconceptions about the sending of the recruits were inevitable, given the lack of any detailed official explanation of why they had been sent. Asquith knew the full story. But in his concern at his son's account of the sufferings of the recruits, he had disregarded several important facts. He himself had explained to the King that at that particular moment of the crisis there were no other troops available either on the Continent or in England capable of playing any part at all in the defence of Antwerp. Asquith knew that on October 4, in his telegram to Kitchener, Churchill had explicitly requested the Naval Brigades to be sent, 'minus recruits'; all subsequent arrangements for the despatch of the Brigades had been made at the Admiralty by Prince Louis, and Asquith himself had undertaken to supervise Prince Louis' work during Churchill's absence. The recruits could easily have been held back had Prince Louis or Asquith desired. When, on October 5, Churchill found that the Brigades had come with their recruits, and were about to be exposed to the full weight of a German assault, he had given immediate orders for them to take up a less exposed, defensive position.

Churchill was momentarily cast down by the force of public criticism. But he never doubted that the defence of Antwerp was necessary. On October 15, five days after the city's fall, he wrote privately to Colonel Repington,[1] the military correspondent of *The Times*, in the columns of which he had been under attack. 'The loss of Antwerp was a bitter pang to me,' he wrote. 'But you must not suppose that sentiment dictated our movements. The sudden & total collapse of the Belgian resistance, & the diversion of the promised French aid, were factors that destroyed a good & reasonable chance of saving the place— even at the last moment. I take the fullest responsibility for my share, but of course I only acted with & within the fullest authority.' This was

[1] Charles à Court Repington, 1858–1925. Entered Army, 1878. Lieutenant-Colonel on Kitchener's staff at Omdurman, 1898. Forced to resign his commission because of a personal indiscretion involving another officer's wife. Military Correspondent of *The Times*, 1904–18. Military Correspondent of the *Daily Telegraph*, 1918–25.

not the interpretation of his actions which his critics or even his colleagues accepted. The Conservatives saw Antwerp as proof of their contention that Churchill was not to be trusted. On October 14 Bonar Law wrote to Sir Joseph Larmor [1] that the defence of Antwerp had been 'an utterly stupid business', and that Churchill seemed to have 'an entirely unbalanced mind which is a real danger at a time like this'. Even Lloyd George, who had originally congratulated Churchill on his efforts, soon expressed doubts. On October 23 his Private Secretary, Frances Stevenson,[2] recorded in her diary that Lloyd George was 'rather disgusted with Winston still about Antwerp, and think that the PM is too. Having taken untrained men over there, he left them in the lurch. He behaved in rather a swaggering way when over there, standing for photographers and cinematographers with shells bursting near him, & actually promoting his pals on the field of action.'

Churchill's actions at Antwerp, both real and imaginary, confirmed for many the description A. G. Gardiner had published in 1913, in a volume of biographical sketches, *Pillars of Society*. 'He will write his name big on our future,' Gardiner had written, 'let us take care he does not write it in blood.' And he continued:

He is always unconsciously playing a part—an heroic part. And he is himself his most astonished spectator. He sees himself moving through the smoke of battle—triumphant, terrible, his brow clothed with thunder, his legions looking to him for victory, and not looking in vain. He thinks of Napoleon; he thinks of his great ancestor. Thus did they bear themselves; thus, in this rugged and most awful crisis, will he bear himself. It is not make-believe, it is not insincerity: it is that in that fervid and picturesque imagination there are always great deeds afoot with himself cast by destiny in the Agamemnon rôle.

During the first two months of the war Churchill had worked energetically at what he believed were wise policies and necessary measures. He had hoped that his actions as First Lord would show both hostile Tories and suspicious Liberals that their earlier distrust of him need survive no longer, and that they could rely on his judgement at a time of national emergency. The way in which he saw his efforts at Antwerp misrepresented convinced him that his hopes were in vain. War had brought no truce, no transformation. Churchill learned that

[1] Joseph Larmor, 1857–1942. Lucasian Professor of Mathematics, Cambridge, 1903–32. Knighted, 1909. Conservative MP for Cambridge University, 1911–22. President of the Royal Society, 1914–15.

[2] Frances Louise Stevenson, 1888–   . Schoolteacher. Private Secretary to Lloyd George, 1913–43. She married Lloyd George in 1943. Countess Lloyd-George of Dwyfor, 1945.

even a successful wartime administration would not obliterate the scars of his earlier enmities. Even the majority of his Cabinet colleagues did not have access to enough of the facts to form an independent view. It was a bitter time. Self-confidence and ebullience ebbed away. In this melancholy mood he told Haldane that he contemplated resigning altogether from public life. Churchill had always respected Haldane's opinion, and on this occasion Haldane acted as a steadying influence. 'I have been thinking over our talk,' he wrote on October 19. 'You must not ever consider leaving the Admiralty at this period of crisis. You are unique & invaluable to the nation—full of courage and re-source. Do not pay the least attention to the fools who write & talk in the press. It is this real thing that counts, & the nation thoroughly believes in you.'

Churchill received further encouragement from Sir John French. 'I don't understand the attitude of the French in this Antwerp affair——' the Commander-in-Chief wrote on October 21 from his new Head-quarters at St Omer; 'at least I should say I *do* understand it—but am necessarily so much accustomed to their vagaries that I have ceased hoping to probe the causes! . . . You did splendid work at Antwerp. When are you coming to me again? For God's sake don't pay attention to what those rotten papers say.' The advice of Haldane, the encourage-ment of Sir John French and the pressure of new events aided the recovery of Churchill's spirits. But his optimism of August and Septem-ber had died. 'It wd be affectation,' he wrote to J. L. Garvin on October 23, 'to pretend that I do not feel the kind of systematic & malicious undermining of which we are now the object. But I hope I am strong enough to overcome my feelings.' 'Antwerp was a bitter blow to me,' he wrote to French three days later, 'and some aspects of it have given a handle to my enemies, and perhaps for a time reduced my power to be useful.'

In his letter to French on October 26 Churchill declared: 'I clear my heart of all hostile reflections and sterile controversies. It is vain to look backwards.' But he was not allowed, either by the Press or the public, to concentrate entirely upon the future. Even some Naval officers whose confidence was essential if Naval morale were to be upheld were sceptical, interpreting Antwerp as proof of Churchill's inability to restrict his activities to his proper sphere, of his rashness and unreliability. Sir David Beatty's reaction was typical. On October 18 he wrote to his wife:[1] 'The man must have been mad to have thought

---

[1] Ethel Newcomb Field, 1873–1932. Only daughter of the Chicago department store owner and millionaire, Marshall Field. She married Beatty (her second husband) in 1901.

he could relieve [Antwerp] . . . by putting 8,000 half-trained troops into it.' A day later he wrote again: 'If he would either leave matters entirely alone at the Admiralty which wd be the best thing to do, or give it his entire and complete attention, we might get forward, but this flying about and putting his fingers into pies which do not concern him is bound to lead to disaster.' And on October 20 he wrote yet again: 'If we only had a Kitchener at the Admiralty we could have done so much and the present state of chaos in naval affairs would never have existed. It is inconceivable the mistakes and blunders we have made and are making.'

5

The Return of Lord Fisher

WITHIN a week of occupying Antwerp, the Germans reached the Channel coast and seized Ostend. The French Government believed that they would at once advance along the coast to Dunkirk and Calais, disrupting communications between France and Britain, and turning the seaward flank of the Allied forces. On October 16 Joffre appealed for British help to prevent such an advance. He wanted the Royal Navy to bombard German positions along the coast between Ostend and Nieuport. Kitchener put the request to Churchill, who immediately ordered the bombardment of the German-held coast to begin on October 17, and detailed his Naval Secretary, Admiral Hood, to take charge of the operation. In the course of the next ten days British Naval activity along the coast was fierce and continuous. Churchill did not restrict the coastal activities to naval bombardment. On October 15 he had already ordered a small military force, based on Dunkirk, to make a series of overland sorties in the direction of Ostend. This force was part of the combined Marine and Yeomanry detachment which he had been deploying in the area of Dunkirk and Cassel before the siege of Antwerp. On October 16 he wrote to his brother, who had been with the force since it reached France:

My dearest Jack,
    My heart marched with you down the road from Dunkirk. God guard you and bring you safe home. I feel about this war that it will devour us all—& for my part I am willing when the time comes to pay the price. I know you will do just what is right—not forgetting the responsibilities of a squadron leader, & not failing to discern the real opportunities which flash up here & there in war & lead to glory.
    I sent some armed cars etc for you all & hope you are well fitted out as the result of yr sojourn under the Admiralty.
    I heard the crack of their shells for 4 days at Antwerp, & I cd be quite content, I can assure you, to ride along in my place with you all. . . .

I have told French you are with the regiment: & have warned him of the limitation of yr training in field work. That all honour & good fortune may go with you is the sincere & profound wish, of your loving brother.

W

PS I have just given S. Grey & Marix the DSO for their wonderful attack on the Zeppelin Sheds at Dusseldorf & Cologne.

En avant. How long is it since John Churchill fought at Lille![1]

The ships continued their bombardment for nearly two weeks. The Yeomanry and their armoured cars were busy on the German flank. Every night during the battle Churchill spoke on the telephone with the British Liaison Officer with the Belgian Army, his friend Colonel Bridges.[2] But this joint naval and military enterprise failed to drive the Germans from the Belgian coast, or to make possible the recapture of Antwerp. On October 26 Churchill wrote to Sir John French, stressing the important long-term objectives:

I do trust you realize how damnable it will be if the enemy settles down for the winter along lines which comprise Calais, Dunkirk or Ostend. There will be continual alarms and greatly added difficulties. We must have him off the Belgian Coast, even if we cannot recover Antwerp.

I am getting old ships with the heaviest guns ready, protected by barges with nets against submarines, so as to dispute the whole seaboard with him. On the 31st instant Revenge, four $13\frac{1}{2}$-inch guns, will come into action if required, and I have a regular fleet of monitors and 'bomb-ketches' now organized which they all say has hit the Germans hard, and is getting stronger every day.

By the end of October it was clear that no British flanking movement, however well supported from the sea, could reach Ostend, far less Antwerp. 'Risks must be run,' Churchill instructed Hood on October 27. But despite Hood's efforts, the Germans could not be dislodged from the coast. During the last week in October it was the British themselves who were in danger further inland. German troops were pressing upon the Ypres salient, and all Sir John French's energies were concentrated upon preventing them from breaking through Ypres and pouring

[1] Churchill's ancestor, John Churchill 1st Duke of Marlborough, opened the siege of Lille—then the capital of French Flanders—on 13 August 1708. The city surrendered on October 22; over 5,000 allied troops, and 5,000 Frenchmen were killed.

[2] George Tom Molesworth Bridges, 1871–1939. Entered Royal Artillery, 1892. Lieutenant-Colonel 4th Hussars, 1914. Head of British Military Mission, Belgian Field Army, 1914–16. Major-General, commanding the 19th Division, 1916–17. Wounded five times. Lost a leg at Passchendaele. Head of British War Mission, USA, 1918. Head of British Mission, Allied Armies of the Orient, 1918–20. Knighted, 1919. Governor of South Australia, 1922–7.

down upon Dunkirk and Calais from the rear. British eyes focused upon the Battle of Ypres, and Churchill's coastal activities went almost unnoticed. Nevertheless the naval action did help to provide the Allied forces with a secure sea flank. By the end of October, the western front was finally established. Henceforth no flanking movement either by sea or land was to dislodge the Germans from their increasingly strong entrenchments for nearly four years, nor were the Germans to advance any further westwards along the coast.

Critics of Churchill's intervention at Antwerp were equally angered by the continued activities of the 'Dunkirk Circus'. 'I trust that Winston will learn by experience,' Asquith wrote to Venetia Stanley on October 13, 'and now hand over to the military authorities the little circus which he is still running "on his own" at Dunkirk—Oxfordshire Yeomen, motor-buses . . . armoured cars &c &c. They have really nothing to do with the Admiralty, which ought to confine its activities to the sea & the air.' Lord Fisher was another critic of Churchill's land activities, informing Pamela McKenna[1] in mid-October that 'Winston has surrounded himself with third class sycophants, and is so autocratic! and is taking charge of Dunkirk instead of the Navy!' Ironically, Churchill was being criticized for undertaking responsibilities which Kitchener had asked him to undertake, and for which the French, or as at Antwerp the Belgian, Government had appealed. Because there was no established method of co-operation between the British and French forces, it was left to the initiative of individual Ministers to work out the most effective means of co-ordination. The daily danger of a German breakthrough, the difficulties of communication when front lines were fluid, and the shortage both of men and materials, added to the difficulties of anyone who undertook such responsibilities.

The limited but important success of the 'Dunkirk Circus' in helping to halt the German advance at the mouth of the Yser, less than ten miles to the east of the Franco-Belgian border, and the continued reconnaissance activities of the naval pilots, did nothing to curb the continuing Press criticisms of Churchill's mission to Antwerp. As well as the naval activity off Ostend, the 'Dunkirk Circus', and echoes of Antwerp, Churchill had to face further criticism during October because the German ship *Emden*, loose in the Indian Ocean, was sinking a series of British merchant ships and eluding all attempts to track her down.[2]

[1] Pamela Jekyll, 1889–1943. She married Reginald McKenna in 1908.

[2] While at large, the *Emden* sank fifteen unarmed merchant ships and captured eight. She also sank a Russian cruiser and a French destroyer inside Penang harbour, and bombarded the oil depot at Madras. She was sunk by an Australian light cruiser, the *Sydney*, on 9 November 1915.

He had also to seek to allay Kitchener's fears of an imminent invasion. At Cabinet, Kitchener not only spoke of invasion as a possibility but asserted that Britain would be unable to repel it. Churchill wanted Kitchener to be more specific. He was angry to find that Kitchener's fears were not backed up by any detailed analysis of possible German action, but that they nevertheless gave many Cabinet Ministers the impression that Churchill had not made proper preparations. Churchill wrote sternly to Kitchener on October 19:

My dear Kitchener,
   . . . The problem of invasion must be studied in detail. You have at yr disposal probably the best experts in the world. Let them make a plan for the landing of 150,000 men (a) on a beach, (b) at a port, anywhere on the East Coast, with the necessary artillery, vehicles & ammunition columns of a German Army on that scale. Let them work out the number of transports, the number of men in each, the number of horses, the number of waggons, the tonnage of supplies and ammunition etc etc. Let them select their beach, or say which harbour they can get into, making sure that the ships are the right draught to get into it. Choose any day in the past month. Assume (a large assumption) that yr Armada has reached the English coast without being detected. Calculate exactly the time taken to land the men, guns, vehicles, horses, stores, under all the limitations of actual physical conditions. Leave out the chance of weather. Assume it all goes perfectly, & that we only get notice when your ships are sighted from the shore. Assume that the whole German Fleet supports this operation. Make any dispositions you like for them & keep them secret.
   The Admiralty will then say what force we can bring to bear, or could have brought to bear, on a particular day at 3, 6, 12, 24 hours respectively,? what our positions wd be at the end of that time. You will be able to see whether any, & if so what changes are required in our arrangements.
   It really is no use dealing with the subject in general terms. All the same, you ought to have the military force to deal with 70,000 men in this country.' This is the deterrent on which we rely to give us a proper target or immunity.
                                                            Yours sincerely
                                                            Winston S. Churchill

   Kitchener did not like to be lectured to about his duties. During the Cabinet of October 21 he repeated his demand that Churchill should make more specific naval dispositions against a possible German invasion. 'Winston made a very good defence of his policy,' Asquith wrote to Venetia Stanley, 'which is (in a word, or at least a few words) that the function of the Great Fleet is not to prevent the landing of an invading force (which is the business of the torpedo flotillas & submarines) but to strike at & destroy the enemy's covering fleet.' But

Churchill did agree, as Asquith reported, 'to have a lot of sheltered or protected harbours wh no submarine can penetrate, & in which some battleships & cruisers can lie in safety'. Churchill told French of his dispute with Kitchener on October 26.

Kitchener is strangely alarmed about invasion . . . we have witnessed an absolute reversal of roles—the WO declaring the country not safe and an invasion of 250,000 a possibility, and the Admiralty reassuring them, or trying to. You know how carefully I have examined that position, and how I have never minimized the risks. But now that we are face to face with realities, I am not alarmed, and my policy is that you should be reinforced by any effective division that can be formed and maintained; and that the Navy will prevent any invasion of a serious character. The Prime Minister is solid as a rock; but waves of nervousness pass over others, and may result in some retardation of your reinforcements.

It was not the British Government alone which worried about the German successes. After the *Emden* had bombarded the oil tanks at Madras, the Indian Government telegraphed urgently for greater British activity in tracking her down. When the Viceroy of India, Lord Hardinge,[1] had complained to Lord Crewe, the Secretary of State for India, that the British Navy were not doing enough to help, Churchill had minuted, on September 23: 'Hampshire, Yarmouth, one French & one Japanese cruiser are hunting Emden in the Bay of Bengal at this moment. There is no other enemy ship within thousands of miles of India. All tendencies to panic should be repressed by authority & example.'

In Cabinet, Kitchener continued to express his fears about the imminence of invasion. Every day news reached London of the slaughter in the Ypres salient. There was a general feeling in the Press that all possible measures were not being taken to ensure the most vigorous prosecution of the war. At the Cabinet on October 23 there was a nervous tone to many of the utterances. Asquith suddenly found Churchill's optimistic pugnacity less vexatious. 'Grey & Haldane were very fussy & jumpy,' he wrote to Venetia Stanley, 'lest the Germans should establish a base at Ostend and keep there a new nest of submarines. Winston (I think with perfectly good reason) derides this, and declares that to-morrow (if necessary) he will shell Ostend into ruins &

---

[1] Charles Hardinge, 1858–1944. Entered Foreign Office, 1880. Knighted, 1904. Ambassador at Petrograd, 1904–6. Permanent Under-Secretary of State for Foreign Affairs, 1906–10. Created Baron Hardinge of Penshurst, 1910. Viceroy of India, 1910–16. Reappointed Permanent Under-Secretary of State for Foreign Affairs, 1916–20. Ambassador to Paris, 1920–3.

make it uninhabitable. I wish some people (EG for instance) had more sense of proportion and perspective.'

Churchill was worried about the increasing public scepticism of the Admiralty's ability to take decisive action. His activities at Antwerp were being judged a failure. He wanted some plan for naval action which would restore public confidence by a definite success. He decided to discuss possible plans of action with Richmond, whom he knew was keen to see the Fleet take the initiative. On October 24 Richmond wrote in his diary:

> Last night, at 8 o'clock, when I was on my way upstairs to dress for dinner, a telephone message came from Churchill asking me to dine. So I took a cab & got there in time. He was in low spirits. There is bad news from South Africa where the rebellion[1] is spreading. . . . From the continent the news was neither good nor bad: but the 1st Lord was rather oppressed with the impossibility of *doing* anything. The attitude of waiting, threatened all the time by submarines, unable to strike back at their Fleet which lies secure behind the dock gates of the Canal, Emden or Wilhelmshaven, and the inability of the Staff to make any suggestions seem to bother him. I have not seen him so despondent before.

Churchill and Richmond discussed a series of possible initiatives. One of them caused Richmond some alarm: 'He wanted to send battleships—old ones—up the Elbe; but for what purpose except to be sunk I did not understand: & as I did not wish to oppose & be counted among the do-nothings I let it alone. . . .'

On October 23 Churchill learned that his cousin Norman Leslie[2] had been killed at Armentières. Leslie, who was twenty-eight years old, was the first of Churchill's relatives to die in the war. On October 24 he wrote to Norman Leslie's mother:[3]

My dear Leonie,

I am so sorry for you and grieve more than I can say for your bitter sorrow. The ever widening conflagration of this war devours all that is precious;

---

[1] A Boer rebellion in support of Germany began in September 1914. It was crushed by loyal South African forces led by General Botha in December 1914.

[2] Norman Jerome Beauchamp Leslie, 1886–1914. 2nd Lieutenant, Rifle Brigade, 1905. Served in Egypt, 1908–10 and Bengal, 1912–14. Captain, May 1914. Killed in action, 18 October 1914.

[3] Leonie Blanche Leslie, 1859–1943. Sister of Lady Randolph Churchill. Married Colonel John Leslie, 1884.

and the end is far away. It is a big enough war about a big enough cause for anyone to go out on. And those who flash away in the conflict doing their duty in good company are not the most unhappy. You must be very brave my dear. My heart bleeds for you. We must at all costs win. Victory is a better boon than life and without it life will be unendurable. The British army has in a few weeks of war revived before the whole world the glories of Agincourt and Blenheim and Waterloo, and in this Norman has played his part. It rests with us to make sure that these sacrifices are not made in vain.

With deepest sympathy, Yours affectionately

Winston SC

On October 27 Jellicoe telegraphed to Churchill that one of Britain's most powerful ships, the Dreadnought *Audacious*, had been sunk by a German mine off the northern coast of Ireland. The loss of this powerful battleship, which had been launched shortly after Churchill had become First Lord, was a serious blow to the Admiralty. 'Winston came here before lunch in a rather sombre mood,' Asquith wrote to Venetia Stanley during the afternoon; 'Strictly between you & me, he has suffered to-day a terrible calamity on the sea, which I *dare* not describe, lest by chance my letter should go wrong; it is known only to him & me, and for a long while will & must be kept secret.' The call for secrecy had come from Jellicoe, who feared that when the news became known it could lead to a loss of morale throughout the Fleet. 'Submit every endeavour should be made to keep Audacious incident from being published,' Jellicoe telegraphed to Churchill at 4.35 that afternoon. 'Hope loss can be kept secret,' he telegraphed again at 10.10 pm. But secrecy was difficult to ensure. A passenger liner, the *Olympic*, had witnessed the sinking, and it could not be long before stories and even photographs were readily available throughout the world. 'It will be very difficult to keep Audacious secret,' Churchill telegraphed in reply to Jellicoe's first appeal. Jellicoe was much perturbed. At 1.00 am on October 28 he telegraphed again: 'Hope that in any case press may be requested not to publish anything on the subject at all'; to which Churchill replied: 'Will consult Cabinet about suppression.' He had himself already telegraphed shortly after midnight, in an attempt to allay Jellicoe's anxieties:

I am sure you will not be at all discouraged by Audacious episode. We have been very fortunate to come through three months of war without the loss of a capital ship. I expected three or four by this time, and it is due to your unfailing vigilance and skill that all has gone so well. The Army too has held its own along the whole line, though with at least 14,000 killed and wounded. Quite soon the harbours will be made comfortable for you. Mind you ask for all you want.

When the Cabinet met on October 28, Churchill told them of Jellicoe's request for secrecy, and gave it his support. After a long debate, in which Lloyd George was among those who deplored any attempt to conceal what had happened, it was decided that the news should be kept secret. Kitchener, who had always been averse to military losses on a similar scale being made public, supported Jellicoe's plea. Asquith, who informed Venetia Stanley that he thought it was 'bad policy on the whole not to take the public into your confidence in reverses as well as in successes', agreed to keep the news secret, but felt uneasy about doing so. He did feel able, however, to give her more information about the sinking itself on October 28:

> The disaster of wh I wrote to you in veiled language yesterday was the sinking of the Audacious—one of the best & newest of the super Dread-noughts, with a crew of about 1,000 and 10 13·5-inch guns. . . . The Olympic came up & took the Audacious in tow. She remained afloat for about 8 hours and the whole of her crew except one man were safely landed. But the ship itself sank before reaching the coast. It is far the worst calamity the Navy has so far sustained, as she cost at least 2½ millions. It is cruel luck for Winston.
> Poor boy he has just been here pouring out his woes. . . .

It took over two weeks before the Germans learned definitely that the *Audacious* had been sunk. On November 14 an American newspaper, the *Philadelphia Public Ledger*, published a photograph of the *Audacious* sinking, taken from the *Olympic*. Churchill's critics were quick to seize upon the attempts to censor the news as a sign of his lack of perspective. On December 8 Margot Asquith recorded in her diary a conversation with one of Asquith's Private Secretaries, Eric Drummond,[1] who told her that such concealment 'was always dangerous as it led the British public to think other naval disasters had happened and been kept dark'. Margot Asquith asked her husband about it; he told her, she wrote in her diary, 'that at the Cabinet he and Lloyd George were strongly of the opinion that nothing should be kept dark . . . but that the whole Cabinet were against them'. Asquith stressed that Jellicoe, not

---

[1] James Eric Drummond, 1876–1951. Entered Foreign Office, 1900. Private Secretary to H. H. Asquith, 1912–15. Secretary-General to the League of Nations, 1919–33. Ambassador to Italy, 1933–9. 16th Earl of Perth, 1937. Chief Adviser on Foreign Publicity, Ministry of Information, 1939–40.

Churchill, had been the principal advocate of secrecy. Margot Asquith approved the need for secrecy, telling Drummond that 'from what I had heard keeping it quiet was not a bad thing to do, as our men were very exhausted at that time in the long Ypres–Calais coast line and that the news had it reached the Germans would have cheered them up dangerously'.

On October 28 Kitchener and Lloyd George quarrelled violently over Kitchener's reluctance to set up a specifically Welsh regiment. Kitchener believed that no body of men recruited entirely from Wales could be relied upon. Lloyd George appealed to Churchill, who supported him. That afternoon Lloyd George wrote enthusiastically:

My dear Winston,
    I feel deeply grateful to you for the way you stood up for fair play to my little nationality this morning.
    I am in despair over the stupidity of the War Office. You might imagine we were alien enemies who ought to be interned at Frimley until we had mastered the intricacies of the English language sufficiently to be able to converse on equal terms with an East End recruit.
    I enclose copy of the order issued by the WO about the Welsh Army Corps. Under these conditions further recruiting is impossible.
    Does K want men? If he does not let him say so then we will all be spared much worry & trouble.
    Why cannot he give us 18 battalions out of the 30 new battalions already formed in Wales. We could then send another division.
                                                        Ever sincerely
                                                        D. Lloyd George

Asquith reported this 'royal row', as he called it, to Venetia Stanley. He believed that Kitchener was 'much the most to blame' having spent 'so much of his life in an Oriental atmosphere that he cannot acclimatize himself to English conditions'. As on other occasions when Kitchener quarrelled, the Prime Minister turned to Churchill for assistance. 'I have told Winston to go and see him,' he wrote to Venetia Stanley, 'and try to infuse some sense of proportion.'

By the end of October Churchill's position had become critical. Many newspapers were beginning to describe his conduct of the war at sea as a succession of disasters. The escape of the *Goeben* and *Breslau* to Turkey, the sinking of the *Hogue*, *Cressy* and *Aboukir*, the attempt to prolong the siege of Antwerp, the failure to track down the *Emden* in the

Indian Ocean, and finally the 'secret' loss of the *Audacious* led many journalists to doubt whether Churchill ought to remain as First Lord. These criticisms were linked together in a general accusation that Churchill continually interfered with the conduct of Admiralty business, that he did not allow the expert advice of the Sea Lords to influence his policy, and that he had converted the once harmonious Board of Admiralty into a mere platform for his own erratic exuberance. On October 21 the *Morning Post* informed its readers:

It is a remarkable thing that while the nation trusts the War Office at this juncture grave doubt is expressed on every hand as to the composition of the Board of Admiralty. In the War Office we have a soldier in whom the Army and the nation have confidence, and therefore there is no nervousness as to our military position. In the Admiralty, upon the other hand, there is a First Lord who is a civilian, and cannot be expected to have any grasp of the principles and practice of naval warfare. This position would not in itself be dangerous if the First Lord recognised that his proper function was to represent the Government in the Admiralty and the Admiralty in the Government, and to be guided in matters of warfare by his expert advisers. But we have now sufficient evidence to demonstrate that the First Lord seeks to guide operations of war.

On October 22 the *Morning Post* predicted that there would be 'further mistakes and further disasters' if Churchill remained in charge of the Admiralty, warning that these might involve 'the destruction of the Empire'. On the following day Asquith informed Venetia Stanley that H. A. Gwynne, whom he described as 'the lunatic who edits the Morning Post' had written him 'a long private letter this morning urging the supersession of Winston by Jellicoe'.

Public confidence in the Navy was ebbing away. On October 19 Haldane had written to Churchill that if Lord Fisher and Admiral of the Fleet Sir Arthur Wilson[1] returned to the Admiralty, it would 'make our country feel that our old spirit of the Navy was alive and come back'. Churchill seized upon this advice. He had long felt that Fisher's return as First Sea Lord would help to restore the nation's confidence in the conduct of naval affairs. He also felt that both Fisher

---

[1] Arthur Knyvet Wilson, 1842–1921. Entered Navy, 1855. Fought in the Crimean War. Awarded the VC in 1884 during the Sudan Campaign. Commander-in-Chief of the Home and Channel Fleets, 1901–7. Knighted, 1902. Admiral of the Fleet, 1907. First Sea Lord, 1910–11. Worked at the Admiralty without any formal post, October 1914–June 1918. He declined a peerage on his retirement.

and Wilson would support his activities with enthusiasm. Prince Louis had been a reluctant ally during the defence of Antwerp, going so far as to tell Sir Francis Hopwood that he might resign in protest against Churchill's activities. Churchill needed the confidence of his First Sea Lord. He wanted more support for his own ideas, and more ideas pouring in from outside, than Prince Louis provided.

Churchill had a profound respect for Fisher's judgement, and felt a strong personal affection towards him. From the moment of their first meeting seven years before he had frequently sought Fisher's advice and companionship. On 1 January 1914 he had written to Fisher: 'Contact with you is like breathing ozone to me.' 'Tomorrow old Fisher comes down to the yacht with me,' he wrote to his wife on July 15. 'This always has a salutary effect.' Churchill admired the Admiral's lack of pomp, his sense of fun, and his total, obsessive, devotion to naval affairs. In an unpublished note written in 1916 he described how, in October 1911, when he became First Lord, 'many of the most important early decisions I took as to the changes in commands, & the Board, & the 15-inch gun & oil—were the result of discussions with him . . . he was always an intimate and trusted counsellor—off the stage'. None of Churchill's existing advisers seemed to him to possess Fisher's abilities. 'The others did not originate much,' he added, 'though Battenberg was very good on the war staff question, and Jellicoe a splendid man of business.' In October 1914 Churchill needed someone who would 'originate much'. He hoped that if Fisher returned to the Admiralty public discontent with naval inactivity would cease, and the continuing criticisms of Antwerp come to an end.

Since the outbreak of war Fisher had seen Churchill on many occasions, and had bombarded him with enthusiastic letters. On September 15 he had written:

Dear Winston,
    I was in a hurry yesterday to see a soldier in hospital (*such tales at first hand I am preparing for you on the war!*) so I did not mention the two following points but it is more than probable they have been very fully considered:—
I The movements of the German Fleet will be dictated from the Army Head Quarters (just as Villeneuve was sent to sea by Napoleon from Cadiz). It will in no wise be naval conditions that will actuate the movements of the German Fleet. *Therefore* totally unlikely naval conditions may see it emerge to fight.
II Why is standard of recruits raised *3* inches to 5 feet 6? It's criminal folly! I think Nelson was only 5 feet 4, and the Ghurkas less! What d—d folly to discard supreme enthusiasm because it's under 5 feet 6. *We are a wonderful*

nation! astounding how we muddle through!—There's only one explanation:—We are the lost 10 Tribes!

'Time and the Ocean and some Guiding Star
In high Cabal have made us What we are'[1]

Yours
F

In his other correspondence Fisher castigated Churchill's senior advisers, writing to one of them, the Additional Civil Lord, on September 25: 'The fact is my beloved Hopwood that Winston has got the wrong lot altogether round him, but I owe him so much for putting Jellicoe where he is that I am loathe to blast the d—d fools that surround him.' On October 21 Fisher sent Churchill encouraging news:

Dear Winston,

Something interesting! After leaving you I had an appointment with an American lady returned last night from Germany. I have employed her on secret service to communicate with my daughter who with her husband are prisoners at Bad-Nauheim near Frankfurt. (He has been in a convict's cell! but now well treated.)[2]

(1) This American lady tells me there is REAL PANIC caused by our heroes who burnt the Zeppelin at Dusseldorf—and people are clearing out of Dusseldorf because expecting another English raid. *The military also are scared!*

(2) The Commander-in-Chief of the Frankfurt Military District (Major-General de Graaf,[3] who has an American wife) asked her if she knew anything of Russian soldiers having passed through England to France!

(3) She also heard the Germans were feeling uncomfortable about the fighting in the neighbourhood of Metz.

(4) Major-General de Graaf said to her that *I* was thought to be of consequence in Germany! . . .

Yours till death
F
Trafalgar Day

[1] From Sir William Watson, *Ode on the Coronation of Edward VII* (published 1902). Watson had written 'fostering' not 'guiding'.

[2] On December 3 *The Times* reported that on President Wilson's personal initiative (through the American Ambassador in Berlin, James W. Gerard) the Germans had agreed to release Fisher's daughter Beatrix and her husband, Rear-Admiral Reginald Rundell Neeld (1850–1939), without asking for any equivalent concession from Britain. They returned home in mid-December, and for four years Mrs Neeld wrote personally and sent clothing to British merchant seamen imprisoned in Germany.

[3] Heinrich (Hendrik) de Graaff, 1857–1924. Born in The Hague. Military Cadet, Berlin, 1873. Lieutenant-General Commanding Frankfurt Military District, August 1914–April 1915. Chief of Staff, 3rd Army Corps, 1915–18. His wife, Elizabeth Virginia Kremelberg, was born in Baltimore, USA.

In the postscript to this letter Fisher wrote: '10 years ago *to-day* I became 1st Sea Lord!'

Churchill deliberated about whether he could trust the judgement of a man of seventy-four, and rely on him not to be borne down by the heavy strains of war. He knew that the removal of Prince Louis would be a controversial event and that Fisher's return would be a risk, however much he might defend it in the naval and national interest. He did not act without much thought about the seriousness of the step which he wished to take, and about Fisher's capacity to fill the post. In *The World Crisis* he recalled how:

I watched him narrowly to judge his physical strength and mental alertness. There seemed no doubt about either. On one occasion, when inveighing against some one whom he thought obstructive, he became so convulsed with fury that it seemed that every nerve and blood-vessel in his body would be ruptured. However, they stood the strain magnificently, and he left me with the impression of a terrific engine of mental and physical power burning and throbbing in that aged frame. I was never in the least afraid of working with him, and I thought I knew him so well, and had held an equal relationship and superior constitutional authority so long, that we could come through any difficulty together. I therefore sounded him in conversation without committing myself, and soon saw that he was fiercely eager to lay his grasp on power, and was strongly inspired with the sense of a message to deliver and a mission to perform.

On October 20 Churchill saw Asquith at 10 Downing Street. 'I think Battenberg will have soon to make as graceful a bow as he can to the British public,' Asquith informed Venetia Stanley later that day; 'Winston has a grandiose scheme (entre nous) for bringing in both Fisher & Sir A. Wilson!' Asquith approved of Churchill's scheme. He himself had not found it easy to work with Prince Louis during Churchill's absence at Antwerp.

On October 27 Churchill called to see Asquith. The two men discussed Prince Louis' weakness as First Sea Lord. Churchill did not want to delay the changes any longer. 'He has quite made up his mind that the time has come for a drastic change in his Board,' Asquith wrote to Venetia Stanley; 'our poor blue-eyed German will have to go, and (as W says) he will be reinforced by 2 "Well-plucked chickens" of 74 & 72.' Asquith and Churchill had, as Asquith reported, 'both enlarged on the want of initiative & constructive thought of the present naval advisers: if they had had any real insight, they wd have begun 2 months ago devising "hen coops" & "shoes", & other protective devices (eg torpedo-proof harbours and refuges) against the submarine.' There were other criticisms of Prince Louis circulating. 'He is the best fellow in the world,' Margot Asquith wrote in her diary on November 7, 'but *not clever*, and the patrolling of our coasts has not been well done.'

Since the outbreak of war Prince Louis had been increasingly depressed by scurrilous attacks upon him in the Press because of his German birth. These attacks had been virulent and sustained, affecting his powers of work. He found it difficult to bear the daily strains of wartime administration. On October 3 Fisher had written to Pamela McKenna that one of Britain's 'damnable war difficulties' was 'our directing Sea Lord played out'. Churchill realized the extent of the strain on Prince Louis resulting from the vicious innuendoes against him, and sympathized with him in his distress. When Lord Charles Beresford had been reported to him at the end of August for having said that although Prince Louis was 'an exceedingly able officer', nothing could alter the fact 'that he is a German, and as such should not be occupying his present position', that he had German servants, and property in Germany, Churchill had acted swiftly and pugnaciously on Prince Louis' behalf, warning Beresford not to make such remarks again. 'The interests of the country,' Churchill wrote, 'do not permit the spreading of such wicked allegations by an officer of your rank, even though retired.' Prince Louis' powers of concentration were affected by the attacks on his loyalty, and he asked Churchill to release him from his post. On October 27 Churchill went to Windsor to inform the King that Prince Louis wished to resign from the Board of Admiralty. According to Lord Stamfordham's formal record of the audience, written that day, Churchill told the King that the attacks on Prince Louis on account of 'his name and parentage' and the anonymous letters with which he had been assailed, had added to the heavy existing strains upon him. 'The exacting duties and heavy responsibilities of his office,' Churchill continued, 'have no doubt affected his general health and nerves, so that for the good of the service a change had become necessary.' The King accepted this advice. Returning to the Admiralty Churchill wrote to Prince Louis:

Most Private

My dear Prince Louis,

The Prime Minister thought & I agree with him that a letter from you to me indicating that you felt that in some respects yr usefulness was impaired & that patriotic considerations wh at this juncture must be supreme in yr mind wd be the best form of giving effect to yr decision. To this letter I wd on behalf of the Govt write an answer. This correspondence cd then be made public and wd explain itself.

I cannot tell you how much I regret the termination of our work together, & how I deplore the harsh and melancholy march of events wh leads to yr temporary withdrawal from active employment. I am sure however that you consult yr own happiness by the sacrifice wh you make.

Will you consider vy carefully whether there is any way in wh I can be of service, & will you tell me of any point wh I shd make in the letter wh I shall write.

No incident in my public life has caused me so much sorrow.

Yrs v sincerely
WSC

'Winston's real trouble,' Asquith wrote to Venetia Stanley on October 28, 'is about Prince Louis & the succession to his post. He *must* go, & Winston has had a most delicate & painful interview with him— the more so as his nephew Prince Maurice[1] was killed in action yesterday. Louis behaved with great dignity & public spirit, & will resign at once.' That same day Prince Louis wrote the formal letter of resignation for which Churchill had asked. 'I have lately been driven to the painful conclusion,' he wrote, 'that at this juncture my birth & parentage have the effect of impairing in some respects my usefulness at the Bd of Admy. In these circumstances I feel it to be my duty, as a loyal subject of HM to resign the office of First Sea Lord, hoping thereby to facilitate the task of the Admn of the great service to wh I have devoted my life, & to ease the burden laid on HM Ministers.'

Prince Louis also wrote a private letter to Churchill on October 28:

Dear Mr Churchill,

I wd like to add a few words to my public letter, in response to yr kind invitation—If on quitting office I cd receive some sign indicating that I still can command the confidence & trust of the King & his Govt, it wd have a gt effect on my position in the country.

I am ashamed to have already so many initials after my name,[2] & there is hardly anything left in Honours.—What I shd value above all else wd be to be admitted to the Privy Council.—I may say that one or two of my predecessors were so honoured in their time.

As regards my successor: Ld Fisher as 1st with Sir A. Wilson as COS wd

---

[1] Prince Maurice Victor Donald of Battenberg, 1891–1914. Lieutenant, King's Royal Rifle Corps, 1914. Grandson of Queen Victoria; son of Prince Henry of Battenberg. He died of wounds received in action in France.

[2] At the outbreak of war Prince Louis had the following initials after his name: GCB, GCVO, KCMG. He became a Privy Councillor on 5 November 1914.

be ideal. If impossible, then Sir A. Wilson shd be ISL rather than Ld F.—
The entire Navy wd subscribe to this I am sure. With you wd rest the task of
overruling his well known obstinacy.

Yours as ever

LB

Churchill had already decided to make Fisher First Sea Lord. It
was this aspect of the change, and not Prince Louis' removal, which had
agitated the King at the audience with Churchill on October 27.
Stamfordham's record outlined their conversation:

> This proposal was a great surprise to the King who pointed out to Mr
> Churchill his objections to the appointment. Lord Fisher has not the con-
> fidence of the Navy: he is over 73 years of age. When 1st Sea Lord he no
> doubt did much for the Navy but he created a state of unrest and bad feeling
> among the officers of the service.
>
> Mr Churchill represented that there was no one in the Admiral's rank
> fitted for the post in the present exceptional circumstances. Sir Hedworth
> Meux[1] was spoken of, but Mr C declared that he could never work with
> him. His Majesty mentioned Sir Henry Jackson[2] but the First Lord, while
> admitting his scientific and intellectual capacity did not think he would do
> —The King also spoke of Sir Frederick Sturdee now Chief of the Staff as
> suitable for the Board but Mr Churchill did not agree—His Majesty con-
> cluded by saying he could not give his approval to the appointment until he
> had seen the Prime Minister.

The King was determined to refuse Fisher's nomination. Stamfordham's record described how, on October 28, he went to 10 Downing
Street and told Asquith: 'His Majesty knows the Navy and considers
that the Service mistrusts Lord Fisher and that the announcement of
the proposed appointment would give a shock to the Navy which no one
could wish to cause in the middle of this great War.' Stamfordham also
pointed out that it was 'stated that Lord Fisher had become aged; he
talked and wrote much but his opinions changed from day to day'.
Asquith defended Churchill's choice. He denied having heard of these
charges before. The existing Admiralty Board, he asserted, 'was weak

---

[1] Hedworth Lambton, 1856–1929. Entered Navy, 1870. Rear-Admiral, 1902. Knighted,
1906. Vice-Admiral and Commander in-Chief, China, 1908–10. Changed his name to Meux,
1911. Admiral, 1911. Commander-in-Chief, Portsmouth, 1912–16. Admiral of the Fleet,
1915. Conservative MP for Portsmouth, 1916–18.

[2] Henry Bradwardine Jackson, 1855–1929. Entered Navy, 1868. A pioneer of wireless
telegraphy. Knighted, 1906. Chief of the Admiralty War Staff, 1912–14. Admiral, 1914. In
August 1914 he was put in charge of planning the seizure of German colonies. First Sea Lord,
May 1915–December 1916. President of the Royal Naval College, Greenwich, 1916–19.
Admiral of the Fleet, 1919.

and incapable of initiative'. Fisher alone, said Asquith, could fill the post with distinction. Asquith asked Stamfordham whom he would suggest in Fisher's place; then he objected strongly to each of Stamfordham's suggestions. Stamfordham's account of this interview continued:

Lord S said the appointment of Lord Fisher would place the King in a very painful position as the Navy would think His Majesty should not have sanctioned it. The PM replied that he himself would be in an equally awkward position as the refusal of Lord F would mean the resignation of Mr Churchill.

Lord S pointed out that from what Mr Churchill had said to the King on the previous day he would not be sorry to leave the Admiralty as its work was uncongenial to him: he wanted to go to the War & fight and be a soldier. The Prime Minister scouted the idea and said Mr Churchill has a most intimate knowledge of the Navy & his services in his present position could not be dispensed with or replaced.

Churchill's veiled threat of resignation failed to influence the King's opposition to Fisher's return. On October 29 Asquith was summoned to Buckingham Palace to discuss the impasse. Immediately after the interview he wrote an account of it to Venetia Stanley:

After lunch I went to see the King, on Winston's business. As you will see in your morning papers, the resignation of Prince Louis is a fait accompli. . . . It was a much more difficult job to persuade the Sovereign to consent to his being succeeded by Jacky Fisher. He gave me an exhaustive & really eloquent catalogue of the old man's crimes & defects, and thought that his appointment would be very badly received by the bulk of the Navy, & that he would be almost certain to get on badly with Winston. On the last point, I have some misgivings of my own, but Winston won't have anybody else, and there is no one among the available Admirals in whom I have sufficient confidence to force upon him. So I stuck to my guns, and the King (who behaved very nicely) gave a reluctant consent. I hope his apprehensions won't turn out to be well founded.

During the afternoon of October 29 the King signed Fisher's appointment. But he did not abandon his protest, writing to Asquith immediately afterwards:

Dear Prime Minister,

Following our conversation of this afternoon, I should like to note that while approving the proposed appointment of Lord Fisher as First Sea Lord, I do so with some reluctance and misgivings.

I readily acknowledge his great ability and administrative power but at the same time I cannot help feeling that his presence at the Admiralty will not inspire the Navy with that confidence which ought to exist especially when we are engaged in so momentous a War.

I hope that my fears may prove to be groundless.

George R.I.

Asquith did not take the King's protest too seriously. Sovereigns, he informed Venetia Stanley, 'have to be humoured and brought in'. Churchill made every effort to lessen the blow of Prince Louis' departure. Asquith agreed to make him a member of the Privy Council. Churchill also told the Prince that he would do his utmost to give him the Portsmouth command once the war was over.[1] On October 29 Churchill sent his formal letter accepting the First Sea Lord's resignation:

My dear Prince Louis,

This is no ordinary war, but a struggle between nations for life or death. It raises passions between races of the most terrible kind. It effaces the old landmarks and frontiers of our civilization. I cannot further oppose the wish you have during the last few weeks expressed to me, to be released from the burden of responsibility which you have borne thus far with so much honour and success.

The anxieties and toils which rest upon the naval administration of our country are in themselves enough to try a man's spirit; and when to them are added the ineradicable difficulties of which you speak, I could not at this juncture in fairness ask you to support them.

The Navy of today, and still more the Navy of tomorrow, bears the imprint of your work. The enormous impending influx of capital ships, the score of thirty-knot cruisers, the destroyers and submarines unequalled in modern construction which are coming now to hand, are the results of labours which we have had in common, and in which the Board of Admiralty owes so much to your aid.

The first step which secured the timely concentration of the Fleet was taken by you.

I must express publicly my deep indebtedness to you, and the pain I feel at the severance of our three years' official association. In all the circumstances you are right in your decision. The spirit in which you have acted is the same in which Prince Maurice of Battenberg has given his life to our cause and in which your gallant son is now serving in the Fleet.

I beg you to accept my profound respect and that of our colleagues on the Board.

I remain, Yours very sincerely
Winston S. Churchill

[1] Prince Louis did not receive the Portsmouth Command. Churchill, like all Cabinet Ministers, could not commit his successors to specific appointments.

The resignation letters were published in the Press. *The Times* wrote critically of Churchill's letter. 'Honest men,' it declared, 'will prefer the brevity of the retiring Admiral to the rhetorical document which accepts his decision.'[1] Prince Louis himself was less censorious, writing to Churchill on October 29:

My dear friend,

I am deeply touched by your letter, which shall be treasured by my sons.[2]

I beg of you to release me. I am on the verge of breaking down & I cannot use my brain for anything.

The COS can help you to carry out the War adm, 2 SL can sign any routine paper.

Do me the favour to assemble the Board for five minutes this afternoon. If you would merely read my letter to you & to say that you have accepted it, not another [word] need, or indeed should be spoken & I can leave the room after a silent farewell handshake with my colleagues.

Yrs as Ever
Louis Battenberg

On the morning of October 30 Fisher spent an hour with the King at Buckingham Palace. The visit was a success. 'He seems as young as ever,' the King recorded in his diary. Fisher and the King agreed to meet regularly once a week. 'He is already a Court Favourite,' Churchill wrote to Asquith and Grey after Fisher's return from his audience.

Sir Arthur Wilson also returned to the Admiralty. He refused any official position or salary, but from a room which he was given at the Admiralty he prepared schemes for attacks on Heligoland and the German North Sea coast. Rear-Admiral Oliver, after only two weeks as Churchill's Naval Secretary in succession to Hood, succeeded Sturdee as Chief of Staff with the rank of Vice-Admiral. Oliver found nothing unusual in working fourteen hours a day, including Sundays. He was

[1] Edward Marsh was much upset by this remark of *The Times*, writing angrily to the editor, Geoffrey Robinson, on October 31 that he was 'undermining the public confidence by an innuendo against the honour of a national leader at a time of crisis'.

[2] Prince George Louis Victor Henry Sergius of Battenberg, 1892–1938. Prince Louis' elder son. Entered Navy, 1905. Lieutenant, 1914. Present at the battles of Heligoland, 1914; Dogger Bank, 1915; Jutland, 1916. Knighted, 1916. Styled Earl of Medina, 1917. Succeeded his father as 2nd Marquess of Milford Haven, 1921.

Prince Louis Francis Albert Victor Nicholas of Battenberg, 1900–   . Prince Louis' second son. A Naval Cadet, 1913–15. Midshipman at Jutland, 1916. Assumed the surname of Mountbatten in 1917. Supreme Allied Commander, South-East Asia, 1943–6. Created Viscount Mountbatten of Burma, 1946. Viceroy of India, 1947. Created Earl, 1947. Governor-General of India, 1947–8. First Sea Lord, 1955–9. Admiral of the Fleet, 1956. Chief of the Defence Staff, 1959–65.

not quite fifty, and had been Fisher's Naval Assistant from 1908 to 1910; Fisher held him in high esteem.

Churchill and Fisher embarked upon an intimate and constructive partnership. On November 1 Fisher wrote to Lord Esher:

SECRET *Burn*
My beloved Friend,
   Thanks for your dear letter! Isn't it fun being back?
   Some d—d fools thought I was dead & buried! I am busy getting even with some of them! I did 22 hours work yesterday but 2 hours sleep not enough so I shall slow down!
   SECRET The King said to Winston (I suppose dissuading!) that the job would kill me. Winston was perfectly lovely in his instant reply:
         'Sir, I cannot imagine a more glorious death'!
   Wasn't that delicious? but burn please!

Yours for ever more
Fisher

Fisher's return was widely approved. *The Times* believed that he would serve as a restraining influence on Churchill's impetuosity. 'Undoubtedly the country will benefit by having Fisher and Wilson back again at the Admiralty,' Lord Esher wrote in his diary on November 4; 'more driving power was required, and they will supply it.' Sir David Beatty believed that the change was for the good, writing to his wife on November 2:

They have resurrected old Fisher. Well, I think he is the best they could have done, but I wish he was ten years younger. He still has fine zeal, energy, and determination, coupled with low cunning, which is eminently desirable just now. He also has courage and will take any responsibility. He will recognise that his position is absolutely secure and will rule the Admiralty and Winston with a heavy hand. He has patriotism, and is a firm believer in the good qualities of the Navy, that it can do anything and will go anywhere, and please God we shall change our present method for a strong offensive policy.

Fisher brought a new energy into Admiralty business. 'Let everyone be optimistic,' he wrote to Jellicoe on November 17, 'and *shoot the pessimists!*' 'It's *NOT* numbers that tell, but *GUNNERY!*' he wrote to Beatty on November 19; '*Gunnery, gunnery, gunnery!* All else is twaddle. Hit the target!' Fisher exulted in his new-found authority. On December 17 he wrote to Esher:

SECRET

My beloved E,

. . . Everyone including the Prime Minister (with whom I was lunching yesterday & danced with his wife to a Moody & Sankey Hymn! *SUCH A LOVELY VALSE*!!!) consider I am Winston's facile dupe!

I am in the position of entering into a game of chess (against a good player) which has been begun by bloody fools! . . .

Fisher's energy was impressive. But there were warning signs that it was an energy which might easily explode. It was not long before his volcanic methods and frequent threats of resignation brought an added strain to Churchill's daily tasks. Shortly before the end of the war Fisher recalled one such incident in a letter to the shipowner, Lord Inchcape.[1] 'In November 1914, when I was First Sea Lord of the Admiralty,' Fisher wrote, 'I went to Lord Kitchener and demanded of him there and then an order to his subordinates to cease enticing away men from our shipyards, and told him I would resign that day at 6 pm my post as First Sea Lord and give my reasons in the House of Lords. . . . He wrote the order there and then, without hesitation.'

On November 3 Fisher summoned the principal Admiralty officials to his room, and demanded that they make arrangements for the immediate construction of six hundred ships of all types; never before had so many vessels been planned at the same time. If anyone thwarted him, he declared, he would make his wife a widow and his home a dunghill. Fisher ensured that contracts were obtained with remarkable speed, and that construction began promptly. But his energy was combined with a flood of threatened resignations and a limitless, incautious correspondence which were to some a warning of a dangerous instability. The public confidence, and Churchill's own delight, were offset by a growing uneasiness among naval officers. On November 2 Beatty had written to his wife, as a second thought: 'I cannot see Winston and Jack Fisher working very long together in harmony. They will quarrel before long.'

There was thirty-five years difference in age between Churchill and Fisher; and yet, despite the anxieties of sailors like Beatty, there seemed no issue in the wide spectrum of naval affairs on which they were not in

[1] James Lyle Mackay, 1852–1937. Shipowner. President of the United Kingdom Chamber of Shipping, 1893, 1918 and 1919. Member, Legislative Council of the Viceroy of India, 1891–3. Knighted, 1894. Member, Council of the Secretary of State for India, 1897–1911. Created Baron Inchcape, 1911. Chairman of the Committee Responsible for Rates of Hire for Vessels Chartered by the Government, 1914–19. Responsible for the sale of war prize vessels, 1920–7. Created Viscount, 1924. Created Earl, 1929.

harmony. 'We were always very intimate & cordial,' Churchill later wrote in an unpublished note. 'Never at any time has any recrimination verbal or literal taken place between us. We worked together in the closest comradeship. . . . Our compact was that neither did anything of importance without the other. On this basis, as I worked till about 12.30 am and he began at 4 am—the Admiralty ran on a twenty hours day.' The compact which they had reached, and the hours which they worked, ensured that a vast flow of work was done, and their combined skills put to constant use. But even these two forceful personalities, confronted every day with unexpected problems, sudden crises and the need to make desperate decisions, could not withstand the strain indefinitely.

Fisher's return to the Admiralty coincided with Britain's only serious naval defeat of the war. On the declaration of war the Commander of the German Far Eastern Squadron, Admiral Count von Spee,[1] had set out from the German naval base at Tsing-tau on the China coast with his flagship the *Scharnhorst*, a second battle-cruiser the *Gneisenau* and the light cruiser *Nürnberg*, all of them fast and heavily armed ships. Despite the activities of the Australian Navy, which throughout August was systematically capturing the many German islands in the South Pacific and destroying their wireless stations, von Spee managed to reach Easter Island in mid-October, and was joined by two further light cruisers, the *Leipzig* and the *Dresden*. These, like his other three powerful vessels, were capable of 23 knots and were heavily armed. The Admiralty soon realized that this small armada was making for the coast of Chile. The commander of the British naval forces off South America, Rear-Admiral Sir Christopher Cradock,[2] was informed by Admiralty telegram on October 5: 'It appears from information received that Gneisenau and Scharnhorst are working across to South America. A Dresden may be scouting for them. You must be prepared to meet them in company. Canopus should accompany Glasgow, Monmouth and Otranto, and should search and protect trade in combination.'

[1] Maximilian von Spee, 1861–1914. Entered German Navy, 1878. Chief of Staff, German North Sea Command, 1908–12. Commanded the German Far Eastern Squadron, 1912–14. Drowned, Battle of Falkland Islands, 8 December 1914.

[2] Christopher Cradock, 1862–1914. Entered Navy, 1875. Rear-Admiral, 1910. Knighted, 1912. Commanded the North American and West Indies station, 1913: his command extended from the St Laurence river to Brazil. Drowned at the Battle of Coronel, 1 November 1914.

BRAVO WINSTON!

The Rapid Naval Mobilisation and Purchase of the Two Foreign
Dreadnoughts Spoke Volumes for your Work and Wisdom.

MR. WINSTON CHURCHILL, FIRST LORD OF THE ADMIRALTY

AND (INSET) HIS CHARMING AND BEAUTIFUL WIFE

1. Churchill on the eve of war, when First Lord of the Admiralty. *Inset,*
Clementine Churchill. Photographs published in the *Tatler,* 12 August 1914

2. 'Full Steam Ahead': cartoon of Churchill by Poy, 4 August 1914

4. Field-Marshal Earl Kitchener
of Khartoum in 1914

3. H. H. Asquith, at the end
of 1915

5. Churchill and Field-Marshal
Sir John French, summer 1914

6. Prince Louis of Battenberg,
January 1914

7. Churchill and Sir Edward Grey, 1914

8. The British armoured train in action at Antwerp, October 1914

9. A bus used by the Royal Naval Division, September–October 1914, and captured by the Germans at Antwerp, October 1914. This photograph and caption were published in *The Times History of the War 1914*

A LONDON MOTOR OMNIBUS TAKEN IN ANTWERP BY THE ENEMY.
Motor Omnibuses have done excellent service in the transport of troops and supplies.

WINSTON IN THE WAR

He is only Forty!

By T. P.

COLONEL SEELY AND MR. CHURCHILL DRIVING THROUGH THE STREETS OF BESIEGED ANTWERP.

10. Colonel J. E. B. Seely and Churchill at Antwerp, October 1914. This photograph was first published in *Great Deeds of the Great War* on 12 December 1914

11. Churchill at Antwerp, October 1914

12. Churchill, Lord Kitchener and David Lloyd George: cartoon
by Poy on Churchill's birthday, 30 November 1914

13. Churchill Family Portrait, September 1914.
Left to right: Winston, Diana, Clementine, Sarah (on lap), Randolph, Lady
Randolph, Peregrine (on lap), Lady Gwendeline, John-George, Jack

The *Canopus* was the only British battleship in South American waters with 12-inch guns. These were far larger than any of the armaments on any of von Spee's ships. But she was an old ship with a maximum speed of only 17 knots; hence the Admiralty's insistence that Cradock should keep all his ships together. *Glasgow, Monmouth* and *Otranto* might more easily seek out and chase the German ships, but without *Canopus* they would be at the mercy of the heavier German guns. On October 18 Cradock telegraphed to the Admiralty: 'I fear that strategically the speed of my squadron cannot exceed 12 knots owing to Canopus, but shall trust circumstances will enable me to force an action.' The import of this telegram seemed clear to the Admiralty: *Canopus* would continue with the Admiral's squadron, and would determine its speed. But on October 27 Cradock telegraphed again that he considered it was impossible, on account of *Canopus'* slow speed, 'to find and destroy enemy's squadron', and that *Canopus* would be employed 'on necessary work of convoying colliers'. Churchill was puzzled by the obscurity of this telegram, minuting to Admiral Oliver on October 28: 'I do not understand what Admiral Cradock intends and wishes.' Oliver replied on the following day that Cradock's ships 'should keep within supporting distance of each other'; those were his instructions. But Cradock acted otherwise. Having left *Canopus* behind in order to guard the colliers, he steamed with his other ships northward along the Chilean coast, eager to intercept von Spee, and determined to destroy the only significant German naval force outside the North Sea.

On the morning of November 1 the first ship in Cradock's line, the *Glasgow*, sighted the *Leipzig*. The *Canopus* was then two hundred miles to the south. In his eagerness to bring the German squadron to battle, Cradock decided that he did not wish to return to seek the protection of his one superior ship. Shortly after six o'clock he telegraphed to the distant *Canopus*: 'I am going to attack the enemy now.' The attack was a disaster. Cradock's squadron was silhouetted against the setting sun, presenting a series of easy targets for the long-range German guns. Both the *Good Hope* and the *Monmouth* were sunk. Over fifteen hundred British sailors, including the Admiral, were drowned. On November 3, before news of the disaster reached London, Fisher, who had just replaced Prince Louis as First Sea Lord, had decided to send reinforcements to Cradock. With Churchill's approval he telegraphed that evening that 'Defence has been ordered to join your flag with all despatch. . . . You should keep touch with Glasgow concentrating the rest of your Squadron including Canopus.' During November 3 Churchill and Fisher sent a further telegram to the Japanese Admiralty:

'We are concentrating Glasgow, Good Hope, Canopus, Monmouth & Defence on the SW Coast of S America, hoping to bring them to battle. We hope that the Japanese Admiralty may now find it possible to move some of their Squadrons Eastward in order to intercept the German Squadron and prevent its return to Asiatic or Australian waters.'

At seven o'clock on the morning of November 4 Churchill began work as usual in his bedroom at the Admiralty. Among the telegrams in his box was one from the British Consul-General at Valparaiso, Allan Maclean,[1] which had reached the Admiralty during the night:

Chilean Admiral just informed me that German Admiral states his ships met Good Hope, Monmouth, Glasgow and Otranto at sunset on Sunday North of Coronel. . . . Fight ensued.

After about one hour's action Monmouth turned over and sank. Good Hope, Glasgow and Otranto drew off into the darkness. Good Hope on fire. An explosion was heard. It is believed she sank. German ships engaged included Scharnhorst, Gneisenau, Nurnberg.

Churchill informed Asquith, who was bewildered by Cradock's actions, writing to Venetia Stanley on November 4:

If the Admiral had followed his instructions he would never have met them with an inferior force, but would have been by now on the other side of South America, with the Canopus & Defence, in overwhelming superiority. I am afraid the poor man has gone to the bottom: otherwise he richly deserves to be court-martialled. . . . As I told Winston last night (and he is not the least to blame) it is time that he bagged something, & broke some crockery.

The Cabinet were equally bewildered by news of this defeat. No one could understand Cradock's decision to fight von Spee without the support of *Canopus* and her 12-inch guns. 'I am very sorry to hear of the unfortunate Valparaiso action,' Kitchener wrote sympathetically to Churchill on November 5; 'what could the Admiral have been thinking of to take on such a vastly superior force in guns.' Churchill replied at once to Kitchener's enquiry:

My dear Kitchener,
    Many thanks for the kindness of your letter.
    Admiralty orders were clear. The Canopus battleship was sent him for his protection. He was told to keep concentrated & said himself he wd avoid

[1] Allan Maclean, 1858–1918. Entered Consular Service, 1893. Consul at Casablanca, 1893–1905; Bilbao, 1906; at Danzig, 1910. Consul-General, Valparaiso, 1913–18.

division of force. Keeping together and scouting with the Glasgow he had a good chance of finding & holding them till reinforcements arrived.

As it was he had no chance at all.

It is vy disappointing. We had 7 separate forces awaiting them at different points, each of wh properly handled & concentrated cd have fought them well.

A good many moves are necessary in consequence of this contretemps.

The Cabinet met on November 5. Churchill gave his colleagues an account of what he knew. 'The Cabinet are of opinion,' Asquith wrote to the King, 'that this incident, like the escape of the Goeben, the loss of the Cressy & her two sister-cruisers, and that of the Hermes[1] last week, is not creditable to the officers of the Navy.' Lloyd George took a more personal view of the disaster, telling Frances Stevenson that day, as she recorded in her diary, that 'Churchill is too busy trying to get a flashy success to attend to the real business of the Admiralty. Churchill blames Admiral Cradock for the defeat in South America—the Admiral presumably having gone down with his ship & so unable to clear himself. This is characteristic of Churchill. . . .'

The return of Fisher to the Admiralty did not protect Churchill from the accusation that he was to blame for the defeat off Coronel. It was argued that Cradock ought to have been given, instead of the slow and old *Canopus*, a fast Dreadnought which would have given him automatic superiority as soon as von Spee appeared off South America. A year later, on 4 September 1915, Churchill set out his defence in a private letter to three Conservative members of Asquith's Coalition Government who had been critical of his conduct of naval affairs, Lord Selborne,[2] Sir Edward Carson and Walter Long:

The obligations upon us at that time, when we had to escort the whole of the great Indian and great Australian convoys and be ready at the same time to meet Von Spee in any of five or six different theatres, strained our resources, great though they were, to the absolute limit. We could not provide fast homogeneous modern cruiser squadrons of superior strength at all these points. We had to eke out our strength with old battleships, under whose heavy guns our cruiser forces could, if need be, take refuge till the whereabouts of the enemy was known. Cradock was given the *Canopus* for this

---

[1] The *Hermes* a seaplane carrier, was torpedoed eight miles west-north-west of Calais on October 30. Nearly all her crew were saved.

[2] William Waldegrave Palmer, 1859–1942. Liberal MP, 1885–6. Liberal Unionist MP, 1886–92. 2nd Earl of Selborne, 1895. First Lord of the Admiralty, 1900–5. High Commissioner for South Africa, 1905–10. President of the Board of Agriculture, May 1915–July 1916.

purpose in ample time. He was told to concentrate and keep concentrated a force superior to Von Spee. He said clearly that he was going to do so and had he done so he would have been safe. . . . But carried away by his fearless and adventurous nature, he divided his forces and then finding himself in the presence of an enemy equal in numbers though vastly superior in strength, he did not find it compatible with his honour or the traditions of the service not to attack.

The Admiralty cannot take any responsibility for this decision, but, as we believe that the Admiral hoped not indeed to win but to inflict such damage upon an enemy unprovided with dockyards or any means of repair as would cripple him, and that this was not an impracticable hope, we have never at any time thrown blame upon him. At the same time he ought not to have done it, and when the records as well as the whole world disposition of the Fleet at that time are studied this will be found indisputable. When Von Spee arrived, after a 5,000 mile voyage across the Pacific, he took 3 or 4 weeks to get the necessary coal supplies, and had Cradock kept his ships together with the *Canopus* he could have observed Von Spee with the *Glasgow* and kept pushing him along from place to place with his stronger though slower force, while all the time British reinforcements would have been hastening from many quarters to the scene. There was therefore a thoroughly good game to play, instead of which a most painful disaster, relieved only by its daring and gallantry, took place.

The public shared the Cabinet's distress at the naval disaster. Reinforced by Fisher's zeal, and sustained by the natural desire of all his subordinates to avenge Cradock, Churchill set about planning von Spee's defeat.

Throughout the week during which the Admiralty was occupied with the disaster at Coronel, Churchill was also much concerned about his brother Jack. On November 2 he learned from Frederick Guest that as a result of the heavy casualties at the battle of Ypres, the Queen's Own Oxfordshire Hussars had, on Sir John French's orders, been put into the front line, and that his brother Jack would soon be under fire. Churchill wrote at once, asking his brother to tell the Regiment that 'I should be proud to be with them', and that he was 'sure no part of the front will be more firmly maintained'. Five days later, on learning of their success in action, he wrote again:

My dear,
    I knew you wd distinguish yrselves. Tell my sqn how glad I am their first contact with the enemy was so creditable to them. . . . I expect it is a stiff experience to stand up for a long time to that shell fire. . . .

I have my own troubles; but have no doubt we shall get the better of them.
Keep a little in touch with French wh you get the chance.

With our best love, Yours always
W

On the following day Churchill received a detailed account of the
action from his brother. A month earlier the sight and sound of battle
at Antwerp had stimulated his desire for military command. Now this
mood was revived. On November 9 he wrote again to his brother:

My dear,

I read yr letter with the deepest interest & pleasure. It is a great source of
regret to me not to be with my squadron now. I feel so acutely the ignoble
position of one who merely cheers from the bank the gallant efforts of the
rowers. But I cannot stir. The combinations at this moment are of the highest
interest and importance. Perhaps in a few weeks I may come & have a day
with you all.

You must feel proud of the way in wh the regiment has taken its place in
the line. . . .

All goes well. Have no fear for the result. We have got the dirty dogs tight.
The end is a long way off: but it is certain tho' not in sight.

Goonie is vy good & brave. She is I think happy here and you cannot
write to her (or me) too often. Every word is precious. . . .

My dear I am always anxious about you. It wd take the edge off much if
I cd be with you. I expect I shd be vy frightened but I wd dissemble.

With fondest love, Yours always
W

'Jack is having a lot of hard service,' Churchill wrote to Sir John
French on November 17, 'and I feel very anxious about him.' Before
this letter reached French, Churchill learned that his brother had been
transferred from his regiment to the Staff, and would henceforth serve at
Headquarters with the Commander-in-Chief. 'French has taken Jack
on to the Staff,' Churchill wrote to his wife as soon as he learned the
news. 'He has done this of his own accord & neither Jack nor I have
ever asked for it. But I am vy thankful, because although there is always
danger, the risk is less & the work more interesting. Jack has done a lot
of hard service & is quite entitled to use his good fortune.'

Sir John French, who felt isolated at his Headquarters, continued to
welcome Churchill as a sympathetic friend who would be his advocate
in Cabinet. The presence of Churchill's cousin Frederick Guest, and from
November of his brother Jack, on French's staff, provided further cause
for personal contact. Guest had written to Churchill on September 8,

after Kitchener's appearance in uniform had caused French such unhappiness: 'I feel sure that you will see his point and understand his frame of mind, and take care that he is not hurt again.' Churchill often put French's point of view to his colleagues, able to explain it more persuasively than the Commander-in-Chief could do from France. By November 9, French was writing to Churchill: 'My dear Winston, If I am too familiar in addressing you like this, forgive me! I write as I feel— you have shown yourself to be one of the greatest friends I ever had in the world.'

But even between French and Churchill all did not go smoothly. The strains imposed by the daily demands of war were severe. On November 14 French sent Churchill a typewritten letter informing him that in future the Royal Flying Corps, not the Royal Naval Air Service, would be in charge of attacking Zeppelin sheds in Germany, and that he himself would decide 'the times at which attacks on Zeppelin sheds should be delivered'. Churchill was infuriated by this proposal to deprive him of authority over the air bases which he had set up in France. He suspected that Sir John French had been persuaded to send this letter by someone at GHQ hostile to him. 'I must frankly say,' he wrote on November 15, 'that the letter signed by you about the naval airmen is very disappointing to me. . . . The Naval Air department look upon the decision conveyed in this letter as a very poor recognition of the dangerous work which they have done. . . .' This letter was not sent. French was technically in the right. The Army could claim to exert aerial responsibility in France whenever it chose. Only at Dunkirk could Churchill insist upon maintaining a base for Admiralty purposes. He therefore bowed to French's demands, writing tersely that evening:

If the Military wing would assume sole responsibility for preventing Zeppelin bases being established in Belgium naval wing could be relieved of this duty. But I hope it is realised that there is no effectual means of dealing with a Zeppelin raid in England after it has started & unless they are destroyed in their bases in Belgium or Germany serious injury may be done to London & our dockyards. At present Admiralty is held responsible.

Apart from this Admiralty feel it imperative to keep a squadron of aeroplanes on the French coast so long as Ostende & Zeebrugge are in German occupation for this is our only means of watching the development of their submarine bases there and other dangerous naval preparations, as well as spotting for British naval fire wh may be again required at any moment.

In these circumstances we propose to withdraw all naval aeroplanes and armoured cars to Dunkirk so as to keep quite clear of the British army and its communications. . . .

Churchill was also hurt to discover that French saw little use for his armoured cars, which served as a mobile shield for the air bases, and had been used successfully against German cavalry on several occasions. Under Josiah Wedgwood the armoured cars had played a significant part at Antwerp, and by November, four squadrons, consisting in all of 127 armoured cars, were operating in northern France.[1] A British intelligence report circulated to senior Cabinet Ministers on November 15 quoted a German in Cologne as emphasizing the value of these cars, which had, it said, caused heavy German losses. On November 17 Churchill wrote to French sharply:

I was sorry to see in your recent telegram that you now attach vy little value to armoured cars. Certainly this does not tally with the information we have received from every quarter in wh ours have been engaged. General Rawlinson & the Cavalry vie with the reports of the enemy . . . in testifying to their effectiveness. No doubt during this period of deadlock & siege lines there is no scope, but the moment you move forward or back the use & convenience of these engines shd be apparent.

At any rate I am too far in to go back; & if when the force is completed you do not desire to have it with you, it can work with the Belgians. Perhaps you will let me know.

The latest types are vy well designed & stand all bullets.

During the last week of November the Cabinet sanctioned a joint military and naval attack along the Belgian coast. Both Churchill and Sir John French were enthusiastic about this further attempt to drive the Germans from the sea; French even agreed to make full use of the armoured cars. But while the operation was being planned he became embroiled with Kitchener over details of the attack, and came to interpret almost every caution and comment which Kitchener made as a criticism of his command. Churchill tried to soothe relations and speed the operation. On December 6, with Kitchener's support, he crossed the Channel to French's Headquarters at St Omer, and explained Kitchener's intentions. As soon as he was back in London he put French's objections to Kitchener, reporting back to French on December 8: 'Nothing cd exceed the urbanity of "our mutual friend" on my return. . . . I have purred like a cat, & shall continue to do so. We *must* all work together for the result.'

Churchill kept Sir John French informed of developments in an almost daily exchange of letters. He tried to make French feel that he

[1] The cars consisted of 45 Rolls-Royces, 42 Talbots and 40 Wolseleys.

was part of the policy discussion of the new operation. On December 9 he wrote again beginning his letter '*Personal & most Secret*':

Kitchener is sending you a copy of the telegram we have fired off at the Fr Govt. I enclose the answer so far recd. Burn it please. I hope you will find means to press the policy on Joffre. Here everyone informed—5 only—is convinced & ready to press vy hard indeed. Please God we succeed. A good & brilliant operation is in sight, conducent immediately to the safety of this country & the general success of the war.

Meanwhile all the naval preparations are going forward; & I will tomorrow write to you in some detail abt them. The Admirals here are red hot for it.

If Joffre 'insists' that it is impossible to replace you in the line, wd it be conceivable to come round with part of yr force on to the sea-flank? I hazard this suggestion, because if the operation were successful, subsequent clearing up wd always be possible.

The combined naval and military operations against Ostend were planned for December 15. Churchill made arrangements to watch them from Dunkirk with Sir Arthur Wilson, and the two men planned to cross the Channel on the evening before. On December 13 Churchill asked French to send a motor-car for him, so that he and Wilson 'could come and join you for a few hours and watch what is going on'. Bad weather forced the operation to be postponed. Churchill was disappointed. In order to ensure that Sir John French remained enthusiastic about taking up the coastal attack on some future occasion, Churchill decided to visit him on December 18. He wanted to see action in France, to feel that he was not a mere spectator, and to get away from the carping and innuendo of both politicians and the Press. It may have been on the eve of this intended visit that he wrote to F. E. Smith, in an undated letter: 'My dear—I am coming over (D.V etc) in Saturday night. . . . I am getting on all right here in spite of some of your party *swine*. Your affectionate friend, W.'

'I propose if you see no objection,' he wrote to Asquith on December 17, 'to go over to Dunkirk tonight & spend tomorrow night at French's H.Quarters, returning Sunday. The clearance of the coast is a most serious matter for the Admiralty & I want to further it if possible.' Asquith sent a single sentence in reply: 'I do not think that you ought to go again to French without first consulting Kitchener & finding that he approves.' Churchill could no longer avoid taking the matter to the Secretary of State for War, and returned Asquith's letter with a note in red ink across it: 'I have always done this, and will do so now. I shall not go till tomorrow afternoon.' Churchill then wrote to Kitchener:

I propose to go tomorrow to Dunkirk to see what the position is.

Have you any objection to my staying with French as he wd like, or to my discussing with him the questions connected with naval co-operation on the sea-flank? . . .

This letter failed to convince Kitchener that Churchill should see French again. On the morning of December 18 the Secretary of State for War went to 10 Downing Street to complain about the visit. Asquith, influenced by Kitchener's protest, wrote to Churchill early that afternoon. He marked his letter 'Secret':

My dear Winston,

There can, of course, be no objection to your going to Dunkirk to look into naval matters, but after talking with Kitchener, who came to see me this morning, I am clearly of opinion that you should not go to French's headquarters or attempt to see French.

These meetings have in K's opinion already produced profound friction between French & himself, & between French's staff & his staff, which it is most desirable to avoid.

Questions of concerted naval & military action can be best discussed and arranged here.

Yrs always
HHA

Churchill was offended by such a questioning of his movements. On receiving Asquith's letter, he wrote immediately to Kitchener: 'The question I asked was one wh you cd easily have answered yourself; & it was one upon wh yr wishes shd naturally prevail. It was not necessary to trouble the Prime Minister; & some of the statements you appear to have made to him are not well founded, & shd certainly in the first instance have been made to me.' Kitchener was much angered by this letter. He returned to 10 Downing Street, and showed it to Asquith, who informed Venetia Stanley that Churchill's letter was 'a rather childish performance'. Kitchener showed Asquith the reply which he had drafted:

My dear Churchill,

I cannot of course object to your going over to discuss naval co-operation with Sir J. French; but at the same time I think I ought to tell you frankly that your private arrangements with French as regards land forces is rapidly rendering my position and responsibility as S of S impossible. I consider that if my relations with French are strained it will do away with any advantage there may be to the country in my holding my present position and I foresee that if the present system continues it must result in creating grave difficulties between French & myself. [I do not interfere with Jellicoe nor do I have a personal correspondence with him.]

I am suggesting to the PM that you should take the WO and let Fisher be 1 Lord then all would work smoothly I hope.

The sentence in square brackets had been crossed out by Kitchener himself. The suggestion that Churchill should be made Secretary of State for War in his place, and Fisher become First Lord, was to have been sent. But on Asquith's insistence, Kitchener agreed to hold the letter back. He explained that he had done so in a letter to Churchill on December 19; the visits to Sir John French were a subject, he wrote, 'that has caused me considerable anxiety'. Churchill replied that same day, stating that he had 'on every possible occasion & by every possible means promoted that good will & confidence between you which I regard as of the highest importance to the country'. He warned Kitchener that 'there was no need to make charges and statements' of the sort which he had made to Asquith: 'They are very unfair to a colleague who has worked with you with the utmost loyalty.'

Churchill could not overcome Kitchener's hostility to his visits to France. Kitchener's threat of resignation had led Asquith to intervene directly in order to prevent future cross-Channel excursions. 'Kitchener, who spent the best part of an hour with me this morning, rather deprecates these frequent visits of W to the front,' Asquith had written to Venetia Stanley earlier that month, on December 4; 'the Army think that he mingles too much in military matters, & the Navy that he is too much away in what may be critical moments for them. I am so far disposed to agree that I think, after this, I shan't allow him to go again for a long time.' Venetia Stanley suggested to Asquith that Churchill should be told to limit his activities to concerting naval and military action in England rather than continue his visits across the Channel; on December 18 Asquith informed her that he had written to Churchill 'as we agreed' and that despite his being upset, 'of course he acquiesced in the decision'. The Prime Minister's veto was final; Churchill gave up all plans to visit Sir John French. He and Kitchener never regained the mutual confidence of the first months of war. Kitchener believed that Churchill had deliberately gone behind his back and sought to undermine his authority. Churchill felt that Kitchener had become oversuspicious of something quite harmless, and would always try to foil his activities when they touched on military matters.

On December 19 Frederick Guest wrote to Churchill from French's Headquarters announcing that his Chief was about to visit London:

Dear Winston,
. . . He is anxious to keep his visit and his whereabouts absolutely secret so do not send any letter addressed to him except by really trustworthy messenger. I am very anxious that he should be put au fait with all the European situation and should hear first hand either from the Foreign Office or the PM all there is to know about Russia etc. At present he only receives K's impressions which seem ill digested & pannicky. . . .

Guest also appealed to Churchill to continue his mediation between Sir John French and Kitchener:

. . . It is because you are so much the cleverer man of the three that the responsibility rests with you to keep the triumvirate together. Also you are the only politician of the group and can see further ahead. Our only consideration is how to 'beat the Bosche'—Forgive me writing plainly but an onlooker often sees most of the game & I have been watching & trying to help you all since the show began. Good bye little man & God bless you.
Yrs
Freddie

French arrived in England on December 20. From Dover he went immediately to see Asquith at Walmer Castle. That afternoon the Prime Minister wrote to Venetia Stanley of how 'I spoke very frankly to Sir J. F. about Winston's visits, & his intervention in military matters. I found that he was substantially of the same opinion, & with all his affection & admiration for W, estimates his judgement as "highly erratic".' Churchill knew nothing of the tone of this exchange. He was busy using the opportunity of French's visit to instil greater enthusiasm for a renewed coastal attack towards Ostend. On December 21 he wrote to Kitchener:

Most Secret
My dear Kitchener,
   . . . We ought to settle tomorrow or Wed either to do the flank thing or simply to stick it out on the existing line. If we decide yes on merits, the Govt ought to grapple with the *French (les Français)* & get our army on the flank for the job. Now is the time, & it will take a good deal of doing. You must say. But if we miss this chance, then all we can do is to hold on—& I expect we can do this—till the Spring.
   I hope you will get a decision taken one way or the other in the next 48 hours. These sporadic attacks of 40 officers a time, & 300 yards (lost again the next day) may keep the enemy on the *qui vive*, but they are a gloomy way of waging war. . . .

Yrs vy truly
WSC

Churchill continued, despite the difficulties involved, to send Sir John French information about events at home and to discuss with him every aspect of military policy. On December 28 he wrote with personal advice: 'I hope you will take good care of yr health & not let yrself be vexed by trifles—like I am fool enough to be. But still I try. All will go well: & the day will come when we shall have "finally beaten down Satan under our feet". Till then in all directions, & on all occasions, count on yr sincere friend.' 'Our friendship,' Churchill wrote four days later, 'though begun late has grown strong and deep, & I feel sure it will stand with advantage all the tests of this remarkable time.' Churchill still wanted to cross over to France. 'I wonder when I shall be able to come to see you again,' Churchill wrote in his letter of January 1. 'I must not put myself in a weak position vis-à-vis "our mutual friend". Here—within my own ramparts—I have a vy strong line whether for defence or offence. Yet it wd be a great relief to me to talk over with you the ideas wh are now coming to the fore, & wh will determine the scope and character of the war in the summer. Well perhaps a chance will come.'
   Although Churchill now stayed in England, his friendship with French continued to bedevil relations with Kitchener. But he did not allow the friendship to sway his judgement. At the beginning of January 1915 he supported Kitchener against French in a dispute about the best method of incorporating the new armies into the existing system. 'Do

not be vexed or discouraged,' Churchill wrote to French on January 8 to soothe him. 'We are on the stage of history. Let us keep our anger for the common foe.'

Parliament, having adjourned on August 28, had not been recalled until November 11. Many Conservatives believed that Asquith had decided not to reconvene the House during October solely to prevent any critical discussion of the Antwerp expedition. During the debate on the address on November 11 Bonar Law had demanded 'a fuller explanation' of what had happened at Antwerp. He asked why Churchill, 'who surely has plenty to do in his Department?' had gone to the city. 'Why,' he questioned, 'was it not Lord Kitchener, or someone delegated by him?' He also demanded an explanation of the defeat off Coronel: 'It certainly is a subject on which we have a right to expect a full explanation from the Government.' Bonar Law's criticisms were answered by Asquith himself. The Prime Minister emphasized that the responsibility for what was done at Antwerp 'was the responsibility not of any individual Minister, but of the Government as a whole', and that 'in particular the Secretary of State for War was consulted and that everything that was done was done with his knowledge and approval'. Asquith went on to try to reassure the House that the expedition was a 'material and most useful factor in the conduct of this campaign'.

The House of Commons insisted upon discussing Antwerp. Liberals were as anxious as Conservatives to know more of the details of the despatch of the two Naval Brigades, of their previous training and of their readiness for war. Bonar Law raised this question in his speech on November 11, and a number of questioners followed it up. Two Liberal backbenchers pressed Churchill on points of detail:

Mr HOGGE[1] asked why sailors at the Crystal Palace have to buy their own oilskins, collars, and silkies?
MR CHURCHILL: Oilskins are not part of a sailor's compulsory kit. All ships and naval establishments, including the Royal Naval Division Depot at the Crystal Palace, are allowed a certain number of oilskin suits or long waterproof coats for the use of those on exposed duty, and the men may purchase waterproof coats for their personal use from Government stocks. Blue jean collars and black silk handkerchiefs are not part of the kit laid down for the recruits, Royal Naval Division.

[1] James Myles Hogge, 1873–1928. Liberal MP, 1912–24.

MR HOGGE: Will the right hon Gentleman make oilskins part of the kit, or, failing that, will he see that all the men are supplied with winter overcoats and not confine them to men who have been sent to camp?
MR CHURCHILL: I will look into it.
MR WATT:[1] Have no extras been given to these men on account of the War in the way of clothing?
MR CHURCHILL: Yes, the whole question of the winter clothing of the Navy has been most carefully studied, and a very large percentage amounting, I think, to more than £300,000, has been incurred in extra warm clothing.

Churchill could answer those critics who raised points of detail in order to try to test him. But Lord Charles Beresford's criticisms were intended to embarrass Churchill rather than to elicit information:

LORD CHARLES BERESFORD asked the First Lord of the Admiralty whether he can state what are the numbers, what the composition, and what the cost to the country of the Naval and Marine Brigades, a portion of which was recently employed at Antwerp in land service; and whether he can state how many officers and men of the original brigades are interned in Holland, giving the men's ratings?
MR CHURCHILL: The German Admiralty have not published the strength and composition of the Naval and Marine Brigades they are now employing in Belgium, and I see no reason why a similar reticence should not be practised here. I shall be happy to give the Noble Lord, as honorary colonel of one of the brigades, the fullest details of its composition. The names of all officers and men interned in Holland were published in the Press on the 26th of last month.

In common with all Ministers, Churchill declined to give any detailed explanation of specific incidents. When a Liberal MP, John Hugh Edwards,[2] pressed for more information about the escape of the *Goeben* and *Breslau*, Churchill replied: 'A partial explanation would be of no value, and the time has not yet come when all the facts can be published without prejudice to vital interests.'

Churchill did not speak until November 16. Criticism had been widely raised both in Parliament and the Press that the Admiralty had sent naval cadets from Dartmouth to sea with the Fleet, and that young trainees should not be exposed to the risks of war.[3] Churchill was called

---

[1] Harry Anderson Watt, 1863–1929. Liberal MP, 1906–18.
[2] John Hugh Edwards, 1869–1945. Liberal MP, 1910–22; 1923–9.
[3] Some naval cadets went to sea at fourteen. Thus Eric Bush, born on 12 August 1899, had his fifteenth birthday at sea on board the *Bacchante*, was present at the Battle of the Heligoland Bight sixteen days later, and served as a Midshipman in charge of a picket boat during the Gallipoli landings of 25 April 1915. (Promoted Captain, 1939, he commanded an assault group at the Normandy landings, 1944.)

upon to defend Admiralty policy. 'The decision to send the naval cadets from Dartmouth to sea in time of war,' he said, 'was arrived at a considerable time ago. It was felt that young officers of their age would be of great use on board His Majesty's ships, and that they would learn incomparably more of their profession in war than any educational establishment on shore could teach them. They are a regular part of the ship's complement.'

Churchill did not understand why the use of sixteen-year-olds in battle shocked many people, while the use of seventeen-year-olds seemed acceptable. Lord Crewe had asked him about the employment of naval cadets on October 1; Churchill had set out his views in more detail when he replied on the same day:

My dear Crewe,

It wd be a vy harsh measure to deprive these young boys of an experience wh they will always look back to, & from wh their professional value is sensibly increased. We have had piteous appeals from the parents of the Osborne cadets to allow their boys to go.

I am assured they render useful services. It has always been the custom of the Navy; & for myself I cannot see much difference in the tragedy of a young life cut short at 16 or at 17.

I have satisfied myself that naval opinion supports the present Admiralty practice. I asked that it shd be carefully re-considered; but we were found united in keeping the lads at sea to take their chance. . . .

Yours vy sincerely
Winston S. Churchill

Churchill's support for boys of sixteen and seventeen going into action was not restricted to those who were in the Navy. In a letter to Lord Kitchener on October 21 he had written:

My dear Kitchener,

Repeated evidence comes in about Germans using boys of 17 in the war. Would it not be wise in the near future to recruit special corps or companies of boys of 17 or 18 here, which cd train on without rifles for the first 8 months, & next year be ready to undergo final training before filling gaps in yr army? If you cd get a couple of hundred thousand of these, you wd have a fine fund for drafts from the end of 1915 onwards.

Napoleon's young soldiers did him very well at Lutzen & Bautzen. . . .

Yours vy truly
Winston S. Churchill

Churchill was greatly encouraged on November 21 by the successful raid by naval aviators on the German hydrogen factory and Zeppelin sheds at Friedrichshafen, on the shore of Lake Constance. Early in November the Admiralty had asked Noel Pemberton Billing[1] to take charge of the raid, which had been suggested by the British Military Attaché in Berne, Colonel Granet.[2] On 10 November 1914 Pemberton Billing headed the small party which had assembled during the day at Southampton: two pilots, eleven air mechanics, four aeroplanes packed up in crates, a motor-car and supplies. The expedition crossed to Le Havre, were transferred to a special train, and went direct to Belfort, in south-eastern France. Men and machines were then moved by motor-car to an airship shed. The crates were unpacked and the aeroplanes put together. By the afternoon of November 14 they were ready for action. But it was not until twenty-four hours later that the remaining pilots arrived, having driven across France with some difficulty, owing to the constant road checks. For two days a strong east wind prevented the aeroplanes from taking off. When the weather improved the first machine to taxi on to the runway smashed its propeller, buckled its left wheel and damaged a wing. By the time repairs were completed, the high winds had returned. It was not until November 21 that the weather improved sufficiently to enable the attack to begin. The first three aeroplanes left the ground safely; the fourth skidded at take off, damaging its tail. The three airborne pilots reached Friedrichshafen and dropped their bombs, despite German anti-aircraft fire. Nine bombs were released in all. Two of the pilots, Flight Commander Babington[3] and Flight Lieutenant Sippe,[4] returned safely. The third, Commander Briggs,[5] was shot down by German machine-gun fire and shrapnel, and captured. On November 22 French troops paraded at Belfort and

---

[1] Noel Pemberton Billing, 1880–1948. Founder and editor, *Aerocraft*, 1908–10. Squadron-Commander, Royal Naval Air Service, 1914–16. Unsuccessfully contested Mile End in support of a strong Air Policy, January 1916. Elected as an Independent MP for East Herts., March 1916. Remained in Parliament until 1921.

[2] Edward John Granet, 1858–1918. Lieutenant, Royal Artillery, 1878. Colonel, 1906. Military Attaché, Rome and Berne, 1911–15. Brigadier-General, 1915.

[3] John Tremayne Babington, 1891–   . Entered Navy, 1908. Lieutenant, Royal Naval Air Service, 1914–15. Air Representative to the League of Nations, 1929–34. Air Officer Commanding-in-Chief, Technical Training Command, 1941–3. Knighted, 1942. Head of Royal Air Force Mission in Moscow, 1943. Assumed the surname of Tremayne, 1945.

[4] Sidney Vincent Sippe, 1884–   . Lieutenant, Royal Naval Air Service, 1914. Flight Commander, 1915. Captain, Royal Air Force, 1918.

[5] Edward Featherstone Briggs, 1882–1963. Entered Navy, 1905. Transferred to Royal Naval Air Service, July 1914. Squadron-Commander, Dunkirk, August 1914. Captured by the Germans, 21 November 1914; prisoner of war in Germany. Escaped, April 1917. Promoted Wing-Commander while a prisoner of war.

pinned the Legion d'Honneur on the two successful pilots. On the following day the planes were crated up again and returned by train to Le Havre, and by boat to Southampton.

The success of the raid was made known by a Swiss engineer who had witnessed it from a hotel near the Zeppelin shed. According to his report, which was published in a Swiss newspaper, 'the bombs made the town tremble, and the military officers lost their heads and gave con-

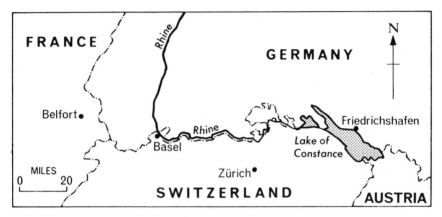

AIR RAID ON FRIEDRICHSHAFEN, 21 NOVEMBER 1914

tradictory orders to the troops'. On November 24 Asquith wrote to Venetia Stanley: 'Winston is quite pleased with his raid on the Lake of Constance: a hydrogen factory wrecked, one Zepp probably destroyed, and 2 out of the 3 aeroplanes safely back.' But a complaint had come from the Swiss Government that, while flying to Germany, the British pilots had flown over Swiss territory, and also that a Swiss had been killed in Friedrichshafen. Churchill was impatient of such complaints, writing to Grey on November 23: 'The strictest instructions were given not to fly over Swiss territory; & we do not believe it was violated at any point. At a great height the position of a machine flying near the frontier might easily be "mistaken" by an ignorant or Pro-German observer. No bomb was dropped on Swiss territory: & if a Swiss was killed in the Zeppelin factory, it serves him right.' To Churchill's disappointment, it was the 'violation' of Swiss territory, rather than the success of the raid itself, which provoked Parliamentary comment. On November 26 a Liberal back-bencher, Frederick Handel Booth,[1] asked

[1] Frederick Handel Booth, 1867–1947. Liberal MP, 1910–18. Chairman of the Yorkshire Iron and Coal Company Ltd.

why neutral territory had been flown over. Churchill explained that instructions had been given to the Naval Flying officers to avoid neutral territory, and that 'the course drawn on the maps supplied to them should have taken them well clear of Switzerland'. But he pointed out, drawing on his own recent experience of flying, that 'when machines are flying at a great height it is almost impossible for any but a skilled observer to determine with any accuracy the course the aircraft are taking unless he is directly beneath them'.

On November 27 Grey told Churchill that the British Government would have to apologize to the Swiss for the incident. Churchill replied:

I hope not too much 'unqualified regret'.
The Swiss in these parts are vy pro-German.
Switzerland is lucky to have Englishmen fighting the battle of the small states. The least she can do is not to be querulous. Everyone else is daring & struggling & suffering—& it is no time for hedging neutrals to give themselves airs.
Our position is that no British aviator crossed Swiss territory: & that even if so the international law on the subject is indeterminate.

Churchill believed that he had every reason to be self-confident. The attack on Friedrichshafen had been a remarkable feat of aerial initiative. He was disappointed that the pioneering efforts of his pilots made less impact upon the public than a technical incident which may or may not have taken place, and annoyed that criticism of his policies seemed to excite people more than did praise of his airmen. He believed that the raid was a British initiative which, if followed up, could have significant repercussions for the war effort. He was dispirited that his constructive ideas did not win popular approval.

To Churchill's annoyance, the raid on Friedrichshafen continued to excite adverse comment in the diplomatic sphere. On November 30 the British Minister in Berne, Evelyn Grant-Duff,[1] telegraphed to Grey that 'if excuses are going to be made I suggest that it should be done quickly as the President[2] says that Eastern Swiss Press is getting restive'. Unaware that on November 27 Parliament had adjourned for two months, Grant-Duff suggested that 'a few words in the House of

[1] Evelyn Mountstuart Grant-Duff, 1863–1926. Entered Diplomatic Service, 1888. Consul-General, Budapest, 1911–13. Minister to the Swiss Confederation, 1913–16. Knighted, 1916.
[2] Hermann-Arthur Hoffman, 1857–1927. Lawyer and parliamentarian. Head of the Swiss Radical Party. Member of the Council of States, 1896–1911; and of the Federal Council, 1911–17. Minister for Foreign Affairs, 1914–17. President of the Swiss Federation, 1914.

Commons would have a good effect'. Grey sent a copy of this telegram to Churchill, who was annoyed that this incident persisted to take up time, and replied on December 2 in a note marked '*Secret*':

1) The international Conference of 1910 reached no agreement on the subject of aeroplanes flying over neutral territory. There is therefore no international law on the subject, & no question can arise of breach of neutrality. It is vy important that this point shd be maintained, as we shall have to fly across the 'Maestricht appendix' of Holland in order to attack Essen, in a few weeks time on a vy large scale.
2) Nevertheless the Br aviators honestly tried to avoid Swiss territory, because the route across German territory was the best & shortest. They believe they succeeded.
3) We must not pay too much attention to pro-German Swiss.
4) Tell them to go & milk their cows.

Later that day Edward Marsh sent Grey a small correction. 'Winston asks me to send you this revised version of his minute of this afternoon,' he wrote. 'After studying the map, he feels obliged to withdraw the words "and shortest"! But the rest of his argument holds good.' It seemed impossible to bring the incident to an end. On December 3 Grant-Duff telegraphed once more from Berne that 'delay in answering Swiss protest creating bad impression here where any violation of Swiss neutrality much resented. As Government at present friendly it seems pity to delay apology. Press agitation increasing.' Grey returned Marsh's letter to him with the note: 'I must see Winston tomorrow. The matter is getting very serious & we shall have a real row with Switzerland.' In a private telegram to Sir Arthur Nicolson,[1] Grant-Duff confided that it was important to close the incident as quickly as possible 'as the Swiss are just now very sensitive about their neutrality and Germans are exploiting matter'. Grey sent this telegram to Churchill with a covering note. 'I ought to have our aviators' version,' wrote the Foreign Secretary, 'but my impression is that unless they are positive they did not fly over Swiss territory I had better suppress report. We don't want to claim the right to go over Swiss territory, nor to alienate Switzerland.' Churchill had now had enough of what he had

---

[1] Arthur Nicolson, 1849–1928. Entered Foreign Office, 1870. Knighted, 1888. 11th Baronet, 1899. Ambassador, St Petersburg, 1906–10. Permanent Under-Secretary for Foreign Affairs, 1910–16. Created Baron Carnock, 1916.

come to regard as something of a charade. 'I have sent an answer on other papers,' he minuted in the margin of Grey's note. Grey's eventual apology to the Swiss went no further than Churchill wished.

Towards the end of November Asquith decided to convene a meeting of senior Ministers and their advisers in the form of a War Council. Their tasks would be to discuss general war policy, and to reach decisions which would be binding upon all Departments. The first War Council met on November 25.[1] The only Cabinet Ministers present were Asquith, Lloyd George, Grey, Kitchener and Churchill. Fisher came to the meeting as the Admiralty representative, and the new Chief of the Imperial General Staff, Lieutenant-General Sir James Wolfe Murray[2] as the War Office representative. A. J. Balfour was invited, not as the nominee of the Opposition, but in his personal capacity as elder statesman. Hankey was established as Secretary, and for the first time in British history formal notes were taken of ministerial discussions. Cabinet discussions remained unrecorded.

Asquith opened the War Council's first meeting by asking both Churchill and Kitchener to explain what had been done at the Admiralty and the War Office to prepare Britain against a German invasion. Churchill gave a detailed account of the preparations which he had made. There were two hundred and sixty vessels, including battleships, cruisers, torpedo craft, submarines and gunboats, in readiness at different points around the coast. In addition to this armada, sixteen destroyers were being recalled from the Mediterranean as reinforcements. Four minefields had been laid along the east coast. Ten aeroplane stations were in constant readiness, the largest, at Hendon, possessing twelve aircraft. This defence system, Churchill pointed out, was 'entirely distinct' from Jellicoe's Fleet, and did not weaken it. Kitchener spoke next, describing the military arrangements which had been made at the War Office; he told the War Council that in his

---

[1] There had been an earlier meeting of selected Ministers at 10 Downing Street on November 2—to discuss closing the North Sea to all ships not sanctioned by the Admiralty. Writing to Venetia Stanley that midnight, Asquith had described the faces of those present: 'K's brick-red, short-nosed, blue-eyed; Fisher strangely un-English, twisted mouth, round-eyed, suggesting the legend (which I believe quite untrue) that he had a Cingalese mother: Jellicoe, small, alert robin-eyed, of (it is said) gipsy parentage; Winston, whom most people wd. call ugly, but whose eyes, when he is really interested, have the glow of genius; and Grey with his well-cut, hawk-like visage, now rather pinched & drawn.'

[2] James Wolfe Murray, 1853–1919. Entered Royal Artillery, 1872. Knighted, 1902. Lieutenant-General, 1909. Chief of the Imperial General Staff, October 1914–September 1915. Special Mission to Russia, 1915–16.

opinion it was 'unlikely that any considerable force would ever succeed in effecting a landing'.

After only two weeks in session, Parliament was adjourned on November 27 for two months. During the motion for the adjournment Lord Charles Beresford rose to discuss the conduct of the war at sea. 'There is a doubt in the public mind,' he proclaimed, 'and a want of confidence in the Navy to carry out its duties.' With the patriotism and zeal of an Admiral of the Fleet, he reminded the House that 'loss of confidence, in my opinion, is absolutely unwarrantable. . . . We have got to support authority with all the energy and ability in our power. . . . This is not the time to criticise, if mistakes were made.' Ignoring his own injunction, he then referred to each of the incidents which had caused disquiet—the sinking of the three cruisers, the escape of the *Goeben*, the defence of Antwerp, and the defeat at Coronel. Beresford urged that although Churchill should continue, as was his duty, to lay down naval policy, he should no longer 'tell the Admirals in command how they are to carry out that policy'.

Churchill answered Beresford's criticisms:

Before it is possible to form a judgment it is necessary that the orders should be disclosed, that the telegrams which have passed should be disclosed, and that the dispositions which prevail, not only at the particular point, but generally throughout the theatre of war, should also in their broad outline and even in considerable detail be made known. That is clearly impossible at the present time. It would be very dangerous for the Minister representing the Admiralty to be drawn into what would necessarily become a controversial, and what might easily become an acrimonious discussion of these matters. And, above all, to disclose partially what has taken place would only lead to demands for fuller and further publication, which would be very prejudicial, not only to actual conduct of the War but to the general interest of the Naval Service, during the course of the War.

Military security made it impossible, Churchill continued, either for the public or for the House of Commons 'to form any judgment on these matters'. He claimed that the Admiralty had given out as much information as was possible, without prejudice to national interests. But because he saw the way in which this constant withholding of information was creating a gulf between those responsible for war policy, and those who could only watch the war from afar and form partial and possibly erroneous views, he devoted a part of his speech to a careful soothing of Press and Parliamentary opinion. He emphasized 'the acute discomfort under which our great newspapers are living at the present time' and expressed the Admiralty's 'very great debt to the Press . . . for the way in which it has helped, with inconsiderable exceptions and with only momentary lapses, the course of the military operations, and has upheld the interests of the country'. He also thanked the House of Commons for 'not pressing for information on many matters in which the keenest interest is taken, and upon which there is a natural desire to arrive at conclusions and to pronounce judgment'.

Churchill advised the House not to put too much emphasis on particular incidents which, he said, were only 'a very small proportion of the work which is going forward all over the world'. He warned that 'it would be a great pity if the mind of the public were disproportionately concerned with particular incidents, and if the departments concerned were occupied in defending themselves or in justifying themselves in regard to these incidents'. He then explained in some detail the specific activities of the Navy since the outbreak of the war, the dangers that had been averted and the success which had been achieved. He ended his statement, which was the last ministerial speech before Parliament adjourned, with an appeal for public confidence both in the Navy, and in the general outcome of the war:

I have thought it right to offer these few remarks of a general character to the House because despondent views are prejudicial to the public interest, and ought not to be tolerated by persons in the responsible position of Members of Parliament while they are in any public situation. There is absolutely no reason whatever for nervousness, anxiety or alarm. . . .

There is every reason for complete confidence in the power of the Navy to give effect to the wishes and the purposes of the State and the Empire. We have powerful Allies on the seas. The Russian Navy is developing in strength; and the French Navy has complete command of the Mediterranean, and the Japanese Navy has effective command of the Pacific, and the utmost cordiality characterises the working of the Admiralties of the four countries.

But even if we were single-handed, as we were in the days of the Napoleonic wars, we should have no reason to despair of our capacity. No doubt we should suffer discomfort and privation and loss. But we should have no reason to despair of our capacity to go on indefinitely, drawing our supplies from wherever we needed them, and to continue this process with a strength which would grow stronger with each month the War continued until, in the end, and perhaps not at any very distant date, the purposes for which we are fighting are achieved.

Churchill had one reason for his confidence which he could not reveal to the House of Commons, or indeed to any colleague except Asquith. On September 6 he had learned from the Russian Government that after the German light cruiser *Magdeburg* had run aground in the Gulf of Finland—on August 26—the Russians had found the secret cipher and signal book of the German Navy on the body of a drowned German signalman. In November the Russians sent this priceless information to the British Admiralty, and on November 8 a special intelligence branch was set up at the Admiralty, in Room 40, under a former Director of Naval Education, Sir Alfred Ewing,[1] to decode the messages. On November 29 Churchill completed the organization of this secret section by appointing Commander Hope[2] to sift and vet the telegrams once they had been decoded. By the end of November Room 40 was able to discover in advance many of the German ship movements in the North Sea and elsewhere. One copy only of each intercepted message was made; this copy was then circulated to Churchill, Fisher, Wilson and Oliver in an envelope marked 'Exclusively Secret', after which it returned to Room 40. Churchill always told Asquith when news had been received of important German ship movements. Asquith sometimes told Grey about them, but not always; he did, however, regularly pass on the news to Venetia Stanley.

On November 30 Churchill celebrated his fortieth birthday. That night Margot Asquith set down in her diary her reflections upon his career:

What is it that gives Winston his pre-eminence? It certainly is not his mind. I said long ago and with truth Winston has a noisy mind.

Certainly not his judgment—he is constantly very wrong indeed (he was strikingly wrong when he opposed McKenna's modest naval programme in 1909 and roughly speaking he is always wrong in his judgment about people). It is of course his courage and colour—his amazing mixture of industry and enterprise. He can and does always—all ways put himself in the pool. He

[1] James Alfred Ewing, 1855–1935. Professor of Mechanisms and Applied Mechanics, Cambridge, 1890–1903. Director of Naval Education, 1903–16. Knighted, 1911. In charge of Admiralty department dealing with enemy cipher, 1914–17. Principal, University of Edinburgh, 1916–29.

[2] Herbert Willes Webley Hope, 1878–1968. Entered Navy, 1892. Commodore, Admiralty War Staff, 1914. Captain, 1915. Rear-Admiral, 1926. President, Woolwich Ordnance Committee, 1928–31. Vice-Admiral, 1931. Admiral, 1936.

never shirks, hedges, or *protects* himself—though he thinks of himself per-petually. *He takes huge risks.* He is at his very best just now; when others are shrivelled with grief—apprehensive, silent, irascible and self-conscious morally; Winston is intrepid, valorous, passionately keen and sympathetic, longing to be in the trenches—dreaming of war, big, buoyant, happy, even. It is very extraordinary, he is a born soldier.

When he came back from Antwerp he sent in his resignation to Henry saying he wanted to join the Army and have a command of some sort—he did not care what. He confided this to Freddy Guest who spoke to me of it with grave anxiety. I reassured him by telling him Henry would not dream of accepting Winston's resignation.

The fall of Antwerp was a cause of real sadness to Winston.

He was subjected to violent abuse in long letters to the Morning Post from Walter Long and other Unionists—the first departure from the political truce—but this did not affect him one hair, he is quite unsensitive which is also a help!

Despite the anxieties and criticisms which war had brought, Churchill still had reason to believe that his career was on an upward path. For his first ten years in Parliament his premature success had made him many enemies, for whom successful youth was as much a sin as any particular political mistake. By 1914 it was no longer his youth but his fervour, rising at times it seemed to callousness, which upset his col-leagues. He seemed over-concerned with too many aspects of the war, too little aware of the jealousies which his activities aroused, too insensitive to the effect of his constant questionings and enthusiasms, too exuberant, when grief and disillusion were widespread.

Since the fall of Antwerp, and with the arrival of German troops at Ostend and Zeebrugge, Churchill believed that a vigorous offensive policy should be adopted. Fisher shared this view. At the second meeting of the War Council, which was held at 10 Downing Street on December 1, Hankey produced a report on the principal factories exposed to attack from the sea, Churchill suggested that, rather than try to build up a defence system 'sufficiently strong at every vulnerable point on the coast', a better policy, and the best means of defence, would be to seize an island off the German coast. This, he believed, could be used as a base with which to blockade the German naval bases at the mouth of the Jade, the Weser and the Elbe. He explained that in his view a German island could be seized by twenty thousand men, and that this should be done as soon as possible. Balfour wondered whether such a plan, although it would 'obviously be worth doing', would provide an effective substitute for Home Defence. Hankey's minutes record Churchill's reply:

MR CHURCHILL pointed out that the seizure and occupation of a suitable island might render possible the establishment of a flying base, by means of which the movements of the German fleet would be kept under constant observation. It would also enable us to keep large numbers of submarines and destroyers, including the older as well as the newer classes, constantly off the German ports. We could also drop bombs every few days. In these circumstances it would be very difficult for the Germans to prepare for invasion without our knowledge, or to escape from the North Sea ports. Invasion could then only come from the Baltic.

Fisher had always believed in the need for offensive action. Long before the war he had considered the seizure of one of the German coastal islands an essential part of British war strategy. Making his first intervention at the War Council, he stressed 'the importance of adopting the offensive' and warned the assembled Ministers that 'the present defensive attitude of our fleet was bad for its *moral*, and did not really protect it from the attacks of submarines'. The War Council authorized the Admiralty to examine the question in detail, but came to no final decision about whether the raid should go ahead. On December 2 Churchill drafted an eight-page memorandum on the advantages of an invasion of Sylt. The idea of seizing a German island excited him, and he pressed it continually upon his Admiralty officials during the ensuing weeks. But they were not impressed. On December 21 Churchill wrote to Fisher despondently:

The key to the naval situation is an oversea base, taken by force & held by force: from wh our C class submarines, & heavily gunned destroyers can blockade the Bight night & day: & around wh and for wh a series of desperate fights wd take place by sea & land, to the utter ruin of the enemy.
But I cannot find anyone to make such a plan alive and dominant: & tell them our situation is as I have told you & as you justly say, that of waiting to be kicked, & wondering when & where.

At the War Council on December 1 Balfour had questioned Churchill at some length about Britain's defensive position. As the meeting was

coming to an end he asked whether the Admiralty had provided adequate protection for oil tanks and other places which were vulnerable to
German attack. He expressed surprise that the Germans had not as yet
made any air raid on the Woolwich Arsenal or on the naval oil depot at
Thameshaven. Churchill replied that it was, in his opinion, 'impossible
to provide effectually by means of passive defences for every vulnerable
point liable to aircraft attack. The best plan was to attack the sheds and
bases of the enemy's aircraft, and this policy was being actively pursued.'

Throughout November the Admiralty planned revenge for the disaster at Coronel. Within a few hours of learning of Cradock's death,
Fisher had suggested that in order to confront von Spee with overwhelming force, the fast battle-cruisers *Invincible* and *Inflexible* should be
sent at once to South America. Churchill at first believed that one battle-
cruiser would be enough. But he accepted Fisher's judgement. At 12.40
pm on November 4, less than six hours after learning of Coronel, the
two men telegraphed to Jellicoe: 'Order Invincible and Inflexible to fill
up with coal at once and proceed to Berehaven with all despatch. They
are urgently needed for foreign service.' Churchill and Fisher worked in
harness to bring about von Spee's destruction. Further telegrams despatched from the Admiralty on November 4 mobilized British resources
and prepared them for battle. The first was sent to the armoured cruiser
Carnarvon at 1.35 pm:

> In view of reported sinking of Good Hope and Monmouth by Scharnhorst
> and Gneisenau off Coronel November 1st, armoured ships on SE Coast
> America must concentrate at once.
> Carnarvon Cornwall should join Defence off Montevideo. Canopus
> Glasgow Otranto have been ordered if possible to join you there. Kent from
> Sierra Leone also has been ordered to join your flag via Abrolhos.
> Endeavour to get into communication with them. Enemy will most likely
> come on to the Rio trade route. Reinforcements will meet you shortly from
> England.

At 2.30 the light cruiser *Glasgow* and the armed merchant-cruiser
Otranto were informed: 'You should make the best of your way to join
Defence near Montevideo. Keep wide of track to avoid being brought to
action by superior force.' A few moments later the *Canopus* was ordered
to join the *Defence* near Montevideo: 'Keep wide of track to avoid being
brought to action by superior force. If attacked however Admiralty is

confident ship will in all circumstances be fought to the last as imperative to damage enemy whatever may be consequences.'

That evening Churchill appointed the former Chief of Staff, Vice-
Admiral Sir Frederick Sturdee, as Commander-in-Chief, South Atlantic
and Pacific. Fisher had already begun, with characteristic spleen, to
blame Sturdee for the faulty staff organization at the Admiralty which,
he alleged, had been responsible for Coronel.

Before the two 'greyhounds', as the *Inflexible* and *Invincible* were
known, could start for South America, they had first to go to Plymouth
for urgent repairs. Churchill and Fisher waited anxiously for them to be
made ready. After four days, impatient at having heard nothing, they
telegraphed to the Admiral Superintendent at Devonport, Rear-
Admiral Mundy,[1] to ask when the ships could sail. Mundy replied by
telegram on November 9: 'The earliest possible date of completion . . .
is midnight 13th November.' Churchill and Fisher were exceedingly
angry at the proposed delay. Shortly after midnight Churchill replied:

Invincible and Inflexible needed for war service and are to sail Wednesday
11th November. Dockyard arrangements must be made to conform. You are
held responsible for the speedy despatch of these ships in a thoroughly efficient condition. If necessary Dockyard men should be sent away in the ships,
to return as opportunity offers.

The Admiralty order was obeyed. Sturdee sailed for South America
on November 11 with dockyard workmen still on board. Battle was
joined at the Falkland Islands on December 8. All the German warships
except the *Dresden* were sunk: and she too was tracked down within four
months, and blew up in Chilean waters. On December 8 Von Spee went
down with his flagship, the *Scharnhorst*. A naval victory had come at last,
after so much disappointment. Coronel was avenged. Fisher's return to
the Admiralty seemed justified beyond expectation. Churchill was the
first to rejoice, writing to Fisher on December 10:

My dear,
This was your show and your luck.
I should only have sent one greyhound and Defence. This would have
done the trick.

[1] Godfrey Harry Brydges Mundy, 1860–1928. Entered Navy, 1873. Admiral Superintendent Pembroke Dockyard, 1908–11. Rear-Admiral, 1912. Admiral Superintendent
Devonport Dockyard, 1913–16. Vice-Admiral, North Atlantic Convoy, 1917–18. Admiral,
1920.

But it was a niggling coup. Your flair was quite true. Let us have some more victories together and confound all our foes abroad—and (don't forget)—at home.

Yours ever
W

Elated by the victory of the Falkland Islands, Churchill drafted a detailed and jubilant communiqué to be published in the Press. In the communiqué he intended to give the details not only of the victory at the Falkland Islands but also of Cradock's defeat and of the escape of the *Dresden*. Churchill believed that this frank communiqué would cheer those who, having expected the war to be over by Christmas, were beginning to ask whether all was well with the Allied cause, on land or at sea. Fisher opposed publication, and on Christmas Day sent Churchill a word of warning:

I suggest to you to hold your hand about Cradock & the Falklands. No doubt the Dresden told all but yet there are always lingering doubts till you hear the other side. We ourselves unintentionally gave away the Invincible and Inflexible in our first communique and doubtless Tirpitz saw it! But that is not the point—the point is there is inexplicable folly in the escape of the Dresden and the murder of Cradock best left alone—and you will also have to go back and explain similar past criminal follies also which time has eaten up. Hawke,[1] Cressy, Aboukir, Hogue, Pegasus,[2] the Singapore butchery, the Goeben all will be resuscitated. So let your facile pen have a Christmas rest!

Churchill acquiesced. The details which he had wished to reveal were withheld. On 16 February 1915 Stamfordham asked Fisher when the Falkland Island despatches were going to appear. 'I told him I could not say,' Fisher wrote to Churchill, 'and asked him in return if the Germans ever published their despatches and whether we were really at War? He looked glum and spoke no more. It will take the gilt off the gingerbread when the despatches are published.'

Exactly a week after Fisher's letter listing the 'past criminal follies' of the Admiralty, a further disaster, the torpedoing of the battleship *Formidable* off the south Devon coast, in which six hundred of her eight hundred crew were drowned, added to the catalogue of misfortune with which Churchill's wartime administration was marred.

---

[1] A British cruiser, torpedoed in the North Sea on 15 October 1914. 500 lives were lost; only the captain survived.

[2] A light-cruiser sunk off Zanzibar on September 20 by the German light-cruiser *Königsberg*. The *Königsberg* was eventually tracked down and blocked in at the mouth of the Rufigi river, East Africa, on October 31.

To avert a repetition of the triple tragedy of the *Hogue*, *Cressy* and *Aboukir*, the Captain of the *Formidable*, Arthur Loxley,[1] had signalled to another ship not to stand by lest she herself should be torpedoed. On the day after the sinking, Sir Lewis Bayly, who had only been appointed Commander-in-Chief of the Channel Fleet sixteen days before, was ordered to haul down his flag. Shortly afterwards Churchill appointed Bayly President of the Royal Naval College at Greenwich; 'not for his own sake', he explained to Jellicoe on 11 January 1915, 'but because to terrorize Admirals for losing ships is to make sure of losing wars'.

Fisher's return to the Admiralty in October 1914 had served Churchill's purpose. The public felt that the highest professional standards of naval conduct would be pursued with the utmost vigour. Fisher's age was ignored. So too were his cantankerous methods, which had for so many years brought division and controversy to the Navy. The public responded to Fisher's return as they had done to Kitchener's two months earlier, finding reassurance in the figureheads of history and legend. At the Admiralty Fisher served as the spark to ignite a hundred trains of powder. His outbursts, his enquiries, his minutes and memoranda, his green pencil, his exclamation marks, his triple underlinings, were the exact opposite of Prince Louis' business-like decorum; and a necessary part of the war spirit which Churchill required. The victory at the Falkland Islands seemed Fisher's personal triumph.

With no specific appointment, without publicity and without controversy, Sir Arthur Wilson worked on in his room at the Admiralty, silent and unobserved. Churchill, Fisher, Wilson and Oliver became the inner council responsible for the most secret aspects of naval affairs. '*AKW and dear Oliver are mules!*' Fisher wrote to Churchill on 23 March 1915, '—besides they diverge for days on some side issue. . . . Oliver so overburdens himself he is 24 hours behind with his basket of papers.' They were assisted by Churchill's new Naval Secretary, Commodore de Bartolomé.[2] Sir Frederick Hamilton, Rear-Admiral Tudor[3] and Cap-

---

[1] Arthur Noel Loxley, 1874–1915. Entered Navy, 1889. Sub-Lieutenant, 1894. Appointed to command HMS *Formidable* in the rank of Captain, 2 September 1914; drowned at sea, 1 January 1915.

[2] Charles Martin de Bartolomé, 1871–1941. Entered Navy, 1885. Commodore, 1914. Churchill's Naval Secretary, October 1914–May 1915. Third Sea Lord, 1918–19. Knighted, 1919. Rear-Admiral, 1919.

[3] Frederick Charles Jones, 1863–1946. Entered Navy, 1876. Assumed surname of Tudor, 1891. Director of Naval Ordnance and Torpedoes, 1912–14. Rear-Admiral, 1913. Third Sea Lord, 1914–17. Commander-in-Chief, China Station, 1917–19. Knighted, 1918. Admiral, 1921. President, Royal Naval College, 1920–2.

tain Lambert[1]—the Second, Third and Fourth Sea Lords—George Lambert,[2] the Civil Lord, and the Additional Civil Lord, Sir Francis Hopwood, were all restricted to routine administration, and excluded from this War Group, which met each day to discuss policy with Churchill. Fisher described the new system to Jellicoe on November 17:

> I listen with great interest day by day to A. K. Wilson, old Oliver and Bartolomé discussing your battle line. (We meet daily for an hour or two to discuss the world 'from China to Peru!'). Old AKW wrote to Winston and the Prime Minister that he was now '*Fisher's slave*'! *Can you imagine AKW being a slave!!!* But he works like a horse all day at all sorts of plans for the Belgian and German coast attack.

Fisher was not easy to work with. His moods were unpredictable and he was given to castigating all around him. 'We have a regular menagerie of "charity admirals" . . .' he wrote to Jellicoe on November 20, 'totally unfitted for the work they are employed on—as the Admiralty is quite full of young Naval officers who ought to be at sea—doing simply clerk's work at the Admiralty. The corridors are crowded with them as I walk along!' Above all, Fisher delighted in writing to his correspondents about his relationship with Churchill. This was the theme of dozens of his letters. 'Winston says I am full of the four S's now!' he wrote to Sir David Beatty on December 7: 'Secret, Silent, Saturnine, Sinister.' On December 13, when Lady Randolph Churchill invited him to dine, he replied, in green crayon: 'I can't dine out—I go to bed at 9.30—I get up at 3.30—I don't go anywhere. Winston is quite enough dissipation for me. I want no more!' On December 20 Jellicoe was sent a more critical outburst, which opened with the instruction 'Please burn at once':

> My beloved Jellicoe,
> . . . Winston has so monopolised all initiative in the Admiralty and fires off such a multitude of purely departmental memos (*his power of work is absolutely amazing!*) that my colleagues are no longer '*superintending Lords*', but only '*the First Lord's Registry*'! I told Winston this yesterday and he did not like it at all, but it is true! and the consequence is that the Sea Lords are atrophied and their departments run really by the Private Office. . . .
> Yours always
Fisher

---

[1] Cecil Foley Lambert, 1864–1928. Entered Navy, 1877. Captain, 1905. 4th Sea Lord, 1913–16. Rear-Admiral, 1916. Knighted, 1920.

[2] George Lambert, 1866–1958. Liberal MP, 1891–1924; 1929–31. Civil Lord of Admiralty, 1905–15. Chairman of the Liberal Parliamentary Party, 1919–21. Liberal National MP, 1931–45. Created Viscount, 1945.

Churchill himself was the most frequent recipient of Fisher's letters. Sometimes they gave shrewd advice, as on December 8, when Churchill returned from one of his visits to France. 'Welcome back!' Fisher wrote. 'I don't hold with these "outings" of yours! I know how you enjoy them! Nor am I afraid of responsibility while you're away! But I think its too venturesome! Also it gives your enemies cause to blaspheme! However, the leopard can't change his spots nor the Ethiopian his skin!' Most frequently, Fisher called for action. On December 21 he set out his thoughts on ships and scrapheaps:

Dear Winston,
. . . We have got to get rid of our multitude of 'Canopi' *ET HOC GENUS OMNE*! Scrap them all! The scrapheap cries aloud! A multitude of splendid seamen butchered in ships that can neither fight or run away! . . .
Look at the murdered Pegasus! All over the world we distributed Tortoises to catch Hares. *Bring them home and put them in the Zoological Gardens as specimens!*
Those minelayers of ours will be butchered if they go out. Send the mines in the 'L' class of destroyers—*they are all fitted to lay mines! The whole 'L' class to be ALWAYS OUT SINGLY, INDEPENDENTLY distributing bouquets of mines at the Amrum Light and far out to sea! LOCK the Germans up! DO SOME-THING!!!!! We are waiting to be kicked! ! !* Next kick this week!

Yours
F

Behind all Fisher's letters, however eccentric, was a lifetime of naval thought and expertise. Churchill encouraged him to give vent to all his feelings, and to probe all aspects of the naval war. As a result of Fisher's activities, Churchill was free to range over the wider subjects which interested him, and which were outside the scope of purely Admiralty affairs. National policy, strategy and invention excited his mind; he was impatient to give them his time. Fisher's presence served both as a relief and a stimulus. Clementine Churchill was apprehensive of the relationship between them. 'How good & vigorous Fisher's letter is,' she wrote on November 18, having read one of the First Sea Lord's letters to her husband: 'I hope he is not like the curate's egg!' Beatty was more certain that the relationship would be short-lived. 'The situation is curious,' he wrote to his wife on December 4; 'two very strong and clever men, one old, wily, and of vast experience, one young, self-assertive, with a great self-satisfaction but unstable. They cannot work together, they cannot both run the show.'

6

The Turkish Puzzle

THREE weeks after the assassination of the Archduke Franz Ferdinand at Sarajevo on 28 June 1914 the flag of the Royal Navy was to be seen at Constantinople, a symbol of British power. The flag was that of a British Rear-Admiral, Arthur Limpus,[1] who for two years had trained and organized the Turkish Navy. Limpus was a popular figure at Constantinople; he represented Britain's desire to help Turkey recover her strength after the crushing defeat of 1912 at the hands of the Balkan States. It was Churchill who had sent him to Constantinople as Head of the British Naval Mission. Although many English Liberals echoed Gladstone's indignant outbursts[2] against Turkish atrocities in Bulgaria and Armenia in the 1880s, Churchill believed in friendship between the British and Ottoman Empires. He respected the motives and admired the courage of the Young Turks, who in 1908 had overthrown the despotic Sultan, Abdul Hamid,[3] and sought to establish a Europeanized regime. Churchill's interest in Turkey had been further stimulated a year later, when he was at German military manoeuvres at Würzburg and had met the universally admired Turkish leader, Enver Pasha.[4] Churchill had been attracted to Enver who, although only twenty-seven years old, was virtual ruler of Turkey and to whom the

---

[1] Arthur Henry Limpus, 1863–1931. Entered Navy, 1876. Rear-Admiral, 1910. Naval Adviser to the Turkish Government, 1912–14. Admiral-Superintendent, Malta Dockyard, 1914–16. Knighted, 1916.

[2] William Ewart Gladstone, 1809–98. Prime Minister, 1868–74; 1880–5; 1886; 1892–4. In a pamphlet *The Bulgarian Horrors and the Question of the East* (published, 1876), he wrote: 'Let the Turks now carry away their abuses in the only possible manner, namely by carrying off themselves . . . bag and baggage . . . from the province they have desolated and profaned.'

[3] Abdul Hamid, 1842–1918. Sultan of Turkey, 1876–1909. Prorogued Parliament, 1878; ruled autocratically for thirty years. Forced to restore the Constitution by the Young Turks, 1908. Deposed, 1909.

[4] Enver Pasha, 1881–1922. Member of the Young Turk triumvirate, 1908. Military Attaché, Berlin, 1909. Commanded Turkish units in the Libyan and Balkan Wars, 1911–13. Minister of War, 1914. Commanded the Turkish forces against the Russians in eastern Turkey, 1915. Fled to Russia, 1918. Killed leading an anti-Bolshevik movement in Turkestan.

new Sultan, Mehmed V,[1] was entirely subservient. In February 1910 Churchill met Enver in London.

Soon afterwards, in September 1910, while cruising in the Mediterranean with F. E. Smith, Churchill had spent five days in Constantinople. There he met several other Young Turks, including Talaat Pasha[2] and Djavid Bey[3] for both of whom he developed an immediate liking. These contacts led him to follow Limpus' reports from Constantinople with sustained interest. Churchill did not accept the prevailing political fashion, agreeable to Asquith and Grey, of looking upon the Turkish Empire as the 'sick man' of Europe whose disintegration was inevitable and might lead to direct territorial advantage to Britain. But he was vexed when Enver turned to Germany for military advice, writing to Lloyd George on 4 October 1911: 'What fools the Young Turks have been to put their money on Germany.'

Alone among senior Cabinet Ministers, Churchill tried to encourage an actively pro-Turkish policy before 1914. When the Italians invaded the Turkish Province of Libya in 1911 he had felt strong sympathy for the Turks. The Turkish Government appealed to Britain for support against Italy. Churchill had wanted the Foreign Office to make some positive response; 'I cd not help feeling,' he wrote to Grey on 4 November 1911, 'that our colleagues were rather inclined to treat a little too lightly the crude overture wh the T Govt have made.' Churchill believed that 'Turkey has much to offer us', and continued:

In fixing our eyes upon the Belgian frontier and the North Sea we must not forget that we are the greatest Mahometan power in the world.[4] We are the only power who can really help her and guide her. And if she wants to turn to England and Russia, and if R herself is anxious for an assocn wh shd carry T in some sort of way into the system of the Triple Entente, the proposition ought not to be lightly pushed aside. We must ask ourselves whether we have not more to gain from Turkish friendship than from Italian policy; and still more whether we have not more to apprehend from the consequence of throwing T than of throwing Italy into the arms of Germany. T is the greatest land weapon wh the Germans cd use agst *us*.

Churchill concluded that the time had come to develop 'a purely Br

[1] Mehmed Reshad Effendi, 1844–1918. Succeeded his elder brother Abdul Hamid as Sultan, 1909. Known as Mehmed V. He had no influence on Turkish policy, which was firmly under the control of the Young Turks.

[2] Mehmed Talaat, 1874–1921. Member of the Young Turk Triumvirate, 1908. Minister of the Interior, 1913–17. Grand Vizier, 1917–18. Fled to Europe, 1918. Assassinated in Berlin.

[3] Mehmed Djavid, 1875–1926. Teacher of political economy. Minister of Finance and Public Works, 1914. Hanged for conspiring to assassinate Mustafa Kemal.

[4] There were an estimated 20 million Muslims in Turkey in 1910. In British India there were 62 million Muslims (census of 1901); there were a further 10 million Muslims in Egypt (census of 1907).

policy in the Orient'. When, early in November 1911, he had received a letter from Djavid asking whether the time might not have arrived 'for a permanent alliance between the two countries?', Churchill had wanted to send an encouraging reply. But the Foreign Office, while prepared to send something 'mellifluous', Grey wrote on 9 November 1911, would not agree to anything substantial.

Churchill was undeterred by Grey's reluctance to contemplate an active pro-Turkish policy. Spurred on by the increasing German military and diplomatic influence at Constantinople, he instructed Limpus to co-operate with the Turkish Navy as closely as possible. Those Turks who were against too great a reliance on German help and goodwill reciprocated with enthusiasm. In 1911 the Turkish Admiralty purchased a dreadnought, then being built at Barrow-in-Furness. This powerful vessel, the *Reshadieh*, was launched in September 1913. But the Turks had no dock suitable for the warship, nor did Constantinople contain the facilities necessary for her upkeep. 'Their arsenals in the Golden Horn,' Limpus wrote to Churchill on 29 October 1913, 'are crumbling—have nearly crumbled—to decay. They need capable management, workmen, and money.' Limpus persuaded both Armstrong Whitworth and Vickers to make an offer to the Turkish Government to build the necessary installations for the new battleship. Both firms sent their leading negotiators to Turkey, Vickers sending Sir Vincent Caillard,[1] and Armstrongs sending a former Director of Naval Intelligence, Sir Charles Ottley.[2] After negotiations with Djavid Bey and other Ministers an agreement was reached on 3 December 1913. This agreement, Limpus wrote to Churchill on that same day, could become 'a really vital nucleus for the building up of a large industry in Turkey. . . . and if I do not mistake, undesirable aliens are shut out for 30 years. . . . It is bad to shout too soon, but the appearance of the infant is so healthy that the temptation to cheer a little is strong.' At first Limpus' optimism seemed justified. Within a month of this agreement for a British-built dock, the Turkish Ambassador in London, Tewfik Pasha,[3]

[1] Vincent Henry Penalver Caillard, 1856–1930. President of the Council of Administration of the Ottoman Public Debt, 1883–98, during which time he reconstituted the Turkish silk, salt and wine industries, and was responsible for securing British financial participation in the Bagdad railway. Knighted, 1896. Joined Messrs Vickers, 1898; Financial Director, 1906–27.

[2] Charles Langdale Ottley, 1858–1932. Entered Navy, 1871. Present at the bombardment of Alexandria, 1882. Senior Naval Officer at Constantinople, 1898. Captain, 1899. Director of Naval Intelligence, 1905–7. Knighted, 1907. Secretary to the Committee of Imperial Defence, 1907–12. Retired from Navy with rank of Rear-Admiral, 1912. Director of Armstrong Whitworth, 1912–19.

[3] Ahmed Tewfik Pasha, 1845–1936. Turkish Ambassador to Berlin, 1885–95. Foreign Minister, 1895 and 1908–9. Grand Vizier, 1909. Ambassador to London, 1909–14.

opened negotiations for the purchase of a second battleship from Armstrongs. The Greeks were also keen to purchase the ship, whose role in the Aegean promised to be decisive. Negotiations took only eight days. The Turks were able to raise the money, the Greeks were not; and on December 28 Armstrongs concluded their agreement with the Turkish Government. The Turks announced that the new battleship would be even larger than the *Reshadieh*. It would be called the *Sultan Osman I*, after the founder of the Ottoman Empire, and with the *Reshadieh*, would be ready for action in 1914. At the end of July both ships were ready to sail to Turkey. A further strengthening of Anglo-Turkish relations took place during July, when Vickers and Armstrong Whitworth took over the Government Naval Construction works in Constantinople. Ottoman Government Guaranteed Bonds were issued to finance the undertaking. On July 21 Caillard circulated the British Press with the prospectus of the Bond issue, and asked them to give it publicity: 'Practically the whole of this loan,' Caillard explained to H. A. Gwynne, 'shall be directly or indirectly spent in this country.' Through battleships and finance, Britain and Turkey were being brought closer together.

On 27 July 1914 Admiral Limpus put to sea to conduct a special exercise of the Turkish Navy. He intended to sail through the Dardanelles, whose defences he had advised the Turks to strengthen, and then to escort the first of the new Turkish battleships to be ready, the *Sultan Osman*, back through the Dardanelles to Constantinople. The imminent arrival of both these ships, which had been paid for by public subscription raised throughout Turkey,[1] would be an important moment for British prestige, a serious challenge to German influence and the day of glory for the Turkish Minister of Marine, Djemal Pasha.[2] The *Sultan Osman* was due to leave England on August 16. Five hundred sailors had come from Constantinople, and on July 29 waited on board a steamer on the Tyne before transferring to their resplendent warship. But Limpus never carried out his assignment. Churchill could not risk such a powerful vessel, armed with ten 13·5-inch guns and capable of $21\frac{1}{2}$ knots, leaving British waters on the eve of what might be a European war. No one could guarantee that Turkey would remain neutral.

On July 29 Eyre Crowe informed the Admiralty that Grey had just learned 'from a reliable source' that the *Sultan Osman* 'is being equipped with coal today and is under orders to proceed to Constantinople as

---

[1] The two battleships cost the Turks a total of £3,680,650.
[2] Ahmed Djemal, 1872–1922. Member of the Young Turk triumvirate, 1908. Military Governor of Constantinople, 1913. Minister of Marine, 1914. Commanded the IVth Army in Syria, November 1914. Fled Turkey, 1918. Assassinated by Armenians in Georgia.

soon as possible, though still unfinished'. Churchill acted with speed, informing Prince Louis and the Third Sea Lord, Admiral Moore:[1] 'The builders shd by every means prevent & delay the departure of these ships while the situation is strained: & in no case shd they be allowed to leave without express permission. If necessary authority will be given to restrain them.' Churchill asked the Foreign Office if they had any objection to holding the ships in British waters. On July 30 Eyre Crowe minuted to Grey: 'I think we must let the Admiralty deal with this question as they consider necessary, and afterwards make such defence of our action to Turkey as we can.' Grey agreed. On July 30 Moore informed Churchill that 'Messrs. Armstrong have been pressed to put all difficulties in the way of hoisting the flag'. Churchill approved Moore's action, and the *Sultan Osman* was boarded by British sailors on August 1. On learning this, Tewfik Pasha went to the Foreign Office and protested to Sir Arthur Nicolson, who recorded their conversation for Grey:

> The Turkish Ambad. called to enquire why the Turkish battleship had been 'embargoed' by the Admiralty. I told him that in view of the serious situation abroad it was not possible to allow a battleship to leave these waters and pass into the hands of a foreign buyer. Of course had she been here on a visit it would have been different, but it was considered that in the present tension it was not right to hand over to the buyer a newly built battleship. The Admiralty had, I believed, taken possession temporarily of her—as it would have been discourteous to have taken any steps once the Turkish flag had been hoisted and a Turkish crew placed on board. The Ambad. seemed puzzled—and said three million pounds had been paid for the ship. I told him he would not lose the money. He asked for how long the ship would be detained. I told him we were before the unknown—& it was impossible to say.[2]

On July 31 the Cabinet had accepted Churchill's argument that both the *Sultan Osman* and the *Reshadieh* should be taken over by the Royal Navy for use against Germany. His colleagues recognized that commandeering the ships of a foreign power was a necessary means of safeguarding British naval superiority in a time of crisis. In Constantinople the

[1] Archibald Gordon Henry Wilson Moore, 1862–1934. Entered Navy, 1875. Naval assistant to Fisher, 1907–8. Director of Naval Ordnance and Torpedoes, 1909–12. Rear-Admiral, 1911. Third Sea Lord, 1912–14. Commander of 2nd Battle Cruiser Squadron, 1914; present at the actions in the Heligoland Bight, 28 August 1914, and Dogger Bank, 23 January 1915, after which relieved of his command on Jellicoe's insistence. Knighted, 1914. Admiral, 1919.

[2] Neither ship was returned to Turkey. The *Sultan Osman* was renamed HMS *Agincourt*, the *Reshadieh*, HMS *Erin*; both served with the Royal Navy throughout the war, and after Turkey's surrender on 30 October 1918 remained in British possession.

seizure seemed an act of piracy, which the Germans were quick to exploit. It had also greatly angered Talaat, Djavid and several other prominent Young Turks who had until then been suspicious of German intentions in the Balkans and Near East, and were advocates of Turkey pursuing a neutral, or even a pro-British policy. The arrival off Constantinople of the *Goeben* and the *Breslau* a week later confirmed the Turks in their high estimate of German power, and helped to ensure that Enver's pro-German policies would prevail. The British Government was unaware that Enver had already committed his country to Germany by a secret Treaty which he had signed with the German Ambassador, von Wangenhein,[1] on August 2. This Treaty was unknown even to the neutralist and pro-British members of the Turkish Cabinet. It did not commit Turkey to enter the war at Germany's side, but gave the Germans the overriding influence in the Turkish capital. In the event of war between Russia and Turkey, Germany agreed to act as Turkey's ally. The Russians sensed what was impending; on August 8 their Ambassador, Count Benckendorff,[2] told Grey of their fears that the Austrian Fleet, then in the Adriatic, would be allowed through to the Black Sea 'with the connivance of Turkey' to attack Russian ports. But this hint of potential Turkish hostility made no impression in Whitehall. To the Foreign Office it seemed inconceivable that Turkey would risk the disintegration of its Empire by entering the war. But on August 11, while the *Goeben* was still in the Sea of Marmara, Admiral Souchon,[3] who was unsure of what his ships were to do when they reached Constantinople, had received the following secret instructions from Berlin: 'It is of the greatest importance to go to Constantinople as quickly as possible in order thereby to compel Turkey to side with us on the basis of the treaty that has been concluded.' Later that day, when Souchon had reached Constantinople, the Turks agreed to his request that the commodore of the British flotilla, Lieutenant Boothby,[4] should not be allowed to return to the Turkish ship on which his flag was flying.

On August 11, as soon as Churchill learned that the *Goeben* and

[1] Hans Freiherr von Wangenheim, 1859–1915. German diplomat. Attaché, St Petersburg, 1887–8. Served at Copenhagen, Madrid, Luxemburg and Lisbon. 1st Secretary, Constantinople, 1899–1904. Councillor, Mexico, 1904–8; Athens, 1908–12. Ambassador in Constantinople from May 1912 until his death in October 1915.

[2] Alexander Count de Benckendorff, 1849–1917. Entered Imperial Russian diplomatic service, 1869. Ambassador to London, 1903–17.

[3] Wilhelm Souchon, 1864–1933. Rear-Admiral commanding the German Mediterranean Squadron, 1913–14. Appointed Commander-in-Chief of the Turkish Navy, September 1914.

[4] Evelyn Leonard Beridge Boothby, 1876–1937. Entered Navy, 1890; retired as a Lieutenant, Royal Marines, 1912. Lieutenant, Turkish Mission, 1914. Lieutenant-Commander, in command of an Armed Yacht, 1914–16. Commander, in command of a Light Cruiser, 1916–18. Captain, 1918.

Breslau had reached the Dardanelles, he telegraphed to Sir Berkeley Milne: 'You should establish a blockade of Dardanelles for the present but be on the lookout for mines.' To this Milne replied that afternoon asking if he should stop all ships, or only German ships, from entering or leaving the Straits. 'If a formal blockade is to be established,' he added, 'will declaration be issued by home government?' Churchill had no authority to declare a blockade at the Dardanelles; such an action would certainly have been a bellicose one, likely to provoke a Turkish declaration of war. The Admiralty replied at once to Milne that the use of the word 'blockade' in Churchill's earlier telegram had been a mistake; that what was intended was 'only to carefully watch the entrance in case enemy's cruisers came out'. This Milne did; but the two German ships remained off Constantinople throughout August.

The Germans, fearing that the presence of the *Goeben* and *Breslau* off Constantinople might lead to Britain taking action against the Turks, announced that they had sold the ships to Turkey.[1] This attempted deception was discussed by the British Cabinet on August 12. The British Ministers had no option but to insist that all German officers and men must leave the ships immediately and return to Germany. Only if the Turks replaced the German crew by an all-Turkish crew, it was argued, would it be safe to assume that Turkey did not intend to go to war with Britain. Churchill decided to reinforce the Cabinet request by a personal appeal to Enver. On August 15 he sent Grey the draft of the telegram which he wanted to send:

I hope you are not going to make a mistake wh will undo all the services you have rendered Turkey, and cast away the successes of the second Balkan war. By a strict and honest neutrality these can be kept secure. But siding with Germany openly or secretly now must mean the greatest disaster to you, your comrades, and your country. The overwhelming superiority at sea possessed by the navies of England, France, Russia, and Japan over those of Austria and Germany renders it easy for the four allies to transport troops in almost unlimited numbers from any quarter of the globe, and if they were forced into a quarrel by Turkey, their blow could be delivered at the heart.

The personal regard I have for you, Talaat, and Djavid and the admiration with which I have followed your career from our first meeting at Würzburg alone leads me to speak these words of friendship before it is too late.

'Don't jump,' he wrote to Grey in a tactful covering note, 'but do you mind my sending this personal message to Enver. I have measured this

---

[1] On becoming part of the Turkish Navy, the name of the *Goeben* was changed to *Jawuz Sultan Selim*, and that of the *Breslau* to *Midilli*.

man & am sure it will do good. But of course your "NO" is final.'[1]
Grey had no objection to Churchill entering into direct communication
with Enver. But he wanted to give the Turks a more attractive induce-
ment than the threat of military attack. He therefore drafted, in the
third person, an extra paragraph guaranteeing the territorial integrity
of the Turkish Empire if Turkey would remain neutral. Grey's offer
read: 'I know that Sir E. Grey who has already been approached as to
possible terms of peace if Germany & Austria are beaten has stated that
if Turkey remains neutral an agreement to respect the integrity of her
territory must be a condition of any terms of peace that affect the near
East.'[1] Churchill inserted Grey's paragraph into his draft and the whole
message was sent as if from him. But Grey was in some ways as threatening
as Churchill. On August 6 he telegraphed bluntly to the British Ambassador in Constantinople, Sir Louis Mallet:[2] 'You should make it
quite clear . . . that if Turkey sides against us there are no limits to the
loss that she may incur.'

Churchill was still in an aggressive mood when the Cabinet met on
August 17. Asquith wrote to Venetia Stanley:

Turkey has come into the foreground, threatens vaguely enterprises against
Egypt, and seems disposed to play a double game about the Goeben and
the Breslau. Winston, in his most bellicose mood, is all for sending a torpedo
flotilla thro' the Dardanelles—to threaten & if necessary to sink the Goeben
& her consort. Crewe & Kitchener very much against (in the interest of the
Moslems in India & Egypt) our doing anything wh could be interpreted as
meaning that we were taking the initiative agst Turkey. She ought to be
compelled to strike the first blow. I agreed to this. But the Turks must be
obliged to come out & tell us whether they are going at once to dismiss the
German crews.

On August 18 Sir Louis Mallet telegraphed optimistically to Grey
that Enver was 'delighted' with the offer of respect for Turkish territorial integrity. Public feeling in Turkey, Enver had told him, would
be 'affected immediately' if the British Government would declare
publicly that the *Reshadieh* and the *Sultan Osman* would eventually
be returned, and that Britain would pay an indemnity for having
seized them. Grey at once sent Mallet's telegram to Churchill, with no
other comment than 'The FO will send any answer that Mr Churchill

---

[1] Churchill's letter to Grey and Grey's draft are reproduced in facsimile on pages 828, 829.
[2] Louis du Pan Mallet, 1864–1936. Entered Foreign Office, 1888. Private Secretary to Sir
Edward Grey, 1905–7. Under-Secretary of State for Foreign Affairs, 1907–13. Knighted,
1912. Ambassador at Constantinople, 1913–14.

ordains'. Churchill immediately telegraphed once more to Enver. He offered to pay full recompense for the two ships on condition that the German crews of the *Goeben* and *Breslau* returned to Germany, as already insisted upon by the Cabinet:

> I deeply regretted necessity for detaining Turkish ships because I knew the patriotism with which the money had been raised all over Turkey. As a soldier you know what military necessity compels in war. I am willing to propose to His Majesty's Government the following arrangement:
> (1) both ships to be delivered to Turkey at the end of the war after being thoroughly repaired at our expense in British Dockyards; (2) if either is sunk we will pay the full value to Turkey immediately on the declaration of peace; (3) we will also pay at once the actual extra expense caused to Turkey by sending out crews and other incidentals as determined by an arbitrator; (4) as a compensation to Turkey for the delay in getting the ships we will pay £1,000 a day in weekly instalments for every day we keep them, dating retrospectively from when we took them over.
> This arrangement will come into force on the day when the last German officer and man belonging to the Goeben and Breslau shall have left Turkish territory definitely and finally, and will continue binding so long as Turkey maintains a loyal and impartial neutrality in this war and favours neither one side nor the other.
> Do you agree?

Churchill knew that Enver had the power to accept this proposal. As neither Asquith nor Grey contemplated a direct appeal, Churchill realized that the initiative must come from him. Knowing that such a proposal from a First Lord to a Minister of War might appear to be going over the head of his opposite number, Djemal Pasha, Churchill telegraphed immediately to Admiral Limpus: 'Will you please take an opportunity of showing Minister of Marine the telegram I have sent to Enver Pasha & telling His Excellency that had I had the pleasure of his acquaintance I shd have addressed myself directly to him.'

Churchill's mediation came too late. Despite a last-minute approach to Russia for territorial guarantees to Turkey in return for Turkish neutrality, Enver decided, without the full support of his colleagues, that Turkey must march with Germany. He refused to receive Churchill's message. When the Cabinet discussed the Turkish situation on August 21, Asquith reported to Venetia Stanley that Churchill was 'violently anti-Turk'. German officers and German crews remained on board the two warships, making a mockery of the alleged sale of the ships to Turkey, and accentuating Churchill's anger at their escape from their British pursuers. While the *Goeben* and *Breslau* remained in neutral Turkish waters and under German command, Churchill felt a personal sense of responsibility for their escape. He realized the danger which they could pose to Russia should Admiral Souchon be instructed to take them to the Black Sea. Enver's refusal to receive his proposals made it certain that the Turkish Government would allow the Germans to remain in command of the two ships. Although Churchill was the foremost British minister to advocate a positive policy of conciliation with Turkey, his ultimate concern and responsibility was German naval strength. Once Turkish action effectively increased that strength in waters where the Entente was weak, he had no alternative but to put the severest possible pressure on Turkey to do what he had previously believed he could do by negotiation and personal persuasion. On August 22 he wrote to Grey to explain his feelings:

We must stick to our point about *all* German ratings from Goeben & Breslau going home at once. If necessary to a friendly Turkey we wd provide the skilled ratings wh are indispensable ourselves.

We must extirpate the Germans from the Turkish Fleet, & above all from German ships transferred illegally to the Turkish flag.

This is of course only the Admiralty view.

Grey decided that as he had already stated the Cabinet's demands about the German sailors, no further action was necessary. German influence in Turkey continued to increase. When the officers and men who were to have manned the *Reshadieh* and the *Sultan Osman* reached Constantinople from Tyneside on August 22, Enver had a further means of stimulating anti-British feeling. On the following day twenty-eight German military officers reached Turkey from Germany. During the last week of August Churchill asked the British Ambassador in Constantinople whether any German sailors were on their way to Turkey. 'In reply to your enquiry,' Mallet telegraphed direct to the Admiralty on August 26, '90 German sailors passed through Sofia yesterday on their way to Constantinople. I have protested strongly but Grand Vizier[1] is unable to control the situation which is dominated by the German Ambassador and Generals.'[2] Churchill minuted on Mallet's telegram: 'The evident intention of the Turkish Government

[1] Mehmed Said Halim, 1863–1921. Grandson of Mehmet Ali of Egypt. Appointed to the Ottoman Council of State, 1888. President of the Council of State, 1912. Grand Vizier, 1913–17. Assassinated by Rumanians in Rome.

[2] In 1913 a German Military Mission led by the Prussian General of Cavalry, Liman von Sanders, arrived in Turkey. There were five hundred German officers on the mission by August 1914. In October 1914 von Sanders was appointed Commander of the Turkish Fifth Army, whose command included the Gallipoli Peninsula.

to put their Fleet as well as their army into German hands and to let the Germans use Turkish ships as well as German ships (wh ought to have been interned), as an effective part of the German naval forces can only have one significance.' That same day the British Minister in Bucharest, Sir George Barclay,[1] telegraphed to the Foreign Office with the news that according to his French colleague,[2] the 'Turks are contemplating some mischief with Goeben and Breslau'. Also on August 26, Admiral Limpus informed Churchill that, despite a new law forbidding any foreign wireless installations to operate in Turkish territorial waters, three German ships still had their wireless aerials up and one at least was in direct communication with Germany. Limpus continued:

In fact I consider that Constantinople is almost completely in German hands at this moment.

It appears to me that Enver and the Army wish and intend this. That Djavid knows that anything but neutrality means ruin; that Talaat *probably* understands this; that the Grand Vizier certainly does; and that Djemal is —a little uncertain—but has French leanings.

The lesser Ministers and the bulk of the people are on the whole adverse to the Germanophile policy of the few: but so long as the Army remains German they cannot do much.

Limpus was still trying to persuade the Turks to remain absolutely neutral, believing that their only chance of retaining their vast and troubled Empire lay in a strict neutrality. 'I continue to use what influence I can wield,' he continued, 'to keep Turkey from finally committing suicide.' Limpus was a sincere friend to Turkey. He believed that the Turkish Empire could not survive a war with Britain. He explained this in the same letter to Churchill:

In giving my reasons to the authorities here why Turkey should not join the German Group I have studiously omitted all talk of action that England might take, such as keeping the requisitioned ships without payment, and fomenting Arabian and Persian Gulf troubles against Turkey: or might encourage Greece to take, such as a landing between Smyrna and the Dardanelles, taking the forts on the south side of the Straits, admitting Torpedo Craft to the Marmora, cutting off and starving first the Gallipoli Peninsula, and soon after cutting all communications between Constantinople and the

---

[1] George Head Barclay, 1862–1920. Entered Diplomatic Service, 1886. 2nd Secretary at Constantinople, 1898–1902. Councillor, Constantinople, 1906–8. Knighted, 1908. Minister to Rumania, 1912–20.

[2] Jean Camille Blondel, French Minister, Bucharest, 1907–16.

South. But they are each and all things which, methodically undertaken and persistently carried out, would succeed, and would annihilate the remaining power of Turkey.

In this brief survey of Turkish weakness the Admiral accurately fore-shadowed the plans and enterprises which were to follow. On August 27 Mallet telegraphed to the Foreign Office with a report from his Military Attaché, Major Cunliffe-Owen,[1] which likewise anticipated direct British action against the Turks. Cunliffe-Owen reported that the *Goeben* was expected to be ready for sea on September 2. He believed that there was 'little practical chance of German personnel being re-moved'; the Turkish Fleet was believed to be completely under the con-trol of German officers, and several German merchant vessels in the Bosphorus were being 'prepared as armed cruisers'. He continued with a proposal for British naval and military action:

It may be advisable to consider question of our fleet entering the Straits.

In respect of this, if mines can be negotiated, there should be little appre-hension of difficulty in running past the shore defences and once off Stamboul, position would be a commanding one, completely paralysing all military movements between European and Asiatic shore.

On the other hand reconstructed Turkish fleet would have also to be dealt with, and a mere fleet entry is not calculated to have any permanent effect nor might fleet be able to remain without simultaneous action on the part of Russian fleet at Bosphorus and Russian military occupation of adjoining country. Personally, except for giving Russia immediate assistance and possibly casting a balance in Balkans on our side, I should be against a fleet enterprise only. Probability is that it might succeed, but to command situa-tion properly at Dardanelles, requires also use of military force and point arises whether substantial enterprise should be attempted in quite a sub-sidiary theatre of war.

After this survey of the problems and opportunities of a naval and military attack on the Dardanelles, Cunliffe-Owen concluded with a brief sentence that military operations against the Turks 'would be far easier in Persian Gulf or Syria where Turkish forces are almost negli-gible'. Both Limpus and Cunliffe-Owen, with first-hand experience of

[1] Frederick Cunliffe-Owen, 1868–1946. Entered Army, 1888. Major, 1903. Attached to the Greek Army during the Balkan Wars, 1912–13. Military Attaché to Turkey, 1913–14. Lieutenant-Colonel, October 1914. He left Constantinople on 2 December 1914. Brigadier-General commanding the Royal Artillery of the Australian and New Zealand Army Corps, Gallipoli, 1915. Served with the British forces in Iraq, 1920. Member of the Refugee Settle-ment Commission, Greece, 1923–6.

Turkey's naval and military strength, were prepared to give an attack at the Dardanelles serious consideration, fully aware as they both were of the many difficulties of such an operation.

By the end of August Churchill was convinced, as were most of his colleagues, that Turkey would in a short time join the Central Powers. But he did not fear Turkish participation in the war. It might be possible, at the outset, for the Turks to make advances into northern Persia, a Russian sphere of influence, or even against Russia itself in the Caucasus. But these attacks could in all likelihood be met by superior Russian forces, while at the same time the strong British positions at two of the extremities of the Turkish Empire, in Egypt and in the Persian Gulf, could be used to put pressure upon the Turks if necessary. For Churchill, the entry of Turkey into the war was of importance entirely because of the effect it could have upon the fortunes of the war in Europe. He was not alone in realizing that the best method of persuading the Balkan States to join the Allies would be in alliance against their common and traditional enemy, the Turk. Such a combination would be important, not because it would lead to the defeat of Turkey but because it would enable these Balkan States, once united and under the flag of the Allies, to move against Austria-Hungary.

Among Churchill's colleagues, Lloyd George was the most enthusiastic at the idea of the joint armies of Rumania, Bulgaria, Greece, Serbia, and even Montenegro, moving northwards to strike at the heart of the Habsburg Empire. With such a massive addition to Allied strength, threatening Austria from the south, there seemed little doubt that the war might be brought to an end within a year, if not sooner. Churchill believed that the best way of forcing the Balkan States to resolve their quarrels and join the Allies as a united bloc, was for Britain to take an immediate initiative against Turkey, ideally at the Dardanelles. He explained this to the Dardanelles Commissioners[1] in 1916:

It is obvious that the ideal action against Turkey, if she came into the war, was at the earliest possible moment to seize the Gallipoli Peninsula by an amphibious surprise attack and to pass a fleet into the Marmora. This operation could be covered by serious feints on the Syrian coast or at Alexandretta,

[1] The Dardanelles Commission of Inquiry was set up by Asquith on 20 July 1916. It took evidence from all those involved in the planning and execution of the attack on Turkey at the Dardanelles and Gallipoli, except Kitchener (who had been drowned early the previous month). The Commission published three reports in 1917. But it did not release its full Proceedings, which included the evidence and cross-examinations on which the reports were based. These Proceedings, which were voluminous, only became available to the public on 1 January 1968, under the Public Record Act of the previous year.

or even at Smyrna. The Turkish seaboard is peculiarly liable to naval and amphibious attack. No one could tell, till the expedition actually sailed, where it would strike. The Turks could not possibly have sufficient forces at every point which was threatened. All points are, in fact, equally and simultaneously threatened from the sea. But the Gallipoli Peninsula, giving access by water to Constantinople, exposed, if taken, the heart of Turkey to a fatal stroke.

Churchill was convinced that Turkey could be defeated by such an attack. At the end of August it seemed that the Greeks would provide the necessary military force if Britain organized the naval attack, even though Grey had persuaded the Cabinet to turn down a Greek offer of alliance which had reached London on August 18. For Churchill, Greek participation was only the first step towards the goal of a League of all the Balkan States which, built upon common hatred of Turkey, would be used as the decisive catalyst in Europe. At that moment Noel Buxton,[1] an influential backbench Liberal MP, was setting off with his brother Charles[2] to visit the Balkans. He sought official encouragement, but found Grey sceptical. Lloyd George and Churchill, however, were both enthusiastic about his visit. On August 31 Churchill wrote Buxton a letter intended to influence political leaders in the Balkan States. During the day, Edward Marsh sent the letter to Grey for his approval, adding: 'It must reach Buxton by 10.30 tonight so it is urgent.' But Grey did not want the letter sent, replying: 'I am afraid I don't much like letters of this kind being given to be shown in the Balkans—words wont influence them. I should like to see Winston about it tomorrow.' But Churchill refused to be deflected by Grey's hesitations and gave Buxton the letter that evening. In it he wrote:

. . . The creation of a Balkan Confederation comprising Bulgaria, Servia, Roumania, Montenegro, and Greece, strong enough to play an effective part in the destinies of Europe, must be the common dream of all their peoples. The result of this war is not doubtful. Sooner or later, Germany will be starved and beaten. Austria will be resolved into its component parts. England has always won in the end; and Russia is unconquerable. England has been the friend of every Christian State in the Balkans during all their years of struggle and suffering. She has no interests of her own to seek in the Balkan Peninsula. But with her wealth and power she will promote and aid

[1] Noel Edward Buxton, 1869–1948. Liberal MP, 1905–6; 1910–18. Labour MP, 1922–30. Minister of Agriculture and Fisheries, 1924; 1929–30. Created Baron Noel-Buxton, 1930.
[2] Charles Roden Buxton, 1875–1942. Liberal MP, 1910. Labour MP, 1922–3; 1929–31. In October 1914, while in Bulgaria, he was shot through the lung by a Turkish would-be assassin. Treasurer of the Independent Labour Party, 1924–7.

every step which is taken to build up a strong union of the Christian peoples, like that which triumphed in the first Balkan War. By acting together in unity and good faith the Balkan States can now play a decisive part, and gain advantages which may never again be offered. By disunion they will simply condemn themselves to tear each other's throats without profit or regard, and left to themselves will play an utterly futile part in the destinies of the world. I want you to make your friends in Greece and in Bulgaria realize the brilliant but fleeting opportunity which now presents itself, and to assure them that England's might and perseverance will not be withheld from any righteous effort to secure the strength and union of the Balkan peoples.

On September 22 Churchill gave public encouragement to the Balkan States, and to the minority nationalities of Austria-Hungary, in an interview with Calza Bedolo of the *Giornale d'Italia*, published in *The Times* on September 24. 'We want this war to reform the geography of Europe according to national principles,' Churchill said; 'we want liberty of the races, the integrity of nations and the diminution of armaments.' Churchill maintained these views. On 21 January 1915 he wrote to Kitchener that 'the case for settling generally on ethnographic principles is a strong one and a hard rule for Austria and Germany'.

Churchill realized that it was not the Balkan States alone which hoped to take advantage of the defeat of Turkey and Austria, but that even Italian neutrality might be overborne if Italy saw an opportunity for territorial gains in the eastern Mediterranean and Adriatic. Grey had informed Churchill of the Greek offer of troops to be used to attack the Gallipoli Peninsula. The offer seemed a firm one. Churchill cast about for yet further sources of man-power. Even the Far East came within his survey. On August 29 he drafted a note to Grey suggesting that Japan send a battle squadron to the Mediterranean. But the Japanese were unwilling to part with either ships or men. The Greeks alone seemed certain to co-operate.

On the last day of August Churchill talked over the Turkish situation in detail with Kitchener. They agreed that two staff officers from the Admiralty and two from the War Office should meet immediately. Their aim, Churchill wrote to General Douglas, the Chief of the Imperial General Staff, on September 1, was to 'examine and work out a plan for the seizure by means of a Greek army of adequate strength of the Gallipoli Peninsula, with a view to admitting the British fleet to the Sea of Marmora'. Churchill asked Douglas to organize such a meeting immediately 'as the matter is urgent, and Turkey may make war on us at any moment'. At six that evening the Director of Military Operations, Major-General

Callwell,[1] and a General Staff officer at the War Office, Colonel Talbot[2] went to the Admiralty, where they discussed the possibility of a Gallipoli landing with the Director of Transport, Graeme Thompson,[3] Captain Lambert—the Fourth Sea Lord—and Captain Richmond. According to a memorandum prepared by Talbot on September 5:

> The representatives of the Admiralty stated that with 6 weeks warning they could collect sufficient transport to convey 40000 to 50000 men to the selected landing places. Ships of war could also be provided to cover the landing with their fire. The D.M.O. stated that, considering the strength of the Turkish Garrison & the large force already mobilised in European Turkey, he did not regard it as a feasible military operation & that he believed this to be the War Office view.

On September 2 Callwell was asked to return to the Admiralty for further talks. This time Lambert and Richmond were joined by Churchill and Prince Louis. 'The matter was thrashed out again,' Talbot recorded, with the result that Callwell submitted a report to Kitchener on September 3 in which, while emphasizing that any attack on Gallipoli was 'likely to prove an extremely difficult operation of war', he nevertheless now considered that with a force of sixty thousand men such an attack would be justifiable. How far Churchill had prevailed on Callwell to reverse his opinion by the weight of evidence, how far by an assertion of his authority, is not clear. Although Churchill quoted Callwell's report of September 3 in *The World Crisis*, he made no reference to their meeting on the previous day, nor to Callwell's abrupt change of mind.

On September 4 Churchill telegraphed to the British Admiral who

---

[1] Charles Edward Callwell, 1859–1928. Entered Army, 1878. Intelligence Branch, War Office, 1887–92. Attached to the Greek Army during the Graeco-Turkish War, 1897. Colonel, 1904. Angered because several of his contemporaries were appointed to General Officer over his head, he retired from the Army in 1909. Satirized Army procedure and War Office routine in *Service Yarns and Memories*, published in 1912. Recalled to the active list, 1914. Acting Major-General, August 1914. Director of Military Operations and Intelligence at the War Office, 1914–16. Special Mission to Russia, 1916. Adviser on ammunition supply, Ministry of Munitions, 1916–18. Major-General, 1917. Knighted, 1917. Military historian.

[2] Milo George Talbot, 1854–1931. Entered Royal Engineers, 1873. On Kitchener's Headquarters Staff during the Sudan campaign, 1897–9. Director of Sudan surveys, 1900. Retired with rank of Colonel, 1905. Recalled to the War Office for special duties, August 1914.

[3] Graeme Thomson, 1875–1933. Entered Admiralty, 1900. Director of Transports, 1914–17. Director of Shipping at the Admiralty and Ministry of. Shipping, 1917–19. Knighted, 1919. Colonial Secretary of Ceylon, 1919–22. Governor of British Guiana, 1922–5. Governor of Nigeria, 1925–31. Governor of Ceylon, 1931–3.

commanded the Greek Navy, Mark Kerr,[1] suggesting that he open discussions with the Greeks on the question 'of the right war policy to be pursued if Great Britain and Greece are allies in a war against Turkey'. Churchill explained to Kerr the basis upon which he should begin discussions with the Greeks, and the importance of Greek military participation:

> In principle, Admiralty would propose to reinforce the Greek Fleet by a squadron and a flotilla strong enough to give decisive and unquestionable superiority over the Turkish and German vessels. They would propose that the whole command of the combined Fleets should be vested in you, and that you should hoist your flag in the British battle-cruiser Indomitable. They will reinforce you to any extent and with any class of vessel that circumstances may render necessary. The right and obvious method of attacking Turkey is to strike immediately at the heart. To do this, it would be necessary for a Greek army to seize the Gallipoli Peninsula under superiority of sea predominance, and thus to open the Dardanelles, admitting the Anglo-Greek Fleet to the Sea of Marmora, whence the Turco-German ships can be fought and sunk, and where in combination with the Russian Black Sea Fleet and Russian military forces the whole situation can be dominated.
>
> Admiralty wish that these conceptions should be immediately examined by the Greek naval and military experts in consultation with you. They wish to know at once the general views of the Greek Government upon this enterprise, and what force they think would be necessary on the assumption that safe transportation is assured. To what extent and in what time could Greece provide the necessary transports, or should we do so? Or what are their alternative suggestions?

On September 2 the Cabinet had agreed, as part of its Balkan policy, to give financial help both to Rumania and to Serbia. The Cabinet had also decided, according to Asquith's report to Venetia Stanley, 'to sink Turkish ships if they issue from the Dardanelles'. In his letter, Asquith did not explain the reason for this provocative decision. Nor did he say who were its advocates; only that it was a Cabinet decision, from which he did not dissent. Yet it must have been clear to the Cabinet that such a belligerent act might easily force Turkey into war. But Asquith believed that Turkish neutrality was more likely to be secured by such warning gestures than by moderation. That day J. A. Pease recorded in his diary that in Cabinet Churchill had favoured, in

---

[1] Mark Edward Frederic Kerr, 1864–1944. Entered Navy, 1877. Naval Attaché, Athens and Constantinople, 1903–4. Admiral, 1913. Commander-in-Chief of the Greek Navy, 1913–15. Commander-in-Chief of the British Squadron in the Adriatic, 1916–17. Major-General, Royal Air Force, 1918. Deputy Chief of the Air Staff, 1918. Poet and naval historian.

the event of war with Turkey, 'landing Greek force on isthmus on west side of Dardanelles [i.e. the Gallipoli Peninsula] & controlling Sea of Marmara. Ships were now at Besika Bay.'

On September 3 the Cabinet agreed that the two Indian Divisions then on their way to Europe should be held for a few days in Egypt before continuing to Marseilles; a decision partly reached, Asquith explained to Venetia Stanley, 'as a warning to the Turks to keep quiet'. Following these two Cabinet meetings, Grey asked the Russians whether they might consider joining in an Allied attack on Turkey. The reply was not encouraging. The German armies were at that very moment marching towards Paris, and Russia can have had little faith in Anglo-French prospects. Grey wrote to Churchill on September 6:

You will see from the telegram from St Petersburg that Russia can give no help against Turkey. If things go very badly in France, Italy may come out on the wrong side & the French fleet may be paralyzed by the way things go in France. I don't like the prospect in the Mediterranean at all, unless there is some turn of the tide in France.

Churchill was anxious to find troops for a Gallipoli landing. He still hoped to influence the Russians in favour of participation. He therefore replied to Grey's pessimistic note in positive terms, asking him to tell the Russians of the possibilities as he saw them:

There is no need for British or Russian anxiety abt a war with Turkey. Even if the Greek army were paralysed by Bulgarian & Turkish attack, a Russian Army Corps cd easily be brought from Archangel, from Vladivostok, or, with Japanese consent, from Port Arthur, round to attack the Gallipoli position. No other military operations are necessary. The price to be paid in taking Gallipoli wd no doubt be heavy, but there wd be no more war with Turkey. A good army of 50,000 men & sea-power—that is the end of Turkish menace.

On the evening of September 6 Grey received an encouraging telegram from the British Minister at Athens, Sir Francis Elliot,[1] reporting

---

[1] Francis Edmund Hugh Elliot, 1851–1940. Entered Diplomatic Service and appointed Attaché at Constantinople, 1874. Consul-General at Sofia, 1895–1903. Minister at Athens, 1903–17. Knighted, 1904. Employed in the Foreign Trade Department of the Foreign Office, 1917–19.

on his discussion with the Greek Prime Minister, Eleutherios Venizelos.[1]
According to Elliot:

He is not afraid of single-handed attack by Turkey by land as General
Staff is confident of being able to deal with it. Greek Government have
received from Sofia positive assurances of definite neutrality but do not trust
them. They would however be satisfied with a formal protest by Bulgarian
Government against violation of Bulgarian territory by Turkish troops proceeding to Greece. If however Bulgaria joined Turkey while Servia was
occupied with Austria situation would be critical.

It is in my opinion highly desirable to let Turkey know that if she attacks
Greece we shall support latter. This would do more than anything to keep
Turkey quiet.

On September 8 Churchill informed Admiral Troubridge that his
'sole duty' in patrolling the waters at the mouth of the Dardanelles was
'to sink the Goeben and Breslau under whatever flag, if they come out
of the Dardanelles'. He was worried lest the reappearance of these two
men-of-war in the Mediterranean would imperil the safety of troopships
carrying Indian, Australian and New Zealand soldiers from Port Said
to Marseilles. He therefore instructed Troubridge to use his whole
force, including submarines, in order to keep the Dardanelles under
strict surveillance, and if necessary to destroy the two ships 'at all costs
by night or day'. Turkey continued to ignore the British demand that
all German officers should leave the ships, and that their 'sale' to
Turkey should be made manifest by the appearance of all-Turkish
crews on board. The German commander, Admiral Souchon, remained on the *Goeben*, flying the flag of the Turkish Commander-in-
Chief, and at least one German officer was reported to have gone on
board every Turkish ship. According to Limpus, who wrote to Churchill
from Constantinople on September 8, 'the number of German workmen, sailors and coast defence gunners imported since the Goeben's
arrival has now risen to about 800'. Many of these men had been sent
to man the forts of the Dardanelles and Bosphorus. But Limpus also
reported that even Djemal Pasha was still reluctant to see Turkey committed to Germany, and resented the dominance of Enver over the
navy as well as the army. 'A revolt against German domination,' Limpus continued, 'may come at any moment. The only question is—have
the Germans got too firm a grip to be ousted? Personally I think not.'

[1] Eleutherios Venizelos, 1864–1936. Prime Minister of Greece, 1910–15. Forced to resign
by King Constantine, May 1915. Prime Minister for the second time, August to October
1915. Subsequently Prime Minister 1917–20, 1924, 1928–32 and 1933.

But on September 9, while Limpus' letter was on its way to London, Churchill, who believed the German grip to be absolute, sent him a telegram bringing his mission to an end:

Now that the Turkish Navy is paralysed by German intrigues Admiralty consider your mission at an end. You and your Officers have laboured faithfully and well to raise the efficiency of the Turkish Navy to a level which would make it an effective weapon of war. It is not your fault that these efforts have not been crowned with success. You have borne with patience and loyalty the continued disappointments of your task, and I am glad now to be able to release you from a position which was ceasing to be in accordance with what is due to the Royal Navy.

Churchill asked Limpus to show this telegram to Djemal. Despite its active search for allies in a war against Turkey, the British Government still hoped that Turkish neutrality might be preserved. Even Churchill believed that the threatened withdrawal of the naval mission might strengthen the arguments of the Turkish neutralists. Unknown to the British, Enver himself had become alarmed at Germany's eagerness to push Turkey into war, and on September 8 he refused a German request to close the Dardanelles to all Allied shipping. Arguing that Turkish neutrality could still be preserved, Mallet persuaded Grey that Limpus, whose expert knowledge of Turkish naval affairs, and special acquaintance with the defences of the Dardanelles would make him a most effective commander against Turkey, ought not, if withdrawn, to be put in charge of the British naval forces in the eastern Mediterranean. Mallet wanted Limpus to go instead to Malta. Such a peaceful action, Mallet believed, would convince the Turks that Britain still wanted peace. Churchill was exceedingly angry at the decision not to allow Limpus to command the eastern Mediterranean forces. On September 11 he wrote in protest to Grey:

Sir Edward Grey,
The First Sea Lord independently informed me that he regarded Limpus' position as an insult to the British Navy. Mallet said that this was the right time of all others for the withdrawal of the mission. Orders have been given accordingly with yr full approval. Now it appears that Turkey not only can injure our whole naval position by a flagrant breach of neutrality about the Goeben, but also is to have a veto on Admiralty appointments; & the squadron wh occupies so critical a station at the present time is to go without a Commander. Mallet's telegram is a tangle of contradictions. He must indeed be hard up for arguments against us when he complains of our 'letting

the Goeben escape'. I do not myself believe that the withdrawal of the mission, the delivery of my message, & the appearance of the Admiral in command of the Meditn Sqn, wd have any other effect, than to cow and embarrass the Turks.

If Mallet thinks he is dealing with a Govt amenable to argument, persuasion, & proof of good faith, he is dreaming. Factions are struggling for ascendancy, & are only actuated by considerations of force & fear, & only restrained by their great doubt as to who is going to win in Europe. The right course wd be to have presented my message to the Minister of Marine as I originally intended, when I believed, and still believe they wd have implored Adl Limpus to remain.

Nothing appeals to the Turkish Govt but force; & they will continue to kick those who they think are unable or unwilling to use it against them. You must decide. There is no question of any other appt for Limpus. He never wd have got this chance but for the fact that he was the only man on the spot, & that it was urgently necessary to fill the place. If he is to be vetoed, another Admiral must go from home at once. In case you take Mallet's view, the mission had better remain until the Germans decide to make it prisoner of war. I shall not say any more.

WSC

Grey would not allow Limpus to raise his flag at the Dardanelles. Under the influence of Mallet's telegrams, he still believed that it might be possible to reach agreement with the Turks. Churchill, conscious of the gravity of the mounting German influence at Constantinople, doubted whether Turkey could preserve its neutrality much longer. On September 16 he wrote again to Grey:

I must repeat that grave injury has been done to our naval position by the flagrant violations of neutrality committed by the Turks. The British naval mission was ordered off the ships entrusted to them & has now after many humiliations resigned.

The appointment of a German C in C of the Turkish Fleet as well as of the Turkish army may not lead directly to war; but the whole attitude of Turkey has been & still is to look for a chance of striking at us if she dares.

We ought to have absolute freedom to deal with her at the peace as the general convenience & interests of the allies require. I earnestly trust that freedom will not be compromised.

Believing war with Turkey to be inevitable, Churchill realized the importance of an Anglo-Greek alliance, and wanted British foreign policy to become more sympathetic to Greece. On September 9 he had received a reply to the telegram which he had sent to Admiral Kerr.

The Admiral reported on his discussions with the Greek General Staff:

> They are of opinion, and I agree, that force at disposal of Greece is sufficient to take Gallipoli if Bulgaria does not attack Greece. It is not sufficient guarantee for Bulgaria to undertake to remain neutral. They will not trust her unless she also attacks Turkey at the same time with all her force.
>
> The plan for taking the Straits of the Dardanelles is ready if above conditions obtain.
>
> Greece has sufficient transports to convey troops. Assistance of a British squadron of two battle-cruisers, one armoured cruiser, three light cruisers and flotilla of destroyers and mine-sweepers will be needed.

Churchill was stimulated by the implications of Kerr's telegram. The thought of action against Turkey excited him. He no longer shared Grey's hope that a peaceful settlement was still possible. He therefore acted independently, justifying his more hostile approach by reference to the Cabinet decision of September 2 to sink Turkish ships if they issued from the Dardanelles. Bowing to Grey's veto on Limpus, he appointed Vice-Admiral Carden[1] to command the squadron at the Dardanelles; but his first instructions to Carden were not at all in the spirit of Grey's advice. On September 21 Churchill telegraphed to Carden:

> Assume command of the squadron off Dardanelles. Your sole duty is to sink Goeben & Breslau, no matter what flag they fly, if they come out of Dardanelles. We are not at war with Turkey but German Admiral Souchon is now C in C Turkish Navy and Germans are controlling and largely manning it. Turks have been told that any Turkish ships which come out with Goeben & Breslau will equally be attacked by us. You are authorized to act accordingly without further declaration or parley. You must deal at yr discretion with any minor Turkish war vessel which may come out alone from Dardanelles, either ordering her back or allowing her to proceed as you may think fit, remembering that we do not want to pick quarrel with Turkey unless her hostile intention is clear.
>
> Indomitable will be diverted from convoy off Crete, & ordered to join yr squadron. French C in C has been requested to send 2 battleships of Patrie class to reinforce yr flag.

---

[1] Sackville Hamilton Carden, 1857–1930. Entered Navy, 1870. Rear-Admiral, 1908. Admiral Superintendent, Malta Dockyard, 1912–14. Vice-Admiral in command of the Anglo-French Squadrons in the Eastern Mediterranean, and at the Dardanelles, 20 September 1914 to 15 March 1915, when ill-health forced him to retire. Knighted, 1916. Admiral, 1917.

Grey was still influenced by the reports from Mallet which arrived daily. The Ambassador continued to insist, as he said in his telegram of September 22, 'that a majority is against war and that peace party is gaining strength'. Believing this to be untrue, Churchill returned this extract from Mallet's telegram to Grey, with yet another strong personal appeal:

My dear Grey,

I must write you a line about Turkey. Poor Mallet's telegrams are in the main mere repetitions of the paragraph attached. We are suffering very seriously from Turkish hostility. Our whole Mediterranean Fleet is tied to the Dardanelles. We are daily trying to buy Turkish neutrality by promises and concessions. Meanwhile the German grip on Turkey tightens and all preparations for war go steadily forward. But all this would in itself be of minor consequence but for the fact that in our attempt to placate Turkey we are crippling our policy in the Balkans.

I am not suggesting that we should take aggressive action against Turkey or declare war on her ourselves, but we ought from now to make arrangements with the Balkan States, particularly Bulgaria, without regard to the interests or integrity of Turkey. The Bulgarians ought to regain the Turkish territory they lost in the second Balkan War, and we ought to tell them that if they join with Roumania, Greece, and Servia in the attack upon Austria and Germany, the allied powers will see that they get this territory at the peace. We always said that Adrianople should never fall back into Turkish hands and the strongest possible remonstrances were addressed to the Porte by you at the time. There is therefore nothing wrong or inconsistent in our adopting this position. If we win the war we shall be quite strong enough to secure this territory for Bulgaria, and Turkey's conduct to us with repeated breaches of neutrality would release us from any need of considering her European interests.

Like you, I sympathise deeply with Mallet in the futile and thankless task on which he is engaged. I do not know what the result will be but I am sure it is not worth while sacrificing the bold and decisive alternative of throwing in our lot frankly with the Christian States of the Balkans to get the kind of neutrality which the Turks have been giving us, and for which we are even asked to pay and be grateful. The whole tone of the telegrams from Roumania and Bulgaria are hopeful. I do most earnestly beg you not to be diverted from the highway of sound policy in this part of the world, both during the war and at the settlement, by wanderings into the labyrinth of Turkish duplicity and intrigue. All I am asking is that the interests and integrity of Turkey shall no longer be considered by you in any efforts which are made to secure common action among the Christian Balkan States.

At a Cabinet meeting held on September 23, Churchill and Kitchener argued out what policy ought to be adopted towards the Turks.

Churchill wanted Britain to make a specific offer to Bulgaria of the Turkish fortress of Adrianople, in return for immediate Bulgarian participation should war break out between Britain and Turkey. Kitchener wrote to Churchill in a note passed across the Cabinet table:

I agree that Turkey is behaving so disgracefully that she ought to be informed we shall not forget it after the war is over—I am doubtful whether we should tell Bulgaria that she shall have Adrianople after the war—This would definitely tie us down to action that might be unpleasant to carry out —I quite agree Turkey should be punished but I would not say definitely how this is to be done—

Churchill replied: 'I don't want vengeance *after* the show is over—but *aid* of a Balkan confedn now.' Kitchener doubted if Churchill's proposed offer would be enough as, in his opinion, 'they want Servian land & Greek'. Churchill did not disagree. 'Well,' he reiterated, 'all I ask for is no more consideration for Turkish interests if we can get any advantage with Bulgaria.' To which Kitchener noted, 'I agree'. In his Cabinet letter to George V, Asquith reported on the differing views, and on Grey's determined attitude:

A long conversation took place on the unsatisfactory situation in Turkey, Mr Churchill, Mr Masterman & others expressing a strong opinion that as Turkey was behaving so badly, we ought at once to free ourselves from any obligation as to her future, and make common cause with the Balkan States. Lord Kitchener repeated his opinion that the important thing is to win over Roumania, and with that object induce Russia to offer her the restoration of Bessarabia. In the end a proposal of Sir E. Grey was adopted that he should instruct Sir L. Mallet to inform the Porte, that while not contemplating for the moment hostile measures, we are grievously dissatisfied with the recent action of the Turkish Government, which has resulted in placing Constantinople under German, and no longer under Turkish control. Unless the 'peace party' soon succeeds in getting the upperhand we shall be compelled to adopt an attitude of hostility & to take measures accordingly.

Throughout the last two weeks of September the Turkish leaders hesitated to commit their country to war. This was the testing time for the new Turkey. Armenians, Greeks and Arabs all clamoured for greater privileges and dreamed of independence. The Russians wanted to expand their control to Constantinople, anxious as always for an ice-free outlet into the Mediterranean which would not depend upon the Turkish power to close the Dardanelles. The Greeks and Bulgarians, who had won their independence from Turkey by force of arms over the previous fifty years, still nursed territorial ambitions at Turkey's expense, and shared with Russia the desire to control at least some part of the Gallipoli Peninsula. If Turkey were to make the wrong decision, its large Empire, already much reduced since the apogee of Ottoman rule three hundred years before, might disintegrate altogether. After the war Djemal Pasha recorded, in *Memories of a Turkish Statesman*, how he and his colleagues sensed even then what war might mean:

> If the English, French, and Russians, who knew perfectly well that we had not a single man at the Dardanelles, in Constantinople, or on the Russian frontier, made a sudden attack on the Dardanelles and the Bosphorus, simultaneously advanced on Erzerum, and after occupying Constantinople and Erzerum approached the interior of Anatolia through Sivas, our army would be unable to complete its mobilisation during the war, and the downfall of the Ottoman Empire would be decreed at the very outset.

Admiral Limpus had reported to Churchill at length on how the senior officers in the Turkish Navy shared Djemal's fears in heightened form. Nor was the Turkish Army immune from doubts, despite the strong German influence exerted by the German military mission. The Turkish military attaché in Sofia, Mustafa Kemal,[1] had protested to Enver about the dangers to Turkey if she followed too closely a German-dictated policy. But Enver had been so impressed by German power that he denied the possibility of a German defeat.

Throughout September the Dardanelles had been busy with Allied merchant shipping. Despite the German influence in Constantinople, there was no interference with this trade. At German insistence, mines were laid across the Narrows, but a small channel was left open and the flow of merchant shipping was undiminished. Ships took on a special pilot at Chanak to sail through the mined areas. Passage through the Dardanelles was essential to Russia. Only by the export of wheat could Russia build up a favourable trade balance by which arms and ammunitions could be bought from Britain, and war debts paid off.

On September 27, as a direct consequence of the Cabinet decision of September 2 to prevent any Turkish ships from leaving the Dardanelles, Vice-Admiral Carden's squadron stopped and examined a Turkish torpedo boat which wished to enter the Aegean. German sailors were

[1] Mustafa Kemal, 1881–1938. Served in the Libyan and Balkan campaigns, 1911–13. Military Attaché in Sofia, 1913–14. Served at Gallipoli, 1915, in the Caucasus, 1916, and in Syria, 1917. Assumed command of the Turkish national movement, 1919. First President of the Turkish Republic from 1922 until his death. Known as Atatürk.

found on board, a clear breach of Turkish neutrality. The boat was therefore ordered to turn back. The German officer in charge of the fortifications at the Dardanelles, Colonel Weber,[1] issued immediate orders to seal the waterway. The minefields across the Straits were completed by September 29. Thenceforth, despite those Treaty obligations intended to secure permanent use of the Straits to all nations not at war, the Dardanelles were closed. Russia lost her one ice-free link with the West. British military supplies could no longer reach Russia except by the hazardous northern route to Archangel.[2] Russian wheat, upon which that Empire depended for so much of its foreign income, could no longer be exported to its world markets. But, despite this serious challenge, the Allied powers could not afford to retaliate. The Germans had been checked at the Marne and Paris saved; but the outcome of the battle on the western front was still uncertain. It was in the forts surrounding Antwerp, and on the low hills to the east of Ypres, that the decisive action seemed to turn during early October. The Turks also welcomed the respite. Enver, Talaat, Djemal and Djavid continued to argue the respective merits of neutrality and intervention.

On October 21, nearly two months after Noel Buxton had set off for the Balkans, he sent two telegrams from Bucharest outlining the results of his enquiries. In the first, to Grey, he set out the territorial demands which each Balkan State would require before committing itself to the Allied cause. In particular he wanted a statement by the Allies that they would support Bulgaria's claims to parts of Serbian Macedonia, Serbia to be compensated for the loss of this territory by much larger gains at Austria's expense. Buxton sent his second telegram direct to Churchill:

With reference to idea of military scheme for Balkan States which you asked me to work for, situation [is] Roumanian action hitherto obstructed by late King's wishes now being possible. Only remaining difficulties are fear of Bulgaria and uncertainty of European situation. . . . Public opinion would be most powerfully affected by a lead from outside especially from England. I beg to suggest utterance by yourself expanding your recent speech would

[1] Erich Weber, 1860–1933. Entered German Army 1878. Colonel, 1913. Inspector-General of Corps of Engineers and Pioneers, German Military Mission Constantinople, 1914. Appointed to command the Turkish defences at the Dardanelles, August 1914. Ordered the closure of the Straits, September 1914. Major-General, April 1915. Commanded the Turkish forces south of Achi Baba during the second battle of Krithia, 4–10 May 1915. Lieutenant-General, June 1920.

[2] Russia was heavily dependent upon British supplies; between August 1914 and October 1917 she bought 3,000 million rounds of ammunition, $8\frac{1}{2}$ million hand grenades, 1 million rifles, 200,000 tons of explosives, 27,000 machine guns, nearly 1,000 aeroplanes and aeroplane engines and 750 heavy and medium guns.

greatly help to secure co-operation and it would be reported verbatim. All steps in support of your policy at Sofia are believed to be deprecated by our Government even when desired by France and Russia.

Churchill received this telegram on the morning of October 23, and wrote at once to Grey: 'I shd like to talk to you about this. I am vy unhappy about our getting into war with Turkey without having Greece as an ally. This was the least to be hoped for. Surely it is not too late.' Grey replied two days later: 'Glad to discuss when we meet'; and the two men met that evening. But Grey advised Churchill against making any such open statement of support for Balkan ambitions.

On October 23 the Turkish puzzle became more complex. That day the Cabinet discussed detailed military intelligence reports which suggested that the Turks were planning an invasion of Egypt. If true, this was a sign of a serious development in Turkish policy which no one had expected. At the Cabinet meeting on October 28 Grey was in an uncompromising mood. Like Churchill, he no longer regarded Turkey as a genuine neutral. On a sheet of 10 Downing Street notepaper he drafted a blunt telegram to Mallet:

It is reported that four Turkish gunboats are intending to proceed from Alexandretta.

You should warn Turkish Government that, as long as German officers remain on 'Goeben' and 'Breslau' and Turkish fleet is practically under German control, we must regard movement of Turkish ships as having a hostile intention, and should Turkish gunboats proceed to sea we must in self defence stop them.

As soon as Turkish Government carry out their promise respecting German crews and officers and observe the laws of neutrality with regard to 'Goeben' and 'Breslau' and free the Turkish fleet from German control, we shall regard Turkish ships as neutral, but till then we must protect ourselves against any movements that threaten us.

Churchill approved Grey's tone, and initialled the telegram. Whether it was read to the Cabinet is not known. But the Cabinet were not convinced that Turkey could be threatened. It seemed more likely that evidence of German successes on the western front would be a strong argument for war against Britain, and that British threats would be dismissed as bluff. One of the reasons which influenced Ministers to agree to suppress all reference to the sinking of the *Audacious* was their belief that if news of this disaster were made public, it might influence the Turks to join an obviously victorious Germany. The Cabinet's caution came too late. At the very moment when the discussion at 10

Downing Street focused upon means of keeping Turkey out of the war, a stealthy but irrevocable decision was being taken at Constantinople. Without consulting his colleagues, Enver agreed to the German request that the *Goeben* and the *Breslau* steam into the Black Sea.

On the morning of Thursday October 29 the *Goeben* and *Breslau*, commanded by Admiral Souchon but flying the Turkish flag, bombarded the Russian Black Sea ports of Odessa, Nikolaev and Sevastopol. Later that day Grey telegraphed to Mallet that unless the Turks made 'immediate reparation to Russia', he did not see how war could be avoided; but he assured the Ambassador that Britain would not 'take the first step'. On October 30, however, he sent Mallet an ultimatum for transmission to the Turks, demanding the dismissal of the German military and naval missions and the removal from the *Goeben* and *Breslau* of all German personnel within twelve hours. If this was refused, Mallet was instructed to 'ask for your passports and leave Constantinople with the staff of the Embassy'.

When the Cabinet met on October 30, fears of an imminent Turkish attack on Egypt were still uppermost in Ministers' minds. Steps were accordingly authorized, as J. A. Pease recorded in his diary, 'to hold or fire on Turkish gunboats outside Alexandria and prevent their passing into Red Sea'. But the Cabinet saw no reason for a formal declaration of war. They preferred, Asquith reported to George V, 'to wait for the developments of the next few days before taking ourselves, or suggesting to other powers, a new departure'. Churchill wanted an immediate demonstration of British power. That day he asked Lord Fisher—who had become First Sea Lord on the previous day—to enquire of Sir Edmond Slade[1] 'his opinion on the possibility & advisability of a bombardment of the sea face forts of the Dardanelles'. In his letter Churchill explained to Fisher: 'It is a good thing to give a prompt blow.'

Later that day Slade sent Churchill a short plan of bombardment. He advised against a sustained bombardment of the forts, which, he wrote, offered 'very little prospect of obtaining any effect commensurate with the risk to the ships'. But he added: 'A little target practice from 15 to 12 thousand yards might be useful.' Churchill underlined this sentence in red. Slade also advised sending a ship to the Turkish port of Akaba, 'to shell the wells and the stores said to be collected there'; Churchill noted on Slade's memorandum that the light cruiser *Minerva*

[1] Edmond John Warre Slade, 1859–1928. Entered Navy, 1872. Director of Naval Intelligence, 1907–8. Commander-in-Chief, East Indies, 1909–12. Knighted, 1911. Vice-Admiral, 1914. On Special Service in connection with Oil Fuel Supplies, 1912–14. Admiralty-nominated Director, Anglo-Persian Oil Company, 1914. Chairman, Diversion of Shipping Committee, 1916. Admiral, 1917.

should be allocated for this task, and that night her Captain, Percival Warleigh,[1] was ordered to sail from the Red Sea to the Gulf of Akaba, and to await further instructions. On October 31 Asquith sent Venetia Stanley an account of the situation:

The Turk has now under German pressure taken a hand, and interesting developments ought to follow. Greece is quite likely to come in, & it will become increasingly hard for Italy & Roumania to keep aloof. Few things wd give me greater pleasure than to see the Turkish Empire finally disappear from Europe, & Constantinople either become Russian (which I think is its proper destiny) or if that is impossible neutralised and made a free port.

Sir Louis Mallet telegraphed from Constantinople on October 31 pleading against retaliation for the bombardment of the Russian ports. He believed that it was still not too late for the anti-German Ministers in the Turkish Government to prevail. But Grey wanted British action to be in accordance with Russian policy, and once Russian cities were under bombardment there could for him be no doubt what action Britain should take. France, likewise, could not hesitate under the terms of her formal alliance with Russia. Grey therefore ordered Mallet to leave Constantinople.

Neither the Cabinet, nor any inner conclave of Ministers, had formally decided on war with Turkey on October 31. But Churchill was convinced that it was only a question of hours before war would be declared. 'We ought to have a means of striking them ready prepared,' he wrote to Fisher that morning. Fisher at once minuted to Oliver: 'Have we anything prepared?' No plans for a bombardment could be found at the Admiralty, beyond Slade's brief outline, hurriedly put together on the previous day. Nevertheless, with the British 'ultimatum' having expired at noon, Churchill felt free to take independent action. At five o'clock that afternoon he telegraphed to Carden: 'Commence hostilities at once against Turkey.' Carden made no immediate move; he had no instructions as to what he should do, nor had any plans been prepared in advance. No act of war therefore took place that evening. But in a 'Secret & Pressing' note Sir Graham Greene wrote to Sir Arthur Nicolson: 'I am commanded by My Lords Commissioners of the Admiralty to acquaint you, for the information of the Secretary of State for Foreign Affairs, that orders have today been given to His Majesty's Fleet to commence hostilities against Turkey.'

Just before midnight on October 31 the Foreign Office issued an

---

[1] Percival Henry Warleigh, 1873–1933. Entered Navy, 1886. Captain, 1913. Placed in command of HMS *Minerva*, 4 August 1914. Retired with the rank of Captain, 1922.

announcement to the Press Bureau. It made no reference to a state of war existing between Britain and Turkey, but declared boldly that 'the British Gvt must take whatever action is required to protect British interests, British territory, and also Egypt from attacks that have been made and are threatened'. Grey and Churchill were both convinced that British interests had been threatened already; Grey because during the day he had received reports that the British Consul at Basra[1] and several British subjects there had been arrested by the Turks; Churchill because the Turks were believed to be laying mines off the coast of Sinai, near the port of Akaba, and because a large Turkish yacht carrying mines was reported to be about to set sail from Smyrna harbour.

On November 1 Grey, who had already, during October, expressed support for Russian claims to Constantinople, telegraphed to Buchanan[2] in Petrograd a secret message for the Russian Government. 'Turkey has shown herself incorrigible and impossible,' he declared, 'and deserves and should receive no consideration.' Britain, Grey added, gave up 'all plea' for consideration of Turkish territorial integrity. That day, on Churchill's instructions, the Turkish yacht in Smyrna harbour was challenged by two British destroyers, *Wolverine* and *Scorpion*,[3] and blew herself up, together with her mines. The destroyers finished the work of destruction which the Turks had begun, and the ship was sunk.

On November 2 the *Minerva* reached Akaba. The small Turkish garrison was asked to surrender, but refused. Captain Warleigh thereupon bombarded the fort, the post office and several government buildings. Later he sent a landing party ashore, and the post office was destroyed. The inhabitants of the town had fled, as had the garrison. The sailors, having posted a proclamation assuring the absent citizens that they were in no danger, returned to their ship. There had been no British or Turkish casualties. 'Tewfik should be told tomorrow,' Grey minuted to Nicolson, 'that the only way to stop further hostilities is to inform his Govn't to send away the German missions.'

Churchill did not regard the actions at Smyrna and Akaba as of great

[1] Francis Edward Crow, 1863–1939. Entered Consular Service, 1885. Consul, Basra, 1903–14. Arrested by the Turkish authorities at Basra, October 1914. Employed at the Foreign Office London, November 1914–August 1919. Consul-General, Isaphan, 1919–23; Salonica, 1923–27.

[2] George William Buchanan, 1854–1924. Entered Diplomatic Service, 1882. Knighted, 1905. Ambassador in Petrograd, 1910–18; in Rome, 1919–21.

[3] The Captain of the *Scorpion*, Lieutenant Andrew Browne Cunningham (1883–1963), was later Commander-in-Chief, Mediterranean, 1939–42; First Sea Lord and Chief of Staff, 1943–6; Admiral of the Fleet, 1943; created Viscount Cunningham of Hyndhope, 1946. The Captain of the *Wolverine*, Commander Osmond James Prentis (1889–1915), was killed in action at the Dardanelles, 28 April 1915.

significance. It was at the Dardanelles, he believed, that Britain could show most clearly its power to harm Turkey. On November 2, he therefore telegraphed, with Fisher's approval, to Carden:

Without risking the ships demonstration is to be made by bombardment on the earliest suitable day by your armoured ships and the two French battleships against the forts at the entrance of the Dardanelles at a range of 14,000 to 12,000 yards. Ships should keep under way approaching as soon after daylight as possible retirements should be made before fire from the forts becomes effective. Ships' guns should outrange older guns mounted in the forts.

On November 3, in accordance with Churchill's instructions, Carden's squadron, assisted by two French ships, bombarded the outer forts on either side of the Dardanelles for a period of ten minutes and at a range of slightly more than seven miles. A shot which hit the magazine of the fort at Sedd-el-Bahr destroyed almost all its heavy guns. Admiralty critics of the bombardment, and also Lloyd George, later declared that it alerted the Turks, and caused them to move their main defences closer to Chanak, in the greater security of the Narrows. But no serious work was done on the Turkish fortifications between this initial bombardment and the Allied attack over four months later. The Dardanelles was so obvious a point of attack for any enemy wishing to crush Turkey that it did not need a brief Allied bombardment to stress the importance of defending this one sea access to Constantinople. The German fortifications experts who had already arrived at the Dardanelles in September and October 1914 had been sent for the specific purpose of strengthening its land defences. They needed no warning from the Allies of where the major attack was likely to come. The principal Turkish problem was a severe shortage of guns, mines and ammunition: but even before the Allied bombardment of the outer forts the majority of all supplies reaching Turkey was sent direct to the Dardanelles. The installation of three torpedo tubes at Kilid Bahr was not the result of the bombardment of November 3, but of a suggestion which Limpus himself had made while head of the naval mission, responsible, among his duties, for advising on the naval defences of the Dardanelles.

On the morning of November 4 Britain had still not declared war on Turkey. 'We do not propose to issue declaration of war at once,' Grey telegraphed to the acting High Commissioner in Egypt, Milne Cheetham,[1] 'but Turkish Ambassador here is being told that in view of

---

[1] Milne Cheetham, 1869–1938. Entered Diplomatic Service, 1894. Counsellor of Embassy, Cairo, 1911–19. Chargé d'Affaires, Cairo, in Kitchener's absence, 1914. Knighted, 1915. Minister to Peru and Ecuador, 1919–20; to France, 1921–2; to Switzerland, 1922–4; to Greece, 1924–6; to Denmark, 1926–8.

hostile Turkish preparations and forcible detention of British consul and subjects at Basrah, as well as of what has happened in Black Sea, I must give him his passports and continue to take what measures are necessary for our protection and that of Egypt, unless he can satisfy us that German missions at Constantinople will be dismissed.'

The Cabinet met later that morning. They could not ignore the facts: the *Wolverine* and *Scorpion* had sunk a Turkish ship in Smyrna harbour; the *Minerva* had destroyed public buildings in the Turkish port of Akaba; Admiral Carden had bombarded the outer forts of Turkey's main sea defences at the Dardanelles. Britain had clearly been making war on Turkey for almost forty-eight hours. 'The Cabinet came to the conclusion,' Asquith reported to George V, 'that a formal declaration of war against Turkey could no longer be postponed.' On the following day, November 5, Sir Arthur Nicolson sent a note to Sir Graham Greene, informing him 'that a state of war exists between Great Britain and Turkey'. The note was headed 'URGENT'. Greene commented on it, before circulating it to the Sea Lords: 'It is not known why the F.O. have thought it necessary to send out this at this date.' Britain and Turkey were at war. The Cabinet had been little consulted, the Admiralty and Foreign Office seeming to regard hostilities against Turkey as mere inter-departmental business. Power had passed from the twenty men at the Cabinet table to the heads of two departments. Even Kitchener seemed little concerned. Asquith made no protest; he did not regard the idea of a third enemy with alarm. Like Grey and Churchill, who had from the start taken the initiative, he saw no insuperable difficulties in defeating Turkey, and much advantage to the Allies in Turkey's defeat. To Venetia Stanley, if not his Cabinet colleagues, he had revealed his hopes that with Britain and Turkey at war, Italy, Greece and Rumania—three neutral powers—would be tempted to join the forces of the triple entente. The Turks had been hustled into war. 'I don't mind—' Margot Asquith wrote in her diary on November 9, 'I *loathe* the Turk and really hope that he will be wiped out of Europe. Germany blackmailed Turkey till it went over but except for threatening Egypt I doubt if it will bother us much.'

The effects of the bombardment of November 3 were studied by Admiral Sir Henry Jackson early in the New Year, and used by him to form the basis of plans for a major naval assault. The damage done to the fort at Sedd-el-Bahr was never repaired. No one at the Admiralty questioned the main implication of the bombardment, which was that naval guns were capable of demolishing land forts. Since the outbreak of war many conventional theories and expectations of war had been challenged. 'Like most other people,' Churchill told the Dardanelles Commissioners in 1916, 'I had held the opinion that the days of forcing the Dardanelles were over; and I had even recorded this opinion in a Cabinet paper in 1911.[1] But this war had brought many surprises. We had seen fortresses reputed throughout Europe to be impregnable collapsing after a few days' attack by field armies without a regular siege.'

Admiral Oliver had also witnessed, and been impressed by, the impact of German guns on the massive forts at Antwerp only a month earlier. Following the Dardanelles bombardment of November 3, Churchill began discussions with Fisher, Jackson and Oliver on the best method of forcing the Dardanelles, using some of the many old battleships which, while of no value to Jellicoe and the Grand Fleet, could still fire their guns against a static land target, and fight a weak naval power like Turkey, possessing no dreadnoughts—except those already seized by the British Government. Churchill was convinced that the Dardanelles was the only point in Turkey at which a decisive action could be fought. At the first meeting of the newly formed War Council on November 25, Churchill had an opportunity to express his conviction. Grave news had come from Egypt. Military Intelligence reports made it clear that a large Turkish army was indeed moving south through Palestine and would soon be in a position to attack the Suez Canal. Hankey's notes recorded in detail the subsequent discussion:

MR CHURCHILL suggested that the ideal method of defending Egypt was by an attack on the Gallipoli Peninsula. This, if successful, would give us control of the Dardanelles, and we could dictate terms at Constantinople. This, however, was a very difficult operation requiring a large force. If it was considered impracticable, it appeared worth while to assemble transports and horse boats at Malta or Alexandria, and to make a feint at Gallipoli, conveying the impression that we intended to land there. Our real point of attack might be Haifa, or some point on the Syrian coast. The Committee of Imperial Defence in 1909 had recommended that a serious invasion of Egypt could best be met by a landing at Haifa.

The discussion turned upon whether sufficient ships were available to assemble a large force, as Churchill wished. Fisher intervened in the discussion to ask 'whether Greece might not perhaps undertake an attack on Gallipoli on behalf of the Allies'. Grey then explained some-

---

[1] In a memorandum printed for the Cabinet on 15 March 1911, as part of his argument against the need for a strong British naval force in the Mediterranean, Churchill had written: '. . . it is no longer possible to force the Dardanelles . . . nobody would expose a modern fleet to such perils.'

thing of the complexities of Balkan diplomacy. The King of Greece[1] had refused to endorse his Prime Minister's unconditional offer of sixty thousand Greek troops for such an attack. The hostility of Bulgaria and Serbia towards Greece 'held out', said Grey, 'no hopes of an accommodation between the several Balkan States', and had led him to the conclusion that Britain ought not to count on Greek co-operation. The early hopes of Greek participation were clearly illusory. Henceforth Greek policy veered between the pro-Allied passions of the Prime Minister, Venizelos, and the pro-German inclinations of King Constantine,[1] whose wife Sophie[2] was a sister of the Kaiser.

At the War Council Churchill had stressed the need for a large military force in any operations against the Dardanelles. On November 30 Oliver suggested that troop transport should be kept in Egypt sufficient to transport a division of troops to the Dardanelles should it become possible to assemble the men in future. Churchill immediately passed on this request to Kitchener with the note: 'Had we not better keep enough transports congregated for 40,000 men, or shall we disperse them ready to assemble at short (? what) notice?' Kitchener minuted in reply: 'I will give Admiralty full notice. I do not think transports need be detailed in Egypt yet.'

The first military action taken against Turkey came at the suggestion, not of the Admiralty, but of the Viceroy of India, Lord Hardinge. On November 7, on Hardinge's orders, the Indian Government landed a military force at Fao, at the head of the Persian Gulf, occupied the Persian oilfields near Ahwaz, and advanced on the Turkish town of Basra, which was captured on November 22. An Indian Army officer, Major Brownlow,[3] was appointed British Military Governor at Basra, and took up residence in what had been the German Consulate. On December 7 British control of the area was completed with the surrender of the Turkish garrison of over a thousand men at Kurna, at the confluence of the Tigris and the Euphrates. In this first month of war with Turkey five British and sixty Indian soldiers had been killed; there were at least three hundred Turkish dead.

[1] Constantine, 1868–1923. Became King of Greece in 1913, when he was created a Field-Marshal in the German Army. Vetoed Greek co-operation in the Dardanelles campaign, 1915. Refused to help the Allied Army at Salonika, 1916–17. Forced to leave Greece by the Allies, 1917. In exile, 1917–20. Returned as King, 1920. Abdicated after a military revolt, 1922.

[2] Sophie, Princess of Prussia, 1870–1932. A granddaughter of Queen Victoria; George V was her first cousin. She married Constantine in 1889. Duchess of Sparta, 1899–1913; Queen, 1913–22.

[3] D'Arcy Charles Brownlow, 1869–1938. Entered the Indian Army, 1891. Major, 1907. Military Governor of Basra, 1914–15. Lieutenant-Colonel, 1915. Brigadier-General, Base Commandant, Mesopotamia, 1916–19.

On December 11 the Admiralty authorized further action against Turkey. The Commander of the East Indies station, Sir Richard Peirse,[1] who had transferred his flag to the Suez Canal at the beginning of the month, was instructed to watch the Turkish Syrian ports and to harass all Turkish troops movements along the coast. Churchill and Kitchener hoped to be able, by use of a small naval force, to interrupt any Turkish plans to transfer troops from Anatolia to Sinai, where they could threaten the Suez Canal and Egypt. Peirse detailed the light cruiser *Doris*, commanded by Captain Larken,[2] to carry out the Admiralty's instructions. On December 18 Larken arrived off Alexandretta; that night a party of sailors went ashore and cut the railway line from Anatolia. An hour later a train coming from the north was derailed. On the following morning Larken ordered a second landing, and a railway bridge was destroyed. By flag of truce, he entered into direct negotiations with the local Turkish authorities. On December 20, under threat of bombardment from the *Doris'* 6-inch guns, the Turkish authorities agreed to blow up their two railway engines and several military stores. Having no explosives, they asked Larken to send some of his own ashore. Larken agreed; and while the Turks watched, British sailors laid the explosive charges. The Turks then supervised the actual destruction, under the beam of the *Doris'* searchlights. Later that evening the *Doris* sailed away.

This incident, with its comic co-operation between attacker and attacked, appeared proof that the Turks were not serious opponents, and encouraged the hope that no great military effort would be needed to force Turkey out of the war. In September 1916 Churchill told the Dardanelles Commissioners:

. . . the incident is not without its significance, because it had helped to form the opinion in our mind as to the degree of resistance which might in all circumstances be expected from Turkey. What kind of Turk was this we were fighting? . . . I must say that it was always in my mind that we were not dealing with a thoroughly efficient military power, and that it was quite possible that we could get into parley with them.

[1] Richard Henry Peirse, 1860–1940. Entered Navy, 1873. Vice-Admiral Commanding-in-Chief, East Indies Station, 1913–16. Knighted, 1914. Commanded Allied Naval Forces on the Suez Canal, 1914–16. Naval member, Board of Invention and Research, 1916–18. Admiral, 1918.

[2] Frank Larken, 1875–1953. Entered Navy, 1889. Lieutenant, Naval Intelligence Department, 1910. Captain commanding the light cruiser *Doris*, 1914–15. Rear-Admiral commanding the 2nd Cruiser Squadron, Atlantic Fleet, 1927–9. Vice-Admiral commanding the Reserve Fleet, 1930–1. Knighted, 1932. Admiral, 1933.

British forces had bombarded one extremity of the Turkish Empire and occupied another. They had also landed on the coast of Syria and persuaded the Turks to co-operate in their anti-Turkish activities. These actions were not followed up. The troops at Basra entrenched themselves on the edge of the desert, and made no attempt to advance up either the Tigris or the Euphrates, whose junction they controlled. No further landings were made on the Syrian coast. The failure of Greece to produce its sixty thousand men brought to an end all ministerial discussions of occupying the Gallipoli Peninsula and capturing Constantinople. Impressed though Churchill had been about the effect of guns on forts, he had no reason to believe that the Dardanelles could be forced by ships alone. Easy though the landings at Alexandretta had been, the number of troops required for a landing of significance, particularly on the Gallipoli Peninsula, remained a matter for speculation and study. Churchill himself had already mentioned three different figures essential for success at Gallipoli, 60,000, 50,000 and 40,000. But throughout December, with no troops at all available, both the Dardanelles and the Gallipoli Peninsula were left unmolested. This did not please Churchill. 'His volatile mind,' Asquith wrote to Venetia Stanley on December 5, 'is at present set on Turkey & Bulgaria, & he wants to organise a heroic adventure against Gallipoli and the Dardanelles: to wh I am altogether opposed. . . .'

7

'Our troops are rotting'

THROUGHOUT November the military situation in Europe grew daily worse for the Allied cause. The British succeeded in stabilizing the front line at Ypres only at tremendous cost. In the east, Russia's swift initial advances were halted; at the Battle of Tannenberg at the end of August the Germans had asserted their military superiority. Towards the end of November the Austrians began an offensive against Serbia which British observers felt could only lead to the swift destruction of the one Allied state in the Balkans. On November 29 Asquith reported to Venetia Stanley that 'desperate efforts are being made to find some territorial formula which will bring Bulgaria and Rumania into the fighting line along side of Servia and Greece'. But Greece was not yet in the fighting line, and Bulgaria and Rumania were little disposed to support an Allied cause which seemed to offer so small a chance of success. On December 1 the Austrians occupied Belgrade. From that moment, if armies were to be found in excess of the men needed on the western and eastern fronts, they were more likely to be used to try to save Serbia, than to attack Turkey. Lloyd George pressed the Cabinet to send British military help to Serbia. But Kitchener insisted that no spare troops were available, either from the western front, or from the new Divisions under training in England. The Serbs reoccupied Belgrade on December 14, taking forty thousand Austrian prisoners and establishing an uneasy period of truce along their northern border. But few believed that such a triumph would be secure for long, and elsewhere the war news was depressing. Russian military efforts continued to be ineffective against the German advance. Rumania intimated that she was not yet ready to commit herself to the Allies. The Italians spoke cautiously of not being able to make a decision before the spring.

On December 21 the British Military Attaché in Petrograd, Lieutenant-Colonel Knox,[1] sent a secret report of the Russian military situation to the War Office. The report, which Kitchener circulated to senior Ministers, spoke of an alarming shortage of ammunition, of Generals with no previous military experience in command of fronts, of 800,000 recruits ready to go to the front but with no rifles to equip them, of 'panic retirements' from the front line, and of neglect of arms and ammunition. Knox reported disillusioned officers saying that 'their men could live on what they picked up locally—frozen potatoes and turnips—they could stick the frost but ammunition did not grow in the fields'. During the last week of December fear of Russia's collapse haunted those British Ministers who knew the truth. Cabinet discussion centred upon the flimsy hope of combining the Balkan States, and even Italy, to march against Austria. This alone, it was believed, could take pressure off the Russian front. Asquith wrote to Venetia Stanley on December 27 that the intervention of Rumania and Italy 'would put an end to Austria' but that on the information which he had received there was no prospect of such intervention until at least the end of January.

Churchill followed these depressing developments with apprehension. He too cast about for some means of relieving the pressure on Russia. During December he resurrected from among the secret plans of the Admiralty one which had for many years been Fisher's favourite: a direct attack on Germany across the North Sea. This plan was in five phases: first, seizure of the island of Borkum; second, using Borkum as a base, the invasion of Schleswig-Holstein; third, the occupation of the Kiel Canal and the winning of neutral Denmark to the Allied cause; fourth, a naval attack through Denmark and the Kiel Canal into the Baltic; and finally, a military landing on the Pomeranian coast from which Allied troops would march the hundred miles to Berlin, supported by the Russians from the east. Churchill examined these plans again in the third week of December. 'The Baltic,' he wrote to Fisher on December 22, 'is the only theatre in wh naval action can appreciably shorten the war. Denmark must come in, & the Russians be let loose on Berlin.' On December 29 Churchill put his views to Asquith:

My dear Prime Minister,
     When Kitchener declared there was nothing in front of us but 'boys and old men', he was wrong; and when you and I agreed there was a fine and

[1] Alfred William Fortescue Knox, 1870–1964. Entered Army, 1891. ADC to Lord Curzon, 1899–1900 and 1902–3. General Staff, War Office, 1908–11. Lieutenant-Colonel, 1911. Military Attaché, St Petersburg (Petrograd), 1911–18. Liaison officer with the Russian Army, 1914–17. Chief of the British Military Mission to Siberia, 1918–20. Knighted, 1919. Conservative MP, 1924–45.

terrible army in our front, we were right. It has taken 5,000 men and more, in killed and wounded, to prove the simple fact. . . .

I think it quite possible that neither side will have the strength to penetrate the other's lines in the Western theatre. Belgium particularly, which it is vital to Germany to hold as a peace-counter, has no doubt been made into a mere succession of fortified lines. I think it probable that the Germans hold back several large mobile reserves of their best troops. Without attempting to take a final view, my impression is that the position of both armies is not likely to undergo any decisive change—although no doubt several hundred thousand men will be spent to satisfy the military mind on the point. . . .

On the assumption that these views are correct, the question arises, how ought we to apply our growing military power? Are there not other alternatives than sending our armies to chew barbed wire in Flanders? Further, cannot the power of the Navy be brought more directly to bear upon the enemy? If it is impossible or unduly costly to pierce the German lines on existing fronts, ought we not, as new forces comes to hand, to engage him on new frontiers, and enable the Russians to do so too? The invasion of Schleswig-Holstein from the sea would at once threaten the Kiel Canal and enable Denmark to join us. The accession of Denmark would throw open the Baltic. British naval command of the Baltic would enable the Russian armies to be landed within 90 miles of Berlin; and the enemy, while being closely held on all existing lines, would be forced to face new attacks directed at vital points and exhaust himself along a still larger perimeter. The essential preliminary is the blocking of the Heligoland debouch. . . .

Churchill ended this letter with a plea for action. He could no longer disguise his growing dismay at Asquith's apparent reluctance to lead his Cabinet forward with a decisive war policy:

Co-operation between the Admiralty and the War Office is difficult, owing to causes of which you are fully aware. The action of the allies proceeds almost independently. Plans could be made now for April and May which would offer good prospects of bringing the war to its decisive stage by land and sea. We ought not to drift. We ought now to consider while time remains the scope and character we wish to impart to the war in the early summer. We ought to concert our action with our allies, and particularly with Russia. We ought to form a scheme for a continuous and progressive offensive, and be ready with this new alternative when and if the direct frontal attacks in France on the German lines and Belgium have failed, as fail I fear they will. Without your direct guidance and initiative, none of these things will be done; and a succession of bloody checks in the West and in the East will leave the allies dashed in spirit and bankrupt in policy.

Yours &c
WSC

During November and December Churchill had received several first-hand accounts of the military confrontation from friends at the front. His personal experience of warfare over twenty years, from his subaltern days on the North-West frontier of India to the siege of Antwerp in October 1914, enabled him to interpret what he was told about conditions on the western front, and to sense the ugly realities which even blunt words could not adequately describe. Towards the end of November he had received a letter from his friend Valentine Fleming,[1] who was serving on the western front, which gave a clear and dismal picture of the war zone:

First and most impressive the absolutely indescribable ravages of modern artillery fire, not only upon all men, animals and buildings within its zone, but upon the very face of nature itself. Imagine a broad belt, ten miles or so in width, stretching from the Channel to the German frontier near Basle, which is positively littered with the bodies of men and scarified with their rude graves; in which farms, villages, and cottages are shapeless heaps of blackened masonry; in which fields, roads and trees are pitted and torn and twisted by shells and disfigured by dead horses, cattle, sheep and goats, scattered in every attitude of repulsive distortion and dismemberment. Day and night in this area are made hideous by the incessant crash and whistle and roar of every sort of projectile, by sinister columns of smoke and flame, by the cries of wounded men, by the piteous calls of animals of all sorts, abandoned, starved, perhaps wounded. Along this terrain of death stretch more or less parallel to each other lines of trenches, some 200, some 1,000 yards apart, hardly visible except to the aeroplanes which continually hover over them menacing and uncanny harbingers of fresh showers of destruction. In these trenches crouch lines of men, in brown or grey or blue, coated with mud, unshaven, hollow-eyed with the continual strain unable to reply to the everlasting run of shells hurled at them from 3, 4, 5 or more miles away and positively welcoming an infantry attack from one side or the other as a chance of meeting and matching themselves against *human* assailants and not against invisible, irresistible machines, the outcome of an ingenuity which even you and I would be in agreement in considering unproductive from every point of view. . . .

Fleming ended his letter: 'It's going to be a *long long* war in spite of the fact that on both sides every single man in it wants it stopped *at once.*' Churchill sent this letter to his wife, who was still recuperating by the sea from Sarah's birth, and added in his covering note: 'What wd happen I wonder if the armies suddenly & simultaneously went on strike and said some other method must be found of settling the dispute!

[1] Valentine Fleming, 1882–1917. Captain, Queen's Own Oxfordshire Hussars, 1909; Major, 1914. Conservative MP, 1910–17. Killed in action. Churchill wrote his obituary notice in *The Times*, 25 May 1917.

Meanwhile however new avalanches of men are preparing to mingle in the conflict and it widens and deepens every hour.' Churchill's anxieties were shared by all his colleagues. 'I am profoundly dissatisfied with the immediate prospect,' Asquith wrote to Venetia Stanley on December 29. The war, he told her, was 'an enormous waste of life and money day after day with no appreciable progress'.

The social world in which both Asquith and Churchill moved had in a few months been shattered by the deaths of so many of its young men. By early December Churchill's cousin Norman Leslie, and his friends Hugh Dawnay and Riversdale Grenfell,[1] were dead. Lord Lansdowne[2] had lost a son, the Duke of Westminster a brother,[3] Lord Stamfordham and Lord Crewe had lost sons-in-law,[4] Prince Louis a nephew. But the patriotism of the first months of war derided all thought of making peace. The one alternative to the slow extinction of the nation's youth seemed to be the discovery of a new sphere of action, where victory might bring the war to a swift conclusion. Churchill believed that a Baltic operation would have this effect, and pressed the scheme with determination. 'This plan,' Asquith wrote to Venetia Stanley on December 30, '(apart from other difficulties) implies either the accession of Denmark to the Allies, or the violation of her neutrality.' But Churchill believed Denmark's neutrality a small sacrifice, if by it Britain could enable Russia to land troops only ninety miles from Berlin.

Lloyd George was also searching for an alternative war zone. On January 1 Asquith informed Venetia Stanley that he had received long memoranda on the conduct of the war from both Churchill and Lloyd George. 'They are both keen on a new objective & theatre as soon as our new troops are ready,' he told her. 'W, of course, for Borkum and the Baltic; LG for Salonika to join in with the Serbians, and for Syria!'

---

[1] Riversdale Grenfell, 1880–1914. Known as 'Rivy'. A financier, he lost his fortune early in 1914 when his family firm went bankrupt. Lieutenant, 9th Lancers. Embarked for France with his twin brother Francis, 15 August 1914. Killed in action, 11 September 1914. Francis Grenfell was killed in action in France on 13 May 1915.

[2] Henry Charles Keith Petty-Fitzmaurice, 1845–1927. 5th Marquess of Lansdowne, 1856. Governor-General of Canada, 1883–8; Viceroy of India, 1888–93; Secretary of State for War, 1895–1901; Foreign Secretary, 1900–5. Minister without Portfolio, May 1915–December 1916. In 1917 he publicly advocated a negotiated peace with Germany. His second son, Lord Charles George Francis Mercer Nairne was killed in action in France, 30 October 1914.

[3] Lord Hugh William Grosvenor, 1884–1914. Captain, Household Cavalry. Reported missing, 7 November 1914.

[4] Arthur Edward Bruce O'Neill, 1876–1914. Crewe's nephew. Entered Army, 1897. Captain, 1902. Unionist MP, 1910–14. Killed in action, 4 November 1914; he was the first MP to be killed in the war.

[4] Henry Robert Augustus Adeane, 1882–1914. Stamfordham's nephew. Captain, Coldstream Guards. Reported killed, 5 December 1914.

In his memorandum Lloyd George asserted that a few more months of trench warfare of the sort seen at Ypres 'will inevitably destroy the *moral* of the best of troops'. He believed that 'any attempt to force the carefully-prepared German lines in the west would end in failure and in appalling loss of life'. A definite victory, he asserted, was only possible somewhere other than in France, and would alone 'satisfy the public that tangible results are being achieved by the sacrifices they are making, and decide neutrals that it is at last safe for them to throw in their lot with us'. Lloyd George proposed two separate attacks. The first was against Austria. The Serbs, Montenegrins, Rumanians and Greeks, with some British support, would form an allied army of as many as 1,600,000 men, and fight Austria along her southern, most vulnerable frontier, where the population was made up largely of Slavs 'who hate both the Germans and Magyars'. The second attack would be against Turkey. Lloyd George suggested that operations against Turkey might take the form of landing a hundred thousand men in Syria. By such a move 'the pressure upon Russia at the Caucasus would be relieved', and the victory would have the advantage of taking place 'in territory which appeals to the imagination of the people as a whole'. Lloyd George concluded:

If a decision were come to in favour of some such plan of campaign as I have outlined, it will take weeks to make the necessary preparations for it. . . . It would take some time to collect the necessary intelligence as to the country, so as to decide where to land the Army and what shall be the line of attack. Transport would have to be carefully and secretly gathered. Large forces might have to be accumulated in the Mediterranean, ostensibly for Egypt. It might be desirable to send an advance force through Salonica to assist Serbia. Military arrangements would have to be made with Roumania, Serbia, Greece, and, perhaps, Italy. All this must take time. Expeditions decided upon and organised with insufficient care and preparation generally end disastrously. And as similar considerations will probably apply to any alternative campaign, I urge the importance of our taking counsel and pressing to a decision without delay.

Lloyd George was not alone in reviving the idea of a possible attack on Turkey as a strategy capable of breaking the stalemate on the western front. Over the Christmas holiday Hankey had also brooded upon the situation. On December 28, in a memorandum which, at Asquith's suggestion, he circulated to Crewe, Grey, Kitchener, Fisher, Churchill and Lloyd George, Hankey put forward a number of arguments for an attack outside the western front. After examining a series of schemes,

Hankey expressed the view that 'Germany can perhaps be struck most effectively and with the most lasting results on the peace of the world through her allies, and particularly through Turkey'. His memorandum continued:

Has not the time come to show Germany and the world that any country that chooses a German alliance against the great sea power is doomed to disaster? Is it impossible now to weave a web round Turkey which shall end her career as a European Power?

Greece and Roumania have hitherto hesitated to enter the war because Bulgaria, brooding on her wrongs, is supposed to be watching her opportunity to make good the gains she considers herself cheated of after the recent Balkan wars. Left to themselves these Balkan States, all of whom stand to gain from the ejection of Turkey from Europe and from the dismemberment of Austria, will be unable to realize their overwhelming opportunity, so great is their mutual distrust.

But supposing Great Britain, France, and Russia, instead of merely inciting these races to attack Turkey and Austria were themselves to participate actively in the campaign, and to guarantee to each nation concerned that fair play should be rendered. If the whole of the Balkan States were to combine there should be no difficulty in securing a port on the Adriatic, with Bosnia and Herzegovina, and part of Albania, for Servia; Epirus, Southern Albania, and the islands, for Greece; and Thrace for Bulgaria. The difficult Dardanelles question might perhaps be solved by allowing more than one nation to occupy the north side and by leaving Turkey on the south, the Straits being neutralised.

If Bulgaria, guaranteed by the active participation of the three Great Powers, could be induced to co-operate, there ought to be no insuperable obstacle to the occupation of Constantinople, the Dardanelles, and Bosphorus. This would be of great advantage to the allies, restoring communication with the Black Sea, bringing down at once the price of wheat, and setting free the much-needed shipping locked up there.

It is presumed that in a few months time we could, without endangering the position in France, devote three army corps, including one original first line army corps, to a campaign in Turkey, though sea transport might prove a difficulty. This force, in conjunction with Greece and Bulgaria, ought to be sufficient to capture Constantinople.

If Russia, contenting herself with holding the German forces on an entrenched line, could simultaneously combine with Servia and Roumania in an advance into Hungary, the complete downfall of Austria-Hungary could simultaneously be secured.

Hankey's scheme for the defeat of two of the three powers with whom Britain was at war made a strong impression upon those who read it. It offered prospects of victory without enormous bloodshed, and in a short period of time. The clarity of Hankey's thought, the calm tone, and the lack of any special departmental or ministerial pleading, struck a new note of authority, reflecting Hankey's own growing abilities as an adviser, and strengthening his influence. Having read Hankey's memorandum, Churchill still believed that the Baltic scheme offered the best chance to break the deadlock, and that the defeat of Germany should be the immediate objective. He felt that the difficulties of finding sufficient men to carry out an attack on Turkey were greater than they had been in November. But he recognized that he and Hankey were working together in their search for an alternative war zone. When he wrote to Asquith on December 31, he expressed yet again his frustration at the Prime Minister's reluctance to force the pace in search of new policies:

My dear Prime Minister,
. . . I have talked to Hankey. We are substantially in agreement and our conclusions are not incompatible.

I wanted Gallipoli attacked on the Turkish declaration of war. But Kitchener does not work far afield or far ahead, *vide* Antwerp. Meanwhile the difficulties have increased.

I look forward to yr Memo. But I think the War Council ought to meet daily for a few days next week. No topic can be pursued to any fruitful result at weekly intervals. . . .

Yours always
Winston SC

'Please have your detailed plans put in hand at once,' Asquith replied from Walmer Castle on January 1. But before Churchill could do so, and before Asquith himself could produce a memorandum on the situation, events outside British control imposed their own pattern on subsequent decisions. On Wednesday December 30 the Grand Duke Nicholas had informed the Chief of the British Military Mission with the Russian Army, Sir John Hanbury-Williams,[1] that Turkish troops were seriously threatening the Russians in the Caucasus, and asked for British help in reducing the Turkish pressure which endangered the Russian military effort against the Germans. Hanbury-Williams at once

[1] John Hanbury-Williams, 1859–1946, Entered Army, 1878. Military Secretary to Sir Alfred Milner, 1897–1900. Knighted, 1908. Major-General, General Staff, War Office, 1914. Chief of British Military Mission, Russian Army in the Field, 1914–17. In charge of British Prisoners-of-War Department, The Hague, 1917–18; Berne, 1918.

informed the British Ambassador in Petrograd, Sir George Buchanan, of what the Grand Duke had said. On the afternoon of January 1, Buchanan telegraphed to Grey, outlining the Grand Duke's request '. . . for Lord Kitchener to arrange for a demonstration of some kind against Turks elsewhere, either naval or military, and to spread reports which would cause Turks, who he says are very liable to go off at a tangent, to withdraw some of the forces now acting against Russia in the Caucasus, and thus ease position of Russians'. The Russian appeal reached the Foreign Office in the early hours of January 2. Grey sent it to Kitchener, who passed it on to Churchill with a covering letter: 'You have no doubt seen Buchanan's telegram about the Russians & Turks, if not FitzGerald[1] is taking it over. Do you think any naval action would be possible to prevent Turks sending more men into the Caucasus & thus denuding Constantinople.'[2]

Churchill later recalled in *The World Crisis* that before he could reply, Kitchener had come to see him at the Admiralty, determined to do something to relieve the Russian distress. 'Could we not, for instance,'' Kitchener asked, 'make a demonstration at the Dardanelles?' He spoke of an entirely naval demonstration. But Churchill, doubting the possibility of anything but a combined naval and military assault, pressed Kitchener to find troops for the military side. Kitchener returned to the War Office, where he put Churchill's request to his advisers. But they were convinced that no extra soldiers were then available for action against Turkey; every man who could be mustered was needed on the western front. As soon as Kitchener heard the War Office view, he wrote:

My dear Churchill,

I do not see that we can do anything that will very seriously help the Russians in the Caucasus.

The Turks are evidently withdrawing most of their troops from Adrianople and using them to reinforce their army against Russia probably sending them by the Black Sea.

In the Caucasus and Northern Persia the Russians are in a bad way.

We have no troops to land anywhere.

A demonstration at Smyrna would do no good and probably cause the

---

[1] Oswald Arthur Gerald FitzGerald, 1875–1916. Lieutenant, Indian Army, 1897. A member of Lord Kitchener's staff, 1904–16. Lieutenant-Colonel, August 1914. Personal Military Secretary to Lord Kitchener, 1914–16. Drowned with Kitchener in HMS *Hampshire*.

[2] Kitchener's letter to Churchill is reproduced in facsimile on page 830.

slaughter of Christians. Alexandretta has already been tried[1] and would have no great effect a second time.

The coast of Syria would have no effect.

The only place that a demonstration might have some effect in stopping reinforcements going East would be the Dardanelles—particularly if as the Grand Duke says reports could be spread at the same time that Constantinople was threatened.

We shall not be ready for anything big for some months.

Yours very truly
Kitchener

The Russian appeal supplanted all other considerations. If Russia were forced out of the war, the German armies then on the eastern front would be free to reinforce their comrades in the west, and would completely outnumber, and overwhelm, the British, French and Belgian forces. Serbia's doom would also be sealed. Once Russia were defeated the Turks could turn their forces against Egypt, where Britain, if pressed desperately on the western front, would be most weak. Churchill and Kitchener were the only two Ministers, in a Cabinet of twenty-four, authorized to plan and conduct all acts of war. Kitchener's insistence that the War Office could undertake no immediate military action threw the burden of responsibility upon the Admiralty. Under the pressure of unforeseen events and dire possibilities Churchill took up the very plan which until then he had believed to be impossible. A naval demonstration had to be made on Russia's behalf. Kitchener's reiteration that it must be at the Dardanelles coincided with his own belief that it was at the Dardanelles that Turkey was most vulnerable. Churchill summoned his Admiralty War Group on the morning of January 3. There was general pessimism, which he shared, about the feasibility of a purely naval attack. Were such an attack to take place it would have to be with old battleships not needed by Jellicoe in the North Sea. Before the war Churchill had allocated some of his Naval Estimates to maintaining these old ships in a fit state to fight, and Parliament had approved of this policy. This gave the War Group confidence that some plan might be worked out for naval action within the next few months, assuming that the commander of the Blockading Squadron at the Dardanelles, Vice-Admiral Carden, felt that the enterprise had

---

[1] A reference to Captain Larken's exploits with the light cruiser *Doris*, 18–20 December 1914 (see page 222).

some chance of success. Churchill telegraphed to Carden shortly after midday:

> Do you consider the forcing of the Dardanelles by ships alone a practicable operation.
> It is assumed older battleships fitted with minebumpers would be used preceded by colliers or other merchant craft as bumpers and sweepers.
> Importance of results would justify severe loss.
> Let me know your views.

In response to Asquith's request, Churchill had prepared a memorandum on naval action in the North Sea, against the island of Borkum. On January 3 he circulated it to Fisher, Wilson and Oliver. 'All necessary appliances,' he wrote, 'and any likely to be useful, should be ordered *now*.' Two dates seemed to him possible for the attack, March 1 and April 15. After elaborating on the details of the attack he concluded: 'A resolve to have the island at all costs, coupled with exact and careful preparations, should certainly, with our great resources, be successful within three days of fire being opened.'

While the Admiralty waited for Carden's reply about the Dardanelles, Fisher, who had been much impressed by Hankey's memorandum of December 28, was evolving his own plan of action in the eastern Mediterranean. '*I CONSIDER THE ATTACK ON TURKEY HOLDS THE FIELD!*' he wrote to Churchill on January 3; 'But *ONLY* if it's *IMMEDIATE*.' Then he outlined what he called 'the Turkey plan':

I. Appoint Sir W. Robertson,[1] the present Quartermaster-General, to command the Expeditionary Force.
II. Immediately replace all Indian and 75,000 seasoned troops from Sir John French's Command with Territorials, etc, from England (as you yourself suggested), and embark this Turkish Expeditionary force ostensibly for protection of Egypt! *WITH ALL POSSIBLE DESPATCH* at *Marseilles*! And land them at Besika Bay direct, with previous feints before they arrive with troops now in Egypt against Haifa and Alexandretta, the latter to be a *REAL* occupation because of its inestimable value as regards the oil fields of the Garden of Eden, with which by rail it is in direct communication, and we shove out the Germans now established at Alexandretta with an immense

---

[1] William Robert Robertson, 1860–1933. Entered Army as a Private, 1877. 2nd Lieutenant, 1888. Intelligence Department, War Office, 1900–7. Brigadier-General, 1907. Major-General, 1910. Commandant of the Staff College, 1910–13. Director of Military Training, War Office, 1913–14. Knighted, 1913. Quarter-Master-General, British Expeditionary Force, 1914–15. Chief of Staff, British Expeditionary Force, 1915. Chief of the Imperial General Staff, 1915–18. Commander-in-Chief, Home Forces, 1918–19. Commander-in-Chief, British Army of Occupation on the Rhine, 1919–20. Created Baronet, 1919. Field-Marshal, 1920.

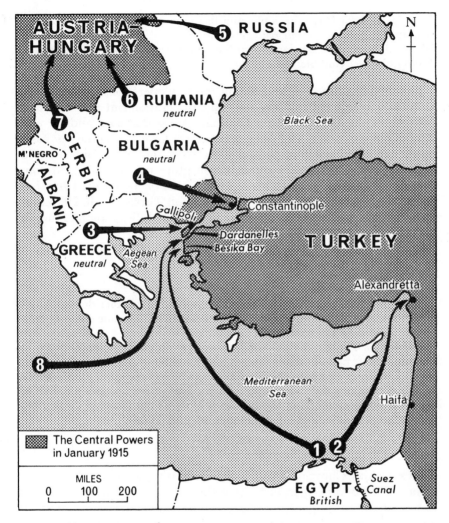

LORD FISHER'S EIGHT-POINT PLAN OF ATTACK,
3 JANUARY 1915

Turkish concession—the last act of that arch-enemy of England, Marschall
von Bieberstein.[1]

III. The Greeks to go for Gallipoli at the same time as we go for Besika, and

---

[1] Marschall von Bieberstein, 1842–1912. German Ambassador to Constantinople, 1897–
1912. His influence over Turkish policy was considerable. In 1908 Lord Kitchener entertained
hopes of being sent to Constantinople as British Ambassador to counter von Bieberstein's
influence.

the Bulgarians for Constantinople, and the Russians, the Servians and Rou-
manians for Austria (*all this you said yourself!*).
IV. Sturdee forces the Dardanelles at the same time with 'Majestic' class and
'Canopus' class! God bless him!

Fisher had outlined eight different military operations. Not only did
he want a combined military and naval operation but also a Grand
Alliance of the Balkan States. Churchill knew that so grandiose and
formidable a scheme as Fisher wanted could never come to pass;
Kitchener could not find the men nor Grey the allies. Only the old
battleships which Fisher wanted to constitute the British naval contribution were available. In his reply to Fisher on January 4 Churchill
revealed his own doubts as to any attack upon Turkey at all. He reiterated his persistent hopes for action in the North Sea, commenting in
his covering note, 'We never seem to settle anything':

Secret
My dear Fisher,
    We must be agreed on certain points:—
    . . . Borkum is the key to all Northern possibilities, whether defensive agst
raid or invasion, or offensive to block the enemy in or to invade either Olden-
berg or Schleswig-Holstein.
    Ask that a regular division of Infantry be assigned to the capture of
Borkum, & that plans be made on that basis for action at the earliest moment.
    . . . I think we had better hear what others have to say about the Turkish
plans before taking a decided line. I wd not grudge 100,000 men because of
the great political effects in the Balkan peninsula: but Germany is the foe,
& it is bad war to seek cheaper victories & easier antagonists. . . .
                                                        Yours ever
                                                Winston S. Churchill

That same day Churchill wrote to Jellicoe setting out the arguments in
favour of a Borkum operation. 'It is the key,' he explained, 'not only
to satisfactory naval policy but to future military action. . . . I am sure
we ought to make the attempt, & am also confident that success will be
attained.' On January 4 the Admiralty War Group began examining
Churchill's Borkum scheme in detail. Oliver gave a copy to Richmond,
who wrote in his diary with characteristic hostility: 'It is *quite mad*. The
reasons for capturing it are NIL, the possibilities about the same. I
have never read such an idiotic, amateur piece of work as this outline
in my life. Ironically enough it falls to me to prepare the plans for this
stupendous folly. Yet Sea Lords like Wilson (for he is in effect a Sea
Lord) enter no protest. It remains with the army, who I hope will refuse

to throw away 12000 troops in this manner for the self-glorification of an ignorant & impulsive man.' Fisher did not share Richmond's scepticism. The Borkum plan was one he had long believed in. But on January 4 he had no time for Churchill's preference for action in the north. That day Fisher wrote to A. J. Balfour to press upon him 'the peculiar merit of Hankey's Turkey Plan', urging: 'I do hope you will give it all your support.' Fisher also wrote again to Churchill to impress upon him that: 'The naval advantages of the possession of Constantinople and the getting of wheat from the Black Sea are so overwhelming that I consider Colonel Hankey's plan for Turkish operations vital and imperative and very pressing.'

No amount of correspondence within the confines of Whitehall could resolve the argument. All future plans depended upon the view of the Admiral on the spot. When Carden's reply arrived early on the afternoon of January 5 it surprised everyone at the Admiralty, including Churchill and Fisher; for Carden declared that he might be able to force the Dardanelles by ships alone. His telegram read: 'With reference to your telegram of 3rd inst, I do not consider Dardanelles can be rushed. They might be forced by extended operations with large number of ships.'

The War Council met later that afternoon. The Baltic project was still uppermost in Churchill's mind. Carden's telegram, suggesting the possibility of an exclusively naval effort at the Dardanelles, had not deflected Churchill's overriding belief that it was on the northern sea flank that Germany must be defeated, and that with the seizure of Borkum and the invasion of Schleswig-Holstein all other theatres of war and all other strategic possibilities would lose their urgency. During the War Council many different points of attack were discussed. Asquith had also been in correspondence with Sir John French on this matter, and had spoken that morning to F. E. Smith, who was on leave from the western front. At midnight he sent Venetia Stanley a survey of current opinion. 'We have now a lot of alternative objectives,' he told her; '(1) Schleswig (Winston) (2) Salonika or Dalmatia (Ll George—curiously enough, French in his letter to me suggests that we might send a diversion to help the Montenegrians) (3) Gallipoli & Constantinople (Kitchener) (4) Smyrna & Ephesus (FE & others—I rather like this).'

Kitchener pressed his colleagues for action at the Dardanelles. Churchill was able to give some support to Kitchener's appeal by reading out to the War Council the telegram which he had received from Carden an hour before. When Churchill returned to the Admiralty after the War Council he found that the 'extended operations' which Carden favoured were supported both by Oliver and Jackson. Jackson, who had been impressed by the effects of the bombardment of November 3, believed that a systematic bombardment from the sea, fort by fort, would enable ships alone to force the Dardanelles even though the operation might take some time. That night Asquith dined with the Churchills at Admiralty House. The others present were F. E. Smith, Frederick Guest and Sir Archibald Sinclair.[1] F. E. Smith was worried about the severe climatic difficulties which were affecting the performance of the Indian soldiers in France and was, Asquith told Venetia Stanley, 'keen for sending them with a stiffening of regulars and territorials to Smyrna—to make their way sooner or later to Constantinople'. Here again was the mirage of troops. But Churchill had to work with urgent realities. Kitchener refused to withdraw the Indians from France, arguing that the balance of military forces seemed too precarious even to send away troops who might fight more successfully elsewhere. On the following afternoon, January 6, supported by the specific enthusiasm of Oliver and Jackson, sustained by the desire of Kitchener and the War Council to follow this slim opportunity, and with Asquith's eastern interest of the night before clear evidence of the importance of the new scheme, Churchill telegraphed to Carden: 'Your view is agreed with by high authorities here. Please telegraph in detail what you think could be done by extended operations, what force would be needed, and how you consider it should be used.'

The exchange of telegrams with Carden was the first tentative move towards a possible naval attack at the Dardanelles. By themselves, these telegrams decided nothing, and committed no one. Meanwhile Admiralty business continued. On Fisher's insistence, naval construction was accelerated. Steps had to be taken to try to meet the threat of German submarine attacks on unarmed merchant ships in the North Sea, the Channel and the Atlantic Ocean. It was two months since Fisher's return as First Sea Lord. His energies and enthusiasm gave Churchill powerful support. But suddenly, on January 4, Fisher announced his intention to resign. At Christmas the Germans had made two air raids on England; a Zeppelin dropped a bomb on Dover on

[1] Archibald Henry Macdonald Sinclair, 1890–1970. Entered Army, 1910. 4th Baronet, 1912. ADC to Colonel Seely, 1915–16. Captain, 1915. 2nd in Command of the 6th Royal Scots Fusiliers, while Churchill was in command January–May 1916. Squadron-Commander, 2nd Life Guards, 1916–17. Major, Guards Machine Gun Regiment, 1918. Served under Churchill, Ministry of Munitions, 1918–19. Churchill's personal Military Secretary, War Office, 1919–21. Churchill's Private Secretary, Colonial Office, 1921–2. Liberal MP, 1922–45. Secretary of State for Scotland, 1931–2. Leader of the Parliamentary Liberal Party, 1935–45. Secretary of State for Air, 1940–5. Created Viscount Thurso, 1952.

December 24 and an aeroplane flew up the Thames on December 25. On January 4 Fisher protested to Churchill, to whom Kitchener had passed the responsibility for defending London against aerial attack, about the urgent danger to London from Zeppelin raids. Twenty Zeppelins, Fisher asserted, were about to raid the capital, each carrying a ton of explosive. A single ton, he wrote with alarm, 'would completely wreck the whole of the Admiralty building', and twenty tons would cause a 'terrible massacre' in the centre of London. The only defence against this danger, he declared, was for the British Government to announce beforehand that, if any bombs were dropped, reprisals would be taken by shooting German prisoners of war. In his letter of January 4 Fisher wrote:

> . . . *As this step has not been taken I must with great reluctance ask to be relieved in my present official position as First Sea Lord*—because the Admiralty under present arrangements will be responsible for the massacre coming suddenly upon and unprepared for by the Public.
>
> *I have allowed a week to elapse much against my judgment before taking this step* to avoid embarrassing the Government I cannot delay any longer.

Churchill replied on the same day:

My dear Fisher,

The question of aerial defence is not one upon wh you have any professional experience. The question of killing prisoners in reprisal for an aerial attack is not one for the Admiralty and certainly not for you to decide. The Cabinet alone can settle such a matter.

I will bring your views to their notice at our meeting tomorrow. After much reflection I cannot support it. I am circulating a paper giving the facts about a Zeppelin raid as far as we can estimate them.

I hope I am not to take the last part of your letter seriously. I have always made up my mind never to dissuade anyone serving in the department over wh I preside from resigning if they wish to do so. Business becomes impossible on any other terms.

But I sympathise with your feelings of exasperation at our powerlessness to resist certain forms of attack: and I presume I may take your letter simply as an expression of those feelings.

Yours vy sincerely
Winston S. Churchill

Fisher agreed to withdraw his resignation. But the incident cast a gloom over Admiralty business. Such outbursts did not make Churchill's work easy; particularly when the question of defending Britain against attack from the air was an entirely novel one, demanding, if it were to be dealt with successfully, a high degree of ingenuity and co-operation among those responsible. At the War Council which met at noon on January 7, only three days after Fisher's threat to resign, Churchill gave his colleagues a survey of the air defence situation, and tried to allay their fears that London could not be defended. He explained that there was in his opinion an active as well as a passive aspect to aerial defence. It was in order to prevent German airship bases from being built in Belgium that he had stationed the special detachment of aeroplanes at Dunkirk. The pilots had been instructed to attack any Zeppelins which landed in Belgium for refuelling and supplies while on their way to Britain. He also explained the system which he had devised to meet any Zeppelins which came direct from Germany. He had assembled sixty aeroplanes at different airports between London and Dover. He gave the War Council a survey of his preparations:

The moment a hostile airship was sighted the alarm would be given and the aeroplanes would ascend. Those on the coast would probably not be able to rise sufficiently high to attack the airships on their approach, but would be ready for them on their return; those at Hendon, however, should be ready to attack the airships as they neared London. These aeroplanes were armed with rifles firing incendiary bullets, which, in the course of experiments, had proved their capacity to destroy a balloon. In addition, he believed that some flyers were prepared to charge a Zeppelin. Within the same triangle there are 9 3-inch, 39 6-prs, and 28 pompom guns—a total of 76 anti-aircraft guns. In London itself there are 2 3-inch, 4 6-pr, and 5 pompoms, with 13 searchlights. The 3-inch is a powerful and accurate long-range gun. The pompoms were now being provided with incendiary shell.

Notwithstanding these preparations, if the enemy thought it worth while to attack London merely for the purpose of injuring and terrorising the civil population and damaging property, there was no means of preventing it. In order to reduce the loss of life to a minimum, instructions had been published by the police warning the populace to remain indoors. The Fire Brigade had worked out careful plans for meeting a simultaneous outbreak of a number of fires.

The members of the War Council questioned Churchill in detail about his aerial preparations. They then turned to the question of general war policy. Churchill had been evolving a new scheme of attack on Germany which would make use of naval power. He wanted Kitchener to send reinforcements to Sir John French so that the Expeditionary Force could advance along the German-held Belgian coast with naval support, capture Zeebrugge and cut off all German access to the North Sea. Without such an offensive, he argued, 'the communications of the army and British commerce up channel were jeopardized'. Kitchener declared that there was insufficient artillery ammunition to enable such a scheme to be put into operation. Lloyd George intervened, questioning Churchill's assumption that as soon as extra troops had been raised they should be sent to the western front, and making a strong appeal for an entirely new zone of action:

If our army on the Continent was to be thrown away and shattered in an operation which appeared to him impossible, the war might continue indefinitely, or at any rate for two or three years more. Was it impossible, he asked, to get at the enemy from some other direction, and to strike a blow that would end the war once and for all? If some new plan should be decided on, every man would be required for it in April or May, and the loss of some fifty battalions of Territorial troops would be very severely felt.

Churchill defended his advocacy of an attack on Zeebrugge, explaining that it would be a combined military and naval operation, in which the troops would receive constant protection from the guns of the fleet, so that, as he told his colleagues, 'we should not shatter our armies on wire entanglements, but would advance in co-operation with the fleet'. At the end of the meeting Churchill again tried to impress upon his colleagues the importance which he attached 'to the seizure of an island on the German coast'. This, he believed, would enable the Navy to limit the operations of the German Fleet in such a way as to make possible further offensive activity towards Zeebrugge or even against the German mainland. There was, he told his colleagues, 'only one suitable such island'; the island of Borkum. He believed that they should address themselves to its capture:

Unquestionably certain risks of loss would be run, but this would not involve serious risk to our main fighting fleets. If an island were occupied, the whole of the B and C class submarines, which at present were unable to be employed on the German coast, could be based on it; and the dangers of any German ship which put to sea would be correspondingly increased. The island would also be a useful base for aircraft, which could reconnoitre the German ports. Invasion would then become impossible, and the risk of raids enormously reduced, as we should soon discover if preparations of this kind were in progress. It was anticipated that about a division of troops would be the largest force that could be employed in the enterprise, and, if it succeed, the Army would be fully recouped by the greater security of and the fewer troops required for Home Defence. A large amount of detailed work would be required before the plans were ready. . . .

Fisher then elaborated on Churchill's explanation, telling the War Council that the Navy could be ready to carry out the operations within three months. After some discussion the War Council approved in principle the proposed attack, and authorized the Admiralty 'to proceed with the making out of plans'. Churchill had nothing further to report about the Dardanelles; Carden had not yet had time to send his detailed proposals for a naval attack. After the meeting Asquith gave Venetia Stanley an account of its discussions:

We had between noon & 2 pm a sitting of our War Council—quite a good body. Self & AJB—Winston, with his two septuagenarian Sea Dogs Fisher & Wilson, E. Grey, Haldane, Crewe, Hankey. . . . W pressed his scheme for acquiring a base at Borkum (wh we have agreed always to speak of & if possible think of as *Sylt*[1])—a big business, as it is heavily fortified, and the necessary preparations will take till near the end of March. We gave him authority for this.

Churchill now had a clear objective, approved by his colleagues, which would enable him to make use of the surplus naval strength whose non-participation in the war was a constant source of concern to him. The Borkum plans were set in motion. Churchill still hoped that Zeebrugge would also be approved. Once these two operations were under way, the Navy would be fully occupied, and some positive advantage might be shown for so many years of preparation.

After the War Council, Churchill remained at 10 Downing Street where he had a long discussion with Asquith, and sought further assurance that the invasion of Borkum would be begun as soon as possible, particularly as Kitchener had unexpectedly agreed to spare a whole division of troops to take part in the landing. Churchill pressed Asquith to treat as a matter of urgency his proposed naval and military attack on Zeebrugge. He also sought assurance from the Prime Minister that no unnecessary offensive would be launched against the German trenches on the western front. After their meeting he put in writing his overriding concern for the harsh conditions of trench warfare: 'If we are to remain on the defensive,' he wrote, '*Query* ought we not to get

[1] I can find no evidence to suggest that the Borkum scheme was ever referred to as 'Sylt' again. It was, however, referred to as 'Danzig' in a memorandum by Captain Richmond in February 1915, in order to keep the typists in ignorance of the real objective.

into a more comfortable, dry, habitable line—even if we have to retire a few miles. (Our troops are rotting.)'

The War Council met again on the following day, January 8. Kitchener opened the discussion with a gloomy warning that a fresh German offensive was imminent on the western front. But before the War Council could address itself to this grim prognostication, Lloyd George made yet another strong appeal in favour of some alternate sphere of action. He saw no victory in trench warfare, reminding the War Council that 'as far back as 1879 the Russians, under one of the best generals they ever had,[1] had been held up by the Turks at Plevna' and that since then 'the power of the defensive' had enormously increased. To attack the German lines and to fail would, in his opinion, 'produce the worst possible physical and moral effect on the Allied armies'. Lloyd George then explained his thoughts in detail:

Was there, he asked, no alternative theatre in which we might employ our surplus armies to produce a decisive effect? He suggested that an attack on Austria might produce the desired effect. This would extend the front of the enemy and enable the superior forces at the disposal of the Allies to be brought to bear. Austria was the weakest part of the hostile combination and had already suffered heavily. There were great racial antagonisms in the Austrian Empire. The population of the south was largely Slavonic in origin and hated the Teutons.

If a British Expeditionary Force landed in Southern Austria it might expect to receive a sympathetic greeting. Further it would have to encounter a nation inferior to Germany in military efficiency and from the point of view of staff and training. An attack on Austria would probably compel Roumania and Italy to join in the war in order to obtain their share of the spoils. In fact, we ought to make it clear that no nation that declined to take part in the war should derive any benefit from it. This plan, therefore, would enormously increase the military strength of the Allies by bringing in other nations.

The result of these combinations would be that Austria would have to withdraw her armies from the north to meet the menace in the south. This would materially assist the Russian plan, enabling them to invade Silesia, as at present it was the Austrians who stood between Russia and Silesia.

The moment Austria was knocked out, Germany would be entirely isolated. Not only would she lose the military strength of Austria, but she would be cut off from her supplies of Hungarian wheat and Roumanian oil.

Kitchener replied by giving the War Council the gist of a letter which he had received from Sir John French six days previously, in

[1] Mikhail Dimitrievich Skobelev, 1843–82. Lieutenant-General at the siege of Plevna, September–December 1877. Defeated the Turks near the Shipka Pass, January 1878. A leading panslavist, in 1882 he forecast a desperate strife between Teuton and Slav.

which the Commander-in-Chief denied that the German lines in France were impenetrable. He quoted French's belief that no attempt should be made elsewhere 'until the impossibility of breaking through on this side was proved'. Asquith declared that French's letter 'was a very able statement of the case against action outside France'. Churchill, though still unconvinced of the need for action against either Austria or Turkey, suggested that the proposals for an attack in the south 'should form the subject of careful Staff examination'. Kitchener did not see the need for further scrutiny of the alternatives, and gave the War Council a brief deprecatory survey of the different possible points of attack favoured by Lloyd George. Trieste and Fiume, he said without explanation, 'might be ruled out'. Ragusa 'was an impossible sea base'. The railway bridges north of Salonika 'would be liable to attack' by bandits. Kitchener saw only one possible alternative outside the western front, and appealed to his colleagues for their support. 'The Dardanelles,' he said, 'appeared to be the most suitable objective, as an attack here could be made in co-operation with the Fleet. If successful, it would re-establish communications with Russia; settle the Near Eastern question; draw in Greece and, perhaps, Bulgaria and Roumania; and release wheat and shipping now locked up in the Black Sea.'

Hankey supported Kitchener, making one of his first interventions in War Council business. Success at the Dardanelles, he asserted, 'would give us the Danube as a line of communication for an army penetrating into the heart of Austria and bring our sea power to bear in the middle of Europe'. Kitchener tried to make Hankey's plan seem within the range of possibility by asserting that 150,000 men might be sufficient for the capture of the Gallipoli peninsula. Lloyd George 'expressed surprise at the lowness of the figure'. Churchill felt that any future Mediterranean operation must be the subject of careful study rather than generalized discussion. His own thoughts were still dominated by the northern theatre:

MR CHURCHILL said he fully agreed in the proposal to study the suggested operations in the Mediterranean. He urged, however, that we should not lose sight of the possibility of action in Northern Europe. As an instance of the attractiveness of such operations, he mentioned that the distance from Emden to Berlin was exactly half the distance from Sir John French's headquarters to Berlin. Was there no possibility that Holland might enter the war on the side of the Allies? He understood that earlier in the war Holland had considered the matter, but had declined. Possibly, however, if given a military guarantee that we could bring a certain force into the field, Holland would change her mind. There were indications that Germany was very anxious about Holland, and Dutch public opinion was only held from declaring for the Allies by fear of the consequences. If Holland could be induced to enter the war the advantages would far outweigh those of the Mediterranean; we could then have an island as a naval base without fighting for it, and our armies, in conjunction with the Dutch, could attack towards Essen.

Kitchener, without abandoning his strong advocacy of a Gallipoli landing, said he agreed with Churchill that the effect of a landing in Holland would be 'decisive'. Grey declared that he was willing 'to sound the Dutch Government' as soon as Britain was in a position to guarantee military assistance on a sufficient scale and to satisfy Holland 'that there was no prospect that she would share the fate of Belgium'. Once again, the northern possibilities were more attractive, and more immediate, than the southern. First Borkum, then Zeebrugge, now Holland, engaged the War Council's attention and seemed the most realistic means of achieving victory. Fisher was also an enthusiast for action through Holland. In a letter to Churchill on January 9, after urging him to approve Kitchener's plan for the seizure of Alexandretta '& press him for instant action' against the Turks in the eastern Mediterranean, he continued:

I don't think that you at all realise that your Dutch project will sweep the board on May 1st (when all chance of Holland being frozen is past!) All other schemes will be swallowed up by it & it will mean the END OF THE WAR! provided we put our shoulders to the wheel & prepare our Transport arrangements & their convoy for 750,000 men being landed at Antwerp, Rotterdam, Amsterdam & all the other spots (however small) along the Dutch Coast— LAND EVERYWHERE! *at once! sudden—secret—subtle*—our 3 watchwords!

Churchill and his wife spent January 10, a Sunday, at Walmer Castle on the coast of Kent, as the guest of Lord Beauchamp.[1] The Castle was the official home of the Warden of the Cinque Ports, and one of Asquith's favourite weekend retreats. At dinner the discussion turned to the question of who should succeed Lord Hardinge as Viceroy of India. There had been rumours that Churchill coveted the appointment, which he had seriously hoped for in 1910, when Hardinge was appointed. Margot Asquith recorded in her diary:

WINSTON said to me: I've given up all desire for that now (he used to say he would like this above all things)—do you think this is a sign of more modesty or more ambition?

[1] William Lygon Beauchamp, 1872–1938. 7th Earl Beauchamp, 1891. Governor of New South Wales, 1899–1901. First Commissioner of Works, 1910–14. Lord Warden of the Cinque Ports, 1913–33. Lord President of the Council, August 1914–May 1915.

MARGOT: More ambition certainly—no one sinks into greater insignificance than a retired viceroy (aged in arteries, pickled by the climate, poor and bewildered by another kind of political public life—he retires to a small and drab quarters in Eaton Place).
WINSTON: My God! This, this is living History. Everything we are doing and saying is thrilling—it will be read by a thousand generations, think of that!! Why I would not be out of this glorious delicious war for anything the world could give me (eyes glowing but with a slight anxiety lest the word 'delicious' should jar on me). I say don't repeat that I said the word 'delicious'—you know what I mean.

While at Walmer Castle Churchill discussed the problem of the deadlock on the western front with Asquith. On January 11 he wrote to Sir John French, warning him that neither he nor Asquith thought that it was wise for the British to take over a further sector of line from the French, as the Commander-in-Chief wished. 'It is a bleak & dreary role,' Churchill wrote, 'for the Br Army simply to take over more & more of this trench warfare, so harassing to the troops & so unrelieved by any definite success.' Churchill told French that he shared his belief that it would be wrong to desert 'the decisive theatre & the most formidable antagonist to win cheaper laurels in easier fields'. He then outlined his own wider plans for the Baltic, and explained the importance of the Zeebrugge operation, for both these schemes were uppermost in his mind:

. . . I favour remaining in the N[orthern] theatre, but endeavouring, as our numbers & resources increase, to lengthen the G[erman] line & compel him to expose new surfaces to the waste of war. It is clear that there are 4 possible lines of activity in this direction: (1) if we cd get command of the Baltic, the Russian armies cd threaten the whole Baltic shore, & Berlin at close quarters. (2) A landing in Schleswig wd directly threaten the Kiel Canal, & bring Denmark out on our side. (3) a landing at Emden wd strike at Wilhelmshaven & at the German heart. Yr headqrs are twice as far from Berlin as Emden is.
All these 3 operations depend on a naval situation not yet realized. But the capture of Borkum (always to be referred to as 'Sylt') was approved in principle by the War Council; & if this cd be achieved in March or April, it may be found possible to establish a control on the German rivermouths vy different from that wh now exists. Therefore I do not exclude these possibilities; tho it is premature to build on them now.
But after all the greatest hope in the N[orth] is (4) bringing Holland in. If in the summer we are in a position to offer Holland the protection of an army of 700,000 or 800,000 men, it is by no means impossible that she might

join the Allies. Her fate is bound up in our victory. One of the reasons why I favour the Coast opern is that it is a step in the direction of Holland & that every yard of Belgian soil cleared shows the Dutch that England never deserts her friends. It is not until all the Northern possibilities are exhausted that I wd look to the S of Europe as a field for the profitable employment of our expanding milty forces. But plans shd be worked out for every contingency.

Writing to Jellicoe on the same day, Churchill explained at length his North Sea proposals. The capture of Borkum would be, he wrote, 'the first step in an aggressive warfare wh wd, as it proceeds, cow the enemy, beat him into his ports, & mine and wire him in there'. Jellicoe had told Churchill of his worries about the German superiority in torpedo craft. 'But suppose,' Churchill wrote, 'we establish ourselves at this island . . . strongly enough to make the surrounding waters *our* torpedo-infested area, wd not the unfavourable situation be offered to the Germans?' Once established at Borkum, he continued, Britain could confront Germany 'with all the ugliest propositions. If he sends mine-sweepers out, destroyers will sink them. If he sends transports covered by bombarding battleships, what more cd our S/Ms ask?' The capture of Borkum, Churchill stressed, 'is the only aggressive policy wh gives the Navy its chance to apply its energy & daring, & in 6 weeks of fierce flotilla warfare we cd beat the enemy out of the North Sea altogether'.

Such was Churchill's opinion on January 11. Germany was the principal foe; her northern flank the primary and most vulnerable objective. Fisher remained an eastern enthusiast. That day he discussed the possibility of an attack on Turkey with Grey's Private Secretary, William Tyrrell. The Foreign Office wanted to know, Tyrrell explained, what chance there was of Britain capturing Constantinople, as the diplomatic advantages of such a victory would be considerable, and Britain's bargaining position with Russia greatly enhanced. On the following day Fisher wrote to Tyrrell that 'if the Greeks land 100,000 men on the Gallipoli Peninsula in concert with a British naval attack on the Dardanelles I think we could count on an easy and quick arrival at Constantinople . . .'.

8

By Ships Alone

O N the morning of January 12 Vice-Admiral Carden's reply reached the Admiralty from the Dardanelles. Instead of posing innumerable difficulties for a naval attack on the Straits, Carden outlined what in his view constituted an entirely effective means of breaking into the Sea of Marmara by ships alone. Nor was this to be such an extended operation of war as his initial telegram had suggested. On reflection he felt that it might be possible to force the Dardanelles in about a month. Churchill later told the Dardanelles Commissioners that Carden's telegram was '*the* most important telegram. Here was the Admiral, who had been for weeks sitting off the Dardanelles, who presumably had been turning this thing over in his mind again and again, wondering on the possibilities of action there, who produced a plan, and a detailed plan and a novel plan.' In his telegram Carden outlined four phases of action:

(A) Total reduction of defences at the entrance.
(B) Clear defences inside of Straits up to and including Kephez Point battery No 8.
(C) Reduction of defences at the Narrows Chanak.
(D) Clear passage through mine field, advancing through Narrows reducing forts above Narrows and final advance to Marmara.

The Admiral proceeded to describe in detail the method by which he would carry out these steps. He listed the ships which he would require, envisaging, as the end of the operation, a large flotilla, including four battleships, two battle-cruisers and twelve destroyers, securely inside the Sea of Marmara. The impact of Carden's plan was immediate, its implications wide. The Navy could achieve by itself a master stroke of the war. By ships alone the pressure on Russia could be relieved. The British, without recalling troops from the western front, would turn the southern and weakest flank of the Central Powers, and make it certain that Greece, Bulgaria and Rumania hasten to join the Allied cause.

248

Up to this moment Churchill had doubted the possibility of forcing the Dardanelles without troops. But he had never doubted that once the Dardanelles were forced, naval power alone would suffice to encompass the Turks' defeat. The force which Admiral Carden proposed to take into the Sea of Marmara would inevitably defeat the puny Turkish Fleet, even with the *Goeben* and *Breslau* at its head. Many tantalizing prospects followed. If the arrival of the *Goeben* and *Breslau* off Constantinople had turned the balance in Germany's favour at the outbreak of war, it seemed impossible that the Turks could resist the overwhelming strength of Admiral Carden's armada. Churchill believed that Enver's followers would abandon the German cause when confronted with so powerful a demonstration of British superiority, and that Enver himself might perhaps take the lead in shaking Turkey from the German grip. The surrender of Turkey did not appear to depend only upon a change of mood among the Turkish leaders. The whole Turkish war-making power was at Constantinople, exposed to attack from the sea. The only shell factory in Turkey was on the shore of the Sea of Marmara, just outside Constantinople. The principal gun and rifle factory was likewise vulnerable to naval attack. The railway linking Constantinople with the important railway junction at Kuleli Burgas, the fortress of Adrianople and the fortified lines of Chatalja ran partly along the shore as far as Kuchuk Chekmeje, ten miles to the west of the city. On the Asian shore, the railway into Anatolia did likewise. Both could be bombarded easily from ships in the Sea of Marmara. Churchill's advisers shared his excitement at the one conclusion which could be drawn from Admiral Carden's telegram: the Royal Navy was in a position to destroy Turkey at a single blow, to relieve Russia, to provide the bait with which to force each Balkan State to turn against the Central Powers, and by the rapid exploitation of victory on the southern flank to bring the whole war to an end. All this could be done, the Admiralty War Group believed, by battleships that were too old to be of use to Sir John Jellicoe in the North Sea, and which were surplus to British naval requirements elsewhere.[1]

On January 12 the War Group—Fisher, Wilson, Jackson and Oliver, assisted by de Bartolomé—discussed every aspect of Carden's proposals.

---

[1] The ships which the Admiralty War Group had in mind had all been launched before 1906, when the launching of the first of the new Dreadnought class meant that older ships would be a liability in any engagement with a Fleet which also had Dreadnought-class ships. The pre-Dreadnought battleships sent to the Dardanelles by 18 March 1915 were: *Majestic* (launched in 1895), *Prince George* (1896), *Canopus* (1899), *Ocean* (1900), *Irresistible* and *Vengeance* (1901), *Cornwallis*, *Swiftsure* and *Triumph* (1904). Also sent were *Agamemnon*, *Inflexible* and *Lord Nelson* (all launched in 1908), which were all of pre-Dreadnought design.

Neither Jackson nor Oliver, who subsequently criticized Carden's plan before the Dardanelles Commission, did so that day. Fisher made no protest. Jackson not merely concurred in the proposals but urged their rapid implementation. Each member of the War Group realized the enormous difficulties involved; each turned his own knowledge and expertise to the search for methods of overcoming the difficulties. The victory at the Falkland Islands six weeks before, by completing the destruction of German naval power outside German waters, released large numbers of ships for the new enterprise. Fisher therefore suggested that in addition to the old ships which Carden considered sufficient, the newest and most powerful ship in the fleet, the *Queen Elizabeth*, should be sent out to the Dardanelles. Her 15-inch guns had not yet been fired but could be tested, Fisher argued, not on dummy targets in the North Sea but on Turkish forts. On January 12 Fisher wrote to Oliver, sticking at the top of his letter a large pink label with the word RUSH in bold gold capitals:

> I've told Crease[1] to find out from Percy Scott and the Gunnery Experts if anything to prevent Queen Elizabeth giving all her ammunition at the Dardanelles Forts instead of uselessly into the ocean at Gibraltar and to let you know. If this is practicable she could go straight there, hoist Carden's flag & go on with her gunnery exercises and free the Indefatigable to go to Malta to refit and allow Inflexible to come straight home from Gibraltar to join the Second Battle Cruiser squadron.
> Perhaps you'll think over this. . . .

'This had not occurred to me before,' Churchill told the Dardanelles Commissioners in 1916, 'but the moment it was mentioned its importance became apparent. We all felt ourselves in the presence of a "new fact". Moreover the Queen Elizabeth came into the argument with a cumulative effect.'

Churchill sent copies of Carden's detailed proposals to Asquith and Kitchener during the early afternoon of January 12. He also put on paper an outline of his own view of the aim and method of the operation, which he sent immediately to Fisher, who approved it. Churchill wrote to Fisher of how glad he was that, as a result of the Admiral's suggestion, the *Queen Elizabeth* would be 'firing all her ammunition at the Dardanelles forts instead of uselessly into the sea'. His outline was in four parts:

---

[1] Thomas Evans Crease, 1875–1942. Entered Navy, 1889. Retired with rank of Commander, 1910. Naval Assistant and Secretary to Lord Fisher, both as First Sea Lord, 1914–15, and as Chairman of the Board of Invention and Research, 1915–16. Private Secretary to the First Lord of the Admiralty, 1917–19. Captain, 1918.

(1) The forcing of the Dardanelles as proposed, and the arrival of a squadron strong enough to defeat the Turkish Fleet in the Sea of Marmora, would be a victory of importance, and change to our advantage the whole situation of the war in the East.

(2) It would appear possible to provide the force required by Admiral Carden without weakening the margins necessary in home waters . . . no capital ship would be ordered from home waters, except four already ordered to be dismantled.

(3) The above takes no account of four French battleships on the spot, and six others reported available. . . .

(4) Operations could begin on February 1, by long-range fire from Queen Elizabeth on forts at the entrance. It is not necessary to develop the full attack until the effect of the first stage of the operation has become apparent. . . .

Definite plans should be worked out accordingly.

The War Council met at noon on January 13. Churchill argued that when new troops were available they should be sent to France and used in the joint military and naval operation against Zeebrugge for which he had argued at the War Council of the previous week. Sir John French, who had come over from France in order to be present at the meeting, agreed that if the Fleet 'would bring enfilade and reverse fire to bear on the enemy's trenches', he himself would be able 'to force his way along the coast'. Churchill believed that the clearance of the Belgian coast would be 'a first class victory', and would constitute 'a material and inestimably valuable protection to the lines of communication'. Grey was enthusiastic in support, feeling that the operation was worth attempting, even if it resulted in the loss of what he called 'only 8,000 men'. Lloyd George doubted the relevance of the advance to the general issue of the war, declaring that it would only be 'a minor operation', pushing back the line a little way, but without the power to break German resistance. No decision was reached.

After discussing the question of artillery ammunition, and the relative numbers of the combatant armies, the War Council adjourned for lunch. On reassembling it turned again to a discussion of the Zeebrugge plan. In answer to a question from Balfour, Churchill said that if Zeebrugge continued to be developed as a German naval base, 'it entailed great disadvantages on the Navy', and that there would probably be a series of 'depressing incidents' involving the sinking of Allied ships by German submarines. Nevertheless, he agreed that from a naval point of view the proposed operation was not one of 'absolutely vital importance' since 'the possession of Zeebrugge by the Germans would not kill our naval supremacy'.

It was not until after sunset that the War Council turned its attention to the Dardanelles, and Churchill outlined the details of Carden's plan. He explained that the three modern and twelve old battleships which Carden believed necessary could be spared for the task 'without reducing our strength in the main theatre of war'. He described the discussions that had already taken place at the Admiralty, and expressed his belief 'that a plan could be made for systematically reducing all the forts within a few weeks'. The effects of this action would, he believed, be impressive: 'Once the forts were reduced, the minefields would be cleared and the Fleet would proceed up to Constantinople and destroy the Goeben.' Hankey recalled in his memoirs, *The Supreme Command*: 'The idea caught on at once. . . . The War Council turned eagerly from the dreary vista of a "slogging match" on the Western Front to brighter prospects, as they seemed, in the Mediterranean. . . . Even French . . . caught something of the tremendous enthusiasm.' According to Hankey's minutes of the meeting, Lloyd George declared that he 'liked the plan', and Kitchener said that he 'thought it was worth trying'. Kitchener added that if the bombardment were ineffective the attack could always be called off.

Discussion then turned to other matters. Grey wanted the Navy to attack the Austrian port of Cattaro on the Adriatic, in an attempt to influence Italy to join the Allies. Churchill suggested that 'it would be awkward for the British Fleet to take any action there' as the French Fleet was already strongly represented in Adriatic waters. Lloyd George raised again the question of a major attack on Austria, and persuaded French to admit 'that complete success against the Germans in the Western theatre of war, though possible, was not probable' and that it would be desirable 'to seek new spheres of activity—particularly in Austria'. At this point Churchill tried to turn the War Council's attention once more to action in the North Sea. 'We ought not to go South,' he stated, 'until we are satisfied that we can do nothing in the North.' 'Was there, for example,' he asked, 'no possibility of action in Holland?' But Grey insisted that Britain should make no approach to Holland until the War Office were in a position to provide at least 300,000 British soldiers for such an expedition. Lloyd George spoke again in favour of a campaign against Austria. He wanted rolling stock to be manufactured for the Salonika railway 'and perhaps barges built for the Danube'. Churchill agreed that these preparations should be made. 'At the worst,' he said, 'they would be a good feint.'

The War Council had listened to a variety of suggestions. Everyone was agreed that plans must be made to cover new points of attack: the

Dardanelles, Holland, Salonika, Cattaro, the Danube, each had come into the discussion. Asquith then drafted the War Council's conclusions, the second and third of which read:

That the Admiralty should consider promptly the possibility of effective action in the Adriatic—at Cattaro, or elsewhere—with the view (inter alia) of bringing pressure on Italy.

That the Admiralty should also prepare for a naval expedition in February to bombard and take the Gallipoli peninsula, with Constantinople as its objective.

The War Council then broke up, and Asquith wrote to Venetia Stanley:

. . . The Council is now over, having arrived harmoniously at 4 conclusions suggested by me which will keep both navy and army busy till March. . . .

I maintained an almost unbroken silence till the end, when I intervened with my conclusions. But, except for one or two furtive glances at your letter (which only arrived at 3) I kept a careful watch on the rest. . . .

Winston (if such a phrase is possible) showed a good deal of rugged fluency.

The War Council was to meet again within the next few weeks to scrutinize their plans for action at the Dardanelles. During the interval Churchill and his advisers examined the details of the naval attack. The War Council's decision to take this risky action on Russia's behalf was reached, by coincidence, on January 13, the Russian New Year, and Churchill took the opportunity to send a message to the Russian people. 'Our resources,' he told them, 'are within reach and inexhaustible; our minds are made up. We have only to bend forward together laying aside every hindrance, keeping nothing back, and the downfall of German ambition is sure.' During the afternoon of January 13 Churchill sent Fisher and Oliver a long minute about the Mediterranean plan, which, he wrote, 'will always be referred to as "Pola"',[1] for secrecy; Sir Percy Scott would be travelling as far as Gibraltar on the *Queen Elizabeth* to help regulate her guns; because Sir Henry Jackson had been taken sick, Oliver would draft the orders for the concentration of the ships and the regulation of the gunnery; ships should begin at once to sail for various Mediterranean ports; a landing place for aeroplanes should be established on the island of Tenedos; to avoid alerting anti-

[1] I can find no evidence that the attack on the Dardanelles was ever referred to as 'Pola' again, either by Churchill's advisers, or by Churchill himself.

aircraft guns, the French should be asked not fly over the Dardanelles; the vessels Carden has asked for should be put under orders; Malta dockyard should prepare to fit ships with mine-bumpers; and finally:

Admiral Carden's proposals should be carefully analysed by an officer of the War Staff in order to show exactly what guns the ships will have to face at each point and stage of the operations, the character of the guns, and their range; but this officer is to assume that the principle is settled, and all that is necessary is to estimate the force required.

This enterprise is regarded by the Government as of the highest urgency and importance. A telegram should be drafted to Admiral Carden approving his proposals and informing him of the forces which will be placed at his disposal. No order should go out to him or anyone else until his answer about ammunition expenditure is received, and until the whole scheme can be considered finally in draft.

Commodore de Bartolomé will keep in touch with the details on my behalf. I hope that definite orders may be issued in 2 or 3 days.

At one in the morning of January 15 Churchill telegraphed to Carden that the War Council had authorized plans to go ahead and that he would be in command of the attack:

Your scheme was laid by the First Sea Lord and myself before the Cabinet War Council yesterday and was approved in principle.

We see no difficulty in providing the force you require including the QUEEN ELIZABETH by the 15th February.

We entirely agree with your plan of methodical piecemeal reduction of forts as the Germans did at Antwerp.

We propose to entrust this operation to you.

Admiral de Robeck[1] will probably be your second in command.

The sooner we can begin the better.

You will shortly receive the official instructions of the Board.

Continue to perfect your plan.

In addition to authorizing Churchill to plan for an attack at the Dardanelles, the War Council had also instructed him to make plans

---

[1] John Michael de Robeck, 1862–1928. Entered Navy, 1875. Rear-Admiral, 1911. Commanded the 9th Cruiser Squadron, charged with protecting British merchant ships in the mid-Atlantic, 1914–15. 2nd in command of the Allied naval forces at the Dardanelles, February–March 1915. Vice-Admiral commanding the Allied naval forces at the Dardanelles, March 1915–January 1916. Knighted, 1916. Commanded the 2nd Battle Squadron in the North Sea, 1916–18. Created Baronet, 1919. Commander-in-Chief of the Mediterranean Fleet, 1919–22. Admiral, 1920. High Commissioner at Constantinople, 1922. Commander-in-Chief of the Atlantic Fleet, 1922–4. Admiral of the Fleet, 1925.

for an attack on Austrian naval positions in the Adriatic. Churchill discussed the possibility of action in the Adriatic with Fisher and Oliver. Fisher minuted on January 14 that the French Admiralty might be persuaded 'to be more active than hitherto'. Both Fisher and Oliver felt that any British naval involvement in the Adriatic might weaken the chances of success at the Dardanelles. On January 15 Churchill put their objections to Asquith, Grey and Kitchener:

We consider that no useful means can be found of effective naval intervention in the Adriatic at the present time. The French have a large superiority of naval force there now, including Dreadnoughts and large numbers of destroyers. Their operations make no progress. . . .

The attack on the Dardanelles will require practically our whole available margin. If that attack opens prosperously it will very soon attract to itself the whole attention of the Eastern theatre, and if it succeeds it will produce results which will undoubtedly influence every Mediterranean power.

In these circumstances we strongly advise that the Adriatic should be left solely to the French and that we should devote ourselves to action in accordance with the third conclusion of the War Council, viz:—the methodical forcing of the Dardanelles.

Agreeing with Fisher's minute, Churchill ended his letter: 'Pressure shd be put upon the French to be more active.' Asquith accepted the Admiralty case. Kitchener and Grey agreed that plans for naval action in the Adriatic should be abandoned. For several months there had been total disagreement as to which plan should be followed. Now agreement had been reached. Asquith was eager that the attack on Turkey should succeed. On January 15 he saw Noel and Charles Buxton, who had just returned from the Balkans. Both were convinced that, by substantial offers of Austrian and Turkish territory, the Balkan States could without exception be persuaded to join the Allies. Asquith wrote to Venetia Stanley that such a Balkan combination 'with our Gallipoli enterprise, of wh of course I did not tell them, might conceivably make a huge & even decisive diversion. It wd certainly compel Italy to come in.'

For the next two weeks the Admiralty War Group concentrated its attention upon the Dardanelles. Every aspect of the attack was examined in detail. Churchill encouraged Carden to report all his needs and problems. A series of telegrams passed between them. On January 15 Sir Henry Jackson, who had recovered from his illness, prepared a memorandum based on Carden's proposals, and saying that previous Admiralty appreciations of forcing the Dardanelles 'differed only in

small details'. He then went into detail about the nature of the operation, urging that minesweepers and munitions 'should be despatched
without delay' and that some experiment in bombardment should be
begun without delay. In a secret and personal telegram to Carden on
January 25 Churchill showed his determination to send Carden every
support, and to give the operation priority:

> . . . I am expecting detailed requirements from you as regards mine-
> sweepers, mine-bumpers, and all such appliances. If possible, these may be
> executed by Malta, but Malta's resources will be supplemented from
> England.
> This is a great opportunity, and you must concentrate absolutely upon it.
> You will have enough ships to be independent of the French. Your plans are
> in principle agreed with by Sir Henry Jackson, who examines for the Board
> all naval questions connected with the East.
> All your wants that cannot be supplied locally should be fully reported by
> telegram. Queen Elizabeth's departure is being expedited as much as
> possible.

Churchill scrutinized the intelligence reports which arrived regularly
from Turkey and the Balkans, sending Carden all the information
which he could extract which bore upon the operation. These reports
dealt with Turkish military strength and morale. He also procured a
Russian plan of the Dardanelles fortifications, which was sent to
Carden on January 30, and which he was instructed to compare with
his own maps.

At the start of the war, on 6 August 1914, the British Government had
agreed that the Mediterranean should be predominantly an area of
French naval activity. Churchill had therefore to persuade the French
to accept a British enterprise there. He also hoped that they would take
a direct part in the operation, for French participation, even on a small
scale, would ensure that Britain did not strain its naval resources in the
event of the attack requiring extra strength. Churchill outlined the
British plan and sought the support of France in a telegram to the
French Minister of Marine, Victor Augagneur.[1] Asquith, Kitchener,
Grey and Fisher all approved the draft, and the telegram was sent on
January 18:

> The British Government find it necessary to take offensive action against
> Turkey in the near future. The Admiralty have in consequence decided to

[1] Victor Augagneur, 1855–1931. A distinguished French pathologist and colonial administrator. Minister of Marine, 1914–18.

attack the Dardanelles forts and force, if possible, a passage into the Sea of Marmora. It is proposed to achieve this by a gradual and methodical reduction of the forts by naval bombardment taking three or four weeks, if necessary, and using a number of the older battleships supported by 2 battle-cruisers & the very long-range fire of the 15-inch guns of the Queen Elizabeth. In all, 15 battleships or battle-cruisers, 3 light cruisers, 16 destroyers, 6 submarines, 1 sea-plane ship and a large number of mine-sweepers & auxiliaries, are required, having regard to the expected casualties & the need of fighting the Turco-German Fleet immediately on entering the Sea of Marmora. This Fleet will be assembled between the 7th and 15th February, and it is hoped that the attack will follow immediately. The scheme of these operations has been prepared by Vice-Admiral Carden, now commanding the Allied Fleets at the Dardanelles.

The Admiralty do not wish, in view of this very important operation, that any change in the local command in that portion of the Mediterranean should be made at the present time. They hope however that the squadron of French battleships, together with the French submarines and destroyers and the sea-plane ship Foudre, will co-operate under a French Rear-Admiral.

Augagneur agreed to send a French naval force to the Dardanelles, but wanted the French to have overall command of the attack. Churchill insisted that the British should control the operation, and was strongly supported by Asquith and Grey. Augagneur agreed to cross over to London before the next meeting of the War Council to resolve the dispute, refusing to commit himself as to whether a French or British Admiral should command. But Churchill proceeded with his plans on the assumption that the French would accept a subsidiary role.

The next War Council was summoned to meet on January 28. In preparation, Churchill issued a series of minutes, all of them approved by Fisher, covering the technical problems involved in the attack. Unwilling to rely upon French seaplanes for intelligence work, Churchill decided to keep the Ark Royal in readiness with her eight seaplanes. He instructed his advisers to analyse Carden's proposals in order to show exactly which Turkish guns each ship would have to face, and to examine their character and range. On January 15 Sir Henry Jackson suggested that the outer forts of the Dardanelles ought to be attacked as soon as possible, 'as the experience gained would be useful' in the subsequent attacks on the Narrows. On January 16 Captain Richmond returned to his idea of a demonstration against the Turkish coast, writing in his diary: 'I spoke again to General Callwell about it at lunch today: he said Kitchener couldn't or wouldn't make up his mind. The French naval attaché is very keen to do something there—preferably to force the Dardanelles. This Oliver has proposed, and Sir H. Jackson has I believe prepared the outline of a plan. So have I.' Richmond saw merits in the Dardanelles scheme: 'With our modern long range heavy guns we can outrange the Turkish forts & a useful bombardment can be carried out. If we can force the passage we have Constantinople open, & the result will I hope be a revolution in Turkey.' The snag, Richmond believed, was that Churchill's true interests were elsewhere. In his diary he confided: 'Meanwhile Winston is busy thinking out pinpricks in the shape of air raids which he seems to think will produce wonderful results, & fails to appreciate that their proper value is reconnaissances, & no more. He also has still his silly Borkum scheme in mind & wants [it] worked out. I have made one or two remarks upon it which I hope will go some way towards damning it.'

Determined to undermine the Borkum scheme, Richmond sent Oliver a strong memorandum on January 19. 'The condemnation of the whole scheme . . .' he wrote, 'lies in the fact that it violates the simple and well established law that you cannot make an oversea expedition of troops until you have command of the sea over which the troops have to pass.' Richmond recorded in his diary that when he saw Oliver that day 'I told him I thought the whole thing impracticable & that it ought not to be done. He agreed. I therefore hope that it will be squashed.' Richmond did not know that Churchill had already turned away from Borkum. Indeed, on January 18, Fisher had appealed to Churchill not to forget the northern theatre:

I have no wish whatever to cold-douche any projects for our being trouble-some to the enemy in the following remarks. . . .

But I desire to emphasize the necessity of sticking to the enemy's vitals! I am not minimizing the coming Dardanelles operation, but I wish to aggrand-ize the great big fact that 750,000 men landed in Holland, combined with intense activity of the British Fleet against, say, Cuxhaven, would finish the War by forcing out the German High Sea Fleet and getting in rear of the German Armies! The First Lord has twice put before the War Council the Dutch Project and no one 'gainsaid' it! Is it going to be done? Great prepara-tions are involved. The frost so deadly to Holland is over in May.

Fisher knew that if sixty thousand men could not be spared for the Dardanelles, it was unlikely that three-quarters of a million would be ready to send to Holland by May. But he now plunged into an orgy of discontent. He feared that the Dardanelles would absorb too much time, and too many ships, to the detriment of Britain's strong naval position in the North Sea. This fear was prompted by a series of letters from Jellicoe, who was pessimistic about the superiority of the Grand Fleet. On January 19 Fisher wrote:

PLEASE BURN
My dear Jellicoe,
 . . . It's amusing how Winston makes out that in all types you are ever so much stronger than when you assumed command of the Fleet. I simply keep on reiterating, '*He has only 29 battleships available at present.*' He can't get round that fact! So goes off on another attack on your arrangements: 'Why do you send so many away at once for repairs and refit?' Because you can't help it! Then the complaint is that you run the ships to death! that they never get rest! etc, etc. And now the Cabinet have decided on taking the Dardanelles solely with the Navy, using 15 battleships and 32 other vessels, and keeping out there three battle cruisers and a flotilla of destroyers—*all urgently required at the decisive theatre at home!* There is only one way out, and that is to resign! But you say '*no*', which simply means I am a consenting party to what I absolutely disapprove. *I don't agree with one single step taken*, so it is fearfully against the grain that I remain on in deference to your wishes. . . .

On January 20 Fisher poured out his woes to Hankey, who passed them on to Asquith, who at once informed Venetia Stanley:

Hankey came to see me today to say that Fisher, who is an old friend of his, had come to him in a very unhappy frame of mind. He likes Winston personally, but complains that on purely technical naval matters he is frequently overruled ('he out-argues me'), and he is not by any means at ease about either the present disposition of the fleets or their future movements. Though I think the old man is rather difficult, I fear there is some truth in what he says.

It was eight days since Fisher had seen Carden's plan of attack. That day he sent Churchill his first dissenting minute, pressing for the return of the British destroyer flotilla from the Dardanelles, and suggesting its replacement by French ships. He also argued that an Australian submarine which had just reached the Dardanelles was wanted urgently in the North Sea and that it was 'inexcusable to waste her on the Turks'. Fisher did not argue that the Turks could not be defeated at sea; he believed, as he wrote in his minute, that 'the whole Turkish force is quite a negligible quantity even with German officers'. Fisher wanted Churchill to ask the French Government to take the necessary action against the Turks, while Britain concentrated its full naval strength upon action in the North Sea and in the Baltic. But the War Council's decision to proceed with an attack on the Turks at the Dardanelles was not one with which Fisher had the authority to quarrel. It had been reached for wide-ranging diplomatic and military reasons. Writing again to Jellicoe on January 21, Fisher was profoundly distressed by his lack of authority but returned once more to his initial plea for soldiers:

... This Dardanelles operation, decided upon by the Cabinet, in its taking away Queen Elizabeth, Indefatigable and Inflexible and Blenheim, with a flotilla of destroyers arranged to have been brought home, is a serious interference with our imperative needs in Home waters, and I've fought against it 'tooth and nail'. But, of course, if the Government of the Country decide on a project as a subject of high policy, one can't put oneself up to govern the diplomatic attitude of the nation in its relation with foreign powers, and apparently the Grand Duke Nicholas has demanded this step, or—(I suppose he would make peace with Germany . . .).

I just abominate the Dardanelles operation, unless a great change is made and it is settled to be made a military operation, with 200,000 men in conjunction with the Fleet. I believe that Kitchener is coming now to this sane view of the matter.

Fisher failed to inform Jellicoe that during the War Council on January 13, Kitchener, under close questioning from his colleagues, had stated categorically that no troops were available for the Dardanelles. There is no other evidence to suggest, as Fisher did in his letter, that Kitchener's views had begun to change on this subject, for Kitchener reiterated his belief at the War Council on January 28; and in early February, while still in favour of forcing the Dardanelles by ships alone, proposed to use the first spare Division which could be assembled for a landing, not at the Dardanelles but at Salonika. Everyone concerned with the attack, including Churchill, would have liked to land troops on the Gallipoli Peninsula in conjunction with the naval bombardment. But Kitchener had made it clear that no troops were available, and Carden had shown himself keen to make the attack with ships alone. There could be no going back on the War Council decision of January 13 unless Fisher could show that despite the ships available and despite the detailed plans which had been worked out, the chances of success were remote. No member of the Admiralty War Group made such an assertion. Fisher's private letters to Jellicoe were no substitute for official memoranda, circulated to his colleagues, and open to discussion by all those at the Admiralty concerned with the operation. 'He is old & worn out & nervous,' Richmond wrote of Fisher in his diary on 19 January 1915. 'It is ill to have the destinies of an empire in the hands of a failing old man, anxious for popularity, afraid of any local mishap which may be put down to his dispositions.'

The eager hopes which turned all minds increasingly to the Dardanelles were forgotten for a brief moment towards the end of January.

On Saturday January 23 Churchill was in his room at the Admiralty when Sir Arthur Wilson and Admiral Oliver strode in. They brought exciting news: an intercepted German message had revealed that the High Sea Fleet would leave its harbour that night. The three men discussed what action to take. A telegram was drafted to Jellicoe, alerting him and wishing his ships all good fortune in the coming battle. The three men then took this telegram, together with naval charts, to Fisher, who was in his room at Archway House, adjoining the Admiralty, confined to bed with a severe cold. Fisher was overjoyed at the prospect of a great naval victory. 'We shared our secret with none,' Churchill later recorded in *The World Crisis*. 'That night I attended a dinner which the French Ambassador was giving to Monsieur Millerand,[1] then Minister of War and in London on a mission of consequence. One felt separated from the distinguished company who gathered there, by a film of isolated knowledge and overwhelming inward preoccupation.'

All Sunday morning the telegrams poured in to the Admiralty announcing that off the Dogger Bank battle had begun. The excitement at the Admiralty was intense. Unable to curb his patience, Churchill sent a messenger along the Mall to Buckingham Palace with the following note, marked 'secret':

Sir,
An action is in progress in the North Sea between the British & German battlecruisers with light cruisers & destroyers on both sides. We have a good superiority, plenty of daylight and plenty of sea-room. I will send Your Majesty a further report presently.

I remain Your Majesty's devoted servant
Winston S. Churchill

By early afternoon the battle was over. Although it had not been as decisive as Churchill had hoped, the German battle-cruiser *Blücher* with twelve hundred men on board had been sunk. The other German ships had returned in haste to port. The public acclaimed the victory. British supremacy in the North Sea seemed undisputed. 'Glorious!' wrote

[1] Alexandre Millerand, 1859–1943. Elected to the French Chamber of Deputies as a Radical Socialist, 1885. Minister of War, January 1912–January 1913; and again from January 1914 to October 1915. He resigned following accusations that he had failed to find sufficient heavy artillery. Prime Minister, 1920. President of the Republic, 1920–4.

Haldane. 'What an answer to silent prayers! I congratulate you with my whole soul. It is well deserved.' But Churchill himself was disappointed. 'Today a chance offered:' he wrote to Sir John French, 'but only one forfeit cd be exacted. I had hoped for more. We hit them vy hard. But their strong armour protected their motive power: & they fled so fast, we cd not obtain a decision.'

A naval success had been won in the North Sea with insignificant loss. But at the Dardanelles none could promise that victory would be so cheap. Fisher feared that unnecessary risks taken at the Dardanelles would impair Britain's naval superiority. Churchill could not agree. In 1916 he explained his point of view in his evidence to the Dardanelles Commissioners:

It is not right to condemn operations of war simply because they involve risk and uncertainty. Some operations can and ought to be made certainties. Others belong to the class where one can only balance the chances, and action must proceed on a preponderance of favourable chances. For instance, the naval attack on the Dardanelles in its final and decisive phase was, of course, a sharp hazard of war. But so were a great many other things we had done successfully since the outbreak. Sending the fleet to its war station on 29th July by the eastern route instead of northabout was a risk. Throwing the whole British Army across the Channel in the early days of August was a supreme risk, both military and naval. Carrying the 7th Division and 3rd Cavalry Division to Zeebrugge in October, 1914, in the teeth of the enemy's submarines, was a most serious risk well run by Prince Louis of Battenberg in my absence at Antwerp. Withdrawing two battle-cruisers from the Grand Fleet to the Falklands to destroy von Spee was a risk. Every time the Grand Fleet has swept down to the German coast there is a heavy risk. Sending two entire brigades of infantry in a single ship (Aquitania) to the Dardanelles through submarine-infested waters, which was run both in my time and in my successor's time, was a very serious risk. Fighting the Battle of Jutland in the enemy's waters was a tremendous risk. All these operations, on which the successful prosecution of the naval war has been founded, were pervaded by grave elements of risk in matters of superior importance to the naval attack on the Dardanelles. Therefore it is idle to condemn operations because they involve hazard and uncertainty. All war is hazard. Victory is only wrested by running risks.

Fisher listened to such arguments from Churchill many times during January. Although he could not always answer them, they roused his instinctive suspicion. In *Winston Churchill As I Knew Him*, Violet

Bonham Carter,[1] who knew both Churchill and Fisher well, drew a perceptive picture of how the Admiral's mind was working:

He lived by instincts, hunches, flashes, which he was unable to justify or sustain in argument. Though words poured from his lips and from his pen he was no match for Winston as a dialectician. In trying to defend his own position he trumped up reasons and pretexts of no substance which Winston easily demolished. . . . His personal intimacy with Winston and affection for him increased his sense of helplessness in standing up to him.

When argument seemed of no avail, Fisher usually resorted to threats of resignation. But now he decided to fight the matter out. On January 25 he drafted a long memorandum of protest which he sent to Churchill with a covering note: 'I have no desire to continue a useless resistance in the War Council to plans I cannot concur in, and I would ask that the enclosed may be printed and circulated to its members before the next meeting.'

In his memorandum Fisher declared that the Dardanelles operation would impair the 'present superiority' of the British fleet in the North Sea, asserting that 'even the older ships should not be risked, for they cannot be lost without losing men, and they form the only reserve behind the Grand Fleet.' Fisher said nothing about the practicability or otherwise of the Dardanelles operation itself. He concentrated entirely upon the dangers to British naval superiority in the North Sea which he believed would arise if ships were sent either to the Mediterranean, or to support Churchill's other plan, a military attack towards Zeebrugge:

We play into Germany's hands if we risk fighting ships in any subsidiary operations such as coastal bombardments or the attack of fortified places without military co-operation, for we thereby increase the possibility that the Germans may be able to engage our fleet with some approach to equality of strength. The sole justification of coastal bombardments and attacks by the fleet on fortified places, such as the contemplated prolonged bombardment of the Dardanelles forts by our Fleet, is to force a decision at sea, and so far and no further can they be justified. . . .

Ours is the supreme necessity and difficulty of remaining passive, except in so far as we can force the enemy to abandon his defensive and to expose his fleet to a general action. In the French wars we aimed at this by cutting off the enemy's trade and by joint naval and military operations against his territory. . . .

[1] Violet Asquith, 1887–1969. Asquith's eldest daughter, by his first wife. In November 1915 she married Asquith's Private Secretary, Maurice Bonham Carter. Active in Liberal politics throughout her life. Created Baroness Asquith of Yarnbury, 1964.

It has been said that the first function of the British Army is to assist the fleet in obtaining command of the sea. This might be accomplished by military co-operation with the Navy in such operations as the attack of Zeebrugge, or the forcing of the Dardanelles, which might bring out the German and Turkish fleets respectively. Apparently, however, this is not to be. The English Army is apparently to continue to provide a small sector of the allied front in France, where it no more helps the Navy than if it were at Timbuctoo.

Replying on January 26, in a memorandum circulated to members of the War Council, Churchill agreed that 'the foundation of our naval policy is the maintenance in a secure position of a battle fleet with all ancillary vessels capable at any time of defeating the German High Sea Fleet in battle'. But he insisted that this principle 'has been and will be fully and strictly observed'. He set out a table showing the respective naval strengths of Britain and Germany and pointed out that even the detailing of ships for the Dardanelles in no way weakened the necessary British naval dominance in the North Sea; not only was Jellicoe's Fleet strong enough to meet any German challenge, but the other function of the Navy, 'the protection of trade and the control of sea communications', was also entirely unaffected by the Dardanelles operation. Churchill then turned to Fisher's complaint that there would be insufficient ships to deal with German raiders:

All German cruisers and gunboats abroad have been sunk, blocked in, or interned (as shown in the margin), with the exception of the Karlsruhe and Dresden, which are hiding. There are great doubts as to the efficiency of the Karlsruhe,[1] of whom nothing has been heard for nearly three months. There are believed to be 2 German armed merchantmen at large (the Kronprinz Wilhelm and Prinz Eitel Friedrich). All the rest of the 42 prepared for arming, and which it has been intended to let loose on the trade routes, have been blockaded, interned, sunk, or captured. To deal with the 2 German cruisers and the two armed liners which are not yet run down, there are now, apart from Home Waters and the Mediterranean, the following British vessels:—

10 armoured or large cruisers.

31 light cruisers (including 2 in Suez Canal).

19 armed merchant cruisers (4 in Red Sea included).

19 self-defensive armed merchantmen.

In addition to the British ships available, there is the Japanese Navy and such French and Russian ships as are outside the Mediterranean and their respective home waters.

[1] The *Karlsrühe*, which from August to October 1914 had sunk 16 British merchant ships in the Caribbean, had in fact been destroyed by an internal explosion on November 4. News of the loss, which only reached Germany in December, was kept secret for several months.

Churchill continued by pointing out that it was not at the Dardanelles alone that surplus ships must eventually be used. There would always be 'objectives of great strategic and political importance' in which the Royal Navy would be involved. Now it was the Dardanelles, and possibly Zeebrugge; another contingency which might arise was the seizure of Borkum and the launching of the Baltic scheme Fisher had always favoured. Churchill insisted that naval actions of this sort need never involve the use of ships which were needed to maintain the superiority of the Grand Fleet. Of the risk of loss of ships and life, Churchill wrote:

It is believed that with care and skill losses may be reduced to a minimum, and certainly kept within limits fully justified by the importance and necessity of the operations. It cannot be said that this employment of ships which are (except the 'Duncans') not needed and not suited to fight in the line of battle, conflicts with any of the sound principles of naval policy set forth by the First Sea Lord. Not to use them where necessary because of some fear that there will be an outcry if a ship is lost would be wrong, and, if a certain proportion of loss of life among officers and men of the Royal Navy serving on these ships can achieve important objects of the war and save a very much greater loss of life among our comrades and allies on shore, we ought certainly not to shrink from it.

This reply completed, Churchill sent Fisher a personal appeal:

There is no difference in principle between us. But when all your special claims are met, you must let the surplus be used for the general cause.

I suggest I show your Memo & my comment to the Prime Minister: instead of printing & circulating the documents. You & I are so much stronger together.

Fisher wanted both his protest and Churchill's reply circulated to the War Council. But Asquith, who strongly supported the Dardanelles operation, refused to allow either of them to be printed. The result was that the War Council were never informed of Fisher's specific objections to the plan, nor of Churchill's answers. Churchill was glad that Asquith had upheld his ministerial authority. Fisher felt cheated that his objections had not been treated as seriously as he had wished.

The planning of the operations continued unchecked. On January 25 Oliver had completed a comprehensive scheme for the rapid concentration of ships at the Dardanelles. *Canopus* had left South America and was nearing Cape St Vincent. *Albion* had left St Helena, *Triumph* was taking on supplies at Colombo, *Ocean* and *Swiftsure* were in Egypt.

Rear-Admiral de Robeck, who had been appointed Carden's second-in-command, was at Gibraltar, awaiting the arrival of his flagship *Inflexible*. At British naval stations all over the world ships were likewise being assembled, fitted and supplied. Despite his strong protest of the previous day, it was Fisher himself who suggested adding two further battleships, *Lord Nelson* and *Agamemnon*. They too were ordered to proceed to the eastern Mediterranean. During January 25 Churchill sent Asquith, Grey and Kitchener a copy of these naval movements, noting that 'Arrangements sh'd enable fire to be opened on Feb 15'.

On the morning of January 26 Grey sent Churchill the text of a message from the Grand Duke Nicholas which had just reached the Foreign Office from Petrograd, regretting that the Russians could take no naval initiative in the Black Sea during the Dardanelles operation. Their fleet, the Grand Duke explained, was 'not more than the equal of the Turkish Fleet' and the Turkish guns at the entrance to the Bosphorus 'as compared both in number and power with those placed in Russian ships were such as to give little hope of a successful attack'. The Grand Duke believed that British action was now imperative. 'A successful attack against Turkey,' he explained, 'would react on the principal enemy (German) line; it would paralyze Turkey; and would infallibly be a deciding factor in determining the attitude of Neutral States in the Balkans.' This telegram reached the Admiralty while Churchill was in conference with Augagneur, who had just arrived from Paris to settle the disputed details of French naval co-operation. With the Grand Duke's Memorandum, Grey sent a covering note:

This is the Russian reply about Dardanelles. It shows that, though Russia cannot help, the operation has her entire goodwill and the Grand Duke attaches the greatest importance to its success.

This fact may be used with Augagneur to show that we must go ahead with it and that failure to do so will disappoint Russia & react most unfavourably upon the military situation, about which France & we are specially concerned just now. . . .

Augagneur accepted that the British were determined to control the naval attack, and agreed to French participation in a subsidiary role. The opportunity for French territorial gains along the Syrian coast, and particularly at Alexandretta, had not been overlooked in Paris. At midday Churchill was able to send an outline of the terms which Augagneur was willing to accept to Grey and Kitchener:

1) The British to have the command at the Dlles & to undertake the operation at their discretion. The French sqn there will cooperate, but the extent

of its cooperation will be defined after the French naval authorities have examined the general plan.

2) The British Vice-Admiral will continue to command in Egypt, but a French VA will command in the Levant, not only as I had proposed from Latakia to Jaffa, but including Alexandretta. Any military operation on the Levantine coast shd be a subject of discussion first between the two govts & the French wish to participate in any occupation of Alexandretta.

Lord Kitchener informs me that he cannot now fix any date for the Alexandretta expedition, so it appears unnecessary to make precise conditions about it.

I think it would be a good thing if you both had a talk with M. Augagneur.

Grey was keen to exploit the French Minister's territorial aspirations, writing to Churchill during the afternoon:

I think it important to let the French have what they want in this Memo even about Alexandretta. It will be fatal to cordial co-operation in the Mediterranean & perhaps everywhere if we arouse their suspicions as to anything in the region of Syria. I hope you will close with this proposal. If it is not agreed to I foresee very untoward consequences.

Churchill reached formal agreement with Augagneur that same day. The Royal Navy would be responsible for planning the Dardanelles operation; a British Admiral would command it; the French would co-operate, obeying British orders. Both Churchill and Augagneur believed that even without Russian help, the enterprise would succeed, and that success would draw more eager Allies, and new ones, into its orbit. But if the Anglo-French squadron failed to force the Dardanelles, the operation could be abandoned. This feature of the all-naval attack had appealed particularly to the War Council, and was also much in Churchill's mind. He had not overlooked the possibility of failure. Should that occur, he was in favour of taking up another of Kitchener's projects, the capture of Alexandretta, and had already written to Kitchener on January 20:

Secret
My dear Kitchener,

Until the bombardment of the Dardanelles forts has actually begun, we cannot tell how things will go. We must guard against the appearance of a serious rebuff: & we shall therefore at the outset only use the battleships needed for the initial stage, keeping the rest of the fleet spread between Malta, Alexandria & Alexandretta, whence they can concentrate vy quickly. It is also vy desirable that the Alexandretta operation shd be so timed as to be practically simultaneous with the attack on the Dlles, so that if we are checked at the Dlles, we can represent that opern as a mere demonstration to cover the seizure of Alexandretta. I believe this aspect is important from an oriental point of view.

Cd you therefore arrange this and let me have yr Alexandretta dates? We are aiming at the 15th Feb for opening fire on the Dlles.

Yours sincerely
WSC

PS I am sending a copy of this to the PM to keep him informed.

All the arrangements, naval and diplomatic, were complete. Only the final approval of the War Council remained. But without warning, on January 28, the day the War Council was to meet, Fisher protested once more, writing to Asquith that morning:

Private and Personal
My dear Prime Minister,

I am giving this note to Colonel Hankey to hand to you to explain my absence from the War Council. I am not in accord with the First Lord and do not think it would be seemly to say so before the Council. His reply to my memorandum does not meet my case. I say that the Zeebrugge and Dardanelles bombardments can only be justified on naval grounds by military co-operation, which would compensate for the loss in ships and irreplaceable officers and men. As purely naval operations they are unjustifiable, as they both drain our naval margin—not too large in view of collisions, such as Conqueror and Monarch, mines and submarines, such as Audacious and Formidable, and other previous great losses, and fools as admirals, such as Bayly and others, who you can no more account for beforehand than for Sir Redvers Buller,[1] who, with a Victoria Cross, was seized with mental paralysis on the field of battle at Colenso and Spionkopf! We are at this moment vitally in want of destroyers, wrongly kept at the Dardanelles in opposition to my representations. We are sending our best submarine to the Dardanelles and our largest and most valuable battleship, the Queen Elizabeth, with the only 15-inch guns ready at present, besides sending other battle cruisers now there against my protest. What will our officers and men say to me if I agreed to those 15-inch guns being in Asia Minor when at any moment the great crisis may occur in the North Sea and the German High Sea Fleet be driven to fight by the German Military Headquarters as part of some military operation?

---

[1] Redvers Henry Buller, 1839–1908. Entered Army, 1858. Received the Victoria Cross in 1879, during the Zulu War. General, commanding the forces in South Africa, 1899–1900. His attempts to relieve Ladysmith were checked by the Boers on 15 December 1899 at Colenso, and on 24 January 1900 at Spion Kop.

I am very reluctant to leave the First Lord. I have a great personal affection and admiration for him, but I see no possibility of a union of ideas, and unity is essential in war, so I refrain from any desire of remaining as a stumbling block.

The British Empire ceases if our Grand Fleet ceases. No risks can be taken.

Yours truly

Fisher

Fisher also sent a letter of resignation to Churchill; it was waiting for him when he reached his desk that morning:

Keep strictly Private & Personal

My dear Winston,

I entreat you to believe that if as I think really desirable for a complete *'unity of purpose'* in the War that I should gracefully disappear and revert to roses at Richmond (*The heart untravelled fondly turns to home*) that there will not be in my heart the least lingering thought of anything but regard and affection and *indeed much admiration* towards yourself.

Late last night quite spontaneously I got these words (*absolutely unsolicited*) from Jellicoe to whom I had said not one word about the Inflexible being detailed to Dardanelles or about the Indefatigable or Destroyers or submarines AE2 or indeed anything beyond the Elizabeth going to the Mediterranean for gun practice & why shouldn't she use her practice shots on the Dardanelles etc and the possibilities flowing from it.

'The Battle cruiser action shewed very conclusively the absolute necessity for a *big* preponderance of this type of ship and I hope will at any rate result in no diversion of ANY "Queen Elizabeths" or ANY Battle Cruisers FROM THE DECISIVE THEATRE. It might easily have been a disaster. Had we lost the *Lion* victory would have been turned into a defeat.'

Yours

F

My position is quite clear:—

I make no objection to either Zeebrugge or Dardanelles if accompanied by military cooperation on such a scale as will permanently hold the Belgian coast to the Dutch Frontier and our permanent military occupation of the Dardanelles Forts pari passu with the Naval bombardment. Simultaneous Military & Naval actions but no drain thereby on Grand Fleet Margin so therefore no modern vessels at Dardanelles.

I shall not as arranged with you attend the War Council and am going down to Richmond.

On receiving Fisher's resignation Churchill hurried across the Horse Guards' Parade to 10 Downing Street. Asquith was furious at Fisher's threat to leave London altogether. A stern summons was sent at once to Admiralty House:

Private
My dear Fisher
    The Prime Minister considers your presence at the War Council indispensable, & so do I. He will receive us both at 11.10 so that we can have a talk beforehand.
    You have assented to both the operations in question & so far as I am concerned there can be no withdrawal without good reason from measures wh are necessary, & for wh preparations are far advanced.
    I wd infinitely sooner work with you than with Sturdee who will undoubtedly be forced upon me in the eventuality of wh you write so lightheartedly.

Yours ever
W

Fisher agreed to put his objections before Asquith. Together with Churchill, he presented himself at 10 Downing Street twenty minutes before the War Council of January 28 was to begin. Fisher's object was to stop both the Dardanelles and Zeebrugge. Churchill recorded in *The World Crisis* that he had argued that 'both Zeebrugge and the Dardanelles scheme should be undertaken, but that if either were to be dropped it should be Zeebrugge . . . The Prime Minister, after hearing both sides, expressed his concurrence with my views, and decided that Zeebrugge should be dropped but that the Dardanelles should go forward.' Asquith's decision left the Dardanelles plan intact.

    Asquith, Fisher and Churchill went downstairs from the Prime Minister's study to join the War Council in the Cabinet Room. The members of the War Council were not told of Asquith's decision. Kitchener began the meeting by telling his colleagues that a Turkish force had crossed the Sinai desert and was within thirty miles of the Suez Canal. The Commander-in-Chief in Egypt, Sir John Maxwell,[1] was preparing to resist. There could no longer be any question, Kitchener declared, of transferring troops from Egypt elsewhere. Discussion turned to the recent publication in the *Daily Mail* of an account of ship movements in the North Sea, which gave important information to the Germans. It emerged that several papers had been indiscreet.

[1] John Grenfell Maxwell, 1859–1929. Entered Army, 1879. Governor of Pretoria, 1900–2. Knighted, 1900. Major-General, 1906. Lieutenant-General commanding the forces in Egypt, 1908–12, and 1914–15. Commander-in-Chief, Ireland, 1916; Northern Command, 1916–19. General, 1919. A member of Lord Milner's mission to Egypt, 1919–20.

Hankey pointed out that *The Times* had actually disclosed the where-abouts of the base of the British Battle Cruiser Squadron. After a long dis-cussion about the Press, the War Council turned briefly to the Zeebrugge scheme. Asquith said nothing about his having made Fisher accept either Zeebrugge or the Dardanelles, and of his own choice of the latter. There was a brief outburst of anti-French feeling. Lloyd George said that the French 'never appeared to have taken us into their confi-dence as to what forces they disposed of', and asked sarcastically 'whether the French intended to attack the German army'. Zeebrugge was then forgotten; the War Council were deflected towards discussing the size and intentions of the French army. After further discussion about the co-ordination of Allied effort in France, Churchill described the French and Russian reactions to the Dardanelles project, and asked 'if the War Council attached importance to the operation, which undoubtedly involved some risks'. At this moment Fisher made his only interjection, stating that 'he had understood that this question would not be raised today, and that the Prime Minister was well aware of his own views in regard to it'. Asquith insisted that in view of the steps which had already been taken both at the Admiralty and in conjunction with the Allied Governments, 'the question could not well be left in abeyance'. There then occurred an incident which, for all its drama, was appar-ently not noticed by many of the members of the War Council. It was described after the war by Fisher himself in *Memories*, in the third person:

> Thereupon Lord Fisher left the Council table. He was followed by Lord Kitchener, who asked him what he intended to do. Lord Fisher replied to Lord Kitchener that he would not return to the Council table, and would resign his office as First Sea Lord. Lord Kitchener then pointed out to Lord Fisher that he (Lord Fisher) was the only dissentient, and that the Dar-danelles operations had been decided upon by the Prime Minister; and he urged on Lord Fisher that his duty to his country was to go on carrying out the duties of First Sea Lord. After further talk Lord Fisher reluctantly gave in to Lord Kitchener and went back to the Council table.

As soon as Fisher and Kitchener were seated, Asquith invited members of the War Council to answer Churchill's question as to what import-ance they attached to the operation. Hankey recorded their answers in the official record of the meeting:

LORD KITCHENER considered the naval attack to be vitally important. If successful, its effect would be equivalent to that of a successful campaign fought with the new armies. One merit of the scheme was that, if satisfactory progress was not made, the attack could be broken off.

MR BALFOUR pointed out that a successful attack on the Dardanelles would achieve the following results:

It would cut the Turkish army in two;

It would put Constantinople under our control;

It would give us the advantage of having the Russian wheat, and enable Russia to resume exports;

This would restore the Russian exchanges, which were falling owing to her inability to export, and causing great embarrassment;

It would also open a passage to the Danube.

It was difficult to imagine a more helpful operation.

SIR EDWARD GREY said it would also finally settle the attitude of Bulgaria and the whole of the Balkans.

Churchill explained to the War Council that Carden 'had expressed his belief that it could be done' and that he would need from three weeks to a month to carry out the operation. Balfour asked whether there was any danger of Austrian submarines from the Adriatic reaching the Dardanelles. Churchill assured him that the French Government thought this unlikely, as they were keeping close and effective watch on the exit from the Adriatic. Haldane asked if the Turks had any submarines. Churchill replied that it was believed they had none. He went on to say that he did not minimize the difficulties of the enterprise. Although the actual bombardment would involve little loss, 'in sweeping for mines some losses must be expected'. 'The real difficulties,' he said, 'would begin after the outer forts had been silenced, and it became necessary to attack the Narrows.' Churchill then explained the plan on a map. Grey said that he thought 'that the Turks would be paralysed with fear when they heard that the forts were being destroyed one by one'. Throughout this discussion Fisher maintained what Asquith described to Venetia Stanley as 'an obstinate and ominous silence'.

Churchill next outlined his general views of the war at sea. 'The ultimate object of the Navy,' he still believed, 'was to obtain access to the Baltic.' He went on to describe in some detail the plans which were being made at the Admiralty for the Baltic operation. Germany, he asserted, had always been 'very nervous of an attack from the Baltic'. For the purpose of invading the Pomeranian coast, Fisher had designed two special light cruisers, each armed with four 15-inch guns, with light draught and capable of a speed of 33 knots. These would cost about a million pounds each. As soon as Churchill mentioned these two new ships, Fisher's despondency left him. Resignation was forgotten. Constructing ships was his life's blood. Confronted by a challenge in this sphere, nothing could restrain his exuberance. Turning enthusiastically upon the War Council he declared that 'if the usual formalities of tenders etc could be dispensed with', these cruisers could be built in eleven months, and that two firms had already offered to complete them within this period. Lloyd George agreed to sanction the expenditure, and with this decision the War Council adjourned.

Despite the welcome change of atmosphere at the end of the War Council, Churchill was apprehensive as to what had passed between Kitchener and Fisher at the beginning of the meeting. In order to find out what was wrong, he called Fisher to his room early that afternoon. When he learned of Fisher's continuing discontent, he tried once more to convince him of the need for the Dardanelles operation. After more than an hour's turbulent discussion, Fisher agreed to support it. When, two years later, Churchill informed the Dardanelles Commissioners of this discussion, Fisher confirmed that he had indeed given his consent. 'When I finally decided to come in,' he told the Commissioners, 'I went the whole hog, totus porcus.'

At four that afternoon a Sub-committee of the War Council met under Kitchener's chairmanship at the War Office. Churchill, Lloyd George and Balfour were its other members: the Chief of the Imperial General Staff, Sir James Murray, and the Director of Military Operations, General Callwell, were also present. The War Council had set up this Sub-committee to discuss where British troops should be sent if the position on the western front reached a stalemate during the spring. Uppermost in all minds was the plight of Serbia. Although the Serbs had repulsed an Austrian attack the previous December, it was obvious that Austria would soon be ready, in conjunction with Germany, to strike again at this isolated, vulnerable state whose other neighbours, Rumania, Bulgaria and Greece, seemed little disposed to come to her aid. Kitchener suggested that as the Serbian Army was short of mounted troops British troops should make up the deficiency. There was, he said, no shortage of British cavalry for other fronts. Lloyd George suggested that in order to persuade the Bulgarians not to stab Serbia in the back during the Austrian invasion, a British force should join with Bulgaria and attack the strong Turkish fortress of Adrianople. This, Lloyd George explained, would draw Bulgaria into the war on the Allied side. While Serbia was fending off Austrian attacks, Bulgaria would face the other way and strike at Turkey. The Serbian rear would be secure. The British would have an ally in their action against the Turks.

During the course of a long discussion, Kitchener, Lloyd George, Churchill and Balfour agreed that help to Serbia was a paramount British interest, and that if any military force were to become available it should be landed, not at the Dardanelles but at Salonika. When the War Council reassembled that evening Serbia dominated its discussion. Kitchener believed that 'there was danger in undue delay as, if we do not move in time, Serbia might be crushed and we might fail to draw in the other Balkan States'. When troops could be spared, Kitchener believed that it was to Serbia they should be sent. Balfour hoped that a brigade would be sent to Salonika at once, but Kitchener feared that 'the effect would soon evaporate if the brigade was not supported by other troops, and its arrival might precipitate an Austro-German attack'. During all these discussions about sending a military force to Serbia, no one suggested that any troops that became available might be sent, as priority, to the Dardanelles. It was assumed throughout the discussion that the Dardanelles could be forced by ships alone, and that if troops were needed it would only be after the naval success, when Britain would enter Constantinople as the victorious power, police the shattered Turkish Empire, and defeat any final outposts of dwindling resistance which might remain. According to his evidence before the Dardanelles Commissioners in 1916, Churchill now wanted the Navy to act alone and doubted whether a military landing would offer any better chance of success. He explained his changed feelings to them.

A landing in force under fire on the Gallipoli Peninsula, now that the Turks were fully awakened, seemed to me to involve a greater stake, though offering a greater expectation, than a naval attack with the old ships as proposed. And the chance of the naval attack succeeding, and producing revolutionary effects at Constantinople and throughout the Balkans, seemed to me to make it worth while to try the naval plan even though, if it failed, a subsequent military operation would be rendered more difficult.

No longer believing that it was necessary to land troops simultaneously in order for the Dardanelles to succeed, Churchill pressed the War Council to despatch the first available brigade to Salonika. By this means, he asserted, the Greeks could be persuaded to join the Allied cause. If, as Churchill believed, the appearance of no more than ten thousand British soldiers were to result in 180,000 Greek soldiers hurrying into action, Serbia's survival would be assured.

Grey declared that five thousand men sent to Salonika would convince Bulgaria as well as Greece of the wisdom of joining the Allies.

The Bulgarian Army, with its war strength of 300,000 and its record of success against the Turks in 1912, would constitute a grave threat to Turkey's remaining possessions in Europe, particularly if, in conjunction with a Bulgarian land attack, the Allied fleet were to reach the Sea of Marmara and cut all communication between European and Asiatic Turkey. The Bulgarian Army would provide a more than adequate substitute for the troops which Kitchener could not find, and which both Churchill and Kitchener realized might be needed to follow up any naval success.

The dinner hour was approaching. For the first time since the war began Asquith found himself presiding over a united War Council, and with a determined war policy ready to be harnessed to the many departmental machines upon which action would depend. That evening it only remained for some method to be found of informing Sir John French that he was not to receive his reinforcements, and that the attack on Zeebrugge had been abandoned. Kitchener, discarding his previous embargo, suggested that Churchill himself should cross over to France and tell the Commander-in-Chief of these decisions. Fisher then announced that he would assemble his subordinates at the Admiralty on the following morning, and set to work in search of the best design for Danube gunboats. Finally, amid the general euphoria, Churchill informed the War Council that, with Fisher's approval, given that same afternoon, the Admiralty had decided 'to undertake the task with which the War Council has charged us so urgently', and would immediately 'push on with the project approved at the meeting held on 13th January, to make a naval attack at the Dardanelles'. On behalf of the Admiralty War Staff, Admiral Oliver gave a brief survey of how the operation would proceed: 'The first shot would be fired in about a fortnight. Ships were on their way, and the intensity of the attack would increase.' Having listened to Oliver's account with enthusiasm, the War Council dispersed.

9

The Search for Men

I N the week following the War Council of January 28, detailed
instructions were worked out at the Admiralty for the naval attack at
the Dardanelles. The first set was completed on February 5 and sent at
once to Carden. His immediate objective was to destroy the forts at the
entrance to the Dardanelles by naval guns. Once these were silenced, his
minesweepers were to clear a channel which would enable his other
ships to proceed methodically towards Chanak, destroying the forts
within the Narrows one by one. He was urged to take special precautions against floating mines, to avoid large risks and to shun heavy
losses. Speed was not essential. The operation should, he was told,
develop 'into a slow methodical progress of perhaps a mile a day', and
no attempt should be made to 'rush' the Narrows. The keynote of the
instructions was caution. They also laid stress on a point which Grey
had made at the War Council, that the 'slow relentless creeping forward
of the attacking force mile after mile will tend to shake the morale of the
garrisons of the forts of Kephez Point, Chanak and Kilid Bahr, and will
have an effect on Constantinople'.

Carden was told that two battalions of marines were to be made
available 'for any small landing operations of a temporary nature'
designed to complete the destruction of forts already seriously damaged
by the Navy. But he was warned that these marines 'should not be
landed against superior forces or entrenched positions in circumstances
where they cannot be efficiently supported by the ships' guns without
first obtaining Admiralty sanction'.

Neither Churchill nor Fisher felt that the proportion of small ships to
large ships available at the Dardanelles was large enough. The French
Admiralty was therefore asked to provide as many small cruisers,
destroyers, seaplanes and submarines as they could spare; but Carden
was instructed to begin the bombardment as soon as possible, and not
necessarily to wait for the entire armada to be assembled.

While these plans were being worked out by the Admiralty War Staff, Churchill crossed over to France, and at the request of the War Council pressed Sir John French to release some of his troops for action in the Balkans. French was unwilling to weaken the British Expeditionary Force in any way, and, as Churchill reported to Kitchener on January 31, was opposed to 'a diversion in S.E. Europe' on strategic grounds. But after two days of discussion Churchill was successful; French agreed to hold two divisions of reserve troops at the disposal of the British Government 'from the middle of March onward' for use, the War Council had decided, at Salonika. Daily telegrams from the Balkans, which Grey circulated to members of the War Council, warned of the danger to Serbia from both Austrian and Bulgarian attack. On February 2, having returned from France, Churchill wrote to French to show him how much troops were needed at Salonika: 'I have had the enclosed pile of Balkan telegrams prepared for you to look through. They will show you why a sabre stroke is needed to cut the tangle. Pray let me have them back after you have looked through them, for I have no other copy. . . . "Dardanelles" goes forward steadily and all the ships are sailing.' On that same day Grey, to whom Churchill had sent a draft of Carden's instructions, gave Churchill his opinion of the benefits to be gained by a naval victory at the Dardanelles, and urged speed:

To my lay mind the operation seems to be well planned. I hope however that these detailed plans will be communicated to as few persons as possible here outside the Admiralty.

The sooner they can be put in execution the better as some striking offensive is necessary to counteract the effect that the presence of German troops on the Balkan frontiers is having in the Balkans.

The Austro-German objective now is to overawe Roumania and Greece, to attract Bulgaria & to steady the Turks by an offensive against Serbia. If we can succeed in forcing the Straits, or even creating a scare at Constantinople before this offensive can make headway we shall have done much to discourage if not to paralyze it.

'I agree with above,' Kitchener noted on February 3.

Churchill was determined to ensure Serbia's survival. On January 29 Lloyd George had written to him of his fears that Britain was looking on complacently 'whilst a catastrophe was being prepared for the Allies in the Balkans'. Churchill shared these fears. It seemed to both him and Lloyd George that Grey, Kitchener and Asquith were doing nothing to avert the imminent crisis. On February 6 the British Minister in

Sofia, Sir Henry Bax-Ironside,[1] telegraphed to Grey that 'German and Austrian policy now is to crush Serbia as soon as possible. . . . It would seem more than ever desirable to render Serbia effectual support.' His telegram reached the Foreign Office during the morning of February 7, reinforcing Churchill's fears. Later that day Churchill protested to Asquith:

> More than three weeks ago you told me of the vital importance of Servia. Since then nothing has been done, & nothing of the slightest reality is being done. Time is passing. You may not yet feel the impact of the projectile. But it has already left the gun & is travelling along its road towards you. Three weeks hence you, Kitchener, Grey will all be facing a disastrous situation in the Balkans: & as at Antwerp it will be beyond yr power to retrieve it. Unless we are prepared to run a risk & play a stake the Balkan situation is finished fatally for us.

In the original draft of this letter was a final sentence which read: 'Surely in your position you cannot be content to sit as a judge pronouncing on events *after* they have taken place.' On the following day Churchill was invited to a lunch given by Grey for the French Foreign Minister, Théophile Delcassé.[2] Serbia was the principal theme of the discussion. Asquith reported to Venetia Stanley that afternoon:

> I had rather an interesting luncheon at Edward Grey's: Delcassé, Cambon, Kitchener & Winston. Winston was very eloquent in the worst French you or anyone has ever heard: '*s'ils savent que nous sommes gens qu'ils peuvent conter sur*' ('count on') was one of his flowers of speech.[3] We were all agreed that (1) the Serbian case is urgent (2) we must promise to send them 2 divisions—1 English 1 French—as soon as may be to Salonika, & *force in* the Greeks & Roumanians (3) we must try our damnedest to get the Russians to join if possible with a corps, not of their good troops, but drawn from the vast reservoir they can't at present get to the front or use against Germany & Austria. Ll George thinks he has got Sir J. French's assent to this; but I have told K to send for him & he is coming over to-night in one of Winston's Destroyers.

In the days leading up to the first bombardment at the Dardanelles Churchill was in daily contact with Carden, whom he encouraged to deal directly with him should any problems arise. 'Do not hesitate to

[1] Henry George Outram Bax-Ironside, 1859–1929. Entered Diplomatic Service, 1883. Minister at Sofia, 1910–15. Knighted, 1911.

[2] Théophile Delcassé, 1852–1923. French Minister of Foreign Affairs, 1898–1908 and 1914–19. Principal French architect of the Anglo-French *Entente* of 1904.

[3] Asquith may have misheard Churchill saying 'compter sur', which is correct French usage for 'to count on'.

send full telegraphic reports, and inform me of all your difficulties,' he signalled on February 6. 'Is everything progressing satisfactorily, and are all your wants being supplied? I attach great importance to fire being opened punctually on the 15th, by which time Queen Elizabeth should have arrived.'

On February 3 a Turkish force of about twenty-five thousand troops led by the former Minister of Marine, Djemal Pasha, crossed the Sinai Desert and reached the Suez Canal. Although they began bridging operations in order to cross the Canal, their attack was driven off. Kitchener circulated a number of reports on the success of the action to members of the War Council, in which Sir John Maxwell, the commander in Egypt, estimated that over four hundred Turks had been killed, and also a German officer. In a counter-attack the British captured four hundred Turkish prisoners, three machine-guns and ninety camels laden with ammunition and stores, and during the ensuing retreat over two thousand Turks were estimated to have been killed. The British force lost a hundred and sixty men, mostly Indian troops. On February 7 a telegram from Maxwell, implying the Turks were not serious opponents, was circulated to the members of the War Council:

Numbers of Anatolian Turks of good quality well clothed, fed and equipped, are deserting. All say large numbers wish to desert from fourth Army Corps and few wish to fight English or invade Egypt. They state officers are bad and do not look after men, and also that the intention is to retire to Bir Saba, reorganise and come on again, but they do not think the men will follow.

This view of Turkish weakness was widely held. On February 8 Captain Larken's report of his exploits with the Doris seven weeks before was circulated to the Cabinet as a Confidential Print entitled 'HMS "Doris": Report of Proceedings off Syrian Coast, 14th to 27th December 1914'. Neither at Alexandretta nor in Sinai did the Turks seem capable of serious opposition. On February 9 Captain Richmond recorded in his diary a conversation with Oliver about a possible use of the Royal Naval Division, which had seen no action since Antwerp, four months before: 'Oliver suggested that it was "about time that the naval division earned its keep" & should go out en masse for the business. They are pretty rotten, but ought to be good enough for the inferior Turkish troops now at Gallipoli: & a bit of work would finish off their training properly & make them fit for service on the Continent later.'

The news from the Balkans was bad in the first week of February, overshadowing the Turkish preparations, and complicating them.

Bulgaria seemed on the verge of abandoning her neutrality and attacking Serbia. On February 7 and 8 Grey had circulated members of the War Council with telegrams from Sofia and Petrograd. Bax-Ironside reported from Sofia on February 6 that the Bulgarians had borrowed money from Germany, and that the Germans in Bulgaria were announcing with confidence that Serbia would be crushed by the middle of July. Sir George Buchanan telegraphed from Petrograd on February 7 that Russia 'could not divert any troops beyond a regiment of Cossacks for service in Balkans', and that the Russian Minister for Foreign Affairs, Sazonov,[1] believed that only an immediate offer of Turkish or Serbian territory could stop Bulgaria joining the Central Powers. The chances of saving Serbia seemed slim. Even the token British force might not arrive in time. Churchill later explained to the Dardanelles Commissioners the extent to which Serbia dominated his thoughts in early February:

> You cannot have a worse situation or a more urgent and painful one. You must remember Serbia had been brought almost to death in the end of the previous year and was practically finished, and then by almost a miracle, a wonderful effort, she had thrown back the Austrians with 40,000 prisoners taken. The apprehension of this thing beginning again and this small Power being again struck down was one of the many factors which I kept continually in view, regarding it as a matter of great urgency to procure relief for them, and it explains to some extent the readiness to run risks in the Dardanelles.

Asquith was similarly convinced of the urgency of success at the Dardanelles. On February 9, just before the meeting of the War Council, he wrote to Venetia Stanley to tell her why:

> The main question of course will be how soon & in what form we are to come to the aid of Serbia . . . I can't help feeling that the whole situation in the Near East may be vitally transformed, if the bombardment of the Dardanelles by our ships next week (*Secret*) goes well. It is a great experiment. . . . If it is successful, it will smash up the Turks, and, incidentally, let through all the Russian wheat wh is now locked up & so lower the price of bread. But it is full of uncertainties.

On the evening of February 8 Churchill had gone to Buckingham Palace to give George V an account of the impending operation. The

---

[1] Sergei Dmitrievich Sazonov, 1866–1927. Russian Minister of Foreign Affairs, 1910–15. Dismissed by the Tsar in November 1915 following his advocacy of Home Rule for Poland. Chief Representative Abroad of Admiral Kolchak, 1919–20. In exile in France from 1919 until his death.

King noted in his diary: 'Saw Winston Churchill and we had an interesting conversation.' Churchill must have expressed his anxiety over the maintenance of secrecy, for that evening he received the unusual compliment of a letter from Buckingham Palace in the King's own hand:

Secret
My dear Churchill,
   Your mind can be entirely at rest. I have not mentioned our conversation of this evening to a soul & I quite realise the extreme importance of secrecy in regard to the operation in the Mediterranean. Any information you give me of a confidential nature is quite safe with me. The only persons I should ever speak to on these subjects are the 1st Sea Lord & sometimes Stamfordham who is absolutely trustworthy.
   I was much interested by all you told me this evening & I only hope that our various schemes for overcoming the enemy may prove successful.
Believe me very sincerely yrs
George R.I.

The War Council met on February 9. Kitchener presented full details of the Turkish failure on the Suez Canal, and stressed the increasing danger to Serbia. Churchill gave a report on the preparations for the naval attack at the Dardanelles, and explained that negotiations were proceeding satisfactorily with the Greek Prime Minister, Venizelos, to enable the island of Lemnos to be used as a base for the operations. The island's inland harbour, Mudros, would provide an ideal shelter for the Allied fleet. The War Council passed swiftly to the main business of the evening, Serbia. After two hours of discussion, they decided that the only British action likely to be of use was the immediate despatch of a Division of Regular troops to Salonika, from which port they could march rapidly north to the Serbian border. Delcassé, the French Foreign Minister, had already agreed while in London on February 6 that if Britain sent a complete Division of twenty thousand men, France would do likewise. Kitchener insisted that only the best British troops ought to go to the east. He therefore proposed sending the 29th Division, which had previously been earmarked for France. Sir John French, who was present at the War Council, 'rather demurred' at this, the minutes of the meeting recorded, expressing his doubts as to whether British troops could fight under the same conditions of hardship and privation that Serbian troops were used to. French declared that he was only prepared to release the 29th Division if he had an assurance that both the Rumanian and Greek armies would also be marching at the side of the Allies. The War Council then discussed the advantages of the 29th Division going initially only to Salonika. Asquith pointed out that as a result of even a limited use of British troops, 'Greece would be brought into the war . . . the hostile attitude of Bulgaria would be paralyzed', and 'in all probability Roumania would be drawn in'. Kitchener believed that the presence of British troops at Salonika might further weaken Turkish morale at the Dardanelles. If it were necessary to send troops to Turkey after the success of the naval attack, men of the 29th Division, Kitchener added, would be near at hand. The War Council then concluded that the 29th Division should be offered to Greece.

On February 11, while the ships detailed to bombard the Dardanelles assembled off Cape Helles, Churchill became embroiled in a domestic merchant-shipping problem. That day, in the House of Commons, Bonar Law accused the Admiralty of making inefficient use of merchant ships commandeered for war service. He told MPs of a ship which in the opinion of its owner had been kept idle for over a month with 400 tons of coal on board, with orders to steam, apparently aimlessly, from Cardiff to Cromarty and from Cromarty to Cardiff. On reading Bonar Law's remarks on the morning of February 12, Churchill telegraphed: 'Please enable me identify ship to which you referred last night so that I may have actual facts investigated.' He followed his telegram with a letter:

Dear Bonar Law,

I hope you will be able to give me the facts. It is always vy unfair to state a case in detail & then refuse to let the details be checked.

Vy likely you are right, & a better procedure shd have been adopted. But a 'hard case' apart from the actual facts is absolutely intangible.

The Admiralty Transport Department were inclined to think they had done rather well—if only the facts were known—; & 'incapacity' is a severe expression. I am bound to look after their claims to consideration, otherwise believe me I wd not trouble you.

Yours sincerely
Winston S. Churchill

On the following day Bonar Law replied, asking that 'a really competent shipowner' should be put at the head of the Department dealing with chartered ships, and suggesting that the shipowner whom he had quoted would be an ideal choice. Churchill pressed for the shipowner's name. After some hesitation, Bonar Law agreed to reveal it. His nominee was Sir Joseph Maclay.[1] Churchill answered Bonar Law's criticisms publicly in the House of Commons on February 15:

> We are at war with the second Naval Power in the world. When complaints are made that we have taken too many transports or armed too many auxiliary cruisers, or made use of too many colliers or supply ships, I must mention that fact. The statement that the Admiralty have, on charter, approximately about one-fifth of the British Mercantile Marine tonnage is correct. With that we discharge two duties, both of importance at the present time; first, the supply, fuelling, and replenishing with ammunition of the Fleets; second, the transport of reinforcements and supply for the Army in the Field, including the return of wounded. It must be remembered in regard to the Fleet that we have no dockyard or naval port at our backs, and that the bases we are using during the War have no facilities for coaling from the shore. We are not like the Germans, living in a great naval port at Wilhelmshaven, on which £15,000,000 or £16,000,000 has been spent. . . . Everything, therefore, required to keep the Fleet in being—supplies, stores, and, above all, fuel—has to be not only carried but kept afloat in ships. What are called the 'afloat reserves'—the great mobile reserves of fuel and stores maintained at the various bases used by the Fleet—are those which are fixed by the War Staff and approved by the Board of Admiralty. . . .
> It is necessary that there should be sufficient colliers to enable all the Fleet units at a particular base to coal simultaneously with a maximum rapidity twice over within a short interval, and extensive naval movements at high speed may at any moment necessitate this being put to the test. . . .
> We cannot possibly run any risk of having the Fleet rendered immobile. We must make assurance doubly sure. The life of the State depends upon it.

Bonar Law spoke immediately after Churchill during the debate. He alleged that the civil servants who ran the Admiralty Transport Department were given work which 'they are incapable of performing adequately, while there are others who might be available who would be capable of doing that work'. He again raised the details of the steamer which he had mentioned before. Churchill rose from his place:

> Really the right hon Gentleman, if I may say so with great respect, does not understand the facts. The fact that the ship had been waiting about doing nothing does not mean that she was not usefully employed. She has been carrying a portion of the indispensable fixed floating reserve of coal which is kept continually available at the different bases. If she was not carrying it,

---

[1] Joseph Paton Maclay, 1889–1951. Shipowner. Created Baronet, 1914. Minister of Shipping, 1916–21. Created Baron, 1922. Of his three sons, one, Ebenezer (born 1891), was killed in action in France, 1918; another, William Strang (born 1895), died of wounds received at Gallipoli, 25 June 1915.

some other ship would have had to be carrying it. The whole of these ships, coal ships, ammunition ships and supply ships, are always waiting about until a sufficient quantity of the commodity in question has been accumulated, and is maintained regularly in a floating position.

Bonar Law continued to express his discontent. That evening Churchill wrote to him again:

> . . . I am vy anxious you shd have every opportunity of satisfying yourself about the collier question: you must realize that it is vital to us to keep something like 400,000 tons of coal afloat, 'idle', in reserve at the various fleet bases. This of course is wholly wasteful & uneconomic. It is merely necessary. I don't wish to obtrude confidential information upon you, in case it might hamper yr freedom of criticism. But if you like I shall be glad to send you a full memorandum on the general collier question as well as on the particular points you have mentioned; and if there are any points in this wh require further explanation, I shall be vy happy to put you in contact with persons who can give you the fullest information.

The dispute was not resolved, nor did the correspondence abate. Bonar Law remained convinced, as he wrote to Churchill on February 17, that 'immense sums of money could be saved' if the Admiralty would adopt what he considered a proper business approach. Churchill was depressed that, despite the agreement between the political parties to minimize wartime criticism, Tory hostility towards him personally had transformed the collier question from a technical detail to an acrimonious dispute.

Angered by what he believed was unfair obstruction on the part of the merchant shippers, Churchill proposed a drastic measure. 'The time has now come,' he wrote to Asquith on February 13, 'when we ought to do what it would have been well to have done at the beginning, namely, to take over the whole British mercantile marine for the period of the war for national purposes.' Churchill explained to Asquith that only a fifth of all private tonnage had been requisitioned by the Government and that, owing to the rise in freight charges since the outbreak of war, 'the profits made by shipowners where vessels have not been requisitioned, promise to be greatly in excess of those obtained for the Govt under requisition charters'. The Government, he believed, already offered 'a fair and even a handsome profit'. Private profit in excess of this created, he claimed, 'a feeling of injustice in practice; and it is detrimental to national interests'. Asquith took the matter no further. Churchill, angry that the Government saw no need to restrict war profits, was led to propose, in a memorandum circulated to the Cabinet on March 5, a general tax on war profits. Called 'Seven Practical Steps', his memorandum envisaged a fifty per cent tax on all wartime profits which exceeded the average profit of the last three peacetime years. This was a radical departure in fiscal policy for which there was no precedent. It did not excite Asquith's enthusiasm; it too was taken no further.

During his speech of February 15 Churchill had warned the House of Commons against too much criticism of naval losses:

If any mood or tendency of public opinion arises, or is fostered by the newspapers, or given countenance in this House, which makes too much of our losses, even if they are cruel losses, and even if it may be said that they are in some respects avoidable losses, then I say you will have started on a path which, pressed to its logical conclusion, would leave our Navy cowering in its harbours, instead of ruling the seas.

Churchill had been upset by the recurring Press and public accusations of Admiralty negligence. He believed that his wartime administration deserved praise, not censure, telling the House of Commons:

When I think of the great scale of our operations, the enormous target we expose, the number of ships whose movements have to be arranged for, the novel conditions to which I have referred, it is marvellous how few have been our losses, and how great the care and vigilance exercised by the admirals afloat and by the Admiralty Staff, and it appears to me, and it will certainly be regarded by those who study this War in history, as praiseworthy in the highest degree.

In his conclusion, Churchill pointed out the burden which war imposed upon those in charge of the nation's affairs:

The stresses and strains of this War are not imperceptible to those who are called on to bear a part in the responsibility for the direction of the tremendous and terrible events which are now taking place. They have a right to the generous and indulgent judgment and support of their fellow countrymen, and to the goodwill of the House of Commons.

We cannot tell what lies before us, or how soon or in what way the next great developments of the struggle will declare themselves, or what the state of Europe and the world will be at its close.

But this, I think, we can already say, as far as the British Navy is concerned, that although no doubt new dangers and perplexities will come upon us continuously, and anxiety will make its abode in our brain, yet the dangers and anxieties which now are advancing upon us will not be more serious or more embarrassing than those through which we have already successfully made our way. For during the months that are to come the British Navy and the sea power which it exerts will increasingly dominate the general situation, will be the main and unfailing reserve of the allied nations, will progressively paralyse the fighting energies of our antagonists, and will, if need be, even in default of all other favourable forces, ultimately by itself decide the issue of the War.

The full meaning of Churchill's peroration about the future use of naval power was lost on a House of Commons unaware of the enterprise which was about to begin. Nor could they realize the cause of his concern for indulgence, or the reason for the worry which underlay his warnings. But he knew that already, six days before, a setback had occurred at the Dardanelles. As Asquith had informed Venetia Stanley on February 10:

A secret telegram came this morning, wh has only been seen by Winston, Grey, K & me, from the Admiral (Carden) that the business out there, wh was to have been begun next Monday, has had to be postponed for a few days, as the requisite mine-sweepers could not be got together sooner. I hope it won't be delayed any longer, as it is all important as a preliminary to our démarche in the Balkans. So far it has been on the whole a well kept secret.

Further problems arose that week, for doubts had arisen in many minds as to the wisdom of a purely naval attack. On February 13 Hankey sought out the Prime Minister, who gave Venetia Stanley an account of their conversation:

I have just been having a talk with Hankey, whose views are always worth hearing. He thinks very strongly that the naval operations of which you know should be supported by landing a fairly strong military force. I have been for some time coming to the same opinion, and I think we ought to be able without denuding French to scrape together from Egypt, Malta & elsewhere a sufficiently large contingent.

If only these heart-breaking Balkan States could be bribed or goaded into action, the trick wd be done with the greatest of ease & with incalculable consequences. It is of much importance that in the course of the next month we should carry through a *decisive* operation somewhere, and this one would do admirably for the purpose.

On February 14 Captain Richmond, in a memorandum entitled 'Remarks on Present Strategy', insisted that 'the bombardment of the Dardanelles, even if all the forts are destroyed, can be nothing but a local success, which without an army to carry it on can have no further effect'. Richmond sent his memorandum to Hankey, who wrote: 'Your Memo. is absolutely A.1 and is most opportune. I am sending it to Jacky. You are preaching to the converted but it may ginger him up.' Fisher was impressed by Richmond's reasoning, writing on February 15: '*YOUR PAPER IS EXCELLENT.*' In his diary for February 14 Richmond had recorded his dissent in detail: 'Thirty thousand men at the Dardanelles next week would make more impression on the continental campaign than five times that number on the banks of the Yser.'

On February 15 Sir Henry Jackson circulated a memorandum in which, while describing in detail how the forts could be destroyed, he concluded that ships alone could not be decisive in ensuring the defeat of Turkey. 'The naval bombardment is not recommended as a sound military operation,' he wrote, 'unless a strong military force is ready to assist in the operation, or, at least, follow it up immediately the forts are silenced.'

Churchill realized the force of these criticisms. He himself had originally insisted upon the need for a large military force in any attempt to reach Constantinople. But for a month he had based his plans upon Carden's belief that ships alone might be sufficient, a belief which suited a situation in which troops were not available. The War Council had instructed him to proceed on this basis. The criticisms of Richmond and Jackson caused him to wonder whether he had been right to accept Carden's assessment. He therefore looked again for some possible source of troops. By a coincidence, on the day he received Jackson's memorandum, the Greek Government turned down the British offer of an expedition to Salonika. Although Venizelos wanted to support, and win advantage from, the Allied cause, King Constantine refused to be drawn into war against his German relation. With the Salonika plan abruptly ended, the Dardanelles became the only immediately available alternative theatre of war in the east, and the 29th Division, designated for Salonika, could be sent instead to the Gallipoli Peninsula. In the early hours of February 16 Fisher added his warning to those of Richmond and Jackson. 'Not a grain of wheat will come from the Black Sea,' he wrote to Churchill, 'unless there is a military occupation of the Dardanelles, and it will be the wonder of the ages that no troops were sent to co-operate with the Fleet with half a million soldiers in England.'

An emergency meeting of the War Council was called on February 16. Before it began, Kitchener called one of his intelligence officers,

Wyndham Deedes,[1] to his room at the War Office. Deedes had formerly been attached to the Turkish Army. Kitchener asked him what prospects he saw in a purely naval attack at the Dardanelles. Deedes replied that in his view such an operation was fundamentally unsound. Kitchener turned on him angrily while he was developing his arguments, telling him that he did not know what he was talking about and bringing the interview to an abrupt end. But Deedes' arguments and experience made a strong impression on Kitchener, who, at the emergency meeting of six of the ten members of the War Council a few hours later, agreed that the 29th Division, now denied its role at Salonika, should go to Lemnos 'at the earliest possible date', sailing from England 'within nine or ten days'. It was also agreed by those present—Asquith, Kitchener, Lloyd George, Grey, Churchill and Fisher—that, if necessary, the Australian and New Zealand troops then in Egypt should go to Lemnos, and that 'the whole of the above forces in conjunction with the battalion of the Royal Marines already despatched' should be available 'in case of necessity to support the naval attack on the Dardanelles'. Churchill was instructed to assemble special transports in order to convey and land 'a force of 50,000 men at any point where they may be required'. He was relieved that troops would be used in conjunction with ships, and that the doubts of Hankey, Richmond, Jackson and Fisher were thereby set to rest.

The decision to send regular British troops, reinforced by the Australian and New Zealand Corps—the ANZACs—to the Dardanelles altered the whole nature of the operation. Churchill and Kitchener became colleagues in a joint military and naval enterprise. Kitchener accepted that his troops would only be needed after Churchill's ships had passed the Narrows. 'The Dardanelles are to be tried three days hence,' Lord Esher wrote in his diary that day. 'A landing force will be composed of the 29th Division, but they cannot be there in time. Lord K's words to Winston were: "You get through! I will find the men." ' Churchill and Kitchener were agreed that the Fleet should go through the Narrows before the troops need be used. But Churchill feared delay in finding the men, writing to Kitchener on February 18: 'If our operations at the Dardanelles prosper, immense advantages may be offered wh cannot be gathered without military aid. . . . I think at least 50,000 men shd be within reach at 3 days notice, either to seize the

[1] Wyndham Henry Deedes, 1883–1956. 2nd Lieutenant, 1901. Employed with the Turkish Gendarmerie, 1910–14. Captain, War Office, 1914–15. Intelligence Officer, attached to the 29th Division, Gallipoli, 1915. Military Attaché, Constantinople, 1918–19. Director-General of Public Security in Egypt, 1919–20. Chief Secretary to the Administration, Palestine, 1920. Knighted, 1921.

Gallipoli Peninsula when it has been evacuated, or to occupy C'nople if a revolution takes place. We shd never forgive ourselves if the naval operations succeeded & the fruits were lost through the army being absent.' Churchill asked Kitchener to send the 29th Division to the eastern Mediterranean at once.

The planning of this enterprise on which so much depended needed the joint efforts and enthusiasm of Churchill and Kitchener. But on February 17 the 'stresses and strains' to which Churchill had referred in Parliament two days before came without warning to a new climax. On that day Churchill received a letter from Asquith, marked '*Secret*', which heralded an abrupt end to the newly achieved ministerial unity. It had nothing to do with the Dardanelles:

Kitchener has just been to see me in a state of some perturbation. He has just received two official letters from French, in which he announces that you have offered him a Brigade of the Naval Division, and 2 squadrons of armoured cars. Kitchener is strongly of opinion that French has no need of either. But, apart from that, he feels (& I think rightly) that he ought to have to have been told of, & consulted about, the offer before it was made.

I hope you will go & see him & put things right.

That evening Asquith mentioned the new crisis to his wife. According to her diary he expostulated: 'Of course Winston is intolerable. It is all *vanity*—he is devoured by vanity. . . . It's most trying as K and he had got a modus vivendi.' Churchill defended himself against Kitchener's charges, replying to Asquith on the same day:

Kitchener's obvious course would have been to send me copies of French's official letters and ask me what I had to say about them. Until I see them I cannot discuss them. If Kitchener raises the subject with me I shall be delighted to go into it with him, and I suggest to you that you should recommend him to do this.

The whole thing is a mare's nest. I have no power to offer any troops to Sir John French. All I can do is to hand over to the War Office, when they ask me for them, any Admiralty units which may be thought to be of use to the Army in the field.

As a matter of fact I have been contemplating, as you know and as Kitchener knows, quite a different destination for the naval brigades.

I wish you had heard what I had to say before assuming that I was in the wrong. This is not the first time that Kitchener has troubled you about matters which a few moments' talk with me would have adjusted. I do not remember that I have ever claimed your aid against any colleague otherwise than in Cabinet.

In the final draft of this letter Churchill deleted the sentence: 'I think you are rather precipitate in assuming I have transgressed the strictest limits of inter-departmental etiquette.' But the tone of the letter as sent was firm enough. Churchill waited a day before writing on February 18:

My dear Kitchener,

With regard to the armoured cars, I told French that if he wanted them, and you approved, I shd be delighted to hand two squadrons over to the War Office. They were made originally for the Army abroad, & some time ago you told me that when he wanted them he shd have them. The matter rests with you, and I see French says in his letter that it is 'subject to the concurrence of the Army Council'. My conversation with French was of course quite unofficial. . . .

You must know what care I have taken in these last few months to avoid anything wh cd cause difficulties with the WO. Even little things, such as whether Adl Bacon[1] shd go over to France to find out where French wanted the howitzers put, or whether Capt Guest shd go to the Dlles, I have sent specially over to obtain yr permission.

Asquith's sympathies were with Kitchener. During the morning he wrote to Venetia Stanley:

I am rather vexed with Winston who has been tactless enough to offer Sir John F (behind K's back & without his knowledge) a brigade of the Naval Division, and 2 squadrons of his famous Armoured Cars which are being hawked about from pillar to post. K came to me & complained very strongly both of the folly of the offer itself & of its being made without any previous consultation with him.

French was evidently very puzzled what to do with these unwelcome gifts[2]—the Naval battalions being still raw & ragged, and the only use he would suggest for the cars being to remove from them their Maxim guns for the use of his troops. The whole thing is a bad bêtise.

---

[1] Reginald Hugh Spencer Bacon, 1863–1947. Entered Navy, 1877. Started the Submarine Service, 1903. Naval Assistant to Sir John Fisher, 1905. First Captain of the *Dreadnought*, 1906. Director of Naval Ordnance and Torpedoes, 1907–9. Rear Admiral, 1909. Retired from the Navy to become Managing Director of the Coventry Ordnance Works, 1910–15. Colonel commanding Royal Marine Heavy Howitzer Brigade, 1915. Vice-Admiral commanding the Dover Patrols, 1915–18. Knighted, 1916. Admiral, 1918. Controller, Munitions Inventions, 1918–19. Naval historian; biographer of Lord Fisher.

[2] Not so unwelcome to the Belgians, who in May asked the Admiralty for the loan of an armoured car squadron, which was sent to Belgium in July. On September 21 Balfour, then First Lord, commented: 'It is curious that our armoured cars should seem so valuable to the Belgians and so worthless to the British in Flanders.'

Tempers were becoming badly frayed. On February 19, the third day of the quarrel, Churchill wrote once more:

My dear Kitchener,

You have known for months past of the armoured cars & the naval battalions, & what was the intention with which they were called into being. It has always rested & now rests exclusively with you when & how they shall join the Army.

So far as the cars are concerned I shd be glad if you found it possible to send over 2 squadrons. I have heard indirectly that one of the Cavalry Generals—Rimington[1]—is vy anxious to work them with his cavalry division so as to be able to make use of them if the armies begin to manoeuvre.

However if you do not wish them to go—please tell me—as I will try to find some other employment for them. . . .

It wd be a great pity to have an argument on the letter of a phrase. If his letters had begun 'I have heard that there are some armoured cars available which the Admiralty have prepared & etc' instead of talking about 'the offer of the First Lord of the Admiralty' this whole wearisome incident wd have been avoided. . . .

Yours sincerely
Winston S. Churchill

February 19 was a bad day for such a quarrel to reach its climax. That afternoon the full War Council was to meet to confirm the decision of three days earlier to send the 29th Division to the Dardanelles. The acrimonious exchanges over armoured cars had created an atmosphere of tension and distrust. The War Council met before Asquith could soothe the disputants. The effect of the quarrel was immediately apparent. At the start of the meeting Kitchener declared that Australian and New Zealand troops could go to the Dardanelles instead of the 29th Division. The War Council minutes recorded:

LORD KITCHENER said that the latest information from Egypt was that the Turks were retiring from the Canal. There appeared to be no intention of an advance by the Turks in greater force than before. For repelling such attacks, or even stronger attacks, the garrison of Egypt was sufficient without the assistance of the Australians and New Zealanders, who numbered 30,000 in all, and were regarded as an army corps. He was inclined to substitute

[1] Michael Frederic Rimington, 1858–1928. Entered Army, 1881. Major-General, 1910. Inspector-General of Cavalry, India, 1911–15. Lieutenant-General commanding the Indian Cavalry Corps in France, 1915. Commanded the Reserve Cavalry Centre attached to Headquarter Units, France, 1916. Knighted, 1921.

these troops for the 29th Division in support of the naval attack on the Dardanelles. . . . In view of the recent Russian set-back in East Prussia, he was
averse to sending away the 29th Division at present.

Churchill was totally unprepared for such a volte-face. It was only three
days since Kitchener had agreed to release the 29th Division without
detriment to the European situation. Churchill was now convinced that
first-class regular troops were needed to ensure the success of the
Dardanelles operation. He at once appealed to the War Council to
confirm the decision of February 16 to send out the 29th Division:

MR CHURCHILL said . . . the attack on the Dardanelles was a very heavy
naval undertaking. It was difficult to over-rate the military advantages which
success would bring. Its importance could only be appreciated by considering
the question as a whole from the point of view of the Allies. In France there
was a complete deadlock; the Russians were arrested. At what point, then,
could a favourable blow be struck by the Allies? The reply was the Dardanelles. In his opinion it would be a thrifty disposition on our part to have
50,000 men in this region. The Russian estimate of the force necessary to
capture Constantinople and open the Dardanelles and Bosphorus was two
army corps. He had hoped strongly, therefore, that we should have 50,000
men within reach of the Dardanelles, which could be concentrated there in
three days. He was sending out the ten trained battalions of the Naval Division. Neither these, however, nor the Australians and New Zealanders, could
be called first-rate troops at present, and they required a stiffening of regulars.
He did not insist that the troops must be landed at Lemnos. He would be
quite content if they were sent to Alexandria, where the men and horses
could be landed for exercise while the heavy gear was left on board. We
should never forgive ourselves if this promising operation failed owing to
insufficient military support at the critical moment.

Kitchener refused to release the 29th Division. All he would agree to
was that 'in case of emergency more troops might be spared from
Egypt'. Churchill believed that no troops would be an adequate substitute for the 19,000 trained men of the 29th Division. When Balfour
queried the need for so many troops, Churchill again insisted that 'it
was necessary to have a sufficient reserve of men on the spot'. Kitchener
warned the War Council that the German successes against Russia
might make it dangerous to send the 29th Division away from Europe;
if the Germans inflicted a decisive defeat on the Russians they would
at once send 'great masses of troops from the Eastern Front to France'.
Lloyd George shared Kitchener's fear that 'Russia might receive a
knockout blow', but he believed that the victorious German troops

would be sent, not against the western front, but against Serbia. For this reason, he accepted Churchill's proposal that a large number of troops should be sent to the east, and told his colleagues that it was important that they should be available 'either for Constantinople or, if that operation failed, to support the Serbians'. Asquith agreed; the most effective way to support Serbia, he told the War Council, would be 'to strike a big blow at the Dardanelles'.

Kitchener, confronted by the combined persuasive powers of Asquith, Churchill and Lloyd George, appeared to relent. If holding back the 29th Division, he said, 'would in any way jeopardize the success of the attack on the Dardanelles', he was willing to let it go; nevertheless, in his opinion, the Australian and New Zealand Divisions already in Egypt would be 'sufficient at first' for any attack on the Gallipoli Peninsula. Lloyd George did not agree. He wanted Kitchener to try to send to the east twice as many troops as Churchill wished to send, asserting that it was worth while 'to take some risks in order to achieve a decisive operation, which might win the war'. Lloyd George believed that 97,000 men could be made available; 39,000 Australian and New Zealand troops, 19,000 troops of the 29th Division, 10,000 Royal Naval Division, 4,000 Royal Marines, 15,000 French and 10,000 Russian troops. The general drift of the discussion favoured Churchill's argument for the despatch of troops:

SIR EDWARD GREY said that a great deal in the Balkans was staked on our attack on Constantinople. If there was a fair prospect of success it would be worth taking some risk.

LORD KITCHENER said that his point was that we had enough troops to ensure success, provided that the navy was successful, without sending the 29th Division.

MR BALFOUR suggested that, if the 29th Division was sent to Malta, it would be available either to reinforce the troops sent against the Dardanelles or to go to France, arriving at either destination within a few days.

... THE PRIME MINISTER said that the general situation would be vitally affected by the issue of the Dardanelles operation. Success would probably change the attitude of the Balkans, which, from our point of view, was very unsatisfactory.

MR CHURCHILL suggested that all preparations for the despatch of the 29th Division should go forward. The fitting of the transports, which had already commenced, should be continued. In four or five days we should have made some impression on the forts, and should have a good idea as to whether we were likely to achieve success by naval means. He wished, however, to lay stress on the fact that the navy could only open the Straits for armoured ships, and could not guarantee an unmolested passage for merchant ships unless the shores of the Dardanelles were cleared of the enemy's riflemen and field guns.

THE PRIME MINISTER then read some extracts from CID Paper 92-B, dated the 20th September 1906, on the subject of 'The Possibility of a Joint Naval and Military Attack upon the Dardanelles,' tending to show that military co-operation was essential to success.[1]

As a result of Asquith's intervention, the War Council were at last made aware of the view of the General Staff over eight years before that even a military landing was so full of risks that they were 'not prepared to recommend its being attempted'. But the then Director of Naval Intelligence, Captain Ottley, had challenged this conclusion in a note accompanying the memorandum of 1906, believing that there was 'no reason to despair of success'. Asquith had read to the War Council only the General Staff appreciation of 19 December 1906; he had made no reference to the meeting of the Committee of Imperial Defence of 28 February 1907, at which the appreciation had been discussed. Fisher had been among those present at the discussion of 1907, but had said nothing. Haldane, then Secretary of State for War, had stressed that 'the operation of landing on the Gallipoli Peninsula with a view to the capture of the forts overlooking the Dardanelles would be highly dangerous and would involve great risks . . . in the event of a rupture occurring with Turkey we should not attempt such a landing.' Grey had suggested that 'the forcing of the passage of the Dardanelles should be ruled out as an impracticable operation. He hoped that other means of bringing pressure to bear on Turkey would be considered. The meeting of 28 February 1907 had concluded 'that the operation of landing an expeditionary force on or near the Gallipoli Peninsula would involve great risk, and should not be undertaken if other means of bringing pressure to bear on Turkey were available'.

Hankey later told the Dardanelles Commissioners that at the War Council on February 19 it was felt that the General Staff pessimism of 1906 did not apply to the circumstances existing in 1915. In a memorandum of 1 September 1916 he told the Commissioners that the following points of contrast had been brought forward by those present at the meeting:

(i) Turkey in 1915, in addition to having to defend Constantinople, was at

---

[1] The paper to which Asquith referred was in fact circulated to the CID on 20 December 1906. It had been written the previous day, signed by General Sir Neville Lyttelton (1845–1931), Chief of the General Staff, 1904–8.

war on three other fronts—namely, the Caucasus, Egypt, and Mesopotamia.

(ii) Since the General Staff Memorandum was written, Turkey had suffered
severe defeats in the Balkan wars, and had shown herself much less
formidable as a military Power than had previously been assumed.
Politically also it was known that there were important elements in the
Turkish nation that were opposed to the Government.

(iii) The conditions in the Balkans in 1915 were likely to be favourably influenced by a successful attack.

(iv) There had been considerable development of naval *matériél* since
1906.

(v) The fall of the Liége and Namur forts had led to the belief that permanent works were easily dealt with by modern long-range artillery,
and this was confirmed by the fall of the outer forts.

(vi) The utilisation of aircraft had led to the hope that, in a comparatively
confined space like the Gallipoli Peninsula, the value of naval bombardment, particularly by indirect laying, would be enormously
increased.

(vii) The development of submarines led to the hope that the main Turkish
communications to the Gallipoli Peninsula, which run through the Sea
of Marmora, would be very vulnerable.

Whatever arguments were used, the pessimistic conclusions of 1906
were set aside. Churchill took up the discussion once more:

MR CHURCHILL recalled the various phases of the question. The first
proposal was to send no troops at all, leaving the Dardanelles to be dealt with
by the Navy. The next phase was that the 29th Division only was to be sent
to Salonika in the view of thereby involving Greece in the war. Then the
situation had again changed by the Russian defeat in the East, and it became
desirable to ensure success in the Dardanelles. If this operation was successful,
it was possible that the Greeks might change their minds, and that a complete
change might be brought about in the Balkans.
LORD KITCHENER said that the Russian reverse in the East might be
followed by further defeats, and this might react in the West in such manner
as to make us very short of men. Nevertheless, if events should show it to be
necessary, he was prepared to send the 29th Division to the East.
. . . MR CHURCHILL said that no one could foretell the results of success
in a country like Turkey. He did not ask for troops actually to be sent to the
Dardanelles, but only that they should be within hail. It might give us a
tremendous opportunity. Some risks must be run in any military operation.
In his opinion, the main risk in this case was that the horses and men of the
29th Division would get out of training through being cooped up on board
ship.

A certain optimism now entered the discussion. Balfour asked 'what would be the precise political effect of an occupation of the Gallipoli Peninsula combined with naval command of the Sea of Marmora':

MR CHURCHILL said it ought to give us control of Turkey.
LORD KITCHENER expected that in this event the Turkish army would evacuate Europe altogether.
MR BALFOUR asked if we should be bound to afford military protection to the Christian population of Constantinople.
SIR EDWARD GREY said that they would have to take their chance.

Although everyone at the War Council was agreed that the battle at the Dardanelles would be of major importance, and that it stood a greater chance of success if troops were available, no final decision was taken on February 19 as to whether or not the 29th Division should be sent to the East. The decision of February 16 was thereby set aside. The only concession to Churchill's arguments was a formal conclusion that transports should be prepared to convey the Australian and New Zealand troops from Egypt to Lemnos, and to take the 29th Division to the Mediterranean at some unspecified future date, 'if required'.

Churchill still hoped that if Carden succeeded in his first attempt to force the Dardanelles, the Turkish collapse would be swift and the need for troops secondary. But it was no longer possible to plan, as both he and Kitchener had originally done, to call off the naval attack altogether if the operation proved too costly or too difficult. The worsening situation on the Russian front, where it had suddenly become possible to talk of a German 'knock-out blow', intensified the importance of the Dardanelles operation. Were it to fail, the Allied situation, already cursed by stalemate on the western front and gloom on the eastern front, might prove untenable. Defeat at the Dardanelles could be a grave blow to Allied morale. Success could mark the turning point of Allied fortunes. Without any serious assessment of Britain's naval or military capabilities, the War Council of February 19 had established the importance of forcing the Dardanelles as a major operation of war. It had also failed to commit to that operation troops of a quality sufficient to make success more certain.

On February 18 the French Government, which had also had second doubts about the chances of a purely naval attack, urged the British Government to suspend the naval operations until the arrival of troops at the Dardanelles. But with Kitchener's approval Churchill informed Grey, for transmission to Paris: 'The naval operations having begun cannot be interrupted but must proceed continuously to their conclusion, every day adding to the dangers of the arrival of German or Austrian submarines & any lull in the attack prejudicing the moral effect on the Turkish Capital.'

Churchill was pressing his officials to expedite arrangements for the transfer of troops to Lemnos, sending the civil Director of Transport, Graeme Thomson, detailed proposals on the morning of February 20:

Secret Please return

1. Transports should be provided for seven battalions and details of the RND, approximately 8,000 men, leaving Avonmouth on Saturday the 27th for Lemnos.

2. All preparations are to be made to embark the 29th Division independently of the above with the least possible delay. The despatch of this Division is not, however, finally decided.

3. There should be accumulated at Alexandria by Saturday the 27th inst, sufficient transport to carry 8,000 or 10,000 infantry. This may be wanted in a hurry if the Dardanelles operations take a favourable turn. This transport must be found locally. The transports which carry the two Marine battalions and some of the ships in the Egyptian Prize Courts might be available.

4. The emergency action provided for in par 3 may not be required, as the operations in the Dardanelles may take a leisurely course. In that event the ships collected for the emergency would form part of a larger fleet of transports which is to be collected without delay for the transport of approximately 40,000 men, details of which will be given by the War Office.

Graeme Thomson noted on the bottom of these instructions: 'Action is proceeding with all possible dispatch.'

Admiralty and War Office co-operation was poor. Serious errors were made in loading the ships. When they reached Alexandria it was discovered that supplies had been packed in the wrong order, and great confusion took place at the time of disembarkation. Guns had been separated from ammunition, primers from shells. In examining this serious error, the Dardanelles Commissioners were confronted by conflicting testimony. Graeme Thomson put the responsibility on the War Office's shoulders, informing them: 'When we get our indents from the War Office we propose which units and which stores should go into what ships. If the War Office accept that I am afraid the War Office must take the responsibility for any dislocation that ensues.' The War Office contended that they had expected the official concerned with the problems of transport to submit workable proposals. Churchill had appointed Thomson Director of Transport in December 1914 against the arguments of both Oliver and Graham Greene. Oliver later maintained that Thomson 'knew the City end of the work and all about taking up ships etc but nothing about war' and that had an abler man been appointed 'the transports for the Dardanelles would have been properly loaded and arrived in the proper order'.

In making arrangements for troops to be stationed on the Greek island of Lemnos, and for ships to anchor in Mudros Bay, Churchill appointed Rear-Admiral Wemyss to be Governor of the island. Grey only learned of this indirectly, when he received the copy of a telegram which had been sent from Cyprus to the Colonial Office. He was much angered, writing to Churchill on February 20:

Dear Churchill,
    I am aghast at this telegram. Do please remember that all Greece agrees to is the use of the harbour at Lemnos by our ships. We do not take charge of the Island & no Governor must be appointed or official steps announced to take over the Island.
    A real catastrophe may be provoked if you go beyond the agreement with Greece & I may have to say that my position is impossible & I must resign.
    Our ships can use the harbour that is all we have at present from Greece & I warned you verbally the other day that no Governor must be appointed by us. To appoint a Governor won't help us to take the Dardanelles: we want the use of the harbour without titles & other useless things.
                                                            Yrs sincerely
                                                            E. Grey

Grey had also complained to the Colonial Office, minuting on the Cyprus telegram: 'Sir Edward Grey is unaware that any British Governor or Official is to be appointed to Lemnos, and strongly deprecates any such announcement.' Churchill had confidence in what he had done. That afternoon he defended his action:

My dear Grey,
    The original telegram from the Greeks said that they wd go out on the 22nd leaving their batteries all standing, & that they wished us to look after the guns. Lemnos is also to be used for a British & probably a French Division to concentrate at. It is therefore quite clear that something must be meant beyond the use of the waters of Mudros Bay, & that the shore landing places, camping grounds, & defensive positions round that bay are also comprised.

In these circumstances it was thought that the Admiral appointed to look after the base & harbour, which will be used by a fleet of nearly 70 British ships apart from French, shd have at his hand some skilful official versed in the problems of a Turco-Greek island. The Chief of the Staff therefore telegraphed to the Vice-Admiral advising him to apply to the Governor of Cyprus[1] for some competent official.

Shortly after this another telegram arrived from Greece, speaking of the transference being limited to Mudros Bay; & I also had my talk with you about a Governor. In consequence, Adl Wemyss was told that he wd not be appointed Governor of Lemnos, but merely Senior Naval Officer at Mudros; & all that you wished in this respect is being done.

Admiral Carden will be informed accordingly.

At the same time it seems clear that there must be some governing authority in this island, especially if it is to be used as a cantonment for troops, as all sorts of questions as between Turks & Greeks, British & French, will have to be settled by the SNO; & it is certainly desirable that he shd have the advice of people who understand this part of the world.

The only workable theory is that Lemnos is a Turkish island in British naval occupation. Any theory that it is a Greek island, or a Turkish island in Anglo-Greek occupation, is plainly inadmissible.

Yours very sincerely
Winston S. Churchill

Having explained his position, Churchill submitted to Grey's authority, enclosing with his letter a telegram to Carden which strictly limited Weymss' status. That evening Grey replied:

Dear Churchill,

The telegram to Carden will meet the case. Let everything in the way of administration be as informal as possible & nothing said about it outside.

For years the Admiralty (notably Fisher) have spoken of having Lemnos & if we announce urbi et orbi (Marsh will translate) that we have appointed a Governor not only the Greeks but the French & Russians will think we have bagged Lemnos & mean to keep it & that we are out for grab & not for the common cause & the very success of our operations at the Dardanelles will be watched with suspicion by our own friends. So do make your Admirals careful to keep all their actions at Lemnos within the limits necessary to use the island for strategic purposes & to say as little as possible. I have suggested an addition to the telegram to Carden for this purpose.

I enclose a minute for the CO, to correct one that I sent there in haste this morning. . . .

Churchill's eagerness to press forward with what he believed to be

[1] John Eugene Clauson, 1866–1918. Entered Army, 1885. Major, 1900. Assistant Secretary, Committee of Imperial Defence, 1904–6. Lieutenant-Governor, Malta, 1911–14. Knighted, 1913. High Commissioner and Commander-in-Chief, Cyprus, 1914–18.

the necessary preparations had led him to go further than Grey would accept. Although he had no territorial motive in what he had done, and did not share Fisher's reiterated enthusiasm for the annexation of Lemnos as a permanent British base,[1] he had failed to anticipate Grey's reaction, and, as had happened before, friction and time-consuming correspondence had been the result.

At eight o'clock on the morning of February 19 Carden had begun his bombardment of the outer forts at the Dardanelles. Asquith awaited the news at Walmer Castle. 'I had hoped to have heard this morning from Winston . . .' he wrote to Venetia Stanley on February 20. 'So far nothing has come. The forts at the entrance of the straits are I fancy the toughest & best armed. If all goes as well as possible the operation of reducing the forts up to Gallipoli will take the best part of a fortnight.' That morning Churchill received Carden's first report. Although the fire had been heavy and prolonged, there had been no direct hits on the guns or their mountings. But the magazines of two of the forts had been blown up, and their communications with their control positions destroyed. It was a modest beginning. On February 20 and 21 a strong south-westerly gale and low visibility prevented any further operations. On February 22 Carden telegraphed that the gale was abating and that he hoped to resume operations on the following day; also that the *Queen Elizabeth* and the *Agamemnon* had arrived at the Dardanelles. Some damage had been caused to the *Vengeance* by four shots from one of the Turkish forts, but apart from that, and despite two of the forts maintaining a rate of fire of one round per gun every ninety seconds, 'enemy fire was inaccurate'.

Churchill was anxious to see troops on their way, and to stir Kitchener into a firm and immediate military commitment. 'The operations at the Dardanelles may go much more rapidly than has been expected,' he wrote on February 20. 'In this case it will be vital to have enough men to hold the lines of Bulair. There will be 2,000 Marines at Lemnos, but that is not enough & I ask you to organize in Egypt 8,000 or 10,000 men who cd in an emergency be despatched much earlier than the others.' Churchill also pressed for the appointment of a General to command the troops who had not yet been despatched, writing on February 22: 'There ought to be a good general at Carden's side as soon

---

[1] The question of annexing Lemnos was much discussed at the Admiralty. On February 19 Limpus had written to Churchill from Malta: 'I venture to suggest that we ought to acquire Lemnos Island. It is more valuable to us as a Sea Power than is Cyprus. The time of turmoil & general War seems to present a better opportunity of acquiring it than peace time would.' On March 2 Churchill himself joined the annexationist school, writing to Fisher and Oliver: 'If Russia has C'ple & Straits, we ought to have Lemnos.'

as possible. You spoke the other day of Hunter-Weston.[1] Could not he or someone equally competent be sent to take command of whatever troops arrive including the Royal Naval Division. He will then be able to judge what ought to be done & what force is required.'

On February 23 the low visibility and strong gale continued at the Dardanelles. Carden signalled that he had again ordered the bombardment to be postponed as a 'great waste of ammunition would be involved by any bombardment under these conditions'. The War Council met at 10 Downing Street on February 24. In answer to a question from Haldane, as to whether the Turks could be driven out of Gallipoli by naval attack, Kitchener declared that in his opinion 'if the Fleet succeeded in silencing the forts, the garrison of Gallipoli would probably be withdrawn'. Otherwise, he said, 'they would run the risk of being cut off and starved out'. When the discussion turned to Mesopotamia, Lloyd George suggested that 'the Mesopotamian expedition was merely a side issue' and that the whole Mesopotamian force ought 'to be withdrawn and concentrated on the Dardanelles'. Hankey thought that it would be 'a very proper use to make of our sea-power', that having already drawn sixty thousand Turkish soldiers down into Mesopotamia, Britain should now withdraw from Basra and concentrate on the Dardanelles which, in his own words, 'was at present the decisive point in the East'. Churchill argued against giving up the Mesopotamian conquest, which he felt should be reinforced from India. He then asked that the 29th Division should be sent to the Eastern Mediterranean as soon as possible. While he believed that 'with a comparatively small number of troops we might be in Constantinople by the end of March', he felt that the result of such an operation might be so far-reaching that as many troops as possible would be needed to follow it up. Churchill told the War Council that he:

. . . would like to send out at once all the available troops, concentrating there the 29th Division, a Territorial Division, the Naval Division, two divisions from Egypt, a French and a Russian Division, making altogether more than 100,000 men. It was not a question of sending them immediately to the Dardanelles, but merely of having them within reach. If an immediate decision was taken, all these troops would be in the Levant by the 21st March.

[1] Aylmer Hunter-Weston, 1864–1940. Entered Royal Engineers, 1884. Served on Kitchener's staff in the Sudan, 1898. Chief Staff Officer to Sir John French's Cavalry Division in South Africa, 1900. Brigadier-General commanding the 4th Division, August 1914; promoted Major-General for distinguished service in the field. Commanded the 29th Division at the landing on Cape Helles, April 1915; promoted Lieutenant-General for the successful landing. Commanded the VIIIth Corps at the Dardanelles and in France, 1915–18. Knighted, 1915. Conservative MP, 1916–35.

Kitchener spoke against Churchill's proposal. The 29th Division could not be spared. The attack on the Dardanelles had been planned as a naval one; did Churchill now contemplate, he asked, a land attack as well? The minutes of the War Council record Churchill's reply:

MR CHURCHILL said he did not; but it was quite conceivable that the naval attack might be temporarily held up by mines, and some local military operation required. He asked how 2 divisions could make the difference between success and failure in the Western theatre of war, especially as, by the middle of April, 4 divisions of new army would be available.

Kitchener then asked Churchill what 'these large forces' would do when they had reached the Dardanelles.

MR CHURCHILL said they would have several choices. If the fleet got through the Dardanelles, they could be put into Constantinople. Or they could be put into European Turkey towards the Bulgarian frontier; Bulgaria could then be invited to take possession up to the Enos-Media line as a condition of joining the Allies. The Allied forces could then be sent up through Bulgaria to Nish. Another plan would be to send them to Salonica in order to influence the Balkan States. Or they might be sent up the Danube if Roumania joined the Allies.

Churchill's demand for troops received further support from the Chancellor of the Exchequer:

MR LLOYD GEORGE agreed that a force ought to be sent to the Levant, which could, if necessary be used after the Navy had cleared the Dardanelles, to occupy the Gallipoli Peninsula or Constantinople. He wished to know, however, whether, in the event of the naval attack failing (and it was something of an experiment), it was proposed that the Army should be used to undertake an operation in which the Navy had failed.

Churchill replied that there was no intention to send any Army if the naval attack failed, but that he could conceive a case where the Navy had almost succeeded 'but where a military force would just make the difference between failure and success'. Lloyd George warned against using the Army 'to pull the chestnuts out of the fire for the Navy' and believed that if the Dardanelles were to fail 'we ought to be immediately ready to try something else' in the Near East.

Kitchener declared that although he was willing to 'risk a good deal in order to open up the Dardanelles', he could not understand the purpose 'for which so many troops were to be used'. He reiterated his belief that once the British Fleet had forced its way through the Dardanelles—indeed, as soon as the forts 'were clearly being silenced one by one'—the Turkish garrison on the Gallipoli Peninsula would evacuate its position, and that 'the garrison of Constantinople, the Sultan, and not improbably the Turkish army in Thrace, would also decamp to the Asiatic shore'. Victory would be achieved by naval guns alone. With patience and wise negotiation the remaining Turkish forces in Europe 'would probably surrender'. Why then was it necessary, he asked, to send out to the Dardanelles 'the large forces contemplated by Mr Churchill'. Before Churchill could answer, Grey spoke in support of Kitchener, emphasizing the moral effect of large naval guns. Once success were achieved at the Dardanelles, he said, 'we might have a coup d'état in Constantinople'. This would obviate the need for any military activity against the Turks, who would presumably return to their former neutrality, or even agree to join with the Allies against their German masters.

All those who spoke at the War Council were agreed that failure must be averted. 'The effect of a defeat in the Orient,' Kitchener told his colleagues, 'would be very serious.' Grey said that if the naval attack failed it would be 'morally equivalent to a great defeat on land'. Churchill took up this harping upon the moral impact of success to urge once more the need for a large Army. Up to now, he said, our diplomacy 'had been paralysed because we had had nothing to offer'. If Britain could offer the Balkan States the prospect of victory against the Turks, it might bring a million Balkan soldiers into the Allied Army. Surely, he asked, the presence of a hundred thousand British troops would be worth while if it achieved this objective? He himself, he declared, 'would be willing to send a quarter of a million men to effect this result, if we had them'. Kitchener could not be convinced. He did not envisage a strong Turkish resistance. When Asquith asked whether the Australians and New Zealanders 'were good enough' for an important operation of war, Kitchener replied 'that they were quite good enough if a cruise in the Sea of Marmora was all that was contemplated'.

Kitchener's obstinacy was decisive. To Churchill's chagrin, the War Council decided to postpone their decision about the 29th Division until the next meeting. The most that Kitchener would agree to was that those troops already in the Eastern Mediterranean should be assembled immediately in Egypt and the Aegean to await the outcome of the naval attack. There were ten thousand of these in all. Neither Asquith nor Churchill believed that they would be adequate. But Kitchener's opposition was final.

Asquith shared Churchill's desire to send a large military force to the

Dardanelles. He agreed with Lloyd George that all available troops should be concentrated upon the expedition. But he was unwilling to overrule the Secretary of State for War. As soon as the War Council ended he wrote to Venetia Stanley:

We are all agreed (except K) that the naval adventure in the Dardanelles shd be backed up by a strong military force. I say 'except K', but he quite agrees in principle. Only he is very sticky about sending out there the 29th Division, which is the best one we have left at home. He is rather perturbed by the strategic situation both in the East & West, and wants to have something in hand, in case the Germans are so far successful against Russia for the moment, as to be able to despatch Westwards a huge army—perhaps of a million—to try & force through Joffre & French's lines.

One must take a lot of risks in war, & I am strongly of opinion that the chance of forcing the Dardanelles, & occupying Constantinople, & cutting Turkey in half, and arousing on our side the whole Balkan peninsula, presents such a unique opportunity that we ought to hazard a lot elsewhere rather than forgo it. If he can be convinced, well & good: but to discard his advice & overrule his judgment on a military question is to take a great responsibility. So I am rather anxious.

Returning to the Admiralty an extremely disappointed man, Churchill immediately telegraphed to Carden, explaining that the naval attack must still be self-contained, and that even the troops which were assembling were intended not to assist the operation, but to follow it up should it prove successful:

The operation on which you are engaged consists in forcing the Dardanelles without military assistance, as generally described in your telegram No 19 of the 11th January and in the structions sent you from the Admiralty. It is not proposed at this stage to use military force other than parties of Marines landed to destroy particular guns or torpedo tubes.

On the other hand, if your operation is successful, we consider it necessary that ample military force should be available to reap the fruits. The following military forces are, therefore, being moved or held ready to move to within striking distance:—

Two Australian Divisions ...	...	30,000
The Royal Naval Division ...	...	8,500
A French Division ...	...	18,000

It is also possible that the 29th regular Division of 18,000 will be sent from England. Full details of these movements will be sent you, but your immediate operations are not affected by them. Ten thousand troops should be held ready, part in Egypt, part in Lemnos, for unexpected contingencies, should your operations proceed more rapidly than had been estimated. But it is not intended that they should be employed in present circumstances to assist the Naval operations which are independent and self-contained.

General Birdwood,[1] who will command the army, is leaving to-night in the 'Swiftsure' to join you. You should discuss the whole position with him, and if you are of opinion that the army can help your operations, you may make recommendations.

In a further telegram that day Churchill again warned Carden that major military operations were not to be embarked upon. 'Occupation of the southern end of the peninsula . . .' he explained, 'is not considered by the War Office essential for insurance of success of first main object, ie, destruction of the permanent batteries.'

Balfour shared Churchill's chagrin at the holding back of troops. After the War Council he set down his reasons in a memorandum which was circulated on the following day. 'We *must* send as many troops as may be required to make the Bosphorus operation, to which we are now committed, a success,' he wrote. If Greece and Rumania would be more likely to join the Allies, if 110,000 rather than 40,000 were troops sent, 'then it might be proper', he asserted, 'to take risks in the West and to send every man we can spare to aid in the Balkan operations'.

The naval bombardment was resumed on February 25. The four outer forts of the Dardanelles were silenced. Carden began making plans for the second stage of the operations, clearing the minefields and destroying the intermediate forts, which he hoped to do at the beginning of March. While the outer forts were being destroyed, Churchill and his wife went to Blandford where the Royal Naval Division was being reviewed by the King before setting off to the Dardanelles. At the review were Asquith's son 'Oc' and Rupert Brooke, both officers of the Division. Margot Asquith, who was present, described the review in her diary:

The whole 9,000 men were drawn up on the glorious downs and Winston walked round and inspected them before the King arrived. I felt quite a thrill when I saw Oc and Rupert with walking sticks standing in front of their men looking quite wonderful! Rupert is a beautiful young man and we get on

[1] William Riddell Birdwood, 1865–1951. Lieutenant, Royal Scots Fusiliers, 1883. General Officer commanding the Australian and New Zealand Army Corps (ANZAC), 1914–18. Lieutenant-General commanding the ANZAC landing, 25 April 1915. Commander-in-Chief of the Allied forces at the Dardanelles, October 1915–January 1916. Knighted, 1913. Field-Marshal, 1925. Commander-in-Chief, India, 1922–30. Master of Peterhouse, Cambridge, 1931–8. Created Baron, 1938.

well, he has so much intellectual temperament and nature about him. He told Oc he was quite *certain* he would never come back but would be killed—it didn't depress him at all but he was just *convinced*—I shall be curious to see if this turns out to be a true instinct.

When we had been standing doing nothing for hours Colonel Quilter[1] let all the men ease off and smoke. Goony and I stood by a few motors and chaises which had collected on the down side and stray people and watched the march past: the King having arrived 11.30 by special train and stood just in front of me with Sir Charles Cust,[2] Winston and Commodore de Bartolomé.

The latter was much annoyed by Cust crabbing the Naval Division. I asked him why he minded what Cust said! Sailors who give up the sea for the Court were hardly critics to be frightened of! (Cust is something in the King's household.)

They marched past perfectly. I saw the silver band (given to the Hood Division by Winston's constituents) coming up the hill and the bayonets flashing—I saw the uneven ground and the straight backs—'Eyesssssss RIGHT!!!—and the darling boy had passed.

The King was pleased and told me they all marched wonderfully.

On the following day Asquith, who had stayed in London, sent Venetia Stanley a report of Clementine Churchill's intervention to improve the medical organization of the Hood Battalion: 'At the eleventh hour it seems to have been discovered that they were without either doctor or drugs, & Clemmie showed a good deal of resource, with the result that they will pick up some necessary "details" at Malta, but it doesn't look as if the organisation was well thought out.' Later that day Asquith wrote again to Venetia Stanley of the apparent good fortune of his family's young friends to be going on the expedition: 'How lucky they are to escape Flanders & the trenches and be sent to the "gorgeous East".'

Churchill returned from the review at Blandford on the evening of February 25. That night he sent Asquith, Lloyd George and Balfour a memorandum which he hoped they would read before the War Council met on the following day. Expressing his doubts as to whether Russia would collapse as easily as War Office Intelligence seemed to suggest, he also reiterated his belief that the trench system on the western front would maintain the stalemate, and that a large military force could

---

[1] John Arnold Cuthbert Quilter, 1375–1915. Entered Army, 1897. Major, 1904. Retired, 1913. Lieutenant-Colonel, Grenadier Guards, 1914. Appointed to command the 7th (Hood) Battalion of the Royal Naval Division, August 1914. Served at Antwerp. Killed at Gallipoli, 6 May 1915.

[2] Charles Leopold Cust, 1864–1931. 3rd Baronet, 1878. Equerry to George V, 1892–1931. Knighted, 1911.

therefore be assembled for action in the east. If the War Council would agree to full military and naval co-operation with these large forces, he continued, 'we can make certain of taking Constantinople by the end of March'. Churchill listed the military forces which he wanted made available:

(in England) 29th Division Another Territorial Div^n	...	36,000 men	
(under orders for Lemnos) RN Division	...	12,000	
(from Egypt) 2 Australasian Div^{ns} ...	...	39,000	
French Div^n	(say)	20,000	
Russian Brigade	(say)	8,000	

Total   115,000

Churchill concluded:

All these troops are capable of being concentrated within striking distance of the Bulair Isthmus by March 21st if orders are given now. If the naval operations have not succeeded by then, they can be used to attack the Gallipoli Peninsula & make sure that the fleet gets through. As soon as the Dlles are open, they can either (a) operate from Constantinople to extirpate any Turkish forces in Europe, or (b) if Bulgaria comes in at our invitation to occupy up to the Enos-Midia line, they can proceed through Bulgaria to the aid of Serbia; or (c) if Bulgaria is merely confirmed in a friendly neutrality, but Greece comes in, they can proceed through Salonica to the aid of Serbia.

The War Council met at 10 Downing Street on February 26. Kitchener, who opened the discussion, once more drew attention 'to the serious position in Russia'. He reported that the Russians had represented to him 'that they were short of nearly everything, especially rifles and artillery ammunition'. He made no reference to the 29th Division. But as the discussion progressed he made it clear that he believed troops were unnecessary at the Dardanelles. According to the Minutes, Kitchener said that, 'once the fleet was through the Straits, the Bulair lines would become untenable, and the Turks would probably evacuate the Gallipoli Peninsula.' A few moments later he spoke again. 'If the forts were reduced,' he said, 'the requisite military effect would be gained.' Churchill intervened with a vehement appeal for an immediate decision to send the 29th Division:

He (Mr Churchill) wished to make the strongest possible appeal that the 29th Division would not be withheld. In three weeks' time Constantinople might be at our mercy. We should avoid the risk of finding ourselves with a force inadequate to our requirements and face to face with a disaster. At the previous meeting Lord Kitchener had asked him what was the use to be made of any large number of troops at Constantinople.

His reply was that they were required to occupy Constantinople and to compel a surrender of all Turkish forces remaining in Europe after the fleet had obtained command of the Sea of Marmora. With an army at hand this could be accomplished either by fighting, or by negotiation, or by bribery. The Chatalja lines would be occupied from the reverse side, the flanks being commanded by men-of-war. Subsequently, if Bulgaria joined the Allies, we should be in a position to push the troops up through Bulgaria to Serbia. Or, if Roumania came in, they could be sent up the Danube or by rail through Roumania. The actual and definite object of the army would be to reap the fruits of the naval success.

This appeal was in vain. Kitchener declined to weaken what he described as 'the only troops we had available as a reserve to send over to France' until the Russian situation was more clear. He declared his belief that the naval attack would in itself secure victory. He was convinced, he said, 'from his knowledge of Constantinople and the East, that the whole situation in Constantinople would change the moment the fleet had secured a passage through the Dardanelles'.[1] Balfour, completely reversing the arguments of his memorandum of the previous day, spoke in Kitchener's support, optimistic that a naval attack would achieve the War Council's purpose:

MR BALFOUR suggested that, if the purely naval operation were carried out, the following results would be attained: the command of the Sea of Marmora would be secured; the Turkish troops remaining in Europe would be cut off; the arsenal and dockyards at Constantinople could be destroyed; the condition of the Turks would become worse every day they held out; the Bosphorus could be opened; a line of supply for war-like stores opened up with Russia, and wheat obtained from the Black Sea.

Churchill could not agree. He pointed out that if the Turks were still in possession of the shores, only armoured ships would be able to go through the Dardanelles, and that even troopships could only go through with difficulty. If men were needed to occupy Constantinople, they might have to be transported over land at Bulair, exposed to

_____

[1] Kitchener spoke with an authority on eastern questions which his colleagues could not easily challenge. He had first visited the Turkish Empire—attached to the Palestine Exploration Fund—in 1874, when he learned Arabic; in 1879 he served as a British Vice-Consul in Anatolia. Both as Commander-in-Chief, India (1902–9), and as British Agent in Egypt (1911–14), he had been much concerned with Muslim problems.

Turkish fire. Hankey intervened with a powerful plea in Churchill's support. His own Minutes recorded his intervention:

LIEUTENANT-COLONEL HANKEY suggested that the probable main use of troops at Constantinople was to open the Dardanelles and Bosphorus to all classes of ship. First it might be necessary to clear the Gallipoli Peninsula. Once this was accomplished, the forces could be withdrawn from there, unless it was necessary to defend the Bulair lines. Next it might be necessary to clear out the position south of the Dardanelles. Probably no very large force could be brought here by the enemy, as the line of communication along the south of the Sea of Marmora was long and difficult, and the normal route for supplying the troops in this region, which was by sea, would not be available. With the advantage of free movement by sea it ought not to be difficult to cut off and isolate the Turkish troops south of the Dardanelles. Once this was done the passage of the Dardanelles would be safe for all traffic, though it might be necessary to leave behind a small force to secure it. Similar operations might be necessary in the Bosphorus.

Kitchener was adamant. He did not believe the Turks would try to defend the southern side of the Dardanelles. Churchill retorted that it was probable they already had an army of forty thousand men there. Hankey again supported Churchill. But Kitchener was determined to minimize the need for military action against the Turks, and in reply to a question by Balfour as to whether the Turks were likely to fight 'with their backs to the wall', he replied that it was more likely that 'the Sultan, the Government, and the principal generals would evacuate Constantinople and go over to Asia. The Turkish army would be deserted, and would probably surrender.' Once more, Kitchener's policy was based upon the low opinion he had formed of Turkish morale. Lloyd George intervened in support of Churchill, saying that he doubted whether victory would come as easily as Kitchener imagined. Churchill insisted that 'if we had insufficient troops the Germans would soon discover it and would tell the Turks, and we should accomplish nothing'.

The discussion became heated. Lloyd George repeated his appeal that as many men as possible should be sent to the east, 'in order to bring Greece into the war' and declared that 'the despatch of 100,000 men, following close on the fall of the Dardanelles, ought to produce a great effect in the Balkans'. Churchill continued to insist that the 29th Division must be sent in order to make the total number of troops up to a minimum of eighty-five thousand. Asquith supported Churchill's request, believing that the quality of the 29th Division was of particular importance, and telling the War Council: 'Man for man they were probably far superior to any other troops who would be engaged', and that they were 'the only first-class seasoned men available'.

Kitchener appealed once more to his colleagues not to weaken the position on the western front. Finding himself supported by both Grey and Balfour, he declared with emotion that he would not accept responsibility for giving up the power to reinforce Sir John French. Kitchener's refusal was decisive. Churchill could do no more. Frustrated, angry, morose, he made one final intervention:

MR CHURCHILL said that the 29th Division would not make the difference between failure and success in France, but might well make the difference in the East. He wished it to be placed on record that he dissented altogether from the retention of the 29th Division in this country. If a disaster occurred in Turkey owing to the insufficiency of troops, he must disclaim all responsibility.

Churchill's plea failed. The support of Lloyd George, Hankey, and even Asquith, had done nothing to help him. The War Council decided to keep the 29th Division in England. Asquith wrote to Venetia Stanley: 'We accepted K's view as right to the immediate situation, to Winston's immense and unconcealed dudgeon.' Hankey was also disappointed, writing to his wife that evening: 'They are getting on better at the Dardanelles again. I am afraid though that K won't do what I want. He is apparently in a funk that the Russians will get badly hammered, and that the Germans will be able to bring a lot of men westward.'

Asquith, angered by Churchill's 'noisy, rhetorical, tactless and temperless—or full' mood at the War Council, as he described it to Venetia Stanley, had taken the unusual step of calling him to his study when the meeting ended. 'Winston was rather trying to-day,' he wrote, '& I felt constrained to talk to him afterwards a little for his soul's good: a task wh as you know I do not relish, & in which I fear I do not excel.' In a letter to his brother that evening, Churchill gave vent to his feelings:

. . . The Dardanelles delay through weather from the 19th to the 24th inclusive was vy vexatious to me, & hard to bear. But now they have moved forward again, & so far everything shows the soundness of the plan. I have had many difficulties in trying to keep people up to the scratch. The capacity to run risks is at famine prices. All play for safety.

The war is certainly settling on to a grim basis, & it is evident that long vistas of pain & struggle lie ahead. The limited fund of life & energy wh I possess is not much use to influence these tremendous moments. I toil away. LG has more true insight & courage than anyone else. He really sticks at nothing—no measure is too far reaching, no expedient too novel.

On the following morning, convinced that his argument was sound, Churchill drafted a further protest, which he asked Hankey to circulate to the War Council, but which, realizing that too much reiteration could weaken his advocacy, he held back:

I must now put on record my opinion that the military force provided, viz, two Australasian divisions supported by the nine naval battalions and the French division, is not large enough for the work it may have to do; and that the absence of any British regular troops will, if fighting occurs, expose the naval battalions and the Australians to undue risk.

Even if the Navy succeed unaided in forcing the passage, the weakness of the military force may compel us to forgo a large part of the advantages which would otherwise follow.

Churchill's optimism had momentarily disappeared; but he now believed in the paramount importance of action at the Dardanelles, and the vital need to capture Constantinople. He continued to argue fiercely about the means; he no longer doubted the ends. Only by defeating Turkey, and offers of Turkish territory, could Britain persuade the neutral Balkan States—Greece, Rumania and Bulgaria—to join forces in attacking Austria-Hungary. Churchill had helped to add to the War Council's self-deception by his earlier willingness to make the operation purely naval; he now believed that ships alone would be inadequate, and that the more troops that could be found, the greater chance there would be of victory. But he so believed in the need for victory that he was prepared to go ahead with the plans for an entirely naval attack. However much he continued to argue that these plans might fail, by agreeing to go ahead with them, he made himself responsible for the very disaster that he forecast.

10

The Assumption of Victory

THE War Council's decision on February 26 to hold back the 29th Division demonstrated that Kitchener's veto was all-powerful. Although Churchill had been supported by Asquith, Lloyd George and the increasingly influential Hankey, his plea had failed. No one found it easy to argue with Kitchener at the War Council. Facts did not seem to sway him. His attitude to questioning was aloof. When he thought his military judgement was being criticized he quickly took umbrage. As Commander-in-Chief during the reconquest of the Sudan in 1898 he had acted unchallenged in drawing up his plans, and in carrying them out. As Commander-in-Chief in India from 1902 to 1909 he had dominated the counsels of a subcontinent, forcing Lord Curzon[1] into resignation. As British Agent and Consul-General in Egypt, the post he had been holding at the outbreak of war, his authority had been absolute. These were the experiences on which he had to draw. If he would not bend or reconsider, his colleagues had to support him. If he would not read or listen, they could not command him. The Liberal Government could not afford to lose its hero. Kitchener's presence as Secretary of State for War protected the vulnerable War Office from serious Conservative attack, the reverse effect of Churchill's presence at the Admiralty. In 1916 Churchill gave the Dardanelles Commissioners his impression of the decisve influence which Kitchener had exerted:

His prestige and authority were immense. He was the sole mouthpiece of War Office opinion in the War Council. Everyone had the greatest admira-

---

[1] George Nathaniel Curzon, 1859–1925. Conservative MP, 1886–98. Under-Secretary of State for India, 1891–2; for Foreign Affairs, 1892–8. Viceroy of India, 1898–1905. Created Earl, 1911. Lord Privy Seal, May 1915–December 1916. President of the Air Board, 1916. Lord President of the Council and Member of the War Cabinet, 1916–19. Secretary of State for Foreign Affairs, 1919–22. Created Marquess, 1921. Lord President of the Council, 1924–5.

tion for his character, and everyone felt fortified, amid the terrible and incalculable events of the opening months of the war, by his commanding
presence. When he gave a decision it was invariably accepted as final. He
was never, to my belief, overruled by the War Council or the Cabinet in any
military matter, great or small. No single unit was ever sent or withheld contrary, not merely to his argument, but to his advice.

Scarcely anyone ever ventured to argue with him in Council. Respect for
the man, sympathy for him in his immense labours, confidence in his professional judgment, and the belief that he had plans deeper and wider than
any we could see, silenced misgivings and disputes, whether in the Council
or at the War Office. All-powerful, imperturbable, reserved, he dominated
absolutely our counsels at this time.

Twenty-four hours after the War Council of February 26 dispersed,
another serious dispute broke out between Churchill and Kitchener.
Although the War Council had accepted Kitchener's argument that
the 29th Division should be held back in England, at its earlier meeting
on February 19 it had agreed to Churchill's request that transports
sufficient to take the Division to the eastern Mediterranean should
nevertheless be held together in readiness. On February 27 Churchill
asked Graeme Thomson in what state of preparation the transports
were. He learned to his horror that a week earlier, on Kitchener's
orders, the War Office had instructed the Admiralty Transport
Department that as the 29th Division was not to go to the east they
could cancel the orders for the collection and fitting of transports.
Churchill had not been informed of this. Graeme Thomson had
assumed that such drastic orders would not have come from the War
Office unless Churchill had previously approved them. Churchill wrote
at once to the Secretary of State for War:

My dear Kitchener,

The War Council on the 19th instructed me to prepare transport inter alia
for the 29th Division, and I gave directions accordingly. I now learn that on
the 20th you sent Col FitzGerald to the Director of Transport with a message
that the 29th Division was not to go, and acting on this the transports were
countermanded without my being informed. It is easy to see that grave inconvenience might have resulted from this if it had been decided at Friday's
Council to send this Division at once.

I have now renewed the order for the preparation of the transports; but I
apprehend that they cannot be ready for a fortnight. It now seems very likely
that the passage of the Dardanelles will be completed before the end of
March, and perhaps a good deal earlier.

May I also ask to be informed of any instructions given to the French

Division? I understand that the War Office do not wish them to come to Lemnos. The absence of any British regulars seems to make the presence of the French specially necessary; and I trust they may not be prevented from coming until at any rate the matter can be discussed in Cabinet.

Yours very truly

WSC

Kitchener agreed that preparations for assembling transport ships which could take the 29th Division to the east, if it were released, should again be taken in hand. But the delay in assembling the ships adversely affected all subsequent troop movements, and made impossible any serious attempt to co-ordinate a military landing with the naval attack.

During a week of intense planning, from February 19 to February 26, Churchill had been buoyed up by the belief that a large British force would be able to watch over the naval attack, support it if things went wrong, and take immediate advantage by land of any success at sea. Kitchener's refusal to part with the 29th Division, and the countermanded orders about troop transports, threw him back upon a plan about which he had expressed serious doubts. The War Council of February 26 had made it clear that it was imperative that the naval attack should go on, whether or not sufficient troops were ready to support it. Churchill had the power to refuse to take the responsibility for a purely naval attack. Had he taken his objections to the point of resignation, the emasculated plan could not have gone on. Either Kitchener would have had to agree to send substantial numbers of troops, or Carden have been instructed to give up the bombardment. But Churchill had originally been impressed by Carden's plan for ships alone. When, on February 25 and 26, Carden successfully destroyed the outer forts, Churchill's earlier optimism for a purely naval attack was revived. Only two full days of bombardment had sufficed to achieve the first objective: British ships could now enter the mouth of the Dardanelles at will. Churchill allowed himself to be swayed by these facts; as a result, he minimized the attendant dangers, including those of which he himself had warned so strongly. Yet he never gave up his search for troops. 'Make it clear to W.O.,' he wrote to Oliver on February 27, 'that Admiralty desire the whole French division at Lemnos without delay.'

The news of the successful bombardment of the outer forts on February 25 had flashed through the Balkans with a mesmeric effect. Churchill was excited by the prospects of a rapid naval victory. 'The progress of an attack on *Dlles* is encouraging & good,' he telegraphed eagerly to the Grand Duke Nicholas on February 27, '& we think the Russian Black Sea Fleet shd now get ready at Sebastopol to come to the entrance of the Bosphorus at the right moment, of wh we will send notice. Any Russian troops that can be spared shd also be ready to embark. Although the hardest part of the task is not yet begun, progress may be quicker than we expected.' The Grand Duke replied on the following day: Russia would attack Constantinople with its Black Sea Fleet and an army of over forty-seven thousand men as soon as the Allies had penetrated into the Sea of Marmara; but no sooner.

Churchill's enthusiasm did not wane. On February 28 he turned his mind to the conditions of Turkey's surrender, writing to Grey:

Secret
My dear Grey,
 Shd we get through Dardanelles, as is now likely, we cannot be content with anything less than the surrender of everything Turkish in Europe. I shall tell the Admiral after destroying the Turco-German fleet to push on at once to attack Bosphorus, & thus cut off the retreat of the army. Their capitulation is then only a question of time. The terms of an armistice might be considered as follows:—
1. Surrender as prisoners of war of all Turkish forces in Europe.
2. Surrender of all arms, arsenals, armaments, ships etc in Europe.
3. Surrender of fortress of Adrianople & military positions affecting the control of the Bosphorus.
4. Allies to occupy & administer militarily the Turkish territories in Europe.
5. Bulgaria to occupy the Enos-Midia line by leave of the Allies.
6. Surrender of all German officers & men in Turkey whether in Europe or Asia as prisoners of war.
7. Subject to the above, an armistice for Turkey in Asia. All troops on both sides to advance no further; to retire if convenient; & no hostilities to take place, pending the general settlement.
 I look forward with much hope to the delivery of Adrianople by the British to the Bulgarian army. But celerity & vigour are indispensable.
 Remember C'nople is only a means to an end—& the only end is the march of the Balkan States against the Central powers.

Yours always
WSC

On February 29 the first of the wavering Balkan States seemed at last determined to take advantage of Britain's impending triumph. Violet Bonham Carter recalled in *Winston Churchill As I Knew Him* how, on the evening of March 1, 'I was sitting with Clemmie at the Admiralty when

Winston came in in a state of wild excitement and joy. He showed us, under many pledges of secrecy, a telegram from Venizelos promising help from the Greeks. . . . Our joy knew no bounds.' Remembering that the King of Greece had a German wife and German sympathies, Violet Asquith asked whether he was 'sound'. 'Yes,' replied Churchill, 'our Minister said Venizelos had already approached the King and he was in favour of war.' Violet Bonham Carter's account continued:

> Winston totted up our combined forces: we now had the Anzac Army Corps on the spot, the Royal Naval Division on the way, the French division, the promise of three Greek divisions, and the Russian Army Corps at Batoum. The 29th was still in the balance. In the background Bulgaria, Roumania and Italy were waiting—ready to pounce—all determined to play a part in the fall of Constantinople. All these tremendous consequences had flowed from our united naval enterprise. . . .
> I went back across the Horse Guards treading on air. Turkey, encircled by a host of enemies, was doomed, the German flank was turned, the Balkans for once united and on our side, the war shortened perhaps by years, and Winston's vision and persistence vindicated.

Even without the 29th Division, the military effect of sixty thousand Greek troops, with a further fifty thousand Russians, would undoubtedly have been overwhelming. 'Winston is breast high about the Dardanelles,' Asquith wrote that evening to Venetia Stanley. On the same day Hankey wrote to his wife that 'we hear on all hands the sensation in the Near East is colossal'. Churchill himself completed plans for sending Commander Samson's squadron of twelve naval aeroplanes and Commander Wedgwood's squadron of armoured cars for service at the Dardanelles. 'Please don't leave me in this country now,' Wedgwood had written to Churchill on February 19 from the armoured car base in Norfolk, '. . . I do want to get at them again.'

Churchill hoped to exploit the revived Greek enthusiasm by persuading the Greeks to contribute ships as well as men. 'Admiralty sharply urge that Greece shd give naval as well as military aid in operation now proceeding at the Dardanelles,' he wrote to Asquith on March 1. 'The Greek battleships and cruisers, the excellent & efficient Greek flotillas of destroyers, the Greek submarines and other small craft, can play a useful part, & if they come immediately will share the credit of the victory. Now is the time, not a day should be lost, as the Turkish resistance is less than was expected.' Asquith gave this letter to Grey, who telegraphed at 11.30 that evening to Sir Francis Elliott in Athens: 'Proposed co-operation of a Greek Army Corps in Gallipoli peninsula would be readily accepted. Admiralty strongly urge that Greece should give naval as well as military aid . . .', and went on to repeat almost word for word the rest of Churchill's letter to Asquith.

Churchill's belief that the blow against Turkey ought to be direct and immediate was reinforced by a letter which Sir Mark Sykes,[1] with many years' experience of Turkey and the Balkans, had sent him on February 26:

I see by the papers that there has been liveliness in the vicinity of the Dardanelles, though what it portends I know not, but as you bore with me the last time, I venture again to write of certain things passing through my mind. . . .

Owing to the affair in East Prussia and the German financial manoeuvre in Sofia, I feel Constantinople and the Dardanelles becomes more and more important, but also do I feel that the blow delivered there should be hard, decisive, and without preamble. Morally speaking every bombardment which is not followed by a passage of the Dardanelles is a victory in the eyes of the mass of Turkish troops around the Marmora. It is worth considering that the Turks are accustomed to thinking in terms of passive defence—Plevna, Erzerum, and Chatalja each make Turks think a long resistance or repulsed attack all that can be wished for.[2] Therefore do I think that 'reconnaisance' and 'harassing' are things to be used as sparingly as tactical requirements will allow. Turks always grow formidable if given time to think, they may be lulled into passivity, and rushed, owing to their natural idleness and proneness to panic, but they are dangerous if gradually put on their guard.

During the Balkan war, they were at one moment ready to abandon Constantinople but in 18 days they had recovered and were ready to fight to their last man. . . .

Abdul Hamid's reign inured the Ottoman mind to demonstrations and manoeuvres. Also I am growing convinced that Bulgaria will not move until she sees some reason for doing so—at present she knows of no real allied success on land—why should she even negotiate with people who cannot touch their enemies' territories. The Bulgarian only knows that Servia is pretty well done up, that France is invaded, that Belgium is overrun, and that the Russian frontier is not intact—and in spite of an attack on the Suez

[1] Mark Sykes, 1879–1919. Travelled widely through Turkey at different times between 1898 and 1904. Honorary attaché at Constantinople, 1905–7. Conservative MP, 1910–19. Raised a reserve battalion, Yorkshire Regiment, 1913–14. 6th Baronet, 1913. Lieutenant-Colonel, on special duties in Serbia, Bulgaria, Egypt and India, 1915–16. British negotiator of an inter-Allied territorial settlement for the Near East, known as the Sykes–Picot agreement, 1916. Member of the British Delegation at the Paris Peace Conference, 1919.

[2] During the Russo-Turkish war (1877–8) the Turks tenaciously defended Plevna (July–November 1877), Erzerum (October–November 1877) and the Chatalja Lines (January 1878), but were defeated at each.

Canal and an invasion of the Caucasus, the Dardanelles and Constantinople are not threatened. . . . Daily I become more and more sure that the war will not end until the Balkan States are mobilised against Austria. . . . As time goes on without any results, the people of this country will grow sick and irritable, and there will be more and more danger of a feeling of suspicion and friction growing up between the French and English. No doubt we can starve Germany out, and will do in the end if no other means avail, but one can never forget that the starving out of Germany will not be retarded by gaining successes and strategic advantages in the Mediterranean and Marmora—Wellington's campaign in the Peninsula was no mistake in our Napoleonic war, and here is another Peninsula far easier of access with far greater prizes in it. . . .

If one has spent from the age of 9 to 37 watching & wondering & listening, one cannot help being interested in the sequel to Gibbon's Decline & Fall, particularly when one sees the pages of the last chapter turning over.

During the night of March 1 minesweeping operations at the Dardanelles were carried out to within three thousand yards of Kephez Point. Carden reported that a small party of Marines had landed, at the entrance to the Dardanelles, and, in the wake of the naval bombardment, had destroyed nineteen heavy guns, eleven light guns, four Nordenfelts and two searchlights. All the Marines returned safely to their ships.

On the morning of March 2 the members of the War Council, who were to meet on the following day, received a seven-page printed memorandum from Hankey entitled: 'After the Dardanelles. The Next Steps.' Written on March 1, it set out in detail the methods which Hankey believed should be followed in order to gain the greatest possible advantage from a naval victory. Principal of these was a British naval advance up the Danube, both to protect Serbia, and to take the offensive against Austria-Hungary:

A British force, supported by a powerful flotilla, would form the centre of the Allied army. On the left the Serbians and Greeks would penetrate into Bosnia and Herzegovina. On the right the Roumanians would form a connecting link with the Russian armies in the Carpathians. The British forces would turn the flank of the enemy's forces opposing the Roumanians, which would enable the Roumanians to threaten the communications of the enemy's forces operating in the Carpathians. All the time the Franco-British armies would be exerting continual pressure in the west, and the Russians, even if driven back to the line of the Bug, should be able to contain considerable armies of observation.

In a later section of his memorandum, Hankey dealt in detail with how the British ships, once through the Dardanelles, could force Turkey to surrender. He was confident that this could be done. He reminded the War Council that Turkey's three principal arsenals were situated on the shore of the Sea of Marmara, vulnerable to naval gunfire; that the road and rail links between Constantinople and European Turkey ran for some way along the shore; and that all Constantinople's contact with Asia could be cut by naval guns once Carden's fleet were in the Sea of Marmara. Hankey concluded with some thoughts on how negotiations with Turkey would be carried out, and what specific terms ought to be a part of the armistice:

(a) The final settlement to be left in abeyance for the present.
(b) The Turkish fleet and all naval material to be surrendered to the Allies.
(c) The defences and material of the Dardanelles and Bosphorus to be surrendered to the Allies. All Turkish troops to be withdrawn from the Dardanelles and Bosphorus.
(d) The Turkish expeditions in the Caucasus and against Egypt and Mesopotamia to be at once recalled.
(e) The demobilisation of the Turkish army.
(f) The hire for the period of the war, or sale to the Allies, of Turkish rifles and other weapons.
(g) The Turkish naval dockyard, arsenal, powder factory, shell factory and clothing factory to be placed under officers appointed by the Allies and worked in their interest.
(h) The persons of all German and Austrian born officers in the army and navy, and of all German and Austrian born officials in any branch of the Turkish administration (whether such persons are Turkish subjects or not) to be handed over to the Allies as prisoners of war. Lists of all other persons of German and Austrian origin in Turkey to be compiled and handed over to the Allies, such persons to be dealt with as decided by the Allies.
(i) All German and Austrian concessions in Turkey to remain in abeyance for the duration of the war. Such concessions to be worked under the supervision of the Allies in the interest of Turkey.
(j) German officials to be replaced by nominees of the Allies (eg, by Belgians).
(k) Free passage up the Dardanelles by the ships of the Allies.
(l) The Allies to have the right to place a garrison in Constantinople during the war.

As a footnote to points (b) and (c) Hankey wrote: 'If this is rejected, purchase might be offered, or it might be merely requisitioned or borrowed for the tenure of the war to "save the face" of the Turkish negotiators.'

Churchill, confident of the outcome, again approached Grey as to the post-war settlement, writing on March 2:

We must not disinterest ourselves in the final settlement of this region. In principle of course Russia's claims are recognised. But if they are to be satisfied the Br Naval position in those waters must also be safeguarded. It is not the time to talk of Lemnos. I consider we shd keep to the rule that all territorial accessions can only be settled at the general peace.

It was a pity that we let the Russians talk of 'giving' us Egypt. We have had it for years *in fact*, & wanted no victorious war to give it to us *in form*.

Certainly we must not let ourselves be pushed out of all interests here by the statement that Egypt is our prize. That wd be paying for Egypt twice over.

I am having an Admy paper prepared abt the effect of a Russian control of the Straits & Cple. I hope you will not settle anything further until you can read it. English history will not end with this war.

Churchill wrote nearly four months too late. On 12 November 1914 Grey had informed the Russian Government: 'We regard the conduct of the Turkish Government as having made a complete settlement of the Turkish question including that of the Straits and Constantinople in agreement with Russia inevitable'. Since 1908 Grey had based his eastern policy upon eventual Russian control of the Straits. 'We must carry out our promises of 1908 . . . in terms acceptable to Russia,' he wrote to Sir Francis Bertie on 18 December 1914; and on 14 January 1915 he had assured the Russian Foreign Minister, Sazonov, that whatever territorial changes took place in Turkey, 'all I said . . . about the settlement of Constantinople and the Straits at the end of the war holds good as far as we are concerned'. Neither the War Council nor the Cabinet had been informed of Grey's commitment to Russia. Early in February he had even refused to encourage an anti-German *coup d'état* in Constantinople by Turks who were willing to leave the war, in return for an Allied promise that Turkey would suffer no territorial or financial loss. On February 10 he explained to Buchanan: 'I shd not propose to negotiate any conditions which would impair or qualify what I said to Minister for Foreign Affairs [Sazonov] about the straits and Constantinople.' In return for giving Russia Constantinople, Grey expected the Russians to halt the southward pressure of their influence in Persia, and to impose no territorial demands in eastern Europe which would lead Germany to refuse a negotiated settlement with Britain, should satisfactory terms be obtainable in the west. Constantinople was to be the British gift to Russia in return for which she must agree to press no further claims. It was also powerful pressure to ensure that Russia did not make a separate peace with Germany. As a diplomatic achievement, the results of promising Russia Constantinople was much in Britain's interest; but it did commit Grey to pressing, for reasons which he did not disclose, for a swift attack on Turkey with Constantinople as the objective.

The War Council met on March 3. Churchill opened the meeting by reading two telegrams from Carden, in which the Admiral announced that he was in the process of destroying forts eight and nine, and that all the forts at the entrance to the Dardanelles 'had been practically demolished'. Churchill then informed the War Council that in order to prevent the Turkish port of Smyrna from being used as a submarine base, instructions had been sent out the previous evening for two battleships and an armoured cruiser to bombard the forts at the entrance to its harbour. The Admiralty orders had made it clear that no troops were to be landed. Balfour suggested that the British Government should ask Greece to attack Smyrna. Churchill pointed out that the Greek Fleet had not yet been put at Britain's disposal, whereas it was absolutely necessary to put the forts out of action immediately, lest Austrian submarines from the Adriatic reach the port and use it as a base for attack on the ships at the Dardanelles. His action was approved.

The War Council turned to a discussion of 'the future of Constantinople'. Grey informed his colleagues of the Russian request for control over the Straits. 'It was absurd,' he said, 'that a huge empire such as Russia should have only ports that were icebound part of the year,' or ports such as those in the Black Sea which could be closed by another power in time of war. Balfour and Haldane both approved of giving Russia a privileged position at the Dardanelles: Churchill did not. 'We should stick to our general principle,' he insisted, 'that the settlement of all territorial questions should be left until the end of the war.' He was unwilling to do anything more than to announce 'sympathy with Russian aspirations'. But Grey said that he doubted whether the question could be left in abeyance much longer. Russia wanted an immediate decision. Haldane pointed out that unless the British made a definite offer, Germany would seize the opportunity to conclude a separate peace with Russia. Balfour advocated the internationalization of the Gallipoli Peninsula. Kitchener proposed that the Peninsula should be 'handed over to Greece'. Fisher suggested that provided Britain 'obtained possession of Lemnos' it did not matter who occupied the Dardanelles, as Britain would then be able to control the exit.

The War Council then considered what Britain's policy should be once the Fleet had forced the Dardanelles. Churchill pointed out the large number of troops that were now available to follow up the naval success. There were 140,000 in all, made up of the Russian army corps ready to embark at Batum, three Greek divisions promised by Venizelos, a French division, the British troops gathering in Egypt, the Royal Naval Division which was on its way to the Mediterranean, and the two thousand Marines already at Lemnos. But Kitchener asked the War Council to delay a decision on the despatch of the British troops from Egypt for another week, when he hoped to have heard from General Birdwood, the acting Commander of the forces being assembled.

Churchill informed the War Council that some time previously he had advised the Foreign Office to prepare a leaflet, announcing that Britain did not come in any hostile spirit but only to root out the pernicious German influence and restore Turkey's former independence and self-respect. Kitchener believed 'that it would be a good plan to announce that we were coming as the ancient friend of the Turks', and suggested that this information should be dropped in leaflet form from aeroplanes. Grey deprecated such an approach. He thought that a leaflet 'would be either very misleading or so offensive as to fail in its object'. It would certainly have been difficult for any leaflet to reconcile Britain's claim to be arriving as a liberator with any ensuing partition of Turkish territory not only to Russia but also to Greece and Bulgaria, and even perhaps to Rumania and Italy.

The discussion turned to the means of preventing a Turkish attack upon the Europeans in Constantinople. Balfour suggested a British promise not to damage mosques or private buildings in return for the docility of the inhabitants. Kitchener preferred sending the Europeans away by ship under the aegis of the American Ambassador, Henry Morgenthau.[1] Churchill disliked the idea of entering into a bargain with the Turks, and believed that once the Fleet was through the Dardanelles the military situation would so favour the Allies that no

[1] Henry Morgenthau, 1856–1946. Born in Germany. Emigrated to the United States, 1865. President, Central Realty Bond & Trust Company, 1899–1905. President, Henry Morgenthau Company, 1905–13. Chairman, Finance Committee of the Democratic National Committee, 1912 and 1916. United States Ambassador, Constantinople, 1913–16; in charge of the interests of Britain, France, Russia, Belgium, Serbia and other belligerents, 1914–16. Honorary knighthood, 1920. Chairman, League of Nations Commission for the Settlement of Greek Refugees, 1923.

such bargains would be necessary. The War Council minutes recorded Churchill's outline of the action which he felt could be taken by the Fleet once it reached the Sea of Marmara:

The first thing to be attempted would be the capture or destruction of the Turco-German fleet. A battle might take place either in the Dardanelles or the Sea of Marmora, or the enemy might seek to escape into the Black Sea. He hoped in this latter event that its egress would be barred either by mines or by the Russian fleet. The second step would be the destruction of the defences of the Bosphorus. This was not so easy as appeared at first sight, owing to the difficulty in attacking some of the forts from a distance. As soon as the fleet was through the Dardanelles, the Turkish lines of communication would be cut at Bulair, and the garrison of the Gallipoli Peninsula would be isolated. In addition, it might be possible to cut some of the bridges on the line between Adrianople and Constantinople by means of aircraft. The prize we ought to seek from this action was nothing less than the occupation by the Allies of Turkey in Europe. All must pass into our hands, and we ought to accept nothing less.

Later in the discussion Churchill told his colleagues that in his view the main importance of the fall of Constantinople was that it would bring the Balkan States into the war against Austria. He did not rule out the possibility of co-operation with Turkey as soon as the Allies had been successful. He even suggested to the War Council 'that we ought to hire the Turkish army as mercenaries', and send them against Austria. Lloyd George deprecated such a move. The Turks 'had never been any use as mercenaries', he said, and although they fought well in their own country, they were not so good elsewhere.

Asquith raised the one pessimistic note of the meeting. 'The Turks and their German masters,' he said, 'would not give in easily.' But the War Council had little time for cautious counsel. Grey announced his hope that 'from the Balkan point of view . . . we should get through the Dardanelles before the Russians met with another reverse'. Fisher declared that 'it was even more important to get through before the arrival of Austrian submarines'. Grey then described how, once the defences at the Narrows were destroyed, he would invite the Bulgarians to advance across Turkey in Europe 'on condition that they joined the Allies', and would also 'get in touch with Italy' at such a moment.

Churchill had emerged as a leading supporter of action at the Dardanelles. But he still believed that the decisive act of war must take place against Germany. In answer to a question from Balfour as to what progress was being made on preparations for a British military and naval advance up the Danube once Turkey was defeated, Churchill stressed what he still believed to be the true perspective of all these plans. The minutes of the War Council recorded:

MR CHURCHILL said that we ought not to make the main line of advance up the Danube. We ought not to employ more troops in this theatre of war than are absolutely essential in order to induce the Balkan States to march. He was still of the opinion that our proper line of strategy was an advance in the north through Holland and the Baltic. This might become feasible later on when our new monitors were completed. The operation in the East should be regarded merely as an interlude.

The War Council of March 3 ended; its members agreed to meet again a week later. Meanwhile the naval action at the Dardanelles moved forward to what was anticipated would be a speedy conclusion. On March 3 Sir Henry Jackson sent Churchill notes on 'Ultimate Terms of Peace Settlement in the Middle East—Assuming that the Entente Powers are Victorious in the Present War': among his suggestions were that Russia, Rumania, Bulgaria, Turkey and Greece should each be given 'ports inside the Dardanelles', and that Britain should annex Lemnos. That same day Lord Hardinge, the Viceroy of India, telegraphed enthusiastically to his Secretary of State, Lord Crewe: 'Knowing every yard of the Dardanelles as well as I do,[1] I am very hopeful that before you get this letter we shall be in possession of the Straits and our Fleet before Constantinople. This will make an immense difference in this country and in Mesopotamia.'

March 4 brought encouraging news. Carden reported that despite minor setbacks, almost entirely the result of rough weather, he believed that he could enter the Sea of Marmara after fourteen more days of bombardment. Churchill asked Kitchener to expedite the military side. 'It seems to me,' he wrote, 'we ought now to fix a date for the military concentration so that the arrival of troops can be timed to fit in with the normal fruition of the naval operation.' Churchill hoped that the transport arrangements which he had already made would enable Kitchener to fix an early date for a military landing, either at Gallipoli or at Constantinople. His letter continued:

The transports for the 30,000 troops from Egypt, less those already taken to Lemnos, will all have arrived at Alexandria between the 8th and the 15th, that is to say the troops could be landed at Bulair, or alternatively, if practic-

---

[1] As a member of the Diplomatic Service, Hardinge had been an attaché at Constantinople in 1881–4 and 2nd Secretary there 1889–90.

able, taken through the Straits to Constantinople, about the 18th instant. By the same date the transports conveying the 8,000 men of the Naval Division from England could also reach the same points. In addition there are, I understand, in Lemnos 4,000 Australians and 2,000 Marines of the Royal Naval Division. Therefore I suggest for your consideration, and for the proper co-ordination of naval and military policy, that we fix in our own minds the 20th March as the date on which 40,000 British troops will certainly be available for land operations on Turkish soil. To make sure of this date it will perhaps be better to give all orders as for the 17th or 18th; we should then have a little in hand. I think the French should be given this date (20th) as their point, and should rendezvous at Lemnos not later than the 16th. We should also inform the Russians and the Greeks, and ask them what dates they can work to (assuming they are coming). It is necessary for me to know what your views and plans are in these matters.

Churchill emphasized that 'the naval operations in the Dardanelles cannot be delayed for troop movements, as we must get into the Marmora as soon as possible in the normal course'. He asked Kitchener to make a decision about the 29th Division by March 10, as transport would be ready five days later. 'The need of one good division of regular infantry in an army composed of so many different elements,' wrote Churchill, 'and containing only British and Australian troops raised since the war, still appears to me to be grave and urgent.'

On March 3 Churchill had heard that Kitchener intended to appoint General Sir Ian Hamilton to command the forces in the eastern Mediterranean. Churchill and Hamilton had known each other since 1897, when Churchill had been in India. 'No choice could be more agreeable to the Admiralty, and to the Navy,' Churchill wrote to Kitchener on March 4. But Hamilton's dashing, chivalrous manner, which had appealed so much to Churchill during their eighteen years of friendship, did not impress everyone. Clementine Churchill later recalled to the author her distrust of Hamilton's staying power, and her fears that his appointment had been a mistake. After lunching with Hamilton six months previously, Asquith had written to Venetia Stanley, on 30 September 1914: 'He is a sanguine enthusiastic person, with a good deal of *superficial* charm . . . but there is too much feather in his brain.'

Churchill continued with his efforts to stimulate Britain's allies. Twice on March 4 he sent his suggestions to Grey. His first letter was about Greece:

Mr Venizelos shd be told *now* that the Admiralty believe it in their power to force the Dardanelles without military assistance, destroying all the forts as they go. If so, Gallipoli Peninsula cannot be held by Turks, who wd be cut off & reduced at leisure. By the 20th inst 40,000 British Infantry will be available to go to C'nople, if the Straits have been forced, either by crossing the Bulair Isthmus, or going up the Dardanelles. A French Divn will be on the spot at the same time. M. Venizelos shd consider Greek military movements in relation to these facts.

In a second letter to Grey, Churchill asked him to pass on the same information to Russia to serve as 'a guide to the Russian military pre-p^{ns}, bearing in mind that bad weather may delay, & a Turkish collapse may shorten, the military operations'.

On March 4 two parties of marines landed at the forts on either side of the entrance to the Straits. Their object was to demolish the remaining fortifications. But they were not entirely successful. Carden explained what had happened in his telegram to the Admiralty on March 5:

Enemy posted in the villages engaged both parties directly they landed. No progress could be made by the party at Seddul Bahr after its attack, and at 1.30 pm they vacated and were withdrawn. Four Nordenfelts[1] had, however, been discovered and destroyed by them.

The party on the Asiatic shore reached the position under Fort No 4, where they were forced to retire by the enemy, whom they encountered in a well-concealed position.

The ship's covering fire was only partially effective, as the seaplane had not succeeded in locating the enemy, in spite of frequent reconnaissances.

Fisher remained sceptical of the whole operation. '*The more I consider the Dardanelles,*' he wrote to Churchill on March 4, '*the less I like it!*' But despite Fisher's sense of foreboding he agreed to the Admiralty telegram sent to Carden that same day, outlining the action to be taken once Carden had forced the Dardanelles:

In the event of your entering the Sea of Marmora, the first task is destruction of Turko-German Fleet wherever it may be. This accomplished, vessels should be sent to cut—by fire or landing parties, according to circumstances—the railway from Scutari to Ismid and the railway and road connecting Constantinople and Kuchuk-Chekmeje.

Our policy is to cut off as much as possible of the Turkish Army on the European shore, and to oblige them to capitulate later.

The forts of the Bosphorus are next to be attacked. A memorandum on this subject by Sir Henry Jackson is being sent you in sections by telegram. Use this as a guide and not as a rule.

When you see yourself within four days of entering the Sea of Marmora,

---

[1] A Swedish machine-gun, in use in the 1880s; obsolete by 1914.

'Askold'[1] should be used to telegraph to the Russian Fleet at Sevastopol to proceed to blockade the Black Sea mouth of the Bosphorus and to attack outer forts with long-range fire. This telegram should be repeated to us in duplicate. Our wish is that the Russians should block the exit, and by opening fire simultaneously with your attack increase the moral effect. No decisive operation from them is expected by us at this stage. . . .

The number of ships at your command will probably admit of Constantinople being summoned [to surrender] when the Turko-German Fleet has been destroyed, without prejudice to the other warlike movements just described against the Bosphorus and railways. The peaceful surrender of the city is our object, and if it appears expedient to you and likely to prevent massacre or futile resistance, you can, at any time after you have entered the Sea of Marmora, assure the American Ambassador or other neutral or Turkish authorities accessible to you that prompt obedience and the orderly surrender of the city will safeguard all private property against injury, and all religious buildings, especially mosques, and objects venerated by Moslems will be treated with the utmost respect. . . .[2]

It was not only the Balkan States which were influenced by the prospect of the fall of Constantinople. From several Ambassadors in the capitals of Europe came news that Italy, which had been brought with such care into the German alliance system in the 1880s, but which had remained neutral on the outbreak of war, was on the verge of committing herself to the Allied cause. On March 5 Churchill urged Grey to take advantage of this fact. 'The attitude of Italy is remarkable. If she cd be induced to join with us the Austrian Fleet wd be powerless & the Mediterranean as safe as an English lake. Surely some gt effort shd be made to encourage Italy to come forward. From leaving an alliance to declaring war is only a step. . . .' Grey noted on Churchill's letter: 'I will neglect no opportunity!' Negotiations with Italy were in fact already well advanced.

[1] The *Askold* was a Russian light cruiser put at the disposal of the British Admiralty on the outbreak of war in August 1914, when she was in the Western Pacific. She took part in the search for the German cruiser *Emden* in the Indian Ocean, September 1914; was in the Suez Canal attached to the British naval force intended to protect Egypt from Turkish attack, November 1914; joined Vice-Admiral Carden's fleet at the Dardanelles, January 1915; and operated off the Bulgarian port of Dedeagatch after the outbreak of war with Bulgaria, October 1915. The ship's main function in 1915 was to ensure direct wireless communication with the Russian Black Sea Fleet.

[2] In 1899, in *The River War*, Churchill censured Kitchener for ordering the destruction of the Mahdi's tomb, the holy place of the Dervishes at Khartoum. 'To destroy what was sacred and holy to them,' he wrote, 'was a wicked act. . . .' Were such conduct to be characteristic of the Government of the Sudan, he continued, 'then it would be better if Gordon had never given his life nor Kitchener won his victories'.

On the morning of March 6 an encouraging telegram from Carden led Churchill to ask Grey if he could telegraph direct to the Russian Commander-in-Chief with the good news, and with an enquiry from Kitchener about Russian co-operation. 'Progress was good on the 5th,' Churchill had written in his draft, 'and 3 principal forts at Kilid Bahr were damaged. . . . We should like to know by what date Russian Fleet will be ready to co-operate and when Russian army corps will be ready to embark'; Grey asked Churchill to hold back his telegram. For two days he had been receiving increasingly bad news from Russia. On March 3 Buchanan had telegraphed from Petrograd that the Russian Government 'could not consent to Greek participation in operations at the Dardanelles'. On the following day Bertie telegraphed from Paris a warning from Delcassé that the Russian Government 'will not at any price accept co-operation of Greece in Constantinople expedition'. The Russian veto on Greek participation was final and absolute. The Russians had dreamed of ruling Constantinople and controlling the Straits for too many centuries to contemplate at this moment of fulfilment a Greek army reaching the city before them. They knew well the emotions with which the Greeks talked of the city of Constantine, and realized that once a large Greek army were in occupation, with all the authority of an Allied and victorious power, no amount of Russian diplomacy could dislodge them. On March 6 Lloyd George urged Grey to take an immediate initiative by going at once to Salonika to meet the French and Russian Foreign Ministers, instead, as Hankey recorded in his diary, 'of going fishing for a holiday'.

Churchill was shattered at the idea of Greek support being cut off. It had been so hard to obtain; its uses were to have been decisive; its training and experience were to have been the one acceptable substitute for the 29th Division. Like Lloyd George, he was afraid that Grey would not exert himself to overrule the Russian veto. Just before midnight on March 6 he wrote in anguish:

My dear Grey,

I beseech you at this crisis not to make a mistake in falling below the level of events.

Half-hearted measures will ruin all—& a million men will die through the prolongation of the war.

You must be bold & violent. You have a right to be. Our fleet is forcing the Dardanelles. No armies can reach Constantinople but those wh we invite. Yet we seek nothing here, but the victory of the common cause. Tell the Russians that we will meet them in a generous and sympathetic spirit about Cple.

But no impediment must be placed in the way of Greek co-operation. We must have Greece & Bulgaria, if they will come.

I am *so* afraid of your losing Greece, & yet paying all the future into Russian hands. If Russia prevents Greece helping, I will do my utmost to oppose her having Cple.

She is a broken power but for our aid: & has no resource open but to turn traitor—& this she cannot do.

Yours ever
W

PS If you don't back up *this* Greece—the Greece of Venizelos—you will have another wh will cleave to Germany.

This letter was never sent. When Churchill reached his room shortly after dawn he found a Foreign Office telegram, from Elliot, informing Grey that the King of Greece had refused to accept Venizelos' pro-Allied policy, and that the Greek Prime Minister, whose support the Allies had rejected in November, and which now they were so anxious to solicit, had resigned. Churchill could hardly believe that the much-needed Greek assistance was lost. 'Whatever happens I trust we shall stand by Venizelos,' he wrote to Grey on the bottom of Elliot's telegram. 'We must have Greece. The accession at this stage in the war of a new ally is a vital matter.' But Greece was lost: no Greek ship was to participate in the Dardanelles bombardment; no Greek soldier was to set foot on the Gallipoli Peninsula.

On March 7 Asquith was at Walmer Castle. Talking to his wife, he described Churchill as 'far the most disliked man in my Cabinet by his colleagues'. He had just received a letter from Edwin Montagu[1] very critical of Churchill. 'Montagu hates him,' Asquith told his wife; and in her diary Margot Asquith recorded the subsequent conversation:

MARGOT: Why does Monty hate Winston? He is rather lovable I think, and though he often bored me before the war I've liked him very much since. I *love* his spirit of adventure—it suits me—and I love his suggestiveness.

[1] Edwin Samuel Montagu, 1879–1924. Liberal MP, 1906–22. Financial Secretary to the Treasury, February 1914–February 1915; May 1915–July 1916. Chancellor of the Duchy of Lancaster, February–May 1915; January–June 1916. Minister of Munitions, July–December 1916. Secretary of State for India, June 1917–March 1922. He married Venetia Stanley in July 1915.

HENRY (irritably): Oh! he is intolerable! *Noisy*, longwinded and full of perorations. We don't want suggestion—we want wisdom. Crewe, K and McKenna are far the best just now. Grey is tired out and hysterical, Runciman in his own way admirable, Simon getting better and of more use as the war goes on. . . . One of the reasons of Montagu's letter to me is he is in terror of Winston going to India [as Viceroy].

Churchill could not know of Asquith's outburst. It was little more than a month since Haldane had written to him on January 23: 'I saw the PM this afternoon. He spoke with great & intelligent appreciation of your work and untiring energy in it.' Churchill was unaware of Asquith's less appreciative comments. It was Tory suspicions, not Liberal doubts, that he feared, and sought to allay. On March 7 he appealed to F. E. Smith, then in France attached to the Indian corps: 'I wish you could manage to come over here in the near future for a few days. . . . I am sorry that you are away. In your absence Bonar Law is surrounded only by persons who wish to revive party bitterness at the earliest possible moment. Your influence here in politics would be invaluable and the services you could render to the country would be far greater than any you can render in the ungrateful sphere in which you move. . . .' But F. E. Smith remained in France, unable to leave his military duties. Tory hostility towards Churchill, and towards his hopes for coalition, was unassuaged. Liberal criticisms remained unsuspected and underground, yet Churchill gave repeated cause for them. While at Walmer Castle on March 7 Asquith had told his wife that Lloyd George, Kitchener and Churchill had suggested imprisoning men who would not work in wartime. Margot Asquith recorded in her diary:

I felt paralysed by the amazing crass stupidity of such a method!
H: (to me) I've had a tiring and painful cabinet—K. understood when the situation was explained to him at once.
M: The idea that you will get more work out of men by imprisoning the tired ones is the high water mark of folly!! (like trying to put down suicide by the police).
Winston is a Tory and knows *nothing* of the British workman. He looks on him as a mere machine to whom high wages make the whole difference. . . .

At the Dardanelles the bombardment continued during the second week of March, but with increasing difficulty. Long-range firing was frequently made impossible by poor weather conditions and low visibility. The Turkish mobile howitzers were hard to locate and inflicted continuous if unspectacular damage. Each attempt to clear the minefields during the night was met by persistent Turkish fire skilfully directed by searchlights. Target-spotting by seaplanes was erratic and unreliable. Two telegrams from Carden outlined this slow and uncertain activity. The first was received at the Admiralty on March 7:

Operations 6th March. Indirect bombardment of Fort No 20 was continued by Queen Elizabeth with Agamemnon and Ocean in support. Interference was caused by howitzers, which found her range at once and made accurate shooting. This necessitated Queen Elizabeth changing her berth twice, finally to position 21,000 yards from fortress attacked. Only eight rounds were in consequence fired by her. Howitzers could not be located, and engine trouble prevented seaplanes attaining sufficient height for observation.

Batteries 7 and 8 were fired on by Vengeance, Albion, Prince George, Majestic, and Suffren inside the Straits. A number of concealed guns attacked these ships. No 13 fort, which also opened fire, was engaged and hit by 12-inch shells.

Queen Elizabeth was hit, also most of the ships inside, without casualties or serious damage occurring.

Carden's second telegram reached the Admiralty on March 9:

Operations 8th March. Wind South, with rain and fog. Queen Elizabeth with Vice-Admiral entered Straits supported by Vengeance, Albion, Irresistible, and Canopus, and attacked Fort 13. On account of failing light only fired eight rounds, of which three hit. Howitzers which could not be located bombarded ships, projectiles falling close. Vengeance and Albion were hit once each, but damage was slight, and there were no casualties.

Seaplane went up, but conditions unfavourable for observation of fire. . . .

Carden's news of the slow progress was disturbing. So much depended upon success. 'Constantinople is only a means to an end,' Churchill wrote to Jellicoe on March 9, 'and that end is the marching against Austria of the five re-united Balkan states.' 'The whole situation in the Balkans is in the melting pot,' Hankey wrote to Esher on the same day: 'Very much depends upon whether the Fleet can get through, and as you know, I personally have always regarded this as a speculation, unless a biggish army was at hand to take the forts in reverse.'[1]

The War Council met on March 10. Kitchener opened with an

---

[1] This was also General Birdwood's opinion. 'I consider the admiral's forecast is too sanguine . . .' he had telegraphed to Kitchener on March 6; 'I doubt his ability to force the passage unaided.'

optimistic account of the progress of the war. To the surprise of all present, he then announced 'that the situation was now sufficiently secure to justify the despatch of the 29th Division'. Here was the decision for which Churchill had pressed so hard, and which had mocked him when it had been most needed. The delays had been such that the Division could not possibly reach and be ready for action at the Dardanelles in less than a month. Meanwhile all were agreed that the naval action must go on. Churchill thereupon described the course of the various bombardments which had taken place during the previous week. He reported that the *Inflexible* was being sent to Malta to change the guns in her fire-turret, and that this would take six days, so that Admiral Carden 'did not expect to get through the Straits for a week or two'. Meanwhile the forts would be 'thoroughly broken up'. 'There was no hurry,' Churchill said, particularly as the Admiral could not sweep up the mines in the Narrows until he had destroyed the Turkish batteries covering them. But once the Turkish batteries were destroyed, 'the clearing of the minefields would, Admiral Carden said, only take a few hours'. Churchill told his colleagues that the Admiralty still believed 'that they could effect the passage of the Straits by naval means alone'. But they were glad to know that military support was available 'if required'. He later told the Dardanelles Commissioners that he had by this time become convinced that if troops were used to occupy the Gallipoli Peninsula there would not only be a dangerous delay but also a far greater loss of life than if the action was an entirely naval one. He still believed that if the naval action were to fail, the ships could be withdrawn immediately and the enterprise abandoned.

The War Council then discussed the future of Constantinople. It was agreed that Russia's claim both to the city and to the Straits should be accepted, provided, as Asquith wrote to Venetia Stanley, 'that both we & France should get a substantial share of the carcase of the Turk'. Lloyd George pointed out to his colleagues that 'the Russians were so keen to obtain Constantinople that they would be generous in regard to concessions elsewhere'. Both Asquith and Kitchener jumped at the chance of pressing Britain's claim for the annexation of Alexandretta, which had, said Kitchener, a military as well as a naval importance.

Because of the significance of these territorial questions Asquith had invited Bonar Law and Lansdowne to be present during this stage of the discussion, wanting any territorial decisions to be given an aura of all-Party acceptance. But Bonar Law was against giving Russia 'exactly what she wants immediately', and Lansdowne supported his leader, fearing that 'if Russia was granted all she wished for now, the result might be to choke off Italy and the Balkan States'. Grey was anxious to see Britain's terms formulated at once. Lloyd George agreed, and so too did Churchill, who had changed his mind since the previous week, and argued that 'after the war there might be mutual jealousies and heartburnings' and that it was therefore 'very desirable to block in the general lines of the terms we required'. He feared that if this were not done, Britain would be at loggerheads with France when the war was over, as some of their respective claims, particularly over Alexandretta, overlapped.

The hopes of an imminent naval success at the Dardanelles led the War Council on to much rambling speculation. Lloyd George suggested that rather than quarrel with France over Alexandretta, they should give it to France. A good alternative, he suggested, 'owing to the prestige it would give us', would be Palestine. Kitchener declared dogmatically 'that Palestine would be of no value to us whatsoever', and pressed the claim for Alexandretta. Fisher strongly supported Kitchener, and argued that Alexandretta had 'a special importance as an outlet for the oil supplies of Mesopotamia and Persia'. McKenna wanted to turn the discussion to questions of 'compensation outside the Mediterranean', and although his colleagues appeared to ignore this interjection, Grey later returned to the point, asking what would be the fate of the German Colonies. The only Minister who seemed at all interested in acquiring the German Colonies was the Colonial Secretary, Lewis Harcourt,[1] who suggested annexing German East Africa 'in order to settle the question of Indian emigration'. But all other opinion was against him:

LORD KITCHENER said it would be a mistake to acquire more of these than we could avoid, as it would more than anything else interfere with the future establishment of goodwill between Germany and ourselves after the war.
SIR EDWARD GREY agreed. He was strongly opposed to the acquisition of German colonies, but feared that South Africa and Australasia would never allow us to cede German South-West Africa and the Pacific colonies.
. . . MR CHURCHILL was strongly opposed to the acquisition of German East Africa. He also said that Egypt ought not to form part of the bargain. The question of Egypt had been decided long ago when it was bartered for Morocco. We ought not, as it were, to have to buy it over again.[2]

[1] Lewis Harcourt, 1863–1922. Liberal MP, 1904–17. Secretary of State for the Colonies, 1910–15. First Commissioner of Works, May 1915–Dec. 1916. Created Viscount, 1917.
[2] In 1904, under the Anglo-French Entente, Britain recognized France's paramountcy in Morocco in return for French recognition of the 'permanency' of the British occupation of Egypt of 1882.

The War Council found itself discussing, for the first time since the war began, Britain's war aims. Churchill spoke of British naval interests:

MR CHURCHILL asked what was to happen about the German fleet and the Kiel Canal? The destruction of the fleet and the removal of the Canal from German control were great objects of British policy. It was essential that we should not come out of this war leaving Germany the power to attack us again in a few years' time. He also pointed out the enormous strategic value of the Kiel Canal, which enabled Germany to transfer the fleet within a few hours from the Baltic to the North Sea and *vice versa*. Ought we not, he asked, to demand the surrender or destruction of the German fleet?

Support for Churchill came from each of the three Conservatives present: Bonar Law believed that 'the first condition of peace was the elimination of the German fleet'; Balfour was in favour of the neutralization of the Kiel Canal; Lansdowne pointed out that Russia would be as keen as Britain to see the German Fleet destroyed and the Kiel Canal removed from German control. Fisher interjected with the proposal that if, after the war, Germany began to build a new fleet, 'we ought to go and smash it at once'. Kitchener thought the way to stop Germany building a new fleet was by finance, and that Britain should 'inflict an indemnity to be paid over a long term of years'. Only Haldane spoke on an idealistic note, hoping 'that the possibility of some agreement for the restriction of armaments would not be abandoned'. This digression on war aims was brought to a close by Asquith, who reminded the meeting that the main subject of their discussion was Russia's desire for Constantinople and the Straits. They ought, he said, to be considering what Britain wanted in return. Crewe then took up Churchill's point that 'if we did not block out what we want we might get left in the lurch'. But the only specific proposal came from Harcourt, who suggested that Britain should acquire, as a preferable alternative to Alexandretta, the little-known port of Marmarice, on the Turkish mainland north of the Italian island of Rhodes.

It was finally agreed that Russia would be informed that Britain accepted her demand for Constantinople and the Straits, subject to Britain herself obtaining her own territorial desiderata, which would be put forward 'as soon as there has been time to consider them'. Asquith thought it would be wise to remind Russia 'that a large section of public opinion in this country' would be opposed to this decision. In deference to the free trade susceptibilities of Liberalism, and as a stimulus to British trading interests, Grey hoped that Constantinople would become a free port for goods in transit. The meeting ended. At their own request, Bonar Law and Lansdowne were never asked to a meeting of the War Council again.[1]

Churchill still hoped that, although Britain must bear the initial burden of the attack at the Dardanelles, it would within hours of its success lead to the formation of an allied Balkan Confederation, which had for so long been a complement to all his plans, and a central object of Grey's diplomacy. There was a glimmer of hope in a telegram, received that evening from Sir Henry Bax-Ironside in Sofia, which Grey at once sent over to the Admiralty. The British Minister reported:

I discussed the political situation with Prime Minister[2] yesterday. He will not be convinced as yet of possibility of forcing of Dardanelles, but our persistent action is having a good effect on urban population, as is also arrival of considerable numbers of refugees from Constantinople. It is reported here that they are also going to Bucharest.

Confidential. King of the Bulgarians[3] is much upset at prospect of our success.

Two telegrams from Greece had indicated a possible change of attitude on the part of the Greek Government. Elliot had telegraphed from Athens on February 28 that 'Operations against the Dardanelles are followed with intense interest here and there is a rapidly growing feeling that capture of Constantinople ought not to take place without Greek co-operation'. Churchill knew that the Russian veto made any Greek

---

[1] Thirteen years later, while reading the proofs of Lord Beaverbrook's book, *Politicians and the War*, Churchill set down his own recollection of why the Conservative leaders had been invited: 'The unexpected successful destruction of the Outer Forts at the Dardanelles, gave me a momentary ascendancy. I immediately recurred to the Coalition plan: & I persuaded the PM to invite the leaders of the opposition into council—ostensibly on the future destination of Cple, but really to broach the idea of bringing them into the circle. The conferences were not a success: for the good reasons given:—the Oppn leaders sat silent and hungry & Mr Asquith did not press forward. Not until he was forced by disaster wd he consent to treat Tories as equals.'

[2] Vasil Radoslavov, 1854–1929. Leader of the Bulgarian Liberal Party. Minister-President of Bulgaria, 1913–18. A leading architect of the German orientation of Bulgarian policy, 1915. In exile in Germany from 1918 to his death.

[3] Ferdinand Maximilian Karl Leopold Maria, 1861–1948. Born in Saxe-Coburg. Lieutenant, Austrian army, 1885. Elected Prince of Bulgaria, 1887. Proclaimed the Independence of Bulgaria, 1908, and took the title of King (or Tsar). Commanded the Bulgarian Army which defeated the Turks, 1912–13. Deeply resentful of Britain's role in preventing Bulgaria from gaining the fruits of victory. Proclaimed the neutrality of Bulgaria, November 1914. Allied to Germany, October 1915. Abdicated, 1918. In exile in Bavaria; ornithologist and entomologist.

co-operation impossible. But when he saw Elliot's telegram he could not resist writing to Grey on March 9: 'Sir F. Elliot ought surely to say to the King that this was the moment when the assistance of Greece and of the Greek flotillas wd have been especially valuable. This ought surely to be made known to the Greek people.' On March 9 Elliot telegraphed again. The Greek King, he told Grey, spoke with enthusiasm of Greece's benevolent neutrality. Churchill wrote again with bitterness to Grey late on March 10. 'Admiral Carden is asking for more destroyers to protect the Fleet from submarine dangers,' he wrote. 'We have none to send him. The Greek flotillas wd have been of inestimable value now. The Russian discouragements have vy likely been a determining factor against fresh aid. If you see an opportunity you shd bring this point home to the Russians. They have put a spoke in our wheel.'

Not all Churchill's advisers shared his hope that Carden could force the Dardanelles without waiting for troops, or that once a major naval bombardment opened upon the inner forts Turkish resistance would collapse. On March 11 Sir Henry Jackson, in a minute to Admiral Oliver, set out his reason for wanting immediate military participation:

To advance further with a rush over unswept minefields and in waters commanded at short range by heavy guns, howitzers and torpedo-tubes, must involve serious losses in ships and men, and will not achieve the object of making the Straits a safe waterway for the transports. The Gallipoli Peninsula must be cleared of the enemy's artillery before this is achieved, and its occupation is a practical necessity before the Straits are safe for the passage of troops as far as the Sea of Marmora.

I suggest the Vice-Admiral be asked if he considers the time has now arrived to make use of military forces to occupy the Gallipoli Peninsula, and clear away the enemy artillery on that side—an operation he would support with his squadrons.

With the Peninsula in our possession, the concealed batteries on the Asiatic side, which are less formidable, could be dealt with more easily from the heights on shore than by ships' guns afloat, and the troops should be of great assistance in the demolition of the fortresses' guns.

At the meeting of the Admiralty War Group on March 11, Jackson's minute was discussed at length. Churchill explained that there was no question of asking Carden to advance 'with a rush' or 'over unswept minefields'. His orders were to continue with the methodical piecemeal reduction of the forts, and to advance his battleships only when he was certain that the minefields had been cleared. Churchill had expected Fisher to make use of Jackson's argument in order to turn against the whole plan. But that morning the Admiralty had intercepted several German wireless messages, which revealed that the forts at the Dardanelles were seriously short of ammunition for their big guns, and that this ammunition could not reach the Dardanelles for some weeks. From these intercepted messages, Fisher believed that the moment had come to press the attack. So great was his excitement that he offered to leave at once for the Dardanelles and personally to take command of the naval forces in place of Admiral Carden, declaring that the responsibility was so great that it could only be borne by the highest authority.

In 1916 Churchill explained to the Dardanelles Commissioners that it was the knowledge of Turkish ammunition deficiency 'that led Lord Fisher and me, with the assent of those whom we were consulting over it, to change the methodical advance and the step by step bombardment . . . into a more decided and vehement attempt to quell and smash up the fortresses at the Narrows and force them to use their ammunition, and to sweep up the Kephez minefield'. That day Churchill, with Fisher's enthusiastic approval, telegraphed to Carden:

Your original instructions laid stress on caution and deliberate methods and we approve highly the skill and patience with which you have advanced hitherto without loss.

The results to be gained are however great enough to justify loss of ships and men if success cannot be obtained without. We wish you now to feel quite free to press the attack vigorously as you suggest. The forts at the narrows are your immediate objective. It is desirable to bring them under decisive fire as soon as possible. The movable Howitzers cannot be wholly cured and the best thing is to remain under their fire as short a time as possible while concentrating overwhelming attack upon the heavy guns. The above can do the ships mortal injury by gunfire.

The turning of the corner at Chanak may decide the whole operation and produce consequences of a decisive character upon the war.

And at the proper moment with favourable weather conditions, you should not hesitate to use your whole force at one time to swell that portion of the defence. We do not wish to hurry you or urge you beyond your judgement, but we recognise clearly that at a certain period in your operations you will have to press hard for a decision and we desire to know whether you consider that point has now been reached. We shall support you in well conceived action for forcing a decision even if regrettable losses are entailed. We wish to hear your views before you take any decisive departure from the present policy.

Although that day Fisher had heard an alarming rumour that Germany was sending submarines in sections to Constantinople by rail through Rumania and Bulgaria, he was not deterred from his new-found enthusiasm. In a minute to Churchill he suggested 'that immediate action be taken with Roumania and Bulgaria to prevent so unfriendly an act being permitted'. Fisher's imagination had been stimulated by the thought of victory at the Dardanelles. In a letter to Churchill on March 12, having first pointed out that British submarines were afraid to leave Dover Harbour in case they were rammed at sight by British merchantmen, he continued:

Moral:—*Carden to press on!* and Kitchener to occupy the deserted Forts at extremity of Gallipoli and mount howitzers there! . . . Invite Bulgaria by telegram (direct from Sir E. Grey) to take Kavalla and Salonica provided she *at once* attacks Turkey and tell Greece '*Too late*'! and seize the Greek Fleet by a '*coup*' later on. They wd probably join us now if bribed! All the kings are against all the peoples! Greece, Bulgaria, Rumania! *What an opportunity for Democracy!*

On March 10, six days after Churchill learned that Sir Ian Hamilton was to command the Mediterranean Expeditionary Force, Kitchener told Hamilton himself of his appointment. 'K has just seen me,' Hamilton wrote at once to Churchill, 'and told me he intends me to go to the Dardanelles. I have no instructions yet, or staff, but I mean to be off to Marseilles as soon as possible. For this I feel myself everlastingly in your debt.' Contrary to Hamilton's belief, Churchill had at no time pressed for his appointment, although he had welcomed Kitchener's choice and given it Admiralty approval. Hearing the news, he tried to hustle forward the General's departure, writing to Asquith at midnight on March 11, with Fisher's support:

My dear Prime Minister,

The ISL & I attach the greatest importance to Ian Hamilton getting to Lemnos at the earliest possible moment. The naval operations may at any moment become intimately dependent on military assistance. In view of the exertions we are making we think we are entitled to a good military opinion as to the use of whatever forces may be available. The enclosed telegrams will show you what the position is.

I trust you will be able to represent this to Kitchener.

Too much time has been lost already for nothing.

Yours ever

W

To underline the sense of urgency Churchill worked all that night and into the morning, devising a timetable by which Hamilton might leave Charing Cross Station at five o'clock on the afternoon of March 12, take a fast destroyer from Dover to Calais, cross France by train, take a 30-knot cruiser at Marseilles and be at the Dardanelles within four days. Kitchener was nonplussed by this all-night exertion. 'Hamilton cannot leave until we have thoroughly studied the situation with which he may be confronted,' he wrote to Churchill on March 12. 'I hope we will get him off Saturday night. "More haste less speed".'

Churchill did not limit his plans to the transportation of the Commander-in-Chief to the scene of action. He also asked whether his brother Jack could join his Staff, and Hamilton agreed. Jack Churchill wrote in his diary on March 12:

About 12 Winston rang up on the telephone. Would I like to go elsewhere? Would I not! A letter is coming over asking the C. in C. to let me go and Sir Ian Hamilton will take me on his Staff. He leaves at once for the Dardanelles: I must be quick! At 2.30 the mail arrived—brought on by Sunny Marlborough and I obtain the letter. Then I seize a car, a rush to Hazebrouck to find Sir John French. . . . My leave was granted at once. Sir John did not know Sir Ian was going to start. He asked about the 29th Division. Was it going to be sent also? He wanted it badly and said he did not think there would be much fighting at the Dardanelles. He said he wanted every man to help to push here and he grudged anybody going elsewhere. He said he thought the War would finish in five or six months! I went back to St. Omer and telephoned again. I have to leave at once and so after dinner I motored to Calais. There I found a destroyer the 'Saracen' and so off to London. . . .

One of the problems which Hamilton had failed to resolve at his first meeting with Kitchener was the need for aeroplanes at the Dardanelles. At one point in the discussion General Braithwaite,[1] who was also present, suggested that a good air service was needed and begged the Field-Marshal to fit out a contingent of aeroplanes, pilots and observers. Hamilton later recorded in his 'diary':[2] 'K turned on him and rent him, saying, "*Not one!*" ' Hamilton saw Kitchener again on

---

[1] Walter Pipon Braithwaite, 1865–1945. Entered Army, 1886. Director of Staff Duties at the War Office, 1914–15. Chief-of-Staff to Sir Ian Hamilton at the Dardanelles, 1915. Major-General, 1915. Knighted, 1918. Lieutenant-General, 1919. Commander, Western Command, India, 1920–3; Scottish Command, 1923–6; Eastern Command, 1926–7. Adjutant-General, 1927–31.

[2] For the origin of Hamilton's 'diary', see p. xxiv.

March 12. When he returned to his home at Hyde Park Gardens he wrote to Churchill:

My dear Winston,

Just back from a three hours talk (!) at the WO. Lord K has decided I start *tomorrow* at 5 pm. I fought hard for today but as the first idea was that I must wait a full fortnight, tomorrow is something substantial in gain of time.

I have got Jack Churchill's name duly registered by Colonel Callwell, Director of Military Operations, as one of my special service officers so the moment he comes back he has only to go to him and get his sailing orders. He is the only officer I am drawing from France as it is thought at the WO French may prove touchy at the idea of anyone going of their own free will from France to another theatre.

I must not in loyalty tell you too much of my WO conversation but I see I shall need some courage in stating my opinions as well as in attacking the enemy; also that the Cabinet will not be quite eye to eye whatever I may have to say!!

I am sending off a Staff Officer to see your people in order that I may know if it will still be all right about the train and the cruiser.

Yours ever
Ian Hamilton

When Churchill saw Hamilton at the Admiralty later that day he explained that, although he was confident that the Navy could force the Straits alone, he would welcome a simultaneous military attack with whatever troops Hamilton had available and before the arrival of the 29th Division, whose presence Kitchener now insisted was essential before any military action could begin. Churchill hoped that when Hamilton reached the Dardanelles he would agree to immediate military participation and thereby force Kitchener's hand. When Hamilton saw Hankey later that day he told him of this discussion. 'He is in an embarrassing position,' Hankey wrote in his diary, 'as Churchill wants him to rush Straits by a *coup de main* with such troops as are available in the Levant (30,000 Australians & 10,000 Naval Division). Lord K on the other hand wants him to go slow, to make the navy continue pounding the Straits, & to wait for 29th Division.'

Churchill was stimulated by the thought of action to ask Kitchener direct to authorize the troops already assembled to assist the forthcoming naval action. He still feared disaster if troops were not ready to follow up a naval success. Kitchener's answer was negative and decisive.

He no longer belittled the ability of the Turks to resist; now he feared that they were too strong. On March 13 he wrote to Churchill:

Most Secret
1st Lord
    In answer to your question, unless it is found that our estimate of the Ottoman strength on the Gallipoli Peninsula is exaggerated and the position on the Kilid Bahr Plateau less strong than anticipated, no operations on a large scale should be attempted until the 29th Division has arrived and is ready to take part in what is likely to prove a difficult undertaking in which severe fighting must be anticipated.

K

Churchill was disappointed by this reply. Throughout March 13 he worried lest the absence of troops made it impossible to secure a complete naval success. At five o'clock that afternoon Churchill saw Hamilton off from Charing Cross station. Hamilton's instructions, which Kitchener had optimistically headed 'Constantinople Expeditionary Force' and which Hamilton changed to 'Mediterranean Expeditionary Force', made it clear that no military action was to take place until the 29th Division had arrived, and that even then the utmost restraint and caution was to be used, both at the Dardanelles, and at Constantinople. Hamilton decided that in view of his long friendship with Churchill, and to prevent friction between Churchill and Kitchener, he ought not to write to the First Lord from the Dardanelles. Later he regretted this decision, realizing that it might have been to his advantage to have someone at the centre of events with whom he could discuss his problems in complete frankness. Churchill did not look forward to being cut off so completely from a friend at the head of an enterprise which meant so much to him. His one link with what was happening at Hamilton's headquarters was his brother Jack. But, for as long as Churchill remained First Lord, Hamilton maintained his resolve. He wrote only once, on March 14, while still in the train going through France:

My dear Winston,
    Just a tiny personal line to tell you we are all going strong and that the fact of you and yours coming down to see us off has given us, morally, the finest possible fillip.
    Jack seems very cheery and fit and will be a great addition to our little band of adventurers. I hope he will always mess with me when we get our mess established and so I shall be able to keep a close eye upon him. I have

been reading all the papers in the train & I must say I don't see how these concealed howitzers are to be tackled without storming the plateau. Only, if we could smash up the search lights they would be no use at night. I feel though it won't be easy to make up one's mind until we have had a thorough aeroplane reconnaissance.

Deep salaams to Mrs Winston,

Yours ever
Ian Hamilton

As a result of Churchill's efforts, Hamilton hoped to arrive at the Dardanelles in time to witness the naval attack on the Narrows, even though the bulk of the troops he was to command was still being assembled in England and Egypt. Churchill had arranged for Hamilton to join the fast cruiser *Phaeton* at Marseilles. Before the General set off, Churchill had taken steps to give him naval aeroplanes in place of the military machines which Kitchener had refused to provide, and to take on board as many officers as possible, telegraphing to the captain of the *Phaeton*, Captain Cameron,[1] in the early hours of March 13:

In addition to Sir Ian Hamilton & his staff you shd embark as many seaplanes and aeroplanes, with their personnel, as can reach you before the time of sailing, and for which you have room. You must make arrangements to take as many officers as possible of the Staff, & also aeroplane officers. Apart from the General & the Senior officers, you need not trouble about Cabins. Active service conditions must prevail, the officers sleeping on mattresses on deck or in hammocks. Make what arrangements are necessary for their food, but the point is to carry them to Lemnos, & nothing else matters except for the General.

On March 13 Churchill received a disappointing telegram from Carden. 'Operations inside Dardanelles during daylight confined to destroying floating mines and preventing enemy moving guns,' Carden signalled. 'Sweeping operations last night not satisfactory owing to heavy fire, no casualties.' Churchill could not understand why an operation which had caused no casualties should be considered unsatisfactory. He marked Carden's last sentence with a cross and sent it to Fisher with the note: 'The sentence at X makes me squirm.' With Fisher's approval, he replied on the same day, seeking an answer to his telegram of March 11 in which Carden had been asked 'to press the attack vigorously . . . even if regrettable losses are entailed'. He was worried by the implications of Carden's telegram:

[1] John Ewen Cameron, 1874–1939. Entered Navy, 1887. Captain, HMS *Phaeton*, 1914–18. Rear-Admiral and Senior Officer, Yangtse river, 1925–7. Vice-Admiral, 1929.

I do not understand why minesweeping should be interfered with by fire which causes no casualties. Two or three hundred casualties would be a moderate price to pay for sweeping up as far as the Narrows. . . .

Secondly, we have information that the Turkish Forts are short of ammunition and that the German Officers have made desponding reports and have appealed to Germany for more. Every conceivable effort is being made to supply ammunition. It is being seriously considered to send a German or an Austrian submarine but apparently they have not started yet. Above is absolutely secret.

All this makes it clear that the operations should now be pressed forward methodically and resolutely by night and day the unavoidable losses being accepted. The enemy is harrassed and anxious now. Time is precious as the interference of submarines would be a very serious complication.

Thirdly, Sir Ian Hamilton leaves to-night to command the Army and will be with you on Tuesday 16th. Take him fully into your confidence and let there be the most cordial co-operation. But do not delay your own operations on his account.

Churchill ended his telegram with the encouraging news that Fisher had ordered two further battleships, the *Queen* and the *Implacable*, 'to sail tonight to strengthen your Fleet and provide further reserves for casualties'.

While the final location and sweeping of the Turkish mines continued at the Dardanelles prior to the main naval attack, the Government were becoming increasingly excited at the prospect of a quick success. Many schemes were being mooted for the partition of the soon-to-be-defeated Turkish Empire. Asquith outlined the views of three of his Cabinet colleagues when he wrote to Venetia Stanley from Walmer Castle on March 13:

H. Samuel had written an almost dithyrambic memorandum urging that in the carving up of the Turks' Asiatic dominions, we should take Palestine, into which the scattered Jews cd in time swarm back from all the quarters of the globe, and in due course obtain Home Rule. (What an attractive community!) Curiously enough, the only other partisan of this proposal is Lloyd George, who, I need not say, does not care a damn for the Jews or their past or their future, but who thinks it would be an outrage to let the Christian Holy Places—Bethlehem, Mount of Olives, Jerusalem &c—pass into the possession or under the protectorate of 'Agnostic Atheistic France'! Isn't it singular that the same conclusions shd be capable of being come to by such different roads? Kitchener, who 'surveyed' Palestine when he was a young Engineer, has a very poor opinion of the place, wh even Samuel admits to be not larger than Wales, much of it barren mountain, & part of it waterless &, what is more to the point, without a single decent harbour. So he (K) is all for Alexandretta, and leaving the Jews & the Holy Places to look after themselves.

On March 12 Lord Crewe had informed Lord Hardinge of the various territorial schemes under discussion in London. 'The fighting departments consider it important to hold a strong position on the flank of our direct road to the East,' he wrote, 'and they regard Alexandretta as the most favourable place. I can quite believe in its merits; but if its possession means holding the whole of the Euphrates valley, above Aleppo to Urfah, on to Baghdad, and thence to the Gulf, it is a large proposition in itself; which if Russia takes Armenia, Italy Adana, France Syria, and Greece wants Smyrna, the Turks remain with Anatolia and little else. This may be inevitable. . . .' Such territorial speculations indicated how widespread was the belief that Turkey's defeat was near. 'The Dardanelles seems too good to be true,' F. E. Smith wrote to Churchill from France on March 15. The good auguries increased daily. On March 12 the Russians had confirmed their desire to attack the Turks by sea and by land once Carden's fleet reached Constantinople. The Grand Duke Nicholas sent Churchill a summary of the instructions which had been given to the Russian Admiral Eberhardt.[1] The instructions read:

First period: While the Allied Fleet is operating in the Dardanelles the rest of the Black Sea Fleet will consist of purely naval demonstrations.

Second period: When the Allied Fleet appears before the Princes Islands a serious attack against the fortifications of the Bosphorus will be undertaken by the Black Sea Fleet. Forcing of the passage to Constantinople by the Russian Squadron without the assistance of the Allied Fleet is considered at Headquarters to be impossible.

Third period: Landing previously arranged will follow destruction of the Turkish Fleet and the junction of the Allied and Black Sea Fleets. Admiral Eberhardt is, however, authorised by these instructions to carry out any advice which Admiral Carden may desire to forward to him.

Such proposals could not help the actual attack. Nor did they lift the Russian veto on Greek help. Churchill replied on March 14, asking the

[1] Andrei Avgustovich Eberhardt, 1856–   . Commander, Russian Black Sea Fleet, 1911–16. In March 1916 he discussed with the Grand Duke Nicholas a combined naval and military attack on Trebizond, but was relieved of his command in June 1916, before this could be put into effect.

Grand Duke whether it would be possible, now that the Allies had agreed to give Russia Constantinople, for the Russians to accept Greek co-operation. Without Greek naval and military assistance, Churchill insisted, 'the progress and even the success of the attack may be affected'. But the Russians still refused to accept Greek participation in any form.

Keen to see the naval operation succeed, Hankey applied his mind to the minesweeping dilemma. 'Spent almost whole day trying to devise for Churchill method of creating smoke blanket for covering sweeping operations in Dardanelles,' he wrote in his diary on March 15: 'Saw Lord Fisher in morning who showed me telegrams that minesweepers are losing heavily & unable to carry out operations owing to fire from light guns wh cannot be located. Suggested use of oil residue mixed with saw dust & anthracene & other variants. In the evening took draft of telegram to Churchill who was very friendly.' Hankey was enthusiastic in his efforts to help the enterprise, but sceptical about the way it was being carried out. When Esher wrote to him that 'the finest stroke delivered in this war, so far, is at the Dardanelles', Hankey replied on March 15, with a reasoned critique of all that had gone wrong since the operation had begun:

Secret
My dear Lord Esher,
    . . . Although on general principles this operation is brilliantly conceived, and quite correct, I am not at all satisfied that it is being carried out in the best possible manner. Troops ought to have been there, or at any rate, within a day or two's reach, when the bombardment began. There ought to have been no blatant Press announcement at the outset, and the bombardment ought to have been announced merely as a demonstration. While the bombardment was commencing the transports ought to have appeared at some entirely different point of the Turkish Coast, such as Alexandretta, Haifa, or elsewhere. Then the troops ought to have come in as a bolt from the blue, immediately following the collapse of the outer forts, and closely supported by the Fleet, to have captured the plateau overlooking the forts of the Narrows by a coup-de-main. I urged this at the outset, but my suggestions fell on deaf ears. Now we have given the Turks time to assemble a vast force, to pour in field guns and howitzers, to entrench every landing place, and the operation has become a most formidable one. Please burn this.[1]
                                                                    Yours ever
                                                                    M. P. A. Hankey

    [1] Perhaps fearing that Lord Esher would obey this injunction, Hankey took the precaution of keeping a carbon copy.

Fisher was also convinced that military co-operation was essential; he was equally eager for instant action. During March 15 he asked Churchill:

> . . . *Are we going on with Constantinople or are we not?*
> If *NOT*—then don't send half a dozen Battleships to the bottom which would be better applied at Cuxhaven or Borkum. If *YES*—then push the military co-operation with all speed & make the demonstration with all possible despatch at *both* extremities of the *Gallipoli Peninsula*—and telegraph at once for the Egyptian Transports to leave with all despatch.
> Anyhow they are safer in Mudros protected by net defence than at Alexandria without it & subject also to being torpedoed *en route* when the Austrian submarines from the Adriatic arrive (*WHICH THEY SURELY WILL*! If not Germans also from England!)
> Everything points to instant action by a collective vote & decision of the War Council with the Opposition joined in. . . .

Churchill was unwilling to put the matter before the War Council, fearing further delays and complications. He wanted Hamilton to join forces with Carden as soon as possible, and anticipated danger if troops were to be held off any longer. He replied at once:

> Secret
> My dear Fisher,
> I don't think we want a war council on this. It is after all only asking a lot of ignorant people to meddle in our business. I expect K will do what we want about the troops being concentrated at Mudros, if you & I see him together. But if not there is nothing for it but to wait for Hamilton's report wh shd reach us Wednesday. Meanwhile the naval operations are proceeding within safe & sure limits.
>
> Yours ever
> W
>
> PS I am counting much on Hamilton.

On March 14 Churchill had already made a strong effort to enlist Kitchener's support for a speedy assembly of troops, writing, with Fisher's approval:

> . . . Fisher is very insistent, and I agree with him, in asking you to have the troops in Egypt which are available sent to rendezvous at Mudros Bay with the French who arrive on the 18th and the 16,000 men who are already there. We do not wish in any way to prejudice any decision which you may take as to the use of the troops after Hamilton has studied the situation with Carden and reported definitely to you. Mudros Harbour has been protected by a boom and nets against submarines, and can accommodate safely the

whole transport fleet. We think it is only asking for a reasonable precaution that the forces now available should be concentrated there.

The naval operations of engaging the forts and sweeping the approaches to the Narrows will proceed steadily. They cannot be delayed, because of the increasing danger of submarines arriving, and of heavy howitzers being mounted. . . .

Whatever the outcome of the movement of troops to Lemnos, and whether or not Hamilton would be authorized, as Churchill wished, to take military action before the arrival of his entire force, it was certain that the first attempt to force the Dardanelles would be a purely naval one. In 1916, Hamilton told the Dardanelles Commissioners that the only instructions he had been given before the naval attack were those he had received from Kitchener before his departure, and that they amounted to this: 'We soldiers were clearly to understand that we were string number two. The sailors said they could force the Dardanelles on their own, and we were not to chip in unless the Admiral definitely chucked up the sponge.' But once the Admiral had 'chucked up the sponge' there would be little likelihood of the War Council asking the Army to intervene. At no time did Kitchener suggest either the possibility or the need for a combined military and naval action, of the sort for which Churchill had argued so vehemently in January and February, and which he had tried to press upon Hamilton before his departure. Even with substantial numbers of troops available Kitchener looked to ships alone. But when Churchill telegraphed to Carden on March 15 he asked him to concert with Hamilton 'in any military operations on a large scale which you consider necessary', pointing out that fifty-nine thousand men would be available after March 18. Churchill told Carden that he approved the Admiral's proposal 'to put the forts at the Narrows effectively out of action by engaging them at a decisive range', and then attacking the forts beyond. 'No time is to be lost,' he telegraphed, 'but there should be no undue haste.' Churchill expressed his concern that Carden should not try to 'push the passage' prematurely. 'No operations of the nature,' he concluded, 'should be decided upon before consulting us. Before undertaking it careful study will be required of the parts to be played by the army and navy in close co-operation, and it might then be found that a naval rush would be costly, without decisive military action, to take the Kilid Bahr plateau.'

In the early hours of March 16 Fisher sent Churchill a plea for action in the North: 'The decisive theatre remains and ever will be the North Sea—our attention is being distracted—Schleswig Holstein, the Baltic,

Borkum are not living with us now! Your big idea of 3 British armies in Holland in May obliterated by Bulair! and so to bed (as Pepys would say!)'

On March 16, while Carden completed his plans, Churchill crossed over to France, hoping to relieve the tension by a visit to Sir John French's Headquarters, and to several sectors of the front line. As soon as he arrived, he received a telegram from Carden, announcing that on the advice of his medical officer he had been compelled to go on the sick list and give up his command. The man who had agreed to the original attack by ships alone, who had worked out its demands and co-ordinated its planning with both the Admiralty and the French, had collapsed under the strain. Churchill had at once to find a successor to take command of the attack that was about to start. The most senior naval officer in the eastern Mediterranean was Rear-Admiral Wemyss, but he was too deeply concerned with the transport operations at Lemnos, upon which any subsequent military action would depend, to be moved. Junior to Wemyss, but intimately associated with all naval operations so far, was Carden's Second-in-command, Rear-Admiral John de Robeck. Churchill telegraphed to Wemyss who at once agreed to accept de Robeck's promotion as Commander-in-Chief. Churchill then telegraphed to de Robeck to make sure that he was in agreement with the plans now so near to completion: 'If not, do not hesitate to say so.' De Robeck replied that he accepted the existing plans, and was willing to begin the attack on the inner forts on March 18. The quite unexpected change of command, which might have been disastrous to the timing, and even the continuation, of the whole enterprise, resulted in only a single day's delay. Churchill had further cause for satisfaction when he learned that Kitchener had received a telegram, sent on March 17, from the head of a special British military mission then in Bulgaria, Sir Arthur Paget,[1] reporting that 'Operations in the Dardanelles have made deep impression . . .' and that 'all possibility of Bulgaria attacking any Balkan state that might side with the Entente is now over, and there is some reason to think that shortly Bulgarian army will move against Turkey to co-operate in the Dardanelles operations.'

If the Bulgarians, despite the pro-German feelings of their king and Prime Minister, could be so impressed by the state of affairs at the Dardanelles so far, a successful action on March 18 would indoubtedly win further adherents to the Allied cause. Any State which wanted to

---

[1] Arthur Henry Fitzroy Paget, 1851–1928. Entered Army, 1869. Knighted, 1906. Commanded the Forces in Ireland, 1911–14: played prominent part in the Curragh incident, March 1914. General, 1913. On special missions to the Balkans, 1914–15.

14. Admiral of the Fleet Lord Fisher, 1915

15. Admiral Sir John
Jellicoe, 1914

16. Vice-Admiral
Carden, 1914

17. General Sir Ian Hamilton and Vice-Admiral de Robeck at the
Dardanelles, 1915

19. Talaat Bey, Turkish Minister
of the Interior

18. Djavid Bey, Turkish
Minister of Finance

20. Enver Pasha, Tur-
kish Minister of War

21. King George V and Churchill arriving at Blandford to inspect the Royal Naval Division before its departure to the Dardanelles, 25 February 1915

22. H.M.S. *Irresistible* foundering at the Dardanelles, 18 March 1915

23. Jack Churchill, while a Major on Sir Ian Hamilton's staff at Mudros, 1915

24. Lieutenant-Commander Wedgwood, MP, 17 September 1914; a friend of Churchill's, severely wounded at Gallipoli, when in command of an armoured car detachment

25. Major-General Braithwaite and General Sir Ian Hamilton going ashore, the Gallipoli Peninsula, 1915

26. British Armoured Motor Cars at Helles, Gallipoli Peninsula, 1915

27. Churchill, February 1915

annex a part of Turkey would have to show some immediate reason why Britain should take its claims seriously. Bulgaria would have to march across European Turkey, breaking any Turkish resistance which survived and cutting off Constantinople from the north. Greece would have to show an immediate intention of helping Serbia to resist the impending Austrian attack. Rumania would have to commit its large army of 350,000 men, to its grain and its oil the Allied reserves. Italy would also have to make a final break with former allies. Even India expected to gain. On March 11 Hardinge had informed Crewe that if the attack on the Dardanelles were successful, 'and a stream of grain came from the Black Sea', India's difficulties in obtaining adequate food would be 'much alleviated'. On March 18 he wrote again, worried because of increasing Turkish and German influence in Persia, which threatened the security of the North-West Frontier. 'The situation in Persia is undoubtedly serious,' Hardinge wrote; 'that is why I am particularly anxious to hear of an early success in the Dardanelles, for I believe that the capture of the Dardanelles and the impending fall of Constantinople will have a strong effect in Persia and Afghanistan, and on the Mahomedans of this country.'

Victory on March 18 would have many strategic advantages. Lloyd George had set out several of these in a memorandum circulated to his colleagues on February 22. 'To bring Bulgaria, Roumania and Greece in with Serbia,' he wrote, 'means throwing an aggregate army of 1,500,000 on to the Austrian flank. This will not only relieve the pressure on Russia, but indirectly on France. It will tend to equalize things, and thus give us time to re-equip the Russian Army.' On March 16 Kitchener circulated a memorandum to the Cabinet stressing future strategic advantages to be gained once Turkey were defeated. Believing that after the war 'old enmities and jealousies which have been stilled by the existing crisis in Europe may revive . . .' and that Britain might find itself 'at enmity with Russia, or with France, or with both in combination', he advocated the annexation of Alexandretta and Aleppo. He also warned that 'if we do not take Mesopotamia, the Russians undoubtedly will sooner or later . . .'. 'If the Ottoman Empire is to be wholly or partially broken up,' he declared, 'it is imperative that Mesopotamia should become British.' Sir Henry Jackson added a further strategic plea. 'From the naval point of view,' he wrote in a memorandum also circulated to the Cabinet on March 16, 'it is most undesirable that any other powerful nation should develop Alexandretta . . .'

In his 'notes for evidence' which Hankey submitted to the Dardanelles Commissioners on 1 September 1916, he outlined the economic arguments which had influenced the War Council in favour of an attack at the Dardanelles:

Prominent among these was the shortage of shipping, which, though less acute than it became later, was already making itself felt, and which rendered very desirable the release of the British, allied, neutral, and interned enemy shipping locked up in the Black Sea, amounting in the aggregate to 120 steamships, with a total of 347,880 gross tons.

Akin to this was the need for the export of Russian wheat, the withdrawal of which compelled Italy and Greece to draw their supplies from America, involving (owing to the longer voyage) a greater demand for shipping, raising freights, and increasing the shortage. The opening of the Russian wheat supplies was also very desirable in order to lower prices in this country and in France.

In this category also fall the Russian exchanges, which had depreciated owing to Russia's inability to export, and which rendered difficult the payment of the interest on the Russian loans, in which so many French families were concerned, involving in consequence, a possible adverse influence on the willingness of France to face a prolonged war.

Relief for Russia, encouragement for France, food for India, salvation for Serbia, doom for Austria-Hungary, isolation for Germany, a swift and almost bloodless triumph for the Allies, new territory for the victors—these shadowy hopes of January offered themselves up on the eve of the naval attack as realities within grasp. For Churchill, the outcome of the attack would be decisive to his whole future. Despite his original strong preference for a joint military and naval operation, and his many anguished and at times angry efforts to obtain a large army to co-operate with his ships, he had nevertheless been willing to offer victory by ships alone. If the battleships assembled at the mouth of the Dardanelles could blast their way past the forts and mines of the Narrows into the Sea of Marmara, and thence to Constantinople, Churchill's impetuosity, his pushing, his petulance, his ambition, his youth, would find their vindication.

11

18 March 1915: The Naval Attack

THE naval attack at the Dardanelles began at ten forty-five on the morning of March 18. Six British and four French battleships entered the Straits, opened fire on the Turkish forts and batteries on the European and Asian shores, and for over two hours subjected the Turks to a massive bombardment. By a quarter to two not one of the Turkish forts under attack was able to continue firing. At a cost of less than forty men killed and wounded, de Robeck had put the principal Turkish defences covering the minefields of Kephez Bay out of action, although the smaller mobile howitzer batteries were still unscathed, and some of the forts needed only ammunition to fire again. The time had come for the minesweepers to clear a passage, and for the battleships to advance to the final set of forts at Chanak and Kilid Bahr. The first line of battleships was ordered to withdraw, to make way both for the minesweepers and for the second line of ships.

As the French battleship *Bouvet* was leaving the Straits, shortly before two o'clock, there was an explosion, a cloud of smoke and steam, and within a few minutes the ship had disappeared. Over six hundred of her sailors were drowned. At the time it was not known whether a mine, or a Turkish shell, had caused the explosion. De Robeck assumed that it was a heavy shell exploding in her powder magazine, not a previously unlocated Turkish mine; he therefore ordered the other ships to continue operations without a break. For two more hours the ships maintained a continuous and fierce bombardment. Confidence grew; 'At 4 pm,' de Robeck subsequently telegraphed, 'the forts of the Narrows were practically silenced; the batteries guarding the minefield were put to flight and the situation appeared to be most favourable for clearing the minefields.' The senior French officer present, Rear-Admiral Guépratte,[1] accepting the loss of the *Bouvet* as part of the necessary

[1] Emile-Paul-Aimable Guépratte, 1856–1939. Entered the French Navy, 1871. Rear-Admiral commanding the French naval forces at the Dardanelles, February–October 1915. Vice-Admiral, October 1915. Knighted, 1915. Subsequently Préfet Maritime at Brest and Commander-in-Chief and Préfet Maritime in Algeria–Tunisia.

hazard of the operation, urged his other ships to greater exertions. Orders were given to sweep the minefields of Kephez Bay and move forward, before dusk, to Chanak itself. At that moment, Sir Ian Hamilton, who since dawn had been sailing off the Aegean shore in the cruiser *Phaeton*, examining possible landing places for a future military assault, entered the Straits. A year later he recalled in his 'diary':

I had promised de Robeck not to take his fastest cruiser, fragile as an egg, into the actual Straits, but the Captain and the Commander[1]. . . were frightfully keen to see the fun, and I thought it fair to allow one mile as being the *mouth* of the Straits, and *not the* Straits. Before we had covered that mile we found ourselves on the outskirts of,—dream of my life—a naval battle! Nor was the reality unworthy of my dream. Here it was; we had only to keep on at thirty knots and we should be in the thick of it! And who would have the courage to say stop!!!

In truth the world did suddenly appear to me quite fantastic; as if it had gone mad! A mile and a half above us was the enormous 'Queen Elizabeth' spouting flame and smoke; the echoes of these detonations mingling with minor explosives of every calibre, the whole strange orchestra making the everlasting hills quiver to their foundations. At the same time we realised the majesty and force of the 'Queen Elizabeth' we felt her also out of her true setting; at a sad disadvantage on such narrow waters, creeping with mines, torpedoes and every description of devilment.

Above the 'Queen Elizabeth' again, making slowly backwards and forwards up almost in the Narrows, were several other men-of-war belching forth fire and smoke at the forts. These were answering in a very half-hearted manner; it seemed as though they were beat, but the concealed mobile guns from the Peninsula and from Asia were busy and apparently unspotted.

At eleven minutes past four the *Inflexible* struck a mine. Three minutes later the *Irresistible* likewise began to list and seemed unable to move. The *Phaeton* moved as close to the *Inflexible* as its captain dared. Hamilton recalled in his 'diary': 'Even as we gazed spellbound no one knew whether the great ship might not dive into the depths. . . . All the crew and stokers were in a mass standing at attention on the main deck . . . silent, orderly in their ranks, facing the imminence of death.' Most of the men on both the *Inflexible* and the *Irresistible* were saved, and the British, more fortunate than the French, had only seventy-three men killed or wounded during the whole day's action. But the apparent presence of mines which had not been previously located, and the sudden, almost simultaneous crippling of two of his battleships, led de

[1] Robert Reynolds Rosoman, 18 ?–1953. Entered Navy, 1898. Lieutenant-Commander, 1907; Commander, 1918. Retired with the rank of Captain, 1922.

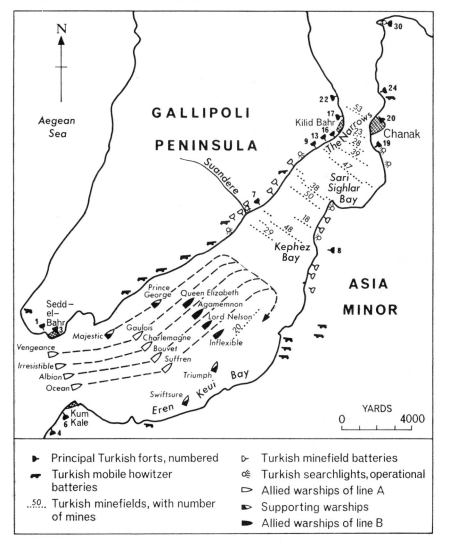

THE ANGLO-FRENCH NAVAL ATTACK AT THE
DARDANELLES, 18 MARCH 1915

Robeck to order an immediate halt to the day's operations. Misfortune continued. While covering the rescue of the *Irresistible*, the *Ocean* also struck a mine. That night both the *Irresistible* and the *Ocean* sank beneath the waters of the Dardanelles. As the remaining ships left the scene of action, Admiral Guépratte reported that the *Gaulois*, badly damaged by gun-fire, had been beached on a nearby island. At six that evening Hamilton wrote to Kitchener from on board the *Phaeton*: 'This has been a very bad day for us judging by what has come under my own personal observation. . . . The scene was what I believe Naval writers describe as "lively". . . . Certainly it looks at present as if the Fleet would not be able to carry on at this rate, and, if so, the soldiers will have to do the trick.'

Churchill returned to England from France during the night. At half past eight on the morning of March 19, after he had begun work at the Admiralty, he received a telegram from de Robeck giving a factual account of the action. He later told the Dardanelles Commissioners how he had 'regarded it as only the first of several days' fighting, though the loss in ships sunk or disabled was unpleasant. It never occurred to me for a moment that we should not go on, within the limits of what we had decided to risk, 10 or 12 ships had been mentioned, till we reached a decision one way or the other.' Churchill found both Fisher and Wilson in the same mood as himself. 'Both met me that morning,' he told the Dardanelles Commissioners, 'with expressions of firm determination to fight it out.' 'De Robeck really better than Carden,' Fisher wrote to Churchill later that day, 'so Providence is with us.'

Fisher showed his enthusiasm by immediately ordering two more battleships, the *London* and the *Prince of Wales*, to reinforce de Robeck's fleet. Two other battleships, the *Queen* and the *Implacable*, were both already on their way to the Dardanelles with Fisher's approval. During the morning news reached the Admiralty that Augagneur was sending another battleship, the *Henri IV*, to replace the *Bouvet*.

The War Council met at eleven o'clock that morning. Churchill read out the telegrams from de Robeck, announcing the sinking of the *Irresistible*, the *Ocean* and the *Bouvet*, the grounding of the *Gaulois*, and the disablement of the *Inflexible*. In answer to a question from Lloyd George, Sir Arthur Wilson said that as far as could be gathered from the telegrams the forts 'had only been temporarily silenced'. Churchill said that if the War Council agreed, he would instruct de Robeck 'to use his discretion in continuing the operations'. Unable to reveal the existence of intercepted German wireless messages, Churchill could only tell them vaguely of 'information that the Turks were short of ammunition and mines'. Some discussion followed on the danger of ammunition being smuggled through Rumania and Bulgaria from Germany. Although these countries were neutral, they had always to remember, Grey pointed out, 'the possibility of the bribery of officials in these Balkan States'. Without further discussion, the War Council authorized

Churchill to inform de Robeck 'that he could continue the operations against the Dardanelles if he thought fit'.

After some discussion about the western front, and about drunkenness in munition factories, the War Council began to discuss the implications of the setback at the Dardanelles. No one wanted to call off the naval attack. Fisher said that a loss of twelve battleships would have to be expected 'before the Dardanelles could be forced by the Navy alone'. Asquith asked whether any plan had been worked out for the landing of troops. Kitchener replied that the War Office 'had not sufficient information to form a detailed scheme of disembarkation', and that any plan would have to be devised by Sir Ian Hamilton himself. There was no further discussion as to the nature or timing of any possible military landing. No one asked whether a second naval attack ought not to be postponed until the Army were ready to land. One attraction of the naval attack had been that it would be possible to break it off entirely if the enterprise failed. No one pointed out that this might be the moment to cancel the attack altogether; no one argued that to break off a military attack once a landing had been effected would be a much more difficult undertaking.

As always when the Dardanelles were under discussion, the minds of Ministers wandered into the territorial sphere. No one felt that they were in the shadow of a naval disaster. They eagerly devised schemes of partition and control which presupposed victory. Grey was anxious to make a good impression upon Britain's Moslem subjects by setting up an independent Moslem State in the Arab Provinces of the Turkish Empire—Arabia, Syria and Mesopotamia. Crewe reported that the India Office were divided in their enthusiasms for such a scheme. Kitchener wanted to transfer Mecca, the centre of the Islamic world, from Turkish to British control, rather than let the Turkish Empire remain intact and thereby make it possible for the Holy Lands of Islam to fall under Russian domination. He pointed out that India 'would expect some return for her effort and losses in Mesopotamia', at which Crewe declared that 'all shades of opinion in the India Office' agreed that the Turkish Province of Basra 'must form part of the British Empire'.

Haldane was once more the only member of the War Council who took a long-term view, urging that 'in the interests of a lasting peace' we should not crush the Germans and Turks at the end of the war. 'Napoleon,' he told the War Council, 'had failed in the attempt to crush nations, and since 1870 Germany had failed to crush the nationality out of Alsace and Lorraine. All experience showed that a permanent peace could not be obtained except by general consent.' Balfour denied that there was any comparison with the War Council's proposals to partition Turkey and 'the Napoleonic plan of crushing nations'. In Europe, he said, territory could of course be divided according to nationality, but in Asia 'we had to deal with countries which had been misgoverned by the Turks'. Churchill returned to his view that such discussions were premature, and should be postponed. 'We should say to France outright that we had not made up our mind'; Britain and France 'should both agree to a self-denying policy in regard to the acquisition of territory' until the matter could be discussed in detail. Grey insisted that the War Council make up its mind about the future of the Turkish Empire. Lloyd George warned that if Germany were weakened too much, she would be unable to act as a counterweight to Russia's growing predominance in the future; he therefore hoped that the War Council would not rule out the possibility 'of giving Germany a bone of some sort' out of the Turkish Empire. Crewe pointed out that it would be 'very dangerous to put the Germans back on the Baghdad Railway'. Churchill, despite his earlier declaration, suddenly hurled himself into the partitionist campaign. 'Surely,' he burst out, 'we did not intend to leave this inefficient and out-of-date nation, which had long misruled one of the most fertile countries of the world, still in possession! Turkey had long shown herself to be inefficient as a governing Power, and it was time for us to make a clean sweep.' These extreme sentiments were in direct and violent contrast to Churchill's earlier sympathies for the Young Turks and their revolution.

Asquith agreed with Churchill's argument, feeling that he and his colleagues would 'not be doing our duty' if they were to leave other nations 'to scramble for Turkey without taking anything ourselves'. The only formal decision reached by the War Council was that 'after the Straits had been forced, and Constantinople had passed into the hands of the Allies, our first desideratum would be the establishment of a Moslem entity. It would have to include Arabia, and the question would arise as to what was to go with it. In the meantime, it would be premature to discuss the partition of Turkey.'

After the War Council Churchill returned to the Admiralty with Fisher and Wilson. An optimistic telegram from de Robeck awaited them: 'With the exception of ships lost and damaged,' the Admiral signalled, 'Squadron is ready for immediate action but the plan of attack must be re-considered and means found to deal with floating mines many of which appear to be given whitened buoys and then attached to floats; those floating are easily dealt with by picket boats. I much regret the heavy casualties in personnel and material. . . .'

Churchill, Fisher and Wilson were encouraged by de Robeck's claim that his ships were ready 'for immediate action'. But they soon realized that it would take some time to repair the damaged ships, for in a further telegram received at the Admiralty that afternoon de Robeck asked for the immediate despatch of materials and dockyard labour from England to carry out the necessary repairs. Although the Admiral contemplated further action by the Navy alone, he was shaken by the loss and damage of so many ships. Immediately after halting the action he had telegraphed to Admiral Wemyss that the Navy had experienced 'a disastrous day'. In a telegram to Kitchener on March 19, Hamilton expressed his doubts about the possibility of a purely naval success. 'I am being most reluctantly driven to the conclusion,' he declared, 'that the Straits are not likely to be forced by battleships as at one time seemed probable and that, if my troops are to take part, it will not take the subsidiary form anticipated. The Army's part will be more than mere landings of parties to destroy Forts, it must be a deliberate and progressive military operation carried out at full strength so as to open a passage for the Navy.'

During the afternoon of March 19 Churchill and Fisher received news which dispelled their gloom at the suspended action, for it pointed to the chance of certain victory as soon as de Robeck renewed the attack. Naval Intelligence had intercepted a message from the Kaiser to Admiral Souchon begging him at all costs to hold out at the Dardanelles and promising to send ammunition at the first opportunity. From the Kaiser's message it was clear that there must have been some panic among the German officers, and a grave shortage of ammunition in the forts of the Dardanelles. As soon as the message was decoded the Director of Naval Intelligence, Captain Hall,[1] took it to Churchill's room, where he found the First Lord standing with Fisher by the fireplace. Hall wrote a somewhat melodramatic account of what happened in an unpublished memoir fifteen years later:

'First Sea Lord,' said I, 'we've just received this.'
Lord Fisher took the message, read it aloud, and waved it over his head. 'By God,' he shouted, 'I'll go through tomorrow!'

[1] William Reginald Hall, 1870–1943. Entered Navy, 1883. Captain, Royal Navy, 1913. Commanded the *Queen Mary*, 1913–14. Forced to give up his sea command after three months of war because of uncertain health. Director of the Intelligence Division at the Admiralty, 1914–18. Rear-Admiral, 1917. Knighted, 1918. Conservative MP, 1919–23; 1925–9. Conservative Party Principal Agent, 1924.

Mr Churchill, equally excited, seized hold of the telegram and read it through again for his own satisfaction. 'That means,' he said, 'they've come to the end of their ammunition.'

'Tomorrow!' repeated Lord Fisher, and at that moment I believe that he was as enthusiastic as ever Mr Churchill had been about the whole Dardanelles campaign. 'We shall probably lose six ships, but I'm going through.'

The First Lord nodded. 'Then get the orders out.'

And there and then Lord Fisher sat down at Mr Churchill's table to draft out the necessary orders.

The telegram which Fisher drafted was sent to de Robeck in the early hours of the morning of March 20. It was not quite as decisive as Hall had recalled:

We regret the losses you have suffered in your resolute attack. Convey to all ranks and ratings Their Lordships' approbation of their conduct in action and seamanlike skill and prudence with which His Majesty's ships were handled. Convey to the French squadron the Admiralty's appreciation of their loyal and effective support, and our sorrow for the losses they have sustained.

Queen and Implacable should join you very soon; and London and Prince of Wales sail to-night.

Please telegraph any information as to damage done to forts, and also full casualties and ammunition expended.

It appears important not to let the forts be repaired or to encourage enemy by an apparent suspension of the operations. Ample supplies of 15″ ammunition are available for indirect fire of Queen Elizabeth across the peninsula.

That same day de Robeck telegraphed to Churchill: 'it is hoped to be in a position to commence operations in three or four days. . . . In the meantime feints at landing in various places will be made in order to draw off some of the enemy's field guns.' In a further telegram sent a few hours later de Robeck declared that the French Squadron had been 'quite undismayed by their heavy loss', and that in both the British and French battleships 'Officers and men are only anxious to re-engage the enemy'.

Captain Hall had been about to return to his office on the evening of March 19 when Churchill asked him whether, as part of his secret activities, he was in direct contact with Constantinople. Hall explained that he had already initiated negotiations, through two British emissaries,[1] with Talaat Bey, the Turkish Minister of the Interior. According to his Intelligence Reports from Constantinople, he said, 'many of its most influential citizens would welcome an immediate break with the Germans', and prayers were even being offered up in the mosques of the city for the arrival of the British Fleet. Hall told Churchill of his emissaries' efforts:

'They have with them,' I told Mr Churchill, 'a letter from me guaranteeing a large sum of money in the event of a successful outcome of the negotiations.'

He stared at me.

'Four million pounds,' I added, and as I mentioned the figure it did seem to be an extraordinarily large sum.

He was frowning. 'Who authorised this?' he demanded.

'I did, First Lord.'

'But—the Cabinet surely knows nothing about it?'

'No, it does not. But if we were to get peace, or if we were to get a peaceful passage [of the Dardanelles] for that amount, I imagine they'll be glad enough to pay.'

It was one of those moments when dropped pins are supposed to be heard. Then Mr Churchill turned to Lord Fisher who was still busily writing. 'D'you hear what this man has done? He's sent out people with four millions to buy a peaceful passage! On his own!'

'What!' shouted Lord Fisher, starting up from his chair. 'Four millions? No, no. I tell you I'm going through tomorrow.'

Fisher was determined to have a naval victory. Turning to Hall he said: 'Cable at once to stop all negotiations. All. No. Offer £2,000,000 for the Goeben and £1,000,000 for the Breslau. But nothing else. We're going through.' Remaining in Churchill's room, Hall drafted the necessary telegrams. Churchill shared Fisher's enthusiasm at the prospect of an immediate and decisive naval victory, and Hall had to abandon his plan for a negotiated peace. 'In view of Lord Fisher's emphatic statement and the First Lord's concurrence,' he later wrote, 'I could not see how the large sum of money which was involved could ever be approved by the Cabinet, if the naval operation now being

---

[1] Hall's emissaries were Griffin Eady, a civil engineer who had been living for some years in Constantinople working on the construction of the railway to Bagdad, and Edwin Whittall, a businessman who had lived in Turkey all his life. Eady and Whittall met a Turkish emissary at Dedeagatch on 15 March 1915. Hall informed Hankey of these negotiations on March 4. On 7 October 1937 Hall sent an account of the negotiations to Captain (then Sir Herbert) Richmond, confirming that 'I had no Cabinet authority for the money then'.

ordered were successful.' Churchill and Fisher were insistent that de Robeck renew the attack as soon as possible. Because of the Turkish shortage of ammunition and the inability of the Germans to make the shortage good for at least a week, victory seemed to them inevitable. On the evening of March 22, Asquith reported to Venetia Stanley that 'Winston is fairly pleased with the situation in the Dardanelles, and K (who has just been here for a talk) appears to be not dissatisfied'.

On March 20 Hamilton told de Robeck that he wished to move his base to Egypt because of the poor facilities at Mudros. De Robeck asked him to delay moving his troops 'until our attack is renewed in a few days' time'. The Admiral was in an optimistic mood. The *Gaulois* was refloated on the afternoon of March 20, after British naval ratings had effected temporary repairs to the damage below her water-line. On March 21 de Robeck reported to the Admiralty that 'preparations for [mine]sweeping are progressing but practice with new crews and of destroyers which is essential to ensure success is impossible at present, weather having broken. . . . Good progress being made with Inflexible, some spaces have been already pumped.'

Fisher did not doubt de Robeck's ability to force the Narrows when the attack was renewed. But he was again worried about Britain's naval strength in home waters, writing to Churchill during March 20:

I count up 28 Destroyers & Torpedo boats at Dardanelles and in view of the very narrow entrance of the Dardanelles and restricted area of operations this is infinitely a bigger proportion than we have at home—but all the same we ought to press the French to send more Destroyers and more light cruisers. It's ridiculous what little the French do! and what good their keeping a force on the Syrian Coast? I have only one anxiety the German and Austrian submarines—*when they appear the game will be up!* That's why I wish to press on the military co-operation and get a base at Cape Helles anyhow. It will be 3 weeks before the military can do anything according to present arrangements.

Churchill replied at once, praising Fisher for his arguments at the War Council in favour of a second attempt to break through the Narrows:

My dear Fisher,
    I do not think you have any need to be anxious about our strength at home. Nothing has changed since you & AKW [Sir Arthur Wilson] were anxious that a 13·5 ship shd go to D'lles—except that the Warspite is nearly ready: & will be ready before the German fleet concentrates again.

Irresistible has hardly lost anybody. I doubt if all told we have 150 casualties.[1]

Remember we cannot man the monitors & the new ships without laying up most of the old battleships. As long as the crews are saved there is no cause for serious regret.

You & AKW were splendid yesterday.

This is a vy hard war to win.

Yours always
W

Towards the end of March Asquith was beset by rumours of dissention in the Government, and of an intrigue against him. Writing from Walmer Castle on Sunday March 21 he told Venetia Stanley that the Chancellor of the Duchy of Lancaster, Edwin Montagu, was 'a good deal exercised by the ascendency which he thinks AJB is gaining over LG as well as Winston. He regards AJB as secretly but genuinely hostile to me.' Montagu told the Prime Minister that Lloyd George and Churchill were pouring 'all their grievances against K and the rest of their colleagues' into Balfour's ears and that Churchill had 'gone so far as to suggest . . . that he (AJB) could be put in charge of the Foreign Office when Grey goes next week for his fishing holiday!' Margot Asquith recorded her husband's reaction to Churchill's suggestion in her diary on March 21:

'Young puppy,' said Henry, 'let him come and suggest this to me and I'll tell him what I think of him! he really is the greatest donkey! he goes gassing about, abusing K to Arthur and I've no doubt abusing me, giving him much too much information. He thinks he knows Arthur Balfour, he has not the foggiest idea of what Arthur really is. . . .'

Asquith told his wife that Balfour was a man with a 'futile feminine brain' who, when his Party is in the depths, 'takes his hat off, says he is ill and leaves his unfortunate friends to be led by a man of fifth rate quality like Bonar Law'. On March 24, the editor of the *Nation*, H. W. Massingham,[2] called on Margot Asquith with a story which he swore he

---

[1] Fifty British sailors died on March 18; 33 from the *Inflexible*, 14 from the *Irresistible* and one each from the *Albion*, *Majestic* and *Ocean*. A further 23 sailors were wounded.

[2] Henry William Massingham, 1860–1924. Editor of the *Daily Chronicle*, 1895–9, resigning because of the unpopularity of his opposition to the South African War. Editor of the *Nation*, 1907–23. In 1909 he wrote an introduction to an edition of Churchill's speeches, *Liberalism and the Social Problem*. Supported Lord Lansdowne's advocacy of a negotiated peace, 1917. Joined the Labour Party, 1923.

could prove to be true. She passed it on at once to Asquith, who informed Venetia Stanley that same day:

. . . Winston is 'intriguing hard' to supplant E. Grey at the Foreign Office & to put AJB in his place. I gave you the other day a milder version of the same story, which the suspicious mind of the Assyrian [Montagu] had treasured up. There is no doubt that Winston is at the moment a complete victim to B's superficial charm; he has him at the Admiralty night & day, and I am afraid tells him a lot of things which he ought to keep to himself, or at any rate to his colleagues.

Since I began the last sentence, Ll George has been here. . . . I asked him what he thought of the Massingham story, & rather to my surprise he said he believed it was substantially true. He thinks that Winston has for the time at any rate allowed himself to be 'swallowed whole' by AJB on whom he, LG, after working with him for a week or two, is now disposed to be very severe.

It is a pity isn't it? that Winston hasn't a better sense of proportion, and also a larger endowment of the instinct of loyalty. As you know, like you, I am really fond of him: but I regard his future with many misgivings. Your little Indian plan for him commands I am afraid no favour in any quarter: the mere mention of it makes the Assyrian foam at the mouth, and is received with less demonstrative but equally emphatic disapproval by the 2 or 3 others to whom I have casually hinted at it. He will never get to the top in English politics, with all his wonderful gifts; to speak with the tongue of men & angels, and to spend laborious days & nights in administration, is no good, if a man does not inspire trust.

As Balfour was a member of the War Council, Asquith could hardly prevent Churchill from seeing him; as Balfour was among the foremost supporters of an active policy at the Dardanelles, he and Churchill could be expected to discuss the diplomatic aspects of the war, and to be critical of Grey's activities. It was not only between Churchill and Balfour that intrigue seemed to be rustling during the last week of March. McKenna brought Asquith another story on March 29. 'The idea is,' Asquith reported to Venetia Stanley, 'that Northcliffe (for some unknown reason) has been engineering a campaign to supplant me by LlG! McK is of course quite certain that LlG & perhaps Winston are "in it". Which I don't believe. . . . I lunched with the Assyrian, tête à tête, and his loyalty is a certain & invaluable asset. Of course he is rather anti-McK, whom he suspects as a mischief maker. I asked him what wd happen if the so-called "intrigue" were to come off, & I was supposed to go. He replied without a moment's hesitation that the *whole* Cabinet, including LlG & Winston, would go with me, & make any alternative impossible.'

Asquith saw quite clearly that general discontent, whether voiced by Churchill or Lloyd George, McKenna or Montagu, did not amount to intrigue and did not threaten his position. On March 30 he summoned Lloyd George and McKenna for a direct confrontation. Lloyd George said that McKenna had inspired an article in the *Daily Chronicle* on 'Intrigue against the Prime Minister' and proceeded to accuse McKenna of always seeing imaginary plots, as in Churchill's 'supposed campaign against Grey'. Lloyd George had invited Churchill to this meeting, but he had refused to come. 'I had a most characteristic letter from Winston, just before dinner,' Asquith wrote to Venetia Stanley that night. 'He said he had refused LlG's invitation to come to our interview this afternoon: because (as he said) "I feel that my case is safe in your hands". That bears out what you said in your most darling letter—that (whatever happens) W is really loyal to me. I am sure, & have never doubted, that he is. So that silly "plot" is done with.'

'I am spoiling to have at it again,' Keyes wrote to his wife from on board the *Queen Elizabeth* on March 21. De Robeck was more hesitant to renew the attack, for he had come to the conclusion that before he could send his ships through the Narrows the Army must go ashore and demolish the Turkish forts. On the morning of March 22 de Robeck called Hamilton and Birdwood to a conference on board the *Queen Elizabeth*, and asked them how soon the troops could be ready for a joint operation, explaining that he would need the help of all of them if the forts lining the Dardanelles were to be put out of action, and the shore of the Peninsula securely in British hands. Birdwood wanted the Army to participate without any further delay, telling de Robeck, as Hamilton later recorded in his 'diary', 'that we ought to land at once, even without ship-shape band-o-bast, and make good the south point of the Peninsula'. Hamilton believed that there was 'a lot to be said' for Birdwood's view—'he has been longer on the spot than I'—but he did not feel able to go against Kitchener's orders, which were, he wrote, 'most specific. I am not to make a piecemeal occupation. . . . The 29th Division is our pièce de résistance and it will be hardly here, complete, for another three or four weeks. By that time I can get all in order for a smashing simultaneous blow.'

Hamilton informed de Robeck that his troops would not be ready for action until April 14. De Robeck at once telegraphed to the Admiralty, explaining that as he felt he could only attack again when the Army was ready, he must suspend operations:

At meeting today with Generals Hamilton and Birdwood the former told me army will not be in a position to undertake any military operations before 14th April. In order to maintain our communication when the Fleet penetrates into the Sea of Marmora it is necessary to destroy all guns of positions guarding the Straits. These are numerous and only small percentage can be rendered useless by gun fire. The landing of demolishing party on the 26th February evidently surprised enemy. From our experience on the 4th March it seems in future destruction of guns will have to be carried out in face of strenuous and well prepared opposition.

I do not think it a practicable operation to land a force adequate to undertake this service inside Dardanelles. General Hamilton concurs in this opinion. If the guns are not destroyed any success of Fleet may be nullified by the Straits closing up after the ships have passed through and, as loss of material will possibly be heavy, ships may not be available to keep Dardanelles open.

The mine menace will continue until the Sea of Marmora is reached being much greater than was anticipated. It must be carefully and thoroughly dealt with both as regards mines and from floating mines. This will take time to accomplish but our arrangements will be ready by the time Army can act. It appears better to prepare a decisive effort about the middle of April rather than risk a great deal for what may possibly be only a partial solution.

This telegram reached the Admiralty at six-thirty on the morning of March 23. All morning the Admiralty War Group discussed de Robeck's desire to suspend naval operations until military co-operation was available. In 1916 Churchill gave the Dardanelles Commissioners an account of Fisher's arguments: 'Lord Fisher took the line that hitherto he had been willing to carry the enterprise forward, because it was supported and recommended by the Commander on the spot. But now that Admiral de Robeck and Sir Ian Hamilton had decided upon a joint operation, we were bound to accept their view.' Churchill recognized the strength of this argument, but did not accept it. He told the Dardanelles Commissioners his reasons:

I believed then, as I believe now, that we were separated by very little from complete success. Although at the outset I should have rejoiced at the provision of an army, I saw the disadvantages which would attend its employment after what had happened. I had a great desire to spare the army the heavy cost of the military operation. Landing on and storming the Gallipoli Peninsula, now that the Turks were fully alarmed, seemed to be a formidable business. It seemed to me a far more serious undertaking than the naval attack. It would commit us irrevocably if it failed, in a way no naval attack could have done. The risk was greater. The stakes were far higher. I knew how far behind the 29th Division was, and above all I feared the inevitable delay.

Both Sir Arthur Wilson and Sir Henry Jackson supported Fisher. But Churchill was determined on a second naval attack. He had been fired by de Robeck's initial enthusiasm after March 18 to renew the attempt to force the Narrows. The intercepted German telegrams also continued to influence him. 'We knew, from a source which we could trust absolutely,' he told the Dardanelles Commissioners, 'that the Turks were very short of big-gun ammunition, and that they and their German advisers were in the greatest apprehension.' This shortage was a fact; the Turks did not have enough heavy ammunition for another full day's firing. Churchill was convinced that another attack, pressed forward with determination, and not broken off in mid-course as that of March 18 had been, would have a strong chance of success. Nor were de Robeck's own doubts shared by all his subordinates at the Dardanelles. Commodore Keyes, his Chief of Staff, was convinced that a further naval attack could not fail. But even Keyes felt the need for a longer delay than Churchill had suggested, in order to reorganize the minesweeping force which had fared so badly on March 18.

Convinced that the Navy could succeed alone, Churchill drafted a telegram to de Robeck insisting upon a renewed naval action:

In view of dangers of delay through submarine attack and of heavy cost of army operation, and possibility that it will fail or be only partly effective in opening the Straits, and that the danger of mines will not be relieved by it, we consider that you ought to persevere methodically but resolutely with the plan contained in your instructions . . . and that you should make all preparations to renew the attack begun on the 18th at the first favourable opportunity. You should dominate the forts at the Narrows and sweep the minefield and then batter the forts at close range, taking your time, using your aeroplanes, and all your improved methods of guarding against mines. The destruction of the forts at the Narrows may open the way for a further advance. The entry into the Marmora of a fleet strong enough to beat Turkish Fleet would produce decisive results on the whole situation, and you need not be anxious about your subsequent line of communications. We know the forts are short of ammunition and supply of mines is limited. We do not think the time has yet come to give up the plan of forcing Dardanelles by a purely naval operation. . . .

This telegram was never sent. Although two members of the Admiralty War Group, Oliver and de Bartolomé, agreed with Churchill, the three senior naval officers, Fisher, Wilson and Jackson, were entirely opposed. Churchill therefore brought the matter before the Cabinet on March 23. Both Asquith and Kitchener agreed with Churchill. During the meeting, Kitchener drafted two telegrams to Hamilton in strong support of Churchill's policies. The first read: 'I am informed you consider the 14th April as about date for commencing military operations if fleet have not forced the Dardanelles by then. I think you had better know at once that I consider any such postponement as far too long, & shd like to know how soon you cd [get?] on shore.' The second read:

Undoubtedly silenced guns should be destroyed and the forts demolished and for this purpose the Admiral should call upon the army authorities to provide landing parties of considerable force whenever necessary for the purpose—It is important to keep up the bombardment and all attempts to pass the narrows by ships. Once ships are through, the Gallipoli military position ceases to be of importance.

Asquith also supported a renewed attack, writing to Venetia Stanley that afternoon:

We had a longish Cabinet this morning. The news from the Dardanelles is not very good: there are more mines & concealed guns than they ever counted upon: and the Admiral seems to be rather in a funk. Ian Hamilton has not yet sent his report, but the soldiers cannot be ready for any big concerted operation before about 14 April. I agree with Winston & K that the Navy ought to make another big push, so soon as the weather clears. If they wait & wait, until the army is fully prepared, they may fall into a spell of bad weather, & (what is worse) find that submarines, Austrian or German, have arrived on the scene.

A further argument against delay was the effect of any hesitation upon Italy. Much of the Cabinet's time was spent, Asquith wrote to Venetia Stanley, 'in discussing how cheaply we can purchase the immediate intervention of that most voracious, slippery, & perfidious Power'. Victory at the Dardanelles was expected to act as the final spur to Italian participation against Austria.

Churchill returned to the Admiralty. Throughout the afternoon of March 23 he argued with his naval advisers. But Fisher, Wilson and Jackson reacted strongly against his proposed telegram to de Robeck. Churchill appealed to Asquith for the second time that day, but Asquith was unwilling to overrule the advice of the three distinguished Admirals, despite his personal support for Churchill's policy. Churchill contemplated resignation. But he finally decided to take the advice of his leading advisers. He explained his decision in *The World Crisis*:

If by resigning I could have procured the decision, I would have done so without a moment's hesitation. It was clear, however, that this would only have made matters worse. Nothing that I could do could overcome the Admirals now they had definitely stuck their toes in. They had only to point to the losses of ships which had been incurred, and every one would have sided with them. I was therefore compelled under extreme duress to abandon the intention of sending direct orders to Admiral de Robeck to renew the attack.

Some reply had to be sent to de Robeck's request for delay. During the morning of March 24 Churchill drafted a personal telegram setting out his reasons for wanting a renewal of a purely naval attack, and urging de Robeck to reconsider his decision. Fisher was against putting any pressure on de Robeck, even of a personal nature. On reading Churchill's proposed telegram he wrote at once to protest: 'Although the telegram goes from you personally, the fact of my remaining at the Admiralty sanctions my connection with it, so if it goes I do not see how I can remain.' Churchill was not to be deterred by such a threat. Nor was he influenced by a second letter from Fisher on March 24 cast in more genial mood:

. . . *You are very wrong to worry and excite yourself!* do try and remember that *we are the lost ten tribes of Israel!* We are sure to win! I know I am an optimist! —*always have been! THANK GOD!* A vituperative woman once called me a 'Sun-Dial'!

> 'There he stands amongst the flowers
> Counting only sunny hours
> Heeding neither rain nor mist
> The Brazen-faced old optimist'! . . .

In his postscript Fisher wrote: '*Send no more telegrams! Let it alone!* . . .' But Churchill could not 'let it alone'. The plan in which he believed, and upon which so much still seemed to depend in the political and military sphere, was now in jeopardy. At seven thirty-five that evening his personal telegram was finally, and with Fisher's reluctant consent, sent to de Robeck. It was headed 'Personal and Secret':

It is clear that the army should at once prepare to attack the Kilid Bahr plateau at the earliest opportunity, and Lord Kitchener hopes that April 14 can be ante-dated. This is a matter for the War Office. But the question now to be decided by Admiralty is whether the time has come to abandon the naval plan of forcing the Dardanelles without the aid of a large army. It may be necessary to accept the check of the 18th as decisive and to admit that the task is beyond our powers, and if you think this you should not fail to say so. But before deciding, certain facts must be weighed; first the delay and the consequent danger of submarines coming and ruining all; second the heavy losses at least 5,000 which the army would suffer; third the possibilities of a check in the land operations far more serious than the loss of a few old surplus ships; fourth the fact that even when the Kilid Bahr plateau has been taken by the army and the Kilid Bahr group of forts rendered untenable, the Asiatic forts will be still effective and most of the mine danger which is now your principal difficulty will menace you in the long reaches above the Narrows.

These must be balanced against the risks and hopes of a purely naval undertaking. You must not underrate the supreme moral effect of a British fleet with sufficient fuel and ammunition entering the Sea of Marmora provided it is strong enough to destroy the Turco-German vessels. The Gallipoli Peninsula would be completely cut off if our ships were on both sides of the Bulair Isthmus. It seems very probable that as soon as it is apparent that the fortresses at the Narrows are not going to stop the Fleet a general evacuation of the peninsula will take place; but anyhow all troops remaining upon it would be doomed to starvation or surrender. Besides this there is the political effect of the arrival of the Fleet before Constantinople which is incalculable and may well be absolutely decisive.

Assuming that only the minimum good results follow the successful passage of the Fleet into the Marmora, namely, that the Turkish army on Gallipoli continues to hold out and with forts and field guns closes up the Straits, and that no revolution occurs at Constantinople, then perhaps in the last resort the army would have to storm Kilid Bahr plateau and secure a permanent re-opening of the Straits. It would be possible with the ships left behind at the entrance, and with those in Egypt, to give the necessary support to the military operations, so that at the worst the army would only have to do, after you had got through, what they will have to do anyhow if your telegram 256[1] is accepted. While on the other hand the probability is that your getting through would decide everything in our favour. Further, once through the Dardanelles, the current would be with you in any return attack on the forts,

[1] The official number given to de Robeck's telegram of 22 March 1915, quoted on p. 364.

and the mining danger would be practically over. Therefore danger to your line of communications is not serious or incurable.

What has happened since the 21st to make you alter your intention of renewing the attack as soon as the weather is favourable? We have never contemplated a reckless rush over minefields and past undamaged primary guns. But the original Admiralty instructions and telegram 109[1] prescribed a careful and deliberate method of advance, and I should like to know what are the reasons which in your opinion render this no longer possible, in spite of your new aircraft and improved method of minesweeping. We know the forts are short of ammunition. It is probable they have not got many mines. You should be able to feel your way while at the same time pressing hard.

I cannot understand why as a preliminary step forts like 7 and 8 should not be demolished by heavy gun fire, first at long range and afterwards at short range, now that you have good aeroplane observation.

I wish to hear further from you before any official reply is sent to your 256. You may discuss this telegram with General Hamilton if he is with you, and then telegraph fully. Admiralty will then give their decision.

You must of course understand that this telegram is not an executive order but is sent because it is most important that there should be no misunderstandings at this juncture.

On the morning of March 25, before this appeal reached the Dardanelles, Churchill received a telegram from de Robeck in which the Admiral expressed his willingness 'to resume a vigorous offensive' before the army was ready, but added the proviso that he did not want to have to pass into the Sea of Marmara. Instead, he sought Churchill's approval for three more limited objectives:

Firstly, completely clearing the area in which Squadron must manoeuvre in order to cover the minesweeping vessels operating in Kephez minefield.

Secondly, with assistance of aeroplanes systematic reconnoitring both shores in order to locate and destroy gunfire of howitzers and other concealed guns and carry out indirect attack on Chanak Forts by Queen Elizabeth with aeroplanes spotting.

In Gulf of Xeros French Squadron will endeavour to attack Gallipoli and camps near Bulair with their aircraft, British seaplanes if available attacking Turkish supply depots at Maidos and vessels above Chanak some of which are said to be loaded with mines.

As soon as he received this proposal, Churchill realized that de Robeck was unlikely to reply to his personal telegram of March 24 with anything as ambitious as he had hoped for. He wrote at once to Fisher,

---

[1] The official number given to Churchill's telegram of 15 March 1915, quoted on p. 347.

accepting that it was no longer possible to give orders for anything of much greater magnitude than de Robeck suggested, but clearly hoping that such a limitation would be temporary:

Secret
My dear Fisher,
The Prime Minister seemed disappointed last night that we had not sent de Robeck a definite order to go on with his attack at the first opportunity, and he expressed his agreement with the telegram to that effect wh I drafted yesterday morning. I explained that the gale was rendering all operations impracticable & that nothing wd be lost by a full interchange of views, such as wd be effected by my 'Personal & Secret' of yesterday afternoon.

Mr Balfour also pointed out to me that de Robeck shows that he anticipates getting through if he tries and that his anxiety now is for his communications after he has got through. This anxiety I am convinced is not well grounded. The arrival of 4 or 5 ships in the Marmora decides the issue.

My own feeling is that de Robeck shd try to clear the Kephez minefield and to smash the forts at the narrows, according to our plans, that any question of going further cd only arise after very marked success had been achieved in the above task.

This is not a vy great extension of what he proposed in this telegram, just received: but it means that we have not abandoned our undertaking, or set definite limits to our sea efforts, & that we shall press on methodically but resolutely with it, and hold ourselves free & ready to profit by any success that may be reaped.

Meanwhile the Army will go ahead with their preparations to begin at the earliest moment.

I hope we shall be together in this.

Yours ever
W

The vision of British ships steaming triumphantly across the Sea of Marmara faded. Ships had been lost by striking mines whose presence had been unknown. The minesweeping force of March 18 had proved inadequate. Further minefields lay ahead. Churchill could not ignore these facts. Dropping his sights from the skyline of Constantinople to the lurking hazards of the Kephez minefield, he drew up a detailed memorandum giving his proposals on how to sweep up moored and drifting mines. It was a sign of Churchill's complete determination not to overlook a single possibility that he should have been able, at the moment when his plan for a naval victory was being shattered, to focus his attention upon minute technical details. He hoped that by instructing the Admiral in an aspect of his work he might even then make the

Admiral's task seem less onerous and encourage him to agree to force his way into the Sea of Marmara, despite his doubts.

But Churchill's technical inventiveness came too late, and was in vain. The arguments had turned against a renewal of the naval attack. On March 25 his brother Jack, then on his way from Mudros to Alexandria with Sir Ian Hamilton, wrote in support of de Robeck's cautious attitude:

We are up against a very tough proposition. Since the 18th many people have altered their views. The sailors are now inclined to acknowledge that they cannot get through without the co-operation of troops. Long range fire on forts is no good unless infantry occupy the fort afterwards and maintain themselves there. Stronger mine sweepers are necessary against the current. The aeroplane spotting is very bad & at present does not help very much. Half the targets are concealed and the ships have the greatest difficulty in locating and firing at the mobile guns. The spotters have little experience. . . . Some of the experienced army airmen 'spotters' are prayed for.

De Robeck behaved very well during the 18th. He never showed any anxiety and remained most calm and cheerful until the evening. When it was all over he is reported to have said 'I suppose I am done for'. . . . Saving the men from the Ocean and Irresistible was a wonderful feat. One destroyer came out with 650 men! De R is very popular in the fleet, and there is some fear that he may be superseded. Hamilton considers him a very sound pusher & they are entirely in agreement. H asked me to write privately to you to say that everyone had confidence in him in spite of the 18th. I said I thought it was unnecessary. . . . We call this expedition the last 'Crusade' and shall expect a papal cross for it!!

On March 25 the *Morning Post* published a newspaper report from Constantinople which seemed a clear warning that Turkish weakness might not be long lasting:

During the last fortnight about 150 mines, any amount of ammunition, guns, &c, have been coming through Roumania from Germany. Six weeks ago, when 40 officers arrived en route for the Suez Canal, they brought with them cases and cases full of ammunition, all marked Red Cross; now, however, there is no attempt at concealment; the ammunition comes through quite openly, and there is nothing to prevent the Germans from bringing in even big guns.

Fisher sent Churchill this extract during the morning. Churchill was horrified to learn that Rumania was allowing the Germans to abuse her neutrality in this way, and sent the press-cutting on to Grey. 'The seriousness of this cannot be overstated,' he wrote in a covering letter. 'I think you ought to make a real row. Do try and make them realise what a grave step they are taking.' During the day a military intelligence report from Petrograd confirmed that the Rumanians were allowing their territory to be used for the transit of German weapons, and added that Bulgaria was doing likewise. Churchill wrote again to Grey:

. . . The facts shd surely be investigated in the most stringent manner with the Roumanian & Bulgarian Governments; & we shd say plainly that the forwarding of any war material to Turkey at this juncture wd be regarded as a grave step, & if this is discovered later when the allies enter Cple the impression produced upon the Allied Governments will be vy painful, etc.

They are playing a double game. But now is the time to stop the war material. This is vital.

Grey spoke at once to the Rumanian and Bulgarian Ministers,[1] but to no avail. The Balkan States were no longer so certain that Britain would be able to defeat the Turks. A sense of imminent disaster seemed to threaten even the War Council's unity of purpose, and political loyalties were suddenly at risk. On March 24 Margot Asquith had written to Lloyd George:

Do warn Winston (*DON'T* give me away) to be careful of what he tells Arthur Balfour. I cd feel at lunch yesterday & when he came to tea 2 evenings ago alone with me that Arthur is really au fond *hostile—VERY* hostile. You & Winston don't know AJB as well as I do. That cool grace, easy mind & intellectual courtesy takes the eye off like the 3 card trick. He is a bitter party opponent.

Amid these doubts and suspicions, Kitchener preserved his calm determination to secure a victory over the Turk. On March 30 Hamilton telegraphed to de Robeck to tell him of Kitchener's apparent hopes for a naval victory, and encouraging him to persevere in his attack:

War Office still seems to cherish hope that you may break through without landing troops. Therefore, as regards yourself I think wisest procedure will be to push on systematically though not recklessly in attack on Forts. It is always possible that opposition may suddenly crumple up. If you should succeed be sure to leave light cruisers enough to see me through my military attack in the event of that being after all necessary. If you do not succeed then I think we quite understand one another.

[1] In 1915 the Rumanian Minister in London was Nicolae Mişu (later a Rumanian delegate at the Paris Peace Conference). The Bulgarian Minister was Pantcho Hadji-Mischef.

During 1916 Hamilton was blamed by several naval enthusiasts for influencing de Robeck to delay his attack. He resented this accusation, and on 23 August 1916, on finding the above telegram among his papers, he sent it to Churchill with the note: 'Several times during our conversations I have gathered the impression that you thought that, in some way or another, to some degree or another, I had influenced de Robeck in his abandonment of purely naval attacks upon the Narrows. Roger Keyes and naval forwards generally have seemed to me sometimes inclined to hold the same view. There is no foundation whatsoever for such an impression, and this message of mine cabled to the Admiral on the 30th of March should give the idea its coup de grâce.'

'We are pushing on preparations for land operations,' Kitchener wrote to Churchill on March 25. 'In the meantime I hope the navy will continue to engage the forts as vigorously as possible and thus induce the Turks to expend their ammunition.' Harcourt was another Minister who had not been deterred by the shadow of defeat. On March 25 he circulated a memorandum to his colleagues entitled 'The Spoils', in which he advocated the annexation of Mesopotamia as 'an outlet for Indian immigration', and suggested offering the Holy Places as a mandate to the United States.

During March 24 Churchill turned his mind away from the Dardanelles, drafting a lengthy scheme for the project which had so excited him two months before, the capture of the German island of Borkum. The attack on Borkum, he wrote, could begin 'as soon as the weather is favourable after May 15th'. Success could lead to Holland joining the Allies. Berlin could be threatened by troops landing from the North Sea, and marching across Germany. On March 25 Fisher spent some time with Churchill discussing this memorandum, and elaborating these plans as if the Dardanelles were dead. On the morning of March 26 Churchill, who had been feeling ill the day before, stayed in bed. Among his morning's correspondence was a cheerful note from Fisher: 'I hope you'll stop in bed! You have got Influenza and *won't admit it* & why I haven't caught it from you is just a wonder! Was I two hours with you yesterday? I shall d—n Borkum if I get Influenza!'

No reply had reached London from de Robeck by the morning of March 26. That morning a grave alarm much nearer Britain threatened to bring the Dardanelles enterprise to an abrupt end. The British Consul-General in Rotterdam, Ernest Maxse,[1] telegraphed to the Foreign Office just before noon that Dutch troops had been ordered to

[1] Ernest George Berkeley Maxse, 1863–1943. Vice-Consul, Algiers, 1890, 1891. Consul-General in Holland and Admiralty Convoy Officer at Rotterdam, 1914–19.

rejoin their regiments along the German frontier: 'General impression among merchant classes seems that Germany is trying to force Holland to declare for or against her. German General Staff is believed to be pressing for violent solution.' An invasion of Holland seemed imminent. That afternoon Churchill wrote to Grey and Kitchener:

In this matter, should it come to anything, time is vital. The success of the German coup wd depend on swallowing Holland or nearly all of it before anyone was alive to the danger; so that they might have another skin to sell instead of merely another army to fight.

It appears to me that FO shd without delay speak to the French & thereafter to the Dutch on the basis of British military help, & that WO shd have all its plans ready for the eventuality. We want to be able to tell Holland that if she is attacked or goes to war, we will put immediately (say) half Sir J. French's army plus whatever Ld K can assign from England at her disposal, & that they can arrive at certain points by certain dates. This means the French must agree to send some of Joffre's reserve army to fill our places on the northern flank. . . .

The vital point to realise is this—that if the Germans can overrun Holland, very quickly, they will have gained a great advantage; whereas if they are held up at or near the frontiers, they will be ruined.

There is no need for action now—only the most minute preparations. The blow may come very quickly if it comes at all.

I am having the naval aspect thoroughly examined.

Fisher and Churchill discussed the naval aspect together. Any substantial naval assistance to Holland could only be given if the Dardanelles Fleet, already weakened by its losses of March 18, were further depleted. The need to help Holland overrode all urgency for the defeat of Turkey. At two o'clock that afternoon Fisher wrote to Churchill:

The following points emerge from a first glance at the Dutch situation:—
1. The English Troops will land at Hook of Holland as the Germans can so easily cut the railway from Flushing & isolate it.
2. That subject to Dutch advice—Terschelling will be our submarine & Destroyer base as being the nearest suitable position to the German Frontier out of range of German guns.
3. That our 3 Monitors (proposed to be stopped at Malta) would be of inestimable value in the Zuyder Zee.
4. That directly Bethell's men return from leave his squadron should go to the Swin to practise gunnery ready for bombarding Zeebrugge &c—
5. That the Grand Fleet will come from Scapa Flow to a . . . [illegible] . . . intercepting German High Sea Fleet.

6. That even now at the 11th hour it would be a wise project for the British Army (re-inforced) to advance along the Belgian Coast to the Dutch Frontier and so close Antwerp.

7. That the Germans can over-run all Holland up to the inundations in a few hours by means of the enormous mass of motors they possess and of which Mr Deterding told me a little time ago as being massed along the Dutch frontier with large stores of Petrol at defended depôts.

An hour after receiving Fisher's note, Churchill was handed de Robeck's answer to his personal telegram. The Dutch danger already jeopardized any future naval initiative at the Dardanelles. De Robeck's telegram effectively destroyed it:

I do not hold check on the 18th March decisive but having met General Hamilton on the 22nd March and heard his proposals I now consider a combined operation essential to obtain great results and object of campaign. . . .

To attack Narrows now with Fleet would be a mistake as it would jeopardise the execution of a better and bigger scheme. . . .

Full appreciation of the situation in the Dardanelles is being prepared and will be telegraphed.

Churchill awaited de Robeck's full appreciation. At three the next morning Fisher sent Churchill his further thoughts on the Dutch situation:

It is awful our having at this juncture to send Destroyers and submarines to the Dardanelles and we want Inflexible & Queen Elizabeth in the North Sea. . . .

There's no doubt the moment is most opportune for Germany to seize Holland when they *now* have nearly a million of German soldiers to dispose of and it is an immense asset the acquiring of such a big whack of fresh territory untouched by war and full of war resources and more rich territory to bargain when peace comes!

De Robeck's full reply reached the Admiralty shortly before dawn on March 27. It left no doubt about his views, for he set out the detailed reasons for opposing further naval action without full military support:

. . . The original approved plan for forcing the Dardanelles by ships was drawn up on the assumption that gunfire alone was capable of destroying forts. This assumption has been conclusively proved to be wrong when applied to the attacking of open forts by high velocity guns; for instance

Fort 3 has been frequently bombarded at distant and close ranges, the damage caused is possibly one gun disabled. Shells which hit either expended their destructive power uselessly on the parapet or destroyed some unimportant building in the background of the fort; to obtain direct hits on each gun has been found impracticable even at ranges of 700 to 800 yards as was attempted in the case of forts 3 and 6. One gun in fort 4 was found loaded and fit for service on 26th February although the fort had been heavily bombarded for two days at long range and at short range.

The utmost that can be expected of ships is to dominate the forts to such an extent that gun crews cannot fight the guns; any more permanent disablement could only be carried out with an excessive expenditure of ammunition at point blank range. . . . Conclusions drawn from the attack on the cupola forts at Antwerp by heavy howitzers are quite misleading when applied to the case described above.

To engage forts 7 and 8 at close range entails ships coming under fire of forts at the Narrows, these have therefore to be silenced with consequent heavy expenditure of ammunition which cannot be spared. Further wear of the old guns is causing me some anxiety; on the 18th there were several premature bursts of cannon shell and guns were out of action from time to time.

It would be the worst policy to carry out bombardment which could not be brought to a decisive result. To destroy forts therefore it is necessary to land demolishing parties. To cover these parties at the Narrows is a task General Hamilton is not prepared to undertake and I fully concur in his view. To carry the demolition out by surprise is impracticable.

The mine menace being even greater than anticipated the number of torpedo tubes, by all reports, having been added to, combined with the fact that they cannot be destroyed, materially increases the difficulties of clearing passage for the Fleet which has to be carried out while the forts are kept silenced by gunfire.

The result of Naval action alone might in my opinion be a brilliant success or quite indecisive. Success depends largely on the effect that the appearance of the Fleet off Constantinople would produce on the Turkish army which appears to control the situation in Turkey at present and which is itself dominated by the Germans, but if the Turkish army is undismayed by the advent of the Fleet into the Sea of Marmora and the Straits are closed behind it the length of time which ships can operate . . . and maintain themselves in that Sea depends almost entirely on the number of Colliers and ammunition which can accompany the Fleet and as the passage will be contested the percentage of large unprotected ships which can be expected to get through is small. The passage of supply ships for the Fleet through the Dardanelles with the forts still intact is a problem to which I can see no practical solution. In such a case it would be vital for the Army to occupy the Peninsula which would open the Strait as guns on Asiatic side can be dominated from the European shore sufficiently to permit ships to pass through.

The landing of an army of the size contemplated in the face of strenuous opposition is in my opinion an operation requiring the assistance of all Naval forces available. A landing at Bulair would not necessarily cause Turks to abandon Peninsula and there could be no two opinions that a Fleet intact outside the Dardanelles can do this better than the remains of a Fleet inside with little ammunition.

With Gallipoli Peninsula held by our Army and Squadron through Dardanelles our success would be assured. The delay possibly of a fortnight will allow co-operation which would really prove factor that will reduce length of time necessary to complete the campaign in Sea of Marmora and occupy Constantinople.

Churchill did not oppose the Admiral's measured decision. 'I had hoped that it would have been possible to achieve the result according to original plan without involving the Army,' he telegraphed that morning, 'but the reasons you give make it clear that a combined operation is now indispensable. . . . All your proposals will therefore be approved.' De Robeck waited for Hamilton and his army to return from Egypt. On its return he acted solely as its subordinate. The responsibility for all subsequent operations fell upon Hamilton and Kitchener. Every decision for action subsequently taken at Gallipoli was taken at the War Office or by Hamilton. During the military action which Kitchener planned for April, and during the subsequent nine months of fighting, the Navy never attempted either to sweep the Kephez minefield or to break through the Narrows into the Sea of Marmara.

Churchill continued to argue that a second naval attack could have been successful, and that de Robeck could have entered the Sea of Marmara with decisive results before the Army was ready to land. 'It still seems to me,' he told the Dardanelles Commissioners in 1916, 'that the War Council having deliberately decided on a purely naval attack, the Admiralty having undertaken to make the attempt, the heavy losses having been fully foreseen and provided for, we ought to have put the matter to the supreme test and reached an absolute decision one way or the other.' But Churchill's willingness to take risks, although shared in this instance by Asquith, was of no avail against the professional caution of his advisers, to whose skills and experience he felt he must defer. The apparent German threat to Holland on March 26 gave de Robeck's telegram an added strength. When Hankey saw Churchill on the evening of March 26, he found him, as he recorded in his diary, 'very depressed' about the Dardanelles and 'very anxious about possibility of German attack on Holland'. On March 27 Hankey sent Churchill his suggestions for 'immediate action, if Germany violates Dutch territory', beginning with the blocking and mining of the Scheldt. 'Should the Monitors on the way to the Dardanelles be recalled?' Hankey asked. Churchill realized the gravity of the problem. That day he wrote a memorandum setting out the reasons which he believed could indeed lead Germany to invade Holland; the principal of these being their desire to control 'the coveted mouths of the Rhine and the Scheldt'. That night Fisher saw Churchill again to discuss in greater detail what naval action Britain should take if she became Holland's ally: where to land and how to strike. Both Churchill and Fisher knew that to gain advantage over Germany as a result of a German attack on Holland was an opportunity compared with which the Dardanelles hardly signified. On the morning of March 28 Fisher wrote to Churchill, stressing that help to Holland would be severely hampered if the Dardanelles Fleet remained at its existing strength:

First Lord,

I noticed some indications in the 'secret papers' (after seeing you last night) that something big may be brewing after March 29th, and it may well be very serious when taken in conjunction with the recent very sudden and quite unexpected hostile German attitude towards Holland. Then there is the appointment of Kuhlmann[1] to the Hague as German Minister; also the reported intention of the German General Staff to press for an immediate termination of Dutch neutrality; then the deliberate and apparently premeditated seizure of five Dutch ships in the last few days, and, above all, the sinking of the Dutch ship Medea when laden only with oranges and her Dutch nationality proved by her papers to be undoubted; and also, as you have so clearly pointed out in your own paper (read by Lord Kitchener and Sir E. Grey last evening), all favours your view that immense benefit will accrue to Germany by Holland being forced out of her neutrality at this special moment, when Germany has a great number of troops available— and can strike at once and gets five-sixths of Holland and also Antwerp and the Scheldt.

All this naturally re-acts on the Dardanelles business. We have, or shall have, sixteen Destroyers there that are very badly wanted indeed at home; the three Monitors have gone: the Reliance (new repair ship); so also the Adamant and three submarines, besides the Australian new submarine detained out there; also all sorts of home resources largely drawn on—eg

---

[1] Richard von Kühlmann, 1873–1949. Entered the Berlin Foreign Office, 1893. Counsellor of the German Embassy in London, 1908–14. On missions to Turkey and Scandinavia, 1915–17. Secretary of State for Foreign Affairs, 1917–18. An advocate of a negotiated peace, he tried to arrange for negotiations with Sir William Tyrrell in Holland in the summer of 1918, and was dismissed by the Kaiser.

Samson and his aircraft; nets; mine sweepers, etc, etc; and finally, the chief anxiety of all—the large expenditure of big gun ammunition, and, as pointed out by de Robeck, the serious anxiety as to the continuing efficiency of the big guns in the old ships. They will be certainly all worn out. The Inflexible hors de combat and about to be towed to Malta. The Elizabeth with only one engine (and so always a cause of anxiety) the Ocean and Irresistible sunk, and Lord Nelson and Agamemnon requiring repair.

If the Germans decide (as well they may)—influenced largely no doubt by our having so large a force away from the decisive theatre—on some big thing at home, there is (you must admit) much cause for anxiety, especially with the German and Austrian submarine menace to the yet unlanded troops and our Dardanelles fleet.

What is Ian Hamilton's report as to probable success? Admiral de Robeck does not look forward to disabling the Turkish guns.

Is the capture of the Gallipoli Peninsula going to be a siege? We should have the military opinion on this.

Is Ian Hamilton assured of the sufficiency of his force?

We know Admiral de Robeck to be a brave man, and he talks assuredly; but his assurance is really based on military co-operation and especially on the demolition of all the guns, thus assuring him of his safe communication with the sea and safe passage of his storeships, colliers and ammunition supplies. . . .

Fisher ended his letter with a postscript: 'I am not blind to the political necessity of going forward with the task, but before going further forward let the whole situation be so fully examined that success is assured while safety in the decisive theatre is not compromised.' Churchill realized that even if he could persuade Fisher not to weaken de Robeck's fleet, he would have to fight for any further reinforcements which it would need for a renewed attack, or even to remain up to its existing strength.

The Dutch alarm proved false. But for Fisher it emphasized the need to guard against allowing reinforcements to go to the Dardanelles at the expense of naval strength in the North Sea. He had become convinced that in an emergency, the Grand Fleet would be unable to take decisive action if the Dardanelles absorbed any more of the naval surplus, or took up any new construction.

The attack of March 18 had failed to achieve its objective. Yet while preparing his evidence for the Dardanelles Commission a year and a half later, Hankey felt it necessary to mention what he believed were the positive results achieved. The Turks, he wrote in his 'notes for evidence' of 31 August 1916, by having to divert troops from the Caucasus to Gallipoli, were forced to abandon their offensive against the

Russians planned for April. The Bulgarians hesitated to commit them-selves to Germany, so that, 'if it did nothing else', Hankey wrote, 'the naval attack . . . gained a breathing space for Serbia for the great ordeal to come'. Above all, in his opinion, the moral effect on Russia was con-siderable. Russian mistrust of the Allies, 'owing to their failure to make progress in the Western theatre', was removed, and the danger of Russia making a separate peace with Germany was averted.

The enterprise to which Churchill had committed so much of his energy and on which he had come to base so many of his hopes, was clearly at an end. Without any massive naval disaster, without any of the harsh slaughter which had become common on the western front, without any conclusive sign that a naval victory was impossible, he had to abandon the most glittering opportunity of his life. He continued to advocate the need to defeat Turkey; he pressed for military action on the Gallipoli Peninsula at the earliest opportunity and with the maxi-mum force. But from the moment that military preparations began, the power to act passed from Churchill's hands. As Secretary of State for War, Kitchener controlled all military initiatives at the Dardanelles.

12
25 April 1915:
The Gallipoli Landings

NO longer at the centre of planning, Churchill was depressed. In the weeks after March 27 he became increasingly frustrated at not knowing what plans were being made. Asquith summoned no War Council to discuss the advisability of a full-scale military attack at Gallipoli; nor were senior ministers given an opportunity of arguing for or against it. 'It did not rest with me to convene a War Council,' Churchill explained in a letter to Lord Cromer,[1] on 5 October 1916; 'nor was I responsible for the conduct of military operations. But I was of course vy glad that Lord Kitchener had decided to use the army; & had the matter been discussed at a War Council, I sh'd no doubt have supported him on the general policy.' Kitchener was zealous in guarding the secrets of his activities, and the projects which were evolved for landing men upon the Gallipoli Peninsula were not sent for Churchill's scrutiny. Churchill had the responsibility of getting the men on shore. But where they landed, and what they did once they had landed, was the concern of the War Office. Few of the decisions associated with the military landings on Gallipoli were shown to him for comment or approval. But Churchill's increasing remoteness from the planning of the Gallipoli landing did not cause him to lose faith in its outcome; he remained a vociferous and optimistic advocate of pressing the attack on Turkey to a conclusion.

At the War Office Kitchener worked to perfect his plans for the military assault, believing, as Churchill did, that the enterprise was a necessary one, and that it would succeed. Fisher continued to write to

[1] Evelyn Baring, 1841–1917. Entered Army, 1858. Private Secretary to Viceroy of India, 1872–6. British Agent and Consul-General, Egypt, 1833–1907. Created Baron Cromer, 1899; Earl, 1901. Chairman of the Dardanelles Commission, 1916–17. He died on 29 January 1917, before the Commission had completed its work.

Churchill about the now restricted operations. Sometimes his letters were disturbingly contradictory. On April 2 he wrote with apparent enthusiasm: 'Let us hope that the Dardanelles will be passed & over by the desired date to your honour & glory and that these d—d Greeks will be jolly well sold by the Bulgarians being first in & so getting *Salonika* & *Kavalla* and *Macedonia generally* as their reward! *I EARNESTLY HOPE THIS MAY RESULT!* Had the Greeks come in all would have been well without doubt!' But Fisher ended his letter with a stern warning:

> *We cant send another rope yarn even to de Robeck.* WE HAVE GONE TO *THE VERY LIMIT!* And so they must not hustle and should be distinctly & most emphatically told that no further re-inforcements of the Fleet can be looked for! *A failure or check in the Dardanelles would be nothing. A failure in the North Sea would be RUIN!* but I dont wish to be pessimistic! . . .

On the same day Fisher wrote tersely to Jellicoe: 'Forgive haste and pencil. *This Dardanelles entirely exhausts my time.*' But with the Navy now acting as Kitchener's landing instrument, its activities were determined, not by Admiralty policy but by War Office requirements. Churchill continued to press de Robeck for information, and to stimulate him to co-operate with Hamilton. 'Please telegraph fully what preparations are being made to land the army,' he asked on April 2, 'and give a clear account of what is proposed. Report also progress of your own preparations for minesweeping.' De Robeck replied on the following day that he could not arrange his final plans until Hamilton returned from Egypt some time after April 7, but that preparations were going well:

> Briefly plan aims at decisive and overwhelming attack on the Narrows, in which Navy and Army can mutually assist each other to the utmost, the first duty of the Navy being to cover landing and advance of Army; second, to attack the Narrows in conjunction with the Army. General Hamilton and I have refrained from communicating by telegraph any details on account of danger of leakage. . . .
>
> As regards Naval preparations our minesweeping service is well organised with Naval ratings in all trawlers now here. Our nets here are nearly ready which with those being sent will be placed across the Dardanelles south of Suandere River before attack commences. This should largely defeat attack by drifting mines on battleships when bombarding inside Straits. Present intention is to use Queen Elizabeth for indirect fire from Gabatepe with observers on shore when Army is landed. . . .
>
> Present delay has been most beneficial: many guns required coppering removed and other defects made good. Expect all ships to be ready by 14th.

Enemy not active, reconnaissance pointing to his placing more guns to protect minefields. If so, satisfactory as they are probably withdrawn from hills towards entrance. Aerodrome at Tenedos now in excellent order, and, with good machines that have arrived, our knowledge of enemy's dispositions should be much improved.

De Robeck ended his telegram with a personal appeal to Churchill to help him obtain more officers. He had already asked Fisher for them, but without success. 'Matter is urgent and time passes,' he stressed.

A telegram from de Robeck on April 4 gave details of the method by which the Admiral proposed to help the troops to land. But he could not develop these plans in detail because, as he explained to Churchill, 'General Hamilton has not informed me yet whether the covering force will land at night and attempt a surprise or by day and obtain maximum assistance from gun fire of Fleet.' Nevertheless, despite his lack of information, de Robeck did everything possible to plan for either a day or night landing. He also reported that minesweeping preparations were making good progress, that seventeen trawlers were available each commanded by a naval officer, that sixteen destroyers were being fitted with minesweeping apparatus and that 'all are practised daily and sweep inside Dardanelles to keep clear area in which ships will manoeuvre primarily'. De Robeck again asked for more personnel. 'Supply of Officers is chief difficulty,' he telegraphed. Churchill supported his request, but Fisher refused to allow further naval personnel to be sent to the Dardanelles, even at de Robeck's repeated request.

Asquith continued to believe in the importance of persevering at the Dardanelles. At Churchill's request, he had drafted a strong telegram to both the French and Russian Governments on April 3, informing them that 'the attack by the allied forces on the Dardanelles will be pressed to a decision' and asking them to agree to a further British request for Greek co-operation. Asquith suggested to the French and Russians that the Greeks should be told that 'unless such co-operation is offered now, there will be little or no opportunity left for Greece to advance claims for compensation in the Smyrna region at the end of the war'. Churchill was delighted at Asquith's forceful attitude. But few of his other colleagues shared it.

Churchill was not always easy to work with. On April 5 he quarrelled with Lloyd George. Frances Stevenson recorded the quarrel in her diary three days later, referring to Lloyd George as C, for Chancellor:

... C was discussing the drink question with Churchill, & Samuel & Montagu were also present. Churchill put on the grand air, and announced that he was not going to be influenced by the King, and refused to give up his liquor—he thought the whole thing absurd. C was annoyed, but went on to explain a point that had been brought up. The next minute Churchill interrupted again. 'I don't see . . .' he was beginning, but C broke in sharply:—

'You will see the point,' he rapped out, 'when you begin to understand that conversation is not a monologue!'

Churchill went very red, but did not reply, & C soon felt rather ashamed of having taken him up so sharply, especially in front of the other two minions.

Later that evening Lloyd George wrote to heal the breach:

Dear Winston,

I am sorry that in our conversation this afternoon I got angry & said what I ought not to have allowed myself to say.

I was very rattled altogether after a most disappointing interview with K. That is my only excuse but it is an inadequate one at best.

I am altogether disappointed at the way we are facing—or rather not facing our difficulties.

Pray accept my apology.

Yours ever
D. Lloyd George

Churchill was relieved and moved, replying at once:

My dear David,

It was *I* who was churlish & difficult.

It is vy kind indeed of you to write as you do.

I admire & value intensely the contribution of energy, courage & resolve wh you are making to the progress of our affairs at their crisis. I share your anxieties, & am not at all removed in thought from your main policy.

Yours always
W

'The two are very fond of each other I believe,' Frances Stevenson noted in her diary.

Early in April Fisher's increasingly erratic behaviour became a problem for Churchill, for Fisher seemed to forget that the Narrows were no longer to be forced without the Army having first landed on the Peninsula and begun its advance towards the high ground overlooking the Narrows, and that de Robeck's task was initially limited to helping the Army get ashore. On April 4 Fisher tried to agitate Jellicoe's mind about the Dardanelles, hoping that Jellicoe would transmit his worries to Churchill: 'I have time for little else now but increasing anxiety over the Dardanelles situation,' he wrote. 'I know so very little of de Robeck and Ian Hamilton that I am not able to rely on their judgement, and Keyes is very shallow and has not shined so far! No good purpose would be served by my resigning. My opinions are known.' Churchill had several times assured Jellicoe that the Grand Fleet would not be depleted because of the Dardanelles. He did not want to enter into a time-wasting dispute with the Commander-in-Chief. But on April 5, disturbed by the pressure Fisher was applying, he drafted a 'Secret and personal' answer to Fisher's complaints:

My dear Jellicoe,
Our main attack on the Dardanelles should take place about the middle of this month. If this is successful the Queen Elizabeth will be able to return home at once. . . .
I have always done my best to strengthen your Fleet in every way, & have taken a great deal of trouble during the last 3 months to secure you the Australia, to collect as many powerful armoured cruisers as possible for you, & to equip you with light cruisers of both 'Town' and 'Arethusa' classes. Your position is now a very strong one, far stronger than at the beginning of the war. . . .

Churchill was vexed by what he believed to be unnecessary alarms: 'I am so great an admirer of the skill & care with which you handle the immense Fleet now under your command,' he continued, 'and of the efficiency of yr work in every branch, that I cannot help feeling sorry when I see the Admiralty records filling up with a long series of letters of complaint full of pessimism & alarms for which there is no warrant in the circumstances.' But on reflection, Churchill decided not to send this letter, realizing that Fisher, not Jellicoe, was the real source of the growing dissatisfaction.[1] On April 5 Fisher complained once more to Churchill about his absorption with the Dardanelles, repeating his belief that the Germans were about to occupy Holland, and demanding a British force which would forestall them. 'We ought to have every detail organized to move in a moment . . .' he wrote. 'You are just simply eaten

---

[1] Churchill was never able to develop friendly relations with Jellicoe. Their mutual reservations inhibited frank exchanges of views on naval strategy. There is an example of Churchill's attitude in a note about naval air policy which he wrote on 24 June 1914: 'Jellicoe—as usual —laborious in demands of all kinds for men and money. Sterile in larger administrative proposals and real reforms.' But to Lady Jellicoe, on 1 August 1914, Churchill was able to write: 'We have absolute confidence in his genius and devotion. We shall back him through thick & thin. Thank God we have him at hand.'

up with the Dardanelles and cant think of anything else! D—n the Dardanelles! They'll be our grave!'

On April 6 Asquith, Churchill and Kitchener met at 10 Downing Street. Hankey, who was present, took a note of their discussion, which he described as 'an informal meeting of the War Council'. Kitchener read out extracts from the telegrams he had received from Hamilton, who said he had not yet received a complete plan of attack. Churchill read out de Robeck's report, telling in detail what had happened on March 18, and asked that the military landings 'should be pressed home vigorously'. Kitchener agreed that the landings would have to be made. When Hankey said that 'the difficulty would be to land the troops at all' because of opposition from howitzers in the many ravines on the Gallipoli Peninsula, Churchill disagreed. Hankey reported in the minutes that Churchill 'anticipated no difficulty in effecting a landing'. After some further discussion, which Hankey did not record, the meeting concluded that the military landings were to take place as soon as Hamilton was ready. On this point, Churchill and Kitchener were in agreement. But they were unable to work in harmony for long. On that same day yet another dispute threw them against each other. Churchill had on several occasions pressed Kitchener for details about ammunition supplies, so that he could adjust his naval requirements accordingly. But as he wrote to him after their meeting at 10 Downing Street:

My dear Kitchener,
On the 16th of February the Admiralty wrote an official letter to the WO asking for information about the anticipated deliveries of Trotyl & picric acid month by month to the end of December next as compared with naval & military requirements. An early reply was asked for on the 1st & 18th of March, & again on the 2nd of April. Up to the present no answer has been given us.
I am afraid I must ask you for this information without wh it is impossible to arrange about the ammunition of the Fleet, the supply of mines, bombs, explosive sweeps etc.

Churchill did not relish these disputes. To avoid causing unnecessary offence he deleted the four concluding paragraphs of his letter, which gave a better indication of his feelings:

I cannot possibly accept the responsibility while remaining in ignorance on a vital matter like this.

It adds enormously to the labour of official work when reasonable & necessary inquiries by one department are not taken any notice of by the others.

I will have to ask at the Cabinet tomorrow for a decision whether I shd be informed of the exact state of supplies of army ammunition & explosives.

I am vy sorry indeed to trouble you personally; but it is really not my fault.

Churchill and Kitchener bore between them the full responsibility for Britain's military, naval and aerial effort. Churchill was aware of the extent to which a quarrel between them could disrupt the brittle fabric of essential co-operation. On April 7, after angry words had been spoken at the Cabinet table about munition deficiencies, he sent an immediate apology. 'I am distressed to have got into a dispute with you this morning,' Churchill wrote. 'It was far from my intention to do so, & I am vy sorry I allowed myself to become angry and hope you will dismiss from your mind anything wh I may have said unjustly.' In his postscript Churchill added: 'This is a vy anxious time & we all have our worries.'

Churchill became absorbed in the technical problems which would face de Robeck when he helped the troops to get ashore. So much had gone wrong during the naval attack; the unexpected had so disrupted the plans for a swift success that nothing could be taken for granted. On April 6 Churchill asked de Robeck what arrangements were being made to protect ships from floating mines, and suggested the use of nets suspended from frames, or 'Mine-Bumpers' as he called them. He also asked the Admiral whether he had considered using a smoke-screen 'to cover landings, or blanket off particular portions of the defence either from inside or outside the Straits?' Churchill was reduced to supervising plans for a naval operation that was to be a subsidiary one. If the Navy's part in the landings were badly done, it could prove disastrous to the whole campaign. But if well done, it might be no more than a routine operation before a swift and decisive land victory.

The idea of a new land campaign was causing unease in London. 'Hankey has just been in,' Asquith wrote to Venetia Stanley on April 7, 'very anxious about the Dardanelles, which he says Robertson (Chief of French's staff) describes as the stiffest operation anyone cd undertake. Now that things look better with Italy & Roumania, Hankey strongly urges postponement—lest a check there shd set back the whole situation. There is a great deal of force in this: what do you think?' Also on April 7, the Second, Third and Fourth Sea Lords, Sir Frederick Hamilton, Captain Lambert and Rear-Admiral Tudor, who were not members of the Admiralty War Group, and therefore took no part in policy discussions about the Dardanelles, expressed their collective doubts about the enterprise in a memorandum to Fisher. In one paragraph of his reply Fisher put forward the strongest possible argument in favour of continuing with the combined military and naval action. 'The Dardanelles operation,' he wrote, 'is undoubtedly one, the political result of which, if successful, will be worth some sacrifice in materiel and personnel; it will certainly shorten the period of the war by bringing in fresh Allies in the Eastern theatre, and will break the back of the German–Turkish alliance, besides opening up the Black Sea.' But three paragraphs later Fisher partly endorsed the Sea Lords' unease about sending de Robeck further reinforcements:

I am of opinion at the present time that our supremacy is secure in Home Waters and that the forces detached are not such as to prejudice a decisive result should the High Sea Fleet come out to battle. But at the same time I consider that we have reached the absolute limit, and that we must stand or fall by the issue, for we can send out no more help of any kind. I have expressed this view very clearly to the First Lord, and should there at a later period be any disposition on the part of the Cabinet to overrule me on this point, I shall request my Naval colleagues to give their support in upholding my view. . . .

I am satisfied with the position at present and in the near future, but shall of course, be more satisfied when we get the battleships back from the Dardanelles.

Churchill believed that if the Gallipoli landings were to be properly supported, de Robeck's requests must be accepted. De Robeck was at the Dardanelles and it was he who could see clearly what was needed. The Army had to be put ashore safely. Whatever broad strategic problems Fisher might worry about, his also was the task to ensure that this specific operation did not fail through lack of effective support. When Fisher tried to impose restrictions upon de Robeck's use of the *Queen Elizabeth*, the *Agamemnon* and the *Lord Nelson*, Churchill rejected Fisher's demands, arguing that these battleships had to support the Army when it landed, as de Robeck had planned.

Fisher's protests were determined by his calculation of the number of ships and men which could be spared from action outside what was for him the 'decisive theatre', the North Sea. He had no doubts that de

Robeck would be able successfully to escort the troops to their landing beaches. A more comprehensive opposition came from Hankey, whose enthusiasm for the Dardanelles had evaporated, and who was busy trying to create an effective opposition. On April 8 he persuaded Captain Richmond to suggest to Fisher that a sudden attack on Haifa and Beirut would be a more sensible operation than to continue at the Dardanelles. Like Hankey, Richmond no longer believed that the Dardanelles could be a quick success. He feared that further setbacks there would discourage Italy from joining the Allies. That same day he sent Fisher a formal proposal 'to abandon the Dardanelles expd' and advocating an attack by eighty thousand troops elsewhere in Turkey: 'The place I would suggest is Haifa, to be followed by the capture of Damascus. . . . Italy's decision would then be placed beyond all shadow of doubt and the Dardanelles could be dealt with after the Turkish Syrian army had been starved or destroyed.' Fisher was impressed by Richmond's suggestion: he put it to Churchill, who rejected it. On the same day, April 8, Hankey tried another line of approach to make his dissent. Finding Balfour sceptical about the chances of a military attack on the Dardanelles, he persuaded him to dictate a letter to Churchill expressing their common doubts. In his letter to Churchill, Balfour made no reference to Hankey's promptings:

. . . As you know, I cannot help being very anxious about the fate of any military attempt upon the Peninsula. Nobody was so keen as myself upon forcing the Straits as long as there seemed a reasonable prospect of doing it by means of the fleet alone—even though the operation might cost us a few antiquated battleships. But a military attack upon a position so inherently difficult, and so carefully prepared, is a different proposition: and, if it fails, we shall not only have to suffer considerably in men, and still more in prestige, but we may upset our whole diplomacy in the Near East, which, at the present moment, seems to promise so favourably.

If you can get your submarines through, we shall evidently be able to blockade the 70,000 Turks now massed in the Peninsula. They will not be able to get supplies by sea and the only road can be absolutely denied them by ships in the Gulf of Xeros. If, and when, an arrangement could be come to with Bulgaria, quite a small force would lock up the whole of the Turkish garrison until they surrender from starvation or panic; and in the meanwhile, without at all abandoning our scheme, it would, I should have thought, be worth considering whether we should not delay its completion till we have destroyed the Turkish Army in Syria. Compare Napoleon in 1805![1]

---

[1] In 1805 Napoleon had defeated the Austrians at Ulm (October), before fighting, and defeating, the Russians at Austerlitz (December).

Churchill was not impressed by this argument for delay. He had always accepted that the attack might have to be postponed if Italy had still not decided to join the Allied Powers. But, as he pointed out to Balfour when he replied on the same day, it was expected that Italy would make her decision by April 14 and that therefore the attack could take place on the first favourable day after that. Another reason for speed, he told Balfour, was the 'fatal danger' that German submarines might soon reach the Aegean, where so far the British ships had been able to operate without any naval opposition. Churchill ended his letter:

You must not be unduly apprehensive of the military operation. The soldiers think they can do it, & it was their influence that persuaded the Adl to delay the renewal of his attack till their preparations were completed. The military attack is in addition to, & not in substitution for, or derogation from, the naval attack. Both attacks mutually aid each other; & either by succeeding wd be decisive.

It seems vy difficult to believe that with the naval artillery support wh can be brought to bear upon the flank & rear of every position from both sides of the Peninsula the army will not be able to advance comfortably at least as far as the Suandere River, & maintain themselves there indefinitely. This in itself cd be a success, & wd greatly aid the naval attack upon the narrows. A 15″ howitzer will be there by the 20th to bombard the forts from a stable platform.

No other operation in this part of the world cd ever cloak the defeat of abandoning the effort against the Dlles. I think there is nothing for it but to go through with the business, & I do not at all regret that this shd be so. No one can count with certainty upon the issue of a battle. But here we have the chances in our favour, & play for vital gains with non-vital stakes.

Churchill felt cause for optimism; among the telegrams that reached him on April 8 was one from de Robeck which gave increased hope for the naval part of the enterprise:

. . . I do not anticipate difficulties in protecting ships against mines floating on the surface; picket-boats can, and did on the 18th March, deal with these effectually, they will also keep special watch for mines with slight negative buoyancy suspended from floats.

Mines drifting below surface are the chief dangers, and against these I must rely upon the tunny nets and indicator nets with reduced mesh; these will be laid across Straits above area in which ships will manoeuvre to attack forts in the Narrows and defences of Kephez minefield. Malta is despatching an additional 2 miles of tunny nets which have a depth of 30 feet. There will be enough nets to completely span Straits.

De Robeck assumed that the military operation would go well enough for him to get into the Sea of Marmara. 'While Fleet advances through Narrows,' he telegraphed confidently, 'ships fitted with mine bumpers and net defences against torpedoes will lead.' Churchill passed on this encouraging news to Asquith, who in turn informed the King. It was a measure of the continuing expectations that on that same day Asquith set up a committee whose instructions were 'to consider the nature of British desiderata in Turkey-in-Asia in the event of a successful conclusion of the war'. Under the Chairmanship of a former British Ambassador to Austria-Hungary, Sir Maurice de Bunsen,[1] the Committee was composed of Sir Henry Jackson, Sir Mark Sykes, Sir Hubert Llewellyn Smith,[2] Sir Thomas Holderness[3] and Major-General Callwell, with Hankey as secretary. The underlying assumption of its work was that Turkey would be defeated. Churchill was no longer concerned with territorial speculation. The setback of March 18 had impressed on him the need to concentrate upon the technical problems of the operation. Both he and Fisher hoped to take advantage of the first military successes at Gallipoli to land a 15-inch howitzer which could then bombard the forts at Chanak from a fixed and stable point on the Peninsula. Sir John French was reluctant to see such an important weapon removed from his control. On April 8 Churchill approached Kitchener for support:

Secret
My dear Kitchener,
    If the military attack is checked at the Killid Bahr position, sites can be found for the 15-inch howitzer which will enable the forts at the Narrows to

[1] Maurice William Ernest de Bunsen, 1852–1932. Entered the Diplomatic Service, 1877. Secretary of Embassy at Constantinople, 1897–1902. Knighted, 1905. Ambassador, Vienna, 1913–14. Created Baronet, 1919.

[2] Hubert Llewellyn Smith, 1864–1945. Entered the Board of Trade as First Commissioner of Labour, 1893. Permanent Secretary at the Board of Trade, 1907–19. Knighted, 1908. General Secretary at the Ministry of Munitions, 1915. Chief Economic Adviser to the Government, 1919–27.

[3] Thomas William Holderness, 1849–1924. Entered Indian Civil Service, 1872. Secretary to the Government of India, Revenue and Agricultural Department, 1898–1901. Secretary, Revenue Statistics and Commerce Department, India Office, 1901–12. Knighted, 1907. Permanent Under-Secretary of State, India Office, 1912–19. Created Baronet, 1920.

be bombarded with all the accuracy of fire attainable only in a shore gun. We think therefore it is a necessary precaution at this stage to get the gun on the way, and one which if we are checked may materially assist the Fleet passing the Narrows. All the arrangements have been made for ship and train. Admiral Bacon anticipates no difficulty whatever in getting the gun ashore, and in conveying it to a firing position. The fourth gun is now practically ready at Sheerness and will be over in France to replace this gun before French can want it.

In these circumstances the First Sea Lord and I wish most strongly that the despatch of the gun should go forward with the utmost speed as has been arranged.

I should be glad if you would send the following to Sir John French from First Lord:—'We regard the immediate despatch of the gun as an imperative precaution at this juncture. We can replace it within a week by the fourth gun now finishing proof at Shoebury. . . .'

Yours sincerely
Winston S. Churchill

Kitchener accepted Churchill's request. His own preparations were gathering momentum. On April 8, having completed the necessary reorganization of supplies, Hamilton set sail from Egypt for Lemnos. After seeing Kitchener on April 9, Fisher reported to Jellicoe that the Field-Marshal 'seems quite certain of success at the Dardanelles!' But it was still not certain where Hamilton's troops would land. General Birdwood, who commanded the ANZAC forces, wanted to ignore the Gallipoli Peninsula altogether and land further north, between Enos and the head of the Gulf of Xeros. Another plan which Birdwood put forward was to land on the Asiatic shore and march to Chanak across the plain of Troy. Hamilton opposed this latter plan because, as he told Birdwood, he had no roving commission to conquer Asia Minor. General Paris, who was in command of the Royal Naval Division, suggested that the main landing should be at Smyrna. But as the discussion between these military men progressed, the Gallipoli Peninsula emerged as the most favoured landing place. As soon as Hamilton reached Lemnos on the morning of April 10 he went on board the *Queen Elizabeth* to put these problems to de Robeck, Wemyss and Keyes. These naval officers, he later wrote in his 'diary', were 'all against any further delay or standing by'. Encouraged by this enthusiasm, Hamilton took the view, as he later wrote, that 'the first and foremost step towards a victorious landing was to upset the equilibrium of the Turk so that he should be unable to concentrate either his mind or his men to meet our main attacks. . . . Prudence here is entirely out of place. There will be and can be no reconnaissances, no half measures, no tentatives. At a given moment we must stake everything on the one hazard.' He decided therefore to make the landings not only opposite Maidos, at the waist of the Peninsula, but at 'as many places as we can south of Achi Baba'.

Technical discussions between the admirals and generals began at Mudros on April 11. The plan which they evolved was for two simultaneous landings, one at Cape Helles and the other at Gaba Tepe. The Navy would put the Army on shore at a number of different beaches, and then provide a shield of fire behind which the troops would advance inland. Once the Gallipoli Peninsula were occupied, the Turkish defences at the Narrows would be attacked both by de Robeck from the Straits and by Hamilton from the high ground above Kilid Bahr. Such a combination, they all believed, would drive the Turks from Chanak and leave the way open for de Robeck to take his ships unmolested into the Sea of Marmara. Jack Churchill sent his brother an encouraging account of the relations between the senior officers, and of de Robeck's feelings following the setback of March 18:

Dear Winston,

We are back again in Mudros Bay and things are at last moving rapidly. Every two or three hours a great transport arrives full of troops and this time they have been properly embarked and are ready to disembark in proper order. I had a long talk to Keyes yesterday. He and De R are very pleased at their treatment by the Admiralty. Particularly the latter, who fully expected to be superseded. He has always been rather against you & your policy etc but since all the things he has asked for, have been given, he has become an ardent admirer. They all appear to be in the best of spirits but no longer talk of it as being an easy job. . . .

My friend gets on very well with the sailors and has formed a very high opinion of De R. Keyes tells me that on the 18th it would have been possible to have got through, but that the Admiral knew if he did so, he might never get out again until troops landed. He thought he might save himself from being superseded by going through, but was prepared to go under rather than do a spectacular thing which might have necessitated another fleet coming here to cover the troops landing. When he retired on the 18th he fully believed it was his last day in command. Wemyss is working very hard and behaving most loyally to De R.

Fisher was determined to continue in his opposition to the naval aspects of the enterprise. On April 11 he opposed de Robeck's request for a number of naval officers to be sent out immediately to the

Dardanelles to co-operate with the Army during the landings. Churchill tried to dissuade Fisher from imposing restrictions which would hamper de Robeck. Fisher agreed to withdraw his opposition. But Churchill was upset by the incident, writing on April 11:

Seriously, my friend, are you not a little unfair in trying to spite this operation by side winds and small points when you have accepted it in principle? It is hard on me that you should keep on like this—every day something fresh: and it is not worthy of you or the great business we have in hand together.

You know how deeply anxious I am to work with you. Had the Dardanelles been excluded, our co-operation would have been impossible. It is not right now to make small difficulties or add to the burden which in these times we have to bear.

Excuse frankness—but friends have this right, and to colleagues it is a duty. . . .

Fisher replied on the following day:

Never in all my whole life have I ever before so sacrificed my convictions as I have done to please you!—*THAT'S A FACT!* . . . Off my own bat I suggested the immediate despatch of Lord Nelson and Agamemnon (hoping they would shield Elizabeth and Inflexible!). De Robeck will hoist his flag in the Lord Nelson you may be sure, instead of the Vengeance, his former Flagship. For the work in hand the Vengeance quite as good for close action. Nevertheless I say no more. The outside world is quite certain that I have pushed you, and not you me! So far as I know the Prime Minister is the solitary person who knows to the contrary. I have not said one word to a soul on the subject except to Crease and Wilson and Oliver and Bartolome, and you may be sure these four never open their mouths.

Indirectly I've worked up Kitchener from the very beginning via Fitzgerald.

I think it's going to be a success, but I want to lose the oldest ships and to be chary of our invaluable officers and men for use in the decisive theatre.

In anticipation of such a success as Fisher now envisaged, the Italian Government drew nearer to a final commitment. Many glittering territorial prizes were offered by the Allies if Italy were prepared to abandon her neutrality. Britain and France were both prepared to offer Italy a large part of Austria's Adriatic coastline, control over the Muslim state of Albania, a sphere of influence stretching across the whole southern coast of Anatolian Turkey and a share in any future division of German territory in Africa. Asquith feared that a further setback at the Dardanelles might cool the Italian ardour, writing to Churchill on April 11:

Secret

My dear Winston,

We have confidentially told both the French & the Russian Govts that active offensive operations will not be resumed at the Dardanelles while the Italian negotiation is trembling in the balance. I hope it may come to a good end in the course of a few days. But meanwhile it is of the utmost importance that neither the naval or military people on the spot shd brusque the situation.

Yrs always

HHA

Neither Churchill nor Kitchener wished to postpone the attack. Churchill replied on the same day giving the Admiralty and War Office view:

. . . The operations at the Dardanelles will probably be delayed a few days from various causes, & when they begin the first phase, though delicate, is not the decisive one. At the point to which these operations have now reached, military considerations & favourable weather shd rule. Kitchener & I wd deprecate any check on non-military grounds to the normal development of what must certainly be a task extending over some considerable time. There is no question of an immediate decisive attack, with consequent risk of flagrant failure, occurring at present. Therefore I hope matters there may be allowed to take a purely military course.

On April 15 Churchill sent Asquith, Grey and Kitchener an encouraging letter which had just been received at the Admiralty from a Greek merchant,[1] who had written from Corfu on March 30:

The disagreement among the Young Turks in power is complete. Enver Pasha, who is left alone with the German officers, is said to demand a fight to the bitter end. Talaat Bey, Minister of the Interior, and a more reasonable man than his opponent, advises peace with the object of saving what remains of Turkey. Notwithstanding the reverse sustained by the Allied fleet in the Dardanelles on the 18th March, the population of Constantinople remains exasperated at the danger to which Enver's policy exposes the country. The

---

[1] The merchant was a regular informant; for the sake of his family I have thought it right not to disclose his name.

Sultan himself, thinking that the policy of Bulgaria is open to suspicion, is said to be very anxious. . . .

One is driven to the conclusion that the Sultan and his sorely tried people have reason for anxiety seeing that it is well known in the City that:—

1. Munitions of war are failing in every branch of the Turkish army.
2. The rout of the Turkish army in the Causasus, Mesopotamia and on the Suez Canal is due to disagreement between the Turkish and German officers.
3. The Austrians on whom the Turks counted are continually defeated by the Russians.
4. The Envoy Extraordinary of Great Britain General Baquot [Paget] is working steadily in Belgrade and Sofia to bring about the reconciliation of these two Slav races.
5. If the Germans give help to their Allies it is certainly their neighbours the Austrians and not the Turks who will be favoured.

Here was the information which Churchill and his colleagues wanted to believe. From the outbreak of war with Turkey five months previously they had been continually buoyed up by the belief that Turkish unity was a myth and that success at the Dardanelles, even by ships alone, would lead to revolution in Constantinople and a neutral, or even allied, Turkey emerging within days.

Churchill was confident, from what little he could learn of Kitchener's plans, and from all he knew of de Robeck's arrangements, that the landings would be a success. On April 19 he telegraphed to his brother:

I am sure forts will be quelled if we go on steadily for two or three days hard action. We know they are running short of ammunition, particularly for the 14-inch guns. The vital thing is not to break off because of losses but to persevere. This is the hour in the world's history for a fine feat of arms and the results of victory will amply justify the price. I wish I were with you. It would be easier than waiting here. All my thoughts are with you. Give every good wish to all my friends and particularly to your Chief. I rejoice he and de Robeck and Keyes get on so well together. They may put full confidence in the loyalty of those at home.

On the evening of April 19 Hankey dined with the Churchills at Admiralty House, describing Churchill in his diary as 'extremely optimistic about Dardanelles operation'. The auguries for success seemed favourable. The armoured cars and aeroplanes under Commander Samson had reached Lemnos and their crews were eager for action. Josiah Wedgwood, in command of the armoured cars, was delighted to leave the tangled disputes which had begun to stifle his activities on the western front for an enterprise where his help might be more welcome, and perhaps decisive. Samson likewise found a more congenial atmosphere at the Dardanelles. The Gallipoli Peninsula could be flown over from the Aegean to the Sea of Marmara in a few minutes. The mines which were such a danger to the Fleet could be spotted from the air. Turkish troops and ammunition could be located moving along the road from Bulair. Before the naval attack of March 18, spotting had been good, except for the twenty mines laid on March 17, which had not been seen from the air—or indeed looked for—and which had sunk the *Irresistible*, the *Ocean* and possibly the *Bouvet*, and damaged the *Inflexible*.

Hamilton's plans for the landing were completed by April 20. On the following day he issued his orders to the troops. 'Together with our comrades of the fleet,' he declared, 'we are about to force a landing upon an open beach in face of positions which have been vaunted by our enemies as impregnable.' De Robeck had completed his plans to put the troops ashore and to provide them with all possible support from his naval guns. As soon as the wild seas and harsh currents were at rest the attack could begin; all that was needed was two days of clear weather.

De Robeck was conscious of the enormous difficulties with which he would be faced. In the early hours of April 20 he telegraphed a request for another old battleship, the *Goliath*, to be sent to him as soon as possible: 'To ensure success . . . require every ship and man we have got. Goliath will be welcome addition. Request she may be sent here at once. It is a huge undertaking to land, on open beach in face of opposition, 10,000 men almost simultaneously followed by 65,000. Greatest energy displayed by all ranks. Everything working well.' Churchill immediately ordered the *Goliath* to proceed to the Dardanelles from Alexandria. Fisher approved this new addition to de Robeck's strength; the *Goliath* formed no part of Jellicoe's fleet. But on April 20 he wrote to Hankey that he was 'more depressed than ever about prospects of the Dardanelles attack', and that he interpreted the reconnaissance reports from the Peninsula with foreboding. On the following day he wrote to Jellicoe: 'You *MUST* have aeroplanes and undoubtedly they can (*if you have a sufficient number*) defend you against the Zeppelins. You should write direct to First Lord and ask for them at once, before they are all sent to the Dardanelles, where they are now going by dozens!'

On April 21 de Robeck telegraphed that he hoped to begin operations on the morning of April 24 if the weather allowed. On the following day, in a conversation which Sir George Riddell recorded in his *War Diary*, Churchill explained why the operation must go on, despite its obvious and increasing difficulties:

He said that the Turks had now fortified positions formerly unfortified and that the lives of many of our men might be lost in consequence. He said that his calculations had in a measure been put out by the mobility of the Turkish guns, which enabled them to train readily on the ships which were confined in a narrow area. Originally it had been thought that the attack might be successful by sea alone, but this had proved impracticable. This war could not be won by sitting still, as some people thought. Offensive operations were necessary, but before deciding on a plan which might, and probably would, result in the loss of many valuable lives, Winston had given the whole subject most anxious consideration. If the operation is successful, its effects will be most important. They are worth the risk. It is better to risk lives in this way than to allow the war to drag on indefinitely. If the operation is unsuccessful, Winston recognises that the effect on his career may be serious. 'They may get rid of me,' he said. 'If they do, I cannot help it. I shall have done my best. My regiment is awaiting me.' He seemed calm, but no doubt is feeling the strain.

The Dardanelles campaign was beginning to come under public criticism. It was first criticized in the House of Commons on April 22, by Lord Charles Beresford, who had already written to Asquith to protest against the operation, but whose letter had, on Churchill's suggestion, been ignored:

LORD C. BERESFORD asked the Prime Minister if he will inform the House who is responsible for the operations in the Dardanelles; whether it was intended to be in the nature of combined naval and military operations, and whether the ultimate success of the operations will be considerably delayed owing to the naval attack having been delivered before the Army was landed?

Asquith replied that the operations were 'being jointly conducted by the Navy and Army in co-operation, under the responsibility of His Majesty's Government', and that it was 'not desirable at the present stage to say anything further'. That same day Asquith was sent yet another sharp criticism of Churchill from the editor of the *Morning Post*, H. A. Gwynne, who wrote:

When I had the honour of writing to you on October 16, 1914 regarding the Antwerp expedition, I pointed out to you that I did not consider the First Lord of the Admiralty a man who should be in charge of the Fleet during this war. I considered that the Antwerp expedition thoroughly justified this opinion, and the recurrence of the same lack of study, the same desire to rush on without due preparation, and the same ignorance of strategic and tactical principles in the Dardanelles expedition confirms this opinion. What I ventured to prophesy in October has come to pass in March, and it is for the Government over which you preside to consider whether the First Lord of the Admiralty should continue to hold that office. I would like to point out that I have no personal animosity whatever against the First Lord of the Admiralty; indeed I have a great admiration for his political talents and his perseverance and energy . . .

The complaints of Beresford and Gwynne were evidence of the mounting criticism of Churchill in Parliament and the Press. At the Admiralty itself not all officials were friendly. On April 22 Captain Richmond wrote angrily in his diary: '. . . there is really no settled policy. Old Fisher is useless & will not express an opinion if he can help it. Winston is ignorant: & Oliver's advice is not taken. . . . It is quite useless to advise: I only get snubbed when [I] put forward my opinions.'

Churchill was upset at the quick acceptance which criticisms gained by all who heard them. On April 24 he wrote a memorandum which was circulated to the Cabinet on the following day. 'I have heard,' he wrote in his covering note, 'that unfavourable comment has been made on the alleged "failure of the Admiralty to foresee the dangers to which ships operating in the Dardanelles would be exposed from floating mines". I therefore append an extract from the original orders issued from the Admiralty to Admiral Carden.' Carden's orders of February 5 had included the paragraphs:

Vessels covering the mine-sweepers will be exposed to attack by drifting mines especially when at anchor. Torpedo nets will be some protection against pairs of mines, connected by lines, coming alongside when the connecting rope takes across the stem.

It may be advisable to prepare buoys to be laid ahead of vessels anchoring in the Dardanelles to catch drifting mines and also to make use of fishing nets between buoys to intercept mines. Concrete blocks could be used as moorings for the buoys.

Drift nets have been found efficacious in the North Sea as a means of clearing away moored mines. They are allowed to drift with the tide, and foul the mines and break them adrift.

Nets might be laid at night by shallow-draught vessels or picket boats above the minefields to drift down with the current.

There may be considerable difficulty in dealing with observation mines owing to the depths at which they may be moored.

The cables will probably have to be crept for with explosive grapnels, but it may be possible also to sweep with mine-sweeping vessels to a sufficient depth.

Rumours and complaints could not always be halted by the circulation of documents. Many of the most outspoken critics were not privy to the evidence, and grasped at chimeras for their criticism. 'Now that the Dardanelles are not doing well,' a misinformed General Wilson wrote in his diary on April 23, 'Winston & Fisher are preparing plans for landing a force in the Baltic and another 8 Divs at Rotterdam. It is incredible.'

For those who knew that only a change in weather stood between all the plans upon which so much depended and the military landings on the Gallipoli Peninsula, the approach of battle acted as a stimulant. 'If a success,' Fisher wrote to Jellicoe on April 22, 'it undoubtedly will be an immense coup to have got to Constantinople.' On April 23 he wrote to Jellicoe again: 'Let us hope for the best, *and the unexpected always happens in war*. The German General in command[1] may make a mess of it, or the Turkish ammunition may fail. The Germans have sent their best Generals and Admirals there. *SECRET*. We have got hold of communications to them! But yet they may fail. *Even Homer nodded!*'

The weather at the Dardanelles had cleared. On April 22 de Robeck informed the Admiralty that the landings would begin on April 25. During April 22 two intelligence reports reached London; one caused alarm, the other provided encouragement. Both were from Russia. The first report, sent by the British Ambassador, Buchanan, reported a total of twelve German submarines converging on the Dardanelles. If this news were true, it was unlikely that the Navy could land Hamilton's army. Churchill was sceptical, writing to Oliver: 'I have asked for more precise information as to source. Meanwhile I do not wish this "scare" message reported to V. Admiral.' Churchill then asked Grey to send a telegram to Buchanan, which was despatched that afternoon: 'We must know character of source of your information about submarines. It appears to us incredible, but if true wd be very serious.' Buchanan's reply made it clear, as Churchill wrote to Fisher and Oliver on the following day, that 'This is obviously a Germanic lie, & part of their regular attempt to conceal the weakness & scarcity of munitions from which we know they are suffering. No need to report to VA [i.e. de Robeck].' The second intelligence report was more credible. Its source was a Russian secret agent in Constantinople who had seen a telegram sent from the Austro-Hungarian Embassy at Constantinople to the Ministry of War at Vienna. Sazonov sent the contents to Grey. 'In consequence of expenditure of large quantity of ammunition,' the

[1] On March 24 Enver had appointed Liman von Sanders to command the Turkish Fifth Army at the Dardanelles, with his headquarters at the town of Gallipoli.

Austrian Embassy had reported, 'Turks have now not enough to repulse two similar attacks.' Churchill sent de Robeck this encouraging news with a covering note, suggesting a renewed attempt to destroy the forts.

This agrees with our information, and importance of forcing forts to fire as often and as long as possible, in order to exhaust their ammunition, will doubtless have occurred to you. I have consulted Lord Fisher before sending this telegram, but, of course, you are free to act as you think fit, so I mark this telegram personal, as intention of all we say is merely to be helpful and a guide, and not a hard and fast instruction.

De Robeck had no intention of going back on his decision of March 22 to take no independent action. Since then he had concentrated all his plans upon the needs of the Army, and to those needs he remained steadfast.

Before leaving Cairo for Lemnos, Sir Ian Hamilton had asked Rupert Brooke to join his Staff. But Brooke shared the eagerness of his colleagues for action and turned down the offer. While still in Egypt he was taken ill with sunstroke, but wrote confidently to Violet Asquith that he hoped to be well enough 'for our first thrust into the fray', even though he expected he would only be able to 'give my Turk, at the utmost, a kitten's tap'. From Egypt, Brooke proceeded with the Royal Naval Division to the Dardanelles, but he did not recover. 'There is bad news of Rupert,' Edward Marsh telegraphed to Violet Asquith on April 22; 'he is ill with blood-poisoning on French hospital ship. Condition grave. I am hoping and will wire directly I hear more.' Two days later Brooke was dead. The news reached London on the eve of the Gallipoli landings. Churchill, who had met Brooke socially at 10 Downing Street, knew how great a friend he was both to Edward Marsh and to Violet Asquith; he was upset by Brooke's death, and angry with Marsh for not having introduced them sooner. A month later he was still angry; at dinner on May 24 he began, as Marsh wrote to Violet Asquith the next morning, 'to abuse me quite angrily, as he has done several times, for not bringing them together sooner'. On April 26 *The Times* published an obituary of Brooke written by Churchill:

Rupert Brooke is dead. A telegram from the Admiral at Lemnos tells us that his life has closed at the moment when it seemed to have reached its springtime. A voice had become audible, a note had been struck, more true, more thrilling, more able to do justice to the nobility of our youth in arms engaged in this present war, than any other—more able to express their thoughts of self-surrender, and with a power to carry comfort to those who watched them so intently from afar. The voice has been swiftly stilled. Only the echoes and the memory remain; but they will linger. . . .

Violet Asquith wrote at once:

Dearest Winston,

I must write one word to tell you how beautiful I thought your tribute to our beloved Rupert in to-day's Times.

All those who loved him must be grateful to you for it.

I feel heart-broken. He was the most radiantly perfect human being I have ever known—so flawless that one sometimes wondered whether he quite belonged to this ragged scheme of things—whether he hadn't strayed here out of some faery land.

He obviously belonged to the 'predestined'—so obviously that one could not but hope that even Fate might shrink from so cruel a platitude as his destruction.

He never had a doubt about his death himself. Not only did he often speak to me of it in those last days at Blandford—& Avonmouth—but in 2 of the letters I have had from him since he started, he refers once indirectly—& once quite directly to it (telling me not to mind too much).

He had so much left to give the world.

Poor Eddie—my heart aches for him—his whole life pivoted on Rupert.

Goodbye dear Winston—bless you.

Yrs ever
Violet

The military attack on the Gallipoli Peninsula began at first light on April 25. During the day over thirty thousand men, including those of the 29th Division, were landed on a series of narrow beaches at Cape Helles and Gaba Tepe. They reached none of their objectives, but by nightfall held precarious positions on the fringe of the Peninsula. At Gaba Tepe, by a mistake of navigation, the whole force was landed too far north, at Ari Burnu. De Robeck had wanted to land at dawn, to avoid just such an error. Instead of finding themselves on a sandy beach, faced only by low hills and an almost flat plain, the men were confronted by steep slopes, dense undergrowth and high cliffs. The reinforcements sent ashore frequently lost their way, units were inextricably mixed, orders were unclear, essential messages mislaid. During the day a series of uncoordinated attacks exhausted the men without achieving any success. In the confused tension, men fired on their fellow-attackers. Communication between the troops and their commanders was at

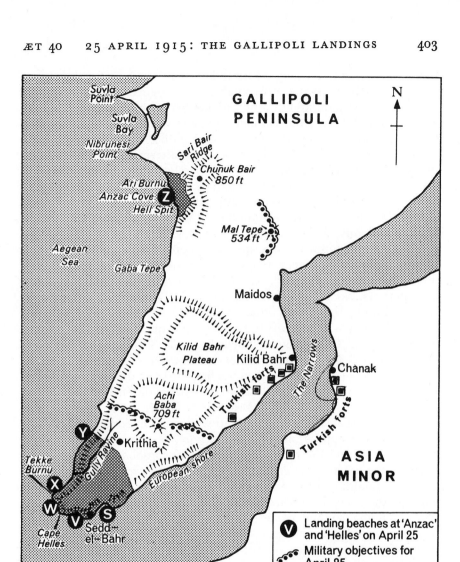

THE ADVANCES ON THE GALLIPOLI PENINSULA,
25 APRIL 1915

times non-existent. Lacking accurate knowledge of how far the troops had advanced, the Navy were unable to give effective covering fire. By 8 am eight thousand troops had landed with only five hundred Turks to check them; but rumours that the whole force was to retire spread rapidly through the ravines and gullies, causing many men to flock back to the beaches throughout the afternoon. By dusk fifteen thousand were ashore, while the Turks who had rushed men forward still had less than five thousand in the area; but confusion and exhaustion combined to prevent any advantage being taken of this.

Like the landings at Ari Burnu, those at Cape Helles were plagued by muddle and folly. At Y Beach no Turks at all faced the attackers, who reached the cliff-top without a single shot being fired against them; but from that moment all went wrong. A message asking what they should do next was never answered. No further orders arrived from divisional headquarters. No advance was made inland. Twelve hours after the Y beach landing, the Turks attacked. After a stubborn resistance the Turkish force was driven off; but an urgent request for reinforcements was not replied to or even acknowledged. At X Beach the first men ashore reached the cliff-top without a casualty. The 12-inch naval guns of the *Implacable* had terrified the few Turks guarding the cliff-top. But once on the cliff-top the attackers halted. No orders had been given to them to link up with the Y Beach or S Beach force. Instead, they established a defensive perimeter, and waited. The landing at S Beach met only slight opposition; but once ashore, no advantage was taken of the success, and the men were ordered to consolidate the position. None of the advantages gained at Y, X and S were exploited. Easy landings, minimal resistance, numbers far greater than those of the Turks in the whole Helles area, were of no value if neglected. Yet at the two remaining landing places, W Beach and V Beach, where fierce opposition had been encountered, any advances from Y, X and S might have weighed the balance against the Turk decisively. At W Beach the men were shot at while still wading through the water.[1] Once ashore, poor maps caused more confusion than the remaining Turkish resistance. Compasses and field-glasses having been made useless while in the water, the muddle was not corrected, and when the W Beach landing had succeeded, it proved impossible to follow it up, or to help the men at V Beach, whose landing was a disaster. There, the collier *River Clyde*, made to look like a deserted ship, was run aground with two

---

[1] Among those killed during the W Beach landing was Thomas Hugh Colville Frankland (1879–1915), who had been captured with Churchill in the armoured train ambushed by the Boers in 1899, and imprisoned with him.

thousand men aboard. But the moment they tried to land, the Turkish defenders, firing with great accuracy, caused a slaughter. Many men, wounded while still wading through the water, stumbled and drowned. Some, unwounded, were drowned by the weight of their equipment. Those who reached the shore were exposed to continual Turkish fire, and could not get further than a low ridge of sand a few yards inland. The combined guns of the *Queen Elizabeth*, the *Albion* and the *Cornwallis* were unable to destroy the Turkish positions. At the slightest sign of movement, Turkish rifle and machine-gun fire would burst out, accurate and fatal.

Jack Churchill witnessed the aftermath of the landings from the *Queen Elizabeth*, and on April 27 sent his brother an account of the first day's battles. He began with his impressions of the naval bombardment. 'Half-way between Gaba Tepe and C Helles the spectacle was wonderful,' he wrote; 'Ahead of us and behind us lay enormous fleets of ships of all sorts. All the men-of-war were in action. It sounded like a continuous royal salute from the whole fleet at Spithead.' The *Queen Elizabeth* then sailed past the beaches at Y and X:

Things seemed to be going well. Here was the weather—the one thing that even optimists feared—perfect, and 3 beaches out of six successfully accomplished. We steamed on, slowly turning to port. Cape Helles came into view. Clearly W party had also landed and made good considerable ground. I could see that the ruin of the Helles lighthouse was occupied by our men. Infantry were lying down all along the top of the cliff. A mass of wire entanglements could be seen in front of them. Some little figures ran about and crouched. They also were under fire. All ships continued to fire rapidly.

Passing Cape Helles, the *Queen Elizabeth* came into view of the village of Sedd-el Bahr.

In the little bay between these two points we could see the 'Wooden Horse', otherwise the River Clyde. It soon became clear that all was not well here. The boat had done well and was piled up on the shore. The lighters formed a pier from her bows to the beach, but she was still full of men. Under a little ridge, where the sand joined the mainland, crouched a couple of hundred men. Evidently they had landed and could not make any progress. As I watched 2 or 3 men tried to get back into the ship. At once the beach and water all round them sprang into the air, and the rat, tat, tat, of a couple of maxims broke out. Inland 20 yards beyond the men more wire could be seen. The situation was clear. It was an amphi-theatre. The 'Wooden Horse' and her advanced party were in the centre of the stage. The semi-circular 'house' was 'full'. Any man who moved on the stage received the 'applause' of everyone from the stalls, 20 yards in front of that beastly wire, from the 'stage boxes' which contained maxims on each flank, and from the 'dress circle and gallery', who occupied various trenches all up the steep slope. . . .

At 8 we could see little figures from W party extending on the cliff tops to their right. If only they could have gone another ½ mile, they would have worried the 'gallery' of the amphi-theatre. But again there was more wire and heavy rifle fire. The little figures suddenly fell flat and remained taking what cover they could. . . .

Something had to be done to help the poor 'Wooden Horse'. She had promised to give us a 'star turn' and was in a bad way, with Achilles looking at her from his tomb exactly opposite! And so at 8.20 the Queen E fired a 15″ into Seddel Bahr. I was on the searchlight bridge at the time and was taken by surprise. My cap went one way and my note book another. My pipe fell to the floor and after a gulp or two, I looked at the village in front. About 150 yards of houses seemed to suddenly rise in the air in a great cloud of smoke and dust. It was two or three minutes before the debris settled. A shrapnel burst near our bows and we fired again. We closed in near the shore and must have been well within rifle shot, but I saw no sign of any bullets directed at us. We were now well into the straits. What a situation! In front of me the great 15″ shells were blowing the last village in Europe to hell, and behind the French melinite was blasting great holes in Asia! . . .

At 10 the fire into the amphi-theatre had increased. The audience were having their money's worth. But they would not go and the maxim could still be heard whenever anyone tried to leave the 'Wooden Horse'. The situation continued unchanged. Seddel Bahr had been blown to bits, but still the beach party could not advance. . . .

The W party could be seen again working to their right. They only had a little way to go to reach point 138, but a heavy fire held them up. At 3 o'clock I saw the Worcesters advance along the top of the cliffs. Suddenly the leading company began to run. The men bent double and were evidently under fire. They reached wire and fell down to take cover. Then two little figures rose and calmly began to cut the wire. Two more joined them and soon they were through. It was a wonderful sight and we all watched with baited breath, expecting every moment to see them fall. But they got through and were followed by the remainder of the company. A few figures fell in the wire and remained there, but another company ran up and through with their bayonets fixed. . . . We remained watching the V position, which was unchanged. At 6.30 a few men crawled to the foot of the old Seddel Bahr fort on the sea front. The Worcesters made a determined attempt to get further to the right, but failed, and at 7 I could see some of them running back. At 7.20 visibility became impossible, but a rippling fire continued.

On the morning of April 26 de Robeck telegraphed to Churchill: 'On 5 beaches the landing was immediately successful though vigorously opposed by an enemy well entrenched and covered by barbed wire entanglements running in all directions.' Only at V Beach were the soldiers still pinned to the sand by Turkish fire. But when the attack was renewed on April 26 V Beach was secured. Substantial ground was gained at every point. But the increased Turkish resistance during the day still prevented Hamilton's army from reaching its initial objectives, the heights of Achi Baba and Sari Bair. At Y Beach the Turks attacked at seven in the morning of April 26, but were driven off. They never returned, but panic set in among the men, and within three hours all of them were embarked, and the position abandoned. There had been more British troops ashore at Y Beach than there were Turks in the whole Helles area; but for the twenty-nine hours during which the men were ashore they had been ignored by their Divisional Headquarters, only twenty minutes away by destroyer. No reply had been sent to their many urgent appeals for reinforcements; no Officer of the Divisional Staff had been sent ashore to gain personal knowledge of the position. Not only were there no Turks at Y Beach during the evacuation, but when Keyes went ashore afterwards to look for wounded, he remained on the battlefield for an hour without a shot being fired at him.

The eighteen thousand Australian and New Zealand troops who had landed by nightfall north of Gaba Tepe, on a beach soon known as Anzac Cove, were demoralized by shrapnel fire and exhausted. General Birdwood signalled to Hamilton that evening that there was 'likely to be a fiasco' unless they were embarked, and advised the Commander-in-Chief to abandon the whole Anzac position. But in the early hours of April 26 Hamilton replied that 'there is nothing for it but to dig yourselves right in and stick it out. . . . You have only to dig, dig, dig—until you are safe.' When Jack Churchill saw the ANZAC attackers from the *Queen Elizabeth* on the morning of April 26 he reported to his brother that they were 'holding a little triangle near the shore, and I could see them clinging on to the scrubby ridges'. Turkish fire from the higher ground which surrounded them was constant and effective and no further advance was possible.

At four-thirty in the afternoon of April 26 the *Queen Elizabeth* steamed past V Beach. The crisis there was over, and Jack Churchill wrote to his brother of its aftermath:

As we approached the point I was gazing at the back of the old castle of Seddel Bahr, when suddenly I saw little men standing round it in the open! There could be no doubt, only English soldiers would stand about like that. Clearly the ridge behind Seddel Bahr was ours. And if so—then V beach was relieved from pressure. The line must be complete and W, V, S could join hands! Sir Ian came up from tea and as he passed asked whether there was anything new. I told what I could see and that I believed the coast line was all ours. He was very excited and doubtful of any such good fortune. But the position was soon clear. A few minutes later the whole plateau above Helles and Seddel Bahr came into view. It was covered with men standing up and walking about, in spots where three hours ago I had seen skirmishers crawling under fire. The amphi-theatre had been taken and the whole of Seddel Bahr was in our hands. The whole situation was greatly relieved and the danger of the landing had been overcome. It was a great relief to everyone. The whole position had been one of great danger, but now the coast was held and guns were disembarking. It would take a great deal to shift that 29th Division and the Turks had evidently retired.

'The Navy have never had such a time,' Jack Churchill ended his letter; 'They dug great chunks out of the hills with their lyddite. Things are going very well, and I hope ships will be in the Sea of Marmora in a fortnight. I think de Robeck will have a try to get through as soon as possible.'

On April 29 Jack Churchill added a postscript to his letter, giving his brother a description of the ANZAC landing and position. On April 28, three days after the landing, the Australians had 'found 5 men in our uniforms among their supports. They were Turks and were shot at once. A sniper was found in the middle of their camp sitting in some dense scrub with 30 days of food and water and 1,000 rounds of ammunition.' In his final postscript Jack wrote:

By the way the wire on shore is terrible stuff—very thick and closely barbed. It is fixed to iron stanchions instead of wooden posts. It is mostly at the spots indicated in Sir Ian's secret orders!!

A letter found on a Turk shows that the Austrians told the Turks to expect our attack on the 21st. It is the very day which was originally fixed!!

Churchill received another account of the battle from Josiah Wedgwood, who had spent all of April 25 and 26 on board the *River Clyde*, using his machine-guns from the prow of the ship to protect the men ashore. Wedgwood described how:

. . . We ran ashore on 'V' beach at 6.30, being shelled on the way by 6″ guns from the Asiatic side. The hopper ran aground in the wrong place. The fire from the shore was heavy, & the original plan could not be worked to.

Five tows of 5 boats each with some 30–40 men in each came on to 'V' beach simultaneously with ourselves, & in 10 minutes there were some 400 dead and wounded on the beach & in the water. Not more than 10% got safe to shore & took shelter under the sand edge. Some of the Munster Fusiliers tried to land from the River Clyde about 7 am after some sort of connection had been made with a spit of rock. Very few of them got safely to land, & Genl Napier[1] & his Brigade Major[2] were killed on the lighter. Thereafter the wounded cried out all day & for 36 hours;—in every boat, lighter, hopper & all along the shore. It was horrible & all within 200 yards of our guns trying to find & shoot the shooters. . . .

That night we landed the rest of the Munsters & the Hampshires (some 1000 in all). The losses then were small. For 3 hours I stood on the end of the spit of what had been rock in 2 feet of water helping the heavily laden men to jump ashore on to submerged dead bodies & trying to persuade the wounded over whom they had to walk that we should soon get them aboard. This is what went on monotonously 'Give me your rifle'; '& your shovel'; 'your left hand'; 'jump wide'; 'it's all right, only kits' 'keep clear of that man's legs, can't you'. And all the time the gangway along one boat worked to & fro on wounded men; & wounded men were brought to the end of the spit & could not be got aboard because the other stream was more important & never ending, & there they slowly sank & died. . . .

So far we had had little help from the fleet, but on Monday morning, all our men (say 3000 reduced to 2000) being ashore, the Queen Eliz & others made the semicircle of hills, & village & fort a lyddite ruin & our Munsters, Dublins & Hampshires, helped on the left by some who had landed at 'W' beach, won the hills. So we now hold 1 mile from the beach all round, the village, castle & crest. I have just come down from the picket line where we have been standing to arms, shooting all night long,—my 3rd sleepless night. . . .

You may be very well satisfied with your 3rd Squadron of 'armoured cars'. As soon as they & we are rested we are going forward on foot with the 29th Division. . . .

I am going to lie down & sleep, the first sleep for 3 eternal days & nights.

As soon as Churchill learned of Hamilton's failure to reach either of his objectives, of the heavy casualties and of the exhaustion of the men who had landed, he felt compelled to intervene in the military arrangements which Kitchener guarded so jealously. On April 26 he wrote out a letter to the Field-Marshal:

I hope you will not cut Hamilton too fine. A loyal man like that will go

[1] Henry Edward Napier, 1861–1915. Entered Army, 1882. Colonel, 1911. Officer commanding No. 11 District, Irish Command, 1914–15. Brigadier-General commanding units of the 88th Brigade, V Beach landing, Gallipoli, 25 April 1915.
[2] John Henry Dives Costeker, 1879–1915. Entered Army, 1898. Staff Captain, Irish Command, 1914. Brigade Major, 4 September 1914 until his death on 25 April 1915.

on with what he has got & never say a word till he cracks up. The easy good fortunes of a beginning may depart again.

I should feel very much happier if you could manage to have another 20,000 in the offing—even if they were never landed. It would be a great insurance; & surely at a pinch you could spare them from Egypt for a fortnight. Do not brush this aside with confident scorn. The things that have to be done are very difficult and a sincere opinion deserves to be considered.

Do consider this. Don't run short of stuffing behind your attack—even if you never need it. My feeling is you are running it very fine.

Don't be vexed with me for bringing this up. It costs so little to have a shot in the locker.

Don't wait till he asks you. It is sure to be too late then.

On reflection, Churchill decided not to send this appeal, feeling that he was powerless to influence Kitchener by his exhortations. Nor did he send the letter which he had written at the same time to Colonel Fitzgerald, Kitchener's private secretary, in which he declared: 'A valiant & successful attack like this may go well for a time; but there must be *stuffing* behind & inside it. . . . Remember every minute of this is history: and every attack requires backing.' The danger of too few men at the scene of action worried Churchill throughout April 26. That night he wrote out a telegram to his brother: 'I refrain from rejoicing till results are further defined but I hope your friend will ask in good time for more men if he wants them. There must be another 20,000 available at a pinch in Egypt. I am sure he would be supported if he asked through the regular channels. I only refer to this by way of precaution. Show this only to your friend.' The telegram was sent from the Admiralty shortly after midnight. In order not to depress his brother, he deleted the first ten words. Churchill's worries were not shared by the Prime Minister. 'Today's news of the Dardanelles is quite good,' Asquith wrote to Venetia Stanley on April 28, '& illustrates the truth that in this extraordinary war all the oldest, as well as the most modern, devices come in. The Trojan Horse, for instance, 2,000 soldiers who were unable to land were shut up in a collier, the decks covered with coal, & the sides made openable & flappable. And then when night came on, she was run ashore, and they emerged from their cupboard, & were all safely landed. . . . It is quite one of the romantic by-episodes of the War.'

13

Crisis

―――――――

EVEN sceptical onlookers were moved by the heroism of Sir Ian Hamilton's army. Hamilton himself believed that when the attack was renewed the ANZAC forces would reach the summit of Sari Bair and the 29th Division stand triumphant on Achi Baba. Hankey, who had throughout disliked the idea of an operation which, he wrote to Esher on April 26, was 'a gamble on the supposed inferior fighting qualities and lack of ammunition of the Turks', felt that there was 'a chance it may succeed . . . they have made a very good start'. On April 29 Churchill discussed the landings with Sir George Riddell. Leaning over an atlas, Churchill traced the position on the map with his finger. In his *War Diary*, Riddell recorded Churchill's words:

This is one of the great campaigns of history. Think what Constantinople is to the East. It is more than London, Paris, and Berlin all rolled into one are to the West. Think how it has dominated the East. Think what its fall will mean. Think how it will affect Bulgaria, Greece, Rumania, and Italy, who have already been affected by what has taken place. You cannot win this war by sitting still. We are merely using our surplus ships in the Dardanelles. Most of them are old vessels. The ammunition, even the rifle ammunition, is different from that which we are using in France—an older type—so there is no loss of power there. I am not responsible for the Expedition; the whole details were approved by the Cabinet and Admiralty Board. I do not shirk responsibility, but it is untrue to say that I have done this off my own bat. I have followed every detail.

Churchill's final remark to Riddell was that 'Fisher and I have a perfect understanding'. This was over-sanguine; although Fisher had made no protest about the military landings, he viewed their failure to reach their objectives with alarm. Churchill tried continually to stiffen Fisher's resolve, writing to him on May 3: 'It is clear that the favourable turn to our affairs in S.E. Europe arose from the initial success of our attack on the Dardanelles, was checked by the repulse of the 18th, & can only be restored by the general success of the operations. It is thus necessary to fight a battle, (a thing wh has often happened before in war) & abide the consequences whatever they may be.'

Evidence of the impact of the landings reached London from Athens. In several telegrams during the last week of April, Sir Francis Elliott reported that the Greeks were once more asking whether Britain would accept Greek military support. The pro-German sympathies of the Greek King could not prevail against the hopes of those who saw a prospect of territorial advantage following in the wake of an Allied victory, even if the Russians were still to prevent a Greek occupation of Constantinople. Churchill advised Grey not to respond to the new Greek mood, writing on April 30:

> The Gk telms show that the Dlles medicine is working with its usual efficiency. In a couple of days all the artillery of the Dlles army will be landed, & in action. The southern force will assault Achi Baba. The Sari Bair force ought to make progress against the Turkish communications. I think you wd be wise to await the result of these operations before relieving this recreant Govt & unfriendly King from their profound disquietude.
>
> We have won the 1st coup twice over now, but we have never won 2 coups running yet. Bulgaria, not Greece, ought to be our objective now. The distress of the Greek Govt is evident from the telegrams attached.
>
> Their help cannot arrive in time, unless we have a check, when it will certainly be withheld.

Much depended upon the ability of the Army to reach the high ground of Sari Bair and Achi Baba. On April 29 de Robeck reported that little progress had been made on either the Cape Helles or Anzac fronts 'owing to the exhausted condition of troops who have been fighting continuously since dawn on 25th'. Nevertheless troops and stores were being landed successfully. Maidos, the largest town on the European side of the Narrows, had been set on fire by shells from the *Triumph* and had burnt for several hours. On May 1 de Robeck reported that the troops had been 'resting and entrenching'. Turkish shelling of their trenches had been light. At Anzac there had been slight advances. Fires had been started in Chanak by long-distance bombardment from the *Lord Nelson*. In the early hours of May 2 de Robeck reported that during May 1 the Army had been 'consolidating its positions preparing for advance'. The Indian Brigade had landed at Helles and was digging in. That night the Turks attacked the Helles positions, but were driven back by British counter-attacks. A further Turkish attack at Helles was repulsed on the night of May 3. North of Gaba Tepe the ANZACs made slight gains. There was a lull in the fighting on May 4 when the Turks buried their dead and collected their wounded. On May 5, de Robeck reported that one of the battalions of the Royal Naval Division had done good work on the previous night when a panic among black French troops from Senegal had left a gap in the Allied line. Hamilton planned to launch a major attack on Achi Baba to begin on May 6.

Churchill's satisfaction at the slow but hopeful course of events was not shared in Conservative circles. At question time in the House of Commons on May 4, Lord Charles Beresford raised again his acerbic criticism:

LORD C. BERESFORD asked the Prime Minister whether the attack on the Dardanelles has developed a new and serious situation; whether the ships, munitions of war, and officers and men of both Services have been diverted to the Dardanelles; and whether, seeing that the Government have informed the public that every man, gun, and munition that can possibly be provided are required for the campaign in Flanders, and in order to allay anxiety with regard to the strain upon our resources for the new campaign in the Dardanelles, he will make a statement on the subject?

Asquith replied that 'The Noble Lord will agree that it is not advisable to deal with this matter by question and answer. A general statement at the present time would be premature.'

The next question came from a Liberal MP, Frederick Kellaway,[1] who wanted to find out more about the rumoured disagreements between Churchill and Fisher and asked 'whether Lord Fisher was consulted with regard to the March attack on the Dardanelles by the Fleet; and whether he expressed the opinion that the attack ought not to be made in the circumstances in which it was made?' According to parliamentary procedure, Kellaway's question had been submitted beforehand. Wanting to scotch rumours of dissension within the Admiralty, Fisher had taken the unusual step of drafting the answer which he wanted Churchill to give:

I must decline in the interests of the proper prosecution of the War to answer this or any similar question. It cannot be permitted that all the various considerations connected with war operations should be fully discussed and

[1] Frederick George Kellaway, 1870–1933. Liberal MP, 1910–22. Joint Parliamentary Secretary, Ministry of Munitions, 1916–21; Secretary, Department of Overseas Trade, 1920–1.

some particular item selected for a malignant attack. I am desired by Lord
Fisher to state that he associates himself fully in this reply. If the insinuation
contained in the question were correct Lord Fisher would not now be at the
Admiralty.

However, Churchill merely replied: 'the answer to the first part of the
question is in the affirmative, and to the second part in the negative'.

In a letter to his brother on May 5, Jack Churchill expressed doubts
about the wider aspects of the Gallipoli landings:

Here we are a comparatively small force clinging on to the end of the
Gallipoli Peninsula and having the prospect of fighting the whole Turkish
Empire! Amiable people who might help us, show no signs of doing so. The
Turk can bring his men from Asia Minor, etc—for nothing threatens him,
and most important of all—he can release the divisions from Constantinople
and send them down here to crush us. Russia is still far off and no one seems
to threaten him nearer home. However, the force here will do its best to get
on—and in the meanwhile we pray that diplomacy and the big cheque will
do something to help us. Such is the position and you must realise the feelings
of the responsible people with the force committed, the front only two miles
inland, and the stores and landing places still under intermittent shell fire.

Churchill left London on May 5 for Paris, together with Sir Henry
Jackson, to take part in the final secret negotiations for Italy's participation in the war. Because Grey was ill, Asquith took charge of the
diplomatic side of the negotiations in London. Travelling under the
name of Spencer, Churchill stayed at the Ritz, and for three days
discussed the intricate details of Anglo-Italian naval co-operation. The
pace of events was wearing, even for him; the effects of his influenza
could not easily be shaken off amid the daily pressure of events. 'Saw
Winston at St Pol,' General Wilson noted in his diary on May 7; 'he
looked ill and unhealthy.'

On May 6 Hamilton launched a massive attack along the whole
Allied front at Helles. His aim was to drive the Turks from the high
ground of Achi Baba, which had been the objective on April 25. Once
this prominent landmark were under Allied control, the Turkish position
on the Gallipoli Peninsula would be seriously weakened. The 15-inch
howitzer which Churchill had caused to be sent to the Dardanelles
would be able to fire on to the forts of the Narrows from a fixed position.
De Robeck had been unable to destroy these forts because of the minefields which protected them. If the howitzer could do the work which
had earlier been assigned to naval guns, the Allied battleships could

once more advance. ANZAC troops had been brought down from the Anzac landing area by sea to add to the forces already assembled. For four days there was savage fighting. But at the end of it no progress had been made, and less than five hundred yards of scrubland had been gained by the Allied troops. By May 9 it was clear that Achi Baba could not be wrested from the Turks. Even the village of Krithia remained in Turkish hands. The Army could do no more; it was exhausted. 'I might represent the battle as a victory,' Hamilton telegraphed to Kitchener, 'as the enemy's advance positions were driven in, but essentially the result has been failure, as the main object remains unachieved.'

The Royal Naval Division had been in the centre of the Helles fighting. Asquith's son was wounded. 'Oc Asquith has had a wonderful escape,' Jack Churchill wrote to his brother on May 9. 'The bullet passed through his knee without touching the bone or injuring the joint. I saw him just before he sailed for Alexandria, he was quite cheery. Another fellow was hit the same day almost in the same place and has had his leg amputated!' Josiah Wedgwood was also wounded on May 9. 'I am coming home,' he wrote to Churchill ten days later from the Royal Naval hospital at Malta. 'I've done my turn and got it comfortably in the balls. So I can respectably retire from a glove fight & bury myself in archeology.'

In his letter of May 9 Jack Churchill described the fighting of May 6:

... The infantry did their best and until dark at 7.30 rushes forward were continuous. But they were always stopped. Machine gun fire swept the front rank away—while clouds of shrapnel burst beautifully over the supports and reserves. Everybody tried—the French, the Senegalese, the RND, the Australians, and the 29th Division—but it was no use and it was obvious that the attack had failed.

On the afternoon of May 7 Jack Churchill had sat in a trench at the top of the cliffs at Helles looking across the plain towards Achi Baba. In front of him the British troops moved slowly forward through a barrage of Turkish shell and shrapnel, while to the right he saw French infantry in their light blue uniforms and Senegalese troops in dark blue advancing towards the Turkish trenches:

Suddenly on the ridge in front a whole line of Turks rose and started running to the rear. It was a most exciting moment. I could see the French break into a run behind them. Their bayonettes flashed and I could see the officers

in front waving their swords. It was just like the cinematograph that you and
I used to take Johnnie to. The film came to an end with the same abruptness.
The picture was obliterated with appalling suddenness. A gigantic explosion
seemed to take place and for several minutes nothing could be seen but clouds
of black smoke, ever growing thicker. When it cleared nothing was left but a
few French running back to the shelter of their trench. The Turks had poured
in a terrible fire of heavy guns—I suspect 'Jack Johnsons' as in France—they
did not spare their own men and Turk & French were blown to bits together.

All that he had witnessed on May 6 and 7 made Jack Churchill pessimistic about the military future on the Gallipoli Peninsula. 'It has been
siege warfare again as in France,' he told his brother:

> Trenches and wire beautifully covered by machine gun fire are the order
> of the day. Terrific artillery fire against invulnerable trenches and then
> attempts to make frontal attacks in the face of awful musketry fire, are the
> only tactics that can be employed. . . . We shall have to fight every yard and
> to do this we must have lots more men. Can we have them? We certainly
> cannot get on without. . . .
> I do not think another push will be attempted until reinforcements arrive.
> We shall have to dig in and withstand the Turks' attacks.

'In this war,' Jack Churchill wrote in his letter of May 9, 'the wounded
are very prominent. As you land you have to step over stretchers on the
little improvised jetty, and there seem to be blood and bandages all over
the beach.' Churchill, the negotiations in Paris having ended successfully, had also spent May 9 in a battle zone, watching the massive,
unsuccessful British attack at Aubers Ridge. He too had seen what he
later described as 'the hideous spectacle' of wounded men at the height
of a battle, recalling in *The World Crisis*:

> More than 1,000 men suffering from every form of horrible injury, seared,
> torn, pierced, choking, dying, were being sorted according to their miseries
> into the different parts of the Convent at Merville. At the entrance, the
> arrival and departure of the motor ambulances, each with its four or five
> shattered and tortured beings, was incessant: from the back door corpses
> were being carried out at brief intervals to a burying party constantly at
> work. One room was filled to overflowing with cases not worth sending any
> farther, cases whose hopelessness excluded them from priority in operations.
> . . . An unbroken file of urgent and critical cases were pressed towards the
> operating room, the door of which was wide open and revealed as I passed
> the terrible spectacle of a man being trepanned. Everywhere was blood and

bloody rags. Outside in the quadrangle the drumming thunder of the cannonade proclaimed that the process of death and mutilation was still at its height.

On May 9 de Robeck called a naval conference on board the *Queen Elizabeth*. Having witnessed for three days the failure of the Army to capture Achi Baba, the sailors discussed the possibility of renewing the purely naval attack. Commodore Keyes was particularly vehement that this ambitious project should be taken up again. The sailors felt dissatisfied at the small amount of help they had been able to give the Army during the previous three days, despite the enormous number of ships gathered on the fringes of the Peninsula. De Robeck's instructions had called for a simultaneous military and naval attack; but during the battle the Navy had made no attempt to bombard the forts or advance towards the Narrows. Although de Robeck had called off the naval attack on March 18 because of his heavy losses, he had never entirely given up the thought of renewing the attack once those losses had been made good, and his ability to deal with mines improved. In a private letter to Churchill on April 28 he had written: 'The fleet are all ready to have another attack on the Chanak defences & only await the right moment. We are sweeping up a good many mines still. Whether they have been laid or those drifted out of the mine field after our explosive creeps have parted their moorings is hard to say. . . . Thank you for all your support & believe me when I say I appreciate it from the bottom of my heart. . . .'

On April 30 de Robeck had sent Churchill details of the ammunition which he had used, noting that 'the main advance of the army and fleet attack at Narrows is before us' and asking for extra supplies of ammunition for the purpose. News of a Russian bombardment at the mouth of the Bosphorus on May 3 had further stirred de Robeck to contemplate resuming the naval attack, and on May 10 he telegraphed to Churchill to ask whether the Navy could 'by forcing the Dardanelles ensure the success of the operations' which had gone so badly on land. But in asking whether he ought to pursue a purely naval attack, de Robeck also expressed his doubts about the ability of the Army to follow up a naval success. 'From the vigour of the enemy's resistance it is improbable that the passage of the Fleet into the Marmora will be decisive,' he telegraphed, 'and therefore it is equally probable that the Straits will be closed behind the Fleet. This will be of slight importance if the resistance of the enemy would be overcome in time to prevent the enforced with-drawal of the Fleet owing to lack of supplies.' The stubborn Turkish resistance during the three days of battle did not give much encourage-ment to the belief that the Turkish capital would surrender at the sight of British warships. 'The temper of the Turkish army in the Peninsula,' de Robeck continued, 'indicates that the forcing of the Dardanelles and subsequent appearance of the Fleet off Constantinople will not, of itself, prove decisive.' De Robeck therefore asked for a decision: 'If the navy were to suffer a reverse, which of necessity could only be a severe one, would the position of the army be so critical as to jeopardize the whole of the operations?'

Churchill returned to London from Paris and the western front on May 10. Although more than two months had passed since his first enthusiasm for a naval attack, during which time he had constantly pressed for action and bowed only with the greatest reluctance to Admiralty opposition, he now realized that new conditions had arisen which seriously affected his earlier enthusiasm. The presence of a large army on the Gallipoli Peninsula which depended for its survival upon total naval mastery in the Aegean, without which its supplies of food and ammunition would be in instant jeopardy, and the suspected arrival in Aegean waters of German submarines which might at any moment disrupt communications, made it almost impossible to set the Navy on a potentially disastrous course, or to send ships into the Sea of Marmara which might then have their retreat cut off and be unable to help the Army in its slow advance. During the negotiations in Paris, Churchill had been obliged, as part of the Allied bargain with Italy, to promise the immediate despatch of four British battleships and four light cruisers to assist the Italian Fleet in the Adriatic. The strength of Jellicoe's forces in the North Sea could not be weakened; this Adriatic squadron would have to be deducted from de Robeck's armada. It was difficult to encourage the Admiral to attack while simultaneously weakening his force. Yet Churchill was reluctant to dampen de Robeck's revived enthusiasm for a renewed naval attack. Unwilling to endanger the Army by a naval advance beyond the Narrows, Churchill decided that the most he could encourage de Robeck to try was to clear the Kephez minefield, and advance as far as the Narrows, destroying the Turkish forts as he advanced. Fisher was opposed to any independent naval action, however limited. On May 11 this conflict of views led to acrimonious exchanges at the Admiralty. 'I used every argument which the situation presented,' Churchill wrote in an unpublished note after the war, 'and made every appeal that our long and intimate association rendered possible. I encountered an absolute refusal, accompanied by signs of the most extreme distress.'

Fisher's distress had a personal cause. When Churchill had left for France on May 5 the responsibility of the daily conduct of Admiralty affairs had fallen automatically upon Fisher's shoulders. The strain had been a heavy one. Clementine Churchill later recalled in a conversation with the author that she had tried to persuade her husband not to go at all, arguing that the old Admiral would not be able to bear the strain. But Churchill's mission to Paris was part of the delicate negotiations intended to bring Italy into the war, and could not be put off. Fisher found himself in sole charge of Admiralty business. The responsibility agitated him. In an effort to soothe him, Clementine Churchill invited him to luncheon at Admiralty House. All went well, and the Admiral departed in a cheerful mood. But some moments later, when she herself was leaving, she found him still lurking in the corridor. 'What is it?' she asked. 'You are a foolish woman,' he replied. 'All the time you think Winston's with Sir John French he is in Paris with his mistress.' Clementine Churchill was stunned by such a wounding remark. It was for her a sure sign that Fisher's mind was unbalanced. She reported all this to her husband on his return, fearing that Fisher might break down. The Admiral, she later recalled, was 'as nervous as a kitten'.

During his discussion with Fisher on May 11 Churchill limited his demands to an attack on the Kephez minefield and the forts. Fisher feared that if this limited operation were successful, Churchill would be in a strong position to urge de Robeck to go further, and try to break through into the Sea of Marmara. By noon deadlock had been reached. In a combative mood Fisher went to see Hankey and asked for his help in preparing a memorandum objecting to any independent naval action at the Dardanelles. Hankey agreed to do so. 'At Fisher's request,' he wrote in his diary that day, 'I prepared memo for him to give the First Lord, setting forth his objections to separate naval action and declining to be in charge of it.' Fisher sent the memorandum to Churchill that afternoon with a covering letter. 'With much reluctance in view of our conversation of this morning,' he wrote, 'I feel compelled to send you the enclosed formal memorandum of my views respecting the Dardanelles, as it is essential that on so vital a point I should not leave you in any doubt as to my opinion.' Fisher added a postscript: 'I have had no communication with Sir A. Wilson or Sir H. Jackson on the subject whatever.' He made no reference to the aid he had received from Hankey. The memorandum stated that an attack by the Fleet on the Dardanelles forts, 'in repetition of the operations which failed on

March 18, or any attempt by the Fleet to rush by the Narrows, is doomed to failure, and, moreover, is fraught with possibilities of disaster utterly incommensurate to any advantage that could be obtained therefrom'. Both Fisher and Hankey believed that military success was essential before the Navy could resume any operations. 'The sweeping of the mines in the Narrows,' the memorandum continued, 'is an operation which, in my opinion, experience has shown not to be possible, even after the batteries have been silenced, until the heights on either side have been occupied by the military.' The memorandum concluded with a threat of resignation:

I cannot, under any circumstances, be a party to any order to Admiral de Robeck to make an attempt to pass the Dardanelles until the shores have been effectively occupied. I consider that purely Naval action, unsupported by the Army, would merely lead to heavy loss of ships and invaluable men, without any reasonable prospect of a success in any way proportionate to the losses or to the possible further consequences of those losses. I therefore wish it to be clearly understood that I dissociate myself from any such project.

Having sent this memorandum to Churchill, Fisher gave Hankey a verbal message for Asquith. 'At F's request,' Hankey recorded in his diary, 'saw PM just before lunch and told him F would resign if such action was taken.' Asquith told Hankey that he thought 'it was a very foolish message'. He nevertheless authorized Hankey to say that 'separate naval action would not be taken without F's concurrence'. Churchill was not informed of Asquith's promise to Fisher. This promise, given to calm Fisher, made him believe that he had received a veto power over Churchill. But only the Prime Minister possessed the power to overrule a member of the Cabinet. As First Sea Lord, Fisher could never have been entitled to such power.

When Churchill received Fisher's memorandum and covering note, he recognized at once the seriousness of the situation. In his reply he used strong arguments:

My dear Fisher,
    You will never receive from me any proposition to 'rush' the Dardanelles; & I agree with the views you express so forcibly on this subject. It may be that the Admiral will have to engage the forts & sweep the Kephez minefield as an aid to the military operations; & we have always agreed in the desirability of forcing them to fire off their scanty stock of ammunition. But in view of Hamilton's latest telegram this is clearly not required now. And it is my most earnest hcpe on public & still more on personal grounds that

any real issue when presented will find us as always hitherto—united. That shall be my only endeavour.

We are now in a vy difficult position. Whether it is my fault for trying or my misfortune for not having the power to carry through is immaterial. We are now committed to one of the greatest amphibious enterprises of history. You are absolutely committed. Comradeship, resource, firmness, patience, all in the highest degree will be needed to carry the matter through to victory. A great army hanging on by its eyelids to a rocky beach, and confronted with the armed power of the Turkish Empire under German military guidance: the whole *surplus* fleet of Britain—every scrap that can be spared—bound to that army and its fortunes as long as the struggle may drag out: the apparition of the long-feared submarine—our many needs and obligations—the measureless advantages—probably decisive on the whole war—to be gained by success.

Surely here is a combination & a situation wh requires from us every conceivable exertion & contrivance wh we can think of. I beg you to lend your whole aid & goodwill, & ultimately then success is certain.

Yours ever
W

Buoyed up by the belief that Asquith would stand by him, Fisher rejected Churchill's appeal. On May 12 he behaved with all the confidence of a man determined not to compromise. 'I met F near the D of York's Column,' Sir Francis Hopwood told Prince Louis over a year later, on 24 June 1916, '& he at once took me into the Atheneum, into a private room at the back and said: "I have resigned and I am off. I've asked for rooms at Nice . . . and I'm off there in the morning. I'm not going to do another stroke of work with that little fellow." I tried to dissuade him & argued for some time, but to no effect, and we parted.' Fisher then called on Hankey at his office in Whitehall Gardens and showed him Churchill's letter, which Hankey described in his diary as 'rather a slippery one'. Fisher told Hankey that the letter had 'much dissatisfied him', and proposed sending his memorandum to Asquith, if Hankey and Hopwood advised him to do so. Hankey accordingly discussed the matter with Hopwood. 'We agreed to advise Fisher to send memo,' Hankey recorded in his diary, 'as it was absolutely necessary to bring Churchill to his bearings.' Encouraged by Hankey and Hopwood, Fisher sent his memorandum to Asquith. Then he replied to Churchill's letter:

My dear Winston,

Until the Military Operations have effectively occupied the shores of the Narrows &c no naval attack on the minefield can take place. But your letter does not repudiate this and therefore in view of our joint conversation with the Prime Minister prior to March 18 I have sent him a copy of my memorandum to you—

With reference to your remark that I am absolutely committed—I have only to say that you must know (as the Prime Minister also) that my unwilling acquiescence did not extend to such a further gamble as any repetition of March 18 until the army had done their part.

Yours truly
Fisher

Churchill did not reply. 'This if acted on,' he wrote to Masterton-Smith the next day, 'wd prevent VA De Robeck from supporting the advance of the Army on the Kilid Bahr plateau and wd therefore rupture the whole plan. But the point can better be dealt with when the moment arrives.' That afternoon Churchill saw Fisher. In an attempt to placate him, and to avert his resignation, Churchill agreed that the *Queen Elizabeth* should leave the Dardanelles, to be replaced by two monitors with 14-inch guns. Churchill knew that it was the presence of this powerful battleship at the Dardanelles which, although originally suggested by Fisher himself, now most agitated the Admiral's mind, particularly as German submarines were reported to have reached the eastern Mediterranean. The return of the *Queen Elizabeth* to home waters must, Churchill believed, lessen Fisher's discontent. During the afternoon of May 12 Churchill sent Fisher a summary of the concessions which he was prepared to make. He also sent a copy to Oliver:

The arrival of German S/Ms in the Eastern Meditn, & the terms of the Anglo-Franco-Italian naval convention, necessitate a readjustment of our forces at the Dlles. The army must now advance slowly towards its goal. An additional army corps is being despatched & cannot reach the scene for nearly a month. A lull must therefore occur in the operations affording an opportunity for the necessary readjustments. I propose to you the following movements:—

1) Q. Elizabeth is to sail for home at once with all despatch & utmost secrecy and to join the Grand Fleet.

2) Venerable & Exmouth to sail with all despatch for Dlles (long range 12″).

3) Queen, Prince of Wales, Implacable, London, to proceed to Malta under RA Thursby[1] as soon as according to the Anglo-Franco-Italian Convention the French sqn is raised to 6 battleships. This sqn will act with the Italian

---

[1] Cecil Fiennes Thursby, 1861–1936. Entered Navy, 1874. Rear-Admiral, 1911. In charge of naval operations at the 'Anzac' landing, 25 April 1915. Commanded British Adriatic Squadron, 1915–16. Knighted, 1916. Vice-Admiral commanding Eastern Mediterranean, 1917–18. Admiral, 1919. Commander-in-Chief, Plymouth, 1919–20.

Fleet under the general command of the Italian C in C[1] after Italy has declared war.

4) Admiral Farragut & Stonewall Jackson to proceed at the earliest possible moment with all despatch to the Dlles to replace Q. Elizabeth.

That evening Kitchener was invited to a conference at the Admiralty and told of this decision. When he learned that the *Queen Elizabeth* was to be withdrawn he became extremely angry. Churchill described his anger in *The World Crisis*: 'His habitual composure in trying ordeals left him. He protested vehemently against what he considered the desertion of the army at its most critical moment.' Now it was Fisher's turn to grow angry, as Churchill recalled: '*The Queen Elizabeth* would come home,' he insisted; 'she would come home at once; she would come home that night, or he would walk out of the Admiralty then and there.' Kitchener was unconvinced either by Fisher's threat to resign or by Churchill's careful explanations, writing to Asquith as soon as he had left the Admiralty that: 'We may have to consider under these circumstances whether the troops [had] better not be taken back to Alexandria, as there may be a Moslem rising in Egypt, and we have denuded the garrison to help the operations.' Kitchener's sarcasm had no effect. Asquith had already committed himself not to take any action of which Fisher disapproved.

Churchill had always sustained de Robeck's needs. He could do so no longer. At nine-thirty that evening he telegraphed:

. . . Arrival of German submarines in Turkish waters makes it undesirable to expose Queen Elizabeth. We are therefore sending you at once instead Exmouth and Venerable; and also before the end of the month the first two new monitors Admiral Farragut and Stonewall Jackson with two 14-inch guns apiece, an effective range of 20,000 yards firing a 1,400 pound high explosive shell, 10 foot draught and special bulges against mine and torpedo.

You will be able to use the two monitors much more freely for all purposes as they have been specially built for this work.

Queen Elizabeth is to sail for home at once with all despatch and utmost secrecy. You should make out she has gone to Malta for a few days and will return. . . .

In the same telegram, Churchill informed de Robeck of the consequences of the Anglo-Italian agreement: four more of his battleships were to be withdrawn, to be replaced by French vessels. Twenty minutes later Churchill sent de Robeck a personal message

[1] Luigi Amadeo Giuseppe Maria Ferdinando Francesco, 1873–1933. Duke of Abruzzi; Prince of Savoy. Arctic and African explorer. Commander-in-Chief of the Italian Navy, 1915–17.

in an attempt to cushion the depressing effect of his previous telegram:

I hope you will not be discouraged by the recall of the Queen Elizabeth and the unavoidable changes in your fleet consequent on the Italian Convention.

The two monitors will go anywhere, and you will be able to use them with freedom.

They are the last word in bombarding vessels.

I am determined to support you and the army in every way to the end of your task, and I am quite sure that the result will amply repay the sacrifices and anxieties of the struggle.

That night, increasingly confident of his ability to stop any further naval activity at the Dardanelles, Fisher wrote to Asquith, whose support he now believed was absolute, reminding him of his protest against the Dardanelles immediately before the War Council on January 28. 'With extreme reluctance,' he continued, 'and largely due to earnest words spoken to me by Kitchener, I, by not resigning (*as I see now I should have done*), remained a most unwilling beholder (and indeed a participator) of the gradual draining of our naval resources from the decisive theatre of the war.'

For several days, Churchill's visit to France for the secret Italian negotiations had been the subject of Conservative criticism. Asquith was asked about it in the House of Commons on May 12:

LORD ROBERT CECIL: May I ask the Prime Minister whether his attention has been called to the statement that the First Lord of the Admiralty has recently been at the Front: whether the statement is true; and, if so, what were the duties which the First Lord was carrying out there on behalf of the Government?

THE PRIME MINISTER: My right honourable friend visited Paris last week on important Admiralty business, and on the way back spent the Saturday and Sunday at Sir John French's headquarters at the Commander-in-Chief's invitation.

LORD ROBERT CECIL: Do I understand that the right honourable gentleman was not discharging any duties on behalf of the Government when he was at headquarters?

THE PRIME MINISTER: No, none.

HONOURABLE MEMBERS: Joy ride!

SIR FORTESCUE FLANNERY:[1] Was the First Lord of the Admiralty carried across the channel in a destroyer?

[1] John Fortescue Flannery, 1851–1943. Liberal Unionist MP, 1895–1906. Knighted, 1899. Created Baronet, 1904. President of the Institute of Marine Engineers, 1897. Conservative MP, 1910–22.

THE PRIME MINISTER: I am sorry such a question should be asked. The First Lord went on most important Admiralty business to Paris. Since the beginning of the war he has not been absent from the Admiralty more than fourteen days during the whole of these nine months.

Asquith's defence was not enough. The Tories wanted to use Churchill's visits to France in order to discredit the Government. Most Conservatives saw the visits as symbolic of Churchill's irresponsibilities, his vagaries, his immaturity, his inability to restrict himself to his proper sphere. Some Liberals took alarm, fearing that Churchill's frequent visits to Sir John French's Headquarters were part of an intrigue against Kitchener. Lord Esher received two letters which typified these suspicions. 'Winston has been over here for a few days on a SECRET visit which is known to everyone in France,' his son Maurice Brett[1] wrote from Paris on May 8; 'Why can't he stick to his own job? He is becoming an object of amusement and some scorn here. The French are beginning to shrug their shoulders when he is mentioned—a bad sign.' Esher passed on his son's comments to Buckingham Palace, from where Lord Stamfordham replied on May 14: 'I was interested in what you said about the criticism among French responsible authorities at Winston's frequent absence from England in France and surprised at the PM's announcement that this amounted to only 14 days since August!'[2]

During the night of May 12 the battleship *Goliath* was sunk off Sedd-el-Bahr by a Turkish torpedo boat which had skilfully slipped down from Chanak stern first. Five hundred and seventy sailors were drowned. For Fisher, the torpedoing of the *Goliath* was proof that he had been right in insisting upon the recall of the *Queen Elizabeth*. On May 13, increasingly confident that his argument could now prevail, he insisted upon firm instructions being sent to de Robeck, deprecating any

[1] Maurice Vyner Baliol Brett, 1882–1934. 2nd son of 2nd Viscount Esher. Entered Army, 1902. ADC to Sir John French, 1904–12. Lieutenant-Colonel, British Intelligence Mission to France, 1914–16. Deputy Assistant Adjutant General, 1916. Assistant Keeper and Librarian, the London Museum, 1919–34.

[2] When Sir Max Aitken (then Lord Beaverbrook) wrote in *Politicians and the War*, that Churchill's frequent absences in France had greatly embarrassed Asquith, Churchill wrote in the margin of Beaverbrook's proofs: 'All this I regard as injurious and misleading. Altogether I was absent on Dunkirk business three separate single days. During my 10 mths war tenure of Adm I was 16 days on the continent—including Antwerp five, a mission to France two, & the Anglo Italian naval convention three. All of wh were at the direct request of Kitchener or of the War Council.'

further independent naval initiative whatsoever. Churchill insisted that if de Robeck considered it feasible to advance to the Narrows in conjunction with the Army, he should be allowed to do so.

That afternoon, at Hankey's suggestion, Fisher went to 10 Downing Street to explain to Asquith why he was refusing to give de Robeck the discretion for which he had asked, and for which Churchill insisted. Fisher was waiting in Asquith's Private Secretary's room when Margot Asquith came in. She recorded their conversation in her diary:

M: How are things going?
LORD F: As badly as they can, 30,000 casualties in the Dardanelles, 16,000 English, 14,000 French, 60 percent of the French engaged. I was always as you know against this mad expedition. The North Sea is the place where we can beat the Germans, we ought to have taken the island of Borkum, landed these Dardanelles fellows there and got into Berlin.
M: You know you have talked too much—all London knows you are against the Dardanelles expedition. Why didn't you resign at the time?
LORD F: It's a lie—I've seen no one, been no where, I'm far too busy.
M: But you've talked to a few—enough for all to know.
LORD F: . . . It's Winston that talks to AJB and F. E. Smith. You can ask AJB if I wasn't against this expedition—taking all our men out there and our ships will have to go too. It will bleed us white.
M: Well, we're in for it and *must* see it through.
LORD F: Oh, yes, it may turn out all right but I doubt it.
M: It's helped to bring Italy in—Has she good ships?
LORD F: Mere organ grinders! No use whatever,[1] but it's no good looking backwards. Why, look at Lot's wife, she looked backwards!! . . . Come along and have a valse.
He seized me by the waist in Bongy's [Maurice Bonham Carter] little room and we valsed round. The old boy is a fine dancer. His last words were 'I'm very glad you told me what they say'.

Fisher then went to see Asquith. After the meeting he told Hankey that 'he had had the most satisfactory interview of his life'. On May 14 he wrote to Hankey that Asquith had said: 'Rely on me. I will never fail you.' While Fisher was at 10 Downing Street giving Asquith his reasons

---

[1] Churchill's opinion of the Italians was no higher; on February 8 Margot Asquith had recorded in her diary his description of Italy as 'the harlot of Europe'. She also reported the French Ambassador, Paul Cambon, as saying of the Italians: 'Ils voleront au secours des vainceurs.'

for wishing to restrict de Robeck's activities, Kitchener was explaining to Sir George Riddell at the War Office how necessary the enterprise was. As part of his task as liaison officer between the Government and the Press, Riddell sent an account of Kitchener's views to all editors:

Lord Kitchener said there is much misapprehension about the expedition to the Dardanelles, which was of the greatest importance from a political point of view. The effect upon the Balkan States and South Europe had been remarkable. Had it not been for those operations it is impossible to say what would have happened in these areas. Lord Kitchener remarked that the magnitude of the operations and the loss of life are matters for regret, but that they were unavoidable incidents of a necessary campaign. The naval and military operations will be vigorously pushed to a conclusion, but all due precautions will be exercised to insure that men and munitions required for the war in the west are not diverted to the east. Lord Kitchener spoke in strong terms about the necessity of impressing the Balkan States and Southern Europe, and I understood that the Germans view our proceedings in the Dardanelles with much anger and apprehension.

Fisher was unable to stanch the flow of his criticism. No sooner had he returned from 10 Downing Street to the Admiralty than he wrote to Asquith, reiterating his views, and threatening resignation yet again:

Instead of the whole time of the whole of the Admiralty being concentrated on the daily increasing submarine menace in home waters, we are all diverted to the Dardanelles, and the unceasing activities of the First Lord, both by day and night, we are engaged in ceaseless *prodding* of everyone in every department afloat and ashore in the interest of the Dardanelles fleet . . . *I feel my time is short.*

Churchill knew nothing of Fisher's meetings and correspondence with Asquith. Throughout May 13 he concentrated upon the problems which would arise should operations at the Dardanelles continue for some time. He was determined to anticipate all conceivable difficulties. During the day he wrote to Fisher:

Although there is good reason to hope that a speedy termination may be reached, it would now be prudent to assume that the operations against the Dardanelles will not take less than three months, and to make all preparations on that basis. If success is obtained earlier, so much the better; but let us make sure that it is not deferred longer. The operations have now reached a point where they may easily develop into a great siege similar to that of

Port Arthur,[1] though not so formidable. Our preparations should therefore consider and cover the following points:—

1. The provision of siege artillery which could be used against the semi-permanent works, and the mounting on shore of heavy long-range naval guns which can from the existing positions held by our troops, bring accurate fire to bear on the permanent defences.

2. The provision of landing stages of a semi-permanent character at Seddul Bahr and Gaba Tepe with cranes, lines of railway, and all other facilities for handling large and heavy traffic.

3. Protection against the enemy's submarines by means of the establishment . . . of regular lines of indicator nets watched by drifters, joining up Imbros with the Gallipoli Peninsula, and providing permanent protection along the western coast. In these tideless waters, and with the great quantity of indicator nets coming to hand, there should be no difficulty in this.

4. The battleships of the bombarding fleet should go by turns to Malta and there be fitted with the best steel trellis work protection against mines which can be devised. While the present lull in the operations continues, there can be no need to keep the whole fleet at the Dardanelles, and every opportunity should be taken to afford the ships the necessary protection.

5. The question should now be considered whether it is not worth while to move the two Russian army corps now unable to be transported to the Black Sea northwards by rail to Archangel, and ship them round to land at Enos. A timetable should be prepared showing what would be possible in this respect.

6. . . . 70 aeroplanes and seaplanes will be required, and preparations must be made to work up to this. Some of the heaviest seaplanes capable of carrying and dropping 500 lb bombs are to be included. I will settle the details of this last provision personally with DAD [Director Air Dept.].

In the final version of these proposals as sent to Fisher, Churchill deleted paragraph five, which was not Fisher's concern, but which would have to be taken up with Kitchener and Grey.

During the afternoon Churchill continued to try to persuade Fisher to send an encouraging message to de Robeck. They had not yet replied to de Robeck's telegram of May 10 seeking guidance on future operations. Fisher refused to countenance even a limited attempt to sweep the Kephez minefields, and pressed Churchill to give de Robeck the order: 'You must on no account take decisive action without our permission.' Churchill refused, writing to Fisher late that afternoon:

I cannot agree to send a telegram which might have the effect of paralysing

[1] The Japanese siege of Port Arthur (1904–5) lasted 157 days, after which the Russians surrendered; Allied troops were on the Gallipoli Peninsula for 259 days, after which they withdrew.

necessary naval action as judged necessary by the responsible Admiral on the spot. The telegram I have drafted is quite sufficient, but I have made a small amendment in an attempt to meet your wishes. It is dangerous to delay sending the telegram, and I have therefore directed the secretary to send it in this form.

The telegram as finally sent to de Robeck shortly after half past eight that evening read:

We think the moment for an independent naval attempt to force the Narrows has passed and will not arise again under present conditions. The army is now landed, large reinforcements are being sent and there can be no doubt that with time and patience the Kilid Bahr plateau will be taken. Your role is therefore to support the Army in its costly but sure advance and reserve your strength to deal with the situation which will arise later when the Army has succeeded with your aid in its task. We are going to send you the first six monitors as they are delivered and you will find them far better adapted to this special work than the old battleships. You will later receive telegrams about increased provisions of nets against submarines about fitting special anti-mine protection to some of your battleships and about landing heavy guns.

Churchill had given way entirely to Fisher's demands. Three days of long argument and bitter recriminations were, he hoped, at an end. But Fisher ignored the extent of his success, and was still determined to give the impression that Churchill had been unreasonable. Immersed in complaints about Churchill's conduct, he wrote to Hankey early the next morning, May 14:

BURN
My beloved Hankey,
    AGAIN last evening Winston sent off another telegram to de Robeck when Bartolome had told him I objected! So I had to go to him at 5.30 pm and say it was a '*casus belli*' and then he cancelled the telegram & sent the one I had given to Bartolome—and then once again at 7 pm he re-asserted his conviction that after all in six weeks time the Fleet would have to do it *ALONE*! '& would I remain on anyhow quiet for these six weeks'!!! *That is to say I am to aid and abet for 6 weeks?*
    What is one to do with such a determined mad Gambler?—ask *MCKENNA*! *SECRETLY*—and the Prime Minister says to me 'Rely on me' 'I will never fail you,' but Winston ignores the lot & sends the telegrams from *himself*—'Surely I can send a private letter to a friend without showing it to you'!!!! That's his argument!—'A private telegram of friendship, cordiality and encouragement' (as he terms it).
                                Yours till death
                                    F

On the morning of Friday May 14 *The Times* hurled a stick of dynamite at the feet of the Liberal Government. The headline declared:

NEED FOR SHELLS
BRITISH ATTACK CHECKED
LIMITED SUPPLIES THE CAUSE
A LESSON FROM
FRANCE

According to the paper's military correspondent, Colonel Repington, the reason for the failure of the offensive against Aubers Ridge on May 9 had been the lack of high explosive shells. Repington's despatch had been written at the instigation of Sir John French himself. The Commander-in-Chief had also sent his two ADCs, Brinsley Fitzgerald[1] and Frederick Guest, to London in order to put his grievances before Lloyd George, Bonar Law and Balfour. French was determined to expose what he considered to be Kitchener's failure. He and his staff had been much angered by a speech which Asquith had made at Newcastle on April 20 in which he had asserted that there was no shortage of ammunition. Asquith had based his assertion upon an assurance from Kitchener in which he wrote, on April 14, that French was confident that 'with the present supply of ammunition, he will have as much as his troops will be able to use in the next forward movement'. But three weeks later, in the midst of battle, French claimed, in his book *1914*: 'I could see that the absence of sufficient artillery support was doubling and trebling our losses in men. I therefore determined on taking the most drastic measures to destroy the apathy of a Government which had brought the Empire to the brink of disaster.'

French and his staff were also angered by Kitchener's enthusiasm for the military operations at the Dardanelles. They did not want to deplete their own forces on behalf of an expedition which they believed to be a mistake. On May 13 General Wilson had written in his diary: 'Sir J told me that he thought it quite likely that K's second army would go to Gallipoli. This *must* be stopped.' The drain of ammunition to the Dardanelles was another source of their anger. On May 9, at the very moment when his forces were being hurled against the German positions on Aubers Ridge, French had received two telegrams ordering him to send 250,000 rounds of eighteen-pounder ammunition and a hundred

[1] Brinsley John Hamilton Fitzgerald, 1859–1931. Stockbroker. ADC and Private Secretary to Sir John French 1900; 1914. Lieutenant-Colonel, 1915.

rounds of heavy ammunition to the Dardanelles. He had replied saying
that as 'a great action' had just begun he could not allow the ammunition to go. Kitchener thereupon sent him a peremptory order, and the
ammunition was sent off from France on May 10. General Wilson noted
in his diary: 'This is a real object lesson in the value of minor operations
& Squiff's lie about ammunition.'

The War Council met at 10 Downing Street on the morning of May
14, its first meeting since April 6. Repington's despatch was a direct
challenge to Asquith, and sought to undermine confidence in Kitchener.
The War Council sat all morning. 'Lord K very gloomy,' Hankey wrote
in his diary; 'Winston Churchill as talkative as ever.' Kitchener reported
a series of bad tidings: the Russians had been defeated in Galicia, the
Germans had held off the British attack on the western front, and Sir
Ian Hamilton's army had been brought to a standstill on the southern
slopes of Achi Baba. Worse than all this, proof that he was not being
supported by his colleagues, a sign of the treachery with which the
Government was surrounded, the *Queen Elizabeth* had been withdrawn
from the Dardanelles. The Army fighting so bravely on shore was without its principal protector. The Admiralty had let him down. They had
lost faith in the enterprise which they had launched. Fisher was not
prepared to listen to charges of bad faith. Though normally silent at the
War Council, having no Ministerial responsibility, he now interrupted
Kitchener's recital, informing the War Council that 'he had been
against the Dardanelles operations from the beginning' and that 'the
Prime Minister and Lord Kitchener knew this fact well'. He said no
more. 'This remarkable interruption,' Churchill later wrote in *The
World Crisis*, 'was received in silence.' To those at the War Council it
was the final proof that Churchill and Fisher were at odds, and that
Admiralty business was being conducted in an atmosphere of crisis.

Kitchener continued with his survey of the war. His pessimism
was undiminished. He warned his colleagues of the danger of a German
invasion. Britain, he asserted, was ill-defended and as soon as new
divisions were ready to fight they should be reserved not for Sir John
French or for the Dardanelles but for home defence. He then warned
that once the New Armies had gone to France, the troops remaining in
Britain would no longer be 'an effective weapon' against a German
invasion. 'If a great disaster similar to that which had happened in
Russia should occur to the French,' he said, 'the trained men of the
New Armies would have to be sent out of the country, which would
increase the danger at home. He asked that a part of the New Armies
should be kept in England for an emergency. But he believed that it was

for the Admiralty 'to take such steps' as would prevent the German Army from landing in Britain. If this were done, he could release the New Armies for service abroad. Churchill did not believe in the danger of a German invasion. He was angry that Kitchener should raise the question now in an attempt to hold back newly trained armies in England. 'There was absolutely no need for anxiety,' he told his colleagues. The armies in France should remain on the defensive; the whole British military effort should be concentrated at Gallipoli.

Lloyd George spoke sceptically of the outcome of the Gallipoli campaign. He believed that the Turks would always be able to meet any British reinforcements by sending additional men of their own to the Gallipoli Peninsula, and asked 'if we could ever send enough men to drive 150,000 Turks out of their position?' Later in the discussion he warned that 'we had under-estimated the resisting power of the enemy at the Dardanelles' and he 'begged that we should not do it again'. He pointed out that the Turks appeared to be fighting well on the Gallipoli Peninsula, and were 'extremely well led by good German officers'. Without wishing to commit himself to a policy of abandoning the enterprise, he wished 'to ascertain exactly the dimensions of the problem, and to decide whether we could do it or not'. It would be very dangerous, he warned his colleagues, 'to go on from day to day merely drifting'.

Kitchener announced that if the War Council decided not to continue the operation without 'the forces required to render success absolutely certain', then he had no doubt that the enterprise ought to be abandoned. He could not promise to make forces on such a scale available. On the other hand, he saw grave danger in withdrawal, particularly 'of a rising in the Moslem world', and declared that 'the only way of getting free from the Dardanelles was to push through'. Crewe also believed that the psychological effect of withdrawal overrode the military difficulties involved in success. 'It was impossible to contemplate the abandonment of the enterprise,' he told his colleagues, 'owing to its effect in India.' Balfour alone spoke of the outcome with a certain degree of hope:

MR BALFOUR said it would be a great mistake to abandon the enterprise unless we were absolutely obliged to. Our position was not a favourable one, but the position of the Turks was by no means pleasant. He suggestion was that we should hold the line which we now occupied, and be content with slow progress, avoiding any operations involving heavy losses. If by withdrawal we could obtain a striking success elsewhere he would agree to it, but there appeared to be no prospect of this. Our immediate course seemed perfectly clear, namely, to maintain our troops in the Peninsula up to the full strength, to make them as comfortable as possible, and to prepare landing places.

Churchill was upset by the mounting doubts of his colleagues. The occupation of the Gallipoli Peninsula, he told them:

. . . would result in rivetting the Turks there, and it had already relieved the pressure on the Russians in the Caucasus. It also rivetted the attention of the Balkan States and of Italy. In his opinion, the outlook was by no means gloomy, and it certainly was not regarded as such by the people on the spot. As regards the alleged drain on ammunition supplies, he pointed out that the 29th Division was the only portion of the troops engaged there which required Mark VII ammunition. Further, a proportion of the artillery was not armed with the 18-pr gun, and the Australians had brought their own ammunition, and the rifles were not the same rifles as we used in France.

Kitchener, Haldane and Lloyd George all raised further brief objections. Churchill spoke again:

MR CHURCHILL said that we had now 560,000 men in France, and, say, 80,000 men in the Dardanelles, a total of 644,000 British troops. Every month new armies were getting nearer completion, and every month the ammunition position was improving. He understood that we already turned out new rifles more rapidly than the French. The Dardanelles enterprise was a very small affair compared with our total resources. He did not share or understand Lord Kitchener's grounds for pessimism with regard to the general situation. He did not see the smallest reason for believing that either the British or French lines in France could be pierced. He objected strongly to despondency.

Churchill's intervention was effective. As Hankey recalled forty years later in *The Supreme Command*: 'His stout attitude did something to hearten his colleagues.' The War Council ended at midday, having decided that Hamilton should be asked 'what force he would require in order to ensure success at the Dardanelles'. This meant that the Dardanelles would go on.

Churchill had been angered by Fisher's outburst that 'he had opposed the Dardanelles operations from the beginning'. The two men had parted amicably on the evening of May 13. Churchill had agreed to the withdrawal of the *Queen Elizabeth*, despite both his own doubts and Kitchener's anger. He had accepted Fisher's refusal to allow a renewed naval attack. Churchill did not know the extent to which Fisher had in the past two days canvassed the support of Asquith, Hankey, Hopwood and McKenna. But he sensed the strange mood that had come over the First Sea Lord. As soon as he returned to the Admiralty he therefore wrote to Asquith in the strongest terms:

I must ask you to take note of Fisher's statement to-day that 'he was against the Dardanelles and had been all along', or words to that effect. The First Sea Lord has agreed in writing to every executive telegram on which the operations have been conducted; and had they been immediately successful the credit would have been his. But I make no complaint of that. I am attached to the old boy and it is a great pleasure to me to work with him. I think he reciprocates these feelings. My point is that a moment will probably arise in these operations when the Admiral and General on the spot will wish and require to run a risk with the Fleet for a great and decisive effort. If I agree with them, I shall sanction it, and I cannot undertake to be paralysed by the veto of a friend who whatever the result will certainly say, 'I was always against the Dardanelles'.

You will see that in a matter of this kind *someone* has to take the responsibility. I will do so—provided that my decision is the one that rules—and not otherwise.

It is also uncomfortable not to know what Kitchener will or won't do in the matter of reinforcements. We are absolutely in his hands, and I never saw him in a queerer mood—or more unreasonable. K will punish the Admiralty by docking Hamilton of his divisions because we have withdrawn the Queen Elizabeth; and Fisher will have the Queen Elizabeth home if he is to stay.

Through all this with patience and determination we can make our way to one of the great events in the history of the world.

But I wish now to make it clear to you that a man who says, 'I disclaim responsibility for failure', cannot be the final arbiter of the measures which may be found to be vital to success.

This requires no answer and I am quite contented with the course of affairs.

That afternoon Fisher again asked Hankey to come to see him at the Admiralty. Perhaps he would have heard further complaints against Churchill, and further threats of resignation. But Fisher was an old man, and had been at work since five that morning. When Hankey reached the Admiralty, he wrote in his diary, 'I found him asleep, tired out, so slipped out again . . . there is a horrible muddle with all this bickering & intriguing between Churchill & Fisher. Why cannot all work honestly for their country only? I am sick of them.'

On waking during the afternoon Fisher summoned his Naval Secretary, Captain Crease. In a memorandum which he wrote in 1923 Crease recalled Fisher's anxieties:

He felt he could not remain much longer at the Admiralty because of the continual drain of the Dardanelles, firstly on the Fleets in Home Waters, in regard to which he was continually receiving personal protests from the Fleets, and secondly on the reserves of ammunition in respect of which the other Sea Lords had recently expressed their uneasiness. He continued, that he knew the Dardanelles operations would go on making further and further demands for ships of all kinds from home, which would prevent all possibility of certain other operations nearer home being carried out, to which he attached very great importance, and since he could not stop the Dardanelles he was beginning to think that he had better clear out and let Mr Churchill carry on.

Churchill believed that he could heal the breach between himself and Fisher. Late that afternoon he went to Fisher's room and for several hours they discussed in detail the position at the Dardanelles. Churchill explained precisely what reinforcements he felt were necessary to enable de Robeck's fleet to continue adequately to support the Army. Fisher agreed that de Robeck should be reinforced with a 15-inch howitzer and two 9·2-inch guns; that nine heavy monitors and six 9·2-inch monitors should be sent to the Dardanelles, and that four ships of the *Edgar* class, specially protected against mines and torpedoes, should go out as soon as possible. For his part, Churchill was willing to bring back more battleships to home waters once the monitors had reached the Dardanelles and to consider the release of the *Chatham*[1] once the *Edgars* were ready. Churchill restricted his request to those things he felt Fisher would accept, and was prepared to limit his requirements to those points which Fisher found acceptable. In a letter to Churchill on 23 October 1923 Crease, who had been present, recalled Churchill's words as he left Fisher's room: 'Well, good night, Fisher. We have settled everything, and you must go home and have a good night's rest. Things will look brighter in the morning and we'll pull the thing through together.' Crease was glad to witness the amicable end of this discussion, writing in his memorandum of 1923:

When Mr Churchill left I could see that he was much relieved. Lord Fisher at once called for me, and said that he wanted to sign his papers and get home,

---

[1] The Light Cruiser *Chatham*, launched in 1911, was not recalled from the Dardanelles either by Churchill or by his successor, but took part in the Suvla landing, August 1915, and was the flagship of Admiral Weymss during the evacuation of the Peninsula. She served with the Grand Fleet, 1916–18, and with the New Zealand Navy, 1920–4.

and he then told me that he had had a very satisfactory discussion with the First Lord, that they had peaceably settled what ships and reinforcements should go to the Dardanelles, and that things were amicable again, and he added, quite cheerily, 'but I suppose he'll soon be at me again'.

Fisher left the Admiralty early that evening. Churchill remained in his room, working on the proposals on which he and Fisher had agreed. By eleven o'clock he had worked them out in detail. As a final point, which on reflection he felt was necessary, he added two more submarines to the reinforcements to be sent to the Dardanelles, 'in view of the request of the VA'; for de Robeck had several times during the previous week urgently requested more submarines. Five new submarines were to be completed in England by the end of May. Churchill felt it reasonable to send two of them to the Dardanelles. This addition to the minute did not commit Fisher in any way. Like the points which they had discussed together during the afternoon, this was a proposal, not an order. Churchill wanted to make this clear to Fisher; he therefore thought it wise to add a personal covering note:

My dear Fisher,
    I send this to you before marking it to others in order that if any point arises we can discuss it. I hope you will agree.

Yours ever
W

Shortly before midnight Masterton-Smith took Churchill's proposals to Crease, with instructions that they should be given to Fisher first thing in the morning. Crease later recorded in his memorandum of 1923 that he had told Masterton-Smith 'that in my opinion Lord Fisher would resign immediately if he received it. . . . Knowing his frame of mind I felt sure that these new proposals, coming just at that moment, would be the last straw.' After some discussion, Masterton-Smith agreed to take the proposals back to Churchill, and to explain Crease's anxieties. Churchill was occupied with urgent business. The Italian Naval Attaché, Lieutenant-Commander Villarey,[1] had called on him to settle the outstanding points of Anglo-Italian co-operation, which was to begin on the following day when Italy's adherence to the Allies was to be announced. It was some time before Churchill could see Masterton-Smith. On hearing of Crease's doubts, he told Masterton-Smith to go back with the proposals and to tell Crease that he was

---

[1] Carlo Rey de Villarey, 1874–1932. Italian Naval Attaché, London, 1913–18. Lieutenant-Commander, 1914; Commander, 1916.

certain Fisher would not object to them, and that 'it was necessary in any case that they should be made'. In his covering letter Churchill had taken care to point out that these proposals were not even to be circulated to the other members of the Admiralty War Group before the two men had discussed them once more. Nor had his ending, 'I hope you will agree', been in the nature of an order. It was well past midnight, and Churchill went to bed.

May 14 had been a day of crisis; but it had ended more calmly than it had begun. Churchill had reason to be content. He had removed some of the gloom instilled by Kitchener at the War Council. He had impressed upon Asquith that future action at the Dardanelles could not be jeopardized by Fisher's eccentric behaviour. He had reached agreement with Fisher on specific reinforcements needed for the Dardanelles, and had put his new proposals in a moderate and cautious form. The weekend would see the Italian alliance made public, a first-fruit of the Dardanelles operation.

Churchill was not unduly borne down by the strain of daily disagreements with Fisher. He remained confident that a successful outcome was possible at the Dardanelles, given the maximum military effort on the Gallipoli Peninsula. On May 11, with Kitchener's increasing determination to secure a victory adding to his confidence, Churchill had sent an official message of encouragement to Hamilton, praising 'the wonderful feats of arms the army has accomplished under your command' and assuring the General that he could rely 'on the utmost aid the navy can give until complete success is won'. Hamilton's reply reached the Admiralty on the morning of May 15:

Your message does me good. Wish you were here. Jack invaluable asset as well as sympathetic friend. You may be proud of Naval Division as a whole. . . . Navy has spared no effort to help us and without them we could neither have landed nor maintained ourselves. . . . Your motor banditti doing well and accounted for many Turks yesterday with their machine guns.

At about nine o'clock that morning Churchill went to the Foreign Office, where he spent some time discussing the Anglo-Italian agreement, the conclusion of which was now further delayed. In *The World Crisis* he later recalled how he was returning to the Admiralty across the Horse Guards' Parade when Masterton-Smith hurried up to him with the words: 'Fisher has resigned, and I think he means it this time.' Masterton-Smith then handed Churchill Fisher's letter of resignation, written in the early hours of the morning:

First Lord

After further anxious reflection I have come to the regretted conclusion I am unable to remain any longer as your colleague. It is undesirable in the public interests to go into details—Jowett[1] said 'never explain'—but I find it increasingly difficult to adjust myself to the increasingly daily requirements of the Dardanelles to meet your views—as you truly said yesterday I am in the position of continually veto-ing your proposals.—

This is not fair to you besides being extremely distasteful to me.

I am off to Scotland at once so as to avoid all questionings.

Yours truly
Fisher

Fisher had threatened resignation so many times before that Churchill was not particularly alarmed. He returned to the Admiralty intending to discuss whatever the new cause for resignation was with Fisher himself. But on reaching the Admiralty, he searched for Fisher in vain. He was not in the Admiralty building, nor in his own quarters at Archway House, over the Mall. All Crease knew was that Fisher had said he was going to Scotland that very morning. Churchill recrossed the Horse Guards' Parade, this time to 10 Downing Street. There he told the Prime Minister what had happened and showed him Fisher's letter. Asquith wrote immediately to Fisher: 'In the King's name, I order you at once to return to your post.'[2] Not knowing Fisher's whereabouts, Asquith sent his Private Secretary, Maurice Bonham Carter, to search London for him in order to give him the letter. It was some time before Fisher could be found. With great reluctance he agreed to see the Prime Minister. When he arrived at 10 Downing Street Asquith was not there: he had gone to the wedding of Geoffrey Howard,[3] a Liberal Whip, at St Margaret's, Westminster. While Fisher was waiting at 10 Downing Street for Asquith's return, Lloyd George arrived. In his *War Memoirs* he recalled how he was 'struck by a dour change' in Fisher's attitude:

A combative grimness had taken the place of his usually genial greeting; the lower lip of his set mouth was thrust forward, and the droop at the corner

---

[1] Benjamin Jowett, 1817–93. Master of Balliol College, Oxford, 1870–93.

[2] Asquith's letter to Fisher is reproduced in facsimile on page 831.

[3] Geoffrey William Algernon Howard, 1877–1935. Son of the 9th Earl of Carlisle. Liberal MP, 1906–10; 1911–18; 1923–4. Parliamentary Private Secretary to H. H. Asquith, 1910. Temporary Captain, Royal Marines, Flanders, 1914. Junior Lord of the Treasury, 1915–16. He married Ethel Christian, daughter of Field-Marshal the 3rd Baron Methuen (1845–1932: Governor and Commander-in-Chief, Malta, 1915–19).

was more marked than usual. His curiously Oriental features were more than ever those of a graven image in an Eastern temple, with a sinister frown.

'I have resigned!' was his greeting, and on my inquiring the reason he replied, 'I can stand it no longer.' He then informed me that he was on his way to see the Prime Minister, having made up his mind to take no further part in the Dardanelles 'foolishness', and was off to Scotland that night.

Lloyd George tried to persuade Fisher to stay at the Admiralty until the following Monday, when he could put his complaints before the War Council. Fisher 'declined to wait another hour'. Lloyd George became quite stern, reminding him that so far as the War Council was concerned 'he had never expressed any dissent from the policy or the plans of the expedition' and that certainly he himself had 'not heard one word of protest from him'. Fisher ignored Lloyd George's reasoning and insisted that he would leave for Scotland immediately. At that moment Asquith returned from the wedding, and with some difficulty persuaded Fisher not to leave London. But he could not persuade him to withdraw his resignation, or to return to the Admiralty building. Fisher then left 10 Downing Street, informing no one of where he intended to go. Asquith sent for Churchill, and they discussed how to persuade Fisher to return. Asquith believed that a letter from Churchill might bring Fisher back to his post. They realized that, unless Fisher returned, the political crisis which they feared would be inevitable.

Fisher would have to be placated. He would need some specific reassurance that naval reinforcements sent to the Dardanelles would be limited to the needs of the Army. The actual proposal which Asquith and Churchill had in mind is not known. Neither of them wrote about it afterwards. Nor did Churchill's letter give any specific details: its intention was to bring Fisher back physically to the Admiralty:

My dear Fisher,
The only thing to think of now is what is best for the country and for the brave men who are fighting. Anything which does injury to those interests will be vy harshly judged by history on whose stage we now are.

I do not understand what is the specific cause wh has led you to resign. If I did I might cure it. When we parted last night I thought we were in agreement. The proposals I made to you by minute were I thought in general accord with your views; & in any case were for discussion between us. Our personal friendship is & I trust will remain unimpaired.

It is true the moment is anxious & our difficulties grave. But I am sure that with loyalty & courage we shall come through safely & successfully. You cd not let it be said that you had thrown me over because things were for the time being going badly at the Dardanelles.

In every way I have tried to work in the closest sympathy with you. The men you wanted in the places you wanted them, the ships you designed—every proposal you have formally made for naval action, I have agreed to. My own responsibilities are great, & also I am the one who gets the blame for anything that goes wrong. But I have scrupulously adhered to our original agreement that we shd do nothing important without consulting each other. If you think this is not so surely you shd tell me in what respect.

In order to bring you back to the Admiralty I took my political life in my hands with the King & the Prime Minister—as you know well. You then promised to stand by me and see me through. If you now go at this bad moment and thereby let loose upon me the spite and malice of those who are your enemies even more than they are mine it will be a melancholy ending to our six months of successful war and administration. The discussions which will arise will strike a cruel blow at the fortunes of the Army now struggling on the Gallipoli peninsula, & cannot fail to invest with an air of disaster a mighty enterprise which with patience can & will certainly be carried to success.

Many of the anxieties of the winter are past. The harbours are protected, the great flow of new construction is arriving. We are far stronger at home than we have ever been, and the great reinforcement is now at hand.

I hope you will come to see me tomorrow afternoon. I have a proposition to make to you, with the assent of the Prime Minister, wh may resolve some of the anxieties & difficulties wh you feel about the measures necessary to support the army at the Dardanelles.

Though I shall stand to my post until relieved, it will be a vy great grief to me to part from you: and our rupture will be profoundly injurious to every public interest.

Yours ever
W

That evening Lloyd George told Frances Stevenson that if Fisher's resignation were accepted, Churchill would also have to leave the Government. She recorded Lloyd George's words in her diary as follows: 'It is the Nemesis of the man who has fought for this war for years. When the war came he saw in it the chance of glory for himself, & has accordingly entered on a risky campaign without caring a straw for the misery and hardship it would bring to thousands, in the hope that he would prove to be the outstanding man in this war.' These were harsh sentiments; many people shared them.

Fisher remained in hiding throughout May 15. Churchill's letter only reached him at ten o'clock that evening. In his reply, sent early on the following morning, Fisher reminded Churchill of his 'extreme reluctance in the Prime Minister's room in January to accept his decision in regard to the Dardanelles' and stated that 'the series of fresh naval arrangements for the Dardanelles you sent me yesterday morning convinced me that the time had arrived for me to take a final decision— there being much more in those proposals than had occurred to me the previous evening when you suggested some of them'. Here then was Fisher's reason: Churchill's addition of two further submarines to the Dardanelles reinforcements which they had discussed together on May 13. He had ignored Churchill's covering note that 'I send these to you . . . in order that if any point arises we can discuss it'; his reply was uncompromising. He paid no attention to Churchill's reference to a 'proposition'. He refused a further meeting:

YOU ARE BENT ON FORCING THE DARDANELLES AND NOTHING WILL TURN YOU FROM IT—NOTHING—I know you so well! I could give no better proof of my desire to stand by you than my having remained by you in this Dardanelles business up to this last moment against the strongest conviction of my life. . . .

You will remain and *I SHALL GO*—It is better so. Your splendid stand on my behalf with the King and Prime Minister I can *NEVER* forget when you took your political life in your hands and I really have worked very hard for you in return—*my utmost*—but here is a question beyond all personal obliga- tions. I assure you it is only painful having further conversations. I have told the Prime Minister I will not remain. I have absolutely decided to stick to that decision. Nothing will turn me from it.—You say with much feeling that '*it will be a very great grief to you to part from me*'. I am certain you know in your heart no one has ever been more faithful to you than I have since I joined you last October. *I have worked my very hardest.*

During the morning of May 16 Fisher made his arrangements to leave the Admiralty altogether. 'We shall take rooms at an hotel on Tuesday,' he informed Crease; 'the Ritz, I think, as the Manager[1] is my devoted friend—I got him the billet—£4,000 a year and all found for his family living at the hotel. *I was a d—d fool not to take it myself! ! !* Can't you see me in the restaurant in a white waistcoat and frock-coat!!!' Fisher also instructed Crease to show copies of his reply to Churchill to Sir Francis Hopwood, and to the Second, Third and Fourth Sea Lords. He then wrote to Reginald McKenna:

My beloved Friend,
    I late last night at 10 pm got a long letter from Winston marked 'Private

[1] In May 1915 the Manager of the Ritz was T. Kroell. I have been unable to obtain further biographical information about him; the records of the Ritz were disposed of in the salvage campaign of the Second World War.

and Confidential', so I do not forward it, nor shall I show it to a soul. I won't remark on it to you, but it absolutely *CONVINCES* me I am right in my *UNALTERABLE DECISION* to resign! *In fact I have resigned!* (He talks of a mighty enterprise which will certainly be carried to success!) *Nothing will turn him!* At every turn he will be thinking of the military and not the naval side— *he never has done otherwise.* His heart is ashore, not afloat! *The joy of his life is to be 50 yards from a German trench!*

I want you kindly to tell the Prime Minister distinctly and definitely that *I am no longer First Sea Lord. There is no compromise possible!*

I enclose copy of my letter to Winston to show the Prime Minister. I am not going to see Winston again or anyone else on the subject. And I so much hope you will lead the Prime Minister to see that it is wasting his precious time to have me up before him again on Monday. I have turned over my work to the Second Sea Lord, as is the usual custom. Nothing could have exceeded the kind, I might say affectionate, words to me of the Prime Minister, and I honestly believe that Winston loves me—'*but kind words butter no parsnips*'! I have an honourable reputation, and though I feel like 20, yet I'm 74 and so no time to make a fresh reputation if I lose the present one!

Yours

F

McKenna received this letter late that afternoon. He took it at once to Asquith, who pointed out that Fisher's resignation was void until he had accepted it. McKenna returned from Downing Street to his home in Smith Square, Westminster, and wrote to Fisher that, before Asquith could accept his resignation, 'I am satisfied that he is bound to have your precise grounds definitely formulated in writing and presented to him'.

During the morning of May 16 Churchill received Fisher's reply; he wrote once more, still hoping to persuade the Admiral to return:

My dear Fisher,

I am touched by the kindness of your letter. Our friendship has been a long one. I remember how in 1908 you tried to bring me to the Admiralty as First Lord. When I eventually came in 1911 I proposed to the Prime Minister that you should return to your old position, and only the difficulties which your enemies were likely to make at that time prevented the accomplishment of my first wish. As it was I followed your guidance in the important decisions which have given us the 15-inch gun & Jellicoe today.

Six months ago in the crisis of this great war you came to my aid: since then we have worked together in the very closest intimacy. One difficulty after another has been surmounted; vast schemes of new construction have been carried through; and tremendous reinforcements are now approaching the Fleet. Over the whole range of war-policy and naval administration there is nothing that I know of on which we are disagreed—except the series of events which have led us into the 'Dardanelles'. Even then we were agreed upon the immediate steps, for I shall not press my wish about reinforcements beyond the point to which you were willing to go—namely the 6 earliest monitors. We are now fully agreed that the fleet is not to attempt to rush the Narrows but is to support the Army in its gradual advance upon the forts by land. Orders in this sense have been given with which you were in complete accord.

It seems to me that the only course now is to hold on, to go slow, putting as many ships as possible in Malta and the Canal, out of harm's way, and using the destroyers which are out there to hunt the submarines and convoy the army corps which is now starting. If you came into the Admiralty tomorrow for the first time and looked at the problem as it now is, you would advise this as the only practical course. You must feel as I do & as the War Council decided—that whoever may be responsible for the original step, to withdraw now cannot be contemplated.

The announcement of your resignation at this juncture will be accepted everywhere as proof that the military operations as well as the naval at the Dardanelles have failed. The position of the Army which has suffered a loss of 30,000 men in a joint operation will be jeopardized. The admission of failure at the Dardanelles, for so your resignation would be exploited all over the world, might prove the deciding factor in the case of Italy now trembling on the brink. The knowledge of these facts forces me, not for my own sake (for the fortunes of individuals do not matter now), to appeal to you not to make your resignation operative until at least Italy has declared herself for which the latest date is the 26th. Meanwhile Sir Arthur Wilson could if you desire it do your work.

There ought to be no reproaches between us, and you, my friend, must at this moment in your long career so act that no one can say you were unmindful of the public interests and of the lives of the soldiers and sailors.

In any case whatever you decide I claim in the name of friendship and in the name of duty a personal interview—if only for the purpose of settling what explanation is to be offered to Parliament.

Fisher refused the personal interview. 'Please dont wish to see me,' he wrote in reply; 'I could say nothing as I am determined not to. *I know I am doing right.*'

Fisher had not resigned in order to be ordered back to his post by Asquith, or asked by Lloyd George to stay until Monday's War Council, or told by Churchill that it would be helpful for him to remain until the Italian agreement were signed. He wanted to be given effective control over naval policy. To his chagrin, none of those in authority had approved his course. His friend McKenna had shown no enthusiasm. Nor did the other Sea Lords, whose support he took for granted, sustain his arguments when they were informed of his resignation on May 16. 'However dissatisfied we may feel with the present procedure,' they wrote collectively to both Churchill and Fisher that day, 'we recognize that we are faced with a national crisis of the first magnitude and that the disastrous consequences which must inevitably follow on Lord Fisher's resignation must be averted. Whatever differences of opinion or defects in procedure may have arisen or become apparent should be capable of adjustment by mutual discussion and concession. . . .'

Fisher had not been content to embarrass and threaten the Liberal Government from within. In the early hours of Saturday May 15 he had sent an anonymous message to Bonar Law, the Leader of the Opposition. The envelope was addressed in Fisher's familiar handwriting. Inside was nothing more than a cutting from an old issue of the *Pall Mall Gazette*, in which Fisher had marked the sentence: 'Lord Fisher was received in audience of the King and remained there about half an hour.' Bonar Law deduced that Fisher wanted him to know that he had resigned. Although on this occasion Fisher had not seen the King, the hint was an obvious one.

Having failed to persuade Fisher to withdraw his resignation, or even to see him, Churchill took the prudent course of finding out whether the other members of the Board of Admiralty were prepared to remain at their posts. During May 16 he learned from Sir Arthur Wilson that the Second, Third and Fourth Sea Lords were all willing to stay on. Churchill asked Wilson whether he himself would be willing to replace Fisher as First Sea Lord. Wilson asked for an hour to consider the matter, and then said that he would do so. Churchill had good reason to believe that he had averted a serious crisis. The news of Fisher's resignation had not yet reached the Press. Nor, as far as Churchill knew, was it known to anyone outside the Admiralty except the Prime Minister, McKenna, Lloyd George and Hankey. As a result of Wilson's willingness to serve as First Sea Lord, Churchill felt certain that it would be possible to present Parliament on Monday May 17, not with an unresolved crisis but with one that was already over. He therefore drove to The Wharf at Sutton Courtenay, where Asquith was spending Sunday. 'I told him that Lord Fisher's resignation was final,' Churchill recalled in *The World Crisis*, 'and that my office was at his disposal if he required to make a change. He said, "No, I have thought of that. I do not wish it, but can you get a Board?" I then told him that all the other Members of the Board would remain, and that Sir Arthur Wilson would take Lord Fisher's place. I understood him to assent to this arrangement.'

The crisis seemed almost over. But while Churchill was at The Wharf the Prime Minister's Private Secretary, Maurice Bonham Carter, who was also there, told him that the combination of Fisher's resignation and Repington's despatch to *The Times* about the shell shortage in France was so serious that Asquith might have to consult the Conservatives. 'I saw from this,' Churchill wrote in *The World Crisis*, 'that the crisis would not be by any means confined to the Admiralty.' After dining with Asquith he returned to London late that night. He still believed that if he announced his new Board with the minimum of delay, and explained the reasons for Fisher's resignation to Parliament, a political crisis could be averted; certainly one in which he would be involved.

On the morning of Monday May 17 he asked to see Balfour, and informed him both of Fisher's resignation and Wilson's willingness to become First Sea Lord. He recorded their subsequent conversation in *The World Crisis*:

I said that if these arrangements were finally approved by the Prime Minister that afternoon, I would make an immediate announcement to the House of Commons and court a debate. Mr Balfour was indignant at Lord Fisher's resignation. He said that it would greatly disturb his Unionist friends and that he would himself go and prepare them for it and steady their opinion. Nothing could exceed the kindness and firmness of his attitude.

Balfour left on his placatory mission to the Conservative leaders. Churchill concentrated upon the speech which he intended to make in Parliament. He knew that he would be challenged in the debate, but welcomed the opportunity which it would present, believing that he could answer all criticisms effectively. But while he prepared his speech, confident that he could limit the issue to one of Admiralty policy and thereby circumvent a more serious political crisis, events were taking place which were to sabotage his plan.

On receiving Fisher's obvious clue, Bonar Law had acted with remarkable speed. Early on Monday morning, before Balfour could reach him, he called on Lloyd George at the Treasury and asked him directly whether Fisher had in fact resigned. Lloyd George described the course of their conversation in his *War Memoirs*:

On being told by me that his information was correct Mr Bonar Law emphasised the grave nature of the political question raised, especially as he was convinced that the Government were misinformed about the shell situation. His party had supported the Government consistently throughout the months of the War, without seeking party advantage, but there was a growing discontent amongst Conservatives at this attitude of unqualified support, especially over the treatment of alien enemies, the deficiency of shells, and the failure of the Dardanelles expedition. Matters indeed, had come to such a pitch that it would be impossible for him to restrain his followers, and yet it was essential to avoid any division in the nation in face of the enemy. He was specially emphatic as to the impossibility of allowing Mr Churchill to remain at the Admiralty if Lord Fisher persisted in his resignation. On this point he made it clear that the Opposition meant at all hazards to force a Parliamentary challenge.

Lloyd George saw the force of Bonar Law's threat. He knew the dangers which a sustained parliamentary onslaught upon the Government might involve. During the grave political crisis of 1910 he had argued that a Coalition was preferable to open conflict, and the risk of political defeat. Asking Bonar Law to wait at 11 Downing Street for a few minutes, Lloyd George went along the corridor to see Asquith at No 10, and, as he later wrote, 'put the circumstances quite plainly before him'. Lloyd George argued forcefully in favour of an immediate Coalition, in order to forestall the Conservative onslaught. Asquith had the power to resist Lloyd George's arguments and to rebuff Bonar Law. He knew that Churchill had been able to reconstitute his Board with only one change, and that with Fisher's departure the smooth flow of Admiralty business would no longer be disrupted, and might even be enhanced. He knew that Churchill was capable of explaining the naval position to Parliament successfully. But Asquith agreed at once with Lloyd George's advice, and declared that he would ask the Conservatives to join his administration. 'This decision,' Lloyd George recalled in his *War Memoirs*, 'took an incredibly short time.'

Asquith had wearied of the fight. Unknown to Churchill, Lloyd George, Bonar Law or Balfour, Asquith's power of decision had been temporarily impaired. Venetia Stanley, whose affections he had sought and pursued with intensity for over nine months, had informed him three days before, on Friday May 14, of her intention to marry Edwin Montagu. 'This is too terrible,' he had written to her that midnight; 'no hell could be so bad.' Her news shattered him. The letters which he had received from her, and the daily hope of further meetings and further letters, had sustained him at every crisis. The confidence he had reposed in her, the secrets he had told her, the grave political problems he had discussed with her; all this, so essential to his peace of mind, was over. He himself had already realized the effect that her marriage might have on him. On May 5, he had written to her: 'You give me the life blood of all that I do, or can ever hope to do.' Two days later he wrote that anyone who wished to exercise the power to get rid of him could exercise it 'effectively, & without a moment's delay, when any veil is dropped between me & you—soul of my life'. Asquith pleaded with Venetia Stanley to write to him, but in vain. She cut herself off from him completely. His torment undermined his resolve. When Bonar Law threatened controversial debate, he refused the challenge. When Lloyd George proposed the formation of a Coalition, he acquiesced. On the morning of May 17, alone for a moment after Lloyd George had gone, he wrote to Venetia Stanley:

... never since the war began had I such an accumulation (no longer shared!) of anxieties ... one of the most hellish bits of these most hellish days was that you alone of all the world—to whom I have always gone in every moment of trial & trouble, & from whom I have always come back solaced and healed & inspired—were the one person who could do nothing, & from whom I could ask nothing. To my dying day, that will be the most bitter memory of my life. . . .

I am on the eve of the most astounding & world-shaking decisions—such as I wd never have taken without your counsel & consent. It seems so strange & empty & unnatural: yet there is nowhere else that I can go, nor would I, if I could.

Churchill knew nothing of Asquith's intense personal distress, or of his abrupt decision to accept a Coalition. Early that afternoon he went to the House of Commons to deliver his explanatory speech, confident that he could save the Liberal Government from further embarrassment. On reaching the Houses of Parliament he went to see Lloyd George, who told him that in his view a Coalition was absolutely necessary. Churchill admitted that he too had always supported the idea of coalition, but that he hoped that any change in the form of Government would be delayed until he had reconstituted the Admiralty Board. But Lloyd George insisted that coalition must be delayed no longer. Churchill then went to Asquith's room, hoping to persuade the Prime Minister to let him make his speech. But Asquith at once made it clear that he no longer wanted a debate. Churchill recalled in *The World Crisis* that no sooner had he given Asquith the names of his new Board, than the Prime Minister told him: 'No, this will not do. I have decided to form a National Government by a coalition with the Unionists, and a very much larger reconstruction will be required. . . . What are we to do for you?'

Churchill was no longer to remain at the Admiralty.

14

'I thought he would die of grief'

THE confrontation between Asquith and Churchill in Asquith's room at the House of Commons on May 17 marked the end of Churchill's career as First Lord. Fisher's resignation, Asquith's personal tragedy, Bonar Law's determination to force a crisis, and Lloyd George's advocacy of coalition, had taken events beyond the point where Churchill could influence them. He realized that as a result of Asquith's decision, his own future was suddenly and totally in jeopardy. He felt that he had no means of insisting that he remain at the Admiralty; in *The World Crisis* he recalled how he had told Asquith that he would favour Balfour as his successor, and that Balfour's appointment 'would be far the best that could be made'. Asquith asked him whether he would like to take office in the new Coalition Government or 'prefer a command in France?' Before Churchill could answer, Lloyd George entered the room, and Asquith asked him for his opinion. 'Why do you not send him to the Colonial Office?' Lloyd George replied; 'there is great work to be done there.' Churchill was indignant, refusing to contemplate any position in the Government which would cut him off from effective conduct of the war, saying he would prefer to take a military command in France. At that moment a telephone message from Masterton-Smith was brought in to Asquith's room, calling Churchill back to the Admiralty as a matter of urgency. Ten minutes later he was at his desk. He was told that an intercepted German wireless message made it almost certain that the German High Sea Fleet was about to sail into the North Sea. 'The political crisis and my own fate in it passed almost completely out of my mind,' he wrote in *The World Crisis*. In Fisher's continued absence, he sent for Oliver, Wilson and the Second Sea Lord, Sir Frederick Hamilton; together they issued orders for the Grand Fleet and all other available forces to proceed to sea. 'I was determined that our whole power should be engaged if battle were joined, and that the enemy's retreat should be intercepted.'

At the moment when Churchill knew that he was no longer to remain at the Admiralty, it had become his duty to supervise the naval battle so long awaited, and which the Admiralty were confident would result in the destruction of the German Fleet. For five hours Churchill remained at the Admiralty supervising every detail of the impending battle. He alerted all British ships. He ordered the Grand Fleet to prepare for sea. He sent the light cruisers, destroyers and submarines from coastal waters to their war stations. Shortly after eight o'clock that evening he telegraphed to Jellicoe: 'It is not impossible that to-morrow may be The Day. All good fortune attend you.' The prospect of a decisive naval battle entirely absorbed Churchill's energies. He asked both Sir Arthur Wilson and Sir Frederick Hamilton to sleep that night in Admiralty House, so that with the dawn the three of them could study the battle together.

The crisis at sea could not blot out the crisis at home. Late that evening, in common with all Cabinet Ministers, Churchill received a formal note from Asquith announcing that a Coalition Government was to be formed. Desperate to be retained in the Government, Churchill replied immediately, taking the opportunity of advising Asquith about other appointments:

My dear Prime Minister,

I am sure LG will not do for WO. Balfour with LG doing Munitions as well as Treasury wd be a far sounder arrangement.

So far as I am concerned if you find it necessary to make a change here, I shd be glad—assuming it was thought fitting—to be *offered* a position in the New Government. But I will not *take* any office except a military department, & if that is not convenient I hope I may be found employment in the field.

I am strongly in favour of a National Government & no personal claims or interests shd stand in its way at the present crisis. I shd be sorry to leave the Admiralty where I have borne the brunt but shd always rely on you to vindicate my work here.

Yours always
W.

Having sent this letter by messenger to 10 Downing Street, Churchill went to bed. May 17 had been an extraordinary day for him. 'In the morning,' he recalled in *The World Crisis*, 'I had prepared for a Parliamentary ordeal of the most searching character; in the afternoon for a political crisis fatal to myself; in the evening for the supreme battle on the sea. For one day it was enough.'

During May 17, Geoffrey Robinson decided that *The Times* could no longer remain silent over what he considered to be the principal cause of the crisis. The editorial which was published on May 18 singled out Churchill for criticism:

What long ago passed beyond the stage of mere rumour is the charge, which has been repeatedly and categorically made in public, that the First Lord of the Admiralty has been assuming responsibilities and overriding his expert advisers to a degree which might at any time endanger the national safety. Though well aware of this charge, we have hitherto refrained from discussing it. . . . We have also refrained as a rule from commenting upon those aspects of Mr Churchill's disquieting personal adventures on the Continent, which have been repeatedly mentioned in Parliament. So long as it was possible to do so, we remained silent, because we preferred to remember the high state of efficiency to which Mr Churchill brought the Fleet before the war, and the promptness with which he mobilized it.

It is no longer possible to keep silence. . . . In this vital and deadly conflict in which we are engaged all considerations affecting individuals must disappear. When a civilian Minister in charge of a fighting service persistently seeks to grasp power which should not pass into his unguided hands, and attempts to use that power in perilous ways, it is time for his colleagues in the Cabinet to take some definite action.

These censures, published on May 18, encouraged Churchill's critics to advance into the open. But he had no time to worry about Press censure that morning. At dawn he was in the Admiralty War Room. He, Sir Arthur Wilson and Sir Frederick Hamilton waited for news from Jellicoe that the British and German Fleets were engaged in battle. For several hours there was no news. At seven o'clock a message came which implied that the German Fleet was turning away from the British forces assembled to catch it. But the watchers in the Admiralty War Room still hoped that the Germans might turn again towards Jellicoe's rapidly advancing Fleet. At eight that morning, while still in doubt as to what the outcome would be, Churchill sent Asquith a letter, asking to be allowed to stay at the Admiralty, penitent that he had refused the Colonial Office so abruptly during their meeting on the previous day:

My dear Prime Minister,

I could not measure the situation yesterday as it concerned me. If an office like the Colonies which was suggested were open to me I should not be right to refuse it. I think there will be great difficulties about the military command, and for me to leave now altogether unless you wish it would be to throw unmerited discredit upon the work I have done here. You invited me to say what my wishes were and therefore I do so.

Above all things I should like to stay here and complete my work, the most difficult part of which is ended. Everything has been provided for and the naval situation is in every respect assured. After 4 years administration and 9 months war I am entitled to say this.

If Balfour were to go to the War Office the two departments would work with perfect smoothness. I hope in any case I may have a talk with you this morning.

The German Fleet are out in full strength and all our ships are at sea. It is possible the afternoon may produce events.

Yours always
W

Asquith did not see Churchill that morning. But he did tell Lloyd George that Churchill had wanted to discuss the situation with him. 'Which means,' Asquith explained, 'the situation as it concerns Churchill personally—how far he is likely to be affected. The situation for Churchill has no other meaning but his own prospects.' Lloyd George reported this cynical observation to Frances Stevenson, who recorded it in her diary on the following day.

The naval victory which might have saved Churchill from catastrophe never took place. By half past ten that morning it was certain that the German Fleet was returning to its harbour. 'The episode was over,' Churchill recalled in *The World Crisis*. 'All our fleets, squadrons, and flotillas turned morosely away to resume their long-drawn, unrelenting watch, and I awoke again to the political crisis. But my hour had passed.'

None of those concerned with the discussions about the formation of the Coalition took Churchill into their confidence. It was the first time for over five years that he had not participated at the centre. He began to say farewell. In a telegram to the Dardanelles on May 18 he asked General Paris to tell the Royal Naval Division how much their efforts were appreciated: 'I deeply regret their losses,' he added, 'but they will not be in vain. The shortest road to a victorious peace runs through the Dardanelles.' At midday he telegraphed to his brother:

Fisher has chosen to resign at this awkward moment largely on Dardanelles questions and very large changes involving my leaving the Admiralty are in progress. But I am quite sure that your two friends will be well supported, that the enterprise will be carried through, and that the results will pay for all. I shall be in a position to help indirectly. My very best wishes to our friends. Tell them not to be disheartened in any way or to think that they are not going to be properly backed. Tell the Admiral that I am very glad we have been able to work together so well.

Asquith had not yet formally accepted Fisher's resignation. There were some who believed that Fisher would take Churchill's place as First Lord. Such a course was advocated publicly by *The Times*, and supported by many who were unaware of the inner story of the crisis. The Colonial Secretary, Lewis Harcourt, who was not a member of the War Council, wrote enthusiastically to Lord Esher on May 18: 'I think Jacky has triumphed.' Fisher himself believed that with Churchill's demise he was about to emerge supreme. During May 18 he sent Captain Crease the 'instant orders' which he intended to issue as soon as he had returned to the Admiralty. The Dardanelles would be the first victim of Fisher's new regime. He would transport Sir Ian Hamilton's army from Gallipoli to Haifa in order to use it for the conquest of the Holy Land. '*Keep secret. TELL NO ONE,*' he emphasized. But on Wednesday May 19 he made his position known to Asquith, sending him the six conditions under which he could 'guarantee the successful termination of the war':

1. That Mr Winston Churchill is not in the Cabinet to be always circumventing me, nor will I serve under Mr Balfour.
2. That Sir A. K. Wilson leaves the Admiralty and the Committee of Imperial Defence and the War Council, as my time otherwise will be occupied in resisting the bombardment of Heligoland and other such wild projects. Also his policy is totally opposed to mine, and he has accepted the position of First Sea Lord in succession to me, and thereby adopting a policy diametrically opposed to my views.
3. That there shall be an entire new Board of Admiralty, as regards the Sea Lords and the Financial Secretary[1] (who is utterly useless). *New measures* demand *new men.*
4. That I shall have complete professional charge of the war at sea, together with the absolute sole disposition of the Fleet and the appointment of all officers of all ranks whatsoever, and absolutely untrammelled sole command of all the sea forces whatsoever.
5. That the First Lord of the Admiralty should be absolutely restricted to policy and parliamentary procedure and should occupy the same position towards me as Mr Tennant, MP,[2] does to Lord Kitchener (and very well he does it).
6. That I should have the sole absolute authority for all new construction and

---

[1] Thomas James Macnamara, 1861–1931. A schoolteacher. Editor, *Schoolmaster*, 1892. Liberal MP, 1900–18. Parliamentary and Financial Secretary to the Admiralty, 1908–20. Minister of Labour, 1920–2. National Liberal MP, 1922–4.

[2] Harold John Tennant, 1865–1935. Margot Asquith's brother. Known as 'Jack'. Private Secretary to Asquith, 1892–5. Liberal MP, 1894–1918. Parliamentary Secretary, Board of Trade, 1909–11. Financial Secretary, War Office, 1911–12. Under-Secretary of State for War, 1912–16. Secretary for Scotland, 1916.

all dockyard work of whatever sort whatsoever, and complete control of the whole of the Civil establishments of the Navy.

In a postscript Fisher added: 'These six conditions must be published verbatim so that the Fleet may know my position.' He appended a list of the new men whom he intended to appoint, and changes in the structure of Admiralty organization. These included the abolition of Admiral Oliver's post of Chief of Staff, which Fisher intended to take over himself. The existing Second, Third and Fourth Sea Lords were all to be replaced.

Asquith did not inform Churchill of these amazing demands, with the result that Churchill had no idea of the full extent to which Fisher had struck out against him.[1] He continued to believe that it was specific disagreements, limited to the Dardanelles, which had caused Fisher's sudden defection. He therefore imagined that he could still win Fisher's support by friendship, persuasion, and if necessary by offering some compromise in their official Admiralty relationship.

Early on the morning of May 19 Fisher showed his ultimatum to Hankey. 'Lord Fisher madder than ever,' Hankey wrote in his diary. 'This morning he arrived early at office with a most preposterous letter of "terms" on which he would return. . . . I remonstrated & told him his terms were impossible and no self-respecting Minister would look at them. I saw him again in the evening & persuaded him to abate his terms. But it was too late, they had been sent to the PM and greatly incensed him.' Lord Stamfordham, who saw Asquith at one o'clock that afternoon, sent the King an account of the Prime Minister's reaction:

He was very severe in his comments and thinks Fisher's mind is somewhat unhinged, otherwise his conduct is almost 'traitrous'! He has not only not objected but concurred in every order which has been issued by the Admiralty until some recent minor question about sending 2 or 3 submarines to the Dardanelles—and was elated by and entirely approved of the first bombardment of the Dardanelles; . . . He has sent in a paper giving the conditions upon which he would remain on in office . . . he wishes to have absolute control. The Prime Minister thinks this paper indicates signs of mental aberration!

---

[1] Churchill first saw Fisher's conditions twelve years later, when Asquith, who was then writing his memoirs, sent him a copy, commenting that the letter was 'Fisher's death-bed ultimatum. . . evidence of the *megalomania* which overclouded his judgement at the time of his resignation'. Churchill replied: 'The document seems to show that Fisher used the uncertain course of events at the Dardanelles as a means of making a bid for supreme Naval power. Considering that he had agreed to every step taken and issued every order, it seems to me his conduct was rather treacherous.'

'I expect Churchill will go to Colonial Office,' Stamfordham wrote the King on May 19, 'but Beauchamp tells me feeling among his colleagues is that he is primary cause of trouble and should be first to go instead of others who will lose their seats in Cabinet.' During the afternoon the King sent his version of events to Queen Mary:[1] 'Personally I am glad the Prime Minister is going to have a National Government. Only by that means can we get rid of Churchill from Admiralty. He is intriguing also with French against K, he is the real danger.' Even more elaborate versions of Churchill's alleged intrigues were soon to circulate. Three weeks later, on June 10, the Postmaster-General, Charles Hobhouse,[2] sent a composite account of these intrigues to the Governor-General of South Africa, Lord Buxton,[3] alleging that 'the two villains of the piece' were Churchill and Lloyd George, who had been plotting 'with the help of their Tory friends' to oust Kitchener and Grey and bring in a Coalition in which they would be supreme. Both Hobhouse and the King were wrong; Churchill had not tried to advance his political position by intrigue. He had been content to serve as First Lord, believing this to be the position in which he could most effectively influence the conduct and outcome of the war. He had put his faith in the success of his conduct of Admiralty affairs, and above all in a naval victory, either in the North Sea or at the Dardanelles.

No public announcement had yet been made of Government changes. Churchill remained in charge of the Admiralty, working each day at his desk, living in Admiralty House, dealing with the telegrams which arrived each hour from the Fleets at sea, and from the Dardanelles. He tried to maintain a cheerful countenance. On May 18 he was at the House of Commons. One of his constituency newspapers, the Dundee *Advertiser*, captured his mood in its report from Westminster published the next day:

While the Whisky Bill was under discussion, Mr Churchill came in behind the Speaker's chair. He looked anything but the 'fallen Minister' some people would have us believe him to be. Talking to a group of his Liberal and Unionist friends, he appeared in the highest good humour. The group broke up in a burst of subdued laughter, and Mr Churchill left the House. A little

[1] Victoria Mary Augusta Louise Olga Pauline Claudine Agnes, 1867–1953. Daughter of the Duke of Teck. Wife of George V.

[2] Charles Edward Henry Hobhouse, 1862–1941. Liberal MP, 1892–5, 1900–18. Chancellor of the Duchy of Lancaster, 1911–14. Postmaster-General, 1914–15. Succeeded his father as 4th Baronet, 1916.

[3] Sydney Charles Buxton, 1853–1934. Liberal MP, 1883–5, 1886–1914. Postmaster-General, 1905–10. President of the Board of Trade, 1910–14. Created Viscount, 1914. High Commissioner and Governor-General, South Africa, 1914–20. Created Earl, 1920.

later he returned more radiant than ever, and strolling to the Treasury Bench, he sat down beside Mr Lloyd George, planted his feet hard up against the table in an attitude that suggested security of tenure, and engaged the Chancellor in lively conversation. Whatever the truth may be, Mr Churchill in the House looked the picture of happiness and contentment.

On the evening of May 18 Churchill asked F. E. Smith and Max Aitken to call on him at Admiralty House, and talked almost the whole night with them. 'That Tuesday night,' Aitken later recorded in *Politicians and the War*, 'he was clinging to the desire of retaining the Admiralty as if the salvation of England depended on it.' Aitken believed that Churchill would 'even have made it up with Lord Fisher' if by such a means he could have remained First Lord: 'He was anxious that the Tories should support him in this, although it was obvious that it was precisely the Tory backing of Lord Fisher that had thrown him down. He negotiated with Lord Balfour to act as intermediary and as his interpreter to the Tory leaders. Balfour in his new role was unfavourably received and in fact severely criticised by his colleagues.' Aitken told Churchill plainly that he had no hope of Tory support. Early on May 19, unwilling to give up hope, Churchill wrote direct to Bonar Law, sending him a set of official telegrams dealing both with the loss of the three cruisers in September 1914 and with Cradock's defeat off Coronel six weeks later. These disasters had provoked serious Conservative criticism of Churchill's competence as First Lord:

Secret
My dear Bonar Law,
Now that there is I rejoice to think good prospect of our becoming colleagues, I feel entitled to send you the enclosed papers.
I have borne in silence all these anxious months the charge that I am to blame by my interference with the naval experts for the loss of the 3 cruisers & the faulty dispositions wh led to the action off Coronel.
I also send you the telegram wh as it happened—tho this was good luck— had such a decisive effect on the operations culminating in the action at the Falklands.
You must not suppose that in sending you these I want to claim all the credit or avoid the blame, only hitherto the principle has been that the blame only came to me.

Yours sincerely
Winston S. Churchill

In his postscript Churchill declared that 'this great event of a National

Government must be made lasting'. Bonar Law was not to be deflected from his distrust by a selection of documents. Churchill believed that the facts, if known, would enable him to remain as First Lord. During May 19 he went to see Grey and Lloyd George, showing them a long statement which he had decided to publish in the Press, defending his Dardanelles policies. Lloyd George begged him not to publish it, as there was as yet no public knowledge that the success of the Dardanelles operation was seriously in doubt, but that by publishing a defence Churchill would imply that it was. Churchill agreed to hold the statement back. Later in the discussion, when he realized that Grey and Lloyd George both took it for granted that he would be leaving the Admiralty, he lost his temper. 'You don't care,' he told Lloyd George, 'what becomes of me. You don't care whether I am trampled under foot by my enemies. You don't care for my personal reputation. . . .' 'No,' said Lloyd George, 'I don't care for my own at the present moment. The only thing I care about now is that we win in this war.' Frances Stevenson reported this bitter exchange in her diary that day.

Churchill tenaciously persisted in trying to maintain his position as First Lord. During the evening of May 19 he turned to the idea of offering Fisher some special position; enhancing Fisher's powers, he believed, would enable him to feel that, like Kitchener, he was on equal terms with the politicians whose power to overrule him had become a cause of frustration and annoyance. 'In the evening,' Hankey wrote in his diary, 'Churchill offered Fisher any terms he liked including a seat in the Cabinet, if he would stay with him at Admiralty. The message was brought verbally by Lambert the Civil Lord, while I was with Fisher at his house in the evening.'

Fisher did not hesitate to inform the Conservatives of this extraordinary offer. For him it was proof that not only the Press and the public but even the man whose career he was shattering, still believed that it was vital for him to return to the Admiralty. That same evening he wrote to Bonar Law: '*Private & Personal . . . Please burn and don't mention.* Very *SECRET AND PRIVATE.* This evening Winston sent Lambert, the Civil Lord of the Admiralty, to offer me a seat in the Cabinet if I would return as First Sea Lord with him (Winston) as First Lord! I rejected the 30 pieces of silver to betray my country.'

Neither Fisher nor Churchill retained the confidence of those who had seen the effects of the crisis clearly. That night Hankey dined with Maurice Bonham Carter and Masterton-Smith. 'We had a very long discussion,' he wrote in his diary, 'and finally agreed that Churchill & Fisher must both go. . . .' On the following morning, May 20, while seeking out further opinions, Hankey discovered that most senior Admiralty officials favoured Balfour as First Lord, with either Sir Arthur Wilson or Sir Henry Jackson as First Sea Lord; and that there was, he wrote in his diary, 'a consensus of opinion that Churchill & Fisher must go'. Sir Frederick Hamilton had, on May 17, taken the extraordinary course of urging the Director of Naval Intelligence, Captain Hall, to pass on to Asquith his view, and that of the Third and Fourth Sea Lords that if Fisher were to go, they believed Churchill should also leave the Admiralty, or that naval morale would collapse. Hall had explained Hamilton's fear to Lord Reading,[1] who had passed it on to Asquith.

On May 20 Sir George Riddell called on Churchill at the Admiralty, and recorded in his *War Diary*:

He looked very worn out and harassed. He greeted me warmly and said, 'I am the victim of a political intrigue. I am finished!' I said, 'Not finished at forty, with your remarkable powers!' 'Yes,' he said. 'Finished in respect of all I care for—the waging of war; the defeat of the Germans. I have had a high place offered to me—a position which has been occupied by many distinguished men, and which carries with it a high salary. But that all goes for nothing. This is what I live for. I have prepared a statement of my case, but cannot use it. The foreign situation prevents me from doing so. I will show you the statement.' He then obtained it from his secretary. I read it. Shortly the effect was that every disposition of ships and the decision on every question of policy had been sanctioned by Fisher, and that the naval attempt to force the Dardanelles had been advised by Admiral Carden and confirmed by Admiral de Robeck, his successor.

Churchill told Riddell that to his surprise Sir Arthur Wilson, who on May 16 had agreed to serve under him as First Sea Lord in succession to Fisher, had, three days later, refused to serve under anyone else. On May 19 Wilson had written to Asquith:

In view of the reports in the papers this morning as to the probable reconstruction of the Government, I think I ought to tell you that although I agreed to undertake the office of First Sea Lord under Mr Churchill because it appeared to me to be the best means of maintaining continuity of policy under the unfortunate circumstances that have arisen, I am not prepared

[1] Rufus Daniel Isaacs, 1860–1935. Liberal MP, 1904–13. Knighted, 1910. Solicitor-General, 1910. Attorney-General, 1910–13. Entered Cabinet, 1912. Lord Chief Justice, 1913–21. Created Baron Reading, 1914; Viscount, 1916; Earl, 1917. Special Ambassador to the USA, 1918. Viceroy of India, 1921–6. Created Marquess, 1926. Secretary of State for Foreign Affairs, 1931.

to undertake the duties under any new First Lord, as the strain under such circumstances would be far beyond my strength.

On May 20, as soon as Churchill learned of Wilson's attitude, his spirits revived. He wrote at once to Asquith in renewed hopes that he could remain at the Admiralty:

My dear Prime Minister,

I have learned with great surprise that Sir Arthur Wilson yesterday informed the Naval Lords that while he was prepared to serve as First Sea Lord under me, he was not prepared to do so under any one else. This is the greatest compliment I have ever been paid.

The three Naval Lords are also ready to serve under me. They take a vy serious view of Lord Fisher's desertion of his post in time of war for what has now amounted to six days, during wh serious operations have been in progress. They feel that shd he return to the Admiralty their positions will be made vy difficult as also will be those of many officers of the department who have been associated with me & will become objects of resentment.

Yrs vy s

W

Asquith knew, from Captain Hall's mission to Lord Reading, that the Sea Lords were not willing to serve under Churchill if Fisher were to go. He also knew that it would not be difficult to find both a First Lord and a First Sea Lord acceptable to them. Sir Arthur Wilson's loyalty to Churchill was irrelevant to Asquith's considerations, and could not save Churchill's position. Wilson's reputation was not as universally impressive as Churchill believed. On May 22, when the rumour that Wilson might succeed Fisher reached Major-General Callwell at the War Office, he wrote at once to H. A. Gwynne hoping that Gwynne would inform the Conservatives of what might happen, and exert his influence to prevent it:

My dear Gwynne,

I had Jacky Fisher here this morning. I should say that Squiff will not accept what he calls his terms and that there must be a new 1st Sea Lord. Do you think that Bonar Law and the Unionist leaders know that there is not the slightest question in the Admiralty as to who should be First Sea Lord? It is Sir Henry Jackson, who is there for the asking. Above all let it not be A. K. Wilson who is a man of quite inferior calibre and who backed up Winston in his folly over the naval attack on the Dardanelles. AKW is all right at knocking down Fuzzy Wuzzies with his fists[1] or getting a cable round a bollard, but the idea that he is a strategist of the first water has no foundation in fact and he is dumb at War Councils and institutions of that character. . . .

Yours ever
Chas E. Callwell

Asquith chose not to circulate Wilson's letter. Churchill, who only learned of the letter confidentially, could not use it to strengthen his position. Clementine Churchill was incensed by Asquith's behaviour towards her husband, writing to him on May 20:

My dear Mr Asquith,

For nearly four years Winston has worked to master every detail of naval science. There is no man in this country who possesses equal knowledge capacity & vigour. If he goes, the injury to Admiralty business will not be reparable for many months—if indeed it is ever made good during the war.

Why do you part with Winston? unless indeed you have lost confidence in his work and ability?

But I know that cannot be the reason. Is not the reason expediency—'to restore public confidence'. I suggest to you that public confidence will be restored in *Germany* by Winston's downfall.

There *is* no general desire here for a change, but it certainly is being fostered by the press who have apparently made up their minds. I trust they are not making up yours for you.

All you have to do is to stand by Winston and the Board of Admiralty and Sir Arthur Wilson.

If you throw Winston overboard you will be committing an act of weakness and your Coalition Government will not be as formidable a War machine as the present Government.

Winston may in your eyes & in those with whom he has to work have faults but he has the supreme quality which I venture to say very few of your present or future Cabinet possess, the power, the imagination, the deadliness to fight Germany.

If you send him to another place he will no longer be fighting. If you waste this valuable war material you will be doing an injury to this country.

Yours sincerely
Clementine S. Churchill

Asquith did not reply; but that day, in one of his last letters to Venetia Stanley, he reported that he had received 'the letter of a maniac' from her cousin Clementine. Pressure against Churchill's retention in the

---

[1] In 1884, during the Sudan campaign, Arthur Wilson had been awarded the Victoria Cross after a brief skirmish inland when he had beaten off several Arab attackers with his sword.

Government mounted. Also on May 20 Asquith was sent a letter by a former Under-Secretary of State for the Colonies, Lord Emmott, who had become Director of the War Trade Department after the outbreak of the war. Emmott wrote as a self-appointed emissary of the Colonial Office:

My dear Prime Minister,

It is only under a very strong sense of duty that I venture to write to you at this time.

I do not know whether, in the reconstruction of the Cabinet, Harcourt will have to leave the CO. I hope not; but if he must, I do implore you for the sake of the Dominions not to put Churchill there.

An office revolt might be the first result. That could be faced even if it took place; but the effect on the Dominions would be lamentable and possibly disastrous. He has neither the temperament nor manners to fit him for the post. I was at the CO for two years & a half and I am so convinced of the truth of what I write that I am willing to risk your displeasure rather than remain silent about it.

Yours sincerely
Emmott

A Liberal backbencher, W. M. R. Pringle,[1] also wrote to Asquith on May 20, telling him of the belief circulating among his colleagues that Churchill had been involved in an anti-Asquithian intrigue. According to Pringle:

A number of your supporters have been driven to the conclusion that the present crisis has been brought about by the actions of Mr Churchill. I do not only refer to his differences with Lord Fisher but we believe that he was privy to the intrigue which resulted in the Repington disclosures.

In these circumstances we regard his presence in the Government as a public danger. It is only fair therefore that you should know, before any arrangement is concluded, that the attitude of a considerable number of members will be determined by this conviction.

The belief that Churchill had helped Repington compile his despatch on shell shortage had no justification. But it circulated widely in Liberal circles, bewildered by the sudden emergence of a Coalition, and by the arrival of the Tories as equals. Churchill had become the scapegoat. One member of the Liberal Party who was unwilling to be influenced by mounting Press and Party criticism was Churchill's Con-

---

[1] William Mather Rutherford Pringle, 1874–1928. Liberal MP, 1910–18; 1922–4.

stituency Chairman, Sir George Ritchie,[1] who wrote from Dundee on May 20:

> I hope the present situation has not been brought about by the action and abuse of the yellow press. Many here think it would have been in the interest of the Country to suspend the Times and Morning Post long ago.
> I don't care for Coalition of any kind, and I question very much if the one now in the process of formation will be the success expected.
> It is quite impossible for an outsider to form a fair and accurate judgement on such information as is available and I must just wait. What I do feel personally is the apparent injury that is to be done you in the readjustment of Offices. We are all patriots and will make the needed sacrifice for the best interests of the country. All the same one resents the unjust outcry and its apparent success.

During May 20 Churchill made a second attempt to obtain Conservative support. That evening, in a long discussion with Bonar Law, he tried to explain his conduct of Admiralty affairs, and in particular of the Dardanelles. Bonar Law had long been the victim of Churchill's patronizing and vituperative attacks. Their quarrels over Ireland had been intense. Churchill had always underrated Bonar Law's abilities. These were not good precedents for seeking Bonar Law's support. The evening discussion was of no avail. On the following morning Churchill sent Bonar Law a final appeal, refusing to accept that his chances of remaining at the Admiralty had been destroyed:

> The rule to follow is what is best calculated to beat the enemy, and not what is most likely to please the newspapers. The question of the Dardanelles operations and my differences with Fisher ought to be settled by people who know the facts and not by those who cannot know them. Now you and your friends, except Mr Balfour, do not know the facts. On our side only the Prime Minister knows them. The policy and conduct of the Dardanelles operations should be reviewed by the new Cabinet. Every fact should be laid before them. They should decide and on their decision the composition of the Board of Admiralty should depend,
> It is not in justice to myself that I am asking for this; but primarily because of the great operation which is in progress, and for which I bear a tremendous responsibility. With Sir Arthur Wilson's professional aid I am sure I can discharge that responsibility fully. In view of his statement to the Prime Minister and to the naval Lords that he will serve as First Sea Lord under me,

[1] George Ritchie, 1849–1921. Grocer's apprentice, 1865. Opened his own wholesale grocery and provision business in the 1880s. Elected to the Dundee Town Council, 1889. Finance Convenor, 1892–3. City Treasurer, 1895–1906. President of the Dundee Liberal Association, 1907–21. Knighted, 1910.

and under no one else, I feel entitled to say that no other personal combination will have so good a chance.

If this view of mine should prove to be true, it affects the safety of an Army now battling its way forward under many difficulties, and the success of an operation of the utmost consequence for which more than 30,000 men have already shed their blood: and I suggest to you that it is your duty to refuse to judge so grave an issue until you know the facts.

My lips are sealed in public, but in a few days all the facts can be placed before you and your friends under official secrecy. I am sure those with whom I hope to work as colleagues and comrades in this great struggle will not allow a newspaper campaign—necessarily conducted in ignorance and not untinged with prejudice—to be the deciding factor in matters of such terrible import.

Personal interests and sympathies ought to be strictly subordinated. It does not matter whether a Minister receives exact and meticulous justice. But what is vital is that from the outset of this new effort we are to make together we should be fearless of outside influences and straight with each other. We are coming together not to work on public opinion, but to wage war: and by waging successful war we shall dominate public opinion.

Churchill asked Bonar Law to show this letter to the other Conservatives who would be joining the new Coalition Cabinet, adding for them several specific points about his naval administration:

I was sent to the Admiralty 4 years ago after the Agadir crisis with the express duty laid upon me to put the Fleet in a state of instant readiness for war with Germany. I have always been supported by high professional advice: but partly through circumstances and partly no doubt through my own methods and inclinations, an exceptional burden has been borne by me. I had to procure the money, the men, the ships and ammunition; to recast with expert advice the war plans; to complete in every detail that could be foreseen the organisation of the Navy.

Supported by the Prime Minister, I had last year for 4 continuous months of Cabinet meetings to beat down the formidable attack of the Chancellor of the Exchequer backed by three-fourths of the Cabinet upon the necessary naval estimates. On the approach of war I had to act far in excess of my authority to make the vital arrangement for the safety of the country. I had to mobilise the Fleet without legal sanction and contrary to a Cabinet decision. I have had to face 9 months of war under conditions no man has known, and which were in the early months infinitely more anxious than those which confront us now.

Many Sea Lords have come and gone, but during all these 4 years (nearly) I have been according to my patent 'solely responsible to Crown and Parliament' and have borne the blame for any failure: and now I present to you an absolutely secure naval position; a Fleet constantly and rapidly growing in strength, and abundantly supplied with munitions of every kind; an organisation working with perfect smoothness and efficiency, and the seas upon which no enemy's flag is flown.

Therefore I ask to be judged fairly; deliberately and with knowledge. I do not ask for anything else.[1]

While waiting for Bonar Law's reply on the morning of May 21, Churchill sent Asquith a much more emotional appeal, a blunt testimony to his desperate worries:

My dear Prime Minister,

What makes me so anxious is the arrival of German Submarines in the Eastern Mediterranean. One has reached Cattaro, & has been told 'as a first objective' to attack the covering battleships at Gaba Tepe. Others will be sent, for it wd be wise for the Germans to suspend the submarine warfare against merchant men until they have more submarines—thus pleasing the Americans[2]—and to turn their energies against the vast fleet of Battleships, transports, storeships etc upon wh the life of the Dardanelles army depends. This danger can be dealt with if the proper measures are taken now. But if it were not dealt with, losses might be incurred wh—if the Admiralty were in uninstructed or unfriendly hands—might lead to the abandonment of the whole Dardanelles operation—which otherwise is a certainty; & then on my head for all time wd be the blood of the 30,000 brave men who have fallen, killed or wounded or sunk in deep water.

My responsibility is terrible. But I know I cd sustain it, & without the slightest impairment of our margin here, cd bring this vast Dardanelles business safely through in spite of the submarines. Arthur Wilson & I together can do it. We alone know the whole position.

But fancy my feelings if, at this critical moment—on mere uninformed newspaper hostility—the whole intricate affair is to be taken out of our hands & put into the hands of a stranger without the knowledge, or worst of all in the hands of a deadly foe to the whole plan.

It is no clinging to office or to this particular office or my own interest or advancement wh moves me. I am clinging to my *task* & to my *duty*. I am

---

[1] Sir Max Aitken, who took this letter from Churchill to Bonar Law, later decided to publish it in *Politicians and the War*. 'You make me tear open old wounds,' Churchill wrote to him on 22 March 1928, 'and their sting returns. . . . Don't you think there is a good deal to be said for the theory that life is only a nightmare and that we shall wake up soon?'

[2] On May 13 the United States Government had protested to Germany about the torpedoing of the *Falaba* (March 28), the *Cushing* (April 28), the *Gulflight* (May 1) and the *Lusitania* (May 7); each ship had been unarmed, and US subjects were drowned. There was a lull in the sinkings until the torpedoing of the *Arabic* (August 19), the *Hesperian* (September 4) and the *Ancona* (November 7); each with the loss of US lives.

straining to make good the formidable undertaking in wh we are engaged; & wh I know—with Arthur Wilson—I can alone discharge.

I did not believe it was possible to endure such anxiety.

None of the ordinary strains of war—wh I have borne all these months—have been comparable to this feeling. It grows upon me each of these long drawn days.

I cannot defend myself. My naval lords & advisers here—all behind me—cannot say anything. My Tory friends who are coming into the government—with whom in a fortnight I shall be on the best of terms—do not know except what they have read in the newspapers.

But *you* know. You alone know the whole situation and that it is my duty to carry this burden safely: and that I can do it.

I can only look to you. Let me stand or fall by the Dardanelles—but do not take it from my hands.

In the near future my aid to you in this strange government will be important: the political combination is one wh in the nature of things is extremely favourable to me. But now—you alone can do me justice & do justice to the military need.

Yours always
W

Churchill had not seen Asquith for several days. Nor had Asquith asked to see him. In his postscript to this letter Churchill wrote: 'I have not come to see you though I shd like to; but it wd be kind of you to send for me some time today.' Asquith did not send for him, but wrote simply and with finality:

My dear Winston,

I have your letters. You must take it as settled that you are not to remain at the Admiralty. I am sure that you will try to take a large view of an unexampled situation. Every one has to make sacrifices; no one more than I, who have to part company with valued and faithful colleagues, who have served me loyally & well. I hope to retain your services as a member of the new Cabinet, being, as I am, sincerely grateful for the splendid work you have done both before and since the war.

I cannot, of course, make any definite offer of any particular place, until I am able to realize and appraise the competing claims of others.

Yrs always
HHA

Receiving this, Churchill knew that his career as First Lord could not be retrieved. A few hours later a brief note from Bonar Law ended all chance of Conservative support:

My dear Churchill,

I thank you for your letter which I shall show to my friends beginning with Austen Chamberlain but believe me what I said to you last night is inevitable.

Yours sincerely
A. Bonar Law

On May 21 Bonar Law sent Churchill's appeal to Austen Chamberlain, who replied that same day that it was 'impossible' for Churchill to remain at the Admiralty: '1st because he has not the confidence of *either* the Navy or the Country. 2ndly because it demands a full enquiry by a Cabinet, & there is no Cabinet to conduct it & we cannot wait to appoint a 1st Lord till *after* a Cabinet has been formed & enquired.'

On the afternoon of May 21 Churchill accepted that Asquith's decision was absolute. Six days of self-torment were at an end:

My dear Prime Minister,

I am very sorry for yr troubles, and sorry to have been the cause of a situation wh has enabled others to bring them upon you—I will accept any office—the lowest if you like—that you care to offer me, & will continue to serve in it in this time of war until the affairs in which I am deeply concerned are settled satisfactorily, as I think they will be.

Yours always
W

Asquith replied within a few hours:

My dear Winston,

I was delighted to receive your letter of today this afternoon, and I recognise with gratitude, but without surprise, the spirit in which it is written.

We have all for the moment to put up with unwelcome new facts, and nothing is more unwelcome than the disappearance of old comrades, and the process of transplantation from one place to another, especially from one of greater to one of lesser interest.

I know you will ply a stout & labouring oar, whatever seat in the boat may be assigned to you.

Yrs always
HHA

Balfour was to be the new First Lord. Churchill sent Asquith a final acceptance of defeat, his sixth letter to Asquith in five days:

My dear Prime Minister,

All right, I accept your decision. I shall not look back.

I have tried my hand but without success to persuade Sir Arthur Wilson to hold himself at Mr Balfour's disposition. In these circumstances I wd advise Sir Henry Jackson. But a complete understanding exists between me & Mr Balfour, & I daresay he will let me talk to him about it.

I must wait for the march of events at the Dlles.

I am grateful to you for yr kindness to me & belief in my vision of things.

Count on me absolutely—if I am of any use. If not, some employment in the field.

Yours vy sincerely
WSC

On the following day, May 22, Asquith saw Churchill briefly, writing to Venetia Stanley that it was 'a most painful interview to me: but he was good & in his best mood. And it ended all right.' But Asquith still had no office for him. 'What a satire,' Margot Asquith wrote in her diary on May 24, 'if the coming Coalition Government of which Winston has gassed so much should not contain him! I know Henry too well to suppose this but there is no doubt if Henry wanted to make himself supremely popular with every party *ours and the others* he would exclude Winston. I would not wish this, there is something lovable in Winston and he is a real pal but I should not be surprised if he wrecked the new Government.'

Throughout the crisis Northcliffe's *Daily Mail* had been demanding Lord Kitchener's dismissal. In contemplating his new Government Asquith had himself thought of removing Kitchener, whose secretiveness at the War Office, and whose lethargy over munitions, had troubled him, and much angered Lloyd George, for some months. But the attacks in the *Daily Mail* were so virulent that there was a fierce public reaction in Kitchener's favour; copies of the *Daily Mail* were burned on the floor of the Stock Exchange. Asquith later announced that Kitchener was to remain as Secretary of State for War. The Order of the Garter was also conferred on him. Churchill wrote to Kitchener on May 21:

I have not written to you on business for two or three days, and soon I shall have no occasion to trouble you with business. But I must tell you how much I regret the odious tone of a section of the press in their calculated attack upon yr work. With gt difficulties you have achieved incredible results. We have not always agreed; but—having been under yr displeasure as a subaltern, I shall always look back with satisfaction to having been yr colleague. I think Dlles will come out all right.

In a postscript Churchill added: 'Fisher went mad.' Kitchener replied on the following day that he did not mind the abuse, but that 'the attempt to make bad feeling between French and myself is a very low down game which will not succeed . . .'. As for the Dardanelles, he reported, 'All seems cheerful.'

On May 22, when it became known that Balfour was likely to succeed Churchill as First Lord, Fisher, still in London, told Hankey that he would serve under neither. To Jellicoe, Fisher wrote on May 22: 'Balfour and Winston are inseparable and have been so since the mad gamble of the Dardanelles was first mooted. Balfour is really more to blame than Winston.' That morning Fisher informed McKenna that as Balfour was to be First Lord, 'I shall be off to Scotland.' But Fisher's departure to Scotland was no easy matter. Hankey recorded in his diary later that day:

Spent most of morning in getting pressure put on Lord Fisher from various quarters to go right away to Scotland away from journalistic influences, as he may do himself and the nation great harm by an indiscretion in his present excited state. I saw him and took the line that he ought to adopt the role of the 'strong, silent man', injured, but still keeping silent. I reminded him that he had given this advice to Kitchener with excellent results, and told him it was his one chance of getting back to the Admiralty. It was 12.30 before he agreed and his train was at 2 pm. Then I remembered that technically, as his resignation had not been accepted, he was First Sea Lord and ought not to quit his post without leave, so I undertook to square this with the PM. Unfortunately the PM was with the King and did not get back until nearly 2 pm. He came back rather flustered and irritable, and when I broached the question of Fisher's leave he said he ought to be shot for leaving his post! This was awkward for me as I had given Lord Fisher a personal guarantee that I would make matters right, and it required some tact to induce Asquith to let me send a wire to Lord Fisher approving his leave. McKenna & Captain Crease were acting with me in getting Fisher away, which, I am sure, was the right course.

During the afternoon of May 22 Churchill said goodbye to the officials at the Admiralty. Many of them had read that morning the opinion of the Naval Correspondent of *The Times*, Commander Robinson,[1] that 'the news that Mr Churchill is leaving the Admiralty has been received with a feeling of relief in the Service, both afloat and ashore', and that although he had introduced a 'breezy atmosphere'

---

[1] Charles Napier Robinson, 1849–1936. Entered Navy, 1861. Retired with rank of Commander, 1882. London Naval Correspondent of the *New York Herald*, 1885–1920. Naval correspondent of *The Times*, 1893–1936. Editor of Brassey's *Naval Annual*, 1929–36:

into naval affairs there had been 'a sense of uneasiness lest those very qualities of his which might be of advantage to the State in other circumstances, should lead him into making some false step, which, in the case of the Fleet, upon which our all depends, would be irretrievable'.

Conservative and naval relief at Churchill's departure was shared by many Liberals. On May 23 the Dundee *Advertiser* informed its readers 'that many Liberals have thought it their duty to make representations through the Whips Department, urging that the Member for Dundee should be excluded altogether from the Cabinet on the ground, as they contend, that he is in a large measure responsible for precipitating the present state of affairs'. 'There is no section in the country, so far as I can see,' Frances Stevenson wrote in her diary on May 24, 'that wishes him to stay at the Admiralty. Masterton-Smith, Winston's own private secretary, told the PM that on no account ought Churchill to be allowed to remain at the Admiralty—he was most dangerous there.' Masterton-Smith's hostile opinion was, if true, surprising. But Frances Stevenson may have exaggerated what she heard, or been told an exaggerated story; for on May 21 Hankey had recorded in his diary: 'I find that Masterton Smith still hankers after Churchill as First Lord, owing to his great driving power & capacity for work.'

During the weekend of May 22–23, Asquith offered Churchill a minor post in the Cabinet, the Chancellorship of the Duchy of Lancaster. Churchill accepted the offer. 'I gather that you have been flung a bone on which there is little meat,' wrote his cousin the Duke of Marlborough on May 24; 'the fare is poor but I suppose you will think it wisest to live on emergency rations pro tem.' Although Churchill was deprived of any departmental influence, Asquith allowed him to retain his place on the War Council, which gave him the right to listen to and to participate in discussions of high policy. 'I have accepted Chancellor of the Duchy of Lancaster with a seat in the Cabinet & on the War Council,' he telegraphed to his brother that Sunday, May 23. 'This will enable me to watch over Dardanelles fortunes. Mr Balfour follows me here to my great relief & Fisher does not return. Although I am down the policy goes on & will be well supported.'

That Sunday, in one of the few friendly press comments throughout the crisis, J. L. Garvin wrote in the *Observer*:

However bitter the moment, Mr Churchill will, we trust, be able to regard it, neither as a blemish on his well-won reputation, nor as a blow to his career, but as the supreme sacrifice which he is called upon to make for his country in the hour of her gravest peril. There is, and can be, no question of failure. Opposed to the most formidable foe it has ever met since the days of the old Royal Navy of France, our sea-power has obtained in ten months a more unchallengeable mastery of the sea than it ever obtained in centuries past after years of successful warfare. The brain and hand of Lord Fisher forged the instrument; but to Mr Churchill, and to Mr Churchill alone, belongs the praise for having used it at the very outbreak of hostility so promptly and so resolutely that the decisive victory was won before a shot had been fired. That can be said even now, and there will be much more to say.

We have suffered losses; there have been, no doubt, mistakes. Mr Churchill may have made his share. But that he should have been malignantly and ungenerously attacked and made the scapegoat for all of them is an injustice which must rouse the blood of any man with a spark of the sense of justice. His mouth has been closed, and must remain closed for a long time to come. He is without present means of defence, yet no sense of fair-play such as Englishmen are supposed to love has prevented his assailants from laying upon him the responsibility for incidents which, for aught they know, may have been attributable to the faults of others. When the day comes for a full revelation of all that has happened in the past ten months, the facts then revealed will cover his traducers with shame.

If the nation is yet able to appreciate great qualities it will testify in no uncertain way its appreciation of the zeal, courage and tireless devotion which Mr Churchill has displayed during the war. He has earned its undying gratitude; he has set an example of faith and resolution which none of the arm-chair critics who have assailed him can ever hope to approach. . . .

He is young. He has lion-hearted courage. No number of enemies can fight down his ability and force. His hour of triumph will come.

On May 25, while he was waiting at the Admiralty to be formally relieved of his office, Churchill received a ministerial visitor, Lord Kitchener. 'He asked what I was going to do,' Churchill recalled in *The World Crisis*. 'I said I had no idea; nothing was settled. He spoke very kindly about our work together. He evidently had no idea how narrowly he had escaped my fate. As he got up to go he turned and said, in the impressive and almost majestic manner which was natural to him, "Well, there is one thing at any rate they cannot take from you. The Fleet was ready." After that he was gone.'

Asquith had not found it easy to form a Coalition Government. The Conservatives wanted an equal part in the prosecution of the war, but this he denied them. On May 25 his new Government was complete. Kitchener remained at the War Office and Grey at the Foreign Office. McKenna became Chancellor of the Exchequer, Simon Home Secretary, Lloyd George Minister of Munitions, Crewe Lord President of the Council. Lord Buckmaster, the former head of the Press Bureau, became Lord Chancellor. Balfour, who had always been a member of the

Liberal Government's War Council, succeeded Churchill at the Admiralty. Other Conservatives had to be content with lesser rank. Bonar Law became Colonial Secretary, Curzon Lord Privy Seal, Selborne President of the Board of Agriculture and Fisheries, Austen Chamberlain Secretary of State for India, Lansdowne Minister without Portfolio, Walter Long President of the Local Government Board. A Labour MP, Arthur Henderson,[1] became President of the Board of Education, the first member of the Labour Party to receive office in a British Cabinet. The most controversial appointment was that of Sir Edward Carson, whose raising of the banner of civil war in Ulster less than a year earlier had made him a hated figure to most Liberals; Asquith made him Attorney-General. F. E. Smith was appointed Solicitor-General, an office not in the Cabinet. Another Conservative friend of Churchill's, Lord Robert Cecil, became Under-Secretary of State at the Foreign Office.

May 26 was Churchill's last day at the Admiralty. His thoughts were still at the Dardanelles. During the morning he wrote to Kitchener: 'You ought to send *at once* to Dardanelles the best helmets & the best gas-making outfit you have. The terrain is so restrictive here that the use of gas on either side might be decisive.' Churchill was a persistent advocate of the use of gas at Gallipoli; but Hamilton, when asked for his opinion by Kitchener, doubted whether gas would be effective in dislodging the Turks from their positions, and it was not used on the Peninsula. Churchill also wrote on the morning of May 26 to Balfour, giving him his thoughts 'for what they are worth' about the Dardanelles, and urging him not to underrate the growing danger of a German submarine attack against de Robeck's Fleet. Unless this danger could be controlled, he wrote, 'there are no limits to the evil consequences. For nearly a fortnight I have not had the authority to make important decisions. Your fresh and calm judgement will give the impulse wh is necessary.' Churchill enumerated seven points for Balfour's consideration:

1. The military operations shd proceed with all possible speed so that the period of danger may be shortened. Whatever force is necessary, can be spared and can be used shd be sent at once, & all at once.

[1] Arthur Henderson, 1863–1935. Labour MP, 1903–18; 1919–22; 1923; 1924–31. Chairman, Parliamentary Labour Party, 1908–10. Chief Whip, Labour Party, 1914; 1921–4; 1925–7. President of the Board of Education, May 1915–August 1916. Paymaster General, August–December 1916. Minister without Portfolio, December 1916–August 1917. Government Mission to Russia, 1917. Home Secretary, 1924. Secretary of State for Foreign Affairs. 1929–31. President of the World Disarmament Conference, 1932–3.

2. Until decisive operations on land can be resumed the Fleet must remain in the safety of Mudros Harbour or the Suez Canal. Such ships as are required to cover the troops shd until the netted lighters arrive be protected by colliers & empty transports lashed alongside.

3. As soon as possible ships must be provided wh are immune from torpedo attack. As specified in my minute of the 13th inst to the First Sea Lord, the 6 heavy monitors shd go out as soon as each is ready: & the 4 Edgars wh have been fitted with bulges and wh supply the medium battery for bombarding purposes, shd be sent at once—nearly a fortnight has been lost in regard to the Edgars by the interregnum here. Until these vessels arrive, & while no decisive land operations are in progress the exposure of the ships shd be kept to the absolute minimum.

4. At least 100 trawlers & drifters with 100 miles of indicator net; & 8 more destroyers wh shd on the way out escort transports, shd be sent; in addition to all the other measures wh have been taken & of wh you will be told.

5. The protection agst submarines must take the form of developing a great netted area around the top of the Gallipoli peninsula, occupied by large numbers of armed trawlers with destroyers & seaplanes always ready. I want to emphasise the fact that action must be drastic & on a large scale. Much less has been done already.

6. The measures to watch & net the mouth of the Adriatic, & to search for submarine bases in Asia Minor, to mine in likely bases, to develop a system of intelligence regardless of expense, all of wh are now in progress must be pressed forward.

7. Punishment must be doggedly borne.

'From the bottom of my heart,' Churchill ended, 'I wish you success in this & all other anxious business wh has been thrust upon you, & wh you have loyally & courageously undertaken.'

Two telegrams to the Dardanelles marked Churchill's last acts as First Lord. 'I hope our friend will ask for all the troops he needs,' he telegraphed to his brother. Kitchener, he informed him, 'is vy friendly to the Dardanelles and means to make it go through; but I am afraid of troops moving in so slowly that you will have to fight the whole Turkish army in relays. Therefore I strongly urge that all that is wanted shd be asked for boldly. New Cabinet will be partial to broad decisions and now is the time. Above is absolutely secret.' Churchill then telegraphed to de Robeck: 'I must now say good-bye & good luck. You will know how to cut the narrow line between upholding the army & exposing your ships to submarines. I think you will be well supported now.' Churchill's farewell reached de Robeck at a tragic time. Only forty-eight hours separated two naval disasters which occurred at the Dardanelles in the last week of May. At noon on May 25 the battleship *Triumph* was torpedoed by a German submarine off Gaba Tepe and seventy-three of her crew were killed. Early on the morning of May 27— Balfour's first day at the Admiralty—the battleship *Majestic*, at anchor off Cape Helles, was also torpedoed by the same submarine, and 40 of her crew were killed. 'I never, never want to see a sight like that again,' Captain Dawnay,[1] an officer on Sir Ian Hamilton's staff, wrote to his wife after witnessing the sinking of the *Majestic*. 'It was horrible— and somehow intensely pathetic as well. The great ship sorely wounded and then her death!'

During May 26 Edwin Montagu called at Admiralty House. 'I went by request to see poor Mrs Winston,' he wrote to Venetia Stanley that day. 'She was so sweet but so miserable and crying all the time. I was very inarticulate, but how I feel for her and him.' On returning to the Treasury Montagu wrote to Clementine Churchill:

My dear Mrs Winston,

My heart bled to see you so unhappy and I came back from your house to write a line in the hope of atoning for my lack of capacity to express myself verbally.

It is a hard time and it is true that Winston has suffered a blow to prestige, reputation and happiness which counts above all. All that is not worth arguing.

But it is also indisputably true that Winston is far too great to be more than pulled up for a period. His courage is enormous, his genius understood even by his enemies and I am as confident that he will rise again as I am that the sun will rise tomorrow, yes and in a far shorter time than you think possible. He will begin to be missed before he is well out of the Admiralty and he will be soon busy adding fresh lustre to the marvellous accumulation he has obtained in so wonderfully short a life.

The reaction in his favour among those who were the hardest critics is already beginning and he will gain new friends every day by his humility under undeserved rebuffs and by the courage with which you and he are facing all that is happening.

Be as miserable as you must about the present; have no misgivings as to the future; I have none, Winston I am sure has none and I know that in your

[1] Guy Payan Dawnay, 1878–1952. Entered Army, 1895. Captain, staff of the Committee of Imperial Defence, 1910–13. General Staff Officer, War Office, September 1914–March 1915. General Staff Officer at Sir Ian Hamilton's headquarters, March–November 1915. Major, October 1915. Lieutenant-Colonel, June 1916. Brigadier-General, General Staff, Egypt, October 1916, and at GHQ, France, 1917–19. Major-General, 1918. Subsequently a director of several companies, Vice-Chairman of the Financial Times Ltd and Chairman of Gordon Hotels Ltd. He married Cecil Buxton (1880–   ) in 1906,

heart and amid your gloom you have undaunted confidence in the man you love.

And the infinite kindness which you and Winston have always shown me gives me the proud right and ability to share your unhappiness and the joyful prospect of sharing in your triumph.

Yrs ever to command
Edwin S. Montagu

On the morning of Thursday May 27 Churchill went to Buckingham Palace, where, after a meeting of the Privy Council, he was received in separate audience by the King, who handed him the seal of the Duchy of Lancaster. For the first time in seven years, he was without executive power. He had no ministerial problems, no vast apparatus of secretaries, no departmental minutes and memoranda. He could attend the War Council debates, but he lacked both the power to inaugurate action and the responsibility to see it through. In the months that followed he was almost unable to believe that he had lost his commanding position at the centre of war policy, or that his influence, at both the Admiralty and the War Council, was effectively at an end. He brooded upon the many facets of the crisis, rehearsing, from his own partial knowledge of what had happened, possible alternatives which might have led to his preservation. It was all in vain. Power had passed from his hands. But the wound and the brooding remained. The Dardanelles had not yet failed. The military and diplomatic opportunities offered by success were still tempting. The cost in life was still far lower than for any equivalent operation on the western front. The climatic conditions were still bearable. New troops were still arriving. The Commander-in-Chief still believed in the possibility of victory. 'The Dardanelles haunted him for the rest of his life,' Clementine Churchill later recalled to the author: 'He always believed in it. When he left the Admiralty he thought he was finished. . . . I thought he would never get over the Dardanelles; I thought he would die of grief.'

15

Loyalties

CHURCHILL's fall from power had been sudden and complete. The speed of the crisis had prevented him from seeing all its aspects, and he had been bewildered by the course of events. Only one fact seemed undisputed: the immediate crisis had begun with Fisher's sudden departure from the Admiralty building on the morning of May 15. Most contemporaries believed that Fisher had gone because he opposed the Dardanelles. Churchill's immediate demotion to the Duchy of Lancaster seemed to confirm that the crisis had arisen because the Dardanelles had failed, and that it was because of this failure that Churchill had been removed from the Admiralty. But there had been throughout a deeper grievance in Fisher's mind than the Dardanelles. Ambition and delusion, not strategy, had led him to his ninth, and final, resignation of six and a half months as First Sea Lord. His letter to Asquith of May 19, in which he had set out the conditions upon which he was willing to return to the Admiralty, revealed the absurd, limitless nature of his aspirations. It was not the Dardanelles policy that would have to change, but all policy. It was not Churchill's methods of conducting the operation which would have to be revised, but all methods different from his own. Only a cypher as First Lord would satisfy him. Impulse, not calculations of policy, dictated Fisher's actions during the crisis. It was the impulse of a man determined to test his own strength and advance his own power, believing that he alone understood the needs of the Navy.

The naval situation at the Dardanelles had not worsened significantly, if at all, on May 15. Churchill had already agreed to abandon any immediate plans for a further naval attack. The Navy had already taken a secondary position. The *Queen Elizabeth* had already been recalled. Kitchener was already planning further assaults inland. It was no new development at the Dardanelles, but Fisher's mental state, that brought the crisis to its climax on May 15. Churchill's absence in Paris for the Italian negotiations had put a heavier burden of work and responsibility on Fisher than he had ever borne before. To be temporarily in charge of Admiralty affairs in time of war, worried not only by submarine dangers at the Dardanelles, but also by the threat of a German invasion of Holland and the possibility that a naval action might begin in the North Sea, demanded nerves of steel. Fisher was unable to preserve the necessary calm. He was seventy-four years old, and the strain of war administration was too much for him.

Churchill had seen no reason why Fisher's resignation on May 15 should lead to the disintegration of the Government, or to his own departure from the Admiralty. He believed that had Asquith wanted to make an effort to preserve his Government intact he might have succeeded, if not in averting, then in postponing the day of coalition. But the concerted pressures for coalition, coming at the moment when Asquith's power of decision had broken down, determined the outcome. Asquith had lacked the strength to resist. Henceforth, Churchill blamed Lloyd George for forcing Asquith to form a coalition, and resented what he regarded as Lloyd George's patronizing tone towards his future place in the Government; hence his ill-judged letter to Asquith informing him that Lloyd George would not make a suitable Secretary of State for War.

Lloyd George knew the extent of Churchill's abilities. He also feared his egoism and distrusted his judgement. He knew that Churchill hoped to emerge as a hero of the war; that he wanted to obliterate past political enmities and wear down persistent Press hostility by successful war policies. Before the war he had often listened to Churchill's dreams. A young Treasury official, Ralph Hawtrey,[1] later wrote to the author of an occasion which he himself witnessed:

When I was private secretary to Lloyd George in 1910–11, he and Churchill drove down one weekend to his house in Brighton, and I in the car had the opportunity of listening. Churchill began to talk about the next war. He described how, at the climax, he himself, in command of the army, would win the decisive victory in the Middle East, and would return to England in triumph. Lloyd George quietly interposed, 'And where do I come in?'

The May crisis had given Lloyd George his chance to 'come in'; the initiative which he was widely believed to have taken in insisting upon coalition gave him a link with the Conservatives which Churchill had

[1] Ralph George Hawtrey, 1879–   . Civil Servant, Admiralty, 1903–4; Treasury, 1904–45. Director of Financial Enquiries, Treasury, 1919–45. Knighted, 1956. Author and economist.

always craved. For Clementine Churchill, Lloyd George was henceforth a Judas, whose demand for coalition had destroyed her husband's
position, and whose 'Welsh trickiness', as she later described it to the
author, had shattered her husband's career. She was not the only
member of the family who singled out Lloyd George for censure. The
Duke of Marlborough wrote to Churchill on May 24: 'Pro tem LG
has done you in.' But once Asquith had accepted coalition, Churchill's
position was weakened beyond the point where Lloyd George could
strengthen it.

As soon as Churchill had realized that Asquith was not prepared to
take any political risk to keep him at the Admiralty, he had appealed
to the leaders of the Conservative Party for support. Many of those
who watched the crisis believed that the Conservatives had refused to
join the Coalition at all unless Churchill were removed from the Admiralty. This was not so. Asquith had decided to move Churchill out
several days before he began consultations with the Conservative
leaders to discover their preferences and prejudices. Churchill appealed
to Bonar Law because, although their relationship had never been good,
it had never been so bad as to exclude at least an outside chance of co-
operation. Only when Churchill received Bonar Law's negative reply
did he realize that the Conservative suspicions built up during ten years
of savage political fighting could not be dispelled, and that if the Conservatives were to play a prominent part in the Administration, he
could not look to them for high office.

As soon as the Government was reconstructed, Churchill sent his new
Conservative colleagues a large number of official documents, outlining
his Admiralty record, hoping thereby to show them how wrong they
were to believe him to have been an irresponsible First Lord. But
Conservative hostility could not be assuaged by such methods, however
detailed or well-documented they might be. Coronel, Antwerp and the
Dardanelles were the proofs of something they had believed for a long
time. Neither the irreverence of his earlier attacks upon them, nor the
vitriol of his speeches against the House of Lords could be pardoned.
His Irish policy had angered them even more. As one of the most vocal
and provocative advocates of Home Rule between 1911 and 1914,
Churchill had, in Tory view, betrayed the cause of Ulster. Bonar Law,
Carson, Austen Chamberlain and Long, all members of the new
Coalition, had been the leading advocates of Ulster. The memories of
Churchill's Irish policies were recent and indelible. For the Conserva-
tives, Churchill's career since 1904 had provided repeated proof of his
irresponsibility, lack of balance, and loyalty only to himself.

Liberal opinion was divided in its assessment of Churchill's character. 'He never gets fairly alongside the person he is talking to,' Asquith had written to Venetia Stanley on 4 February 1915, 'because he is always so much more interested in himself and his own preoccupations & his own topics than in anything his neighbour has to contribute, that his conversation (unless he is made to succumb either to superior authority or to well-directed chaff) is apt to degenerate into a monologue. It is the same to a certain extent in the Cabinet.' But it was not Churchill's method alone, but his judgement that seemed at fault to those Liberals who did not know him as well as did Asquith. Since the siege of Antwerp in October 1914 the backbenches of the Party had pullulated with growing distrust of Churchill's judgement. This hostility had burst through to Cabinet level early in March 1915 when the editor of the Liberal weekly the *Nation*, H. W. Massingham, had told Asquith that Churchill was the leader of an intrigue aimed at replacing Grey by Balfour at the Foreign Office. At the end of March further suspicions had been voiced by the Home Secretary, Reginald McKenna. Asquith did not treat these rumours seriously, realizing that they were the product of long-standing Liberal suspicions of Churchill's loyalty; but even Asquith could not always shake himself free of doubts. On April 16, following an attack in Cabinet by Lloyd George and Churchill on Kitchener, Asquith, weary of Churchill's outbursts, had written to Venetia Stanley: 'he is impulsive & borne along on the flood of his all too copious tongue'. By May 1915 there were many Liberals, particularly among backbench MPs and junior Ministers, who believed that Churchill was aiming to break the Liberal Government altogether in an attempt to enhance his own powers. Among the stories which Hobhouse sent to Lord Buxton on 10 June 1915 was the statement that Churchill's objective in the May crisis, had been 'a new Ministerial office, a sort of Department of Public Safety' which would give him supreme control of war policy. Churchill knew nothing of this particular charge. But he realized the extent of Liberal hostility. Many Liberals who admired his energy and courage still had doubts as to whether he ought to remain a member of the Government. John Burns,[1] who had resigned from the Cabinet on the outbreak of war, was a typical example. Between 1908 and 1910, while President of the Local Government Board, Burns had been in constant and constructive contact with Churchill at the Board of Trade; nearly twenty years older

[1] John Elliot Burns, 1858–1943. Trade union leader. Independent Labour MP, 1892–1910. Liberal MP, 1910–18. President of the Local Government Board, 1905–14. President of the Board of Trade, 1914, resigning on the outbreak of war.

than Churchill, he had always taken a friendly interest in his career. On May 24 he wrote in his diary:

It looks as if poor Winston was doomed to go. In a way a great pity. He is patriotic (not in Johnsonese sense). He is energetic and at times inspired to great thoughts and noble expression but at heart he is dictatorial and in his temper demoniacal (note his look coming from Admiralty in papers); he alternates in his passions between blood lusts against the foreigner, and brain storms against his rivals which would be better if they burst upon them instead of devouring himself. I have always been fair, at times indulgent, to him and I see his displacement with regret, because he is brave.

Many Liberals shared Burns' alarm at Churchill's 'dictatorial' tendencies. Others were jealous of the extent to which Asquith had come to rely upon a man whom they believed did not share the deepest instincts of Liberalism. Asquith's relationship with Churchill was a complex one. For many years he had been attracted by Churchill's imagination and energy. He had advanced Churchill's career so swiftly that on the outbreak of war, aged only forty, Churchill had reached a peak of political office and influence. When Asquith became Prime Minister in April 1908 he had immediately brought Churchill into his Cabinet as President of the Board of Trade. Each subsequent advancement had been on Asquith's initiative. Churchill's transfer from the Home Office to the Admiralty had been at Asquith's instigation. He supported Churchill's work at the Admiralty against strong Liberal criticism on the backbenches, in the Press and in the Cabinet. On the outbreak of war, Asquith had brought Churchill into the inner sanctum of power. The Prime Minister had deliberately limited his discussion of war policy at the highest level to an even smaller number of Ministers than were in the Cabinet or, from November 1914, on the War Council: Churchill had been one of this number. Asquith had turned to him as a mediator when Cabinet dissensions threatened to disrupt Government unity. He had used him to placate the Press and the House of Commons. He had entrusted him with delicate naval negotiations, first with France, then with Italy.

Churchill had reciprocated Asquith's confidence. He had no other patron of such power in British politics. The Churchills had been taken into Asquith's family circle, and for several years had been frequent guests at 10 Downing Street, The Wharf and Walmer Castle. But by April 1915 Churchill saw in Asquith a man whose powers of concentration were waning, and felt that he lacked the ruthlessness needed to pursue an effective war policy. When the question of a second naval attempt to force the Dardanelles had arisen in March, Churchill believed, as he later wrote in *Great Contemporaries*, that Asquith 'was resolute to continue', but that 'unhappily for himself and for all others he did not thrust to the full length of his convictions'. From that moment Asquith's patronage had been withdrawn. In giving Fisher a veto power over the Dardanelles reinforcements, as he had done on May 12, Asquith had effectively withdrawn his earlier support for Churchill's actions. Without Asquith's support, Churchill was entirely vulnerable. Had Asquith not had doubts about Churchill's reliability, he would have found it easier to reject Fisher's pressure.

In May 1915, despite these recent and growing doubts, Asquith did not welcome the crisis as a means of removing Churchill from the Admiralty. In a single Party government, Asquith knew that he could control Churchill's enthusiasms. But as soon as a coalition had to be formed, Churchill was no longer manageable. The Conservatives would either win him over by their greater zeal for an active war policy, or rebel against his exuberance and thrusting. It was clear to Asquith from the moment that he decided to form his Coalition that Churchill's presence would lead to dissension. He wanted to control his new Government with the maximum authority. He could not risk Churchill's presence in high office.

Churchill saw Asquith as the man ultimately responsible for his fall. Clementine Churchill shared his belief. Her cousin Sylvia Henley[1] later told the author that Clementine Churchill had, during the crisis, declared that her one remaining ambition was to dance on Asquith's grave. For Churchill, the change in Asquith's behaviour towards him rankled far more than Fisher's resignation, Lloyd George's advocacy of coalition, Conservative acrimony, or Liberal innuendo. He resented above all Asquith's refusal to let him defend the Dardanelles policy. Because Asquith had removed Churchill from the Admiralty, critics of the Dardanelles assumed that Asquith shared their criticisms. Churchill's dismissal was seen as a punishment for launching an enterprise which, although it had not yet failed, was regarded by many as doomed. Kitchener's responsibility for the military landings of April 25, and for all subsequent fighting on the Gallipoli Peninsula, was overlooked. Because Churchill alone had suffered demotion, he alone was thought to be responsible. Asquith's personal support for the Dardanelles expedition was unknown to the public. Yet Asquith, eager for the

[1] Sylvia Laura Stanley, 1882–   . Daughter of the 5th Baron Stanley of Alderley. Clementine Churchill's cousin. In 1906 she married Brigadier-General Anthony Morton Henley, who died in 1925.

enormous benefits to be brought by success, had at every stage given the enterprise the support without which it could not have been begun, or been continued. For many months, at the War Council, and at smaller meetings of three or four Ministers, Asquith had encouraged the Dardanelles to go forward as a matter so secret and so urgent that it need not be debated in full Cabinet. It was Asquith who, on January 28, had persuaded Fisher to give up the Zeebrugge operation and support the Dardanelles in its place. But it was not until 1917, when he was no longer Prime Minister, that Asquith publicly revealed his feelings about the Dardanelles. Speaking in the House of Commons on 14 March 1917 he said: 'It saved the position—absolutely saved the position—of Russia in the Caucasus; it prevented for months the defection of Bulgaria to the Central Powers; it kept at least 300,000 Turks immobile; and, what is more important, it cut off, annihilated, a corps d'élite, the whole flower of the Turkish Army. They have never recovered to this moment from the blow inflicted upon them.'

Churchill had taken it for granted that Asquith would support him after Fisher's resignation, and was exceedingly bitter when he did not. He was unaware of the reservations in Asquith's attitude towards him, which had been present even before the war, and which were aggravated and magnified by the war itself. The constant proximity of the two men, their daily political and personal contact, only twice interrupted—during the siege of Antwerp and the Paris negotiations—by more than forty-eight hours' separation, had led by May 1915 to an increasingly sceptical attitude towards Churchill on Asquith's part. The intensity of Churchill's exhortations had begun to tire him. He found Churchill's eagerness to do and dare, his insistent calls for speed and action, his repeated desire to be in the war zone, his changing and exhausting moods, his emotional appeals to the stage of history, too frequent always to be taken seriously.

As the war progressed a more serious charge was levelled against Churchill than that of personal ambition. Many people began to see in him a man of blood. For those who saw him every day he was the 'happy man' at the outbreak of war, the frustrated soldier thirsting for action at Antwerp, the naval enthusiast willing to throw away ships and men in spectacular enterprises, the Cabinet Minister keen to see the war continue in order to provide opportunities for his own fertile imagination. Churchill seemed to have a lust for battle. On 14 September 1914 Asquith had written to Venetia Stanley: 'I am inclined almost to shiver when I hear Winston say that the last thing he would pray for is Peace.'

Despite his enthusiasm for conducting and directing war policy,

Churchill was under no illusions about what fighting meant to the soldiers and sailors who bore the brunt of it. 'Much as war attracts me,' he had written to his wife from German Army manoeuvres in 1909, '& fascinates my mind with its tremendous situations—I feel more deeply every year—& can measure the feeling here in the midst of arms—what vile & wicked folly & barbarism it all is.' Churchill had seen the cruel side of action at Antwerp as well as on the distant frontiers of India. During his visit in May to the western front he had heard the piteous cries of savagely wounded men at the casualty clearing station, a sight the horrors of which he was never to forget. But he believed that the war had to be fought until victory was secured, and felt that if victory demanded losses and suffering, they must be accepted. Efficiency, determination and ruthlessness were the qualities he prized. But he had also a sincere desire to prevent needless slaughter. This was not evident to those who were repelled by his enthusiasm for directing war policy.

In the immediate aftermath of his dismissal, Churchill saw how great was the gap between the reality of war policy and public beliefs about it. Watching as rumours about him changed in the telling from near plausibility to complete nonsense, he feared that his many achievements during nine months of war would remain unknown until they could no longer help his career. In later years he looked back with pride upon what he regarded as major achievements: the preparation of the Navy in the years leading up to war, the mobilization of the Fleet, its successful and secret transfer from the Channel to the North Sea, the safe transport of troops from Britain and the Empire to the zones of war, the hunting down of von Spee, the clearing of the German raiders from the oceans, the maintenance of Britain's naval and maritime supremacy, the check to the German advance at Antwerp, the success of the armoured cars and the naval airmen, the confidence provided by his public speeches and the fertility of his private counsel. But in May 1915 all he felt was that he had been thrown over by the Prime Minister cruelly and unnecessarily, that he had been singled out from among his colleagues as a scapegoat for the Dardanelles, and that even over the Dardanelles he was cut off from all the plans on which he had worked, and from any chance to further those plans effectively. The offensive against Germany in the North Sea would be for others to carry out. Others would maintain Britain's naval supremacy. Others would deploy Britain's naval power in search of victory. Others would win the acclaim for victory when it came.

16

The Duchy of Lancaster

CHURCHILL was no longer at the centre of war policy. But he could not accept the limitations which his loss of influence entailed. He continued to believe that his opinions would be taken seriously, that if expressed forcefully enough they would prevail, and that the new Conservative Ministers would welcome his advice. In a series of memoranda, in discussion at Cabinet and in his correspondence, he acted as if he still retained some control over war policy. But he was deceiving himself. His was a voice which no longer had to be listened to; for that reason, he found few listeners. At first he did not realize the extent of his isolation and was always hoping that with time he might regain his full former powers.

When news of his demotion to the Duchy of Lancaster was known Churchill received a flood of letters. Admiral Limpus wrote from Malta on June 7: 'We say farewell—for the present—with a heavy heart. But you are yet young & will be needed again.' Rear-Admiral William Pakenham[1] recalled the time when he had been on the Admiralty Board, writing on June 1 that there had been 'no improvement of the conditions of service of officers and men, or in material, which did not emanate from you'. General Sir John Brabazon,[2] who had been Churchill's first commanding officer, wrote on June 5:

Dear Winston,
    I felt much inclined to write to you some days ago, and then I thought it would have the appearance of a letter of condolence and I want you to

---

[1] William Christopher Pakenham, 1861–1933. Entered Navy, 1874. Captain, 1903. Fourth Sea Lord, 1911–13. Rear-Admiral commanding the 3rd Cruiser Squadron, 1913–17. Knighted, 1916. Commanded the Battle Cruiser Fleet, 1917–19. Commander-in-Chief, North America and West Indies, 1920–2.

[2] John Palmer Brabazon, 1843–1922. Entered Army, 1862. Commanded 4th Hussars, 1893–6. Commanded Imperial Yeomanry in South Africa, 1900. Major-General, 1901. Knighted, 1911. Colonel, 18th Hussars, 1913–22.

understand that I am *not* condoling with you, because I with very many others think you did magnificently well.

One can not win battles or campaigns by acting entirely on the defensive and you are the only one who has shown the least initiative.

Moreover you saved the situation, and in my opinion the Nation, at the beginning of the war, or rather before the war began. If other Ministers had been as bold and far seeing as yourself we should have been in a different position today.

It is not pleasant to be superseded by men whom one feels are inferior to oneself but you have never done anything better in your life than in accepting the very inadequate position they offered you.

But you will come out top dog yet, and old as I am I hope to live to see it.

Ever your very sincere old friend
J. P. Brabazon

Josiah Wedgwood wrote on May 19 from the Royal Naval Hospital at Malta, where he was recovering from the wound he had received on the Helles front at the beginning of the month:

My dear Churchill,

I cannot tell you with what indignation I learn that you have ceased to be First Lord. The jackals have got you down at last. Don't imagine that I care a damn about you, except as the sharpest weapon available against those German hounds. It is their rejoicing which puts the lid on the folly of the change.

I suppose they will now make you High Commissioner of S Africa or Governor of Queensland, & you will take it for a living. Then they can make peace & kiss Wilhelm's boots. . . .

Of course there is just a chance that you may choose to stick it & keep the non-party humbug up to the scratch in Parliament. If so count me in every time.

Yours very gratefully
Josiah C. Wedgwood
Lt Com

On May 29 Jellicoe wrote to Churchill 'of the whole hearted manner in which you have lived for the navy for 3 years'. Churchill replied on June 1 with his thoughts on Fisher, the Dardanelles and his own work as First Lord:

My dear Jellicoe,

My separation—quarrel there was not—from our august old friend is among the most painful things in my life. I have been looking through all the letters he wrote me, musing regretfully upon the vanished pleasures of his comradeship & society. The Dardanelles has run on like a Greek tragedy— our early successes converting what was originally launched only as an experiment into an undertaking from wh it was impossible to recede; the awful delays of the army, week after week consumed while the Germans taught the Turks to entrench, & submarines seemed ever drawing nearer; his growing anxiety when checks & losses occurred; his increasing dislike of the whole business; the imperious need to go forward to victory—you can fill in the rest. But you see it must be 'Aye' or 'No' in war.

Now the long-dreaded arrival of submarines complicates gravely the situation, & the military operation continually expands. But on the other hand the monitors are approaching, & Mr Balfour with his cool quiet courage will not leave undone any possible thing. And at least we have Italy as a first-fruits.

I have tried not to think of myself in these days, but to keep my mind steadily fixed upon the enemy. Yr vy kind letter gives me much pleasure. I hope my work here taken altogether may stand the test of after-examination. We have not always agreed as you say, but I have always felt quite safe with you at sea. Your patience inexhaustible, yr nerve untired, your practice & experience unequalled. I feel almost entitled to say the gravest & most critical period is past. In a few months anyhow when the new construction flows in all will be well—even according to yr exacting standards.

All good wishes to you in yr great command.

Yours sincerely
Winston S. Churchill

As Chancellor of the Duchy of Lancaster Churchill's only serious duty was to appoint County magistrates, a diminutive patronage following upon his enormous responsibilities at the Admiralty. 'The Duchy of Lancaster has been mobilized,' he wrote to Jack Seely on June 12; 'A strong flotilla of magistrates for the 1915 programme will shortly be laid down.' Even with such an insignificant official task, Churchill received several direct requests from his colleagues. Lewis Harcourt, whose constituency was in Lancashire, wrote to ask whether he could submit a few names for magistrates. Like most of his predecessors at the Duchy, Churchill had no intention of becoming involved in the complex cross currents of local political patronage, replying on June 16 with a letter drafted in the Duchy Office which served for all future patronage seekers. Applications, he wrote, should come 'from a *non-political* source', and should go direct to the Lord-Lieutenant of Lancashire, Lord Shuttleworth.[1] On May 31 Shuttleworth wrote to Churchill,

[1] Ughtred James Kay-Shuttleworth, 1844–1939. Liberal MP, 1869–80; 1885–1902. Chancellor of the Duchy of Lancaster, 1886. Created Baron Shuttleworth, 1902. Lord-Lieutenant of Lancashire, 1908–28.

offering to put his 'experience & knowledge of Lancashire & its affairs' at Churchill's disposal. Henceforth all the official work of the Duchy was in Shuttleworth's hands.

After the formation of the Coalition, the War Council became known officially as the Dardanelles Committee, although it continued to discuss the European as well as Asiatic aspects of war policy. Churchill attended all its meetings. But he had little power to influence its decisions. His new office contained no facilities for a Minister at the centre of affairs; there was not even a messenger attached to it. On June 18 he asked Edwin Montagu if the Treasury could let him have 'a room for myself & two smaller rooms for a Private Secretary & shorthand writer with the necessary conveniences. . . . It is also necessary that I should have a messenger.' The Treasury agreed to give him rooms at 19 Abingdon Street, opposite the House of Lords, and much nearer Whitehall than the Duchy Office off the Strand, and to let him retain the services both of Edward Marsh, and of his Admiralty shorthand writer Henry Beckenham.[1] With this minuscule staff Churchill turned his attention from the affairs of the Duchy to matters of national importance. Despite his diminished influence, he could not abandon his earlier concerns, and still felt the need to push and prompt those who now had power over war policy. On May 29, three days after he had left the Admiralty, he wrote to Masterton-Smith with several important points which he wished to be put to Balfour. These included the proposal to send two extra submarines to de Robeck, over which Fisher had resigned. Balfour agreed with the need to send them to the Dardanelles, and soon decided that even more should be sent. Sir Henry Jackson, who had succeeded Fisher as First Sea Lord, concurred in Balfour's decision. Churchill also wrote to Masterton-Smith about plans for deep-keel pontoons, about which he felt responsible:

It makes me very unhappy to think that this project actually received Treasury approval and that I subsequently allowed myself to be turned from it. If we had these vessels now, as we should have done had the order been given at the time, they would afford a complete protection against submarines to ships bombarding the Gallipoli Peninsula. Six months have been lost and I reproach myself for having abandoned a project about which I felt so strongly; but the moral of this war is not to be afraid of making long plans, and that it is never too late in it to begin making them afresh.

[1] Henry Anstead Beckenham, 1890–1937. Entered Admiralty, 1910. Assistant Private Secretary to Churchill, 1912–15; to Sir W. Graham Greene, 1916; to Jellicoe when First Sea Lord, 1917; to Wemyss when First Sea Lord, 1918; to Churchill, 1918–22. Secretary to the British Empire Exhibition, Wembley, 1923–5.

On May 30 Churchill circulated a paper to the Cabinet showing the increase in British naval strength since the outbreak of war, and giving details of the progress that had been made in the manufacture of ammunition and torpedoes, the supply of coal and oil, and the development of the Royal Naval Air Service, which had expanded from 98 officers and 595 men in August 1914 to 895 officers and 8,039 men in May 1915, and which would have 1,200 aircraft by the end of the year. This was his first exercise since leaving the Admiralty in the defence of his record as First Lord. 'There is no reason for anxiety,' he declared, 'about our superiority in the decisive theatre.' On June 1 Churchill sent leading Ministers a memorandum in which he set out his views of the futility of renewed frontal assaults on the western front:

Although attacks prepared by immense concentrations of artillery have been locally successful in causing alterations of the line, the effort required is so great and the advance so small that the attack and advance, however organised and nourished, are exhausted before penetration deep enough and wide enough to produce a strategic effect has been made. The enemy must always have some knowledge of the concentration before the attack. They will always have time to rectify their line afterwards. At an utterly disproportionate cost the line will be merely bent; and bendings of the line at particular points do not appear to compromise other parts. I expect we have lost more than 50,000 men since the beginning of April—two-thirds in attempts at the offensive—without appreciable results. . . .

We should be ill-advised to squander our new armies in frantic and sterile efforts to pierce the German lines. To do so is to play the German game. As long as the process of attrition works evenly on both sides we are on the road to victory. But a few weeks of an attempted offensive may inflict irreparable injury upon our newly gathered military power.

Churchill could not turn his mind for long from the Dardanelles. He was distressed and angered by what was happening on the Gallipoli Peninsula. There, he wrote in his memorandum, the longer the battle lasted, 'the more dangerous it will become'. He believed that the delays in beginning the military operations, and the piecemeal manner in which troops had been despatched, had 'already given time for the Turks to make elaborate defensive preparations'. Churchill warned his colleagues:

If we delay longer in sending the necessary reinforcements, or send them piecemeal, we shall have in the end to send all, and more than all, that are now asked for, and we shall run the double risk of fighting the whole Turkish army in relays around the Kilid Bahr plateau, and of being seriously harassed by numbers of German submarines, which will certainly be attracted to the spot by the success which has attended the first one. It seems most urgent to try to obtain a decision here and wind up the enterprise in a satisfactory manner as soon as possible.

Churchill then set out his own plan for a rapid conclusion at the Dardanelles. First, the Army was to advance across the Kilid Bahr plateau in order to dominate the Turkish forts on the Asian shore with its artillery. This alone, he now believed, would ensure that the Fleet could enter the Sea of Marmara. Once this was done it would only be 'a few hours steam to Constantinople', and to victory. Churchill ended his memorandum with a survey of how victory could be achieved:

The Turco-German fleet can then certainly be destroyed. Its destruction removes the menace which has hitherto prevented a Russian army from crossing the Black Sea and attacking Constantinople from the north. Although the Russian army which had been held ready to profit by our success has now been drawn away by more urgent interim needs, the Russians certainly will not let Constantinople fall without their participation. Bulgaria cannot remain indifferent to the movement and approach of these events. She will be inevitably forced to march on Adrianople, and with Bulgaria the whole of the Balkans must come out on our side. Any Turkish troops in other parts of the Gallipoli Peninsula will be incidentally cut off as soon as the Fleet severs the water communication with Chanak and closes the Bulair isthmus from both sides.

But the position of all the Turkish forces in Europe, whatever their numbers, is by the same series of events decisively affected. Their homes are in Asia, their food comes from Asia, their Government will have fled to Asia. They must fall into our hands with all their stores and artillery, as a mere by-product of the main operation. And all this depends on the conquest of 3 or 4 miles of ground! Where else in all the theatres of the war can we look during the next three months for a decisive victory, or for results of this extraordinary character?

The Liberal Ministers felt that they had heard these views before. The Conservatives did not want to be distracted by someone whose place in the Cabinet was peripheral. The only Conservative Minister who circulated a memorandum supporting Churchill was Lord Selborne, a former First Lord whom Asquith had appointed President of the Board of Agriculture and Fisheries. 'At the very worst fortune of the war for us,' Selborne wrote sceptically on June 4, the Gallipoli Peninsula, Constantinople and the Bosphorus could be given to

Germany in exchange for the re-establishment of an unoccupied and neutral Belgium.

Churchill no longer regarded victory at the Dardanelles as either easy or inevitable. On June 2, in reply to a friendly letter of farewell from Hankey, Churchill explained what he believed were the reasons for his failure:

No one knows better than you the difficulties of carrying through a positive enterprise with only partial control. If I have erred, it has been in seeking to attempt an initiative without being sure that all the means & powers to make it successful were at my disposal.

The Lost opportunities of this war from Antwerp to the Dardanelles are a tragic catalogue. No where has there been design or decision. I have tried & Fisher with me, but even our comradeship was not proof agst the ugly situations wh circumstances in the control of others have produced.

Now it will be a hard & stern test to carry through the Dardanelles: & without decision & design very terrible catastrophe may ensue.

Hankey replied two days later that he had 'not the smallest desire to shirk any measure of responsibility which can fairly be attributed to me for the Dardanelles operation. Strategically it has always appeared, and still appears, to me to be the right thing to do.'

On June 5 Churchill went to Dundee to make a public speech about his work as First Lord. He devoted much effort to defending past actions. He described how, since going to the Admiralty in 1911, he had borne a 'heavy burden', responsible in the 'real sense' of the word, in that he had had to take 'the blame for everything that has gone wrong'. Nevertheless he believed that he had done everything possible to secure success, and that 'the archives of the Admiralty will show in the utmost detail the part I have played in all the great transactions that have taken place. It is to them that I look for my defence.' Churchill then summarized the Navy's achievement of which, he said, 'I shall always be proud to have had a share.' This was his claim and pride:

The terrible dangers of the beginning of the war are over, the seas have been swept clear; the submarine menace has been fixed within definite limits; the personal ascendancy of our men, the superior quality of our ships on the high seas, have been established beyond doubt or question; our strength has greatly increased, actually and relatively from what it was in the beginning of the war, and it grows continually every day by leaps and bounds in all the classes of vessels needed for the special purpose of the war. Between now and the end of the year, the British navy will receive reinforcements which would be incredible if they were not actual facts. Everything is in perfect order. Nearly everything has been foreseen, all our supplies, stores, ammunition, and appliances of every kind, our supplies and drafts of officers and men—all are there. Nowhere will you be hindered. You have taken the measure of your foe, you have only to go forward with confidence. On the whole surface of the seas of the world no hostile flag is flown.

These were the words which Asquith had not let him speak in the House of Commons on May 17.

Churchill then spoke briefly about the Dardanelles, pointing out that in nearly every case where a ship had been sunk 'the precious lives of the officers and men are saved', and that the naval losses had been 'exaggerated in the minds both of friend and foe'. It was essential, he said, not to forget what victory at the Dardanelles would bring:

When I speak of victory, I am not referring to those victories which crowd the daily placards of any newspaper. I am speaking of victory in the sense of a brilliant and formidable fact, shaping the destinies of nations and shortening the duration of the war. Beyond those few miles of ridge and scrub on which our soldiers, our French comrades, our gallant Australians, and our New Zealand fellow-subjects are now battling, lie the downfall of a hostile empire, the destruction of an enemy's fleet and army, the fall of a world-famous capital, and probably the accession of powerful Allies. The struggle will be heavy, the risks numerous, the losses cruel; but victory when it comes will make amends for all.

There never was a great subsidiary operation of war in which a more complete harmony of strategic, political and economic advantages has combined, or which stood in truer relation to the main decision which is in the central theatre. Through the narrows of the Dardanelles and across the ridges of the Gallipoli Peninsula lie some of the shortest paths to a triumphant peace.

Churchill had been distressed during the May crisis by the virulent and continuing Press attacks upon himself. To this subject, which had so upset him, he then turned. He believed that it was wrong for newspapers to be allowed 'to attack the responsible leaders of the nation' or to write in a manner 'which is calculated to spread doubts and want of confidence in them'. If there was to be criticism, it ought to be in Parliament. If secret matters had to be criticized, Parliament ought to meet behind closed doors. But it was essential in the national interest 'that irresponsible or malicious carping should not continue'.

Although a member of the Cabinet and the War Council, Churchill appealed to the Government to bring to an end what he believed were the debilities which had cursed Asquith's previous administration, and hampered his own work as First Lord:

I ask myself this question—What does the nation expect of the new National Government? I can answer my question. I am going to answer it in one word—action. That is the need, that is the only justification, that there should be a stronger national sentiment, a more powerful driving force, a greater measure of consent in the people, a greater element of leadership and design in the rulers—that is what all parties expect and require in return for the many sacrifices which all parties have after due consideration made from their particular interests and ideals. Action—action, not hesitation; action, not words; action, not agitation. The nation waits its orders. The duty lies upon the Government to declare what should be done, to propose to Parliament, and to stand or fall by the result. That is the message which you wish me to take back to London—Act; act now; act with faith and courage. Trust the people. They have never failed you yet.

Churchill ended with an appeal to the nation:

Above all, let us be of good cheer. . . . I have told you how the Navy's business has been discharged. You see for yourselves how your economic life and energy have been maintained without the slightest check, so that it is certain you can realise the full strength of this vast community. The valour of our soldiers has won general respect in all the Armies of Europe. The word of Britain is now taken as the symbol and the hall mark of international good faith. The loyalty of our Dominions and Colonies vindicates our civilisation, and the hate of our enemies proves the effectiveness of our warfare. Yet I would advise you from time to time, when you are anxious or depressed, to dwell a little on the colour and light of the terrible war pictures now presented to the eye. See Australia and New Zealand smiting down in the last and finest crusade the combined barbarism of Prussia and of Turkey. See General Louis Botha[1] holding South Africa for the King. See Canada defending to the death the last few miles of shattered Belgium. Look further, and, across the smoke and carnage of the immense battlefield, look forward to the vision of a united British Empire on the calm background of a liberated Europe.

Then turn again to your task. Look forward, do not look backward.

---

[1] Louis Botha, 1862–1919. Commandant-General of the Boer forces in the South African war, 1900. First Prime Minister of the Union of South Africa, 1910–19.

Gather afresh in heart and spirit all the energies of your being, bend anew together for a supreme effort. The times are harsh, the need is dire, the agony of Europe is infinite, but the might of Britain hurled united into the conflict will be irresistible. We are the grand reserve of the Allied cause, and that grand reserve must now march forward as one man.

Churchill's speech was widely reported. Its final appeal was much praised. According to the Liberal London evening newspaper, the *Star*: 'Mr Churchill has spoken the words the nation wanted to hear. He has swept away the gadflies and blowflies. He has done justice both to the spirit of the nation and to the gallantry of its youth. His words are thrice welcome, seeing that the axe-grinding pessimists for weeks have been supreme.' A flood of letters brought Churchill the congratulations of both friends and strangers.

A veteran member of the Liberal Party, Lord Channing of Welling-borough,[1] wrote on June 9:

Dear Churchill,

Though I fear to write to men in the thick of the great work and great anxiety, I must write one word to thank you for your noble, generous and magnificent speech, the best and most inspiring of any speech during this war.

Without intruding on your obvious and generous desire to say nothing, I will say that I cannot comprehend the ungenerous and stupid failure of some of the Press to understand and appreciate your services in giving the Country an invincible fleet, a splendid water plane and air plane service and I will go farther, in showing that touch of genius in facing great risks wh has scared some people.

I know from old talks with great experts the enormous risks you took in the Dardanelles. But if your plan succeeds, as it will, I earnestly hope, it will mean much to the decisive ending of the war. As one of the old hands I venture to send you my warm thanks for all you have done and dared.

Yours very sincerely
Channing of W

Churchill was encouraged by so much praise. 'I am now master of myself & at peace;' he wrote to J. L. Garvin on June 7, '& yesterday I was conscious that I was not powerless.'

[1] Francis Allston Channing, 1841–1926. Born in the United States of America. Tutor, fellow and lecturer in philosophy at University College, Oxford, 1866–70. Naturalized as a British subject, 1883. Liberal MP, 1885–1910. Created Baron Channing of Welling-borough, 1912. A prominent backbencher, the champion of tenant farmers and agricultural labourers.

Since the outbreak of war the British Army had filled its ranks with volunteers. The New Armies being raised by Lord Kitchener depended entirely upon voluntary enlistment. Many Conservatives believed that only a system of compulsory military service would provide sufficient manpower to win the war. Now that the Conservatives had moved from the obscurity of a silent Opposition to the centre of Government, the conscription issue was likely to be raised in increasingly insistent form within the Cabinet itself. Churchill shared the general Liberal dislike of compulsory service. During his Dundee speech he had pointed to the successful mobilization of millions of British and Empire citizens by the voluntary method, which he described as 'one of the most wonderful and inspiring facts in the whole history of this wonderful island'. If there were to be compulsory service, he felt that it would 'cast away this great moral advantage which adds to the honour of our Armies and to the dignity of our State'. Conscription, he declared, would have the effect 'of hustling into the firing line a comparatively small proportion of persons, themselves not, perhaps, best suited to the job'. Such a policy, he felt, would be 'unwise in the extreme'.

While firmly opposed to military compulsion, Churchill saw another area of national life in which conscription could be of value. 'But service at home,' he said, 'service for home defence and to keep our fighting men abroad properly supplied and maintained' seemed to him to be another matter:

We are locked in a mortal struggle. To fail is to be enslaved, or, at the very best, to be destroyed. Not to win decisively is to have all this misery over again after an uneasy truce, and to fight it over again, probably under less favourable circumstances and, perhaps, alone. Why, after what has happened there could never be peace in Europe until the German military system has been so shattered and torn and trampled that it is unable to resist by any means the will and decision of the conquering Power.

For this purpose our whole nation must be organised, must be socialised if you like the word, must be organised, and mobilised. . . . I think there must be asserted in some form or other by the Government, a reserve power to give the necessary control and organising authority and to make sure that every one of every rank and condition, men and women as well, do, in their own way, their fair share. Democratic principles enjoin it, social justice requires it, national safety demands it, and I shall take back to London, with your authority, the message: Let the Government act according to its faith.

On returning to London from Dundee, Churchill drafted a Parliamentary Bill intended to introduce national service for all non-combatants. Under his Bill, the Government would be empowered 'to direct any person to perform any duty necessary for the prosecution of the war or the safety of the State; and to prescribe the hours and conditions of such a duty'. Churchill circulated this draft Bill to his colleagues on June 9. But Asquith did not think that the time had come for such drastic measures.

On leaving the Admiralty, Churchill's salary dropped immediately from £4,500 to £2,000 a year. Asquith, realizing the financial difficulties which would result, offered to let him go on living at Admiralty House with his family. But Clementine Churchill did not want to be dependent upon the Prime Minister's charity, and they turned down his offer. His cousin Lord Wimborne[1] let him move into 21 Arlington Street for a short while. Churchill decided that it might be prudent to move with his family into his brother's house at 41 Cromwell Road, immediately opposite the Natural History Museum. It was a large house, and with his brother away at the Dardanelles, Lady Gwendeline Churchill was alone there with her two sons. 'It seems to me,' Churchill wrote to his brother on June 12, 'that in the uncertain situation during the war we must not have two establishments and that the families must live together. Clemmie & Goonie are so fond of each other, that this is very attractive & easy.' But the financial difficulties which had threatened to follow the sudden fall in salary were unexpectedly relieved almost at once, for the Coalition Government decided on a new salary system for the duration of the war, whereby Ministerial salaries would be pooled, and shared on an almost equal basis. Under this scheme Churchill received £4,360 a year. But he could not tell how long he would remain a member of the Coalition, and still deemed it prudent for his family and his brother's to join forces. 'We shall probably all pack into Cromwell Road for economy's sake,' he wrote to his brother on June 19, and he and his family moved there at the end of the month.

Since leaving the Admiralty at the end of May, Churchill had spent his weekends at a Tudor farmhouse in Surrey, which he had rented for the summer. The house had been converted into a country residence by Edwin Lutyens[2] fifteen years before. Known as Hoe Farm, it lay in a secluded wooded valley a few miles from Godalming. Churchill was

---

[1] Ivor Churchill Guest, 1873–1939. Conservative MP, 1900–6. Liberal MP, 1906–10. Created Baron Ashby St Ledgers, 1910. Paymaster-General 1910–12. Lord in Waiting, 1913–15. 2nd Baron Wimborne, 1914. Lord Lieutenant of Ireland, 1915–18. Created Viscount Wimborne, 1918. In August 1914 Asquith had been much angered when Churchill pressed him to appoint Wimborne a Civil Lord of Admiralty.

[2] Edwin Landseer Lutyens, 1869–1944. Architect. His best-known work, the design of the Viceroy's house and central buildings of New Delhi, was begun in 1913. Knighted, 1918.

so attracted by the area that he even thought for a while of buying a nearby farmhouse as a permanent residence. Hoe Farm itself was quiet and remote, providing a refuge from the noise and strains of London. But he could not shake off his depression at the change in his political fortunes; often, alone, he would pace up and down the grass path at the top of the garden, from the copse of young trees at one end to the small wooden summerhouse at the other, stooped in anxious thought.

The Dardanelles Committee held its first meeting in Asquith's room at the House of Commons on June 7. Hankey was not present, and no notes were taken. But at a Cabinet meeting two days later Asquith told his colleagues, as he reported to the King, that the Committee had reached 'a unanimous decision' to reinforce Hamilton with three Divisions from the first of the New Armies, and that these would reach Gallipoli in July. De Robeck was to receive extra cruisers and monitors. The Dardanelles Committee met again at 10 Downing Street on June 12. On the previous day Churchill had sent Asquith, Balfour, Bonar Law and Curzon a memorandum suggesting that a landing on the Bulair Isthmus might be decisive, as an alternative to the frontal attacks at Helles and Anzac, and that it ought to be carried out by fresh troops sent out specially for the purpose. 'It seems vital to us now,' Churchill insisted, 'to consider this operation in detail. . . . Ought we not now to put these possibilities to Sir Ian Hamilton by telegraph fully and plainly?'

Asquith took the chair at the Dardanelles Committee meetings, as he had done at the War Council. Kitchener, Balfour, Crewe and Churchill were the only other members of the old War Council present. The new Conservative Ministers were represented by Bonar Law, Curzon and Lord Lansdowne. Churchill hoped to influence the new Tory Ministers present in favour of persevering at Gallipoli, and at the meeting he reiterated a view which he had frequently expressed while at the Admiralty, that once Allied troops occupied the high plateau above Kilid Bahr, 'it would mean a great disaster to the Turkish army in Gallipoli and the whole position would fall into our hands'. Once Hamilton's forces had advanced that far, he asserted, the naval attack could be renewed with a much greater chance of success. During the discussion he found that Kitchener was in agreement with his contention that troops should be landed on the Bulair Isthmus. Such a landing, Churchill stressed, would seriously endanger the Turkish supply routes, for Turkish sea communications would already be disrupted once Balfour had carried out a proposal of his own to send eight submarines into the Sea of Marmara. Kitchener agreed with Churchill's suggestion that Hamilton should be consulted; indeed, on the evening of June 11 he had already telegraphed asking him for his views on Bulair, and on the afternoon of June 12 he telegraphed again. But Hamilton did not believe that his troops were capable of the extra effort involved, or that the operation stood any real chance of success. It was therefore abandoned, to Churchill's chagrin.

Churchill realized that whatever contribution he might make to the discussion at the Dardanelles Committee, the future of the expedition itself was firmly in the hands of Kitchener and Balfour. He was already looking beyond the political horizon. 'I remain here for the present in the Cabinet,' he wrote to Jack Seely after the Dardanelles Committee, 'as I seem to be able to influence events in wh I am greatly interested & for wh I bear a burden. But I do not propose to shelter myself in this sinecure indefinitely, fat tho' it be.' Churchill gave Seely an account of the political situation:

LG is making a strong gas attack on GHQ supported by the Northcliffe batteries heavy & light, & hopes to capture the position in the course of the summer. His successive failures in the Marconi, Anti-Navy, Anti-War and Prohibition operations do not seem at all to have affected his prestige or morale. I occupy a detached position en potence covering GHQ & maintaining communications with the Belgians who have lately come in to line on our left. I am not at all exposed to fire now and my units are reorganising.

Churchill's interest in a military career was not entirely fanciful. On the same day that he wrote to Seely implying that he might give up politics, the Commanding General Southern Command, Lieutenant-General Campbell,[1] wrote to ask him whether he wished to take command of a battalion of the Oxfordshire Hussars. 'Dear Major Churchill,' he wrote from his Headquarters at Salisbury, '. . . You may not be so busy politically just now, and it might suit you.' But Churchill still believed that he could play some part in the political decisions which had yet to be made about the Dardanelles. Despite Bonar Law's rebuff in May, he saw the new Conservative Ministers, the 'Belgians' of his letter to Seely, as potential allies. Even Asquith was making an

---

[1] William Pitcairn Campbell, 1856–1933. Entered Army, 1875. Lieutenant-General commanding Southern Command, 1914–16. Knighted, 1915. General Officer Commanding-in-Chief, Western Command, 1916–18.

effort to mitigate the blow of Churchill's loss of influence. On June 12 Churchill wrote to his brother:

My dearest Jack,

... The political situation is favourable to me. The Prime Minister much concerned to look after me: the new men good & vy friendly: the public sympathetic. It has been resolved to carry Dlles through coute que coute, & the critical period in wh you cd have been injured by pessimism is past. Mind you ask for what is really necessary. The might of Britain is behind your enterprise & everyone is determined to carry it through. Meanwhile I sit here at the centre thinking only how I can watch over your interests & make sure that you are supported & aided and that our friends have full justice done them in all circumstances.

Poor Naval Division.[1] Alas the slaughter has been cruel. All are gone whom I knew. It makes me wish to be with you. But for the present my duty is here where I can influence the course of events.

Your loving brother
W

Henceforth Churchill was torn between the desire to be at the front and what he believed to be his watching brief over the Dardanelles. In an effort to ensure that any new offensive would not fail through lack of men, he wrote to Kitchener on June 15 with a strong plea:

... Suppose the three fine divisions now under orders do a great deal, but not all, & after 3 or 4 days fighting are brought to a standstill with 10 or 15000 casualties, both they & the enemy being exhausted: suppose two or three fresh divisions are then needed to carry the business through to complete success: & suppose there is nothing nearer than England wh means a month's delay, by the end of wh you wd have to begin all over again! There is my fear.

Prudence now wd surely keep these extra divisions in Egypt under yr own control, so that you can, if they are needed, put them in in a few days: & if not needed how easy to bring them back!

My feeling is that you now have the opportunity & the means of settling this business, but that if this chance fails, it will be very bad for the Govt & for the country.

Kitchener replied on the following day that the troops were being sent out as quickly as ships could be found to take them, and that plans had

---

[1] During the second battle of Krithia, from 4 to 6 June 1915, the Royal Naval Division lost forty officers and six hundred men. The losses were so severe that two of the Battalions of the Division, the Benbow and the Collingwood, had to be disbanded, its men being absorbed into the remaining three Battalions, the Hood, the Howe and the Anson.

been made until well into July. 'Later,' he wrote, 'we will make up a further programme, if necessary, but it would be as well to see how things go before doing so.'

The Dardanelles Committee met again on June 17. Balfour explained that it was difficult to find sufficient escort vessels to get the necessary men to Gallipoli much before the end of August. Kitchener, Curzon and Churchill all protested:

LORD CURZON said that this information put the whole operation in a different perspective. Hitherto we had imagined that the attack would take place in the second week in July. Now, however, the whole operation would have to be postponed until the end of August.
LORD KITCHENER said that it might even happen that two divisions would have to be used instead of three for the assumption of the offensive. He personally would be satisfied if the date could be advanced until the end of July, but waiting until the end of August would seriously cripple our troops.
MR CHURCHILL said that he could not understand why these delays should be necessary. He knew that there was a very large amount of transport in the Mediterranean area. At one time there were no less than five divisions on the water simultaneously. He suggested that perhaps some French transports might be obtained.

Later in the discussion Churchill warned that 'though he himself was admittedly as impatient as anyone could be to push on, he would prefer to delay action while sufficient troops and ammunition were accumulated to ensure success, rather than to risk a premature attack'. He warned his colleagues of his fear that although good progress would be made at the beginning of any advance from Anzac, 'the troops would be worn out with fatigue and that insufficient reserves would be available to carry the operation to a successful conclusion'. He suggested that two territorial divisions should be sent to Malta or Alexandria, as a permanent reserve within forty-eight hours sailing distance of the Dardanelles. Kitchener supported him, and Balfour promised to press his expert advisers further on the possibility of accelerating transport. Later in the discussion Churchill suggested that until five divisions could be sent to the Dardanelles 'our offensives should be postponed'. A premature attack with insufficient troops, he warned again, had no chance of success.

Churchill was not content to express his views in council. He wanted to give Balfour the advantage of his experience at every point. But he was nervous of approaching Balfour direct, and found himself asking

Masterton-Smith to put his points for him. The fears which he had of transport delays leading to a dangerous delay in troops reaching Gallipoli led him to follow up his plea at the Dardanelles Committee with a letter to Masterton-Smith, elaborating a number of detailed schemes for troop movements. He ended on a personal note: 'Be very careful how you use this letter, because I am so anxious not to give any offence; & of course I have not the material for making a true picture of the shipping. Yours ever, W.'

On June 18 Churchill circulated the members of the Dardanelles Committee with a lengthy memorandum arguing once more that it was still possible, with determination, to achieve victory at the Dardanelles. He stressed again the futility of a renewed offensive on the western front, pointing out that in the previous two months the British had lost at Ypres, Aubers Ridge and La Bassée four thousand officers and ninety-six thousand men, and that as a result of such sacrifice, out of 'approximately 19,500 square miles of France and Belgium in German hands we have recovered about 8'. He commented scathingly that during eight months of trench warfare 'ingenuity seems to have had so little success in discovering means of offence and advance'. He reminded his colleagues that it was nearly six months since he, Lloyd George and Hankey, 'all working independently', had pressed upon Asquith the need for an alternate zone of war, or for some mechanical means which would help achieve a break-through.

In his memorandum Churchill emphasized French and Russian weakness. It was necessary for one of the Powers to speak 'with the indispensable prestige of victory', and this Britain alone could do. 'She commands the sea. . . . She wields the power of the purse. She is becoming an important arsenal of munitions. . . . She only requires victory to give her the ascendancy, without which no good common action is to be expected.' Victory could be obtained most rapidly, Churchill concluded, by success at the Dardanelles:

There can be no doubt that we now possess the means and the power to take Constantinople before the end of the summer if we act with decision and with a due sense of proportion. The striking down of one of the three hostile Empires against which we are contending, and the fall to our arms of one of the most famous capitals in the world, with the results which must flow therefrom, will, conjoined with our other advantages, confer upon us a far-reaching influence among the Allies, and enable us to ensure their indispensable co-operation. Most of all, it will react on Russia. It will give the encouragement so sorely needed. It will give the reward so long desired. It will render a service to an Ally unparalleled in the history of nations. It will multiply the resources and open the channel for the re-equipment of the Russian armies. It will dominate the Balkan situation and cover Italy. It will resound through Asia. Here is the prize, and the only prize, which lies within reach this year. It can certainly be won without unreasonable expense, and within a comparatively short time. But we must act now, and on a scale which makes speedy success certain.

While Churchill was setting out for his colleagues this plea for decisive action at the Dardanelles, Sir Ian Hamilton, no longer feeling bound by his embargo not to write to Churchill on official policy, sent him a long account of the prospects as he saw them:

My dear Winston,

I have been simply thirsting to write to you ever since my last letter. The time that has elapsed is so long that you must credit me with a camel's resistance to thirst, but still there it is, you know the perpetual strain on a Commander. Especially in such a show as this.

There may come a moment, for instance, when you have so knocked the enemy that you are, humanly speaking, certain he will lie quiet for 2 or 3 days. The sea may be so glassy calm that you feel for 24 hours at least you have, humanly speaking, respite from the deadly submarine. All's well. You light your pipe, stretch out your legs, and prepare for the siesta when suddenly—bang!—a Taube[1] has dropped his cursed egg within less than no distance of your tent!

In all the world's history surely this is the queerest of all military situations that has ever arisen. We have turned Gallipoli into a cockpit, whereunto we have drawn to ourselves, as if with a magnet, all the best available resources of a vast, if decaying, empire.

The advantages are obvious. We are attacking Constantinople instead of defending Cairo. Were it not for us Basra would have fallen before the Turks and Van would not have fallen before the Russians. The object lesson also to the Balkan States is near at hand and contagious. All these are *broad* considerations. From the *narrow technical* point of view, nothing in the world could suit the Turks better than to have both flanks resting on the sea (yet in ground so conformed that they cannot be bombarded from the sea) so that their stupid, but exceedingly brave, infantry can be set down to fight with perfectly simple orders to stick where they are at all costs, and shoot anyone who advances against them.

The idea has been suggested from home that we might use our reinforcements to make a separate operation on the Asiatic side of the Straits. I have not answered yet. The project is enormously attractive to me seeing there are not many troops on the Asiatic side at present, and that such a move

[1] Taube, the German for 'dove': the name applied to all German Rumpler biplanes. The design of their wings gave them a dove-like appearance.

would relieve our backs and right flank from this cursed Asiatic shelling, which is going on at the moment I write to you—one heavy gun per 30 seconds. Men killed in hospital and officers killed in their dug-outs: all this is not too pleasant, though it is as yet on a small scale and therefore not a prime factor. . . .

But, on the other hand, three separate operations with three separate lines of communications and bases from the Naval point of view are not really practical politics, even for a nation like Great Britain, in view of the existence of the submarine. Moreover, by splitting our force into three, I am so afraid the result might be that each of the three operations would get more or less hung up against entanglements etc, and this would be in the last degree vexatious. No, I think I shall stick to my Gallipoli Peninsula, and handle it in a way which I must not commit to paper, even to you. . . .

Hamilton sent Churchill encouraging news about the Royal Naval Division; despite the heavy losses they had suffered, 'you would not recognise the men if you saw them again now. They have filled out and got a splendid, bold, martial appearance that would delight your heart. They are all good, but the best of them are the miners from the north, Durham and York.'

Churchill had assumed that Hamilton would not abandon his ban on correspondence while he was still in the Cabinet. On June 19, before he received Hamilton's letter, he sent his brother a full account of his feelings about future operations at the Dardanelles, obviously intended to be shown to the General:

The education of the new men proceeds, & most of the important Unionists are now fully convinced not only of the obligation to carry the Dardanelles policy through, but of the wisdom of the enterprise in strategy & politics. But I have had a hard battle all these weeks & have been fighting every inch of the road. . . .

I was vy much attracted by the Bulair project & I think the naval objections cd have been overcome: but of course the Anzac line of attack if it succeeded wd be instantly decisive. My anxiety is lest you have not enough men to carry it through: & that if a check occurred another long wait wd be necessary for reinforcements. That is why I want 2 more divisions, (besides the 2 corps) held in Egypt or somewhere else at hand, to give the added weight & sustained drive to the attack. It seems to me it will be a vy severe operation, & while delay is unpleasant, nothing really matters so much as making sure that the move when it comes will do the trick. K always says the troops in Egypt are available as a reserve & that they can come over for an emergency. I hope that every scrap of force that can be laid hands on will be used when the time comes, and that the General will not hesitate to ask for all he requires. . . .

We hope great things from the submarine blockade of the Marmara. One of the points on wh Fisher went was my request for 2 more E boats. The new Board have however sent 6 or 7: & are trying to get 2 French of large size besides. It shd be vy difficult to feed the Turkish army via Bulair or from Asia & still more difficult to supply it with ammunition, if sea transit both with Panderma & Mudania is cut off. All intelligence reports received here show gt anxiety & depression in Cple. We must never forget the enemy suffers as well as we do. I have derived the impression that the pace of the war has been rather too hot for the Turks. . . .

In a more personal note, Churchill revealed to his brother a growing sense of anxiety:

The war is terrible: the carnage grows apace, & the certainty that no result will be reached this year fills my mind with melancholy thoughts. The youth of Europe—almost a whole generation—will be shorn away. I find it vy painful to be deprived of direct means of action, but I bear the pangs, because I see & feel the value of my influence on general policy. I do not think the present arrangement will last for ever, and I hope to regain a fuller measure of control before the end of the year.

The impotence which Churchill felt at being unable to influence policy gnawed at him day by day. He wanted a ministerial challenge to absorb his wasted energies. He began to advocate the establishment of a special Air Department, independent of both the Admiralty and the War Office; a Department which he was confident he could organize effectively himself. Early in June he sent Asquith a four-page, type-written memorandum entitled 'Notes on the Formation of an Air Department'. It was a strong hint for re-employment. Churchill ended with a confident assertion: 'It ought not to be impossible before the end of the year to make the British Air Service indisputably the largest, most efficient and most enterprising of any belligerent power.' But Asquith took no action.

Churchill could not drive Gallipoli from his mind. Only the weekends offered the chance of a brief escape. 'I am now off to Hoe Farm for the Sunday,' he wrote to his brother on June 19, 'where I shall see JG & Peregrine [1] disporting themselves with my flotilla. How I wish you cd be there. It really is a delightful valley and the garden gleams with summer jewelry. We live vy simply—but with all the essentials of life

[1] Henry Winston Spencer Churchill, 1913–   . Known as Peregrine. Jack Churchill's younger son.

well understood & well provided for—hot baths, cold champagne, new peas, & old brandy.' But even at Hoe Farm there was no real escape from anguish. Nothing could distract him. His wife despaired of ever seeing him unworried. His depression frightened her, and not even the weekends out of London seemed able to bring him comfort or relaxation. His sister-in-law Gwendeline Churchill stumbled upon a possible solution. She had set up her easel in the garden and begun to sketch. Churchill was fascinated. Seeing this, she realized that if she could persuade him to take up painting, he might be amused and distracted. That Sunday she suggested that he use her sons' watercolour paints. He responded at once. Hoe Farm provided him with inspiration. There was much to paint: the pond in front of the house, the winding, tree-lined drive, the rambling house itself with its jumble of roofs and chimneys, the dark timbered rooms, the sloping lawns, the pasture rising behind the house, the woods beyond.

Churchill's experiments that Sunday were the beginning of a new experience which was to bring him comfort until the last years of his life. He found that he could concentrate upon painting to the exclusion of politics. He painted in silence, absorbed entirely by the problem of transferring his subject to the canvas. Edward Marsh, who was with him during the first experiments, recalled in *A Number of People* that 'the new enthusiasm . . . was a distraction and a sedative that brought a measure of ease to his frustrated spirit'.

On June 21 Churchill returned to London. Worries about the Dardanelles flooded back. When the Dardanelles Committee met on the following Friday, June 25, he begged Balfour to make arrangements for a reserve of small craft in Egypt which would be invaluable, he insisted, 'if any landing was contemplated at any time'. He also clashed with Kitchener, who argued that the Turkish supplies of small arms ammunition 'were unlimited'. Churchill claimed that this was not so, and 'that the Turks would fire away the whole of their available ammunition' in the course of the Gallipoli campaign. But he repeated his conviction that 'the attack ought to be postponed until there was ample ammunition' for Hamilton's troops.

Churchill had not forgotten the previous weekend's experiment, and decided to try to paint in oils when next he was at Hoe Farm. After the Dardanelles Committee meeting at 10 Downing Street on June 25 he bought his first easel. Four days later he bought a mahogany palette, oil, turpentine, paints and brushes. On July 2 he returned to Hoe Farm. In an article first published in the *Strand Magazine* in December 1921 Churchill recalled the next stage in his new adventure:

The palette gleamed with beads of colour; fair and white rose the canvas; the empty brush hung poised, heavy with destiny, irresolute in the air. My hand seemed arrested by a silent veto. But after all the sky on this occasion was unquestionably blue, and a pale blue at that. There could be no doubt that blue paint mixed with white should be put on the top part of the canvas. One really does not need to have an artist's training to see that. It is a starting-point open to all. So very gingerly I mixed a little blue paint on the palette with a very small brush, and then with infinite precaution made a mark about as big as a bean upon the affronted snow-white shield. It was a challenge, a deliberate challenge; but so subdued, so halting, indeed so cataleptic, that it deserved no response.

The challenge seemed to have failed:

At that moment the loud approaching sound of a motor-car was heard in the drive. From this chariot there stepped swiftly and lightly none other than the gifted wife[1] of Sir John Lavery. 'Painting! But what are you hesitating about? Let me have a brush—the big one.' Splash into the turpentine, wallop into the blue and the white, frantic flourish on the palette—clean no longer—and then several large, fierce strokes and slashes of blue on the absolutely cowering canvas. Anyone could see that it could not hit back. No evil fate avenged the jaunty violence. The canvas grinned in helplessness before me. The spell was broken. The sickly inhibitions rolled away. I seized the largest brush and fell upon my victim with Berserk fury. I have never felt in awe of a canvas since.[2]

The change in Churchill's daily life between May and June was complete. The daily conferences with the heads of a powerful Department of State were over; so also was the incessant interdepartmental activity, the notes and minutes sent across to the Foreign Office and War Office, the scrutiny of plans submitted daily from experts and intermediaries, the challenge of parliamentary questions, the opportunity for important policy speeches. Gone was the thrill and responsibility of daily contact with the inner secrets of war policy: the

[1] Hazel Trudeau Lavery, c. 1887–1935. Second wife of the painter Sir John Lavery, 1856–1941. The Laverys lived at 5 Cromwell Place, a few yards from the Churchill house at 41 Cromwell Road.

[2] The *Strand Magazine* article was called 'Painting as a Pastime'. It was twice reprinted: in a volume of essays entitled *Thoughts and Adventures* (Thornton Butterworth, 1932), and in *Painting as a Pastime* (Odhams Press and Ernest Benn, 1948). In 1966 David Coombs compiled a catalogue of Churchill's paintings, *Churchill his paintings* (Hamish Hamilton, 1967). This catalogue included four paintings done at Hoe Farm in 1915: number 23 (the inner hall: incorrectly described in the catalogue as 'the inner hall at Breccles c. 1928'), number 146 (Lady Gwendeline Churchill in the garden), number 148 (the drive and pond) and number 149 (view of the house and garden).

intercepted German wireless messages, the tantalizing reports from neutral capitals, the information collected by British agents and the planning of attacks too secret to divulge to any but the Prime Minister. For each fifty letters which he had received while First Lord, there were only one or two addressed to him at the Duchy. A few letters still trickled in from Admirals wishing to console their former chief. A few requests for patronage came his way. Bonar Law, who had once pressed the First Lord to give his two nephews an opportunity of serving at the Dardanelles, now asked the Chancellor of the Duchy to appoint a nominee of his to the Bootle Bench. The longest and most frequent letters which Churchill received came from his brother and from Hamilton at the Dardanelles.

On June 26 Jack Churchill sent an account of the continued fighting on the Helles front. The 29th Division had not rested for two months, and 'although the men are still splendid, everybody's nerves have been strained by being always under shell fire'. Jack Churchill shared his brother's frustration at Britain's failure to obtain Balkan allies. 'We had hoped that Greece would have been moving by now. But our diplomacy is rotten,' he wrote. 'If the Balkans are useful to us—why did they not send out good men—the best they could find—to all these places on the declaration of war. Venezelos had come in with a big war majority, but finds his hands tied for some time, because the Germans have bought most of the senior military officials! Surely we ought to be able to compete in the bribing market.' Jack Churchill reported that the Royal Naval Division had once again had 'a very bad time'; their best officers and men had been killed, and the few officers remaining were too sick to fight.

One member of the Coalition who was enthusiastic about the Dardanelles was Lord Robert Cecil, the new Under-Secretary of State at the Foreign Office. He wrote several times to Churchill with information which had been received at the Foreign Office, and with encouragement. On June 20 he sent news of Balkan developments, asking tersely of the Bulgars: 'Why dont they march straight on Constple?' Three days later he wrote again, worried that not enough artillery was being sent to Gallipoli: 'We ought to devote whatever efforts are necessary to success.' On July 3 he sent Churchill a printed sheet giving extracts from intercepted private letters revealing much hardship inside Austria. These letters, Cecil wrote, confirmed his view 'that we should press on our attacks on Austria i.e. the Dardanelles'. But Cecil's encouragement contrasted with a letter which Churchill received from Carson, the new Attorney-General, written on June 21. 'All anticipations in the Dardanelles have been falsified by events,' Carson declared. 'I quite agree,' he went on, 'that to gain a victory in the Dardanelles whilst there is apparently a checkmate in Flanders would give a very helpful and hopeful turn to the War, but I do not want the obvious advantages of this step to influence our judgements in the direction of miscalculating the difficulties.'

Churchill began to tire of arguing about Gallipoli. He wanted to go there; to lead a brigade fighting the Turks, instead of bickering with his colleagues on the Dardanelles Committee. He expressed these thoughts to Gwendeline Churchill, who passed them on to her husband. But Jack Churchill did not approve. 'I hope you will not attempt such a thing,' he wrote on July 3. 'You would sacrifice such a lot and gain so little. You would have a wonderfully interesting 10 days, and then you would have long periods with nothing to do but be shelled. There are no exciting movements—how can there be with a four mile front and the sea on each flank. A brigadier or even a div-general has a poor show. I am quite sure as far as this show is concerned, you would be twice as useful at home as here.' Jack Churchill had another idea. 'Why don't you get 3 weeks leave,' he wrote, 'and get sent out to report on the situation to the Cabinet!! You could see every inch of the position in 3 days. But I suppose it would raise a shriek!' Churchill was attracted to Jack's suggestion and a number of incidents at the end of June and early in July reinforced his distaste for remaining in London.

At the end of June there was a sharp division of opinion among Cabinet Ministers on what attitude Britain ought to adopt towards Bulgaria. Crewe, who was acting as Foreign Secretary while Grey was ill, doubted very much whether Bulgaria could be brought into active co-operation with the Allies. He felt that far from there being a possibility of a grand Balkan alliance concerting action against Turkey and Austria, it was more likely that a new Balkan war would break out between Serbia and Greece on one side, and Bulgaria on the other. Churchill had always been a pro-Bulgarian. The precipitant Greek reversal of her offer of troops to take part in the Dardanelles operation had destroyed his original plan for a joint military and naval attack on Turkey. He believed that Bulgarian support, could it be obtained, would be more consistent, and indeed more useful. Lloyd George, who shared Churchill's pro-Bulgarian sympathies, was equally frustrated by what appeared to both men to be a lack of initiative on the part of the Foreign Office. 'I am all for playing the game right out to get Bulgaria,' Churchill wrote to Lloyd George on June 25. 'She is the real prize, & it is only if and when we know she will not come that we shd consider Greek & Servian interests.' On the following day Churchill wrote direct to Cecil at the Foreign Office that it would be wrong to threaten Bulgaria in any way by using 'take it or leave it methods'. The Foreign Office should not 'whittle away the definite offers which have been made to her. . . . For the present we are in the Bulgarian camp: let us stay there. She is worth all the rest put together, and she would bring all the rest in too.' At the Cabinet on June 30 Churchill and Lloyd George acted in unison. Asquith sent an account of the discussion to the King on July 1:

Some members of the Cabinet—especially Mr Lloyd George & Mr Churchill—were strongly of opinion that a high price (at the expense mainly of Greece) was worth paying to secure the prompt adhesion of Bulgaria. Others inclined to the Italian proposal to delay any definite answer to the last Bulgarian note until Italy has declared war against Turkey. Finally, it was agreed that a complete dossier of the whole negotiations should be prepared by the Foreign Office, and a definite decision put off until Friday's Cabinet, or the early part of next week.

Churchill hated such delays, knowing them to be but the prelude to further procrastination. At the beginning of July he asked Asquith if he could go with him to the forthcoming discussions on inter-Allied strategy to be held at Calais; but Asquith said no.

On July 4 Balfour asked Fisher to become Chairman of an Admiralty Committee, the Board of Inventions and Research. Churchill learned of Fisher's appointment when he read about it in the newspapers on July 5. He went at once to complain to Balfour, who told him that Asquith had approved. On July 6 he went to see Asquith and to protest. Asquith told him that as Fisher had apologized for his behaviour in May, there was no reason why he should not have been given the new appointment. Churchill returned to the Duchy of Lancaster Office and wrote angrily:

My dear Prime Minister,

Fisher resigned his office without warning or parley. He assigned no reason except inability to work with me. The only points of policy under discussion were of minor consequence, & all have been settled by the new Board as I had proposed. You ordered Fisher to return to his post in the name of the King. He paid no attention to yr order. You declared that he had deserted his post in time of war; & the facts are not open to any other construction. For ten days or more the country was without a First Sea Lord as Fisher did not even do his duty till his successor was appointed; & during that period events occurred wh might have led to the decisive battle of the naval war. You have repeatedly assured me that in view of these facts you wd not consent to this officer's employment under the Admy.

It was therefore with surprise that I read in the newspapers of Monday's appointment, & still more that I heard from Mr Balfour that you had approved it beforehand. Yesterday you explained to me that Fisher had expressed regret for his conduct & had excused himself by saying that his mind was at the time seriously affected, & that in view of his 'contrition' you had thought it possible to give him the appt.

Considering that it was Fisher's unreasonable & extraordinary action that led you to remove me from the Admiralty in time of war, & thus to humiliate me before the whole world & deprive me of the fruits of my work when they were being gathered, I do not think that this light & easy explanation ought to have been so readily accepted by you; & I feel that I as still a colleague deserved at least the consideration of being consulted before it was accepted.

Fisher's expressions of regret & admissions of nervous or mental weakness will remain unpublished. His appointment is all that will be known. Meanwhile I have remained silent & the truth is undisclosed.

Our friendship has been the light in wh I have forced myself to view a very puzzling series of events [largely incomprehensible to me]. But I must now frankly say that I think this last incident required somewhat different treatment, & that if expressions of regret have been tendered by Fisher, some of them at least were due to me.

Churchill crossed out the phrase in square brackets. Then he decided not to send the letter at all. Instead, he wrote to Masterton-Smith of his anger at Fisher's appointment. Masterton-Smith spoke to Balfour, who wrote to Churchill on July 8, pointing out that Churchill himself had often spoken of Fisher's 'great gifts as an inventor' and of his 'originality of mind and his consuming energy'. These qualities were, as Balfour wrote, 'too valuable at such a time as this to be thrown away'. Churchill replied on July 9, repeating the arguments which he had intended to use in his letter to Asquith, and continuing:

On other grounds I am sure the step which has been taken will be productive of inconvenience and unrest, in the Admiralty office and to a less extent in the Fleet. Every officer who is under Fisher's ban—and they are many—or who did not actively support him, will fear that he is shortly to return to power. As the result two parties will be formed in the Admiralty, one of which will count on Fisher's resumption of office, and the others will endeavour to prevent it at their peril. The position of the Third Sea Lord and of the officers of the technical departments will be specially embarrassed. A newspaper campaign will be set on foot—has already begun. Losses when they occur will be used to prove the need of Fisher's return to real control. Successes will be attributed to his influence behind the scenes.

All this must be viewed in relation to a very old man, without the nerve to carry on war, not quite sane in moments of crisis, and perfectly unscrupulous.

In all my conduct in these recent affairs I have tried to act with loyalty and simplicity. I have striven to do everything that care for the public interests could suggest. I therefore am not actuated by personal feelings, when I say that I am very sorry you did not give me an opportunity of being heard before your decision was taken.

Churchill's protest was in vain. Fisher took up his new appointment, presiding over a team of scientists who examined all suggestions put forward, and authorized research on those inventions which impressed them.

The Dardanelles Committee met again at 10 Downing Street on July 5. Churchill took little part in the discussion. The arguments used by his colleagues were those he had often put forward himself. Lloyd George declared that 'he attached the utmost importance to a proper supply of high explosive ammunition at the Dardanelles' and argued that the appropriate quantity of such ammunition ought to be sent to Gallipoli 'even if we could not supply sufficient for the much larger Army in France'. Kitchener said that the war would be over 'as soon as the Gallipoli Peninsula was captured. Once you got to Constantinople the Turkish resistance would collapse.' Curzon advocated sending out a fifth division to the Dardanelles. Lansdowne and Balfour both agreed that further reinforcements were needed.

As a result of several weeks' pressure from Curzon, Lansdowne, Balfour, Lloyd George and Churchill, Kitchener agreed that two territorial divisions should be sent as reinforcements to the eastern Mediterranean. On July 7 Churchill sent Hamilton the good news:

My dear Hamilton,

I rejoice to say that on Monday (after 3 weeks work) the War Council definitely decided to add 2 territorial divisions to your army making in all 6 divisions not yet engaged. I rejoice also at the punishment you are inflicting on the Turks, at the evident distress of their army & their capital, & at the progress made in gaining ground. My confidence in the future & in the wisdom of the policy wh has launched this operation remains unshaken.

Well done & with good luck or mistakenly done & with bad luck, if done in the end it will repay all losses & cover all miscalculations in the priceless advantages wh will rise for the Allied cause. Everything in troops & ships that I can think of or you & de Robeck have asked for has now been given. It seems to me that whereas hitherto you have been fighting against numerical superiority & with little HE [high explosive] shell, your next important effort shd be made with a superiority of nearly 2 to 1 & with plenty of HE shell; & further that it will be made upon an enemy army much enfeebled & dispirited by losses & defeats, and short both of food & ammunition.

In these circumstances, I cannot help feeling hopeful, & that there are just grounds for hope. Moreover the monitor fleet will have arrived & will be able to give you a support far more effective than you have had hitherto.

It has been a remarkable experience to me watching opinion slowly & steadily consolidating behind this enterprise, & to see the successive waves of opposition & surrender—feeling baffled & surmounted one after another. Ignorance, pessimism in high places, the malice of newspapers, the natural jealousies & carping of the Flanders army, & of the French soldiers have all failed to prevent the necessary reinforcements by land & sea from being sent. And now you are equipped with all that you have asked for—& more, the next great effort can be made.

I never look beyond a battle. It is a culminating event, & like a brick wall bars all further vision. But the chances seem favourable & the reward of success will be astonishing. Your daring spirit and the high qualities of your nature, will enable you to enjoy trials and tests under wh the fleshly courage of commonplace commanders wd quail. The superb conduct & achievements of the soldiers wd redeem even a final failure: but with a final success they will become a military episode not inferior in glory to any that the history of war records.

Then there will be found honour for all who have never flinched & never wavered. God go with you.

Your sincere friend
Winston S. Churchill

Victory over the Turks continued to excite the mind of annexationists, of whatever political party. The Report of the Committee on Asiatic Turkey, which Asquith had called for in April, was made available to members of the Dardanelles Committee on July 8. Five separate schemes were each considered in detail. Under the most ambitious of the proposals, Britain would control the whole of the Tigris and Euphrates valley and extend her sovereignty from Alexandretta in the eastern Mediterranean to Basra at the head of the Persian Gulf. Under each of the five schemes, Russia would annex Constantinople and occupy the Gallipoli Peninsula.

Churchill had lost interest in these discussions. They seemed to him to be a game played by people who were not necessarily prepared to commit themselves to the action needed to see their plans come true. The thought of going out to Gallipoli continued to excite his imagination. At the beginning of the second week of July, to Churchill's surprise, Kitchener suggested that he go on an official visit to the Dardanelles. Asquith and Balfour both gave their approval. Kitchener wanted a senior ministerial opinion on the conditions and prospects of the Gallipoli Peninsula. Asquith and Balfour felt sympathy for Churchill in his political impotence. They realized that a visit to the scene of action would give them an opportunity to hear about the situation from someone who had followed their discussions from the start. It was a task which Churchill welcomed. On July 16 he asked Asquith for a formal letter 'expressing your wish & that of my colleagues that I should go'. Asquith replied the same day:

My dear Winston,
   I believe that your visit to the Dardanelles will secure for the Cabinet valuable information & suggestions in regard both to the future of the campaign & to our policy in that theatre of the War.
   Your object will be to survey & report upon the situation, after Conference with the Commanding Officers. You will no doubt make it clear to ·the General & the Admiral that your mission is not dictated by any want of confidence in them, but by a wish to get into closer touch, so far as they are concerned.
   They both enjoy, as they have deserved, our gratitude & trust.

Yours always
H. H. Asquith

Churchill proceeded to make the necessary arrangements. First he drafted a telegram to Hamilton, which Kitchener sent under his own name on the following morning: 'Churchill is coming out on behalf of the Cabinet to confer with you generally upon the situation and to watch the impending operations. He will start on ·Tuesday morning and will bring one officer & a secretary with him.' Hamilton replied to Kitchener on July 18: 'With reference your telegram I had hoped we were too far off for visitors but you know that in all circumstances you can rely on my loyalty to you.' Churchill was not shown this reply.

   The Allied positions on the Gallipoli Peninsula were all within range of Turkish artillery. Churchill would therefore need extra insurance cover for the duration of his visit. On July 16 he asked his insurance broker, W. H. Bernau,[1] to call on him at the Duchy of Lancaster Office. During the meeting Bernau took the following notes:

Going to Dardanelles on private mission. No-one to know. Thorough inspection (as a civilian) in order to report fully to the Cabinet on entire position after conference with Sir I H. He undertakes not to take part in any military operations; he will inspect landing of troops and inspect the trenches. He will 'run no risks'. He expects to be gone about 3 or 4 weeks. He suggests the policy should cover two months as he may call at the scene of warfare in France on return journey.

On the following day Churchill wrote to Bernau to reassure him that he would not take 'an active part in the fighting', but adding: 'It is possible however that my mission may in certain circumstances be extended, and that I may have to visit the Balkan States.'

Churchill realized that he might be killed during his visit to Gallipoli. On July 17 he wrote out a letter 'to be sent to Mrs Churchill in the event of my death':

Darling,

Cox holds about £1000 worth of securities of mine (Chiefly Witbank Collieries): Jack has in his name about £1000 worth of Pretoria Cement Shares & Cassel has American Stocks of mine[2] wh shd exceed in value my loans from him by about £1000. I believe these will be found sufficient to pay my debts & overdraught. Most of the bills were paid last year. Randolph Payne & Lumley are the only two large ones.[3]

The insurance policies are all kept up & every contingency is covered. You will receive £10,000 and £300 a year in addition until you succeed my mother. The £10,000 can either be used to provide interest ie about £450 a year or even to purchase an annuity against my mother's life, wh wd yield a much larger income at the expense of the capital. Of course it wd be much better to keep the £10,000 and live on the interest than to spend it on the chance of my mother living a long time. But you must judge.

I am anxious that you shd get hold of all my papers, especially those wh refer to my Admiralty administration. I have appointed you my sole literary executor. Masterton Smith will help you to secure all that is necessary for a

---

[1] William Henry Bernau, 1870–1937. Started work at Cox & Co., bankers, 1889; in charge of the Insurance Department, 1910–35; retired, 1935.

[2] Sir Ernest Cassel's Administration held, on Churchill's behalf, $10,000 United States Steel Corporation 5% Sinking Fund Bonds, and $10,000 Atchison Topeka and Santa Fé Railway 4% Convertible Bonds.

[3] In July 1915 Churchill owed Randolph Payne & Sons, wine merchants, nearly £500 (having already paid £100 in June). Lumley & Lumley were his solicitors; he owed them £180 (having already paid £100 in April).

complete record. There is no hurry; but some day I shd like the truth to be known. Randolph will carry on the lamp. Do not grieve for me too much. I am a spirit confident of my rights. Death is only an incident, & not the most important wh happens to us in this state of being. On the whole, especially since I met you my darling one I have been happy, & you have taught me how noble a woman's heart can be. If there is anywhere else I shall be on the look out for you. Meanwhile look forward, feel free, rejoice in life, cherish the children, guard my memory. God bless you.

Good bye
W

On the following day Churchill set out formally, in a letter to Asquith, his reasons for the visit, and also raised the question, which he had mentioned to his solicitor, of a possible extension of his mission:

The two reasons wh have led me to undertake this journey are first: in case the coming attack does not succeed, or succeeds only partially, I wish to be able to advise the Cabinet with the fullest knowledge upon the new & grave situation wh will then arise. I can acquire this knowledge only upon the spot, & no one else will have the same advantages for acquiring it. Secondly—if a decisive victory is won, I shall be at hand shd the Govt decide to send a special mission to Sofia or Athens, in order to reap to the fullest extent the fruits of the victory.

Of this you must judge *quickly*, if & when the circumstances arise.

I shall of course be careful to run no unnecessary risks; but it will not be possible for me to appreciate the position without landing on the Gallipoli peninsula & in consequence coming under fire. If any mischance shd occur I consider that my wife shd receive the pension prescribed for a general officer's widow; & I rely on you to see to this.

I am looking forward vy much to this most interesting expedition.

While Churchill's plans went forward, Kitchener was beginning to doubt the wisdom of his going to the Dardanelles unaccompanied. 'I wish you would send Hankey with him,' he wrote to Asquith on July 17; 'I am sure it would be a wise step & very useful to me.' Asquith at once agreed to Kitchener's request. On Sunday July 18 Churchill went to Hoe Farm for a day with his family before leaving. On Monday July 19 he spent his final day in London. Grey sent him a friendly note from the Foreign Office: 'I am so sorry to have been so busy this afternoon. In case I don't see you before you go I send this line to say that all my good wishes & kindest thoughts go with you.' Stamfordham wrote from Windsor Castle that the King was 'glad to hear' of Churchill's mission to the Dardanelles and quite understood that he could not ask for an audience before his departure.

Churchill had reckoned without his new Conservative colleagues. The Cabinet had met on the morning of July 19. When it had ended, Asquith, Kitchener and Grey remained in the Cabinet room, and Churchill said goodbye to them. As he was shaking hands, and being wished good luck, Curzon unexpectedly returned. Where, he asked, was Churchill going, that he needed to be wished good luck? Curzon had to be told; he gave the visit his blessing, but hurried off to inform his fellow Conservative Ministers about it. The visit seemed to them so unwise that Bonar Law informed Asquith that a serious crisis might develop if Churchill went on with it. Confronted by this opposition, Churchill wrote to Asquith that night that he did not feel he could undertake the mission. Hankey would go alone. Asquith replied at once to Churchill:

Private
My dear Winston,
Thanks for your letter. I was under the impression, as I know you were, that your mission was approved with practical unanimity by all our colleagues. I was therefore much surprised (and annoyed) to find last evening that several of them were quite of a contrary opinion. Nor do I think, after what some of them said, that I or others wd succeed in overcoming their objections.
In the circumstances, I think you are right in saying that you would not undertake such a task in the face of any serious division of opinion.
I am *extremely* sorry, believing, as I do, that you would have been able to render a very real service to the Government & the country.

Yours always
HHA

On July 20 Curzon wrote to explain why he had opposed Churchill's departure:

Confid.
My dear Winston,
I would like to be quite above board with you in this as in all things.
Yesterday morning when I learned for the first time that you were going to the Dardanelles on behalf of the Cabinet (who had never been consulted) I gave to you my startled acquiescence in the project. Later in talking it over with several of our colleagues, who knew as little about it as I did, I found that we shared a doubt as to the wisdom of sending out a Cabinet Minister to the scene of war & as to the reception that public opinion might give to such an act, for which the Govt would be held collectively responsible. . . .

Yrs ever
Curzon

On July 21 Kitchener saw Lord Esher, and told him of the Conservative veto. 'He laughed over it a good deal,' Esher wrote in his diary, 'and admitted that he would not have been sorry to get rid of Winston for a while.' Churchill's disappointment was intense. On July 22 he wrote angrily to Balfour about reported aeroplane deficiencies at the Dardanelles, which were, he said, if true, 'very discreditable to the Naval Wing', and showed in his opinion 'a failure on the part of the Air Department to grasp the importance of the aviation service at the Dardanelles and the scale on which they require to be maintained'.

Churchill did not feel confident that Balfour was working at full stretch. He believed that there were better methods of using air power at the Dardanelles than had yet been tried. Without the power to institute action, he thrust his ideas before Balfour with a persistence which annoyed rather than convinced. One idea of which Churchill wrote in his letter of July 22 was for a comprehensive bombing policy:

The field of operations for aircraft in offensive action in the Dardanelles is very wide, and many important objectives are open. It has occurred to me that now that several submarines will be operating in the Marmora it would be easy for seaplanes to fly across from the Gulf of Saros and join the submarines in the Marmora, refill there, and then deliver attacks on Constantinople. The submarines could carry within limits the comparatively small supplies of petrol which seaplanes require, and have appliances to make the simplest repairs in an emergency. We might therefore organise half a dozen seaplanes working in the Marmora in conjunction with our submarines: scouting for them, making bomb attacks on Constantinople, on the munition factories, on bridges, and on the railways supplying Constantinople. There is a reference in the Foreign Office telegrams to the important effect which would be produced by a bomb attack on Constantinople. The 100-lb bombs would be very effective for smashing up railway bridges, and there can be no great quantity of anti-aircraft guns to prevent the machines flying low enough for accurate aim. In the event of a machine breaking down, or having to make a forced landing, the presence of several submarines in the Marmora in touch with the seaplanes would afford safety to the pilots, who could be taken off in the submarines and the seaplanes scuttled in the same way as we have done in the Heligoland Bight on several occasions.

I hope this project will receive your attention and that of your advisers.

At the Dardanelles Committee on July 24 Churchill spoke with bitterness of the failure to reach a clear policy over the future of the Gallipoli campaign:

MR CHURCHILL pointed out that in case the main operation now under preparation did *not* succeed, it was necessary to settle now, *beforehand*, what our course was to be. Were any more troops to be sent? And if so, were the necessary arrangements for their transport being made? On many occasions it was impossible to look beyond the next battle, but contingencies had to be surveyed.

A few moments later he intervened again:

MR CHURCHILL said that to him there seemed a chance of being able to take Constantinople, but that the Turks might have been bringing up reinforcements as well as we. We ought to consider the possibility of making some progress, but of being then checked. Did we mean to take Constantinople? We had the reserves; but if we did not hurry to do so the Germans would before us.

Churchill's questions received no answer. His isolation was complete. It seemed that his chance of controlling a fighting department could never come again. On July 30 he took matters into his own hands, drafting a personal and private telegram which he wished to send to Hankey, who would by then have arrived at the Dardanelles. 'General sh'd not hesitate,' the draft telegram read, 'to ask for more High explosive ammunition in addition to what is now being supplied. . . . More is available here & wd probably be sent overland if he pressed for a larger supply as a precautionary measure.' Kitchener told Balfour that no such exhortation was needed; Hamilton had just been told that three train-loads of guns and ammunition were on their way to him. Masterton-Smith wrote to Edward Marsh later that day: 'Mr Balfour hopes therefore that Winston will agree with him that the proposed message to Hankey is not now necessary.' Churchill held back the telegram. But although Kitchener had agreed to send the ammunition, he did not tell Churchill either when it was sent off, or by what route. Churchill wanted to know, not trusting Kitchener to carry out his promise. On August 2 he wrote to Masterton-Smith, his only contact with Dardanelles policy: 'Your note about the 3 trains of ammunition for Dlles was comforting. But will you please find out if they have really gone or when they are to go. Creedy[1] cd tell you on the telephone, or

---

[1] Herbert James Creedy, 1878–   . Entered War Office as a Clerk, 1901. Private Secretary to successive Secretaries of State for War, 1913–20, including Lord Kitchener, August 1914–June 1916, Lloyd George, July–December 1916, and Churchill, January 1919–February 1920. Knighted, 1919. Secretary of the Army Council, 1920–39. Permanent Under-Secretary of State at the War Office, 1924–39. Chairman of the Security Executive, 1943–5.

General Callwell or even Glyn.[1] Probably you know at Admy because of the ship wh meets them. Send me a wire to let me know if it is all right.' On the following day Churchill wrote to his brother:

There are so many 'able men' in this cabinet that it is vy difficult to get anything settled. The parties hold each other in equipoise. The tendency to the negative is vy pronounced. Never mind. They are in the Dardanelles up to their necks now, & you have only to go forward. Afterwards we will talk about it all. I expect this letter will reach you in the midst of events. Well! A battle is a gamble. It cannot be anything else. We must suspend judgement till after the coup. All my heart is with you & your chief. No great offensive in this war ever offered so much to the Allied cause. Never was there a moment when victory wd be sweeter & more timely.

I am soberly hopeful. I think you will have a good superiority: & they have suffered heavily. The losses will no doubt be cruel: but better there when victory will be fruitful than in the profitless slaughter pit of Ypres.

This time last year I was fortunate in getting the Fleet safely into its station; & now I think we ought to have another gleam of sunlight.

It was only three days before Sir Ian Hamilton was to launch a new attack on the Turkish position. Churchill did not believe that Balfour was taking all possible steps to ensure that the operation succeeded. On August 3 he wrote again to Masterton-Smith:

I cannot help feeling unhappy about the 12″ Monitors not being at the Dardanelles. The more my mind turns over the situation there, the more I feel that 4 armoured Monitors may prove just not quite enough to pass the forts and dominate the Marmora. There is really no margin for casualties. There must have been a great slowing down in the production of 12″ Monitors, if only 2 are ready now. The department loves to tinker at ships till they are absolutely faultless, forgetting the end in perfecting the means. However, the coup must obviously be played without them now.

On August 5, less than twenty-four hours before the new offensive was to start, Hamilton wrote to Churchill:

My dear Winston,
    Standing once more on the brink of the unknown, and about to take a

[1] Ralph George Campbell Glyn, 1885–1960. Lieutenant, Rifle Brigade, 1904. Secretary, Unionist Reorganization Committee, 1911. Employed at the War Office, 1912–14. Captain, on Missions to Serbia and Russia, 1914–15. Liaison Intelligence Officer between the War Office and GHQ France, May–August 1915. Served Gallipoli and Salonika, 1915–16; France, 1917–18. Major, 1918. Conservative MP, 1918–22; 1924–53. Joint Parliamentary Private Secretary to Ramsay MacDonald, 1931–7. Created Baronet, 1934. Created Baron Glyn of Farnborough, 1953.

plunge which will be as vital in its consequences as the first landing, I want just to stretch out a hand to one who has been a steadfast patron to this expeditionary force and all that it stands for. Whatever happens; whether we fail or whether we succeed, we have done a big thing. And if, by the help of God, we can carry it one step further then your perspicuity will be vindicated and the world will understand that where the great Achilles once fought and conquered lies the Achilles heel of that horrible German Empire.

All the troops are in good heart, with the possible exception of one Division whose Commander is not the fount of energy and confidence a Commander should be. Still, take it all round, the troops are quite wonderful, and as ready as they were on the first day of landing to storm hostile trenches and redoubts.

. . . We have no castles here or Rolls-Royce motor-cars, or millionaires gratefully pressing exquisite vintages upon their soldier hosts. On the contrary, dust and sand is our portion mixed with flies and French vin ordinaire. . . .

In his postscript Hamilton wrote:

Now is the moment I would have loved you to be here. I am sure you would have done everyone good going down the trenches and cheering up the men. This was my first feeling and is also my last. Between the two phases of thought was a moment when I felt that from your own point of view it was better not seeing the handle your many venomous rivals might manufacture out of the visit—However—there it is!

Churchill was convinced of the need to persevere at Gallipoli; but he was pessimistic about the planning and the outcome. In his letter of August 2 to Masterton-Smith he had recalled the very different circumstances of the previous August:

We were in the middle of it a year ago: & how tremendous it seemed. Now slaughter is commonplace, & destruction has become the order of the day.

I am anxious about the D'lles, because the delay of 3 weeks taken in making up the mind of the new Cabinet has enabled the Turks to bring up large reinforcements. History will hold a strict account of every days indecision.

17

Unheeded Counsel

SIR IAN HAMILTON'S renewed attack at the Gallipoli Peninsula was launched on August 6. Its purpose was to capture the ridge of Sari Bair which rises up to nearly a thousand feet in the centre of the Peninsula and holds a dominant position overlooking the Dardanelles. Hamilton hoped that once his troops were astride the ridge they would plunge down to the northern shore of the Dardanelles. The Turks on the Helles front would be cut off. The Navy would be able to renew its assault on the Narrows without fear of artillery opposition from the European shore. None of these benefits came to pass. After six days of savage fighting the Turks still held the commanding heights. Churchill received a detailed account of the battle from his brother. Two days after the landings at Suvla Bay, Jack Churchill had gone ashore with Hankey and Colonel Aspinall[1] in search of Sir Frederick Stopford,[2] who was in charge of that sector. Neither the General nor his Chief-of-Staff, General Reed,[3] had yet been on shore. Throughout August 7 and 8, while the army fought its way across the dry salt lake and towards the Anafarta hills, its senior commanders remained on board ship in Suvla Bay. Having landed successfully, the troops halted. Although at that moment there was hardly any Turkish opposition

[1] Cecil Faber Aspinall, 1878–1959. Entered Army, 1900. Major, May 1915. Served on Sir Ian Hamilton's Staff at Gallipoli. Chief General Staff Officer during the evacuation of the Peninsula, 1915–16. Chief Staff Officer to the Royal Naval Division in France, 1916–17. Retired with rank of Brigadier-General, 1920. Assumed surname of Aspinall-Oglander, 1927. His official history, *Military Operations Gallipoli*, was published in 2 volumes, 1929 and 1932.

[2] Frederick William Stopford, 1854–1929. Entered Army, 1871. Knighted, 1900. Major-General commanding London District, 1906–9; received no further military command until 1915. Lieutenant-General commanding the IX Corps in the landing at Suvla Bay, 6 August 1915. Relieved of his command, 16 August 1915.

[3] Hamilton Lyster Reed, 1869–1931. Entered Army, 1888. Awarded the Victoria Cross, South African War, 1899–1902. Military Attaché with the Turkish forces in the Balkan War, 1912–13. Brigadier-General, 1914. Senior Staff Officer of the IX Corps at the Dardanelles, 1915. Commanded the 15th (Scottish) Division, 1917–19. Major-General, 1919.

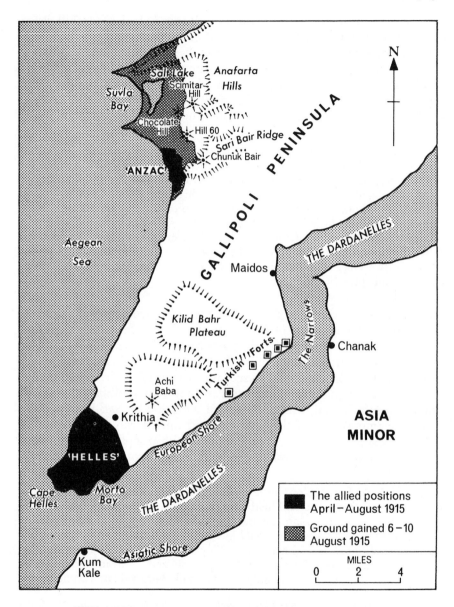

THE MILITARY LANDINGS ON THE GALLIPOLI
PENINSULA, 6–10 AUGUST 1915

in the plain or foothills, they had not advanced. Jack Churchill asked the Chief-of-Staff why the men were digging in instead of advancing. 'Reed explained,' Jack Churchill wrote to his brother on August 11, 'that of course troops could not advance without heavy artillery, which could not be landed yet. From where he was—part of the shore was obliterated by the great 14" guns of the monitor & by the cruisers waiting for a target' Jack Churchill had then landed on the plain itself:

There was no musketry anywhere and with the exception of the occasional tick-tok, which reminded me of the advanced guard in S Africa which we used to do; there appeared to be nothing in front of us. In the plain troops were moving about in the open—no shells being fired at them. I talked to one or two regimental officers. They were quite pleased with themselves. They thought there was little in front of them & that an advance would soon take place. . . . We found the GOC 11th div.[1] He seemed apathetic. I understood that the Brigadiers had said that they could not do any more and so on. Everybody seemed to have 'turned it down'. . . . The apathy of the senior officers had spread to the men.

For another twenty-four hours no forward movement was made. It was only on the morning of August 10 that Sir Frederick Stopford and his officers were willing to begin the advance. By then the Turks had taken up positions on all the hills. To the south a small number of allied troops had almost reached the summit of Chunuk Bair. But they did not receive adequate reinforcements in time to consolidate their position. Mustafa Kemal, who commanded the Turks on Sari Bair, saw the strategic importance of this summit, and hurled wave after wave of Turkish soldiers against it. By noon the British troops had been driven off by sheer weight of numbers. Jack Churchill wrote:

It has been Spion Kop[2] over again. The same Knob on a ridge—the key of the position taken and held for a short time after terrific fighting. The same lethargy on the plain below. The same fighting on a small narrow front, when a broad advance would have enabled the men at the important point to hold on & make good what they had gained. It is a terrible disappointment. A new advance is being organized. . . . But the splendid surprise has gone and we shall only gain Chunuk Bair again at a terrible cost.

[1] Frederick Hammersley, 1858–1924. Entered Army, 1876. Major-General, 1914. Commanded the 11th Division at the Suvla Bay landing, 6 August 1915. Relieved of his command, 23 August 1915.

[2] A mountain in Natal; on 24 January 1900 the British forces under Sir Redvers Buller were defeated there by the Boers.

By August 11 it was clear that the attack had failed. Jack Churchill wrote to his brother that day: 'The golden opportunity has gone, and positions that might have been won with a little perspiration would only be gained now by blood.' In his letter, Jack Churchill tried to explain what had gone wrong:

We are all trying to understand what on earth has happened to these men and why they are showing such extraordinary lack of enterprise. They are not cowards—physically they are as fine a body of men as the regular army. I think it is partly on account of their training. They have never seen a shot fired before. For a year they have been soldiers and during that time they have been taught only one thing. Trench warfare. They have been told to dig everywhere and have been led to expect an enemy at 100 yds range. From reading all the stories of the war they have learnt to regard an advance of 100 yards as a matter of the greatest importance. They landed and advanced a mile & thought they had done something wonderful. Then they had no standard to go by—no other troops were there to show them what was right. They seemed not to know what they should do. Was it right to go on so far— might they be cut off or suddenly walk into a trap. Was an occasional bullet only a sniper or was a hidden trench bristling with rifles waiting for them? . . .

The 10th & 11th had nothing to go by. They showed extraordinary ignorance. A shell burst near a working party—at least $\frac{1}{2}$ a mile away. Officers & men stopped work rushed to the low beach cliffs and lay down taking cover! A land mine exploded and the men near all lay flat and remained there thinking they were being shelled! I have just heard that the 53rd are no better. A few shots sent them retreating pell mell from Chocolate hill! Blaming the senior officers must be left to the people who can give effect to their opinions. But there is no doubt that these divisions were completely out of hand.

Jack Churchill reported that as a result of the four days' battle 'all the tricks were lost'; and that Hankey, who had arrived in time to see the battle begin, Hamilton and himself had 'all been going about tearing our hair for the last three days to see such a glorious victory thrown away'. Hamilton was willing to try yet another attack. But, as Jack Churchill wrote, he 'seems to think that it would be dangerous to press them too much at the moment'. On August 12 Jack Churchill added a further page to his letter. 'We still hope to do a lot of good,' he wrote, 'but the chance of a real coup has gone I am afraid.' He was right. Never again were the armies clustering at Helles and Anzac to advance in full force, or to reach any of the objectives which had been set, either for the original landings of April 25 or for the renewed battle of August 6.

On learning of Hamilton's failure, Churchill at once pressed for extra reinforcements to be sent to him. He was convinced that victory could be secured by one further massive effort. At least twenty thousand of the fifty thousand British troops in Egypt, he believed, ought to be sent to Gallipoli for the next offensive. These troops, he wrote to Asquith on August 12, 'could swiftly return the moment the push is over or if an emergency arose in Egypt'. He also believed that 'strong drafts should be sent from here to replace casualties which are, I fear, very heavy'. Churchill had failed to obtain detailed information from Kitchener about what reinforcements were likely to be sent to Gallipoli. 'Kitchener is, I know, doing something in this direction,' he wrote to Asquith, 'how much, I do not know. An enquiry from you would accelerate and augment the flow, as well as secure the information.' Churchill also pressed Asquith to ensure that three or four train-loads of ammunition were sent out as quickly as possible to Marseilles, and thence by sea to the Dardanelles. He ended his letter: 'We are so near a great victory that nothing humanly possible should be neglected to secure it.'

Kitchener was as keen as Churchill for a further advance. On August 14 he wrote to Churchill that he had just learned from Hamilton that the reason for the failure was that General Stopford and his two Divisional Generals, Hammersley and Mahon,[1] had done badly. 'It is most annoying,' Kitchener wrote; 'I am taking steps to have these Generals replaced by real fighters as quickly as possible.[2] Nothing has gone wrong but they have missed the chance of pushing on & Ian Hamilton says he feels reluctantly obliged to give them further time for rest and reorganization. It is very disappointing.'

The Dardanelles Committee met on August 19. Kitchener was absent in France. An acrimonious discussion took place. Bonar Law declared that Hamilton 'was always *nearly* winning'. When Churchill pointed out 'the difficulties of the task set him', Grey remarked tersely 'that we should deal with facts and accept them'. Asquith said that it

[1] Bryan Thomas Mahon, 1862–1930. Entered Army, 1883. Lieutenant-General, 1912. Knighted, 1912. General Officer commanding the 10th (Irish) Division, 1914–15. Commanded the Division at the Suvla Bay landing, 6 August 1915. Resigned his command, August 15. Resumed command, August 23. Commanded the Salonika Army, 1915–16. Commander-in-Chief, Ireland, 1916–18. Senator of the Irish Free State, 1922–30.

[2] Sixteen years later, when writing *Military Operations Gallipoli*, Aspinall-Oglander learned that the Cabinet wished to suppress all critical references to the Suvla generals. On 23 November 1931 he wrote to Churchill: 'The truth is that if the generals who failed are whitewashed the blame comes back (*a*) to you, and (*b*) to the unfortunate troops who, till Stopford & Co had choked them in a fog of defeatism, were perfectly ready & capable to do everything required.'

'was not easy to see' why Hamilton remained confident, despite having lost twenty-three thousand men. Bonar Law declared 'that a further attack would be a useless sacrifice'; Carson agreed with him. Churchill suggested an alternative to further attacks, which was 'making a separate peace with Turkey'. He proposed that Britain should offer to make peace on the basis of the Straits being kept open, Turkish independence guaranteed by Britain and the Germans expelled from Turkey. Grey said the Russians would never agree to such terms. Later in the discussion Churchill urged that if Hamilton thought he could still reach the crest of Chunuk Bair, 'he should be allowed to do it'.

The Dardanelles Committee met again on August 20, after Kitchener's return from France. The Secretary of State for War declared that in his opinion Hamilton 'would now be in a position to master the situation'. Discussion turned to the western front. Kitchener suggested urging upon Joffre the need for an early offensive, 'as delay was dangerous'. Churchill opposed any new offensive on the western front:

MR CHURCHILL expressed his regret at such a course. The German forces on the Western front had not been reduced, and were some 2,000,000 against the Allies 2,500,000. This amounted to a superiority for the Allies of five to four, which was inadequate for the offensive. Since our last offensive effort the relative strengths had not altered, while the German defences had been continually strengthened, and heavy guns and ammunition had not been correspondingly accumulated by the Allies.

It seemed to him that in the hope of relieving Russia and to gratify our great and natural desire to do so, the Allies might throw away 200,000 or 300,000 lives and ammunition and might possibly gain a little ground. The attack of the 9th May (Festubert-Arras) had been a failure, and the line had not been altered by it. *After* an expenditure of lives and ammunition in this way by us the Germans would have a chance worth seizing; and it would be worth their while to bring back great forces from the East. A superiority of two to one was laid down as necessary to attack, and we (the Allies) had not got it.

LORD KITCHENER admitted that there was a great deal of truth in what Mr Churchill had said, but unfortunately we had to make war as we must, and not as we should like to. There was another point unconnected with the actual strategy, and that was that trench work was becoming very irksome to the French troops, and than an offensive was necessary for the *moral* of the French army, amongst the members of which there was a good deal of discussion about peace.

Once more the fear of a negotiated peace on the part of an ally dictated British war policy. Early in 1915 fears of Russian and French defeatism had been a factor in pressing on with the Dardanelles operation; now they were the stimulus to further frontal attacks against an enemy numerically almost as strong and much more securely dug-in, and to denying to Hamilton the reinforcements which he believed might bring victory on the Gallipoli Peninsula.

On August 21, as Kitchener wished, a further attack was launched towards the high ground dominating the Gallipoli Peninsula. Hamilton had decided to attack in the afternoon so that the infantry could advance with the sun on their backs and the defenders blinded by its glare. But shortly after midday the sun disappeared unexpectedly behind a bank of cloud, and the Turkish positions were hidden by the haze. The preliminary artillery bombardment failed to touch the Turkish front line. At the outset of the advance most battalions lost their officers, and many their guides. The result was confusion. The immediate objectives, Scimitar Hill and Hill 60, were scenes of bitter fighting. Of the 14,300 men who took part in the fighting around Scimitar Hill, over 5,300 were killed or wounded by nightfall. The battle for Hill 60 continued for seven days. Throughout the fighting the crest of the hill remained in Turkish hands. By August 28 it was clear that no further progress could be made. The troops at Anzac and Suvla had exhausted all their energy. No further attack was possible. The Turks remained in complete control of the Sari Bair ridge, and despite their own severe losses, maintained their dominance over the Peninsula.

Writing to Asquith, Kitchener and Balfour on August 21, Churchill had argued that the time had come to look again at the possibility of a renewed naval attack. He begged them to believe that the military operations had failed, and pointed out that Hamilton's army, 'though five times as large as the original force', was in the General's opinion 'inadequate to the essential task'. Churchill feared that 'the possibility of the German Armies overawing Roumania, crushing Servia, and seducing Bulgaria comes nearer every day', and that to maintain a large army on the Gallipoli Peninsula during the winter would be extremely difficult and costly. The naval risks, he argued, would be far smaller:

Even the unfortunate operations of the 18th [March]—foolishly treated as a 'stupendous event'—only entailed to the British the loss of 2 old battleships and about 100 men. The question now arises whether, in view of all the above considerations, the naval operation begun on the 18th March should not be resumed, pressed to a decision, and fought out, as it has never yet been; and in these circumstances it is worth while examining the new facts which have developed in the naval situation.

Churchill stressed three such facts which increased the possibility of a naval success. The first fact was that the Turkish Army on the Gallipoli Peninsula had become so large, and the land route to it so inadequate, that once a squadron of British ships were in the Sea of Marmara 'the Turkish army must either be starved or so reduced that our army can overpower them'. The second fact was that any British squadron which reached the Sea of Marmara would no longer have to be so strong, for the *Beslau* was known to be out of action and the *Goeben* to be in a dilapidated condition. At the same time there were a number of British submarines continually in the Sea of Marmara, making Turkish naval communications with Gallipoli almost impossible, and forcing the Turkish Army to move almost all its stores and men over the land route, which at the Bulair isthmus was largely exposed to naval guns. The third fact was that special naval vessels had been designed by the Admiralty, 'protected against torpedoes by their structure' and so shallow in draught 'that they should be able to pass over the Kephez minefield without danger'. Four of them were ready for action. Churchill then set out in detail how he proposed that the naval operation could take place. 'There is no reason why the losses should be severe,' he concluded. 'But they could not in any case be weighed for a moment against the vast and fatal catastrophe towards which we may be drifting. The risks to be avoided and the prizes to be won, are incomparably greater than the risks and stakes which would be involved. And before we resign ourselves to the failure of all our hopes, this effort ought certainly to be made.'

When the Dardanelles Committee met on August 27 Balfour reported that the Admiralty, 'after a special investigation of the matter, are adverse to sending monitors or other ships under existing conditions into the Sea of Marmora'. Kitchener declared that Hamilton was satisfied that the forty-seven thousand troops that were being sent to reinforce him were 'sufficient to make it unnecessary for him to abandon any of his 3 positions [Helles, Anzac and Suvla] or to contract his lines'. 'For what it was worth,' Kitchener added, 'the trend of all the reports pointed to the fact that we should hang on, for the Turks could not last much longer.' On August 30 Hankey circulated a memorandum to the members of the Dardanelles Committee reporting on his visit to the Gallipoli Peninsula, and declaring that in his opinion 'there is good ground for hoping for another success in the Anzac region'. On the following day he gave the Dardanelles Committee a verbal report on his visit, reiterating his belief that if Hamilton were reinforced, a further offensive, and the chance of a victory, was possible, and that until the offensive, 'we should hang on to all three landing places'. The Dardanelles Committee met again on September 3. The discussion ranged over the best means of helping Hamilton, either by reinforcements or by a further landing, possibly on the Asiatic shore. The French wanted a landing at Besika Bay. Churchill pressed Kitchener to concentrate on Gallipoli and 'to discourage, by every means, the prosecution of a violent offensive in France'. Kitchener replied that such a policy 'would break the Anglo-French alliance'. Lloyd George supported Churchill with strong remarks, which brought the meeting to a close:

MR LLOYD GEORGE pointed out that an attempt should be made at one operation or the other and not at both at the same time. He thought that we had the men to give our troops a fair chance in the Dardanelles, but if we frittered away our strength and split them between two theatres, we ran a great chance of meeting with failure in both. He thought it was important to persuade the French to postpone the offensive in the West, and to send any excess in men and munitions to the Dardanelles, where we already had some superiority.

During early September Churchill began to press his colleagues to make a careful provision for the coming of winter weather at the Dardanelles. In Cabinet he asked Balfour to circulate a report on weather conditions, and Balfour agreed to do so. But when no report was circulated, Churchill was provoked to anger, writing to Balfour on September 5:

Generally, I am very anxious about the provision which is being made for the winter campaign on the Peninsula. The sanitary conditions in the wet weather require extraordinary study and exertion. The trenches and living shelters should have been long ago properly cemented. Good reservoirs should be made, and a complete system of wire-haulage and tramways established. These last are no doubt not your affair, but still I hope they will not be out of your mind.

Neither Balfour nor Kitchener was willing to be influenced by any of Churchill's schemes or anxieties. Since July, Kitchener had been making plans for a further offensive on the western front. On July 6 and 7, at the Anglo-French conference at Calais, the British Ministers present —Asquith, Balfour and Crewe—believed that they had obtained a veto on further attacks in the west in 1915; unknown to them, Kitchener and

Joffre had agreed on the necessity of launching a British as well as a French offensive on the western front during September.

Since the middle of August Churchill had been a member of the War Policy Committee of the Cabinet, whose task was to examine Ministers and civil servants in order to report on the need for conscription, and on whether munitions output made conscription possible. Lord Crewe was Chairman of the Committee; Curzon, Austen Chamberlain, Selborne and Arthur Henderson its other members with Churchill. They held twelve meetings. On August 16 they examined Lloyd George, who told them: 'You will not get through without some measure of military compulsion or compulsion for military service. The longer you delay the nearer you will be to disaster. I am certain you cannot get through without it. . . . To send a number of men who are obviously inadequate is just murdering our own countrymen without attaining any purpose at all.'

Churchill had, since June, come to accept Lloyd George's argument, and tried privately to persuade Grey that conscription was needed. But Grey was appalled at the idea, writing to Churchill on August 18:

I cannot understand your passion for uncontrolled Recruiting. It is madness unless I am mad.

The Germans carefully exempt from military service the people necessary to carry on the life of the country: if they had not done so they would have had a break down by now.

We on the other hand recruit without regard to the trades necessary to keep the country alive & even to supply military & naval needs.

There are two possible ways of being beaten in this war: one is to be defeated on land & sea by the enemy: the other is to commit suicide at home. It seems to me that we are heading straight for the latter & quite unnecessarily, for I believe that we cannot in this war be beaten by anybody but ourselves.

Kitchener's frequent denials that compulsory service was needed had been based, not on moral but on military grounds. But Major-General Callwell, Director of Military Operations and Intelligence at the War Office, knew that Kitchener's denials were not based upon the military facts. 'The truth is I am afraid,' Callwell had written to H. A. Gwynne on July 7, 'that K is not letting his colleagues know the state of things, and that he wants to be able to say at the end of the business that he

produced an army of so many divisions by the voluntary principle.' The
War Policy Committee examined three of Kitchener's subordinates:
Major-General Montgomery[1] on August 17, Sir Reginald Brade[2] on
August 19 and Callwell on August 20. Each gave assurances that
Kitchener's faith in voluntary service was justified by the facts of the
military situation. Neither Montgomery, Brade nor Callwell felt able to
oppose their chief. Callwell had lied to maintain Kitchener's position.
He expressed his guilt in a letter, undated, to H. A. Gwynne:

By his opposition to Compulsory service he is antagonising the bulk of the
Cabinet and they will, sooner or later, find out the difficulties we are in and
the imposture which these 'New Armies' are. We can keep going possibly
for a time with three in the field, besides all the old stuff; but after that there
must come a collapse it seems to me. . . . At the present moment, when
I. Hamilton is far below establishment, we are only dribbling out about half
the drafts he requires to make him up to strength, and by the time those are
there he is bound to have lost a lot more. In dealing with Cabinet Committees
it is very difficult not to expose the business. I am not a good liar—the spirit
may be willing but the flesh is weak—and you cannot fool people like Curzon
& Winston who know the business. Northcliffe may get hold of the facts
because Repington somehow has very useful sources of information, and if he
does he may make trouble much more effectually than he did on munitions.
K trusts to bluffing them all; but he may not succeed. . . .

On August 24 Kitchener himself appeared before Crewe's Committee. He declared that men could always be obtained by a voluntary
appeal. Churchill warned that he might be mistaken:

. . . the time is coming when very heavy taxation will have to be imposed,
which will perhaps touch the working classes, and when prices will rise still
higher, and when the idea that nobody is to be worse off by the war will
long have passed away, and when the war may be very unpopular. A series
of unbroken disasters and of very very heavy losses might create a situation
such that when you come forward and are ready to stake everything on it,
you may find the opposition much greater than it is now, because based
upon the general unpopularity of the war.

To this Kitchener replied: 'I do not feel competent to form an opinion
on such a subject.'

[1] Robert Arthur Montgomery, 1848–1931. Entered Royal Artillery, 1868. Major-General,
1902. Commanded the 22nd Division, 1914–15. Director-General of Recruiting, 1915.
[2] Reginald Herbert Brade, 1864–1933. Entered War Office as a Clerk, 1884. Secretary of
the War Office and Army Council, 1914–20. Knighted, 1914.

Lord Crewe reported to Asquith on September 7 that the Committee had been unable to reach a conclusion on the basis of what they had heard. Kitchener and Lloyd George had adopted irreconcilable positions, and their evidence had been contradictory. Churchill, Curzon, Selborne and Chamberlain submitted a dissenting 'Supplementary Memorandum' in which they, a majority of the Committee, declared that 'the times are so grave, and the crisis of our national fortunes so urgent, that it is our duty to set forth in explicit terms . . . the conclusions to which we have come'; these were that conscription was absolutely necessary, and a workable proposition. They quoted Lloyd George's remarks verbatim to prove their point. Asquith took no action on this majority report.

Since joining the Government as Attorney-General, Sir Edward Carson had been appalled by the way in which important war business was conducted. He disliked the casual way in which his colleagues brushed aside carefully prepared arguments, and resented too strong or emotional an appeal on some major war question. Provoked by Kitchener's unwillingness to admit that more troops were needed at Gallipoli to ensure success, and by his refusal to gather together the largest possible number of men available, Carson expressed his anger in a letter to Churchill on September 9. The two men had come into vitriolic conflict on the Irish issue immediately before the outbreak of war. The war itself found them of like mind, and Carson knew that Churchill would be sympathetic:

. . . What I feel so acutely about is that all our calculations (if we can dignify them by that name) are absolutely haphazard—we are always told what we can send & not how many are necessary & this I think leads to minimum calculations so as to get what the general on the spot thinks is the best we can expect—we cannot win on these principles & I feel it criminal to waste insufficient forces simply on the grounds that it is the best we can do under the circumstances.

I have not yet been at any Cabinet when anything was properly or usefully decided ie in such materials as we wd require in deciding the usual questions which arise in ordinary business matters. Nor do I see how it even can be so in a cabinet of 22 meeting for a fixed & definite time & with no plans properly worked out when they are submitted.

Is there no way in which we cd have the whole question of the present system raised? or wd it seem to be a reflection on the PM who has formed the Cabinet? A good war staff working daily at war problems only & submitting to the Cabinet the duty of finding the means is as far as I can see the solution. The Cabinet to be vy small 5 or 6 & sitting daily to consider the problems.

Carson ended his letter on a pessimistic note: 'Personally I look on all our Cabinet Meetings as useless & waste of time & I earnestly wish I could humbly retire.'

Churchill received much news and encouragement from his friends in France. On August 10 Sir John French had written from his Head-quarters to say how sorry he was that the Dardanelles visit had not taken place. 'I hope you are coming to see me again some day!' he wrote; 'I often—very often—think of you.' It was exactly three months since Churchill had last visited the western front. During September his thoughts turned to something more challenging than a brief visit to the General Headquarters or a short tour of the trenches. On September 10 he asked Asquith if he could leave the Government and command a Brigade in France. Asquith was sympathetic; he knew how frustrated Churchill felt at the Duchy. But neither of them could overcome Kitchener's hostility. Kitchener did not mind Churchill going on a Cabinet mission to the Dardanelles; he did object to him taking up a permanent post in his own armies. Churchill had therefore to give up the idea, writing to Asquith on September 13: 'I was too much influenced by French who is always so kind to me; & I saw—for a moment—an escape from a situation wh on various grounds public & private I dislike increasingly as the days pass by. Many thanks for the interest which you took in my feelings.'

A senior military command was clearly impossible. Churchill tried instead to arrange for a prolonged visit to the western front. On September 14 he wrote to W. H. Bernau about extra insurance cover. 'I may require to go to France in the near future on the same sort of conditions of liberty as were arranged for my visit to the Dardanelles,' he explained. 'I shd like to pay an extra premium to cover say 15 days actually in the zone of the armies though not serving as a soldier; these days to count as they occur.' Churchill did not give up hopes for some military activity. Kitchener might refuse to give him a senior post. But he could always go out as a major in the Queen's Own Oxfordshire Hussars. 'In the event of my later on in the same year wishing to pay the regular £5.5.0% of full war risk,' he wrote to Bernau, 'I shd like this partial fragment to be counted towards the total. Can this be done?'

That night Churchill dined with Lloyd George and Curzon. His contempt for both Asquith's and Kitchener's direction of war policy was complete. Lloyd George reported the dinner conversation, and his own thoughts, to Frances Stevenson, who recorded in her diary later that week:

They had a most important talk, and Curzon says the Tories are going to approach the PM & say that they cannot proceed any longer under the present state of things. They will demand conscription and the removal of K from the WO, as being incompetent and having failed to grasp the military situation. D [Lloyd George] & Churchill will throw in their lot with Curzon & his followers, for D says he cannot possibly be a party any longer to the shameful mismanagement and slackness. He says that things are simply being allowed to slide, and that it is time someone spoke out. As I said before, however, he hates going against his party, & he fears that the Liberals will hate him violently if he goes against them now. He fears Churchill, too. He is not sure whether Churchill will come too, or whether he will remain & get the PM to put him into D's shoes in the Munitions Office. D says that Churchill is the only man in the Cabinet who has the power to do him harm, and he does not trust him when it comes to a matter of personal interest.

Churchill sensed Lloyd George's distrust. He felt quite friendless in political circles. The trenches seemed to him the only escape. But he did not want his departure for the front line to be interpreted as an escape from criticism of his time as First Lord. He was tired of being the recipient of all the innuendo and odium connected with his wartime months at the Admiralty. On August 10 Josiah Wedgwood had given Churchill the draft of a letter which he had wanted to send to Oliver Locker-Lampson.[1] In his letter Wedgwood described a rumour that was beginning to circulate to the effect 'that Prince Louis of Battenberg did everything that was right & C only what was wrong'. Wedgwood believed that he and Lampson were 'not the only people who are rather "fed up" with this utterly unjust treatment of almost the only man with push enough to be a leader', and had proposed to distribute publicly a memorandum setting out the 'Charge' against Churchill, followed by the 'Facts' of the three cruisers, Antwerp, Coronel and the Dardanelles. For each of the incidents which he mentioned, Wedgwood had written out the facts as he saw them. Churchill kept Wedgwood's proposed letter, and no memorandum was published. Churchill realized that the initiative in any attempt to vindicate him would have to come from the Government. On September 15 he wrote to ask Asquith to pub-

---

[1] Oliver Stillingfleet Locker-Lampson, 1880–1954. Conservative MP, 1910–45. Lieutenant-Commander, Royal Naval Air Service, December 1914; Commander, July 1915. Commanded the British Armoured Car detachment in Russia, 1916–17. Parliamentary Private Secretary to Austen Chamberlain, 1918–21.

lish 'the truth' about Antwerp, the sinking of the three cruisers and the defeat off Coronel:

> ... I am repeatedly made the object of vy serious charges in all these matters, wh have never been contradicted, & seem in some way to be confirmed by my leaving the Admiralty. Sometimes the charges appear in print ... but much more are they kept alive by conversation, or by constant references in newspaper articles; & there is no doubt whatever that the belief is widespread that I personally acted in these events wrongfully & foolishly.
>
> You know the facts. I have made them known to some of my colleagues. But that does not help me outside, & I still remain under the shadow of utterly false aspersions wh are a serious injury to me.
>
> For a long time I have been content to do nothing, but I am now convinced that action is necessary. In justice to me, & also I may add to your late Government the truth must be published; & I am determined not to let this session slip away without this being done. I am sure that you wd not wish to treat unfairly one who has been so long yr colleague & friend.

Churchill suggested one of three courses: Parliament could be given a digest of the actual telegrams and minutes; Asquith could give a detailed written answer to a Parliamentary question; or Churchill himself could make a full personal explanation. The Dardanelles presented a particular difficulty, as Churchill explained in his letter.

> Here again my only wish is that everything shd be published. These operations are however still proceeding in the same circumstances & on the same ground, & discussion of them might be harmful. There is a clear line of demarcation between past & current operations. It will be all the easier to maintain this line if we show ourselves ready to make a full disclosure of what has happened in the past, & if Parliament sees how good our case is in that respect.

While waiting for Asquith's reply, Churchill received another appeal from Carson on September 19:

> Are we going to allow everlasting drift on the policy of the Dardanelles?
> I read daily in the dispatches & news the effect which delay & failure is having in Russia & the Balkans & this delay & failure is daily changing the situation & making success more & more difficult. In my opinion we are guilty of criminal folly to the nation in this policy of drift. . . .
> Surely outside a Cabinet such delay & want of policy wd not be tolerated in any business.
> Now you know I always speak vy plainly—I daresay rudely—but I am going to say that no one is held more responsible for the Dardanelles policy than yrself! Now if the clear policy of certain victory at any cost is adopted by

the Cabinet I will back it, but it must be no narrow margins nor estimates framed 'to do the best we can' & for Generals who are only looking to see how far they can please.

I feel every day more inclined to retire altogether, not because of any particular policy but because there is *none*—absolutely *none*, & I feel ashamed when I see the H of C & the country misled about it. . . .

Please do not answer this. I will be in town on Tuesday morning & will see you at another futile Cabinet!

Asquith does not appear to have answered Churchill's letter of September 15. On September 23 Churchill wrote to him again, enclosing 'papers which I have prepared about Cradock and the three cruisers' and urging the publication at least of the Cradock documents, as no secrecy was involved. Over Antwerp, Churchill wrote that as the French Government was involved, and as he regarded their role as rather discreditable, 'I regret that I do not feel able to ask for its publication', although, as he told Asquith, the story of Antwerp was from his point of view '. . . the best of all'. Asquith was unwilling to institute any enquiry about past events. Churchill wanted retrospective vindication. But Kitchener, Grey and the Prime Minister himself still held the positions which they had held then, and any open scrutiny of their actions might lead to loss of public confidence. All Churchill could do, in default of open publication, was to circulate the documents of his Admiralty administration to his Cabinet colleagues as part of his right as a Cabinet Minister. This he proceeded to do. The Conservative Ministers had seen none of these documents before; many of the Liberals had not had access to them at the time. Both had relied upon second-hand reports, or upon the Press, for their information. Churchill proceeded to send them a series of folders. On September 29 he circulated a bulky set of telegrams concerning Antwerp; on October 14 what he described in his covering note as 'the facts about certain episodes of past Admiralty administration which have been the subject of criticism, and with regard to which misconception exists'; on October 29 thirty-three pages of telegrams relating to the Dardanelles; on November 12 a further short set of papers about the Dardanelles, with the pathetic covering note: 'My colleagues may like to have these odd papers for their Gallipoli collection.'

Clementine Churchill had begun war work of her own, helping to set up canteens for munition workers, whom the YMCA provided with cheap meals. She asked her husband to speak at one of her canteens, and he did so, at Enfield Lock, on September 18. It was three months since his previous public speech, at Dundee. He spoke twice, first to the men about to go on the night shift, and then to the men coming off the day shift. Both speeches were reported fully in the national press. Churchill emphasized the many disappointments of the war in the previous months. But of Gallipoli he was confident, 'that we have only to persevere with resolution and unflinching courage, to move forward to a conclusion which, when it is achieved, will repay all the heavy cost and losses we have endured'. He ended his speech with a rousing peroration:

Our situation is a serious one. We have it in our power by our exertions to carry this war to a successful and a decisive conclusion, but we have it in our power to do so only if we exert our strength to the utmost limit of human and national capacity.

After all we did not seek this struggle. We did not desire as a nation, or as a generation, to have imposed upon us this terrible ordeal. We cannot understand the inscrutable purposes which have plunged these evils upon the world, and have involved all the nations of Europe in a catastrophe measureless in its horror. But we know that if in this time of crisis and strain we do our duty, we shall have done all that it is in human power to do—and we shall so bear ourselves in this period—all of us, whatever part we play on the stage of the world's history—we shall bear ourselves so that those who come after us will find amid the signs and scars of this great struggle that the liberties of Europe and of Britain are still intact and inviolate; when those looking back upon our efforts such as they have been, will say of this unhappy but not inglorious generation, placed in a position of extraordinary trial, that it did not fail in the test, and that the torch which it preserved lights the world for us today.

I cannot but express most sincerely my gratitude for all the exertions which are being made, and I earnestly trust you will not flag or slacken in these, so that by your efforts our country may emerge from this period of darkness and peril once more into the sunlight of a peaceful time.

Since the beginning of the war Churchill had been much exercised by the unequal contest between men and machines, to which all his soldier friends bore witness. On 23 September 1914, in a memorandum to Colonel Ollivant and Captain Sueter, he asked for work to be begun on a trench spanning car: it was his first formal proposal for a mechanical device to influence trench warfare. 'It is most important,' he wrote, 'that the motor transport and armed motor-cars should be provided to a certain extent with cars carrying the means of bridging small cuts in the road, and an arrangement of planks capable of bridging a ten- or twelve-feet span quickly and easily should be carried with every ten or twelve machines. A proportion of tools should also be supplied.' Admiral Bacon, at that time Manager of the Coventry Ordnance Works, and a naval gunnery expert, worked on the design. Within two months Bacon had designed a machine such as Churchill envisaged. Unfortunately the bridge device was found unable, after tests at the War Office, to negotiate a double line of trenches, and was abandoned. Colonel Swinton,[1] the War Office Eyewitness at the Headquarters of the British Expeditionary Force in France, had come independently to the same conclusion that Churchill had reached. He too believed that a trench-crossing weapon might be decisive in securing victory for the side which possessed it. Swinton had taken his idea to Hankey, who at the end of December 1914 circulated several members of the Cabinet, including Churchill, with a paper on the need for some trench-crossing mechanical device. As soon as Churchill read Hankey's memorandum he wrote to Asquith, on 5 January 1915, urging him in the strongest possible language to take immediate action:

It would be quite easy in a short time to fit up a number of steam tractors with small armoured shelters, in which men and machine guns could be placed, which would be bullet-proof. Used at night, they would not be affected by artillery fire to any extent. The caterpillar system would enable trenches to be crossed quite easily, and the weight of the machine would destroy all wire entanglements.

Forty or fifty of these engines, prepared secretly and brought into positions at nightfall, could advance quite certainly into the enemy's trenches, smashing away all the obstructions, and sweeping the trenches with their machine-gun fire, and with grenades thrown out of the top. They would then make so many *points d'appuis* for the British supporting infantry to rush forward and rally on them. They can then move forward to attack the second line of trenches.

Churchill had wanted Asquith to authorize the necessary expenditure to prepare a prototype. 'The cost would be small,' he wrote. 'If the experiment did not answer, what harm would be done? An obvious measure of prudence would have been to have started something like this two months ago. It should certainly be done now.' Asquith sent

[1] Ernest Dunlop Swinton, 1868–1951. Entered Army, 1888. Assistant-Secretary to the Committee of Imperial Defence, 1913–14, and to the War Council, 1915. Colonel, 1916. Raised Heavy Section, Machine Gun Corps (tanks), 1916–17. Major-General, 1918. Knighted, 1923. Chichele Professor of Military History, Oxford, 1925–39. Colonel Commandant, Royal Tank Corps, 1934–8.

Churchill's letter to Kitchener, who set in motion a certain amount of design work at the War Office. But this did not satisfy Churchill, who felt that the military authorities were not really convinced either that the machine could be made, or that it would be of much value once it were completed.

In February 1915 Churchill had dined with his friend the Duke of Westminster. Among the guests were some officers of the Armoured Car Division of the Royal Naval Air Service, in which the Duke was then serving. One of these officers, Major Hetherington,[1] who knew something of the experiments which had already been carried on at the War Office, declared his complete conviction, not only that such vehicles could be made but that they would win the war. During the dinner he told Churchill that he believed a very large cross-country armoured car could be designed which could carry guns, and be able to surmount most obstacles. Churchill instructed Hetherington to submit his plans to him. On the following morning he sent for one of his leading ship designers at the Admiralty, Captain Eustace Tennyson D'Eyncourt,[2] and showed him Hetherington's proposals. Churchill asked D'Eyncourt to go into the question exhaustively, and try to design 'a land ship'. Captain Seuter was also brought into the discussion. Hetherington and Seuter examined the possibility of a caterpillar type of propulsion. To mystify those who might see the designs or early experiments in progress, the new weapons were called 'water carriers for Russia' and it was put about that they were some new method of bringing water forward in large quantities to the troops in the battle area. Colonel Swinton, seeing that they would probably be abbreviated in the War Office to 'WCs for Russia', suggested that they should be called 'tanks'.

The first formal Admiralty conference to discuss the best methods of proceeding with the tank was held on 20 February 1915, in Churchill's bedroom, as he was suffering from a bad attack of influenza. As a result of this meeting a Land Ship Committee was formed with D'Eyncourt as Chairman. It held its first meeting on February 22, and submitted its proposals to Churchill, who accepted their recommendations, minuting on February 24: 'As proposed & with all despatch.' An order for the

---

[1] Thomas Gerard Hetherington, 1886–1951. Joined Royal Flying Corps on its formation, May 1912. Attached to the Royal Naval Air Service for experimental work, 1914–15. Air Attaché, Washington, 1926–30; Rome, 1931–5.

[2] Eustace Henry William Tennyson-d'Eyncourt, 1868–1951. A naval architect, 1898–1912. Director of Naval Construction and Chief Technical Adviser at the Admiralty, 1912–23. Knighted, 1917. Vice-President of the Tank Board, 1918. Managing Director of Armstrong Whitworth's shipyards at Newcastle, 1924–8. Director of the Parsons Marine Steam Turbine Company, 1928–48. Created Baronet, 1930.

first tank was placed with Messrs Fosters of Lincoln, a firm of agricultural engineers, one of whose Directors, William Tritton,[1] joined the Land Ship Committee. It was Tritton who suggested using a tractor as the model for the new machine.

By the end of February Churchill, having obtained Asquith's approval for his experimental activities, gave the Committee £70,000 from Admiralty funds to pursue its developments with as much speed as possible. The first designs were submitted to Churchill by the Committee on March 9, and he minuted: 'Press on.' Twelve days later he received a further progress report and a request from D'Eyncourt to proceed with the construction of eighteen separate prototypes. Churchill minuted on March 20: 'Most urgent. Special report to me in case of delay. . . .'

When Balfour succeeded Churchill as First Lord a new mood descended upon the Admiralty. Churchill described this in a letter to the Royal Commission on War Inventions in 1919:

> The new Board of Admiralty included three out of the four naval members of the Old Board. They appear to have viewed the financial commitments which had already been incurred to an extent of about £45,000 either as undesirable or wholly beyond the sphere of Admiralty interests. They, therefore, proposed to terminate the contracts and scrap the whole project.

In his memoirs, *A Shipbuilder's Yarn*, published in 1948, D'Eyncourt recalled how Balfour summoned him and said: 'Have not you and your Department enough to do in looking after the design and construction of ships, without concerning yourself about material for the Army?' But D'Eyncourt did not despair. He went at once to Churchill and warned him of what was about to happen. Churchill immediately appealed directly to Balfour, who agreed to allow experiments to continue.[2] But the enthusiasm which Churchill had imparted

---

[1] William Ashbee Tritton, 1875–1946. Member of the Firm of Tritton, Foster & Co. of Lincoln. Knighted, 1917, for his part in the development of the tank.

[2] In its Report of 17 November 1919, the Royal Commission on War Inventions stated that 'it was primarily due to the receptivity, courage and driving force' of Churchill that the idea of using the tank as an instrument of war 'was converted into a practical shape'. Churchill refused any monetary payment. The Commission granted £1,000 to Swinton, £1,000 to Tennyson d'Eyncourt, and £7,500 to Tritton, as well as making several other payments. Its Report concluded with a note about the claim of Mr L. E. de Mole: '. . . We consider that he is entitled to the greatest credit for having made and reduced to practical shape as far back as the year 1912 a very brilliant invention which anticipated and in some respects surpassed that actually put into use in the year 1916. It was this claimant's misfortune and not his fault that his invention was in advance of his time, and failed to be appreciated and was put aside because the occasion for its use had not then arisen. We regret exceedingly that we are unable to recommend any award to him. . . .'

to the project was gone. On 23 September 1915 he wrote to Arthur Steel-Maitland,[1] the Under-Secretary of State for the Colonies, expressing his mounting frustration:

My dear Maitland,

I ordered a dozen of these machines as an experiment when I was at the Admiralty—tho' they were no business of mine. I believe that they are *one* way of taking trenches. There are parts of the Dlles terrain in wh they cd be used.

But the effect now of fostering the idea is I fear beyond my present resources. If you want to help you shd study the problem for yourself or ask Captain Hetherington of the RNAS to tell you about it, & then if you are still pleased with the project, you shd try to convince your Chief.

Remember the elephants of Roman times. These are mechanical elephants to break wire & earthwork phalanges.

I am intimately acquainted with the general aspect of the machine. Its merits will be appreciated after the war is over.

Yours vy truly
Winston S. Churchill

'It is odious to me,' Churchill had written to Jack Seely three days before, 'to remain here watching sloth & folly with full knowledge & no occupation.'

The Dardanelles Committee met on September 23. Its members discussed the imminent danger of an Austro-German attack on Serbia, and whether there was anything Britain could do. Lloyd George suggested holding on to Anzac and Helles, but withdrawing from Suvla Bay, and sending the forty-five thousand troops there to Salonika. Britain, he insisted, 'must not make the same mistake that we had always made so far in dealing with the Near East, that is, of being too late with our proposals'. Churchill supported Lloyd George, believing that 'by sending four divisions now rotting at Suvla we might be able to prevent the Austro-German incursion'. But later in the discussion he spoke with bitterness against Lloyd George:

MR CHURCHILL said that both Mr Lloyd George and Mr Bonar Law wished to abandon the Dardanelles, and this was their real aim in the proposal to move four divisions from Suvla Bay. Not to send the promised four French divisions and two British divisions meant throwing up the

[1] Arthur Herbert Drummond Ramsay Steel-Maitland, 1876–1935. Conservative MP, 1910–29. Parliamentary Under-Secretary for the Colonies, 1915–17. Created Baronet, 1917. Joint Parliamentary Under-Secretary of State, Foreign Office, and Parliamentary Secretary, Board of Trade, 1917–19. Minister of Labour 1924–9.

sponge at the Dardanelles. It would be very hard to explain, particularly in the case of Australia, a sacrifice which had been incurred with no result, and to decide to do so in a hurry would be fatal. There was also to be considered the fate of the troops at the Dardanelles. He inquired if the operations based on Salonica were to take the place of those suggested on the Asiatic side of the Dardanelles.

MR LLOYD GEORGE said that the operation based on Salonica had no point if the Austro-Germans did not attack; and if the Austro-Germans did attack in Europe, what was the good of having troops in Asia? By holding Anzac and Helles we would, on the other hand, keep some of the Turks in occupation.

MR CHURCHILL said that he would not be a party to abandoning the Dardanelles.

On the following day the Dardanelles Committee met again. The six Conservative Ministers present, Lansdowne, Curzon, Bonar Law, Balfour, Selborne and Carson, and the five Liberals, Asquith, Crewe, Churchill, Grey and Lloyd George, with Kitchener's approval, agreed on 'the importance of pushing on arrangements for a winter campaign in the Gallipoli Peninsula'. That day Kitchener telegraphed to Hamilton: 'I need hardly say there is no intention of abandoning Dardanelles.'

The British offensive on the western front, against which the Calais conference in July had seemingly decided, and against which Churchill had warned, began on September 25. The objective was the village of Loos, and the high ground a mile beyond. Within two days, more than fifteen thousand British soldiers had been killed. The Germans lost five thousand. The offensive had failed; the German line was intact.

On September 10 an officer on Sir Ian Hamilton's staff, Captain Dawnay, had arrived in London from the Dardanelles. He was at once asked his opinion about the chances of victory on the Gallipoli Peninsula, not only by Kitchener but also by Churchill and other Ministers. On September 14 Dawnay saw Churchill, recording in his diary that Churchill had said 'that the resources of the Admiralty in small craft, etc—were ample to meet any demands that might be made. He also raised the question of the evacuation of Suvla Bay, and expressed himself as very much averse to the adoption of this measure.' On September 16 Dawnay breakfasted with Steel-Maitland and Bonar Law, recording in his diary that he 'contradicted Bonar Law's pessimism about Suvla and the situation generally'. On September 21 he discussed the military situation with Carson and Churchill at the War Office, recording:

> Sir Edward Carson and Mr Churchill pressed the question of the prospects of a renewed offensive. . . .
>
> Mr Churchill pressed the project of an expedition on the Asiatic side of the Straits. By this time, information from French Headquarters had been received, which made it begin to appear improbable that the French would after all undertake an expedition there. Mr Churchill, therefore, proposed to tell the French that if they did not undertake the task we would do so—even to the point of withdrawing a number of divisions from France. His view and that of Sir Edward Carson was that, if done at all, it should be done on the amplest scale. Mr Churchill proposed that 10 divisions should be landed, completely mobile, so as to ensure that the force should be sufficient to sweep aside all possible opposition to a dash on Chanak, in combination with a renewal of our attack on the Sari Bair and towards Maidos.

Callwell, who was present, pointed out the great amount of time that would be needed to land up to 200,000 men on an open beach, but no detailed discussion took place. Dawnay saw Churchill again three days later, when they discussed the new 'Stokes trench Mortar' which Dawnay believed could be effective at Gallipoli. On the following day, September 25, Callwell informed Churchill that Dawnay had seen the Stokes gun in action 'and came back immensely impressed with its capabilities, especially for work in the Dardanelles . . .'. Callwell added that 'there seems to be a good deal of delay about adopting this weapon'. Churchill promised to use his influence to hasten its production, entering into a long and at times acrimonious correspondence with Lloyd George's Parliamentary Secretary at the Ministry of Munitions, Dr Christopher Addison.[1] On September 30 Dawnay saw Churchill for the last time before returning to Gallipoli, and recorded in his diary Churchill's bitter comment: 'He said that he thought the operations in Champagne had definitely failed to achieve any vital success, and said that with one quarter of the military effort which has been needed to take the village of Loos, we should have been able to get

[1] Christopher Addison, 1869–1951. Hunterian Professor of Anatomy, 1901. Liberal MP, 1910–22. Parliamentary Secretary to the Board of Education, 1914–15. Parliamentary Secretary, Ministry of Munitions, 1915–16. Minister of Munitions, 1916–17. Minister in Charge of Reconstruction, 1917. President of the Local Government Board, 1919. Minister of Health, 1919–21. Minister without Portfolio, 1921. Labour MP, 1929–31; 1934–5. Minister of Agriculture and Fisheries, 1930–1. Created Baron, 1937; Viscount, 1945. Secretary of State for Commonwealth Relations, 1945–7. Paymaster-General, 1948–9. Lord Privy Seal, 1947–51.

through the Narrows.' Churchill's belief that the Gallipoli campaign had not yet failed was reinforced by all that Dawnay told him.

On October 1 Churchill lunched with Lloyd George. The comparison between the western and Gallipoli fronts was uppermost in his mind. The editor of the *Manchester Guardian*, C. P. Scott,[1] who was present at the lunch, made a note of their conversation immediately afterwards:

> Both very hostile to the policy of attack now being carried out on Western front, any considerable success from which they regard as impossible. The whole of Cabinet had been opposed to it except one man—Kitchener. . . .
>
> Both Lloyd George and Churchill insisted on the far greater possibilities of the Eastern front. As Churchill put it the same effort and expenditure which had given us the village of Loos would have given us Constantinople and the command of the Eastern world. Our policy in the Balkans had been persistently futile. We had missed some six excellent diplomatic chances. Even now we were without a considered policy and merely waiting on events. Bulgaria was obviously only playing for time till the Central powers were ready to attack.

When the lunch was over, Churchill took Scott back to the Duchy of Lancaster Office, where they had a further talk. Scott noted:

> . . . spent an hour with him in going through the confidential papers relating to (1) the loss of the 3 cruisers in the North Sea (2) Cradock's defeat in the Pacific (3) the Antwerp expedition (4) the attack by sea on the Dardanelles. He made out a conclusive case for himself on the first two and a fairly good defence on the other two. At first he offered to let me take away the papers to study, but thought better of it. He is chafing desperately at having virtually no work to do and spoke of perhaps resigning and joining his regiment. He said that so far as his difference with Lord Fisher was concerned the Prime Minister had promised to back him, but when at the same time, in face of the munitions scandal, Lloyd George forced on a coalition Government it was inevitable that he should be sacrificed. He did not complain of that—it was the fortune of war. What he did strongly resent was that he should be held responsible for errors which he had done his best to prevent and he longed for the day when he could publish the whole of the facts.

Since leaving the Admiralty, Churchill had continually pressed upon Balfour the need to accelerate the despatch of Monitors to the Dardanelles. His greatest faith lay in Monitors armed with 14-inch guns,

---

[1] Charles Prestwich Scott, 1846–1932. Editor of the *Manchester Guardian*, 1872–1929. Liberal MP, 1895–1906. A friend of Lloyd George, who often sought his advice.

which he believed would be able to force the Narrows without difficulty. While First Lord he had sent de Robeck two 14-inch-gun Monitors, believing that they would exert a decisive influence on the naval campaign. On September 29 Balfour asked Masterton-Smith to send Edward Marsh an extract from a letter he had received from de Robeck, commenting on the Monitors. 'Mr Balfour thinks that Winston should see the enclosed,' Masterton-Smith wrote to Marsh that day. The extract from the letter, which was undated, read:

Each class of monitor has her own particular trouble; 14″, the steering engines are too weak; 9·2″, the exhaust fumes in the funnel; 6″, weakness of decks under the guns; but they are mostly being successfully dealt with by 'Reliance', where Engineer-Captain Humphreys[1] is worth his weight in gold and never makes a difficulty.

We must not expect too much from these monitors, especially the 14″, which could not navigate the Dardanelles without tugs, so the question of forcing the Narrows with monitors is, I am afraid, for the present not a workable proposition.

This was depressing information, made all the more galling by Churchill's realization that Balfour had no intention of taking him into his confidence, and was content to use de Robeck's letter to increase his sense of isolation.

Churchill could not make up his mind whether to abandon politics or not. Asquith was contemplating setting up a smaller war policy group, and told Churchill that he would try to find a place on it for him. When he wrote to his brother on October 2, he was therefore more optimistic about his power to influence events. 'I am slowly gathering strength & influence in council,' he wrote, 'in spite of the sombre course of your Dardanelles operations. I shall do my best to see you through.' Churchill passed on one complaint which, 'if just', he felt should be put right, 'viz that the General is not enough seen by his troops on the mainland & remains a remote figure on an island'. The war overshadowed all other considerations. 'Alas, the world is getting vy grey,' he ended. 'Courage we shall not fail, but at every cost to this generation & to ourselves will conquer. Also I am sure we shall carry the Dardanelles to ultimate victory. Do not despair whatever happens, or let others do so. I wish I were with you so much. Here with full knowledge & now

[1] Henry Humphreys, 1864–1924. Entered Navy, 1884. Engineer-Captain, 1913. Served at the Dardanelles, 1915. Engineer Rear-Admiral, 1918. Knighted, 1919.

lots of time on my hands it is damnable. But for the present this is my post.'

There was little Churchill could do in his 'post' but write a series of lengthy memoranda and closely argued letters. On October 4 he sent Asquith a series of 'definite proposals for action' against Turkey through a new zone of attack, based either on Salonika or the Asiatic coast of Turkey. He feared that nothing would be done while Kitchener remained at the War Office, informing Asquith that in his opinion:

1. Kitchener shd command the British armies in France.
2. French shd command the British armies against the Turks.
3. A French General of proved reputation shd command the army operating with the Greeks & Serbians in the Balkan peninsula.

Churchill went on to warn Asquith of the danger of defeat unless new policies were adopted:

The time has clearly come when nothing but bold & drastic changes in persons and broad regroupings of armies in accordance with a coherent & positive plan will save the allies from disaster & probable defeat. We must first make up our own minds & then come to a complete agreement with the French Government. But every day that passes without a policy carries us nearer to a fatal conclusion.

I feel it my duty to write to you upon Lord Kitchener's position from another point of view which is also a vy grave one.

The experiment of putting a great soldier at the head of the War Office in time of war has not been advantageous. In the result we have neither a Minister responsible to Parliament nor a General making a plan. In spite of his splendid qualities wh in their proper sphere wd achieve success, we have suffered most terribly during the war from his control of the War Office. The composition of our new armies, the preparation of munitions, the strategic & professional advice at the disposal of the Cabinet are three salient examples. Nearly all our principal colleagues including those who have joined us from the Conservative party are convinced that the present arrangement is thoroughly bad: and you had yourself determined to change it as long ago as the formation of the Coalition. These are not times when one is at liberty to shrink from most disagreeable tasks, or when vital state policy can be conducted upon what is known to be an unsound foundation by all who are acquainted with the facts. I therefore feel bound, unpleasant though it is, to put my conviction plainly before you—being anxious to do my duty as I see it now. I urge you to revert to the intention you told me of when the new Government was formed and to put Lloyd George at the War Office as Secretary of State with the best & strongest general staff that can be found.

[Sir Douglas Haig[1] in spite of his feeble powers of speech is incontestably the most highly educated & intellectually gifted soldier we possess; & he has solid achievements in the field behind him. His science with Lloyd George's drive and penetrating insight wd make what] we now lack altogether—viz an efficient *composite* brain for war direction of military affairs.

In his draft Churchill then crossed out the passage in square brackets; later he decided to hold back these final three paragraphs altogether. His views were expressed with conviction, but he knew that they would not influence Asquith. He therefore concentrated upon more practical suggestions, writing to Asquith again on October 5 proposing four separate possible alternative attacks which, in the event, as then seemed likely, of Bulgaria invading Serbia, he believed should be examined and compared by the General Staff of the War Office:

(i) Entry into action on the left of the Greek Army. Objective: the Bulgarian Army, Sofia, & the railway communications between Austria & Turkey. Base Salonica.

(ii) Entry into action on the right of the Greek Army, ie the seaward flank. Objective: the Bulgarian Army, the Turkish Army in Thrace & the railway communications between Tirnova & Kuleli-Burgas. Bases: Salonica & Cavalla, & later Dedeagatch and Enos.

(iii) An operation detached from the Greek Army by direct landings at Dedeagatch & Enos. Objective: the Turkish Army in Thrace & the railway communications between Adrianople & Constantinople, & secondarily the land communications in Thrace with the Bulair Isthmus.

(iv) A landing on the Asiatic shore. Objective: Chanak, or some point on the Dardanelles, & the Turkish Army in the Gallipoli Peninsula.

Churchill found it galling to be making proposals for war against Bulgaria. He and Lloyd George had both believed, from the early days of the war, that of all the Balkan States, Bulgaria could most easily be brought into the Allied orbit. Such was his anger at what he regarded as a major failure of British diplomacy that on October 6 he circulated to the Cabinet a memorandum which he had written the previous July, insisting upon the need to win Bulgarian support. 'We must get Bulgaria now,' he had written; 'Bulgaria is strong, her army

[1] Douglas Haig, 1861–1928. Entered the Army, 1885. Knighted, 1909. Chief of Staff, India, 1909–11. Lieutenant-General, 1910. Commander of the 1st Army Corps, 1914–15. His successful defence of Ypres, 19 October–22 November 1914, made him a national figure. Commanded the 1st Army at Loos, November 1915. Succeeded Sir John French as Commander-in-Chief, British Expeditionary Force, 19 December 1915. Field-Marshal, 1917. Created Earl, 1919.

CHURCHILL'S FOUR-POINT PLAN OF ATTACK AGAINST
BULGARIA, 5 OCTOBER 1915

is ready.' But none of the territorial offers which Churchill had then
outlined in his memorandum to win Bulgaria had been offered, and
Bulgaria had turned to Germany for patronage. Churchill felt that the
Bulgarian failure was but a single example of overall neglect. In a bitter
covering note he lashed out at the Government for its inept war policy:

The enclosed memorandum was written by me in the middle of July. I
showed it to Curzon and Mr Lloyd George; but did not circulate it generally,
because I felt it would be useless then to add to the views I had already
expressed in Council. Since then, from the 6th to 9th August, the battle in
Gallipoli has been fought without success. This battle could have been

fought a month earlier if the decisions ultimately come to had been taken in time. The loss of a month enabled at least five fresh Turkish divisions to reach the Peninsula, and thus our reinforcements were countervailed before they arrived. On the 12th August Sir Ian Hamilton reported the failure of his attempt and asked for large reinforcements, and for drafts to raise his units to full strength. It is now the 6th October.

Nearly three months have passed since the plan of sending Allied troops to the Vardar [i.e. to Salonika] was favourably entertained by the Cabinet. But the four Powers were still corresponding on the point when the Bulgarian mobilisation occurred. Every suggestion made by any one of them has been pulled to pieces by the others; and the obvious remedy for this state of things, viz., that we should send a person of the highest consequence as an envoy to the Balkans—so often urged—was never adopted.

In July we were assured that the Germans were about to begin a great offensive in the west, and were actually concentrating large armies for that purpose in the neighbourhood of Cologne. So far from this being true, it is we who have taken the offensive. The wise decisions of the Calais conference were thrown to the winds by the generals. Our action in the Balkans and at Gallipoli has been paralysed at the very moment when it was most urgent and would have been most fruitful. It will soon be possible to measure what we have gained instead in France, and what those gains have cost in life and limb.

When the new Government was formed the belief was widely held that some form of national service would be introduced. More than $4\frac{1}{2}$ months have passed and the Cabinet has never yet ventured to discuss the subject. During the last two months our losses have greatly exceeded our recruiting, and the total of the British armies instead of growing has already begun rapidly to dwindle.

My object in now circulating this paper is not to make reproaches nor to boast superior foresight, but to implore my colleagues to rouse themselves to effective and energetic action before it is too late.

In a further memorandum written on October 6, entitled 'Gallipoli', Churchill tried to put his colleagues' minds at rest about reports of growing Turkish ammunition supplies reaching the Dardanelles. He believed that these reports were exaggerated, and that it was well within the Army's powers to deal with an increased artillery bombardment. He was particularly scathing at how little had been done on the Peninsula to meet such a contingency: 'Had the Germans held the positions we have been holding for all these months, a system of subterranean habitations, lighted by electric light, lined with concrete, and properly warmed and drained, would have been in existence.' Churchill believed that the prospects at Gallipoli were still hopeful, that the artillery danger was less than in the Ypres salient, 'where positions

subject to every military vice . . . have been held month after month
in spite of the fire of batteries incomparably heavier and more numerous, and far more abundantly supplied with ammunition . . .'. He felt
that the artillery danger would be reduced by the use of smoke screens,
and that, as the rains came, greater efforts should be made to trap and
conserve the water. Churchill did not prejudge the question of evacuation: 'Whether it is desirable to leave an army of these dimensions indefinitely to waste by fire and sickness on the Gallipoli Peninsula, without
hope of an offensive or any plan to relieve it, is another question. But if
it is decided to take that course, there is no reason at the present time
to doubt our ability to maintain ourselves, in spite of losses, for an
almost indefinite period.' Churchill ended his argument by warning
against allowing the artillery threat to dictate a premature policy of
withdrawal:

When dangers are a long way off and it is desired to emphasise the need
for immediate action, one is often led to speak of those dangers in exaggerated
and too sweeping terms. For instance, the approach of the submarine was
regarded by me with the utmost dread, and I had even gone so far as to
write that their arrival would be fatal. In fact, however, when the danger
came, it was successfully grappled with by the Admiralty and reduced to its
proper dimensions. The landing and supply of far larger armies on the
Gallipoli Peninsula has been successfully accomplished since the arrival of
the German submarines than we had ever attempted beforehand. Our own
resources grew with the resources of the enemy, and the warfare in this
theatre gets more thoroughly understood. We must not be in a hurry to yield
to the prospect of dangers and difficulties which, when stoutly confronted,
will not be found to contain any decisive element.

In his third letter to Asquith in three days, Churchill suggested on
October 6 that he and Lloyd George should be appointed as a special
sub-committee of the Committee of Imperial Defence, with Hankey
as their secretary, to report to the Dardanelles Committee about the
whole future of the Gallipoli operation. He feared that the War Office
was neglecting its duty to the troops on the Peninsula. 'Kitchener is far
too busy to make a special study of these things,' he wrote. 'Subordinates do not know what data to work on nor what weight to assign to
each part of them. I believe LG is seeking the truth on this point, &
although we approach it from different poles, I think we cd together
thrash it out thoroughly. You cannot do this in the War Council. What
is required is the patient canvassing & study of the whole case as presented by the soldiers, by 2 of us.' Churchill asked Asquith to propose

this arrangement when the Dardanelles Committee met on October 7. But Asquith refused to support it.

Churchill's desire to see a renewed naval attack had been stimulated by a letter which his brother-in-law, William Hozier[1] had sent him from Mudros on September 21. Hozier reported that 'it is the opinion of some senior officers here that a well organized attempt would meet with success in forcing the narrows'. Hozier then outlined a possible plan of attack, whereby 'the Bosphorus would be forced and a junction made with the Russian Fleet & Constantinople raised to the ground by half a dozen ships left for that purpose'. He argued that 'things so far have been half done & have therefore failed'. A renewed attempt, he declared, 'would be gladly welcomed out here. There is a feeling of despair at present owing to our helpless inactivity.'

On October 6 Churchill wrote to Balfour pleading for an examination of the possibility of a renewed naval attack, and telling him not to give too much weight to de Robeck's hesitations:

. . . You should not overlook the fact that Admiral de Robeck is deeply committed against this by what has taken place, and his resolution and courage which in other matters are beyond dispute, are in this case prejudiced by the line he has taken since the beginning. Could he have foreseen after the 18th the terrible course and vast expansion of the military operations, it is inconceivable that we would not have renewed the attack. But in those days the loss of four or five thousand men was the most expected and a swift victory was counted upon. Since then probably 150 thousand French and British troops have been killed or wounded on the Peninsula. The Admiral is therefore in a very difficult position. The naval attack is admittedly a great hazard. If it fails there is a heavy loss; if it succeeds he would be stultified. Is it not natural that in these circumstances his opposition to it should be deep-seated?

The Cabinet met that day. The discussion was dominated by Gallipoli. After heated arguments, Asquith agreed to set up a committee of naval and military experts[2] to examine, as a matter of extreme urgency, the respective merits of the western and Gallipoli fronts. The Committee sat throughout the weekend, and on Monday October 9 circulated its conclusion to the Cabinet, recommending that all military

---

[1] William Ogilvy Hozier, 1888–1921. Clementine Churchill's brother. Entered Navy, 1904. Lieutenant, 1909. Commanded the Torpedo Boat Destroyers *Thorn*, 1914–15, and *Nubian*, 1915. 1st Lieutenant on board the Cruiser *Edgar*, 1915–16. Commanded the *Clematis*, 1916–18. Lieutenant-Commander, 1917.

[2] The Committee consisted of members of the Admiralty and War Office Staffs headed by the First Sea Lord, Sir Henry Jackson, and the Director of Military Operations and Intelligence, Major-General Callwell.

effort should be concentrated on the western front. On that same Monday, events in the Balkans made this conclusion worthless. German and Austrian forces crossed the Danube and entered Belgrade. Serbia's days of independence seemed numbered. Two days later the Bulgarians abandoned their neutrality and mobilized their army on Serbia's eastern border. On October 11, the day of Bulgarian mobilization, the Dardanelles Committee met at 10 Downing Street. Bulgaria's action destroyed any lingering hopes that the unified Balkan States could be persuaded to join the Allied cause. With Bulgaria committed to the Central Powers, Turkey had little to fear of a stab in the back in Thrace or on the Gallipoli Peninsula. Greece had every reason to refuse to succumb to Allied blandishments. Rumania, flanked on all but her northern border by hostile powers, had even greater cause to cling to her neutrality. At the Dardanelles Committee Carson asked scathingly what the British forces were now supposed to do at Gallipoli: 'Was it to hold on and to prepare to resist the Bulgarians, Germans and Turks?' Grey suggested that whatever happened, Gallipoli must be evacuated: 'One way was to advance and carry the Peninsula, and then having saved our prestige, we might withdraw without danger. The second way was to evacuate the Peninsula whatever the cost.' Churchill asked 'whether we had the force' to capture the Gallipoli Peninsula; if not, he too favoured evacuation. But Kitchener was appalled at the thought of leaving the Gallipoli Peninsula:

LORD KITCHENER said . . . that abandonment would be the most disastrous event in the history of the Empire. We should lose about 25,000 men and many guns. He thought also that Egypt would not stand long. The troops along the canal would not be able to hold on; the Western borders were open to attack anywhere. He considered that the dangers of abandonment were, therefore, very grave, but he would like to liquidate the situation.

Carson wanted troops to be sent at once to help Serbia. Curzon was also anxious to help the Serbs, hoping that a rapid British decision might even then cause the Bulgarians to hesitate in their advance. The strongest plea for Serbia came from Lloyd George:

MR LLOYD GEORGE . . . wanted to know why the Roumanians and Greeks had hesitated so far. He thought it was the reputation we had gained for neglecting our Allies and friends. It was only necessary to look at Belgium, whose safety we had guaranteed, lying trampled on in the mud, and it seemed as if Serbia would be treated in the same way. He thought that if Great Britain abandoned Serbia, the whole of the East would point to the way she abandoned her friends, and that Germany was the country to be followed. He did not think that people who thought and said these things were to blame. It was a question of self-preservation for them. It seemed to him a very serious thing to abandon Serbia; it also seemed that it would be a great disaster to withdraw from Gallipoli, but at the same time if we made another effort there which failed, it would double the number of men we might lose.

The question turned upon how long it would take to send British troops to Salonika. Lloyd George spoke with passion that 'we had always been two or three weeks late for everything. . . . He thought that the Germans would have reached Gallipoli by the third week in November.' When Asquith pointed out that the Germans, too, might be late, Lloyd George replied, 'that it so happened that the Germans were not often late'.[1] Churchill said little during the long and acrimonious discussion which proceeded between Lloyd George and the Prime Minister. Curzon suggested a third alternative to the Salonika or Gallipoli plans, that Britain might 'come to terms with the Turks'. He thought that despite the British promise of Constantinople to Russia, 'we might guarantee the Young Turk Party the retention' of their capital. Curzon reminded his colleagues that the immense sacrifice made by the British on the Gallipoli Peninsula had been made 'partly on Russia's account' but that they had now come to such a stage 'that it was unavoidable that we should endeavour to make some arrangement with the Turks'. The discussion then veered away from the question of peace to the question of reinforcements. Towards the end of the discussion Churchill tried to focus his colleagues' attention upon the three points which he felt needed urgent decisions:

1. Whether to send an army to Salonica to help the Serbians.
2. Whether to send a force to Gallipoli.
3. Whether to abandon the whole proposition in Gallipoli.

Asquith, declaring that he 'was of an open mind', told his colleagues that two of these proposals seemed 'out of the question': to abandon Gallipoli, and to throw a body of troops into Serbia. The only conclusion that the Dardanelles Committee was able to reach was that 'a

---

[1] Two months after this outburst, speaking in the House of Commons on 20 December 1915, Lloyd George repeated this theme of 'too late' with great effect: 'Too late in moving here!' he declared. 'Too late in arriving there! Too late in coming to this decision! Too late in starting with enterprises! Too late in preparing! In this war the footsteps of the Allied forces have been dogged by the mocking spectre of "Too Late"; and unless we quicken our movements damnation will fall on the sacred cause for which so much gallant blood has flowed. I beg employers and workmen not to have "Too Late" inscribed upon the portals of their workshops!'

specially selected General' should proceed without delay to the Near East 'to consider and report as to which particular sphere and with what particular objective, we should direct our attention'. Lloyd George felt that Churchill had used unfair pressures to influence Asquith in favour of remaining on the Gallipoli Peninsula. 'He is sick with Churchill,' Frances Stevenson wrote in her diary that night, 'who will not acknowledge the futility of the Dardanelles campaign. He (Churchill) prevents the Prime Minister from facing the facts, too, by reminding him that he too is implicated in the campaign, & tells him that if the thing is acknowledged to be a failure, he (the PM) as well as Churchill will be blamed.'

On the following day Lloyd George told Frances Stevenson of a further attempt, in which he believed Churchill was implicated, to influence the Gallipoli policy by unfair means. The Dardanelles Committee of October 11 had been circulated a War Office General Staff memorandum which advocated sending a further 150,000 men to Gallipoli. But Frances Stevenson recorded in her diary on October 12 that 'Carson was told by a member of the General Staff that this plan was not approved by them, that it was not in the memorandum and that it must therefore have been inserted by the Prime Minister at the instigation of Churchill'.

Lord Esher recorded in his diary on the same day another version of the same story:

Last night, Lloyd George and Winston swooped down on Lord K with a telegram to Greece and Rumania that they were very anxious to send. The gist of the telegram was this, that if they would come in on the side of the Allies, we would send at once 150,000 men to Salonika. They then added the interesting information that we are giving 500,000 rifles to Russia, and that the Russians will be ready immediately to attack the Bulgarians. Lord K was tired, and would not struggle with them. They then went on to Asquith, and obtained his sanction.

Churchill persevered in the inconclusive daily discussions, in which he could only advise on policy, not initiate it. He believed that if he could argue clearly in favour of a particular course of action, his colleagues might be convinced. But throughout this period there were those who advised him to leave the Government. 'If you can not see your way clear to help the country in the capacity of a minister,' Frederick Guest had written to him on July 21, 'why not leave the Government and become its saviour as a free lance and a powerful patriot critic?' On October 10 Guest wrote again, asking him to consider four points that Lord Rothermere[1] had put to him on the telephone that morning:

1. That some sort of a collapse or fall of the Government will take place this week and that you will not only go down with it but will be irretrievably out of future business—
2. That you will be made the scapegoat for the failure of foreign diplomacy by being saddled with the Dardanelles from which (they will still say) all our Eastern troubles have come.—
3. That you have only 2 or 3 days in which to clear your self of all the misrepresentation that has been showered upon you—
4. That if you do so now & leave the Government on grounds of general mushiness & want of confidence in the War Office, that in less than 6 months you may be at the head of the state.

Guest believed that Rothermere's brother, Lord Northcliffe, shared these alarmist views. His letter continued:

It is not too late to break away now as the ship is not sinking actually—only it has a heavy list. Later on when things get much worse you perhaps could not do it—

I dont know why he thinks a collapse inevitable—He must know something to have rung me up here this morning.

To my mind the whole thing is pitiable, every body knows but no one will say & so I fear it will go on to the end. How unfair it is on all those gallant, trusting, men who hold the trenches and assault impossible places, that so much should be rotten behind them at home; and how uncomfortable must or should be the conscience of anyone who knows it & has the power to remedy & yet does not do so.!

Truth is indestructible & always wins eventually, nothing else matters now.

Churchill rejected this advice. He knew that Asquith was in no serious danger, and still hoped to influence the Cabinet from within.

Early on the morning of October 14 Bulgarian troops crossed into Serbia, advancing rapidly. When the Dardanelles Committee met at 10 Downing Street that day it discussed at length what Britain's reaction should be. The former British Military Attaché at Sofia,

[1] Harold Sidney Harmsworth, 1868–1940. Younger brother of Lord Northcliffe, with whom he had helped to establish the *Daily Mail* and *Evening News*. Created Baronet, 1912. Proprietor of the *Daily Mirror*, 1914. Created Baron Rothermere, 1914. Launched the *Sunday Pictorial*, 1915. Director-General of the Royal Army Clothing Factory, 1916. President of the Air Council, 1917–18. Created Viscount, 1919.

Colonel Napier,[1] proposed a landing of British troops at the Turkish port of Enos, from which they might, after by-passing the Turks, attack Bulgaria, a plan similar to one of those which Churchill had suggested to Asquith nine days before. Grey declared that in the Foreign Office's opinion, 'we were entitled to commence hostilities' against Bulgaria. Sir Henry Jackson, who had succeeded Fisher as First Sea Lord at the end of May, proposed a direct bombardment of the Bulgarian port of Dedeagatch. Kitchener stated that such a bombardment 'might be of some value'. Bonar Law felt we should bombard the Bulgarian port 'at once and show definitely that we were at war'. But Balfour said that he would prefer to let Russia take the lead against Bulgaria. Kitchener then proposed simultaneous action by Russia against Varna and by the British against Dedeagatch. No decision was reached.

Churchill only entered the Committee's discussion when Asquith raised the question of recalling Sir Ian Hamilton on the grounds that he 'had lost the confidence of the troops under him'. In a letter to Curzon on October 2 Churchill had opposed Hamilton's recall on the grounds that the failures at Gallipoli had been largely due to the 'unnecessary delays in supplying him with reinforcements . . . the failure to keep his units up to their proper strength by the supply of drafts, the poor quality of the troops sent him, the lack of any proper proportion of regular troops, and, lastly, the character of the subordinate Generals'. But by October 14 these considerations had been set aside, and no Minister was willing to insist that Hamilton be retained in his command. Churchill acknowledged that Hamilton had lost the confidence of his men, but intervened briefly on his friend's behalf:

MR CHURCHILL said that it must not be forgotten what appalling difficulties Sir I. Hamilton had had to contend with, in the task of landing a small army and maintaining himself in the face of the growing strength of the enemy. Though he had failed to retain confidence, he had never failed to plan the *coup* and to attempt what was demanded of him. The failure was partly due to inexperienced officers, to the fact that he had under him only one Regular division, and that he had been prevailed upon by his staff to keep aloof. He had made most strenuous efforts and Mr Churchill trusted that his recall would be effected without casting a slur on him.

It was decided to recall Hamilton from the Dardanelles. On October 16

[1] Henry Dundas Napier, 1864–1941. Entered Army, 1884. Military Attaché, Sofia and Belgrade, 1908–11. Lieutenant-Colonel, 1912. Military Attaché, Sofia, 1914; Bucharest, 1915. Captured by a German submarine in the Adriatic, 1915. Prisoner of war in Austria, 1915–16. Military Representative, Sofia, 1918.

he received his orders to return to England. He left the Dardanelles on the following day, handing over his command temporarily to Birdwood until his successor, Sir Charles Monro,[1] reached Mudros on October 28.

The discussion at the Dardanelles Committee of October 14 returned to the repeated question of what should be the next military development on the Gallipoli Peninsula. Churchill accused Kitchener of having done 'practically nothing' to send out the troops which the Dardanelles Committee had agreed to send. Kitchener protested 'that no time had been lost and that everything had been done except the actual despatch of troops'. He defended himself by explaining that he had 'asked Sir J. French to send off six divisions and two Indian divisions as soon as possible, and had asked General Joffre to take over the extent of line now held by the two southern British divisions as soon as his offensive was over. There had been no delay.'

Later in the discussion Churchill told his colleagues that 'he personally would not for a moment shrink from the evacuation of Gallipoli if he was certain that everything else had been tried'. Lloyd George believed that everything had been tried. 'The notion that we are satisfying the needs of this critical situation by making another attack on the Gallipoli Peninsula is, to my mind,' he wrote in a memorandum that evening, 'an insane one. We have failed repeatedly when the Turks were short of ammunition. Are we now to succeed when they are reinforced with heavy German guns and abundance of ammunition? It is by no means improbable that the Turks, thus re-equipped, might drive us into the sea before reinforcement ever reached our army on that Peninsula.' Churchill could not make up his mind as to whether Lloyd George's argument was entirely valid. On the following day, October 15, he drafted a lengthy memorandum dealing with the whole question of evacuation, pleading for a decision one way or the other:

Nothing leads more surely to disaster than that a military plan should be pursued with crippled steps and in a lukewarm spirit in the face of continual nagging within the executive circle. United ought not to mean that a number of gentlemen are willing to sit together on condition either that the evil day of decision is postponed, or that not more than a half-decision should be provisionally adopted. Even in politics such methods are unhealthy. In war they are a crime.

[1] Charles Carmichael Monro, 1860–1929. Entered Army, 1879. Lieutenant-General commanding the Third Army in France, 1915. Knighted, 1915. Commanded the Mediterranean Expeditionary Force, October 1915 to January 1916. Commanded the First Army in France, 1916. Commander-in-Chief, India, 1916–20. Created Baronet, 1921. Governor and Commander-in-Chief, Gibraltar, 1923–8.

There is no disgrace in honest and loyal decisions, however the incalculable event may subsequently fall. Even withdrawals and capitulations if they are necessary should not be flinched from. But there would be enduring shame in impeding a decision, in hampering military action when it is decided on, in denying a fair chance to a warlike enterprise to which the troops have been committed, or in so acting, even unconsciously and unintentionally, that an executive stalemate is maintained until disaster supervenes.

Every war decision must be forced to a clear-cut issue, and no thought of personal friendship or political unity can find any place in such a process. The soldiers who are ordered to their deaths have a right to a plan, as well as a cause.

I have done my utmost to co-operate with those who seek to bring effective aid to Serbia, and I believe that the gaining of Greece and Roumania to our side now is a more urgent and a more important objective than forcing the Dardanelles—would indeed, if attained, carry the Dardanelles with it. But whether this plan will succeed will be settled in a few days. Then we must make up our minds one way or the other about Gallipoli, without compromise of any kind.

Churchill's instinct remained in favour of continuing the attack at Gallipoli. He was concerned about the effect of withdrawal upon Russian morale, and Russia's ability to continue the war. 'The one great prize and reward which Russia can gain,' he wrote, 'is Constantinople. The surest means of re-equipping her, the one way of encouraging her efforts, is the opening of the Dardanelles and the Bosphorus. With the evacuation of the Gallipoli Peninsula that hope dies.' Churchill decided not to circulate this memorandum to his Cabinet colleagues. He knew that support for remaining at Gallipoli was waning. But in an attempt to influence one Liberal newspaper, the *Westminster Gazette*, he sent his memorandum to its editor, J. A. Spender.[1] But Spender was unimpressed, replying on October 18: 'The main point is that we failed with the August offensive . . . the war will be ended by killing Germans & in no other way.'

On October 20 Churchill circulated a further memorandum to the Dardanelles Committee pointing out that large German installations of poison gas had arrived at Constantinople. It was a matter of urgency, he wrote, 'to send out a complete new outfit of the latest [gas] helmets' to Gallipoli. He also argued in favour of the Allies themselves using poison gas against the Turks, a policy which had been opposed at the Dardanelles Committee on the grounds that the Turks, being Muslims,

---

[1] John Alfred Spender, 1862–1942. Editor of the *Westminster Gazette*, 1896–1922.

would find this method of warfare repellent. Churchill drew no distinction between Christians and Muslims. In his memorandum, he gave his reasons for wanting to extend the practice of the western front to Gallipoli.

I trust that the unreasonable prejudice against the use by us of gas upon the Turks will now cease. The massacres by the Turks of Armenians and the fact that practically no British prisoners have been taken on the Peninsula, though there are many thousands of missing, should surely remove all false sentiment on this point, indulged in as it is only at the expense of our own men. Large installations of British gas should be sent out without delay. The winter season is frequently marked by south-westerly gales, which would afford a perfect opportunity for the employment of gas by us.

During October Kitchener became the object of a sustained attack by those Ministers who were outraged at his apparent neglect of military policy, both at Gallipoli and on the western front. Conscription became the issue on which his opponents decided to challenge him. Kitchener had declared himself entirely opposed to any system of compulsion. His recruiting policy had relied for over a year on the personal appeal to the patriotic conscience of every able-bodied man with posters insisting: 'Your country needs YOU.' When the Cabinet had met on October 12, Kitchener had defended the adequacy of voluntary recruitment. Five Ministers had argued that the voluntary system was inadequate: Lansdowne, Curzon, Lloyd George, Walter Long and Churchill. 'Very odd position,' Hankey wrote in his diary after the Cabinet meeting, 'Churchill, Curzon, Selborne & the other conscriptionists, who have for a long time been attacking Lord K, are now basing a tremendous National Service push in the Cabinet on a Memo of Lord K's.' This memorandum was a survey by Kitchener of military needs, which he claimed proved his case, and which the advocates of conscription were convinced sustained theirs. On October 15 Margot Asquith wrote to Hankey warning him against a 'plot' led by Lloyd George, Churchill and Curzon:

Dearest Col Hankey,
    Does Arthur Balfour realize what is happening? It is clear as day that LlG, Curzon & Winston are going to try & wreck the Gov.
    . . . *Inside* we know LlG, Winston & Curzon—outside the same lot led by Northcliffe who loathes our Lib Gov—are they to break the Coalition??

Do be brave & go & see Balfour. Directly you get this & just say to him: 'You've read LlG's, & Winston's, & K's memorandums, it must be clear to you that things are rocking—if you don't support the PM & stand close to Grey, Crewe & the PM you play into the hands of LlG & Co.'

You are the only person who can do this—you shd also see K or Fitz-Gerald on this subject. . . .

Yours affectionately
MA

Three days later Margot Asquith wrote direct to Kitchener:

. . . Remember you, Henry, Grey, Crewe, Arthur Balfour, McKenna & Runciman can beat Curzon, F. E. Smith, Winston & Ll George if you show courage & above all do it at once. Get hold of them & talk it all out.

This is what I hear Curzon is going to do. He is going to bring it before the Cabinet backed by Ll George & Winston (the country campaign paid for & organised by Northcliffe). If the Cabinet go against them they threaten to resign. Now there is only one thing to do which is to make it quite clear to *everyone* what you & the Prime Minister wish over the question of conscription. If you wish it then LlG, Curzon & Co will have triumphed, it is for you to say to my husband 'There is no need in *my* mind for conscription now everything possible is being done & I will back you'. . . .

The Ministers who were challenging Kitchener's authority did so because they believed that he was no longer fit to hold a responsible position at the centre of Government policy. His secretiveness appalled them. Often, at meetings of the Dardanelles Committee, he took up contradictory positions almost simultaneously. He had a tendency of ascribing to his Generals opinions which they did not always hold. He was often reluctant to divulge important statistics, without which the Dardanelles Committee could not possibly form a clear opinion. He did not always seem to consult, or fully to understand, the telegrams which were arriving from the western and Gallipoli fronts. At the Cabinet meeting immediately after the German and Austrian armies had invaded Serbia, several Ministers had asked Kitchener whether the attacking force had actually crossed the Danube. Kitchener said that he had received no news. But when Asquith's secretary telephoned the War Office to ask if news had been received since Kitchener had left for the Cabinet, it emerged that the War Office had learned twenty hours previously that the Danube had been crossed. Carson wrote to Lloyd George across the Cabinet table: 'K does not read the telegrams —& we don't see them—it's intolerable.'

On October 12 Carson resigned, angered by Britain's failure to help Serbia, and convinced that Kitchener's tenure of the War Office was leading to disaster. But Carson's resignation did not precipitate the Government's collapse, nor were the conscriptionists able to use his resignation as a lever against Asquith. On October 5 Asquith had appointed Lord Derby[1] as Director of Recruiting, with instructions to find an alternative to compulsory service, and Derby's plan was ready by October 15. It completely undermined the position adopted by those who were trying to use Kitchener's faith in voluntary recruiting as a means of ousting him. Under the Derby scheme every man between the age of eighteen and forty-one was asked to 'attest'; that is, to pledge himself to volunteer when his 'class' was called for. There were two classes, single and married men, each class subdivided into twenty-three age groups. Kitchener believed that as a result of this scheme, the voluntary system which he so prized could be preserved, and would provide sufficient men to meet all the needs of war. His critics could not prevent the scheme from being given its chance, and Churchill had to acquiesce in something which he believed could not succeed.

Churchill was finding it increasingly difficult to obtain information from Kitchener which, as a member of the Dardanelles Committee, he needed in order to join in its discussions effectively. On October 19 he sent Kitchener a long and terse note asking for specific details which until then Kitchener had failed to provide, about the troops being sent to Salonika.[2] 'What operation does the General Staff advise?' Churchill ended curtly. Kitchener did not reply. When the Cabinet met on October 21 the atmosphere was tense. Asquith was unwell, and Crewe presided. It was felt by all present that the Dardanelles Committee was too large to be effective. The need for a series of rapid decisions on war policy demanded a much smaller group. After the Cabinet meeting, all the members of the Dardanelles Committee except Kitchener remained behind. They came to the conclusion that Kitchener was no longer fit to remain Secretary of State for War. On October 22 Churchill prepared an account of the discussion for Asquith. On reflection, he did not send it, but it expressed his angry feelings:

---

[1] Edward George Villiers Stanley, 1865–1948. Conservative MP, 1892–1906. Postmaster General, 1903–5. 17th Earl of Derby, 1908. Director-General of Recruiting, October 1915. Under-Secretary of State at the War Office, July–December 1916. Secretary of State for War, December 1916–18. Ambassador to France, 1918–20. Secretary of State for War, 1922–4.

[2] On October 5 an Anglo-French expedition had landed at Salonika. The French troops were commanded by General Sarrail, the British by Sir Bryan Mahon. The force advanced northwards towards the Bulgarian border, but by mid-December had been pushed back almost to Salonika.

My dear Asquith,

Crewe will have written to you about the opinion unanimously expressed in Cabinet yesterday that the executive conduct of the war shd be vested forthwith & publicly in a vy small committee of Ministers, & of our sincere wish that no personal claims or considerations shd stand in the way of this being done. After the Cabinet the members of the War Committee remained behind to settle some points left over from our morning meeting, & Mr Balfour then informed us that he could not serve upon a Committee so small as three because of Kitchener's unsuitability to the duties of Secretary of State for War. The reasons wh Mr Balfour gave were most serious & were not disputed by any one present. They are well known to you. They seem to me to apply with equal force to a Committee of five or six. There is no doubt whatever that the present Administration of the War Office does not command the confidence of any of your principal colleagues, & that a speedy change is required in the highest interests of the State. You were yourself of this opinion as far back as the date of the formation of the Coalition. You know how much the same feeling influenced Sir Edward Carson in his decision to resign. This is not a time when disagreeable duties must be flinched from. The peril to our cause & natural fortunes is grave in the extreme & does not permit us to build upon unsound foundations. There are no doubt other steps wh shd be taken, but all of these are of minor importance compared with this prime necessity viz a competent civilian Secretary of State for War responsible in a real sense to Parliament & sustained by the strongest General Staff wh can be formed.

Churchill felt so strongly that Kitchener ought to be removed that he had intended to end his letter by making his own Cabinet position dependent upon Kitchener's departure:

In these circumstances I feel it my duty to inform you that I for one cannot continue in the Government unless a change in the control of the War Office is made or is about to be made.

It is with the greatest sorrow on personal grounds that I shd take leave of you. Our close friendship has never been disturbed by the political stresses & storms of nearly ten years official work at your side & under your leadership. That friendship was specially prized by me because it revived the older one wh existed between you & my father. I am sure that the course to wh I now feel bound by the strongest sense of duty & wh I must pursue no matter at what cost to myself will not impair it. . . .

Yours always
Winston S.C.

Asquith refused to dismiss Kitchener, even on the recommendation of so many senior Ministers. He had no intention of leaving the War Office open for Lloyd George. Margot Asquith discussed the crisis with

Eric Drummond, her husband's former Private Secretary, and since May 1915 Secretary to Grey at the Foreign Office. Drummond wrote to her on November 1, setting out several points which he felt should be borne in mind, and suggesting that Asquith take over the War Office:

1. That K's position in the country is still quite inassailable. He may be a wooden idol but he is still worshipped, and if Lloyd George tries an attack on him even with Tory support, he will fail as badly as Northcliffe did. It follows from this that he can only be induced to leave the War Office entirely of his own free will and any idea of pressure is very dangerous. He can, I am afraid, almost dictate his own terms to the Cabinet and the Prime Minister must therefore keep his own side.

2. L.G. in War Office is fatal. He destroyed the Treasury and the Munitions office is chaos. The ideal solution is that he should have some job like the Duchy of Lancaster and be on the War Committee, where he would be of value because his brain is very fertile.

. . . I believe the best solution for the W.O. would be that the P.M. should take it over with Bob Cecil and Edwin Montagu under him—one for military and the other for financial questions. . . .

Asquith curbed the criticisms of Government inefficiency by announcing his intention to end the Dardanelles Committee almost at once, to set up in its place a small policy-making Committee of three—himself, and the heads of the two military Departments, Kitchener and Balfour. Balfour agreed to serve with Kitchener.

Once the Dardanelles Committee were no longer in existence, Churchill would lack all contact with war policy. In Cabinet he spoke openly of resignation. 'I hope you may still decide to stay,' Harcourt wrote to him during one Cabinet meeting. This was also the advice of the Conservative MP, Sir Edward Goulding,[1] a close friend of F. E. Smith, who wrote to him on October 24: 'You are wanted in England. Stick to your guns and remember your Father's great mistake.'[2] Carson's resignation, Goulding pointed out, was 'a failure—24 hrs talk & no permanent effect'. But Churchill was determined to go unless he could have fuller powers. Hankey thought up one job he might do, writing in his diary on the evening of October 22: 'Suggested to PM to send Winston Churchill to Russia to buck up communications of

[1] Edward Alfred Goulding, 1862–1936. Known as 'Paddy'. Conservative MP, 1895–1906; 1908–22. Created Baronet, June 1915. Created Baron Wargrave, 1922.

[2] Lord Randolph Henry Spencer-Churchill, 1849–95. Secretary of State for India, 1885–6. Appointed Chancellor of the Exchequer, June 1886. He resigned in December 1886 and received no further political office.

Archangel & Vladivostok for importation of rifles and munitions.' But nothing came of this suggestion.

For a week Churchill waited to see whether Asquith might offer him some worthwhile employment. No such offer was forthcoming. In the last week of October Churchill wrote a 1,400-word statement of his air policy when First Lord, as an answer to what he described as 'inaccurate or partial accounts' circulating; he was bitter that Balfour had not corrected these accounts. He believed that his work with the Royal Naval Air Service clearly showed his abilities, and that these should not now be discarded. 'When the whole story,' he wrote in his statement, 'of the wonderful creation in so short a space of time of an entirely new arm on the largest possible scale can be told, the country will not deny to those concerned in it the recognition and goodwill which are their due.' He sent the statement to Balfour for his comments. 'Mr Balfour has read the statement . . .' Masterton-Smith wrote to Edward Marsh on October 25, 'and has no objection whatever to Winston making any use of it he intends.' Churchill did nothing further with it. No appeal to history could help him to regain the influence he had lost in May. On October 25 Churchill wrote a further memorandum on the Dardanelles, pleading yet again for a renewed naval attack against the Narrows. 'Mere sentiment in regard to the loss of vessels,' he wrote, 'is exercising an altogether undue influence.' Failure at the Dardanelles, he concluded, 'may easily be the decisive struggle between England and Germany'. On October 27 Churchill sent Asquith, Kitchener and Balfour a 'most secret' seven-point proposal 'for recovering the initiative in the Near East'. He wanted an immediate advance against Turkey and Bulgaria by an Anglo-French force, reinforced by 150,000 Russians, armed by Britain with Japanese rifles. No other Cabinet minister sought either to champion or to contest Churchill's suggestions. On October 30, realizing he had no means of asserting his claims to take part in determining war policy, he wrote to Asquith resigning his office:

My dear Asquith,

I had hoped to see you yesterday, to tell you that our ten years work in office together must now end.

I agree with the principle of a war executive composed of the Prime Minister & the heads of the two Military Departments; but the change necessarily deprives me of rendering useful service.

After leaving the Admiralty five months ago I have only remained in the Government at your request in order to take part in the work of the War Council. It would not be right for me at this time to remain in a sinecure.

The views I have expressed on war policy are on record, and I have seen with deep regret the course which has been followed. Nor could I conscientiously accept responsibility without power. The long delays in coming to decisions have not been the only cause of our misfortunes. The faulty & lethargic execution and lack of scheme and combination over all military affairs, & of any effective concert with our Allies are evils wh will be not cured merely by the changes indicated in yr memorandum—good though these are in themselves.

I therefore take my leave of you not without many regrets on personal grounds but without any doubts. There is one point however on which it would perhaps be well for us to have a talk. It is now necessary for the truth to be made public about the initiation of the Dardanelles expedition.

Asquith had planned to make a policy statement to Parliament on November 2. On the grounds that this would include a full explanation of the Dardanelles, he persuaded Churchill to withhold his resignation at least until then. Churchill hoped that Asquith would rebut the charges that had been made against him. At the same time, Kitchener's removal was again the subject of much discussion, and this too might affect his decision. On November 1 Hankey recorded in his diary that Asquith told him 'that the Cabinet were unanimous that Lord K ought to leave War Office, principal reason being that he will not tell them the whole truth'. Asquith decided to ask Kitchener to go to the Near East as Commander-in-Chief of all British forces outside France. Kitchener refused. It was finally decided, by Asquith, Balfour and Kitchener himself, that Kitchener, while remaining Secretary of State for War, should go to Egypt and Gallipoli to report on the situation.

On the evening of November 1 Churchill telephoned Hankey and asked if he would come and see him, to help him draft a statement about the Dardanelles operation which Asquith could deliver in Parliament on the following day. 'He was in a very excited state,' Hankey recorded in his diary, 'and told me he had only stayed in the Government for this.' On November 2 Asquith made his statement to the House of Commons. In it he defended the Dardanelles operation in general terms. He did not use the material Churchill had provided, nor did he defend Churchill from the charges levelled against him. It was the removal of Kitchener, if only for a short while, which was Asquith's overriding worry. By sending him to the Dardanelles and Egypt, Asquith explained to Lloyd George on November 3, they were avoiding 'the immediate supersession of K as War Minister, while attaining the same result'.

Ministerial discussion centered upon the question of the evacuation of the Gallipoli Peninsula. The arguments were turning against any further effort to remain. On October 31 Sir Charles Monro, who had taken up his command at the Dardanelles three days previously, had telegraphed to Kitchener that he could see no military advantage in remaining on the Peninsula, and that steps ought to be taken to evacuate it.[1] 'It must be remembered,' he added, 'that the whole of the troops on the Peninsula have been very seriously affected in the matter of health, and that few of them could now be regarded as really strong men capable of great physical exertion.' On November 2 Monro had telegraphed again, at Kitchener's request. His advice was unchanged. 'The longer the troops remain on the Peninsula,' he asserted, 'the less efficient they will become.' Bonar Law, who was a leading advocate of immediate evacuation, wrote to Asquith on November 5 echoing these views. The Gallipoli positions, he wrote, were 'untenable' and the delay in reaching a decision which Kitchener's visit involved 'is in my opinion a fatal error'.

The Dardanelles Committee met for the last time on November 6. No conclusion was reached about Gallipoli, and the Committee's work was over. Churchill was excluded from its successor, the Cabinet War Committee. He realized that he could no longer exercise any influence upon war policy. That evening Hankey recorded in his diary a conversation with Balfour:

Winston Churchill had asked the PM to make him Governor-General and British Commander-in-Chief in British East Africa and had given him a scheme for attacking the Germans with armoured cars. He added that perhaps if he succeeded in this the military objections to his resigning a high post of command would disappear. All this tickled Mr Balfour so much that he positively pirouetted on one foot, looking very odd in his long frock coat, so that Masterton-Smith and I fairly roared with laughter.

On November 11 Asquith informed the King that a new Cabinet War Committee had been set up. It would have five members, not three: himself, Lloyd George, Balfour, Bonar Law and McKenna. Kitchener was not to be a member. He had left London on his special Cabinet mission to the Dardanelles, to report on whether or not the Gallipoli campaign should continue. There were no changes in the

---

[1] Churchill wrote scathingly of Monro in *The World Crisis*: 'General Monro was an officer of swift decision. He came, he saw, he capitulated.' Keyes recorded in his *Naval Memoirs* that Monro had told him that 'every man not employed in killing Germans in France and Flanders is wasted'.

composition of the Cabinet. That same day Churchill sent off his second and final letter of resignation:

My dear Asquith,

When I left the Admiralty five months ago, I accepted an office with few duties in order at your request to take part in the work of the War Council, and to assist new Ministers with the knowledge of current operations which I then possessed in a special degree. The counsels which I have offered are upon record in the minutes of the Committee of Imperial Defence, and in the memoranda I have circulated to the Cabinet: and I draw your attention at the present time to these.

I am in cordial agreement with the decision to form a small War Council [i.e. the Cabinet War Committee]. I appreciated the intention you expressed to me six weeks ago to include me among its members. I foresaw then the personal difficulties which you would have to face in its composition, and I make no complaint at all that your scheme should be changed. But with that change my work in the Government comes naturally to a close.

Knowing what I do about the present situation, and the instrument of executive power, I could not accept a position of general responsibility for war policy without any effective share in its guidance and control. Even when decisions of principle are rightly taken, the speed and method of their execution are factors which determine the result. Nor do I feel in times like these able to remain in well-paid inactivity. I therefore ask you to submit my resignation to the King. I am an officer, and I place myself unreservedly at the disposal of the military authorities, observing that my regiment is in France.

I have a clear conscience which enables me to bear my responsibility for past events with composure.

Time will vindicate my administration of the Admiralty, and assign me my due share in the vast series of preparations and operations which have secured us the command of the seas.

With much respect, and unaltered personal friendship, I bid you good-bye.

Yours very sincerely
Winston S. Churchill

Asquith accepted Churchill's resignation, replying on November 12:

My dear Churchill,

I hoped that you would reconsider your decision and regret to learn from your letter that you have not felt able to do so.

You have rendered services, both in Council and in Administration, which no one is better able to appreciate than myself, in regard to the conduct and direction of the war, and I am sincerely grieved that you should think it your duty to leave the Cabinet.

I am certain that you will continue to take an active and effective part in the prosecution of the war.

As you know well, on personal grounds I feel acutely the severance of our long association.

Yours always sincerely
H. H. Asquith

Churchill's letter of resignation and Asquith's reply were published in the newspapers on November 13. For the first time in ten years Churchill was without political office. He still hoped that he might be offered the command of the British forces fighting against the Germans in East Africa. Balfour had found the idea absurd, but it received support from an unexpected quarter. On November 12 Bonar Law wrote to Asquith:

I wish you would not definitely decide against Churchill going to East Africa without consulting some of your military advisers as to the wisdom of it. I suggest Callwell or Brade or both. I thought of Callwell, to whom of course I have not spoken on the subject, because he quite approved of trying to get Smuts[1] when K was against it.

I am certainly influenced by sympathy with W, but one of the things from all I hear about the operations in France, I feel most strongly is we are suffering from the want of brains in the higher commands; and if the responsibility were mine alone I think I should rather entrust East Africa to Churchill than to any officer whom we are likely to get.

As regards Parliamentary and Press criticism, it is I think true that, while the appointment would be attacked as a job, there is another strong stream of criticism against the incapacity of our generals, and this appointment could be defended on the ground of capacity. I spoke to Carson today about it and he thinks and would say in the House that though when he entered the Cabinet he had the strongest prejudice against Churchill he was so impressed by his ability that he would regard the giving of such an appointment to him as an indication that the Government were trying to make use of available ability and were not bound by red tape.

I only press this idea to the extent of asking you to find out how it would be regarded by some of your intelligent advisers at the WO.

News of the possibility of Churchill commanding in East Africa reached the Press. On November 14 the pilot Spenser Grey sent him

---

[1] Jan Christian Smuts, 1870–1950. Born in Cape Colony. General, commanding Boer Commando Forces, Cape Colony, 1901. Colonial Secretary, Transvaal, 1907. Minister of Defence, Union of South Africa, 1910–20. Second-in-command of the South African forces that defeated the Germans in South West Africa, July 1915. Honorary Lieutenant-General commanding the imperial forces in East Africa, 1916–17. South African Representative at the Imperial War Cabinet, 1917 and 1918. Prime Minister of South Africa, 1919–24. Minister of Justice, 1933–9. Prime Minister, 1939–48.

notes on a Royal Naval Air Service wing which could be set up in East Africa, and hoped that he would soon be serving under Churchill again. 'I imagine,' he wrote, 'and sincerely hope that you are not really going to Flanders as Major of your Regiment. It doesn't seem to offer you a very large scope for your energies.'

Asquith declined to give Churchill the East African appointment, which would undoubtedly have aroused Parliamentary criticism. The only opportunity open to Churchill for active service was therefore to go to France as a Major in the Queen's Own Oxfordshire Hussars. This he decided to do. Among the first letters which he received when his decision to go to France was known was one from Violet Asquith, who wrote from 10 Downing Street on November 13:

Dearest Winston,

... Fate has been very blind & very cruel—any day she may veer & change & show us a golden face again—but meanwhile you are going out to France—away from us all & away from the great theatre in which you have played so great a part—to an even greater arena—where perhaps an even greater rôle may await you. *I* trust your star—but star or no—it is a *splendid* thing to do—& for one who knows as you do what he has to offer the world— it is a very great thing to risk it all as you are doing. So fine a risk to take that I can't help rejoicing proudly that you should have done it—tho' I don't for a minute think you should have been allowed to. . . .

Goodbye dearest Winston & God bless you—come back to us very soon & remember that England trusts & needs you.

Always yrs
Violet

On November 15, following the custom of all resigning Ministers, Churchill made a personal statement in the House of Commons. 'No other Minister,' he stated, 'who does not hold a laborious office, and is not on the War Council, has been so closely connected as I have been with the conduct of the War for its first ten months.' He then spoke of each of the episodes for which he had been criticized during his Admiralty administration. 'I am not the cause of any withholding of papers from publication,' he pointed out. 'It is not in my interest that they are withheld.' Referring to Lord Fisher, Churchill told the House: 'I did not receive from the First Sea Lord either the clear guidance before the event or the firm support after which I was entitled to expect.' The essence of his criticism was that 'If the First Sea Lord had not approved the operations, if he believed they were unlikely to take the course that was expected of them, if he thought they would lead to undue losses, it was his duty to refuse consent. No one could have prevailed against such a refusal. The operation would never have been begun.' Later in his speech Churchill turned to strategic considerations:

All through this year I have offered the same counsel to the Government— undertake no operation in the West which is more costly to us in life than to the enemy; in the East, take Constantinople; take it by ships if you can; take it by soldiers if you must; take it by whichever plan, military or naval, commends itself to your military experts, but take it, and take it soon, and take it while time remains.

The situation is now entirely changed, and I am not called upon to offer any advice upon its new aspects. But it seems to me that if there were any operations in the history of the world which, having been begun, it was worth while to carry through with the utmost vigour and fury, with a consistent flow of reinforcements, and an utter disregard of life, it was the operations so daringly and brilliantly begun by Sir Ian Hamilton in the immortal landing of the 25th April.

Towards the end of his speech, Churchill reiterated the belief which he he had held since the start of the war, that the Allies must win in the end:

There is no reason to be discouraged about the progress of the War. We are passing through a bad time now, and it will probably be worse before it is better, but that it will be better, if we only endure and persevere, I have no doubt whatever. Sir, the old wars were decided by their episodes rather than by their tendencies. In this War the tendencies are far more important than the episodes. Without winning any sensational victories, we may win this War. We may win it even during a continuance of extremely disappointing and vexatious events. It is not necessary for us to win the War to push the German lines back over all the territory they have absorbed, or to pierce them. While the German lines extend far beyond their frontiers, while their flag flies over conquered capitals and subjugated provinces, while all the appearances of military successes attend their arms, Germany may be defeated more fatally in the second or third year of the War than if the Allied Armies had entered Berlin in the first.

Churchill ended with an appeal to the neutral States which still hesitated to decide whether or not to intervene in the conflict:

It is no doubt disconcerting for us to observe the Government of a State like Bulgaria convinced, on an impartial survey of the chances, that victory will rest with the Central Powers. Some of these small States are hypnotised by German military pomp and precision. They see the glitter, they see the episode; but what they do not see or realise is the capacity of the ancient and mighty nations against whom Germany is warring to endure adversity, to put up with disappointment and mismanagement, to recreate and renew their strength, to toil on with boundless obstinacy through boundless suffering to the achievement of the greatest cause for which men have fought.

Churchill knew that his vindication could not come until Asquith allowed the full story to be told. For over five months he had watched his influence slip away. As Chancellor of the Duchy there had not been a single opportunity for him to speak to Parliament. His resignation speech gave him the occasion to show the House once more his grasp of events. His sense of perspective was unimpaired; his confidence in the outcome clear. Perspective and confidence were two qualities which the House appreciated, and which it seldom received. But this was a speech of farewell. Nothing could be built upon it. Churchill won sympathy by it; but it could not retrieve his lost influence. Asquith gave a brief reply, before passing on to other business:

The House is always accustomed, and properly accustomed, to give great latitude, and even to expect great latitude, to explanations from a Minister of the Crown who has resigned his office, and my right hon Friend has taken advantage of that privilege in a manner which, I think, will be generally appreciated and admired.

I only wish to say two things. I think my right hon Friend has dealt with a very delicate situation not only with ability and eloquence, but also with loyalty and discretion. He has said one or two things which I tell him frankly I had rather he had not said, but, on the other hand, he has necessarily and naturally left unsaid some things which, when the complete estimate of all these transactions has to be taken, will have to be said. But that does not affect his personal position at all. . . .

I desire to say to him and of him, having been associated with him now for ten years in close and daily intimacy, in positions of great responsibility and in situations varied and of extreme difficulty and delicacy, I have always found him a wise counsellor, a brilliant colleague, and a faithful friend.

I am certain, Sir, he takes with him to the new duties which he is going to assume, having with great insistency abdicated those he has hitherto discharged, the universal goodwill, hopes, and confident expectations of this House and of all his colleagues.

During the debate that followed, a number of members referred to Churchill's resignation. Bonar Law spoke with evident sympathy:

I entered the Cabinet, to put it mildly, with no prejudice in favour of the right hon Gentleman. I have now been his colleague for five months. He has the defects of his qualities, and as his qualities are large the shadow which they throw is fairly large also, but I say deliberately, in my judgment, in mental power and vital force he is one of the foremost men in our country. . . .

He is a man still young who has had some little experience of the Army, and who is resuming his old profession. We know his capacity, and I for one trust that the Commander-in-Chief will find some means of utilising his great ability.

The Irish Nationalist MP, T. P. O'Connor,[1] declared that it was a 'national tragedy' to remove from the Government's counsels 'a man with such courage, genius and insight as my right hon Friend the Member for Dundee'. That night Frances Stevenson wrote in her diary: 'I am rather sorry for him, as it must be a terrible experience for one who has had so much power in his hands. But all the same I think he deserved it.'

During his speech Churchill had referred to the Dardanelles as 'a legitimate gamble'. This phrase horrified some MPs, and became the subject of continuing critical comment in the Press in later months. The phrase 'legitimate gamble' was frequently quoted by those who thought that he lacked moderation and shunned caution; for them his departure was acceptable, and indeed welcome.

On the morning following Churchill's speech, J. A. Spender, the editor of the *Westminster Gazette*, wrote to Lord Esher: 'Winston was less mischievous than was expected &, if the egotism can be pardoned, the performance was effective though essentially unfair to Jackie & the experts. It is all very well to say that "discussions were frequent & no adverse opinions were expressed", but we all know who discussed & what happened to the exponents of adverse opinions.'

Following his resignation, Churchill received a great number of letters of sympathy and encouragement. Most of them were from strangers. Sir Charles Coke,[2] who had commanded the British squadron on the coast of Ireland while Churchill was First Lord, wrote from his home in Exeter on November 13:

Two days ago I was returning from London, in the train was a young Flying officer who did not know I was an Admiral, he remarked 'Where

---

[1] Thomas Power O'Connor, 1848–1929, Irish Nationalist MP, 1885–1929. Journalist and biographer.

[2] Charles Henry Coke, 1854–1945. Entered Navy, 1868. Rear-Admiral, 1908. Knighted, 1911. Vice-Admiral commanding on the coast of Ireland, 1911–15.

would the Naval Flying Service have been but for Mr Churchill's energy &
foresight' & went on to say how the whole Naval Flying Corps owed you a
deep debt of gratitude; It is not often that I enter into conversation in the
train, but could not help cordially agreeing & remarked that—'Mr Churchill
not only deserved the gratitude of the RN Air Service, but that of the entire
service & the country, for his untiring efforts both before & after war was
declared'.

Lloyd George wrote on November 16:

Dear Winston,
    . . . Your speech yesterday was amazingly clever both in substance &
tone.
    Under the circumstances you are right to go. All the same it is a blunder—
a stupid blunder—to let you off. Here your special knowledge & gifts would
be invaluable. I cannot help thinking that you must soon return.
    In a hurry. Good luck to you.

                                            Yours sincerely
                                            D. Lloyd George

Violet Asquith, who had heard the speech, also wrote on November 16:

Dearest Winston,
    One line to say I thought your speech *quite* flawless—I have seldom been
more moved—It was a fine and generous speech—*How* thankful I am you
said what you did about that wicked old lunatic.
    Is there anything you *haven't* got for the Front? Compass? Luminous
wristwatch? Muffler & Tinderlighter? If there is any lacuna in your equipment let me fill it.
    Goodbye and good luck—God bless you—

                                            Yours
                                            Violet

Grey also wrote on November 13, expressing his own feeling about the
war. 'Your going is a great wrench,' he wrote, 'it adds to my hatred
of the war—I shall look back upon it if I survive it, as a time of horrible
memory. I hated it beforehand & I hate it now, though I do not see
how it could have been avoided. . . .'
    Churchill decided to go at once to join his regiment in France. He
knew that he would be made welcome in the Oxfordshire Hussars, and
that some position would be found for him in the regiment. On November 16 he gave a farewell luncheon at 41 Cromwell Road. Violet and

Margot Asquith, Gwendeline Churchill, Nellie Hozier[1] and Edward Marsh were among the guests. Violet Bonham Carter later recorded her impressions in *Winston Churchill As I Knew Him*:

Clemmie was admirably calm and brave, poor Eddie blinking back his tears, the rest of us trying to 'play up' and hide our leaden hearts. Winston alone was at his gayest and his best, and he and Margot held the table between them. . . .

For most of us it was a kind of wake. My heart ached for Clemmie, and Eddie was very pathetic. Winston was not unmindful of his plight and had asked my father to take him on as an extra Private Secretary as he could not bear to think of poor Eddie being plunged back into the bowels of the Colonial Office, sans personal function, sans friends, sans anything. So he was coming to us at No 10 to be put in charge of Civil List Pensions, which we hoped would make him feel a little less of a motherless child.

On the following evening Max Aitken called at 41 Cromwell Road. 'The whole household was upside down while the soldier-statesman was buckling on his sword,' he later wrote in *Politicians and the War*. 'Downstairs, Mr "Eddie" Marsh, his faithful secretary, was in tears. . . . Upstairs, Lady Randolph was in a state of despair at the idea of her brilliant son being relegated to the trenches. Mrs Churchill seemed to be the only person who remained calm, collected and efficient.' On the morning of Thursday November 18 Churchill crossed to France. That evening James Masterton-Smith, who had been his Naval Secretary throughout his three and a half years as First Lord, wrote to Clementine Churchill from the Admiralty:

It is half after ten of the clock and the shutters of the old familiar Private Office are just going up, but I cannot let this day pass without telling you that you no less than Winston have been much in the thoughts of many of us. Not even the high gods (whether their home be Fleet Street or Mount Olympus) can make things that have been as if they had never been, and to those of us who know and understand, Winston is the greatest First Lord this old Admiralty has ever had—or is likely to have.

With those of us who shared his life here he has left an inspiring memory of high courage and tireless industry, and he carries with him to Flanders all that we have to give him—our good wishes.

[1] Nellie Hozier, 1888–1957. Clementine Churchill's sister. Served as a nurse in Belgium, 1914. Captured by the Germans but released almost immediately. She married Colonel Bertram Romilly in 1915.

18

'The Escaped Scapegoat'

CHURCHILL crossed over to France on 18 November 1915 to join the Oxfordshire Hussars. No sooner had he reached Boulogne than higher authorities intervened, for Sir John French had sent a car to meet him, and take him to the General Headquarters of the British Expeditionary Force at St Omer. This summons was totally unexpected. On the way to GHQ Churchill persuaded the driver to take him to the Regimental Headquarters of the Oxfordshire Hussars at Bléquin, where he spent a few hours. That night he dined with the Commander-in-Chief at St Omer.

French suggested that Churchill should either become one of his ADC's at St Omer, or that he should take command of a Brigade. Churchill at once opted for the Brigade, and the Commander-in-Chief said he would arrange it as soon as he could. The offer of a Brigade meant much to Churchill. Here was the military responsibility for which he had often longed. Before accepting a Brigade, Churchill asked to have some experience of trench warfare, and suggested that if French could arrange it, he would like to have his training with the Guards. That night Churchill wrote to his wife:

> . . . I am staying tonight at GHQ in a fine chateau, with hot baths, beds, champagne & all the conveniences. Redmond[1] has been dining here—very agreeable, & admits I am absolutely right to leave the Govt. They are descending into the abyss. I am sure I am going to be entirely happy out here & at peace. I must try to win my way as a good & sincere soldier. But do not suppose I shall run any foolish risks or do anything wh is not obviously required.
>
> I will write to you again tomorrow my dearest pet as soon as my plans are finally settled.

[1] John Edward Redmond, 1851–1918. MP, 1881–1918. Chairman of the Irish Parliamentary Party at Westminster.

On November 19 Sir John French asked Lord Cavan,[1] the Commander of the Guards Division, to come to St Omer, and put Churchill's request to him. Cavan agreed that Churchill should have his training with the Grenadier Guards. During the day Churchill wrote to his brother, who was still at the Dardanelles, explaining why he had decided to abandon politics, which were still much on his mind:

My position at home since I left the Admiralty has been one of such responsibility without control & I have watched all these weary months folly, sloth & indecision ruining large conceptions. I have made up my mind not to return to any Govt during the war except with plenary & effective executive power: & this is a condition not likely to be satisfied. So I propose to do my utmost to win my way in the Army wh is my old profession & where as you know my heart has long been. . . .

I am extremely happy & have regained a peace of mind to wh I had long been a stranger.

On November 19 Churchill drove the twelve miles from St Omer to La Gorgue, the headquarters of the Guards Division, where he was introduced to the senior officers of the Division. He returned to St Omer for the night, writing to his wife:

Midnight
My dearest soul,
(this is what the gt d of Marlborough used to write from the low countries to his cat) All is vy well arranged . . . but as I do not know to wh battalion I am to be sent, I cannot tell the rota in wh we shall go into the trenches. But I do hope you will realise what a vy harmless thing this is. To my surprise I learn they only have about 15 killed & wounded each day out of 8,000 men exposed! It will make me vy sulky if I think you are allowing yourself to be made anxious by any risk like that. You wished me to write & tell you & therefore I do—to satisfy you, & not because I attach any importance to so ordinary & average an experience. I went this afternoon to see my regt: also my Brigadier.[2] They were caressing. They highly approved of my course of action & thought it vy right & proper. Altogether I see that the Army is

---

[1] Frederick Rudolph Lambart, 1865–1946. Entered Army, 1885. 10th Earl of Cavan, 1900. Major-General commanding the 4th (Guards) Brigade, September 1914–June 1915. Commanded the Guards Division, August 1915–January 1916. Commanded the XIV Corps in France and Italy, January 1916–18. Commander-in-Chief, Aldershot, 1920–2. Chief of the Imperial General Staff, 1922–6. Field-Marshal, 1932.

[2] Geoffrey Percy Thynne Feilding, 1866–1932. 2nd Lieutenant, Coldstream Guards, 1888. Lieutenant-Colonel, 1912. Wounded during retreat from Mons, October 1914. Brigadier-General commanding 1st (Guards) Brigade, August 1915–January 1916. Major-General commanding Guards Division, January 1916–October 1918. General Officer Commanding, London District, 1918–29. Knighted, 1919.

willing to receive me back as 'the prodigal son'. Anyhow I know what they think right, and mean to do it. . . .

I am vy happy here. I did not know what release from care meant. It is a blessed peace. How I ever cd have wasted so many months in impotent misery, wh might have been spent in war, I cannot tell.

In the intervals between going into the trenches I shall come back for hot baths etc to GHQ where I have been told to consider a place always open. French tells me he has written to you today. He is a good friend.

Always your loving husband

W

Sir John French's letter was brief but sympathetic:

Dear Mrs Churchill,

I am just sending a line to tell you that Winston has come out and that I am going to do all I can to help him. I want you to know that I will do all I can for him & to take care of him.

Forgive me for writing to you but I know how you must have felt parting with him and I am hoping this line may make you feel happier.

Yours very sincerely

J. French

Churchill spent the morning of November 20 at GHQ and then returned to La Gorgue for lunch with Lord Cavan, who told him that he had been attached to the 2nd Battalion of the Grenadier Guards, commanded by Lieutenant-Colonel Jeffreys.[1] The Battalion was to go into the line near Neuve Chapelle that afternoon. Churchill drove with Cavan to Jeffreys' headquarters. Most of the Battalion was already on its way to the front. Cavan returned to La Gorgue; Churchill set off with the officers of the Battalion's headquarter staff to the front. In *Thoughts and Adventures* he recalled:

It was a dull November afternoon, and an icy drizzle fell over the darkening plain. As we approached the line, the red flashes of the guns stabbed the sombre landscape on either side of the road, to the sound of an intermittent cannonade. We paced onwards for about an hour without a word being spoken on either side.

[1] George Darell Jeffreys, 1878–1960. Known as 'Ma'. 2nd Lieutenant, Grenadier Guards, 1897. Lieutenant-Colonel commanding the 2nd Battalion, Grenadier Guards, 1915. Commanded the 58th, 57th and 1st Guards Brigades, 1916–17, and the 19th Division, 1917–19. Major-General, 1919. Commanded London District, 1920–4. Knighted, 1924. General Officer Commanding-in-Chief, Southern Command, India, 1932–6. General, 1935. Created Baron, 1952. Colonel of the Grenadier Guards, 1952–60.

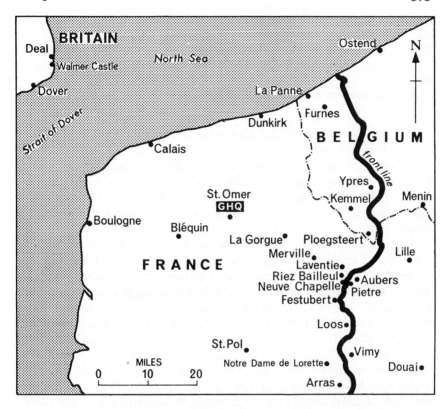

THE OSTEND TO ARRAS SECTOR OF THE WESTERN
FRONT, NOVEMBER AND DECEMBER 1915

Then the Colonel: 'I think I ought to tell you that we were not at all consulted in the matter of your coming to join us.'

I replied respectfully that I had had no idea myself which Battalion I was
to be sent to, but that I dared say it would be all right. Anyhow we must
make the best of it.

There was another prolonged silence.

Then the Adjutant:[1] 'I am afraid we have had to cut down your kit rather,
Major. There are no communication trenches here. We are doing all our

[1] Wilfred Russell Bailey, 1891–1948. 2nd Lieutenant, Grenadier Guards, 1911. Lieutenant,
2nd Battalion Grenadier Guards, October 1914; Adjutant, November 1914. Captain,
September 1915. Lieutenant-Colonel commanding the 1st Battalion, Grenadier Guards,
October 1918. Succeeded his father as 3rd Baron Glanusk, 1928. Commanded the Training
Battalion of the Welsh Guards, 1939–42. Colonel, 1942.

reliefs over the top. The men have little more than what they stand up in. We have found a servant for you, who is carrying a spare pair of socks and your shaving gear. We have had to leave the rest behind.'

I said that was quite all right and that I was sure I should be very comfortable.

We continued to progress in the same sombre silence.

The 2nd Battalion of the Grenadier Guards had suffered greatly during the first year of the war. Of the twenty-four officers of the Battalion who had fought in the first Battle of Ypres at the end of October 1914, eight had been killed and six wounded by the time the battle had ended in mid-November. When Churchill joined them a year later Jeffreys was almost the only surviving officer of the original band.

At dusk on the evening of November 20 the Battalion reached the front line. Battalion headquarters was situated in what Churchill described in *Thoughts and Adventures* as 'a pulverized ruin called Ebenezer Farm', behind whose broken walls a few sandbagged rooms had been constructed. He recalled that at dinner that night in Ebenezer Farm the officers drank 'strong tea with condensed milk', not a drink to which he was addicted; and that under Jeffreys' stern gaze there was little conversation: 'His subordinates evidently stood in the gravest awe of their Commanding Officer, and very few remarks were made except on topics which he himself initiated.' 'At about eight o'clock,' Churchill recalled, 'a dead Grenadier was brought in and laid out in the ruined farmhouse for burial next day.' When dinner was over, Churchill had to decide where to sleep. He was offered first a place in the signal office at Ebenezer Farm. On inspection, he found that the office was only eight feet square, stifling hot, and already 'occupied by four busy Morse signallers'. The only alternative was a rough dugout two hundred yards from the farm. This, he discovered, was 'a sort of pit four feet deep, containing about one foot of water'. He therefore decided to sleep in the signal office.

It was not a comfortable existence, even in a static line. For most of November the ground had been hard with frost. With each brief thaw, it was clogged up with mud and water. A surfeit of rats added to the discomfort.

'The trenches here have been damnably neglected by the troops whom we succeeded,' Churchill wrote to his wife on November 21, 'and the Guards are working hard to make the defences strong and safe.' He himself had been put to hard work. A young Machine Gun officer,

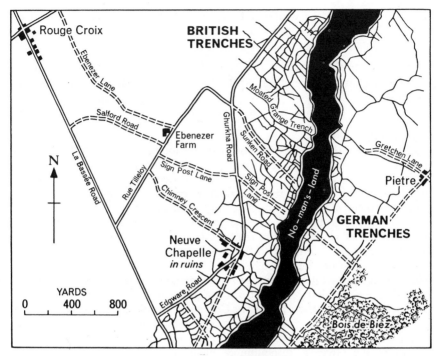

BRITISH AND GERMAN TRENCHES, NEUVE CHAPELLE
NOVEMBER AND DECEMBER 1915

Ralph Bingham,[1] later recorded, in a letter to the author, the impression
Churchill's arrival made on the Guards:

I was a MG officer in the 1st Guards Brigade MG Company. We were in
the front line near—I think—Laventie. It was winter and cold and wet; if I
remember rightly. Churchill came out to the front to learn the routine of trench
warfare, and was attached to the 2nd Bn Grenadier Guards for instruction.
As soon as they heard that Churchill was coming to them, they rubbed their
hands together and said 'By Jove we're getting one of those damned politicians to teach. We'll walk him off his so-and-so feet!' Which they did. They
walked poor Winston round and round the Trench system until he was
practically stone cold—it was a somewhat tiring job unless you were used

[1] Ralph Charles Bingham, 1885–   . Lieutenant, First Life Guards Reserve of Officers,
July 1914. Captain, Machine Gun Corps, October 1915. Wounded on the Somme, September
1916. Lieutenant-Colonel commanding 4th Battalion City of London Regiment, 1934–7.
Clerk of the Cheque and Adjutant of the Yeoman of the Guard, 1950–5.

to it—especially in the winter. Of course, the Grenadiers quickly got over their 'damned politician' point of view.

In his letter of November 21 Churchill gave his wife an account of his experiences in the trenches, and of the opinion he had formed of Jeffreys:

My darling,

Here I am in the line. Except for heavy cannonading the results of wh do not come near us, everything is vy quiet. A few men are hit now & again by stray bullets skimming over the trenches, or accurate sniping. But we are able to walk right into the trenches without crawling along a sap, & even in the fwd trenches of the front line there is gt tranquillity. We came in last night on a 48 hours spell, then 48 hours in support, & then into the front line again up to a total of 12 days at the end of wh we are entitled to 6 days rest in Divisional reserve. I am attd to the 2nd Battalion of the Grenadier Guards, wh once the gt d of Marlborough served in & commanded. I get on vy well with the officers—though they were rather suspicious at first—& all the generals are most civil & kind. I am not going to be in any hurry to leave this regt while it is in the 1 line, as its Colonel is one of the vy best in the army & his knowledge of trench warfare is complete & profound. All his comments and instructions to his men are pregnant with military wisdom; & the system of the Guards—discipline & hard work—must be seen at close quarters to be admired as it deserves. Altogether I look forward to an extremely profitable spell of education.

The conditions of life though hard are not unhealthy, & there is certainly nothing to complain about in them—except for cold feet. . . .

The artillery fire is dying away now as the light fades; & per contra there is a certain amount of maxim & rifle fire beginning. I am writing from a dugout a few hundred yards behind the trench where the Colonel & Adjutant are. . . .

Churchill appealed to his wife for supplies, sending her a numbered list of the things which he wanted her to despatch '*with the utmost speed*' to St Omer. The list was comprehensive:

1. A warm brown leather waistcoat.
2. A pair of trench wading boots. Brown leather bottom, & water proof canvas tops coming right up to the thigh.
3. A periscope (most important).
4. A sheepskin sleeping bag; that will either carry kit, or let me sleep in it. . . .
   In addition Please send me

5. 2 pairs of Khaki trousers (wh Messrs Tautz forgot to pack).
6. 1 pair of my brown buttoned boots.
7. 3 small face towels.
   Voila tout!
   Your little pillow is a boon & a pet.

Churchill's one night in the signal office at Ebenezer Farm had been enough for him. He had not come to the western front to listen to the noise of signallers tapping out their morse messages, or to partake of the restrained regime of a Battalion headquarters. He wanted to be where the action was, and decided to spend the next night in the trenches. Edward Grigg,[1] whom he had known before the war, was commanding the Battalion's Number One Company in a forward trench. Churchill asked Grigg if he could spend the night in his dugout. Grigg was delighted, as indeed was Churchill, for among the other contrasts with Ebenezer Farm, whisky was allowed in the forward trenches as a comfort in such cold conditions. Churchill spent the night of Sunday November 21 with Grigg's Company. 'This gives me the opportunity,' he wrote to his wife two days later, 'of seeing & learning thoroughly. It is not more dangerous than at battalion headquarters, because frequent walks to & from the trenches over an area where stray bullets are skimming are avoided.' But the front line was, he told her, 'a wild scene'; the trenches which Grigg's Company were holding had been built along the ruins of older trench lines taken from the Germans, and then built up again without too much care. A great deal of time was spent, Churchill wrote, 'cleaning everything up' and trying to strengthen the trenches and parapets. This was unpleasant work, made more difficult by increasing shelling and firing, by cold winds and intermittent snow. 'Filth & rubbish everywhere,' Churchill wrote to his wife, 'graves built into the defences & scattered about promiscuously, feet & clothing breaking through the soil, water & muck on all sides; & about this scene in the dazzling moonlight troops of enormous bats creep & glide, to the unceasing accompaniment of rifle & machine guns & the venomous whining & whirring of the bullets wh pass over head.' 'Amid these

---

[1] Edward William Macleay Grigg, 1879–1955. Editorial staff of *The Times*, 1903–5; 1908–13. Served in the Grenadier Guards, 1914–18. Military Secretary to the Prince of Wales, 1919. Knighted, 1920. Private Secretary to Lloyd George, 1921–2. National Liberal MP, 1922–5. Governor of Kenya, 1925–31. National Conservative MP, 1933–45. Parliamentary Secretary, Ministry of Information, 1939–40. Financial Secretary, War Office, 1940. Joint Parliamentary Under-Secretary of State for War, 1940–4. Minister Resident in the Middle East, 1944–5. Created Baron Altrincham, 1945. Editor of the *National Review*, 1948–55.

surroundings,' he continued, 'aided by wet & cold, & every minor discomfort, I have found happiness & content such as I have not known for many months.'

During Churchill's first forty-eight hours in the trenches, two men were killed and two wounded. There was spasmodic shelling and sniping. From both sides of no-man's-land snipers watched intently to catch the slightest movement, and to fire. The Battalion held a front seven hundred yards long, from Moated Grange Trench to Sign Post Lane. Between these two positions a maze of trenches nearly four hundred yards long transformed what had once been farmland into a sunken chaos of dugouts and strong points which gave the men whose task was to kill a brief and uncertain safety.

On the evening of November 22 the Battalion marched to its reserve billets at Bout Deville, three miles behind the line. On November 23 the Battalion's war diary recorded laconically: 'Wet and muddy. Poor billets.' Churchill sent his wife a fuller description of his new surroundings: 'We are near enough to hear rifle fire but out of range of everything except the artillery, wh will not be likely to bother about the cottages & farms in wh we are living. I have spent the morning on my toilet & a hot bath—engineered with some difficulty. . . .' He was becoming increasingly absorbed in Battalion life: 'I have lost all interest in the outer world and no longer worry about it or its stupid newspapers.' That afternoon he had been to see Asquith's son Raymond[1] who was in billets about six miles away. 'We had a pleasant talk & some tea,' Churchill told his wife; 'he is quite a soldier now, & much improved by the experience.' Returning to his Battalion's reserve billets, Churchill sent her his further reflections about the Guards:

I am making friends with the officers & the Colonel, and it is pleasant to see their original doubts & prejudices fading away. The discipline & organisation of their battalions are admirable. In spite of losses which have left scarcely a dozen of the original personnel remaining, and repeated refills from various sources, the tradition & the system of the Guards asserts itself in hard work, smartness & soldierly behaviour. It will always be a memorable experience to me to have served with them.

It was sixteen years since Churchill had submitted to the rigours of military cooking. Since then he had become accustomed to eating well. He had no intention of accepting army food without also trying to summon help from home. In his letter of November 22 he had asked his

[1] Raymond Asquith, 1878–1916. Asquith's eldest son. Called to the Bar, 1904. Lieutenant, Grenadier Guards, 1915–16. Killed in action, 18 September 1916.

wife to help satisfy his culinary demands: 'Will you send now regularly once a week a *small* box of food to supplement the rations. Sardines, chocolate, potted meats, and other things wh may strike your fancy. Begin as soon as possible.' This letter ended with a reflection on his new status: 'Do you realize what a vy important person a Major is? 99 people out of every 100 in this gt army have to touch their hats to me. With this inspiring reflection let me sign myself, Your loving & devoted husband, W.' In his postscript Churchill wrote: 'Kiss Randolph, Diana & that golden Sarah for me.'

In London the Cabinet had decided to evacuate the Gallipoli Peninsula. 'Personally I felt desperately depressed at this decision,' Hankey wrote in his diary on November 23. 'I believe it to be an entirely wrong one. Since Churchill left the Cabinet and the War Council we have lacked courage more than ever.'

On November 24, while still in reserve, Churchill wrote to his mother. It was the first personal letter he had written to her for some time. It marked a renewal of their correspondence, which had languished since his marriage seven years before. During his earlier army days he had found his mother's letters the principal source of that encouragement which he so much needed when cut off from the people who made up the world in which he moved. By his note to her he seemed to invite her once more to write to him as of old:

Dearest Mamma,

Clemmie will I am sure have shown you my letters to her, so that I only write a few lines by way of supplement.

I am vy happy here & have made good friends with everybody now. I always get on with soldiers, & these are about the finest.

I do not certainly regret the step I took. I am sure it was right from every point of view. Also I know I am doing the right thing out here. Mind you write to me & tell me all your news & what plans you are making with Clemmie & Goonie. Keep in touch with people who can be useful & are friendly.

With fondest love.

Your loving son
Winston

In his postscript Churchill wrote: 'Do you know I am quite young again.' Lady Randolph had not needed his letter in order to take up her pen. She not only wrote to her son frequently while he was at the front, sending him her strange blend of good cheer and gossip, but also began to busy herself on his behalf. In London she brought together at her dinner table a small group of politicians and friends who still believed that her son's true place was not in the trenches but in Parliament. On November 21 she wrote to him with news of Kitchener, who was still on his Cabinet mission to the Dardanelles, and with a favourable report of her son's resignation letter of November 11 and his House of Commons speech four days later. Only a week had passed since his last Parliamentary appearance:

My dearest Winston,

You venturesome fellow! But I might have known that 50 miles behind the firing line was not your particular style—I can understand that you want to study sur place this new phase of warfare. It is no use my saying 'be careful'. It is all in the hands of God—I can only pray & hope for the best. . . . I have no doubt you have found plenty of friends & they are making a fuss over you —but that was a certainty. . . .

They tell a story of K of K telegraphing that as his job was finished, he wd now return—but the whole Govt frantically looked for something else to keep him out there.

Clemmie will have told you of our arrangements for the moment. I am trying to let the house for 6 months or a year—I have some one coming to see it tomorrow but unless I let it for a certain sum it wd not repay me— Meanwhile until I do I propose to contribute towards the housekeeping at C Rd [Cromwell Road] as much as I can. I had tea there today with all the children—Great darlings.

While I have the house I mean now & then to have a dinner. Goonie is coming on Thursday & I have asked Bonar Law & George Curzon. I wish you were going to be here—it is like Hamlet without Hamlet. I will write to you how it all goes off.

Ld Ribblesdale[1] came to see me today. I reproached him for making a rash speech in the H of L—on the evacuation of Gallipoli. He thought yr letter & speech splendid & thought you were quite right to defend yrself and until yr speech he—like many others blamed you. . . .

I saw the Laverys today—I haven't seen as yet your chef d'oeuvre of Goonie. She tells me that Jack is now at Salonika. . . .

Best love—write to me sometimes & let me know if you want anything— or want me to find out anything—Bless you

Your loving
Mother

Lady Randolph's letters were enthusiastic and gossipy, but hardly gave Churchill the support he needed; it was his wife's letters that

[1] Thomas Lister, 1854–1925. 4th Baron Ribblesdale, 1876. Lord-in-Waiting to Queen Victoria, 1880–5. Master of the Queen's Buckhounds, 1892–5.

provided him with the information, advice and comfort upon which he depended, and helped to reduce his sense of isolation.

Writing from 41 Cromwell Road on November 21, Clementine Churchill sent an account of all she was thinking, and of the many things that she had done. 'I long for you to have a Brigade,' she wrote, '& yet not too soon for fear of partly dimming the "blaze of glory" in which you have left the country.' She reported that wherever she went, 'I find people awestruck at your sacrifice'. She was particularly worried that he was going into the trenches too quickly, and 'that you may get pneumonia or an internal chill unless you get gradually hardened'. At the end of the letter, above the sketch of a cat, she signed herself, 'your loving lonely Clemmie'. On the following day she wrote again, warning him that he must be inoculated '*as soon as possible* . . . as it would be terrible if you had typhoid or enteric'. Edward Marsh had lunched with her that day, and was, she wrote, 'much excited at your going with the Guards'. On November 23 she wrote again to say that she had received his second list of requirements, and had sent them all off 'with the exception (alas) of the trench wading boots. London seems to be emptied of these, but I am going to make a fresh try this morning & if I fail I shall send you pro tem a pair of rubber waders which they say is the next best thing.' It made her so miserable, she continued, to wake up at night and think of him shivering in the trenches. She also told him that his son Randolph wanted to buy a spade so that if a bomb fell on his father's trench he could dig himself out sideways.

Three days earlier Clementine Churchill had dined with her cousin Venetia Montagu. Everyone at the dinner, she continued, 'was thrilled at your having joined the Grenadiers'. Augustine Birrell,[1] who was present, 'was most sympathetic & has invited me to dine with him tonight which is I know a great honour as he does not ask many people'. She also reported that J. L. Garvin was dining that night with Lady Randolph, and that she herself was disappointed not to have been asked in time. Nevertheless, she had arranged to see Garvin soon at 41 Cromwell Road, to enlist his support for her husband's actions. She wrote also of a young soldier who had just returned from the front, and had told her sister Nellie Hozier 'that it was common knowledge that you had refused a Brigade & wished to go in the trenches'. The young man had told Nellie Hozier that 'everyone thought this splendid as the general expectation among the rank & file of officers was that you would join your regiment for a week or a fortnight; that you would then be put

[1] Augustine Birrell, 1850–1933. Liberal MP, 1889–1900; 1906–18. Chief Secretary to the Lord Lieutenant of Ireland, 1907–16.

on some staff while the regiment was given some interesting work & that you would then be given a Brigade'. Clementine Churchill's letter ended on a sad note, for this was the beginning of an unhappy time for her. 'My darling,' she wrote, 'I think of you constantly & I do hope that when you think of me, it is not a picture of a harsh arguing scold, but your loving & sad Clemmie. I love you very much more even that I thought I did—for Seven years you have filled my whole life & now I feel more than half my life has vanished across the channel. . . .' There had been many occasions during their seven years of marriage when Churchill and his wife had not been together. Churchill's work had often called him away from London. But this was the first time that they had been apart for any length of time. Both knew that they might never meet again.

On November 26 Churchill's career nearly came to an abrupt end. He had returned to the trenches the previous day, and was sitting in the headquarters dugout of No 1 Company with Edward Grigg eating some lunch, when an urgent message arrived from far behind the lines. It read: 'The Corps Commander wishes to see Major Churchill at four o'clock at Merville. A car will be waiting at the Rouge Croix crossroads at three fifteen.' The Corps Commander was Lieutenant-General Haking,[1] whom Churchill had known for many years. If he were to be appointed to the command of a Brigade, it might well be one under Haking's command. Churchill described what then happened in a letter to his wife on the following day:

. . . I thought it rather a strong order to bring me out of the trenches by daylight—a 3 miles walk across sopping fields on wh stray bullets are always falling, along tracks periodically shelled. But I assumed it was something important and anyhow I had no choice. So having made myself as clean as possible, I started off just as the enemy began to shell the roads & trenches in revenge for the shelling he had been receiving from our provocative and well fed artillery.

I just missed a whole bunch of shells wh fell on the track a hundred yards behind me; and arrived after an hour's walking, muddy wet & sweating at the rendezvous where I was to meet the motor. No motor! Presently a Staff

[1] Richard Cyril Byrne Haking, 1862–1945. Entered Army, 1881. Brigadier-General commanding the XI Corps, 1915–18. Knighted, 1916. Commanded British Military Mission to Russia and the Baltic Provinces, 1919. High Commissioner, League of Nations, Danzig, 1921–3. General Officer commanding the British troops in Egypt, 1923–7.

Colonel turned up—saying he had lost the motor wh had been driven off by shells. He added that the general had wanted to have a talk with me but that it was only about things in general & that another day wd do equally well. I said that I was obeying an order, that I regretted leaving the trenches at a moment when they were under bombardment, that if I was not wanted for any official duty I wd return at once. And this I did—another hour across the sopping fields now plunged in darkness. As I walked I cd see our trenches in the distance with great red brilliant shells flaring over them in fours & fives & cd hear the shriek of the projectiles rising like the sound of a storm. It looked fierce & formidable but by the time I got near silence had descended. You may imagine how I abused to myself the complacency of this General— though no doubt kindly meant—dragging me about in rain & wind for nothing.

I reached the trenches without mishap & then learned that a quarter of an hour after I had left, the dugout in wh I was living had been struck by a shell which burst a few feet from where I wd have been sitting; smashing the structure & killing the mess orderly who was inside. Another orderly and one officer who were inside were shaken & rattled, & all our effects buried in mud & debris. When I saw the ruin I was not so angry with the General after all.

My servant too was probably saved by the fact that I took him with me to carry my coat. Now see from this how vain it is to worry about things. It is all chance and our wayward footsteps are best planted without too much calculation. One must yield oneself simply & naturally to the mood of the game and trust in God wh is another way of saying the same thing.

These are commonplace experiences out here wh do not excite wonder or even interest. . . .

This near escape from death was one on which Churchill often reflected. 'In war,' he later wrote in *Thoughts and Adventures*, 'chance casts aside all veils and disguises and presents herself nakedly from moment to moment as the direct arbiter over all persons and events. . . . You may walk to the right or to the left of a particular tree, and it makes the difference whether you rise to command an Army Corps or are sent home crippled or paralysed for life.'

Churchill remained with the Guards for another four days. He spent a further forty-eight hours in the front line, exploring the trench system, learning how saps were constructed and parapets strengthened, gaining an impression of the power of snipers and the force of exploding shells, watching men under stress, and sharing their dangers. 'I continue to make friends with these Grenadiers,' he wrote to his wife on November 26, 'and really I have had no time to think of larger things than those I see.' He found himself drawn towards leniency and towards compassion. 'I keep watch during part of the night so that others may sleep. Last night I found a sentry asleep on his post. I frightened him dreadfully but did not charge him with the crime. He was only a lad, & I am not an officer of the regiment. The penalty is death or at least 2 years.' The hazards of war did not disturb him unduly. 'This morning we were shelled & I expect there will be more tonight,' he wrote to his wife on November 26. 'It has not caused me any sense of anxiety or apprehension, nor does the approach of a shell quicken my pulse, or try my nerves or make me about to bob as do so many. It is satisfactory to find that so many years of luxury have in no way impaired the tone of my system. At this game I hope I shall be as good as any.'

Churchill felt that he had learned a great deal in five days, and that his experiences would serve him well once he had been given a Brigade. 'I feel I understand the conditions and shall not be at sea if I take a command,' he wrote to his wife. 'Nothing but direct personal experience as a company officer cd have given me the knowledge. Few generals have drawn their water from this deep spring.' The Battalion marched to its reserve billets on the evening of November 26. In that brief period of holding the line two men had been killed outright, two had died of wounds and eight others had been wounded. The wintry conditions had not abated: 'Cold and raw with a little snow during the night,' the Battalion's war diarist had recorded on November 25. Writing from reserve billets at Riez Bailleul, Churchill tried to reassure his wife that he was not disturbed by his new surroundings: 'I do not mind the discomfort at all & do not think it will affect my health in any way. . . . I feel vy much master of myself & superior to the ordinary material considerations.' Two days later, on November 28, he wrote again:

. . . We came out of the line last night without mishap, & marched in under brilliant moonlight while the men sang 'Tipperary' & 'The Farmer's boy' and the guns boomed applause. It is like getting to a jolly good tavern after a long day's hunting, wet & cold & hungry, but not without having had sport. The discipline of this battalion is vy strict. For the slightest offence— a sulky word, a single crouch under the parapet at the wrong time, a small untidiness, men are sharply punished. But the results are good. The spirit is admirable. The men are better than most of the officers. The officers are quite up to the mark.

A total indifference to death or casualties prevails. What has to be done is done, & the losses accepted without fuss or comment. But for the fact that I ought to do what is most useful, I cd be quite content with a company in this fine regiment.

In reserve, Churchill had time to reflect, for the first time since he had left London, on politics, and on his own future. 'I do not feel the least revolt at the turn of events,' he had written to his wife in his letter of November 27. 'LG & McK [McKenna] & the old block [Asquith] are far away & look like mandarins of some remote province of China. If I survive the war, I shall have no difficulty in taking my place in the House of Commons & it must ever be a good one.' He had a number of commissions for her to carry out: 'Garvin, Scott, Rothermere & others shd be cultivated. They are loyal friends of quality & power. Keep in touch with the Government. Show complete confidence in our fortunes. Hold your head vy high. You always do.' There followed a more personal reflection: 'Above all don't be worried about me. If my destiny has not already been accomplished I shall be guarded surely. If it has been there is nothing that Randolph will need to be ashamed of in what I have done for the country.'

During his forty-eight hours in reserve, Churchill received a letter from Lord Lansdowne, who had written on November 20: 'If I had a regiment to rejoin I should very likely have followed your example, but having none I suppose I must remain where I am. It cannot be for long, and when you come back to political life you will find me—if still in any sense alive—beyond all doubt politically extinct.' Churchill replied on November 27, encouraging Lansdowne not to resign:

Your vy kind letter has just reached me on coming out of the trenches, & I take advantage of a day in support to answer it—& to thank you for it.

It was a gt pleasure to me to find that we were so often in agreement on the questions of the war; & I feel that you understood fully & to a large extent shared my point of view. I hope you will not think of leaving the Government. My position & commitments were quite different to those of any other Minister. I took pains to point this out when I spoke in Parliament. It wd be a cause of regret to many out here if you were to stand aside—without a reason of supreme importance. The only thing that really matters is to persevere obstinately in the war. For that you stand as the representative of the Conservative party more than any one else. Method & policy are quite subordinate to this.

I am being vy kindly received & treated by the soldiers, & am happy to be free from cares, serving in the line with the Grenadiers. Later on they may find something else for me to do, but it is only possible to learn the conditions of trench warfare by living under them.

This was the first political letter Churchill had written for over a week.

On November 28 Lord Cavan asked Churchill to lunch with him at his Headquarters at La Gorgue. 'He talked everything over quite freely,' Churchill wrote to his wife that night, '& invited me to do the same.'

Cavan told Churchill that it was no longer necessary for him to return to the trenches, that after a week's concentrated experience of the front line—most unusual for a man of his age—the time had come for him to remain at Brigade headquarters until he was appointed to command a Brigade of his own. But Churchill refused this offer. 'I said I wouldn't miss a day of it,' he wrote to his wife. 'Nor did I. I also scorned the modest comforts of Battalion HQ & lived in the wet & the mud with the men in the firing line. My physique is such that I support these conditions without the slightest ill effect. Of course I have seen vy little, but I have seen enough to be quite at my ease about all the ordinary things.'

On the night of November 28 the 2nd Battalion returned to the trenches. Once more Churchill slept in a front line dugout with Grigg's Company. 'A quiet night. Casualties one man slightly wounded,' the Battalion diarist reported. Very little happened throughout the next day, except rain. On the morning of November 30 there was more activity. It was Churchill's forty-first birthday. 'We had a good deal of shelling . . .' he wrote to his wife, '& for about 3 hours the trenches were under bombardment at about 2 shells a minute. I had a splendid view of the whole entertainment. Splinters & debris came vy close—*inches*—but we only had 2 men hurt in the company. They were all vy glad to be relieved however, & on our return celebrated my birthday with a most cheery dinner.'

The 2nd Battalion spent the next eight days in reserve billets at Merville. Churchill accepted Sir John French's invitation to return to St Omer as his guest.

Edward Grigg had found Churchill absorbed by army life. On December 2 he wrote to his mother:[1]

Winston was attached to the Company again for all the last period in the firing line. It was very cold and very wet—first a bitter frost, and then rain, sleet and thaw, which put us up to the calf in mud and slime. That part of the line is in bad order, too, and we had nothing but a small dug-out about 2 ft 6 high with a wet mud floor to live and sleep in, and we all got kinks in our spines getting in and out of the beastly thing. But Winston accepted the situation with great cheerfulness and we had quite a good time. He has forgotten his political legacy from Lord Randolph, and thinks much more, I am sure, of the military instincts which have descended to him from the great Duke of Marlborough. The result is that he is strictly amenable to discipline,

---

[1] Elizabeth Deas Thomson, 1836–1920. Married, 1870, Henry Grigg, Indian Civil Service, who died in 1895, aged 54.

and salutes the Commanding Officer as smartly as any of us when he comes round. It's a funny world.

Churchill reached St Omer on the evening of December 1. Lord Esher,[1] who arrived earlier on the same day, wrote in his diary that night that Churchill had amused the inhabitants of GHQ by referring to himself as 'the escaped scapegoat!'. The atmosphere at Sir John French's headquarters was tense. The Commander-in-Chief had just been recalled to London, and for several days those who believed themselves privy to the secrets of Government spoke openly of his imminent removal from his high command. 'Sir John is in a state of dégommé,' wrote Sir Henry Wilson in his diary on November 30. Both Wilson and Esher gave Churchill their views on the political situation, and were pleased to find someone new with whom they could exchange confidences. But Churchill was disturbed by all they told him. He had hoped to be able to forget politics and to become a soldier. Their information would not allow him to do so. Esher told Churchill about the latest situation on the Gallipoli Peninsula, recounting further details about the incident of which his mother had written; of how Kitchener, despatched to the East by the Cabinet in order to report personally on the situation, had returned precipitately to London, having first demanded and then opposed an end to the whole Gallipoli enterprise. London and Paris were buzzing with rumours of the imminent departure of the whole Allied force from the Gallipoli Peninsula. 'The idea of evacuating Gallipoli infuriates him,' Esher recorded in his diary, 'and he declares that if this is decided upon, he will go back to the House of Commons and denounce his colleagues. Of these, without exception, he has no great opinion. Apropos of the War Council, from which he was excluded, he said, "I was one of HM's servants, but not one of his upper servants." He has lost nothing by being in the trenches, not even his brilliant conversational powers.'

A day at St Omer surrounded by political talk wrenched Churchill's thoughts from parapets to politics. Not only the Gallipoli evacuation,

[1] Esher's status in France was obscure. 'Nobody knows what he does here exactly,' Northcliffe later wrote to Geoffrey Robinson from Paris, on 8 August 1916. 'The Ambassador does not know, and asked me. He is dressed as a colonel and wears the Grand Cross of the Legion of Honour all day long and probably all night too. He is always going backward and forward between Paris and the French G.H.Q., writes for the papers, sees everybody who comes to Paris directly they arrive, is mixed up with some very queer Jews, but is really, I believe, only a busybody. Still what he says, as the Americans say, "goes" among the French. His visiting card is a most extraordinary production; it is in French—"Le Vicomte Esher, Member of the War Council (or some such words), Governor of Windsor Castle, Commissioner of the Red Cross." There are about seven lines of it.'

but the difficulties on both the Salonika and Mesopotamian fronts upset him. He also learned of the appointment of Sir Horace Smith-Dorrien[1] to the East African command which he had so wanted. Two days later, on December 3, he wrote to his wife:

... The news I get here from the generals & Esher reveals a continuance of the same utter inability to take a decision on the part of the Government. What they settle one day is upset the next. Months have now passed in this condition: & now the great twin disasters at Gallipoli & Salonika are drawing near. The story when told, as told it shall be, will be incredible to the world: & the guilt of criminality attaches to those responsible. . . . There is I fear no doubt that the Baghdad operation has been heavily checked. There again 4 precious weeks were wasted making up the Cabinet mind after the victory of Kut-el-Amara.[2]

Kitchener returns after 25 days of futile banging about the Near East and making silly proposals. It seems likely that to get rid of him a large number of troops will be diverted to Egypt & locked up there. Old Smith-Dorrien for East Africa! Bravo Henry!

Rumour placed Churchill at the centre of many cabalistic combinations. A journalist, James Douglas, wrote to Fisher on December 2: 'I hear that Beresford & Carson are forming a "National" Party to provide an Opposition and an alternative Government. This is Churchill's pet scheme, and the idea is that he would come back and join the cabal. Churchill and Beresford would be a dangerous combination with Carson. May heaven preserve us from that!'

Churchill was not privy to such eccentric plots. On the morning of December 2 he rode with Sir Henry Wilson. 'We have made friends again after some serious differences in the past,' Churchill wrote to his wife on December 3. 'He was much impressed with my ideas & at his suggestion I have spent today embodying them in a paper. . . .' Wilson drew Churchill into talk of an anti-Asquith movement. 'I

---

[1] Horace Lockwood Smith-Dorrien, 1858–1930. Entered Army, 1876. Served on Lord Kitchener's Staff at Omdurman, 1898. Major-General, 1901. Knighted, 1904. General commanding the IInd Corps, 1914–15; the 2nd Army, 1915. Removed from his command by Sir John French, May 1915. Commanded the 1st Army for Home Defence, May–November 1915. Appointed to command the forces in East Africa, December 1915, but invalided home with pneumonia on reaching Cape Town. (The command was given to General Smuts.) Governor of Gibraltar, 1918–23.

[2] In July 1915 a British Expeditionary Force advanced from Basra towards Bagdad. Kut-el-Amara, 100 miles from Bagdad, was captured on September 29. Advancing to Ctesiphon, 13 miles from Bagdad, the Force was defeated on November 24, and retreated to Kut, having lost in killed or wounded over one-tenth of its men.

asked him why he did not go home, join forces with Milner[1] & Carson, & knock Squiff off his perch,' Wilson wrote in his diary on December 2: 'He was quite open about these things. He was going to wait for Gallipoli and Salonica disasters & then try to jump in.' This was an incomplete interpretation of Churchill's feelings. Although he was not averse to denouncing Asquith's conduct of the war should it seem to be leading to disaster, he did not believe that an outsider could ever overthrow a Prime Minister so well entrenched as Asquith. Only widespread popular revulsion with the war policy, based upon genuine concern, could lead, in his opinion, to effective political change, and tempt him home. Wide-ranging power, not partial involvement, was what he wanted, as he had explained to his brother two weeks before. Milner and Carson could not give him that. He therefore turned his attention to the mechanics of war.

The ideas which he had discussed with Wilson were centred upon his search for something to break the deadlock on the western front; preferably some mechanical means which would end the stalemate and offer swift victory, while at the same time reducing considerably the loss of life which trench warfare entailed. Churchill wrote down his ideas that evening and during most of the following day. He then had them typed out at GHQ in the form of a memorandum which he called 'Variants of the Offensive'. His memorandum examined methodically a series of possible attacks other than by the 'bare breasts of men'. His first proposal was for shields: 'For the specific object of protecting men from machine gun bullets during the short walk across from trench to trench *shields*[2] are indispensable.' These shields could be carried by single men 'or pushed by several men'; they would be 'lined along the parapet and picked up by the men on the signal to advance'. Churchill suggested the use of a collective shield, capable of covering between five and fifteen men, 'pushed along either on a wheel or still better on a Caterpillar'. This collective shield on Caterpillar tracks would be fifteen feet broad and four feet high. Faced in the direction of German machine-guns, which would fire at it in vain, the men behind it would complete any cutting of the German barbed wire which the artillery had failed to demolish. Churchill wanted five such composite

[1] Alfred Milner, 1854–1925. Under-Secretary for Finance, Egypt, 1889–92. Chairman of the Board of Inland Revenue, 1892–7. Knighted, 1895. High Commissioner for South Africa, 1897–1905. Created Baron, 1901. Created Viscount, 1902. Member of the War Cabinet, December 1916–18. Secretary of State for War, 1918–19; for the Colonies, 1919–21.

[2] In 1914 Sir Frederick Hamilton, the Second Sea Lord, designed a model steel screen 12 ft long by 6 ft high which would take six infantrymen abreast and give protection to at least twenty-five men as they advanced. On 2 January 1915 he wrote to Churchill: 'As I have been an advocate of this principle & have been trying to find any flaw in it for the last 20 years I make no apologies for indicating how I think they should be used.'

shields used in front of a Battalion during the attack, and 'slewed around to face the fire' forty or fifty yards in front of the attacking units.

Churchill suggested that some seventy shields should be completed before a single one was used in battle. Then they would be 'disposed secretly along the whole attacking front two or three hundred yards apart. Ten or fifteen minutes before the assault these engines should move forward over the best line of advance open, passing through or across our trenches at prepared points. They are capable of traversing any ordinary obstacle, ditch, breastwork or trench. They carry two or three maxims each and can be fitted with flame apparatus. Nothing but a direct hit from a field gun will stop them.'

The memorandum went on to examine what the Caterpillar could do once it reached the German wire; its tracks could turn to left or right, running parallel to the trench, sweeping its parapet with fire, crushing and cutting its barbed wire, and making the gaps through which 'the shield-bearing infantry will advance'. The Caterpillars could also be designed so that they could cross the trenches, climb slopes and, with armoured machine-guns on top of them, act as an offensive as well as a protective weapon. The Caterpillar trench-cutting and firing machine would be used suddenly and unexpectedly, but it should not be used alone. The collective shield and individual shields should be used simultaneously. While the Caterpillar machine was cutting the wire, individual soldiers would be at work with special wire-cutting implements. In a footnote to his memorandum Churchill commented:

In the dockyards one frequently sees men cutting steel plates with a jet of flame as if they were brown paper. Could not a rod be made which a soldier could carry with the necessary gas cylinder which would enable him to fuse *instantly* the wire in his front? If so, no invention would appear to be more urgently required.

Churchill also envisaged what he called 'the attack by the spade'. Instead of isolated saps pushed out in front of particular trench lines, the soldiers of several Battalions would dig, on a two- to three-mile front, some three hundred saps, dug simultaneously towards the enemy lines, and themselves interconnected. Once they reached within sixty yards of the enemy's parapet, they would be immune from his artillery.

Churchill discussed his ideas with all those within range. Having spent the morning riding with Sir Henry Wilson on December 2, he then drove out for lunch with his friend Jack Seely, at the headquarters of the Canadian Cavalry Division near Kemmel, and after the lunch, he, Seely and Seely's ADC Sir Archibald Sinclair examined the cavalry positions. That same night, back at St Omer, Valentine Fleming came to dinner, and once more Churchill expounded his ideas. Absorbing himself in these technical problems, Churchill did not let himself be over troubled by so much talk of politics. He had made up his mind to have no part in the schemes of those he met. 'I am jolly glad to be out of it,' he wrote to his wife on December 3. 'It has indeed distressed & unsettled me to come again for a few days into the area of secret information. The able soldiers there are miserable at the Government's drifting. Some urge me to return and try to break them up. I reply no—I will not go back unless I am wounded; or unless I have effective control.'

Clementine Churchill continued to write to her husband while he was at St Omer, comforting, advising and warning him as best she could. 'Poodle darling,' he had written to her on November 27, 'I love yr letters and it is a delightful thought to me that you are there at home with your 3 kittens thinking of me & feeling that I am doing right.' On November 28 she was still worried that he was 'staying longer in the trenches than your duty requires', and that he might suffer from having gone 'at one swoop from an atmosphere of hot rooms, sedentary work & Turkish baths to a life of the most cruel hardships & exposure'. She was worried too about how his reputation might be affected should his trench experiences end in disaster: 'If you were killed & you had over exposed yourself the world might think that you had sought death out of grief for your share in the Dardanelles. It is your duty to the country to try & live (consistent with your honour as a soldier).' She was disturbed by his description of the rats which swarmed everywhere in the front line. 'I should mind the rats even more than the bullets,' she wrote; 'Can you kill them or would that be wasting good ammunition?' She was also sad that 'for the first time for seven years besides being parted from you I am cut off from the stream of private news & have to rely upon the newspapers and *rumour*, so that I am in a state of suspended animation'. The only political news she could impart was on December 1, when she reported that 'Simon yesterday made a long attack on Northcliffe which would certainly have been very damaging if it had not been made by a prig and a bore'. Her principal pride was that he was on active service: 'Since you have re-become a soldier I look upon civilians of high or low degree with pity & indulgence. The wives of men over military age may be lucky but I am sorry for them being married to feeble & incompetent old men.'

These sturdy sentiments hid a deeper anguish. In her letter of November 28, which she hoped would reach him on his birthday, but which in fact arrived a day late, she wrote of how lonely she was without him. Not even their daughter Sarah, who looked so like him, could fill the gap caused by his absence. Nor could her fears be dispersed by his own self-confidence, or her forebodings by his optimism. It was a terrible time for her, uncertain, cold and overshadowed by the knowledge of the dangers of the front-line. Too many of their relations and friends were dead already, too much mutilation had occurred, too many lives made unbearable by sudden loss, for her to shake off the desperate fear which so many women had now to live with.

On November 30 Violet Asquith married Maurice Bonham Carter, her father's Private Secretary. To everyone's surprise, for they all believed that he was still in the eastern Mediterranean, Kitchener arrived to sign the register. The Churchills were also represented at the ceremony. Clementine Churchill reported the next day: 'Randolph officiated as one of the pages and looked *quite* beautiful in a little Russian velvet suit with fur. His looks made quite a sensation & at Downing Street afterwards he was surrounded & kissed & admired by dozens of lovely women.'

On November 27 Churchill's mother sent him a long account of her activities. She reported dinner gossip to the effect that Churchill had been offered the command of a Brigade, but had refused it; that she had dined with Garvin and Curzon on the previous Thursday; that she was trying to arrange a further dinner for Bonar Law and Balfour; that Curzon 'was full of you, he wants to write to you & I gave him yr address'. She also told her son that she was writing literary articles which brought her £50 a month, and that she would give all her earnings to her two daughters-in-law. She was concerned about her son's welfare. 'I am sending you a pair of oil silk stockings,' she wrote, 'to be worn sandwiched between two woolly ones. They say they keep yr feet at the same temperature as when you put on the stockings—*not* very healthy but better than frost bites. Let me know how they do and I will send you some more—I hope this will reach you in time for your birthday. . . .' Her faith in her son's future was unshaken:

Please be sensible. I think you ought to take the trenches in small doses after 10 years of a more or less sedentary life—But I am sure you won't 'play the fool'—remember you are destined for greater things than even in the past. I am a greater believer in your star—& I know that you are doing absolutely the right thing. We shall all of us 'hot up' your friends & keep the ball rolling. . . .

Churchill replied to his mother on December 1: 'The return of K delights me. What a world of shams it is! Well I am thank God only a spectator now, so I am better situated to see the humour of the play.' Of her offer to 'hot up' his friends, he wrote: 'You are quite right to keep in touch with our friends—also with our pseudo-friends. My attitude towards the Government is independent not hostile, & yr tone sh'd be salt not bitter.'

At the end of November Edward Marsh had written to Churchill reporting that a Duchy of Lancaster key was missing. 'Eddie dear,' Churchill replied on December 1, 'I have no split key—nor any key— except the key to heaven.' His letter continued: 'Tout va bien ici. I am now "resting" after 10 days in the line. I had a lot to live down with the Grenadiers, having been so long in the Government: but I parted from them this morning for two or three days as if from home. . . . You would enjoy yourself out here, if I could find you a coign. . . . Best love. Write sometimes.'

On December 3, Clementine Churchill received a visit at 41 Cromwell Road from General Bridges, who had just seen her husband at GHQ and spoke appreciatively of his military future. 'It is nectar to me,' she wrote after Bridges had gone, 'to feel & see generous admiration & appreciation of you, which for so long have been denied unjustly.' Her scorn for Asquith was undiminished. On December 3 she reported how, after Violet Asquith's wedding, she had been standing with Haldane in the hall at 10 Downing Street, when Asquith appeared: he merely 'muttered a few civil words & shuffled off sniffing nervously'. There was also family news from home. On December 4 her sister Nellie Hozier married Bertram Romilly.[1] On the previous day she had reported that 'Randolph, Diana and Johnny are terribly excited as they are to carry Nellie's train arrayed in white satin'. But there was sad news too. No family could escape the toll of war. Churchill's first cousin, Clare Sheridan,[2] had lost her husband,[3] and was distraught. Clementine Churchill wrote in anguish: 'My darling I don't know how one bears such things. I feel I could not weather such a blow. She has a beautiful little son 8 weeks old, but her poor "black puss" sleeps in Flanders. You *must* come back to me my dear one—(you are now my orange pug again . . .).'

[1] Bertram Henry Samuel Romilly, 1878–1940. 2nd Lieutenant, Scots Guards, 1898. Colonel, attached to the Egyptian Camel Corps, 1914–17. Military Governor, Province of Galilee, 1919–20. Chief Instructor, Cairo Military School, 1925–8.

[2] Clare Consuelo Frewen, 1885–1970. Sculptress.

[3] William Frederick Sheridan, 1879–1915. Known as Wilfred. Grandson of Richard Brinsley Sheridan. Businessman. Married Clare Frewen, 1910. 2nd Lieutenant, 11th London Regiment, September 1914. Captain, 2nd Rifle Brigade, 1915. Killed in action at the battle of Loos, 25 September 1915, five days after the birth of his son.

19

The Seven-day General

CHURCHILL spent December 3 at St Omer, confident that when Sir John French returned that evening he would be given a formal offer of higher military employment. He was relieved to have left the hostile atmosphere of London, but did not intend to neglect his few supporters. After he resigned, C. P. Scott had sent him a note of encouragement. 'It is something of a calamity,' Scott had written on December 1, 'that you should be lost to our politics at the time when they stand most in need of your qualities.' Churchill welcomed the *Manchester Guardian* as an ally. The *Observer* had been his most consistent supporter; to its editor, J. L. Garvin, Churchill wrote on December 4, telling him of Scott's letter and adding: 'I hope you will keep in touch with him. Two virtuous pens may save the nation. Who else is there?'

Like the others who had gathered at GHQ, Churchill was concerned to learn the future of Sir John French himself—for it was common knowledge at GHQ that the Commander-in-Chief no longer had the confidence of the Cabinet, and his dismissal was believed to be imminent. But when French returned to St Omer that Friday evening, he was still in command of the British forces in France. As such, he remained responsible for all promotion, and was Churchill's patron. That night Churchill dined at GHQ as the Commander-in-Chief's guest, and learned of what had passed in London. 'Asquith clearly wants him to go, & go without any kind of friction,' Churchill reported to his wife. 'French wants to stay but also to behave with dignity. Asquith has so left the case that French is free to stay & is all the time tortured by the sense of utter insecurity. For three weeks no one has thought of the enemy. 'Tis cruel. Anyhow I don't expect any immediate change.'

French pressed Churchill to accept a Brigade at once. He already had full confidence in Churchill's abilities to take one; but he also had a further reason for wanting to settle the matter quickly, knowing that within three weeks he would no longer be Commander-in-Chief. 'I have acquiesced,' Churchill wrote to his wife on December 4. It was now certain that in a week or two he would be a Brigadier-General. Meanwhile he decided to stay on at St Omer, to visit other sectors of the front, and to go into the line once more with the Grenadiers before taking up his command. In his letter of December 4 he continued:

. . . I have just got back from a vy long walk with French—talking about all things in heaven & earth. I am so sorry for him. No man can sustain two different kinds of separate worries—a tremendous army in the face of the enemy: a gnawing intrigue at the back. He seems to have told a good many people of my refusal of a Brigade and insistence on going to the trenches. He said the PM spoke with emotion about me. But Asquith's sentiments are always governed by his interests. They are vy hearty & warm within limits wh cost nothing.

While at St Omer Churchill had made friends with a young cavalry captain, Edward Louis Spiers,[1] whom he had first met before the war at the home of Venetia Stanley's sister, Sylvia Henley. Spiers, who was serving as liaison officer between GHQ and the French 10th Army, offered to take Churchill to the 10th Army's sector of the line in front of Arras on December 5. During the journey he was stimulated by Spiers' interest in him. The admiration of this young man, whose bravery Sir John French had praised, encouraged him to spill out his bitter thoughts about the Dardanelles, the conduct of the war and Grey's Balkan diplomacy. Spiers recorded in his diary that evening:

. . . WC talked of everything. . . . Failure in Aug in Gallipoli was due to our thinking one div was as good as another one—we were within a few 100 yards of the ridge which meant success & 16 or 17 Divs prisoners. Says Serbia was non accommodating & refused to give Bulgaria Bulgarian country even against heavy compensations elsewhere. Believes it is a war of men & therefore we must not lose men fighting Bulgaria etc. Told me we had achieved the impossible, i.e. a union between Bulgar & Turk with a fair chance of Greece chipping in against us as well. All due to our hesitations. Believes we ought to leave Salonika at once as news bad. . . . Thinks we will have

[1] Edward Louis Spiers, 1886– . Joined Kildare Militia, 1905. Captain, 11th Hussars, 1914. Four times wounded, 1914–15. Liaison officer with French 10th Army, 1915–16. Head of the British Military Mission to Paris, 1917–20. In 1918 he changed the spelling of his name to Spears. National Liberal MP, 1922–4; Conservative MP, 1931–45. Churchill's Personal Representative with French Prime Minister and Minister of Defence, May–June 1940. Head of British Mission to General de Gaulle, 1940. Head of Spears Mission to Syria and the Lebanon, 1941. First Minister to Syria and the Lebanon, 1942–4.

disasters in Serbia, Dardanelles & Bagdad—but we will win in end as ruin is better, so all England thinks, than a bad peace—and above all Russia has been given breathing space.

Churchill and Spiers reached the French front line at noon. 'I was received with much attention,' Churchill wrote to his wife that night, 'more so in fact than when I went as 1st Lord.' Spiers showed him round the battlefields where, in the fighting two months before, a hundred thousand men had been killed. Churchill wanted to set her mind at rest about the danger. The Germans, he wrote, 'considerately refrained from shelling as usual, & I was able to visit all the celebrated spots'. He was photographed, at the French General's[1] insistence, against a background of German prisoners, and for the photograph he wore a French steel helmet, which General Fayolle had given him. He kept the helmet, whose superior safety virtues he at once recognized. 'I have been given,' he told his wife, 'a true steel helmet by the French wh I am going to wear, as it looks so nice & will perhaps protect my valuable cranium.' The two men then drove off. Once again Churchill confided in Spiers, who recorded in his diary:

. . . On return journey WC said French spoke v highly of me to him. Said I was most gallant & able. He told me Sir John wd probably go & be replaced by Robertson. Sir J might get big job in London as adviser to the government. Meanwhile had offered WC a Brigade! WC said he wd prefer a Bn but Sir J advised him to take what he offered. WC consulted me & all things considered I advised a Bde—after all Seely has one. He then said he had asked Sir J for me as Bde Major!! Sir J said I had been wounded twice & [had no] right to expect more, further that I cd ill be spared. WC put the question to me. Well I said I was anxious enough to fight—& because it was put to me that it was a come down to accept, wd not say no. Flattered in a way but anxious & don't quite think it right.

Later that evening Spiers had further thoughts:

On thinking it over think it wd be absurd—a politician as Brigadier, a cavalryman as Bde Major! Poor Brigade. I know nothing of what wd be required, no details—& yet I wd practically have 6 Bns to command. . . .
WC has no doubts. Quietly spoke of it having been proposed he should command the force going to E. Africa.

<hr />

[1] Marie Emile Fayolle, 1852–1928. Entered the French Army, 1875. Professor, Ecole de Guerre, 1897–1907. General of Brigade, 1910. Commanded the 33rd Corps, 1915–16; the 6th Army, 1916–17; the Centre Group of Armies, 1917; the Group of Armies of Reserve, 1917–18; the French Occupation Forces on the Rhine, 1918–20. Marshal of France, 1921.

Although Sir John French had persuaded Churchill to bypass the humbler sphere of Battalion Commander, Clementine Churchill did not think this was a wise move. On December 6, as soon as she heard of the proposed promotion, she wrote to dissuade him:

> . . . I hope so much my Darling that you may *still* decide to take a battalion first, much as I long for you to be not so much in the trenches. I am absolutely certain that whoever is C in C, you will rise to high commands. I'm sure everyone feels that anything else would be wasting a valuable instrument. But everyone who *really* loves you & has your interest at heart wants you to go step by step whereas I notice the Downing Street tone is 'of course Winston will have a brigade in a fortnight'—Thus do they hope to ease their conscience from the wrong they have done you, and then hope to hear no more of you. I have the fear that if you are now suddenly given a brigade & Sir John shortly afterwards goes, you might perhaps stick there as his successor might feel stodgy & that enough has been done for you. Sir John loves you & wants *himself* to have the joy of doing something for you, but I believe in Lord Cavan's advice—you & he should make a very strong combination & if he gets a corps I feel sure you wld soon get a division under him. Do get a battalion *now* & a brigade later.

Churchill had already made up his mind to take a Brigade. While at St Omer he had talked several times to Sir John French about his future staff. He was determined to have Spiers as his Brigade Major, and Sinclair as his ADC. The Commander-in-Chief argued that Spiers might not think Brigade Major a promotion. But on December 6 Churchill wrote to his wife that 'Spiers yesterday of his own initiative asked me to let him come to me in any command I obtained: & if they will let him go I shall certainly get him'. On December 7 Sir John French was in Paris. There was still no definite news of Churchill's promotion. 'General Instability is in command,' Churchill wrote to his wife on December 8. He had decided to spend another day with Spiers, and on December 7 they had gone to La Panne on the Belgian coast, to see the extreme sea-flank of the Allied line. During the drive they had discussed a variety of topics. Spiers recorded in his diary that night:

> Met W Churchill at C in C's house at 8. W angry at my own car being late. Set off in one of C in C's Rolls Royces to La Panne. Lovely day & pleasant run. Told WC of my lack of experience as a Bde Major, of how important it was etc. He poo-hooed the idea—if it comes off & I fail he was warned.
> We talked literature. Mostly French & politics—I made out a case for the house of Lords & he downed it—no agreement reached. He said some fine

things about democracies, their answer to finer calls. Talk on religion—told him my views & he his—he believes he is a spirit which will live, without memory of the present, in the future.

When they reached La Panne, Churchill and Spiers were met by General Bridges, who took them to see the trenches running down to the sea. On returning from the coast Churchill and Spiers visited Maxine Elliot,[1] Churchill's friend of many years, who was supervising a reception centre for Belgian refugees from a barge which she had made her headquarters and her home. Spiers was fascinated by this diversion from the rigours of military life. 'Tea with Maxine Elliot on her barge,' Spiers wrote in his diary, 'nice clever woman, must have been v beautiful. . . . Played 3 handed bridge. WC lost 20 f & I 11 f. WC v entertaining. Full of stories. Has one for every event. Dwelt on his cleverness in leaving Cabinet when they meant to sacrifice him & before the disasters he foretells occur—Salonika, Dardanelles & Bagdad.' Churchill had greatly enjoyed the visit. 'Such a jolly place,' he wrote to his wife, '& Spiers after so many months of war weariness & danger found it quite hard to climb the ladder wh led out into the night. . . . Maxine was absolutely alone—& vy lonely. She has done good work & is a really fine woman—tho' she must be judged by special standards.'

Churchill and Spiers drove back to St Omer. 'I like him vy much,' Churchill told his wife, '& he is entirely captivated.' In Spiers, Churchill found something that he greatly needed; someone who would listen to his plans without trying to denigrate them; someone who would be excited to hear of what he had done as First Lord, and would not belittle the things which he believed were achievements; someone who could give him the affection which he so needed at this moment of uncertainty and loneliness. It had been a tiring day; but throughout the return journey Churchill continued to tell Spiers of the plans and stratagems which he had devised when he was First Lord:

. . . WC said when we got to sea we shd have understood we had turned G's flank. Clever. Said we shd have forced Holland in at beginning & landed troops there. Said it had been thought of landing at Borkum & making naval & submarine base there to watch G fleet, our short range submarines wd then have come in & 1 Div wd have been landed forcing enemy to garrison whole coast & forced G fleet to fight. Forgets Borkum within range of land & water shelling. Wd be true of Heligoland but disastrous there. Said we

[1] Jessie Dermot, 1868–1940. Born in Maine, USA. She adopted the name 'Maxine Elliot' for her stage career. In 1914 she organized a Belgian Relief Barge, from which, in fifteen months, she fed and clothed some 350,000 refugees.

cd then have put a few big ships in Baltic not to fight a fleet but destroy units & joining hand with Russians. Spoke of torpedoes fired from seaplanes.

Late that night Churchill and Spiers reached St Omer, but the day was not over. For some while Lord Curzon had been pestering Clementine Churchill about the apparent non-arrival of a letter which he had sent Churchill on November 30, together with some apparently indiscreet enclosures. When she had told him that there was nothing in her husband's letters to indicate he had received it, Curzon was alarmed, and afraid that it had been intercepted by the military censor, a serious matter, as it contained an account of the Government's dilemma over the evacuation of Gallipoli. But the letter was not lost. On returning to GHQ with Spiers, Churchill found it waiting for him.

In the letter, which Churchill opened in front of Spiers, Curzon revealed a number of disturbing and extraordinary things: that the Cabinet had been divided by the issue of whether or not to evacuate the Gallipoli Peninsula; that a serious political crisis threatened; that Asquith had favoured evacuation; that Curzon had led the protest against it; that Lansdowne, Selborne and Crewe had supported Curzon; that a forceful report had been circulated to the Cabinet from Admiral Wemyss in which he insisted that a further naval attack, on the scale of that of 18 March 1915, could turn the balance in favour of a combined military and naval victory. Curzon reported that Bonar Law, 'who with Lloyd George is the leader of the Scuttle', had demanded immediate evacuation. But that the combined influence of Lansdowne, Selborne, Crewe and Curzon had forced Asquith to give a pledge of a week's delay before any decision was reached. Curzon believed that this delay, though short, was 'a powerful factor operating against abandonment'. But he also told Churchill that 'B. Law and Ll George will fight to the finish'. Of Balfour's attitude he wrote with acerbity: 'Balfour is as usual an inscrutable factor, sitting silent and detached as though he were a spectator on Mars, observing through a powerful telescope a fight between the astral inhabitants of Saturn.' Most extraordinary of all, according to Curzon, were Kitchener's antics:

. . . A new and uncertain factor has been introduced on to the scene by the reappearance of Kitchener. It now transpires that he took away with him the Seals of Office, apprehending that they would be taken in his absence and transferred to Ll George! He is said to have scented a conspiracy against him and to have returned deliberately in order to defeat it. The most pathetic telegrams were sent to him by the PM pointing out how urgently his services were required to steady Egypt and straighten out Salonica or inspire some third place. But he always managed to receive these telegrams just too late to act upon them. And after a characteristic tour in which he hobnobbed with the various warrior kings and was cheered at the Continental railway stations, he reappeared last night, just in time to sign the register at Violet Asquith's wedding today.

His telegrams from the Aegean were almost fatuous, being contradictory, unbalanced and destitute of grasp or foresight. Starting from pronouncements against evacuation, he then wobbled, proposed a great Alexandretta move, and when this was refused became obsessed with an Egyptian nightmare, under the stress of which he came down on the side of evacuation at Gallipoli. I expect, if he were sent back again to carry it out, he would sing to a different tune. In the meantime his friends (or is it his enemies?) say that he is conscious that his days as S of S are numbered, and is resolved on getting out, through the Viceroyalty of India. Asquith took advantage of his absence to appoint Smith Dorrien to British E. Africa, and to hand over the remaining ordnance departments to Ll George [as Minister of Munitions], which I do not suppose will have sweetened his temper. . . .

Curzon ended his letter on an expectant note, hinting at Churchill's return to politics: 'I miss you very much—and so I am sure do many others. For as regards the Dardanelles I have only caught your mantle, as it fell from the fiery car of Elisha; and as regards Compulsion—we shall stand in urgent need of your advocacy and alliance.' This was the first time since Churchill's departure that a colleague had implied that there was still a place for him at the centre of political discussions. His first instinct was to return at once. Spiers, to whom he showed Curzon's letter and read Wemyss' report, was astonished at Churchill's reaction. 'Seemed furious,' he wrote in his diary, '. . . said things were moving fast and he might have to go to London.' But when morning came Churchill was less certain that his opportunity had come. He was thrilled that Wemyss had advocated a renewed naval attack, which he himself had always believed could be decisive. But he did not see how his personal position could really be rescued by his return. That evening he wrote to his wife:

. . . It wd not have been any good my joining in these discussions. A fresh uncompromised champion like Curzon had a better chance than I cd ever have had: & he has started the case as well as I cd have done. Please lock up all these papers after reading them, & never say you have seen them. Also keep in touch with Curzon & others. Don't fail to keep the threads in yr fingers. Let me know who you see. Curzon's letter & enclosures have of course revived distressing thoughts. My scorn for Kitchener is intense. If they evacuate in disaster—all the facts shall come out. They will be incredible to the world. The reckoning will be heavy & I shall make sure it is exacted.

Churchill knew that there was no part for him in the renewed Gallipoli discussions. All he could do was to try to encourage Curzon to persevere, and to rehearse his own reasons for remaining in France, writing to him on December 8:

My dear George,

I have read yr papers (wh reached me last night only) & as you may imagine with deep emotion. You have fought a splendid fight, & coming into it fresh & uncompromised, were better armed than I cd ever have been. I am absolutely content with your advocacy & do not desire to add or alter a word. By now I expect the decision will have been taken; but yr story breaks off at the climax & I must wait for the sequel.

The situation is no longer capable of the good solutions wh were open some months ago: but I do not think the right decisions wd be difficult, if any one had the necessary authority. Broadly speaking my views are yours: withdraw from Salonica: hold on at Gallipoli: use the Salonica and Egyptian forces to renew the attack by land both at Suvla & on the Asiatic side at the earliest moment, in conjunction with a resolute effort by the Fleet. I shd also persevere with the Bagdad expedition and make a further *barrage* there to the Oriental ambitions of Germany. It is needless to say that energy & efficiency in *execution* are as important as good decisions in principle.

I do not feel any prick of conscience at being out here. I did not go because I wished to disinterest myself in the great situation or because I feared the burden or the blow: but because I was and am sure that for the time being my usefulness was exhausted & that I cd only recover it by a definite & perhaps prolonged withdrawal. Had I seen the slightest prospect of being able to govern the event I wd have stayed. But in the circumstances I was not only free but bound to claim release.

And what a release! Except for the distressing thoughts wh yr papers & letter revive I have been entirely happy & free from care. I do not know when I have passed a more joyous three weeks; & to let that tremendous melancholy situation of our affairs all over the world slide from one's mind after having fixed it so long in mental gaze, has felt exactly like laying down a physical load. . . .

It is a jolly life with nice people; & one does not seem to mind the cold & wet & general discomfort; nor do I seem to be affected by them. Also as one may be killed at any moment—tho' I hope not—worries great & small recede to remote & shadowy distances.

I am not far away: but vy good reasons wd be required before I cd return. If such a break up on conscription as you indicate were to occur I cd not refuse my aid to an opposition, if it were desired. But I hope & believe this corner will be turned without a smash. I shall be painfully interested in your letters, but vy grateful for the kindness wh impels & inspires them. Give them to Creedy who will put them in French's bag—as long as there is a French! The uncertainty of the command out here & the rumours of change do great harm, & paralyse military thought. It wd be better to let things alone.

Yours ever
W

Curzon's letter had given Churchill a night of anticipation and uncertainty. But he soon realized that it was impracticable to act upon it. Clementine Churchill had also been thrilled to learn that Curzon had emerged in Cabinet as an advocate of renewed effort at Gallipoli. She had always fervently believed in the importance of victory at the Dardanelles. Writing to Curzon from 41 Cromwell Road on December 9, she took the initiative in trying to strengthen the new friendship:

My dear Lord Curzon,
    I have just heard from Winston—a long letter telling me of your letter to him.
    All you have told him has revived distressing thoughts & agitated him. But he says:—'It would not have been any good my joining in these discussions: a fresh uncompromised champion like Curzon had a better chance than I could ever have had.' He adds that you have stated the case better than he could have done. I should much like to see you—I wonder if you would lunch with me here on Saturday at 1.30?
    I have always felt you liked Winston, but now that I know you both think alike it is another bond in common.

Yours always sincerely
Clementine S. Churchill

In her postscript Clementine Churchill wrote: 'The news in W's letter has moved me deeply; since he went away I have heard nothing of what has been going on in your councils, & have tried not to think or feel too much.' Although Churchill's thoughts of politics had been stirred by Curzon, the call to London never came. Nor was he entirely certain that it really would, or that he was not better off in France. When he wrote to his mother on December 8, urging her to 'keep in good touch with all my friends'—including Curzon and Garvin—he declared emphatically that 'All I hear confirms me in my satisfaction to be freed from my share in the present proceedings.' To J. L. Garvin he wrote with acerbity that same day:

28. Churchill as Chancellor
of the Duchy of Lancaster.
Photograph printed in the
Bystander, 2 June 1915

29. Churchill,
Lord Lansdowne and
Lord Curzon, 1915

30. Churchill and
A. J. Balfour, 1915

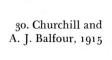

31. Sir Edward Carson and F. E. Smith, before 1914

32. Andrew Bonar Law

33. Sir Max Aitken, 1916

34. Churchill and his wife
arriving at Enfield

35. Churchill and his wife at Enfield, 18 September 1915, when Churchill addressed munitions workers. During his speech he told them:
'We cannot understand the inscrutable purposes which have plunged these evils upon the world, and have involved all the nations of Europe in a catastrophe measureless in its horror. But we know that if in this time of crisis

and strain we do our duty, we shall have done all that it is in human power to do —
and we shall so bear ourselves in this period — all of us, whatever part we play on the
stage of the world's history — we shall bear ourselves so that those who come after us
will find amid the signs and scars of this great struggle that the liberties of Europe
and of Britain are still intact and inviolate; when those looking back upon our
efforts such as they have been, will say of this unhappy but not inglorious generation, placed in a position of extraordinary trial, that it did not fail in the test, and
that the torch which it preserved lights the world for us today.'

36. A Sopwith biplane which Churchill had just piloted, 1913: biplanes of this type were used on the western front and at the Dardanelles, 1914–16

37. Wing-Commander Samson, 1915. One of Churchill's flying instructors before 1914, he commanded the aeroplane squadron at Dunkirk, 1914–15, and the Dardanelles, 1915

38. Churchill and Lloyd George at Wormwood Scrubs, 28 June 1915, watching a trial of the Killen-Strait barbed-wire cutter, a forerunner of the tank. Churchill is half-hidden behind the post, Lloyd George is in bowler hat

39. Evacuation of a gun and men from the Gallipoli Peninsula, December 1915

40. Lloyd George and Churchill, autumn 1915

K. is unspeakable & I thought I took leave of a comrade & a hero—whatever his blunders. I am glad not to have been present at the return of a booby.

Events will now take charge in both these theatres; & these events it seems to me must be decisive in the case of A & K. I suppose a system a la L.G. will have its trial then. There is no virtue there: but at least there will be an effort and a plan. I do not like holding Salonika, even if it is not impossible as many declare. . . . The Balkans must be left to stew in their own bitter juice. Germany will not find them tractable or harmonious. . . . But you must erect a barrage further east against the German advance; & I consider the Bagdad operation shd be vigorously persisted in.

. . . The military indictment wh cd be made on the operations of the last 6 months wd be—shall I say—will be—incredible to the world. There is also no equal to it in the history of war; & those who have wielded the power must bear the burden. At the right time, Parliament will have to be informed of the whole sequence of events. . . .

Keep in touch with Scott.

During December 8 Churchill was able to telephone the Admiralty from GHQ. Helped by Masterton-Smith, he had managed to speak for a few moments to his wife. 'I rejoiced to hear your voice over the telephone,' he wrote two days later; but as a Staff Officer had stayed in the room, 'I cd not say much & even feared you might think I was abrupt. One cannot really talk down it.' 'It was wonderful . . . to hear your voice on the telephone,' she had written on December 9, 'but very tantalising, as there is so much I want to say to you which cannot be shouted into an unsympathetic receiver!' It had been a strange experience for her, returning to the Admiralty after six months' absence. 'Masterton very nice & amiable—I think he manages the whole show,' she wrote. 'Colonel Hankey came out of "your" room where he had been speaking to Mr Balfour & was then wending his way to Downing Street. He said to me "In these moments of anxiety & difficulty I miss your Husband's courage & power to take a decision." '

On December 9 Churchill left St Omer and returned to the Grenadiers in their front-line trenches near Neuve Chapelle. 'Ma' Jeffreys offered to make him acting second-in-command of the Battalion. He was flattered; but his hopes for higher things had been so stimulated by Sir John French's request that he stay on at GHQ, that he returned to St Omer that evening. There he learned exciting news. He was definitely to become a Brigadier-General. Sir John French had chosen the Brigade, and his friend Tom Bridges was to be his Divisional General. In his letter of December 10 he wrote:

I am to be given the command of the 56th Brigade in the 19th Division. Bridges will command the Division—having risen from a squadron at the beginning of the war. The 19th Division is a regular Division in the second new army, & the Bde I shall command comprises 4 Lancashire Battalions. The division has a good reputation, has been out here some time, & is now in the line, next to the guards. It forms a part of the same Army corps—the 11th wh I hope will soon be commanded by Cavan; but is at present under General Haking (the corps commander who led me on such a lucky wild goose chase). Altogether it is a vy satisfactory arrangement.

Churchill feared that his wife would not approve of so swift a promotion, and tried to anticipate the reasons which she would use in urging delay: 'Of course there will be criticism & carping. But it is no good paying any attention to that. If I had taken a battalion for a few weeks, it must equally have been said "he has used it merely as a stepping stone etc". I am satisfied this is the right thing to do in the circumstances, & for the rest my attention will concentrate upon the Germans.' But Clementine Churchill no longer argued against the promotion, replying on December 15 that she was 'thrilled' by the news; but she was also worried that, while the danger from rifle fire would be less, that from shellfire would be greater. Not everyone at GHQ was impressed by Churchill's impending promotion. Sir Henry Wilson recorded in his diary on December 11:

Winston came up this morning to my room & had a long talk. I advised him *not* to take a Brigade as it would be bad for Sir John, Winston and the Brigade, but I did not convince him. He said Squiff had promised him a Division! and that as French's tenure was uncertain he would not adopt my proposal of taking a Battalion first, but would take the Brigade while he could get it.

On December 11 Churchill returned to the Grenadiers for the last time before joining his Brigade. On December 12 he wrote to his wife from the Battalion's reserve billets at Laventie:

I am out here now with the Guards again in a shell torn township whose name need not be mentioned. We go into the trenches tomorrow, & I shall continue doing duty with them till I get other directions. I saw Cavan today & told him what was settled. He seemed quite pleased & has arranged for me to study the supply system tomorrow morning—what they call the Q side of the work—I am to follow the course of a biscuit from the base to the trenches etc. He has written a long memo on my 'Variants of the Offensive' generally in cordial agreement & urging action. If only French were staying —all these thoughts wd take shape and have their fruition in some fine event. That odious Asquith, & his pack of incompetents & intriguers ruin everything.

I am now quite cut off from information and am content to be. I thought it more seemly to come out here, than to wait about at GHQ—comfortable as it was, & civil as was everyone. Really they are nice to me here, & delighted to see me. I rode over to the Divisional HQ this morning, had a talk with Cavan, lunched with the 2nd Guards Brigade. . . . Went to see Raymond [Asquith] whose battalion is in reserve, & then back here, to spend a pleasant evening singing songs (some of a vy sultry character) with Grigg's company & other officers. I dined with Grigg. We had a few casualties yesterday afternoon from shell fire, otherwise all is vy quiet in this section of the front: and the mining game seems to have reached no climax yet. The ground is soaked with water; but the breastworks are not uninhabitable; & we can still go in & out through communication trenches wh saves loss of life.

My Darling the most divine & glorious sleeping bag has arrived, & I spent last night in it in one long purr. Also food boxes are now flowing steadily; & I get daily evidences of the Cat's untiring zeal on my behalf. The periscope was the exact type I wanted. How clever of you to hit it off. My steel helmet is the cause of much envy. I look most martial in it—like a Cromwellian. I always intend to wear it under fire—but chiefly for the appearance.

My dearest one—I have your little photograph up here now—and kiss it each night before I go to bed. . . .

On December 13 the Battalion went into the front-line trenches for forty-eight hours. While they were in the line an extraordinary incident occurred, which Churchill reported to his wife on December 15, after he had returned to St Omer:

10 Grenadiers under a kid[1] went across by night to the German Trench wh they found largely deserted & water logged. They fell upon a picket of Germans, beat the brains out of two of them with clubs & dragged a third home triumphantly as a prisoner. The young officer by accident let off his pistol & shot one of his own Grenadiers dead: but the others kept this secret and

[1] William Alastair Damer Parnell, 1894–1916. Joined 2nd Battalion Grenadier Guards as a 2nd Lieutenant, 21 August 1915. He was awarded the Military Cross for the raid. Killed in action on the Somme, 25 September 1916. His eldest brother, the 5th Baron Congleton (born 1890) was killed at Ypres in November 1914.

pretended it was done by the enemy—do likewise. Such men you never saw. The scene in the little dugout when the prisoner was brought in surrounded by these terrific warriors, in jerkins & steel helmets with their bloody clubs in hand—looking pictures of ruthless war—was one to stay in the memory. *C'est tres bon.* They petted the prisoner and gave him cigarettes & tried to cheer him up. He was not vy unhappy to be taken & to know he wd be safe & well fed till the end of the war.

The Grenadiers had heard of Churchill's promotion before he had reached them. Their reaction pleased him. 'Colonel Jeffreys had heard of my impending move,' he wrote to his wife, '& with a total absence of justifiable jealousy, said he had absolute confidence & really seemed to rejoice in it. I was touched because of all men in the army none had claims so good.' Higher things even than a Brigade were being spoken of at Laventie: 'In the Grenadiers the opinion is that I am to have a division. This they seemed to consider quite reasonable.' Although he was on the verge of generalship, Churchill believed that there would still be a place in it for him in politics when the crisis came. 'The hour of Asquith's punishment & K's exposure draws nearer,' he told his wife. 'The wretched men have nearly wrecked our chances. It may fall to me to strike the blow. I shall do it without compunction.'

London was filled with much hostile comment when news of Churchill's impending Brigade became known. A question had been put down on the House of Commons' Order Paper by a Conservative MP, Sir Charles Hunter,[1] which the Government would have to answer on December 16. Hunter reflected the growing backbench hostility to Churchill's new sphere of activity, for he intended, 'To ask the Under-Secretary of State for War if Major Winston Churchill has been promised the command of an Infantry brigade; if this officer has ever commanded a battalion of Infantry; and for how many weeks he has served at the front as an Infantry Officer.' It was not only parliamentary backbenchers who were critical of Churchill's promotion to the command of a Brigade. When Lord Esher, who had returned to London from St Omer, lunched with Clementine Churchill at the Berkeley

[1] Charles Roderick Hunter, 1858–1924. 3rd Baronet, 1890. Inspector of Musketry, Imperial Yeomanry, 1900. Conservative MP, 1910–18. Divisional musketry and machine gun officer, 1914–16.

Hotel in Piccadilly, she was shocked and disturbed by his outspoken criticisms, which she held back until her letter of December 17:

My darling,
   . . . I will tell you (for what it is worth) what Lord E said. Of course you will know better than I can whether he is in touch with feeling in the Army or not & whether to attach importance & weight to his opinion. He said 'Of course you know Winston is taking a Brigade & as a personal friend of his I am very sorry about it; as I think he is making a great mistake. Of course it's not his fault, Sir John forced it upon him. All W's friends are very distressed about it as they had all hoped he would take a battalion first.'
   He said how tremendously popular & respected you had become in the short time you had been there & repeated to me the story you told me of the Colonel of the Grenadiers receiving you so disagreeably & then being entirely won over.
   This interview took place in the crowded grill-room of the Berkeley. I preserved a calm & composed demeanour, but I was astonished & hurt at his blurting all this out to me. He repeated again & again that the thing was a mistake; I tried at last to head him off by asking him personal questions about you, how you were looking, if you were well.
   He then launched forth again, saying that you had been in the greatest danger, in more than was necessary etc & that French had determined to give you this Brigade as he was convinced you wld otherwise be killed. After this I crawled home quite stunned & heart-broken. . . .

Esher's arguments were crudely stated. It is not surprising that they led Clementine Churchill once again to doubt whether her husband was wise to accept the rapid advancement on which he had decided. But she no longer felt the strength to challenge him. 'My Darling Love,' she wrote in the same letter, 'I live from day to day in suspense and anguish. At night when I lie down I say to myself Thank God he is still alive. The 4 weeks of your absence seem to me like 4 years. If only My Dear you had no military ambitions. If only you would stay with the Oxfordshire Hussars in their billets.' Churchill's new career was a daily source of torment for her. 'I can just bear it,' she wrote, 'feeling that you are really happy. I have ceased to have ambitions for you. Just come back to me alive that's all. Your loving Clemmie.'

Churchill returned late on the night of December 14 to St Omer. Sir John French was no longer there. He had been summoned to London, where Asquith had informed him that his dismissal could no longer be delayed. Churchill already knew that French's fate was virtually sealed. On the following morning a letter from Spiers brought good news: 'Nothing could please me more than to be your Brigade Major,' Spiers wrote. 'Once in the way of it I believe I cd be useful to you & I sd love it.' That morning Churchill wrote to Edward Marsh; the decision to evacuate Gallipoli, a decision he was powerless to influence in any way, had much upset him:

My dear Eddie,
    My information is only good in parts; but distressing letters from various quarters had already apprised me of the decisions wh have at last been reached. You know only too well what I think about them. I was vy glad to be able to occupy my mind with the practical trifles of trench warfare & the bickerings of the rival artilleries. The tale has yet to be told to its con-clusion. . . .

Churchill could not be certain whether French's imminent dismissal would affect his appointment as a Brigadier-General or not. 'I do not know what effect the unhappy recall of my friend will have on my local fortunes,' he wrote to Marsh, 'but I feel superior to them. A Brigade or a company in the Guards is the same or almost the same to me—during the present interlude. I have fallen back reposefully into the arms of fate; but with an underlying instinct that all will be well and that my greatest work is to hand.' Marsh's absence, after nine years of daily intimacy, added to Churchill's sense of isolation. He hoped that once he were formally appointed a Brigadier-General, Marsh would join him:

    I should like to set you free from your present surroundings and if if were in my power to find you a little island here I should not hesitate to propose it to you. Brigades have an 'interpreter' who has a jolly time. Let me know what you feel. I am very glad you found a cigarette case among those wh Clemmie produced wh appealed to you. 'Tis but the poor symbol of a deep affection.

                                                        Yours always
                                                              W

    This letter sealed, Churchill then wrote to his wife:

    I am back here at GHQ to see the last of my poor friend who returns to pack up tomorrow. I don't know what effect this change of command will produce upon my local fortunes: possibly it will throw everything into the melting pot again. Believe me I am superior to anything that can happen to me out here. My conviction that the greatest of my work is still to be done is strong within me: & I ride reposefully along the gale. I expect it will be my duty in the early months of next year—If I am all right—to stand up in my place in Parliament and endeavour to procure the dismissal of Asquith & Kitchener: & when I am sure that the hour has come I shall not flinch from any exertion or strife. I feel a gt assurance of my power: & now—naked— nothing can assail me. . . .

This letter too was sealed, and Churchill waited for the arrival of the King's Messenger who was expected at St Omer that morning, and would take both letters back with him to London during the afternoon. While waiting for the Messenger, he was called to the telephone. It was Sir John French himself, speaking from London. He had something extremely unpleasant to say. That morning he had received a letter from Asquith vetoing Churchill's promotion. The blow was unexpected and severe. At first Churchill could hardly believe it. 'Do not allow the PM to discuss my affairs with you,' he wrote to his wife, after having reopened his letter to add the bad news. 'Be vy cool & detached and avoid any sign of acquiescence in anything he may say.'

Asquith's direct intervention had brought seven days of expectation to an end. Churchill was bewildered by what had happened. 'You will cancel the order for the tunic!' he wrote to his wife in his postscript. That evening he dined at Sir John French's house at St Omer. He had asked Spiers to dine with him, not knowing when he had invited him that his hopes would be so suddenly smashed. On the telephone Sir John French had told him that Asquith had actually written in his letter: 'Perhaps you might give him a Battalion.' Churchill did not want such a narrow sphere of command but if he had to, he would accept. In his diary Spiers described the evening:

Dined at C in C's house. . . . Winston had long talk with me. He likes telling me his affairs. . . . Says things always turn out for best. . . . Spoke of various things. Of danger we all run, of how we wd probably all be killed in next offensive. . . .

At dinner he was brilliant, really fascinating. Told me in private Holland was the only Rd open to us, in public that the Gs wd first use Egypt & attack India by the Turks. Told me Asquith was a man of warm friendship but never let it interfere with duty or even comfort. Told me K of K was played out. Churchill told me he had thought, when still in Government, of going to Russia [1] & taking me! He is of course selfish, likes me but wants to make use of me. He is all right. . . .

[1] Perhaps a reference to the mission to Vladivostock and Archangel which, two months earlier, Hankey had suggested to Asquith as a possible outlet for Churchill's energies. This entry in Spiers' diary is the only contemporary evidence I have found that Churchill may have taken the idea seriously.

By December 17 Churchill felt the full enormity of Asquith's veto. Twice that day he wrote to his wife, with the black thoughts that had taken control of him; a day later he asked her to burn the letters, telling her: 'I was depressed & my thought was not organised. Everyone has hours of reaction, & there is no reason why written record shd remain.' Nor does it.

Desperate to learn the full story of Asquith's abrupt decision, Churchill stayed at St Omer throughout December 17. French returned that evening with orders to hand over his command to his successor, Sir Douglas Haig. As soon as he reached his headquarters he gave Churchill an account of what had happened in London. On the following day Churchill sent his wife an account of what French had reported:

> The position is as follows. He saw Asquith, told him that he had given me a Brigade & Asquith said he was delighted. A few hours later, being I suppose frightened by the question in the House, Asquith wrote a note to French (wh French showed me *vy privately*) saying that 'with regard to our conversation about our friend—the appointment might cause some criticism'—& should not therefore be made—adding 'Perhaps you might give him a battalion'. The almost contemptuous indifference of this note was a revelation to me. French was astonished; but in his weak position he cd do nothing, & now he is no longer C in C. Meanwhile he had told everyone that he had given me a Brigade & is of course deeply distressed at the turn of events.

Churchill could not restrain his bitterness against the Prime Minister:

> To measure Asquith's performance one has to remember that on my leaving the Admiralty he offered me a Brigade: & that when I told him three months ago of the offers that French had made to me if I came out to the front, he advised me to go & assured me that any advancement wh was thought fitting by the C in C would have his hearty concurrence. One has to remember all the rest too of a long story of my work & connexion with him.
>
> Altogether I am inclined to think that his conduct reaches the limit of meanness & ungenerousness. Sentiments of friendship expressed in extravagant terms; coupled with a resolve not to incur the slightest criticism or encounter the smallest opposition—even from the most unworthy quarter. Personally I feel that every link is severed: & while I do not wish to decide in a hurry—my feeling is that all relationship shd cease.

Churchill was not enthusiastic about taking command of a Battalion, and was angered by the suggestion that an appointment to a Battalion involved any generosity on Asquith's part:

With regard to my taking the command of a battalion: there is no use in my doing so unless under a C in C who believes in me & means in a few weeks to promote me. The risk & labour of such a task are vy heavy, & I am a special target for criticism. The appointment is no gift. With my rank & war services I cd have obtained it quite easily had I been an ordinary unknown officer. I shd be practically alone with 1000 amateur officers and untrained men, in a situation of much anxiety and no real scope. I have not asked for anything out here & have only accepted the brigade after considerable hesitation & delay. But having done so, I do not feel called upon to undertake the duties of a batallion commander, unless they are pressed upon me in a manner that leaves me no choice.

The uncertainties of the higher command put Churchill's military future at risk, and he could not tell whether Haig would be helpful:

This afternoon French is to see Haig & intends to tell him the whole story. My action will necessarily depend on the new man's view & disposition. Unless he is inclined to make himself responsible for the decision to wh French had come and takes clearly a favourable & friendly view, I shall remain with the Grenadier Guards as a company officer. I think they will be willing to make an exception to their rule about only Guards commanding Guards & will let me do the work in a regular way. This at any rate is the place of honour and as they will be continuously in the line till the 25th Jany I shd find the service of great interest.

Churchill did not dismiss from his mind the possibility, however remote, that he might return to London without taking up any further military duties. 'I do not think any difficulty would be placed in my way,' he ended his letter, 'if I required to return home for Parliamentary duties if the situation needed my presence.'

In later months and years Churchill was often to brood on his failure to secure a Brigade, and on Asquith's veto. The threat of Parliamentary criticisms had been decisive. During a month in which many members of Parliament believed that the Government was in difficulty over the question of conscription, the Prime Minister did not want to create any opportunity, however trivial, for backbench unrest. When Sir John French informed Asquith of Churchill's impending promotion on December 14, the Prime Minister sensed danger. He acted accordingly, thereby protecting himself from an irritating attack in Parliament. On December 16, when Sir Charles Hunter asked his hostile question, the Parliamentary Under-Secretary of State for War, H. J. Tennant, was able to reply with disingenuous confidence: 'I have no knowledge myself, and have not been able to obtain any, of a promise of command of an Infantry brigade having been made to my right hon and gallant

Friend referred to in the question.' Hunter then asked whether Churchill had been promised command of a Battalion, to which several unidentified MPs called out—'Why not?' A former Indian Army officer, Sir George Scott Robertson,[1] spoke up in Churchill's defence: 'Is not the question absurd on the face of it . . .?' he asked pointing out that as a serving officer under sixty Churchill was qualified to command a battalion. But the last comment was a hostile one. A Conservative MP, Evelyn Cecil,[2] asked: 'Is the right hon Gentleman aware that if this appointment were made it would be thought by very many persons both inside and outside this House a grave scandal?'

At noon on December 18, Sir John French's last day at St Omer, he and Churchill set out from the town by car. Finding a small, secluded cottage in the countryside, they picnicked together. On the drive back they talked at length, as Churchill wrote to his wife, 'about every sort of thing'. They reached St Omer only a short while before Sir Douglas Haig, who was to take over formal command of the British Army in France on the following day. French appealed at once to Haig on Churchill's behalf. Haig wrote in his diary:

> . . . I saw Sir John French at 3 pm. He did not look very well and seemed short of breath at times.
>
> He expressed a wish to help me and the Army in France to the best of his power at home. Then he said that 'there was a delicate personal matter' which he wished to speak about. This was that he had wanted to give Winston Churchill an Infantry Brigade. This had been vetoed but he was anxious that Winston should have a Battalion. I replied that I had no objection because Winston had done good work in the trenches, and we were short of Battalion CO's. I then said goodbye.

Haig asked to see Churchill, telling him that there was no chance of an immediate Brigade, but offering him a Battalion. Churchill accepted. That evening he wrote to his wife of the interview:

> . . . He treated me with the utmost kindness of manner & consideration, assured me that nothing wd give him greater pleasure than to give me a Brigade, that his only wish was that able men shd come to the front, & that I

[1] George Scott Robertson, 1852–1916. Indian Medical Service, 1878–88. Indian Foreign Office, 1888–95. Knighted, 1895. Liberal MP, 1906–16.

[2] Evelyn Cecil, 1865–1941. Grandson of the 2nd Marquess of Salisbury. Conservative MP, 1898–1929. Chairman of the Committee on Public Retrenchment, 1915. Member of the Inter-Allied Parliamentary Committee, 1916–18. Created Baron Rockley, 1934.

might count on his sympathy in every way. He had heard from Cavan of the 'excellent work' I had done in the trenches. Altogether it was quite clear that he will give me a fair chance. In these circumstances I consented to take a battalion—wh one is not yet settled—but it will be one going in the line. I asked for an officer—Archie or Spiers—and he went off and arranged at once that I was to have what I wanted. It is possible even that I shall get the two in a short time. The need of a few competent professionals is really vy great, and every step I take is watched by curious eyes. I must be well supported. I was greatly reassured by his manner wh was affectionate almost. He took me by the arm and made the greatest fuss. I used to know him pretty well in the old days when he was a Major & I a young MP. But I am bound to say the warmth of his greeting surprised me. . . .

Stimulated by Haig's warmth, Churchill decided to ask him if he would be interested to read his memorandum on trench warfare. 'I asked him if he wd like to see "Variants of the Offensive" & he said he wd be "honoured"—! So I am back on my perch again with my feathers stroked down.' That same day Haig told Churchill that he could command the 9th Battalion of the King's Royal Rifle Corps. Later in the afternoon he discovered that the Battalion was about to leave France almost immediately, and wrote apologetically:

Dear Winston,
    V many thanks for the notes which I will read with much interest.
    I had no idea the Battn was about to go abroad.—Please ask the Mil Sec to cancel your posting to the 9th KRR & I'll see to it personally when I have taken over.
    Meantime good luck to you—Excuse hurried line and Believe me,
                                            Yrs vy truly
                                            D. Haig

Churchill's anger towards Asquith intensified in the weeks to come. He did not know whom he could trust, or who would give him confidence in the future. F. E. Smith was the only friend then in the Cabinet to whom he felt he could turn.[1] On December 18 he sent him a sad appeal for support and encouragement:

My dear,
    I am awfully disappointed and so is French. What ill-fortune.
    It is becoming important for me to see you and I trust you will not fail me. I do not know where I shall be; but a rendez-vous can easily be arranged without exposing your uninsured person to danger.

    [1] F. E. Smith had entered the Cabinet on 3 November 1915 as Attorney-General, following Carson's resignation.

A week ago French gave me the command of the 56th Brigade XIXth Division. The Prime Minister however being frighted of the question in the House got this cancelled. Quel homme! The departure of French is a gt blow to me and threatened to leave me vy much en l'air. In these circumstances I had resolved to take a company in the Grenadiers, where I have my footing. But Haig who I saw this afternoon with French treated me with the utmost cordiality and consideration, assured me of his desire to give me a Brigade and to further my interests, and in the circumstances I have consented to take a battalion in the front line. I wd not have done this except under a sympathetic C in C: preferring a company in the Guards, if no advancement were open, to a long spell with strangers, and imperfectly trained men.

Early next week I shall be in the line; and there will be no nice dinners sitting next to the C in C like tonight, which I can offer you; but come and we will make shift somehow.

I have many things to say to you and some to hear from you: and I do hope you will be able to come. GHQ will I am sure facilitate your movements, and you can telegraph to me through Brade. I am suspending certain political action till I see you.

I find myself treated here with good will and I think respect on all sides: though I am usually urged to go home and smash the bloody Government.

Yours always
W

'As for Asquith,' Churchill wrote to his wife in his letter that evening, 'make no change except a greater reserve about me & my affairs. The incident is best ignored; but it need not be forgotten. Don't you tell me he was quite right—or let him persuade you. Esher talks foolishly. It wd not have been a great mistake for me to take a Brigade. There was something to be said either way. But on the whole it was worth taking.'

Churchill asked his wife to comfort Sir John French in his distress, writing in the same letter: 'He is a dear friend. I want you & Goonie to get him to come & dine with you and cherish him properly: & write him a nice letter. My heart bled for him in this wrench.' French spent his last morning at St Omer on December 19. Churchill described the final scene to his wife on the following day:

French's departure was affecting. He saw a long succession of generals etc & then opened his door & said 'Winston, it is fitting that my last quarter of an hour here shd be spent with you'. Then off he went with a guard of honour, saluting officers, cheering soldiers & townsfolk—stepping swiftly from the stage of history into the dull humdrum of ordinary life. I felt deeply his departure on every ground—public & private. It was not I think necessary or right. The French are rather unhappy about it: the army have no real opinion. But Asquith will throw anyone to the wolves to keep himself in office. . . .

Churchill had gone to France to escape the anxieties of political impotence. For four weeks he had found an escape, amid the daily activities of the Grenadiers and the challenge of trying to devise new weapons which could lead to new war tactics. But Asquith's unexpected intervention, ending his chances of a Brigade, brought politics once more to the forefront of his thoughts and worries. It was clear that there could be no escape from political pressures and jealousies; that no military environment could shield him from the ever-clamant demands of political life; and that he himself, however keen to participate in the world of divisions, brigades, battalions and companies, could never really be satisfied by army life. From that moment Churchill aspired, not to advance his military career, but to rebuild his political one. From the isolation of the war zone, from the danger of the front line, from the uncertainties of a crashed career, he turned his energies and introspection to a political objective. A return to Cabinet Office was certainly remote, and probably unobtainable. But for twelve months he sought to return. Sometimes he acted alone, sometimes with colleagues. But wherever he was, however weak his political position, however demanding his military duties, a drastic change in the methods of warmaking became his target.

Waiting at St Omer to learn which Battalion he was to command, Churchill received several letters in which politics predominated. F. E. Smith wrote on December 19 with an account of events in the Cabinet:

My dear Winston,

. . . We fought (Curzon, Selborne, Lansdowne & myself) for the Dardanelles as long as possible & only gave up when every single soldier abandoned us including K and we were told that it was impossible this weather to send the Salonika troops then if we decided that the evacuation at Salonika shd be made to reinforce the Dardanelles.

I am so disappointed at not seeing you. It was a combination of tragic mishaps. You may absolutely rely on seeing me in a fortnight or so and I will make friends with Haig in your interest. BL's star is much in the ascendant & he continues most friendly.

Yours affectionately
F

Lady Randolph also wrote on December 19, with news and questions. She had just spoken to one of Fisher's friends, the journalist Lovat

Fraser:[1] 'He says there is much grumbling in the Navy against AJB—they say he has gone to sleep & everything is left to slide. Fraser also said that K—was the stumbling block at the beginning, & is still so. He ended by saying that you must return at the first good opportunity. . . . Do you know Haig? I mean fairly well? I remember him in the old days. . . . A hard man—& a bit of a bounder—but I imagine a fine soldier. . . .'

The fullest political news came from J. L. Garvin, who hoped to act as a focus of unity for those Liberals and Conservatives who were dissatisfied with Asquith's leadership. He believed that Churchill had an important part to play in any such group. The main reason for dissent during December 1915 was conscription. Asquith was still trying to preserve the voluntary system. But the increasing demand for more men at the front had placed a heavy strain upon voluntary recruitment; a strain which Kitchener could no longer conceal. Lord Derby had been brought in to effect a compromise. But many critics of the Government, led by Curzon inside the Cabinet and Carson outside it, believed no compromise would work, and that if the war were not to be lost, compulsion must be brought in at once. Asquith feared the anger of many Liberals if he abandoned the voluntary system. But it seemed to his critics that it was no longer a question of military tradition or Liberal ethics, but of the urgent needs of war. On December 20 Garvin, himself a compulsionist, wrote to Churchill:

. . .It is impossible to say yet what will happen at home. I think Asquith's confidence in being able to hold on is very considerably shaken. The worst disasters anticipated won't come from all I hear; so that the chance that events themselves might force a drastic solution is deferred, and you have still the situation as unsatisfactory as possible yet it's not difficult to change.

Of course without LG there can be no sufficient change, but he is still singularly isolated on the one hand, while on the other resolved not to jump until he is certain to land on sound ground. His greatest mistake was the breach with you, and sooner or later that estrangement must be composed if only on the principles of a marriage de convenance. He needs alliances. He will get them somehow because others need him as much as he needs them. His power in Opposition would at any time be enormous but specially under unmuzzled conditions after the war. But I think he will 'pig' it with irksome but tenacious patience until he sees the real big chance.

When will it come? Not now as was anticipated by some last week.

[1] Lovat Fraser, 1871–1926. Editor, *Times of India*, 1902–6. On his return to London in 1907 he joined the Editorial Staff of *The Times*, remaining with the paper until 1922. Chief Literary Adviser, *Sunday Pictorial* and *Daily Mirror*, 1922–6.

Asquith is much more likely to come to an agreement with Derby to deal with the residue of single men by a peremptory call that may save the face of voluntaryism.

Garvin informed Churchill of the first stage of the end of the Gallipoli story: 'The news that Anzac troops have been evacuated at last comes today, and the War Office claim that the casualties have been insignificant and that the guns and stores have been saved. . . . It is a bitter amputator of hopes that were as much part of us as limbs, but now we must look right forward, and set our teeth.' Only the troops at Helles remained on the Peninsula.

Jack Churchill, who had witnessed the evacuation from Anzac, sent his brother an account of it on December 22:

My dear,

The arrangements were perfect—but we had to have wonderful good fortune to get away as we did. The enemy suspected nothing, and the embarkation was absolutely unmolested. But the weather was the most important feature. During the operation it remained dead calm—but as soon as it was over a South Westerly gale sprang up, which must have smashed all the old piers and which would have sunk all the small boats & lighters had it occurred a few hours before. As it was—the large army was all withdrawn. With the loss of 2 men wounded! Almost all the munitions and guns were brought away and nothing of value to enemy was left intact. Birdwood carried out the whole operation and I think the Govt & Ld K owe him a great deal. A disaster would have settled the Govt I should imagine, but this will give them a new lease of life.

It was a great feat—but we are all very depressed at having to come away. The Anzacs feel it very much. One man expressed himself 'We have a lot of fellows sleeping in those valleys, and we should never have been told to leave them'.

Best love
Jack S.C.

On 19 December 1915 Sir Douglas Haig took up formal command of the British forces in France. At dinner that evening with Spiers and Sinclair, Churchill spoke optimistically of his own military future. Spiers wrote in his diary: 'Dined with Churchill & his friend Archy Sinclair a particularly nice fellow at Rest Vincente. 2 bottles of Champagne, 2 glasses of Brandy. Rather nice talk. He is to get a Bn & is having Sinclair attached & asking for me as 2nd in Command. . . . WC has Douglas Haig to heel. DH is ready to do anything for him.'

On December 20 Churchill moved from GHQ a few doors further

down the street, taking up quarters with his friend Sir Max Aitken, who
had temporarily left London to take up the post of Canadian Eyewitness
at the Front. It was the beginning of a lifelong intimacy between the
two men. At St Omer, Aitken gave Churchill renewed hope in his
future. Churchill's anger with Asquith over his lost Brigade had swung
his mind violently back to politics; Aitken encouraged him to believe in
his political future. It was a time when Churchill desperately needed
such encouragement. He never forgot how at that moment, when
almost everyone else seemed against him, Aitken held out the hand of
hospitality and hope.

Churchill waited at St Omer for the offer of another vacant Battalion.
Haig had agreed to let him have Sinclair as his ADC. Whether he would
be allowed to have Spiers was still uncertain. On December 20 Churchill
and Spiers had tea together at St Omer, Spiers recording in his diary:

He v interesting describing battle of Coronel & Falkland, how it happened,
Craddock disobeying orders & insisting on fighting & how at the Falklands
the 1st message was that v Spee had come up & that the Brit fleet was coaling.
How Fisher objected to the fast cruisers leaving England on Friday the 13th.
Fascinating. Also dodges to catch submarines, the boat which pretends to
surrender, the crew tumbling overboard & then guns unmasking. . . .

That same afternoon Churchill wrote to his wife, whom he had
hoped would be able to meet him in Paris after Christmas:

. . . I shall know today or tomorrow wh battalion I am to have, & where
it is posted in the line. Archie comes with me, tho I have not yet settled how
to fit him in. I must first see how they all look in their jobs. Afterwards I may
get Spiers. This will be a vy arduous and anxious piece of work, requiring the
whole of my attention. It is not more dangerous than I shd have made a
Brigade command: but of course much depends on the part of the line we
are in. . . .

I am sure there is no chance of Paris for some time yet. I have at least six
weeks of the most strenuous work before me—& that direct responsibility—
like a ship's captain—for the safety of all in my charge.

That evening Churchill received a letter from his wife, dated
December 18, in which she wrote that she was 'astounded at the PM
not backing you for a brigade'. She hoped that Asquith had asked
Haig to give him one 'later on after you have commanded a battalion
for a little while'. 'My own Darling,' her letter ended: 'I feel such absolute confidence in your future—it is your present which causes me agony

—I feel as if I had a tight band of pain round my heart. It fills me with great pride to think that you have won the love & respect of those splendid Grenadiers & their austere Colonel: in happier times you must let me see them all. Perhaps if any of them come home on leave they would come & see me.' Churchill replied at once:

Your 1 a.m. 18th letter has just arrived, & stimulates me to add a little to what I wrote this morning. . . . I am simply waiting d'un pied a l'autre for orders. It is odd to pass these days of absolute idleness—waiting 3 or 4 hours together in tranquil vegetation, when one looks back to the long years of unceasing labour & hustle through wh I have passed. It does not fret me. In war one takes everything as it comes, & I seem to have quite different standards to measure by. As one's fortunes are reduced, one's spirit must expand to fill the void.

I think of all the things that are being left undone & of my own energies & capacities to do them & drive them along all wasted—without any real pain. I watch—as far as I can—the weak, irresolute & incompetent drift of Government policy and turn over what ought to be done in my mind, & then let it all slide away without a wrench. I shall be profoundly absorbed in the tremendous little tasks wh my new work will give me. I hope to come to these men like a breeze. I hope they will rejoice to be led by me, & fall back with real confidence into my hands. I shall give them my vy best.

No battalion command had become vacant by December 22. Churchill took advantage of the delay to make a brief visit to London to see his wife and family.

While Churchill was in London he was caught up briefly but deeply in political speculation, seeing both J. L. Garvin and Lloyd George. At dinner with Garvin the subject of his working once more with Fisher was raised. Garvin sent Fisher an account of the discussion in a letter dated 'Christmas 1915':

Winston is home for a few days leave. I dined with him and went at my old aim with him and you—union for the country's sake. He is willing to bury the hatchet and is out and out for your wonder-ship. Why not reopen the old firm ON AN AGREED PROGRAMME to the accompaniment of throwing up hats throughout the country? There would be glory enough there for two and to spare but to have you and him working under the same administration somehow again is vital. Lloyd George, you, Carson and Winston are a fighting quartette (or Super-Dreadnought Squadron) which can save this country and the allies. I am not sure anything else can. This is the best and most affectionate Christmas card that could be sent to you by yours ever

J. L. Garvin.

Garvin also wrote to Lloyd George on Christmas Day. 'You, Carson, Winston, Fisher,' he declared, 'working together can win this war. Haldane (as I know having dined with him) would join you. . . .'

In a conversation with Lloyd George, Churchill discussed the political crisis which had again arisen over conscription. Lloyd George was bitter against Asquith for the delay in bringing in national service, and held out hopes for a change of government which would enable Churchill to return. On December 27, having returned to France, Churchill wrote to Lloyd George: 'I shall be glad to hear how things go. . . . Don't miss yr opportunity. The time has come.' On his return to St Omer, Churchill could not contain his excitement. On December 28 he saw Spiers, who recorded in his diary:

> Dined with WC at Canadian office, after dinner he v interesting. He thinks there is going to be a political crisis on compulsion. He saw Lloyd George who is going to try & smash the Government when either Bonar Law or LG wd be PM & Churchill get Munitions or Admiralty, the remaining one getting the WO.
>
> He showed me all the Government minutes on the war. Some of his really prophetic & really clever & sound.
>
> Bed after 1. . . .

Clementine Churchill was less certain that the time had come for anti-Government action. 'I know nothing, but I feel the break-up is not yet,' she wrote to her husband on December 28. 'This futile government,' she added, 'will fumble on for a few more months.' On the following day she wrote again, having heard that the conscription crisis was apparently over: 'I feel very sad but not exactly disappointed as I never allowed myself to *really* hope for a break-up.' On December 29 Lloyd George lunched with her at 41 Cromwell Road. That afternoon she sent her husband an account of their conversation:

> LlG has been & gone. As I feared the crisis is over with 'no change' except the extremely unlikely resignations of Runciman & Simon. The PM appeared at the Cabinet yesterday & did *all* the fighting *for* compulsion. LlG & Curzon hardly opened their mouths. Runciman and McKenna argued against it on the ground of injuring the trade of the country, but finally all agreed with exception of Simon & Runciman who are 're-considering' their positions. I asked LlG if he & the other die hards had tried to break the Government; he said there wasn't a chance as the PM had come right over on to their side. He expressed great distress at you not being in the Government. He said repeatedly 'We must get Winston back'. He asked me if you would come back & manage the heavy gun department of the Munitions Office. He has just

been told that 100 of them due in March will not be delivered till later owing to want of drive of the man in charge, 'a first class 2nd rate man' who before the war was earning £15,000 a year with a big armament firm.[1]

Clementine Churchill was surprised at how quickly Lloyd George's pugnacious ardour had cooled. 'LlG is a strange man,' she wrote. 'He was very polite & civil & most friendly, but for the moment the chance of working with you is gone & so his fire is gone and he is more detached than the other day. . . .' On December 30 she wrote again with more political news. Her enthusiasm for Lloyd George had dwindled further:

. . . I forgot to tell you in yesterday's letter that McKenna absented himself from the War Council and sulked down at Munstead which caused a mild flutter, but LlG said that a little flattery and cajolery from the PM would bring him round. I suppose that if compulsion is carried without a single resignation (which seems likely) it will be a feather in the PM's cap & a vindication of his slow state-craft. I am very much afraid this is going to be a 'personal triumph' for him.

I think my Darling you will have to be very patient. Do not burn any boats. The PM has not treated you worse than LlG has done, in fact not so badly for he is not as much in your debt as the other man (i.e. Marconi).[2] On the other hand are the Dardanelles. I feel sure that if the choice were equal you would prefer to work with the PM than with LlG. It's true that when association ceases with the PM he cools & congeals visibly, but all the time you were at the Admiralty he was loyal & steadfast while the other would barter you away at any time in any place. I assure you he is the direct descendent of Judas Iscariot. At this moment although I hate the PM, if he held out his hand I could take it, (though I would give it a nasty twist) but before taking LlG's I would have to safeguard myself with charms, touchwoods, exorcisms & by crossing myself. I always can get on with him &

---

[1] Charles Edward Ellis, 1852–1937. Director, John Brown & Co., Shipbuilders, 1890. Entered Ministry of Munitions, July 1915. Deputy Director-General, Guns and Equipment, 1915–16; Director-General, Ordnance Supply, 1916–17. Knighted, 1917. Head of Paris Establishment, Ministry of Munitions, 1917–18; Liquidator of Contracts, France, Italy, Switzerland, 1919. Member, Royal Commission on Awards to Inventors, 1919.

[2] In 1912, during the 'Marconi affair', Churchill had rendered Lloyd George—who, with Rufus Isaacs, was much implicated—a triple service. He had prevailed on Lord Northcliffe to play the scandal down as much as possible in *The Times* and the *Daily Mail*; he had persuaded F. E. Smith and Sir Edward Carson to appear for Lloyd George and Isaacs in their libel action against *Le Matin*; and he had influenced Asquith, in the Debate on the Report of the Select Committee of the House of Commons, not to use any phrase which might provoke Lloyd George's resignation. Churchill shared his wife's view that Lloyd George was in his debt as a result of this help. Later he was to try get Lloyd George to redeem his debt, but in vain.

yesterday I had a good talk, but you can't hold his eyes, they shift away.

You know I'm not good at pretending but I am going to put my pride in my pocket and reconnoitre Downing Street. . . .

While Clementine Churchill prepared to visit 10 Downing Street, her husband was back in the war zone, from which it seemed he would not easily escape. On December 30 he sent her an account of his three days back in France:

We had a rough passage on the destroyer and I was forced to surrender first my lunch and subsequently my breakfast. In the midst of these pre-occupations the coxswain arrived on behalf of the ship's company to wish me the compliments of the season & express gratitude for past favours to the Lower Deck. A clumsy skipper failed to get us ashore in Dunkirk till after 4 hours of trying—the wind was vy strong—& finally we settled down on a mudbank. Luckily close enough to the quay for me to escape to the land.

The next day I went to see Bridges. . . . I lunched with him & afterwards was taken by his Chief of Staff[1] to see Neuve Chapelle. The Germans oblig-ingly stopped shelling it as we arrived & I was able without much risk to see this part of the line, wh fills in a gap in my now extensive examination of the front. I also saw my old friends of the 2nd Battalion.

Spiers came over and dined with me in the evening, & yesterday we made an expedition to the French lines. I was able to go to the very farthest point we hold on the Vimy Ridge, from which a fair view of the plain of Douai was obtainable.

I believe Spiers & I are the only Englishmen who have ever been on this battle-torn ground. It was pretty quiet. The lines are in places only a few yards apart, but a much less spiteful temper prevails than on the part of the Guards. There you cannot show a whisker without grave risk of death. Here the sentries looked at each other over the top of the parapet: & while we were in the trench the Germans passed the word to the French to take cover as their officer was going to order some shelling. This duly arrived; but luckily it was directed upon the boyau [communication trench] up wh we had just come & not on that by wh we were returning.

Dinner with the corps, and prolonged earnest discussion of the possibilities of the offensive. They _all_ agree with me. These men who have suffered the whole terrible experience of these vain attacks, repeated almost word for word the arguments wh I so unsuccessfully addressed to that weak & foolish Cabinet. My mind is making its way steadily through the vast problem of 'how to do it': without prejudice to my present conviction that 'it might not be done'. I am going to write something soon about it all, wh perhaps may be of use. So far as I can tell from the papers Asquith has had no great

[1] Archie Stewart Buckle, 1868–1916. 2nd Lieutenant, Royal Artillery, 1888. Lieutenant-Colonel, 1914. Explosives expert. Chief-of-Staff, 19th Division, January 1915–January 1916.

difficulty in choosing between his office & his principles, & now I daresay things will run on for some time.

Fifty-five years later, in conversation with the author, Spears recalled the expedition of December 29:

I tried to show him what would interest him. I took him to look down on the plain of Douai. The French would be polite—they always were. But they never took him seriously. He played no part in the military hierarchy, which was the one thing that mattered in the French army.

We were both very struck by the rats that we saw. They were appalling things; they were huge. Winston pointed out that they played a very useful role by eating human bodies—it was quite true. At the time of the German retreat to the Hindenburg line there were 15 to 20 miles of trenches left empty. The rats were everywhere. I have driven over roads where you squashed rats as you went along. Had you fallen in a trench you would never have got out alive. They would have devoured you. One heard them all night running about in the barbed wire.

Mostly Winston looked. If there was a question to be put, he put it. There was a place I took him to at Notre Dame de Lorette. It was a ridge and a declivity. The French kept attacking it, but nobody had ever been known to come back alive. This interested Winston considerably. He wanted to know why, why, why. The Germans had realized the importance of the counter-slope, of having trenches within 15 yards of the top of the hill on the far side, and shooting like rabbits at anyone who popped over the top. It was a terrible place. I got wounded there myself. Winston had an inquiring mind of rare quality. He always turned up with some new invention—once it was a bullet-proof waistcoat. On another occasion a bullet-proof raincoat which would have sunk anyone wearing it in any sea.

Winston was very curious, very inquisitive to see what the French were doing. It was a time when they were experimenting with all sorts of devices, like a moving shield which you pushed along in front of the infantry. But when Winston mentioned the idea of tanks the French said: 'Wouldn't it be simpler to flood Artois and get your fleet here?'

Churchill continued his letter to his wife of December 30 with a request that she buy a silver cigar box which he wanted to present to the Headquarters Staff of the Guards Division. As well as an inscription, he wanted her to get for it 'a photograph of the Blücher[1] turning turtle (you know the one) and have this mounted on the top of the cigar-cigarette box—under glass'. As he explained:

[1] The German battle-cruiser *Blücher* was sunk during the action of the Dogger Bank, 24 January 1915. One thousand of her crew were drowned; two hundred and fifty rescued by British ships.

I have made great friends with them & am anxious to give them a token. Get this done as soon as possible.

Also, my dearest one, send over my hot water bottle. I always forget it.

Today I am off to Boulogne to meet Archie & to pass the time. You will be glad to know I am making a safer expedition.

No Christmas parcels or food have reached me yet. I am not in immediate want of them: but they seem to have gone astray.

Churchill ended his letter 'Tender love my darling, do not be lonely or low-spirited. Everything will come out right in the end: and we shall look back upon these days with satisfaction—even pride. . . .'

Clementine Churchill continued her side of the correspondence, answering all his queries, carrying out all his requests, acting as a moderating influence on his wilder whims, and trying to cheer him. 'In an hour the Cabinet meets,' she wrote on December 27, 'I hope the season of peace & goodwill will not have infected its members'; and on the following day: 'It seems centuries since you have left & a thick pall of fog has settled round me thro' which I can neither hear nor see the conflict. . . . I am absolutely worn out with emotions & the excitement of seeing you & I must have a few days' rest. I can't sleep for anxiety. . . .'[1]

On December 30 Clementine Churchill wrote from Lord Stanley of Alderley's[2] house, Alderley Park in Cheshire: 'I hoped to find Venetia here but she passed me in the train, summoned back to town by the imperious Montagu.' On New Year's Day, while still at Alderley Park she wrote again: 'Venetia the prosperous and the happy, arrived this evening to enliven us & to lift us out of the doldrums. . . . She entertained the PM on New Year's Eve to Beer & Skittles.' Of her husband's request for a photograph of the sinking German battleship to go on the silver cigarette box, Clementine Churchill was not at all certain that this would be a wise present. It was, she wrote, 'a very ghastly picture with all those wretched scorched singed Germans clinging to her & rolling off her'. Another reason against it, she explained, was that it had already been widely published. Had it been a secret, unknown photograph, he might have had an excuse to use it. She was willing, if he still insisted on a gruesome picture, to find a less well known one. But she ended her letter by suggesting that it would be more sensible to use a plain inscription on the box.

[1] This letter is reproduced in full in facsimile, pp. 832–3.

[2] Edward Lyulph Stanley, 1839–1925. Liberal MP, 1880–5. 4th Baron Stanley of Alderley and 4th Baron Sheffield. Clementine Churchill's uncle. Father of Venetia (Mrs Edwin Montagu) and Sylvia (Mrs Anthony Henley).

Churchill bowed to her advice. The photograph of the *Blücher* was abandoned. But he was unconvinced by her letter of December 30 in which she had tried to say a good word for Asquith, replying on January 2:

> . . . You are a vy sapient cat to write as you do in yr last letter. But I feel that my work with Asquith has come to an end. I have found him a weak and disloyal chief. I hope I shall not ever have to serve under him again. After the 'Perhaps he might have a battalion' letter I cannot feel the slightest regard for him any more. LG is no doubt all you say: but his interests are not divorced from mine and in those circumstances we can work together if occasion arises. After all he always disagreed about D'Iles. He was not like HHA, a co-adventurer—approving & agreeing at every stage. And he had the power to put things right with us as regards my policy & myself. But his slothfulness & procrastination ruined the policy, & his political nippiness squandered his credit. However there is no reason why ordinary relations shd not be preserved.

As 1915 came to an end there was still no news of which Battalion he was to go to. Churchill remained at St Omer at Max Aitken's headquarters, brooding on politics and anxious to take up his command.

20

In Training

WHILE he was at St Omer on New Year's Day 1916 Churchill learned that he had been appointed to the command of an Infantry Battalion, the 6th Royal Scots Fusiliers. Military security would not permit him to tell his wife either where his Battalion was to train, or to which part of the front it would be sent; all he could say was that the trenches would be 'a few miles to the left of where I was before'. He told her how glad he was to be leaving St Omer, 'a desert' since French's departure.

The 6th Battalion of the Royal Scots Fusiliers consisted of thirty officers and seven hundred men. It formed a part of the Ninth (Scottish) Division, commanded by Major-General Furse,[1] with whom Churchill dined on January 1 at his headquarters at Merris. The evening was a success, more so than his first evening with the Grenadiers, for, as he wrote to his wife: 'They evidently will like vy much to have me. The general—Furse—is extremely well thought of here and is a thoroughly frank & broadminded man. . . . Most of the staff had met me soldiering somewhere or other, & we had a pleasant evening.' During the dinner Churchill asked about the condition and history of his Battalion. He heard of its gallantry at the Battle of Loos in September 1915, and of its heavy losses, writing to his wife:

More than half the men, & ¾rs of the officers were shot, & these terrible gaps have been filled up by recruits of good quality, & quite young inexperienced officers. I shd therefore be able to bring in my two good officers Spiers & Archie & put them where I like. They will be sorely needed. In spite of its crippled condition the regiment has been for two months in the worst part

[1] William Thomas Furse, 1865–1953. Entered Army, 1884. ADC to Lord Roberts when Commander-in-Chief, India, 1890–3. Brigadier-General commanding the II Corps in France, 1915. General Officer commanding the 9th (Scottish) Division, 1915–16. Knighted, 1917. Lieutenant-General, 1917; Member of the Army Council, 1920.

of the line; but now they are resting & do not go in again till the 20th: & then to an easier post. Thus I will have at least a fortnight to pull them together and get them into my hand.

Churchill's hope of having Spiers with him as his principal support was dashed a few days later when he learned that he could not take him to the Battalion. The work of training seven hundred men and taking them into the line was considered inappropriate for an officer of Spiers' experience, whose liaison activities were assuming increasing significance.[1] But Haig agreed to let Sir Archibald Sinclair join Churchill as his second-in-command.

Churchill entered into his duties as a Battalion Commander with enthusiasm, writing to his wife on January 3, before he had even met his men: 'Now that I shall be commanding a Scottish battalion, I shd like you to send me a copy in one volume of Burns. I will soothe & cheer their spirits by quotations from it. I shall have to be careful not to drop into a mimicry of their accent! You know I am a vy gt admirer of that race. A wife, a constituency, & now a regiment attest the sincerity of my choice!' A day later, on January 4, Churchill was formally appointed to his command. He knew that it would not be an easy task, commanding a Battalion which had suffered so severely, and all of whose senior officers had been killed in battle. 'It will be an exhausting labour,' he wrote to his wife, 'but I expect I shall succeed. I am vy glad to have some work to do: after this long appalling waste of my energies; tho' perhaps some more appropriate outlet cd have been found.' Lieutenant Hakewill Smith,[2] the Battalion's only regular officer in 1915, recalled fifty years later in conversation with the author, the 'horror' with which the news of Churchill's impending arrival was

[1] The friendship built up between Churchill and Spiers during December continued to flourish, and Churchill followed Spiers' career closely. 'I read your name this morning in the casualty list for the 4th time with keen emotion . . .' Churchill wrote to him on 27 October 1916. 'I cannot tell you how much I admire and reverence the brilliant & noble service you are doing & have done for the country. You are indeed a Paladin worthy to rank with the truest knights of the great days of romance. Thank God you are alive. Some good angel has guarded you amid such innumerable perils, & brought you safely thus far along this terrible & never ending road. . . . Thank you so much for the helmet you sent me. It is a fine trophy. But my dear why don't you write. I shd so value yr letters and it wd be such a pleasure to me to receive them.'

[2] Edmund Hakewill Smith, 1896–   . Born in South Africa. Served Cape Town Highlanders, August–September 1914. Royal Military College, Sandhurst, November 1914–June 1915. 2nd Lieutenant, Royal Scots Fusiliers, June 1915. On active service, 1915–18; twice wounded. Major-General, 1942. Director of Organization, War Office, 1942–3. Commanded 52nd Lowland Division, 1943–6. Governor, Military Knights of Windsor, 1951. Deputy Constable and Lieutenant-Governor, Windsor Castle, 1964. Knighted, 1967.

greeted. Another regimental officer, Captain Gibb,[1] recorded in *With Winston Churchill at the Front* the reaction of officers and men alike:

When the news spread, a mutinous spirit grew. . . . Why could not Churchill have gone to the Argylls if he must have a Scottish regiment! We should all have been greatly interested to see him in a kilt and, besides, the Argylls were accustomed to celebrities in their ranks since Ian Hay[2] had celebrated their deeds in his remunerative volume. Or again, we should all have been glad to see him once for all oust and utterly displace the Brigade Commander,[3] who had jarred upon us since the day he stopped the Battalion's leave for a fortnight on finding in our front line a well-rusted bayonet, the property of some migratory and irresponsible sapper. We should even have been glad to see him replace the Divisional General [Furse] who, although popular, was always unduly anxious to involve us in unpleasant and dangerous brawls with the Germans opposite. Indeed, any position at all in the Expeditionary Force seemed not too exalted for Winston if only he had left us our own CO and refrained from disturbing the peace of the pastures of Moolenacker.

On January 5 Churchill set off from St Omer to join his Battalion in its reserve billets near the town of Meteren. He and his small staff were billeted in the village of Moolenacker, which for the next three weeks was to be their home. The gently undulating terrain reminded some of the young Scottish officers of Caithness; 'flat and uninteresting', as Lieutenant McDavid[4] later recalled in a letter to the author, 'with croftlike farms scattered all around. Buildings were dilapidated, occupying three sides of a muddy square, with the inevitable dung-heap in the middle. . . . I can't remember seeing any livestock, other than some-

---

[1] Andrew Dewar Gibb, 1888–   . Called to the Bar, 1914. Officer commanding D Company, 6th Royal Scots Fusiliers, 1915–16, Captain and Adjutant, 1916. He published *With Winston Churchill at the Front* in 1924. Regius Professor of Law, Glasgow University, 1934–58. Chairman of the Scottish National Party, 1936–40.

[2] John Hay Beith, 1876–1952. Novelist, playwright and historian; pen-name, Ian Hay. Captain, Argyll and Sutherland Highlanders, 1914–16, Published *The First Hundred Thousand* in 1915. Member of the British War Mission to the United States, 1916–18. Published *Carrying On* in 1917; several chapters were set in Ploegsteert. Director of Public Relations at the War Office, 1938–41.

[3] Henry Ernest Walshe, 1866–1947. Entered Army, 1889. Crossed to France, 13 August 1914, as a Major with the 2nd Battalion South Staffordshire Regiment. Brigadier-General Commanding the 27th Infantry Brigade, September 1915–April 1916.

[4] Jock McDavid, 1897–   . Enlisted in the Royal Scots Fusiliers, October 1914. 2nd Lieutenant, April 1915. Acting Adjutant, 6th Royal Scots Fusiliers, November 1915. Promoted Lieutenant while serving as Adjutant, December 1915. Gassed, August 1918. Demobilized, October 1919. Area-Manager, Shell-Mex Ltd. 1919–28; Divisional Manager, 1928–34. Subsequently in the brewing and distilling industry.

what decrepit nags and a few mules probably discarded by a remount section previously billeted in the district.' The Battalion was in need of rest. After its severe losses at the Battle of Loos, it had spent some months in the front-line trenches of the Ypres salient before being sent into reserve. 'We had a frightfully bad time at Ypres,' Hakewill Smith recalled, 'with water up to the waist. We were observed and watched by the Boche all the time; they were oppressively close.'

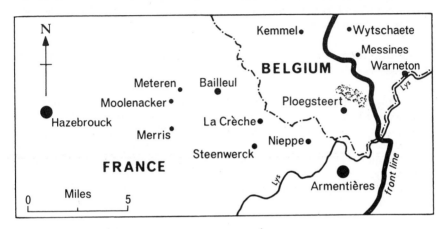

THE WYTSCHAETE TO ARMENTIÈRES SECTOR OF THE
WESTERN FRONT, JANUARY 1916

Before he reached the village of Moolenacker Churchill sent a message forward to say that he wished to meet all the officers at luncheon, after which he would inspect the whole Battalion. 'Just before noon,' Hakewill Smith recalled, 'an imposing cavalcade arrived. Churchill on a black charger, Archie Sinclair on a black charger, two grooms on black chargers followed by a limber filled with Churchill's luggage—much more than the 35 lbs allowed weight. In the rear half we saw a curious contraption: a long bath and a boiler for heating the bath water.' Churchill proceeded to his headquarters at Moolenacker Farm, a farm which, Gibb wrote, was 'a more than usually dirty farm', whose farm people were 'more than usually dirty and unprepossessing'. Some of them had gathered in the orderly room to witness the arrival of the new Commanding Officer. Gibb described the ensuing scene:

Whether by means of the sign-language, or by dint of that reiteration which works such wonders, the dirty ladies of the house had come to understand that the new Colonel was somebody. Winston therefore made fitting entry on this his formal accession to power, for not only was there much clicking and saluting on the part of

- (a) the officers,
- (b) the Sergeant-Major, and
- (c) the prisoners,

but the ladies rose up to the accompaniment of loud whispers of '*Monsieur le ministre!*' '*Monsieur le Colonel!*' '*Ah, c'est lui?*' '*C'est votre ministre?*' and in this way imparted to the proceedings at once an irregular air of friendliness, and an international colour, which produced a most happy effect and one worthy of the occasion.

Churchill then lunched with the officers of his headquarters staff. Hakewill Smith later recalled:

It was quite the most uncomfortable lunch I had ever been at. Churchill didn't say a word: he went right round the table staring each officer out of countenance. We had disliked the idea of Churchill being in command; now, having seen him, we disliked the idea even more. At the end of the lunch, he made a short speech: 'Gentlemen, I am now your Commanding Officer. Those who support me I will look after. Those who go against me I will break. Good afternoon gentlemen.' Everyone was agreed that we were in for a pretty rotten time.

There followed a parade of the whole Battalion, of which Hakewill Smith was again a witness:

The after lunch parade was a farce. The men were at the slope when Churchill appeared on his charger. Captain Gibb reported that all were present. While the troops were still at the slope, Churchill called out: 'Royal Scots Fusiliers! Fix Bayonets!' The command could not possibly be carried out from the slope position. A couple of the chaps put their rifles on the ground and pulled out their bayonets; the rest were merely mystified. Eventually, Gibb persuaded Churchill to call 'Order Arms' and to fix their bayonets in the normal way.

Winston then inspected the men. Having done so, he gave a cavalry order: 'Sections Right!' This meant nothing to the Jocks, who had the sense to stand still and do nothing.

Such were the impressions that Churchill made in his first hours as a Commanding Officer. His own impressions were mixed. There was a more successful drill parade on the following morning. When Churchill wrote to his wife he was enthusiastic and hopeful: 'The young officers are all small middle class Scotsmen—vy brave & willing & intelligent: but of course all quite new to soldiering. All the seniors & all the professionals have fallen. I have spent the morning watching each company in turn drill & handle their arms. They are vy good. . . . The regiment is full of life & strength, & I believe I shall be a help to them.' McDavid was conscious that the Royal Scots Fusiliers had not made quite the same impact upon Churchill as the Grenadiers had done. Later he recalled, in conversation with the author:

The immediate impression which Churchill formed when he reached us was a poor one. He had come from a guards battalion which consisted almost entirely of regular soldiers. These Guardsmen spent only 48 hours in the trenches at any one time, while we were 6 days in and 6 days out. When Churchill joined the 6th Royal Scots Fusiliers he joined a conglomerated mess of young civilians and old reservists, both of whom had experienced hell since they arrived in France in the spring of 1915; the demoralising effects of the Battle of Loos. After Loos there had only been an extremely brief period of rest, followed by the most disastrous winter of the war over in the Ypres Salient. At Ypres we had to walk four miles from our rest billet to the front line, and over half of this was in the slimy mud with exploding shells as a constant danger. Morale was low, understandably so because of the absolutely hellish condition of the Salient trudging mile after mile with mud up to one's thighs, severe frost, poor equipment, and continual bombardment. When Churchill reached us we had only had a week's rest following these demoralising conditions. No wonder we made a poor impression on him.

It was Churchill's task, as Colonel, to rally these men and prepare them for their return to the front line two weeks later. It was a short time and a heavy task. 'I am now deeply immersed in the very small things which fall to my lot,' he wrote to his wife on January 6. 'I do all I can with zest.' On January 7 he sent his wife an account of his first efforts to gain his men's confidence. They were still puzzled by the appearance of a popular politician in their midst:

. . . I made my battalion parade this morning & drilled them myself all together. They have not done this before and I am anxious to make them feel their corporate identity & the sense of my personal control. A colonel within his own sphere is an autocrat who punishes & promotes & displaces at his discretion. The Brigadier is leaving me to myself for these first days in order that I may get all the threads in my hand. It is not hard for me to give orders as you know. . . .
I am quite comfortable, & the mess, as I told you, is clean & well supplied. Everyone is filled with the desire to obey & assist and I feel a growing confidence in the way the machine will work when I take it into action. Athough

the fortnight's further 'repose' is vy valuable for training & gaining control, of course I look forward to its conclusion.

'I am settling down here and gaining control & confidence,' he wrote to his wife again on the following day. 'The young officers are so keen, plucky & intelligent, so ready to obey & to be led, that I feel increasingly sure that we shall stand any ordinary test without discredit.' Two days later, on January 10, he wrote:

> . . . I continue to work at the details of my battalion wh is officered entirely by quite young boys. Archie does a mass of housekeeping work, & I try to make good arrangements & give them all the feeling that there is something behind them & that they are strongly commanded. Of course they yield implicit loyalty & obedience & endeavour to meet or forestall every wish. I am fairly confident of being able to help them to do well, in spite of the woefully attenuated state of the regiment's officers.

After a week with his Battalion, Churchill felt that he had begun to win their confidence. Nor was Brigadier-General Walshe, his immediate superior, dissatisfied. On January 13 Churchill wrote to his wife:

> . . . The Brigadier-General has left me quite alone, tho' civil. He has not meddled at all in my affairs wh I am conducting with confidence. I am pressing hard for the proper promotion of officers wh is shockingly neglected & delayed. I am filling up all the non-commissioned officers vacancies. Yesterday I spent seeing all the officers & NCO's, company by company, & explaining to them how I wish things to be done. It was odd to see these politicians of a year ago—Glasgow grocers, fitters, miners—all Trade Unionists probably, who I have harangued in bygone days in the St Andrews Hall—now all transformed into Sergeants & corporals stiffened by discipline and hardened by war into a fine set of warriors.

Churchill was not enamoured of the reserve billets; 'squalid little French farms', he described them to his wife, 'rising from a sea of sopping fields & muddy lanes'. Even in reserve the war was never far away: 'The guns boom away in the distance,' he told her, '& at night the sky to the Northward blinks & flickers with the wicked lights of war.' On January 13 he gave her an account of the training which he himself was having:

> . . . In the morning Archie & I practised bomb-throwing. It is a job to be approached gingerly. You pull out the safety pin, & then as long as you hold the bomb in your hand nothing happens. But the moment you throw it—or release your hand—the fuse begins to burn & then 5 seconds afterwards there

is real good bang & splinters fly all over the place. As soon as you have thrown it, you bob down behind the parapet, until the explosion has occurred. Sometimes the men are stupid—drop the bomb in the trench or close to it—then the bombing officer—a young Sandhurst kid—deftly picks it up & throws it away with perhaps 2 seconds to spare. Everyone has to learn. It is perfectly safe as long as you do it right.

The 'young Sandhurst kid' was Hakewill Smith, whom Churchill soon renamed the 'bomb boy'. He too recalled the Colonel's training on that cold January morning: 'Churchill wasn't very accurate in his throwing.[1] He threw one bomb and said "That's enough".'

The efforts which Churchill made to fit himself into the military routine made a strong impression upon the men under his command. McDavid recalled:

After a very brief period he had accelerated the morale of officers and men to an almost unbelievable degree. It was sheer personality. We laughed at lots of things he did, but there were other things we did not laugh at for we knew they were sound. He had a unique approach which did wonders to us. He let everyone under his command see that he was responsible, from the very moment he arrived, that they understood not only *what* they were supposed to do, but *why* they had to do it. . . .

No detail of our daily life was too small for him to ignore. He overlooked nothing. . . . Instead of a quick glance at what was being done he would stop and talk with everyone and probe to the bottom of every activity. I have never known an officer take such pains to inspire confidence or to gain confidence; indeed he inspired confidence in gaining it.

The Battalion was due to go forward on about January 20. It had been allocated a sector of the front line near the village of Ploegsteert, on the Belgian side of the Franco-Belgian border. Churchill was surprised to learn that the men of the Ninth Division spent longer in the trenches than the Guards had done. He explained the routine to his wife in his letter of January 13: 'Unlike Cavan's—this division do 6 days in the front line, 6 days in the support line (just as unhealthy) 6 days more in the front line, & then some of them 6 days rest—& begin again. No wonder they wear them out. Compare this with 48 hours in & 48 hours out, 3 times repeated, & then 6 days rest.' On the following day he was able to send her more information about the Ploegsteert sector. 'It is a vy quiet part of the line at present,' he wrote,

[1] In 1896, when going ashore at the Sassoon Dock, Bombay, Churchill had dislocated his shoulder, an injury which inconvenienced him for the rest of his life. He was unable to raise his right arm sharply, and had always to play polo with the upper part of his arm strapped to his body.

'though the general (Furse) means to stir them up. The casualties run only to 5 or 6 a day on the front of the division: wh is no more than are lost in one battalion of the Guards. Also I hear good reports of the trenches—dugouts etc. Not too muddy, & good communications to get into them by.'

On January 13, when less than a week remained before the Battalion was due to go into the trenches, Churchill learned they were to have an extra week in training: 'I am sorry there is this further delay,' he wrote to his wife, 'for a war without action is really a dreary affair. But these boys were evidently delighted. . . .' On the following day he replied to a letter from his brother by sending him an account of life as a Commanding Officer. His Battalion, he said, consisted 'entirely of young boy officers—willing, plucky, intelligent—but of course almost untrained and quite inexperienced'. Their average age, he had calculated, was twenty-three. His brother's news about the evacuation of the Gallipoli Peninsula caused him to brood for a while on the past. Of the Dardanelles he wrote: 'History will vindicate the conception, & the errors in execution will on the whole leave me clear. My one fatal mistake was trying to achieve a gt enterprise without having the plenary authority wh cd so easily have carried it to success.' But now, he wrote, 'the days slip away quickly in the transaction of small things'. Churchill told his brother that after two or three months as a Battalion Commander he expected to be appointed to command a Brigade. But he was no longer worried about attaining the position which had so cruelly mocked him in the previous month; 'I shall be proud to lead this shattered battalion to the assault,' he wrote. He was concerned about his brother's future. After Hamilton's departure from Gallipoli in October 1915, Jack Churchill had been taken on to General Birdwood's staff. 'I often think of you,' Churchill wrote, 'and rejoice you are on the whole not ill-placed in these times. Stick to Birdwood, & don't go into unnecessary danger.' As for the future, he wrote, 'The war plods on slowly & I think it will be all right in the end. But what a weary toil for the millions! After it is over politics will be interesting; & we shall find a clear field. . . . If I am killed, the insurances are quite good & Clemmie & Goonie must hold together till peace comes—not—please God—one day before undoubted victory.'

While his Battalion was at Moolenacker, Churchill rode to Kemmel to see Major-General Lipsett,[1] of the Royal Irish Regiment, who had

---

[1] Louis James Lipsett, 1874–1918. 2nd Lieutenant, Royal Irish Regiment, 1894. Major, attached to the Canadian Army, 1911–14. Brigadier-General, attached to the Canadian Expeditionary Force, 1914–16; Lieutenant-Colonel, Royal Irish Regiment, 1917–18.

been at Sandhurst with him, and was attached to the Canadian forces. Lipsett was the inventor of the 'raid'; a means of taking offensive action within the strictly limited confines of trench warfare. In the first of these 'raids' a group of Canadians had left their front-line trenches, crossed no-man's-land, entered the German trenches facing them, and with the loss of only one of their own men had killed forty Germans. They then returned to their own trenches. Lipsett was keen to show Churchill how his 'raids' worked. 'He is full of ruses and stratagems,' Churchill wrote to his wife on January 14, 'and his revealing his secrets to me is a compliment.' After a day with Lipsett he wrote to her again:

He made a realistic attack with his bombs on a section of our reserve trenches. The splinters flew all over the place. It was like a skirmish: but no one was hurt. Lucky! The Canadians grinned from ear to ear to see me. Wonderful fellows: like leopards. I was made to make them a speech & produced a really good one on the spur of the moment. Meanwhile the Germans threw occasional shrapnel shells wh burst a short distance off without anyone taking the slightest notice.

When Churchill wrote to his wife on January 16 he was under no illusion about the effort still needed to get the Battalion up to the mark:

This battalion is the weakest in the brigade & makes the least good appearance. The young officers have not the command to make their companies drill & march really well. They can do a plain job all right; but the polish is at present lacking. Both Furse & the Brigadier realise fully these difficulties, and I am doing my best to cope with them. Up to the present however, I have been entirely occupied with practice points—gas helmets, rifles in good order, trench discipline & routine etc. As we are going to be a week more out of the line, I shall give them some vy precise drill & marching. It is all helpful.

Churchill's only serious disagreement with his officers was over the question of military discipline. His mind turned instinctively to leniency. 'My dear,' he wrote to his wife, who worried lest he was too severe, 'don't be at all anxious about my being hard on the men. Am I ever hard on anybody? No. I have reduced punishment both in quantity, & method.' Churchill had been much moved by the sufferings of the 6th Royal Scots Fusiliers at Loos. His first question to the first troublemaker who came before him was: 'Were you in the battle?' When the man replied, 'Yes,' the charge against him was dismissed. The officers were surprised by this generous act; and horrified when, as McDavid recalled, 'everyone then said they had been at Loos'. Robert

Fox,[1] one of the Battalion's Lewis gunners, recalled in a radio broadcast in 1964: 'Churchill was scrupulously fair to any man before him on a charge. I remember once, when acting as escort, I heard him cross-examine the NCO giving evidence against the man, with all the skill of a counsel at the Bar. The evidence did not satisfy him, so he dismissed the charge and gave the NCO a homily on the virtues of exactitude.' Gibb believed that Churchill was 'quite wrong' in siding so openly with the rank and file, writing in his book:

It is difficult to see how his ideas on this matter could receive sanction without serious detriment to the one essential of discipline, viz, prompt obedience to orders.

It used to happen that a soldier when ordered say, by a corporal, to perform some duty, did, through laziness or dislike of the corporal or distaste for the order given, refuse to obey that order, at the same time usually inviting the corporal to perform certain notoriously impossible physical feats or proceed to a certain non-existent destination, all in order to show his utter contempt of the corporal and emphasize his determination on no account to do as he was told. Now this is indiscipline in the highest degree, and a man is always 'run in' at once for it, and on the facts being proved against him he is usually heavily punished.

It was however impossible, Gibb recalled, to persuade Churchill to punish such indiscipline according to the rules:

He considered that no man would wittingly incur the serious penalties inevitable in such a case, did he know that his conduct was in fact precisely such conduct as would render him liable to them. In any event, the Colonel used to say, whether or not the man knew, it was only fair to explain the position to him there and then, and there and then to give him a chance to depart from his insubordinate attitude.

Churchill's offer of a second chance appalled the officers. 'I am afraid the men began to realize,' wrote Gibb, 'that they might at least once indulge themselves in the luxury of telling their sergeants to go to hell!'

Despite his officers' disapproval, Churchill persevered in what they considered his unmilitary attitude towards discipline.

---

[1] Robert Fox, 1894–   . Left school at the age of twelve. Worked in mills, factories and shipyards. Enlisted, Royal Scots Fusiliers, 16 August 1914. Crossed to France with 6th Battalion, 11 May 1915. Wounded at Festubert, June 1915. Fought at Loos, September 1915. Wounded on the Somme, August 1916. Wounded near Arras, April 1917. Demobilized, 1919. Subsequently a reporter, proof reader and journalist, working in Paris on the *Chicago Tribune* and the *New York Herald*.

While the Battalion was in reserve, Churchill had continued to badger his wife for supplies. 'Try to get a King's messenger to bring over my new boots when they are ready,' he had written on January 2. When some food parcels were delayed he wrote impatiently, on January 3: 'You must find out from the Post Office what went wrong & also what is the best route & method.' 'Order me a new tunic thicker than the last,' he wrote on January 5, 'with less baggy pockets. . . . Send also 2 spare bits of badge for this regiment: and a Glengarry cap.' On January 8 he wrote from Moolenacker Farm; 'Go on sending brandy (my own) & tinned things of the ordinary types (but good quality). Fantastic tinned things usually mock me in the end.' On the same day, realizing that he was going to be with the Battalion for some time, he wrote: 'Let me have some note paper printed nicely:

6TH ROYAL SCOTS FUSILIERS
IN THE FIELD

It is a good thing to fly the flag at the main.'

On January 13 Clementine Churchill's Christmas hamper finally arrived. He was delighted: 'I never saw such dainties & profusion. We shall eat them sparingly keeping the best for the trenches. It will be a good thing to start off another case on the same lines (esp the cheese & the raisins). If you send it now, it will be here in a fortnight or three weeks & will be vy welcome.' He was full of praise for the sleeping bag which she had sent him: 'I must admit the warmth of the red hot polar bear is delicious to sleep in. It wd just suit you as it seems to have a natural warmth of its own & you cd develop that fierce temperature wh is good for Kats before they plunge into slumber.'

Churchill did not limit the search for comfort to himself alone. On his first afternoon with the Battalion he had addressed the officers with solemn words: 'Gentlemen, we are now going to make war—on the lice.' And this he was determined to do, for, as Gibb recorded:

With these words did the great scion of the house of Marlborough first address his Scottish Captains assembled in council. And with these words was inaugurated such a discourse on pulex Europaeus, its origin, growth, and nature, its habitat and its importance as a factor in wars ancient and modern, as left one agape with wonder at the erudition and force of its author. . . .

Thereafter he created a committee of company commanders to concert measures for the utter extermination of all the lice in the battalion.

The delousing committee was soon busy. 'It was a terrific moment,' McDavid recalled, 'and by God it worked.' The French officer attached to the 9th Division as liaison officer, Emile Herzog,[1] was sent with McDavid to Bailleul to search for baths for the men. Churchill had suggested that brewery vats might be suitable for his Fusiliers. When Herzog and McDavid found a deserted brewery on the outskirts of the town, the men were marched the two miles from Moolenacker to their improvised bath-house. While the delousing committee was at work, Churchill turned to other aspects of the Battalion's comfort. When he addressed the men on the morning after his arrival he spoke sympathetically. 'You men have had a hard time,' he said. 'Now you're going to have it easy for some time—I hope.' Action soon followed, as Robert Fox recalled:

Huge stocks of clothing arrived at the quartermaster's stores. We all needed new rig-outs. We got them. Steel helmets were by then being issued to the British Army. We were among the first to get them. We found, too, a vast improvement in our rations. Bully beef and biscuits were only memories.

There were no parades after mid-day. The rest of the day was given over to rest and recreation. A field was rolled out more or less flat and goal-posts erected. Jerseys and footballs arrived from somewhere. Games were arranged against neighbouring units. The Fusiliers won them all. Churchill took a great pride in his team. He rarely missed a match.

The culmination of these efforts came on January 16, when Churchill arranged a combined sports day and concert. 'The officers & men have taken a lively interest in both affairs,' Churchill wrote to his wife on the great day; 'it is odd no one has got any up for them before.' A piano had been procured from somewhere, new songs were practised and various games were devised with somewhat macabre local touches, such as 'the bomb throwers'. 'I will let you know how it goes off,' he told his wife. 'I think they want nursing & encouraging, more than drill-sergeanting. . . .'

Churchill sent his wife a full account of the day's activities. He was proud of his efforts, and had invited several guests:

The sports were highly successful & the men were really delighted. They were most amusing sports—mule races, pillow fights, obstacle races etc. All

[1] Emile Salomon Wilhelm Herzog, 1885–1967. Lieutenant, French Army, 1914–16. Attached as liaison officer to the 9th Division, 1916. He drew upon his experiences for his first novel, *Silences du Colonel Bramble*, published in 1918 under the name André Maurois. Novelist and historian. Honorary knighthood, 1938. Eyewitness attached to the British GHQ in France, 1939–40.

well organised, & supported by gt keenness & interest. After dark we had
our first concert in a big barn. Such singing you never heard. People sang
with the greatest courage who had no idea either of words or tune. Jack Seely
and other officers came & Jack presented the prizes for the sports, & called
for three cheers for me & an extra one for you, all were most heartily given.
We had quite a banquet in the evening. Jack S, Colonel Holland,[1] some of
the Bde staff, 'Ian Hay' & others. Quite a cheery day. The men enjoyed
themselves immensely. Poor fellows—nothing like this had ever been done
for them before. They do not get much to brighten their lives—short though
they may be. . . .

On the day after the concert, training had to continue, for on January
18 all four Battalions were to take part in a route march, under
Brigadier-General Walshe's critical gaze. 'This morning,' Churchill
wrote to his wife on January 17, 'I have been drilling them vy strictly,
so that tomorrow they may give most satisfaction to the Brigadier, &
work with more style & polish. They seemed to try vy hard & I think
they will do better. However they are not grenadiers & I am not a drill
sergeant.'

On January 17 Churchill rode into Hazebrouck, just over six miles
away, to hear a special lecture by Colonel Holland on the battle of Loos.
This battle was a grim memory for all who had been through it; its
'lessons' would obviously have to be learned before any further attempt
to break through the German trenches were made. Churchill described
the lecture to his wife:

. . . The theatre was crowded with Generals & officers. Jack Seely & I cd
not even get a seat, but stood at the wings of the stage. Tom spoke vy well
but his tale was one of hopeless failure, of sublime heroism utterly wasted &
of splendid Scottish soldiers shorn away in vain. . . with never the ghost of a
chance of success. 6,000 k & w out of 10,000 in this Scottish division alone.
Alas alas. Afterwards they asked what was the lesson of the lecture. I restrained an impulse to reply 'Don't do it again'. But they will—I have no
doubt.

As the days passed, the atmosphere at Moolenacker became more
relaxed. The men realized that their commanding officer was not
going to make life hell for them, or let them down. The 27th Brigade
route march took place on January 18. For the first time since he had

---

[1] Arthur Edward Aveling Holland, 1862–1927. Known as 'Tom'. Entered Army, 1880.
Colonel, 1910. Commanded the Artillery of the 8th Division, 1914–15; of the 1st Division,
1915–16. Major-General commanding the Artillery of the 3rd Army, 1916. Lieutenant-
General commanding the Artillery of the I Army Corps, 1917–18. Knighted, 1918. Conservative MP, 1924–7.

taken command Churchill saw his Battalion exposed to the critical gaze of higher authorities. He was confident that the efforts which he had made during the past two weeks would be successful. Among his special concerns was that his men should sing while they were marching. The route march was to be the first public exhibition of their talents. Gibb remembered this aspect of the route march vividly:

We were second company, and in passing through the village of Merris the men were busy inventing adventures and ever fresh adventures in song for their hero and heroine. Afar off I saw the Colonel coming down the column and my heart leaped, for here was our company singing lustily and I felt sure of praise. Winston's large black horse loomed in sight, and then the amazing thing happened. The first platoon—mine—was seized, for the first and last time in its existence, with a devastating attack of modesty and dried up like a mountain rill in summer. The contagion spread and in a moment the company was marching mute—mute of modesty:

'Why are your men not singing, Captain Gibb?' shouted the Colonel to our Company Commander.

'They *were*, sir, but they think—they thought—they're afraid that——' but Winston had passed on down the column shouting 'Sing, sing' as he went.

Despite this setback, Churchill was satisfied by his Battalion's performance. 'The men did vy well,' he wrote to his wife; 'Their equipment & bearing showed a gt advance. The Brigadier was impressed in spite of himself; & said what a gt improvement had taken place.'

On January 19 Churchill went into Hazebrouck again, together with the other three Colonels of the Brigade. Colonels had been summoned from the whole reserve area. 'All the day I have been at the Machine gun school,' he wrote to his wife, 'with scores of Colonels listening to not vy illuminating lectures.' Among those who travelled in with him on the bus was Cameron of Lochiel,[1] who had been at Harrow and Sandhurst with him, and had raised, and was then commanding the 5th Battalion of the Cameron Highlanders. 'He has done heroically out here,' Churchill wrote to his wife; and he described how, at Loos, 'only he & his adjutant & 100 men survived unhit out of 26 officers & 850 men who charged. These stormed the German trench & held it. Where is Balaclava compared to that.[2] Two distinguished conduct medals were given to the men! Glorious system.'

[1] Donald Walter Cameron of Lochiel, 1876–1951. Entered Army, 1896. Retired with rank of Captain 1906. Raised and commanded the 5th Battalion of the Cameron Highlanders, 1914–16. Commanded the Lovat Scouts Sharpshooters, 1917–18. Knighted, 1934.

[2] On 25 October 1854, at the battle of Balaclava, the Light Brigade lost over 400 of its 673 men.

After the lectures Churchill somehow procured a car, and was driven into St Omer, 'to buy a few stores, & see a few potentates'. On the road to St Omer, he wrote to his wife, 'Quite by chance I met Haig riding on the road 3 miles out. He rode up & shook hands & we exchanged a few banalities.'

On January 20 Churchill paid his first visit to the sector of the line which his Battalion was to hold. This was the area in which he would be living and fighting for several months. He was pleased with what he found:

My beloved,

. . . I have just come back from the line, having had a jolly day. I examined the whole of our front & all its approaches thoroughly. It is much the best bit of line I have yet seen all along the front. Incomparably better on every score than the sector where the Guards were. It is dry—the trenches are boarded & drained. The parapets are thick & bullet-proof. The wire is good. The field of fire clear. There are in most parts plenty of traverses (to localise the effect of shells), good dugouts & good shelter from fire. I think we cd stand a pretty good pounding here with comparatively little loss. Yesterday afternoon in fact hundreds of shells were fired into the trenches, & only *one* got a result. . . .

There was a little shelling today. The weather beautiful in the morning. I shall like this line vy much & shall feel vy proud to take charge of 1000 yards of 'the frontier between right & wrong'. . . .

While returning from his preliminary reconnaissance of his own future sector of the front line, Churchill lunched with Seely. That afternoon they attended one of the many lectures which had become a feature of life behind the lines. This time it was a lecture on the front line, 'illustrated by magic lantern aeroplane photographs,' he wrote to his wife; 'The lecturer was inarticulate, & the photographs indistinguishable, a futile performance'. That night Churchill dined with the Argyll and Sutherland Highlanders with whose Colonel, Henry Pelham Burn,[1] he had already made friends. There were twelve Colonels in the Ninth Division, all of whom had met at the machine-gun school on the previous day. 'I looked the youngest of all . . . & felt so too,' Churchill told his wife, 'yet I was the oldest but 2: & have had more

[1] Henry Pelham Burn, 1882–1958. Entered Army, 1901. Captain, 1910. Adjutant, 1st Battalion the Gordon Highlanders, November 1914. Brigade Major, 8th Infantry Brigade, April 1915. Colonel commanding the 152nd Infantry Brigade, July 1916–April 1918. Served in France and Belgium from 31 October 1914 to 8 April 1918. Brigadier-General, 1918.

worry than the lot put together.' Among those invited to the dinner was Pelham Burn's Divisional General, Arthur Hoskins.[1] 'He was a good sort of General,' Churchill wrote to his wife on January 22, '& like nearly all these fellows had met me campaigning several times, tho' I had forgotten. We sat jawing till 12.30 and Archie dropped asleep.'

Churchill was eager to go into action; Clementine Churchill was less enthusiastic. 'It makes me terribly anxious to feel that your Battalion is so weak,' she wrote to him on January 20; 'It will be a great credit to you if you improve it and bring it up to the mark. Do not think me over-cautious, but don't be too ambitious at first or try your men too high—I wish you were not going so soon with these untried men into the line.' She worried about him all the time, and wanted so much to see him again. She even devised a scheme to go over to Dieppe and meet him there, but nothing came of it. In her letter of January 20 Clementine Churchill wrote of how she often woke up at night thinking of him, and of all the women in Europe who, equally distraught, lay awake praying for their husbands' safety. On the following day his sister-in-law, Lady Gwendeline Churchill, wrote, sharing Clementine Churchill's concern:

My dear Winston,

Five more days before you and your battalion go in to the Trenches—and that fact distresses me—it makes me fidgett on my chair; makes me toss in my bed, makes me bite my nails at meals—I will be lighthearted again when you come out—when will that be? . . .

Keep dodging the bullets—whatever happens don't get shot—you will be wanted here—& for Godsake I hope it will be before the end of the War—before the government have brought the Country down to a stalemate peace—but even my dear, if you are not back before then, you will be wanted then after the corpses of these mediocre worn out extenuéed ministers have been removed & it won't be too late to be at the head of a still vigorous & healthy nation—it will clamour for such a man as you—you are unique in your generation—you are the only one—so dodge the bullets—one ought not to grudge your sojourn at the Front, as long as you keep out the way of obvious danger—it is doing no harm either to yourself or to the Country FOR THE TIME BEING—you have been out barely 2 months—what are a few months in your crowded life or in the life of the Country—though I know that a few days, a few hours count in a War. . . .

---

[1] Arthur Reginald Hoskins, 1871–1942. 2nd Lieutenant, 1891. Served on the Nile Expedition, 1898. Brigadier-General commanding the 8th Infantry Brigade, March–October 1915. Vth Army Corps Staff, October 1915–December 1916. Commander-in-Chief, East Africa, 1917. Knighted, 1919. Principal, Bonar Law College, 1929–38.

How the injustice of all that has happened since last May smarts one—& you in your innermost thoughts have been right ever since the first days of the War—your instincts were right, your Policy, properly carried out, properly supported was absolutely right—energy, decision, forethought, you had them—isn't it extraordinary that you could not down the mediocrities— of course there were too many of them.

You are in the right place just now as it has all turned out—& if only one could make certain that you were bullet proof, it would be alright. . . .

Much love, Yrs affectionately
Goonie

On January 21 Churchill visited the front line again. When he wrote to his wife about his visit on the following day, his account was hopeful and soothing:

I asked a soldier of the Border Regiment who I found yesterday in the trenches we are to hold whether he was not vy glad after three months in the front line to be going to rest. He replied that he was rather sorry, as they wd never get such a good place again. My second examination of the position confirms me in the favourable view I took at first sight. I think we shall be vy comfortable & dry & the trenches generally are well protected against shelling. The two farms in wh I shall live by turns are not far apart; in fact I shall only move back about $\frac{2}{3}$s of a mile from the front line when we are in support & supposed to be 'resting'. Therefore for the next 2 or 3 months we shall all dwell continuously in close range of the enemy's artillery. However in this part of the world the houses have not been knocked about much: & the losses have been small.

Do you remember a great wood I told you about when I paid a visit to the front more than a year ago. I did not expect then that my fortunes wd lead me to live alongside it for months. In the spring it will be beautiful & alive with wild flowers, & the leaf will give good cover all over this flat country to our daily movements.

Orders came for the Battalion to start moving forward on January 24. It was to reach the support area immediately behind the front line on January 25, and take over its section of the front on the following day. 'Brandy & cigars wd be welcome,' Churchill wrote to his wife on the day before leaving; 'Also another of those lifeguard periscopes you were so clever in finding.'

The last week in reserve was spent preparing for the inspection of the

Brigade by the Corps Commander, General Sir Charles Fergusson.[1] The inspection took place on January 22. Churchill wrote to his wife about it on the following day:

The inspection yesterday was a gt success. The Corps Commander (Fergusson) expressed himself astonished at the improvement in the battalion since he last saw it five weeks ago. The men certainly tried vy hard and my battalion drills have taught them a smartness in handling their arms wh was before lacking.

The general was vy polite & friendly, excused himself for not having come to see me, & asked me to ride in & have tea with him. This I did taking Archie to make friends meanwhile with the senior mammon of unrighteousness. I had a long talk with Fergusson. I had met him & most of his staff in the Omdurman campaign. He said he was very sorry I had been sent to this battalion, wh was such a vy weak & shattered one, & that he wd have found me a much better one 'for my purposes' i.e. to learn about regimental work. I said I might be more useful here, & that as long as the difficulties were recognised, I preferred to have a battalion wh wanted helping along. He said there had been a vy gt improvement, & there was no doubt I had done a gt deal of good. I left him a copy of my Variants to ponder over. There is no doubt he is a friend who will help in every way. He spoke with confidence of my having high command etc. However now that we are going into the line I am quite interested here. . . .

Throughout Sunday January 23 the officers prepared the Battalion for its march into action. Colonel Holland gave Churchill lunch at Divisional Headquarters. Furse, Churchill wrote to his wife, 'had been full of praise. So at any rate we go into the line with a good backing.' That same day, writing from 41 Cromwell Road, Clementine Churchill urged her husband to make a careful record of all his experiences once he was in the trenches. She pointed out that even if he did not want to write for the newspapers, he ought nevertheless to write for posterity. She knew that his experiences were shared by millions of soldiers, but she believed that he was one of the very few people who could write 'with genius' on the war. She therefore urged him to make notes every day, and send them to her for safe keeping. Churchill never found time to make these notes. He did, however, find time to write his first letter to his four-year-old son. He wrote, in capital letters:

[1] Charles Fergusson, 1865–1951. Entered Army, 1883. Adjutant-General, Egyptian Army, 1901–3. 7th Baronet, 1907. Brigadier-General, 1907. Inspector of Infantry, 1909–13. Lieutenant-General commanding the II Corps, 1915–16. Military Governor, Occupied German Territory, 1918–19. Governor-General and Commander-in-Chief, New Zealand, 1924–30.

My dearest Randolph,

I am living here in a little farm. It is not so pretty as Hoe Farm, and there are no nice flowers and no pond or trees to play gorilla but there are three large fat dirty pigs. Like the ones we saw in the wood.

The Germans are a long way off and cannot shoot at us here. It is too far. So we are quite safe as long as we stay here. But we can hear the cannons booming in the distance and at night when it is all dark we can see their flashes twinkling in the sky. Soon we are going to go close up to the Germans and then we shall shoot back at them and try to kill them. This is because they have done wrong and caused all this war and sorrow.

Give my very best love to Diana and kiss Sarah for me. Write me a letter yourself soon and I will send you an answer back.

Your ever loving father
Winston S.C.

On the night of January 23 Churchill entertained all the officers of the Battalion to dinner at the Station Hotel in Hazebrouck. He invited Furse and Holland to the dinner. On the following day he described the scene to his wife:

We sat down 20 & had an elaborate feast beginning with oysters & lots of champagne. . . . I made the officers a little speech & the Bde Major[1] told them all about the regiment in the battle; & the pipers played doleful dirges; & we sang Auld Lang Syne and generally there was a scene of much enjoyment. This is the first time they had ever been brought together round a table. Poor lads, they were really delighted. Altogether things have now gone vy well. I put it to Holland & the General (Furse) not to hustle us into raids etc till we had really got a full knowledge of the *terrain* & the enemy; but to lie *doggo* for a fortnight, & then have a whole batch of small enterprises— five at a time—so that if one or two got chopped the success of the others wd carry us through. They were much taken with this idea; & I think they will adopt it.

At eight in the morning of January 24 Churchill left Moolenacker Farm and rode towards the trenches at the head of his Battalion. For two nights he and his men were billeted in the village of La Crèche, half-way between Moolenacker and the front line. Churchill was in reflective mood. It was exactly twenty-one years since his father's death. 'He was only 4 years older than you are now,' Lady Randolph had written to her son the day before. On January 29 Churchill replied: 'I thought much of my father on Jan 24, & wondered what he wd think of it all. I am sure I am doing right.'

[1] Norman McDonald Teacher, 1878–1917. Brigade Major, 27th Brigade, 1916. Commanding Officer, 2nd Royal Scots, 1917. Killed in action in the Ypres salient, 26 September 1917.

21

Ploegsteert

D URING 1915 the Belgian village of Ploegsteert had been transformed by the British into 'Plug Street'. It had become a soldiers' town, a maze of billets and dugouts, canteens and cafés. Eastwards from the village a series of tracks and communication trenches led to the front line, along which the soldiers, moving each day to the trenches, were exposed to a spasmodic ration of German shells and bullets. Going up the line, the men risked death or mutilation long before they had reached their forward trenches. By the time the 6th Royal Scots Fusiliers arrived, several military cemeteries had been opened near the village; the largest, on the Armentières road, was less than a hundred yards from Churchill's headquarters.

The arrival of the 6th Battalion of the Royal Scots Fusiliers at Ploegsteert was a routine matter. Men whom the Army considered fresh were replacing those who were in every way exhausted. The Ninth Division was taking its turn in the forward line. It had done so before, and would do so again. Holding the line at Ploegsteert was not easy or safe work, but it was not 'going over the top'; during the hundred days in which the Battalion was in the trenches under Churchill's command only fifteen men were killed and a hundred and twenty-three wounded. After the horrors of Loos, with its swift, brutal losses, the men accepted Ploegsteert with equanimity, and became attached to it. Those, the majority, who went south to fight on the Somme in July would look back to their time at Ploegsteert with nostalgia.

More than a month had passed since Churchill had been in the trenches with the Grenadiers. Now he was going into the line again, in command of men whom he had trained, and who trusted in him. His Battalion headquarters was the former workshop of the Sisters of Charity[1] on the western side of the road which led from Ploegsteert to Armentières. Churchill knew it as the Hospice. It was situated in a good

[1] A French religious order, they had left France at the time of the anti-clerical legislation of 1900. Their mother superior, Mathilde Désirée Foule, was born in Limoges in 1857.

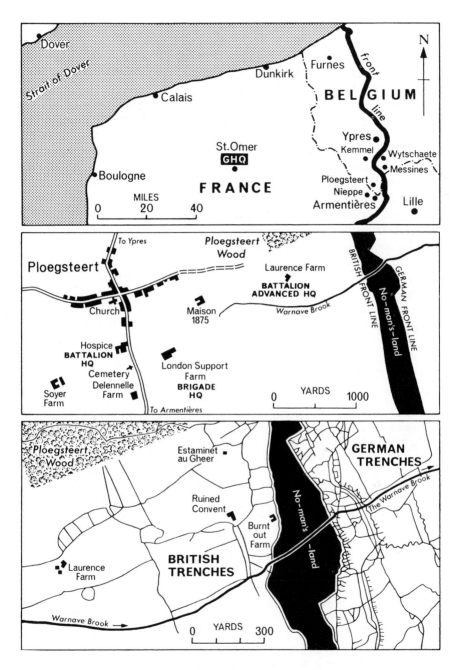

THE PLOEGSTEERT SECTOR OF THE WESTERN FRONT,
JANUARY–MAY 1916

position for the control of a Battalion serving in the line. It was four hundred yards from London Support Farm, in which Brigadier-General Walshe had established Brigade Headquarters.

While in reserve Churchill's companies were lodged in and around three nearby farms. The largest, Soyer Farm, lay directly behind the Hospice, eight hundred yards across the fields. The second, Delennelle Farm, was a thousand yards to the south, beyond the cemetery along the Armentiéres road. The third, known locally as Maison 1875, was five hundred yards in front of the Hospice on the direct line between Churchill and the trenches. When Churchill arrived at Ploegsteert there had been little serious damage done to any of these farms, and the Hospice was intact.

The enormous military machine of which Churchill was so small a cog did not need his experience, his skill or his courage in order to survive. Sir Douglas Haig, at his headquarters twenty-eight miles away had no reason to be aware of anything more than Churchill's existence.[1] The southern end of Ploegsteert was his home, the fields around his base, the defence of a short section of the trenches in front his ultimate concern.

On January 26, his first night at the Hospice, Churchill sent his wife an account of life near the trenches, trying, as he knew he must, to put her mind at rest about the dangers:

I am extremely well-lodged here—with a fine bedroom looking out across the fields to the German lines 3,000 yards away. Two nuns remain here and keep up the little chapel which is a part of the building. They received me most graciously when I marched in this morning, saying that we had saved this little piece of Belgium from the Germans, who were actually there for a week before being driven out. I have made the women at all the billets where I have stayed make their excellent soup for us—wh they do most gladly—so we are free for the moment from 'Maggi' & the rest of the tabloid class. On the right & left the guns are booming; & behind us a British field piece barks like a spaniel at frequent intervals. But the women & children still inhabit the little town[2] & laugh at the shells wh occasionally buff into the old church.

It is vy quiet on the front today, & really from your point of view this is

[1] The only reference in Haig's diary to Churchill at this time is on January 15, when he wrote: 'I received a letter from Admiral Bridgeman telling me that I should be on my guard against Winston Churchill acting as a private reporter to the Cabinet. Personally I feel that I can only do what I judge best, and I have no time, even if I had the inclination, to keep an eye on Winston's writings.'

[2] When, late in 1915, the British military authorities had tried to evacuate the villagers westwards, the villagers petitioned the King of the Belgians to be allowed to stay. Their petition was granted; but in the summer of 1916, after the church had been destroyed and the shelling had intensified, they agreed to move away.

an ideal part of the line. It is vy unlikely to be the scene of a big attack by either side. It has no great concentration of German artillery opposite it. The trenches are good, well wired, with a broad interval between the lines. The houses have been little damaged. Some of the men of the battalion we are relieving call it 'The Convalescent Home'. I think instead of being anxious you ought to set your mind gratefully at peace. The Btn we are relieving has lost 70 men only in 4 months: whereas in one day where I was before the Grenadiers lost 20—doing nothing. . . .

Churchill was confident that, despite the reduced size of the Battalion, it would do its duty as well as any:

. . . We take over the trenches before daylight tomorrow. You must not suppose that they will not be adequately defended. Although we have only 700 men instead of 900 wh our predecessors had, 1,050 wh we ought to have, we have more machine guns—so important. Rest assured there will be no part of the line from the Alps to the sea better guarded. It will be watched with the vigilance that mobilised the Fleet. . . .

Commanding a Battalion was a far cry from being First Lord. This was not the responsibility he had sought, nor the sphere in which he had wished to exercise it. But he tried not to become too depressed at the far drop in his fortunes. From his room at the Admiralty he used to look out over Horse Guards' Parade, across to the windows of the Cabinet Room at 10 Downing Street; from the window of the Hospice he could see, as he wrote to his wife, '2 bright red pigs rooting about among the shellholes'. That evening the Battalion prepared to move forward to its front-line trenches. Churchill called his officers from their farms and gave them a vivid description of how he believed they should behave. He reported the outline of his 'speech' to his wife in the following day:

. . . Don't be careless about yourselves—on the other hand not too careful. Keep a special pair of boots to sleep in & only get them muddy in a real emergency. Use alcohol in moderation but don't have a great parade of bottles in yr dugouts. Live well but do not flaunt it. Laugh a little, & teach your men to laugh—gt good humour under fire—war is a game that is played with a smile. If you can't smile grin. If you can't grin keep out of the way till you can. . . .

Churchill added in his letter home: 'Since Polonius' advice to Laertes there had been nothing like it. I trust they were edified.' 'It was a good pep talk,' McDavid later recalled; Churchill had been careful

to point out that 'although our predecessors had said this was a sanc-
tuary compared with Ypres and Loos, they must not take anything for
granted. They had to be on the qui vive in case the Germans discovered
that a new Division had come up and lay on at least trench raids for
identification purposes.' The officers returned to their companies, and
repeated Churchill's warnings to their NCOs.

That night at the Hospice Churchill found it difficult to sleep. A
succession of orders about the day's move forward arrived at intervals
from midnight onward from Brigade Headquarters. There were last-
minute adjustments insisted upon by the Divisional General, and map
positions to be co-ordinated with the General in charge of artillery. At
3.30 a.m. the Battalion prepared to move. 'The fever was at a very high
level,' McDavid recalled. 'It was possible that word had been put out
that the late First Lord of the Admiralty had arrived among us.' The
men feared some special German action as they moved forward. But
when McDavid put these fears to Churchill, he replied: 'If they
thought I was here they would have devastated the country for twenty
square miles around.' No German bombardment greeted the Battalion
on that tense morning. Shortly after four o'clock the officers moved off
from their farms, the men from their outbuildings, shacks and nissen
huts. It was dark. Military security forbade lamps or lights. Slowly, in
small groups, the companies moved forward along the dark, muddy
tracks and into the sodden communication trenches towards the front
line. At ten minutes to six, while it was still dark, they relieved the
2nd Battalion of the South Lancashires, and were in place.

Churchill reached his advanced headquarters before dawn. Known
as Laurence Farm,[1] it was a small shell-battered farm half-way between
the Hospice and the front line. From this farm to the line itself a series
of ever-deepening trenches ran forward, whose sandbagged security
was protection from all but a direct hit, and which ran so deep that
German rifle and machine-gun fire could not interrupt the continual
passage of men moving forward into the line. Churchill had sent his
wife an impression of Laurence Farm when he had made his brief
preliminary visit a week before:

The battalion HQ . . . is about 500 yards only from the trenches in a farmhouse. This is often good quarters. I have a small room to myself with a little
cellar underneath where Archie thinks of establishing himself.

The mess & orderly rooms are clean and waterproof. The place is however

---

[1] The farm was spelled 'Laurence' on the War Office trench maps of 1916, but 'Lawrence'
in the Battalion's war diary.

a target; & has been hit by perhaps 8 or 10 shells, while many have fallen close around. There is a tolerable shelter in the barn—a corrugated steel-hooped beehive loaded up with sandbags & bags of bricks & able to resist all ordinary shells. In this the HQ population take refuge when things get lively.

As soon as Churchill had established himself and his headquarters' staff in Laurence Farm, and surveyed the position which he was to occupy for each of the six-day periods that his Battalion was in the line, he himself went forward to examine the trenches in which his men had taken up their positions. The line which he and his men were holding stretched two hundred yards from the estaminet at Le Gheer to the Warnarve brook, which ran down from Ploegsteert and through the German lines. The British position consisted of two approximately parallel forward trenches linked by a series of communication trenches. The ground was absolutely flat. On his preliminary visit Churchill had noticed a small shell-shattered convent, and seen some use for it, writing to his wife: 'I am rather attracted by the cellars of a ruined convent right up in the firing line, & if they can be drained & made comfortable they wd be a better and safer HQ especially for fighting purposes than this commodious but conspicuous farm.'

Churchill was proud of the smoothness with which he had moved his Battalion into the line. On January 27, after a busy day both in the sandbagged security of Laurence Farm and in the trenches themselves, looking into the possible uses of the convent cellars, and peering across the front-line parapet at the Germans, he wrote to his wife:

My darling,
The relief was accomplished this morning before daylight with the utmost precision in under 2 hours. I don't think the Grenadiers ever did better. We now hold about 1,000 yards of trenches & I am responsible for this whatever happens. We have so far had no losses—though there has been shelling & sniping & our parapet has at one place been blown in. All is proceeding regularly & the day has been quiet & normal in spite of being the Emperor's birthday. I spent three hours in the trenches this morning deciding on all the improvements I am going to make in them, & looking into the arrangements of the company commanders. It is now dark & we are able to light our fire without being betrayed by the smoke, so that we shall get a hot dinner as usual. Archie is now going round the trenches, & I shall go again after dinner. It takes nearly 2 hours to traverse this labyrinth of mud. . . .

During his first afternoon at Laurence Farm Churchill busied himself with administration. In the evening the Germans began shelling

Ploegsteert, and from the Farm he watched the shells pass overhead and explode in the fields well behind him. Writing to his wife that night he described the organization which was under his control, and returned to his culinary demands, for these remained as persistent in the front line as in reserve:

... I have telephones to each of my companies, to the brigadier, & to the artillery. In 30 seconds I can turn on a horrid blast of shells—if an attack is made. . . . We are vy careful about gas. That is an odious peril: but I am inclined to think more has been put in on our front by the enemy. We never move an inch without 2 helmets.

About food—the sort of things I want you to send me are these—large slabs of corned beef: stilton cheeses: cream: hams: sardines—dried fruits: you might almost try a big beef steak pie but not tinned grouse or fancy tinned things. The simpler the better: & substantial too; for our ration meat is tough & tasteless: & here we cannot use a fire by daylight. I fear you find me vy expensive to keep. Mind you bill me for all these apart from your housekeeping. . . .

Churchill signed himself: 'Your ever loving and devoted—greedy though I fear you will say, W.' Clementine Churchill did her best to satisfy her husband's continuing demands for food, but it was not easy. 'I note your likings as to food,' she replied on January 31, 'but hams are impossible except by the Havre route becos' of weight; the parcel must not be more than 7 lbs. The other day when you asked for Stilton I had to have one cut in half. I will send you a *small* slab of corned beef however—Tell me whether I shall send a ham after all. . . .' Despite the hope of ham and stilton, life at Laurence Farm was far from luxurious. In the trenches the danger of death was ever present. On January 28 he wrote to his wife after having returned from the front:

... While I was passing the convent, a good sized shell burst in its ruins (where the cellars are). A fountain of brickbats went up into the air; & I watched them carefully from 50 yards away, to dodge if any fell near me. Suddenly I saw, almost instantaneously with the explosion, 5 or 6 black objects hurtling towards me—You know how quick thought is.

I had time to think they were splinters, to argue that they could not belong to the same explosion, & to reach out for another solution, before I saw that they were frightened birds! . . .

Churchill remained only two days at Laurence Farm, for his Battalion's first spell in the forward line had been kept deliberately short; all subsequent ones were to last for six days. Churchill was proud

of his powers of organization in bringing his battalion back to Ploegsteert so smoothly, writing from the Hospice on January 29:

The relief went off like machinery. No casualties; & all over in 4 minutes
under the 2 hours I estimated for. Our companies marched into billets in
admirable order going through the village in brisk parade step—unheard of
outside the Guards. There is no doubt that officers & men try vy hard to do
everything I tell them. I am extremely pleased with the officers who are
really working splendidly. I got up at 4 am (no rooster) and on coming in
here at about 7 we had breakfast & attended Mass in the little chapel. The
old *vicaire*[1] was vy gracious. His church is shattered, and the house in wh he
lives is freely shelled: but he sticks to his post & 'flies his flag' in the chapel of
this hospice. The shelling yesterday evening wh was vy persistent was directed
at a battery a few hundred yards away, & was not aimed at any of these
houses, though of course the projectiles passed vy near them. It is satisfactory
that they ignore the houses, & have ignored them so long: for the artilleryman
—particularly the Bosch artilleryman is a creature of habit—& sticks to the
target he sets his fancy on. The guns are so accurate that even a hundred
yards away one is safe or almost so. . . .

As soon as he was back at the Hospice, Churchill set about arranging
the more domestic side of Battalion life:

. . . We have a vy attentive and spruce Belgian[2] officer attached to us as
interpreter—well embusquéd. I have set him and the doctor[3] to work to forage
for fresh mutton; (I am tired of tough frozen beef); vegetables; & dairy produce: & have seduced the nuns (don't be frightened) . . . into culinary pursuits.
We shall make ourselves vy comfortable here I think when we are settled
down. There is a piano too, & several can play it. I have discovered a
splendid bath (portable) & a tolerably hot water supply. I am now going to
sample it, after 3 days of deprivation of that first of comforts. . . .

There was less repose in reserve than Churchill had hoped for. To
his mother, that evening, Churchill wrote of 'a tiresome thing' which
had happened during the afternoon, and which showed that it could
be as dangerous in reserve as in the front line:

. . . There is a battery in the fields behind our house wh the Germans try

[1] Jules-Jean Vynckier, 1855–1941. Curé, Ploegsteert, 1908–36.
[2] Emile Herzog (André Maurois). The French and Belgian interpreters' caps—with 'floche'
—were not dissimilar. Maurois later wrote to the author: 'I cannot hope he noticed that
unknown Frenchman who looked at him with admiring eyes and said little.'
[3] I have been unable to discover to which Medical Officer Churchill was referring. 'We
had several MOs while Winston was with us,' Captain Gibb wrote, 'and he used to discuss
them and compare and contrast their points as enthusiastically as though they had been
specimens of some wild animals which he collected.'

to hit; & this afternoon they put a dozen shells over us in search of it, wh burst with loud explosions at no gt distance. I had just had a splendid hot bath—the best for a month & was feeling quite deliciously clean, when suddenly a tremendous bang overhead, & I am covered with soot blown down the chimney by the concussion of a shell these careless Boches have fired too short & wh exploded above our roof, smashing our windows & dirtying me! Well . . . it is an odd world, & I have seen a gt deal of it. . . .

Churchill gave his mother an account of his new existence:

. . . Commanding a battalion is like being captain of a ship. It is a vy searching test and a severe burden. Especially so when all the officers are young & only soldiers of a few months standing: & when a hundred yards away lies the line of the German army with all its devilments & dodges. One wd not have thought it possible a year ago to put a battalion thus composed in the line. But they will give a good account of themselves & no part of the front will be better guarded. . . .

The next two days in reserve at the Hospice were busy ones. Equipment had to be cleaned and repaired, ammunition collected, sandbagging completed, orders from above scrutinized, artillery support arranged, food supplies perfected. 'I have made a treaty with the mess to make excellent soup etc,' he had written to his wife on January 28; and with the arrival two days later of the brandy and cigars which she had sent from London he felt 'well provided'. The mundane tasks of the Battalion pleased him, as he explained on January 31:

. . . I like this sort of work vy much. It occupies me & I hope to be able to do it well. I don't think there is much difference in safety between the trenches & our 'rest billets'. Both HQrs, advanced & support, are registered & shelled. But it takes an awful lot of shells to do much harm; apart from bad luck. On the whole I prefer the trenches where there is always something going on, & where one really is fighting in this gt war for the triumph of right & reason. No doubt about it—one is doing the real thing—wh has to be done by someone. . . .

Politics and his future were also in his mind: 'If I come through all right my strength will be greater than it ever was. I wd much rather go back to the trenches tonight, than go home in any position of mediocre authority. But I *shd* like to see my beloved pussy cat.'

On February 1 the Battalion returned to the trenches for six days: the longest consecutive period Churchill had yet spent in such proximity to the Germans. Captain Gibb recorded in the Battalion's war diary for the whole six days: 'Very quiet period in the trenches. No men killed, 3 wounded'; a typical example of the laconic approach of an experienced soldier to the daily activities of a static line. Churchill was less laconic. For him there was drama in each day's events. On his first day back at Laurence Farm trenches he wrote:

> . . . Peace all the morning, but at about 4.30 Shells—chiefly on the convent (where the cellars are). I had just passed through it and was 150 yards to the right when they began. Some were white shrapnel, others big black HE [High Explosive] 'crumps': others 'woolly bears' & some make a tremendous cloud of yellowy white smoke—or even plum & black, 30 in all. Having luckily wandered down the right turn, Archie & I had a fine view of this exhibition without being at all inconvenienced. We had 4 men hit—one let his own rifle off by accident in jumping nervously when a shell burst overhead. The doctor (not our own) was joyriding in the trenches—did not return when the shelling began—so 2 of the wounded who were rather badly hurt—did not get the prompt attention they required. I have rebuked him. I ordered artillery retaliation for this German aggression & we gave them a good deal stiffer dose than we received. But of course one cannot tell what results are produced.
>
> Darling—Do you like me to write these things to you? They are the ordinary incidents of life here—they are dangerous; but not vy dangerous. The average risk is not great—I wd not write to you about them if I thought the account wd cause you extra anxiety. But I think you like to know the dimensions of the dangers, & what they are like. . . .

That day Churchill spent several hours in the front-line trenches. He seemed to scorn caution. 'I have seen him stand on the fire step in broad daylight,' Lieutenant McDavid later recalled, 'to encourage the Jocks, and to prove to the man on the fire step how little danger there was of being hit.' Churchill decided to go out that night into no-man's-land, across the open fields, to the Battalion's forward posts, which were situated in the shell craters which pitted the landscape between the two armies. McDavid recalled how:

> The Colonel's first visitation of our posts in No Man's Land nearly brought the whole British Army into action. Clad in his long trench waterproof, shining knee-high trench boots and blue steel helmet, with his revolver and powerful flash-lamp attached to his web-belt, he preceded me on the journey through the wire. All went well until we were within a few yards of the first post. Then enemy machine-gun fire swept the sphere of operations.
>
> We all made a dive for the shelter of the shell crater, which was now somewhat overcrowded, and consequently we had to keep in a crouching position. Suddenly a blinding glare of light appeared from the depths of the hole and

with it the CO's muffled request to 'Put out that bloody light!' It was only a matter of seconds before he realised his crouching posture was responsible for pressure on the contact switch of his own flash-lamp, and corrective action quickly followed.

This excursion into no-man's-land was not an isolated example of Churchill's apparent tendency to flout safety. Hakewill Smith remembered similar incidents:

He would often go into no-man's-land. It was a nerve-racking experience to go with him. He would call out in his loud, gruff voice—far too loud it seemed to us—'You go that way, I will go this. . . . Come here, I have found a gap in the German wire. Come over here at once!' He was like a baby elephant out in no-man's-land at night. He never fell when a shell went off; he never ducked when a bullet went past with its loud crack. He used to say, after watching me duck: 'It's no damn use ducking; the bullet has gone a long way past you by now.'

Churchill did not seek these dangers for their own sake. He wanted his men to feel that he was one of them, that where the danger was there he would be, that when they needed guidance or good cheer or courage he would be at hand, and that he would not fail them in their hour of need. He knew that many of his men were puzzled to find a politician, whose name and features were familiar to them from their newspapers, commanding them in the line. He was determined that they should trust him. German shells exploded round Laurence Farm almost every day. But Churchill seemed imperturbable. 'He used to sit on one side of the farm,' McDavid recalled. 'Hakewill Smith and Kemp[1] put on the hits of the day on a little portable gramophone. He would sit for a while just beating time, just ruminating.' He even set up his easel in the courtyard of the farm and began painting. The officers were amazed. Hakewill Smith remembered the moment:

Winston started painting the second or third time he went up to the farm. Each time we were in the line he spent some time on his paintings. Gradually, too, the courtyard became more pitted with shellholes. As his painting came nearer to completion, he became morose, angry, and exceedingly difficult to talk to. After five or six days in this mood, he suddenly appeared cheerful and delighted, like a small boy at school. I asked him what had happened, and he said 'I have been worried because I couldn't get the shell-hole right

[1] Laurence Kemp, 1891–1956. Signal Officer, 6th Royal Scots Fusiliers, 1916. Invalided home, 1916–17. Served in the Balkans, 1918. Ironmonger. Director of his family's firm, William Kemp & Co, Glasgow, 1929–56 and Chairman, 1949–56.

in the painting. However I did it, it looked like a mountain, but yesterday I discovered that if I put a little bit of white in it, it looked like a hole after all.'

Churchill persevered with his paintings, and even managed to preserve some.[1] While providing distraction for himself, he also remembered his men's needs. Music was the answer, he believed, and summoned the band of the Ninth Division to Ploegsteert. Bandsman Fulton[2] had reason to remember the occasion, writing to the author fifty-five years later:

A figure appeared. It was Winston Churchill. He was carrying his own Chair—it was a ·303 Ammunition Box. He says this will do Lads. We fixed up and started our programme. He sat in the middle. A young lad from the RAMC sang that beautiful old Ballad 'Sunshine of your smile'. Then shelling started some well off the mark and some mighty near accompanied by a few overhead shrapnels. Well with plenty of ducking and a broad smile on Winston's face we got through it. At the end he thanked us all. He said 'Lads I am sorry bringing you into such a precarious position but I am going to let you into a little secret. Last week the Germans had a band at the back of their lines playing to them and our artillery got on them and all you saw was instruments & drums going into the air and I really wanted to see if their artillery were as good marksmen as ours.'

When General Furse visited the Battalion with Colonel Holland on February 2, Churchill took them into the forward trenches and then, as he told his wife, gave them lunch 'in my shattered farmhouse'. It was a quiet day, he wrote, 'profound peace . . . not a shell or a casualty— hardly a bullet'. But on the following day there was further excitement:

My darling one,
    Yesterday (3rd) we had a lucky escape. We had just finished an excellent lunch and were all seated round the table at coffee & port wine, when a shell burst at no gt distance making the window jump. Archie said that at the next one we wd go into our dugout in the barn just opposite & we were discussing this when there was a tremendous crash, dust & splinters came flying through the room, plates were smashed, chairs broken. Everyone was covered with debris and the Adjutant [Jock McDavid] (he is only 18) hit on the finger.

---

[1] There is a colour reproduction of one of Churchill's paintings of Laurence Farm on page 17 of *Churchill his paintings* (Hamish Hamilton, 1967), compiled by David Coombs, and a black and white reproduction of a painting of shells exploding over the village (on page 90). The original of the latter hangs at Chartwell. In 1918 Churchill gave Sir Archibald Sinclair one of his Laurence Farm paintings as a wedding present.

[2] Robert Fulton, 1889–   . Apprentice Ironmoulder, 1904–11. Ironmoulder, 1911–14. Enlisted, Gordon Highlanders, September 1914. Crossed to France with the 9th Division, May 1915. Fought at Loos, September 1915; and promoted to Lance Corporal. Cornet soloist, 9th Division Band, 1916–19. Worked in an ironfoundry, 1919–57.

A shell had struck the roof and burst in the next room—mine & Archie's. We did not take long in reaching our shelter—wh is a good one! My bedroom presented a woe-begone appearance, the nose of the shell passing clean through it smashed the floor and cut a hole in the rear wall. Luckily vy few of my things were damaged. The only serious loss is my milux lamp.[1] . . . I am sending this home as a souvenir, & beg you to send me another *at the vy earliest moment*, as they are indispensable. The wonderful good luck is that the shell (a 4·2) did not—& cd not have—burst properly. Otherwise we shd have had the wall thrown in on us—& some wd surely have been hurt.

I have made them put up another still stronger dugout—quite close, on wh they are now hard at work. I slept peacefully in my tiny war-scarred room last night, after a prolonged tour of the trenches. . . .

There was a respite from shelling on February 4, although Ploegsteert itself was quite heavily bombarded, and some damage was done to the Battalion's supporting billets at Delenelle Farm and Maison 1875. Brigadier-General Ritchie,[2] who commanded the neighbouring Brigade, came to lunch at Laurence Farm on February 5 and was, as Churchill wrote to his wife on the following day, 'much impressed at the damage' of the previous day. He and Ritchie had last met in 1898, during the Sudan campaign. It was a quiet day. Churchill worked on a scheme of front-line defence. Under this scheme there was to be more sandbagging, deeper trenches and stronger dugouts. Ministerial papers were not always so easily approved. 'I took lots of pains about it,' he told his wife; 'it was like one of my Cabinet papers, & it carried all before it.'

During the six days in the trenches Churchill had cleared out the water from the cellars of the convent, and these cellars, which he now named 'The Conning Tower', became what he called his 'Battle Headquarters' while he was in the line. They were only a hundred yards from no-man's-land, seven hundred yards closer than his 'Advance Headquarters' at Laurence Farm and only four hundred yards from the nearest German trench. Clementine Churchill worried about the added danger of her husband being so near the Germans.

---

[1] Churchill had a closer escape than he informed his wife. 'Winston had been toying about with his lamp,' McDavid later recalled to the author. 'He was sitting playing with this thing when the shell came along. A piece of shrapnel almost split the battery holder in two—it lodged in the metal of the battery holder. It was less than two inches from his right wrist. If it had been any nearer it certainly would have taken off his wrist.'

[2] Archibald Buchanan Ritchie, 1869–1955. Entered Army, 1889. Served on the Nile Expedition, 1898. Lieutenant-Colonel, 1913. Brigadier-General commanding the 26th Brigade of the 9th Division, 1915–16. Commanded the 11th Division, 1917, and the 16th Division, 1918. Major-General, 1919. Commanded the 51st Highland Division of the Territorial Army, 1923–7. Knighted, 1927.

Even Laurence Farm did not seem very safe to her as he had described it. '*Please* leave that wretched farm and find a safer place,' she had written on February 2. Sometimes she wrote of coming to see him: 'It wd be so easy & I cd live with the poor French women in a ruined cottage & hoe turnips'—she had forgotten that her husband was in Belgium. He understood her fears, and while continuing to write graphically of the events he witnessed, insisted that he was not really disturbed by the danger. 'It is one long holiday for me,' he wrote, '. . . like my African journey.'[1]

After five weeks as a Lieutenant-Colonel, Churchill's hopes of Generalship were suddenly and unexpectedly raised again. He had always believed that Haig would give him the promotion once he had gained some front-line experience. On the morning of February 6 a telegram reached Laurence Farm from St Omer telling him to proceed at once across the fields to London Support Farm and to take over command of the Brigade. Churchill's first reaction was that Asquith's veto had been overcome, and that his future as a Brigade Commander was assured. But it was not in fact so. What had happened, he explained to his wife on February 6, was that 'I am for the moment actually the senior commanding officer, & the Brigadier—Walshe—is expected back tomorrow'. His was merely a brief and transitory migration to Brigade headquarters: 'I have not therefore attempted to master the detail of the command, but remain here ready to give any broad simple decision that an emergency might (but won't) require. They have now had 4 different men commanding this Brigade in 9 days! Queer folk!' As a result of Walshe's absence, Churchill was temporarily in command of five Battalions—a total of four thousand men—and over two thousand yards of the front line. On reaching Brigade Headquarters on February 6 he received a summons to lunch with General Furse at Divisional Headquarters in Nieppe. To his surprise he found that Curzon was there. It soon emerged that it was only as a result of Curzon's persistent demands to see him that Churchill had been called away from his temporary Brigade duties. Churchill insisted upon showing Curzon the front line. 'I took him out to my shattered farm,' he wrote that night to his wife, '& along my own trenches; & he told me all the news & his view of men & politics in his usual sprightly style. . . . I think he was interested by what he saw. It was vy quiet & we successfully avoided the

[1] In 1908, when Under-Secretary of State for the Colonies, Churchill spent five months travelling with Edward Marsh through Egypt, the Sudan, the Uganda Protectorate and British East Africa. As well as conducting much official business, Churchill hunted rhinoceros, lions and wart-hogs. He wrote an account of his travels for the *Strand Magazine*, later expanded as a book, *My African Journey*, published in December 1908.

shells & the machine gun bullets, both of wh came discreetly & tactfully in the places wh we had left or in those wh we had not reached.'

Curzon went back to Carlton House Terrace, Churchill to London Support Farm. Walshe did not return, as had been expected, on February 7, and Churchill remained in command of the Brigade for another day. 'It is not a vy satisfactory arrangement,' he wrote to his wife on February 8, 'as of course I am only a caretaker and cannot attempt to take a grip of the whole machine. I do the office work and have prepared myself to meet any emergency; but otherwise I wait about from hour to hour. The whole Brigade is now out of the line & in rest billets, so there is nothing going on.' Sinclair telephoned from the Hospice to report heavy shelling on one of the farms which served as a reserve billet, and three men wounded. The Germans had not bombarded the reserve area in this way before. 'They are getting spiteful,' Churchill wrote, '& fire 5 or 6 shells at once without any warning—then wait 20 minutes or so and have another go.'

While he was at Brigade Headquarters, Churchill discovered that the General who had just been appointed to command the Ninth Division artillery, Hugh Tudor,[1] was another friend from the distant past, from subaltern days in Bangalore nineteen years before. On February 7 General Tudor came to see him at London Support Farm. 'We were vy pleased to meet again after so many years—I had not seen him since S. Africa,' Churchill wrote to his wife on February 8. Tudor told Churchill more about the battle of Loos. 'My dear,' Churchill continued, 'what mistakes they made at Loos. You simply cannot believe them possible.' His own thoughts were also critical of the military machine:

. . . there is gt lack of 'drive' throughout the administration of the army. Take the telephone system for instance. It is grotesque. You cannot get through. When you do you cannot hear, there is always a dog fight going on over the wires. They have stuck in the main to the same little field instruments that an army on the move uses instead of making a perfect system wh cd so easily be done. And how vitally important it might be in a battle! If we had been content at the Admiralty to paddle along at that feeble pace, we shd never have mastered the German submarine. Then of course there ought to be 10 times (at least) as many light railways on the front. This war is one of mechanics & brains & mere sacrifice of brave & devoted infantry

[1] Henry Hugh Tudor, 1871–1965. 2nd Lieutenant, Royal Artillery, 1890. Brigadier-General commanding the Artillery of the 9th Division, 1916–18. Major-General commanding the 9th Division, 1918. Knighted, 1923.

is no substitute & never will be. By God I wd make them skip if I had the power—even for a month. . . .

Lieutenant McDavid, the young adjutant who had been wounded in the hand at Laurence Farm, went back to England on leave on February 7. That evening he called at 41 Cromwell Road. 'Such a delightful youth,' Clementine Churchill wrote on the following day, 'bringing with him the nose of the shell which shattered your bedroom, your oiler lamp and photographs of you, also very exciting news, ie that for the present you are a Brigadier—I wonder if you are to be one for good?' Clementine Churchill was worried about the unexpected shelling of the Hospice. 'Write quickly,' she asked, 'and tell me that you have arranged a safer headquarters. I fear so that the Germans in front of you may know you are there.' Churchill had also come to the conclusion that the Hospice was too risky a place for his Battalion headquarters. As soon as he relinquished his temporary command of the Brigade, he moved his Battalion headquarters eight hundred yards further from the front line, to one of his company billets at Soyer Farm.

During his first morning at Soyer Farm Churchill examined the new Battalion arrangements, and inspected the cellar below the entrance hall down which he and his men must dash if the farm were shelled. He hoped they were sufficiently far from Ploegsteert to escape bombardment; but Ploegsteert itself could never escape. From their maps the Germans were able to register their artillery fire with impressive accuracy upon the village crossroads, the church, the curate's house and any other village building which they might choose. That afternoon Churchill, from his study at Soyer Farm, watched the village being bombarded. On the following day, February 10, he wrote to his wife:

The shells hitting the church made enormous clouds of red brick dust wh mingled gaily with their white smoke. Other black & white shrapnel burst over the street & struck the houses. Three of our men who were strolling in the town were hit—one fatally, & another sustained a shock from being near a shell from wh he immediately died. In the last 2 days of 'rest' I have lost 8 men, or more than in 6 days in the front line. I am now reduced to under 600 men instead of 1,000. There are many other battalions like this. . . .

During his first period at Soyer Farm Churchill found time to travel a little behind the lines. On February 10 he and Sinclair went with General Tudor to the far side of Ploegsteert Wood, to watch the progress of a British artillery bombardment. He described it to his wife on the following day:

. . . Two points in the German trenches were selected, & a tremendous fire of 12 inch, 9·2 inch & field guns was suddenly opened on them. This proved a more dangerous expedition than I had expected for I did not think the general commanding all the artillery of a division wd expose himself to undue risks. He took us however (Archie & me) to the front line of our trenches only 100 yards away from the German points attacked, & of course as soon as we began, the enemy replied with vigour. For one hour, by the clock, there was a brief cannonade. Our own guns made so much noise we cd not hear the whistle of the German shells, but they burst all round, striking the parapet, or just skimming over, or bursting in the air with loud explosions & covering us with dirt & debris. It was vy exciting, especially as our own 9·2's put two shells *behind* us by mistake. This was the first really sharp artillery fire I have been under, & certainly it seemed vy dangerous. I was impressed however with the way in wh the trenches gave good protection, & I can quite understand how even the heaviest bombardments can be endured for days on end. Besides the shells, we had bombs from trench mortars thrown at us. These you can see in the air; & after they fall there is an appreciable interval in wh to decide what you will do. I liked these the best of all. I found my nerves in excellent order & I do not think my pulse quickened at any time. But after it was over I felt strangely tired: as if I had done a hard day's work at a speech or article.

That evening Churchill rode over to Divisional Headquarters at Nieppe to dine with Colonel Holland. Even here, three miles from the front line, the German shells could find a target. 'They are in a pretentious chateau surrounded by a moat,' Churchill told his wife. 'It was dusk. Suddenly a loud bang. A shell coming from miles away had fallen in the moat, just outside our window. Presently came 1 more. No one paid the slightest attention to them. It is pure chance, & a shell may come anywhere at any time. . . .'

On February 11 Churchill made a brief excursion across the border into France, when he and Archibald Sinclair rode into Armentières. 'It is a large town almost deserted, & constantly shelled,' he wrote to his wife on February 12; 'The debris of several hits that had occurred half an hour before was scattered in the streets. And every now & again a shell passed overhead. But there were a fair number of shops open, with women serving in them: & a lot of factories smoking away as if nothing was going on.' Sinclair and he were photographed together: 'I will send you some copies as soon as we get them.' He had also discovered that 'good cakes & sweets' could be bought in Armentières, a further incentive to go again. On February 12, while the Battalion remained in reserve at Soyer Farm, Churchill went forward to the trenches to see what damage had been done since he had been in reserve. He described his expedition to his wife that evening:

... Today has brought with it its own risks. I went round the trenches with the Colonel of the Gordons[1] whom we relieve in the line tomorrow morning & saw what work he had done & learned his plans etc. A German aeroplane passed overhead & our guns fired at it. The fragments of the shell as they fell back to earth around us made curious hissing noises quite different from an ordinary projectile. Then on the way back the Gordons' Major[2] (a vy good soldier) insisted on walking across the fields behind the trenches while it was still daylight, & in consequence we were fired upon at no gt distance. Vy foolish I thought, & promptly made for a trench—while Archie & the others scampered about. Finally on the way back to our present HQ the German machine gun 'sprayed' our path with zipping bullets. . . .

There was a further annoyance when he returned that evening to the Hospice: 'And now just as Tudor is coming to dinner in our unprotected but vy comfortable house they have flung 2 shells about 200 yards further up the street. This is a vy bad habit for them to start after dark, & if it continues it will sensibly reduce the amenities of this otherwise admirable dwelling.'

On Sunday February 13 the 6th Royal Scots Fusiliers moved forward once more to Laurence Farm. That night Churchill wrote to his wife, who was staying at Walmer Castle as a guest of the Asquith's:

My beloved,

It is odd thinking of you at Walmer now. I remember so well being there at the end of February last, when all was hope at the Dardanelles & I looked forward to a vy wide sphere of triumphant activity. Everything is changed now—only the old block [Asquith] continues solid & supine.

I am now in the line again and am living in the farm I told you of. I am protecting it in various ways by sandbags etc against a renewed incursion of shells; & I have now 2 vy substantial dugouts—sandbags over steel cupolas —wh will at a pinch accommodate our whole population at HQrs—35 or 40.

This afternoon many aeroplanes overhead, & much shooting at them. I was disgusted to watch 1 German aeroplane sailing about scornfully in the midst of *14* British—none of wh cd or worse still perhaps—*wd* bring him to action. Ours seemed to sheer off time after time, & he went where he pleased for at least an hour & a half. As for our guns they fired hundreds of shells without lifting a feather of this hostile bird. . . .

[1] Alan David Greenhill-Gardyne, 1868–1953. Entered Army, 1888. Lieutenant-Colonel, October 1915. Commanded 8th Battalion, Gordon Highlanders, October 1915–March 1916. Retired invalided, 1920. Big-game hunter and water-colourist.

[2] George J. G. G. Cumine, 1881–1941. 2nd Lieutenant, 1900. Major, 8th Battalion Gordon Highlanders, October 1914–July 1916. Machine Gun Corps, 1917; Tank Corps, 1918. He died in London as a result of enemy action.

Some of my officers have returned from leave. They are vy homesick. No doubt they feel the weight & burden of this business & long for its conclusion. But it will take a long time, & we must not expect quick results. I think I shall take 8 days leave early in March & come home to see you. I am entitled to it & there will be no difficulty. We must give a few nice dinners. I shall do 2 more tours in the trenches first (including this one now beginning) & come away so as to miss a 6 day rest period. I will let you know the exact dates soon. . . .

Kiss the kittens. I think a gt deal about you all. I never expected to be so completely involved in the military machine. It almost seems to me as if my life in the gt world was a dream, & I have been moving slowly forward in the army all these years from subaltern to colonel. Good night my dearest soul.

Your ever devoted

W

That same day Clementine Churchill wrote to her husband from Walmer Castle. She described how 'sitting on the bastion we could distinctly hear the rumble of heavy guns——'; she suspected that it was British ships shelling the Belgian coast. But the contrast with the war zone was complete. She played golf with Asquith, and was annoyed not to have beaten him; it was a victory, she wrote, that she would have relished.

Churchill was back in the forward trenches again on February 14. There was much to do at Laurence Farm:

My darling,

I take up my pen to send you my daily note. Another long day in the trenches has closed, & I sit in a battered wicker chair within this shot scarred dwelling by the glowing coals of a brazier in the light of an acetyline lamp. At 6 I went round my trenches, just as day was breaking and was saluted on my doorstep by a vy sulky bullet. All the morning I laboured in the small business of the battalion & dealt with my Company Commanders & sent off the numerous reports for wh our superiors clamour—patrols, operations, situations, wind, work, fighting strength, enemy's shelling, intelligence etc. . . .

It had been a busy morning, but Churchill's work was not done. For some weeks General Furse had wanted the Ninth Division to take an initiative in trying to break the defensive character of trench warfare. Churchill's sector had been selected for a specially heavy British artillery 'sträfe' organized by his friend General Tudor, who came to lunch at Laurence Farm and explained what was about to happen. As Churchill explained to his wife:

... I had arranged to withdraw all my men from those parts of the line & its approaches on wh I thought the enemy's certain retaliation wd fall, & have had them distributed in safe places along the front line—always the safest. We had a hurried lunch—but excellent & wh was terminated by the arrival of a shell 4·2 wh burst close by, obliging us all to adjourn to the new dugout. ...

Churchill was keen to see Tudor's bombardment clearly. He took the General across the fields to a small ruined farmhouse a hundred yards from his dugouts. The two men clambered on to the roof:

... here we awaited developments. At 2.30 our guns began, & almost immediately the German reply. They fired about 50 shells altogether & we about 150. I had correctly anticipated their intervention & owing to the men having been moved out of the dangerous points and well concealed, *we never lost one*. But several of our trenches were knocked about, particularly a communication trench wh Archie dislikes. It was an odd sensation perched up behind this thin brick wall wh rocked with the mere wind, to see these big shells bursting only a 100 yards away, & to realise that only the caprice of the gunner stood between me and their direct attentions. After half an hour of this we returned to join the others in the dugout: to receive your letter & read it with eager appetite, & to browse about among ungrateful press cuttings & the unfriendly newspapers. ...

Finally Archie & I go up again to the trenches to see the damage, & the officers walk about in them for an hour and a half, & on the way down that same communications trench that Archie dislikes we receive (with thanks) 5 shells wh all keep just outside it. ...

Churchill returned to Laurence Farm; hopefully his day was done: 'darkness has fallen & dinner is almost ready. I shall go round the trenches again tonight, & on the whole when sleep comes, I think I shall have earned my 25 shillings.' The day was not yet over. On February 15 Churchill wrote to his wife of how:

... Last night after writing & after dinner, I had a splendid walk with Archie all over the top of the ground. We left the trenches altogether & made a thorough examination of all the fields, tracks, ruins etc immediately behind our line. You cannot show yourself here by day, but in the bright moonlight it is possible to move about without danger (except from random bullets) & to gain a vy clear impression. Archie was a vy good guide. We also went out in front of our own parapet into the No man's land & prowled about looking at our wire & visiting our listening posts. This is always exciting. Last night also two of my officer patrols went right up to the German wire & cut large strands of it as trophies. One was foolish enough however to leave a Union Jack fastened on to it in bravado. This will only make them more vigilant. Can you imagine such a silly thing. . . .

Churchill got little sleep that night. There was fighting ten miles to the north, just beyond Ypres, and at Laurence Farm, he wrote, 'we cd hear the cannonade splintering & snarling away all through the night'.

Churchill was working out his plans for the leave that was now due to him. He hoped to spend seven days in London, beginning on March 2. 'Of course,' he wrote to his wife on February 15, 'these plans of leave may be altered by my getting a Brigade. . . .' On February 3 his mother had sent him a first-hand report of Asquith himself hinting at a Brigade:

> . . . I dined with Cassel last night—16 of us—& who shd take me in to dinner but the PM! He looked very dubious at first, but I exerted myself to put him at his ease, & we got on all right—No use being nasty, it does not help things, & so I made friends with the Mammon of Unrighteousness! Well! of course he asked after you, & I told him you had just come out of the trenches, & repeated the story about the bath & the bomb. He got quite red with emotion. In the bottom of his heart I really think he is very fond of you —but he is so selfish he wd sacrifice anyone to his own convenience. I told him about your batt: & he said 'Of course this is only the beginning & he will get the next step very soon' those were his words. . . .

These hopes were but chimeras. Neither Asquith nor Haig had any plans to give Churchill the promotion for which he hoped.

On February 16 Churchill wrote to his wife from Laurence Farm of the day's dangers:

> My darling,
> . . . We had only just finished dressing this morning when shells began to arrive in the neighbourhood—just about 200 yards away & then much nearer. Archie & I persevered in our breakfast—till a tremendous bang, clouds of debris & the whizzing of splinters proclaimed our house hit again —this time our dining room was pierced on the other side, & our joint bedroom penetrated in 5 or 6 places. The signal office in the next room completely shattered (mercifully I had just ordered the signallers to take refuge in the dugout). The signal officer, Lieut Kemp, down with 5 wounds (not dangerous) & another man hit. Without knowing all that had happened, we hastily seized our eggs & bacon, bread and marmalade & took refuge in our dugout. Here we remained while perhaps 20 shells were devoted to our farm & its curtilage. Then the 'strafe' being over we emerged and went about our

business. I have now had 2 officers hit out of 5 in my HQ mess: & there is no doubt that we are rather a target. But I do not intend to change these HQrs as they are convenient & it is difficult to find others. Instead I am piling sandbags inside all the walls & on the upper floor & trying to make it proof against the 30 pr shells—if they start with 100 pr I shall have to flit to some hole or other. But till then we remain. . . .

It was odd gobbling bacon & marmalade in the dugout, while the doctor bandaged the gt raw wounds of our poor officer a foot or two away! Archie is vy good—cool, methodical, careful—yet quite fearless. I do not think I mind it vy much. At any rate it does not affect my spirits or my temper. But it is a vy curious life to live.

Your ever loving & devoted
W

Clementine Churchill continued with her war work, helping to organize YMCA canteens for munitions workers in north London. On February 16 she sent him a long account of what she had been doing:

. . . Last night, I mean Monday, that nice boy Mr McDavid dined with Goonie & me & we took him to a Music Hall. He is very small & young & rather loveable. I feel sorry for his Mamma. I think he is too young to have a real sweetheart.[1]

The big Ponder's End Canteen . . . flourishes exceedingly, another wing is to be added for the men, & I have just been told that the Manager is engaging 500 girls (diluted labour) & that he expects me to feed them too! At present I am feeding about 650 people a day in my district, in about 2 months I shall be feeding about 1,800, scattered in different places.

With each of the seven years of their married life, Churchill had become more and more involved in politics. Even his weekends had been filled increasingly with public affairs, or, as in the spring of 1914, with weekends away from his wife while he was learning to fly. She had envied him his capacity to absorb himself so fully in his work that he did not seem to need time with her. She wanted him back, not only from the trenches but also from his obsession with work. In her letter of February 16 she explained her hopes about their future together when the war was over. She longed for the time when they could relax in the country, he painting and playing his 'grizzly bear' game with the children; both of them finding time for leisure. She wanted him to promise that he would put aside for their life together an hour out of every day, a day out of every week and six weeks out of every year.

[1] He did have a real sweetheart, Harriet Murray (1895–1965); they were married a year later.

In her letter Clementine Churchill had gone on to describe how some of his methods had influenced her; how the other women who were organizing the canteens were surprised at the speed with which she got things done, and at her energy in driving forward her fellow-helpers. She began work at nine in the morning and did not finish until seven-thirty at night: 'You have taught me to work outside office hours,' she wrote proudly.

Clementine Churchill's letters meant much to her husband. They made him feel less cut off from London and its daily life. She renewed his vigour; and any delay in the correspondence—inevitable in wartime conditions—depressed him. His own news was almost entirely of shells and sandbags. On February 17 he wrote from Laurence Farm:

My darling,

No letter from you—only one in 4 days has reached me & Mr McDavid who I daresay was the bearer of one as well as of various parcels, is gone in hospital with the effects of anti-tetanus injections.

We were shelled again at this farm at 9, at 11, & at 1 today. Two batteries now take an interest in us—one tries 30 lb & the other 15 pr shells & they shoot from different sides so that they search our weak points vy disagreeably. The house is now much better sandbagged & by tomorrow morning shd be still more so. We were vy punctilious about going into the dugout whenever the bombardment began & waiting for ten minutes without a shell before coming out. No other part of my line has been touched, & no casualties have occurred in the trenches. Other farms in rear of the line are also being made a target—so that there is no reason to suppose there is anything personal in the enemy's attentions. We come out of the line on Saturday morning. These last five days have gone like a flash. The complete absence of worry or strain, of mental work of any serious kind, the good food, & warmth & comfort in wh we live, with lots of open air are vy good for one's health. As a rest cure for the unusual the life is admirable. I expect I am putting on weight.

Some of the others however fret a good deal. The officer who was wounded yesterday morning was given the nose-piece of the shell which wounded him as a *souvenir*. He kissed it! His joy at leaving almost triumphed over the severe pain of his wounds.

I have no more tales to tell you tonight—my dearest soul—so good night & tenderest love

from yr devoted & ever loving
W

The evening's letter was but a brief break in the ever-continuing activity. Churchill was determined to check the increased German shelling by some heavy retaliation. He had made special arrangements that day for some shelling of his own, which he directed late that evening by telephone from Laurence Farm. Robert Fox recalled:

When we saw him in the front line accompanied by two naval officers we knew he meant business. Special observers located the concreted German minenwerfer and machine-gun emplacements and sniper's posts. Twelve-inch naval guns on an armoured train six miles away were to be used against them. As the two front lines were only 80 yards apart in places, we evacuated our forward trenches in case of a shell dropping short. With a noise like approaching express trains these huge missiles hurtled over our heads and crashed into the German line. Each impact was like a miniature earthquake.

'I had to sit at the end of the telephone,' Churchill reported to his wife on the following day, 'so that I did not get much fun out of it. But it worked vy well.' On February 18 rain and mist prevented any German retaliation. Churchill had not decided to take the initiative without anticipating the effects. He looked to expertise to counter them. Earlier that month he had sought the advice of the Major who commanded the Royal Engineer section of the Ninth Division. 'Then long pow-wow with Major Hearn[1]—the engineer,' he wrote to his wife on February 14, 'an Indian acquaintance of mine—fat, shrewd, placid, sensible—a regular koi hai:[2] about wh trenches shd be strengthened or drained & where dugouts shd be built etc. He works with me admirably and helps in every way.' Major Hearn—whom Churchill had met in 1898 during the Malakand expedition—had to return to Divisional Headquarters. But he left behind him a young engineer officer, Lieutenant Napier-Clavering,[3] who took charge of the fortifications.

Churchill was impressed with Napier-Clavering's abilities, and soon became absorbed by the work which the Lieutenant and his engineers were doing. Napier-Clavering later recalled, in a conversation with the author, that as soon as he arrived at Laurence Farm, Churchill had remarked: 'The trouble with these dugouts, is they are not whizzbang proof.' The young officer promised to do his best. Churchill's next

[1] Gordon Risley Hearn, 1871–1953. Entered Royal Engineers, 1890. Inspector of Railways for the Government of India, 1904–14. Major, 1910. Commanded the Royal Engineers of the 9th Division, 1914–18. Knighted, 1926.

[2] A Hindustani phrase, used in British India, for someone who had seen long service there; derived from the way in which servants were summoned in a club—'Koi hai?' 'Is there any one there?'

[3] Francis Donald Napier-Clavering, 1892–1969. Lieutenant, 64th Field Company, Royal Engineers, attached to the 9th Division, 1915–16. Major, 1918. Subsequently an engineer with Robert McAlpine & Sons Ltd.

question was: 'How much earth do you need to stop a bullet?' 'You want at least three feet,' Napier-Clavering replied. 'Well,' said Churchill. 'We'll go up to the front line tonight and have a look. Bring with you a stick three feet long.' After dinner Churchill and Napier-Clavering left Laurence Farm, walked along the communication trench and reached the front line. Once in the forward trench, they climbed up on the parapet and walked along it for the whole length of the Battalion's line. Napier-Clavering had never seen an officer take such a passionate interest in the details of trench engineering, but there was more to come, as he recalled:

Up went a Verey Light. Churchill was on his knees measuring the depth of the earth with the stick. The Hun machine guns opened up, belly high. Why the hell we weren't killed I just don't understand. I didn't want to die; I wanted to kill some of the Hun first. 'For God's sake keep still, Sir,' I hissed. But he didn't take the slightest notice. He was a man who had no physical fear of dying.

During the days that followed, under Churchill's constant surveillance, Napier-Clavering continued his work of improving the parapets, fortifying the dugouts and trying to arrange an effective drainage system for the trenches. In the evenings, when they were dining, Churchill often questioned him about his work, and about how the Royal Engineers ought to be run. Hakewill Smith recalled how on one occasion Churchill asked: 'Why haven't we got a trench digger? We want a trench digger. Something that would crawl along and dig out a trench in five minutes.' Not to be outdone, Napier-Clavering decided to ask his own questions:

I said to him one night, after the necessary number of Ports, 'could you tell us, Sir, what advantage it would be to us to win the war?' There was silence for three minutes. Then for the next twenty minutes he gave us a Parliamentary speech. At the end of each paragraph he looked up, and looked at everybody in the room to see what the effect was. His language was so absolutely marvellous. I was only twenty-two at the time. My eyes were standing out like hatpins.

Churchill was equally impressed by Napier-Clavering. 'This young fellow was lunching with us,' McDavid later recalled. 'Winston started giving a dissertation on a new type of vehicle he was keen on. A "Caterpillar" Winston called it; it could get over the humps and over the wire. He used the various condiment sets to explain what he meant. He had this idea that a tracked vehicle could cut the German wire, or drag it through and make a gap. We all thought it an airy fairy idea.

"If it amuses him, let him go on talking about it," we thought, "but it is a damned silly idea." It was away up in the clouds. But the young engineer officer took it up with him. He was the only one who encouraged him to talk about it. He realized that it was a possibility. They had quite a discussion together about it.'

The effect of trench life on Churchill was profound. As the weeks passed, the conditions under which his men were living impressed themselves harshly upon his mind. At Laurence Farm he could do nothing to express the anger which he felt at the indignities which the war was imposing upon exuberant boys; transforming them into tired men, driving them to despair or killing them needlessly. By personal intervention, by leniency, by kindness, he tried to lessen in some small way the burden which his men bore. They themselves appreciated the efforts which he made on their behalf. A young private, Reginald Hurt,[1] later recorded two examples of Churchill's attitude in a letter to the author. The first incident took place while the battalion was in the trenches:

I was on sentry duty that night, which meant standing on the fire steps of the front line trench, and looking out towards the enemy lines. It was a bitterly cold, wet night and very quiet as regards action, and in a weak moment I stood my rifle up against the parapet; in a corner of the trench. I then marched up and down on the fire step trying to get some warmth into my arms and legs, when suddenly some-one jumped down behind me from the top of the parapet. Fortunately for me and my sleeping colleagues, it was Sir Winston Churchill and his Adjutant, Sir Archibald Sinclair and not a German patrol. The next five or ten minutes were amongst the unhappiest of my life, all because my rifle *was not* in my possession. I received, and deservedly, the most severe reprimand I can recall. Finally he asked me my age, and on learning that I was one of the youngest soldiers in the Battalion, and had been in the trenches at the age of eighteen, his anger evaporated and he became almost paternal. My punishment was much less severe than that meted out to a Corporal on sentry duty in the next bay, found doing almost the same as myself, who was demoted to the ranks, because he was both a time serving soldier and an NCO, and should have set a better example.

The second incident that Private Hurt recalled took place in reserve:

On one occasion, whilst acting as company runner, I was walking along what had been Plugstreet's main road, when I saw the OC coming along in

[1] Reginald Hurt, 1896–   . Employed by the Sheffield Electric Supply Department. Enlisted in the Army, May 1915. Crossed to France, September 1915. Severely wounded, May 1916.

the opposite direction. I gave him the usual smart salute, and had passed along about a dozen paces when he called me back and asked why I was limping. I explained that my feet were sore because of the bad condition of my boots, and that when I had applied for a new pair the quartermaster said they would last another three months. The OC took a letter from his tunic pocket, detached the envelope and wrote on it, 'Quarter-master Sgt. B. Company, supply bearer with one pair of boots *immediately*,' and signed it.

It was not only Churchill's sympathy but also his enthusiasm that caused his men to respond to him. In his book Gibb later wrote:

To see Winston giving a dissertation on the laying of sandbags, with practical illustrations, was to come inevitably to the conclusion that his life-study had been purely of poliorketics and the corresponding counter-measures. You felt sure from his grasp of practice that he must have served apprentice to a bricklayer and a master-mason, while his theoretical knowledge rendered you certain that Wren would have been proud to sit at his feet. . . .

The spectre of a Brigade hovered in front of Churchill throughout February. He was not alone in believing that promotion was still possible. On February 18 Colonel Holland wrote to Clementine Churchill from the Headquarters of the Ninth Division:

Dear Mrs Winston,
    I must just write you a line to say how glad we are to have Winston commanding one of our battalions.
    He is awfully well, better than I have seen him for ages, & full of vigour & vitality & has made his battalion from a moderate one into a d—— good one. He is gradually acquiring the Scotch lingo, which I find very difficult. I always take an interpreter about with me. I hope he will get a brigade soon & have more scope for his energy. . . .

                                                        Yrs sincerely
                                                        A. E. Holland

'I find that everyone has heard of the improvements you have effected in your Battalion,' Clementine Churchill wrote to her husband a few days later. 'Soldiers back from the Front on leave talk about it. This is good, as it prepares the way for a Brigade.'
    On February 19 the Battalion moved back into reserve. Gibb, the Battalion diarist, wrote in the war diary for the six days in reserve: 'Nothing of note to record.' But Churchill had much to describe in his letter home on February 20. He had gone to the Hospice to sleep,

hoping that it would be less noisy than at Battalion headquarters at Soyer Farm:

My darling,

. . . We have been hunted by shells during these two days in 'rest' billets—nine men hit this evening and all our farms shelled repeatedly. Archie & I have had a particularly exciting time. I told you how we decided to leave the uncomfortable & crowded farm & go back to delightful quarters in the little town. Yesterday we differed on policy. Archie was for living in one room and darting into a cellar when shelling began. I was for another room next door . . . and was building a strong sandbag protection there. My principle is that one ought to try to make the ordinary place where one lives fairly comfortable & safe & take the chance there. Archie contended that only the cellar was really safe, & he insisted on my following his plan on two occasions yesterday when things became disagreeable. So we all assembled in the cellar —Archie, I, the 3 signallers, two servants, & the people of the house viz an old man, two women & a jolly little flapper. This plan worried me. I hate having repeatedly to skip into a cellar, & wonder where each shell is coming & whether we ought to move in or not.

Also we always got a shell pretty near going across the courtyard & finally I declared that the cellar was not really safe & that a shell at a certain angle wd penetrate it. He said it was 1000 to 1 against it. Well this morning he went out to visit our companies & I stayed in to write a paper on Air, wh may turn out either as a splash or a letter! I had made up my mind to go to the other room & not use the cellar. At about 11 shelling began: and the buildings all around were hit & other shells burst in the courtyard or stopped just short of us across the road. I concentrated my mind on my air argument and wrote on placidly without any feelings of anxiety. After an hour the shelling stopped & I went out to look at the damage. My dear! Archie's pet cellar! A 30 pound shell had entered our bedroom (where I shd have been writing) passed completely through it, had penetrated the cellar where all the assembly were huddled—& then mercifully failed to burst. Otherwise they wd all have been killed. Archie returned from his walk to abandon his argument. This is now the third time in a fortnight that our bedroom has been pierced by shells—three different rooms. Archie says it is the roughest time in billets he has ever had all the war. You will be glad to hear that I have now moved back 300 yards to this beastly farm; as I am sure they meant to smash the little town to pieces. Yet even here shells came in pursuit, & riding across the ploughed fields shrapnel kept pace with us in the air. One lives calmly on the brink of the abyss. But I can understand how tired people get of it if it goes on month after month. All the excitement dies away & there is only dull resentment.

The church steeple wh had withstood the vicissitudes of 16 months of fighting came down yesterday at the explosion of a big shell. So this evening we are smashing up one of their steeples & they are retaliating by scattering their shells in twos & threes on various points. Meanwhile the German aeroplanes sail about unmolested overhead watching the shooting, & scorning our anti-aircraft guns. There is no doubt who is master of this air! . . .

Goodnight my darling—fondest love
Your devoted
W

Shelled out of the Hospice, Churchill was forced to sleep at Soyer Farm. The Germans turned their attention elsewhere, and there followed two quiet days, with snow, and the sound of heavy shelling somewhere to the south. 'They cannot see to shoot,' Churchill reported to his wife on February 22. 'This unusual interlude is welcome.' He was excited about his coming leave, wanting time to relax and to paint. He asked his wife to make the arrangements: 'I have every hope of coming home on the 2nd. I propose to come to Dover by destroyer & that you meet me at the Lord Warden Hotel where we can lunch & go up to London together. . . . Mind you have a servant ready to look after me, & let him come in time to have everything ready on arrival.'

On February 25 Colonel Holland called on Churchill at Soyer Farm. He had just been promoted to a senior appointment with the 3rd Army. 'His sphere is extended 12 or 15 times,' Churchill explained to his wife the next day. Holland brought good news, which Churchill passed on: 'He told me that General Furse had spontaneously sent in an official recommendation that I shd be selected for a Brigade command; & that he (Holland) was going to impress this upon GHQ where he stays tonight. It is satisfactory anyhow that my immediate superiors have confidence in my work.' Furse's recommendation came to nought. In London society it was assumed that Churchill was already a Brigadier; on the day after Holland's visit Churchill learned from his wife that at dinner one night the Vice-Chamberlain of Queen Alexandra's household, Lord Gosford,[1] had said that he was 'shocked when he heard you were not yet a Brigadier and said he had been told you really were one but it had not been gazetted'.

On February 26 Churchill returned for the fourth time to Laurence Farm, and to the front-line trenches. Napier-Clavering and his sappers had done their work well. 'Our farm is much more protected,' Churchill wrote to his wife, 'and it wd take 5 9-inch guns to smash it up.' Winter

---

[1] Archibald Brabazon Sparrow Acheson, 1841–1922. 4th Earl of Gosford, 1864. Vice-Chamberlain to Queen Alexandra, 1901–22.

conditions had returned, but the British Army was not without resource, nor was Churchill in any particular discomfort:

Snow covers the ground and we do our scouting in calico gowns—almost invisible at 200 yards. I was up till 1.30 in the trenches, as the night was so dark & the price of safety is eternal vigilance. The artillery co-operation was vy loose last night and we took a vy long time to get a response from them.

I like this farm so much better than the one I am in at 'rest'.

Archie & I have a nice little square room together—the ceiling is propped up by timber, & there are 3 layers of sandbags & brick bags on the top, and all the sides are heavily protected. There are a good many things to burst a shell before it actually hits us, & then the sandbags may be counted on to stop the splinters & to keep out the blast. Inside we have a glowing brazier & two comfortable canvas beds . . . we sleep warm and peaceful.

Confident that his farm was well-nigh impregnable, Churchill had persuaded the artillery to lay on another 'sträfe', which he augmented by front-line fire. All did not go well. The British shells, falling short, killed two men and wounded four. A newly arrived officer, 2nd Lieutenant Buchan,[1] was also slightly wounded. A report of this tragedy was sent the next morning to General Tudor at Artillery headquarters at Steenwerck. 'I found on investigation,' Tudor wrote in his diary, 'that the gunners were entirely to blame.' On the following day Tudor lunched with Churchill at Laurence Farm. Then he saw the artillery officer whose 'offending guns' had caused the tragedy. 'He will arrange something . . .' Tudor wrote in his diary, 'to restore confidence.'

Churchill remained at Laurence Farm for the next three days. He did not write to his wife as he would be seeing her before his letters could arrive. The only record of events is in the Battalion's war diary, which was as usual succinct:

27.2.16 LAWRENCE FM (Bn HQ) shelled at noon with 20–30 7·7 cms. 3 signallers working outside were severely wounded—all three eventually died of their wounds.

28.2.16 Bn HQ shelled twice—once at 1 pm & once at 3 pm. Cupola dugouts afforded complete protection. An orderly who was standing at the mouth of one, however, was severely wounded in the head.

29.2.16 A very quiet day with no shelling. Weather still extremely cold.

1st March 1916 Quiet day. No shelling. One private killed.

[1] Alastair Ebenezer Buchan, 1894–1917. Brother of the novelist John Buchan. 2nd Lieutenant, Cameron Highlanders, 1915. Transferred to the Royal Scots Fusiliers, March 1915. Died 9 April 1917 of wounds received at Arras.

At seven in the morning of March 2 the Battalion was relieved by a Battalion of Gordon Highlanders. Churchill left Flanders for London, giving Sinclair command of the Battalion in his absence. He had not been home since Christmas, over two months before. His wife had prepared a careful plan to keep him busy and amused; but it was not a private world that welcomed him back.

22

'You can be Prime Minister'

D URING his first two months in command of the 6th Royal
Scots Fusiliers Churchill had found little time for anything but
his military duties. But fifteen years of intense political activity were not
to be obliterated by mud or noise or danger. Throughout January and
February he had been alerted, not only by the shriek of German shells
but by political news from home. On January 1 the Press had announced
the resignation of Sir John Simon, the Home Secretary, in protest
against the Military Service Bill. Many Liberals feared that the Bill
was the first step on the road to conscription. Churchill's meeting with
Lloyd George at the end of December had given him the brief hope that
the conscription crisis would enable him to rejoin the Government as a
leading advocate of compulsory service. But after some reflection he
saw little likelihood of Simon's resignation leading to any significant
change either in Cabinet policy or personnel. It was a great pity, he
wrote to his wife on January 3, that Simon had not been followed 'by
others who have not got their hearts in the war'. He realized that
by itself Simon's resignation could not weaken Asquith's position;
indeed, during February Asquith skilfully emerged as a supporter of
the growing conscription lobby. Churchill was not impressed by
the Prime Minister's change of view. 'I cannot regard the delay to do
what is now shown to be necessary, & the waste of time & energy entailed, as any triumph for Asquith,' he wrote; 'he has simply played the
party game as long as he cd, while ruling in the name of the nation.'

The failure of the conscription crisis to develop was not Churchill's
only frustration. On the afternoon of January 3 he was summoned to
St Omer by the Operation Division of GHQ, and told that they had
been instructed by the War Office to follow up his idea of a Caterpillar
machine.[1] They 'wanted to know who to apply to in England about

---

[1] The Colonel who summoned Churchill to St Omer was Hugh Jamieson Elles (1880–
1945). Commanded the tanks in action at Cambrai, 1917. Knighted, 1919. Master-General
of Ordnance, 1934–7. Colonel Commandant, Royal Tank Regiment, 1934–45. General,
1938.

them', Churchill wrote to his wife. This made him angry; 'imagine', he continued, that 'after 9 months of actual manufacture and committees unending, there should still be such ignorance and lack of concern'. The combination of Asquith's stratagems over conscription and the War Office's hesitations over the Caterpillar, led him to exclaim to his wife: 'God for a month of power & a good shorthand writer.'

During January Churchill continued to try to overcome his wife's distrust of Lloyd George. 'Keep in touch with LG,' he wrote to her on January 4; 'his necessities will keep him straight if a split occurs. Asquith on the other hand will never have need of me again. It is *need* alone that counts. Nothing else is considered.' After fifteen years in politics, Churchill believed himself a competent judge of political realities. 'I keep turning things over in my mind,' he wrote to his wife on January 6, 'without doing much good. But broadly my conclusion is that nothing but a complete change of regime will require me to return—or be of any use. Asquith will never face the certain demands of opposition hostile to me.' Churchill believed that his chance of Cabinet office depended upon Asquith's overthrow. When this were done, he expected it to be done by others, who would then invite him to return. If it were not done, he could see no future for himself in the political sphere. 'There is little likelihood of my obtaining real power again during the war,' he wrote to Edward Grigg on January 6, '& anything less than that I do not intend to take. It is vexatious to see so many things left undone, or half done, or done too late: but I try with a measure of success to avert my mind from the wide panorama, & close my mental eyes.' He had no doubts about the outcome of the war: 'It will all come right in the end,' he told Grigg, 'though not by the shortest or least costly method.'

On January 7, reading of the continuing conscription crisis, Churchill wrote to his wife in a depressed mood. 'I watch in The Times (6th inst) the movement of political things & I must confess it excites & disturbs my mind,' he explained. 'I try however not to look back too much, having not only put my hand but fettered it to the plough. I must rely on you to keep constant touch with the friends & pseudo-friends I have. I do not like to feel forgotten & deconsidéré out here—especially when I am not in the trenches, but only waiting in reserve billets. . . .' Churchill always looked forward to his periods of duty in the trenches. He wanted to escape the depressed moods which came with reading newspapers, and having the time to reflect and brood upon news from England. The trenches provided him with just such an escape. 'I feel vy much bound on the wheel of things out here,' he told his wife in his letter of January 7, 'and when politics calm down again, I shall yield myself to the inexorable motion with suppleness and placidity. But peace out here & crisis at home are disturbing combinations for my mind.'

Churchill needed his wife's encouragement. It was her commentary on political events at home that enabled him to interpret the information which he read in the newspapers or received from others. He wanted too her personal support and her approval for all that he had done. 'You cannot write to me too often or too long—my dearest & sweetest,' he wrote. 'The beauty & strength or your character & the sagacity of yr judgment are more realised by me every day. I ought to have followed yr counsels in my days of prosperity. Only sometimes they were too negative. I shd have made nothing if I had not made mistakes. Ungrateful country.'

Throughout January Clementine Churchill was busy on her husband's behalf. On January 7 she had tea with Margot Asquith at 10 Downing Street, discovering, as she wrote to her husband that evening, 'great relief in that quarter that the division on compulsion went so well'. She had met the Prime Minister in the hall: 'He looked shy when he first saw me, but thought better of it & I had a little talk to him. . . . He asked after you with compunction in his voice.' She remained dubious about Lloyd George. 'I don't think he has managed very well,' she wrote. 'At one time he abused the Dukes to please the working-men, now he has abused the working-men to please the soldiers.[1] He seems to me very isolated. . . .'

On January 7 Churchill received a letter from his mother in which she gave him news of the conscription debate, and told him that by some accounts 'the PM was very badly received', and that the Speaker[2] had doubted whether things would go well 'notwithstanding the crowds of MPs brought back from the front to vote with the Govt'. This news stirred Churchill to further speculation, for he now saw a way in

---

[1] By the end of 1915 many munitions works were far behind with their deliveries. Speaking in Parliament on December 20 Lloyd George, the Minister of Munitions, had linked the deaths at the front with lethargy in the factories at home. On Christmas Eve 1915 he went to Beardmore's Works on the Clyde to urge the men to speed up deliveries of heavy guns. He was met by the singing of the 'Red Flag'. On the following morning in St Andrew's Hall, Glasgow, the Clydeside workers howled him down. The Trade Unions were determined to resist any dilution of labour which might be caused by military conscription. They were also afraid that the Government would introduce some form of industrial compulsion.

[2] James William Lowther, 1855–1949. Conservative MP, 1883–5, 1886–1921. Under-Secretary for Foreign Affairs, 1891. Speaker of the House of Commons, 1905–21. Created Viscount Ullswater, 1921.

which he could perhaps repair his reputation, if nothing more. On the following day he wrote to his wife: '. . . I am inclined to think that the PM's position is only temporarily strengthened; & that once this conscription corner is turned his utility will be reduced, & his authority stand on a vy lopsided basis. As soon as the Dardanelles episode is finished I propose to invite him to publish papers, including my various forecasts & requests for support.' Churchill believed that if the facts about the Dardanelles were published, they would show that neither the naval failure on March 18 nor the subsequent military disasters had been his responsibility, and that once this were established his political prospects would be much improved. Clementine Churchill did not share this view, replying on January 11:

If you ask the PM to publish the Dardanelles papers let me know what happens. If he refuses or delays I beg you not to do anything without telling me first & giving me time to give you my valuable (!) opinion on it. It is an unequal match between the PM & an officer in the field in war-time—If he dissents I fear you will have to wait. If you insisted on publication against his wish you would have against you all the forces of cohesion and stability including every member of the Cabinet.

On the other hand when the papers are eventually published his refusal to do so earlier will have a very bad effect for him.

But of course the PM may consent. Are you quite certain however that this is the best time for publication, when you are away and not able to speak in the debate which is bound to take place. I am very anxious that you should not blunt this precious weapon prematurely.

Churchill's bitterness against Asquith's treatment of him was unabated. On January 7 he wrote to his mother:

My feeling agst him is due to the fact that knowing my work, & having been a co-adventurer in my enterprises (not merely an approver), he threw me over without the slightest effort even to state the true facts on my behalf; & still more that thereafter in all the plenitude of power he never found for me a useful sphere of acting wh wd have given scope to my energies & knowledge. If I am killed at the humble duties I have found for myself he will no doubt be sorry & shocked. But the fact will remain that he has treated me with injustice, & has wasted qualities wh might have been used in many ways to the public advantage in this time of war.

To his wife, who continued to warn him against Lloyd George, and to beg him not to cut himself off entirely from Asquith, he wrote on January 10:

I cannot see any way in wh Asquith's interests can stand in need of me. However friendly his feelings, his *interests* are best served by my effacement. If I were killed he wd be sorry: but it wd suit his political hand. LG on the other hand wd not be sorry, but it wd not suit his political hand. It is this factor that alone counts in the cruel politics of today. I can feel no sense of loyalty or friendship for Asquith after the revelation of his utter indifference shown by his letter to French. Still here again there is no occasion for a personal breech.

Whenever my mind is not occupied by work, I feel deeply the injustice with wh my work at the Admiralty has been treated. I cannot help it—tho' I try. Then the damnable mismanagement wh has ruined the Dardanelles enterprise & squandered vainly so much life & opportunity cries aloud for retribution: & if I survive, the day will come when I will claim it publicly.

Clementine Churchill continued in her efforts to find out about the political situation, and to give her husband a clear view of what was happening at home. 'To-day, I lunched at Downing Street & for the first time since you resigned talked to the PM,' she wrote on January 9. 'He talked a great deal about you and asked a great many questions. I was perfectly natural (except perhaps that I was a little too buoyant) & he tried to be natural too, but it was an effort. I think it is a good thing to keep up civil relations & it is always interesting to follow the Block's train of thought. He seemed very much pleased at the *Parliamentary* situation, but I expect things must still be very uncertain judging from the fact that this is the 2nd Sunday he has spent in London.' Clementine Churchill was appalled by the lack of serious concern at Downing Street in the conduct of the war. 'The chief topic of social gossip,' she told him, 'is who is to go to India [as Viceroy]. After ranging round the Crewes, Harcourts, McKennas, Islingtons,[1] Sir F. Hopwood etc speculation has narrowed down to two obscurities & it is a dead heat between them—Chelmsford[2] or Balcarres![3] It seems incredible——' On

[1] John Poynder Dickson-Poynder, 1866–1936. Liberal MP, 1892–1910. Created Baron Islington, 1910. Governor of New Zealand, 1910–12. Under-Secretary of State for the Colonies, 1915–16. Under-Secretary of State for India, 1916–19. Chairman, National Savings Committee, 1920–6. Married, 1896, Anne Dundas, a friend of the Churchill family.

[2] Frederick John Napier Thesiger, 1868–1933. 3rd Baron Chelmsford, 1905. Governor of Queensland, 1905–9; of New South Wales, 1909–13. Viceroy of India, 1916–21. Created Viscount, 1921. Married, 1894, Frances Charlotte Guest, eldest daughter of Churchill's uncle Ivor Guest.

[3] David Alexander Edward Lindsay, 1871–1940. Conservative MP, 1895–1913. 27th Earl of Crawford and 10th Earl of Balcarres, 1913. Enlisted as a Private, Royal Army Medical Corps, August 1914, without disclosing his identity. President of the Board of Agriculture and Fisheries, July 1916. Lord Privy Seal, 1916–19. Chancellor of the Duchy of Lancaster, 1919–21. First Commissioner of Works, 1921–2. Minister of Transport, 1922. Chairman of the Royal Fine Art Commission, 1924.

January 11 F. E. Smith sent Churchill discouraging news, declaring that as a result of the conscription crisis: 'The country is overwhelmingly with us & indeed the Bill has a little restored the prestige of the Government.'

Clementine Churchill shared F. E. Smith's interpretation of the conscription crisis, and of Asquith's improved position. 'I'm afraid I can't agree that the PM's position is only temporarily strengthened,' she wrote to her husband on January 11. 'He will always in the end tip down on the side of strong measures after delaying them & devitalising them so as to try and keep everybody together. His method of defeating the enemy is not by well planned lightning strokes, but by presenting to him a large stolid gelatinous mess which he (the enemy) is supposed to pommel in vain.' Clementine Churchill was aware of the terrible pressures which made her husband unhappy. But she believed passionately in his future, and tried always to share his anxieties with him. 'My own Darling,' she wrote on January 12, 'I long so to be able to comfort you. Later on when you are in danger in the trenches you will be equable and contented, while I who am now comparatively at ease will be in mortal anxiety. Try not to brood too much; I would be so unhappy if your naturally open and unsuspicious nature became embittered. Patience is the only grace you need.' She was confident about his future: 'If you are not killed, as sure as day follows night you will come into your own again. I know *you* don't fear death, it is I who dread that. But I am almost glad to be suffering now, becos' I am sure no single soul will be allowed to live thro' this time without sorrow, so perhaps what we are enduring now will be counted and we shall be spared the greatest pain of all.' Recalling August 1914 she wrote: 'I remember quite well when we were at the Admiralty during those wonderful opening weeks of the war, we were both so happy, you with the success of the Naval preparations & with the excitement of swiftly moving events and I with pride at the glamour surrounding you & the Navy. I remember feeling guilty and ashamed that the terrible casualties of those first battles did not sadden me more. I wondered how long we should continue to tread on air.'

'When it is all over,' she believed, 'we shall be proud that you were a soldier & not a politician for the greater part of the war—soldiers and soldier's wives seem to me now the only real people. . . .' Clementine Churchill's letter continued with some personal advice. She did not want him to tell chance visitors his hostile opinion of Asquith's character and policy, suggesting that he use Archibald Sinclair as a safety-valve for his anger, just as she used her sister-in-law Gwendeline.

For the first two weeks of January Sir John Simon had been much abused for having opposed compulsory military service. By resigning, he drew upon himself the odium of a belligerent society. Many people shared F. E. Smith's view that, as he wrote to Churchill on January 11, Simon was pegging out 'a claim in the garbage' by refusing to compromise his principles. Churchill took a different view. When Jack Seely, who had been at the conscription debate, returned to France, he told Churchill that Simon was much upset; so much so that he thought of joining the Army as an ordinary recruit. Churchill was moved by this news, informing his wife on January 13:

> I have written him a note telling him he is vy welcome to come here if he likes. I will look after him & teach him soldiering, & he wd be a pleasant companion to teach me law. I am sorry for him—now he is down. It is vy hard—if one has not the training of a soldier. A cabinet minister can fight in the trenches; but to be drilled by a sergeant in the barrack yard—invests adversity with a squalid air. He cd learn everything out here quite easily.

Seely's account of London politics stimulated Churchill's appetite for political news. 'LG by all accounts is isolated,' he wrote to his wife in the same letter. 'He has been vy foolish in his relations with me, Bonar Law, FE & Curzon. He might have combined us all. As it is he has earned the deep distrust of each, & I who was his friend and had worked with him so long, have now largely by his action been rendered quite powerless for the time being.' Churchill wanted to know more about his wife's meeting with Asquith. '. . . I shd like a *verbatim* report of the Kat's conversation with the old ruffian,' he wrote. 'He has handspiked compulsion as long as he cd, & long after it was needed; & only adopted it in the end, against his deepest convictions, to keep his office—or what is perhaps true—to keep LG out of his office; and for this "statecraft" at the expense of our arms & treasure—he is acclaimed as the saviour of the Nation. . . .'

That evening Churchill read in *The Times* of the previous day, which had just reached Ploegsteert, that the last of the Allied troops at Gallipoli had finally been evacuated from Helles. It was a bitter moment for him. But he was thrilled to learn that Carson had described the Dardanelles as 'admirably conceived' when speaking in the House of Commons on January 11. 'Gradually people will see what I saw so vividly this time last year,' he wrote to his wife on January 14, 'but alas too late forever. Thank God they all got off safe. If things never turn out as well as you expect them, it is also true they never turn out as badly.

There is no culminating catastrophe: only a cruel tale of wasted effort, life & treasure, & opportunity—priceless & unique—gone forever.'

Churchill continued to debate in his own mind whether he had been right to leave London for the trenches. On January 16 he wrote to his wife of 'the wisdom & necessity of my coming out here'. It would have been impossible, he explained, to have 'sat still in England—painting to keep my mind quiet & waiting for the wind to change. Here I have to sit still; but somehow dullness does not fret me.' Nevertheless, there were daily reminders of what he could achieve in politics. Writing to his wife on January 17 he described one such incident:

. . . Air fights have been going on overhead this morning, & I think there has been an air raid on some of the neighbouring townships, as a lot of our machines are up. There is no excuse for our not having command of the air.

Since I left the Admiralty, the whole naval air wing has been let down: & all our precious ascendency has been dissipated. If they had given me control of this service when I left the Admiralty, we shd have supremacy today. Asquith wanted this, but in contact with the slightest difficulty & resistance, he as usual shut up.

Churchill told his wife that he was also worried that the large numbers of British troops at Salonika and Egypt were serving no purpose, and that these expeditions were welcomed by the Germans as a means of keeping these troops idle, 'while they use the Turks to stir up Persia, & later on Afghanistan'; a thought which led him to exclaim in his postscript: 'Imbecile government, and purblind Kitchener. Wait & see.' Every letter which reached him provoked similar painful speculation. Towards the end of January he received a long account from his brother-in-law, William Hozier, who had been at the Dardanelles on board HMS *Edgar*. This letter, dated January 17, had a disturbing effect on Churchill, whose mind was tormented by descriptions of avoidable failure and opportunities cast away by inefficiency and lack of enterprise:

. . . I can now without transgressing the censorship rules give you some idea of the work carried out by the Edgar class and the monitors between the beginning of August and the withdrawal on January 8th and 9th. . . .

The Air Service was not organised sufficiently to cooperate with the ships and there was no responsible head to direct matters and to confer with us.

There was no interchange of ideas between the Generals at Helles and ourselves. . . .

Up to the middle of September our orders were to expend a maximum of 25 rounds a day on some section of Achi Baba. This was always done at the same time and was of little value.

The impression therefore prevailed amongst the soldiers that our only value was a moral one and that naval gunfire was of little use to support an offensive. . . .

August 7th A grand attack by the Helles Army just before the landing at Suvla Bay. RESULT—2,000 casualties: and not an inch of advance. Ships' fire hopelessly ineffective.

Nov 15th An attack by the 8th Army Corps. 50 casualties, 200 yards advance. Supporting ships—Edgar and two 14″ monitors. Edgar firing on twelve different batteries. 14″ monitors firing on trenches and earthworks, and our shore artillery on the remaining four hostile batteries.

I am convinced that had it been realised how the naval gunfire would become effective, the 60,000 troops frittered away at Suvla Bay would have been used in the capture of Achi Baba. Of course many more troops would have been needed to beat the Turkish Army but we could have established ourselves for the winter. . . .

Those who are running this war require more 'ruthlessness' or we shall lose it.

Churchill shared his brother-in-law's fear that without 'ruthlessness' there could be defeat. He felt confident that he himself could provide the necessary driving force. But his isolation was complete. 'You do not tell me in yr letter what the PM said,' Churchill had written to his wife on January 11. She replied on January 16:

He talked a great deal about trivialities & feminities which you know he adores and he asked a good many questions about you and about the detail of your life out there—He *wanted* the answers to be reassuring, & my good manners as a guest forbade me making him uncomfortable which of course I could easily have done. He seemed grateful to me for sparing him——! He is a sensualist & if I had depicted you in a tragic and sinister light it would have ruined his meal and I should probably not be bidden again!

Clementine Churchill remained uncertain as to how far Asquith had behaved dishonourably towards her husband. 'I think one might say,' she wrote in her letter, 'that the PM instead of battling bravely with a hurricane is so anxious to avoid ship-wreck that he never minds how often he tacks, so that he frequently describes a complete circle before reaching his object—with consequent loss to our arms & fortunes.' Churchill was not to be deflected from his bitterness against Asquith. His hope of some political development favourable to himself had been stimulated yet again by a letter from F. E. Smith sent from London on January 18. 'If you write any of your able memoranda,' F. E. Smith encouraged him, 'send me one & I will circulate it above my own august initials to the cabinet.' F. E. Smith wrote that he was dining shortly with Lloyd George and the editor of the *Daily Chronicle*, Robert Donald,[1] '& will tell you if anything happens'. He sent disturbing news about the United States, whose entry into the war, for which Churchill had so wished when he was at the Admiralty, seemed increasingly remote: 'The US swine,' wrote F. E. Smith, 'grow more and more truculent and are apparently almost prepared to slobber over Brother Bosch.'[2] F. E. Smith added that he was going to 'make an effort to come & see you on Friday week if this suits your arrangements. *If not let me know what weekend will suit you.*' On January 23 Churchill wrote to his wife: 'I am enchanted at the idea of FE coming out. Tell him to keep it a secret so as to give no handle for political & newspaper gossip.'

Churchill continued to debate with his wife the merits and failings of the Prime Minister. On January 19 he declared emphatically: 'My precious—I don't take back a word of what I wrote about Asquith. He has cruelly & needlessly wronged me; & even in his power & prosperity has had the meanness to strike at me. No—if I survive—my political life will be apart from him. He passes from my regard.' His letter continued: 'My mind is now filling up with ideas & opinions in many military & war matters. But I have no means of expression. I am impotent to give what is there to be given—of truth & value & urgency. I must wait in silence the sombre movement of events. Still it is better to be gagged than give unheeded counsel.' Dependent upon his wife for almost all the contacts which he wanted to maintain in London, Churchill enlisted his wife's support:

I had a nice letter from Rothermere—saying that 'I had emerged unscathed from Gallipoli'. *Do* I beseech you keep in touch with him, & also through Aitken with Bonar Law. Don't neglect these matters. I have no one but you to act for me. I shd like you to make the seeing of my friends a regular business, like your canteens wh are going so well. It is fatal to let the threads drop. Curzon, FE: BL: Carson; Garvin, Rothermere: Goulding:

---

[1] Robert Donald, 1861–1933. Editor, *Daily Chronicle*, 1902–18. Chairman, Empire Press Union, 1915–26. A Director, Department of Information, 1917. A strong advocate of dropping leaflets over enemy territory. Knighted, 1924. A friend of the first Labour Prime Minister, Ramsay MacDonald, for whom he undertook publicity work.

[2] On 2 January 1916 the unarmed British liner *Persia* had been sunk without warning in the Eastern Mediterranean by an Austrian submarine. Over half of the 350 passengers and crew were drowned. Among the dead were many Americans, including the American Consul at Aden. On hearing the news President Wilson cut short his honeymoon to return to the White House. But despite what *The Times* described on January 5 as 'excitement in Washington' against 'Teutonic savageness', the United States accepted a cash indemnity and remained at peace with the Central Powers.

Alick[1] all these you shd keep in touch with. There is nothing to ask of them —only represent *me* in their circle.

Even while he was writing this letter, Churchill became increasingly disturbed. It was six o'clock in the evening, 'a bad hour for me', he continued; 'I feel the need of power as an outlet worst then; & the energy of mind & body is strong within me.' On the following day he wrote more calmly: 'I expect the Kat will be flustered by my directions to her to keep in touch with so many people. Do only just what comes easily & naturally to you my darling. On the other hand don't simply vanish out of the political circle & plunge into bed & canteens. Do what you can.' Clementine Churchill continued to see her husband's friends and potential allies. She also sent him her own thoughts upon the political scene. 'If tomorrow the PM disappeared Bonar Law would be the successor,' she wrote on January 21. 'He has made a great impression in the House during these last weeks by his skilful handling of delicate topics and this impression will spread to the country—Myself I think Bonar is not a big man, but he is a very skilful one and does not miss his markets. I think Ll-George will remain *perdu* for a bit and then gradually slide away from his "compulsion" attitude towards the working men.' She had just met the new Chancellor of the Duchy of Lancaster and reported: 'Montagu after an absence of 6 months from the Cabinet finds very little change except a greater disinclination to action, the only Warrior is Curzon.'

On January 23, after lunching with Augustine Birrell, Clementine Churchill wrote again. 'Bonar's growing prestige,' she reported, 'is the common table-talk, & also the disappearance of Ll-G "into quarantine".' On the following day she saw Lloyd George, and hoped that her husband appreciated all her efforts on his behalf. 'Now don't scold your Kat too much for being a hermit,' she wrote on January 24. 'Here in two days I have hob-nobbed with Montagu, Birrell, Lloyd George and a South African potentate![2] Tomorrow night I am dining with Cassel. Please send me home the Distinguished Conduct Medal at once & much praise.'

During January Churchill became increasingly distressed at German air superiority on the western front. He often saw German aeroplanes

---

[1] Alexander William Charles Oliphant Murray, 1870–1920. Liberal MP, 1900–5; 1906–10; 1910–12. Under-Secretary of State for India, 1909. Chief Liberal Whip, 1909–12. Created Baron Murray of Elibank, 1912. Director of Recruiting for Munitions Works, 1915–16.

[2] Abe Bailey, 1864–1940. One of the principal mine owners of the Transvaal. Knighted, 1911, for his services in promoting South African Union. Served as a Major on the staff of the South African forces which attacked German South-West Africa, 1915. Created Baronet, 1919.

flying over the British trenches, but there was little corresponding activity from the British side. He was excited when his wife reported speculation in London that the Navy and Army air services—the Royal Naval Air Service and the Royal Flying Corps—might be taken away from their respective Ministries and formed into a united Air Ministry, controlled by some political figure who could unify and vitalize them. This was a task for which Churchill believed himself to be ideally suited. The work he had done in building up the Royal Naval Air Service before 1914, his own flying experience, his responsibilities at the outbreak of war for the aerial defence of Britain, had all prepared him for just such a task. Only a few days before he was due to go into the trenches where he hoped to forget such tantalizing political things, he was confronted by the question of his possible return, and felt anew the frustration of lack of power.

In a letter to his wife on January 23 Churchill commented angrily on Britain's weakness in the air, which upset him greatly. 'They have indeed maltreated the Naval Air Service,' he wrote, 'since my protective ring was broken. The way in which these slugs smile & prosper is astonishing.' Clementine Churchill shared her husband's anger and frustration. 'Everyone "in office" seems to be unbelievably smug,' she had written to him two days before. 'Were we like that when you were in power? There is an atmospheric non-conductive barrier between those whose men are in danger & those whose men are in powerful security at home. . . .' Clementine Churchill had also been excited by the Air Ministry rumours: 'Everyone not in office is much disturbed at the gradual ascendency of the German aeroplane,' she wrote. 'If only, when you left the Admiralty you had been given the "air"! I believe if you had really tried for it you might have got it, as in the press there was a movement in that direction—Do you think there is a chance even now tho' "too late"?' 'Of course I wd take an Air Ministry—if it were offered me,' Churchill replied on January 24, 'provided it carried with it a seat on the War Council. But the PM will never face the minor difficulties of such a departure, & I am sure he knows that his interests are best served by my political or other extinction.' Churchill felt that he had nothing to gain by listening to such speculations. 'I think over a gt many plans,' he wrote to his wife; 'but it is better to go on simply here for a while.'

On January 24 Churchill moved forward with his Battalion towards the trenches. That same day his wife lunched with Lloyd George. That afternoon she sent him an account of their conversation. 'He is very anxious to be amiable,' she wrote. 'He talked about current events; just now he is quite out of it—I brought in Bonar Law's name & said how well he had led the House. He didn't like that much & said that he had estranged more Tories than he had conciliated Liberals—He is going to France next week & says he means to seek you out.' Clementine Churchill was most reluctant for the two men to meet. 'I would never like you to be intimately connected,' she wrote, 'becos' tho' he seems to recover again & again from his muddles & mistakes I am not sure his partner would; he would instead be saddled with the whole lot while Ll-G skipped off laughing.'

Churchill was excited by the imminent arrival of both Lloyd George and F. E. Smith at his headquarters. There was much that he wanted to talk about. Every day provided him with examples of the Government's neglect, filling him with anger and contempt. Reading in *The Times* that Harold Tennant, the Under-Secretary of State for War, had told the House of Commons on January 20 that 'nearly every fight in the air takes place on the German side of the trenches', he wrote to his wife on January 26:

Tennant's answer in H of C about German aeroplanes never coming over our lines reads amusingly here. I saw one flaunting himself 20 miles behind the line yesterday; & 4 of them threw bombs within 50 yards of the party of men I sent on to prepare these billets for our reception. The flying officers tell me a sad tale of their difficulties, & the utter want of knowledge & drive that characterises present War Office administration.

Churchill also tried to answer his wife's criticisms of Lloyd George, explaining that although in his view Lloyd George 'has been vy faithless & is now friendless', the Minister of Munitions had nevertheless 'been more on the true trail than anyone else in this war'. In a letter which he wrote to Lloyd George on January 25 he set out his opinions without reserve, but with a certain desperation at his distance from the centre of power:

Secret & Personal
My dear David,
    How do you come out of all this? I cannot tell, but from this distance it seems to me that you are even more isolated than when we all dined at Rufus's. Asquith is stronger than ever; K still overlays the War Office; you have enthroned McKenna at the Treasury, in the War Council in the confidence of the Liberal party & press. The coalition wh you made brings to

the fore untractable forces & personalities who do not view the world as you do. The Tory dream & intention is a Tory Government. You get the unpopularity of conscription with such elements as oppose it. Others get the credit. Bonar Law particularly has greatly gained & he seems to have effectively assumed the joint Leadership of the House.

Meanwhile what is happening to the war. Germany seeks to present impenetrable fronts in France & Russia, while she raises hell in Asia. She fools us into wasting forces at Salonika & in Egypt while as usual the real movement lies elsewhere. Our initiative seems now to be a choice between two thoroughly unpromising enterprises:—viz either a concerted campaign in gt strength in the Balkans wh means consuming our manhood in killing Bulgars: or more useless slaughter here against fortifications wh daily increase in strength. Even in the air, where at least the defensive has no advantage, we have lost our ascendency. How long ago was it you wrote 'We are slouching to disaster'?

Yet it is true that if you could have had your way last January about Salonika, or in the alternative I cd have had my way last February about the Dardanelles, the whole face of the war wd have been changed. Either plan properly backed would have succeeded. The strategic conceptions were sound and all embracing: & the military forces required at the time were well within our means. The ghosts of Arras, Loos & Champagne cd have altered the history of the world.

Will last years tragedy repeat itself magnified this year? Will a half-measure campaign in the Balkans be the counterpart on a vaster scale of Gallipoli: will the next grand offensive cost us 500,000 instead of only a quarter of a million men. And all this to the tune of Islam triumphant in Asia, and at a cost of five millions a day. There is a will in the conflict. Ponder on these things.

If you come out here on Munition business, come to see me. I cd give you dinner. It is safe enough after dark—unless there is something special on.

Lloyd George did not reply to this appeal. Nor did he accept Churchill's invitation to visit the front line. But he planned to be at St Omer a few days later, and Churchill hoped to see him then. 'I am delighted LG is coming to France,' Churchill wrote to his wife on January 27, 'and I hope we shall meet. I have much to say to him.' At the same time, Churchill learned that F. E. Smith would also be in France, and would make a special effort to go right forward to Laurence Farm on the night of January 28.

Churchill did not hope for any immediate political outcome from these visits. Both he and his wife were becoming increasingly certain that there would be no place for him in the Government until the war was over. He became more and more depressed. Clementine Churchill tried to comfort him. 'Do not fear your political Estate has now vanished,' she wrote on January 27; 'it is all waiting for you when the right moment comes which (Alas for the country) may not be till after the war—if only you come safely thro'.' On January 28, after he had seen a press report that Enver Pasha had admitted that in March 1915 Turkey had been on the verge of defeat, and could not have withstood a renewed naval attack at the Dardanelles,[1] he wrote to his wife:

... It is the truth: & mind you—hereafter Germans & Turks & chancy British naval officers will testify & argue that had we pushed on—we wd have got through. I shall probably get an altogether exaggerated vindication after it is no more good to me—for the purposes of directing this war. However here in the line I am absolutely happy; without care tho' not without caution.

You must not suppose that any of my depressions here have any relation to those terrible and reasonless depressions wh frighten me sometimes. I sorrow only for real things, for gt enterprises cast away needlessly—wantonly—For not having the power wh I cd use better than any other living Englishman to determine the war policy of Britain. It is painful at times: but it is bearable always. ...

Churchill ended his letter: 'Keep in touch with those smug swine at home'; and wrote in the postscript: 'After the war I shall be friends with *Enver* & will make a gt Turkish policy with him. *Perhaps!*'

F. E. Smith could not get to Laurence Farm on the night of January 28. 'On the whole I was relieved,' Churchill wrote to his wife the next day, 'as the path across the fields to my advanced HQ is not free from random & even sometimes spiteful bullets after dark.' His new plan was to meet both F. E. Smith and Lloyd George in St Omer on Sunday January 30 or the following Monday. On January 27 Clementine Churchill dined with F. E. Smith. Two days later she wrote that like Lord Robert Cecil, who had been present at the dinner, F. E. Smith had become 'an absolute mandarin & is enamoured of the Government & all its machinery'. On January 28 she had put on what she described as '3 layers of armour' and went to luncheon in Smith Square with Reginald and Pamela McKenna. Sir Ernest Cassel was among those present and, as Clementine Churchill reported to her husband, she had been 'tickled by the contrast in their attitude towards the war, the red-hot patriotism of the German & the tepid counter-jumping calculation of the Englishman'. She wrote in her letter that she was

---

[1] Churchill made no reference to the rest of Enver's statement—quoted in *The Times* on January 27—that 'even had the British ships got to Constantinople, it would not have availed them much. Our plan was to repair our army to the surrounding hills and to Asia Minor.'

appalled when McKenna told the assembled guests that 'he wld reduce the size of the present army if he had the power', and that he planned for the future 'to pay our allies to do all the fighting while we do all the manufacturing here'. 'He really is a most noxious creature,' she commented. 'Sir Ernest & I walked away from the house much depressed. . . . I am afraid the war will go on for ever at this rate.'

Although disturbed by the lack of dynamism in high places, Churchill saw no opportunity for his return. 'I am increasingly fatalistic in my moods about things,' he wrote to his mother on January 29, '& do not worry at all at the dangers when they come.' But if the bullets did not trouble him, he could not completely accept political impotence, telling his mother:

I only fret when I think of the many things that ought to be done, & my real powers lying unused at this gt time. But the temper of the country seems admirable; & remember we have only to persevere to conquer. In grt or small station, in Cabinet or in the firing line, alive or dead my policy is 'Fight on'.

I am glad you are keeping in touch with some of my friends. I hope that FE & Ll George will pay me visits here during the next few days, & I shall thus learn how the big game does. But this existence contents me & I am happy & at peace now that we are in the line or near it. . . .

During the afternoon of January 29 a telegram reached Ploegsteert from Haig's headquarters at St Omer, informing Churchill that F. E. Smith would be coming out to see him on the following evening. The visit went well. 'We had a jolly good meal,' Hakewill Smith recalled, 'and then sat for hours yarning away. Winston and FE had consumed a considerable amount of brandy: Winston seemed all right, but FE was pretty shot when we went to bed.'

While F. E. Smith and Churchill had been dining at the Hospice, the telephones of GHQ, the 2nd Army, the 9th Division and the 27th Brigade were all unusually active. The cause of the commotion was this: while F. E. Smith had been on his way to Ploegsteert it emerged that he had not received a pass to visit the forward zone, although he had asked for one a few days before. Because he was in military uniform, being a Lieutenant-Colonel in the Queen's Own Oxfordshire Hussars, he was committing a military offence by proceeding to the front without permission. During the evening a telegram was sent from GHQ to the Headquarters of the 2nd Army, the gist of which was: 'Sir Frederick Smith is visiting Lt Colonel Winston Churchill. Ascertain if

he has a pass to enter forward zone. If not then supply him with one.'
Before this telegram reached the 2nd Army Headquarters it had
apparently been altered by some malicious hand, whose identity has
never been traced, and read: 'Sir Frederick Smith is visiting Lt Colonel
Winston Churchill. Ascertain if he has a pass to enter forward zone. If
not then place him under close arrest and return him to GHQ immediately.'[1]

This order for the arrest of a Cabinet Minister was unique. At four
o'clock that morning a Provost Marshal arrived at Ploegsteert, located
the Hospice and put the Attorney-General under arrest. F. E. Smith's
expostulations were of no avail; he was driven off to St Omer. Still under
arrest, he was taken to the Hotel du Commerce and confined to a bedroom.

Churchill was bewildered by F. E. Smith's arrest. He was also
annoyed at being cheated of the long-awaited opportunity for a political
gossip. As soon as F. E. Smith had been driven off, he wrote an angry
letter to Bonar Law, who had just reached St Omer with Lloyd George:

My dear Bonar,
   The arrest of FE in the present circumstances seems to me to be a vy
serious event. I received him here in virtue of a telegram from the ADC to
the C in C transmitted to me through the HQ of the IXth Division in wh I
am serving. Of this I enclose a copy. The act of placing a Cabinet Minister
charged with the ultimate appeal in all Court Martial cases in arrest and
removing him in conditions of indignity is one wh cannot & will not end here
in France. It will become public knowledge and will draw with it many other
things. I am of course resolved to take any steps wh the law allows. And I rely
on you to give the subject your most earnest & immediate attention as his
colleague & friend. You shd show this to Lloyd George.
                                             Yours vy sincerely
                                             Winston S.C.

At eight o'clock that morning F. E. Smith woke up at the Hotel du
Commerce to find two military policemen outside his door. 'What the
Hell are you doing here?' he asked them.

'We are on guard to make sure you don't leave: you are under close
arrest.'

'What will you do if I leave?'

'Shoot you, sir.'

F. E. Smith then walked out of the room and left the hotel. Furious,
he set about seeking redress. He forced his way into the office of the

[1] I am grateful to Major-General Sir Edmund Hakewill Smith for recalling the gist of these
telegrams, and for much of the account of F. E. Smith's arrest.

Adjutant-General, Major-General Macready;[1] but Macready merely asked: 'If you are a civilian, why are you here in uniform? If you are a soldier, why don't you obey the regulations?' F. E. Smith left Macready's headquarters with his temper unabated. He had been technically in the wrong, and was powerless to obtain redress. Nor could he know of the tampered telegram.

Although they were actually at St Omer, Lloyd George and Bonar Law knew nothing of what had occurred during the night. Churchill's letter had not yet arrived. On the previous day they had asked Haig if they could see Churchill, and Haig had agreed. A telegram had been despatched from St Omer asking Churchill if he would meet the Minister of Munitions and the Colonial Secretary at Hazebrouck at ten o'clock that Monday morning. Churchill had for some days been looking forward to meeting Lloyd George; F. E. Smith's arrest added urgency to his journey. Hakewill Smith recalled how, at breakfast:

Winston came in very silent and very angry. There was no sign of FE. Winston demanded a car without delay. I had difficulty in getting one from Divisional HQ. 'Lt Col Winston Churchill is in no mood to be trifled with,' I said. 'It must come in twenty minutes.'

It was a bitterly cold day: about five degrees of frost. To our horror an *open* Vauxhall turned up. Winston was in no mood for badinage. 'Drive as hard as hell to Hazebrouck,' he ordered the driver.

Churchill reached Hazebrouck just before midday. Lloyd George and Bonar Law were waiting for him at Lieutenant-Colonel Newton's[2] extemporized grenade factory, unaware of F. E. Smith's arrest the night before. Churchill told them all he knew. The arrest seemed evidence that GHQ was more prepared to exert itself in order to humiliate a politician than to defeat the Germans.

Lloyd George and Bonar Law, incensed at the treatment which had been meted out to their Cabinet colleague, left the grenade factory and

[1] Cecil Frederick Nevil Macready, 1862–1946. Entered Army, 1881. Major-General, 1910. Knighted, 1912. General Officer Commanding, Belfast, 1914. Adjutant-General, British Expeditionary Force, 1914–16. Member of the Army Council, 1916. Lieutenant-General, 1916. Adjutant-General to the Forces, 1916–18. General, 1918. Commissioner of the Metropolitan Police, 1918–20. Commanded the Forces in Ireland, 1920–2. Created Baronet, 1923.

[2] Henry Newton, 1880–1959. Entered Territorial Force, 1902. Lieutenant-Colonel commanding 2nd Army Royal Engineer Workshops, 1915–17. Deputy Controller, Trench Warfare Department, Ministry of Munitions, 1917. Chief of Design, Mechanical Traction Department, Ministry of Munitions, 1917–19. Among his inventions were the wire-cutting Fuses Nos. 107 and 110; the Newton 6-inch Trench Mortar; the Newton Trench Mortar Bomb; the Newton Pippin rifle and hand grenades; the Newton Universal Military Tractor. Many of these inventions were manufactured at his factory in Hazebrouck.

drove back at speed to St Omer, where they found F. E. Smith at Max Aitken's headquarters. Hakewill Smith was present at the meeting, and later recalled how 'FE was there pacing up and down like a caged lion, in a stinking temper'. Churchill calmed him, and persuaded him to tell them the full story, which he did. 'On hearing this,' Hakewill Smith recalled, 'Winston sat down in a chair and roared with laughter. FE, Bonar Law and Lloyd George then went to lunch with Haig at HQ. They had great difficulty in persuading FE to go as he regarded Haig as the source of his discomfort.' 'He came and sat on my left,' Haig wrote in his diary later that day. 'He did himself very well in the way of liquor and ended up with several glasses of old brandy! After lunch . . . he started a long story which I listened to patiently for three or four minutes, and then asked him what he really wanted. He apologised for having bothered me, and they all agreed it was best to leave the matter as it stood.' Churchill was stirred to make a bitter reflection, writing to his wife on February 1: 'Some of these potentates get more upset about an "incident" of this kind than about sending 1000 men to their deaths.'

In the early afternoon of January 31, Lloyd George, Bonar Law, and F. E. Smith returned to Max Aitken's headquarters, where Churchill awaited them. So many politicians, all of them critics or opponents of Asquith, could not avoid a lengthy political discussion. None of the participants wrote about it afterwards, but Hakewill Smith later recalled that there had been 'full and complete agreement that Asquith had to be got rid of at all costs'. Three of those present were members of Asquith's Cabinet. Lloyd George had hinted that his aim was to become Secretary of State for War. 'I hope he will get it,' Churchill wrote to his wife on February 1, giving as his opinion that the War Office needed 'a civilian's drive & the leadership of a gifted man.' Churchill felt that the politicians who had met accidentally at St Omer were an obvious nucleus of a future government; one in which he believed he would almost certainly find a place. 'The group I want to work with & form into an effective Government instrument,' he wrote to his wife, 'is LG: FE: BL: Carson: & Curzon. Keep that steadily in mind. It is the alternative Government when "wait & see" is over.'

While they were at St Omer, Lloyd George and Bonar Law did Churchill a service which contrasted with Asquith's earlier action. When they saw Haig they told him, as Churchill reported to his wife, 'that if he saw fit to give me a Brigade there wd be no difficulty at home'. This friendly gesture reinforced Churchill's belief that he could rely on Lloyd George and work with him. He still felt that he could do nothing until Asquith were overthrown; but he now saw the makings of a coalition which might lead to just such an end. Politics remained uppermost in his mind. 'My dislike of Asquith & all his works grows steadily,' he wrote to his wife on February 2; 'He is a fatal drag on our success.' That same day Clementine Churchill lunched with Lloyd George, hoping, she wrote, 'to glean from him news of you'. But she learned little, as there were others present. Her dislike of Lloyd George was unabated. 'I don't trust him one bit,' she wrote; 'fair of speech, shifty of eye, treacherous of heart. . . . You may *have* to work with him but never trust him—If he does not do you in he will at any rate "let you down".'

Lloyd George was to open one of Clementine Churchill's YMCA canteens on the following day, at Ponders End. After lunching with him she sent him some notes about the canteens, to help him with his speech. 'I wanted to ask you so much more about Winston,' she wrote in her postscript, 'but I felt shy before company!' Lloyd George spoke to two thousand munitions workers, 'packed like sardines on the workshop floor', Clementine Churchill reported to her husband on February 4. 'They did not cheer when they saw LlG,' she wrote, 'but (don't say I said so) they gave me a beautiful cheer.' Clementine Churchill complained to her husband about Lloyd George's speech. 'The shabby little tike,' she wrote, 'altho' he said he had just returned from the Front never mentioned your name.' Lloyd George had told her privately that Curzon was anxious to become Air Minister, adding: 'I am so surprised . . . I thought perhaps Winston might have done it—do you think he would have liked it?' To this Clementine Churchill had replied: 'Winston would do it better than anyone else.' But Lloyd George said nothing further on the subject. 'This ungenerous cautious streak in his nature,' Clementine Churchill wrote to her husband, 'will in his old age which is fast approaching leave him lonely & friendless— Ishmael! I do not think *you* will ever need him, *he* will need you when he is on the down gradient—& of course you will help him and he knows it.' Frances Stevenson had accompanied Lloyd George to Ponders End. In her diary she wrote of another visitor to the ceremony:

Much to everyone's surprise, Mrs Bonham Carter (Miss Asquith) turned up, though as far as we can make out she had not been invited. D [Lloyd George] is of the opinion that she turned up expecting to see a row. It appears that even Mrs Churchill was uneasy as to how the meeting would go off, as many of the workers are hostile to him at the present moment. . . . 'The

Asquiths and their friends are boasting,' said D to me, 'that Lloyd George cannot hold a meeting with the workers now.' However, she was unpleasantly surprised if she came with that object. One of the speakers referred to D as the man of the moment, & one of the audience shouted: 'Put him in Asquith's place!' . . .

However, Mrs A herself has been heard to declare that 'Nothing but God Almighty himself will drive Herbert out of Downing Street.'[1]

Lloyd George and Clementine Churchill drove back together from Ponders End to London. She sent her husband an account of the drive. Lloyd George had made a poor impression upon her. She contrasted his shabbiness and tiredness with their own strength and vitality. She knew that Lloyd George understood what was in her mind: that he would need her husband in the future, and that in any future scandal such as the Marconi affair, Churchill could be relied upon to help him. The drive with Lloyd George had made her more hopeful about her husband's future. 'I know (DV),' she wrote, 'that you will come back rejuvenated & strengthened from the War & dominate all these decrepit, exhausted politicians.' She ended her letter with a further word for Asquith, still believing that her husband's political future might depend as much upon Asquith's goodwill as upon Lloyd George and the anti-Government forces. 'Don't close your mind to the PM entirely,' she wrote. 'He is lazy but (or perhaps therefore) healthy & anyhow he is not a skunk tho' a wily old tortoise. I must meet him this week and tweak his ear.'

Among Asquith's most vociferous critics in London was Lord Fisher. Churchill knew that Fisher led a faction of discontent, and that he still hoped to return to the Admiralty, for the third time, as First Sea Lord. He believed that if Fisher's opposition were ever to reach serious proportions, Asquith would take effective action. 'I am rather anxious about old Fisher,' he wrote to his wife on February 2. 'I cannot trust the PM not to put him back. He & his press are vy active now. The general apathy at the Admiralty naturally excites dissatisfaction. Fisher without me to manage him wd be disastrous.' Churchill still believed that Fisher could not be trusted to act alone; but in January 1916 the chances of the two men working together again were remote.

[1] A view satirized by Max Beerbohm during 1916:

Filled through and through with British phlegm
(than which no phlegm is phlegmier)
He seems quite likely to be sem-
piternally our Premier

Writing to Hankey on January 7, Fisher insisted upon a change of Government as the prerequisite for his return:

I had an illuminating visit here yesterday from George Lambert MP late Civil Lord corroborating two visits from Lord Northcliffe (—the two as you know being as opposite as the poles are asunder!) in anticipating a big uprising of feeling in the country involving big chances in our conduct of the war. . . .

For myself I tell them and many others in reply to multitudes of letters that it appears to me that Asquith & Balfour are such astute Parliamentarians that no one will turn them out & they are irremovable! That's my belief— *and so long as they are in I shall be out!* . . .

There is certainly apathy in the Admiralty and our shipyards are empty and the Germans will give us shortly a Big Naval Surprise I think!

On January 26 Fisher wrote to Hankey again to complain about 'the very sad "INERTIA" ' which he saw all about him. 'I am getting very sick of it,' Fisher wrote, 'and am contemplating some action.' In his postscript he added: 'The Prime Minister saw me in the Lobby of the House of Commons 3 days ago. . . . He asked about the Naval Situation! I said what was required was *"Push and Go"*! (NOT *"Wait and See"*!). On that he left me! What a lot of old women of both sexes are leading us to ruin!' On the following day Fisher wrote yet again:

Please burn.

. . . It is no use my talking to the Prime Minister—as he would only pass me on to Balfour who would involve me in subtle dialectics and in philosophic doubts! . . . I know perfectly well I could entirely change the face of the Naval situation! YES. COMPLETELY ENTHUSE IT! *instead of the present despair!* King Herod was smitten with worms for bragging so I'm not going to be such an ass! but I have not yet been wrong in any one little detail since June 10 1902 when I became Second Sea Lord!

Fisher enlisted two newspaper editors in his quest for action, J. L. Garvin of the *Observer* and C. P. Scott of the *Manchester Guardian*. Throughout January and February the Admiral cast about for some means to return to the centre of naval and national affairs. 'We want another plan,' he wrote to Lloyd George at the beginning of January; 'none exists! I am not sure even of our coming sea supremacy!' On January 14 he reported to the former Civil Lord of Admiralty, George Lambert, that Geoffrey Robinson, the editor of *The Times*, 'asked to see me urgently yesterday, and he remained two hours', while Bonar Law also was 'very anxious' to see him. But Fisher knew, as he told Lambert, that as long as Asquith and Balfour—'Wait and See' and the 'philosophic doubter'—were still in office, 'I am out of it!' This did not deflate his energies. Early in February he wrote to Bonar Law: 'I propose at an early date to take a drastic step to make the country acquainted with my views. I think I have a case that will necessitate a change.' To C. P. Scott he wrote bitterly on February 2 of Bonar Law's lethargy, at the same time announcing that '*A BIG SMASH IS IMMINENT! A FATAL SMASH.*' Fisher was desperate to return to the centre of war-making policy. Inaction was anathema to him. He felt, he informed Lambert, like Elijah, 'discarded, cast out'. On February 3 he wrote direct to Asquith warning that 'there is grave anxiety and serious misgiving in the Fleet both as to the conduct of the war at sea as well as in the provision for the same'. On February 8 he informed Jellicoe that 'yesterday Hankey came to see me, as he thinks the state of lethargy at the Admiralty is serious'. He also told Jellicoe that he intended to announce 'shortly' in the House of Lords that Balfour's naval administration was 'fraught with vital danger'. In a second letter to Jellicoe on February 8 he used the words: 'If I should become First Lord, which don't seem likely to me (though others think so). . . .'

Fisher believed that it was only Churchill, from whom he had parted so precipitately and with such disastrous results for both of them, who knew his true worth. Churchill's willingness to resign in October 1914 if Fisher were not brought back to the Admiralty had made a deep impression on him. On February 14 he wrote to Lambert that it was the King alone who had stood in his path at that time, and that 'the whole crew, Lloyd George, Bonar Law, Jellicoe, Carson—whatever good intentions—have not the courage of Winston, who said "you be d——d"!'

It was assumed by all that after the disaster of May 1915 neither Churchill nor Fisher would wish to see the other again. Only Clementine Churchill realized that the bond between Fisher and her husband was intimate and indestructible. She dreaded a reunion, knowing how much her husband was excited by Fisher's very presence, and fearing that the old Admiral would poison his judgement, and tempt him to unwise actions. At the beginning of February Churchill had no reason to believe that his path and Fisher's might cross again. He still professed scorn, verging on contempt, for what Fisher had done to him the previous May. He could see no immediate political future for himself, no grouping yet ready to challenge Asquith's control, no sphere in which he might make his mark. 'I wish I could do more,' he wrote to his wife on February 4, 'but after all, I have kept nothing back.' He was at Laurence Farm, drawing up schemes for the defence of his Battalion's front. The needs of his seven hundred men were for the time being uppermost in his mind.

On February 5 Churchill's sister-in-law Nellie Romilly wrote to him of an American schoolboy howler that she had read in the *Daily Mail* on the previous day: ' "Who is Prime Minister of England?" Unanimous reply: "Winston Churchill." ' On February 8 a cutting from a German newspaper, rejoicing that Churchill was no longer in office, reached him at Laurence Farm. These pieces of news set him thinking again about his resignation from the Cabinet in November, and about Fisher. 'While I never doubt the wisdom of my decision to quit office,' he wrote to his wife on February 8, 'I writhe daily at the lack of power to make things move. And so I am sure does the old Malay. The time may come when I shall feel it my duty to go home & make an effective opposition. But not yet.' The letters he received continued to stir him. 'I think that the Admiralty has lost all initiative and push since your departure,' the Duke of Marlborough wrote on February 7, 'and a complete static selfish atmosphere seems to prevail in that Department. An atmosphere congenial to AJB's temperament. It is a pity you are not there to give the officials some inspiration.'

Churchill speculated about his political future. It was not very hopeful. The bulk of the Tory Party remained hostile to him; nor was there any evidence that his brief encounter with Bonar Law at Hazebrouck and St Omer had resulted in a change in the Conservative Leader's unsympathetic attitude towards him. The Liberal backbenchers continued to doubt his reliability; many of them had by February 1916 been convinced, some by Reginald McKenna, some by the backbencher W. M. R. Pringle, that Churchill had intrigued with Sir John French to publicize the 'shell scandal' of May 1915. There remained nevertheless a small group of public men who thought highly of Churchill's abilities, and wanted them used in Government.

On February 6, J. L. Garvin appealed in the *Observer* for a rearrangement of the Government and a more effective war-making Cabinet, giving as his prescription for success that Churchill should become Air Minister and Fisher return to the Admiralty as First Lord. Garvin believed that Churchill and Fisher could work together once more. He felt that these two in tandem ought to be in the Cabinet. He hoped that his suggestion would be widely enough supported to lead to Balfour's removal from the Admiralty. Both Churchill and his wife were taken quite by surprise by Garvin's article. Clementine Churchill was worried because Fisher's name had been linked with her husband's in Garvin's appeal. For her, this was a disaster, not an opportunity; a threat that her husband's return to politics might take place only in some unsuitable and cabalistic combination rather than on its own merits, and with the minimum of controversy. 'I cannot gauge the Fisher danger,' she wrote on February 8; 'He is certainly very active and has a good press, but neither Asquith nor Balfour can possibly want him back—I expect however that some fancy post will be found for him to satisfy the ignorant and famishing public.'

It was not until February 10 that Churchill was able to read the text of Garvin's appeal in the *Observer*. It did not convince him. 'I do not think they will want me for Air,' he wrote to his wife that day. 'The view I take of my duty, renders me powerless at present, as a critic of the government, & consequently Asquith can afford to let me alone. He knows this & will act quite naturally upon it. Garvin's article was vy friendly & I am touched by his loyalty: but it will not count in the decision.'

Parliament was shortly to reassemble, and in the Debate on the Address it was open to any critic of the Government to challenge Asquith's conduct of the war. Had Churchill wished to take this opportunity, there were undoubtedly those who would have been willing to help him gather the necessary material, naval, military, and diplomatic. He believed that with preparation he could rise in the House of Commons, the soldier returned from the trenches, the 'escaped scapegoat' come to demand retribution, the patriot seeking to save his country from ignominious defeat, and that by his speech he could bring together all the disparate elements of dissatisfaction. 'I have meditated profoundly on whether I shd come home,' he wrote to his wife on February 11; '. . . I have decided against it—tho' sorely tempted. The time has not yet come—nor the occasion.'

From the beginning of the year a number of very different, and previously hostile and competing groups, had united in the hope of gaining political advantage from the public dissatisfaction with the conduct of the war. Many of the leading newspaper proprietors were critical of Asquith's leadership. Lord Northcliffe believed that the war would last for at least another five years if Asquith remained at the helm. Three leading editors, C. P. Scott, J. L. Garvin and Robert Donald, were tired of trying to criticize the Government while at the same time having no formal opposition behind which they could throw their support. Lloyd George sensed and reflected the discontent. On January 5 Sir George Riddell, who had spent the day with him, recorded in his *War Diary* Lloyd George's remarks: 'Opposition is in the blood of the people. They must conduct their affairs on those lines. At present they want a leader to voice their views.' Who that leader was to be, no one knew. In January it had seemed that Sir Edward Carson might come forward as an opposition figure capable of offering an alternative to Asquith. But the public did not respond readily to Carson, whose support never spread much beyond the Conservative backbenchers in the House of Commons. Nor had Carson shown evidence of executive ability, upon which so much of a successful war administration must depend.

When Lloyd George lunched with Riddell on February 11 he declared that Fisher ought to be brought back into the Government, though he could not see in what capacity. Lloyd George told Riddell: 'Fisher has a genius for war.'

On February 16, in a debate in the House of Commons on air-raid defence, the Government was severely criticized for not taking adequate measures to protect the civilian population against the increasingly frequent German Zeppelin attacks. Lloyd George told Riddell at breakfast the next morning that had a division been taken, the Government would probably have been defeated. He went on to say that he believed that Churchill should have been made head of an air-raid defence department, but that Asquith would not have it.

Stimulated by Garvin's open support, Fisher and his friends continued to search for some means of influencing Government policy. 'We are at the very blackest period of the war,' Fisher wrote to Garvin on February 19. On the same day he informed C. P. Scott that Northcliffe had been to see him a few weeks before, 'and told me it was essential and vital I should be back, and he intended to have me back!' On February 22 Lambert told the House of Commons that it was 'almost a disaster at the Admiralty' to continue without Fisher as First Sea Lord. To Hankey, on March 2 Fisher wrote: 'No amount of Cabinet or War Council instructions are of the slightest use if those who have to carry them out are totally wanting in "push" and initiative. There must be ginger at the top if you want ginger at the bottom!'

Fisher's supporters could not overcome the fact that the Admiral alone did not constitute a political force. The public may still have believed that only Fisher could restore the Navy to its earlier pitch of readiness and resolve. But in the political arena, in Whitehall and in the Houses of Parliament, Fisher had little strength. A politician was needed to bring together the widely scattered forces of discontent. Yet there was no politician willing to take the lead. Asquith's skill in creating his coalition of May 1915 had neutralized the Conservative opposition without alienating any but the fringe of his Liberal majority. When Riddell had tea with Lloyd George on February 26 he learned of Lloyd George's continuing unease at the conduct of the war. 'He says the PM never moves until he is forced, and then it is usually too late,' Riddell recorded in his *War Diary*. 'He fears we shall not improve matters until we get another leader. He says that at a time like this the PM should lead, not follow. . . . He says Asquith will not face unpleasant facts.' Lloyd George spoke of the possibility of resigning, but told Riddell that because of war secrecy he would be unable to give his specific reasons for doing so.

Churchill knew nothing of Fisher's activities and little of Lloyd George's discontent. On February 13, on reading an attack on Fisher in the *Morning Post*, he wrote to his wife: 'I expect the old rogue will realise increasingly as time passes the folly of his action. Together we cd have ridden out every gale, & sure of our strength, we cd have afforded to run those risks wh alone open the gate to victory.' It was two weeks since the St Omer meeting, two weeks of heavy and continual problems in his Battalion's sector: 'I never expected to be so completely involved in the military machine,' he wrote. The news that Curzon might be made Air Minister prompted him to write to his wife on February 14: 'Well I do not care. I cd have done it well. But I am under the vague displeasure of the press: & Asquith's interests as I told you will best be served by my disappearance temporary or final. But I must confess it riles me to see how ungrateful they are. But for my personal struggles we shd not have had *half* the air service we have today.'

The time had come for Churchill to make arrangements for leave, which he expected to take when his Battalion left the trenches on March 2. He would then have seven days, which, he wrote to his wife on February 15, 'is the only leave I shall get for another 3 months'. He felt that it was therefore important for him 'to see various people: and I shall take decisions about my future plans. . . . I shall review the situation & consider what I ought to do.' On February 16 he received an account of the first trial of the 'tank' from the Director of Naval Construction, Eustace Tennyson-d'Eyncourt. 'You see this idea is bearing fruit,' he wrote to his wife. '. . . But what a toil to get anything done! And how powerless I am! Are they not fools not to use my mind—or knaves to wait for its destruction by some flying splinter? I do not fear death or wounds, & I like the daily life out here; but their impudence & complaisance makes me quite spiteful sometimes.'

During the week before his leave Churchill received a long political letter from his cousin Lord Wimborne, written on February 15. It held out no encouragement to him personally. 'I think this Govt are active and determined,' wrote Wimborne; 'not very prescient perhaps, but dogged and tenacious and are getting bolder too.' Wimborne saw no further opening for Churchill in politics while the war was on. His letter continued: 'But the war must end some day and then the fun will begin. . . . Then will be the moment for a real broad national policy and for the *man* to advocate it.' Churchill did not want to contemplate so distant a future. His one desire was to be asked to take his part again at the centre of war policy. In a letter written on February 14, describing the first testing of the tank, Tennyson d'Eyncourt had explained to Churchill: 'After losing the great advantage of your influence, I had considerable difficulty in steering the scheme past the rocks of opposition & the more insidious shoals of apathy, wh are frequented by red herrings wh cross the main line of progress at frequent intervals'. Churchill felt stirred by this to write direct to Asquith, for the first time in three months, urging him to give the fullest encouragement to d'Eyncourt's activities. 'It interested me very much,' Asquith replied, not to Churchill but to Churchill's wife, on February 19. 'I have heard a great deal about the Caterpillar from those who have seen it on trial, and we hope great things from it.' There was no encouragement here for someone seeking office and responsibility.

Towards the end of February Churchill became increasingly angry at the repeated criticisms in the *Morning Post*, and other Conservative newspapers, which claimed that it was his neglect while First Lord of the Admiralty that was responsible for the lack of air defence against the Zeppelin. This press criticism revived his idea of making some political speech when he came home on leave, in order to defend himself against these allegations. 'The newspapers not knowing the facts,' he wrote to his wife on February 18, 'continue to carp mechanically about the air & my responsibility. On my return I may perhaps deal fully with the whole subject. I intend to take my seat on the Front Opposition Bench—but shall not decide on any action yet.'

Churchill was disappointed to hear from his wife that on her latest visit to the Prime Minister at Walmer Castle there had been no political talk; Asquith clearly had no intention to ask him back into the Government. Clementine Churchill echoed Lord Wimborne's sentiments when she wrote on February 16, 'I am sure you will return to power after the war with increased prestige.' But Churchill did not wish to wait until the war was over. He was frequently distraught by the fear that the war might actually be lost, and by his profound belief that if the situation worsened, his presence could turn the balance from defeat to victory.

Rather than stimulating his political thoughts, the approach of leave seemed to make Churchill more detached and wistful. Reading a rumour that Balfour was about to abolish the Royal Naval Division, he wrote to his wife on February 22, more in sorrow than in anger, of the activities of his successor as First Lord, 'the old grey tabby', as he called him: 'How easy to destroy. How hard to build. How easy to evacuate, how hard to capture. How easy to do nothing. How hard to achieve anything. War is action, energy & hazard. These sheep only want to browse among the daisies.'

On February 19 Clementine Churchill wrote that if he would send her a list of people, 'I will make some little dinner parties in your honour.' His reply on February 22 was more concerned with his painting and his private life than with politics:

You must parcel out the days as well as possible. I will have one dinner at my mother's, at least 3 at home, 2 plays alone with you & one man's dinner out somewhere. Make up a programme on these lines. Also lunches & try to work in all my friends. You can let people know that I am coming home for a week. I leave it all to you. One night I expect to go to the National Liberal Club for the unveiling of my portrait & here I may make a speech. . . .

I will be vy good & keep all my engagements punctually. Time is so short. . . . I put it all in your hands my dearest soul. Arrange whatever you like to amuse us both the most. I much prefer people coming to dine with me than dining out with them. I want to have at least one day's painting in Lavery's studio. Do you know I think that will be a gt pleasure & resource to me if I come through all right.

Before returning to England Churchill received two letters sent from London on February 25. The first, from his wife, contained an account of the dinner arrangements which she had made to entertain the Prime Minister and his wife that evening at 41 Cromwell Road: 'I have had to work like a beaver to get together the 8 indispensable bridge players which are necessary for their comfort and happiness.' It was to be an entirely social occasion, with Lady Gwendeline Churchill, Lord Wimborne and Sir Ernest Cassel among the guests. The second letter from London was from F. E. Smith. Like Wimborne's letter earlier in the month it did not offer Churchill much political hope. 'The Government,' wrote F. E. Smith, 'is not popular but indispensable & I think that the PM is firmer in the saddle than ever. LG is still very much alone.' F. E. Smith, who did not know that Churchill's leave was almost due, encouraged him to return. 'Do come soon,' he wrote. 'I am sure it is a good thing to turn up at the proper intervals & see people.'

Churchill crossed over to England on the evening of March 2. It was not until he reached London that he discovered that Balfour was to introduce the Naval Estimates in the House of Commons on March 7. Suddenly his path seemed clear to him. He would speak in the debate; he would castigate the naval policy of his successor, defend his own record over aerial defence, and outline an effective policy against the Zeppelin. He would show that it was he, not Balfour, who had a true grasp of what was needed in order to avoid disaster at sea and in the air. Throughout Friday March 3 he worked at his speech. His plans for leisure were put aside. He gave up the idea of unveiling his portrait at the National Liberal Club.[1] That night he dined with his mother, who had invited those whom she thought might help him in his attack on the Government. C. P. Scott had been summoned from Manchester by telegram. Garvin and F. E. Smith were also there. Another guest was Sir Francis Hopwood, who had retained his position as Additional Civil Lord of Admiralty on Balfour's Board. Three months later Hopwood gave his recollection of the dinner to Prince Louis, who noted:

That Friday evening Lady Randolph gave a dinner, which included Hopwood, Garvin and several other public men. To these Churchill delivered his speech, which began by recommending the evacuation of Salonika, suggesting other uses for these troops etc. This part of the speech he afterwards dropped on the advice of friends present. Not one word was said about Fisher in this rehearsal, but to Hopwood, who was the last to leave, C suddenly said that he would teach that d——d old Oriental scoundrel F what it meant to quarrel with him.

[1] The portrait had been painted in the autumn of 1915 by Ernest Townsend, paid for by an anonymous donor. It was ready for presentation on 20 December 1915, and was hung temporarily in a Club Committee Room until such time as Churchill could unveil it. No opportunity was found for the ceremony. In 1921, when Churchill was no longer *persona grata* with the National Liberal Club, the Club decided that his portrait should be 'packed and stored in some dry place'. During the Second World War it was taken out of storage and rehung; almost immediately it was damaged by bomb blast. After being restored, it was finally unveiled by Churchill himself in 1941.

In *Winston Churchill As I Knew Him* Violet Bonham Carter recalled that she had heard later that Lady Randolph's guests were said to have told Churchill that he was 'the *homme nécessaire* who alone could save a rapidly deteriorating situation' and that they had urged him 'to take action and lead an Opposition in Parliament'. Churchill had intended no such opposition. He wished to make use of the coincidence of his return to warn the House of Commons that all was not well in the naval war, and to defend his own past actions. But for some of those present at Lady Randolph's dinner, Churchill's decision to speak out against the Government seemed an opportunity of a more decisive sort. Garvin and Scott were the partisans of Lord Fisher. They were the men who had for two months urged Fisher's return to the Admiralty, believing that he still possessed energies and insights for which there was no substitute. Churchill's willingness to speak out seemed to them to provide the opportunity for Fisher to emerge again. But Fisher and Churchill had first to be brought together. Churchill's assertion to Hopwood that he would destroy Fisher once and for all was his last hostile outburst. Fisher's friends arranged a meeting between them. To Clementine Churchill's horror, Fisher was invited to lunch at 41 Cromwell Road. F. E. Smith was also present. There is evidence in F. E. Smith's letter of February 25 to Churchill that at the time of his arrest in January the two men had discussed this very possibility of an accommodation with Fisher, and that F. E. Smith himself had acted as an instrument of reconciliation, through his friend Sir Edward Goulding. 'It has not at present been found possible to do anything for our friend,' F. E. Smith had written, 'nor did Garvin, as usual impetuous, help much by premature publicity. . . . I conveyed your wishes I think with discretion about Fisher to Paddy [Goulding] & he tells me all has been made very plain without committing you.'

F. E. Smith told Margot Asquith about the luncheon, and she told Violet Bonham Carter, who wrote in her book: 'I knew what agony this must have been to Clemmie, who had no illusions about Fisher or the ruin he had brought to Winston's fortunes. According to FE she had said to Fisher at luncheon, "Keep your hands off my husband. You have all but ruined him once. Leave him alone now." ' On the evening of March 5 Fisher and Churchill met again. Churchill read Fisher the speech which he proposed to make during the Naval Estimates debate. Not only did he intend to attack Balfour's conduct of naval affairs; he had also decided that he would end his speech with an appeal for Fisher's immediate return as First Sea Lord. By this appeal Churchill was determined to show Parliament that he was not a man to harbour rancour or malice; that he could overcome his hostility towards his former opponent in the national interest, and for the sake of the war. Fisher was exhilarated by this extraordinary change in their relationship; for him it was a return to the friendship and excitement of earlier times. Churchill was going to bring him back once more. In the early hours of the following morning he wrote feverishly:

4 a.m.!! The Early Bird!
YOU are the *late one*!!
My dear Winston,
I've slept over what you said to me last night—It's THE epoch of your Life!——
I am going to be the humble instrument! So magnificent, a proof OF YOUR SOLE OBJECT BEING THE WAR will have (*justly*) an *immense* effect on your popularity. Ride in on the crest of that Popularity! THE WAR—THE WHOLE WAR—AND NOTHING BUT THE WAR! Do you imagine that if you got up and said '*What are over* half a million of *our* men doing *now* in an unattackable Egypt and in a Salonika where we are being fooled by a few Austrians—*when these half a million men in France are of vital consequence?* Do you imagine you would not topple over the whole present gang? and also ask what a big British Fleet is NOW doing in the Mediterranean? *when the grand Fleet is in danger!!!*' . . .
The Reason the Government are strong is THERE IS NO OPPOSITION LEADER! *Get up every night and batter the box from the Opposition Bench!* No use your sending up one Rocket and then going to have your head '*bashed in*' at the Trenches! Go the whole Hog! *Totus Porcus! Salvation—Here* and *Now!* I repeat what I have said behind your back. *There is no one in it with you to conduct the War—and you can be Prime Minister if you like!*
'*THE NAVY IN DANGER*' *IS THE CRY!* TAKE YOUR OATH, if I ONCE GET IN THERE *WILL BE HELL TILL YOU GET IN!*
I say this from *PURE* belief the present mob are absolutely effete! *Audacity* and *Imagination* are the requirements of successful war—*THEY DON'T NOW EXIST!* It's *NOT* '*Wait and See*' we want but '*Push and Go!* Not '*Asquith and Balfour*', but *Winston and*——'.
May I criticise?

> ('In angels faults conspicuous grow
> The smallest speck is seen in snow')

I think it's too long—your air portion of your speech—it's too much of an apology *and not enough of an Attack!* Say this:——
In the 9 months since you left why have not aeroplanes and seaplanes carried in small craft and submarines been pushed forward? The Aeroplane is the *ONLY* antidote to the zeppelin. Emphasise the zeppelin menace to

the Grand Fleet. The new Zep. has a radius of 600 miles! So why why why has not the aeroplane been developed?

I don't think you say enough of the frightful menace to the Grand Fleet of the new Big German submarines—you can be vague and misty about it but you want to be more mysteriously alarmed!

'Omne ignotum pro magnifico'!

Finally this is absolute fact!

To *win the War and with no other heartfeeling do we two coalesce! We can do it! Come on!*

Yours as heretofore
Fisher

I am at Berkeley Square the *WHOLE*
day if you want me. I am not   My telephone number
going to leave the house.   is Gerrard 8795

Churchill had one more day to reflect upon the course which he had decided to take. Among those who encouraged him to speak in the naval debate were three Liberal MPs who despaired of Asquith's leadership; Sir Henry Dalziel,[1] Sir Arthur Markham,[2] and Sir Alfred Mond:[3] all were friends of Lloyd George.

That afternoon Fisher asked C. P. Scott to strengthen Churchill's resolve to make his speech, and to lead the opposition to Balfour. Fisher warned Scott, as the latter noted, that Clementine Churchill differed from her husband and 'insisted' that he should return to France. Scott went to 41 Cromwell Road, where for more than an hour he tried to persuade Churchill that his place was at Westminster. Scott recorded:

I urged that on political grounds there could be no question that he would be more useful in Parliament—that as regards the navy there was not a day to be lost in making the great and acknowledged deficiencies and the whole movement for that and also for vitalising the army, as to which he had strong views, would collapse if he left. He and Lloyd George and Carson were the only three men in the front rank with the instinct for action and capacity for carrying on a great war. Carson was ill, George was for the time being under

[1] James Henry Dalziel, 1868–1935. Radical journalist. Liberal MP, 1892–1921. Chairman and Managing Director of United Newspapers Ltd; owner of *Reynolds Weekly Newspaper* and the *Pall Mall Gazette*. Knighted, 1908. Chairman of the Committee in charge of German prisoners, 1914–18. Helped Lloyd George to buy the *Daily Chronicle*, 1918. Created Baron Dalziel of Kirkcaldy, 1921.

[2] Arthur Basil Markham, 1866–1916. Liberal MP, 1900–16. Created Baronet, 1911. He died on 7 August 1916.

[3] Alfred Moritz Mond, 1868–1930. Industrialist and financier. Liberal MP, 1910–26. Created Baronet, 1910. First Commissioner of Works, December 1916–21. Joined the Conservative Party, 1926. Created Baron Melchett, 1928.

a cloud and Churchill alone remained. Mrs Churchill was evidently uneasy but acquiesced and Churchill virtually decided to resign his commission.

He then read me the full notes for his speech which wound up dramatically with the demand for the recall of Lord Fisher. He was satisfied with it himself and said if it were the last he was ever to deliver he would be content to stand by it and that was the final test. I found nothing to object to, but Mrs Churchill thought it went at one part rather too much into details which had better not be made public. Churchill said he thought he had better give the Prime Minister notice of what he meant to do (and he would no doubt inform Balfour) so that it might not be said he had taken the Government by surprise. He had asked to see the Prime Minister that afternoon, but had not yet had an answer. In any case Asquith was coming to dinner and he could tell him then that he meant to ask for Fisher's recall, but was not anxious to say more and so bring down protests.

He was not aiming at anything for himself but only at getting what was necessary done. Six months abroad had 'cleaned' him. He had come in contact with the crude realities of life and escape from the atmosphere of scheming and intrigue. Had learned to see things more simply. He had missed the means of self-expression, but on the whole the time of absence had been one of the most contented of his life. He seemed to be indeed stronger and saner than before he went out.

Fisher sent one further exhortation on March 6:

Dear Winston,
    If you dont follow my advice *then* your Future is *RUINED*!
DON'T GO BACK! *Stick to* THE BOX OF THE LEADER OF THE OPPOSITION—your last words are splendid!!
    '*I feel events are so grave in the Navy that my duty is* HERE *with HEALTHY not* HOSTILE *criticism*'!
IT IS NOT TOO LATE!! THEREFORE I SPEAK! ! Otherwise I would have held my tongue. Let me as First Sea Lord be a subsidiary matter—the one to see NOT ONLY the old programme completed but to take fresh gigantic steps for fresh gigantic doings with Big Conceptions that will end the War! *You Winston Churchill yourself ask for nothing! Simply you are there to help!* and feel more use at the opposition leaders box than the unwilling partner of an effete conduct of the war!!!
                                                                    Yours
STICK TO THIS!   F
Don't let Asquith know.

    That night Asquith and his wife dined with the Churchills at 41 Cromwell Road. Churchill made no secret of his intentions to speak in the debate. He said nothing about his detailed criticisms, but did say

that he intended to demand Fisher's return. Asquith's daughter Violet
Bonham Carter wrote in *Winston Churchill As I Knew Him*:

When they returned from this dinner-party Margot, who had sat next to
him, told me that she had said to him that she was sorry he was going to
speak in the debate and that he had replied 'with a glare in his eye': that he
had 'a good deal of importance to say about the Navy'. She said that she
then told him what a 'fine exit' he had made, giving up money and position,
taking his place with his fellows and risking his life for his country, and added,
'Don't go and spoil it all.' Later he asked her whether she thought a proper
Opposition in the House of Commons would be a good, or a bad, thing for
the country. She said she could not see the elements of a good Opposition in
Dalziel, Markham, Mond, Carson, etc, and added that she could not
see him co-operating with the Simon group.[1] . . . She was convinced that
Winston was 'dreaming of an amazing Opposition which he was to lead'.

My father told me that he had had a short private talk with Winston after
dinner and feared that he was going to make a most unwise speech which
could do him nothing but harm. He had done his best to dissuade him from
it but evidently felt that he had failed. I said that I was surprised at not
having had a word or a sign from him since he got back. My father replied,
'That doesn't surprise me in the least in view of his intentions.'

After breakfast on the morning of March 7 C. P. Scott called on
Churchill, recording in his note of the conversation: 'He evidently felt
he was in for a serious enterprise, said he knew he should have to face
obloquy, but once launched on an enterprise he could never hold back.'
Churchill told Scott that making this speech 'needed more courage
than the war of the trenches'. He went on to say that he had not yet
finally decided 'whether to stay or return to France. It would partly
depend on how things went today. He wished he could be here a week
hence for the Army Estimates. He had a good deal to say on the Army
administration which was in many ways old-fashioned and unenter-
prising. Our Army telephones for instance—a vital matter—were mere
toys compared to the Germans.' Fisher lost no opportunity during the
last hours to excite Churchill's mind and seek to push him forward,
having convinced himself that even the Premiership was within
Churchill's grasp. On the morning of March 7, while Churchill was
putting the finishing touches to his speech, Fisher wrote once more:

My Dear Winston—
    Please forgive my d—d reiteration but I am terribly afraid of the
Asquithian cajolery! (*am I already too late?*)

---

[1] A small group of Liberal MPs who, after Sir John Simon's resignation in January 1915,
had united to oppose conscription. In May 1915 they voted against the Military Service Bill.

Providence has placed the Plum bang in your mouth, *Certain Prime Minister!*
You have no Rival as Leader of the Opposition and Such a Cry for assuming the position! ! ! ! so PATRIOTIC! ! ! !

'The Navy in Danger'
'But not "TOO LATE" for Safety'

Ask George Lambert to tell you the inner history of the late East End Election when BOTH the Election Machines working furiously only just avoided defeat 300 Votes! 151 men in that huge constituency could have beaten the Coalition Government![1] *There is seething and wide-spread discontent at the conduct of the War!*
But the People see no one as a new Leader!
There is the Cave of Adullam but no David has come along!
See the 1st Book of Samuel Chap 22 Verse 2

'He became a Captain over them'
'And there with him about 400 Men'!

AINT THAT A GOOD MAJORITY FOR YOU?

SO DONT GO BACK!

Never leave that Box—once you have banged it as you will this afternoon —As meek as Moses you'll say your mission is to help!
YES! Help the War!
YES! 'BIG CONCEPTIONS! QUICK DECISIONS!'
That will be your War Cry!

'THINK IN OCEANS'!

SHOOT AT SIGHT!

That will be your action!

Go in and Win!
Dont Falter
'Aut Caesar Aut Nullus'
accept no post in this Government
They are doomed!
Fate has you in it's Grasp!
Dont wriggle out of it!
D-n Fisher!—You get
Prime Minister!
That will end the War!
Nought else will!
The Country wants a Man!
Every War always wants a Man!
Dont go back—accept nothing![2]

Yours

F

[1] On 25 January 1916, in a by-election at Mile End, the Coalition candidate, Warwick Brookes, was elected as a Unionist MP with 1,991 votes. Pemberton Billing, the only other candidate, received 1,615 votes.

[2] Fisher's letter to Churchill is reproduced in facsimile on pages 834–7.

In the retrospect of more than half a century this letter may seem to bear the mark of lunacy. But for Churchill, cut off from the inner workings of politics, rejected, as he believed, by his former colleagues, denied any place in a Government in which he believed he could play a decisive part, this appeal from the man with whom he had worked so closely and admired so deeply did not depend for its strength upon its logic. Only five days earlier Churchill had been isolated and alone amid what he had described to his wife as 'the strain & severity' of life in the trenches, amid the remoteness of the war zone, and the ever-present chance of death. Now he was told that he was on the verge of a great personal triumph which might lead him forward to power. All the vociferous forces of faction and discontent were pressing him to go forward. He failed to see that he was about to prove to every critic and to most friends that he lacked the mature judgement of statesmanship.

23

Humiliation

TWELVE years had passed since Churchill had last spoken in the House of Commons as the critic of a Government. Then, his had been the lance of youthful anger hurled, always with agility and sometimes with venom, against the Conservative Prime Minister, A. J. Balfour. It had seemed impudence for so young a Member of Parliament to attack the Leader of the ruling Party, from whose back benches he had only just migrated. The impudent young man had himself risen to be a member of the Cabinet, and an able administrator. Since 1906, whatever he had done, he had done as a member of the Government and from a position of increasing political power. When he rose to speak from the front opposition bench late in the afternoon of Tuesday 7 March 1916, it was with the accumulated experience of those twelve years behind him; but it was also with his credibility impaired by the controversies and disasters of the previous year. After twelve years, it was again A. J. Balfour whom he rose to attack.

At the outset of his speech Churchill warned: 'I shall have to strike a jarring note.' He explained that it would be 'a note not of reproach, nor of censure nor of panic, but a note in some respects of warning'. He had nothing but praise, he told the House of Commons, for the sailors at sea, or for their commanders who combined 'the utmost professional skill' with 'unflinching resolution'. His intention was to criticize the inadequacy of the ships, the guns, the ammunition and the supplies which these men had at their disposal. He spoke of the naval programmes for which he, Prince Louis and Lord Fisher had been responsible. 'How are they being executed?' he asked. 'Are they being executed at full blast—are they being executed punctually?' There was, he declared, a serious gap in the survey of the naval situation which Balfour had delivered in the House earlier that afternoon. 'I rather wish that the First Lord had found it possible,' he said, 'to give an assurance to the House that the

716

dates to which Lord Fisher and I were working would be substantially and with inconsiderable exceptions maintained throughout the great new field of new construction.' He expressed alarm that the goals established during the early months of the war, while he was First Lord, and the enormous armada of new ships which had been laid down when Fisher returned to the Admiralty in October 1914, had not been properly pursued. 'I am bound to say,' he warned the House, 'that since I returned to this country I have received from sources, on which I must to some extent rely, impressions of a less completely satisfactory and reassuring kind than would naturally be derived from the annual statement of the Minister responsible.' He contrasted the apparent slackening of effort at the Admiralty under Balfour with what he felt convinced must be the opposite policy in Germany:

We do not know what Germany has done. An impenetrable veil, as the right hon Gentleman knows, has fallen for eighteen months over the German dockyards, naval and commercial. The right hon Gentleman says he does not know what progress is being made there. That is a serious statement—not one in connection with which I make any reproach, but it is a grave fact which we must bear in mind that we do not know what is going on there. But let us be sure of this: something is in progress there. . . .

Can we conceive that the German Government, as we know it to our cost, would be content to allow that Navy to lie impotent and derided in the Kiel Canal without any hope of action? If there were any possibility within the range of their extraordinary military intelligences by which it could be rendered a really effective factor in the course of the struggle, is it likely that they would have acquiesced in the total loss of utility and of all the efforts, organisation, and resources which have made them the second naval Power? We should be most imprudent if we were to act on such an assumption. We are bound to assume that Germany has completed every vessel begun before the War. It may not be so—I dare say it is not so—but we must assume it.

It would be lamentable, Churchill warned, if, confronted by German preparations on a vast scale, 'serious and solid reasons' did not exist for the postponement and delays in the building of British ships. Before the war began, Parliament had sanctioned the construction of fourteen battleships, each armed with 15-inch guns. He wanted to know why these were not yet ready. There was a further point which disturbed him:

We have not only reached a period in the War when all the capital ships begun before the War can certainly be completed, but we are just entering upon a period when new capital ships begun since the War may be ready on either side. Here, again, I know of course what we have done, and that secret is jealously guarded; but we cannot tell what Germany has done. We have left the region of the known, of the declared or defined; we have left the region of naval annuals and almanacks; and we have entered the sphere of the uncertain. We have entered a sphere which is within certain limits not merely uncertain but incalculable. For this reason we cannot afford to allow any delay to creep into the execution of our programme, because we must from now on provide, not only against the known and against the declared ships, but against what will be a continually increasing element of the unknown. . . .

The War is full of surprises to all of us; but so far the Admiralty has kept ahead. But that has not been done—I am very anxious to couch my argument in language which will not be offensive or vexing to my right hon Friend, whose courtesy I have always experienced, but I must say that it has not been done—by easy methods. It was done by rough and harsh and even violent methods, and by a tireless daily struggle. Remember, everything else is in movement too. We see our own great expansion, but remember, everything else around us is expanding and developing at the same time. You cannot afford to indulge even for the shortest period of time in resting on your oars. You must continually drive the vast machine forward at its utmost speed. To lose momentum is not merely to stop, but to fall.

We have survived, and we are recovering from a shortage of munitions for the Army. At a hideous cost in life and treasure we have regained control, and ascendency lies before us at no great distance. A shortage in naval material, if it were to occur from any cause, would give no chance of future recovery. Blood and money, however lavishly poured out, would never repair the consequences of what might be even an unconscious relaxation of effort.

The House of Commons had not heard such a strong indictment of a Government Department since the war began. Violet Bonham Carter, who was present during the debate, recorded in *Winston Churchill As I Knew Him*, that everything Churchill was saying seemed calculated 'to shake the confidence of the House in the energy, initiative and determination of the present Board of Admiralty. And to arouse fears that Germany was secretly outbuilding us.'

Churchill was determined to disturb the conscience of Parliament. He felt that this was the moment in the war when the Government must choose, either to continue in the old way with loss of life and loss of opportunity going hand in hand, or to strike out in a more forceful, a more logical, a more intelligible and, ultimately, a victorious direction.

He asserted that if this opportunity for a radical change were lost, Britain might lose the war:

I have come down here this afternoon to say these things with the deepest sense of responsibility. I say them because I am sure there is time to avoid all these dangers, because I am sure that it is not too late. If it were too late, silence would be vital. It is not; there is time; and I am anxious that the warning and exhortation which I am going to use, and am using, which may possibly excite resentment, but which must, nevertheless, be said, should be spoken while it is quite certain they may produce a useful effect. But I say advisedly that, though there is time, the Admiralty must not think the battle over. They must forthwith hurl themselves with renewed energy into their task, and press it forward without the loss of a day.

Churchill continued his speech with an examination of the details of the naval programme. He had already sought to create doubts about the adequacy of battleship construction; he next turned to the question of destroyers. He drew the attention of the House to the fact that when Fisher had returned to the Admiralty in October 1914, and the two of them had worked together, 'things were not only planned, but done on a scale beyond anything ever thought possible'. He feared that the programme, both of destroyers, and other small vessels, which he and Fisher had launched, had been 'allowed to fall into arrears' and that 'their delivery has been allowed to slide back from month to month'. If this were so, he went on, 'then I say the Navy and the Grand Fleet might find themselves deprived of securities and advantages which we had prepared for them, and which we deemed it indispensible they should receive'. He did not believe that Balfour's survey of naval affairs had given any indication that the naval programme was really being driven forward. 'It is no use saying, "We are doing our best," ' Churchill warned, 'you have got to succeed in doing what is necessary.' He was worried that Balfour had failed to obtain the necessary labour in the dockyards to build the ships as quickly as they could be built. At this point Asquith interrupted, 'He did not say so,' but Churchill persevered in his argument. Balfour had spoken, he said, of bringing men back from the front as if that would be a remedy for labour problems in the docks; 'and I understood', Churchill continued, 'a remedy which has not yet been adopted'. He was disturbed by the labour situation. 'I know my right hon Friend's difficulties, and the toils and burdens upon him, but he must overcome them. The resources of British shipyards are incomparable, and fully equal, if used at the highest possible speed and power. . . .' At this point Balfour interrupted.

His remarks, although inaudible in the Reporters' Gallery and there-fore not recorded in Hansard, made Churchill exceedingly angry. How did Balfour suppose, he retorted, that the fleet of Monitors which he and Fisher had designed—'which have been so improvidently scattered to the world'—had been brought into existence in the course of only six months? 'No one,' he told the House, 'can form any conception of the achievements which can be produced from the British yards if they are really driven to their fullest capacity.'

Churchill's speech gathered in force and foreboding as it continued. He was warning of dangers which no one had warned of in public before. He was voicing the discontent which others had begun to feel. There were, he warned, 'novel dangers requiring novel expedients'. In a naval war 'you must always be asking about the enemy—what now, what next? . . . your measures must always be governed and framed on the basis that he would do what you would least like him to do'. Churchill criticized Balfour for making no reference in his speech to the danger of submarines:

Although the German submarine campaign has up to date been a great failure, and although it will probably continue to be a failure—here again you cannot afford to assume that it will not present itself in new and more difficult forms, and that new exertions and new inventions will not be demanded, and you must be ready with your new devices before the enemy is ready with his, and your resourcefulness and developments must continu-ally proceed upon a scale which exceeds the maximum you expect from him. I find it necessary to utter this word of warning, which for obvious reasons I should not proceed to elaborate.

From the future danger of the submarine, Churchill turned to the existing depredations of the Zeppelin, hinting that had he and Fisher remained at the Admiralty schemes of a bolder and more effective nature might have been adopted to deal with them:

A strategic policy for the Navy, purely negative in character, by no means necessarily implies that the path of greatest prudence is being followed. I wish to place on record that the late Board would certainly not have been content with an attitude of pure passivity during the whole of the year 1916. . . .

We hear a great deal about air raids. A great remedy against Zeppelin raids is to destroy the Zeppelins in their sheds. I cannot understand myself why all these many months, with resources far greater than those which Lord Fisher and I ever possessed, it has not been found possible to carry on the policy of raiding which, in the early days even, carried a handful of naval pilots to Cologne, Düsseldorf, and Friedrichshafen, and even to Cuxhaven itself.

Churchill had completed his criticisms. At times, in the interests of secrecy, he had spoken guardedly, but the culminating result was to raise serious doubts about Admiralty policy. He had made his points simply, confidently and with effect. The House had listened with a growing realization that Admiralty mismanagement could lead to defeat. Churchill had one more point to make. It was an appeal so extraordinary in its implications, so improbable in its advocate, that the House listened in stunned silence, and Violet Bonham Carter, who considered herself his friend, believed that 'he must surely be deranged'. This was his conclusion:

But I have not spoken to-day without intending to lead up to a conclusion. I have not used words of warning without being sure first that they are spoken in time to be fruitful, and secondly, without having a definite and practical proposal to make.

When in November, 1914, Prince Louis of Battenberg told me he felt it his duty to retire and lay down the charge he had executed so faithfully, I was certain that there was only one man who could succeed him. I knew personally all the high officers of the Navy, and I was sure that there was no one who possessed the power, the insight, and energy of Lord Fisher. I therefore made it plain that I would work with no other First Sea Lord. In this way the oppositions, naval and otherwise, which have always, perhaps not unnaturally, obstructed Lord Fisher's faithful footsteps, were overcome. He returned to his old place, and the six months of war administration which followed will, I believe, rank as one of the remarkable periods in the history of the Royal Navy.

I did not believe it possible that our very cordial and intimate association would be ruptured, but the stress and shocks of this War are tremendous, and the situations into which men are plunged expose them to strain beyond any that this generation have had experience of.

We parted on a great enterprise upon which the Government had decided and to which they were committed and in which the fortunes of a struggling and ill-supported Army were already involved; it stood between us as a barrier. I therefore should have resisted, on public grounds, the return of Lord Fisher to the Admiralty—and I have on several occasions expressed this opinion in the strongest terms to the Prime Minister and the First Lord of the Admiralty.

We have now reached an entirely different situation, and I have no doubt whatever what it is my duty to say now. There was a time when I did not think that I could have brought myself to say it, but I have been away for some months, and my mind is now clear. The times are crucial. The issues are momentous. The great War deepens and widens and expands around us. The existence of our country and of our cause depend upon the Fleet. We cannot afford to deprive ourselves or the Navy of the strongest and most vigorous forces that are available. No personal consideration must stand between the country and those who can serve her best.

I feel that there is in the present Admiralty administration, for all their competence, loyalty, and zeal, a lack of driving force and mental energy which cannot be allowed to continue, which must be rectified while time remains and before evil results, and can only be rectified in one way. I am sure the nation and the Navy expect that the necessary step will be taken. . . .

I urge the First Lord of the Admiralty without delay to fortify himself, to vitalise and animate his Board of Admiralty by recalling Lord Fisher to his post as First Sea Lord.

Churchill's appeal for Fisher's return destroyed in a few minutes the whole impact of his speech, turning what had been to that moment one of the most serious and skilful speeches he had ever made into an object of derision. Churchill's hammer blows of criticism were forgotten. The Government, Parliament and, on the morrow, the British public, gaped in amazement. When Violet Bonham Carter reached her father's room in the House of Commons, she found Asquith 'speechless' and Edward Marsh with tears in his eyes. Churchill, Asquith told her, had taken a 'suicidal' step by his appeal for Fisher's return. Yet Churchill had believed that this appeal would strengthen his position as a critic; it would show that the personal animosities and divisive rancour of May 1915 were over, and indicate that he wanted the Navy to be in the hands of the one man whose energy and stature were known to all: proof that he was thinking, not of himself but of the national need. Churchill was deluded. He had aroused in the House the realization that Britain could lose the war; but ending with the appeal for Fisher's return, he had blunted the impact of this warning and made himself appear absurd.

Holding a weapon which Churchill himself had delivered into its hand, the Government acted quickly. Asquith had already shown his usual skill at political manoeuvre by having asked Fisher to attend the War Council that was to meet on the following morning. Of all the national newspapers, only the *Manchester Guardian* decided to treat Churchill's speech as a serious and valid challenge to Government inertia; C. P. Scott having always looked to Fisher's return as a panacea. Churchill received no flood of congratulatory letters. No enthusiastic notes were passed to him along the benches. Violet Bonham Carter wrote to him in bewilderment, asking for a chance to talk to him. Only one correspondent, Fisher, was enthusiastic, writing on March 7:

My dear Winston,
    SPLENDID!!!
You'll have your Reward! All I entreat you now is to entrench yourself as Leader of the Opposition! and wait for the Big thing to come to you!
    C. P. Scott said to me it would come! Your attitude so excellent—a helpful (*not a hostile*) critic. *Anyhow my heart is very full!* I feel the good old times are back!

Yours
Fisher

Don't trouble to answer. Telephone when I can see you after the Council tomorrow and *where*!

Churchill left the House of Commons immediately after his speech. He was quite unprepared for the ridicule which its extraordinary conclusion had drawn upon him. In the debate that followed only one speaker, George Lambert, tried, briefly, to take up the plea for Fisher's return; but Parliament was less interested in discussing whether Fisher should return than in castigating Churchill for having urged them to bring him back. Commander Bellairs[1] spoke bitterly of the dangers to British policy should Churchill control it once more:

Does he mean by an attitude of activity the thing we have been accustomed to in the past, with ship after ship knocking at the Dardanelles, warning the Turks we were coming, when we had embarked on that project without any central scheme of action—is that the sort of activity he means? Does he mean we are to go and bombard Heligoland, and thereby knock out more of those capital ships he considers so necessary? Is not the Navy accomplishing at the present moment every single purpose for which it was devised?

For Churchill to demand that the Government discard its senior naval adviser and bring in someone else was, Bellairs declared, 'an intolerable situation'. 'Hear, hear!' interrupted Balfour.
    The most vitriolic speech that evening came from the Admiral, Sir

---

[1] Carlyon Bellairs, 1871–1955. Midshipman, 1886. Retired from the Navy with rank of a Commander 1902, on the failure of his eyesight. Liberal MP, 1906–9. Conservative MP, 1909–10; 1915–31. An opponent of political honours, he declined a Baronetcy in 1927.

Hedworth Meux, whom Churchill had known for many years. This was his maiden speech:

I had not intended to interpose in this Debate until I had the pain of hearing the speech of the late First Lord of the Admiralty (Colonel Churchill). I think it is well the House should know that if the present First Lord is foolish enough to adopt his suggestion and bring Lord Fisher back to the Admiralty there will be general consternation throughout the Navy.

Some week or ten days ago I had two or three officers in the Grand Fleet say to me, 'For God's sake stop this intrigue which is going on,' and I intend to do what I can.

What is the right hon and gallant Gentleman—I was very sorry not to see him in uniform; he has often seen me in uniform, but I have never seen him —really asking the First Lord of the Admiralty to do? He is asking him to commit harikiri, and not only him, but the Government also. That is the meaning of this intrigue—to turn out the Government, nothing else.

Let us put ourselves in the place of the Grand Fleet—Sir John Jellicoe, captains and officers—when they read this Debate and see what the late First Lord has said. They will say, 'Here is a nice state of things. What has our present First Sea Lord of the Admiralty done? What is the matter with Sir Henry Jackson? What is his fault?' Shall I tell you what is his fault in the eyes of the people who want to turn him out? It is that he does not advertise.
Mr BALFOUR: Hear, hear!
Admiral Sir HEDWORTH MEUX: He does not have correspondents and newspaper people in his place all day. That is really the reason this agitation has been got up. It is because the present Board of Admiralty are doing their work to the satisfaction of the Navy and not boasting about it.

In the first few months of the War, whenever we had a success or whenever the enemy had a slight failure, the whole of the Navy were pained by the vulgar boasting that went on. When we read boasting and foolish condemnation of our enemies—who, in spite of some of their brutalities, are a gallant enemy—a quiver goes through the whole of the Navy. Anybody in the Navy knows what an unlucky thing it is to boast. When the present First Lord's speech is read we shall say, 'Thank heaven, at last we have got a ruler who does not grate upon our nerves!'

The hon and gallant Member is a very old friend of mine, and I have received many kindnesses from him, but there are limits to endurance. When the late First Lord (Colonel Churchill) and Lord Fisher were at the Admiralty they were at daggers drawn, and everybody at the Admiralty knew it. Are we to have all that over again? What did the late First Lord say about Lord Fisher when he made his exculpating speech in this House? Did he not say that he could not get proper guidance from Lord Fisher, and is that the man you want to bring back?

Who has called for Lord Fisher? Has the House called for him? The Navy has not called for him. . . .

Churchill was not present to hear this strident attack, or to answer the serious accusation that he was privy to an intrigue aimed at overthrowing the Government. Meux referred to his absence at the end of his speech, in a savage passage:

I am sorry the late First Lord is not in his place, because, with all due humility, I would like to say to him, 'Rolling stones gather no moss.' I do not know how many posts he has had in his short and brilliant career. He has succeeded in them all. He might always have done better had he stuck to them, but he never has, and I believe what I say now will be approved by a very large number of Members in this House. We all wish him a great deal of success in France, and we hope that he will stay there.

The Press criticisms on the morning of March 8 echoed the views of Bellairs and Meux. Although comment concentrated upon the final appeal for Fisher's return, no newspaper denied that the earlier part of Churchill's speech constituted a clear and powerful indictment of Asquith's administration. Some newspapers expressed surprise that there had been no official answer that evening to the detailed charges which Churchill had put forward. But because Churchill's criticisms had been so unexpected, because he had taken so short a time to prepare them, because he had not sought to enlist the help of a single member of the Government, his speech puzzled more people than it inspired. He had made it without enlisting parliamentary supporters or setting up a Press campaign to set the scene, believing that spontaneity and surprise would give the speech an added strength. His friends, other than Fisher, were bewildered by his action. When Riddell spoke to Lloyd George on March 8, Lloyd George, according to Riddell's *War Diary*, called the speech 'a great error':

He should have stopped after criticising the Administration. When Winston remarked, 'I am now going to make a practical suggestion,' I wondered what he was going to say. Bonar Law whispered to me, 'He is going to suggest the recall of Fisher.' I could not believe it. Of course, if his object was to ruin Fisher's chances, he did his best to achieve it; but I do not believe he would act in such a Machiavellian way. That is not like Winston. On the other hand, if he meant to improve his own position, he made a great mistake.

Churchill realized the damage which he had done to himself by insisting upon Fisher's recall. He could not decide whether to remain in London for further debates, or to return to Flanders. On the morning of March 8 Fisher appeared at 41 Cromwell Road and tried to persuade him to continue with his parliamentary criticisms. Clementine Churchill doubted whether, as a result of his speech, her husband could possibly win parliamentary support. Fisher disagreed, believing that only a few more well-directed blows aimed at naval or military policy would bring Asquith down. Churchill was inclined to agree, and believed that he still had a part to play.

On the afternoon of March 8 Balfour replied to Churchill's speech in the House of Commons. By his speech, he ensured that Churchill's humiliation was complete. Churchill's criticisms, he said, were 'very unfortunate, both in form and substance . . . inspired I know not by whom, or whence . . .'. Balfour proceeded to deal with Churchill's various points, denying absolutely 'slackness, indifference, want of push and drive', and claiming that the Navy 'is far stronger than it was at the beginning of the War, and is, I believe, stronger than it has ever been in its history'. But Balfour did not defend himself against Churchill's criticisms by rational argument. He concentrated instead upon Churchill's final appeal, using ridicule and invective:

Let me say now one word about the remedy which he proposed at the end. I do not imagine that there was a single person who heard my right hon Friend's speech who did not listen to this latter part of it with profound stupefaction.

My right hon Friend has often astonished the House, but I do not think he ever astonished it so much as when he came down to explain that the remedy for all our ills, as far as the Navy is concerned, is to get rid of Sir Henry Jackson and to put in his place Lord Fisher.

My right hon Friend has never made the smallest concealment, either in public or in private, of what he thought of Lord Fisher. Certainly the impression that we all had of what he thought of Lord Fisher was singularly unlike the picture that we should ourselves have drawn uninspired as to the character of a saviour of his country. Because, what did he say when he made what at the time he thought was his farewell speech, when he exchanged a political for a military career? He told us that the First Sea Lord, Lord Fisher, did not give him, when he was serving in the same Admiralty with him, either the clear guidance before the event or the firm support after it which he was entitled to expect. . . .

Then my right hon Friend, with the memory of that speech in his mind, had naturally to frame some explanation of advice which suggested that Sir Henry Jackson should be relieved of his office in order to put in his place the most brilliant and distinguished sailor who had, however, according to the right hon Gentleman, the defect of not giving his chief either the clear guidance or the firm support which his chief had a right to expect. It was not a very easy thing to explain, and I must honestly say not a thing which was very adequately or satisfactorily explained.

All that my right hon Friend said was that he had gone since then to the front, and that with the opportunity for calm meditation which apparently the front presents his mind was cleared.

The great ancestor of my right hon Friend, the first Duke of Marlborough, was always supposed to be more cool, more collected, more master of himself, more clear in thought amid the din of battle than he was in the calmer occupations of peace, and perhaps my right hon Friend shares this hereditary peculiarity. I venture to suggest that that clearness of thought which we all desiderate is bought at a rather costly figure if it involves a European war in order to obtain it. . . .

I cannot follow the workings of the right hon Gentleman's mind. He told us in his speech yesterday, I have not got the quotation, but it came however to this, that he told the Prime Minister when Prince Louis resigned the position of First Sea Lord that the only man he could work with was Lord Fisher.

He seemed dogged by ill-fortune. Is it not a most extraordinary and emphatic coincidence that the only man with whom my right hon Friend could consent to work at the Admiralty was the most distinguished sailor who, after five months, refused to work with my right hon Friend? . . .

I do not know if my right hon Friend is under the impression—perhaps he is—that if the change which he desires to force on the Government were accepted, I should still remain a member of the Government. But let us suppose that that is so, and that I was prepared to take my Board of Admiralty from the right hon Gentleman—rather a violent supposition—why does he suppose that Lord Fisher should behave differently to me from the manner in which my right hon Friend declared Lord Fisher behaved to him? Is it my merits? Am I more happily gifted in the way of working with people than my right hon Friend? Does he think that I could better utilise Lord Fisher's great gifts and avoid this want of harmony which rose between them and which in different circumstances might still have prevailed if Lord Fisher were still First Sea Lord? I do not know whether that is the explanation or not.

The fact remains that the right hon Gentleman, who could not get on with Lord Fisher—I will not say that, but with whom Lord Fisher could not get on—says that Lord Fisher, who according to my right hon Friend neither supported him nor guided him, is nevertheless the man who ought to be given as a supporter and a guide to anybody who happens to hold at this moment the responsible position of First Lord of the Admiralty. It is a paradox of the wildest and most extravagant kind. . . .

My right hon Friend comes forward with this suggestion. He put it in the form of a suggestion that Lord Fisher should come to the Admiralty. There is another form in which it could be put, which is equally veracious. That is that Sir Henry Jackson should go from the Admiralty. . . . I think when the right hon Gentleman comes down to this House, and, without a tittle of evidence, giving us no argument, no ground, suggests to the Government that this great public servant should be turned adrift in order to introduce in his place a man of whom I would never say anything which does not indicate my enormous admiration of the great services he has performed to his country in connection with the creation of our Fleet, but who, according to the right hon Gentleman himself, has not done that which is his first duty as First Sea Lord to do, namely, to give guidance and advice to the First Lord and his colleagues in the Cabinet, seems to me the most amazing proposition that has ever been laid before the House of Commons. . . .

I should regard myself as contemptible beyond the power of expression if I were to yield an inch to a demand of such a kind, made in such a way. . . .

Churchill was stunned by the savagery of Balfour's reply. He answered briefly and with dignity, but to no avail. Balfour, he said, was 'a master of Parliamentary sword-play and of every dialectical art'; his high position in British politics enabled him easily to rebuke those who did not have his authority, and in particular one 'who is so much younger than himself'. 'All the familiar Parliamentary devices,' he said, had been employed against him. He reiterated briefly the points which he had made in his speech on the previous day, and continued:

It is very easy to exaggerate the statements which I made, and then to protest against the form in which they were couched. But the right hon Gentleman ought, I think, not to be unduly offended or vexed at the speech which I made, because, after all, a speech is a very small thing, and a failure of any kind in this matter is a vital thing.

Do not let us be too touchy on the Treasury Bench in regard to matters of that kind. It is right that a note of warning should be sounded, and sounded in time.

Churchill then spoke of his final plea for Fisher's return:

The right hon Gentleman, of course, was very effective in dealing with my relations with Lord Fisher. I made him a present of all the rhetorical and debating retorts which he can derive from that fertile field, and I must say that I do not at all wonder that he was able to rove about in this luxuriant field, so well fitted to the special arts he exercises.

But, after all, what is the real fact? The real fact is that if we could associate in some way or another the driving power and energy of Lord Fisher, with the carrying out of Lord Fisher's programme at the highest possible speed, there is no reason to suppose that great public advantage would not result from that.

Compared with Balfour's attack, Churchill's reply made no impact at all. Balfour had triumphed. Margot Asquith wrote to him later that day from 10 Downing Street:

Dearest Arthur,

I hope & believe Winston will never be forgiven his yesterday's speech. Henry & I were thunderstruck at the *meanness* & the gigantic folly of it. I've never varied in my opinion of Winston I am glad to say.

He is a hound of the lowest sense of political honour, a fool of the lowest judgement & contemptible.

He cured me of oratory in the House & bored me with oratory in the Home!

If it's not cheek I must tell you Henry & I thought you admirable and if H had not had a deputation he said he wd have given Winston 10 of the nastiest minutes of his life he was so *disgusted*.

Everyone delighted with Hedworth.

V devoted
Margot

Margot Asquith's verdict was also for a large part the Parliamentary one. It ignored the anguish which Churchill felt at what he believed to be unpardonable neglect and apathy in high places. But ridicule, wielded effectively, had greater force than reason. By his final plea, Churchill had laid himself open to derisive laughter; it was a gesture as naïve as it was ill-considered. At noon on March 7 Churchill had believed that the challenge which he was about to make could change the course of the war. By noon on March 8 he knew that he had failed. 'My dear Lord Fisher,' Hankey wrote on March 9, 'I fear that Winston, whose conduct is in striking contrast to yours, did not do you much good. He gave AJB a chance he was not likely to miss.' In the House of Lords on March 9, Lord Charles Beresford—who had been created Baron Beresford in January—declared he would halt the mischief caused by Churchill's 'wicked statement'. Not all commentators were hostile. 'Churchill's outburst,' Lord Esher wrote to Sir Douglas Haig on March 11, 'was the culmination of a great deal of discontent in the Fleet itself. . . . It is said that the old peace methods prevail there, as elsewhere, and that the highest degree of efficiency is denied to the Grand Fleet by adherence to procedure that is unsuited to a war of this kind. That Jellicoe is short of certain types of vessels essential to him is, I fear, beyond question.'

Churchill knew that the arguments which he had put forward about the Navy were valid. He felt that equally strong arguments could be used to criticize the conduct of military affairs. He therefore decided to stay in England, and to continue his assault upon Government policy. That day he wrote to the Secretary of State for War from 41 Cromwell Road:

Circumstances have arisen which make it my duty to give undivided attention to Parliamentary and public business for some time to come. I ask you therefore to have me relieved from my command as soon as this can be done without disadvantage to the service. In the meanwhile I should be glad if my leave of absence could be extended—equally without disadvantage, as I must otherwise return to France tomorrow.

Perhaps you will if necessary show this letter to the Prime Minister.

Kitchener took this letter to 10 Downing Street. Asquith agreed to extend Churchill's leave; Churchill was no longer a threat politically either in London or in Ploegsteert. The speech had destroyed his power to harm the Government. By inviting Fisher to the War Council of March 8, Asquith had isolated Churchill even further. 'Five Admiralty officials with masses of paper to swallow me up!' Fisher wrote to Jellicoe after his first reappearance at 10 Downing Street since May 1915. At the War Council Asquith had flattered Fisher, so that he came away believing, as he wrote to Jellicoe, that although 'Balfour & Co tried a lot of red herrings to no purpose!' he and Asquith had been in agreement 'that the position of the Grand Fleet owing to lack of destroyers was "PERILOUS"!' Asquith's impression was very different. At four o'clock that afternoon he saw C. P. Scott at 10 Downing Street, at Scott's request. 'He was silent and grim,' Scott recorded in a note of the interview. Scott told Asquith that he had intended to speak to him about the Navy, but that 'a great part of what I wanted to say had now already been said by Churchill'. Scott pressed for Fisher's return. Asquith told him that when the War Council had asked Fisher what was required to make the Navy more effective his answer had been: 'a contemptuous ejaculation and gesture, casting thumb back over shoulder as though to get rid of dirt'.

Scott recorded that Asquith then rose from his seat and began 'marching to and fro', denouncing both Fisher and Churchill with vehemence. Soon afterwards Scott wrote down the gist of Asquith's remarks:

As for Churchill's speech it was a piece of the grossest effrontery. Did I know that only 3 months ago when Fisher was appointed as head of the Inventions Department both Churchill and his wife had been furious and had denounced it as an outrage, so much so that Mrs Churchill had almost cut him and his wife and would not speak to him. And now suddenly Churchill professed to have discovered Fisher's extraordinary merits and called for his reinstatement. It was a piece of 'impudent humbug'. Why when Churchill and Fisher were together they did nothing but quarrel and Fisher's resignations were a perpetual worry of his life. He had resigned 8 times before the last time. Then he actually deserted his post and went away at a time too of some anxiety. Had he not gone there would, said Asquith, have been no Ministerial crisis and no Coalition. 'He deserved to be shot,' shouted Asquith, 'and in any other country he would have been shot.'

Fisher was a spent force. The War Council, having seen this, could ignore Churchill's challenge. When the War Council was over Hankey sent Fisher a fulsome letter of praise, thanking him for 'dotting the "i's" and crossing the "t's" of Jellicoe's evidence'; he then informed him that the country owed him a debt of gratitude 'not merely for what you have done but for the patriotic manner in which you have avoided any publicity, which might help the enemy, and compelled the highest authority to take the matter up . . .'. This strong hint for continued silence was successful. Fisher decided to give up his idea of putting forward his criticisms in the House of Lords. But he still hoped that Churchill would make the running for him. Of Fisher's friends, Scott, however, influenced by Asquith's outburst, was sceptical of any chance of success for Churchill. Garvin remained optimistic, feeling that Churchill could circumvent the ridicule of his naval speech by a further attack on the Government during the Army Estimates debate on the following Tuesday, March 14. During the afternoon of March 8 Churchill asked Violet Bonham Carter to call to see him at Lady Randolph's house. She recorded her impressions in *Winston Churchill As I Knew Him*:

I found him alone there. He looked pale, defiant, on the defensive. I shall never forget the pain of the talk which followed. I knew better than to criticize, reproach or even ask the question that gnawed at me, 'What possessed you? *Why* did you do it?' I saw at once that, whatever his motive, he realized that he had hopelessly failed to accomplish what he had set out to do. . . . What he had conceived as a great gesture of magnanimity—the forgiveness of the wrongs Fisher had done to him, for the sake of a greater aim, our naval supremacy—had not been interpreted as such. It was regarded instead as a clumsy gambler's throw for his own ends. . . .

I had not seen him since our farewell luncheon at Cromwell Road in November, two days before he left for the Front. My first words were of the joy of his safe return, the miracle of the evacuation of Gallipoli, of his own experience since—but I knew that his attention was perfunctory and his mind elsewhere.

After a pause he said: 'I suppose you are against me like the rest of them.' I said that he knew well that I could never be against him, but that I was strong against reinvesting Fisher with any sort of authority, as he had proved himself quite unfit for it. I could never trust him again and I was amazed that Winston could bring himself to do so. 'You may forgive what he has done to you. You have not the right to forgive the ruin he has brought on others and on the Dardanelles campaign.' He sheered off the Dardanelles and said that he knew from private sources that things were going badly at the Admiralty; that Fisher's fire and drive could put it out of the rut, reanimate it, speed it forward, etc. etc. 'Arthur's never been exactly a dynamo at the best of times.'

I did not pursue the argument, but after a time asked what his plans were. Was it true, as my father had told me, that he thought of resigning from the Army here and now and not returning to France? He said it was. He had come to the conclusion that it was right for him to remain here and exercise what influence he had at the heart of affairs. Many others thought so too. He had many friends and supporters (this rather militantly), including the *Manchester Guardian*. Had I read it that morning?

Fisher remained convinced that Churchill could succeed in over-throwing Asquith if he made a further effort, believing that the Army debate on March 14 offered a major opportunity for a renewed attack on the Government's conduct of the war. On March 8 Fisher wrote urging him to give up his Battalion altogether:

My dear Winston,

For Goodness sake dont hesitate! Write at once and resign! *I beg you to do this!* Garvin is absolutely confident it would be the mistake of your life to leave the House of Commons for a single day! You mark the gravity of the Naval and Military situation by remaining! Fancy losing your splendid opportunity next week on the Army Estimates. . . . Who else but you can rub Kitchener's nose in it? I assure you I am not so much thinking of your personal interests (*immense as they are! because you have the Prime Ministership in your grasp!*) but of saving the country! *Now now now* is the time to save the Country NOT 3 months ahead! As my dear Winston you know better than I do that it's all d——d humbug Asquith weeping on your shoulder and entreating you to go and be shot at!—I feel certain Kitchener and Balfour felt the danger today of your stopping at home when they discussed your letter! I *earnestly EARNESTLY* beg you to *write at once* and resign! *The man who hesitates is lost!* If ever in this world a Leader was wanted—it is *NOW*! and Providence has provided you and given you an automatic opportunity. So once more on my bended knees I implore you to write at once. Delays are Dangerous!

Yours
Fisher

On March 9 Fisher wrote triumphantly to C. P. Scott: 'McKenna told me yesterday (This is most secret!) that if Winston remained he

would turn out the Government. Dead Sure. *SO HE WILL!!!*'
Churchill's speech, he wrote to Jellicoe that same day, 'was really
wonderfully good. *HE HELD THE HOUSE ENTHRALLED.*'

Asquith, having flattered Fisher's ego and obtained his silence, now
tried to persuade Churchill to abandon his opposition. Neither Asquith
nor Churchill left any account of their meeting, which took place on
March 9 at 10 Downing Street. Immediately after it, Violet Bonham
Carter asked her father what had passed between them and later
wrote in *Winston Churchill As I Knew Him*:

> He told me that he had reminded Winston how his father, Lord Randolph
> (to whom my father was devoted), had committed political suicide through
> one impulsive action. He had said, 'If I can, I want to save you from doing
> the same thing. You will know that nothing but affection prompts me. It is
> because I care for you that I shall save you.' He said that Winston had tears
> in his eyes when they parted and that he was sure that he would go back to
> France. He added that it was strange how little Winston knew of the attitude
> of others towards himself. He had spoken to my father, as he did to me, of the
> many ardent supporters who looked to him for leadership and my father had
> said to him, 'At the moment you have none who count at all.' One of the
> things which saddened my father most about this episode was that he was
> always watching and hoping for an opportunity when the climate of opinion
> in the Tory Party would change and enable him to bring Winston back into
> the Government. Alas, 'at this moment he has few political friends inside it or
> outside, nor is there a single office he could be given'. I said the wheel must
> turn—'He will, he *must*, come back some day. If only he isn't killed. . . .
> Supposing that he were killed—what should *we* feel, those of us who have
> urged him to go back?' My father said, 'I could only advise him to do what
> I am sure is right—right above all for his own sake.'

On March 10 an unexpected straw in the wind gave Churchill
further encouragement for political action. At a by-election in East
Hertfordshire the official Conservative candidate, Captain Henderson,[1]
who had the support of the local Liberal organization, was defeated.
The successful candidate was the airman Pemberton Billing, who stood
as an independent in the interests of a strong Air policy. Pemberton
Billing polled 4,590 votes against 3,559 cast for the coalition. That
afternoon Fisher and Garvin went together to see Churchill at 41
Cromwell Road. To their delight, they found that he had already prepared a speech for the Army debate, which he read to them. That
evening Fisher wrote to C. P. Scott, who had returned to Manchester:
'This East Herts Election is a Big Bomb. I believe the Government will

[1] Brodie Haldane Henderson, 1869–1936. Civil Engineer. Served in the Royal Engineers,
1914–18. Captain, 1914. Brigadier-General, 1918. Knighted, 1919.

soon be cleared out if our Friend remains as he should do and discourses on the Army estimates next Tuesday.' Sir Max Aitken also tried to convince Churchill to stay in London. Two weeks later, on March 24, Churchill wrote to him from Ploegsteert: 'I did not feel able after all to take yr advice; for though my instinct agreed with yours I had small but insistent obligations here wh cd not be hastily discarded for the sake of a personal opportunity. . . . I did not feel in me . . . the virtue necessary for the tremendous tasks you indicated. My interests were too evident & one cannot tell how much they sway one's judgement.' What were these 'tremendous tasks'? The leadership of a powerful opposition, drawing in dissidents from both Liberal and Conservative ranks? The overthrow of Asquith? Fisher, who saw Churchill again on the evening of March 10, did not doubt the nature of Churchill's opportunity. 'I think the Government will be turned out in about 3 weeks time,' Fisher wrote to Hankey on March 11: '*There is* SEETHING DISCONTENT *throughout the masses.*' That morning Fisher made a final appeal:

My dear Winston,
    I've slept over it! I've thought of nothing else! If any specious twaddle about honour or Asquithian Juggglery persuades you not to rise from the corner of the Front Opposition Bench next Tuesday to brand the Government with the *massacre* of our *troops* and the utter *ineptitude* of the conduct of the war then I say that *YOU* become the '*Murderer*' because you are the *one and only* man who it is absolutely certain can prevent it and can voice the removal of Kitchener and so if not Prime Minister (which I am *sure* you will be) then you can be War Minister.
    NEVER was there such an Opportunity!
    Fate has led you straight to it!
    Had you the very faintest idea when you left France that the Prime Minister with his own hand had written Jellicoe's condition as
'PERILOUS'
Had you then the faintest idea that both 'Coalition' and 'Labour' would be utterly smashed by the Seething Discontent of the Masses?
    GREAT OCCASIONS NECESSITATE GREAT RISKS! To the public— Balfour has trounced *you*! *You've* got to trounce *him* by another flank movement! *He has got to be discredited!* Or he will be the alternative Prime Minister with Asquith as Lord Chancellor!
VIA THE ARMY ESTIMATES YOU CAN DO IT!
    Stick at nothing!
    Speak on Tuesday!
Yours
F

On March 11 Churchill rehearsed his naval criticisms in a letter to Sir Frederick Cawley,[1] the Chairman of the Liberal War Committee,[2] and an influential backbench figure:

I have, after very careful consideration of all the circumstances, decided to apply to be relieved of my command in order to resume Parliamentary duties. Meanwhile I am returning to France and I wish to restate briefly the main facts about the Admiralty which compelled me to intervene in the recent debate. They are eight in number:—
1. The margin of safety is ample and unimpaired.
2. There has been preventable delay in completing the Fisher war Programme.
3. This delay affects both capital ships and destroyers required for the progressive reinforcement of the Fleets at sea.
4. A new impulse of the utmost vigour must be imparted to the whole volume of our construction, particularly to those units most urgently needed.
5. If this impulse is forthcoming there is still time fully to maintain the position.
6. For this purpose the present Board of Admiralty must be strengthened in whatever way will be most effective regardless of naval or personal feuds.
7. There has been a total lack of initiative in the tactical direction of the Naval Air Service resulting in a cessation for many months of all attempts to destroy German zeppelins in their bases and thus safeguard this country from their attacks.
8. There has been ample time to prepare and organize these counter air raids and to make all the appliances required for them;
It would appear to be the duty of your Committee to take good care that these vital facts are not overlooked.

On that same day Churchill obtained a written promise from Asquith that his eventual return would not be frustrated by any military pressures. 'As you are returning with my full approval to your military functions at the front,' Asquith wrote, 'I wish to assure you that, if

[1] Frederick Cawley, 1850–1937. Liberal MP, 1895–1918. Created Baronet, 1906. Member of the Dardanelles Commission, 1916–17. Chancellor of the Duchy of Lancaster, December 1916–18. Created Baron, 1918. Of his four sons, three were killed in the war: Major J. S. Cawley in the retreat from Mons, August 1914; Captain Harold Thomas Cawley, MP, at Gallipoli, September 1915; and Captain Oswald Cawley, MP, in France, August 1918.
[2] The Liberal War Committee, a group of some forty Liberal MPs anxious about the conduct of the war, who wanted Parliament to take a more active part in war policy. Several of them, including Cawley, joined Lloyd George's Government in December 1916. Its members included Dalziel, Markham and Mond.

hereafter you should find that your sense of public duty called upon you to return to political life here, no obstacle will be put in your way, and your relief will be arranged for, as soon as it can be effected without detriment to the Service.' That evening Fisher and Churchill met again. Fisher insisted that it was Churchill's duty to remain in London. Pemberton Billing's by-election success was, he said, a clear indication of real public discontent with the Government. Churchill had not yet made up his mind. On the morning of March 12 Fisher wrote again:

You said last night you had not given your final answer to Asquith *so I make one more effort not to lose the war!* The very fact of Asquith's intense desire for you to go back coupled with Mrs Asquith's entreaty to F. E. Smith to use all his influence to make you go back and the considered opinion of Asquith's closest friend that you will turn out the Government if you stay and the East Herts Election to support you on Tuesday in your onslaught and the approaching Tigris disaster and possibly a yet bigger disaster that must be *momentarily* dealt with! (*No use then your coming home!*) TOO LATE! I say in view of these facts you are absolutely blind both to Patriotism as well as self-interest to return. *And it is not too late even now! A telegram will do it you know it can!*

Your speech as you rehearsed it on Friday afternoon to Garvin and me was incomparable! And you have yet to say you left France without the very faintest idea that the Navy Estimates were coming on! And you are paying £500 a year extra premium on your Life Insurance, losing £400 a year as MP because serving in the war and only getting £500 a year for your soldiering and Asquith asks you as to your material loss if you go back! A *sorry joke!*

'There's a tide in the affairs of men which taken at the Flood leads on to Fortune . . .'
You know how to finish it! ! ![1]
    Seize the Moment!
Rehearse your Army speech to Carson! but *he won't back you*! WE ARE GOING TO LOSE THE WAR! ! !

That night, Churchill saw Sir Henry Dalziel, one of his few parliamentary supporters, to discuss his political prospects. Dalziel was keen for Churchill to stay in London. But Clementine Churchill persuaded

---

' 1 The quotation, from Shakespeare's *Julius Caesar* (Act 4, Scene 3), continues:
                Omitted, all the voyage of their life
                Is bound in shallows and in miseries.
                On such a full sea are we now afloat;
                And we must take the current when it serve
                Or lose our ventures.

her husband that he must return at once, if only for a short while, to his Battalion duties. By returning, he would not be able to take part in the opening of the Army debate. He hoped that if the debate lasted long enough he might be able to come back later and intervene at its end. On the morning of March 13 he wrote to Dalziel:

I daresay in about a week I shall be able to return to the House of Commons. You must forgive these uncertainties which arise from the difficulty of doing justice to two different sets of obligations.

I am grateful to you for your help and kindness during this tiresome week.

Do you think there is any chance of the army estimates running over into the next Parliamentary week? If so, send me a line and I will once again adjust my mind to the topic that I mentioned to you.

Churchill left for Flanders that morning. On his way to Dover with his wife he rehearsed the arguments in favour of taking up a permanent place with the parliamentary opposition. But Clementine Churchill was sceptical of his chances. Her assessment of the political situation was right. Churchill had no influential supporters. On March 11, having heard of the moves to attack the Government, Northcliffe had telegraphed from Paris to the editor of *The Times*, Geoffrey Robinson: 'Stated here that Churchill lead opposition. Don't give least support. . . .' Robinson obeyed his instructions. Several newspapers still hankered after Fisher's return; none felt compelled to advocate Churchill's.

Churchill was not influenced by his wife's doubts. On reaching Dover he sent Asquith a letter asking to be relieved of his command, and gave his wife a statement for the Press Association explaining his course. Then he crossed over to France. Late that afternoon he reached Ploegsteert, where his Battalion was in its forward trenches. He was exhausted by the week that had passed. He could not judge how far his speech had shattered his chances of leading an effective opposition. He wanted more time to reflect, and realized that it would be too precipitate to return even during the final stages of the military debate. If he failed then to gather sufficient support he would be in a very weak position. He felt on reflection that he had been unwise to send off his letter to Asquith, resigning his command. He wanted to wait longer, to look at the situation more calmly, to understand the nature of his support. He therefore telegraphed that night to Asquith withdrawing his letter. Asquith was relieved, and at once despatched Maurice Bonham Carter to 41 Cromwell Road to retrieve the Press Association statement from Clementine Churchill.

24

'My True War Station'

CHURCHILL returned to the trenches shaken by his Parliamentary humiliation of the previous week. But he no longer doubted that his future must be a political one. He sensed that unless he returned quickly to the political arena he might be cheated of the career which he now knew was the only conceivable one for him. 'My dearest soul,' he wrote to Clementine Churchill on March 13, his first evening back in reserve, 'you have seen me vy weak & foolish & mentally infirm this week. Dual obligations, both honourable, both weighty have rent me. But I am sure my true war station is in the H of C. There I can help the movement of events. I cannot tell you how much I love & honour you and how sweet & steadfast you have been through all my hesitations & perplexity.' He was looking forward to 'a few more days reflection' in the trenches, and declared that he would not write to anyone 'or ask anyone for his advice or opinion'. 'Don't we live in a strange world,' he continued, 'full of wonderful pictures & intricate affairs. Across the troubled waters one can only steer by compass—not to do anything that is not honourable & manly, & subject to that to use my vital force to the utmost effect to win the war—there is the test I am going to try my decision by.'

After seeing her husband off at Dover on March 13, Clementine Churchill had gone at once to Carson's house at Rottingdean. On March 14 she sent her husband an account of the meeting, and of Carson's grave doubts about the wisdom of a precipitate return. 'Carson is a most important factor,' Churchill replied on March 16, '& I am impressed by his misgivings.' But he was not to be deterred in his course. 'That it is right for me to come home is certain,' he insisted. 'What is not clear is when & on what grounds.' General Furse, with whom he discussed the question of what course he should take, had been emphatic, Churchill reported to his wife, 'that my future was at home'. Furse had told Churchill bluntly that 'although it may be easier for you here with a battalion or a brigade & pleasanter, you have no right to think of that'. Churchill had played the devil's advocate. He had argued that a rapid return to politics would brand him with the mark of a change-ling; but Furse had replied: 'The thing is much larger than that.'

Churchill also discussed his problems with Archibald Sinclair, to whom he unburdened himself each evening. 'Archie is a strong advocate of my staying here,' Churchill told his wife in a long letter on March 16. Sinclair saw no point in a precipitate return, or in any action without a definite reason. This was also Clementine Churchill's opinion. 'It is odd,' he told her, 'how similar are the standpoints from wh you and he both view my tiresome affairs.'

During Churchill's first week back in reserve, General Walshe was relieved of his command. A new Brigadier was needed to take charge of the Brigade. There was a chance that Churchill would be promoted to this position, on which he had once set his heart. But Generalship held no attractions for him now. 'Although this matter will in no way *determine* my action,' he wrote to his wife, 'I may as well have its decision before me before I settle.'

Churchill and his men were due to move forward again to the front line on March 20. He felt that by then he might have reached the decision to return. 'Now mind you keep in touch with Garvin, Scott, Dalziel,' he wrote in his long letter of March 16, '& don't let them drift off or think I have resigned the game. Tell them I am taking time to consider, method & occasion, but that in principle I have decided.' She might, he added, have a talk with Sir Frederick Cawley, '& even with the Fiend himself'. Clementine Churchill refused to talk to Fisher, but did everything else that he asked. Churchill appreciated his wife's efforts on his behalf. 'I cannot tell you,' he wrote on March 16, after reading of her visit to Carson, 'how much I treasure & count on yr aid & counsel. It was hard on you to set such exhausting tasks. You dis-charged them famously.'

On March 17 Churchill received the newspaper reports of the Army debate in which he had so wanted to take part. That night he wrote to his wife:

. . . How different I cd have made it! My conviction strengthens & deepens each day that my place is there, & that I cd fill it with credit & public advantage. Meanwhile however the actual step seems so easy to put off—so irrevocable when taken, that I continue to pause on the brink, not undecided but dilatory.

We are elated to have our little town (nameless) mentioned in Haig's daily report as a scene of artillery activity. The odd thing is that this mention occurs *the day before* the shelling took place! How history is written! . . .

One of the last things our late lamented Brigadier did was to rebuke me by memo for 'undue leniency' in punishments. I was preparing statistics to show that since I have commanded the battalion, offences as well as punishments have sensibly diminished. However this will not be necessary now.

This evening Archie & I took a stroll up the lines on our right & went to the HQrs of the battalion there. The same conditions & features reproduce themselves in every section—shattered buildings, sandbag habitations, trenches heavily wired, shell holes, frequent graveyards with thickets of little crosses, rank wild growing grass, muddy roads, khaki soldiers—& so on for hundreds & hundreds of miles—on both sides. Miserable Europe. Only a few rifle shots & the occasional bang of a gun broke the stillness of the evening. One wondered whether the nations were getting their money's worth out of the brooding armies.

Cd I help to a victorious peace more in H of C than here? That is the sole question. Believe me if my life cd materially aid our fortunes I wd not grudge it.

On March 19 Churchill learned that Colonel Trotter,[1] a friend of earlier years, was to succeed Walshe as Brigadier. Trotter's appointment made it clear, he wrote to his wife, 'that I have no prospects'. His reaction was calm: 'I do not mind this a bit,' he told her. 'If I were to stay out here, I cd hardly be better suited than where I am. A Brigade wd give me no more scope & less personal interest. There is no doubt at all in my mind as to what I ought to do.' But on March 19 Churchill delayed his decision to return in order to let Archibald Sinclair go on leave. He prized his friendship with Sinclair. In reserve the two men had spent many hours each day together trying to solve the Battalion's problems, and reflecting on Churchill's political ones. In the front line they shared the ever-present dangers. On March 19 Churchill wrote to his wife to ask her to look after Sinclair while he was on leave:

I want him to stay at Cromwell & you & Goonie to cherish & nourish him. He is all alone in the world,[2] & very precious as a friend to me. I am telling him to come straight to you on arrival—so get my room ready for him in good time. He will tell you all about our life out here; & my disturbing

---

[1] Gerald Frederick Trotter, 1871–1945. Entered Army, 1885. Major Grenadier Guards, 1914–16. Brigadier-General commanding the 27th Infantry Brigade, 17 March 1916 to 4 July 1916. Commanded 51st Infantry Brigade, July 1916–May 1917 Commanded British Military Mission (Instructional) to the USA, 1917–18. Gentleman Usher to George V, 1919–36.

[2] Sinclair's mother (formerly Miss Mabel Sands of New York) died in November 1890, within a month of his birth; his father (Clarence Granville Sinclair) died in 1895.

moods. In order not to interfere with his much needed rest & change, I have put off once again the hour of decision. It wd have been vy hard on him to cut him from his longed-for holiday. . . . He will arrive about 5 pm on 22nd. I think you had better engage him a temporary servant. . . . You must write me every day. I shall be vy much alone while Archie is away.

Churchill returned to Laurence Farm and the front-line trenches on March 20; his desire to return to politics was clamant. That day he explained his feelings to Garvin, in order to put Garvin's mind at rest about his intentions:

I have not in any way altered my view that I shd return to the H of C as soon as possible. On the contrary reflection makes me more than ever convinced that my duty is there. In principle therefore I am decided. But time & occasion still present difficult questions: for to be useful when I come home I must return under good conditions. Also here the days pass easily away absorbed in exercise & small affairs; and one cannot help being reluctant to terminate finally associations so simple & so honourable. Meanwhile I have written to Carson and shall have time to receive an answer from him.

You shd I think continue as occasion serves to prepare the way for the formation of a stronger opposition, & for an increase in the influence of the H of C. These Army debates for instance seem to me to have been quite lifeless & the armies' needs wh claim attention to have found little or no expression. Also the Naval issue shd not pass out of sight—tho' no doubt some of the work that was required is done.

I will write to you again shortly: meanwhile pray write to me. Do not I beg you suppose that I am incapable of facing the perplexities & risks of the Front Opposition Bench, or that I shall shrink from decision. But I am naturally reluctant to quit this scene (the more so oddly enough that I can do so at any moment) and especially am I anxious when I do return to do so in circumstances wh will be most favourable to my usefulness. The decision is for me alone: but to some extent my friends—none a better friend than you—can create & dispose these circumstances.

Fearing that his friends in London might mistake his wife's cautious attitude for his own, Churchill wrote to her on March 21: 'Be careful not to use arguments or take up an attitude in conflict with my general intention, & do nothing to discourage friends who wish for my return. On the contrary labour as opportunity serves to create favourable circumstances.' Clementine Churchill believed that a sudden return to London would stimulate her husband's critics without encouraging his friends. 'With patience and waiting for the right and good opportunity,' she wrote on March 21, the future 'is all yours'. On the following day she wrote again. C. P. Scott had called to see her, and was, she reported, 'very anxious that your return should not make an unfavourable impression'. While at 41 Cromwell Road, Sinclair had told her that her husband might still get a Brigade somewhere else in the line. '*That* is what I *hope*,' she wrote; and she reiterated C. P. Scott's belief that 'the right opportunity should be waited for'. Churchill was certain that it was futile to wait. He believed that if he returned at once he could still make a forceful impression on Parliament. On March 22 he wrote to his wife, rehearsing the arguments against his return, but then declaring:

. . . I do not think any reason is needed beyond the general reason—wh is the true one—that I think it right to resume political & Parlt duties wh are incompatible with holding a military command. It wd of course be a good thing to have some local reason for a break—such as our division going out of the line, or my being offered promotion; but this advantage must be weighed agst opportunities in England. I cannot decide yet. The broad facts may with confidence be submitted to the public. Let us see what they are.

1. I resigned my office & gave up a salary of £4,300 a year rather than hold a sinecure at this time.

2. I shall have served for nearly five months at the front, almost always in the front line, certainly without discredit—discharging arduous & difficult duties to the full satisfaction of my superiors & to the advantage of my officers & men.

3. I have a recognised position in British politics acquired by years of public work, enabling me to command the attention (at any rate) of my fellow countrymen in a manner not exceeded by more than 3 or 4 living men.

4. The period of our national fortunes is critical & grave: and almost every question both affecting war & peace conditions, with wh I have always been foremostly connected, is now raised. I cannot exclude myself from these discussions or divest myself of responsibilities concerning them.

Surely these facts may stand by themselves as an answer to sneers & cavillings. At any rate I feel I can rest upon them with a sure & easy conscience. Do not my darling one underrate the contribution I have made to the public cause, or the solidarity of a political position acquired by so many years of work & power. Gusts of ill-feeling & newspaper attack sweep by. But public men who really are known by the mass of the nation, do not lose their place in public counsels except for something wh touches their private character & honour. My command of the 6th RSF will certainly not unfavourably affect these general conclusions.

Churchill exaggerated the strength of his position. He did not realize the extent of feeling against him. But even with his belief in his own indispensability, he could not resolve the dilemma of when he should act. 'Next time I come home,' he wrote to his wife on March 23, 'it will be with a set purpose & a clear course, & with no wild & anxious hurry of fleeting moments & uncertain plans.' 'When you do return,' his wife warned on March 24, 'the reason should be apparent to the man in the street, tho' he need not necessarily agree with it.' She believed that it would be damaging to his career 'if it got about that you had returned becos' you were dissatisfied with your prospects of promotion and irked by the smallness of your duties in your present position'. She felt that his resignation speech of the previous November 'did not give the impression that you meant to return home after you had made a sufficient interval between your position as a member of the government and as a member of the opposition'. She received support for her view from Carson, who wrote to Churchill on March 23:

. . . I think myself, speaking quite candidly, that having stated in yr resignation you were going to take up active service in the field it will give lots of grounds for criticism if you come back without some opportunity of showing the grave necessity you feel for such a step —& above all things it wd be so hard for yr causes & usefulness if the country got the impression you acted spasmodically or without sound and deliberate judgement. . . .

Clementine Churchill sent this letter on to her husband on March 24. 'You see how anxious he is,' she wrote, 'that you should not blunt or break yourself as an instrument by a premature return.' Churchill rejected Carson's advice. On March 26, as soon as the letter reached him, he wrote to his wife:

. . . Of course if C chooses he can make my path smooth; but smooth or rough I mean to tread it. I am absolutely sure it is the right thing to do—& all these fears of taunts & criticisms shd be treated as if they were enemy's shells—i.e. they shd not deter one from any action wh is necessary in the general interest. As Furse says 'It is bigger than that'. Have a good confidence & do not easily lend yourself to the estimate formed by those who will never be satisfied till the breath is out of my body. All this dawdling is wrong. Manoeuvering for position is only a minor part of war; a strong army & a good cause & plenty of ammunition drives ahead all right. . . .

Nothing will now turn me from my intention. The more I feel myself cool & indifferent in danger here, the more I feel strong for the work that lies before me. . . . If Carson & his whole committee advised against my return —protested even—still I shd come—& at once.

Not all the advice which Churchill received was opposed to his return. When C. P. Scott wrote on March 24 he expressed none of the reservations which he had expressed to Clementine Churchill two days before. Scott was enthusiastic to see Churchill back in the House of Commons:

> . . . I rejoice that you intend to return shortly & I cannot doubt that, so far as the political opportunity is concerned, the need for your presence is immediate. The Opposition—that is the party of energy & of concentration —is leaderless & waits for you to lead it. Any day may bring great events— the reconstruction of the Ministry, or a military folly or misfortune. . . . People may say what they like about you, as they have said & will say, but as long as you do the right thing with a single eye to the public safety nothing can hurt you. Personally—if it's worth while to speak of so small a matter—I have often found myself in antagonism to you & expect I shall again, but that doesn't prevent me from seeing that you may be able to render a great service to the country & from desiring that, with the least possible delay, you shd take the work in hand. Your place is here, not there. . . .

On March 22 Churchill read in the newspapers of the attack made on the Government's air policy by the newly elected Pemberton Billing. 'Our present position in the air,' Billing had told the House of Commons, 'is one that reflects credit neither on our Government, nor on those officers whose duty it has been to prepare, to look forward, and to endeavour to gain for this country supremacy in the air'; and he demanded the creation of an Air Board which would promote an active and unified air policy. 'Billing's air speech strikes me as vy good,' Churchill wrote to his wife on March 25, '& it must disturb the complacency of the Govt—if anything cd.' But Billing had no political strength: Clementine Churchill saw this at once, and told her husband so.

Churchill was driven forward—his wife exhausted—by this daily barrage of uncertainty and doubt. 'These grave public anxieties are very wearing,' she wrote to him on March 23; 'When next I see you I hope there will be a little time for us both alone. We are still young, but Time flies, stealing love away and leaving only friendship which is very peaceful but not very stimulating or warming.' Churchill, shaken by this sad confession, replied on March 26:

> . . . Oh my darling do not write of 'friendship' to me—I love you more each month that passes and feel the need of you & all your beauty. My precious charming Clemmie—I too feel sometimes the longing for rest & peace.

So much effort, so many years of ceaseless fighting & worry, so much excitement & now this rough fierce life here under the hammer of Thor, makes my older mind turn—for the first time I think to other things than action. Is it 'Forty & finished' as the old devil's Duchess wrote? But wd it not be delicious to go for a few weeks to some lovely spot in Italy or Spain & just paint & wander about together in bright warm sunlight far from the clash of arms or bray of Parliaments? We know each other so well now & cd play better than we ever could.

Sometimes also I think I wd not mind stopping living vy much—I am so devoured by egoism that I wd like to have another soul in another world & meet you in another setting, & pay you all the love & honour of the gt romances. Two days ago I was walking up to the trenches & we heard several shells on our left, each shot coming nearer as the gun travelled round searching for prey. One cd calculate more or less where the next wd come. Our road led naturally past the ruined convent (where I have made the 'conning tower') and I said 'the next will hit the convent'. Sure enough just as we got abreast of it, the shell arrived with a screech and a roar & tremendous bang & showers of bricks & clouds of smoke & all the soldiers jumped & scurried, & peeped up out of their holes & corners. It did not make me jump a bit—not a pulse quickened. I do not mind noise as some vy brave people do. But I felt—20 yards more to the left & no more tangles to unravel, no more anxieties to face, no more hatreds & injustices to encounter: joy of all my foes, relief of that old rogue, a good ending to a chequered life, a final gift—unvalued—to an ungrateful country—an impoverishment of the war-making power of Britain wh no one wd ever know or measure or mourn.

But I am not going to give in or tire at all. I am going on fighting to the vy end in any station open to me from wh I can most effectively drive on this war to victory. If I were somehow persuaded that I was not fit for a wider scope I shd be quite content here—whatever happened. If I am equally persuaded that my worth lies elsewhere I will not be turned from it by any blast of malice or criticism.

During the last week of March, Churchill wrote to several friends in England seeking their advice: to F. E. Smith, to Edward Goulding, to Max Aitken, to Carson again and to Sir George Ritchie, the Chairman of the Dundee Liberal Association. On March 27 he dined with General Lipsett. 'He has gone out of his way to be helpful to me out here,' Churchill wrote to his wife on the following day, 'even coming out with me on a prowl in No-man's-land to see if there were any possibilities to bringing off an enterprise agst the German trenches.' They talked about Churchill's future. 'I was interested,' Churchill reported, 'to hear him repeat almost word for word Carson's opinion.' Lipsett's arguments for delay had impressed him. But he still could not believe they were the right ones. Once more he explained his reasoning to his wife:

> . . . His view is that by waiting a month here a good occasion might be found that wd save 2 or 3 months waiting at home before effective work wd be open to me. 'Of course you ought to go home: but you must get the barbed wire cut first.' Cd not Carson or the Liberal war cte [committee] ask you to come etc! You are familiar with all this. Do not suppose I do not feel the force of it. But what if these good conditions cannot be obtained while I remain out of touch—with all my means of action & communication paralysed? Frankly I do not think any really responsible or influential body of MP's are likely to take the responsibility of inviting me to return, without knowing what I mean to do or say. And on the other hand if I wait for a Ministerial crisis, will it not look as if I had come back like a sultan hastening unbidden to a feast. Whereas in spite of all the crabbing abuse wh has always beset me, I cd undoubtedly from the box at Westminster, exercise an influence & command attention to matters of vital urgency & import, wh wd in itself justify retrospectively the step I had taken. Nothing cd I think deprive me of my hold on the public attention. Even a controversy about whether I shd or shd not have come home wd only increase the interest in what I said: and the need for justice & Parly expression is so great & widely felt & so real & so recurring that everything will come right. Therefore if, as I expect, it will not be possible to get the barbed wire cut beforehand, I shall nevertheless try to make my way through it. . . .

This was Churchill's last confident assertion that he could brave the difficulties of a return to politics alone. There now arrived from England several letters which made it absolutely clear that if he came back too soon his position would not only be weak but hopeless. On April 3 he received Sir George Ritchie's assessment of Dundee opinion, written on March 28. Churchill could not ignore the views of a man so close to political realities in the constituency upon whose votes he depended. Ritchie stressed bluntly that many of his constituency supporters regarded the Fisher speech as 'unfortunate'. Dundee opinion, he wrote, was 'quite solid that nothing should be done to cause division'; indeed, 'no movement which would endanger the unity of the Country or the stability of the present Government would have the slightest chance of success'. Ritchie felt that if Churchill opposed Asquith publicly, it would 'put a weapon into the hands of your Enemies who would hurl the charge of instability at you and use it for all it was worth to thwart your advancement'.

Churchill was influenced by Ritchie's letter. He knew that it was based upon careful inquiries and genuine goodwill. 'It makes a serious impression upon me,' he wrote to his wife on April 3. She tried to re-inforce Ritchie's advice, sending her husband a letter which Garvin had sent her on March 28, and which argued against precipitate action. Garvin had written:

... no instant conquests are to be looked for. The less they seem to be sought—when so many enemies are on the qui vive to impute feverish ambition—the sooner they will come. Something like a definite programme of the course to be pursued should be mapped out and adhered to. Then the occasions will lend their aid.

It would be well worth Winston's while to spend a month after leaving the army before reappearing in the House. That would put him back again on the old basis of thorough mental preparation which is his strength; and to the deliberation would attach the sense of power.

If he comes back to play a rather lone hand for a few months, he owes it to himself that people should not be *too* certain of what he is going to say and that his criticisms should have measured power by recognising where the Government have done well, or rather less ill, in some respects than in others. As I am never tired of saying, to be obstructive one must be just. It's abso-lutely true. So much for 'the lone hand' which in a few months would make him much sought after by several sections.

Garvin speculated on the possibility of Churchill joining with Carson, or alternatively of waiting for the possibility of an autumn Election. He continued:

Above all, no hurry. Too much is at stake for the whole of after-life. A month after coming home to study the whole situation, to see people and things as it were from the outside, to make sure of what ground is firm under foot before the quiet vibrating decisive intervention begins. I have *no fear* for the ultimate result: at the worst adversity for six months, a year, two years! What does that matter to the only man of high political rank who has the priceless advantage of being only 41.

Garvin echoed Clementine Churchill's concern for the man himself, for his reputation and for his personal position. Churchill understood such concern. But he was consumed by the desire to return at once to active political life, believing that this could not harm his reputation.

Garvin had ended his letter with an immediate suggestion: 'I believe Northcliffe would take for the Times a series of articles on the "needs of the army", done as Winston could do them.' Churchill was excited by this idea. Because neither of Northcliffe's main daily newspapers, *The*

Times and the *Daily Mail,* were sympathetic to Churchill, he moved cautiously, enlisting the support of Northcliffe's brother, Lord Rother-mere, who encouraged him to follow up Garvin's suggestion. On April 3 Churchill sent his wife a letter for Northcliffe which he asked her to send on once she had read it: 'It can only do good or do nothing,' he told her. But she did not like it, and explained why. 'If it goes,' she warned him on April 6, 'it will form part of your biography in after times and after the way Lord N has flouted you I cannot bear that you should write to him in that vein. Besides I do not think it is as well-expressed as some of your letters. I am sure it is no use writing private letters to great journalists—Even if they do, in consequence decide to run you, they feel patronizing and protective about it and the support then lacks in genuine ardour.' Clementine Churchill realized, on read-ing his letter to Northcliffe, that her husband did not intend to remain at the front much longer. In her own letter she tried to explain her feelings:

My Darling own Dear Winston I am so torn and lacerated over you. If I say 'stay where you are' a wicked bullet may find you which you might but for me escape. . . .

If I were sure that you would come thro' unscathed I would say: 'wait wait have patience, don't pluck the fruit before it is ripe. Everything will come to you if you don't snatch at it.' To be great one's actions must be able to be understood by simple people. Your motive for going to the Front was easy to understand. Your motive for coming back requires explanation.

That is why your Fisher speech was not a success—people could not understand it. It required another speech to make it clear. . . .

Darling don't be vexed with me for writing so crudely. If to help you or make you great or happy I could give up my life it would be easy for me to do it.

Clementine Churchill knew how much her husband was the victim of depression. She had seen him depressed to the point of resignation after his return from Antwerp. She had seen depression settle upon him after his removal from the Admiralty. She had watched while the obsession with Gallipoli threatened to cloud his judgement and alienate his colleagues. In her letter of April 6 she warned him of the danger that if he returned too soon from the trenches, and failed to obtain political office, he risked embittering himself yet again. She was afraid that this time he would not be able to shake off the brooding and the introspec-tion, but that, as she wrote bluntly, he would 'rehearse all the past events over and over again and gradually live in the past instead of in the present and in the great future'.

Clementine Churchill continued to send her husband warnings against too swift a return. She feared that his hatred of Government inaction was an insufficient reason, and might appear to many purely opportunistic. She felt that his isolation in Flanders had led him to exaggerate the public need for his return. Nor did she share his optimism at the effect of Billing's challenge. 'Mr Pemberton Billing does not make headway,' she had written to him on March 29 'tho' I agree with you in thinking his speech good. The newspapers are chary of taking him up. People seem to think he has an axe to grind (being an unsuccessful aeroplane constructor) and so he is suspect. I am afraid he is rather a flashy young man. . . . I really don't think he has harmed the Govt one bit. It needs something far more stern and weighty. He is just out to make people's flesh creep!' But Churchill could not bear to be deflected from his path. 'How completely out of action I am!' he wrote to his wife on March 30. 'How wasted all my knowledge, training, life, energy! Believe me I do all that I can do here usefully. But it wd be folly to continue—now that I see clearly another field opening out.' Clementine Churchill recognized the intensity of his feelings. 'His intention of coming home,' she wrote in her reply to Garvin on March 29, 'is gradually hardening and becoming definite. In fact he has now ceased to discuss the pros and cons. The remaining difficulty with him is the time for taking the step. . . . He may return quite suddenly.'

April 1 was Clementine Churchill's birthday. She was thirty-one; but, she wrote to him, if victory were imminent and he both safe and content, she would feel no older than twenty. But contentment was impossible for him. That same day Sir Arthur Markham, one of his few Parliamentary supporters, wrote urging him to return at once:

My dear Churchill,

You have doubtless many friends & advisers urging you to take a certain decision either to remain in France or return. I will add one more word if I may, though I do not suppose it will influence your decision. I am quite clear your duty is in the House of Commons & that you can do more effective work there for your country than commanding a regiment. No one doubts your courage & that any decision you arrive at will not be influenced by public opinion. To be candid your reply to Balfour was unfortunate, you would have done better to have left him alone or to have remained here pursuing the course you had taken to its logical end; at all events this view is held by most people. All that I want is to see effective opposition for the good of the country. Carson certainly is in better health but if you returned you could both with your voice & pen render I am convinced better service to the country than by remaining in France. The govt drift day by day indecision being their key note, & our poor country has bad days ahead. You ought to be the vigilant watch dog to urge them to make war. I would rather see a multitude of mistakes where we had the initiative than we always should let the Germans have the same. The man who makes no mistakes never makes anything; we all make mistakes. Come back; those who want you, will help you to fight your battle in the House.

Best of wishes, Yrs sincerely
Arthur B. Markham

'My mind is unchanged about returning,' Churchill wrote to his mother on April 3; 'It is only a question of how & when. I expect to decide vy soon now. . . . I will let you know when I come to any decision. Meanwhile try to get hold of Donald of the Daily Chronicle & without telling him my plans try to make him friendly & well-disposed. After all he is a Fisherite—so he ought to be pleased.' 'How & when', he could not decide. 'I am still waiting to hear further from Carson,' he wrote to his wife on April 6, '& I suppose he is still waiting to see how the situation develops.' Later that day he wrote to her again, for he had heard from F. E. Smith of further grumblings in the Cabinet about conscription. 'Try to keep in touch with LG,' he asked her, '& with BL through Max. I don't expect myself that this will come to anything. A [Asquith] will toe the line about compulsion when he sees they mean to have it. He delays these things in order to be able to give them away at the last minute. But I am not in any hurry now, & will certainly "wait & see".'

Throughout April Churchill tried to discover what issues would threaten to bring Asquith's Government down, who were the politicians willing to exploit them, and whether they would be willing to let him work with them, and join them in any new administration. He believed that his principal hope lay in Lloyd George's defection. '*Keep in touch with LG*,' he begged his wife on April 7. It was over the growing demand for conscription that a serious crisis was most likely to arise. Churchill believed that the Tories, led by Bonar Law, Curzon and Lansdowne, might leave the Coalition if Asquith refused to introduce conscription immediately. 'A vy big situation wd be open then,' he told his wife, 'but I am by no means certain how it would affect me.' On April 3 he had written to Curzon to encourage a firm line over conscription. 'Surely there is only one course now with regard to the married man,' he wrote, '—universal compulsion with necessary exemptions. I hope you are pressing this.' Churchill asked Curzon for 'one of your promised letters'; but it never came.

Churchill had great faith that F. E. Smith would represent his interests in London, writing to him on April 6: 'Keep in touch with LG . . . keep him up to the mark about me.' Two days later he wrote again, realizing how much he depended upon F. E. Smith for the successful advocacy of his cause. He was convinced that if Asquith's Government fell, its successor would have need of him. He also believed that the help which he had given Lloyd George during the Marconi affair in 1913 had put Lloyd George politically in his debt. His letter to F. E. Smith of April 8 was frank; so much so that he wanted it burnt, writing:

. . . Generally speaking LG is the key to my position at the moment. However a new system might be formed, it seems to me that LG and I shd be together. If he came in to what must be in substance a Tory Administration, he wd need above all Liberal associates. I think you shd get hold of Rufus [Lord Reading] betimes and put to him vy plainly the personal obligation wh exists. He has always recognised it, and wd have gt weight on that point in that quarter.

I have a feeling that BL and LG have a supreme chance now, if they have the resolution to act. It does not seem to me material whether BL is first or LG War or *vice versa*. Either place wd afford the basis of an effective war organisation—compared to wh nothing matters. Munitions will seem to be the easiest opening for me, tho' of course you know my wishes, if they are attainable.

The party of the future might be formed. I am sorry the crisis comes now— if it does: but in that case it is to you I must look and do look with entire confidence that you will set my affairs first in yr thoughts. Burn this wh is for your secret eye alone.

At a time when Churchill most needed a platform, he had to abandon his plan to write for the Northcliffe press. 'I have heard from Goulding, who I got to sound Northcliffe through a discreet channel,' he wrote to his wife on April 9, 'that the latter was vy hostile to the plan. This wd be serious.' 'The opportunity wh existed after the Navy Row has passed,' he added; 'I think I missed a chance through indecision.' But a new opportunity presented itself unexpectedly on April 10, when Churchill received a letter from Carson, written four days earlier, no longer trying to keep him at arm's length:

. . . I think myself things are coming to a crisis here over the question of universal military service, and my Committee, which is growing very strong, is determined that we should raise the question on a definite motion before Easter, and are indeed growing very dissatisfied with the way everything is drifting. It might be worth your while to consider, when a day is fixed for this, whether it would not be your duty to come over, but you will see how things develop in that direction within the next few days. I am not so sure myself that it will be possible for the present Coalition Government to continue its existence as at present, but I will write to you again if there is any information that I think may guide your judgment.

Fired by Carson's change of mood, Churchill wrote immediately to Lloyd George, to discover if his discontent over the repeated delays to bring in conscription had reached the point of breaking with Asquith:

Secret

My dear David,

It seems to me from what I hear that the situation we had in view before the Derby efforts, & again at Christmas is now again maturing. A decision on the recruiting question is now vital, & the repeated postponements cannot surely be tolerated longer. I think that Asquith will probably give way again at the last moment and thus the crisis will be averted for the time. But if not the moment for you to act has come. We are jeopardizing our chances of winning by a continuance of a Governing instrument wh never acts except upon political expediency, wh never initiates anything, & wh utterly fails to do justice to the resolution & spirit of the country. You have let several good chances go by in hope of a better. I cannot judge events & forces vy thoroughly from here, but I am inclined to think that this is the best opportunity that has yet offered: & that unless a decision to adopt universal compulsion is taken forthwith you ought to resign. The party of the future might then be formed: & in that party we shd be strong enough to secure those special political interests & principles with wh we have been identified after the war is over, as well as driving the war forward with the utmost vigour.

I intend vy shortly to return to the House and I am only delaying from day to day on account of small ties out here wh are being adjusted. I am not however in any hurry & wd much rather return on general grounds at my leisure than on the eve of a crisis. I hold the PM's written promise I shall be relieved whenever I wish. Events however may force my hand. . . .

I shd like vy much to hear from you as soon as you feel able to write freely, & no doubt you can find a safe hand to carry your letter. On the whole I believe our interests are likely to lie together in the near future as they have done so often in the past, & certainly we have a common object wh overrides all others.

Yours vy sincly
Winston S. Churchill

Hoping to secure the support of the Liberal Press for a new alignment in which he would have a part, Churchill also wrote on April 10 to C. P. Scott:

My dear Scott,
   . . . The possibilities of a change in the character & leadership of the Government make me anxious to interchange thoughts with you upon the general & ultimate consequences of such an event. My feeling is that everything that may be necessary to win the war shd be done apart altogether from political peace time opinions: but that it must also be an honourable understanding that after the war our Liberal position on all these questions must be in no way prejudiced, save in so far as the world is changing round us. We have the gt causes of the harmony of the European family of nations, of the rights of nationalities including Ireland, & of a sound & peace tending economic system to safeguard, and we shall need to stand together to discharge these obligations well. Do not let us therefore worry about anything that we may feel necessary to be done now—so long as it is temporary & emergency in its nature. On the other hand we must be strong enough in any new arrangement to secure respect for these enduring interests. You have a considerable part to play at this juncture. See Carson: see Cawley: see also Lloyd George. Show the last if you will this letter.
   The numbing hand of Asquith is over everything, and all initiative & energy seem paralysed. All the time however our money (which is not limitless) and life & limb are being consumed on a cruel scale. If they cd see themselves the actual spectacles they wd perhaps sense themselves. . . .
   Try now with your influence to knit together the forces that may best serve us in the present catastrophe, and preserve our political conceptions, after we have weathered the storm.

Yours vy sincerely
Winston S. Churchill

On April 12 Clementine Churchill begged her husband to change his mind about returning. She did not share his belief in the imminence of a crisis, nor of the ability of Carson, Lloyd George or C. P. Scott to assuage the enmities which her husband had created both as First Lord, and by his continual criticism of Coalition lethargy:

   . . . You say in your letter to me: 'You are deluded if you think that by remaining here and doing nothing, I shall regain my influence on affairs.' That is not what I do think.
   What I do think is that remaining there you are in an honourable, *comprehensible* position until such time as a portion at least of the country demand your services for the state. If you come back before the call you may blunt yourself. People will always try to deny you power if they think you are looking for it. To gain a share of war direction you are contemplating a

terrible risk, the risk of life-long disappointment and bitterness. My Darling Love—For *once only* I pray be patient. It will come if you wait. Don't tear off the unripe fruit which is maturing tho' slowly or check its growth by the frost of a premature return.

I could not bear you to lose your military halo. I have had cause during the 8 years we have lived together to be proud and glad for you so often, but it is this I cherish most of all. And it is this phase which when all is known will strike the imagination of the people: The man who prepared and mobilized the Fleet, who really won the war for England—in the trenches as a simple Colonel. It would be a great romance.

You say you want to be where you can help the war most. If you come home and your return is not generally accepted as correct soldier-like conduct you will not be really able to help the war. You *are* helping it now by example. You are always an interesting figure, be a great one my Darling. You have the opportunity. . . .

Do not be alienated from me by what I write. If I hide what I feel from you the constraint would be unbearable.

Churchill could not take his wife's advice. 'Well,' he replied on April 15 from Laurence Farm, 'there is no use going over the old ground again, nor in darkening this page with my reflections.'

Churchill was not deflected by the weakness of his position. He was determined to return to the centre of policy-making. His feelings about the war intensified during April, strengthening this determination. The prolonged bloothbath of Verdun seemed, he had written to F. E. Smith on April 6, 'to vindicate all I have ever said or written about the offensives by either side in the West.'[1] On April 14 he wrote to his wife setting out the 'definite opinions' he had formed about the war:

First we must now make up our minds that there is no chance of our winning in 1916. That is the beginning of wisdom—we must make our plans for a combined attack in the summer of 1917: & meanwhile only bicker on all the fronts, while improving our armies, piling up munitions and arming the limitless manhood of Russia. Let the Germans attack if they will. Above all no premature offensive by France, or still more by England alone.

My advice wd therefore be with variation the same as last year. No offensive in the West, destroy Turkey. That is all we have the strength to do this year. Next year victory may be won.

[1] The Germans launched an attack on the French fortress of Verdun on 21 February 1916. After four months of intense fighting and artillery bombardment, 650,000 French and German soldiers had been killed, but Verdun remained in French hands. In his book *Verdun*, published in 1930, General Pétain wrote of the young French soldiers returning from the fortress: 'In their unsteady look one sensed visions of horror, while their step and bearing revealed utter despondency. They were crushed by horrifying memories.'

Unhappily I expect the exact opposite of all this will be done: and we shall end the year after bitter losses no further forward than we are today.

I greatly fear the general result. More than I have ever done before, I realize the stupendous nature of the task; & the unwisdom with wh our affairs are conducted makes me almost despair at times of a victorious issue. The same leadership that has waited on public opinion & newspaper promptings for so long, will readily be the exponent of an inclusive peace—if that mood is upward in the nation.

Do you think we should succeed in an offensive, if the Germans cannot do it at Verdun with all their skill & science? Our army is not the same as theirs; and of course their staff is quite intact & taught by successful experiment. Our staff only represents the brain power of our poor little peacetime army—with wh hardly any really able men wd go. We are children at the game compared to them. And in this day to day trench warfare—they lose half what we do in my opinion. On the sea the submarine menace is by no means at an end. Balfour's easy & airy slumbers have after 11 months left us in a worse position than before. Then the danger was new & unfamiliar. I see a lot of ships sunk each day, & they no longer publish any weekly summaries: but far more than in our time. Yet think of the advantage they have over us in resources. Yet no one complains.

You know how often I have been right about this war. I feel now that only a supreme effort of patience, & wisdom, with furious energy straining at the leash will save our cause. Alas I am powerless even to utter my warnings.

Asquith was finding it increasingly difficult to retain the loyalty of his ministers. On April 13 Lloyd George and C. P. Scott had tea with Sir George Riddell. According to Riddell's *War Diary* Lloyd George spoke bitterly against the Coalition. 'There is no grip,' he asserted; 'Asquith and Balfour do not seem to realize the serious nature of the situation.' Lloyd George declared that he might resign and praised Carson for 'managing his little group with great skill'. The discontent mounted. On April 18 Lord Milner appealed in the House of Lords for compulsory military service. He was supported by Lord Morley, who had resigned on the eve of war in protest against British involvement, by Lord Charles Beresford, and by Lord Derby, whose voluntary recruiting scheme Asquith had tried to use as an alternative to compulsion. On April 20 Sir Henry Wilson wrote to Milner: 'If ever a man deserved to be tried and shot that man is the PM. . . . We hope that you and Carson and LG have, at last, got him by the throat. No mercy please.' That same day Asquith offered to explain his recruiting policy to Parliament. But he insisted that his explanation must take place at a Secret Session.

As soon as Lord Milner emerged as a focal point of dissent, Churchill's chances of being called upon faded considerably. Ten years had passed since he had publicly and savagely attacked Milner's conduct of affairs in South Africa. But time could not heal all wounds, and these were deep ones. Milner refused to forgive Churchill for what had passed. Carson tried to act as an intermediary, but in vain. Nor did Churchill receive sufficiently full accounts of how the various centres of dissent were grouping to appreciate their objectives or gauge the part he might play. Until March he had appeared to the dissenters a possible and indeed valuable ally, articulate and persuasive; since his Fisher speech many critics of the Government saw him as a dangerous companion, erratic and unpredictable. Clementine Churchill sensed this new hostility. After a dinner party at 10 Downing Street in the second week of April she talked to Lord Reading. 'He fears your coming back unless sent for would be injurious to your reputation,' she wrote on April 14. There were other Ministers at the dinner. 'Grey terribly aged and worn-looking,' she wrote, 'Kitchener thinner and sad. AJB wan and white, but still purring away.' As for the conscription crisis, Asquith 'seems quite unconcerned. . . . He is like morphia.'

On April 15 Churchill wrote to his wife from Laurence Farm that General Furse, his Divisional General, was coming to dine with him. Many Generals had become disillusioned with the Coalition. 'His only relaxation,' Churchill wrote of Furse, 'is to wish for the downfall of Asquith who he thinks is the cause of all our evils.' Churchill told his wife of his own state of mind: 'when I am not consumed with inward fury at the damnable twists wh I have been served with and chewing black charcoal with all my might, I am buoyant & lively . . .'.

On April 18 Churchill learned of the Secret Session, and decided to seek leave to return to London. This he was granted; but he had to promise to return to his Battalion the moment the debate was over. He reached London on April 19. On April 20 Sinclair wrote encouragingly from Ploegsteert: 'Good luck to you Samson, and if you find your strength has returned, stay where you can most effectively contribute to the damnation of the Philistine.' On reaching London Churchill received a letter dated April 16 from C. P. Scott, replying to his own letter of April 10 and informing him that Lloyd George was on the verge of resignation. Upon this belief Scott had based a plan in which Churchill had a leading part. Lloyd George's departure, Scott believed:

. . . will be the beginning of a new chapter in the history of the war & of our politics. At once, with him & Carson outside the Govment there will be the beginnings of a real Opposition. You will, I take for granted, join them—as soon, I hope, as Parliament meets after the Easter recess—and together you will be formidable & all the more independent and energetic elements in the House will by degrees rally round you. The effect on the Govment will be immediate & in the long run decisive—A real reconstruction will for the first time become possible—one which shall be not merely a re-shuffling of the old elements with the old palsied spirit still pervading, it, but one in the construction of which those at present outside it will have had the chief voice & on which they will be able to impose a new policy—— That is an occasion surely large enough & hopeful enough to recall you to your true place—I desire your return the more because I agree so deeply with the general policy outlined in your letter. There will be those in any combination, old or new, who will be opposed to some of its main ideas & who will be prepared to substitute a tariff war for a war of armies &, so far as in them lies, to divide Europe into two permanently hostile camps—That way lies the destruction & death & the ruin of all our hopes for the future of our country & of the world. Anything rather than that, & if there is to be union it must be a union on terms & in the hope & resolve of a better England which, even during the war, we may join to build up. This part of your letter I read to Lloyd George today & he cordially concurred in the policy expressed. On that basis we can join hands. . . .

Churchill was excited by Scott's plan. He saw Lloyd George, who discussed the possibility of resigning, and of their common action. But in the third week of April, determined to preserve his Coalition, Asquith bowed to the Cabinet's pressure and agreed to an extension of compulsion. Lloyd George had therefore no cause to resign. Scott's hopes for a 'real Opposition' were destroyed. 'Churchill is very sick at the idea of the thing going through quietly,' Frances Stevenson noted in her diary on April 19. 'He is all for a split, and for the forming of a vigorous opposition, in which he would take an active part.' Churchill found himself, not an engineer of Asquith's most serious parliamentary challenge of the war, but a spectator of events which could not bring him advantage. He decided, however, to seek further release from his military duties, and asked for an extra two weeks leave to follow on immediately from the Secret Session. Haig sent a message to say that he had no objection; his Deputy Military Secretary, Major Vesey,[1] wrote enthusiastically to Churchill on April 23: 'Good luck to you in your

[1] Ivo Lucius Beresford Vesey, 1876–   . 2nd Lieutenant, 1897. Major, War Office 1914–15; GHQ France, 1915–16. Director of Recruiting and Organization, War Office, 1919–23. Knighted, 1923. Director of Organization and Staff Duties, Air Ministry, 1923–9. Major-General, 1928. Director of Staff Duties, War Office, 1931–34. General, 1937. Chief of General Staff, India, 1937–9.

work during the next few weeks. I am sure you can do a good deal at home for the Cause.'

No record survives of what was said during the Secret Session of April 25. 'If only your speech had been reported,' Clementine Churchill wrote three days later, 'I feel the Press would urge your recall.' But secrecy, as Asquith realized, acted to the Government's advantage. The Press was necessarily silent, and the public never found out who had spoken, or to what purpose.

On April 27 Parliament met in open session. This was the moment of public confrontation. To his extreme anger, Churchill could not be there. That morning he had received a telegram from Brigadier-General Trotter informing him that General Furse 'does not sanction extension while you are commanding 6 R Scots Fus and your battalion is in trenches'. Churchill returned at once to Ploegsteert. 'It is such a waste having him in a dugout,' Jack Churchill wrote to Lady Randolph that night, 'and it reflects very much on the jealous fools who keep him there. . . .' The debate on conscription took place in Churchill's absence; he could neither influence it, nor gain advantage from it. On April 27 the Government introduced a Bill for a further extension of partial military service. Carson rose as the leader of the opposition and was so successful in demanding a more comprehensive measure that Asquith abandoned the Bill. Five days later the Government accepted the principle of full compulsory service. On May 3 a new Bill was introduced in the House of Commons, making all men between the ages of eighteen and forty-one subject to compulsory enlistment. For fear of civil unrest, Ireland was excluded. On May 25 the Bill received Royal assent. The compulsionists had won. Carson was triumphant. But Asquith remained Prime Minister.

Clementine Churchill was angry that her husband had been recalled so abruptly and unexpectedly to the front. Despite her strong pleas for him not to return prematurely, she now recognized the tremendous opportunity which joint opposition with Carson offered him. 'If only you had been here yesterday & spoken,' she wrote to him on April 28. Her disillusionment with Asquith was complete: 'The Government are in a shameful position,' she wrote. Churchill did not fret. He had made up his mind to leave the Army altogether, convinced that another opportunity for opposition would soon present itself. Plans were being discussed at GHQ to amalgamate the 6th Battalion of the Royal Scots Fusiliers with the 7th Battalion, as there were no longer enough men in either to form two effective fighting units. The amalgamated force was likely to be commanded by the Colonel of the 7th Battalion, Lieutenant-

Colonel Gordon,[1] a regular officer, so that Churchill had no immediate prospect of further front-line employment. Hakewill Smith later wrote to the author that at about this time Churchill had gone to St Omer to see Sir Douglas Haig. On his return he had told the officers of his Headquarters Staff 'that Haig had offered him command of a Brigade; but had said that he could do much more for the war effort by returning to Parliament and using his energy and skill to get conscription through the House. Winston added that he had seen the force of Haig's arguments and had reluctantly agreed to return to England.'

The amalgamation of the Battalions seemed to Churchill an ideal opportunity to quit the trenches. On April 29 he wrote to his wife from Laurence Farm: 'The military were pleased & placated by my return. It is probable that the battalion will be broken up within 10 days, & that we shall not return to the trenches after we leave them on Wednesday morning.' In his postscript Churchill asked his wife to 'explain the position' to Carson, Garvin and Scott, on whom his political hopes centred increasingly. Lloyd George remained in the Cabinet, gaining in power and confidence; he had no need of Churchill's support.

Churchill waited impatiently for confirmation that his Battalion was to be dissolved. 'The Government is moribund,' he wrote to his wife on May 1. 'I only trust they will not die too soon.' Clementine Churchill had become equally impatient for a decision. 'Let me hear that you are coming home for *good* to take up your *real* work,' she wrote from Blenheim Palace on April 30. She was now an active partisan of his swift return. On May 2 Churchill sent her his final letter from Laurence Farm. With his hopes for a rapid return to politics fulfilled, his fretfulness was gone, and he was willing to contemplate relaxation. 'Wd it not be vy nice to go to Blenheim for the Sunday,' he wrote: 'If you arrange this, please get me 3 large tubes of *thin* white (not stiff) . . . also 3 more canvasses: and a bottle of that poisonous solution wh cleans the paint off old canvasses.'

The time had come for Churchill to leave his Battalion. On May 3 he and his men moved out of Ploegsteert, where they had served for more than four months. Dry billets were found a few miles behind the lines. On May 6 Churchill wrote formally to his Corps Commander, Sir Charles Fergusson: 'I do not seek a new appointment at the present time. I desire to attend to my Parliamentary & public duties which

[1] Edward Ian Drumearn Gordon, 1877–1942. 2nd Lieutenant, Royal Scots Fusiliers, 1899. Major, January 1915. Lieutenant-Colonel commanding, 6th/7th Battalion, Royal Scots Fusiliers, June 1916–January 1918; 1st Battalion, January–July 1918. Retired, 1919.

have become urgent. I request therefore that I may be permitted to proceed to England on leave as soon as my command is broken up & that I may await further orders there.' Churchill's request was granted.

During his final days with the 6th Royal Scots Fusiliers Churchill made every effort to help those whose future was uncertain as a result of the Battalion's amalgamation. 'He took endless trouble,' Captain Gibb recorded: 'he borrowed motor-cars and *scoured* France, interviewing Generals and Staff-officers great and small, in the effort to do something to help those who had served under him. Needless to say, the orderly-room was seething with applications of all sorts, possible and impossible, but he treated them all with the utmost patience and good humour.' On May 6 Churchill gave his officers a farewell lunch in Armentières. That afternoon the Battalion entrained for Bethune, and for a rest in reserve, out of the war zone. On May 7 General Furse sent Churchill a note of farewell. 'It seems to me peculiarly up to you and to Lloyd George,' he wrote, 'to concentrate all your efforts on breaking such a futile Govt—and that, immediately. How can anyone suppose that the same men in the same large flat bottomed tub can do any better in the future than they have done in the past? . . . I wish you the best of luck in a task of enormous difficulty and honour.' On the morning of May 7 the Battalion was inspected by Major-General McCracken,[1] the officer commanding the 15th Division to which it was to be transferred. At two that afternoon Churchill summoned his officers to the Orderly Room. 'He told us,' Gibb recalled, 'that he had come to regard the young Scot as a most "formidable fighting animal", and he touched on his other connections with Scotland in the most appreciative fashion. As he rose to shake hands, the Adjutant spoke up and told him what we were all thinking, and what it had been to us to serve under him. . . . I believe every man in the room felt Winston Churchill's leaving us a real personal loss.'

[1] Frederick William Nicholas McCracken, 1859–1949. 2nd Lieutenant, 1879. Major-General, 1914. Inspector of Infantry, December 1914–March 1915. Commanded 15th Scottish Division, March 1915–June 1917. Knighted, 1917. Lieutenant-General commanding Scottish Command, 1918–19.

25

'I am learning to hate'

CHURCHILL's return to London in May 1916 was marked by no upsurge in his political fortunes. Asquith, by accepting compulsory service, had prevented the conscriptionists from destroying the Coalition. Lloyd George, with whom Churchill had hoped to form the nucleus of an opposition, remained in the Cabinet. Of the dissident Tories, Lord Milner still refused to be reconciled to Churchill, and Carson's opposition had been temporarily weakened by Asquith's conscription success. As for Lord Fisher, everyone whom Churchill met spoke disparagingly of the old Admiral, and there seemed no future in a Fisher–Churchill alliance.

Having chosen to resume his Parliamentary duties, Churchill had every intention of speaking as soon as possible, although his wife advised him to bide his time. On May 9, only two days after his return, he spoke in the Commons for the first time since the Secret Session; and for the first time publicly since his Fisher speech. The issue was a serious one, but the occasion unsuited to a major assault on Government policy. In April 1916, the Easter Rising in Dublin had been suppressed by armed force; Asquith therefore decided that, given the excited state of Irish feeling, Ireland should be excluded from compulsory service. A clause was inserted into the Military Service Bill which allowed Ireland to keep the system of voluntary recruitment. Asquith gave the House of Commons only a brief time to debate the Bill, and the Irish exclusion clause received little attention. But Carson, as the champion of Ulster, spoke against special privileges designed to placate the southern catholics, and Churchill, fearing that a shortage of men would create grave danger for the Allies, spoke likewise against the Irish clause. Both he and Carson knew that they could not change Government policy. But, like Carson, Churchill wanted to make his protest known. 'It is a time when men are urgently needed,' he told the House of

Commons, 'and from the British and Imperial point of view the desirability of obtaining fresh and extended supplies from Ireland is clear and patent to the minds of everyone.' Churchill's experience of trench warfare had convinced him of the paramount need for more men. 'This is a time for trying to overcome difficulties,' he insisted, 'and not for being discouraged or too readily deterred by them.' At that moment there was an interruption. An Irish Nationalist MP, Laurence Ginnell,[1] cried out in anger: 'What about the Dardanelles?'

Here was the challenge which would recur month by month and year by year, never to be shaken off. Suddenly Churchill realized that well-argued speeches on subjects about which he felt strongly were not enough to re-establish his political position. He needed to clear his name of a crippling charge. The conscription debate continued. Churchill could not interrupt his speech in order to discuss the Dardanelles. No clever repartee, no brief digression, could answer the allegations which had been built up against him. He knew that it would need a searching enquiry to make the facts known. All he could reply to Ginnell's outburst, almost all he could ever say unless the Government agreed to publish the facts, was a lame: 'I am afraid I should be out of order if I were to deal with that matter.' He continued with his speech. Ireland was the subject, of Ireland he must talk. But the cry, 'What about the Dardanelles?' echoed about the Chamber like a widow's curse.

During Churchill's first week back in London Fisher sent him a letter of welcome. 'This moment I've seen in the paper you are back,' he wrote on May 10; '*Welcome home* for *good I hope!*' A year had passed since Fisher's resignation. 'My dear Fisher,' Churchill replied affectionately on May 14, 'This accursed year has now come to an end, & please God there will be better luck for you & me in the next, & some chance of helping our country to save itself & all dependent on it. Don't lose heart—I am convinced destiny has not done with you yet. Yours ever W.' Fisher replied that day: 'A Big Change is imminent but will it be in time?' He was wrong; no change in Asquith's strength was either imminent or likely. The only organized Parliamentary opposition group, the Unionist War Committee led by Carson, did not feel itself strong enough to divide the House.

[1] Laurence Ginnell, 1854–1923. A Barrister. Nationalist MP, 1906–18. One of the founders of the London Irish Literary Society.

On May 17 Churchill rose again to speak from the opposition benches, this time about an Air Department which the Government had agreed to establish. A Conservative MP, William Joynson-Hicks[1] had brought in a motion calling upon the Government to take without delay 'every possible step to make adequate provision for a powerful Air Service'. Churchill believed that he himself could revitalize the Air Service, enthuse the pilots, and give their frail craft mastery of the air. He had watched with anger the growing German air superiority above his own trenches at Ploegsteert. He listened with apprehension to the Government's plans, which were outlined in the Commons by the Under-Secretary of State for War, Harold Tennant, who explained that an Air Board would be set up, with powers to co-ordinate the air policy of the Admiralty and War Office. Tennant added that Asquith had invited Lord Curzon to accept the presidency of the Board, and that Curzon had accepted. Churchill was dissatisfied with what Tennant had outlined as the Air Board's functions and powers. 'The House will have heard with some feelings of disappointment,' he said, 'the announcement of my right hon Friend of the change which is proposed by the Government. After the many months that this matter has been under discussion, and the repeated postponements in bringing it before the House, we had hoped that a real solution, or a real effort towards a solution, would have been set forth in the Government statement.' Churchill did not criticize the choice of Curzon as President, although many of his listeners knew how much he himself had hoped to be offered the post. He criticized, not the man but the nature of his task. 'Lord Curzon, without adequate powers, will not succeed in altering the present state of affairs,' he declared, 'and in the choice of a policy, judging by the impression made upon me by the statement to which we have just listened, the Government have followed no principle whatever, except the familiar principle of postponing until the last possible moment and then following the line of least resistance.'

Churchill felt the need to defend his own record in the matter of air defence. Without defending each of his Admiralty policies which had been under attack, he could not see how he would ever again be accepted as a serious contender for high office. He believed that the aerial successes won while he was at the Admiralty had been based upon policies which his successor, A. J. Balfour, had subsequently

---

[1] William Joynson-Hicks, 1865–1932. Known as 'Jix'. Churchill's successful opponent at the by-election in North-West Manchester, 1908. Conservative MP, 1908–10; 1911–29. Keenly interested in aeronautics. Chairman, Belgian Field Ambulance Service, 1914–18. Created Baronet, 1919. Postmaster-General and Paymaster-General, 1923. Minister of Health, 1923–4. Home Secretary 1924–9. Created Viscount Brentford, 1929.

neglected; and that the public had never been given the facts about all that he himself had achieved. He defended his record as First Lord:

It is commonly supposed that the Admiralty before the War, at some more or less distant period before the War, under my impulsion rushed into the business of Home defence, snatched it away from the proper authorities, and then mismanaged and neglected it. That is not the truth. The contrary is the truth. Until a month after the war had begun the sole responsibility for the defence of all vulnerable points in England, by gun fire, seaplanes, or any other method against aerial attack, rested with the War Office. . . .

A month after the War had begun—3rd September, I think, was the actual date—Lord Kitchener asked me whether the Admiralty would undertake the general duty of Home defence against aerial attack. . . .

I carefully stated that the Admiralty could not be responsible for Home defence, but could only be responsible for doing the best possible with the material available. On this basis, which was formally accepted by the Government, the Admiralty undertook, very reluctantly for the most part, the thankless—and as it seemed then almost hopeless task. . . . Our available guns and aeroplanes were forthwith disposed to what we considered the best possible advantages, and overseas air bases in France and Flanders were established, and those have proved an effective and almost absolute parry to the attack of German Army Zeppelins coming from Belgium and the Rhine.

The series of offensive enterprises against the Zeppelin sheds began, and on this quest, in spite of their slender resources, the naval arm went to Düsseldorf, to Cologne, and Friedrichshafen, on Lake Constance, and even to Cuxhaven, in the North Sea. Six Zeppelins, it is believed, were destroyed either in the air, or in their sheds by a handful of naval pilots acting, what the First Lord of the Admiralty would now call, 'outside their normal sphere'.

It would be hard to show that all allied airmen and pilots had during all the War succeeded by this method in destroying so many. Moreover, within a few weeks of the Admiralty becoming responsible very large orders were placed for aerial guns and the proper kind of ammunition, and searchlights, and immense orders were distributed for aeroplanes to the utmost productive limit of every aircraft factory in any part of the world not already occupied with Army work. . . .

Such were the circumstances in which the Admiralty became responsible for Home defence, and the manner in which we endeavoured to discharge that responsibility, and I think I am justified in telling them to the House and to the country.

The criticisms levelled at Churchill covered, as he knew, every aspect of his work at the Admiralty; even the phrases which he had used in his speeches. He had once referred to the pilots of the Royal Naval Air

Service as 'hornets'. This description had subsequently been criticized as derogatory to the pilots, and this criticism had been raised again earlier in the debate of May 17. Churchill spoke strongly in his own defence:

My hon Friend the Member for Brentford (Mr Joynson-Hicks) has twitted me this afternoon with my phrase about 'hornets'. I am very glad to come to the 'hornets'. The main defence of England against Zeppelins has consisted since the War began in that formidable 'swarm of hornets' of which I spoke in 1913—that is to say, aeroplanes with skilful pilots held ready with bombs and guns to attack any Zeppelin which approaches our shores. This defence has been effective, up to date, in preventing any attack by Zeppelins coming here by daylight, or even by moonlight.

Churchill continued his defence, angry that his concern to build up the Royal Naval Air Service had become the subject of criticism by those who felt that he should have concentrated his efforts on the Navy:

But for the aeroplane service we had created before the War there would have been nothing to stop Zeppelins from raiding us every fine day; and if they were able to come in daylight they would be able to find their way with certainty to the vital and vulnerable points—to our arsenals, to our magazines, to our oil tanks, to our dockyards, to our munition works, and to drop their bombs with accuracy and deliberation from altitudes beyond the reach of any anti-aircraft gun which, at any rate, existed during the first year of the War.

Our aeroplane defence has restricted Zeppelin attacks to a few nights in certain months, and even then those attacks can only be delivered erring and almost blindfold. The proof of the triumph of the aeroplane is that after twenty-two months of war no object of any military or naval importance among the thousands which exist scattered broadcast throughout the country has yet been struck by any Zeppelin bomb.

Churchill was so embittered by being a victim of misrepresentation, so depressed by the accusations of his rashness and negligence, so convinced that his achievements placed him above almost all his leading contemporaries in foresight and perseverance, that he felt forced to defend himself in detail; otherwise, he believed, he would never be called to office again. Because of the increased German Zeppelin raids, his critics had begun to ask why the Admiralty had refused, while he was First Lord, to build its own airships which could have been the counterpart to the Zeppelin. Churchill's preference for aeroplanes was denounced as a fatal error; proof that he did not understand the realities of national defence. This was a serious indictment, which, if it could be sustained, might greatly damage his political future, certainly for as long as the war lasted. He defended his decision:

. . . who is to pretend that it was in our power, even if we had begun, say, in 1912, to create a Zeppelin fleet approaching in quality or numbers the German Zeppelin fleet—the product of ten years' expense and experiment on the most lavish scale.

Why, Sir, even if any Government had entertained the project—and no Government I have ever seen would have done—even if any Parliament had voted the funds necessary, we could not have hoped to compete with Germany successfully in rigid airships in the time available. We had not the art, we have not the native stores of aluminium which would be accessible in time of war. Our attempts to build experimental machines have been baulked until some months after the beginning of the War by continuous delay and disappointment.

Nearly 100 aeroplanes and their sheds can be obtained for the price of one Zeppelin and its shed.[1] What folly it would have been for us to have squandered the hard-won, grudged, and exiguous money which had to be secured for air defence on Zeppelins, fewer in number, inferior in type, and certainly ineffective for the purpose in hand—the defence of the civil population from Zeppelin raids.

What would our situation have been at the sudden outbreak of war if we had been found with a handful of these frail and feeble monsters, so easily broken by the accidents of weather, instead of with an Army Aeroplane Service, out of which the immense expansion of the present time has developed, or of a Naval Wing which in the emergency guarded securely every vital point in our Islands, and set the military free to go abroad? We should indeed have thrown away the substance for the shadow.

We are all surfeited nowadays with that kind of wisdom which comes after the event, but I do not in the least shrink from applying that unfair test to the policy pursued by the Admiralty and the War Office, partly under my responsibility and with my full agreement, in regard to the building of a Zeppelin fleet before the War.

Suppose by the stroke of a wand we could step back with full knowledge to the year 1912, and suppose that the £8,000,000 or £10,000,000 necessary to establish a good Zeppelin fleet were placed at our disposal as an addition to the ordinary Estimates which were, in fact, voted. Should we be wise to build one? With £10,000,000 you could have had sixty or seventy submarines; you could have had fifty destroyers; you could have had another twenty-five

---

[1] A Zeppelin could cost as much as £500,000. This sum included the cost of the shed and its land, which, because of the Zeppelin's size (and lack of manoeuvrability while on the ground), was much greater than for an aeroplane.

light cruisers; you could have had an Aeroplane Service of absolutely over-whelming strength; you could have had 2,000,000 rifles, which would, per-haps, have meant 3,000,000 more men in the field during the great struggle of last autumn; you could have had 1,000 heavy guns, applied in the earlier stages of the War, might have ruptured the German lines in France.

Is it not clear that, even if we are going to use the light of our present knowledge on the decisions which should have been taken before the War, a great many other competing things would have had to be considered before we came to the question of spending £10,000,000 on Zeppelins? Are we quite sure, after twenty-two months of war, that the Germans themselves might not have made a more formidable investment of the large sums of money which they have spent on their Zeppelins?

At any rate, the story is not yet finished. Events unfold from day to day, and I, for my part, am quite content to await the final judgement which will be passed on these matters when the War can be surveyed in retrospect as a whole.

Churchill had no intention of answering his critics and then sitting down. Confident of his case, he moved into the attack. The true remedy for Zeppelin raids, he said, was to counter-attack the German Zeppelin sheds. This had been his policy as First Lord. He believed that it had succeeded, but that Balfour had not followed it up:

... I can only repeat what I said three months ago—why has it been discontinued?

Why, after a whole year of limitless money, of accumulated experience, and of multiplying resources, has it not been possible to continue this system of attack upon the enemy's air bases?

Why has it not been possible to construct the special types of machines that may be required for each particular objective? ...

No doubt the difficulties have increased, and the enemy's means of defence is continually improving. All the more condemnation to you, I say, for losing so much valuable time, and perhaps for letting such precious opportunities slip by!

Churchill did not accept that the remedy lay in an Air Board such as Asquith had just set up. These plans, he declared, were a feeble subter-fuge:

They seem to be a mere attempt to parry the demand for an Air Ministry by setting up another Advisory Committee with Lord Curzon, instead of Lord Derby, at its head. There is, I gather, to be a Joint Board, and the members of this Board may advise the president, but he need not take their advice, and the president may advise the Admiralty and the War Office, but they need not take his advice. . . .

And if their advice, suggestions, recommendations etc, bear no fruit with the two fighting Departments, who, after all, are busy carrying on the War, and apt to give rough answers on these matters, then the president, I understand, may complain to the War Council——

Here Churchill was interrupted by Bonar Law; but he continued with his charge, pointing out that if Curzon's powers as President of the Air Board were limited to giving general advice, without the power to carry it through into action, he might as well just give it as an advising Cabinet Minister. He warned of the futility of setting up an Air Board without executive powers:

I know the public Departments, and especially the military Departments, of this country well, and I know what their attitude is towards a body which has the opportunity to inquire, to criticise, to offer advice, and to make complaints, but which has not the right to their allegiance and the power to exact obedience to orders.

Either the arrangements now proposed will lead to nothing effective, which will be the case if Lord Curzon shows the great qualities of tact which are likely to be required of the holder of the new office which is created, or—I say quite frankly—they seem to me likely to lead to a first-class row.

If he is going to make his work a reality, it is perfectly clear there will be very great differences, and much friction—the friction which you have been unable to overcome yourselves in making these proposals—will be created. In both cases, whether they produce no result, or whether they lead to trouble, they will lead to delay . . .

Can anyone feel that the proposals are put forward by the Government in the sincere belief that they will really open the way for the conquest of aerial supremacy for this country? Yet I cannot think it difficult.

Churchill had his own solution; an Air Ministry with full departmental powers:

No doubt we shall hear from the Government of the difficulties that stand in the way of an Air Ministry, of the resistance of this and that highly-placed official, and the prejudices of the Departments. No doubt we shall be told of the practical difficulties of calling it into existence in the middle of a great war, as if far greater difficulties have not been overcome, and far greater prejudices worn down, in the creation of a Munitions Department.

I cannot think it difficult myself either to devise or to bring into operation a unified organisation, or to divide on natural and well-marked lines the services of training and supply on the one hand, from the tactical employment of units afloat and in the field on the other hand.

I proposed to the Prime Minister a scheme on those lines nearly a year ago.

Soon, Churchill believed, the Air Service would be 'the dominating arm of war'. It should therefore—'and the sooner the better'—be a 'unified, permanent branch of Imperial defence, composed exclusively of men who will not think of themselves as soldiers, sailors or civilians, but as airmen . . .'.

Churchill knew that he could not change Government policy by his speech, or blot out the hostility which had accumulated against him. But he had no intention of remaining silent. A growing disgust with Government policy, a mounting frustration at his own lack of power, drove him on:

Complete, unquestionable supremacy in the air would give an overwhelming advantage to the artillery of the Armies that enjoyed it. It would confer the greatest benefits upon the Fleet that enjoyed it.

You have not got, in spite of what the right hon Gentleman has said, that complete supremacy now. You have not even got equality. On the contrary, in many respects the Germans have the advantage, and you have lost the superiority which, at the outbreak of war, it was admitted we possessed. But you can recover it. There is nothing to prevent your recovering it.

At sea, the increased power of the defensive in mines and submarines has largely robbed the stronger Navy of its rights. On land, we are in the position of having lost our ground before the modern defensive was thoroughly understood, and having to win it back when the offensive has been elevated into a fine art. But the air is free and open. There are no entrenchments there. It is equal for the attack and for the defence. It is equal for all comers.

The resources of the whole world are at our disposal and command. Nothing stands in the way of our obtaining the aerial supremacy in the War but yourselves. There is no reason, and there can be no excuse, for failure to obtain that aerial supremacy, which is, perhaps, the most obvious and the most practical step towards a victorious issue from the increasing dangers of the War.

It fell to Bonar Law, the Colonial Secretary, to answer Churchill's attack. He reacted as Balfour had done two months before, ignoring Churchill's serious charges but scoring a debating point: 'I really do not understand my right hon and gallant Friend', he said. 'He is in favour of an Air Ministry. Did that never occur to him as a good thing earlier, when he himself was a Member of the Government?' Churchill replied that he had put before Asquith early in June 1915 proposals of that character. Bonar Law replied cheaply: 'If I remember correctly, that was after the right hon and gallant Gentleman had left the Admiralty'; and to Churchill's stunned gasp, went on in similar mocking vein: 'I really do not understand my right hon and gallant Friend. If there was one man who, if an Air Ministry was the right thing, had the power to establish it, it was my right hon and gallant Friend. . . .'

Bonar Law's ridicule was effective. Few MP's were interested in Churchill's defence, or stirred by his anger. The Government's military and air policies were not altered on account of Churchill's criticisms. But he continued to speak in every debate about the war; to defend his own record, to attack that of his successors, to demand a more coherent war policy, and to argue that the endless squandering of human life without plan, or purpose, or prospect of victory, was a wicked policy. On May 23, six days after his attack on the Air Board, he rose again from the opposition bench, speaking immediately after the Prime Minister, as the first opposition speaker. Asquith had asked the House of Commons for a Supplementary Vote of Credit of three hundred million pounds, the identical sum which Parliament had already voted a month before. As during the Air debate, Churchill spoke from a position of political weakness and personal isolation. His speech did nothing to advance his political fortunes. Asquith ignored it; the Tories were not won over by it; no powerful group of dissident backbenchers rallied to him as a result of it.

Churchill appealed for a policy which would enable all able-bodied men to take their place in the fighting line, which would end the discrimination which sent some to the front and some to a leisured post, and which would draw upon the great reserves of manpower which remained neglected or untapped. He was afraid that as a result of the influx of conscripted men, inequalities and unfairness would be created, and the rights of the men themselves neglected. He wished to dwell, he told the House, not on technical matters, but 'on the men who are paid and maintained with the money which Parliament is asked and is willing to vote'. He begged the House to realize that compulsion was a major event. 'We have now reached a point,' he declared, 'when the need of the State is so grave that it has been necessary to compel by law to serve in the field the willing and the unwilling, the married and the unmarried, the young student and the old war-broken soldier, the head of a business and the father of a family.' Parliament, he believed, 'would not have taken these measures if it had not been convinced that they were indispensable to preserving the life of the State in the most serious and deadly crisis in its history'.

Churchill insisted that the men who were conscripted should be used in the most effective, least wasteful manner, and that every other possible source of manpower outside Britain 'should be simultaneously used to its utmost extent'. He drew attention to 'five large reservoirs of men', which he believed were being neglected, thereby throwing an unfair burden on the men in the trenches. The first reservoir was the officers and men who, although actually in France 'in the prime of their military manhood', never, or only seldom, went under enemy fire. Churchill told MPs that he had seen while at the front 'one of the clearest and grimmest class distinctions ever drawn in this world—the distinction between the trench and the non-trench population'. He believed that this distinction ought to be ended at once:

... the trench population lives almost continuously under the fire of the enemy. It returns again and again, after being wounded twice and sometimes three times, to the front and to the trenches, and it is continually subject, without respite, to the hardest of tests that men have ever been called upon to bear, while all the time the non-trench population scarcely suffers at all, and has good food and good wages, higher wages in a great many cases than are drawn by the men under fire every day, and their share of the decorations and rewards is so disproportionate that it has passed into a byword.

I wish to point out to the House this afternoon that the part of the Army that really counts for ending the War is this killing, fighting, suffering part.

The second reservoir of manpower of which Churchill spoke was 'the Army at home', created by the massive response to Kitchener's appeal for volunteers. Many of the volunteers had proved unfit for military service, but had been kept on in the army, forming, as Churchill explained, a 'very large accumulation in our depots, in our hospitals, in our camps, in our training schools, of men who have never been and will never be fit to be put into the field'. Why, he asked, had these men been taken away from productive work in factories and mines, shipyards and other useful employment, drawing army pay and carried on the army's ration strength:

No man should be retained who is not going to be of use. There is no need to try to swell mere numbers now for paper purposes. No man need be taken until he is required, and no man should be taken who can do more to beat the Germans by staying at home than by serving as a soldier.

I have never looked on compulsion as a means to sweep a vast mass into the military net, though it is perhaps the only way in which large aggregate numbers can be obtained. I have regarded compulsion not as the gathering together of men as if they were heaps of shingle, but the fitting of them into their places like the pieces in the pattern of a mosaic. . . .

The case of every man, the employment of every man now in uniform, should be subjected to at least as severe a scrutiny as the case of every man not yet joined. . . .

We hear a great deal, and this is the moral of what I have been saying in the House, about 'comb this industry', or 'comb that', or 'comb this Department or that', but I say to the War Office, 'Physician, comb thyself.'

Churchill then spoke of the third neglected reservoir of manpower, 'the Armies in the East', amounting in all to half a million men. He hoped that one day Parliament would be told why so great an allied Army had ever been sent to the eastern Mediterranean at all: he wanted the story told—'the fullest information and the publication of documents'—as soon as possible. Meanwhile, he asked: 'What have they been doing all these months? What are they doing now? We have a great Army in Egypt. What is it doing? Who is it fighting? We have another great Army at Salonika. What is it doing? Who is it fighting & who is it going to fight? Who can it get at to fight, except the Bulgarians, who do not want to fight?' There were, Churchill believed, enormous tasks which the troops idle in the East could perform:

Used in time, and sent in time, there is no military object in the Eastern theatre which the forces which are now accumulating in the East could not have achieved. But what have they done? What are they doing? Are they threatening Constantinople? Are they helping the Grand Duke? Are they relieving the pressure upon Verdun?

In all these tremendous events they have borne and are bearing absolutely no part. The Government is open to obvious and serious criticism every day that passes without these forces being made to play their part against the enemy.

. . . every day that these Armies are discovered sitting behind their defences and not holding their fighting weight in the conflict, there is a gross and grave misuse and maldirection of our limited military resources, for which there can be no excuse and no adequate explanation.

Churchill's fourth and fifth reservoirs of men, which he likewise accused the Government of neglecting, were those African and Indian troops who had volunteered for service in the Imperial Army, but had not been allotted a war station. He wanted a military camp set up in

Egypt, or somewhere else with a suitable climate, 'where African troops raised in various parts of the Continent would be assembled, drilled and trained, and then passed into the war as individuals or as units in whatever capacity they were best fitted for, and in whatever theatre of war and against whatever enemies the climate and their religion rendered it most suitable for them to be employed'.

Many MPs saw Churchill's proposals as no more than the time-wasting exercises of a man frustrated because he no longer had a part to play in the war. But Churchill spoke with a conviction which, while made more bitter by frustration, drew its strength from his contempt for what he was certain were misguided and dangerous policies:

I would not venture to put such an argument to the House but for the grave situation. I say to myself every day, What is going on while we sit here, while we go away to dinner, or home to bed? Nearly 1,000 men—Englishmen, Britishers, men of our own race—are knocked into bundles of bloody rags every twenty-four hours, and carried away to hasty graves or to field ambulances, and the money of which the Prime Minister has spoken so clearly is flowing away in its broad stream. Every measure must be considered, and none put aside while there is hope of obtaining something from it. . . .

Suppose you get only 100,000 men for your theatres of war. Is that nothing? Suppose you get only 20,000 men. Is that nothing? In this War you will find that at the very best you will have to pay a life for a life. Every man counts, and his case must be counted against the case of someone whom, perhaps, you know. . . .

Here let me point to the great difference which has been made by the enactment of national service in this country.

If we were keeping our manhood out of the struggle and trying to get it fought for us by subject races and mercenary armies, all the old arguments and reproaches with which history is familiar would apply. But when we are engaging every class, when the last man and the last shilling are to be claimed, we have a right and are bound to claim similar exertions, or whatever exertions are possible, from the dependencies which share our fortunes.

The doctrine of equality of sacrifice is not limited by the confines of the United Kingdom.

Churchill turned finally to the aspect of the war which worried him most, the wastage of human life by futile offensives. He had heard so often from the officers of his own Battalion, from the Generals at their headquarters, and from his friends at the front, of the grotesque slaughter of men during the battle of Loos. He did not want further unnecessary bloodshed:

Many of our difficulties in the West at the present time spring from the unfortunate offensive to which we committed ourselves last autumn. My right hon Friend knows that this is no new view of mine taken after the event.

Let us look back now. Only think if we had kept that tremendous effort ever accumulating for the true tactical moment. Think if we had kept that rammer compressed ready to release when the time came—if we had held in reserve the energies which were expended at Loos, Arras, and in Champagne —kept them to discharge at some moment during the protracted and ill-starred German attack on Verdun! Might we not then have recovered at a stroke the strategic initiative without which victory lags long on the road?

Let us not repeat that error. Do not let us be drawn into any course of action not justified by purely military considerations. The argument which is used that 'it is our turn now' has no place in military thought. Whatever is done must be done in the cold light of science. . . .

When you are able to gather round the frontiers of Germany and Austria armies which show a real, substantial preponderance of strength, then the advantage of their interior situation will be swamped and overweighed, and then the hour of decisive victory will be at hand. This hour is bound to come if patience is combined with energy, and if all the resources at the disposal of the Allies are remorselessly developed to their extreme capacity.

Churchill had spoken with passion. He did not believe that Britain could win the war by hurling men continuously to their deaths, and he despised the Government for trying to do so. The premature offensive against which he warned took place on the Somme within six weeks of his speech. On 1 July 1916, the first day of that offensive, twenty thousand men died and sixty thousand were wounded north of the Somme, for gains that were small, and to no perceptible advantage to the Allied cause. Yet no Cabinet Minister replied to Churchill's charges; and the reply which was given, by the Under-Secretary of State at the War Office, Harold Tennant, began with a sneer which echoed Balfour and Bonar Law, and confirmed the pattern for all official answers to Churchill's subsequent appeals. 'There is one thing,' Tennant said, 'which I envy my right hon and gallant Friend, and that is the time which he has in order to prepare his very carefully thought-out speeches. I wish I had the same opportunity.'

Churchill needed political allies, but these were hard to find. George Lambert, the only MP to have openly supported Churchill's appeal for Fisher's return in March, wrote on May 25 asking if Churchill intended to speak again against the wastage of manpower in the War

Office debate of May 31. 'If so,' Lambert wrote, 'I will come up and support you by speech or vote.' Churchill hoped that Lambert's offer of support might tempt a wider alliance of opposition.[1] He therefore sent Lambert's letter to Carson, asking: 'Surely the W.O. vote ought to be made the occasion for pressing for a sound policy of Army Administration. Do your people contemplate any action?' But Carson's Unionist War Committee had no plans to force a vote on May 31. They were guarding their strength. Churchill therefore acted alone. He spoke in the House of Commons again, at length and in great detail, on May 31. In his conclusion he again attacked Government policy:

We feel ourselves grappling with the most terrible foe that ever menaced freedom. Our whole life energies are required. We are trying our best, but are we at present developing the full results of the great effort made by the nation? I cannot think so. . . .

I say the nation has responded to every call, and the force which we have exerted in this War is far greater than any Ally had a right to expect or than any enemy had a right to take into its calculation; but the fact remains that full use has not yet been made and is not now being made of the nation's strength or of the Army's strength, or of the Empire's strength.

We are the only great reserve of the Allied cause, and a proper use of our resources will enable us increasingly to come to the succour of our superb Ally with an Army which grows increasingly in strength and power as our latent resources are realised, and becomes a support for all the losses and exertions to which she has been put.

No one who subjects the present organisation of the Army, either in the field or at home, to searching and dispassionate scrutiny can believe that every measure to that end is being taken at the present time.

Churchill's lone opposition brought him no nearer to high office. He was entirely cut off from Government policy-making. He had no access to the inner sources of discontent. He could not see the telegrams from Ambassadors, the reports from Generals, the estimates drawn up at the War Office and the Admiralty. He knew little of the arguments which were dividing the Cabinet, of the policies in dispute, or of the strategies being devised for future assaults. He had no power to move forward from his belligerent but isolated position to one where his return to the Cabinet might be considered. As soon as the debate of May 31 was over

---

[1] Lambert did not know that in August 1914 Churchill had pressed Asquith to remove him from his post as Civil Lord of the Admiralty, and to give the office to his cousin, Lord Wimborne. Asquith had refused to make the change. 'L is not very competent,' he had written to Venetia Stanley on August 9, 'but to boot him out at this moment wd be cruel.' Haldane had also intervened on Lambert's behalf, writing to Churchill on the same day: 'It would be a humiliation for him at such a period.'

he sat down to write to Fisher, who was likewise isolated from the power he so desired:

My dear Fisher,

Let us meet. You must not be downhearted. I am vy confident that things will right themselves in time. Nothing counts but winning the war. Gt care is needed. I do not deal with the Navy at the moment; because I am gathering strength and now that I am installed here I can measure the situation much more surely than under the disadvantages of a flying visit.

But what a shameful year of cowardice, inertia, futility and insolence has the Arthur Balfour regime presented.

The dead hand lies heavy on our noble fleets: & they even kiss it.

Courage as the gallant French say.

Yours ever
W

The public was impressed by Churchill's parliamentary protest.[1] Many soldiers and soldiers' wives, wrote to express their gratitude that he had spoken out so frankly about the wastage of manpower. One letter, typical of many, came from a servant in the Officers' Mess at the Buller Barracks, Aldershot, H. C. Waterlow,[2] who begged to be given an opportunity to serve overseas. The work which he and his fellow servants were doing, he claimed, could easily be done by women, by men over age, of by those who were unfit. He told Churchill that the male staff at the Barracks, all of military age, consisted of five officers' servants, five clerks, seven waiters, seven kitchen men, six general cleaning men, two men to clean silver, two to wash china, two to attend boilers, one to wash glass, one to clean knives, one for the wine cellar and one for the stores. 'Imagine a club, or a small hotel,' he wrote on June 7, 'with an average of fifty members or visitors, keeping a staff of forty-seven to attend to them.' Mrs Gillespie, the mother of a lieutenant in a Highland Regiment, wrote that her son[3] had been badly wounded at Loos, being hit in no less than five places, twice seriously in the head; but that after six months at home he expected to be sent out again to France. 'Seeing that there are *hundreds* of *thousands* of fit & willing men anxious to go out and do their bit,' she wrote on June 14, 'I certainly consider this returning of wounded men an absolute scandal. These men have been through the mill, and in *few* cases have they much heart for going out

---

[1] Churchill's army speeches of May 23 and May 31 were published on 13 July 1916 by Macmillan as a 32-page penny pamphlet *The Fighting Line*. Five thousand copies were printed.

[2] I have been unable to find further biographical details about H. C. Waterlow.

[3] Five commissioned Gillespies from Highland regiments fought at Loos: two in the Gordon Highlanders, two in the Highland Light Infantry, one in the Seaforth Highlanders. I cannot discover which one was Mrs Gillespie's son.

again.' In the postscript she wrote: 'I may say I expect to have five sons serving by next month.' An earlier appeal, dated May 31, came from Glasgow:

To the Honourable Colonel,

I the Wife of Lance Corp Thomas McKee[1] 7759 I Coy 2nd Scottish Rifles Humble pray your Honour to Interest yourself in my sad case my husband has did his duty for 3 years & four months in South Africa and as soon as this war broke out although time expired went and gave his service for King & Country till shot through the throat at the charge of Neuve Chappel they have sent him to France again from me & his 6 little children & I would nobley make the Sacrifice. But there are so many young men trained for the Past 18 Months who have never Been sent to France to do their Bit my whole 5 Brothers are doing there duty 3 in France one a prisoner in Wattenberg Germany & one at Deal. I asked him not to Leave us again & so many young ones at Home. But he only said I am sorry I did not think they would send me again But I must obey my Superiors. I most humbly pray that your honour will help me & my 6 children.

Mrs Thomas McKee

Asquith knew of the general impact of Churchill's speeches. He had no desire to see Churchill's concern for the soldiers lead to a growth of anti-Government feeling, and two attempts were at once made to involve him in a semi-official manner in the Government's affairs. Curzon asked him to attend a meeting of the Air Board in order to give his opinion of what ought to be done; Balfour, when the first official news of the Battle of Jutland on June 1 had shaken public confidence, asked him to draft a more inspiring communiqué which might steady the public's nerve. Churchill attended Curzon's Board, and drafted Balfour's second communiqué.[2] But these minor contributions did not satisfy his hunger to be involved once more in Cabinet policy.

By the end of May Churchill had come to realize that there was only

[1] I have been unable to trace any further biographical details about Lance Corporal McKee. According to the Ministry of Defence, his records were probably among those destroyed by fire during the blitz of 1940, when the Army Records Centre, Arnside Street, Southwark, London, SE1, was bombed and three-quarters of its records destroyed.

[2] Other than writing this communiqué, Churchill had no part in the Battle of Jutland. There is no contemporary correspondence about it in his papers. On hearing of the battle he had gone at once to see Lord Fisher, who was likewise only a spectator. But in 1927, in volume 3 of *The World Crisis*, Churchill entered into the Jutland controversy, devoting 62 pages to the battle, many of them critical of Jellicoe's conduct. He ended his account: 'The ponderous, poignant responsibilities borne successfully, if not triumphantly, by Sir John Jellicoe during two years of faithful command, constitute unanswerable claims to the lasting respect of the nation. But the Royal Navy must find in other personalities and other episodes the golden links which carried forward through the Great War the audacious and conquering traditions of the past.'

one way in which he could ensure his return; that there was one indispensable step to take, without which his denunciation of Government policy could not be effective. The cry 'What about the Dardanelles?' must be answered. The public would have to be shown the details of what had happened, of what it had been about; and would have to be satisfied that it had not been a lunatic offspring of Churchill's irresponsibility, but, as he believed, a central and carefully thought out part of Government policy. Churchill pressed Asquith to allow the principal documents to be published, as fully as military security would allow. Asquith agreed, and on June 1 Bonar Law announced in the House of Commons that documents relating to the Dardanelles would be laid before Parliament as soon as possible. Churchill was determined to exploit this opportunity for vindication to the full, writing to Asquith on June 2:

Private
My dear Prime Minister,
Wd it not save your time, if you sent Hankey to me to arrange what shd be published about the Dardanelles & Gallipoli operations? I wd explain to him my views with wh I think you will be in general agreement. The series of papers wh I wish to have published cd then be printed provisionally & circulated with those wh others affected may choose. It may be that a few additions will then be thought necessary.

I shd be ready with my papers to see Hankey on Monday morning—if you think this course convenient. . . .

The main point I wish to establish from them is my demand on behalf of the Admiralty on the 27th of Feb for the immediate despatch of the 29th Division & two Territorial Divisions in addition to the other troops. I also think that the decision of each War Council meeting about the Dardanelles shd be shortly stated, with the names of those who were present. This last I think vy important. Nearly everyone of consequence was present when the original decision to begin a purely naval attack was taken. I presume that I may refresh my memory from the records of any meeting in wh I was concerned. . . .

Yours sincerely
W

Fisher was also determined that his story should be told fully. At 1.30 on the afternoon of June 2 he presented himself at 10 Downing Street and handed in the following letter:

My dear Prime Minister,
I see in the Times of this morning that the Government have undertaken to publish papers about the Dardanelles and Gallipoli operations. I have no objection in principle to such a publication provided the papers give a fair

representation of the facts, and I presume I shall be consulted as to any selection that may be made.

Certain striking facts must be incorporated in these published papers that do not of course appear in the written records; but nevertheless they are vital and verifiable by the Participants in the Drama—such, for instance, as my abruptly rising from the War Council Table at 10 Downing Street on January 28th, 1915, and going to the window, determined to terminate my service at the Admiralty, and Lord Kitchener following me to that window with his professional remonstrance appealing to me to continue and carry through the Dardanelles operations, which caused me reluctantly to resume my seat!

There are also other vital incidents not recorded in writing . . .

Fisher appended to his letter a large selection of documents which he had already had privately printed.

Churchill's excitement during the first week in June was intense. He was determined that the story should be published as fully as possible. He wanted every shift and twist in the War Council's decisions, and his own repeated appeals, first for Allies, then for troops, to be made known. In search of documentation he entered into correspondence with Fisher and saw Sir Ian Hamilton, who since his recall to London in October 1915 had little hope of high military command in the field. Fisher, Hamilton and Churchill, each desperate for an active part in the war, made a natural triumvirate, but a feeble one. Each looked to past events for vindication. But those conducting the war were concerned with the present and future. They had not the time to focus on retrospective problems, to reconstruct arguments which had no relevance to the urgent needs of the war. Yet for Fisher, Hamilton and Churchill, only a re-examination of the past seemed to offer any hope of employment in the future. Asquith envisaged the publication of certain selected documents; they wanted the story told in such detail that every subtle shift of policy could be displayed. Fisher continued to have printed documents and reflections which he felt were to his advantage. Hamilton began to dictate to his secretary, Mary Kaye,[1] an elaborate narrative of events, based upon recollection and documents. On June 5 Churchill dined with Hamilton at his home in Hyde Park Gardens. Together they went through some twenty telegrams which Hamilton had sent to the War Office from Gallipoli, in which he had pleaded for high explosive shells to be sent to him at once, instead of the shrapnel shells

[1] Mary Forbes Kaye, 1895–   . Personal Secretary to Sir Ian Hamilton, 1916–47. Married George Eustace Ridley Shield, 1925. Sir Ian Hamilton's Literary Executor, 1947–

which had proved too feeble. Together they examined Hamilton's protests at the holding up in Egypt of a whole Army meant for the Dardanelles on the pretext that Cairo was in grave danger from a possible attack by tribesmen in the Libyan desert. Hamilton later wrote in *Listening For The Drums* of how he had impressed upon Churchill that these appeals, 'had all been bottled up by K of K and not one had been shown to the Cabinet when he had met them during the campaign and professed to expound the situation'.

Churchill was appalled at this evidence of Kitchener's neglect. He felt certain that the public would be amazed by the contrast between his own repeated warnings and Kitchener's neglect. This, he decided, would be the central, unanswerable theme of his case, so well-documented that Kitchener would be unable to controvert it. Churchill asked Hamilton to call on him the next morning at 41 Cromwell Road. He wanted to go through these damning telegrams again, checking that nothing had been omitted, and finalizing the statement which he intended to make as part of his submission of evidence. At midday on June 6 Hamilton drove to Churchill's house. The two men pored once more over the documents. Suddenly they heard a noise in the street. Somebody was calling out Kitchener's name. In *Listening For The Drums* Hamilton recorded the sequel: 'We jumped up and Winston threw the window open. As he did so an apparition passed beneath us. I can use no other word to describe the strange looks of this newsvendor of wild and uncouth aspect. He had his bundle of newspapers under his arm and as we opened the window was crying out, "Kitchener drowned! No survivors!" '

On the previous day Kitchener had left Scapa Flow on board HMS *Hampshire* for a secret mission to Russia, yet another attempt by Asquith to remove him from London. The ship had struck a mine, and sank in a few minutes beneath the icy waters of the North Sea. Kitchener's death sent a wave of horror across the country. The hero had gone; and while those in Government knew that he had for many months been edged away from power, for the British public it was a disaster. There could no longer be any question of Churchill's evidence, or of anyone's evidence, about the Dardanelles depending upon criticism of Kitchener. A legend had been born, which Asquith's Government could not allow to be tarnished; a legend of military skill and wise counsel. 'The fact that he should have vanished,' Hamilton wrote in his book, 'at the very moment Winston and I were making out an unanswerable case against him was one of those *coups* with which his career was crowded—he was not going to answer!'

Hamilton and Churchill went upstairs to lunch. Among the others present were Clementine Churchill and her mother, Lady Blanche Hozier.[1] The two men went into the dining-room. Hamilton later recorded: 'Winston signed to everyone to be seated and then, before taking his own seat very solemnly quoted: "Fortunate was he in the moment of his death!"' It was, Hamilton recorded, 'a nightmare lunch—no small talk—Winston said K might yet turn up but I told the company that he always had a horror of cold water, and that the shock of the icy sea would at once extinguish his life.'

The Secretary of State for War was dead; the struggle for his succession began at once. Lord Milner saw this as his opportunity to lead a phalanx of Tory dissidents forward into the citadel of Government. Asquith thought otherwise, and acted accordingly with his usual skill, delaying the new appointment for over a month, but letting it be known that he was most likely to move Lloyd George from the Ministry of Munitions to the War Office. Churchill believed that Lloyd George's departure from Munitions would be his opportunity. Some months previously Lloyd George had already suggested that he might take charge of the heavy gun department of the Ministry. He believed he could take the whole responsibility into his hands.

On June 7, the day after Kitchener's death was announced, Churchill called to see Lloyd George at the Ministry of Munitions. As he was going into Lloyd George's room, Lord Northcliffe came out. When Northcliffe saw Churchill he said, chaffingly 'I suppose you have come after LG's job.' Many years before, Northcliffe had given Churchill a small white china bust of Napoleon, which had become a most prized possession, and stood upon his desk facing him when he wrote. Stung by Northcliffe's jest, he felt that his desperate desire to serve his country was being turned into an object of jest and derision. Returning home, he wrote to the Press Lord:

Private
Dear Northcliffe,
 You will I am sure understand why I send back this statuette.
 I accepted it as a token of friendship and even when much unfair and ill-informed attack robbed it of that significance, I still regarded it as the gift of a courteous gentleman.
 I can do so no longer.

Yours v. fthfy.
Winston S. Churchill

[1] Lady Blanche Ogilvy, 1852–1924. Daughter of the 10th Earl of Airlie. She married Sir Henry Hozier, who died in 1907. Mother of Clementine, Nellie and William.

Northcliffe sent Churchill's letter to Lloyd George, commenting: 'I think it must be a matter of Health.' Lord Rothermere telegraphed asking Churchill to accept his brother's apology. Northcliffe sent the little Napoleon by special messenger to Blenheim Palace, asking Churchill to receive it back, and writing:

Dear Churchill,

I am sorry that you took a purely chaffing remark so seriously. I had no desire whatever to wound your feelings.

The attitude of my public newspapers toward public men has nothing to do with my private disposition toward individuals. Had I thought that the remark would have wounded you, I would not for a moment have made it; and I ask you to accept an expression of my regret for having said it.

Yours sincerely
N

Churchill replied on June 9:

Dear Northcliffe,

I accept your expression of regret in the spirit in wh it is offered, & I am vy glad indeed that you are able to remove from my mind a painful impression.

I shall not think about it any more. Let my words be forgotten too.

Yours sincerely
WSC

Kitchener's death, Northcliffe's jibe, the impending vacancy at the Ministry of Munitions, each made it more imperative to Churchill that the facts about the Dardanelles should be published fully and quickly. On June 8, while at Blenheim Palace, he wrote to Asquith:

. . . You will readily understand my wish that the truth shd be known. Not a day passes without my being the object of unjust reproach & now that poor Kitchener is gone I cannot see that the fortunes of the Ministry will be in any way prejudiced. The genesis of the operation is the vital point & your interest in showing that it was soberly & carefully entered upon is the same as mine. . . .

Only the facts can tell the tale: and the public ought now to have them.

Churchill tried to show Lloyd George how concerned he was about munitions. On June 8 he wrote asking him to see his friend Pelham Burn, 'one of the best young Colonels in the army who has been through the whole war' and who was in London on leave. 'You can only learn the truth,' Churchill wrote, 'by talking to the men who really do the work. Please send for him. . . . ' On June 13 Lord Reading dined with Churchill at 41 Cromwell Road. They discussed the possibilities of Churchill succeeding Lloyd George as Minister of Munitions. As soon as the dinner was over, Reading sought out Lloyd George, and on the following day sent Churchill an account of their meeting. 'LG was at No 10 when I got back from you,' wrote Reading, 'I saw him afterwards. In a word he thinks it is premature to press you for the post in question—but is very sympathetic and as you wish it, notwithstanding his own views he will push it. Nothing could be better than his reception of the suggestion.'

Churchill knew that Lloyd George's goodwill was not enough. Asquith had no reason to bring him back into the Government while the stigma of the Dardanelles remained upon him. The Government would only invite continued controversy if it had to explain to the public why someone whose judgement it had been taught to distrust was to come back. For the rest of June Churchill pressed upon the Prime Minister the need to publish the Dardanelles documents immediately. But Asquith was becoming increasingly reluctant to have the documents published. On June 20 Churchill learned from Hamilton that the Admiralty were 'jibbing' at the publication of the naval side of the story. That day he wrote to Fisher: 'The refusal on the part of the Government to publish now would be very prejudicial to them. So will the publication.' Churchill correctly assessed the Government's dilemma. The publication of documents might help him to escape from further unfair attacks; but it might equally well bring unwelcome controversy to Asquith. Yet Churchill continued with his pressure, supported by Carson and Dalziel. On June 21 he described the situation, and his own mood, to his brother, who was then serving in France at the Headquarters of the Anzac Corps:

. . . The Press is amazingly vicious & I count only on the publication of the Dlles papers to turn their mood. These will much embarrass the Government. I am sorry that the end of poor old K shd have come at this moment. For his own sake it was a good exit—the glory had departed, the clouds were gathering & night drew near. . . . I am quite resigned to a further period of detachment & do not care vy much one way or the other. But for the war, I wd not dream of acting with these people. . . .

On June 19 Hankey had written to inform Churchill that Asquith had decided not to allow him to use the War Council minutes in the documents which he was selecting for publication. Asquith believed, Hankey wrote, that if these minutes were published, 'it would be very difficult to resist a pressure to publish proceedings in regard to other aspects of the war which might not be in the public interest'. Asquith also feared, Hankey explained, that if the remarks of senior Ministers were 'liable to publication', future discussion might be hampered. Churchill replied direct to Asquith on June 22, pointing out that it was only from the minutes of the War Council that any clear idea could be obtained by the public of how the policy had been evolved, and of his own part in it. It was necessary, he said, to publish the text of what the War Council had discussed on 28 January 1915 in order to show 'the strong support of the naval project given by you, Grey, Kitchener & A. Balfour . . .'. He also demanded that all the War Council minutes for February should be published, showing as they did 'my disclaimer of responsibility if a military disaster occurred through adequate troops not being sent in time'. He felt that it was important that the public should know that his disclaimer 'was not an ordinary incident of discussion, but that I asked formally & at the time that my dissent shd be placed on record'. Surely, he continued, Asquith could see 'that this fact is vy important for a true judgement on the event'? Churchill was afraid that if Asquith refused to allow the publication of the War Council minutes, even in some paraphrased form, the public would never learn of his real part in the evolution of the Dardanelles campaign. 'I am sure,' he ended his appeal, 'your sense of fairness wd not acquiesce in its suppression.'

Hankey's letter to Churchill about the impossibility of publishing the War Council minutes indicated a change in Asquith's attitude towards the whole question of letting the story be told. Realizing this, Churchill mobilized the few forces at his disposal in an attempt to hold the Prime Minister to his pledge. On June 26 Dalziel asked in the House of Commons when the Government would publish the despatches of the Gallipoli campaign. Asquith replied that 'a considerable period must elapse before these papers are likely to be ready'. Churchill believed that delay was a euphemism for cancellation; but when he put this view to Edward Marsh, who was then working in Asquith's private office, Marsh consulted Masterton Smith and replied on July 4 that there was nothing 'sinister' about the hold up in the production of the documents, and that the Admiralty were not trying in any way to prevent publication. 'There are hundreds of telegrams to be gone through,' Marsh wrote 'besides those which figure in your file—the War Staff is at work on them, but it is a matter which *must* take time, & of course they haven't much to spare.' Churchill persevered in his quest for vindication. On July 7, the day of Lloyd George's formal appointment as Secretary of State for War, he wrote to Lloyd George, asking him to allow the documents which he wanted from the War Office files to be published with as few 'omissions and suppressions' as possible. On July 8 he wrote to Asquith that he would be glad to hear from him about whether or not he could quote in his evidence the verbatim minutes of the War Council. He added:

> . . . I am also anxious to obtain from you an assurance that dilatory measures will not be allowed to prevent the publication being made while Parliament is sitting. More than six weeks have already passed since the promise to lay the papers was made to the House of Commons: and if I may judge from reports that have reached me there are some indications that an obstructive attitude is being adopted.
>
> I propose therefore unless I hear from you some reasons to the contrary to put a series of questions on the notice paper.

Four days later Asquith wrote to tell Churchill that the Government had decided not to publish the Dardanelles documents at all. It was a bitter blow. Asquith claimed that his decision had been taken on the grounds of security. But Major-General Callwell, whom Asquith had instructed to go through the War Office files, explained to H. A. Gwynne on July 13 that 'if the papers were laid at all the truth would have to be told about there not being sufficient men available to keep Hamilton up to strength'. On July 13 Dalziel and Carson asked formally in the House of Commons when the documents were to be laid before Parliament. Asquith replied that publication had now been abandoned, as it would not be in the national interest. Churchill wrote at once in protest to Asquith:

> . . . I cannot agree that this decision is justified in the public interest. The pledge of the Government was freely given by the Colonial Secretary speaking with your full and direct authority. The circumstances of the case, the nature of the documents, and their bearing on the course of the war must have been present in your mind, although perhaps there were some which you have over-looked or forgotten. The pledge to publish was not given at my request, though as you know I have always wished that the whole truth should be made known to the nation and to the Dominions, and that nothing essential should be concealed. It was given to the House and we have been left for more than six weeks in the expectation that it would be fulfilled. I do not think that in these circumstances it ought to be departed from on any

vague and general ground. Papers have been submitted to you by me and I understand by other persons affected. There may be passages in these papers which affect allied or neutral powers. Certainly they are few and far between. There is no reason why they should not be omitted, or expressed in a different way by mutual agreement. There may be technical matters which if desired could be suppressed without impairing in any way the proper presentation of the facts of the case.

It is unfair to the House—I do not speak of individuals—that objections founded on a few passages or documents which are not material, and would not be claimed as material to the case by the persons concerned, should be used as a bar to prevent any publication at all. . . .

Churchill was not alone in being angered at Asquith's reversal of the Government's pledge to publish the Dardanelles documents. An increasing number of MPs began to press for a full-scale debate. In an attempt to deflect criticism, Lloyd George suggested that the Government should appoint a secret committee of the House of Commons to enquire into the Dardanelles operation. He discussed his suggestion privately with Churchill, proposing that the report of this committee should be allowed to replace the earlier proposal that the documents themselves should be put before Parliament. Churchill did not approve of this change:

My dear Lloyd George,

. . . First the Government have given a definite promise to the House that the authentic documents shd be published. The matter is one wh therefore concerns the House of Commons, & I have no right to express an opinion on their behalf.

Secondly altho' the pledge was given by Mr Bonar Law, the Prime Minister had intended to give it himself personally & was only prevented from doing so by the unexpected prolongation of the debate on other matters.

Thirdly the pledge of the Government was given after prolonged consideration & with full knowledge both of the facts and of the suitability of the documents for publication at this juncture. In consequence of the pledge of the Government I submitted to the Prime Minister a series of documents wh I conceive are necessary among others to the exposure of the truth, & wh except in minor and immaterial details & passages to the excision of wh no objection cd be taken, cd in any judgment be made public without detriment to the State. These papers had been circulated to the Cabinet more than a year ago. They have been examined lately by an impartial general[1] chosen by the Government, who has reported that their publication in the main wd not be injurious to the State, but that it wd reflect upon the Government. In these circumstances I can well understand the desire of the Government to substitute for a publication of authentic documents on wh the nation can judge, a secret inquiry of indefinite duration by a body selected by themselves.

The personal aspect of this matter is not vy important, except in so far as it affects the behaviour of colleagues to one another. But the public aspect is serious. The nation & the Dominions whose blood has been poured out vainly have a right to know the truth. The Government had decided of their own accord that the truth cd be told & had given a formal promise to Parliament: & now as the time draws nearer they shrink from the task.

If a Committee is appointed I will of course attend and assist its labours in any way that is possible. But the first witness who shd be called before them is the Prime Minister, who alone cd have co-ordinated the naval and military action & given to the war-policy of the country the necessary guidance & leadership. Such a Committee however can be no substitute for the laying upon the table of the House of the papers wh the Government have promised: nor cd I allow it to prejudice in any way my freedom of action & discussion if need & opportunity arise. . . .

Churchill's appeal was in vain. He was angry and depressed not to be allowed to put before Parliament a full documentary statement of what had occurred. Without evidence in profusion, without the clear authenticity of the documents themselves, he knew that he would always remain the scapegoat. Every mistake that had been made, every aspersion that had been cast, every taunt that had been thrown would be a rope holding him back from his chance of exercising power at the centre of national affairs. On July 15 he went to Blenheim Palace with his family, hoping to calm his mind by painting. But he could not do so. In his depression he even thought of returning to the western front as a battalion commander. That evening he wrote to his brother:

Is it not damnable that I should be denied all real scope to serve this country, in this tremendous hour? I cannot tell how things political will turn out: but great instability prevails and at any moment a situation

[1] The General was Callwell. In his book *The Dardanelles*, published in 1919, he concluded: 'Cabinets, War Councils, Dardanelles Committees, and kindred executive gangs are generally composed entirely, or almost entirely, of persons, who if they have any knowledge of war at all, are merely furnished with that modicum of it that is so dangerous a thing . . . governments should leave the contriving of military and naval operations to those who understand them.'

favourable to me might come. Meanwhile Asquith reigns supine, sodden and supreme. LG made a half-hearted fight about Munitions. He is very much alone and none too well qualified for the particular job he has claimed. But very friendly according to the accounts I get from various trustworthy sources.

The Govt have decided to repudiate their pledge to publish the D'Iles papers. My dossier was more than they could face. There will be a row, but there are many good arguments in the public interest against publishing: and many more good arguments in the Government interest!

Tho' my life is full of comfort, pleasure and prosperity I writhe hourly not to be able to get my teeth effectively into the Boche. But to plunge as a battalion commander unless ordered—into this mistaken welter—when a turn of the wheel may enable me to do 10,000 times as much would not be the path of patriotism or of sense. There will be time enough for such courses. Jack my dear I am learning to hate.

26

Cast Aside

ON July 18 the House of Commons debated whether or not the
Dardanelles documents should be put before them. Asquith
announced that 'the presentation of these Papers must be postponed',
and trusted that the House would agree 'that the pledge to publish
them cannot for the moment . . . be fulfilled'. The reason, he said, was
that the Admiralty, the War Office and the Foreign Office were
'unanimously of the opinion that the publication at the present time of
papers could not be made . . . without omissions so numerous and so
important that the papers actually presented would be incomplete
and misleading'. A long debate ensued. Carson took the lead in criticising the Government's decision. Two days later Asquith announced
that the most the Government would agree to was to set up a select
committee 'to inquire into the conduct of the Dardanelles operations'.
Its chairman was Lord Cromer; its other members Field-Marshal Lord
Nicholson,[1] Sir William Pickford,[2] Admiral of the Fleet Sir William
May,[3] Sir Frederick Cawley, James Clyde,[4] Captain Gwynn[5] and
Walter Roch.[6] This was the outcome which Churchill feared: the

[1] William Gustavus Nicholson, 1845–1918. Lieutenant, Royal Engineers, 1865. Major-
General, 1899. Chief of the Imperial General Staff, 1908–12. Field-Marshal, 1911. Chairman
of the Commission on Indian Army Expenditure, 1912–13. Created Baron, 1912.
[2] William Pickford, 1848–1923. Judge of the High Court of Justice, 1907–14. Knighted,
1914. Lord Justice of Appeal, 1914–18. Created Baron Sterndale, 1918. President of the
Probate Division, Admiralty Court, 1918–19.
[3] William Henry May, 1849–1930. Lieutenant, Royal Navy, 1871. Knighted, 1904.
Second Sea Lord, 1907–9. Commanded the Home Fleet, 1909–11. Commander-in-Chief,
Plymouth, 1911–13. Admiral of the Fleet, 1913.
[4] James Avon Clyde, 1863–1944. Solicitor-General, Scotland, 1905–6. Liberal Unionist
MP, 1909–18. Lord Advocate, Scotland, 1916–20. Conservative Unionist MP, 1918–20.
Lord Justice-General of Scotland, 1920–35.
[5] Stephen Lucius Gwynn, 1864–1950. Author and journalist. Nationalist MP, 1906–18.
Joined the Leinster Regiment as a Private, January 1915; Captain, July 1915. Served in
France with the 16th Irish Division, 1915–17.
[6] Walter Francis Roch, 1880–1965. Liberal MP, 1908–18.

committee would undoubtedly publish a fair report; but it would be opinions, not documents; fragments of evidence, not substantial fact. The debate that followed Asquith's announcement was a turbulent one. Many MP's shared Churchill's fears that a Commission of Inquiry would be inconclusive and inadequate. When Asquith proposed that the House adjourn, Churchill spoke with bitterness that it had not been found possible to publish the documents, 'as was originally intended and promised by the Prime Minister, in the name of the Government'. He told the House how, very soon after the Government had made this promise to publish, he had noticed 'a dilatory and destructive tendency'. But he had to accept Asquith's proposal. It was better than nothing. He hoped that the Commission of Inquiry would be given every encouragement to publish as many documents as possible. It was not the solution that he had wanted; but he realized that his political future depended upon the story being known, at least in part. He preferred truncated evidence to no evidence at all. He did not wish to remain the scapegoat for ever.

As soon as Asquith announced his decision to set up a Commission of Inquiry on the Dardanelles, Churchill began to prepare a statement to make before it. He was determined to include as many documents as possible in his own evidence. For five months, from July to November 1916, he worked at his statement, assembling documents, rehearsing arguments and drafting increasingly elaborate narratives.[1] The need to make the statement as comprehensive and as convincing as possible, became his preoccupation.

During July Churchill found a journalistic outlet, writing four articles for Lord Rothermere's *Sunday Pictorial*. He was excited at how much he was to be paid, writing to his brother on 15 July, 'I get 4 or 5 shillings a word for everything I write: and apparently even at this price the newspaper is the gainer. *Sunday Pictorial* circulation is 448,000 in a single day. This beats all records in journalism.' The four articles earned him £1,000, and appeared on four successive Sundays in July. The first two described different aspects of the coming of war in August 1914. On the second Sunday Lord Haldane sent Churchill a note of approval. 'These articles contain far the most penetrating and accurate analysis of the

---

[1] 'Let me say at the outset,' Churchill wrote on the first of several hundred pages of handwritten notes for his evidence, 'that I take full responsibility for all the proceedings of the Adm^y in these affairs during my tenure. I have no complaint to make in regard to any officer serving under the Bd of Adm^y whether afloat or ashore . . . in what I am about to say I do not seek to transfer responsibility to any officer serving under the Admiralty. If I cite the opinions & advice of Admirals & others of high expert authority it is not to relieve myself of responsibility, but to show that that responsibility was properly & carefully discharged.'

situation before the war that I have ever seen,' wrote the former Secretary of State for War, '& I agree with every word you have written in them. . . . What you yourself did will always be historical.' Churchill's third article described the state of the Navy at the beginning of the war, and the role of the Navy in British power. His final article described the changing nature of the war in Europe. 'The chaos of the first explosions,' he wrote, 'has given place to the slow fire of trench warfare: the wild turbulence of the incalculable, the sense of terrible adventure have passed. . . . A sombre mood prevails in Britain. The faculty of wonder has been dulled; emotion and enthusiasm have given place to endurance; excitement is bankrupt, death is familiar, and sorrow numb. The world is in twilight; and from beyond dim flickering horizons comes tirelessly the thudding of guns.' On July 31 Churchill sent Jack Seely copies of his articles, together with a survey of the political position:

My dear Jack,
    . . . There is gt uncertainty here & the position of the Government is not good. Asquith in particular seems to be on the road to pay his debts. L.G. is vy affable and I see a good deal of him. . . .
    You know my views on the offensive too well for me to repeat them here. I trust you will not expose yourself needlessly to danger when not on duty: Look after Jack (my other one) if you come near Anzac H.Qrs.
    Archie has had a good rest, but now has succeeded in getting ordered to France as a Squadron commander in the 2nd L. Guards. I am vy fond of him & shall always remember yr kindness in letting me have him when I was at the war.
    Let me know if there is any way in wh I can serve you. It is vy painful to me to be impotent & inactive at this time: but perhaps a little later on I may find a chance to be useful.
    The Dardanelles Commission will require some of my attention in the near future. I am hopeful that the truth may be published. But failure & tragedy are all that are left to divide.
    This is a morose letter—but do not let it depress you. . . .
                                                    Your devoted friend
                                                              W

Churchill wanted to be heard in Government circles, and at the Cabinet table. He feared a repetition of the Somme offensive, and further bloodshed for objectives which he believed were both ill-considered and unobtainable. He put these fears into a memorandum. F. E. Smith agreed to write an introduction to it, and to have it printed for the Cabinet. Churchill's memorandum, dated August 1, concluded:

So long as an army possesses a strong offensive power, it rivets its adversary's attention. But when the kick is out of it, when the long-saved-up effort has been expended, the enemy's anxiety is relieved, and he recovers his freedom of movement. This is the danger into which we are now drifting. We are using up division after division—not only those originally concentrated for the attack, but many taken from all parts of the line. After being put through the mill and losing perhaps half their infantry and two-thirds of their infantry officers, these shattered divisions will take several months to recover, especially as they will in many cases have to go into the trenches at once.

Thus the pent-up energies of the army are being dissipated, and if the process is allowed to go on, the enemy will not be under the need of keeping so many troops on our front as heretofore. He will then be able to restore or sustain the situation against Russia.

There were some politicians and soldiers who suspected an ulterior motive in Churchill's hostility to the strategy of the Somme offensive. On August 1 Hankey recorded in his diary a talk with Sir William Robertson, the Chief of the Imperial General Staff: 'Robertson told me that F. E. Smith was writing a paper to show that the big offensive in France had failed. I suspect that Ll George & Winston Churchill are at the back of it. Personally I think it is true but it is a mistake to admit it yet.' F. E. Smith circulated Churchill's memorandum to the Cabinet on August 1. The reaction was one of scepticism. Ministers did not want to believe that the Somme offensive should be halted. A copy of the memorandum reached Haig at St Omer within a week; he too was unwilling to accept any limitation to his policy of continual attack. To Northcliffe, who was visiting St Omer, Haig strongly defended the offensive. Northcliffe wrote to Geoffrey Robinson on August 8, from Paris: 'Let me once more say and urge that what is taking place on the Somme must not be measured in metres. It is the first time we have had a proper scientific attack. There are no complaints of bad Staff work, no complaints of lack of ammunition, no muddling. . . . If we wrote communiqués as well as the Germans, we would lay much more stress on the German losses, which are *known* to be immense.' Robinson accepted Northcliffe's judgement. Churchill's criticisms met with no response in *The Times*.

The summer passed. Churchill's opinion was not sought again by the Government. He sat for his portrait by William Orpen.[1] In 1964, a few months before his death, Churchill dined alone with one of his former

---

[1] William Orpen, 1878–1931. Painter. Knighted, 1918. The portrait, which was Churchill's favourite portrait of himself, passed first to his son Randolph and then to his grandson Winston.

Private Secretaries, John Colville,[1] who later recorded, in a letter to the author:

His memory had already faded and conversation was exceedingly difficult. During the first two or three courses at dinner I tried every subject in which I knew him to be interested, without success. . . . Finally, over the savoury, I looked at the Orpen, which was hanging in the dining room behind his chair, and made the not very original remark that it was far and away the best portrait of him which had ever been painted. Suddenly his brain cleared. His voice became exactly as it had been years before. He replied, 'I am glad you think so. I gave him eleven sittings, which is more than I have ever had time to give any other painter. It was in 1916, at a very unhappy time of my life when I had nothing whatever to do. Rothermere gave me the portrait, which was very generous of him, and almost my only occupation was to sit to the artist.' His mind then clouded over again and we had no coherent conversation for the rest of the evening.

On July 24 Asquith introduced the Supplementary Vote of Credit for 1916, asking the House of Commons to vote a further £450,000,000 for the prosecution of the war. Churchill was Asquith's principal critic, speaking immediately after the Prime Minister:

We have not had from the Prime Minister what he alone can give and what his moving these Votes would enable him to give, namely, a broad survey of, or at any rate some reference to, the general progress of the War and the state of the great enterprises for the furtherance of which this money is asked. . . .

Very grave and important events have taken place in the two months that have passed. I had certainly looked forward to hearing from the Prime Minister, in asking for this immense sum of money, some reference to events like the naval battle off Jutland, or the brilliant tactics of General Brusiloff,[2] or the sustained and magnificent defence made by our Allies at Verdun. Even if it were not possible to comment on the other operations which are now in progress, I believe a statement from the Prime Minister on this subject would be bound, as on other occasions, both to instruct the country and to encourage and to gratify our Allies.

[1] John Rupert Colville, 1915–   . A grandson of Lord Crewe. Entered the Diplomatic Service, 1937. Assistant Private Secretary to Neville Chamberlain, 1939–40; to Churchill 1940–1 and 1943–5; to Clement Attlee, 1945. Private Secretary to Princess Elizabeth, 1947–9. Joint Principal Private Secretary to Churchill, 1951–5.

[2] Alexei Alexeievich Brusilov, 1853–1926. Commanded the Russian Armies south of the Pripet Marshes, 1916–17. His successful offensive, launched on 4 June 1916, was halted in September through lack of artillery munitions, having at one point advanced 70 miles. Supreme Commander of the Russian Armies, May–July 1917. Put his services at the disposal of the Red Army during the Russo-Polish war, 1920. Inspector of Cavalry, 1923–4. Head of the State Horse-breeding Establishment, Moscow, 1924–6.

Churchill used the opportunity of this debate to speak caustically against Asquith for not appointing a Secretary of State for War during the thirty days between Kitchener's death on June 6 and Lloyd George's transfer to the War Office on July 7. Throughout that month, Asquith himself had acted as Secretary of State for War; he had therefore been responsible for the conduct of War Office policy both during the final three weeks of preparation and the first disastrous week of battle on the Somme. Churchill attacked Asquith for undertaking this responsibility:

It was impossible that the War Office in time of war should be conducted by the Prime Minister in the odd hours that he could snatch from his own laborious duties, and from adjusting the recurring crises of the Coalition Government. When the office became vacant it ought to have been filled within forty-eight hours in the interests of the War. It ought not to have been left vacant, with only such time as the right hon Gentleman could spare from his already most severe labours. It was not at all a satisfactory event, and I think it is one of those cases which illustrates the undue importance which is attached at the present time to mere political adjustments as compared with effective, energetic means to prosecute the War.

Churchill then raised, in more detail and with added evidence, the points which he had made two months before about the misuse and wastage of manpower. He addressed himself to the new Secretary of State for War, Lloyd George:

What has been done to provide, as far as possible, substitutes for young, fit, military males who are at present engaged in non-combatant services far from the front? What has been done to afford relief to war-worn soldiers, and particularly to wounded men, who are sent back time after time to the trenches which others have never visited at all?

Does my right hon Friend know—I am informed that it is the case and it seems so extraordinary that I put it in interrogative form—that wounded men on being discharged from hospital are immediately placed in what is known as category A? That is to say, they go back to their depots and home units as fit for service.

One would have thought that when a wounded man recovers from injury he would have been put at the bottom of the roster of trained and fit men, and would only have gone out after the whole of the list had been exhausted. . . .

I have heard nothing which indicates that any attempt is being made to use the manpower of India, or India's great resources effectively in the War. The India Office attitude is one of general apathy and obstruction.[1]

What about Africa? I asked before what use was the Government making of the African population, whether for war or for labour? There are the natives of East Africa about whom encouraging reports are spread by those who are acquainted with the country and with the military quality of these men. There are possibilities in South Africa. There is the native population of Nigeria. There are the native populations of the Soudan. All those great fields ought to be developed to the fullest possible capacity, and merely to say, 'Oh, there are great difficulties,' and 'It is difficult to find officers and interpreters,' and so on, is not dealing with the subject as its urgency and importance require.

I am going to ask the right hon Gentleman whether anything has been done to reduce redundant administration training staffs at home.

I am quite certain, if he looks into the condition of some of those large fortresses at home, with depots in them, he will find great overlapping, great confusion and complication of machinery, undue multiplication of persons engaged in the training staff proportionate to the number of recruits they are turning out and handling, and generally the possibilities of reduction in the staffs, which will both save the public purse and liberate more men for the fighting front. . . .

All these matters are serious and urgent. I make no apology for bringing them before the House. We are fighting for our lives, and any useful means of advance towards the strengthening of our war effort is legitimate, and Parliament ought to give its attention to these matters.

Churchill turned to another contentious matter, that of military honours. 'I am not concerned,' he said sarcastically, 'with the honours and rewards of the Staff and of the higher ranks, because, I believe, they are tolerably well provided for at the present time.' His concern was with those men 'on whom we depend for our lives'. 'It is the privates, the non-commissioned officers, and the regimental officers,' he explained, 'whose case requires the sympathetic attention of the House and of the Secretary of State. Honour should go where death and danger go, and these are the men who pay all the penalties in the terrible business which is now proceeding.' Churchill went into further details about awards and decorations. The House was impatient with such minutiae. But Churchill persevered in his attack. 'People who never themselves go into danger,' he said, 'talk airily about cheapening

[1] Between 1914 and 1918 India provided one soldier for every 225 of its inhabitants; New Zealand, 1 for every 5; Great Britain, 1 for every 7; Australia, 1 for every 10; Canada, 1 for every 11; South Africa, 1 for every 44. Of the 1,400,000 Indians under arms, 850,000 left India for the war zones.

the British standard of decoration and reward. If you gave three or four times, or even five or six times, as many as you have given to the lower ranks of the Army, I am certain you could do it without conferring any reward upon a man who would not have gained the highest possible distinction, or, at any rate, marked distinction and notice, in any previous war.' Churchill believed that honours, properly bestowed—not 'handed out with the rations' as many officers joked—would make a difference 'to the lives, the hopes and encouragement' of the men at the front. As for the Military Medal, which had just been introduced, he was annoyed that 'the distribution has been so limited and so niggardly, and the cases in which it has been given promptly so rare and exceptional, that it has practically made no sensible impression at all upon the immense armies we have now got in the field'. Churchill had further advice for the new Secretary of State for War. It concerned promotions. 'I wonder if my right hon Friend is aware,' he asked, 'that promotion in the battalions at home is much quicker than promotion in the battalions at the front?' It was, he believed, 'a very anomalous state of affairs that one man should be a year or a year and a half in the trenches, in continual danger, and should actually make slower progress up the military ladder than his brother who has joined a Home service battalion and has not been ordered to the front'.

Churchill believed that these were important matters. 'Let us never forget,' he urged, 'how much these things are thought of by the people who are risking everything for us.' But he realized that he was amid a hostile audience which did not want to hear such detail. 'I do not believe,' he said, 'that people in this country have any comprehension of what the men in the trenches and those who are engaging in battles are doing or what their sufferings and achievements are.' It was his contention that, despite the obvious lack of parliamentary interest in front-line problems, 'the trench population, these fighting men, are the people who require the care and attention of the House and the Secretary of State'.

Churchill continued his speech by outlining several practical suggestions about the system of communications at the front, a system whose inadequacies he had himself witnessed. He wanted preparations to be made at once for the winter, 'so that our men will have as good a chance as the Germans, so that they may have as much comfort in their life in the trenches as the Germans, so that they will not lose more life than the enemy, and in order that the lines can be held by as few troops as possible, and our Armies have the utmost possible rest during the winter months'. He pressed for a more extensive and elaborate system

41. Churchill
leaving for the
Front, early 1916

42. Sir Archibald Sinclair and Churchill, Armentières, 11 February 1916

43. Captain Gibb, Adjutant, 6th Royal
Scots Fusiliers, April 1916

44. Lieutenant Napier-Clavering,
Royal Engineers, 1916

45. 2nd Lieutenant Hakewill Smith, 6th
Royal Scots Fusiliers, April 1916

46. 2nd Lieutenant McDavid, 6th
Royal Scots Fusiliers, April 1916

47. Captain Spiers (third from left), Churchill, General Fayolle (on right) and a German prisoner (in cap, behind General Fayolle), 29 December 1915

48. Violet Bonham Carter, Clementine Churchill and David Lloyd George, Ponders End, 3 February 1916, at the opening of a canteen for munitions workers

49. German shell exploding above Ploegsteert Wood, 1916

50. Ploegsteert Church, spring 1916

51. British trench in the Ploegsteert sector, after a snowfall, January 1916

52. Churchill, 1916

53. Clementine Churchill, 1915

54. Churchill, summer 1916

55. David Lloyd George, 1916

of light railways to enable trench stores to be brought up more quickly and easily to the front, and kept in constant repair. He then raised the question of the inferior quality of British trench lights. The German light, he said, burned brighter and longer, and went much further; the British light could not even reach the German lines, and the Germans could strengthen their front-line wire without interruption. 'These are very important things for the successful conduct of the War,' he pleaded, 'and there is no excuse for these lights not being as good as the German lights....' Churchill went on to express his anger that the Government had delayed so long in introducing steel helmets, one of which he himself had worn throughout his six months in the trenches. 'Many men might have been alive to-day,' he said, 'who have perished, and many men would have had slight injuries who to-day are gravely wounded had this proposal not been put aside in the early stages of the War.'

During his speech Churchill made one reference to the Admiralty. Here too he was concerned at the unnecessary risk which the men at sea were forced to run. 'The Admiralty,' he insisted, 'ought to press on night and day with every form of new construction. . . . That is, the construction which saves the lives of our men, and does not expose them to needless and hopeless peril.'

In his reply, Lloyd George spoke appreciatively of Churchill's criticisms. They would, he said, be carefully examined, and, where justified, followed up. He subsequently encouraged Churchill to call on him at the War Office whenever he wanted to raise some point of military policy; he listened to Churchill's suggestions and in many cases acted upon them. With Lloyd George at the War Office, Churchill's position as a critic was much weakened. He knew that in any change of Government he would depend almost entirely upon Lloyd George's support for a Cabinet position. Nor did he regard Lloyd George as lacking in the qualities needed to effect a drastic change in war policies.

During August, Lloyd George and Churchill saw much of each other, and talked freely of politics. Christopher Addison recorded in a note of August 4, later published in his memoirs *Four And A Half Years*:

On Tuesday (August 1) had breakfast with L.G.. Churchill and Reading came in. The chief gossip was of Government reconstruction. Churchill, with whom the wish is father to the thought, considered the P.M. would welcome the opportunity of becoming Lord Chancellor and so get rid of his private financial difficulties. I do not see this happening, unless he is obliged: neither, I think, did Reading. The P.M. will sit tight and things will drift on longer.

Lloyd George and Churchill began again to discuss foreign affairs, with the same acerbity as in the summer of 1915. Both were still critical of what they regarded as Grey's lack of foresight, and Asquith's lethargy. Shortly before the German–Bulgarian–Austrian attack on Rumania of 1 September 1916 Lloyd George explained the military situation in detail to Churchill, who recorded in *The World Crisis*: '. . . after we had mutually alarmed each other in a long talk at Walton Heath, he wrote a serious though belated warning to the Prime Minister.' But the warning itself, that the French and Russian Governments should be urged to be more active on Rumania's behalf, came to nothing. Nor could Lloyd George's confidences give Churchill a sense of real participation in war policy.

Churchill tried to find solace in painting. In mid-August he spent a weekend at Hurstmonceux Castle in Sussex, the home of Claude Lowther.[1] Violet Bonham Carter was also there. In *Winston Churchill As I Knew Him* she recalled how Churchill painted in silence, totally absorbed by the canvas:

The spell was only broken once that day by the dull distant thunder of the cannonade in France. He broke off then, laid down his brush and spoke with bitterness of his position; of the unfair attacks upon him for the failure in Gallipoli, of his desire for a public enquiry, in which he could have the chance of vindicating himself, of the Government's duty to lay the relevant papers before Parliament; of his sense of unjust exclusion from the great world struggle in which he knew that he could play an essential part, of all the ideas he could pour into it, now running to waste in the sand. 'They don't want to listen to me, or use me. They only want to keep me out.'

On August 13, while at Hurstmonceux, Churchill wrote to Seely:

My dear Jack,

I think it probable that Asquith will out last the session—& then there is a six weeks holiday. His position is however not at all good. The Tories outside the Gvt despise him: the Irish have lost faith in him & many of the Liberals are estranged or sore. There are vy hostile forces at work in the Cabinet and at any time a collapse is possible.

Meanwhile the Dlles Commission will occupy my immediate attention; & I am hopeful that my case may command their respect when it is fully unfolded. It is a pretty good commission.

[1] Claude Lowther, 1872–1929. Conservative MP, 1900–6; 1910–18. Served with the Imperial Yeomanry in South Africa, 1900. In August 1914 he raised a battalion of Sussex men, known as Lowther's Lambs, whom he commanded in France. In 1915 he raised three more battalions.

When will you come home for a spell of leave? I want vy much to talk to you & learn all yr news. I see a good deal of French and we dwell pleasantly 'upon the days that are no more'. A. Balfour dozes placidly upon the Admiralty throne, & the art of doing nothing with mighty rewards is carried to its finest perfection.

On the whole it looks as if Austria was hard hit. We ought to concentrate all efforts on her destruction. Germany can no more stand without Austria, than we & France cd conquer without Russia. Looking back on this war one sees that its gt decisions arose out of the interplay of forces wh had escaped from human direction—the turn at the Marne—the check on the Yser—the non extinction of Russia as a belligerent in the autumn of 1915; Brusiloff's lightening stroke now—All are imponderable—Why did the Germans attack Verdun? Surely it has been their undoing. Fancy both Germany & Austria coming to the West against us & Italy, & letting that half dead bear rise with renewed & perhaps illimitable strength. Turkey shows weakness now wh is as unexpected to me as her strength was last year. She must have been vy nearly cooked at Gallipoli. A little more energy & resolution, a clear determined policy, & we might so easily have done her in.

Good luck to you my dear—count on me if the moment comes when I am worth anything again.

I can hear the guns here (Sussex) quite plainly thudding away. I am sorry there was no sphere for me out there. It is painful being here idle. But I must just wait. Perhaps another chance of being of some use will come.

Yours always
W

Churchill continued to speak on military affairs. But the military debates no longer provided him with the opportunity he had earlier expected from them. It had been easy to attack War Office policy while Kitchener was responsible for it. But as soon as Lloyd George went to the War Office, a less defective policy was adopted; nor did Churchill relish attacking the one senior political figure sympathetic to his aspirations.

In August the Government introduced a Special Register Bill to determine who would be entitled to vote, should there be a wartime election. Under this Bill, soldiers in France were to have been excluded. On August 16 the President of the Local Government Board, Walter Long, spoke on behalf of the Government. He said that although the Bill had certain weaknesses, it should nevertheless still be passed. Churchill replied with a short, sarcastic speech:

This is what he now says to us: That the Bill is an unseaworthy Bill, an illogical Bill, a bad Bill . . . all these defects, all these evils! Therefore what? Therefore pass it! Pass it at once. Pass it with scarcely any study. Pass it with very little discussion. But pass it with general acclamation!

Surely, Sir, when measures of consequence are put forward in such a very half-hearted fashion, and with such evident lack of conviction behind them, those who make themselves responsible for them should not blame the House if it asks for reasonable time and opportunity, and if it declines to pass propositions of this character without reasonable time and opportunity for considering them.

Churchill's principal complaint was this: 'Is it not perfectly clear that the soldiers who are fighting our battles ought not to be excluded?' But Asquith was determined that the Bill should be passed without further delay, and used the official Whip to press Parliamentary opinion behind it. Churchill again protested. This, he declared, was a flagrant misuse of the Government's Parliamentary powers. Bonar Law, in a sharp and personal reply, which ignored the substance of Churchill's criticism, tried to demolish his credibility by mockery:

I really do not think that any of us who have listened to this Debate have much reason to be proud of the display which the House of Commons is making. The right hon Gentleman who has just spoken has given us two very valuable lessons, which came with great effect from him. One is, that we should all conduct ourselves with becoming modesty, which is good advice wherever it comes from. The other is that we are committing an unpardonable offence in proposing to put on the Government Whips for a Government Bill.

It may be worth while to note in passing that this is the same right hon Gentleman who told us yesterday that all that the House of Commons wanted the Government to do was to give a lead and say what they wanted.

Churchill was stung by these remarks, writing to Max Aitken on August 18: 'It is a pity Bonar shd be *personal* in rejoinders to me. I do not make personal attacks on him or try to decry his personal behaviour or qualities. Surely the wide field of political argument shd afford sufficient scope at the present time, when everything is so uncertain.'

Each debate led to bitterness. Churchill was unable to win the respect of the Tory leaders. The future of Asquith's Government was unclear; the speculation about his successor unnerving. Old wounds began to smart again, old sores to fester; and in such an atmosphere Churchill suffered. A letter which Lord Derby wrote to Lloyd George on August 19 reflected the Tory hostility. Derby had heard that Churchill often called to see Lloyd George at the War Office:

I know your feelings about him and I appreciate very much that feeling which makes you wish not to hit a man when he is down, but Winston is never down or rather will never allow that he is down and I assure you that his coming to the War Office as he does is—not to put it too strongly—most distasteful to everybody in that office. If as I hope there will be a new Party formed at the end of the War which shall break down all the old Party ties, Winston could not possibly be in it. Our Party will not work with him and as far as I am concerned personally nothing would induce me to support any Government of which he was a member. I like him personally. He has got a very attractive personality but he is absolutely untrustworthy as was his father before him, and he has got to learn that just as his father had to disappear from politics so must he, or at all events from official life.

Churchill continued to try to influence the House of Commons. On August 22, in the main speech of the Adjournment debate, he warned the House that all was not going well with the war, despite frequent Government assertions to the contrary. He wanted the Government to intervene in every aspect of war-direction. 'We cannot go on treating the War,' he warned, 'as if it were an emergency which can be met by makeshifts. It is, until it is ended, the one vast, all-embracing industry of the nation, and it is until it is ended the whole aim and purpose of all our lives.' He believed that there was only one solution: 'Everything in the State ought now to be devised and regulated with a view to the development and maintenance of our war power at the absolute maximum for an indefinite period. If you want to shorten the War, do this. If you want to discourage the enemy, let them see that you are doing it. If you want to cheer our own people, let them feel that you are doing it.' The most effective method of disheartening Germany, he asserted, was to make it quite clear that 'her most formidable antagonists, for so we are now coming to have the honour to be, are coldly, scientifically, and systematically arranging their national life for the one supreme business in hand'.

Churchill begged the Government to control the rise in food prices. He warned that if prices continued to rise a collapse of civilian morale was inevitable. Prices could be kept low, he insisted, only if the State took control of the shipping industry and eliminated the profits which shipowners were making as a result of war conditions. Churchill declared emphatically that although the country was able to accept 'every hardship and every sacrifice', he strongly believed that 'the people of this country do require to know that the sacrifices and sufferings they endure arise solely from the needs of the War and of the action against the enemy and that they are not added to by any lack of grip and energy in dealing with the freight problems here or by the accumulation of extortionate profits in the hands of private individuals'.

Churchill had seen each of his recent speeches dismissed by Govern-

ment spokesmen with cheap sneers and sarcasm. In appealing at the end
of this speech for resolute Government action, he implored the House of
Commons to take his criticisms seriously, even though Ministers would
try to dismiss them. 'Ministers are often offended with discussions which
take place in this House . . .' he warned. 'The slightest opposition
renders them indignant, and they are always ready to attribute mean
motives to those concerned in it.' Their duty was to take positive action.
'Let the Government show,' he concluded, 'that they do not merely
hold the offices of State, but that they hold the key to the solutions of the
difficulties with which they are confronted; that they do not need to be
pushed by the House of Commons and by the Press into action on so
many occasions, but that they can go forward spontaneously with good
and well-thought-out arrangements; that they are really the leaders of
the country in its hour of peril. . . .'

From the beginning of June, when Asquith had first promised to put
the Dardanelles documents to Parliament, to the end of July, when the
Commission of Inquiry was set up, and on through the late summer and
autumn, each of the participants assembled his evidence and prepared
to be examined by the Commission. Churchill became increasingly
embroiled in the past. At the end of July, Fisher asked him for help in
preparing his own evidence for the Commissioners. 'My dear Fisher,'
Churchill replied on August 1, 'I really feel gt diffidence in doing what
you ask me. Although I greatly appreciate the confidence you show in
me, I am sure it is much better that in the first instance you shd do it
yrself. Then we can discuss it.' Three days later Fisher sent Churchill his
first draft. It was not at all hostile to the enterprise. 'The gt kindness &
goodwill of yr paper touches me,' Churchill replied at once. 'I will come
& talk to you about it next week. You must set yrself more on public
grounds for every action & you can I think do more justice to yr own
case. But it has the compulsive buoyancy of truth.' Churchill discussed
his own evidence with Hankey on several occasions. On August 3
Hankey wrote in his diary: 'In the evening Churchill called to see me &
ranted for an hour about the Dardanelles, so that I got home very late.'

On August 10 Churchill and Fisher met to discuss the progress of
their respective statements. Fisher was anxious that Churchill should
continue to help him with his evidence. Churchill rehearsed to the
Admiral a possible line of argument to support his hostility to the
Dardanelles. On the following morning Fisher wrote:

My dear Winston,
   You were most convincing last night!

Impossible for me to equal it! So please telephone to Phillips[1] on your return (Gerrard 301) & tell him to send shorthand writer and dictate just as you said it so convincingly last evening. Dont fail! What I enclose puts it on the wrong basis yet I would wish to bring out how you fought for me and how I reciprocated your affection!

All the telegrams & letters I enclose were sent me by Crease (*just as you see them*) as being what he had put by! I never kept letters received or copies of letters sent—I am not sure now that this is not a happy thing! They cant call for what I have not got! So please let me, say next week, have your last evening's excellent narrative.

Yours
Fisher

The two men met again on August 15. Churchill again helped Fisher with his draft, and promised to write down a line of argument for him. A few hours after their meeting Fisher wrote enthusiastically:

3.30 *A.M.*!!!
Private
'The Early Bird *catches the worm*'

Dear Winston,

I did not emphasize the following point yesterday evening made by my acute Duchess[2] LONG SINCE!:—

She has ALL ALONG maintained (*the war being our* ONE *object!*) that your case can be infinitely better stated for YOUR benefit by MY case being put forward on the one sole ground that I was originally drawn to you by your WAR ATTRIBUTES (*unpossessed by any other member of the Government*).

'*Celerity*'
'*Courage*'
'*Audacity*'
'*Imagination*'

So I clung to you! clung against my convictions!

If on that text you unfold my case to the young woman Phillips sends you on application (Gerrard 301 Extension 5) then you'll make a good thing of it!

Yours
Fisher

'I think also YOU made an excellent point,' Fisher wrote in his postscript, 'of enlarging on the Armada of 593 vessels & my reluctance to leave that task unfinished. . . . Also I see the Force of your remark

[1] James Faulkner Phillips, 1871–1933. Deputy Librarian, Admiralty, 1908–31; Librarian, 1931–2. Fisher's Secretary at the Board of Invention and Research, 1915–18.
[2] Nina Mary Benita Poore, 1878–1951. She married, 1901, the 13th Duke of Hamilton, an old shipmate of Fisher's. She was Lord Fisher's friend and ardent supporter. She and her husband made the Admiral welcome at both Hamilton Palace in Lanarkshire and Balcombe Place in Sussex. Vice-Patron, Royal Society for Prevention of Cruelty to Animals, 1903–25.

about bringing in the Falkland Islands, slurred over in all recent emanations from Authority!'

Because Churchill and Fisher had renewed their friendship, Churchill did not build up his evidence, as he might have done, on the basis of Fisher's erratic behaviour between October 1914 and May 1915. Instead, he tried to make their two cases fit together, modifying the fierce conflict which had in reality done so much harm to the planning of the enterprise. Fisher's mental collapse, to which Asquith, Hankey and Churchill had each referred with such conviction in May 1915, and the megalomania of the resignation demands which Fisher had sent Asquith on 19 May 1915, were not referred to once during the six months of the Commission's sittings.

By the middle of August Churchill's evidence was almost ready. On August 12 he had written to the Chairman of the Dardanelles Commission, Lord Cromer, setting out his intentions. The letter was confident in its tone and comprehensive in its demands:

My dear Lord Cromer,

As I expect that the meetings of your Commission are about to commence, I write to say that I desire at an early stage in the proceedings to place the Commission in possession of certain documents and information, and to make a general statement to them in regard to the Admiralty's share in these transactions. I presume that the Prime Minister will probably wish to come before you first, but I should be quite ready to follow him with reasonable notice.

My evidence will be given in three separate phases: (1) the genesis of the Naval and Military operations and their conduct, down to the conclusion of Sir Ian Hamilton's first attempt to carry the Peninsula in the early days of May. (2) The proceedings leading to the Battle of Suvla Bay in August. (3) The policy and conduct of the operations from after the Battle of Suvla Bay to the evacuation of the Peninsula in January 1916.

It is with the first of these phases that I am now alone prepared to deal in detail. I was much less closely concerned with the other two stages, and considerable research among the papers and documents is required to enable me to present the case as I see it to the Commission. If agreeable to you, I should therefore prefer to confine my evidence to the first phase at the present time: but in regard to this I wish to deal both with the naval & military operations & their co-ordination.

With regard to the procedure of the Commission, I presume that I shall be at liberty to be present during the course of the Enquiry. I have a number of witnesses to bring before the Commission. I propose to conduct the case, so far as I am concerned, myself, and not to ask leave to employ Counsel.

Yours sincerely
Winston S. Churchill

Churchill sent a draft of his evidence to a Liberal MP, Alexander MacCallum Scott,[1] who in 1905 had written Churchill's biography, and who was just about to publish another biographical volume, *Winston Churchill in Peace and War*. On August 25 MacCallum Scott sent his suggestions, including advice about the way Churchill should deal with the renewal of the indecisive naval attack of 18 March 1915:

... I suggest you should not emphasise or over-elaborate your own personal view, or insist over much that you would, if it had been left to you alone, have ordered the attack to be renewed. I think you were right; but after all you were not the technical expert, & the Committee is not inquiring into what you might have done under other circumstances but what was done under existing circumstances.

As far as the Commission is concerned the important fact is that the naval attempt was then broken off in view of definitely promised military operations.

You would have preferred pressing the naval assault to the final test but in view of the decision of the technical experts & of your colleagues you deferred.

At all events, I think this part of the story wants careful handling.

During August Lloyd George helped Churchill to obtain material from the War Office files. The Admiralty provided copies of many of the naval signals that had passed between the Admiralty and the officers at the Dardanelles. But a serious problem was caused by Asquith, who still refused to give Hankey permission to send Churchill a complete set of the War Council minutes. Asquith could only suffer if the evidence of his own support for the Dardanelles, or of Kitchener's vacillations, were to become known, and be used as a lever against him by Government critics. Without this essential evidence Churchill's case was incomplete, and in parts much weaker than it might otherwise have been. By the end of August Churchill had done what he could from the materials at his disposal. On August 30 he wrote to Fisher:

My dear Fisher,

I have been working at my statement of the Admiralty case & have vy nearly completed it. I will send it you when it is ready & we can then discuss particular points & documents. . . . I think you will be pleased with it.

I send you a copy I got from the WO of Kitchener's statement to the War

[1] Alexander MacCallum Scott, 1874–1928. Secretary, the Liberal League against Aggression and Militarism, 1900–3. Liberal MP, 1910–22. He published a biography, *Winston Spencer Churchill* in 1905 and a revised edition, *With Winston Churchill in Peace and War*, in 1916. He joined the Labour Party in 1924.

Council of May 13. It will certainly be produced. He was vy angry about the Queen Elizabeth being withdrawn.

The Admiralty papers wh they are putting in consist entirely of Oliver's & Jackson's plans with the reports from the Admirals. You and I do not seem to have existed! I think they are behaving well. In addition there are the telegrams.

Grey has authorised me to have my papers printed at FO & this will be a convenience. I don't expect to be called before Sept 20 or thereabouts. So there is plenty of time.

Yes indeed stagnation, apathy & playing for safety are the orders of the day.

Yours vy sincerely
Winston S. Churchill

The Foreign Office printer worked quickly. On September 8 Churchill received several copies of the first selection of his evidence. He sent one set at once to F. E. Smith, together with the draft of a covering letter which he intended to give to the Commission. To F. E. Smith he wrote:

My dear Fred,

. . . In this letter I have put down what I believe I can prove by documents and witnesses. I have drafted it so that Fisher will probably be able to say, 'I do not disagree with any of the statements of fact, but I must add, etc, etc.' I want you to consider the case from an advocate's point of view. I am under no obligation to put in all these documents, and the question of how big a target should be exposed spontaneously is important. . . .

The great question of tactics seems to be whether I should confine myself exclusively to the Naval part and avail myself of my formal and recorded disclaimers of responsibility for the Military operations. There is no doubt, I think, that the Naval part is very solid, but on the other hand the case as I present it in my draft is the true case.

Another question is whether I should not very early point out that the kind of crude misconceptions which have generally been widely current about the inception of the Naval operations, eg that it was an amateur scheme without proper expert backing, rushed through the War Council without consideration or even with concealment; that the Navy began unbeknown to Lord Kitchener and at dates that the Army did not expect, etc— and should I then when these allegations have been demolished ask the Commission to clear away these misconceptions decidedly? . . .

If you are in London Monday or Tuesday perhaps we could have a talk about these things, and I could then show you some alternative or additional documents about which I am at present undecided. . . .

Yours always
W

It was difficult to reconstruct the past, particularly as much of the evidence was locked away in archives to which Churchill had no access. There were only a few people with whom he could consult. When he sent a draft of his evidence to Sir Graham Greene, the Secretary to the Admiralty, Greene replied on September 9, advising him to moderate his criticisms of Kitchener. 'Although,' Greene wrote, 'so far as I am able to judge your comments are just, I am inclined to think that, having regard to the fact that he is no longer alive and able to speak for himself a little more reserve in referring to him would improve the general impression gained from hearing or reading your memorandum.' Churchill could not challenge the Kitchener myth; he was defeated before he could even present his defence.

Churchill continued his collaboration with Fisher, sending drafts of his evidence to the Admiral, and checking Fisher's drafts. On September 16 he sent Fisher an outline of how he thought Fisher should present his evidence to the Commission:

1. Definite long formed opinion against it.
2. Desire not to close the mind against *new* developments.
3. Overwhelming political need and pressure.
4. Unanimity at the Admiralty and on the spot for it.
5. Me!
6. Loyal and resolute conduct of the operation up to the point where the Admiral on the spot pulled up.
7. Then determination not to go further and desire to break off—if possible.
8. Consequent disagreement with me.
9. Hopeless military indecision and delay.
10. Conviction that you could not put your heart into the further measures —your utility for the time exhausted.
Above all sombre, silent, sphinx.

Churchill ended his letter on a personal note. 'Ah how cruel it is,' he wrote, 'to feel what we could do for these mugs! . . . Still I have not given up hope yet—that things may come right for us both.'

Some of Fisher's friends thought Churchill's collaboration with him unwise, and even Churchill wondered whether it should continue. But F. E. Smith was opposed to any secrecy or concealment. On September 20 Churchill wrote to Fisher:

FE saw no objection to our having a talk or to yr seeing the statement & documents I propose to hand in. On the contrary he thought it right that misunderstanding shd be eliminated where possible between persons who have been responsible for such momentous affairs, so that the truth cd be made clear without confusion or unfounded reproaches. I intend to show Asquith what I am going to say beforehand in pursuance of this advice.

But beset as we are by foes it is better to proceed with the utmost caution. I think you have chosen very wisely in Garvin. I will see him in the first instance and show him what I have prepared. We can postpone our talk till afterwards: & it may not be necessary in the end.

I will send for G today.

Freddy is such a loyal friend that his advice must always be weighed even when it is not endorsed by others.

On September 21, after he had spent an evening with Fisher going through the Admiral's evidence, Garvin wrote to Churchill:

My dear Winston,

. . . The Admiral seems strongly inclined now to discard his 'preamble' and to adopt the alternative statement of his case—with letter January 3rd 1915 and Baltic project for its corner-stones. A vast improvement. I have put to him the point about his offer to go out in Command. He and I are to meet again at Edward Goulding's (Wargrave) for a few hours, and I hope to get him again on Tuesday or Wednesday and to bring him to close quarters with your case. Really he is very amenable and magnanimous. He is convinced that if you were both together again, you could do the Baltic yet and above all *execute now* the letter of January 3—with modifications of course—so as to solve the Balkan–Constantinople business, where the military hitch promises to become again serious & prolonged!!! I must see you after I have seen him, next Monday.

Yours ever
JLG

On September 19 the Dardanelles Commission met to consider Churchill's letter of August 12. On the following day Lord Cromer informed him of their decisions, which were not what Churchill had anticipated:

. . . As regards procedure, you say, 'I presume that I shall be at liberty to be present during the course of the enquiry.' The Commissioners have decided, in respect of all such meetings as are held in secret, not to admit anyone. They are, therefore, unable to comply with your request. But I may add that the evidence of all the witnesses will be printed, and that, should it appear desirable, for whatsoever reason, that any witness who has been already examined should be placed in possession of the evidence of other witnesses, a copy will be confidentially sent to him. Thus, on the one hand, the Commissioners will have an opportunity of recalling a witness should they think it desirable to do so, and, on the other hand, a witness who has been already examined will have an opportunity of requesting that he may be recalled in order to furnish any further explanation which he may wish to make, resulting from the evidence of subsequent witnesses. . . .

A second letter from Cromer on September 21 seemed to imply that the evidence considered by the Commission might not be as detailed as Churchill had wanted. 'As regards the Admiralty papers,' Cromer wrote, 'a very large number of telegrams were put at our disposal. I have not myself seen them but I believe they contain nothing but telegrams. A great many of these deal with points of detail which, for our purposes, are unimportant.' Cromer did not explain how he judged what was unimportant before any of the evidence had been taken. Another member of the Commission, Sir William Pickford, had gone through the file of telegrams, and, Cromer told Churchill, 'selected all those which are of real importance'. This was before a single witness had been examined.

On September 28 Churchill appeared before the Commissioners. He read his statement and answered their questions. He told them that five distinct truths could be drawn from the factual evidence. These were, he said:

1. That there was full authority;
2. That there was a reasonable prospect of success;
3. That greater interests were not compromised;
4. That all possible care and forethought were exercised in the preparation;
5. That vigour and determination were shown in the execution.

The evidence that Churchill produced to substantiate these points was voluminous; but it was never published. When the enquiry was over the Government agreed to publish only a general report. The documents, the submissions and the cross-examination were not made public.

On one of Churchill's visits to the War Office in the summer of 1916 Lloyd George had told him that a small number of the new 'tanks', with the development of which Churchill had been so closely connected, were to be used on the Somme. Churchill was shocked at the idea of the premature use of what he believed would be a decisive weapon if held back until it could be used in quantity, and with an element of surprise. He therefore asked Asquith to see him. Asquith listened so patiently to Churchill's tactical arguments that he came away believing that the tank would not be used until there were sufficient numbers to make an immediate impact; probably early in 1917. But Churchill's arguments had not prevailed. On 15 September 1916 the first few tanks went into action, without any decisive effect, and the element of surprise was lost. 'My poor "land battleships",' Churchill wrote in his letter to Fisher of September 16, 'have been let off prematurely and on a petty scale. In that idea resided one real victory.' Churchill was angered by what he believed to have been a shortsighted policy. But he was also disappointed to gain no political advantage from the widespread public excitement at the appearance of a new weapon of war. Few people knew how closely he had been connected with its development. When Arthur Conan Doyle[1] wrote to him at the end of September with praise for his efforts with the tank, Churchill replied on October 1:

I am vy much obliged to you for yr kindness in writing to me about the caterpillars.

There are plenty of good ideas if only they can be backed with power and brought into reality. But think what a time it took—from February 1915 when I gave the original orders—to Sept 1916 when the first use was made of these machines! And even then I think it wd have been better to wait & act on a much larger scale—having waited so long.

The caterpillars are the land sisters of the monitors. Both are intended to restore to the stronger power an effective means of the offensive. The monitor was the beginning of the torpedo-proof fleet. The caterpillar of the bullet proof army. But *surprise* was the true setting for both.

On October 12 Lloyd George was questioned about the invention of the tank in the House of Commons. He explained that the suggestions had come from D'Eyncourt and Hankey, but that 'these suggestions would never have fructified had it not been for the fact that Mr Churchill, who was then First Lord of the Admiralty, gave practical effect to them by making the necessary experiments, setting up committees for carrying the suggestions into effect, and by putting the whole of his energy and strength towards materialising the hopes of those who

[1] Arthur Conan Doyle, 1859–1930. Historian and novelist. Inventor of Sherlock Holmes. During the First World War he was gathering material for his six-volume history *The British Campaign in France and Flanders*, published at intervals between 1915 and 1920.

had been looking forward to an attempt of this kind'. Lloyd George's praise did not reduce Churchill's isolation.

Press hostility had not diminished since Churchill's return from the trenches. On October 11 H. A. Gwynne, the editor of the *Morning Post*, sent General Rawlinson details of an intrigue which he believed he had uncovered. 'French, Winston, Smith and Lloyd George are all working hand in hand though with different objects,' he wrote. 'Lloyd George is, I think, merely trying to get the Army in the hollow of his hand, and be able to order it about as he did the Ministry of Munitions. The others want to get rid of DH [Haig], but do not have any anxiety about the outcome. I have got satisfactory assurances that the plot will fail entirely, and that it may recoil on the heads of those who planned it. . . . I have taken care that the right people shall be prepared for all the ramifications of this dirty little trick.' To Asquith, Gwynne wrote that same day of 'a sort of plot whose ramifications I am not altogether able to trace. There seems to be on the part of the War Minister, Mr Winston Churchill, Sir F. E. Smith, and Lord French, a common agreement in regard to the capabilities of the Commander-in-Chief of the British Armies in France; and I am about justified in saying that I perceive indications that the form which this understanding is taking is that of exalting the French system of tactics and strategy at the expense of our own.' Churchill's most severe public rebuke came on October 13, when a leading article in Lord Northcliffe's *Daily Mail* challenged his criticism of the renewed offensive in France, and warned him not to pit himself against Haig, or against the Chief of the Imperial General Staff, Sir William Robertson:

There is no Cabinet Minister or ex-Cabinet Minister, not even the most eminent, the most gifted, the most eloquent, the most energetic and most popular, whom this country would allow at this time of day to interfere with the plans of these two men. We have had more than enough of that sort of thing in the present war. The country has seen a Cabinet Minister who had just intelligence enough to know that Antwerp and Constantinople were places of importance and yet was mad enough to embark on adventures in both places with forces and methods that were insanely disproportionate to the enterprises upon which our unfortunate sailors and soldiers were launched in each case. In the Dardanelles affair in particular a megalomaniac politician risked the fate of our Army in France and sacrificed thousands of lives to no purpose.

His duty at the time when he dragged his too pliant officers and experts with him into these reckless and hopeless 'gambles' was simply to supply the Navy with men and with material, and to be answerable to the House of

Commons that it was so supplied. He had no other function whatever, and, if his naval colleagues had been men of the stamp of Sir Douglas Haig and Sir William Robertson, he would not have been allowed to exercise any other function.

Asserting in italics, '*Ministerial meddling means military muddling*', the article continued: 'No politician who remembers the contemptible fiasco of Antwerp and the ghastly blunder of Gallipoli need expect either patience or forgiveness from the British public if he interferes with the soldiers in charge of our operations. . . .' Churchill was familiar with these accusations. He realized that he had little chance of returning to office if, while the whole Dardanelles episode was still being enquired into, he could be pilloried in this way in an influential daily newspaper. On October 17 he wrote to Lord Cromer to protest both about the article in the *Daily Mail* and about the methods adopted by the Dardanelles Commission to obtain evidence:

Whether this article is a proper one to have appeared while matters of this character are sub judice is a question which I do not now refer to; but it shows very clearly the kind of attack to which I am exposed and from which I have every right to defend myself before the Commission. I am doing so however under considerable disabilities. I am not able to examine myself the principal witnesses upon whom I rely to establish the Admiralty case. Many of the questions which are essential to elicit the facts have not yet been put to them. On the other hand adverse witnesses have had a number of leading questions put to them the result of which has been to obtain from them evidence which is open to direct challenge without my having any opportunity of cross-examination. Other questions have been put to witnesses which they have no competence to answer, and their answers are recorded as authoritative pronouncements. I need not point out to the Commission (for it is recognised I believe in nearly every civilised system or procedure) the misleading effects which are certain to follow from very suggestive legal questions when wholly uncorrected by cross-examination. The result of this is that the Commission has not yet been placed in a position to do justice to the Admiralty case especially in its professional and technical aspect.

Churchill persisted with his defence, trying to ensure that the Commission was fully informed of what had actually taken place at the Dardanelles. On October 19 he wrote to its Secretary, Grimwood Mears,[1]

---

[1] Edward Grimwood Mears, 1869–1963. Gave up his practice at the Bar on Government request to investigate allegations of German atrocities in Belgium, 1914–15. Secretary to the Royal Commission appointed to enquire into the causes of the Easter Rising in Ireland, 1916. Secretary to the Dardanelles Commission, 1916–17; he agreed to become Secretary on condition that he was given a knighthood for his services. Knighted, 1917. Assistant to Lord Reading, Washington, 1918–19. Chief Justice, Allahabad High Court, India, 1919–32.

that he intended to bring forward 'sufficient evidence and argument' to prove three points:

(a) That at no time during the Dardanelles operation was the margin of safety of the Grand Fleet compromised or reduced in the slightest degree.
(b) That the ammunition reserves of the Admiralty were in all respects sufficient both for the needs of the Grand Fleet and the Dardanelles operation as planned.
(c) That the old battleships of the Majestic and Canopus class were really *surplus* to all requirements of the Fleet of blue water fighting and were therefore available to be risked in bombarding or in a similar operation.

That day Churchill also wrote to Admiral Oliver, who had been summoned to give evidence to the Dardanelles Commission. 'I think you should be able to give evidence broadly as follows,' Churchill wrote, and then outlined the points which he wished Oliver to stress:

That, like other Naval officers of high standing who have been captains of ships, you have yourself a good general knowledge of naval gunnery and its possibilities. . . .

That you have, during the course of this war, repeatedly made plans or revised plans for bombarding operations of all kinds. . . .

That in Commodore de Bartolomé you had a gunnery specialist of very high order with whom you were in frequent consultation, at regular meetings and at other times.

That your plans were prepared with all possible care and thought in accordance with the directions of the First Lord and First Sea Lord, in close conjunction with the work which was being done by Sir Henry Jackson, and that, of course, the full and accurate information of the Admiralty Intelligence Department was at your disposal.

That you adhere to the general soundness of these plans so far as the calculable factors are concerned, the chief of these being the destruction of permanent forts.

That the degree of Turkish resistance which would be encountered was an incalculable factor, though there were good reasons (vide Doris' proceedings on the Syrian Coast, etc.) for believing that the Turkish resistance would not immediately be of the most efficient character.

That the amount of opposition from mobile guns and its effect upon sweeping the Kephez minefield was also an incalculable factor.

That, for that reason, a gradual method of advance was prescribed, from which we could at any time withdraw, and from which we did, in fact, withdraw.

Oliver agreed to give evidence as Churchill suggested. In a private note on Churchill's letter he commented: 'If all the requirements they consider essential to success had to be met before an operation was undertaken no big operation of war would ever be undertaken. Most operations consist in making the most of a lot of bad conditions.'

On October 27 Hankey wrote in his diary: 'Winston Churchill called in the afternoon. . . . He seems quite satisfied that he made good his case.' That day Churchill wrote to Captain Spiers: 'I am slowly triumphing in this Dardanelles Commission, and bit by bit am carrying the whole case. I am really hopeful that they will free me from the burden wh cripples my action.' On October 28 Churchill wrote to Asquith, pointing out how much of the evidence given to the Commission by the naval experts vindicated his judgement. But he was disappointed by Grey's evidence, which he felt was 'pretty thin'. 'After all,' he reminded Asquith, 'it was a great Foreign Office need that the Admiralty were endeavouring to meet.' The Dardanelles Commission continued to sit throughout November. Churchill absorbed himself in studying the evidence which they took almost every day, and in seeking, where he felt it necessary, to rebut the accusations as they were made against him. In the whole of the British Press there was only one friendly article. It appeared on November 12 in the *Sunday Pictorial*, signed by the proprietor himself, Lord Rothermere:[1]

In the minds of some writers Mr Churchill appears to exercise an omnipresent and ubiquitous influence. They see his shadow in every glass. They search for traces of his identity in any anonymous writings that may for the moment attract more than usual attention. The public departments which he administered in the past are suspected of still echoing his views. Individual Ministers are thought to be susceptible to his influence, while any suggestion in any quarter to the effect that Mr Churchill has performed great and enduring services to the nation is seized upon as evidence of some concerted intrigue to restore him to power.

. . . the attacks on Mr Churchill continue, the object apparently being to discredit him utterly as a politician in the estimation of the public, and to prevent him at any future time from taking any useful share in the public life of the nation.

The majority of these attacks I believe to be sincere and devoid of personal animus. They are based upon the belief that Mr Churchill is by record and temperament unfitted to play any conspicuous part in the councils of the people. A man's character and temperament are expressed by his record in life, by the things which he has done and the things which he has not done,

---

[1] On the following day Rothermere's second son, Vere Sidney Tudor Harmsworth (born 1895), was killed in action in France, while serving as a Lieutenant, Royal Naval Division. His eldest son, Harold Alfred Vyvian St George Harmsworth (born 1894) died of wounds received in action in France on 12 February 1918.

and it is, I believe, because Mr Churchill's opponents are only in partial possession of the facts concerning his administrative career at the Admiralty that they regard him as temperamentally unfitted for the most serious duties of public service.

There followed a detailed examination of Churchill's record at the Admiralty, and the statement that 'it is to Mr Churchill's credit that the outbreak of war after a century of peace found every ship, great or small, of our enormous fleets ready and at their war stations'. Such an achievement, Rothermere concluded, 'may never be repeated in history. It was one of those great specific acts of statesmanship which shape and decide the destinies of wars and peoples. It was an achievement which is alone sufficient to secure for Mr Churchill and all others concerned a grateful recognition in the records and the minds of their countrymen.'

During October, Sir Edward Carson had been busy organizing an effective opposition to Asquith. Over a hundred and fifty Conservative MPs had become associated with his Unionist War Committee, which had been set up at the beginning of the year, and was as critical of Bonar Law as of Asquith. On every possible occasion members of Carson's Committee spoke in Parliament of the need for greater state control: shipping, food distribution and coal were three areas where they believed direct state intervention was necessary in the interests of the proper prosecution of the war. Churchill had sympathy with many of their demands.

On November 8 Carson led the dissidents in their first concerted challenge to the Government, using a debate on the disposal of enemy property in Nigeria as the point of attack. The Government proposed to sell the captured property to any buyers except citizens of enemy countries; Carson demanded that it should be sold only to British buyers. Bonar Law, who defended the Government's policy, insisted that the vote would be one of confidence in the Government. The vote went in the Government's favour. But of those Conservatives who voted, sixty-five supported Carson, as against seventy-one who voted for the Government. Had Carson been supported by only four more Tories, Bonar Law, under the pledge he had given the Conservatives on joining the Government in May 1915, would have had to resign, and the Coalition would have collapsed. Among the others who voted with Carson were eleven Liberals, including Churchill.[1] Bonar Law at once

[1] The Liberals who voted with Carson included Frederick Handel Booth (one of Churchill's critics at the time of the Friedrichshafen raid), Leicester Harmsworth (brother of Lord Northcliffe and Lord Rothermere), Sir Alfred Mond (the only Privy Councillor other than Churchill) and Walter Roch (a member of the Dardanelles Commission).

took measures to protect his position and that of the Coalition, meeting with both Carson and Lloyd George to devise some scheme of reconstruction. Both Bonar Law and Lloyd George were willing that Asquith should remain Prime Minister, but both wanted the daily direction of war policy to be in other hands.

On the evening of November 20 C. P. Scott went to see Churchill at 41 Cromwell Road. He spent two hours alone with him, noting two days later:

He was evidently suffering acutely from his enforced inactivity. 'What fools they are,' he said, smiting the arm of his chair. 'They could get more out of me now in two years of war than in a hundred afterwards.' I urged him to make a business of Parliament and make himself a figure there, but he said the papers (with the exception of the Manchester Guardian) would not report him and on the contrary ill natured remarks were always made, as that 'there were few members present and no one troubled to come in' or 'what a contrast with the old days when his rising was the signal for the House to fill' and so on. Therefore he preferred to find his public in the press. Then at least every word he wished to say was printed and it took him no longer to write an article for the 'Sunday Pictorial' for which he got £250 than to prepare a speech which was not reported. After Xmas he meant to start a new series of articles in which there would be some very plain speaking.

At present he was the best abused man in the country. He was determined, however, to stick it out. He could effect nothing by going back to the Army so he must just 'wait in that chair'—a large and comfortable one—till his chance came. The mistake he had made was in not allowing enough for the power of the press, at a time of suspended party activity, to attack and ruin an individual. He had great hopes from the forthcoming report of the Dardanelles Commission which he had reason to believe would go far to clear him on that issue. . . .

Speaking of the possibility of a reconstructed Ministry he said no change would be material which did not involve a change in the Premiership. Lloyd George, 'with all his faults', was the only possible alternative Prime Minister. I asked if in case George formed a ministry he could count on being included. He said he thought so—that George would desire it and that it would be in his interest.

But when C. P. Scott spoke to Lloyd George's Parliamentary Secretary, David Davies,[1] on November 22, Churchill's chances of office seemed less certain. 'Didn't I think he had had his chance?' Davies asked Scott:

[1] David Davies, 1880–1944. Liberal MP, 1906–29. Commanded 14th Battalion Royal Welch Fusiliers, 1914–16. Parliamentary Private Secretary to Lloyd George, 1916–17. Landed proprietor and company director. Created Baron, 1932.

'And when a man had had his chance and missed it ought he not to be set aside?' Davies went on to say that Churchill was 'anathema in the Army', and that if Lloyd George were involved in giving him office he might incur a share of the unpopularity which would result. Scott did not pass back this gloomy intelligence to Churchill, who seemed unaware of how slim were his chances of gaining advantage from Asquith's fall.

On November 26, when Bonar Law, Lloyd George, Carson and many of those who had been Churchill's Cabinet colleagues in 1914 were concentrating upon the political crisis, Churchill himself published in the *Sunday Pictorial* his first public account of what had happened at Antwerp over two years before. The attack in the *Daily Mail* had stirred him to action. He sensed that the Dardanelles Commission of Enquiry would not publish enough evidence to vindicate, or even to explain, his actions. He therefore began the process of self-defence for the policies over which he had been criticised, not only the Dardanelles, but Antwerp and all naval policy. This process was to take up much of his time in the years to come. But his Antwerp article could not make any serious impression on the public during a week of intense political speculation about the future of the Coalition.

On November 27 Churchill received a further communication from the Dardanelles Commission. It was a copy of the statement submitted to them two days before by one of Kitchener's former Private Secretaries, Sir George Arthur.[1] Churchill was incensed at what he regarded as its blatant falsifications. Arthur had told the Commissioners that, on some unspecified date, Kitchener had been 'invited to a Conference by the First Lord of the Admiralty when the passage of the Dardanelles was the subject of discussion' and that 'he protested vigorously against such an undertaking by the Navy without very strong and very careful support from & co-operation with the Army'. For two days Churchill brooded upon this new challenge to his own honesty. Then, on November 29, he sent his answer. Bitterness broke through in every paragraph:

The only 'Conferences' held on this subject were the various meetings of the War Council the records of which are before the Commission. On no occasion either in Council or in conversation did Lord Kitchener express views of the kind attributed to him by Sir George Arthur. If he held such

[1] George Compton Archibald Arthur, 1860–1946. 3rd Baronet, 1878. Entered Army, 1880. Private Secretary to Lord Kitchener, 1914–16. Assistant to the Director of Military Operations, War Office, 1916–18. On several missions to France; he acted as interpreter between Sir Douglas Haig and General Nivelle before the battle of Arras, March 1917. His publications include *Life of Lord Kitchener* (3 vols, 1920) and *Concerning Winston Spencer Churchill* (1940).

opinions it was his duty to have expressed them at the War Councils in place of the diametrically oppositive views which he expressed both by speech and in writing. The documentary evidence I have laid before the Commission and the records of the War Council are conclusive on this point. Further, Lord Kitchener was in almost daily consultation with the Prime Minister and the Prime Minister has deposed that 'Lord Kitchener was strongly in favour of the Naval undertaking'. . . .

If it were necessary I have no doubt that negative evidence from all the naval and political personages concerned could be adduced to prove first that no such Conference took place and secondly that no such protest was made by Lord Kitchener as is described by Sir George Arthur. I hardly imagine however that in view of the evidence before them the Commissioners will wish to embark on this process. If they decide to do so I would ask their leave to marshal the evidence; and if expressions of Lord Kitchener's opinion made to a responsible person at unnamed dates are to be admitted in evidence I conceive myself in a position to produce evidence that Lord Kitchener expressed private opinions in an entirely contrary sense during the period when the Naval attack showed good prospects of succeeding. . . .

All the facts stated by Sir George Arthur are untrue and without foundation, but I desire to repeat what I have said on several occasions to the Commission—that I take full responsibility for the advice given by me in the name of the Admiralty to the War Council in regard to the Naval operation. I have never tried to throw any of this burden upon Lord Kitchener. As a principal person next to the Prime Minister concerned with the direction of the war, and as a great soldier acquainted with gunnery and quasi-military problems such as the attack of Forts, etc, he no doubt has his responsibility, but I wish to bear my responsibility as the head of the Admiralty so far as I may properly do so myself. In the same way I conceive that the prime responsibility for the inception and conduct of the military operation rests subject to the War Council with the Secretary of State for War. As the Commission know, this last point is one to which I attach importance. . . .

Churchill then raised the question of the origin of the rumours which had been circulating against him:

I have for the last eighteen months been the subject of persistent and damaging attacks in the public press and elsewhere in connection with the Dardanelles operation. It is hardly conceivable that such attacks would have been maintained with so much confidence, if they had not been founded and nourished on statements purporting to emanate from the highest authority of the character of those now brought before the Commission by Sir George Arthur. I cannot believe that Lord Kitchener himself had anything to do with the circulation of such untruthful and unfounded allegations, but that they have been made from time to time by persons in his entourage has long been suspected by me and this suspicion cannot but be confirmed by Sir George Arthur's statement.

Before the Commission began its labours I was frequently asked whether I was in a position to disprove the charge that Lord Kitchener was throughout opposed to the whole Dardanelles policy. There is no doubt that this impression was sedulously fostered and is even now widespread. The fact that at the close of the first phase of the Dardanelles operations which the Commission have now under review, I was removed from my Office as First Lord of the Admiralty while Lord Kitchener was simultaneously invested with the Order of the Garter and continued to be Secretary of State for War until his lamented death has no doubt been accepted as an unanswerable confirmation of such statements. . . .

November 30 was Churchill's forty-second birthday. He spent it at home with his wife and family. It was a year since he had ceased to be a Cabinet Minister. Nearly eighteen months had passed since he had last been the head of a Department of State. His correspondence with the Dardanelles Commission and his articles on the early history of the war took up much time; but they were not what he wanted to use his time for. While he fell back into an angry contemplation of the past, political developments continued on a turbulent course. Conservative and Liberal Ministers alike were discussing how to reduce Asquith's powers, and even to remove him altogether. Some saw Bonar Law, others saw Lloyd George, as the likely successor. Churchill was not consulted about the political upheaval, and was seldom informed of its course. On December 2, the day on which Lloyd George wrote to Bonar Law that 'the life of the country depends on resolute action by you now', Max Aitken met Churchill in London. He recalled in *Politicians and the War* how Churchill was 'almost wistfully eager for news'. Churchill was in a remote position. Yet his career seemed to depend upon the outcome of the political struggle. If Asquith remained in any position of power, or if Bonar Law became Prime Minister, it was unlikely that he could expect any upsurge in his political fortunes. But if Lloyd George emerged either as Prime Minister, or as the real focus of power, he was convinced that there would be a place for him in the new Government. Lloyd George knew the full extent of Churchill's capabilities; he understood his burning desire to help the nation at war, shared his dislike of sloth, humbug and deception, and appreciated his skill at inspiring those who feared defeat. But the only supporter of

Churchill's claims who wrote on his behalf was Sir Abe Bailey, a South African mine owner who wrote on December 2:

Dear Mr Lloyd George,

Am just off after being held up for four days & I only hope to God every-thing goes right & you are elected Prime Minister. Then there is a chance. I shall be awfully sorry if Winston's brain & push have to be left on the shelf for I know & so do you that he is full of ideas, & good ones too. I have no friendships except for the Empire & it is having those feelings that I shall for one deplore the loss of his valuable services. He will I know assist *you* in any case.

Goodbye, good luck & God bless your work.

Yours most sincerely
Abe Bailey

On December 3 Asquith agreed to the joint demands of Lloyd George and Bonar Law for a small War Committee, led by Lloyd George, on which Asquith would not serve, although he would remain Prime Minister. Lloyd George told Churchill of this enormous con-cession by Asquith. Churchill was sceptical, doubting that it would really serve the purpose of a more vigorous direction of the war. In *The World Crisis* he later wrote of how both he and Carson had felt that Lloyd George's position would be a weak and possibly a dangerous one under such a scheme:

On him would fall all the brunt of battling with the naval and military Chiefs. . . . The appeal in all cases would have been to the Prime Minister who, free from the friction of the discussions of the War Committee, yet fully informed on every point, would have been able to decide with final author-ity. On the other hand, Mr Lloyd George, publicly appointed to preside over the Committee actually directing the conduct of the war, would have been held responsible for every misfortune that occurred and there were bound to be many.

It was Asquith, not Lloyd George, who changed his mind, rejecting the arrangement to which he had already agreed. Lloyd George thereupon resigned. On December 5 Bonar Law, Curzon, Austen Chamberlain and Lord Robert Cecil likewise submitted their resignations. Faced with the immediate dissolution of his Government, Asquith tendered his own resignation to the King at seven o'clock that evening. Two and a half hours later the King received Bonar Law at Buckingham Palace, and asked him to form an administration. Lloyd George was in favour of Bonar Law doing so, and willing to serve under him. That evening Lloyd George and Aitken were due to dine with F. E. Smith at Grosvenor

Gardens. Churchill had not been invited; but in *Politicians and the War* Max Aitken gave an account of how, at this late hour of the crisis, Churchill was drawn in:

Birkenhead [F. E. Smith] and Churchill were at the Turkish Bath of the Automobile Club that evening, and Birkenhead had rung up George to remind him of a dinner engagement. He mentioned that Churchill was with him and Lloyd George immediately requested that Churchill should be asked to come too. This suggestion, probably quite carelessly made, produced on Churchill's mind the natural impression that he was regarded as one of the new set of war administrators who were about to grasp the helm. Surely Lloyd George would not ask him to be included in a dinner party on this night of all others if he did not mean to offer him a real post—and a real post to Churchill meant nothing but war-service. . . .

At the dinner, Aitken recalled, the conversation 'turned entirely on the personnel of the new Ministry' and all present—Lloyd George, F. E. Smith, Max Aitken and Churchill—took part in the conversation 'on terms of equality'. Lloyd George had to leave in order to meet Bonar Law on his return from Buckingham Palace. He asked Aitken to accompany him. During the drive he explained to Aitken that enormous pressure was being brought to bear to exclude Churchill from any new administration, and that if Lloyd George himself were to become Prime Minister, even he would not be prepared to run the risk involved in giving Churchill Cabinet office. Aitken's account continued: 'Lloyd George asked me to convey a hint of this kind on my return to the party. . . . He thought Churchill too confident of high office in the new regime. A refusal would be awkward. It would be better if Churchill were dashed a bit first.'

Aitken therefore returned to F. E. Smith's house; he himself expected some position, perhaps a substantial one, in the new administration, and therefore, as he recalled:

I smiled on Churchill as a senior colleague might on an aspiring junior. I still, so to speak, walked warily—but I walked. Churchill also had every reason to suppose that he was sure of high office. We discussed as allies and equals the personnel of the new Government. Churchill suggested that I might be made Postmaster-General—a task suitable to my abilities.

Then I conveyed to him the hint Lloyd George had given me. . . . these are the exact words I used: 'The new Government will be very well disposed towards you. All your friends will be there. You will have a great field of common action with them.'

Something in the very restraint of my language carried conviction to Churchill's mind. He suddenly felt he had been duped by his invitation to the dinner, and he blazed into righteous anger. I have never known him address his great friend Birkenhead in any other way except as 'Fred' or 'FE'. On this occasion he said suddenly: 'Smith, this man knows that I am not to be included in the new Government.'

With that Churchill walked out into the street. . . .

On the evening of December 5, after leaving Buckingham Palace, Bonar Law asked Asquith if he would agree to serve under him. Asquith refused. On the following afternoon, at a meeting of Balfour, Bonar Law, Lloyd George, Asquith and the Labour leader Arthur Henderson at Buckingham Palace, Bonar Law said that if Asquith would not serve under him, he would give up the attempt to form a Government, and that Lloyd George must do so. The Conference broke up. When it was over Asquith again refused Bonar Law's offer. That evening Bonar Law returned to Buckingham Palace and told the King that he declined to try any longer to form a Government. The King then asked Lloyd George to form a Government, and that evening Lloyd George became Prime Minister, with Bonar Law as Chancellor of the Exchequer. Balfour agreed to serve as Foreign Secretary,[1] Lord Curzon as a member of the War Cabinet. Lord Milner and Arthur Henderson also joined the War Cabinet. Lord Derby became Secretary of State for War, Walter Long Colonial Secretary, Dr Christopher Addison Minister of Munitions. F. E. Smith remained Attorney-General and Lord Robert Cecil Minister of Blockade. At a discussion on the personnel of the new Ministry held at the War Office on December 6, Addison drafted a list of possible Ministers. Churchill was not in the list. But Lloyd George wrote in the margin '? Air Winston'. No Air Ministry was established, however; nor did Lloyd George offer Churchill any place in the new Coalition.

Lloyd George wanted to give Churchill a place in his Government. But he had been unable to overcome the strong Conservative opposition to Churchill's inclusion. In his *War Memoirs* he recalled that when he had asked Bonar Law: 'Is he more dangerous *for* you than when he is *against* you?' Bonar Law had replied: 'I would rather have him against us every time.' The attitude of the Conservative Leader was shared by almost all his followers, and by *The Time:* and the *Morning Post*, both

[1] Of Balfour at this time Churchill wrote in *Great Contemporaries*: 'He passed from one Cabinet to the other, from the Prime Minister who was his champion to the Prime Minister who had been his most severe critic, like a powerful graceful cat walking delicately and unsoiled across a rather muddy street.'

for so long his implacable adversaries. Churchill's exclusion became a certainty when, on December 7, Austen Chamberlain, Walter Long, Lord Robert Cecil and Curzon pressed upon Lloyd George, as a condition of their own entry into his Cabinet, that Churchill should be excluded altogether from the administration. Without the support of these four Conservatives, Lloyd George could not have formed a Government. He therefore bowed to their veto. Churchill felt humiliated and betrayed; his critics rejoiced. The public, declared *The Times*, 'learn with relief and satisfaction that Mr. Churchill will not be offered any post in the new Administration'.

The implacable hostility and suspicion of the Conservatives, Asquith's refusal to allow the facts about the Dardanelles to be published, and the isolation imposed by a year without office, combined to keep Churchill from power. Lloyd George's Cabinet colleagues were confident that they could deal with the war without his guidance. That his outspoken public criticisms of Asquith during the previous six months may have helped their cause did not mitigate their hostility or reduce their mistrust. Nor did they consider that his long experience of naval warfare and organization gave him any claim to return to the Admiralty. Carson was appointed First Lord, the post Churchill had wanted for himself.

From May 1915 to December 1916 Churchill had believed that if he had been called upon to direct the nation's affairs, he would have made an effective war leader. He was convinced, he wrote to his wife on 28 January 1916, that he could use power 'better than any other living Englishman to determine the war policy of Britain'. He was confident that he had the ability to drive forward the machinery of Government with vigour and cohesion, and that his ideas for national organization and naval, military and aerial strategy could have averted the disasters and broken the stalemates of 1915 and 1916. Churchill's confidence in his abilities was absolute; as a Cabinet Minister he had shown this confidence to his colleagues, and it had always been a striking feature of his public speeches. It was a strong and vaunted confidence, applauded at first both by his colleagues and by the public, who appreciated and were often inspired by his combination of faith in the outcome of the war and recognition of the difficulties still to come. But to be accepted fully, to be trusted and rewarded, such confidence needed to be set against successful results. The series of failures at the Dardanelles and Gallipoli, however much they could be explained by errors other than Churchill's own, or, as he had come to explain them, by his lack of overall authority, set up a barrier between the confidence which he felt in himself, and the public assessment of him. Nor was it the Dardanelles alone that kept this barrier in place, depriving him of the power which he believed he could use effectively, and relegating him to political impotence. Irrespective of particular successes or failures, in spite of such explanations and documentation which he was able to give, Churchill's contemporaries found in his activities insufficient claim on their respect and trust. He was believed by many to be wanting in certain essential qualities of statesmanship; and was judged more deficient in these qualities by the winter of 1916 than he had been in the autumn of 1914. His wartime work at the Admiralty, for which he believed himself entitled to the praise and support of his fellow-countrymen, was interpreted in such a way as to confirm in many minds the doubts that had already been formed during the previous decade, and to create doubts where none had earlier existed. Churchill believed that his war policies and warmaking zeal had been both unique and beneficial, making him indispensable to any successful wartime administration, and qualifying him for the highest public office. But for others his war policies, and the enthusiasm with which he entered into them, created suspicion and even fear, destroying his chances of directing the war from 10 Downing Street, the Admiralty or the War Office. Any other place he regarded as insufficient challenge to his abilities, and as a waste of his energies.

Churchill did not understand why it was that he created mistrust where he expected to secure approval. He believed that his abilities and achievements were such that only a malicious critic would deny them. Clementine Churchill realized why he did not inspire trust. She saw how far his strident confidence frightened those with whom he worked and to whom he had to look for support. She alone of those closest to him told him of his faults; others, like Asquith and Lloyd George, added to his self-deception by frequent praise and encouragement when they were with him, but by severe censure on him in their private talk and correspondence. Clementine Churchill cautioned him directly. In her letters to him she stressed the danger to his career of the impatience and scorn which he often showed towards those who disagreed with him. She rebuked his tendency to take provocative or unexpected measures without regard to the likely reaction of others. She stressed how much he harmed himself by acting upon ideas which he had not given others time to accept, or which he had failed adequately to explain. She warned him that these weaknesses of character were accentuated by his often brusque and dictatorial manner, and by his overriding impatience. She saw clearly that the ideas which he produced with such extraordinary energy and conviction were seen by others as lacking in judgement; and that the more fiercely he pressed forward with a course of action, the more lacking in perspective he appeared to those colleagues without whose support he could not act.

These criticisms were all justified; Clementine Churchill understood her husband's failure to convince others. But there was a deeper failure than that. Churchill had always to be at the centre; he wanted to be responsible for the principal decisions of the war, and to be known to be. He believed that risks had to be taken and failed to understand why others were repelled by his evident relish for warmaking. While he had been at the Admiralty he had insisted upon swift and bold decisions. Those who hesitated to accept those decisions sensed his disapproval. Those who wanted to wait longer upon events found his scorn direct, outspoken and galling. He showed little sympathy for those who could not make up their minds, or who did so with reservations. As 1915 progressed, his arguments at the War Council became increasingly ineffective. Because of his forceful and assertive manner he often appeared to his colleagues over-simple and over-dramatic. At times his counsel was weighty and sober, but at times it seemed hasty and immature. Unable to explain his diverse moods, his growing obsessions or his seemingly dictatorial approach to dissent, Churchill's contemporaries found themselves making frequent and caustic reference to his ambition, which, they felt, overrode consistency. Asquith and Lloyd George, whose respective patronage had been essential to Churchill for him to remain in Government or return to it, both felt that the imaginative, constructive, hard-working colleague of pre-war years was being eaten up by personal ambition, and that his judgement had been impaired.

The doubts felt by Asquith and Lloyd George kept Churchill from office for nearly two years. These doubts were widespread, making his emergence as a war leader impossible. He believed he could govern the country effectively in time of war; few other people shared this belief. He had no national following and no regional support. No influential section of the Liberal Party considered him their leader. No significant political groups regarded him as their spokesman. The hostilities which he had aroused by the end of 1915 cut him off from all but a small group of isolated allies of no political strength. Churchill craved the allegiance of large numbers, both in Parliament and outside it. He believed that his foresight and his abilities, if fully known by his fellow-countrymen, would win that allegiance for him. But faith in his powers of leadership was held by few; by a small family circle, and by friends who had been captivated by his driving force. They alone felt that his consuming self-confidence, his impatience and his brooding were a necessary counterpart to his positive qualities, and did not undermine them.

Churchill could not dispel the doubts and distrust which he had created. All the faults to which people pointed seem to spring from an egoism which would be dangerous if allowed to control, or even influence, a War Cabinet. Only an overriding concern with self seemed adequate to explain the different phases of his wartime career: his excitement at the preparations for war, his exhilaration when it came, his personal involvement in the siege of Antwerp, his desire to give up the Admiralty for a military command, his growing obsession with the Dardanelles, his gnawing impatience with his reduced powers at the Duchy of Lancaster, his appeal for Fisher's return to the Admiralty in March 1916 and his brooding concern for vindication over each of the disasters of his nine and a half wartime months as First Lord. The selfishness and irresponsibility which these concerns of his seemed to indicate could be set against substantial achievements in naval policy, and wisdom and foresight in counsel. But the mistrust which Churchill aroused prevented these comparisons from being made, and his substantial achievements failed to create public confidence.

During 1916 Churchill saw that he could do nothing to curb the continuous criticisms of his past actions, or to allay suspicions about his motives. He came increasingly to fear that his contemporaries would never recognize what he believed were the extent of his achievements, and of his capabilities. He felt that these had come to be blotted out of the public mind by malice, partisanship and prejudice. His bitterness against Asquith for not publishing the documents about the Dardanelles was acute; his dislike of the Press for condemning him without the evidence was severe. He became convinced that only when the archives of the Admiralty and the War Council were made public would his true worth be known. He believed that, although contemporaries belittled his achievements, historical research would show his actions to have been prudent, wise and remarkable. He fell back upon the belief that, despite the harsh judgement of his contemporaries, the judgement of history would support him. Cut off from power, denigrated, condemned, Churchill saw history as the final refuge of his reputation. But his immediate career, and his influence on the course of the war, depended entirely, not upon the historical, but upon the contemporary verdict; that verdict, in December 1916, was outspokenly hostile and seemingly irreversible.

Facsimiles

1. Winston S. Churchill, 15 August 1914 (see p. 194) 828

2. Sir Edward Grey, 15 August 1914 (see p. 195) 829

3. Lord Kitchener, 2 January 1915 (see p. 232) 830

4. H. H. Asquith, 15 May 1915 (see p. 438) 831

5. Clementine S. Churchill, 28 December 1915
    (see pp. 622, 626) 832

6. Lord Fisher, 7 March 1916 (see pp. 713–714) 834

First draft
handed
15 April 1913

25 . 8 . 14

My dear Grey,

     Don't jump: but do
you mind my sending
this the personal message
to Enver. I have measured
this move & am sure
it will do good. But
of course your ` NO ' is
final .

         Yours ever

         L

I know that Sir E Grey who has
already been approached as to possible
terms if peace if Germany & Austria
has stated that if Turkey remains
neutral an agreement to respect
the integrity of her territory must be
a condition of any terms of peace that
affect the Near. East.

2 · 1. 15·

My dear Churchill

You have no doubt
seen Buchanan's telegram about
the Russians & Turks if not England
is taking it over.
Do you think any naval actions
would be possible to prevent Turks
sending more men into the
Caucasus & thus denuding
Constantinople.

Yours very truly
Kitchener

10, Downing Street,
Whitehall. S.W

Lord Fisher

In the King's name,
I order you at once
to return to your post.

H.H. Asquith

15 May 1915

Dec: 28th

My darling

Your letter from Dover just arrived & I am sending it on at once to H—q. coupled with an invitation to luncheon. It seems centuries since you left & a thick pall of fog has settled round me thro' which I can neither hear nor see the conflict. Something good must come of it — If as I fear the P.M keeps his pledge, at any rate we get Conscription.

Tomorrow I go to Alderley till Monday
I am absolutely worn out with
Emotions & the excitement of seeing
you & I must have a few days'
rest. I can't sleep for anxiety —

I send you one or two letters
& a cutting. I know nothing, but I
feel the break-up is not yet; this
futile government will fumble on
for a few more months.

I could not tell you how much
I wanted you at the Station. I was
so out of ~~the~~ breath with running
for the train. Your loving
Clemmie
with such a headache.

Tuesday Morning. 36 Berkeley Square

My dear Minister.

Please forgive my d—d reiteration but I am terribly afraid of the Asquithian cajolery! (Am I already too late?)
Providence has placed the Plum bang in your Mouth! Certain Prime Minister!
You have no Rival as Leader of the Opposition and Such a Cry for assuming the position !!! So Patriotic !!!!

"The Navy in Danger"
" — But not "too late" for Safety".

Ask George Lambert to tell you the inner history of the late second Election when both the Election Machines

2.

looking furiously on just <ins>avoided</ins> ~~saved~~ defeat
300 votes! . 157 men in that huge Constituency
would have beaten the Coalition Government!
There is seething and Wide-spread
discontent at the Conduct of the war!

But the People see No One as a
new Leader !

There is the Cave of Adullam but
No David has come along.!

See the 1st Book of Samuel Chap 22 Verse 2

"He became a Captain over them"
"And there with him about 400 Men" !

. Aint that a good majority for you?

So dont go back !

3

Never leave that Box. once you
have banged it as you will this
afternoon _ As meek as Moses
you'll say your mission is to help!
Yes! Help the war!
Yes! " Big Conceptions! Quick Decisions!
That will be your War Cry!
   " Think in Oceans "!
            Shoot at Sight!
That will be your action!
      Go in and Win!
         Dont Falter
   " Aut Cæsar aut Nullus "
      accept no pot in this Government They

4

They are doomed !

Fate has you in its' Grasp !

Dont wriggle out of it !

D—n Fisher !— You get
Prime Minister !

That will End the War !

Nought else will !

The Country wants a Man !
Every War always wants a Man !
Dont go back. Accept nothing ! Yours
7.3.16.

THE TURKISH EMPIRE,

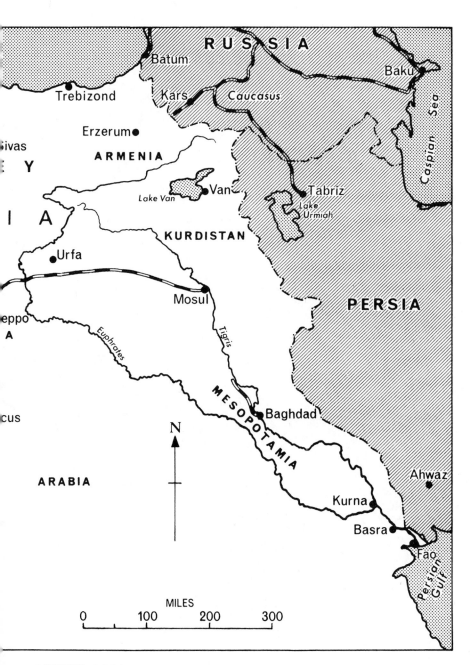

R U S S I A

Batum

Baku

Trebizond

Kars

Caucasus

Erzerum

ARMENIA

Sivas

Van

Tabriz

E Y

Lake Van

Lake Urmiah

I A

KURDISTAN

Urfa

PERSIA

eppo

Mosul

A

Euphrates

Tigris

cus

MESOPOTAMIA

Baghdad

N

ARABIA

Ahwaz

Kurna

Basra

Fao

Caspian Sea

Persian Gulf

MILES

0   100   200   300

AUGUST 1914

THE GALLIPOLI PENINSULA AND THE

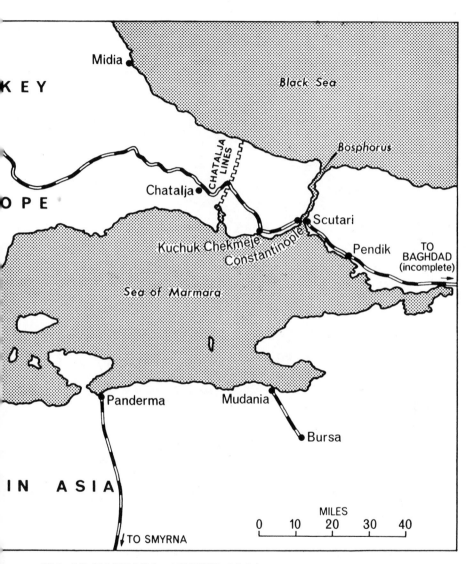

SEA OF MARMARA, AUGUST 1914

THE ALTERNATE WAR ZONES DISCUSSED IN
JANUARY 1915

Index of
Documents Quoted

In this Index I have listed, in chronological order, the 1446 documents quoted in full or in part in this volume. I have given the date on which each document was written, the page on which it is cited in this volume, and the archive in which I found it. For all documents from the Churchill papers, or from the Admiralty, Air Ministry, Foreign Office and War Office papers, I have given specific file references. Whenever the document can be found in the Churchill papers as well as in other collections, I have given the Churchill papers file number.

For six of the documents cited, I have taken the text from a published version, having been unable to find the original source; for two documents, my reference was a facsimile copy printed in a published book. Whenever the date of a document is uncertain, I have indicated this by square brackets.

1906–13

19 Dec. 1906   General Staff memorandum, p. 294. Churchill papers: 2/89

[19] Dec. 1906   Ottley note, p. 294. Churchill papers: 2/89

28 Feb. 1907   Committee of Imperial Defence minutes, p. 294. Churchill papers: 2/74

15 Sept. 1909   Churchill to Clementine Churchill, p. 481. Spencer-Churchill papers

15 March 1911   Churchill memorandum, p. 220. Churchill papers: 21/43

13 Aug. 1911   Churchill memorandum, p. 63. Churchill papers: 24/7

4 Oct. 1911   Churchill to Lloyd George, p. 189. Lloyd George papers

28 Oct. 1911   Djavid Bey to Churchill, p. 190. Churchill papers: 21/95

4 Nov. 1911   Churchill to Grey, p. 189. Copy, Churchill papers: 21/95

9 Nov. 1911   Grey to Churchill, p. 190. Churchill papers: 21/95

29 Oct. 1913   Limpus to Churchill, p. 190. Churchill papers: 13/20

3 Dec. 1913   Limpus to Churchill, p. 190. Churchill papers: 13/20

JANUARY–JUNE 1914

1 Jan. 1914   Churchill to Fisher, p. 145. Fisher papers

22 Feb. 1914   Bayly to Churchill, p. 19. Churchill papers: 13/26

20 May 1914   Churchill to Asquith and Grey, p. 2. Copy, Churchill papers: 13/29

25 May 1914   Grey to Asquith and Churchill, p. 2. Copy, Churchill papers: 13/26

24 June 1914   Churchill note, p. 385. Churchill papers: 13/45

JULY 1914

15 July 1914   Churchill to Clementine Churchill, p. 145. Spencer-Churchill papers

21 July 1914   Caillard to Gwynne, p. 191. Gwynne papers

22 July 1914   Churchill to Grey, p. 3 Copy, Churchill papers: 8/62

24 July 1914   Churchill to Clementine Churchill, p. 5. Spencer-Churchill papers

25 July 1914   Asquith to George V, p. 4. Royal Archives

26 July 1914   Prince Louis to Callaghan, p. 6. Admiralty papers: 137/50

27 July 1914   Clementine Churchill to Churchill, p. 7. Spencer-Churchill papers
                   Churchill to all naval Commanders, p. 8. Milne papers

28 July 1914   Churchill to Callaghan, p. 9. Copy, Churchill papers: 8/63
                   Churchill to Clementine Churchill, pp. 10, 31. Spencer-Churchill papers

29 July 1914   Pease diary, p. 10. Gainford papers
                   Churchill to Lloyd George, p. 12. Lloyd George papers
                   Crowe to Greene, p. 191. Admiralty papers: 137/880
                   Churchill to Prince Louis and Moore, p. 192. Admiralty papers: 137/880

30 July 1914   Churchill to Milne, p. 18. Copy, Churchill papers: 13/31
                   Prince Louis note, p. 18. Cabinet papers: 1/34
                   Churchill to Grey, p. 19. Cabinet papers: 1/34
                   Crowe to Grey, p. 192. Foreign Office papers: 371/2137
                   Moore to Churchill, p. 192. Admiralty papers: 137/880

31 July 1914   Churchill to Clementine Churchill, pp. 11, 18, 21. Spencer-Churchill
                       papers
                   Churchill to George V, p. 14. Royal Archives
                   Fisher to Balfour, p. 16. Balfour papers
                   Fisher to Churchill, p. 16. Churchill papers: 13/28
                   Churchill to Asquith, p. 19. Admiralty papers: 137/452
                   Ponsonby to Churchill, p. 21. Churchill papers: 2/64
                   Churchill to Ponsonby, p. 21. Copy, Churchill papers: 2/64
                   Asquith to Venetia Stanley, p. 22. Montagu papers
                   F. E. Smith to Churchill, p. 22. Churchill papers: 13/26
                   Churchill to Lord Hugh Cecil, p. 22. Quickswood papers

AUGUST 1914

1 Aug. 1914   Clementine Churchill to Churchill, pp. 18, 25. Spencer-Churchill papers
Lord Robert Cecil to Churchill, p. 22. Churchill papers: 2/64
Churchill to F. E. Smith, p. 22. Birkenhead papers
Hankey to Adeline Hankey, p. 23. Hankey papers
Asquith to Venetia Stanley, p. 23. Montagu papers
Henry Wilson diary, p. 24. Wilson papers
Ollivant memorandum, p. 24. Lloyd George papers
Churchill to Lord Robert Cecil, p. 24. Chelwood papers
Nicolson to Grey, p. 192. Foreign Office papers: 371/2137
Churchill to Lady Jellicoe, p. 385. Jellicoe papers

2 Aug. 1914   Churchill to Lord Robert Cecil, p. 25. Chelwood papers
Churchill to Clementine Churchill, p. 25. Spencer-Churchill papers
Churchill to all naval Commanders, p. 26. Copy, Churchill papers: 13/29
Churchill and Prince Louis to Milne, p. 26. Milne papers
Churchill to Milne, p. 28. Milne papers

3 Aug. 1914   Jellicoe to Churchill, p. 14. Copy, Jellicoe papers
Robinson to K. Perfect and M. J. Dawson, p. 24. Quoted, Wrench
Geoffrey Dawson and Our Times p. 105
Churchill to Asquith and Grey, p. 27. Admiralty papers: 137/988

4 Aug. 1914   Jellicoe to Churchill, p. 14. Copy, Jellicoe papers
Clementine Churchill to Churchill, p. 15. Spencer-Churchill papers
Churchill to Asquith and Grey, p. 29. Copy, Churchill papers: 13/37
Churchill to Milne, p. 29. Copy, Churchill papers: 13/31
Asquith to Venetia Stanley, p. 29. Montagu papers
Churchill to all British Ships, p. 30. Milne papers
Churchill to Milne, p. 30. Milne papers
Churchill to Milne (Italian neutrality), p. 30. Milne papers
Churchill to all British ships, p. 30. Milne papers
Churchill to all naval Commanders, p. 31. Milne papers
Walter Long to Churchill, p. 32. Spencer-Churchill papers

[4] Aug. 1914   Beatty to Churchill, p. 14. Copy, Beatty papers

5 Aug. 1914   Carson to Churchill, p. 32. Churchill papers: 2/64
Churchill to Grey, p. 96. Grey papers

6 Aug. 1914   Churchill to Kitchener, p. 34. Kitchener papers

7 Aug. 1914   Gretton to Churchill, p. 33. Spencer-Churchill papers
Kitchener to Churchill, p. 35. Churchill papers: 13/43

8 Aug. 1914   Fisher to Hankey, p. 17. Hankey papers
Benckendorff note, p. 193. Copy, Churchill papers: 13/37

9 Aug. 1914   Clementine Churchill to Churchill, pp. 33, 39. Spencer-Churchill papers
Churchill to Prince Louis, p. 37. Admiralty papers: 137/452
Churchill to Clementine Churchill, p. 39. Spencer-Churchill papers
Asquith to Venetia Stanley, p. 775. Montagu papers
Haldane to Churchill, p. 775. Churchill papers: 28/152

11 Aug. 1914   Churchill to Clementine Churchill, p. 39. Spencer-Churchill papers
Grey to Greene, p. 42. Copy, Churchill papers: 13/43
Churchill to Grey, p. 43. Copy, Churchill papers: 13/43
Grey to Churchill, p. 43. Churchill papers: 13/43
Grey to Churchill, p. 44. Churchill papers: 2/64
Berlin to Souchon, p. 193. Copy, Churchill papers: 29/1
Churchill to Milne, p. 194. Milne papers
Milne to Admiralty, p. 194. Copy, Milne papers
Admiralty to Milne, p. 194. Milne papers

12 Aug. 1914   Churchill minute, p. 46. Copy, Churchill papers: 13/27

[12] Aug. 1914   Clementine Churchill to Churchill, pp. 39, 44. Spencer-Churchill papers

13 Aug. 1914   Churchill to Clementine Churchill, p. 40. Spencer-Churchill papers
Churchill to Yashiro, p. 43. Draft, Churchill papers: 13/27
Churchill to Mensdorff, p. 45. Copy, Churchill papers: 13/5
Mensdorff to Churchill, p. 46. Churchill papers: 13/44

15 Aug. 1914   Churchill to Enver Pasha, p. 194. Copy, Churchill papers: 21/36
Churchill to Grey, p. 194. Churchill papers: 13/45
Grey note, p. 195. Draft, Churchill papers: 13/45

16 Aug. 1914   Churchill to Prince Louis and Sir F. Hamilton, p. 47. Copy, Churchill papers: 13/31
Grey to Mallet, p. 195. Foreign Office papers: 371/2172

17 Aug. 1914   Churchill minute, p. 50. Churchill papers: 13/27
Asquith to Venetia Stanley, p. 195. Montagu papers

18 Aug. 1914   Mallet to Grey, p. 195. Copy, Churchill papers: 13/45
Grey to Churchill, p. 195. Churchill papers: 13/45

19 Aug. 1914   Churchill to the Grand Duke Nicholas, p. 53. Copy, Churchill papers: 13/27
Villiers to Grey, p. 96. Copy, Churchill papers: 13/43
Churchill to Enver Pasha, p. 196. Copy, Foreign Office papers: 371/2137
Churchill to Limpus, p. 196. Copy, Foreign Office papers: 371/2137

20 Aug. 1914   Richmond diary, p. 51. Richmond papers
Churchill to Grey, p. 96. Copy, Churchill papers: 13/43

21 Aug. 1914   Asquith to Venetia Stanley, p. 196. Montagu papers

22 Aug. 1914   Churchill to Kitchener, p. 57. Copy, Churchill papers: 8/65

23 Aug. 1914   Churchill to Grey, p. 197. Grey papers

24 Aug. 1914   Grand Duke Nicholas to Churchill, p. 53. Churchill papers: 13/27
Churchill to Jellicoe, p. 55. Draft, Churchill papers: 13/44
Churchill to John Churchill, p. 55. John Churchill papers

25 Aug. 1914   Churchill to Jellicoe, p. 55. Jellicoe papers
Churchill to Aston, p. 56. Copy, Churchill papers: 8/67

26 Aug. 1914   Asquith to George V, p. 56. Royal Archives
Emmott diary, p. 57. Emmott papers
Pease diary, p. 57. Gainford papers
Churchill to John Churchill, p. 58. John Churchill papers
Mallet to Churchill, p. 197. Admiralty papers: 116/1336
Churchill minute, p. 197. Admiralty papers: 137/880
Barclay to Grey, p. 198. Copy, Admiralty papers: 116/1336
Limpus to Churchill, p. 198. Churchill papers: 13/45

27 Aug. 1914   Prince Louis report, p. 41. Copy, Churchill papers: 13/29
Churchill minute, p. 41. Copy, Churchill papers: 13/29
Cunliffe Owen report, p. 199. Copy, Admiralty papers: 116/1336

28 Aug. 1914   Gwynne to Churchill, p. 33. Copy, Gwynne papers
Churchill to Kitchener, p. 58. Copy, Churchill papers: 26/1
Clementine Churchill to Kitchener, p. 58. Kitchener papers
Clementine Churchill to Keyes, p. 59. Keyes papers

29 Aug. 1914   Churchill to Grey, pp. 44, 202. Copy, Churchill papers: 13/29
Haldane to Churchill, p. 59. Churchill papers: 13/45
Churchill to Beresford, p. 148. Copy, Churchill papers: 13/43

30 Aug. 1914   Arthur Lee memorandum, p. 148. Copy, Churchill papers: 13/43

31 Aug. 1914   Kitchener to French, p. 60. Copy, Kitchener papers
French to Kitchener, p. 60. Kitchener papers
Marsh to Grey, p. 200. Churchill papers: 13/44
Grey to Marsh, p. 200. Churchill papers: 13/44
Churchill to Noel Buxton, p. 200. Copy, Churchill papers: 26/1

[?] Aug. 1914   Tyrwhitt to Mrs Tyrwhitt, p. 49. Quoted, Marder *From the Dreadnought to Scapa Flow*, volume two, p. 54

SEPTEMBER 1914

1 Sept. 1914   Asquith to Venetia Stanley, p. 60. Montagu papers
Samson orders, p. 67. Admiralty papers: 116/1352
Churchill to Douglas, p. 202. Copy, Churchill papers: 26/1

2 Sept. 1914   Churchill to French, p. 60. Copy, Churchill papers: 26/1
Asquith to Venetia Stanley, p. 204. Montagu papers
Pease diary, p. 205. Gainsford papers

3 Sept. 1914   French to Churchill, p. 61. Churchill papers: 26/1
Haldane to Churchill, p. 64. Spencer-Churchill papers
Samson log book, p. 65. Air Ministry papers: 1/724/76/5
Churchill to Sueter, p. 66. Copy, Churchill papers: 8/67
Churchill to Prince Louis, p. 72. Copy, Churchill papers: 8/67
Callwell to Kitchener, p. 203. Copy, Churchill papers: 2/82
Asquith to Venetia Stanley, p. 205. Montagu papers

4 Sept. 1914   Churchill to Prince Louis and Sturdee, p. 52. Copy, Churchill papers: 13/29
Samson to Admiralty, p. 68. Admiralty papers: 116/1352
Churchill to Kerr, p. 204. Copy, Grey papers

5 Sept. 1914   Esher to Churchill, p. 63. Churchill papers: 13/45
Churchill to the Board of Admiralty, p. 66. Copy, Churchill papers: 8/67
Churchill to Prince Louis and Sueter, p. 67. Copy, Churchill papers: 8/67
Churchill to Northcliffe, p. 70. Copy, Churchill papers: 2/64
Churchill Press communiqué, p. 70. Churchill papers: 8/65
Asquith to Venetia Stanley, p. 70. Montagu papers
Asquith to Churchill, p. 71. Churchill papers: 2/64
Grey to Churchill and Kitchener, p. 97. Copy, Grey papers
Talbot memorandum, p. 203. War Office papers: 106/1463

6 Sept. 1914   Fisher to Cecil Fisher, p. 49. Fisher papers
Grey to Churchill, p. 205. Churchill papers: 26/1
Churchill to Grey, p. 205. Copy, Churchill papers: 26/1
Elliot to Grey, p. 206. Copy, Churchill papers: 26/1

7 Sept. 1914   Northcliffe to Churchill, p. 70. Copy, Churchill papers: 28/117
Kitchener to Grey, p. 97. Grey papers
Churchill to Grey (military supplies), p. 97. Grey papers
Churchill to Grey (refugees), p. 97. Grey papers
Churchill to Asquith, Grey and Kitchener, p. 98. Copy, Churchill papers:
    13/58

8 Sept. 1914   Balfour to Marsh, p. 64. Marsh papers
Ian Hamilton to Churchill, p. 64. Churchill papers: 13/45
Guest to Churchill, pp. 71, 162. Churchill papers: 13/45
Balfour to Alice Balfour, p. 72. Balfour papers
Churchill to Lord Robert Cecil, p. 77. Copy, Churchill papers: 13/44
Churchill to Troubridge, p. 206. Copy, Churchill papers: 13/29
Limpus to Churchill, p. 206. Churchill papers: 13/45

9 Sept. 1914   Fisher to Churchill, p. 64. Churchill papers: 13/28
Churchill to Hopwood, p. 100. Admiralty papers: 137/1010
Churchill to Limpus, p. 207. Copy, Churchill papers: 13/35
Kerr to Churchill, p. 209. Churchill papers: 13/27

10 Sept. 1914   Aitken to Churchill, p. 48. Churchill papers: 13/45
French to Churchill, p. 71. Churchill papers: 26/1
Asquith to Venetia Stanley, p. 72. Montagu papers
Sarell to Foreign Office, p. 73. Foreign Office papers: 371/2174

11 Sept. 1914   Churchill speech, p. 76. Churchill papers: 9/50
Lord Hugh Cecil to Churchill, p. 77. Churchill papers: 13/45
Churchill to Austen Chamberlain, p. 77. Austen Chamberlain papers
Churchill to Grey, p. 207. Grey papers

12 Sept. 1914   Churchill to Bonar Law, p. 48. Bonar Law papers
Sarell to Crowe, pp. 69, 73. Foreign Office papers: 371/2174
Austen Chamberlain to Churchill, p. 78. Churchill papers: 13/44
Churchill to Austen Chamberlain, p. 78. Copy, Churchill papers: 13/44

13 Sept. 1914   Churchill to Kitchener, p. 36. Kitchener papers
Austen Chamberlain to Churchill, p. 79. Churchill papers: 13/44
Churchill to Austen Chamberlain, p. 79. Copy, Churchill papers: 13/44

14 Sept. 1914   Churchill to John Churchill, p. 74. John Churchill papers
Austen Chamberlain to Churchill, p. 79. Churchill papers: 13/44
Churchill to Austen Chamberlain, p. 79. Copy, Churchill papers: 13/44
Asquith to Venetia Stanley, p. 480. Montagu papers

15 Sept. 1914   Churchill to Grey, p. 100. Foreign Office papers: 371/2174
Fisher to Churchill, p. 145. Churchill papers: 13/43

16 Sept. 1914   Admiralty Aeroplane Conference minutes, p. 80. Copy, Churchill papers: 13/29
Churchill to Grey, p. 208. Grey papers

17 Sept. 1914   Churchill to Grey, p. 100. Grey papers

18 Sept. 1914   Churchill to Prince Louis, p. 85. Copy, Churchill papers: 13/29

19 Sept. 1914   Asquith to Venetia Stanley, p. 74. Montagu papers
Churchill to Oliver, p. 83. Copy, Churchill papers: 13/29

20 Sept. 1914   Churchill to Seely, p. 83. Mottistone papers

21 Sept. 1914   Churchill to Carden, p. 209. Copy, Churchill papers: 8/72

22 Sept. 1914   Asquith to Venetia Stanley, pp. 74, 90. Montagu papers
Stamfordham to Bonham Carter, p. 86. Asquith papers
Samson log book, p. 88. Air Ministry papers: 1/724/76/5
Gerrard to Admiralty, p. 89. Admiralty papers: 116/1352
Mallet to Grey, p. 210. Grey papers

23 Sept. 1914   Garvin to Churchill, p. 49. Churchill papers: 13/45
Churchill minute, p. 139. Churchill papers: 13/45
Churchill to Grey, p. 210. Copy, Churchill papers: 2/114
Churchill, Kitchener, Cabinet notes, p. 211. Grey papers
Asquith to George V, p. 211. Royal Archives
Churchill to Ollivant and Sueter, p. 534. Copy, Churchill papers: 8/67

24 Sept. 1914   Churchill to Grey, p. 44. Grey papers
Scott to Churchill, p. 90. Kitchener papers
Churchill to Kitchener, and minute, p. 91. Kitchener papers
Churchill to Paris, p. 93. Admiralty papers: 116/1348
Churchill to Villiers, p. 100. Foreign Office papers: 371/2174

25 Sept. 1914   Churchill to Grey, p. 91. Grey papers
Grey to Churchill, p. 91. Grey papers
Fisher to Hopwood, p. 146. Southborough papers

26 Sept. 1914   Churchill to Kitchener, p. 92. Churchill papers: 26/1
Kitchener to Churchill, p. 92. Churchill papers: 26/1
Churchill to Clementine Churchill, p. 92. Spencer-Churchill papers

[26] Sept. 1914   Clementine Churchill to Churchill, p. 92. Spencer-Churchill papers

27 Sept. 1914   Stamfordham to Esher, p. 88. Esher papers

29 Sept. 1914   Asquith to Churchill, p. 93. Churchill papers: 13/44

30 Sept. 1914   Asquith to Venetia Stanley, pp. 101, 325. Montagu papers
[?] Sept. 1914   Samson report, p. 93. Churchill papers: 13/44

OCTOBER 1914

1 Oct. 1914   Churchill to Kitchener, p. 51. Kitchener papers
Dallas to War Office, p. 101. Copy, Churchill papers: 8/181
Asquith to Venetia Stanley, p. 102. Montagu papers
Churchill to Crewe, p. 171. Crewe papers

2 Oct. 1914   Bayly to Sir F. Hamilton, p. 84. Quoted. Marder *From the Dreadnought to Scapa Flow*, volume two, p. 48
Grey to Bertie, p. 102. Copy, Churchill papers: 8/181
Asquith to Venetia Stanley, p. 102. Montagu papers
Villiers to Grey, p. 104. Copy, Churchill papers: 8/181

3 Oct. 1914   Grey to Villiers, p. 105. Copy, Churchill papers: 8/181
Bertie to Grey, p. 105. Copy, Churchill papers: 8/181
Grey to Villiers, p. 106. Copy, Churchill papers: 8/181
Asquith to Venetia Stanley, p. 106. Montagu papers
Churchill to Kitchener and Grey, p. 107. Copy, Churchill papers: 13/58
Fisher to Pamela McKenna, p. 148. McKenna papers

4 Oct. 1914   Churchill to Kitchener, pp. 108, 131. Copy, Churchill papers: 8/68
Littlejohn log book, p. 109. Admiralty papers: 116/1352
Dallas to Kitchener, p. 109. Copy, Churchill papers: 8/181
Richmond diary, p. 110. Richmond papers
De Broqueville to Churchill, p. 110. Churchill papers: 13/58
Churchill to Admiralty, p. 110. Copy, Churchill papers: 8/181

5 Oct. 1914   Churchill to Asquith, p. 111. Beaverbrook papers
Asquith to Venetia Stanley, pp. 112, 113, 130. Montagu papers
Asquith to George V, p. 112. Royal Archives
Rawlinson war journal, p. 114. Rawlinson papers
Churchill to Kitchener, p. 114. Kitchener papers
Kitchener to Churchill, p. 114. Churchill papers: 1/181
Churchill to Kitchener, p. 115. Copy, Churchill papers, 1/181
Hopwood to Stamfordham, p. 119. Royal Archives
Stamfordham to Hopwood, p. 120. Southborough papers
Admiralty to Cradock, p. 156. Copy, Churchill papers: 13/59

6 Oct. 1914   Churchill to Kitchener and Grey, p. 116. Copy, Churchill papers: 1/181
Asquith to Venetia Stanley, p. 117. Montagu papers
Churchill to Kitchener, p. 118. Churchill papers: 13/58
Bentham to Bentham, p. 119. Bentham papers

7 Oct. 1914   Asquith to Venetia Stanley, p. 120. Montagu papers
Grey to Clementine Churchill, p. 121. Spencer-Churchill papers
Haldane to Churchill, p. 121. Spencer-Churchill papers
Lloyd George to Churchill, p. 121. Spencer-Churchill papers

8 Oct. 1914   Paris to Churchill, p. 121. Churchill papers: 29/1
Asquith to Venetia Stanley, p. 122. Montagu papers

9 Oct. 1914   Asquith to George V, p. 122. Royal Archives

10 Oct. 1914 Asquith to Venetia Stanley, p. 124. Montagu papers

11 Oct. 1914 Kitchener to French, p. 124. Copy, Kitchener papers
       Grey to Bertie, p. 124. Copy, Churchill papers: 13/58

13 Oct. 1914 Buckmaster to Churchill, p. 129. Churchill papers: 13/45
       Asquith to Venetia Stanley, pp. 130, 137. Montagu papers

14 Oct. 1914 Churchill to Garvin, p. 127. Garvin papers
       Bonar Law to Larmor, p. 132. Copy, Bonar Law papers

15 Oct. 1914 Churchill to Repington, p. 131. Copy, Churchill papers: 2/64

16 Oct. 1914 Gwynne to Asquith and others, p. 127. Copy, Gwynne papers
       Churchill to John Churchill, p. 135. John Churchill papers

17 Oct. 1914 Spenser Grey report, p. 123. Admiralty papers: 116/1352

18 Oct. 1914 Beatty to Ethel Beatty, p. 134. Beatty papers
       Cradock to Admiralty, p. 157. Churchill papers: 13/31

19 Oct. 1914 Haldane to Churchill, pp. 134, 144. Spencer-Churchill papers
       Beatty to Ethel Beatty, p. 134. Beatty papers
       Churchill to Kitchener, p. 138. Asquith papers

20 Oct. 1914 Beatty to Ethel Beatty, p. 134. Beatty papers
       Asquith to Venetia Stanley, p. 147. Montagu papers

21 Oct. 1914 French to Churchill, p. 133. Churchill papers: 26/1
       Asquith to Venetia Stanley, p. 138. Montagu papers
       Fisher to Churchill, pp. 146. Churchill papers: 13/28
       Churchill to Kitchener, p. 171. Kitchener papers
       Noel Buxton to Churchill, p. 213. Admiralty papers: 116/1336

22 Oct. 1914 Churchill note, p. 93. Draft, Admiralty papers: 116/1351

23 Oct. 1914 Frances Stevenson diary, p. 132. Countess Lloyd-George papers
       Churchill to Garvin, p. 133. Garvin papers
       Asquith to Venetia Stanley, pp. 139, 144. Montagu papers
       Churchill to Grey, p. 214. Admiralty papers: 116/1336

24 Oct. 1914 Richmond diary, p. 140. Richmond papers
       Churchill to Leonie Leslie, p. 140. Leslie papers

25 Oct. 1914 Grey to Churchill, p. 214. Admiralty papers: 116/1336

26 Oct. 1914 Churchill to French, pp. 133, 136, 139. Copy, Churchill papers: 29/1

27 Oct. 1914 Churchill to Hood, p. 136. Churchill papers: 13/40
       Jellicoe to Churchill (4.35 pm), p. 141. Churchill papers: 13/40
       Jellicoe to Churchill (10.10 pm), p. 141. Churchill papers: 13/40
       Churchill to Jellicoe, p. 141. Churchill papers: 13/40
       Asquith to Venetia Stanley, pp. 141, 147. Montagu papers
       Stamfordham record, pp. 148, 150. Royal Archives
       Churchill to Prince Louis, p. 148. Copy, Churchill papers: 13/5
       Cradock to Admiralty, p. 157. Churchill papers: 13/59

28 Oct. 1914   Jellicoe to Churchill, p. 141. Churchill papers: 13/40
                Churchill to Jellicoe, p. 141. Copy, Churchill papers: 13/40
                Asquith to Venetia Stanley, p. 142. Montagu papers
                Lloyd George to Churchill, p. 143. Churchill papers: 2/64
                Prince Louis to Churchill, p. 149. Churchill papers: 13/27
                Asquith to Venetia Stanley, p. 149. Montagu papers
                Prince Louis to Churchill, p. 149. Copy, Churchill papers: 13/27
                Stamfordham record, p. 150. Royal Archives
                Churchill to Oliver, p. 157. Copy, Churchill papers: 13/59
                Grey to Mallet, p. 214. Foreign Office papers: 371/2144

29 Oct. 1914   Asquith to Venetia Stanley, pp. 124, 151, 152. Montagu papers
                George V to Asquith, p. 151. Royal Archives
                Churchill to Prince Louis, p. 152. Copy, Churchill papers: 13/27
                Prince Louis to Churchill, p. 153. Churchill papers: 13/27
                Grey to Mallet, p. 215. Grey papers

30 Oct. 1914   George V diary, p. 153. Royal Archives
                Churchill to Asquith and Grey, p. 153. Churchill papers: 13/27
                Grey to Mallet, p. 215. Copy, Churchill papers: 8/72
                Pease diary, p. 215. Gainford papers
                Asquith to George V, p. 215. Royal Archives
                Churchill to Fisher, p. 215. Admiralty papers: 137/96
                Slade to Churchill, p. 215. Admiralty papers: 137/96

31 Oct. 1914   Churchill minute, p. 66. Copy, Churchill papers: 2/93
                Marsh to Robinson, p. 153. Copy, Marsh papers
                Asquith to Venetia Stanley, p. 216. Montagu papers
                Churchill to Fisher, p. 216. Admiralty papers: 137/96
                Fisher to Oliver, p. 216. Admiralty papers: 137/96
                Churchill to Carden, p. 216. Copy, Churchill papers: 8/72
                Nicolson to Greene, p. 216. Foreign Office papers: 371/2145
                Foreign Office announcement, p. 217. Foreign Office papers: 371/2144

[?] Oct. 1914   Fisher to Pamela McKenna, p. 137. McKenna papers

                                NOVEMBER 1914

1 Nov 1914   Fisher to Esher, p. 154. Esher papers
                Cradock to Canopus, p. 157. Copy, Churchill papers: 13/31
                Grey to Buchanan, p. 217. Foreign Office papers: 371/2080

2 Nov. 1914   Beatty to Ethel Beatty, pp. 154, 155. Beatty papers
                Churchill to John Churchill, p. 160. John Churchill papers
                Asquith to Venetia Stanley, p. 176. Montagu papers
                Grey to Nicolson, p. 217. Foreign Office papers: 371/2145
                Churchill to Carden, p. 217. Admiralty papers: 137/2165

3 Nov. 1914   Fisher to Cradock, p. 157. Copy, Churchill papers: 13/39
                Churchill and Fisher to Japanese Admiralty, p. 158. Copy, Churchill
                    papers: 13/35
                Maclean to Admiralty, p. 158. Churchill papers: 13/39

4 Nov. 1914   Esher diary, p. 154. Esher papers
                Asquith to Venetia Stanley, p. 158. Montagu papers

Churchill and Fisher to Jellicoe, p. 182. Copy, Churchill papers: 13/39
Admiralty to *Caernarvon*, p. 182. Churchill papers: 13/39
Admiralty to *Glasgow* and *Otranto*, p. 182. Churchill papers: 13/39
Admiralty to *Canopus*, p. 182. Churchill papers: 13/39
Grey to Cheetham, p. 218. Foreign Office papers: 371/2145
Asquith to George V, p. 219. Royal Archives

5 Nov. 1914   Kitchener to Churchill, p. 158. Churchill papers: 13/43
Churchill to Kitchener, p. 158. Kitchener papers
Asquith to George V, p. 159. Royal Archives
Frances Stevenson diary, p. 159. Countess Lloyd-George papers
Nicolson to Greene, p. 219. Admiralty papers: 137/96

7 Nov. 1914   Margot Asquith diary, p. 148. Countess Oxford and Asquith papers
Churchill to John Churchill, p. 160. John Churchill papers

9 Nov. 1914   Churchill to John Churchill, p. 161. John Churchill papers
Churchill to French, p. 162. Copy, Churchill papers: 26/1
Mundy to Admiralty, p. 183. Churchill papers: 13/41
Margot Asquith diary, p. 219. Countess Oxford and Asquith papers

10 Nov. 1914   Churchill to Mundy, p. 183. Copy, Churchill papers: 8/70

12 Nov. 1914   Grey to Buchanan, p. 320. Foreign Office papers: 371/2145

14 Nov. 1914   French to Churchill, p. 162. Churchill papers: 13/27

15 Nov. 1914   Churchill to French (not sent), p. 162. Churchill papers: 13/27
Churchill to French, p. 162. Copy, Churchill papers: 13/27

17 Nov. 1914   Fisher to Jellicoe, pp. 154, 186. Jellicoe papers
Churchill to French, pp. 161, 163. Copy, Churchill papers: 26/1
Churchill to Clementine Churchill, p. 161. Spencer-Churchill papers

18 Nov. 1914   Clementine Churchill to Churchill, p. 187. Spencer-Churchill papers

19 Nov. 1914   Fisher to Beatty, p. 154. Beatty papers

20 Nov. 1914   Fisher to Jellicoe, p. 186. Jellicoe papers

21 Nov. 1914   Report on effect of Friedrichshafen raid, p. 173. Admiralty papers: 116/1352

23 Nov. 1914   Churchill to Grey, p. 173. Foreign Office papers: 372/570

24 Nov. 1914   Asquith to Venetia Stanley, p. 173. Montagu papers

25 Nov. 1914   War Council, Secretary's notes, pp. 176, 220. Cabinet papers: 22/1

27 Nov. 1914   Churchill to Grey, p. 174. Copy, Churchill papers: 2/64

29 Nov. 1914   Asquith to Venetia Stanley, p. 224. Montagu papers

30 Nov. 1914   Grant-Duff to Grey, p. 174. Copy, Admiralty papers: 116/1336
Margot Asquith diary, p. 179. Countess Oxford and Asquith papers
Churchill to Kitchener, p. 221. Copy, Churchill papers: 13/27
Kitchener to Churchill, p. 221. Churchill papers: 13/27

[?] Nov. 1914   Fleming to Churchill, p. 227. Spencer-Churchill papers
Churchill to Clementine Churchill, p. 228. Spencer-Churchill papers

DECEMBER 1914

1 Dec. 1914   War Council, Secretary's notes, p. 180. Cabinet papers: 22/1

2 Dec. 1914   Churchill to Grey, p. 175. Admiralty papers: 116/1336
Marsh to Grey, p. 175. Admiralty papers: 116/1336
Churchill memorandum, p. 181. Admiralty papers: 137/452

3 Dec. 1914   Grant-Duff to Grey, p. 175. Foreign Office papers: 372/570
Grey to Marsh, p. 175. Admiralty papers: 116/1336
Grant-Duff to Nicolson, p. 175. Copy, Admiralty papers: 116/1336
Grey to Churchill, p. 175. Admiralty papers: 116/1336
Churchill to Grey, p. 176. Admiralty papers: 116/1336

4 Dec. 1914   Asquith to Venetia Stanley, p. 166. Montagu papers
Beatty to Ethel Beatty, p. 187. Beatty papers

5 Dec. 1914   Asquith to Venetia Stanley, p. 223. Montagu papers

7 Dec. 1914   Fisher to Beatty, p. 186. Beatty papers

8 Dec. 1914   Margot Asquith diary, p. 142. Countess Oxford and Asquith papers
Churchill to French, p. 163. Copy, Churchill papers: 26/1
Fisher to Churchill, p. 187. Churchill papers: 13/28

9 Dec. 1914   Churchill to French, p. 164. Copy, Churchill papers: 26/1

10 Dec. 1914   Churchill to Fisher, p. 183. Admiralty papers: 116/3454

13 Dec. 1914   Churchill to French, p. 164. Copy, Churchill papers: 26/1
Fisher to Lady Randolph Churchill, p. 186. Churchill papers: 28/84

[16] Dec. 1914   Churchill to F. E. Smith, p. 164. Birkenhead papers

17 Dec. 1914   Fisher to Esher, p. 155. Esher papers
Churchill to Asquith, p. 164. Asquith papers
Asquith to Churchill, p. 164. Copy, Asquith papers
Churchill note, p. 164. Asquith papers
Churchill to Kitchener, p. 165. Kitchener papers

18 Dec. 1914   Asquith to Churchill, p. 165. Churchill papers: 26/1
Churchill to Kitchener, p. 165. Copy, Churchill papers: 26/1
Asquith to Venetia Stanley, pp. 166, 167. Montagu papers
Kitchener to Churchill, p. 166. Draft, Kitchener papers
Grey to Bertie, p. 320. Copy, Grey papers

19 Dec. 1914   Kitchener to Churchill, p. 166. Churchill papers: 26/1
Churchill to Kitchener, p. 166. Copy, Churchill papers: 26/1
Guest to Churchill, p. 167. Churchill papers: 26/1

20 Dec. 1914   Asquith to Venetia Stanley, p. 167. Montagu papers
Fisher to Jellicoe, p. 186. Jellicoe papers

21 Dec. 1914   Asquith to Venetia Stanley, p. 95. Montagu papers
Churchill to Kitchener, p. 168. Copy, Churchill papers: 26/1
Churchill to Fisher, p. 181. Fisher papers
Fisher to Churchill, p. 187. Churchill papers: 29/1
Knox to War Office, p. 225. Copy, Churchill papers: 26/5

22 Dec. 1914   Churchill to Fisher, p. 225. Fisher papers

23 Dec. 1914   Churchill note, p. 94. Draft, Admiralty papers: 116/1351

25 Dec. 1914   Fisher to Churchill, p. 184. Churchill papers: 13/43

27 Dec. 1914   Asquith to Venetia Stanley, p. 225. Montagu papers

28 Dec. 1914   Churchill to French, p. 168. Copy, Churchill papers: 26/1
Hankey memorandum, p. 229. Churchill papers: 2/89

29 Dec. 1914   Churchill to Asquith, p. 225. Copy, Churchill papers: 26/1
Asquith to Venetia Stanley, p. 228. Montagu papers

30 Dec. 1914   Asquith to Venetia Stanley, p. 228. Montagu papers

31 Dec. 1914   Churchill to Asquith, p. 231. Copy, Churchill papers: 26/1

JANUARY 1915

1 Jan. 1915   Churchill to French, p. 168. Copy, Churchill papers: 26/2
Asquith to Venetia Stanley, p. 228. Montagu papers
Lloyd George memorandum, p. 229. Churchill papers: 2/74
Asquith to Churchill, p. 231. Churchill papers: 13/46
Buchanan to Grey, p. 232. Copy, Churchill papers: 26/4

2 Jan. 1915   Kitchener to Churchill, p. 232. Churchill papers: 13/46
Kitchener to Churchill, p. 232. Churchill papers: 26/4
Sir F. Hamilton to Carden, p. 591. Churchill papers: 26/3

3 Jan. 1915   Churchill to Carden, p. 234. Copy, Churchill papers: 13/65
Churchill to Fisher, Wilson and Oliver, p. 234. Admiralty papers: 137/452
Fisher to Churchill, p. 234. Churchill papers: 13/56

4 Jan. 1915   Churchill to Fisher, covering note, p. 235. Copy, Churchill papers: 13/46
Churchill to Fisher, p. 235. Copy, Churchill papers: 13/46
Churchill to Jellicoe, p. 235. Copy, Churchill papers: 13/46
Richmond diary, p. 236. Richmond papers
Fisher to Balfour, p. 237. Balfour papers
Fisher to Churchill, p. 237. Churchill papers: 13/56
Fisher to Churchill, p. 239. Churchill papers: 13/56
Churchill to Fisher, p. 239. Copy, Churchill papers: 13/56

5 Jan. 1915   Carden to Churchill, p. 237. Churchill papers: 13/65
Asquith to Venetia Stanley, pp. 237, 238. Montagu papers
Churchill to Asquith, p. 535. Churchill papers: 13/44

6 Jan. 1915   Churchill to Carden, p. 238. Copy, Churchill papers: 13/65

7 Jan. 1915   War Council, Secretary's notes, p. 240. Cabinet papers: 22/1
                   Asquith to Venetia Stanley, p. 242. Montagu papers
                   Churchill to Asquith, p. 242. Copy, Churchill papers: 26/2

8 Jan. 1915   Churchill to French, p. 168. Copy, Churchill papers: 26/2
                   War Council, Secretary's notes, p. 243. Cabinet papers: 22/1

9 Jan. 1915   Fisher to Churchill, p. 245. Churchill papers: 13/56

10 Jan. 1915   Margot Asquith diary, p. 245. Countess Oxford and Asquith papers

11 Jan. 1915   Churchill to Jellicoe, pp. 185, 247. Copy, Churchill papers: 13/46
                   Churchill to French, p. 246. Copy, Churchill papers: 26/2
                   Carden to Churchill, p. 248. Churchill papers: 13/65

12 Jan. 1915   Fisher to Tyrrell, p. 247. Foreign Office papers: 800/220
                   Churchill to Fisher, p. 250. Copy, Churchill papers: 8/78
                   Fisher to Oliver, p. 250. Oliver papers

13 Jan. 1915   War Council, Secretary's notes, p. 251. Cabinet papers: 22/1
                   Asquith to Venetia Stanley, p. 253. Montagu papers
                   Churchill to the Russian People, p. 253. Copy, Churchill papers: 26/2
                   Churchill to Fisher and Oliver, p. 253. Copy, Churchill papers: 2/74

14 Jan. 1915   Fisher minute, p. 255. Churchill papers: 2/82
                   Grey to Sazonov, p. 320. Copy, Grey papers

15 Jan. 1915   Churchill to Carden, p. 254. Copy, Churchill papers: 13/65
                   Churchill to Asquith, Grey and Kitchener, p. 255. Churchill papers: 2/82
                   Asquith to Venetia Stanley, p. 255. Montagu papers
                   Jackson memorandum, pp. 255, 257. Churchill papers: 2/82

16 Jan. 1915   Richmond diary, p. 256. Richmond papers

18 Jan. 1915   Churchill to Augagneur, p. 256. Copy, Churchill papers: 26/3
                   Fisher to Churchill, p. 258. Churchill papers: 29/1

19 Jan. 1915   Richmond memorandum, p. 258. Richmond papers
                   Richmond diary, pp. 258, 260. Richmond papers
                   Fisher to Jellicoe, p. 259. Jellicoe papers

20 Jan. 1915   Asquith to Venetia Stanley, p. 259. Montagu papers
                   Fisher to Churchill, p. 259. Churchill papers: 13/56
                   Churchill to Kitchener, p. 267. Copy, Churchill papers: 13/46

21 Jan. 1915   Churchill to Kitchener, p. 202. Robertson papers
                   Fisher to Jellicoe, p. 260. Jellicoe papers

23 Jan. 1915   Haldane to Churchill, p. 330. Churchill papers: 2/65

24 Jan. 1915   Churchill to George V, p. 261. Royal Archives
                   Haldane to Churchill, p. 261. Churchill papers: 2/65
                   Churchill to French, p. 261. Copy, Churchill papers: 26/2

25 Jan. 1915   Churchill to Carden, p. 256. Copy, Admiralty papers: 137/96
                   Fisher to Churchill, p. 262. Churchill papers: 13/56

Fisher memorandum, p. 262. Churchill papers: 13/56
Churchill to Asquith, Grey and Kitchener, p. 266. Churchill papers: 13/54
Grand Duke Nicholas to Grey, p. 266. Copy, Churchill papers: 26/2

26 Jan. 1915 Churchill memorandum, p. 264. Cabinet papers: 37/137
Churchill to Fisher, p. 265. Fisher papers
Grey to Churchill, p. 266. Churchill papers: 26/2
Churchill to Grey and Kitchener, p. 266. Copy, Churchill papers: 2/74
Grey to Churchill, p. 267. Churchill papers: 2/74

28 Jan. 1915 Fisher to Asquith, p. 268. Copy, Fisher papers
Fisher to Churchill, p. 269. Churchill papers: 13/56
Churchill to Fisher, p. 270. Fisher papers
War Council, Secretary's notes, p. 271. Churchill papers: 2/86
Asquith to Venetia Stanley, p. 272. Montagu papers

29 Jan. 1915 Lloyd George to Churchill, p. 277. Churchill papers: 26/2

31 Jan. 1915 Churchill to Kitchener, p. 277. Copy, Churchill papers: 2/82

FEBRUARY 1915

2 Feb. 1915 Churchill to French, p. 277. Copy, Churchill papers: 26/2
Grey to Churchill, p. 277. Churchill papers: 26/3

3 Feb. 1915 Kitchener note, p. 277. Churchill papers: 26/3

4 Feb. 1915 Asquith to Venetia Stanley, p. 477. Montagu papers

5 Feb. 1915 Admiralty to Carden, pp. 276, 399. Copy, Churchill papers: 2/82

6 Feb. 1915 Bax-Ironside to Grey, p. 278. Copy, Churchill papers: 26/4
Churchill to Carden, p. 279. Copy, Churchill papers: 2/88

7 Feb. 1915 Churchill to Asquith, p. 278. Draft, Churchill papers: 13/47
Maxwell to Kitchener, p. 279. Copy, Crewe papers
Buchanan to Grey, p. 280. Copy, Churchill papers: 26/4

8 Feb. 1915 Asquith to Venetia Stanley, p. 278. Montagu papers
Larken report, p. 279. Churchill papers: 13/58
George V diary, p. 281. Royal Archives
George V to Churchill, p. 281. Churchill papers: 13/47
Margot Asquith diary, p. 426. Countess Oxford and Asquith papers

9 Feb. 1915 Richmond diary, p. 279. Richmond papers
Asquith to Venetia Stanley, p. 280. Montagu papers
War Council, Secretary's notes, p. 281. Cabinet papers: 22/1

10 Feb. 1915 Asquith to Venetia Stanley, p. 286. Montagu papers
Grey to Buchanan, p. 320. Foreign Office papers: 371/2479

12 Feb. 1915 Churchill to Bonar Law, p. 282. Copy, Churchill papers: 13/47
Churchill to Bonar Law, p. 282. Bonar Law papers

13 Feb. 1915 Bonar Law to Churchill, p. 282. Churchill papers: 13/44
Churchill to Asquith, p. 284. Cabinet papers: 37/124
Asquith to Venetia Stanley, p. 286. Montagu papers

14 Feb. 1915   Richmond memorandum, p. 286. Richmond papers
                   Hankey to Richmond, p. 287. Richmond papers

15 Feb. 1915   Churchill to Bonar Law, p. 284. Bonar Law papers
                   Fisher to Richmond, p. 287. Richmond papers
                   Richmond diary, p. 287. Richmond papers
                   Jackson memorandum, p. 287. Churchill papers: 2/82

16 Feb. 1915   Fisher to Churchill, pp. 184, 287. Churchill papers: 13/56
                   War Council, Secretary's notes, p. 288. Cabinet papers: 22/1
                   Esher diary, p. 288. Esher papers

17 Feb. 1915   Bonar Law to Churchill, p. 284. Copy, Bonar Law papers
                   Asquith to Churchill, p. 289. Churchill papers: 13/47
                   Margot Asquith diary, p. 289. Countess Oxford and Asquith papers
                   Churchill to Asquith, p. 289. Draft, Churchill papers: 13/47

18 Feb. 1915   Churchill to Kitchener, p. 288. Copy, Churchill papers: 13/47
                   Churchill to Kitchener, p. 290. Copy, Churchill papers: 13/47
                   Asquith to Venetia Stanley, p. 290. Montagu papers
                   Churchill to Grey, p. 296. Churchill papers: 13/54

19 Feb. 1915   Churchill to Kitchener, p. 291. Copy, Churchill papers: 13/47
                   War Council, Secretary's notes, p. 291. Churchill papers: 2/86
                   Limpus to Churchill, p. 300. Churchill papers: 13/47
                   Wedgwood to Churchill, p. 316. Churchill papers: 13/47

20 Feb. 1915   Churchill to Graeme Thomson, p. 297. Copy, Churchill papers: 2/82
                   Graeme Thomson note, p. 297. Churchill papers: 2/82
                   Grey to Churchill, p. 298. Copy, Admiralty papers: 116/1336
                   Grey minute, p. 298. Copy, Grey papers
                   Churchill to Grey, p. 298. Copy, Admiralty papers: 116/1336
                   Grey to Churchill, p. 299. Admiralty papers: 116/1336
                   Asquith to Venetia Stanley, p. 300. Montagu papers
                   Churchill to Kitchener, p. 300. Copy, Churchill papers: 13/47

22 Feb. 1915   Carden to Admiralty, p. 300. Churchill papers: 2/88
                   Churchill to Kitchener, p. 300. Churchill papers: 13/45
                   Lloyd George memorandum, p. 349. Churchill papers: 21/38

23 Feb. 1915   Carden to Admiralty, p. 301. Churchill papers: 2/88

24 Feb. 1915   War Council, Secretary's notes, p. 301. Cabinet papers: 22/1
                   Asquith to Venetia Stanley, p. 301. Montagu papers
                   Churchill to Carden, p. 304. Churchill papers: 13/54
                   Churchill to Carden, p. 305. Churchill papers: 2/88
                   Balfour memorandum, p. 305. Churchill papers: 2/89
                   Churchill minute, p. 536. Admiralty papers: 116/1339

25 Feb. 1915   Margot Asquith diary, p. 305. Countess Oxford and Asquith papers
                   Churchill memorandum, p. 307. Churchill papers: 26/3

26 Feb. 1915   Asquith to Venetia Stanley, p. 306. Montagu papers
                   Asquith to Venetia Stanley, p. 306. Montagu papers

War Council, Secretary's notes, p. 307. Churchill papers: 2/86
Asquith to Venetia Stanley, p. 310. Montagu papers
Hankey to Adeline Hankey, p. 310. Hankey papers
Churchill to John Churchill, p. 310. John Churchill papers
Sykes to Churchill, p. 317. Churchill papers: 26/2

27 Feb. 1915   Churchill memorandum, p. 311. Draft, Churchill papers: 21/38
Churchill to Kitchener, p. 313. Copy, Churchill papers: 13/46
Churchill to Oliver, p. 314. Oliver papers
Churchill to Grand Duke Nicholas, p. 314. Copy, Churchill papers: 13/47

28 Feb. 1915   Churchill to Grey, p. 315. Copy, Churchill papers: 26/2
Elliot to Grey, p. 334. Admiralty papers: 116/1336

MARCH 1915

1 March 1915   Asquith to Venetia Stanley, p. 316. Montagu papers
Churchill to Asquith, p. 316. Copy, Churchill papers: 13/54
Grey to Elliot, p. 316. Copy, Churchill papers: 26/4
Hankey memorandum, p. 318. Churchill papers: 2/89

2 March 1915   Churchill to Fisher and Oliver, p. 300. Churchill papers: 26/3
Churchill to Grey, p. 320. Copy, Churchill papers: 26/2

3 March 1915   War Council, Secretary's notes, p. 321. Cabinet papers: 22/1
Jackson notes, p. 324. Churchill papers: 26/3
Hardinge to Crewe, p. 324. Crewe papers
Buchanan to Grey, p. 328. Copy, Churchill papers: 26/4

4 March 1915   Churchill to Kitchener, p. 324. Copy, Churchill papers: 13/48
Churchill to Grey, p. 325. Copy, Churchill papers: 13/48
Churchill to Grey, p. 326. Copy, Churchill papers: 13/45
Fisher to Churchill, p. 326. Churchill papers: 13/56
Churchill to Carden, p. 326. Copy, Churchill papers: 13/65
Bertie to Grey, p. 328. Copy, Churchill papers: 26/4

5 March 1915   Churchill note, p. 46. Churchill papers: 13/58
Churchill memorandum, p. 285. Harcourt papers
Carden to Admiralty, p. 326. Churchill papers: 13/65
Churchill to Grey, p. 327. Copy, Churchill papers: 26/2
Grey to Churchill, p. 327. Churchill papers: 26/2

6 March 1915   Churchill to Grand Duke Nicholas, p. 328. Draft, Churchill papers: 13/45
Hankey diary, p. 328. Hankey papers
Churchill to Grey, p. 328. Draft, Churchill papers: 26/2
Birdwood to Kitchener, p. 331. Copy, Churchill papers: 2/88

7 March 1915   Churchill to Grey, p. 329. Churchill papers: 26/4
Margot Asquith diary, pp. 329, 330. Countess Oxford and Asquith papers
Churchill to F. E. Smith, p. 330. Copy, Churchill papers: 2/65
Carden to Admiralty, p. 331. Churchill papers: 2/88

9 March 1915   Carden to Admiralty, p. 331. Churchill papers: 2/88
Churchill to Jellicoe, p. 331. Copy, Churchill papers: 13/48
Hankey to Esher, p. 331. Esher papers

9 March 1915   Churchill to Grey, p. 336. Grey papers
                Churchill minute, p. 537. Admiralty papers: 116/1339

10 March 1915   War Council, Secretary's notes, p. 332. Cabinet papers: 22/1
—   Bax-Ironside to Grey, p. 335. Copy, Admiralty papers: 116/1336
                Churchill to Grey, p. 336. Grey papers
                Ian Hamilton to Churchill, p. 338. Churchill papers: 26/2

11 March 1915   Jackson to Oliver, p. 336. Copy, Churchill papers: 13/54
                Churchill to Carden, p. 337. Copy, Churchill papers: 13/65
                Fisher to Churchill, p. 338. Admiralty papers: 137/1089
                Churchill to Asquith, p. 338. Copy, Churchill papers: 13/48
                Hardinge to Crewe, p. 349. Crewe papers

12 March 1915   Fisher to Churchill, p. 338. Churchill papers: 13/56
                Kitchener to Churchill, p. 339. Churchill papers: 13/48
                John Churchill diary, p. 339. Copy, Churchill papers: 28/139
                Ian Hamilton to Churchill, p. 340. Churchill papers: 26/2
                Crewe to Hardinge, p. 344. Hardinge papers
                Grand Duke Nicholas, instructions, p. 344. Copy, Churchill papers: 2/74

13 March 1915   Kitchener to Churchill, p. 341. Churchill papers: 13/54
                Hankey diary, p. 341. Hankey papers
                Churchill to Phaeton, p. 342. Admiralty papers: 137/109
                Carden to Churchill, p. 342. Churchill papers: 13/54
                Churchill to Fisher, p. 342. Churchill papers: 13/54
                Churchill to Carden, p. 343. Copy, Churchill papers: 13/54
                Asquith to Venetia Stanley, p. 343. Montagu papers

14 March 1915   Ian Hamilton to Churchill, p. 341. Churchill papers: 26/2
                Churchill to Grand Duke Nicholas, p. 345. Copy, Churchill papers: 26/4
                Churchill to Kitchener, p. 346. Copy, Churchill papers: 13/49

15 March 1915   F. E. Smith to Churchill, p. 344. Churchill papers: 2/65
                Hankey diary, p. 345. Hankey papers
                Hankey to Esher, p. 345. Copy, Hankey papers
                Fisher to Churchill, p. 346. Churchill papers: 13/56
                Churchill to Fisher, p. 346. Fisher papers
                Churchill to Carden, p. 347. Copy, Churchill papers: 13/65

[15] March 1915 Esher to Hankey, p. 345. Hankey papers

16 March 1915   Fisher to Churchill, p. 347. Churchill papers: 13/56
                Kitchener memorandum, p. 349. Cabinet papers: 42/2
                Jackson memorandum, p. 349. Harcourt papers

17 March 1915   Churchill to de Robeck, p. 348. Copy, Churchill papers: 13/65
                Paget to Kitchener, p. 348. Copy, Churchill papers: 26/4

18 March 1915   Hardinge to Crewe, p. 349. Crewe papers
                Ian Hamilton to Kitchener, p. 353. Copy, Hamilton papers
                De Robeck to Wemyss, p. 357. Copy, de Robeck papers

19 March 1915   Fisher to Churchill, p. 354. Churchill papers: 13/56
War Council, Secretary's notes, p. 354. Cabinet papers: 22/1
De Robeck to Churchill, pp. 351, 356. Churchill papers: 13/65
De Robeck to Churchill, p. 357. Churchill papers: 13/65
Ian Hamilton to Kitchener, p. 357. Copy, Churchill papers: 2/88

20 March 1915   Churchill and Fisher to de Robeck, p. 358. Copy, Churchill papers: 13/65
De Robeck to Churchill, p. 358. Churchill papers: 13/65
De Robeck to Churchill, p. 358. Churchill papers: 13/65
De Robeck to Ian Hamilton, p. 360. Copy, Churchill papers: 13/65
Fisher to Churchill, p. 360. Churchill papers: 13/56
Churchill to Fisher, p. 360. Fisher papers
Churchill to Fisher, p. 360. Fisher papers
Churchill minute, p. 537. Admiralty papers: 116/1339

21 March 1915   De Robeck to Admiralty, p. 360. Churchill papers: 13/65
Asquith to Venetia Stanley, p. 361. Montagu papers
Margot Asquith diary, p. 361. Countess Oxford and Asquith papers
Keyes to Eva Keyes, p. 363. Keyes papers

22 March 1915   Asquith to Venetia Stanley, p. 360. Montagu papers
De Robeck to Churchill, p. 364. Churchill papers: 13/65

23 March 1915   Churchill to de Robeck, p. 365. Draft, Churchill papers: 13/55
Kitchener to Ian Hamilton, p. 366. Draft, Churchill papers: 26/3
Kitchener to Ian Hamilton, p. 366. Draft, Churchill papers: 26/3
Asquith to Venetia Stanley, p. 366. Montagu papers

24 March 1914   Asquith to Venetia Stanley, p. 362. Montagu papers
Fisher to Churchill, p. 367. Churchill papers: 29/1
Fisher to Churchill, p. 367. Churchill papers: 13/56
Churchill to de Robeck, p. 368. Copy, Churchill papers: 13/65
Margot Asquith to Lloyd George, p. 372. Lloyd George papers
Churchill memorandum, p. 373. Churchill papers: 13/56

25 March 1915   De Robeck to Churchill, p. 369. Churchill papers: 13/65
Churchill to Fisher, p. 370. Churchill papers: 13/56
John Churchill to Churchill, p. 371. Churchill papers: 1/117
Churchill to Grey, p. 371. Admiralty papers: 116/1336
Churchill to Grey, p. 372. Admiralty papers: 116/1336
Kitchener to Churchill, p. 373. Churchill papers: 13/49
Harcourt memorandum, p. 373. Harcourt papers

26 March 1915   Fisher to Churchill, p. 373. Churchill papers: 13/56
Maxse to Foreign Office, p. 374. Copy, Churchill papers: 21/37
Churchill to Grey and Kitchener, p. 374. Copy, Churchill papers: 21/37
Fisher to Churchill, p. 374. Admiralty papers: 116/1350
De Robeck to Churchill, p. 375. Churchill papers: 13/65
Hankey diary, p. 377. Hankey papers

27 March 1915   Fisher to Churchill, p. 375. Churchill papers: 13/56
De Robeck to Churchill, p. 375. Churchill papers: 13/65
Churchill to de Robeck, p. 377. Copy, Churchill papers: 13/65
Hankey to Churchill, p. 378. Admiralty papers: 116/1350
Churchill memorandum, p. 378. Churchill papers: 26/3

28 March 1915   Fisher to Churchill, p. 378. Churchill papers: 13/56

29 March 1915   Asquith to Venetia Stanley, p. 362. Montagu papers

30 March 1915   Asquith to Venetia Stanley, p. 363. Montagu papers
Hamilton to de Robeck, p. 372. Copy, Churchill papers: 2/74
Greek intelligence report to Admiralty, p. 395. Admiralty papers: 116/1336

APRIL 1915

2 April 1915   Fisher to Churchill, p. 382. Churchill papers: 13/57
Fisher to Jellicoe, p. 382. Jellicoe papers
Churchill to de Robeck, p. 382. Copy, Churchill papers: 13/65

3 April 1915   De Robeck to Churchill, p. 382. Churchill papers: 13/65
Asquith to Bertie and Buchanan, p. 383. Admiralty papers: 137/1089

4 April 1915   De Robeck to Churchill, p. 383. Churchill papers: 13/65
Fisher to Jellicoe, p. 385. Jellicoe papers

5 April 1915   Lloyd George to Churchill, p. 384. Churchill papers: 2/68
Churchill to Lloyd George, p. 384. Lloyd George papers
Churchill to Jellicoe, p. 385. Draft, Churchill papers: 13/50
Fisher to Churchill, p. 385. Churchill papers: 13/57

6 April 1915   Hankey note, p. 386. Cabinet papers: 22/1
Churchill to Kitchener, p. 386. Copy, Churchill papers: 13/50
Churchill to de Robeck, p. 387. Copy, Churchill papers: 13/65

7 April 1915   Churchill to Kitchener, p. 387. Kitchener papers
Asquith to Venetia Stanley, p. 387. Montagu papers

8 April 1916   Frances Stevenson diary, pp. 383, 384. Countess Lloyd-George papers
Fisher to Hamilton, Lambert and Tudor, p. 388. Copy, Fisher papers
Richmond to Fisher, p. 389. Copy, Richmond papers
Balfour to Churchill, p. 389. Churchill papers: 13/50
Churchill to Balfour, p. 390. Copy, Churchill papers: 13/50
De Robeck to Churchill, p. 390. Churchill papers: 13/65
De Robeck to Churchill, p. 390. Churchill papers: 13/65
Committee on Asiatic Turkey, instructions, p. 391. Churchill papers: 21/38
Churchill to Kitchener, p. 391. Copy, Churchill papers: 2/88

9 April 1915   Fisher to Jellicoe, p. 392. Jellicoe papers

11 April 1915   John Churchill to Churchill, p. 393. Churchill papers: 1/117
Churchill to Fisher, p. 394. Copy, Churchill papers: 13/57
Asquith to Churchill, p. 395. Churchill papers: 26/2
Churchill to Asquith, p. 395. Copy, Churchill papers: 26/2

12 April 1915   Fisher to Churchill, p. 394. Churchill papers: 13/57

14 April 1915   Kitchener to Asquith, p. 430. Facsimile, *The Autobiography of Margot Asquith* pp. 180–1

16 April 1915   Asquith to Venetia Stanley, p. 477. Montagu papers

19 April 1915   Churchill to John Churchill, p. 396. Copy, Churchill papers: 13/65
                  Hankey diary, p. 396. Hankey papers

20 April 1915   De Robeck to Churchill, p. 397. Churchill papers: 2/88
                  Fisher to Hankey, p. 397. Hankey papers

21 April 1915   Ian Hamilton to his troops, p. 397. Hamilton papers
                  Fisher to Jellicoe, p. 397. Jellicoe papers

22 April 1915   Gwynne to Asquith, p. 398. Asquith papers
                  Richmond diary, p. 399. Richmond papers
                  Fisher to Jellicoe, p. 400. Jellicoe papers
                  Churchill to Oliver, p. 400. Admiralty papers: 137/1089
                  Churchill to Buchanan, p. 400. Admiralty papers: 137/1089
                  Sazonov to Grey, p. 400. Grey papers
                  Churchill to de Robeck, p. 401. Copy, Churchill papers: 29/1
                  Marsh to Violet Asquith, p. 401. Quoted, V. Bonham Carter *Winston
                  Churchill As I Knew Him* p. 380

23 April 1915   Henry Wilson diary, p. 400. Wilson papers
                  Fisher to Jellicoe, p. 400. Jellicoe papers
                  Churchill to Fisher and Oliver, p. 400. Admiralty papers: 137/1089
24 April 1915   Churchill note, p. 399. Churchill papers: 13/58

25 April 1915   Birdwood to Ian Hamilton, p. 407. Hamilton papers

26 April 1915   Violet Asquith to Churchill, p. 402. Churchill papers: 1/117
                  De Robeck to Churchill, p. 406. Churchill papers: 13/65
                  Ian Hamilton to Birdwood, p. 407. Copy, Hamilton papers
                  Churchill to Kitchener, p. 409. Draft, Churchill papers: 13/45
                  Churchill to Fitzgerald, p. 410. Draft, Churchill papers: 13/45
                  Churchill to John Churchill, p. 410. Draft, Churchill papers: 13/45
                  Churchill to John Churchill, p. 410. As sent, copy, Churchill papers:
                  13/65
                  Hankey to Esher, p. 411. Esher papers

27 April 1915   John Churchill to Churchill, pp. 405, 407. Churchill papers: 1/117
                  Wedgwood to Churchill, p. 408. Churchill papers: 21/43

28 April 1915   Asquith to Venetia Stanley, p. 410. Montagu papers
                  De Robeck to Churchill, p. 417. Churchill papers: 13/51

29 April 1915   John Churchill to Churchill, p. 408. Churchill papers: 1/117
                  De Robeck to Churchill, p. 412. Churchill papers: 13/65

30 April 1915   Churchill to Grey, p. 412. Copy, Churchill papers: 13/51
                  De Robeck to Churchill, p. 417. Churchill papers: 13/65

MAY 1915

1 May 1915   De Robeck to Churchill, p. 412. Churchill papers: 13/65

2 May 1915   De Robeck to Churchill, p. 412. Churchill papers: 13/65

3 May 1915   Churchill to Fisher, p. 411. Admiralty papers: 137/1089

[4] May 1915   Fisher draft, p. 413. Churchill papers: 13/55

5 May 1915   John Churchill to Churchill, p. 414. Churchill papers: 1/117
Asquith to Venetia Stanley, p. 446. Montagu papers

7 May 1915   Henry Wilson diary, p. 414. Wilson papers
Asquith to Venetia Stanley, p. 447. Montagu papers

8 May 1915   Margot Asquith diary, p. 31. Countess Oxford and Asquith papers
Maurice Brett to Esher, p. 425. Esher papers

9 May 1915   Ian Hamilton to Kitchener, p. 415. Kitchener papers
John Churchill to Churchill, p. 415. Churchill papers: 1/117
French to Kitchener, p. 431. Quoted Henry Wilson diary, Wilson papers

10 May 1915   De Robeck to Churchill, p. 417. Churchill papers: 29/1
Henry Wilson diary, p. 431. Wilson papers

11 May 1915   Hankey diary, pp. 419, 420. Hankey papers
Fisher to Churchill, p. 419. Churchill papers: 13/57
Fisher memorandum, p. 419. Churchill papers: 13/57
Churchill to Fisher, p. 420. Copy, Churchill papers: 13/57
Churchill to Ian Hamilton, p. 437. Hamilton papers

12 May 1915   Hankey diary, p. 421. Hankey papers
Fisher to Churchill, p. 421. Churchill papers: 13/57
Churchill to Oliver and Fisher, p. 422. Admiralty papers: 116/3491
Churchill to de Robeck, p. 423. Copy, Churchill papers: 13/52
Churchill to de Robeck, p. 423. Copy, Churchill papers: 13/65

13 May 1915   Churchill to Masterton-Smith, p. 422. Churchill papers: 13/57
Fisher to Asquith, p. 424. Asquith papers
Margot Asquith diary, p. 426. Countess Oxford and Asquith papers
Riddell, account of Kitchener's remarks, p. 427. Garvin papers
Fisher to Asquith, p. 427. Asquith papers
Churchill to Fisher, p. 427. Admiralty papers: 116/3491
Fisher to Churchill, p. 428. Crease papers
Churchill to Fisher, p. 428. Crease papers
Churchill and Fisher to de Robeck, p. 429. Copy, Churchill papers: 21/38
Henry Wilson diary, p. 430. Wilson papers

14 May 1915   Stamfordham to Esher, p. 425. Esher papers
Hankey diary, pp. 426, 431, 434. Hankey papers
Fisher to Hankey, pp. 426, 429. Hankey papers
War Council, Secretary's notes, p. 431. Cabinet papers: 22/1
Churchill to Asquith, p. 434. Copy, Churchill papers: 13/52
Churchill to Fisher, p. 436. Cabinet papers: 1/33 part 2
Churchill to Fisher, p. 436. Fisher papers
Asquith to Venetia Stanley, p. 446. Montagu papers

15 May 1915   Ian Hamilton to Churchill, p. 437. Churchill papers: 13/56
Fisher to Churchill, p. 438. Churchill papers: 13/57

Asquith to Fisher, p. 438. Cabinet papers: 1/33
Churchill to Fisher, p. 439. Copy, Churchill papers: 13/57
Frances Stevenson diary, p. 440. Countess Lloyd-George papers
Fisher, envelope and enclosure, p. 444. Referred to, Beaverbrook *Politicians and the War* pp. 105–6 (1960 edition)

16 May 1915 Fisher to Churchill, p. 440. Churchill papers: 13/57
Fisher to Crease, p. 441. Crease papers
Fisher to McKenna, p. 441. McKenna papers
McKenna to Fisher, p. 442. Fisher papers
Churchill to Fisher, p. 442. Copy, Churchill papers: 13/57
Fisher to Churchill, p. 443. Churchill papers: 13/37
Sir F. Hamilton, Lambert and Tudor to Churchill and Fisher, p. 444. Fisher papers

17 May 1915 Asquith to Venetia Stanley, p. 447. Montagu papers
Churchill to Jellicoe, p. 449. Copy, Churchill papers: 13/64
Churchill to Asquith, p. 449. Copy, Churchill papers: 13/52

18 May 1915 Churchill to Asquith, p. 450. Copy, Churchill papers: 13/52
Churchill to John Churchill, p. 451. Copy, Churchill papers: 13/52
Churchill to Paris, p. 451. Copy, Churchill papers: 13/55
Harcourt to Esher, p. 452. Esher papers
Fisher to Crease, p. 452. Crease papers

19 May 1915 Wedgwood to Churchill, pp. 415, 483. Churchill papers: 2/66
Frances Stevenson diary, pp. 451, 456. Countess Lloyd-George papers
Fisher to Asquith, p. 452. Copy, Churchill papers: 2/153
Hankey diary, pp. 453, 456. Hankey papers
Stamfordham memorandum, p. 453. Royal Archives
George V to Queen Mary, p. 454. Royal Archives
Churchill to Bonar Law, p. 455. Bonar Law papers
Fisher to Bonar Law, p. 456. Bonar Law papers
A. K. Wilson to Asquith, p. 457. Copy, Churchill papers: 2/66

20 May 1915 Hankey diary, p. 457. Hankey papers
Churchill to Asquith, p. 458. Copy, Churchill papers: 13/52
Clementine Churchill to Asquith, p. 458. Asquith papers
Asquith to Venetia Stanley, p. 458. Montagu papers
Emmott to Asquith, p. 460. Asquith papers
Pringle to Asquith, p. 460. Asquith papers
Ritchie to Churchill, p. 461. Churchill papers: 5/11

21 May 1915 Churchill to Bonar Law, p. 461. Bonar Law papers
Churchill to Asquith, p. 463. Asquith papers
Asquith to Churchill, p. 464. Churchill papers: 13/52
Bonar Law to Churchill, p. 465. Churchill papers: 2/65
Austen Chamberlain to Bonar Law, p. 465. Bonar Law papers
Churchill to Asquith, p. 465. Copy, Churchill papers: 13/52
Asquith to Churchill, p. 465. Churchill papers: 13/52
Churchill to Asquith, p. 465. Copy, Churchill papers: 13/52
Churchill to Kitchener, p. 466. Copy, Churchill papers: 2/65
Hankey diary, p. 468. Hankey papers

22 May 1915 Callwell to Gwynne, p. 458. Gwynne papers
Asquith to Venetia Stanley, p. 466. Montagu papers

22 May 1915 Fisher to Jellicoe, p. 467. Jellicoe papers
      Fisher to McKenna, p. 467. McKenna papers
      Hankey diary, p. 467. Hankey papers

23 May 1915 Churchill to John Churchill, p. 468. Draft, Churchill papers: 13/52

24 May 1915 Marsh to Violet Asquith, p. 401. Quoted, Hassall *Edward Marsh* pp. 340–1
      Margot Asquith diary, p. 466. Countess Oxford and Asquith papers
      Frances Stevenson diary, p. 468. Countess Lloyd-George papers
      Duke of Marlborough to Churchill, pp. 468, 476. Churchill papers: 2/66
      Burns diary, p. 478. Burns papers

26 May 1915 Churchill to Kitchener, p. 470. Kitchener papers
      Churchill to Balfour, p. 470. Copy, Churchill papers: 2/99
      Churchill to John Churchill, p. 471. Churchill papers: 13/52
      Churchill to de Robeck, p. 471. Copy, Churchill papers: 13/52
      Edwin Montagu to Clementine Churchill, p. 472. Churchill papers: 28/152

27 May 1915 Dawnay to Cecil Dawnay, p. 471. Dawnay papers

29 May 1915 Jellicoe to Churchill, p. 483. Churchill papers: 2/66
      Churchill to Masterton-Smith, p. 485. Cabinet papers: 1/33 part 2

30 May 1915 Churchill memorandum, p. 486. Churchill papers: 13/58

31 May 1915 Shuttleworth to Churchill, p. 485. Churchill papers: 14/1

JUNE 1915

1 June 1915 Pakenham to Churchill, p. 482. Churchill papers: 2/66
      Churchill to Jellicoe, p. 483. Copy, Churchill papers: 2/66
      Churchill memorandum, p. 486. Churchill papers: 2/82

2 June 1915 Churchill to Hankey, p. 488. Hankey papers

4 June 1915 Hankey to Churchill, p. 488. Churchill papers: 21/43
      Selborne memorandum, p. 487. Churchill papers: 2/99

5 June 1915 Brabazon to Churchill, p. 482. Churchill papers: 2/66
      Churchill speech at Dundee, pp. 488, 492. Churchill papers: 9/52

7 June 1915 Limpus to Churchill, p. 482. Churchill papers: 2/66
      Churchill to Garvin, p. 491. Garvin papers

9 June 1915 Channing of Wellingborough to Churchill, p. 491. Churchill papers: 2/66
      Churchill draft Parliamentary bill, p. 493. Churchill papers: 21/39
      Asquith to George V, p. 494. Royal Archives

10 June 1915 Hobhouse to Lord Buxton, pp. 454, 477. Earl Buxton papers

11 June 1915 Churchill memorandum, p. 494. Churchill papers: 2/99

12 June 1915 Churchill to Seely, pp. 484, 495. Copy, Churchill papers: 2/67
      Churchill to John Churchill, pp. 493, 496. John Churchill papers
      Dardanelles Committee, Secretary's notes, p. 494. Churchill papers: 2/86
      Pitcairn Campbell to Churchill, p. 495. Churchill papers: 1/117

15 June 1915   Churchill to Kitchener, p. 496. Copy, Churchill papers: 21/43

16 June 1915   Churchill to Harcourt, p. 484. Copy, Churchill papers: 14/1
Kitchener to Churchill, p. 497. Churchill papers: 21/43

17 June 1915   Dardanelles Committee, Secretary's notes, p. 497. Churchill papers: 2/86
Churchill to Masterton-Smith, p. 498. Cabinet papers: 1/33 part 2

18 June 1915   Churchill to Montagu, p. 485. Copy, Churchill papers: 14/1
Churchill memorandum, p. 498. Churchill papers: 8/89
Ian Hamilton to Churchill, p. 499. Churchill papers: 21/43

19 June 1915   Churchill to John Churchill, pp. 493, 500. John Churchill papers

20 June 1915   Lord Robert Cecil to Churchill, p. 504. Churchill papers: 21/43

21 June 1915   Carson to Churchill, p. 504. Churchill papers: 21/43

23 June 1915   Lord Robert Cecil to Churchill, p. 504. Churchill papers: 21/43

25 June 1915   Dardanelles Committee, Secretary's notes, p. 502. Churchill papers: 2/86
Churchill to Lloyd George, p. 505. Lloyd George papers

26 June 1915   John Churchill to Churchill, p. 504. Churchill papers: 1/117
Churchill to Lord Robert Cecil, p. 506. Copy, Churchill papers: 21/43

30 June 1915   Esher diary, p. 87. Esher papers

[?] June 1915   Churchill memorandum on Formation of Air Department, p. 501. Asquith papers

JULY 1915

1 July 1915   Asquith to George V, p. 506. Royal Archives

3 July 1915   Lord Robert Cecil to Churchill, p. 504. Churchill papers: 21/43
John Churchill to Churchill, p. 505. Churchill papers: 1/117
5 July 1915   Dardanelles Committee, Secretary's notes, p. 508. Churchill papers: 2/86

6 July 1915   Churchill to Asquith, p. 506. Copy, Churchill papers : 13/53

7 July 1915   Churchill to Ian Hamilton, p. 508. Hamilton papers
Callwell to Gwynne, p. 527. Gwynne papers

8 July 1915   Balfour to Churchill, p. 507. Churchill papers: 13/53

9 July 1915   Churchill to Balfour, p. 507. Copy, Churchill papers: 13/53

16 July 1915   Churchill to Asquith, p. 510. Copy, Churchill papers: 21/37
Asquith to Churchill, p. 510. Copy, Asquith papers
Bernau notes, p. 511. Churchill papers: 28/142

17 July 1915   Kitchener to Hamilton, p. 510. Copy, Churchill papers: 21/37
Churchill to Bernau, p. 511. Churchill papers: 28/142
Churchill to Clementine Churchill, p. 511. Spencer-Churchill papers
Kitchener to Asquith, p. 512. Kitchener papers

18 July 1915   Ian Hamilton to Kitchener, p. 510. Kitchener papers
                  Churchill to Asquith, p. 512. Copy, Churchill papers: 21/37

19 July 1915   Grey to Churchill, p. 512. Churchill papers: 1/117
                  Stamfordham to Churchill, p. 512. Churchill papers: 21/43
                  Asquith to Churchill, p. 513. Churchill papers: 21/37

20 July 1915   Curzon to Churchill, p. 513. Churchill papers: 21/37

21 July 1915   Esher diary, p. 514. Esher papers
                  Guest to Churchill, p. 551. Churchill papers: 2/67

22 July 1915   Churchill to Balfour, p. 514. Copy, Churchill papers: 2/99

24 July 1915   Dardanelles Committee Secretary's notes, p. 515. Churchill papers: 2/86

30 July 1915   Churchill to Hankey, p. 515. Draft, Churchill papers: 21/43
                  Masterton-Smith to Marsh, p. 515. Churchill papers: 21/43

AUGUST 1915

2 Aug. 1915   Churchill to Masterton-Smith, pp. 515, 517. Cabinet papers: 1/33 part 2

3 Aug. 1915   Churchill to John Churchill, p. 516. John Churchill papers
                  Churchill to Masterton-Smith, p. 516. Cabinet papers: 1/33 part 2

5 Aug. 1915   Ian Hamilton to Churchill, p. 516. Churchill papers: 21/43

10 Aug. 1915   French to Churchill, p. 530. Churchill papers: 28/152
                  Wedgwood to Locker Lampson, p. 531. Draft, Churchill papers: 2/68

11 Aug. 1915   John Churchill to Churchill, p. 520. Churchill papers: 1/117

12 Aug. 1915   Churchill to Prince Louis, p. 6. Draft, Churchill papers: 2/67
                  John Churchill to Churchill, p. 521. Churchill papers: 1/117
                  Churchill to Asquith, p. 522. Copy, Churchill papers: 21/43

13 Aug. 1915   Prince Louis to Churchill, p. 6. Churchill papers: 2/67

14 Aug. 1915   Kitchener to Churchill, p. 522. Churchill papers: 21/43

16 Aug. 1915   Lloyd George statement, p. 527. Churchill papers: 21/56

18 Aug. 1915   Grey to Churchill, p. 527. Churchill papers: 21/43

19 Aug. 1915   Dardanelles Committee, Secretary's notes, p. 522. Churchill papers: 2/86

20 Aug. 1915   Dardanelles Committee, Secretary's notes, p. 523. Churchill papers: 2/86

21 Aug. 1915   Churchill to Asquith, Kitchener and Balfour, p. 524. Copy, Churchill
                  papers: 2/88

24 Aug. 1915   Churchill, cross-examination of Kitchener, p. 528. Churchill papers: 21/59
                  Kitchener, reply to Churchill, p. 528. Churchill papers: 21/59

27 Aug. 1915   Dardanelles Committee, Secretary's notes, p. 525. Churchill papers: 2/86

30 Aug. 1915   Hankey memorandum, p. 525. Harcourt papers

31 Aug. 1915   Dardanelles Committee, Secretary's notes, p. 526. Churchill papers: 2/86

[?] Aug. 1915   Callwell to Gwynne, p. 528. Gwynne papers

SEPTEMBER 1915

3 Sept. 1915   Dardanelles Committee, Secretary's notes, p. 526. Churchill papers: 2/86

4 Sept. 1915   Churchill to Selborne, Carson and Long, p. 159. Copy, Churchill papers: 21/37

5 Sept. 1915   Churchill to Balfour, p. 526. Copy, Churchill papers: 2/99

7 Sept. 1915   War Policy Committee, supplementary memorandum, p. 529. Harcourt papers

9 Sept. 1915   Carson to Churchill, p. 529. Churchill papers: 21/37

13 Sept. 1915   Churchill to Asquith, p. 530. Copy, Churchill papers: 21/37

14 Sept. 1915   Churchill to Bernau, p. 530. Churchill papers: 28/142
Dawnay diary, p. 539. Dawnay papers

15 Sept. 1915   Churchill to Asquith, p. 532. Copy, Churchill papers: 13/53

16 Sept. 1915   Dawnay diary, p. 539. Dawnay papers

19 Sept. 1915   Carson to Churchill, p. 532. Churchill papers: 21/43

20 Sept. 1915   Churchill to Seely, p. 538. Mottistone papers

21 Sept. 1915   Balfour minute, p. 290. Admiralty papers: 137/1055
Dawnay diary, p. 540. Dawnay papers
Hozier to Churchill, p. 548. Churchill papers: 1/117

23 Sept. 1915   Churchill to Asquith, p. 533. Copy, Churchill papers: 13/53
Churchill to Steel-Matliand, p. 537. Steel-Maitland papers
Dardanelles Committee, Secretary's notes, p. 538. Churchill papers: 2/86

24 Sept. 1915   Dardanelles Committee, Secretary's notes, p. 539. Churchill papers: 2/86
Kitchener to Hamilton, p. 539. Copy, de Robeck papers

25 Sept. 1915   Callwell to Churchill, p. 540. Churchill papers: 21/43

29 Sept. 1915   Masterton-Smith to Marsh, p. 542. Churchill papers: 21/43

30 Sept. 1915   Dawnay diary, p. 540. Dawnay papers

[?] Sept. 1915   Frances Stevenson diary, p. 531. Countess Lloyd-George papers
De Robeck to Balfour, p. 542. Copy, Churchill papers: 21/43

OCTOBER 1915

1 Oct. 1915   C. P. Scott, note, p. 451. Scott papers

2 Oct. 1915   Churchill to John Churchill, p. 542. John Churchill papers
Churchill to Curzon, p. 553. Copy, Churchill papers: 21/43

4 Oct. 1915   Churchill to Asquith, p. 543. Copy, Churchill papers: 21/43

5 Oct. 1915   Churchill to Asquith, p. 544. Copy, Churchill papers: 2/86

6 Oct. 1915   Churchill memorandum, p. 544. Churchill papers: 2/74
Churchill note for the Cabinet, p. 545. Churchill papers: 2/74
Churchill memorandum, p. 546. Churchill papers: 2/99
Churchill to Asquith, p. 547. Churchill papers: 21/43
Churchill to Balfour, p. 548. Copy, Churchill papers: 21/43

10 Oct. 1915   Guest to Churchill, p. 552. Churchill papers: 2/67

11 Oct. 1915   Dardanelles Committee, Secretary's notes, p. 549. Churchill papers: 2/86
Frances Stevenson diary, p. 551. Countess Lloyd-George papers

12 Oct. 1915   Frances Stevenson diary, p. 551. Countess Lloyd-George papers
Esher diary, p. 551. Esher papers
Hankey diary, p. 556. Hankey papers

14 Oct. 1915   Churchill note, p. 533. Harcourt papers
Dardanelles Committee, Secretary's notes, p. 553. Churchill papers: 2/86
Lloyd George memorandum, p. 554. Harcourt papers

15 Oct. 1915   Churchill memorandum, p. 554. Churchill papers: 21/42
Margot Asquith to Hankey, p. 556. Hankey papers

18 Oct. 1915   Spender to Churchill, p. 555. Churchill papers: 21/43
Margot Asquith to Kitchener, p. 557. Kitchener papers

19 Oct. 1915   Churchill to Kitchener, p. 558. Copy, Churchill papers: 21/43

20 Oct. 1915   Churchill memorandum, p. 555. Churchill papers: 2/99

22 Oct. 1915   Churchill to Asquith, p. 559. Draft, Churchill papers: 21/37
Hankey diary, p. 560. Hankey papers

24 Oct. 1915   Goulding to Churchill, p. 560. Churchill papers: 2/67
Churchill memorandum, p. 561. Cabinet papers: 42/3

27 Oct. 1915   Churchill to Asquith, Kitchener and Balfour, p. 561. Copy, Churchill papers: 21/45

30 Oct. 1915   Churchill to Asquith, p. 561. Copy, Churchill papers: 2/67

31 Oct. 1915   Monro to Kitchener, p. 563. Copy, Churchill papers: 2/68

[?] Oct. 1915   Carson to Lloyd George, p. 558. Lloyd George papers
Harcourt to Churchill, p. 560. Churchill papers: 21/37
Churchill statement, p. 561. Churchill papers: 21/43

NOVEMBER 1915

1 Nov. 1915 Drummond to Margot Asquith, p. 560. Countess Oxford and Asquith papers
Hankey diary, p. 562. Hankey papers

2 Nov. 1915 Monro to Kitchener, p. 563. Copy, Churchill papers: 2/68

3 Nov. 1915 Asquith to Lloyd George, p. 562. Lloyd George papers

5 Nov. 1915 Bonar Law to Asquith, p. 563. Copy, Churchill papers: 21/42

6 Nov. 1915 Hankey diary, p. 563. Hankey papers

11 Nov. 1915 Churchill to Asquith, p. 563. Copy, Churchill papers: 28/154

12 Nov. 1915 Churchill note, p. 533. Cabinet papers: 37/137
Asquith to Churchill, p. 564. Churchill papers: 2/68
Bonar Law to Asquith, p. 565. Copy, Beaverbrook papers

13 Nov. 1915 Violet Asquith to Churchill, p. 566. Churchill papers: 28/152
Grey to Churchill, p. 570. Churchill papers: 28/152
Coke to Churchill, p. 570. Churchill papers: 28/152

14 Nov. 1915 Spenser Grey to Churchill, p. 566. Churchill papers: 13/53

15 Nov. 1915 Churchill speech, p. 566. Notes and typescript, Churchill papers: 9/51
Frances Stevenson diary, p. 569. Countess Lloyd-George papers

16 Nov. 1915 Spender to Esher, p. 569. Esher papers
Lloyd George to Churchill, p. 569. Spencer-Churchill papers
Violet Asquith to Churchill, p. 570. Churchill papers: 28/152

18 Nov. 1915 Masterton-Smith to Clementine Churchill, p. 571. Churchill papers: 28/152
Churchill to Clementine Churchill, p. 572. Spencer-Churchill papers

19 Nov. 1915 Churchill to John Churchill, p. 573. John Churchill papers
Churchill to Clementine Churchill, p. 573. Spencer-Churchill papers
French to Clementine Churchill, p. 574. Spencer-Churchill papers

20 Nov. 1915 Lansdowne to Churchill, p. 587. Churchill papers: 28/154

21 Nov. 1915 Churchill to Clementine Churchill, p. 576,578. Spencer-Churchill papers
Lady Randolph Churchill to Churchill, p. 582. Churchill papers: 28/153
Clementine Churchill to Churchill, p. 583. Spencer-Churchill papers

22 Nov. 1915 Churchill to Clementine Churchill, p. 579. Spencer-Churchill papers
Clementine Churchill to Churchill, p. 583. Spencer-Churchill papers

23 Nov. 1915 2nd Battalion Grenadier Guards, war diary, p. 580. War Office papers: 92/1215
Churchill to Clementine Churchill, p. 580. Spencer-Churchill papers
Hankey diary, p. 581. Hankey papers
Clementine Churchill to Churchill, p. 583. Spencer-Churchill papers

24 Nov. 1915 Churchill to Lady Randolph Churchill, p. 581. Churchill papers: 28/120

25 Nov. 1915 2nd Battalion Grenadier Guards, war diary, p. 586. War Office papers: 92/1215

26 Nov. 1915 Churchill to Clementine Churchill, p. 585. Spencer-Churchill papers

27 Nov. 1915 Churchill to Clementine Churchill, pp. 584, 593. Spencer-Churchill papers
Churchill to Lansdowne, p. 587. Lansdowne papers
Lady Randolph Churchill to Churchill, p. 594. Churchill papers: 28/153

28 Nov. 1915 Churchill to Clementine Churchill, pp. 586, 588, 593. Spencer-Churchill papers
2nd Battalion Grenadier Guards, war diary, p. 588. War Office papers: 92/1215

30 Nov. 1915 Churchill to Clementine Churchill, p. 588. Spencer-Churchill papers
Henry Wilson diary, p. 588. Wilson papers
Curzon to Churchill, p. 601. Churchill papers: 2/68

DECEMBER 1915

1 Dec. 1915 Esher diary, p. 581. Esher papers
Clementine Churchill to Churchill, p. 593, 594. Spencer-Churchill papers
Churchill to Lady Randolph Churchill, p. 595. Churchill papers: 28/120
Churchill to Marsh, p. 595. Marsh papers
C. P. Scott to Churchill, p. 596. Churchill papers: 28/154

2 Dec. 1915 Grigg to Elizabeth Grigg, p. 588. Altrincham papers
Douglas to Fisher, p. 590. Fisher papers
Henry Wilson diary, p. 591. Wilson papers

3 Dec. 1915 Churchill to Clementine Churchill, pp. 590, 593, 596. Spencer-Churchill papers
Churchill memorandum, p. 591. Churchill papers: 2/68
Clementine Churchill to Churchill, p. 595. Spencer-Churchill papers

4 Dec. 1915 Churchill to Garvin, p. 596. Garvin papers
Churchill to Clementine Churchill, p. 597. Spencer-Churchill papers

5 Dec. 1915 Spiers diary, p. 597. Spears papers
Churchill to Clementine Churchill, p. 598. Spencer-Churchill papers

6 Dec. 1915 Clementine Churchill to Churchill, p. 599. Spencer-Churchill papers
Churchill to Clementine Churchill, p. 599. Spencer-Churchill papers

7 Dec. 1915 Spiers diary, pp. 599, 602. Spears papers

8 Dec. 1915 Churchill to Clementine Churchill, pp. 599, 602. Spencer-Churchill papers
Churchill to Curzon, p. 603. Curzon papers
Churchill to Lady Randolph Churchill, p. 604. Churchill papers: 28/120
Churchill to Garvin, p. 605. Garvin papers

9 Dec. 1915 Clementine Churchill to Curzon, p. 604. Curzon papers
Clementine Churchill to Churchill, p. 605. Spencer-Churchill papers

10 Dec. 1915   Churchill to Clementine Churchill, pp. 605, 606. Spencer-Churchill papers

11 Dec. 1915   Henry Wilson diary, p. 606. Wilson papers

12 Dec. 1915   Churchill to Clementine Churchill, p. 606. Spencer-Churchill papers

14 Dec. 1915   Spiers to Churchill, p. 610. Churchill papers: 28/152

15 Dec. 1915   Clementine Churchill to Churchill, p. 606. Spencer-Churchill papers
Churchill to Clementine Churchill, pp. 607, 610. Spencer-Churchill papers
Churchill to Marsh, p. 610. Marsh papers
Spiers diary, p. 611. Spears papers

17 Dec. 1915   Clementine Churchill to Churchill, p. 609. Spencer-Churchill papers

18 Dec. 1915   Churchill to Clementine Churchill, pp. 612, 614, 616. Spencer-Churchill papers
Haig diary, p. 614. Haig papers
Haig to Churchill, p. 615. Spencer-Churchill papers
Churchill to F. E. Smith, p. 615. Birkenhead papers
Clementine Churchill to Churchill, p. 620. Spencer-Churchill papers

19 Dec. 1915   F. E. Smith to Churchill, p. 617. Spencer-Churchill papers
Lady Randolph Churchill to Churchill, p. 618. Churchill papers: 28/153
Spiers diary, p. 619. Spears papers

20 Dec. 1915   Churchill to Clementine Churchill, pp. 616, 620. Spencer-Churchill papers
Garvin to Churchill, p. 618. Churchill papers: 2/68
Spiers diary, p. 620. Spears papers
Churchill to Clementine Churchill, p. 621. Spencer-Churchill papers

22 Dec. 1915   John Churchill to Churchill, p. 619. Spencer-Churchill papers

[25] Dec. 1915   Garvin to Fisher, p. 621. Fisher papers
Garvin to Lloyd George, p. 622. Copy, Garvin papers

27 Dec. 1915   Churchill to Lloyd George, p. 622. Lloyd George papers
Clementine Churchill to Churchill, p. 626. Churchill papers: 1/118

28 Dec. 1915   Spiers diary, p. 622. Spears papers
Clementine Churchill to Churchill, pp. 622, 626. Churchill papers: 1/118

29 Dec. 1915   Clementine Churchill to Churchill, p. 622. Churchill papers: 1/118

30 Dec. 1915   Clementine Churchill to Churchill, pp. 623, 626. Churchill papers: 1/118
Churchill to Clementine Churchill, p. 624. Spencer-Churchill papers

JANUARY 1916

Early Jan. 1916   Fisher to Lloyd George, p. 700. Lloyd George papers

1 Jan. 1916   Clementine Churchill to Churchill, p. 626. Churchill papers: 1/118
Churchill to Clementine Churchill, p. 628. Spencer-Churchill papers

2 Jan. 1916   Churchill to Clementine Churchill, pp. 626, 639. Spencer-Churchill papers

3 Jan. 1916   Churchill to Clementine Churchill, pp. 629, 638, 679. Spencer-Churchill papers

4 Jan. 1916   Churchill to Clementine Churchill, pp. 629, 680. Spencer-Churchill papers

5 Jan. 1916   Churchill to Clementine Churchill, p. 639. Spencer-Churchill papers

6 Jan. 1916   Churchill to Clementine Churchill, pp. 632, 633, 680. Spencer-Churchill papers
Lady Randolph Churchill to Churchill, p. 682. Churchill papers: 28/153

7 Jan. 1916   Churchill to Clementine Churchill, pp. 633, 680. Spencer-Churchill papers
Clementine Churchill to Churchill, p. 681. Churchill papers: 1/118
Churchill to Lady Randolph Churchill, p. 682. Churchill papers: 28/120
Fisher to Hankey, p. 699. Hankey papers

8 Jan. 1916   Churchill to Clementine Churchill, pp. 634, 639, 682. Spencer-Churchill papers

9 Jan. 1916   Clementine Churchill to Churchill, p. 683. Churchill papers: 1/118

10 Jan. 1916   Churchill to Clementine Churchill, pp. 634, 682. Spencer-Churchill papers

11 Jan. 1916   Clementine Churchill to Churchill, pp. 682, 684. Churchill papers: 1/118
F. E. Smith to Churchill, pp. 684, 685. Churchill papers: 1/124
Churchill to Clementine Churchill, p. 687. Spencer-Churchill papers

12 Jan. 1916   Clementine Churchill to Churchill, p. 684. Churchill papers: 1/118

13 Jan. 1916   Churchill to Clementine Churchill, pp. 634, 636, 639, 685. Spencer-Churchill papers

14 Jan. 1916   Churchill to Clementine Churchill, pp. 635, 637, 685. Spencer-Churchill papers
Churchill to John Churchill, p. 636. John Churchill papers
Fisher to Lambert, p. 700. Copy, Fisher papers

15 Jan. 1916   Churchill to Clementine Churchill, p. 637. Spencer-Churchill papers
Haig diary, p. 650. Haig papers

16 Jan. 1916   Churchill to Clementine Churchill, pp. 637, 640, 686. Spencer-Churchill papers
Clementine Churchill to Churchill, p. 687. Churchill papers: 1/118

17 Jan. 1916   Churchill to Clementine Churchill, pp. 641, 686. Spencer-Churchill papers
Hozier to Churchill, p. 686. Churchill papers: 1/124

18 Jan. 1916   Churchill to Clementine Churchill, p. 642. Spencer-Churchill papers
F. E. Smith to Churchill, p. 687. Churchill papers: 1/124

19 Jan. 1916   Churchill to Clementine Churchill, pp. 642, 688. Spencer-Churchill papers

20 Jan. 1916   Churchill to Clementine Churchill, pp. 643, 652, 689. Spencer-Churchill papers
Clementine Churchill to Churchill, p. 644. Churchill papers: 1/118

21 Jan. 1916   Clementine Churchill to Churchill, pp. 689, 690. Churchill papers: 1/118
Lady Gwendeline Churchill to Churchill, p. 644. Churchill papers: 28/152

22 Jan. 1916   Churchill to Clementine Churchill, p. 644. Spencer-Churchill papers

23 Jan. 1916   Churchill to Clementine Churchill, pp. 645, 646, 647, 688, 690. Spencer-Churchill papers
Clementine Churchill to Churchill, pp. 647, 689. Churchill papers: 1/118
Lady Randolph Churchill to Churchill, p. 647. Churchill papers: 28/120

24 Jan. 1916   Churchill to Clementine Churchill, pp. 646, 690. Spencer-Churchill papers
Clementine Churchill to Churchill, pp. 689, 691. Churchill papers: 1/118

25 Jan. 1916   Churchill to Lloyd George, p. 691. Draft, Churchill papers: 2/71

26 Jan. 1916   Churchill to Clementine Churchill, pp. 650, 691. Spencer-Churchill papers
Fisher to Hankey, p. 700. Hankey papers

27 Jan. 1916   Churchill to Clementine Churchill, p. 692. Spencer-Churchill papers
Clementine Churchill to Churchill, p. 693. Churchill papers: 1/118
Fisher to Hankey, p. 700. Hankey papers

28 Jan. 1916   Churchill to Clementine Churchill, pp. 654, 656, 693, 823. Spencer-Churchill papers

29 Jan. 1916   Churchill to Lady Randolph Churchill, pp. 647, 655, 694. Leslie papers
Churchill to Clementine Churchill, p. 655. Spencer-Churchill papers
Clementine Churchill to Churchill, p. 693. Churchill papers: 1/118

31 Jan. 1916   Clementine Churchill to Churchill, p. 654. Churchill papers: 1/118
Churchill to Clementine Churchill, p. 656. Spencer-Churchill papers
Churchill to Bonar Law, p. 694. Bonar Law papers
Haig diary, p. 697. Haig papers

[?] Jan. 1916   Churchill to Randolph Churchill, p. 647. Randolph Churchill papers

FEBRUARY 1916

Early Feb. 1916   Fisher to Bonar Law, p. 701. Bonar Law papers

1 Feb. 1916   6th Royal Scots Fusiliers, war diary, p. 656. War Office papers: 95/1772
Churchill to Clementine Churchill, p. 657, 696. Spencer-Churchill papers

2 Feb. 1916   Churchill to Clementine Churchill, pp. 698, 699. Spencer-Churchill papers
Clementine Churchill to Churchill, pp. 660, 698. Churchill papers: 1/118
Clementine Churchill to Lloyd George, p. 698. Lloyd George papers
Fisher to C. P. Scott, p. 701. Scott papers

3 Feb. 1916   Lady Randolph Churchill to Churchill, p. 668. Churchill papers: 28/153
Frances Stevenson diary, p. 698. Countess Lloyd-George papers
Fisher to Asquith, p. 701. Asquith papers

4 Feb. 1916   Clementine Churchill to Churchill, p. 698. Churchill papers: 1/118
Churchill to Clementine Churchill, p. 701. Spencer-Churchill papers

5 Feb. 1916   Nellie Romilly to Churchill, p. 702. Churchill papers: 1/124

6 Feb. 1916   Churchill to Clementine Churchill, p. 660, 661. Spencer-Churchill papers

7 Feb. 1916   Duke of Marlborough to Churchill, p. 702. Churchill papers: 1/124

8 Feb. 1916   Churchill to Clementine Churchill, pp. 662, 702. Spencer-Churchill papers.
Clementine Churchill to Churchill, pp. 663, 703. Churchill papers: 1/118.
Fisher to Jellicoe, p. 701. Jellicoe papers

10 Feb. 1916   Churchill to Clementine Churchill, pp. 663, 703. Spencer-Churchill papers

11 Feb. 1916   Churchill to Clementine Churchill, pp. 663, 703. Spencer-Churchill papers

12 Feb. 1916   Churchill to Clementine Churchill, p. 664. Spencer-Churchill papers

13 Feb. 1916   Churchill to Clementine Churchill, pp. 665, 705. Spencer-Churchill
papers
Clementine Churchill to Churchill, p 666. Churchill papers: 1/118

14 Feb. 1916   Churchill to Clementine Churchill, pp. 666, 671, 705. Spencer-Churchill
papers
Fisher to Lambert, p 701. Copy, Fisher papers
D'Eyncourt to Churchill, p. 706. Churchill papers: 2/71

15 Feb. 1916   Churchill to Clementine Churchill, pp. 667, 668, 705. Spencer-Churchill
papers
Wimborne to Churchill, p. 706. Churchill papers: 2/71

16 Feb. 1916   Churchill to Clementine Churchill, pp. 668, 705. Spencer-Churchill papers
Clementine Churchill to Churchill, pp. 669, 707. Churchill papers: 1/118

17 Feb. 1916   Churchill to Clementine Churchill, p. 670. Spencer-Churchill papers

18 Feb. 1916   Churchill to Clementine Churchill, pp. 671, 706. Spencer-Churchill papers
Holland to Clementine Churchill, p. 674. Churchill papers: 1/124

19 Feb. 1916   Fisher to Garvin, p. 704. Garvin papers
Asquith to Clementine Churchill, p. 706. Churchill papers: 1/124
Clementine Churchill to Churchill, p. 707. Churchill papers: 1/118

20 Feb. 1916   Churchill to Clementine Churchill, p. 675. Spencer-Churchill papers

22 Feb. 1916   Churchill to Clementine Churchill, pp. 676, 707. Spencer-Churchill papers

25 Feb. 1916   Clementine Churchill to Churchill, pp. 676, 707. Churchill papers: 1/118
F. E. Smith to Churchill, pp. 708, 709. Churchill papers: 1/24

26 Feb. 1916   6th Royal Scots Fusiliers, war diary, p. 674. War Office papers: 95/1772
Churchill to Clementine Churchill, p. 676. Spencer-Churchill papers

27 Feb. 1916   Tudor diary, p. 677. Chartwell Library copy
6th Royal Scots Fusiliers, war diary, p. 677. War Office papers: 95/1772

28 Feb. 1916   Tudor diary, p. 677. Chartwell Library copy
                6th Royal Scots Fusiliers, war diary, p. 677. War Office papers: 95/1772

29 Feb. 1916   6th Royal Scots Fusiliers, war diary, p. 677. War Office papers: 95/1772

MARCH 1916

1 March 1916   6th Royal Scots Fusiliers, war diary, p. 677. War Office papers: 95/1772

2 March 1916   Fisher to Hankey, p. 704. Hankey papers

6 March 1916   Fisher to Churchill, p. 710. Churchill papers: 2/72
                Scott note of a conversation with Fisher, p. 711. Scott papers
                Fisher to Churchill, p. 712. Churchill papers: 2/72

7 March 1916   Scott note of a conversation with Churchill, p. 713. Scott papers
                Fisher to Churchill, p. 713. Churchill papers: 2/72
                Fisher to Churchill, p. 723. Churchill papers: 2/72

8 March 1916   Margot Asquith to Balfour, p. 729. Balfour papers
                Churchill to Kitchener, p. 730. Draft, Churchill papers: 2/71
                Scott note of a conversation with Asquith, p. 730. Scott papers
                Fisher to Churchill, p. 732. Churchill papers: 2/72

9 March 1916   Hankey to Fisher, pp. 729, 731. Fisher papers
                Fisher to Scott, p. 732. Scott papers
                Fisher to Jellicoe, p. 732. Jellicoe papers

10 March 1916   Fisher to Scott, p. 733. Scott papers

11 March 1916   Esher to Haig, p. 729. Copy, Esher papers
                Fisher to Churchill, p. 734. Churchill papers: 2/72
                Fisher to Hankey, p. 734. Hankey papers
                Churchill to Cawley, p. 735. Copy, Churchill papers: 2/71
                Asquith to Churchill, p. 735. Churchill papers: 1/124
                Northcliffe to Robinson, p. 737. Northcliffe papers

12 March 1916   Fisher to Churchill, p. 736. Churchill papers: 2/72

13 March 1916   Churchill to Dalziel, p. 737. Copy, Churchill papers: 2/71
                Churchill to Clementine Churchill, p. 738. Spencer-Churchill papers

16 March 1916   Churchill to Clementine Churchill, p. 738. Spencer-Churchill papers

17 March 1916   Churchill to Clementine Churchill, p. 739. Spencer-Churchill papers

19 March 1916   Churchill to Clementine Churchill, p. 740. Spencer-Churchill papers

20 March 1916   Churchill to Garvin, p. 741. Garvin papers

21 March 1916   Churchill to Clementine Churchill, p. 741. Spencer-Churchill papers
                Clementine Churchill to Churchill, p. 741. Churchill papers: 1/118

22 March 1916   Clementine Churchill to Churchill, p. 742. Churchill papers: 1/118
                Churchill to Clementine Churchill, p. 742. Spencer-Churchill papers

23 March 1916   Churchill to Clementine Churchill, p. 743. Spencer-Churchill papers
Carson to Churchill, p. 743. Churchill papers: 2/71
Clementine Churchill to Churchill, p. 744. Churchill papers: 1/118

24 March 1916   Clementine Churchill to Churchill, p. 743. Churchill papers: 1/118
Scott to Churchill, p. 744. Churchill papers: 28/154

25 March 1916   Churchill to Clementine Churchill, p. 744. Spencer-Churchill papers

26 March 1916   Churchill to Clementine Churchill, pp. 743, 744. Spencer-Churchill papers

28 March 1916   Churchill to Aitken, p. 734. Beaverbrook papers
Churchill to Clementine Churchill, p. 744. Spencer-Churchill papers
Ritchie to Churchill, p. 745. Churchill papers: 5/18
Garvin to Clementine Churchill, p. 746. Churchill papers: 2/71

29 March 1916   Clementine Churchill to Churchill, p. 749. Churchill papers: 1/118
Clementine Churchill to Garvin, p. 749. Garvin papers

30 March 1916   Churchill to Clementine Churchill, p. 749. Spencer-Churchill papers

APRIL 1916

1 April 1916   Markham to Churchill, p. 749. Spencer-Churchill papers

3 April 1916   Churchill to Clementine Churchill, p. 746. Spencer-Churchill papers
Churchill to Lady Randolph Churchill, p. 750. Churchill papers: 28/120
Churchill to Curzon, p. 750. Curzon papers

6 April 1916   Clementine Churchill to Churchill, p. 748. Churchill papers: 1/118
Churchill to Clementine Churchill, p. 750. Spencer-Churchill papers
Churchill to Clementine Churchill, p. 750. Spencer-Churchill papers
Carson to Churchill, p. 750. Churchill papers: 2/71
Churchill to F. E. Smith, pp. 751, 754. Birkenhead papers

7 April 1916   Churchill to Clementine Churchill, p. 750. Spencer-Churchill papers

8 April 1916   Churchill to F. E. Smith, p. 751. Birkenhead papers

9 April 1916   Churchill to Clementine Churchill, p. 751. Spencer-Churchill papers

10 April 1916   Churchill to Lloyd George, p. 752. Lloyd George papers
Churchill to Scott, p. 753. Churchill papers: 2/71

12 April 1916   Clementine Churchill to Churchill, p. 753. Churchill papers: 1/118

14 April 1916   Churchill to Clementine Churchill, p. 754. Spencer-Churchill papers
Clementine Churchill to Churchill, p. 756. Churchill papers: 1/118

15 April 1916   Churchill to Clementine Churchill, p. 755. Spencer-Churchill papers

16 April 1916   Scott to Churchill, p. 756. Churchill papers: 2/71

19 April 1916   Frances Stevenson diary, p. 757. Countess Lloyd-George papers

20 April 1916   Henry Wilson to Milner, p. 755. Milner papers
Sinclair to Churchill, p. 756. Churchill papers: 1/124

23 April 1916   Vesey to Churchill, p. 757. Churchill papers: 1/124

26 April 1916   Trotter to Churchill, p. 758. Churchill papers: 1/124
John Churchill to Lady Randolph Churchill, p. 758. Churchill papers: 28/121

28 April 1916   Clementine Churchill to Churchill, p. 758. Churchill papers: 1/125

29 April 1916   Churchill to Clementine Churchill, p. 759. Spencer-Churchill papers

30 April 1916   Clementine Churchill to Churchill, p. 759. Churchill papers: 1/118

MAY 1916

1 May 1916   Churchill to Clementine Churchill, p. 759. Spencer-Churchill papers

2 May 1916   Churchill to Clementine Churchill, p. 759. Spencer-Churchill papers

6 May 1916   Churchill to Fergusson, p. 759. Churchill papers: 1/124

7 May 1916   Furse to Churchill, p. 760. Churchill papers: 1/124

10 May 1916   Fisher to Churchill, p. 762. Churchill papers: 2/72

14 May 1916   Churchill to Fisher, p. 762. Fisher papers
Fisher to Churchill, p. 762. Churchill papers: 2/72

25 May 1916   Lambert to Churchill, p. 775. Carson papers
Churchill to Carson, p. 775. Carson papers

31 May 1916   Churchill to Fisher, p. 776. Fisher papers
McKee to Churchill, p. 777. Churchill papers: 2/71

JUNE 1916

2 June 1916   Churchill to Asquith, p. 778. Copy, Churchill papers: 2/74
Fisher to Asquith, p. 778. Copy, Churchill papers: 2/74

7 June 1916   Waterlow to Churchill, p. 776. Churchill papers: 2/71
Churchill to Northcliffe, p. 781. Copy, Churchill papers: 2/71

8 June 1916   Northcliffe to Lloyd George, p. 782. Copy, Northcliffe papers
Churchill to Asquith, p. 782. Copy, Churchill papers: 2/74
Churchill to Lloyd George, p. 782. Lloyd George papers

[8] June 1916   Northcliffe to Churchill, p. 782. Copy, Northcliffe papers

9 June 1916   Churchill to Northcliffe, p. 782. Copy, Churchill papers: 2/71

14 June 1916   Reading to Churchill, p. 783. Churchill papers: 2/71
Gillespie to Churchill, p. 776. Churchill papers: 2/71

[15] June 1916   George V minute, p. 87. Royal Archives

19 June 1916   Hankey to Churchill, p. 784. Churchill papers: 2/74

20 June 1916   Churchill to Fisher, p. 783. Fisher papers

21 June 1916   Churchill to John Churchill, p. 783. John Churchill papers

22 June 1916   Churchill to Asquith, p. 784. Copy, Churchill papers: 2/74

24 June 1916   Prince Louis, record of conversation, pp. 421, 708. Milford Haven papers

JULY 1916

4 July 1916   Marsh to Churchill, p. 784. Churchill papers: 2/74

7 July 1916   Churchill to Lloyd George, p. 785. Copy, Churchill papers: 2/74

8 July 1916   Churchill to Asquith, p. 785. Copy, Churchill papers: 2/74

13 July 1916   Callwell to Gwynne, p. 785. Gwynne papers
                  Churchill to Asquith, p. 785. Copy, Churchill papers: 2/74

15 July 1916   Churchill to John Churchill, pp. 787, 790. John Churchill papers
                  Haldane to Churchill, p. 790. Churchill papers: 2/71

31 July 1916   Churchill to Seely, p. 791. Mottistone papers

[?] July 1916   Churchill to Lloyd George, p. 786. Copy, Churchill papers: 2/74
                  Churchill, draft statement on the Dardanelles, p. 790. Churchill papers:
                  2/75

AUGUST 1916

1 Aug. 1916   Churchill memorandum, p. 791. Churchill papers: 2/73
                  Hankey diary, p. 792. Hankey papers
                  Churchill to Fisher, p. 802. Fisher papers

3 Aug. 1916   Hankey diary, p. 802. Hankey papers

4 Aug. 1916   Churchill to Fisher, p. 802. Fisher papers

8 Aug. 1916   Northcliffe to Robinson, pp. 589, 792. Dawson papers

11 Aug. 1916   Fisher to Churchill, p. 802. Churchill papers: 2/72

12 Aug. 1916   Churchill to Cromer, p. 804. Copy, Churchill papers: 2/74

13 Aug. 1916   Churchill to Seely, p. 798. Mottistone papers

16 Aug. 1916   Fisher to Churchill, p. 803. Churchill papers: 2/72

18 Aug. 1916   Churchill to Aitken, p. 800. Beaverbrook papers

19 Aug. 1916   Derby to Lloyd George, p. 800. Lloyd George papers

23 Aug. 1916   Hamilton to Churchill, p. 373. Churchill papers: 2/74

25 Aug. 1916   MacCallum Scott to Churchill, p. 804. Churchill papers: 2/75

30 Aug. 1916   Churchill to Fisher, p. 805. Fisher papers

31 Aug. 1916   Hankey notes for evidence (part I), p. 380. Churchill papers: 2/85

SEPTEMBER 1916

1 Sept. 1916   Hankey notes for evidence (part II), pp. 294, 350. Churchill papers: 2/85

8 Sept. 1916   Churchill to F. E. Smith, p. 806. Copy, Churchill papers: 2/74

9 Sept. 1916   Greene to Churchill, p. 807. Churchill papers: 2/74

16 Sept. 1916   Churchill to Fisher, pp. 807, 810. Garvin papers

20 Sept. 1916   Churchill to Fisher, p. 808. Fisher papers
                 Cromer to Churchill, p. 808. Churchill papers: 2/74

21 Sept. 1916   Garvin to Churchill, p. 808. Churchill papers: 2/74
                 Cromer to Churchill, p. 809. Churchill papers: 2/74

28 Sept. 1916   Churchill statement to the Dardanelles Commission, pp. 200, 220, 248,
                 312, 337, 354, 364, 809. Churchill papers: 2/91

OCTOBER 1916

1 Oct. 1916   Churchill to Conan Doyle, p. 801. Conan Doyle papers

5 Oct. 1916   Churchill to Cromer, p. 381. Copy, Churchill papers: 2/74

11 Oct. 1916   Gwynne to Rawlinson, p. 811. Rawlinson papers
                Gwynne to Asquith, p. 811. Copy, Gwynne papers

17 Oct. 1916   Churchill to Cromer, p. 812. Copy, Churchill papers: 2/74

19 Oct. 1916   Churchill to Mears, p. 813. Copy, Churchill papers: 2/74
                Churchill to Oliver, p. 813. Oliver papers

[19] Oct. 1916   Oliver note, p. 814. Oliver papers

27 Oct. 1916   Churchill to Spiers, pp. 629, 814. Spears papers.
                Hankey diary, p. 814. Hankey papers

28 Oct. 1916   Churchill to Asquith, p. 814. Copy, Churchill papers: 2/74

NOVEMBER 1916

22 Nov. 1916   Scott notes, p. 816. Scott papers

25 Nov. 1916   Sir George Arthur statement, p. 817. Copy, Churchill papers: 2/74

29 Nov. 1916   Churchill to Mears, p. 817. Churchill papers: 2/74

DECEMBER 1916

2 Dec. 1916   Lloyd George to Bonar Law, p. 819. Bonar Law papers
   Abe Bailey to Lloyd George, p. 820. Lloyd George papers

6 Dec. 1916   Lloyd George note, p. 822. Facsimile, Addison *Four And A Half Years* pp. 272–3

1918–64

9 March 1918   King Albert of the Belgians memorandum, p. 125. Churchill papers: 15/161

18 Oct. 1918   Fisher to Inchcape, p. 155. Quoted, Marder *Fear God and Dread Nought*, Vol. 3, p. 555

31 Aug. 1919   Churchill to Royal Commission on War Inventions, p. 537. Copy, Churchill papers: 2/109

17 Nov. 1919   Royal Commission on War Inventions, draft report, p. 537. Churchill papers: 2/109

21 Feb. 1921   Art Committee minute book, p. 708. National Liberal Club papers

23 Oct. 1923   Crease to Churchill, p. 435. Churchill papers: 8/48

[Oct.] 1923   Crease memorandum, p. 435. Crease papers

13 Sept. 1927   Asquith to Churchill, p. 453. Churchill papers: 2/153

15 Sept. 1927   Churchill to Asquith, p. 453. Copy, Churchill papers: 2/153

18 March 1928   Churchill to Beaverbrook, p. 25. Copy, Churchill papers: 2/157

22 March 1928   Churchill to Beaverbrook, p. 463. Copy, Churchill papers: 2/157

[Aug.] 1928   Churchill note, pp. 90, 334. Beaverbrook papers

23 Nov. 1931   Aspinall-Oglander to Churchill, p. 522. Churchill papers: 2/177

7 Oct. 1937   Hall to Richmond, p. 359. Richmond papers

1959   Oliver notes, pp. 101, 298. Oliver papers

14 July 1964   Fox broadcast, p. 671. BBC transcript, recording No. T6W 63759

AUTHOR'S RECORDS 1966–71

Field-Marshal Earl Alexander of Tunis: conversation with the author, 28 Dec. 1968, p. 111

Mr Frank Ashton-Gwatkin: conversation with the author, 14 Feb. 1970, p. 43

Mr Ralph Bingham: letter to the author, 11 July 1966, p. 577

Mr J. R. Colville: letter to the author, 11 May 1970, p. 792

Air Vice-Marshal Sir John Cordingley: letter to the author, 27 Dec. 1968, p. 50

Mr Robert Fulton: letter to the author, 20 Dec. 1968, p. 659

Major-General Sir Edmund Hakewill Smith: conversation with the author, 22 Dec. 1966, p. 628 *et seq.*; letter to the author, 3 Jan. 1971, p. 759

Sir Ralph Hawtrey: letter to the author, 10 Nov. 1968, p. 475

Mr Reginald Hurt: letter to the author, 8 March 1970, p. 672

Mr Jock McDavid: conversation with the author, 15 March 1967, p. 633 *et seq.*; letter to the author, 5 March 1970, p. 630; conversation with the author, 24 May 1970, p. 660

The 10th Duke of Marlborough: conversation with the author, 7 Oct. 1969, p. 36

M. André Maurois: letter to the author, 6 Jan. 1967, p. 655

Mr C. J. F. Mitchell: conversation with the author, 6 March 1969, p. 117

Major F. D. Napier-Clavering: conversation with the author, 21 Nov. 1968, p. 671 *et seq.*

Mr Stewart Owler: letter to the author, 5 Feb. 1970, p. 122

Major-General Sir Edward Louis Spears: conversation with the author, 4 May 1970, p. 625

Baroness Spencer-Churchill: conversation with the author, 7 Aug. 1969, pp. 419, 477

Mr Henry Stevens: letter to the author, 14 April 1969, p. 108

Index

Compiled by the Author

Abdul Hamid, Sultan of Turkey: 188, 317

Aboukir (British cruiser): torpedoed (22 Sept 1914), 85–6; loss of, a cause of criticism of Churchill, 143, 184–5, 532

Abruzzi, Duke of: commands Italian navy, 423

Achi Baba (Gallipoli Peninsula): Hamilton decides to land south of, 393; Hamilton's army fails to reach summit of (25–26 April 1915), 407; Hamilton confident that his forces will reach, in May, 411, 413; renewed offensive towards (6–9 May 1915), 414; remains in Turkish hands (May 1915), 415, 431; Churchill learns of failure of ships' fire against, 687; MAPS, 403, 519

Achnasheen (Ross and Cromarty): mystery of a searchlight at, 82–3

Adamant (British submarine Depot Ship): Fisher wants returned to home waters from Dardanelles (28 March 1915), 378

Adana (Turkey): possible area of post-war Italian influence, 244; MAP, 838

Addison, Dr Christopher: Churchill clashes with (Sept 1915), 540; records breakfast discussion between Lloyd George, Churchill and Reading (1 Aug 1916), 797; becomes Minister of Munitions (Dec 1916), 822

Adeane, Henry Robert Augustus: killed in action, 228

Aden: American consul at, drowned at sea, 688n

Admiral Farragut (British monitor): to go to Dardanelles (12 May 1915), 423; at the Dardanelles (Nov 1915), 687

Admiralty, the: Churchill becomes First Lord of (1911), 1; his policy at, 2; conference (25 July 1914) postponed, 4–5; communiqué about Fleet concentration issued from, 7; defensive preparations of (27 July 1914), 8; further preparations of (29 July 1914), 11; Staff meeting at (30 July 1914), 13; relations with War Office, 21, 36, 226; visit of F. E. Smith and Sir Max Aitken to (1 Aug 1914), 24; urged by *Manchester Guardian* to 'trust the people', 38; confident of ability to prevent invasion, 57; purchases flying boats from United States (Nov 1914), 66; conference on aircraft production at (16 Sept 1914), 80; Court of Inquiry on sinking of *Aboukir*, *Cressy* and *Hogue*, 85–6; rubber manufacturers summoned to, 86; 'without a head', 117; tries to reassure War Office that a German invasion can be successfully challenged, 139; special intelligence branch set up at (8 Nov 1914), 179; merchant shipping policy of criticized by Bonar Law (Feb 1915), 282–4; intercepts German messages about shortage of ammunition at the Dardanelfes, 337; Fisher in charge of, during Churchill's absence in France (6–10 May 1915), 419; Churchill learns that he must leave (17 May 1915), 447; Churchill appeals to Asquith to allow him to stay at (20 May 1915), 458; Churchill's last day at (26 May 1915), 470; Churchill speech (5 June 1915) defending his work at, 488–91; and the origin of the tank, 536–8; Churchill sees possibility

Admiralty, the—*continued*
of returning to (Dec 1915), 622;
Churchill criticizes 'feeble pace' of,
under Balfour (Feb 1916), 662; Churchill criticizes Balfour's administration
of (March 1916), 716-22; and the
proposed publication of the Dardanelles documents (June 1916), 784;
Churchill urges greater efforts in new
naval construction upon (July 1916),
797; Carson becomes First Lord of
(Dec 1916), 823

Admiralty Board: Churchill informs of
anti-aircraft and anti-airship needs,
66; Captain Richmond critical of,
110; Asquith not very trustful of, 117;
Churchill alleged to be overruling
advice of, 144; Asquith describes as
'incapable of initiative' under Prince
Louis, 151-2; Churchill urges Balfour
to bring Fisher back to (March 1916),
721-2

Admiralty War Group: composition
of (Nov 1914), 185-6; summoned
to discuss possible attack on
Dardanelles (3 Jan 1915), 233;
examines Churchill's plan for a North
Sea offensive (4 Jan 1915), 236; plans
Dardanelles attack with battleships
surplus to Jellicoe's fleet, 249; discusses
(12 Jan 1915) Carden's proposals for
attack on Dardanelles, 250; Dardanelles plans examined by, 255; discusses (11 March 1915) Sir H. Jackson's appeal for troops to participate
in Dardanelles attack, 336-7; discusses Hamilton—de Robeck decision
to postpone second naval attack until
14 April 1915, 364; Churchill holds back
Dardanelles reinforcement proposals
from, until Fisher can approve them, 437

Adrianople (Turkey): Churchill wants
Grey to offer, to Bulgaria, 210-11;
Turks sending troops against Russia
from, 232; railway to (from Constantinople), exposed to attack by sea,
249; Lloyd George suggests joint
Anglo-Bulgarian attack on, 273; Chur-
hill wants the surrender of, as a condi-

Adrianople (Turkey)—*continued*
tion of peace with Turkey, 315;
Churchill proposes cutting of railway
between Constantinople and, 323,
544; MAPS, 545, 838, 840

Adriatic Sea: approaches watched by
British ships, 26; French blockade of,
46; Hankey proposes Serbian port on,
230; proposed British naval action in,
252-3, 255; Austrian submarines in,
272; Italy wants control of Austrian
coastline of, 395; Churchill suggests
submarine net across the mouth of,
471; MAPS, 29, 842

Adventure (British light cruiser): takes
Churchill to Dunkirk, 92

Advertiser, The (Dundee): on Churchill's
'highest good humour' (18 May 1915),
454-5

Aegean Sea: *Goeben* reaches, 41; Graeco-
Turkish rivalry in, 191; Turkish
torpedo boat prevented from entering
(27 Sept 1914), 212; British troops
being assembled in, 304; fear of German submarines in, 390; MAPS, 29, 235,
545, 838, 840, 842

Afghanistan: probable effect of a British
victory at the Dardanelles on, 349;
possibility of Turkish activity in, 686

Africa: Churchill wants greater use of
troops from (May 1916), 772-3, 794

Agadir (Morocco): crisis at (1911), 1,
63, 114, 462

Agamemnon: Churchill seen as casting
himself in the heroic rôle of, 132

Agamemnon (British battleship): to go to
Dardanelles, 249n, 266; at Dardanelles,
300, 331; needing repair, 379; Churchill rejects Fisher's attempt to impose
restrictions on de Robeck's use of,
388; Fisher recalls that despatch of, to
Dardanelles was his own idea, 394;
MAP (18 March 1915), 353

Agincourt, battle of (1415): Churchill
believes 'glories of' revived in 1914,
141

Ahwaz (Persia): Government of India
occupies oilfields near (Nov 1914),
221. MAP, 839

Air Board: *see* Air Department

Air Department (*or* Air Ministry, *or* Air Board): Churchill proposes establishment of (June 1915), 501; Churchill wishes he had been appointed to, 686; Churchill tantalized by possibility of appointment to, 690; the *Observer* advocates Churchill's appointment to (Feb 1916), 702–3; Curzon said to be the future head of (Feb 1916), 705; Billing asserts need for, in House of Commons (March 1916), 744; Churchill speaks on, in House of Commons (17 May 1916), 763, 767–70; Churchill attends meeting of, 777; Lloyd George and the suggestion of Churchill as head of (Dec 1916), 822

Aircraft Manufacturing Company: Churchill buys American flying boats from, 66*n*

Air Ministry (possibility of): *see* Air Department

Aisne, River (France): British troops to move from (Sept 1914), 81; MAP, 54

Aitken, Allan Anderson: joins Royal Naval Division, 48

Aitken, Sir William Maxwell: and possible Coalition on eve of war, 13; plays Bridge at Admiralty (1 Aug 1914), 24–5; seeks place for brother in Royal Naval Division, 48; quotes Asquith letter critical of Churchill (22 Sept 1914), 90; Churchill defends visits to France to, 425*n*; recalls Churchill's mood of 18 May 1915, 455; takes letter from Churchill to Bonar Law (21 May 1915), 463*n*; and Churchill's departure for the front (Nov 1915), 571; Churchill moves into St Omer headquarters of (Dec 1915), 620, 627; Churchill urges his wife to keep in touch with Bonar Law through, 688, 750; Lloyd George, Bonar Law, F. E. Smith and Churchill meet at St Omer headquarters of, 697; advises Churchill to stay in London and criticize the Government (March 1916), 734, 744; Churchill complains to, about Bonar Law's 'personal' attacks in Parliament (Aug

Aitken, Sir William Maxwell—*continued* 1916), 800; and Lloyd George's emergence as Prime Minister (Dec 1916), 819, 821–2

Aix-la-Chapelle (Aachen, Germany): Churchill proposes air raid on (25 Sept 1914), 91

Akaba (Turkey): Admiral Slade advises naval action against (31 Oct 1914), 215; *Minerva* sails to, 216; British naval bombardment of, 217, 219; MAP, 838

Albania: 230; Italy wants control over, 395; MAPS, 235, 545, 842

Albert Ballin (B. Huldermann): quoted, on Churchill and the coming of war, 5

Albert, King of the Belgians: and the defence of Antwerp (Oct 1914), 104, 106–7, 113, 116, 125, 650*n*

Albion (British battleship): on way to Dardanelles, 265; at Dardanelles, 331, 361*n*; at Gallipoli landings (25 April 1915), 405; MAP (18 March 1915), 353

Aleppo (Turkey): 344; Kitchener advocates annexation of (16 March 1915), 349; MAP, 839

Alexandretta (Turkey): possibility of feints at, 200; Turkish gunboats reported proceeding from (28 Oct 1914), 214; British sailors blow up railway trains and stores at (18–21 Dec 1914), 222–3, 233, 279; Fisher wants feint at, 234; Fisher approves capture of, 245; French desire for, 266; French naval command extended to, 267; and possibility of British seizure of, 267–8; Asquith and Kitchener favour annexation of, 332; Lloyd George prepared; to give to France to avoid a quarrel, 333; Kitchener prefers to Palestine for ultimate British control, 344; Hankey critical of failure to have a feint at, during Dardanelles attack, 345; Kitchener advocates annexation of (16 March 1915), 349; proposed extension of British sovereignty from Persian Gulf to, 509; Kitchener proposes an attack on (Nov 1914), 602; MAPS, 235, 838

Alexandria (Egypt): Turkish gunboats to be intercepted at, 215; Churchill wants troop transports assembled at, 220, 292; mistakes in loading of ships discovered at, 297; British troop transports arriving at, 324, 346; Jack Churchill on way to, 371; Kitchener threatens to withdraw Gallipoli troops to, if *Queen Elizabeth* leaves the Dardanelles, 423; Churchill wants Dardanelles troop reinforcements assembled at (June 1915), 497; MAP, 838

Algeria: 17; MAP, 29

Alsace-Lorraine: Haldane cites German failure to crush nationality of, after 1871, as evidence of need to avoid a punitive peace, 355

Ameland (Dutch island): possible British base, 19, 21; Churchill proposes naval attack on, 37; MAP, 19

Amiens (France): British Expeditionary Force reaches (14 Aug 1914), 47; *The Times* report from (30 Aug 1914), 70; MAP, 54

Amphion (British light cruiser): sunk (6 Aug 1914), 38

Amrum Light (off Schleweig-Holstein): Fisher on need to lay mines at, 187

Amsterdam (Holland): Fisher urges massive British troop landings at (Jan 1915), 245

Anafarta Hills (Gallipoli Peninsula): allied failure to reach (Aug 1915), 518, 520–1; MAP, 519

Anatolia (Turkey): Djemal Pasha records fear of allied advance through, 212; British keep watch for transfer of troops to Sinai from, 222; railway into (from Haydarpasha), exposed to attack from the sea, 249; seen as only part of Turkish Empire likely to remain Turkish after the war, 344; Italy wants control of southern coast of, 395; MAP, 838–9

Ancona (Italian steamship): torpedoed (7 Nov 1915), 463n

Anglo-Portuguese Alliance (1386): 7n

Antwerp (Belgium): Royal Naval Air Service base at (Sept 1914), 89, 91,

Antwerp (Belgium)—*continued*
114, 122–4; problems of the defence of, 96–104; Churchill's mission to (4–6 Oct 1914), 106–19; final stages of siege of, 120–2; surrender of, 124; criticisms of Churchill's actions at, 126–34, 137, 140, 143; Churchill recalls 'crack of their shells' at, 135; little chance of recapturing, 136; effect on Churchill of battle at, 161; expedition to, criticized in Parliament, 169–70, 177; the fall of, 'a cause of real sadness' to Churchill, 180; Fisher wants British troops landed at (9 Jan 1915), 245; Churchill warns Asquith of similar disaster if help to Serbia further delayed, 278; de Robeck explains misleading analogy between Dardanelles forts and, 376; H. A. Gwynne claims Churchill's actions at, demonstrate 'same ignorance of strategic and tactical principles' as at Dardanelles, 398–9; Churchill wants Asquith to publish documents concerning, 531–2, 533; Churchill defends his policy at, in *Sunday Pictorial* (Nov 1916), 817; MAP, 99

Anzac Cove (Gallipoli Peninsula): 407; MAP, 403

Aquitania (British troopship): 'a serious risk' sending to Dardanelles, 262

Arabia: Limpus suggests British action against Turkey in, 198; Grey favours setting up an independent Arab State in, 355; MAP, 839

Arabic (British passenger liner): torpedoed (19 Aug 1915), 463n

Archangel (Russia): possibility of transfer of Russian troops to Ostend from (28 Aug 1914), 58; possibility of transfer of Russian troops to Gallipoli from, 205, 428; Russia increasingly dependent upon, after closure of Dardanelles, 213; Hankey suggests sending Churchill on mission to (Oct 1915), 560–1, 611n

Archway House (London): Fisher not to be found at (15 May 1915), 438

Arethusa (British light cruiser): damaged (28 Aug 1914), 59

Ari Burnu (Gallipoli Peninsula): military landings at (25 April 1915), 402, 404, 407; MAP, 403

Ark Royal (British Seaplane Carrier): to go to Dardanelles, 257

Armenia (Turkey): possible area of postwar Russian control, 344; MAP, 839

Armentières (France): Royal Naval Air Service reconnaissance over (4 Sept 1914), 65, 68; Norman Leslie killed in action at (18 Oct 1914), 140; Churchill and Sir Archibald Sinclair photographed in (11 Feb 1916), 664; Churchill gives his battalion officers a farewell lunch in (6 May 1916), 760; MAPS, 75, 631, 649

Armoured motor-cars: sent to France (Sept 1914), 67, 74; Sir J. French sees little value in (Nov 1914), 163; Churchill and Kitchener quarrel bitterly over use of (Feb 1915), 189–191

Armstrong, Whitworth: and arms for Antwerp, 100; and building of Turkish dockyard facilities, 190–1; instructed to prevent Turkish Admiral hoisting his flag on *Sultan Osman*, 192

Arras (France): battle at (9 May 1915), 523; Churchill visits French front line near (5 Dec 1915), 597; Churchill urges Parliament (23 May 1916) not to repeat battle errors of, 774; MAP, 575

Arthur, Sir George Compton Archibald: Churchill clashes with, over rôle of Kitchener at the time of the Dardanelles, 817–19

Ashton-Gwatkin, Frank Trelawny Arthur: recalls story of Cabinet discussion on Japan, 43

Askold (Russian light cruiser): at Dardanelles, 327

Aspinall, Cecil Faber: at Suvla Bay (8 Aug 1915), 518; his reflections on the failure at Suvla Bay, 522n

Asquith, Arthur Melland (Oc): on his way to Antwerp, 112, 116, 117; his experiences at Antwerp, 130–1;

Asquith, Arthur Melland (Oc)—*continued* departs for Dardanelles, 305–6; wounded at the Dardanelles, 415

Asquith, Emma Alice Margaret (Margot): records Lloyd George's recollections of Churchill's mood at outbreak of war, 31; on the attempt to keep the loss of the *Audacious* secret, 142–3; on Prince Louis' failings as First Lord, 148; Fisher dances with, 155; reflects on Churchill's career and qualities, 179–80; hopes Turks 'will be wiped out of Europe', 219; discusses 'ambition' with Churchill, 245–6; Asquith describes quarrel between Churchill and Kitchener to, 289; her account of the Blandford review (25 Feb 1915), 305–6; discusses Churchill's character with Asquith, 329–30; reports Asquith's reaction to alleged intrigue (21 March 1915), 361; warns Lloyd George of Balfour's hostility, 372; tells Fisher he has 'talked too much' about his hostility to the Dardanelles (13 May 1915), 426; on Churchill and the new Coalition (24 May 1915), 466; and the concerted ministerial attack on Kitchener (Oct 1915), 556–7, 560; and Churchill's departure for the trenches (Nov 1915), 571; Clementine Churchill has tea with (7 Jan 1916), 681; said to have declared 'Nothing but God Almighty himself will drive Herbert out of Downing Street', 699; and Churchill's advocacy of Fisher's return to the Admiralty (March 1916), 709, 712–13, 729; begs F. E. Smith to urge Churchill to return to the trenches (March 1916), 736

Asquith, Herbert Henry: sends Churchill to Admiralty (1911), 1; informs King George V of European crisis (25 July 1914), 4, and of British intention to challenge German aggression, 7; approves Admiralty measures (27 July 1914), 8; approves sending Fleet to North Sea, 9; Churchill urges royal conference upon, 10; Secretary of

Asquith, Herbert Henry—*continued*
State for War, 12; supports Churchill's preparations (30 July 1914), 18; and plans for an offensive against Germany, 20-1; lunches at Admiralty (31 July 1914), 21-2; describes mood at Cabinet (1 Aug 1914), 23; authorizes full naval mobilization (1 Aug 1914), 25; authorizes military mobilization (2 Aug 1914), 26; approves Anglo-French naval co-operation (3 Aug 1914), 27; and Kitchener's appointment as Secretary of State for War, 28; and the chase of the *Goeben*, 29-30; critical of Marine expedition to Ostend, 56; and Churchill's conscription proposal (26 Aug 1914), 57; calls emergency meeting of Ministers (31 Aug 1914), 60; speaks at Guildhall (4 Sept 1914), 62; praises Churchill, 64; asks Churchill to draft Press communiqués, 70-1; Churchill dines with, 72; puts forward Amending Bill on Home Rule, 77-80; approves Churchill's visit to Sir J. French in France, 80; does not wish publicity on cause of sinking of *Aboukir*, *Cressy* and *Hogue*, 86; critical of Churchill's absence in France (22 Sept 1914), 90; relations with Churchill referred to, by Clementine Churchill, 92; advises Churchill to lay mines in North Sea, 93; sees Churchill at work, 95; and defence of Antwerp, 98, 101-3, 106, 111-14, 116-17, 120-2, 124; and criticisms of Churchill's actions at Antwerp, 127, 130-1, 132, 180; reports on Churchill–Kitchener disagreement about invasion, 138-9; praises Churchill's attitude in Cabinet (23 Oct 1914), 139; and sinking of *Audacious*, 141-2; sends Churchill to mediate between Lloyd George and Kitchener, 143; approves of replacement of Prince Louis as First Lord by Fisher, 147, 149; George V protests to about Fisher's appointment as First Lord, 150-2; Churchill reports 'Fisher is already a Court Favourite' to, 153; on battle off Coronel, 158-9; and

Asquith, Herbert Henry—*continued*
Churchill's proposed sixth wartime visit to France (Dec 1914), 164-7; answers Bonar Law's criticisms of Antwerp, 169; convenes first War Council (25 Nov 1914), 176; describes faces of colleagues, 176n; told of all-important intercepted German naval telegrams, 179; A. K. Wilson describes himself as 'Fisher's slave' to, 186; and pre-war Turkish policy, 189; and Turkish 'double game' (17 Aug 1914), 195; reports Cabinet decision to sink Turkish ships coming out of Dardanelles, 204; on warning to Turks 'to keep quiet', 205; tells George V of Britain's need to take hostile measures against Turks, 211; tells George V Britain will not take initiative against Turks, 215; believes Constantinople should be ruled by Russia, 216; does not regard war with Turkey with alarm, 219; 'altogether opposed' to attack on Gallipoli and Dardanelles (5 Dec 1914), 223; Churchill proposes North Sea offensive to (29 Dec 1914), 225-6; describes the war as 'an enormous waste of life and money' (29 Dec 1914), 228; receives plans for alternate war zone from Churchill and Lloyd George, 228-9; Churchill asks for memorandum from, 231; dines at Admiralty House, 238; informs Venetia Stanley of code-name for attack on German island of Borkum, 242; at War Council (8 Jan 1915), 244; at Walmer Castle, 246; Churchill sends Dardanelles plans to (12 Jan 1915), 250; and planning of Dardanelles operation, 256; upholds Churchill's ministerial authority, 265; Fisher protests to, 268-9; mediates between Churchill and Fisher, 270; at War Council (28 Jan 1915), 271-2, 275; Lloyd George critical of, 277; Churchill critical of, 278; explains importance of success at Dardanelles (9 Feb 1915), 280; favours British troops at Salonika, 282; Churchill proposes

Asquith, Herbert Henry—*continued*
wartime nationalization of British mercantile marine to (13 Feb 1915), 284; Churchill proposes tax on war profits to (5 March 1915), 285; informs Venetia Stanley of secret telegram from Dardanelles, 286; at War Council (16 Feb 1915), 288; caught up in quarrel between Churchill and Kitchener (17–19 Feb 1915), 289–91; tells War Council (19 Feb 1915) Serbia could best be helped by 'a big blow at the Dardanelles', 293; hopeful about outcome of naval bombardment (20 Feb 1915), 300; asks whether Anzac troops 'were good enough', 303; asserts importance of forcing the Dardanelles, 304; Churchill urges need for 115,000 troops at Dardanelles on, 306–7; supports Churchill's plea for a minimum of 85,000 troops at the Dardanelles, 309; annoyed by Churchill's 'noisy, rhetorical, tactless' mood, 310; describes Churchill as 'breast high about the Dardanelles' (1 March 1915), 316; believes Sir Ian Hamilton has 'too much feather in his brain', 325; describes Churchill (7 March 1915) as 'the most disliked man in my Cabinet', 329; describes Churchill as 'intolerable', 330; wants Britain to have 'a substantial share of the carcase of the Turk', 332; ends digression at War Council (10 March 1915), 334; unwilling 'to treat Tories as equals' (Churchill in 1928), 335; and Sir Ian Hamilton's departure for the Dardanelles, 338; reports (13 March 1915) differing Cabinet views on Palestine and the Jews, 343–4; asks at War Council (19 March 1915) whether plans exist for a military landing at Gallipoli, 355; believes War Council would not be doing its 'duty' if it took no Turkish territory, 356; and rumours of intrigues against him (end March 1915), 361–3; supports Churchill's desire for a renewed naval attack at the Dardanelles, 366, 367, 370; does

Asquith, Herbert Henry—*continued*
not call War Council to discuss the need for a military landing on the Gallipoli Peninsula, 381; tells France and Russia that Dardanelles attack 'will be pressed to a decision' (3 April 1915), 383; and decision to proceed with military landings on the Gallipoli Peninsula, 386; sets up Committee to examine British territorial needs in Turkey, 391; and Fisher's opposition to the Dardanelles, 394; worried about setback at Dardanelles influencing Italy's decision to join the Allies, 395; receives news (15 April 1915) of dissension among Young Turks in Constantinople, 395–6; answers critics of Dardanelles operation in House of Commons (22 April 1915), 398; and the Gallipoli landings (25 April 1915), 410; and Lord Charles Beresford's criticisms in House of Commons (4 May 1915), 413; Hankey passes on Fisher's resignation message to (11 May 1915), 420; agrees that no 'separate naval action' will take place at Dardanelles without Fisher's approval (11 May 1915), 420, 423; Fisher sends his memorandum of dissent about the Dardanelles to (12 May 1915), 421; Fisher sends further protest about Dardanelles to (13 May 1915), 424; defends Churchill's ninth visit to France in House of Commons (12 May 1915), 424–5; receives threat of resignation from Fisher (13 May 1915), 427; and Fisher's resignation (15 May 1915), 438–43; Churchill visits at Sutton Courtenay (16 May 1915), 444–5; unwilling to fight for the preservation of his Liberal administration (17 May 1915), 446; accepts a Coalition with the Conservatives, 447; and Churchill's Cabinet post in the new Coalition, 448, 449, 450–1; and Fisher's six conditions under which he promises to 'guarantee the successful termination of the war' (19 May 1915), 452–3; Sir Arthur Wilson

Asquith, Herbert Henry—*continued*
informs (19 May 1915) that he will
serve under no other First Lord but
Churchill, 457–8; Clementine Churchill appeals to (20 May 1915), 459;
asked not to make Churchill Colonial
Secretary (20 May 1915), 460; Churchill's appeal to remain as First Lord
(21 May 1915), 463–4; informs Churchill that he cannot remain at
Admiralty, 464, 465; reported as
saying (22 May 1915) that Fisher
'ought to be shot for leaving his post',
467; offers Churchill Chancellorship
of the Duchy of Lancaster, 468; and
the formation of the Coalition (May
1915), 469–70; and the political crisis
of May 1915, 475–81; reports the
decision to reinforce Hamilton's army
at the Dardanelles (9 June 1915), 494;
seems well-disposed to Churchill (June
1915), 495–6; does not agree to Churchill's suggestion to set up an Air
Department (June 1915), 501, 769–
70; reports to George V (1 July 1915)
about Cabinet discussions on Bulgaria, 506; Churchill protests to,
about Fisher's appointment to the
Board of Inventions and Research
(July 1915), 506–8; and Churchill's
proposed visit to the Gallipoli
Peninsula (mid-July 1915), 510–13;
Churchill seeks information about
Gallipoli reinforcements from, 522;
Churchill urges renewed naval attack
to (21 Aug 1915), 524; at Calais Conference (July 1915), 526–7; and
Cabinet views on conscription (Sept
1915), 529; and Churchill's desire to
take up a military command (Sept
1915), 530; and Churchill's desire for
publication of Admiralty documents,
531–3; and the origin of the tank, 533;
and the setting up of a smaller war
policy committee (Sept–Nov 1915),
542, 559–62; Churchill urges new war
policies on (Oct 1915), 543–4; and
the future of the Gallipoli expedition,
547–51; and the ministerial attempt

Asquith, Herbert Henry—*continued*
to remove Kitchener from the Dardanelles Committee, 556–60; Churchill
sends letter of resignation to (30 Oct
1915), 561–2; Churchill sends second
letter of resignation to (11 Nov 1915),
563–4; and possibility of Churchill
commanding the forces in East Africa
(Nov 1915), 565–6; replies to Churchill's resignation speech (15 Nov
1915), 568; seems to Churchill like a
mandarin 'of some remote province
of China' (27 Nov 1915), 587; Clementine Churchill sees (3 Dec 1915),
595; and Sir John French's dismissal
(Dec 1915), 596; his sentiments
'always governed by his interests'
(Churchill, 4 Dec 1915), 597; tries to
delay Kitchener's return to England
(Nov 1915), 601–2; Churchill describes as 'odious', 607; Churchill
believes the hour of his punishment
'draws nearer', 608; Churchill sees
himself as having 'to procure the
dismissal' of, 611; refuses to allow
Churchill to command a Brigade,
611–14; Churchill's growing bitterness against, 616–17, 626–7; Clementine Churchill the guest of (13 Feb
1916), 665–6; Lady Randolph Churchill dines with (2 Feb 1916), 668;
Churchill's criticisms of (Jan 1916),
679–80; reported to have asked after
Churchill 'with compunction' (7 Jan
1916), 681; Churchill and his wife
disagree over, 682–4, 687–90, 699;
Churchill describes as 'stronger than
ever' (25 Jan 1916), 691; his removal
discussed by Lloyd George, Bonar
Law, F. E. Smith and Churchill at St
Omer (31 Jan 1916), 697–8; talks to
Fisher in the House of Commons (23
Jan 1916), 700; growing political dis-
content with (Feb 1916), 703–5, 708,
Churchill writes to, about the tank,
706; and Churchill's advocacy of
Fisher's return to the Admiralty
(March 1916), 709–14, 719, 722, 725,
729, 730–1; and Churchill's continuing

Asquith, Herbert Henry—*continued*
criticisms of his Government (March–April 1916), 734–5, 736, 739, 741, 750, 752–3; and the renewed conscription crisis (April 1916), 755–8, 761; Churchill speaks in House of Commons as principal opposition speaker to (23 May 1916), 770; and Churchill's request to publish the documents about the Dardanelles (June 1916), 777–9, 782–5; and Kitchener's successor at the War Office (June 1916), 781; Churchill protests to, against decision not to publish Dardanelles documents, 785–6; Churchill describes as 'supine, sodden and supreme' (15 July 1916), 787; agrees only to set up Commission of Inquiry on Dardanelles, but *not* to publication of documents, 789–90; Churchill critical of his failure to give the House of Commons a full picture of the war (July 1916), 793; Lloyd George, Churchill, Reading and Addison discuss possible resignation of (Aug 1916), 797; Churchill describes his position as 'not at all good' (13 Aug 1916), 798; and the Special Register Bill (Aug 1916), 799–800; refuses to allow Churchill full access to War Council notes (Aug 1916), 805; Churchill intends to show his Dardanelles statement to, in advance (Sept 1916), 808; and Churchill's attempt to stop the premature use of the 'tank' (Sept 1916), 810; informed of alleged Lloyd George–Churchill–F. E. Smith–Sir J. French intrigue against Sir Douglas Haig (Oct 1916), 811; and Churchill's criticisms of Grey's evidence to the Dardanelles Commission, 814; and his replacement by Lloyd George (Dec 1916), 819–23; his changing attitude towards Churchill, 825

Asquith, Raymond: Churchill visits in reserve billets (Nov 1915), 580, 607

Asquith, Violet: recalls relations between Churchill and Fisher, 263; recalls Churchill's 'joy' at the promise of

Asquith, Violet—*continued*
Greek military help at the Dardanelles (1 March 1915), 315–16; and the death of Rupert Brooke, 401–2; and Churchill's resignation (Nov 1915), 566, 570, 571; marries Maurice Bonham Carter (30 Nov 1915), 594, 595, 602; (*see henceforth* Bonham Carter, Violet)

Aston, Sir George Grey: and British plans against Germany (1913–14), 20; commands Marine Brigade at Ostend (Aug 1914), 56; falls ill (Sept 1914), 73

Atatürk, Kemal, *see* Kemal, Mustafa

Atchison, Topeka and Santa Fé Railway: Churchill owns $10,000 bonds of, 511*n*

Athens (Greece): 205; Churchill willing to go on special mission to (July 1915), 512; MAPS, 838, 842

Aubers Ridge (France): Churchill watches unsuccessful attack on (9 May 1915), 416; Repington blames failure at, on shortage of high-explosive shells, 430; MAP, 575

Audacious (British battleship): sunk by German mine (27 Oct 1914), 141–2; sinking of, kept secret, 144, 214; loss of, impairs British naval margin, 268

Augagneur, Victor: and French naval participation at the Dardanelles, 256–7, 266–7; sends further battleship to the Dardanelles to replace the *Bouvet*, 354

Austerlitz (battle of, 1805): Napoleon defeats Russians at, 389*n*

Australia (Australian battle cruiser): 385

Australian and New Zealand Army Corps (ANZAC): fears for safe transit of, 206; War Council agrees to send to Dardanelles (16 Feb 1915), 288; Kitchener wants at Dardanelles instead of 29th Division, 291; Churchill insists will, require 'a stiffening of regulars', 292; Kitchener considers 'sufficient at first' for an attack on Gallipoli, 293; preparations for sending to Gallipoli, 296; Kitchener believes good enough for 'a cruise in the Sea of Marmora' (24 Feb 1915),

Australian and New Zealand Army Corps (ANZAC)—*continued*
303; being assembled in readiness for Dardanelles, 304, 316; at the Gallipoli landings (25 April 1915), 407; slight advances of (to 29 April 1915), 412; further slight gains (3 May 1915), 413; joins renewed offensive at Helles (6–9 May 1915), 415; and evacuation of Anzac area (Dec 1915), 619; Jack Churchill on headquarters staff of, in France (June 1916), 783

Austria-Hungary: and the crisis of July 1914, 2–3; ultimatum to Serbia, 4, 6; Germany prepared to defend against Russia, 5; British warning to, 7; Balfour about to visit on eve of war, 17; false news of war with Britain, 41; Britain declares war on (12 Aug 1914), 45; Churchill establishes blockade of, 46–7; possibility of uniting Balkan States against, 200–2, 210; occupies Belgrade (1 Dec 1914) but driven from (14 Dec 1914), 224; Lloyd George's repeated proposals for an attack on, 229, 243, 252; proposed dismemberment of, 230; Kitchener deprecates attack on, 244; War Council discuss defence of Serbia against, 273–4; imminence of attack on Serbia by (Feb 1915), 278, 280; Mark Sykes on need to mobilize Balkan States against, 317–18; Hankey favours offensive against by means of British naval attack up the Danube (1 March 1915), 318; Churchill sees capture of Constantinople as prelude to defeat of, 331; hardship in (June–July 1915), 504; attacks Rumania (1 Sept 1916), 797; Churchill asserts importance of concentrating on the destruction of (Aug 1916), 799; MAPS, 29, 545

Avonmouth (Gloucestershire): 402

Babington, John Tremayne: in air raid on Friedrichshafen (21 Nov 1914), 172

Bacchantes (class of British cruiser): patrolling Dogger Bank (Sept 1914), 85–6

Bacon, Reginald Hugh Spencer: 290, 392; and the origin of the tank, 535

Bad-Nauheim (Germany): Fisher's daughter and son-in-law prisoners at (Oct 1914), 146

Bagdad (Turkey): British forces fail to capture (Nov 1915), 590; Churchill forecasts (Dec 1915) disaster in future fighting at, 598, 600; Churchill advocates perseverance in attack on, 603, 605; MAP, 839

Bailey, Sir Abe: Mrs Churchill 'hobnobs' with (Jan 1916), 789; appeals to Lloyd George to give Churchill a place in his government (Dec 1916), 820

Bailey, Wilfred Russell: and Churchill's first day with the Grenadier Guards (20 Nov 1915), 575–6

Bailleul (France): German armoured cars reported near (Sept 1914), 68; brewery vats of, used for delousing of Churchill's battalion (Jan 1916), 640; MAPS, 75, 631

Balaclava (battle of, Oct 1854): Churchill compares losses of, with those of battle of Loos (Sept 1915), 642

Balcarres, 10th Earl of (David Alexander Edward Lindsay): a possible Viceroy of India (1916), 683

Balfour, Alice Blanche: 72

Balfour, Arthur James: learns of naval situation from Fisher (July 1914), 16; enthuses to Fisher about Churchill, 17; at Guildhall (Sept 1914), 62, 63; impressed by Churchill's military prediction of 1911, 64; reports on Churchill's military reflections, 72; defends Churchill in House of Commons against charges of responsibility for sinking of *Aboukir*, *Cressy* and *Hogue*, 86; and Churchill's regulations about promotion to Admiral of the Fleet, 87; at War Council (25 Nov 1914), 176; questions offensive naval policy in North Sea, 181; asks about Britain's sea defences, 181–2; Fisher writes to, of importance of attack on Turkey (4 Jan 1915), 237; at War Council (7

Balfour, Arthur James—*continued*
Jan 1915), 242; at War Council (13 Jan 1915), 251; outlines benefits to be gained by victory at the Dardanelles, 272; agrees on need for military help to Serbia, 273–4; comments on value of armoured car squadrons, 290*n*; asks War Council about political effects of occupation of Gallipoli Peninsula, 296; wants as many troops as possible sent to Dardanelles (24 Feb 1915), 305; Churchill urges need for 115,000 troops at Dardanelles on, 306; favours purely naval attack at Dardanelles, in contrast to his opinion two days earlier, (26 Feb 1915), 308, 310; approves giving Russia a privileged position at Dardanelles in any post-war settlement, 321; and the protection of the Europeans in Constantinople, 322; asks about naval advance up Danube, 323–4; favours post-war neutralization of Kiel Canal, 334; argues at War Council (19 March 1915) in favour of partitioning Turkey, 356; Asquith describes as a man with a 'futile feminine brain', 361, and of 'superficial charm', 362; on the problems of a renewed naval attack at the Dardanelles, 370; Margot Asquith warns Lloyd George of the hostility of, 372; critical (8 April 1915) of a military landing on the Gallipoli Peninsula, 389; Churchill's reply to, 390; Fisher protests at Churchill talking to, 426; Sir J. French puts his grievances to (May 1915), 430; tells War Council (14 May 1915) Gallipoli positions should not be evacuated, 432–3; Churchill appeals to, as an intermediary with the Conservatives (17 May 1915), 445, 455; Churchill suggests, as his successor as First Lord, 448; Churchill suggests, as Secretary of State for War, 449, 451; Fisher refuses to serve under, as First Lord, 452, 467; most senior Admiralty officials favour, as First Lord, 457; to become First Lord, 465; Churchill

Balfour, Arthur James—*continued*
relieved to be succeeded by, 468; Churchill sends seven points to, on future of Dardanelles operation (26 May 1915), 470–1; Churchill describes his 'cool quiet courage', 484; Churchill seeks to influence, over supplies for the Dardanelles, 485, 502; Churchill proposes Bulair landing to, 494; explains shortage of troop escort vessels for Dardanelles, 497; appoints Fisher Chairman of the Board of Inventions and Research (4 July 1915), 506–7; approves Churchill's proposed visit to Gallipoli Peninsula (mid-July 1915), 510; Churchill urges need for greater aerial activity at the Dardanelles on (22 July 1915), 514; Churchill worried about lethargy of (3 Aug 1915), 516; Churchill urges renewed naval attack to (21 Aug 1915), 524; opposes renewed naval attack, 525; Churchill angered by (5 Sept 1915), 526; at Calais Conference (July 1915), 526–7; and the origin of the tank, 537; agrees (Sept 1915) to winter campaign at Gallipoli, 539; and the use of Monitors at the Dardanelles (Sept 1915), 541–2; Churchill proposes renewed naval attack to (Oct 1915), 548; Margot Asquith seeks to alert, against an alleged Lloyd George–Curzon–Churchill plot, 556, 557; believes Kitchener unsuitable to be Secretary of State for War (Oct 1915), 559, 560; and Churchill's defence of his air policy (Oct 1915), 561; and speculation on Churchill's future career (Nov 1915), 563; Lady Randolph Churchill plans to dine with (Nov 1915), 594; and the Gallipoli evacuation (Nov 1915), 601; Lady Randolph Churchill reports 'they say he has gone to sleep' (Dec 1915), 618; and Fisher's attempt to return to the Admiralty (Jan–March 1916), 702–3; Churchill's criticisms of Admiralty administration of (Feb–March 1916), 707–11, 716–36, 749,

Balfour, Arthur James—*continued*
755; Mrs Churchill describes as 'wan and white, but still purring away' (April 1916), 756; Churchill criticizes air policy of (May 1916), 763–4, 767; his sneers echoed by a lesser man, 774; Churchill describes (31 May 1916) 'cowardice, inertia, futility and insolence' of Admiralty regime under, 776; asks Churchill to draft Jutland communiqué (2 June 1916), 777; Churchill writes that he 'dozes placidly upon the Admiralty throne' (Aug 1916), 798; and the emergence of Lloyd George as Prime Minister (Dec 1916), 822

Ballin, Albert: Churchill dines with (24 July 1914), 5

Baltic Sea: Churchill wants Japanese help to secure naval command of (29 Aug 1914), 44, 202; Churchill suggests joint Anglo-Russian action in, 52–3; 84; Churchill wants British naval action in (22 Dec 1914), 225–6, 228, 231, 237, 246; Fisher wants British naval plans concentrated on (20 Jan 1915), 259, 265; Churchill describes 'ultimate object' of Navy as access to (28 Jan 1915), 272; Churchill repeats, action in, is Britain's 'proper line of strategy' (3 March 1915), 324; Fisher insists, it is 'the decisive theatre' (16 March 1915), 348; rumours of a planned British naval offensive in, 400; MAPS, 53, 842

Barclay, Sir George: reports fears of a Turkish attack on Russia, 198

Basra (Turkey): British consul at arrested (Oct 1914), 217, 219; occupied by Government of India troops (Nov 1914), 221, 223; Hankey wants troops at withdrawn, and sent to Dardanelles (24 Feb 1916), 301; the India Office declare that it 'must form part of the British Empire' after the war, 355; Hamilton believes Turks unable to recapture because of the military pressure at Gallipoli, 499; proposed extension of British control from

Basra (Turkey)—*continued*
Alexandretta to, 509; British Force advances towards Bagdad from, 590n; MAP, 839

Battenberg, Prince Louis Alexander of: Churchill discusses European crisis with (25 July 1914), 5; and the halting of the dispersal of the Fleet (26 July 1914), 6–7; and decision to send Fleet to North Sea, 8–9; and replacement of Callaghan by Jellicoe, 14, 16; Fisher's opinion of, 17; at Anglo-French naval discussion (30 July 1914), 18–19; and the *Goeben*, 26, 30, 41; and the British Expeditionary Force, 34; Churchill sends strategic thoughts to, 37; Churchill confers with, after fall of Namur, 55; willing to share responsibility for Admiralty prevention of invasion, 58; Churchill expresses danger of aerial attack to, 72; and orders to discontinue Dogger Bank patrol, 85; enthusiastic about air attack on German Zeppelin sheds, 89; and defence of Antwerp, 103, 104; arranges departure of troops for Antwerp, 109, 115, 262; perturbed by Churchill's absence, 111; Asquith not very trustful of, 117; critical of Churchill's Antwerp mission, 119–20; his work supervised by Asquith, 131; Churchill dissatisfied with, 145; his resignation as First Lord (October 1914), 147–53, 157, 721; contrasted with Fisher, 185; discusses possibility of Gallipoli landings (2 Sept 1914), 203; his nephew killed in action, 228; and revivied criticism of Churchill's Admiralty administration (Aug 1915), 531; receives an account of Churchill's advocacy of Fisher's return to the Admiralty (March 1916), 708–9

Batum (Russia): Russian army corps at, 316, 322; MAP, 839

Bautzen (Saxony) (battle of, 1813): 171

Bax-Ironside, Sir Henry George Outram: reports (6 Feb 1915) Austrian policy is to crush Serbia, 277–8; reports (6 Feb 1915) Bulgarians

Bax-Ironside, Sir Henry George Outram—*continued*
borrowing money from Germany, 280; reports (10 March 1915) possibility of Bulgarian co-operation with the Allies, 335

Bayly, Sir Lewis: Clementine Churchill's advice on, 15; studies possible offensive action against Germany, 19–20; angered by Churchill's phrase 'rats in a hole', 84; ordered to haul down his flag, 185; described as a fool by Fisher, 268

Beauchamp, 7th Earl (William Lygon Beauchamp): 245; reports Liberal Ministers' belief that Churchill 'primary cause of trouble' in crisis of May 1915, 454

Beatty, Sir David: opposes replacement of Callaghan by Jellicoe, 14; Clementine Churchill's advice to her husband about, 15; critical of Churchill's actions at the siege of Antwerp, 134; approves Fisher's return to Admiralty, 154; worried about Churchill and Fisher quarrelling, 155, 187

Beatty, Lady (Ethel Field): 133, 154, 155

Beaverbrook, 1st Baron, *see both* Aitken, Sir William Maxwell *and Politicians and the War*

Beckenham, Henry Anstead: Churchill's personal shorthand writer, 485

Beerbohm, Max: on Asquith's premiership, 699n

Beirut (Turkey): Captain Richmond wants British troops landed at, instead of at Gallipoli, 389; MAP, 838

Beith, John Hay (Ian Hay): serves with the Argyll and Sutherland Highlanders, 630; at Churchill's battalion sports day, 641

Belfort (France): British aviators attack Friedrichshafen from (21 Nov 1914), 172; MAP, 173

Belgian Congo: Churchill distrustful of Belgian policy in, 10

Belgium: independence of, 1; neutrality of, 7, 9–10, 12, 22–4; German intention to invade, 26; Cabinet decision

Belgium—*continued*
about, 27; German invasion of (3 Aug 1914), 31, 53–5; and the British desire to defend Antwerp (October 1914), 96–134; Churchill believes has become 'a mere succession of fortified lines' (by Dec 1914), 226; British pilots attack Zeppelins which refuel in, 240; anxious to use British armoured car squadron, 290n

Belgrade (Serbia): Austrians occupy (1 Dec 1914), but driven out of (14 Dec 1914), 224; Austrians reoccupy (9 Oct 1915), 549; MAPS, 545, 842

Bellairs, Carlyon: opposes Churchill's return to political influence (March 1916), 723, 725

Benckendorff, Alexander Count de: and Russian fears of an Austrian naval attack, 193

Bengal, Bay of: British ships search for *Emden* in, 139

Bentham, John Henry: at Antwerp (Oct 1914), 119

Berard, Edouard: Governor of Calais, 52

Berehaven (Co. Cork): *Invincible* and *Inflexible* ordered to sail to, 192

Beresford, Lord Charles William de la Poer: at Other Club meeting (6 Aug 1914), 35; Fisher willing to co-operate with, 50; and formation of Royal Naval Division, 51; rebuked by Churchill for calling Prince Louis 'a German', 148; asks for details of Royal Naval Division activities at Antwerp, 170; criticizes conduct of the war at sea (27 Nov 1914), 177; questions Dardanelles operation in House of Commons (22 April 1915), 398, and again (4 May 1915), 413; believed to be about to combine with Churchill and Carson (Dec 1915), 590; criticizes Churchill's 'wicked statement' (March 1916), 729; appeals for compulsory military service (April 1916), 755

Berkeley Hotel (London): Lord Esher lunches with Mrs Churchill at (Dec 1915), 608–9

Berlin: Fisher believes 'spy postman' has sent letter to, 49; Churchill proposes Russian advance on (19 Aug 1914), 52; Sir J. French confident of reaching, if he can be reinforced, 61; consternation reported in, after British air raid on Düsseldorf and Cologne (9 Oct 1914), 123; Royal Naval Division prisoners of war near, 125; secret instructions for Admiral Souchon from, 193; Churchill resurrects (Dec 1914) British naval plan to help Russians advance on, 225–6, 228; Churchill wants Sir J. French to land at Emden and advance on, 244, 245; Churchill revives (25 March 1915) plan for attack on, 373; Fisher asserts Dardanelles troops should have been sent to, 426; MAPS, 53, 842

Bermuda: troops cross Atlantic from, 37

Bernau, William Henry: and Churchill's proposed visit to the Gallipoli Peninsula (mid-July 1915), 511; and Churchill's proposed visit to the war zone in France (Sept 1915), 530

Bertie, Sir Francis Leveson: Grey informs, of need for French help at Antwerp, 102; reports Antwerp position not hopeless, 105; Grey informs, of British rôle at Antwerp, 124; Grey informs, of 'promises of 1908' to Russia about the future of Constantinople, 320; sends Grey report of Russian refusal to allow Greeks to join in the attack at the Dardanelles, 328; asks Northcliffe what Lord Esher's status is in France, 589n

Besika Bay (Turkey): British ships at (2 Sept 1914), 205; Fisher wants British military landing at (Jan 1915), 234–5; French Government want military landing at (Aug 1915), 526; MAPS, 235, 840

Bessarabia (Russia): Kitchener believes Russia should restore to Rumania, 211

Bethell, Sir Alexander Edward: 85, 374

Bethlehem (Turkey): Lloyd George does not wish to see, under French control, 343

Bethune (France): 760; MAP, 75

Betteshanger (Kent): Naval Brigade leaves for Antwerp from, 112

Bieberstein, Marschall von: establishes German influence at Alexandretta (before 1914), 234–5

Bignold, Sir Arthur: mistaken for a German spy, 82; innocent, 83

Billing, Noel Pemberton: commands air raid on Friedrichshafen (21 Nov 1914), 172; fails to be elected at Mile End by-election (25 Jan 1916), 714n; elected at East Hertfordshire by-election (10 March 1916), 733–4, 736; attacks the Government's air policy, 744, 749

Bingham, Ralph Charles: recalls Churchill's training with the Grenadier Guards (Nov 1915), 577

Birdwood, Sir William Riddell: acting commander of troops assembling at the Dardanelles, 305, 322; sceptical (6 March 1915) of a naval success at Dardanelles without military support, 331; at conference on board Queen Elizabeth (22 March 1915), 363–4; wants to land the Anzac troops between Enos and Gulf of Xeros, avoiding Gallipoli Peninsula, 392; wants to withdraw from Anzac area on first day of Gallipoli landings (25 April 1915), 407; temporarily replaces Hamilton at the Dardanelles (17–28 Oct 1915), 554; and the evacuation of the Anzac area (Dec 1915), 619; takes Jack Churchill on to his Staff, 636

Birmingham: Churchill agrees to speak at, but then declines (Sept 1914), 77

Birrell, Augustine: 583, 689

Bir Saba (Turkey): Turkish troops retire to, 279

Black Sea: Russian fears of Austrian Fleet in, 193; British fears that Goeben and Breslau will sail into, 197; Goeben and Breslau bombard Russian ports in (29 Oct 1914), 215, 216, 219; need to restore access to, 230, 237; Russia regrets cannot take naval initiative in,

Black Sea—*continued*
266; Fisher insists on military occupation of Dardanelles in order to ensure opening of, 287; Balfour on importance of obtaining wheat from, 308; Allied shipping locked up in, 350; MAPS, 235

Blandford, Marquis of (John Albert Edward William Spencer-Churchill): visits Churchill at Admiralty (Aug 1914), 36

Blandford (Dorset): Royal Naval Division reviewed at, 305–6; Rupert Brooke at, 402

Blenheim, battle of (1704): 'glories of', revived in 1914, 141

Blenheim Palace (Oxfordshire): Churchill refuses to spend Christmas at, 36; Churchill plans to paint at, 759; Northcliffe sends bust of Napoleon to Churchill at, 782; Churchill tries to calm his mind by painting at, 787

Blenheim (British depot ship): Fisher wants in home waters, not at Dardanelles, 260

Bléquin (France): 572; MAP, 575

Blondel, Jean Camille: 198

Blücher (German battle cruiser): sunk in Dogger Bank action (24 Jan 1915), 261; 625

Boer War (1899–1902): Liberal criticisms during, 79

Bombay (British India): troops transported to France from (Aug 1914), 37; Churchill's shoulder dislocated at (1896), 635n

Bône (Algeria): bombarded by *Breslau*, 29; MAP, 29

Bonham Carter, Maurice: 87, 426, 438, 445, 456, 737; marries Violet Asquith (30 Nov 1915), 594

Bonham Carter, Violet (*for earlier references, see* Asquith, Violet): at the opening of Clementine Churchill's Ponders End canteen (3 Feb 1916), 698–9; and Churchill's advocacy of Fisher's return to the Admiralty (March 1916), 709, 713, 718, 721,

Bonham Carter, Violet—*continued*
722, 723, 731–2, 733; recalls Churchill's thoughts about the Dardanelles Commission (Aug 1916), 798

Booth, Frederick Handel: asks in Parliament if naval aviators have violated Swiss neutrality (Nov 1914), 173–4; votes against the Government in the Nigeria debate (Nov 1916), 815n

Boothby, Evelyn Leonard Beridge: Turks do not allow to return to his ship (11 Aug 1914), 193

Bordeaux (France): French Government moves from Paris to, 105, 106

Borkum (German island): possible British base, 19, 21; *Königen Luise* sails from, 38; Churchill resurrects plan for seizure of (Dec 1914), 225, 228, 236, 237, 241–2, 245, 246–7, 265; Richmond determined to undermine Churchill's plan for an attack on, 258; Fisher wants naval action at, 346, 348; Churchill drafts (24 March 1915) lengthy scheme for the capture of, 373; Fisher asserts Dardanelles troops should have been landed at, 426; Churchill recalls (Dec 1915) plans for landing at, 600; MAPS, 19, 842

Born Deep (Holland): possible British base, 21

Bosnia (and Herzegovina): 230; MAP, 842

Bosphorus (Turkey): German merchant ships being armed in (27 Aug 1914), 199; forts manned by German officers, 206; Hankey sees no insuperable obstacle in capture of (Dec 1914), 230; Russia cannot hope to destroy guns at entrance to, 266; Russians believe substantial number of troops needed to capture, 292; Balfour believes naval operations alone sufficient to open (26 Feb 1915), 308; Churchill wishes Admiral Carden to attack, following his entry into the Sea of Marmara, 315, 323, 326–7; Russian plan to attack forts at the mouth of, 344; Russians bombard forts at mouth

Bosphorus (Turkey)—*continued*
of (3 May 1915), 417; Churchill's brother-in-law believes, can still be forced (Sept 1915), 548; MAPS, 838, 841

Botha, Louis: 490

Boulogne (France): 572, 625; MAPS, 575, 649

Bout Deville (France): Churchill in reserve billets at, 580

Bouvet (French battleship): sunk at the Dardanelles (18 March 1915), 351, 354, 397n; MAP (18 March 1915), 353

Bowles, Thomas Gibson: accuses Churchill of responsibility for sinking of *Aboukir*, *Cressy* and *Hogue*, 86

Brabazon, Sir John Palmer: on Churchill's dismissal from the Admiralty, 482–3

Brade, Sir Reginald Herbert: and conscription (Aug 1915), 528; Bonar Law wants Asquith to consult, about sending Churchill to command in East Africa (Nov 1915), 565; at the War Office, 616

Braithwaite, Walter Pipon: asks Kitchener for a good air service at the Dardanelles, 339

Breslau (German light cruiser): British ships keep watch on (2 Aug 1914), 28; bombards Bône (4 Aug 1914), 29; escapes British search, 40–2; escape of, a cause of criticism of Churchill, 143, 170; reaches Constantinople (10 Aug 1914), 193; sold to Turks, 194–5; renamed *Midilli*, 194n; Britain insists on German crew leaving, 196; action against Russia feared (26 Aug 1914), 198; Troubridge instructed (8 Sept 1914) to sink, 206; Carden instructed (21 Sept 1914) to sink, 209; Turkish Government warned about (28 Oct 1914), 214; bombards Russian Black Sea ports (29 Oct 1914), 215; defeat of envisaged, 249; Fisher willing to offer one million pounds for (March 1915), 359; known to be out of action (Aug 1915), 525

Brett, Maurice Vyner Baliol: critical of Churchill's visit to France (6–10 May 1915), 425

Bridgeman, Sir Charles Francis: succeeded by Prince Louis as First Sea Lord (1912), 15n; warns Haig against Churchill (1916), 650n

Bridgeman, Lady: her 'power to do mischief', 15

Bridges, George Tom Molesworth: liaison officer with Belgian army, 136; Clementine Churchill talks about her husband's military future to (Dec 1915), 595; shows Churchill coastal trenches (Dec 1915), 600; Churchill expects to serve under, 606; Churchill lunches with, 624

Briggs, Edward Featherstone: in air raid on Friedrichshafen (Nov 1914), 172

Brindisi (Italy): *Goeben* refused coal at, 26; MAP, 29

British Campaign in France and Flanders, The (A. Conan Doyle): 810n

British East Africa: Churchill's possible military command in (Nov 1915) 563, 565–6, 598; Churchill wants greater use of native troops from 'for war or for labour' (July 1916), 794

British Expeditionary Force: and the Admiralty, 11; Cabinet refuses to send to France (1 Aug 1914), 24; Navy ready to send to France, 34; crosses to France, 37, 39, 40; reaches Amiens, 47; at Mons, 53; retreats from Mons, 54; Churchill sees need for continual reinforcement of, 56–57; in retreat for thirteen days, 62, 69–70; advances across Marne, 71–2; Kitchener fears its position endangered (Oct 1914), 103; Churchill wants advance of, along Belgian coast (Jan 1915), 241; Sir J. French unwilling to send troops to south-east Europe from, 277

Brooke, Rupert: at Antwerp (Oct 1914), 116, 130; departs for Dardanelles, 305; quite certain he will be killed (25 Feb 1915), 306; dies (24

Brooke, Rupert—*continued*
April 1915), 401; Churchill's obituary of (26 April 1915), 401–2

Brookes, Warwick: defeats Pemberton Billing at Mile End by-election (25 Jan 1916), 714*n*

Browne, William Denis: at Antwerp (Oct 1914), 130

Brownlow, D'Arcy Charles: appointed Military Governor of Basra (Nov 1914), 221

Bruges (Belgium): Marine reconnaissance to, 56; problem of refugees from, 97–8; Churchill expected at (3 Oct 1914), 106; General Rawlinson reaches (6 Oct 1914), 115; British forces to be reorganized at, 118; Rawlinson establishes HQ at, 120; MAP, 99

Brusilov, Alexei Alexeievich: his successful Russian offensive (June–Aug 1916), 793, 799

Brussels (Belgium): German troops reach, 75, 101; MAPS, 54, 99

Buchan, Alastair Ebenezer: wounded (Feb 1916), 677

Buchanan, Sir George William: at Petrograd, 217, 232, 280, 320, 328, 400

Bucharest (Rumania): 213; MAPS, 545, 842

Buckle, Archie Stewart: shows Churchill British trenches at Neuve Chapelle (Dec 1915), 624

Buckmaster, Sir Stanley Owen: unwilling to suppress press criticism of Churchill's actions at Antwerp (Oct 1914), 129; becomes Lord Chancellor (May 1915), 470

Bulair (Turkey): Churchill wants sufficient troops to hold the lines of (20 Feb 1915), 300, 307, 308; Hankey on possible need for troops at, 309; proposed cutting of Turkish communications at, 323; Churchill names 18 March 1915 as possible day for landing troops at, 324; Churchill says 20,000 troops ready to land at, by 20 March 1915, 326; Admiral

Bulair (Turkey)—*continued*
Carden instructed (5 March 1915) to prevent movement of Turkish troops across, 327; Fisher worried by Churchill's obsession with, 348; the probable effect of British ships either side of, 368; the French to attack with aircraft, 369; de Robeck does not believe that a landing at would cause Turks to abandon Gallipoli Peninsula, 377; Turkish troop movements at, visible from the air, 397; Churchill proposes (11 June 1915) landing at, 494; Sir Ian Hamilton opposed to landing at, 495; Churchill continues to be attracted by idea of landing at (19 June 1915), 500; Churchill's plan to cut Turks off from (Oct 1915), 544; MAPS, 545, 840

Bulgaria: possibility of action against Austria by (Aug–Sept 1914), 200–2; promises Greece to remain neutral in event of Graeco-Turkish war, 206; Greeks want simultaneous attack on Turkey by, 209; Churchill wants as an ally (Sept 1914), 210, 211; hostile to Greece, 221; Asquith reports Churchill's mind 'set on' (5 Dec 1914), 223; not disposed to join Allies (Dec 1914), 224; importance of in British plans to defeat Turkey, 230, 235, 244, 249, 273–5, 323; Austrian aim to attract, 277, 279–80; Churchill asserts possibility of joint action with, 302, 307, 308; Churchill intends British troops will capture Adrianople for, 315; has no reason to join Allies before some sign of their success, 317; Churchill stresses need for alliance with, 329; German submarines said to be on their way to Turkey via, 338; possibility reported of an attack on Turkey by (March 1915), 348, 349; German ammunition reported in transit for Turkey through, 372; Hankey recalls (Aug 1916) effect of naval attack at Dardanelles on, 380; Fisher wants as an ally in attack on Turkey, and also

Bulgaria—*continued*
on Greece, 382; Balfour wants an 'arrangement' with, 389; reported Turkish fears of attack from, 396; Churchill on importance of alliance with (30 April 1915), 412; Asquith recalls (March 1917) beneficial effect of Dardanelles operation on, 480; Cabinet divided over policy towards (June 1915), 505–6; Churchill fears German armies will seduce (Aug 1915), 524; Churchill's plan for military action against (Oct 1915), 544–5; mobilizes against Serbia (Oct 1915), 549; Grey proposes hostilities against (Oct 1915), 553; Churchill against wasting men in fighting Bulgaria (Dec 1915), 597, and (May 1916), 772; attacks Rumania (1 Sept 1916), 797; MAPS, 235, 545, 838, 840, 842

Bulgarian Horrors and the Question of the East, The (W. E. Gladstone): quoted, 188n

Buller, Sir Redvers Henry: Fisher describes as 'seized with mental paralysis', 268

Burgas (Bulgaria): MAP, 842

Burn, Henry Pelham: Churchill dines with (Jan 1916), 643–4; Churchill sends to see Lloyd George (June 1916), 782–3

Burns, John Elliot: on Churchill's character (May 1915), 477–8

Bush, Eric: serving at sea on fifteenth birthday, 170n

Buxton, Charles Roden: departs on mission for the Balkans (Aug 1914), 201; sees Asquith on return from mission (Jan 1915), 255

Buxton, Edward Noel: departs on mission to the Balkans, 201–2; reports on his mission, 213–14; sees Asquith on return from mission, 255

Buxton, 1st Viscount (Sydney Charles Buxton): 454, 477

Cabinet, the British: meeting (24 July 1914), 3–4; records of, 3n; meeting

Cabinet, the British—*continued*
(27 July 1914), 7–8; Churchill fears to consult, 9; meeting (29 July 1914), 10, 12; Churchill reads F. E. Smith's letter to, 22; rejects full naval mobilization (1 Aug 1914), 23, 462; opposes sending Expeditionary Force to France, 24; ratifies full naval mobilization (2 Aug 1914), 25; and German ultimatum to Belgium, 27; not consulted about Anglo-French naval co-operation, 27–8; refuses Churchill's request to fight *Goeben* before outbreak of war, 30; report of discussion on Japan in, 43; rumour of opposition to formation of Royal Naval Division, 51; approves Churchill's Marine expedition to Ostend, 56; rejects Churchill's arguments for compulsory service (26 Aug 1914), 57; alarmed by Sir John French's decision to fall back behind Paris (31 Aug 1914), 59–60; not informed of Churchill's visit to France (10 Sept 1914), 72; learns of naval problem during one of Churchill's visits to France (22 Sept 1914), 89–90; discusses defence of Antwerp (30 Sept 1914), 101–2; approves sending Naval Brigades to Antwerp, 109; Churchill offers to resign from (5 Oct 1914), 111–12; meeting at which Antwerp discussed (5 Oct 1914), 113; Churchill reports on Antwerp to (7 Oct 1914), 120; Kitchener warns of possibility of invasion (mid-Oct 1914), 138; Asquith reports Grey and Haldane 'fussy & jumpy' (23 Oct 1914), 139; discusses need to keep *Audacious* sinking secret (28 Oct 1914), 142; bewildered by British naval defeat off Coronel, 158; regards Coronel defeat as, in Asquith's words, 'not creditable to the officers of the Navy', 159; sanctions joint military and naval attack along Belgian Coast towards Ostend (end Nov 1914), 163; seizure of Turkish battleships approved at (31 July 1914), 192; discusses sale of *Goeben* and *Breslau* to Turkey (12

Cabinet, the British—*continued*
Aug 1914), 194; Asquith describes Churchill as 'violently anti-Turk' at (21 Aug 1914), 196; agrees to financial aid for Rumania and Serbia (2 Sept 1914), 204; attempts to avert a Turkish attack by holding Indian troops in Egypt (3 Sept 1914), 205; discusses Turkish policy (23 Sept 1914), 210–11; imminent Turkish invasion discussed at (23 Oct 1914), 214; Grey uncompromising towards Turkey at (28 Oct 1914), 214; decides not to take warlike acts against Turkey (30 Oct 1914), 215; insists on need for formal declaration of war against Turkey (4 Nov 1914), 219; reported by Montagu to be entirely loyal to Asquith (March 1915), 362; discusses (23 March 1915) the possibility of a renewed naval attack at the Dardanelles, 366; Churchill and Kitchener in dispute at (7 April 1915), 387; Churchill defends his policy for dealing with mines at the Dardanelles in a memorandum for (24 April 1915), 399; Churchill circulates defence of his policy as First Lord to (30 May 1915), 486; Asquith informs (7 June 1915), of decision to reinforce Dardanelles army, 494; discusses possibility of alliance with Bulgaria (30 June 1915), 506; meets (19 July 1915), 513; War Policy Committee of (Aug–Sept 1915), 527–9; Carson angered by 'waste of time' at (Sept 1915), 529–30, 532–3; meets (6 Oct 1915), 548; meets (12 Oct 1915), 558–9; Churchill speaks of resignation in (Nov 1915), 560; unanimous that Kitchener should leave War Office (1 Nov 1915), 562; decides to evacuate Gallipoli Peninsula (23 Nov 1915), 581; discussion about Gallipoli evacuation in, 601–2, 617; F. E. Smith enters (3 Nov 1915), 615*n*; Churchill describes as 'weak and foolish', 624; F. E. Smith sends Churchill news of discussions in (Jan 1916), 688

Cabinet Ministers, conclaves of: on 1 Aug 1914, 25; on 2 Aug 1914, 26; on 3 Aug 1914, 27–8; on 31 Aug 1914, 60; on 5 Nov 1914, 176*n*; *see subsequently index entries for* War Council *and* Dardanelles Committee

Cabinet War Committee, the: successor to the Dardanelles Committee, 563; Churchill excluded from, 563–4; Fisher attends, 730–1

Cadiz (Spain): Napoleon sends Villeneuve to sea from (1805), 145

Caillard, Sir Vincent Henry Penalver: sent to Constantinople (1913), 190

Cairo (Egypt): MAP, 838

Calais (France): Churchill declines to send Royal Naval Division to, 52, 108; German threat to (Sept 1914), 72; Churchill crosses to (16 Sept 1914), 80; fear of German advance to (Oct 1914), 103, 135, 136; Anglo-French conference at (July 1915), 506, 526–7, 546; MAP, 575, 649

Callaghan, Sir George Astley: given order not to disperse Fleet, 6; given order to send Fleet to North Sea, 9; replaced by Jellicoe (4 Aug 1914), 14–16

Callaghan, Lady: her 'power to do mischief', 15

Callwell, Charles Edward: reports (3 Sept 1914) on possibility of seizure of Gallipoli Peninsula, 203; critical of Kitchener's indecision, 257; attends War Council Sub-Committee (28 Jan 1915), 273; registers Jack Churchill's name for service at Gallipoli, 340; serves on Committee to examine British territorial needs in Turkey, 391; informs H. A. Gwynne of the May crisis (22 May 1915), 458–9; and Dardanelles ammunition supplies, 516; and conscription (July–Aug 1915), 527–8; and Guy Dawnay's visit to London (Sept 1915), 540; examines merits of western and Gallipoli fronts, 548*n*; Bonar Law wants Asquith to consult about appointment of Churchill to East African military command

Callwell, Charles Edward—*continued*
(Nov 1915), 565; explains the reason
for Asquith deciding not to publish
the Dardanelles documents (June
1916), 785; his post-war criticisms of
politicians controlling war strategy,
787n

Calshot (Kent): anti-aircraft flights
based on, 66

Calza Bedolo, Gino: at Antwerp, 115;
Churchill's interview with, on the
minorities question, 202

Cambrai (France): Royal Naval Air
Service reconnaissance over, 65; MAP, 75

Cambon, Paul: 24, 261, 278; his scathing
remark about Italy reported, 426n

Cameron, John Ewen: takes Sir Ian
Hamilton to the Dardanelles, 342; at
the Dardanelles, 352

Cameron of Lochiel, Donald Walter:
his bravery at the battle of Loos, 642

Campbell, Henry Hervey: placed on
half pay, 86

Campbell, William Pitcairn: offers Churchill command of a battalion (12
June 1915), 495

Canada: army volunteers from transported across Atlantic, 37; troops
from, in the first trench 'raids', 636–7;
ratio of troops to inhabitants, 794n

Canadian Cavalry Division: J. E. B.
Seely in command of, 83

Canopus (British battleship): off South
America, 156–60, 182; to go to
Dardanelles, 249n, 265; at Dardanelles,
331

Cape Helles (Turkey): Allied ships
assemble off (Feb 1915), 282; Fisher
urges need for a military base at (20
March 1915), 360; Hamilton decides
on military landing at, 393; military
landings at (25 April 1915), 402–10;
further offensive at (6–9 May 1915),
414–16; MAPS, 403, 519

Cape St Vincent (Portugal): 265

Carden, Sackville Hamilton: appointed
to command at Dardanelles (21 Sept
1914), 209; prevents Turkish torpedo boat leaving Dardanelles (27

Carden, Sackville Hamilton—*continued*
Sept 1914), 212; instructed to 'commence hostilities at once against
Turkey' (31 Oct 1914), 216; bombards
outer forts of Dardanelles (3 Nov 1914),
218, 219; asked about possibility of
forcing Dardanelles (3 Jan 1915),
233–4; his reply reaches Admiralty
(5 Jan 1915), 237–8; his detailed
proposals awaited, 242; his detailed
proposals discussed in London (12
Jan 1915), 248–52; his plan authorized
(14 Jan 1915), 254; and preparations
for naval action, 255–7, 259–60, 266,
272, 276–7, 279, 286–7; bombards
outer forts (19 Feb 1915), 300–1;
instructions to (24 Feb 1915), 304–5;
resumes bombardment (25 Feb 1915),
305; destroys outer forts (25–6 Feb
1915), 314; destroys further forts, 321;
believes he can enter Sea of Marmara
after fourteen more days' bombardment (4 March 1915), 324; reports on
landing of sailors to demolish forts
(4 March 1915), 326; receives instructions (5 March 1915) on what to
do once his ships reach Sea of Marmara, 326–7; reports on slow progress
of bombardment at the Dardanelles,
331, 332; asks for more destroyers,
336; Fisher offers (11 March 1915) to
replace him as commander-in-chief,
337; new instructions to (11 March
1915) urging him to 'press the attack
vigorously', 337; Fisher wants him '*to
press on!*', 338; reports minesweeping
difficulties (13 March 1915), 342;
Churchill urges him to take greater
risks, 343; instructed (15 March 1915)
to concert with Sir Ian Hamilton 'in
any military operations which you
consider necessary', 347; forced by
illness to give up his command (16
March 1915), 348; Fisher believes de
Robeck better than, 354; Churchill's
orders to (5 Feb 1915) about mines, 399

Cardiff (Glamorgan): Asquith visits (2
Oct 1914), 102; Asquith unable to
return in time from, 103

Caribbean Sea: *Karlsrühe* sinks British merchant ships in, 264n

Carnarvon (British cruiser): and preparations for battle of Falkland Islands, 182

Carrying On (Ian Hay): 630n

Carson, Sir Edward Henry: and possible Coalition on eve of war, 13; writes encouragingly to Churchill (5 Aug 1914), 32–3; Churchill sends defence of his naval policy to, 159; becomes Attorney-General (May 1915), 470; and Churchill's Irish policies, 476; warns Churchill not to miscalculate difficulties at the Dardanelles (21 June 1915), 504–5; opposes further Gallipoli offensive (19 Aug 1915), 523; angered by Cabinet procedure (Sept 1915), 529–30, 532–3; agrees (Sept 1915) to winter campaign at Gallipoli, 539; discusses Gallipoli with Guy Dawnay (Sept 1915), 540; against remaining at Gallipoli (Oct 1915), 549; and Gallipoli reinforcements, 551; his resignation from the Cabinet (12 Oct 1915), 558, 559; believed to be about to combine with Churchill and Beresford (Dec 1915), 590; Milner wants Churchill to join (Dec 1915), 591; succeeded as Attorney-General by F. E. Smith, 615n; rejects compromise over conscription, 618; Garvin sees as a 'fighting-quartette' with Lloyd George, Fisher and Churchill (Dec 1915), 621–2; and the Marconi affair (1912), 623n; and the final withdrawal from Gallipoli (Jan 1916), 685; Churchill asks his wife to keep in touch with (Jan 1916), 688; Churchill sees as a future Cabinet colleague, 697; Fisher compares Churchill's 'courage' with, 701; his opposition to Asquith (1916), 704, 711, 713; and Churchill's opposition to Asquith, 736, 738–9, 741, 743, 745–6, 747, 750, 751–2, 753; seeks to mediate between Churchill and Milner (April 1916), 756; seen as a leader with Lloyd George of an opposition to Asquith

Carson, Sir Edward Henry—*continued* (April 1916), 756–7; and the introduction of the Military Service Bill (April 1916), 758; Churchill's political hopes centre on, 759; protests against exclusion of Irish soldiers from the Military Service Bill (May 1916), 761–2; Churchill seeks to stimulate to further criticism of the War Office, 775; presses Asquith to publish Dardanelles documents (June 1916), 783, 785; organizes the first serious parliamentary challenge to Asquith (8 Nov 1916), 815–16; and the fall of Asquith (Nov–Dec 1916), 816–17, 820; becomes First Lord of the Admiralty (Dec 1916), 823

Cassel, Sir Ernest Joseph: Churchill dines with (24 July 1914), 5; holds $20,000 of American stocks for Churchill, 511; Lady Randolph Churchill dines with (2 Feb 1916), 668; Mrs Churchill to dine with (Jan 1916), 689; Mrs Churchill reports on 'red-hot patriotism' of, 693; at a bridge evening with Asquith, 708

Cassel (France): armoured car skirmish near, 68; armoured cars in region of, 93, 135; Royal Marines and armoured cars forced to return to Dunkirk from, 103, 105; MAP, 75

Cattaro (Austria-Hungary): Grey wants British attack on, 252–3; German submarine known to have reached, on way to Dardanelles (21 May 1915), 463; MAP, 842

Caucasus (Russia): possibility of Turkish action against Russia in, 200; Lloyd George wants to attack Turkey in order to relieve pressure on Russia in, 229; Russians appeal for help to reduce Turkish pressure on, 231, 232; Turks routed in, 396

Cavan, 10th Earl of (Frederick Rudolph Lambart): agrees that Churchill can train with the Grenadier Guards (Nov 1915), 573–4; suggests Churchill leaves the trenches until appointed to command a Brigade, 588; Churchill

Cavan, 10th Earl of—*continued*
  hopes to serve under, 606–7; tells
  Haig of Churchill's 'excellent work' in
  the trenches, 615
Cawley, Sir Frederick: Churchill sets
  out his criticism of Balfour's naval
  administration in letter to (11 March
  1916), 735; Churchill asks his wife to
  keep in touch with, 739; Churchill asks
  C. P. Scott to keep in touch with, 753
Cawley, Harold Thomas: killed in
  action at Gallipoli (Sept 1915), 735n
Cawley, John Stephen: killed in action
  during the retreat from Mons (Aug
  1914), 735n
Cawley, Oswald: killed in action in
  France (Aug 1918), 735n
Cecil, Lord Edgar Algernon Robert: on
  Conservative support for Liberal
  policy, 22–3; Churchill informs about
  war crisis, 24, 25; Churchill explains
  need for Home Rule proposals to (8
  Sept 1914), 77; criticizes Churchill's
  ninth wartime visit to France in House
  of Commons (12 May 1915), 424;
  becomes Under-Secretary to Grey at
  the Foreign Office, 470; wants to
  persevere with Gallipoli attack (June–
  July 1915), 504; Churchill advises
  (26 June 1915), not to threaten Bulgaria, 506; suggested as deputy to
  Asquith at War Office (Nov 1915),
  560; Mrs Churchill describes, as
  'enamoured of the Government' (Jan
  1916), 693; and the emergence of
  Lloyd George as Prime Minister
  (Dec 1916), 820; becomes Minister
  of Blockade (Dec 1916), 822; vetoes
  Churchill's inclusion in Lloyd George's
  Cabinet (7 Dec 1916), 823
Cecil, Evelyn: says Churchill's command of a battalion would be 'a
  grave scandal' (16 Dec 1915), 614
Cecil, Lord Hugh Richard Heathcote
  Gascoyne: advocates neutral policy
  for Britain, 22; accuses Churchill of
  responsibility for war, 27; threatens
  strong Conservative opposition over
  Irish Home Rule (11 Sept 1914), 77

Chamberlain, Joseph Austen: in dispute
  with Churchill over Irish Home Rule
  (Sept 1914), 77–80; Bonar Law
  shows Churchill's appeal to (May
  1915), 464; becomes Secretary of
  State for India (May 1915), 470;
  and Churchill's Irish policies, 476;
  and the War Policy Committee of the
  Cabinet (Aug 1915), 527, 529; and
  the emergence of Lloyd George as
  Prime Minister (Dec 1916), 820; vetoes
  Churchill's inclusion in Lloyd George's
  Cabinet (7 Dec 1916), 823
Champagne (France): French military
  offensive in, 540, 774
Chanak (Turkey): Turkish defences at,
  218; Carden's plan to advance ships
  to (12 Jan 1915), 248, 276; Churchill
  stresses to Carden importance of
  'turning of the corner' at (11 March
  1915), 337; British ships ready to
  attempt the advance to (18 March
  1915), 351, 352; Churchill wants 15-
  inch howitzer to bombard from the
  Kilid Bahr plateau, 391; Birdwood
  suggests overland attack across plain of
  Troy on (April 1915), 392; combined
  naval and military plan to drive the
  Turks from, 393; fires started in by
  naval bombardment, 412; Churchill
  wants 'a dash on' (Sept 1915),
  540; Churchill proposes as military
  objective (Oct 1915), 544; MAPS,
  29, 353, 403, 519, 545, 838, 840,
  842
Channing of Wellingborough, Baron
  (Francis Alston Channing): praises
  Churchill's Dundee speech (5 June
  1915), 491
Charlemagne (French battleship): at the
  Dardanelles (18 March 1915), MAP,
  353
Charleroi (Belgium): French troops
  south of, 53; MAP, 54
Chatalja Lines (Turkey): 249, 308, 317;
  MAP, 841
Chatham (British cruiser): Churchill
  willing to recall from Dardanelles (14
  May 1915), 435

Chatham (Kent): Churchill goes with Heligoland Bight victors to, 59

Cheetham, Milne: learns Britain does not mean to issue immediate declaration of war on Turkey (4 Nov 1914), 218

Chelmsford, 3rd Baron (Frederick John Napier Thesiger): to be Viceroy of India (1916), 683

Cherbourg (France): British Admirals urge defence of, 55; MAP, 54

Chicago Tribune: 638n

Chile: von Spee's squadron makes for coast of (Oct 1914), 156

China: Churchill said to have offered, to Japan (Aug 1914), 43

Christian, Arthur Henry: placed on half pay, 86

Chocolate Hill (Gallipoli Peninsula): 521; MAP, 519

Chunuk Bair (Gallipoli Peninsula): Allied troops fail to reach summit of (6–10 Aug 1915), 520; Churchill willing to allow Hamilton to make further attack on, 523; MAPS, 403, 519

Churchill, Clementine: Churchill's letters to (1914–15), 4–5, 10–11, 21, 25, 31, 39, 161, 228; at Cromer (July 1914), 407; Churchill sends impressions of European crisis to, 10–11; her advice about the replacement of Callaghan by Jellicoe, 15–16; on Churchill's mood (August 1914), 18; believes it would be 'a wicked war', 25; on Conservative approval of her husband (Aug 1914), 33; uses Blenheim Palace notepaper to write to Lloyd George, 36; asks about Expeditionary Force, 39; worried about Churchill's tiredness, 39–40; returns ring to wealthy shipowner, 40; reports news of German spies, 44–5; returns to London, 58; welcomes Commodore Keyes after Heligoland Bight action, 59; warns Churchill of danger of his repeated visits to France, 92; Grey praises Churchill to, 121; apprehensive of Fisher's influence over her husband, 187; at Walmer Castle, 245;

Churchill, Clementine—*continued* intervenes to provide Royal Naval Division with adequate medical facilities, 306; at Admiralty when news of possible Greek military help at Dardanelles arrives, 315–16; recalls her distrust of Sir Ian Hamilton's staying power, 325; recalls the strain on Fisher during Churchill's absence in France (6–10 May 1915), 419; appeals to Asquith to allow Churchill to remain at Admiralty (20 May 1915), 459; Edwin Montagu visits (26 May 1915), 472; recalls effect of Dardanelles on her husband, 473; blames Lloyd George's 'Welsh trickiness' for her husband's demotion in May 1915, 476; her one remaining ambition in May 1915, to dance on Asquith's grave, 479; refuses to be dependent on Asquith's charity, 493; moves with her family into 41 Cromwell Road, 493; Churchill's letter to (17 July 1915), to be opened in the event of his death, 511–12; helps to organize canteens for munitions workers, 533–4; and Churchill's departure for France (Nov 1915), 571; Sir John French writes to, 574; writes to Churchill while he is on the western front (Nov 1915–May 1916), 583, 593, 594, 599, 605, 606, 620, 622, 623, 626, 644, 647, 654, 660, 663, 666, 669, 676, 681, 682, 683, 684, 687, 689, 690, 691, 693, 698, 703, 707, 741, 742, 743, 744, 748, 749, 753, 756, 758, 759; writes encouraging letter to Curzon (Dec. 1915), 604; telephoned by her husband from St Omer, 605; lunches with Lord Esher, 608–9; lunches with Lloyd George, 622–3; takes one of her husband's young officers to the Music Hall, 669; dines with F. E. Smith (27 Jan 1916), 693; critical of Reginald McKenna (28 Jan 1916), 693; critical of Lloyd George (2 Feb 1916), 698; and the opening of her canteen at Ponders End (3 Feb 1916), 698–9; opposes reunion of Churchill and

Churchill, Clementine—*continued*
Fisher (Feb–March 1916), 701, 709, 711–12; entertains Asquith to a bridge evening (Feb 1916), 707–8; Asquith tells C. P. Scott of hostility of, 730–1; urges her husband to suspend his criticisms of Asquith, 736–7; visits Carson (13 March 1916), 738; opposes her husband's precipitant return to London, 741–2, 743, 749, 753; urges her husband not to send letter to Northcliffe, 748; dines at 10 Downing Street (April 1916), 756; encourages her husband to return from the trenches to Parliament (April 1916), 758–9; not afraid of telling her husband of his faults, 824–5

Churchill, Diana: at Cromer (July 1914), 4–6; returns to London, 58; 581; to carry train at Nellie Hozier's wedding (Dec 1915), 595; 647

Churchill, Lady Gwendeline: at Cromer, 40, 44; 'vy good and brave', 161; at Blandford review of Royal Naval Division (25 Feb 1915), 306; Churchill family join forces with, 493; rouses Churchill's interest in painting (June 1915), 502; Churchill expresses desire to fight Turks to, 505; and Churchill's departure for the trenches (Nov 1915), 571; Churchill paints, 582; and Sir John French's dismissal, 616; her concern for Churchill's safety and future, 644–5; dines with one of Churchill's battalion officers, 669; Mrs Churchill's safety valve, 684; at a bridge evening with Asquith (Feb 1916), 708; Churchill asks her to look after Sir Archibald Sinclair, 740

Churchill, Henry Winston Spencer (Peregrine): at Hoe Farm (June 1915), 501

Churchill, Lord Ivor Spencer-: visits Churchill at Admiralty (Aug 1914), 36

Churchill, John, 1st Duke of Marlborough: 136, 573, 578, 589, 727

Churchill, John-George Spencer: at Cromer (Aug 1914), 18, 416; at Hoe Farm (June 1915), 501; to carry

Churchill, John-George Spencer—*continued*
train at Nellie Hozier's wedding (Dec 1915), 595

Churchill, John Strange Spencer (Jack): at Cromer (Aug 1914), 18; dines at Admiralty House, 30; Churchill informs, of retreat from Mons, 55; about to leave for France with Oxfordshire Hussars, 58, 74; reaches Dunkirk, 135; under fire near Ypres, 160–1; Churchill expresses his frustrations about the Dardanelles to, 310–11; to join Sir Ian Hamilton's staff at Dardanelles, 339, 340, 341; reports (25 March 1915) on difficulties facing any renewed naval attack at Dardanelles, 371; reports (11 April 1915) on naval preparations at the Dardanelles, 393; Churchill impresses need to persevere on, 396; sends Churchill an account of the Gallipoli landings, 405–6, 407–8; Churchill informs (26 April 1915) of 20,000 extra men in Egypt available for Gallipoli landings if Sir Ian Hamilton asks for them, 410; worried about the prospects of the Army on the Gallipoli Peninsula (5 May 1915), 414; describes renewed Helles offensive (6–9 May 1915), 415–16; Hamilton describes (15 May 1915), as 'invaluable asset', 437; Churchill telegraphs news of his leaving the Admiralty to (18 May 1915), 451; Churchill telegraphs to (23 May 1915), 'the policy goes on', 468; Churchill telegraphs to, that Kitchener 'vy friendly to the Dardanelles' (26 May 1915), 471; Churchill decides to move into house of, 493; Churchill writes to (12 June 1915), 496, and (19 June 1915), 500–1; sends Churchill an account of the continued fighting on the Helles front (26 June 1915), 504; does not approve Churchill's desire to join Hamilton's army, 505; Churchill writes to (3 Aug 1915), 516; sends Churchill an account of the renewed

Churchill, John Strange Spencer (Jack)—*continued*
attack at Gallipoli (6–11 Aug 1915), 518, 520–1; Churchill sends complaint about Sir Ian Hamilton to (Sept 1914), 542; believed to be at Salonika (Nov 1915), 582; reports on evacuation of Anzac area (Dec 1915), 619; Churchill writes to from France, while in reserve, 636; on the 'jealous fools' who keep his brother in the trenches (April 1916), 758; Churchill writes to (21 June 1916), 783; Churchill writes to 'I am learning to hate' (15 July 1916), 787–8, 790; Churchill asks Seely to 'look after', 791

Churchill, Randolph Frederick Edward Spencer: at Cromer (July 1914), 4–6, 18; returns to London, 58; 'will carry on the lamp' should Churchill die, 511; wants to buy a spade to help Churchill protect himself in the trenches, 583; and his father's achievements, 587; a page at Violet Asquith's wedding (30 Nov 1915), 594; to carry train at Nellie Hozier's wedding (4 Dec 1915), 595; Churchill sends his first letter to (Jan 1916), 647

Churchill, Lady Randolph: dines at Admiralty House (4 Aug 1914), 30; Fisher unable to dine with (Dec 1914), 186; and Churchill's departure for the front (Nov 1915), 571; Churchill writes to, from the front, 581, 595, 682, 694, 750; writes to Churchill while he is at the front, 582, 594, 617–18, 647, 668, 681; arranges dinner for C. P. Scott, Garvin, F. E. Smith, Hopwood and others on Churchill's return from the trenches (3 March 1916), 708–9; Violet Bonham Carter meets Churchill at house of (8 March 1916), 731; Jack Churchill writes to, 758

Churchill, Lord Randolph Henry Spencer-: Churchill urged not to repeat resignation mistake of, 560; Churchill said to have forgotten political legacy of, 589; Churchill wonders 'what he

Churchill, Lord Randolph Henry Spencer-—*continued*
wd think of it all' (Jan 1916), 647; Asquith begs Churchill not to repeat the 'one impulsive action' of, 733; he and his son believed by Lord Derby to be 'absolutely untrustworthy', 801

Churchill, Sarah Millicent Hermione: 120, 228, 594, 647; 'that golden Sarah', 581

Churchill, Winston Leonard Spencer
ATTITUDES TO THE WAR:
'I am interested, geared up & happy' (28 July 1914), 31; 'the terrible march of events' (13 Aug 1914), 46; 'We have not entered this business without resolve to see it through' (24 Aug 1914), 55; 'The war will be long and sombre' (11 Sept 1914), 76; '*We* sit still in the steady cold blooded game & can I think keep it up indefinitely' (20 Sept 1914), 83; has 'tasted blood' and is 'beginning like a tiger to raven for more' (reported by Asquith, 7 Oct 1914), 122; 'this war . . . will devour us all' (16 Oct 1914), 135; 'This is no ordinary war . . . it raises passions between races of the most terrible kind' (29 Oct 1914), 152; on the battle of Coronel 'a most painful disaster, relieved only by its daring and gallantry' (Sept 1915), 160; 'I expect I shd be vy frightened but I wd dissemble' (9 Nov 1914), 161; 'our situation is . . . of waiting to be kicked, & wondering when & where' (21 Dec 1914), 181; 'you know what military necessity compels in war' (19 Aug 1914), 196; 'Sooner or later, Germany will be starved and beaten' (31 Aug 1914), 201; 'Are there not other alternatives than sending our armies to chew barbed wire in Flanders?' (29 Dec 1914), 226; 'Germany is the foe, & it is bad war to seek cheaper victories & easier antagonists' (4 Jan 1914), 235; 'long vistas of pain & struggle lie ahead' (26 Feb 1915), 310; 'Half-hearted

Churchill, Winston Leonard Spencer
  ATTITUDES TO THE WAR—*continued*
  measures will ruin all—& a million
  men will die through the prolongation
  of the war' (6 March 1915), 328;
  'This is a vy hard war to win' (20
  March 1915), 361; 'There is no need
  for action now—only the most minute
  preparations' (26 March 1915), 374;
  'Don't run short of stuffing behind
  your attack—even if you never need
  it' (26 April 1915), 410; 'every minute
  of this is history: and every attack
  requires backing' (26 April 1915),
  410; 'Whether it is my fault for trying
  or my misfortune for not having the
  power to carry through is immaterial.
  We are now committed . . .' (11 May
  1915), 421; 'he objected strongly to
  despondency' (War Council notes, 14
  May 1915), 432; '*someone* has to take
  the responsibility' (14 May 1915),
  434; 'I am the one who gets the blame
  for anything that goes wrong' (15
  May 1915), 440; 'one difficulty after
  another has been surmounted' (16
  May 1915), 442; 'I will not *take* any
  office except a military department'
  (17 May 1915), 448; 'the naval situation is in every respect assured' (18
  May 1915), 451; 'The rule to follow
  is what is best calculated to beat the
  enemy, and not what is most likely to
  please the newspapers' (20 May 1915),
  460; 'by waging successful war we
  shall dominate public opinion' (20
  May 1915), 460: 'Let me stand or fall
  by the Dardanelles, but do not take it
  from my hands' (21 May 1915), 464;
  'Punishment must be doggedly borne'
  (26 May 1915), 471; 'the last thing
  he would pray for is Peace' (reported
  by Asquith, 14 Sept 1914), 480;
  'We should be ill-advised to squander
  our new armies in frantic and sterile
  efforts to pierce the German lines'
  (1 June 1915), 486; 'No where has
  there been design or decision' (2 June
  1915), 488; 'You have taken the

Churchill, Winston Leonard Spencer
  ATTITUDES TO THE WAR—*continued*
  measure of your foe, you have only to
  go forward with confidence' (5 June
  1915), 489; 'Trust the people. They
  have never failed you yet' (5 June
  1915), 490; 'The times are harsh, the
  need is dire, the agony of Europe is
  infinite, but the might of Britain
  hurled into the conflict will be irresistible' (5 June 1915), 491; 'our whole
  nation must be organised, must be
  socialised . . .' (5 June 1915), 492;
  'The war is terrible. . . . The youth
  of Europe—almost a whole generation—will be shorn away' (19 June
  1915), 501; 'honour for all who have
  never flinched and never wavered'
  (7 July 1915), 509; 'Death is only an
  incident, & not the most important
  wh happens to us in this state of
  being' (17 July 1915), 511; 'The tendency to the negative is vy pronounced'
  (3 Aug 1915), 516; 'the profitless
  slaughter pit of Ypres' (3 Aug 1915),
  516; 'slaughter is commonplace' (2
  Aug 1915), 517; 'may be very unpopular' (24 Aug 1915), 528; 'this
  period of darkness and peril' (18 Sept
  1915), 534; 'what a weary toil for
  the millions' (14 Jan 1916), 636; on
  the battle of Loos 'hopeless failure . . .
  sublime heroism utterly wasted' (17
  Jan 1916), 641; 'a game that is
  played with a smile . . . . If you can't
  smile grin' (26 Jan 1916), 651; 'one
  long holiday for me' (6 Feb 1916), 661;
  'It will all come right in the end,
  though not by the shortest or least
  costly method' (6 Jan 1916), 680;
  'we have only to persevere to conquer'
  (29 Jan 1916), 694; 'War is action,
  energy & hazard. These sheep only
  want to browse among the daisies'
  (22 Feb 1916), 707; 'To lose momentum is not merely to stop, but to fall'
  (7 March 1916), 718; 'At a hideous
  cost in life and treasure we have
  regained control' (7 March 1916),

Churchill, Winston Leonard Spencer
ATTITUDES TO THE WAR—*continued*
718; 'One wondered whether the nations were getting their money's worth out of the brooding armies' (17 March 1916), 740; 'Do not my darling one underrate the contribution I have made to the public cause' (22 March 1916), 742; 'I greatly fear the general result' (14 April 1916), 755; 'All the more condemnation to you . . . for losing so much valuable time' (17 May 1916), 767; 'Nothing stands in the way of our obtaining aerial supremacy . . . but yourselves' (17 May 1916), 769; 'bundles of bloody rags' (23 May 1916), 773; 'Nothing counts but winning the war' (31 May 1916), 776; 'But for the war, I wd not dream of acting with these people' (21 June 1916), 783; 'excitement is bankrupt, death is familiar, and sorrow numb' (July 1916), 791; 'the accumulation of extortionate profits in the hands of private individuals' (22 Aug 1916), 801; of the tank 'In that idea resided one real victory' (16 Sept 1916), 810

OPINIONS:
'Balkan quarrels are no vital concern of ours' (31 July 1914), 21; 'the world is gone mad—& we must look to ourselves—& our friends' (2 Aug 1914), 26; 'We have not entered this business without resolve to see it through' (23 Aug 1914), 54; 'You have only to endure to conquer' (4 Sept 1914), 63; 'The war will be long and sombre. It will have many reverses of fortune . . .' (11 Sept 1914), 76; 'Victory is a better boon than life and without it life will be unendurable' (23 Oct 1914), 141; 'the ignoble position of one who merely cheers from the bank the gallant efforts of the rowers' (9 Nov 1914), 161; 'it is no time for hedging neutrals to give themselves airs' (27 Nov 1914), 174; 'to terrorize

Churchill, Winston Leonard Spencer
OPINIONS—*continued*
Admirals for losing ships is to make sure of losing wars' (11 Jan 1915), 185; 'Nothing appeals to the Turkish Govt but force' (11 Sept 1914), 208; 'Kitchener does not work far afield or far ahead' (31 Dec 1914), 231; 'It is not until all the Northern possibilities are exhausted that I wd look to the S of Europe for the profitable employment of our expanding milty forces' (11 Jan 1915), 247; 'Unless we are prepared to run a risk & play a stake the Balkan situation is finished fatally for us' (7 Feb 1916), 278; of Lloyd George, 'LG has more true insight & courage than anyone else' (26 Feb 1915), 311; 'the settlement of all territorial questions should be left until the end of the war' (3 March 1915), 321; 'Half-hearted measures will ruin all' (6 March 1915), 328; 'excuse frankness—but friends have this right, and to colleagues it is a duty' (11 April 1915), 395; 'every minute of this is history' (26 April 1915), 410; 'the imperious need to go forward to victory' (29 May 1915), 484; 'without decision & design a very terrible catastrophe may ensue' (2 June 1915), 488; 'The soldiers who are ordered to their deaths have a right to a plan, as well as a cause' (15 Oct 1915), 554; 'Time will vindicate my administration of the Admiralty' (11 Nov 1915), 564; 'Without winning any sensational victories, we may win this war' (15 Nov 1915), 567; 'It is all chance and our wayward footsteps are best planted without too much calculation' (27 Nov 1915), 585; 'If my destiny has not already been accomplished I shall be guarded surely' (27 Nov 1915), 587; 'energy & efficiency in *execution* are as important as good decisions in principle' (8 Dec 1915), 602; 'The Balkans must be left to stew in their own bitter juice', (8

Churchill, Winston Leonard Spencer
OPINIONS—*continued*
Dec 1915), 605; 'That odious Asquith
& his pack of incompetents & intriguers ruin everything' (12 Dec
1915), 607; 'My conviction that the
greatest of my work is still to be done
is strong within me' (15 Dec 1915),
611; 'Asquith will throw anyone to the
wolves to keep himself in office' (19
Dec 1915), 617; 'It is not hard for me
to give orders, as you know' (7 Jan
1916), 632; 'I wd much rather go back
to the trenches tonight, than go home
in any position of mediocre authority'
(28 Jan 1916), 656; 'By God I wd
make them skip if I had the power—
even for a month' (9 Feb 1916),
662; 'God for a month of power & a
good shorthand writer' (3 Jan 1916),
680; 'I shd have made nothing if I
had not made mistakes' (7 Jan 1916),
681; 'It is better to be gagged than give
unheeded counsel' (19 Jan 1916),
688; 'the power which I cd use better
than any other living Englishman to
determine the war policy of Britain'
(28 Jan 1916), 693, 823; 'Are they
not fools not to use my mind—or
knaves to wait for its destruction by
some flying splinter' (16 Feb 1916),
705; 'if my life cd materially aid our
fortunes I would not grudge it' (17
March 1916), 740; 'Nothing cd I
think deprive me of my hold on the
public attention' (28 March 1916),
745; sees his death as 'an impoverishment of the war-making power of
Britain wh no one wd ever know or
measure or mourn' (26 March 1916),
745–6; 'The numbing hand of Asquith
is over everything, and all initiative
& energy seem paralysed' (10 April
1916), 753; 'the unwisdom with
wh our affairs are conducted makes me
almost despair at times of a victorious
issue' (14 April 1916), 755; 'Whatever
is done must be done in the cold light
of science' (23 May 1916), 774; on

Churchill, Winston Leonard Spencer
OPINIONS—*continued*
the Dardanelles, 'only the facts can
tell the tale: and the public ought now
to have them' (8 June 1916), 782; 'the
Nation & the Dominions whose
blood has been poured out vainly have
a right to know the truth' (7 July 1916),
787; 'Asquith reigns supine, sodden
and supreme' (15 July 1916), 787;
'Asquith in particular seems to be on
the road to pay his debts' (31 July
1916), 791; 'stagnation, apathy &
playing for safety are the orders of the
day' (30 Aug 1916), 806; 'there are
plenty of good ideas if only they can
be backed with power and brought
into reality' (1 Oct 1916), 810

CHARACTERISTICS OF, AS SEEN BY HIS
CONTEMPORARIES:
'tingling with life to the tips of your
fingers' (Clementine Churchill, 1
Aug 1914), 18; 'very bellicose and
demanding immediate mobilization'
(Asquith, 1 Aug 1914), 23; 'longing
for a sea fight in the early hours of the
morning' (Asquith, 4 Aug 1914), 30;
his 'grasp of the situation . . . above
all praise' (*The Times*, 4 Aug 1914),
31; 'a really happy man' (Lloyd
George, recalling 4 Aug 1914), 31;
'a statesman who well understands
the nature of war' (*Observer*, 9 Aug
1914), 39; 'Public Enemy No 1' (John
Cordingley, recalling Aug 1914), 50;
'not sane' (Captain Richmond, 20
Aug 1914), 51; 'stupid and boring'
(Lord Emmott, 26 Aug 1914), 57;
'hardly one war was enough for him'
(Lord Birkenhead, recalling 1914), 58;
'the equivalent of a large force in the
field' (Asquith, reported by Haldane
3 Sept 1914), 64; his boasting and
bombast (Sir Lewis Bayly, 2 Oct 1914),
84; his frankness and calm (*Manchester
Guardian*, 2 Oct 1914), 84–5; no longer
believed to be 'a gentleman' (George
V, June 1915), 87; 'the only young

Churchill, Winston Leonard Spencer
CHARACTERISTICS OF, AS SEEN BY HIS
CONTEMPORARIES—*continued*
vital person in the Cabinet' (Clementine Churchill, 26 Sept 1914), 92;
'intrepid' (Asquith, 3 Oct 1914),
106; 'energetic and imperative' (Henry
Stevens, recalling Oct 1914), 109; his
'lunatic hands' (Captain Richmond,
4 Oct 1914), 110; 'tranquilly smoking
a large cigar . . . under a rain of
shrapnel' (Calza Bedolo, Oct 1914),
115; 'quite off his head' (Lord
Stamfordham, 5 Oct 1914), 120;
'genius for war' (Sir Edward Grey,
7 Oct 1914), 121; his 'incompetence'
as First Lord (H. A. Gwynne, 16
Oct 1914), 127; 'initiative, energy,
enterprise' (*Observer*, 18 Oct 1914),
128; 'not . . . a Napoleon' (*Morning
Post*, 19 Oct 1914), 129; 'an utterly
unbalanced mind' (Bonar Law, 14
Oct 1914), 132; 'unconsciously playing
a part—an heroic part' (A. G.
Gardiner, 1913), 132; 'unique and
invaluable . . . full of courage and
resource' (Haldane, 19 Oct 1914), 133;
'must be mad' (Sir David Beatty, 18
Oct 1914), 134; 'autocratic' (Lord
Fisher, mid-Oct 1914), 137; 'cannot
be expected to have any grasp of the
principles and practice of naval
warfare' (*Morning Post*, 21 Oct 1914),
144; 'busy trying to get a flashy success' (Frances Stevenson, 5 Nov
1914), 159; his judgement 'highly
erratic' (Sir John French, 20 Dec
1914), 167; 'intrepid, valorous . . .
dreaming of war . . . a born soldier
. . . quite unsensitive' (Margot Asquith, 30 Nov 1914), 179–80; 'mono-
polized all initiative in the Admiralty'
(Lord Fisher, 20 Dec 1914), 186;
'young, self-assertive, with a great
self-satisfaction, but unstable' (Beatty,
4 Dec 1914), 187; his 'volatile mind'
(Asquith, 5 Dec 1914), 223; 'a good
deal of rugged fluency' (Asquith, 13
Jan 1915), 253; 'a dialectician'

Churchill, Winston Leonard Spencer
CHARACTERISTICS OF, AS SEEN BY HIS
CONTEMPORARIES—*continued*
(recalled by Violet Bonham Carter,
1965), 263; 'intolerable . . . devoured
by vanity' (Asquith, reported by Margot Asquith, 17 Feb 1915), 289; 'far
the most disliked man in my Cabinet'
(Asquith, reported by Margot Asquith,
7 March 1915), 329; 'longwinded . . .
full of perorations' (ibid), 330; 'a
Tory . . . knows *nothing* of the British
workman' (Margot Asquith, 7 March
1915), 330; 'does not inspire trust'
(Asquith, 24 March 1915), 362;
'really loyal' (Asquith, 30 March
1915), 363; turns conversation into
'a monologue' (Lloyd George, 5
April 1915), 385; 'ignorance of strategic and tactical principles' (H. A.
Gwynne, 22 April 1915), 398; 'perseverance and energy' (ibid), 399;
'ignorant' (Captain Richmond, 22
April 1915), 399; 'a determined mad
Gambler' (Lord Fisher, 14 May 1915),
429; saw in the war 'the chance of
glory for himself' (Lloyd George
reported by Frances Stevenson, 15
May 1915), 440; '*The joy of his life
is to be 50 yards from a German trench*'
(Lord Fisher, 16 May 1915), 442;
'overriding his expert advisers' (*The
Times*, 18 May 1915), 450; 'his folly'
(General Callwell, 22 May 1915),
458; 'the power, the imagination, the
deadliness to fight Germany' (Clementine Churchill, 20 May 1915), 459;
neither 'the temperament or the
manners' to be Colonial Secretary
(Lord Emmott, 20 May 1915), 460;
'He is young. He has lion-hearted
courage. No number of enemies can
fight down his ability and force'
(*Observer*, 23 May 1915), 469; 'far too
great to be more than pulled up for a
period' (Edwin Montagu, 26 May
1915), 472; his conversation apt 'to
degenerate into a monologue' (Asquith, 4 Feb 1915), 476; 'borne along

Churchill, Winston Leonard Spencer
CHARACTERISTICS OF, AS SEEN BY HIS
CONTEMPORARIES—*continued*
on the flood of his all too copious
tongue' (Asquith, 16 April 1915),
476; 'dictatorial' (John Burns, 24
May 1915), 478; 'so anxious not to
give any offence' (17 June 1915), 498;
'I remain under the shadow of utterly
false aspersions' (15 Sept 1915), 532;
Carson reported 'so impressed by his
ability' (12 Nov 1915), 565; 'England
trusts and needs you' (Violet Asquith,
13 Nov 1915), 566; 'a wise counsellor,
a brilliant colleague and a faithful
friend' (Asquith, 15 Nov 1915), 568;
'one of the foremost men in our country' (Bonar Law, 15 Nov 1915), 569;
'great cheerfulness . . . strictly amenable to discipline' (Edward Grigg,
2 Dec 1915), 589; 'his brilliant conversational powers' (Lord Esher, 1
Dec 1915), 589; 'selfish' (Captain
Spiers, 15 Dec 1915), 610; 'an inquiring mind of rare quality' (recalled
by Spears, 1970), 625; 'he overlooked
nothing' (recalled by McDavid, 1967),
635; 'you are unique in your generation' (Lady Gwendeline Churchill,
21 Jan 1916), 644; 'I must wait in
silence the sombre movement of
events' (19 Jan 1916), 688; his 'courage' (Lord Fisher, 14 Feb 1916),
701; 'quite spiteful sometimes' (16
Feb 1916), 706; 'stronger and saner'
(C. P. Scott, 6 March 1916), 712;
'deranged' (recalled by Violet Bonham Carter, 1965), 721; 'a hound of
the lowest sense of political honour,
a fool of the lowest judgement & contemptible' (Margot Asquith, 8 March
1916), 729; 'I am not going to give in
or tire at all' (26 March 1916), 745;
'The man who makes no mistakes
never makes anything' (Sir Arthur
Markham, 1 April 1916), 750; his
lack of modesty (Bonar Law, 16 Aug
1916), 800; 'will never allow that he is
down' (Lord Derby, 19 Aug 1916),

Churchill, Winston Leonard Spencer
CHARACTERISTICS OF, AS SEEN BY HIS
CONTEMPORARIES—*continued*
800; 'absolutely untrustworthy' (ibid),
801; '*Celerity, Courage, Audacity, Imagination*' (Lord Fisher, 15 Aug 1916),
803; 'a megalomaniac . . . sacrificed
thousands of lives to no purpose' (*Daily
Mail*, 13 Oct 1916), 811; 'anathema
in the Army' (David Davies, 22 Nov
1916), 817; 'full of ideas, & good ones
too' (Sir Abe Bailey, 2 Dec 1916),
820; 'I would rather have him against
us every time' (Bonar Law, Dec 1916),
822

HIS EVIDENCE TO THE DARDANELLES
COMMISSION:
on the idea of an attack at Gallipoli,
200; on the possibility of forcing the
Dardanelles, 220; on Turkish military
capabilities, 222; on Admiral Carden's suggestions for reaching the Sea
of Marmara, 248; on Fisher's decision
to send the *Queen Elizabeth* to the
Dardanelles, 250; justifies the taking
of risks in war, 262; and Fisher's
support for the Dardanelles operation,
273; and the argument against a
military landing at Gallipoli, 274, 332;
on the relation between the Serbian
danger and the Dardanelles, 280; on
Kitchener's authority at the War
Council, 312–13; and the decision
to take greater risks at the Dardanelles
(11 March 1915), 337; on the naval
losses of 18 March 1915, 354; on
Fisher's decision to oppose a renewed
naval attack (23 March 1915), 364;
and the Turkish shortage of ammunition at the Dardanelles, 365; on the
need for 'an absolute decision one
way or the other', 377

INTRIGUES ALLEGED AGAINST:
to replace Grey by Balfour at the
Foreign Office (March 1915), 361–2;
to replace Asquith by Lloyd George
(March 1915), 362–3; to remove

Churchill, Winston Leonard Spencer

INTRIGUES ALLEGED AGAINST—*continued*
Kitchener (May 1915), 454; to remove Kitchener and Grey (May 1915), 454, 477; to disclose the details of the shell shortage (May 1915), 460; 'to try & wreck the Gov' (Oct 1915), 556–7, 560; to provide an alternate Government (Dec 1915), 590; to remove Haig from Command of the British forces in France (Oct 1916), 811

MEMORANDA AND MINUTES BY
(in chronological order):
On forcing the Dardanelles (15 March 1911), 220; on the nature of a German attack on France (13 Aug 1911), 63; on blockade of Germany and Austria (16 Aug 1914), 46; on the establishment of the Royal Naval Division (17 Aug 1914), 50; on Turkish intentions (26 Aug 1914), 197; on the escape of the *Goeben* and *Breslau* (27 Aug 1914), 41; on aerial strategy (5 Sept 1914), 66; on need to repress 'all tendencies to panic' (23 Sept 1914), 139; on the need for a trench-spanning vehicle (23 Sept 1914), 534; on the surrender of German troopships (22 Oct 1914), 93–4; on ordering flying boats from the United States (31 Oct 1914), 66; on the advantages of an invasion of the German island of Sylt (2 Dec 1914), 181; 'any white flag hoisted by a German ship is to be fired on as a matter of principle' (23 Dec 1914), 94; on the use of British naval power (26 Jan 1915), 264–5; urges tank development forward 'with all despatch' (24 Feb 1915), 536; on need for a substantial number of troops at the Dardanelles (25 Feb 1915), 306–7; on inadequacy of existing troops allocated to Gallipoli (27 Feb 1915), 311; advocates 50% tax on all war profits (5 March 1915), 285; on the effect of the North Sea blockade (5 March 1915), 46; on

Churchill, Winston Leonard Spencer

MEMORANDA AND MINUTES BY—*continued*
need to 'press on' with development of the tank (8 March 1915), 537; on urgency of tank construction (20 March 1915), 537; on importance of capturing the German island of Borkum (24 March 1915), 373; on the possible German invasion of Holland (27 March 1915), 378; on the mine danger at the Dardanelles (24 April 1915), 399; on increase of British naval strength since outbreak of war (30 May 1915), 485–6; on the futility of renewed offensives on the western front (1 June 1915), 486–7; advises military landing on the Bulair Isthmus, Turkey (11 June 1915), 494; on the need to concentrate British military effort against Constantinople (18 June 1915), 498–9; on the need to set up an Air Department and create a powerful 'British Air Service' (during June 1915), 501; on the need for conscription (7 Sept 1915), 530; on the need for Bulgarian support against Turkey and Austria (6 Oct 1915), 544–6; on the prospects at Gallipoli (6 Oct 1915), 546, 547; on the need for a decision on the evacuation of Gallipoli (15 Oct 1915), 554–5; advocates use of gas against the Turks at Gallipoli (20 Oct 1915), 555–6; on the danger of failure at the Dardanelles (25 Oct 1915), 561; on his air policy while First Lord (end October 1915), 560; urges a renewed Franco-Russo-British attack on Turkey (27 Oct 1915), 560; on the need for mechanical devices to break the trench stalemate on the western front (3 Dec 1915), 591–3, 615; on the danger of a new offensive on the western front (1 Aug 1916), 790–1

MILITARY AMBITIONS OF:
writes to his brother 'I shall try to come out too, if there is any use for me' (Aug 1914), 58; telegraphs to Asquith

Churchill, Winston Leonard Spencer
MILITARY AMBITIONS OF—*continued*
from Antwerp 'I am willing to . . .
undertake command' (Oct 1914), 110;
asks Asquith for 'some kind of military
command' (Oct 1914), 121; 'I am
willing when the time comes to pay
the price' (Oct 1914), 135; tells George
V he wants to be a soldier (Oct 1914),
150; writes to Asquith about 'employment in the field' (May 1915), 449;
wishes he were at Gallipoli (June 1915),
496; wants 'an escape' from the Government (Sept 1915), 530; seeks command of British forces in East Africa
(Nov 1915), 566–7; writes to
Seely: 'it is painful being here idle,
but I must just wait' (13 Aug 1916),
799

MILITARY SERVICE OF:
with the Grenadier Guards (Nov–
Dec 1915), chapter 18, 572–94, 605–8;
in command of the 6th Royal
Scots Fusiliers, in reserve (Jan
1916), chapter 20, 628–47; in the
front line (Jan–May 1916), chapter
21, 648–78, 694–8, 737, 744–5, 758–
60

MILITARY EXPERIENCES DRAWN ON BY:
to devise new methods of mechanical
warfare (Dec 1915), 590–3; to assert
importance of extending conscription
to Ireland (9 May 1916), 762; to
stress need for British air supremacy
(17 May 1916), 763, 769; to advocate
proper use of conscripts (23 May
1916), 770–1; to compare the trench
population with the non-trench population (23 May 1916), 771; to allege
'gross and grave misuse' of military
manpower (23 May 1916), 772–3; to
oppose the Somme offensive, 773–4,
791–2, 793–4; to criticize the Government's military policy (24 July
1916), 794–6; to advise against premature use of the tank (Sept 1916),
810

Churchill, Winston Leonard Spencer
VISITS ABROAD OF:
his first wartime visit to France (10
Sept 1914), 72–3; his second (16
Sept 1914), 80; his third (22 Sept
1914), 88, 89; his fourth (26 Sept
1914), 92; his fifth (6 Dec 1914), 163;
his sixth (29 Jan 1915), 277; his
seventh (16 March 1915), 348; his
eighth (5–10 May 1915), 414, 416–17,
418, 424, 425; at the siege of Antwerp,
(4–6 Oct 1914), 106–19

HOPED-FOR MISSIONS ABROAD OF:
to the Calais Conference (July 1915),
506; to the Dardanelles (July 1915),
510–14; to the Balkan capitals (July
1915), 512; to Russia (Oct 1915), 561,
611n; to East Africa (Nov 1915), 563,
565–6, 568

MOODS OF:
'geared up & happy' (20 July 1914),
31; seeks reassurance from Lloyd
George (23 Aug 1914), 55; 'Unless
we win, I do not want to live any
more. But win we will' (24 Aug 1914),
55; 'gloomy & dissatisfied' (Clementine Churchill, 26 Sept 1914), 92;
'very depressed' (Asquith, 8 Oct 1914),
122; cast down by criticisms of his
action at Antwerp (Oct 1914), 130–3;
'It is vain to look backwards', 133;
'I have not seen him so despondent
before' (Captain Richmond, 24 Oct
1914), 140; 'a rather sombre mood'
(Asquith, 27 Oct 1914), 141; 'vexed
by trifles' (28 Dec 1914), 168; disappointed by lack of public enthusiasm for the Friedrichshafen air
raid (Nov 1914), 174–5; elated by
Falkland Islands victory (Dec 1914),
184; 'his most bellicose' (Asquith,
17 Aug 1914), 195; 'violently anti-
Turk' (Asquith, 21 Aug 1914), 196;
'I would not be out of this glorious
delicious war for anything' (reported
by Margot Asquith, 10 Jan 1915),
246; disappointed by limited results

Churchill, Winston Leonard Spencer
MOODS OF—*continued*
of Dogger Bank action (24 Jan 1915), 260–1; impatient with Asquith, Grey and Kitchener (7 Feb 1915), 278; 'the stresses and strains' of the war (15 Feb 1915), 285; 'I wish you had heard what I had to say before assuming that I was in the wrong' (17 Feb 1915), 290; disappointed at failure to obtain troops for the Dardanelles (24 Feb 1915), 304; 'immense and unconcealed dudgeon' (Asquith, 26 Feb 1915), 310; 'breast high about the Dardanelles' (Asquith, 1 March 1915), 316; determined to renew the naval attack at the Dardanelles after the setback of 18 March 1915, 354; frustrated not to be at the centre of planning (March–April 1915), 381; 'It was *I* who was churlish & difficult' (5 April 1915), 384; 'eaten up with the Dardanelles' (Lord Fisher, 5 April 1915), 385–6; 'a vy anxious time' (7 April 1915), 387; 'his stout attitude' (recorded by Hankey, 1961), 432; glad that Fisher 'lived to endure his pangs' (1928), 452*n*; 'in the highest good humour' (*Advertiser*, 18 May 1915), 454; 'worn out and harassed' (Riddell, 20 May 1915), 457; 'I did not believe it was possible to endure such anxiety' (21 May 1915), 463; 'I thought he would die of grief' (Clementine Churchill, 1969), 472; 'master of myself & at peace' (7 June 1915), 490; 'I find it vy painful to be deprived of direct means of action' (19 June 1915), 501; finds a distraction and sedative in painting (June 1915), 502; 'anxious about the D'lles' (2 Aug 1915), 517; 'the truth must be published' (15 Sept 1915), 532; finds it 'odious . . . watching sloth & folly' (20 Sept 1915), 538; finds it 'damnable' without political influence (2 Oct 1915), 542; wants to resign from the Cabinet (22 Oct 1915), 558; resigns from the Cabinet (30 Oct 1915),

Churchill, Winston Leonard Spencer
MOODS OF—*continued*
560–1 and (11 Nov 1915), 563–4; 'I have made up my mind not to return to any Govt during the war except with plenary & effective executive power' (19 Nov 1915), 573; 'I have lost all interest in the outer world' (22 Nov 1915), 580; 'I am quite young again' (24 Nov 1915), 581; 'how vain it is to worry about things' (27 Nov 1915), 585; 'distressed and unsettled' (3 Dec 1915), 593; 'I am thank God only a spectator now' (1 Dec 1915), 595; 'distressing thoughts' (7 Dec 1915), 602; 'worries great & small recede to remote & shadowy distances' (8 Dec 1915), 603; 'quite cut off from information and . . . content to be' (12 Dec 1915), 607; 'I feel a gt assurance of my power: & now—naked—nothing can assail me' (15 Dec 1915), 611; 'I was depressed' (16 Dec 1915), 612; 'my own energies & capacities . . . wasted' (20 Dec 1915), 621; 'I do not think my pulse quickened' (10 Feb 1916), 664; 'the complete absence of worry or strain' (17 Feb 1916), 670; 'disturbing combinations for my mind' (7 Jan 1916), 681; 'try not to brood too much' (Clementine Churchill, 12 Jan 1916), 684; 'I am impotent to give what there is to be given—of truth & value & urgency' (19 Jan 1916), 688; 'I sorrow only for real things' (28 Jan 1916), 693; 'it riles me to see how ungrateful they are' (14 Feb 1916), 705; 'hesitations & perplexity' (13 March 1916), 738; 'my disturbing moods' (19 March 1916), 740–1; 'the longing for rest & peace' (26 March 1916), 744; 'I am powerless even to utter my warnings' (14 April 1916), 755; 'chewing black charcoal' (15 April 1915), 756; 'Not a day passes without my being the object of unjust reproach' (8 June 1916), 782; 'I am learning to

Churchill, Winston Leonard Spencer
   MOODS OF—*continued*
   hate' (15 July 1916), 788; 'It is vy
   painful to me to be impotent & inactive' (31 July 1916), 791; 'They only
   want to keep me out' (Aug 1916,
   recalled by Violet Bonham Carter),
   798; 'It is painful being here idle'
   (13 Aug 1916), 799; 'suffering acutely
   from his enforced inactivity' (C. P.
   Scott, 20 Nov 1916), 816; 'almost
   wistfully eager for news' (Dec 1916,
   recalled by Lord Beaverbrook), 819;
   'righteous anger' (5 Dec 1916, recalled by Lord Beaverbrook), 822

   SPEECHES BY:
   At the Guildhall, London (4 Sept
   1914), 62–3; at the Opera House,
   London (11 Sept 1914), 75–7; at
   Liverpool (21 Sept 1914), 84–5; in
   the House of Commons (27 Nov 1914),
   177–8; in the House of Commons (15
   Feb 1915), 283–6; at Dundee (5 June
   1915), 488–91, 492; at Enfield (18
   Sept 1915), 534; in the House of
   Commons (15 Nov 1915), 566–8;
   in the House of Commons (7 March
   1916), 716–22; in the House of Commons (8 March 1916), 728; in the
   House of Commons (9 May 1916),
   761–2; in the House of Commons
   (17 May 1916), 763–9; in the House
   of Commons (23 May 1916), 770–4; in
   the House of Commons (31 May 1916),
   775; in the House of Commons (24
   July 1916), 793–7; in the House of
   Commons (16 Aug 1916), 799–800;
   in the House of Commons (22 Aug
   1916), 801–2

   UNPUBLISHED NOTES OF:
   on the effect on the Kaiser of not dis-
   persing the Fleet, 7; the Cabinet
   'absolutely against war' (27 July
   1914), 8; on Belgian policy before
   1914 and Belgian heroism in 1914,
   10; on Kitchener's forebodings about
   German high-explosive shells, 11; on
   his fear of a surprise German sub-

Churchill, Winston Leonard Spencer
   UNPUBLISHED NOTES OF—*continued*
   marine attack, 13; on the intolerable
   suspense (1 Aug 1914), 24; on the
   need to make Kitchener Secretary of
   State for War, 28; on Kitchener's
   precipitant cancellation of day-time
   troop crossings of the Channel, 34–5;
   on his anxiety about troop movements at sea, 37; critical of Milne's
   respect for Italian neutrality, 42;
   on the role of Lord Fisher before 1914,
   145; on his relationship with Fisher
   (Oct 1914–May 1915), 156; on
   Fisher's opposition to renewing the
   naval attack at the Dardanelles (11
   May 1915), 418–19
Churchill, Winston Spencer (1940–   ):
   791n
Churchill his paintings (compiled by David
   Coombs): 503n, 659n
'Churchill's Innocent Victims': a nickname for the Royal Naval Division, 48
'Churchill's Pets': a nickname for the
   Royal Naval Division, 48
Clark, Ian Hew Waldegrave Dalrymple:
   drops bomb on Germans near Cambrai
   (3 Sept 1914), 65; reconnaissance
   flight beyond Bailleul, 68
Clauson, John Eugene: 299
Clyde, James Avon: a member of Dardanelles Commission, 789
Coalition: discussed on eve of war, 12,
   22; Churchill fails to advance the
   cause of, although suggesting presence
   of Bonar Law and Lansdowne at
   War Council (10 March 1915), 335n;
   Bonar Law presses for and Asquith
   accepts (17 May 1915), 446; Churchill's Constituency Chairman critical
   of (20 May 1915), 461; Margot Asquith on Churchill and (24 May
   1915), 466; completed (25 May 1915),
   469–70; Churchill's potential strength
   in, 479; Churchill believes it was
   'forced on' by Lloyd George in May
   1915, 541; many Generals disillusioned by (April 1916), 756
Coke, Sir Charles: 569

Colenso, battle of (15 Dec 1899): 268

Collet, Charles Herbert: bombs German Zeppelin shed at Düsseldorf (22 Sept 1914), 89

Cologne (Germany): British air raid on Zeppelin sheds at (22 Sept 1914), 89; second air raid on (9 Oct 1914), 122–3, 136; Churchill refers to air raids on, 721, 764; MAP, 88

Colombo (Ceylon): 265

Colonial Office: Grey protests to about Churchill's actions, 298–9; Lloyd George suggests sending Churchill to (May 1915), 448; Churchill willing to go to, 450; Cabinet Ministers reported reluctant that Churchill should go to, 454; Asquith implored not to send Churchill to, 460

Colville, John Rupert: records a conversation with Churchill about 'a very unhappy time of my life', 793

Committee of Imperial Defence: Kitchener a member of, 9n; its plans for national emergency, 11; General Wilson's demonstration to (1911), 28; discusses Dutch neutrality, 96; Churchill a member of, 114; recommends military landing at Haifa (1909), 220; examination of possible joint military and naval attack on Dardanelles (1906), 294; Fisher insists on Sir Arthur Wilson being dismissed from, 452; Churchill wants special sub-committee of, to report on future of Gallipoli (Oct 1915), 547

Compulsion, see Conscription

Conan Doyle, Arthur: Churchill writes to about the 'tank' (Sept 1916), 810

Concerning Winston Spencer Churchill (Sir George Arthur): 817n

Congleton, 5th Baron (Henry Bligh Fortescue Parnell): killed in action at Ypres (18 Nov 1914), 607n

Conqueror (British battleship): collision with Monarch (27 Dec 1914) impairs naval margin, 268

Conscription: pre-1914 campaign for, 47; Churchill argues in favour of, at Cabinet (26 Aug 1914), 57; the

Conscription—continued
growing pressure for (June 1915), 492; Kitchener attacked for his opposition to (Oct 1915), 556–60; Curzon appeals to Churchill for support over (Nov 1915), 602; its advocates gain in strength (Dec 1915), 618–19; the growing crisis over (Jan 1916), 679–82; the renewed crisis over (April 1916), 750–2, 755–8; Churchill on the need to make proper use of, 770–2

Conservative Party: and the coming of war, 22–3; attitude to Churchill, 32–3; and Home Rule, 77–80; critical of Churchill's visits to France, 90, 424–5; critical of Churchill's actions at Antwerp, 132; Churchill describes certain members of as 'swine', 164; believes Asquith did not reconvene Parliament (Oct 1914) in order to avoid questions on Antwerp, 169; critical of Churchill's policy on the collier question, 284; finds it difficult to attack War Office while Kitchener is Secretary of State, 312; and criticism of Gallipoli landings, 413; denied equal part in prosecution of the war, 469–70; and Churchill's hopes of support from during the political crisis of May 1915, 476–7; the growing call for conscription, 492; Churchill believes its 'dream and intention' a Conservative Government, 692; Asquith waiting for a change in the hostile attitude to Churchill of (March 1916), 733; said by Churchill to 'despise' Asquith (Aug 1916), 798; hostility towards Churchill unabated (Aug 1916), 800; Derby believes, 'will not work' with Churchill, 801

Constance, Lake of: 172, 173; MAP, 173

Constantine, King of Greece: refuses to support Britain against Turkey, 221; refuses to allow British troops to land at Salonika, 287; said to favour helping Britain against Turkey, 316; rejects pro-Allied policy of his Prime

Constantine, King of Greece—*continued*
Minister, 329; talks of benevolent
neutrality for Greece, 336; his influence weakened by prospect of a
British victory at Gallipoli, 412

Constantinople (Turkey): *Goeben* and
Breslau anchor off (10 Aug 1914), 40;
Admiral Limpus at, 188; Churchill
visits (1910), 189; dockyard inadequacies of, 190; dockyard construction in to be under British control,
191; reaction in to the seizure of
Turkish ships, 192–3; Churchill believes vulnerable to attack from the
sea, 201; Russia anxious to extend
control at, 211; Asquith believes
Russian rule of 'its proper destiny',
215; Grey supports Russian claims for,
217; Churchill sees possibility of
Britain dictating peace terms at, 220;
Russia wants reports spread of threat
to, 233; Fisher believes possession of
imperative (4 Jan 1915), 237; F. E.
Smith wants Indian troops to advance
from Smyrna to, 238; Turkish war-
making power at, 249; Richmond
sees, as 'open' to British naval power,
258; Balfour sees Dardanelles victory
as putting 'under our control', 272;
means of effecting morale of Turks
in, 276; Grey's hopes of 'creating a
scare' at, 277; Churchill wants 50,000
troops to occupy in event of revolution
at, 288–9; Russians estimate 50,000
troops needed to capture, 292;
Churchill believes capture of possible
with 'a comparatively small number
of troops', 301; Asquith asserts importance of occupation of, 304;
Churchill wants 115,000 troops for
capture of, 307; Churchill insists capture of is 'only a means to an end',
315, 331; apparently promised to
Russia by Grey as early as 1908, 320;
War Council discusses future of (3
March 1915), 321; Admiral Carden's
instructions (5 March 1915) for the
surrender of, 327; War Council
discusses the future of (10 March 1915),

Constantinople (Turkey)—*continued*
332, 334–5; report of dissension in,
395–6; Churchill on the importance
of the capture of, 411; Churchill
asserts (18 June 1915) that Britain has
the power to capture, 498–9; British
proposal for eventual Russian annexation of, 509; Curzon willing to allow
Turks to keep, in return for peace (Oct
1915), 550; 'take it, and take it soon,
and take it while time remains'
(Churchill, 15 Nov 1915), 567;
Churchill wants troops used to threaten
(May 1916), 772; MAPS, 29, 545, 838,
841, 842

Contemporary Personalities (Lord Birkenhead): quoted, on Churchill, 58

Cordingley, John Walter: recalls hostile
opinions of Churchill, 50

Corfu: 395

Cornwall (British cruiser): and preparations for battle of Falkland Islands,
182

Cornwallis (British battleship): to go to
Dardanelles, 249n; at Gallipoli landings, 405

Cornwallis-West, George Frederick Myd-
delton: commands a battalion in the
Royal Naval Division, 49; at siege of
Antwerp, 122n, 130

Coronel (Chile): prelude to battle off,
156; British squadron defeated at,
157–8; Cabinet bewildered by news
of, 158–9; Churchill defends Admiralty's policy at time of, 159–60;
criticisms of Churchill for British
defeat at, 177, 531; the search to
avenge, 182–4; Churchill sends Bonar
Law documents concerning (19 May
1915), 455; Churchill wants Asquith
to publish documents concerning,
532, 533; Churchill recounts (Dec
1915) defeat of, 620

Costeker, John Henry Dives: killed at
Gallipoli landings (25 April 1915),
409

Council of War: meets on 5 Aug 1914,
33–4

Coventry Ordnance Works, 535

Cox and Company (bankers): 511

Cradock, Sir Christopher: his instructions, 156; defeated by von Spee off Coronel, and drowned (1 Nov 1914), 157; Asquith critical of, 158; Churchill's criticisms of, regarded as suspect, 159; Churchill sends criticisms of, to leading Conservatives, 160; his death avenged, 182–3; Fisher believes there was 'inexplicable folly' in defeat of, 184; Churchill sends Bonar Law documents concerning defeat of, 455; Churchill wants Asquith to publish documents concerning, 533; Churchill shows C. P. Scott documents concerning, 541; Churchill recounts (Dec 1915) his 'insisting on fighting', 620

Crease, Thomas Evans: 250, 394; and the crisis of May 1915, 435, 436, 438, 441, 452, 467; and Fisher's preparation of evidence for the Dardanelles Commission (Aug 1916), 803

Creedy, Herbert James: 515, 604

Cressy (British cruiser): torpedoed (22 Sept 1914), 85–6; loss of a cause of criticism, 143, 159, 184–5, 532

Crete: Indomitable diverted to Dardanelles from, 209

Crewe, 1st Marquess of (Robert Offley Ashburton Crewe-Milnes): at 10 Downing Street (1 Aug 1914), 25; and Churchill's mission to Antwerp, 119; Lord Hardinge complains to, 139; questions Churchill about employment at sea of naval cadets, 171; opposed to taking initiative against Turkey (17 Aug 1914), 195; his son-in-law killed in action, 228; Hankey's proposal for attack on Turkey circulated to, 229; at War Council (7 Jan 1915), 242; Asquith's praise of, 330; at War Council (10 March 1915), 334; informs Hardinge of territorial discussions in London about the future of Turkey, 344; learns of benefits to be gained by India after a British victory at the Dardanelles, 349; at War Council (19 March 1915),

Crewe, 1st Marquess of—continued
355–6; opposes abandoning Gallipoli attack (14 May 1915) because of 'its effect in India', 432; becomes Lord President of the Council (May 1915), 470; at Dardanelles Committee (12 June 1915), 494; doubts possibility of obtaining Bulgaria as an ally (end June 1915), 505; at Calais Conference (July 1915), 526–7; and the War Policy Committee of the Cabinet (Aug 1915), 527–9; agrees (Sept 1915) to winter campaign at Gallipoli, 539; and the growing anti-Kitchener feeling (Oct 1915), 557, 559; opposes Gallipoli evacuation, 601; a possible Viceroy of India (1916), 683

Cromarty (Ross and Cromarty): 282

Cromer, Earl (Evelyn Baring): Churchill recalls (Oct 1916) his attitude towards a military landing on the Gallipoli Peninsula to, 381; Churchill writes to, about procedures to be adopted by the Dardanelles Commission (12 Aug 1916), 804; his reply (19 Sept 1916), 808–9; Churchill protests about Daily Mail accusations to (17 Oct 1916), 812

Cromer (Norfolk): Mrs Churchill staying at, 4, 6, 39, 44–5

Cromwell, Oliver; Churchill unable to name battleship after (1912), 87

Crooks, William: speaks at London Opera House (11 Sept 1914), 75

Crow, Francis Edward: arrested by Turks, 217, 219

Crowe, Sir Eyre: 69, 191–2

Crystal Palace (London): Royal Naval Division Depot at, 169

Ctesiphon (Turkey): British Force defeated at (24 Nov 1915), 590n

Cumine, George J. G. G.: Churchill describes as 'a vy good soldier', but takes risks, 665

Cunliffe, Walter: on City attitude to coming of war, 23

Cunliffe-Owen, Frederick: proposals of (17 Aug 1914), for British action against Turkey, 199–200

Cunningham, Andrew Browne: commands *Scorpion* off Smyrna, 217*n*

Curragh Mutiny (March 1914): J. E. B. Seely resigns after, 83

Curtiss Company: Churchill buys American flying boats from, 66*n*

Curzon of Kedleston, 1st Earl of (George Nathaniel Curzon): Kitchener drives to resignation (1905), 312; becomes Lord Privy Seal (May 1915), 470; Churchill proposes Bulair landing to, 494; at Dardanelles Committee (17 June 1915), 497; wants a further division sent to the Dardanelles (5 July 1915), 508; opposes Churchill's visit to the Gallipoli Peninsula (mid-July 1915), 513; and the War Policy Committee of the Cabinet (Aug 1915), 527–9; discusses conduct of war with Churchill and Lloyd George (Sept 1915), 530–1; agrees (Sept 1915) to winter campaign at Gallipoli, 539; and Churchill's views on Bulgaria, 545; wishes to send British help to Serbia (Oct 1915), 556; believed by Margot Asquith to be part of a Lloyd George–Churchill plot (Oct 1915), 556–7; Lady Randolph Churchill invites to dine (Nov 1915), 482; Lady Randolph Churchill dines with (Nov 1915), 594; informs Churchill of Cabinet crisis (Nov 1915), 601–4; opposed to the evacuation of Gallipoli, 617; rejects compromise over conscription (Dec 1915), 618; Churchill shows front-line trenches to (6 Feb 1916), 661–2; Churchill asks his wife to keep in touch with (Jan 1916), 688; Churchill sees as a future Cabinet colleague, 697; and talk of an Air Ministry, 705; and the renewed conscription crisis (April 1916), 750–1; becomes President of the Air Board (May 1916), 763, 767, 777; and the emergence of Lloyd George as Prime Minister (Dec 1916), 820; vetoes Churchill's inclusion in Lloyd George's Cabinet (7 Dec 1916), 823

Cushing (American steamship): attacked by a German aeroplane (28 April 1915), 463*n*

Cust, Sir Charles Leopold: critical of Royal Naval Division, 306

Cuxhaven (Germany): Fisher wants British naval attack on, 258, 346; Churchill refers to naval air raid on, 721, 764

Cyprus: 298–9, 300*n*; MAP, 838

Daily Chronicle: reports on anti-Asquith intrigues (March 1915), 363; 688, 711*n*, 750

Daily Express: bought by Sir Max Aitken, 13*n*

Daily Mail: critical of Churchill's actions at Antwerp, 126; said to have given important information to Germans, 270; demands Kitchener's dismissal (May 1915), 466; and the Marconi affair (1912), 623*n*; and an American schoolboy howler (Feb 1916), 702; not sympathetic to Churchill (March 1916), 748; describes Churchill as 'a megalomaniac' (Oct 1916), 811–12; Churchill seeks to defend himself against, 817

Daily Mirror: 552*n*

Daily News: publishes defence of Churchill's actions at Antwerp, 128

Dallas, Alister Grant: sent by Kitchener to Antwerp, 101, 103, 107, 108, 109

Dalmatia (Austria-Hungary): Lloyd George favours British attack on, 237; MAP 842

Dalziel, James Henry: and Churchill's criticisms of Asquith (March 1916), 711, 713, 736–7, 739; a member of the Liberal War Committee, 735*n*; presses Asquith to publish Dardanelles documents (June 1916), 783, 784, 785

Damascus (Turkey): Captain Richmond wants British troops to capture, instead of landing at Gallipoli, 389; MAP, 838

Danube, River: Lloyd George anticipates British naval action on, 252–3;

Danube, River—*continued*
Balfour believes victory at Dardanelles will open passage to, 272; Fisher to design gunboats for, 275; Churchill suggests allied force might advance up, 302, 308; Hankey sees British flotilla on, as centre of an allied attack on Austria-Hungary, 318; Austrian forces cross (Oct 1915), 549; MAP, 842

'Danzig': used as code name for attack on Borkum, 242

Dardanelles (Turkey): *Goeben* and *Breslau* pass through (10 Aug 1914), 40, 193–4; Admiral Limpus to escort *Sultan Osman I* through, 191; Limpus refers (26 Aug 1914) to possibility of landing near, 198; Cunliffe-Owen reports (27 Aug 1914) military force needed to command properly, 199–200; Churchill suggests plan for joint Anglo-Greek action against, 204–5; *Goeben* and *Breslau* to be sunk if they emerge from, 206; forts manned by German officers, 206; Enver refuses German request to close, 207; Grey refuses to allow Limpus to command British forces at, 208; Greek plan to capture reported to be ready (9 Sept 1914), 209; British prevent Turkish torpedo boat from leaving, 212; minefield laid across (29 Sept 1914), 213; Admiral Slade advises 'target practice' against forts of, 215; outer forts bombarded (3 Nov 1914), 218; Asquith reports Churchill as wanting 'heroic adventure against' (5 Dec 1914), 223; Hankey discusses territorial future of, 230; Kitchener favours 'demonstration' at (2 Jan 1915), 233; Carden asked about possibility of forcing (3 Jan 1915), 233–4; Carden believes in possibility of forcing, 237–8; Kitchener describes as 'the most suitable objective' (8 Jan 1915), 244; preparations for naval attack on, 248–60, 267; Churchill recalls need to take risks at, 262; Fisher's growing opposition to an attack on, 263–5, 268–71; War Council

Dardanelles (Turkey)—*continued*
(28 Jan 1915) discusses importance of victory at, 271–2; Admiralty work out plans for attack on, 276–7, 279–81; set-back at, 286; criticism of naval plans for, 286–7; the search for troops to be used in attack on, 288–9, 291–8; bombardment of outer forts of (19 Feb 1915), 300; further bombardment delayed, 301; the search for troops continues, 302–5; the bombardment resumed (25 Feb 1915), 305; War Council discusses need for troops at (26 Feb 1915), 307–11; outer forts bombarded (25–6 Feb 1915), 314–15; Churchill wants Greek naval help at, 316; speculation about the territorial future of, 324; Churchill informs Grey of Admiralty confidence to force, *without* military assistance, 325; difficulties of naval progress at, 330–1; shortage of ammunition in forts at (11 March 1915), 337; the naval attack on (18 March 1915), 351–4; the aftermath of the naval attack (March–April 1915), 355–80; Fisher declares (2 April 1915) '*entirely exhausts my time*', 382; Churchill's desire for a renewed attack on (April 1915), 382–6; and the mine danger at, 387, 390–1, 399–400; and Fisher's resignation (April–May 1915), 394–6, and chapter 13, 411–47, 474–5; Churchill's responsibility for, 463–4, 488; possible further attacks at (June–Oct 1915), 496, 498, 500, 516; Churchill's proposed visit to (July 1915), 510–14; Hankey at (Aug 1915), 518; Churchill wants publication of documents concerning (Sept–Nov 1915), 532–3; Churchill refers to attack on as a legitimate gamble (15 Nov 1915), 569; Churchill seeks vindication over (1916), 682; Asquith agrees to publish documents concerning, 778–9, 782–4; Asquith decides *not* to publish documents concerning, but to set up a committee of inquiry into (20 July 1916), 789; MAPS, 235, 353, 519, 838, 840

Dardanelles, The (Sir Charles Callwell): quoted, 786*n*

Dardanelles Commission: Churchill's evidence to, 200, 220, 222, 248, 250, 262, 273, 274, 280, 312, 332, 337, 354, 364, 365, 377; Fisher's evidence to, 273; Sir Ian Hamilton's evidence to, 347; Hankey's memorandum for (1 Sept 1916), 294, 349–50; Hankey's memorandum for (31 Aug 1916), 379–80; Graeme Thomson's evidence to, 297; Asquith agrees to the establishment of, 789–90; Churchill prepares his evidence for, 790–1, 798, 802–8; Churchill appears before (28 Sept 1916), 809; Churchill protests about *Daily Mail* allegations to (17 Oct 1916), 812; Churchill's reaction to the evidence of others to (Oct 1916), 814; Churchill's hopes of vindication from, 816; Churchill protests to about allegations concerning Kitchener's role over the Dardanelles, 817–19

Dardanelles Committee, the: successor to the War Council (q.v.), 485; meets (7 June 1915), 494; meets (12 June 1915), 494–5; meets (17 June 1915), 497; meets (25 June 1915), 502; Churchill tired of bickering in, 505; meets (5 July 1915), 508; meets (24 July 1915), 514–15; meets (19 Aug 1915), 522–3; meets (20 Aug 1915), 523; meets (27 Aug 1915), 525; meets (3 Sept 1915), 526; meets (23 Sept 1915), 538; meets (24 Sept 1915) 539; meets (11 Oct 1915), 549–51; meets (14 Oct 1915), 552–4; Churchill circulates memorandum to (20 Oct 1915) advocating use of gas at Dardanelles, 555; Kitchener's position on, 557, 559; Asquith decides to bring to an end (Nov 1915), 560; final meeting of (6 Nov 1915), 563; replaced by Cabinet War Committee (q.v.), 563

Davies, David: doubts Churchill's chances of office after Asquith's fall, 816–17

Davies, Richard Bell: commands aircraft squadron in France, 67

Dawnay, Guy Payan: sees *Majestic* sink at Dardanelles (May 1915), 472; his visit to London (Sept 1915), 539–41

Dawnay, Hugh: Churchill dines with, at GHQ (16 Sept 1914), 81; killed in action, 228

Dawson, Margaret Jane: 24

de Bartolomé, Charles Martin: assists Admiralty War Group, 185–6, 250, 254; angered by criticism of Royal Naval Division, 306; wants de Robeck to make a second attempt to force the Narrows by ships alone, 366; and Fisher's opposition to the Dardanelles, 394, 429; his expertise cited by Churchill in defence of the Dardanelles operation, 813

de Broqueville, Charles Marie Pierre Albert: appeals to Allies for help in defence of Antwerp, 101–2, 104–8, 110

de Bunsen, Sir Maurice William Ernest: 391

Dedeagatch (Bulgaria): 327, 544, 553; MAPS, 545, 840

Deedes, Wyndham Henry: tells Kitchener purely naval attack at Dardanelles is bound to fail, 288

Defence (British light cruiser): ordered to South America, 157–8, 182

de Forest, Maurice Arnold: summoned to Dover, 11; one of Churchill's Austrian friends, 45; commands armoured car squadron in France, 68

de Graaff, Heinrich: says Fisher is thought to be 'of consequence' in Germany, 146

Deguise, Victor: at Antwerp, 109–16

Delcassé, Théophile: in London (8 Feb 1915), 278; agrees to send French troops to Dardanelles, 281; informs Grey of Russian refusal to allow Greek troops to participate in attack on the Dardanelles, 328

Delennelle Farm (Ploegsteert, Belgium): company billets at, 650; shelled, 660; MAP, 649 de Mole, L. E.: the true inventor of the tank, 537n

Denmark: independence of, 1; Churchill's hope of winning to allied cause, 225–6, 228, 246; MAP 19

Derby, 17th Earl of (Edward George Villiers Stanley): appointed Director of Recruiting (5 Oct 1915), 558, 618, 752; supports Milner's appeal for compulsory military service (April 1916), 755; writes to Lloyd George to protest about Churchill (19 Aug 1916), 800–1; becomes Secretary of State for War (Dec 1916), 822

de Robeck, John Michael: second-in-command of British naval forces at Dardanelles, 254, 266; becomes Commander-in-Chief of naval forces at Dardanelles, 348; and the naval attack of 18 March 1915, 351–2, 354–7; urged not to appear to be suspending operations (20 March 1915), 358; opposes Hamilton's plan to move troops from Mudros to Egypt (20 March 1915), 360; and the decision to delay a second naval attack until at least 14 April 1915, 363–6; and Churchill's desire to influence to renew the attack, 367–70; Hamilton believes to be 'a very sound pusher', 371; Hamilton encourages to renew naval attack, 372–3; informs Admiralty (26 and 27 March 1915), that only a combined naval and military attack can lead to victory at the Dardanelles, 375–7, 379; reports (3 April 1915) on preparations for a combined attack, 382–3; Churchill advises on the problem of floating-mines (6 April 1915), 387; Churchill supports naval requirements of, 388; reports on his preparations against mines, 390; his plans to penetrate into the Sea of Marmara, 391; opposed to further delay at Dardanelles (10 April 1915), 392; will attack forts at the Narrows in conjunction with army, 393; completes plans for landing army on Gallipoli Peninsula, 397;

de Robeck, John Michael—continued
learns of Turkish shortage of ammunition (22 April 1915), 400–1; wants a dawn landing at Gallipoli, 402; reports to Churchill on Gallipoli landings, 406–7; said to be willing to try to penetrate to Sea of Marmara within two weeks of Gallipoli landings, 408; reports (29 April 1915) on military activity at Helles and Anzac, 412–13; contemplates the renewal of a purely naval attack on the Narrows, 417–18; Churchill informs of withdrawal of Queen Elizabeth from the Dardanelles (12 May 1915), 423; Fisher reluctant to allow him to take any further naval initiative (13 May (1915), 425–6, 428; informed (13 May 1915) that 'the moment for an independent naval attempt to force the narrows has passed', 429; Fisher agrees (14 May 1915) to send some reinforcements to, 435; Churchill decides (14 May 1915) to send two further submarines to, 536; Churchill's final telegram to (26 May 1915), 471; Churchill presses Balfour (29 May 1915) to send extra submarines to, 485; Dardanelles Committee decides (7 June 1915) to send reinforcements to, 494; and the use of Monitors (Sept 1915), 541–2; and the possibility of a renewed naval attack (Oct 1915), 548

Deterding, Henri Wilhelm August: Fisher advises Churchill to give him a knighthood, 16–17; on German preparations to invade Holland, 375

Dieppe (France): Clementine Churchill tries to devise scheme to meet her husband at (Jan 1916), 644

Dixmude (Belgium): Marine reconnaissance to, 56

Djavid, Mehmed: Churchill meets (1910), 189; proposes Anglo-Turkish Alliance (1911), 190; angered by seizure of Turkish ships (Aug 1914), 193; said to know that 'anything but neutrality means ruin', 198; argues

Djavid, Mehmed—*continued*
merits of neutrality and intervention, 213

Djemal, Ahmed: his day of glory, 191; Churchill's message to, 196; his reported pro-French leanings, 198; reported reluctant to see Turkey committed to Germany, 206; Churchill seeks to influence, 107–8; records fears of sudden attack by Entente powers, 212; argues merits of neutrality and intervention, 213; leads Turkish military forces against Suez Canal, 279

Dogger Bank: loss of three cruisers from patrol of, 85; naval action in, 261–2

Donald, Robert: 688, 703, 750

Doris (British light cruiser): at Alexandretta (18–22 Dec 1914), 222, 233n; report of action circulated to Cabinet (8 Feb 1915), 279; Churchill cites psychological effect of the exploits of, in defence of the Dardanelles operation, 813

Douai (France): Royal Naval Air Service reconnaissance over, 65; Marine Brigade units at, 73, 75; aircraft and armoured cars based on, 88; Churchill looks across plain of, 624–5; MAPS, 75, 88, 575

Douglas, Sir Charles Wittingham Horsley: receives orders from Kitchener, 34; Churchill asks to examine plan to seize Gallipoli Peninsula, 202

Douglas, James: publishes defence of Churchill's actions at Antwerp, 128; foresees Churchill–Beresford–Carson combination (Dec 1915), 590

Dover (Kent): Kitchener intercepted at, 28; anti-aircraft defence line starts at, 66; Churchill's train recalled to London while on way to (3 Oct 1914), 103; Churchill's train returns to, 105; Arthur Asquith telegraphs from, 112; Churchill returns to from Antwerp (6 Oct 1914), 120; Zeppelin drops bomb on (24 Dec 1914), 238–9; anti-Zeppelin force of sixty aeroplanes assembled between London and, 240; Fisher's reaction to report that British

Dover (Kent)—*continued*
merchant ships are afraid to leave, 338

Dover Strait: Fleet sails secretly through, 9; sealed against German ships, 34, 36

Dresden (German light cruiser): 156; at battle of Falkland Islands, 183–4; in hiding, 264

Drummond, James Eric: against keeping loss of *Audacious* secret, 142; his views on the ministerial crisis (Oct–Nov 1915), 560

Dublin: Easter uprising in (April 1916), 761

Dublin (British light cruiser): attempts to thwart escape of *Goeben*, 41

Duchy of Lancaster: Churchill appointed Chancellor of (May 1915), 468; Churchill handed seals of, 472; Churchill's first weeks at (May–June 1915), 482–5; Churchill frustrated at (Sept 1915), 530; Lloyd George suggested for (Nov 1915), 560; Churchill resigns from, 563; Edward Marsh seeks missing key of, 595

Dundee (Angus): Churchill's speech at (5 June 1915) defending his work as First Lord, 488–91

Dunkirk (France): Royal Naval Air Service base established at, 65, 67–9, 240; German threat to, 72; Churchill's first wartime visit to (10 Sept 1914), 72–3; Churchill's second wartime visit to (22 Sept 1914), 88–90; Churchill's third wartime visit to (26 Sept 1914), 92; Joffre asked to send troops to, 102; Royal Marines forced to return to, 103, 105; Churchill expected at (3 Oct 1914), 106; Royal Naval Division to be sent to Antwerp via, 107, 112; General Rawlinson on way to Antwerp from (5 Oct 1914), 114–15; British forces disembarking at (6 Oct 1914), 116; Churchill's visits to described as 'useless', 119; French fear of German advance to, 135; 'damnable' if Germans reach, 136; Churchill maintains air base at, 162; Churchill proposes to visit (17 Dec 1914), 164–5; MAPS, 75, 575

Durham: miners from, in Royal Naval Division, 500

Düsseldorf (Germany): British air raid on Zeppelin sheds at (22 Sept 1914), 89; second air raid on (9 Oct 1914), 122-3, 136, 146; Churchill refers to air raids on, 721, 764; MAP, 88

Eady, Griffin: negotiating with the Turks, 359

Eastchurch (Kent): Churchill learns to fly at (1912-14), 65; anti-aircraft flights based on, 66

Easter Island (Pacific Ocean): reached by von Spee, 156

East Hertfordshire: by-election at (10 March 1916), 733, 736

Ebenezer Farm: Battalion HQ when Churchill serving with Grenadier Guards (Nov-Dec 1915), 576, 579; MAP, 577

Eberhardt, Andrei Avgustovich: his instructions, 344

Edgar (British cruiser): at the Dardanelles, 686-7

Edwards, John Hugh: asks for details about escape of *Goeben* and *Breslau*, 170

Egypt: and defence of Suez Canal, 9; Kitchener anxious to return to, 12; number of Muslims in, 189n; fear of Turkish threat to (17 Aug 1914), 195; possibility of putting pressure on Turkey from, 200; Indian troops to be halted at to impress Turks, 205; imminent Turkish invasion reported (23 Oct 1914), 214; Cabinet expresses fears for (30 Oct 1914), 215; Margot Asquith not worried about Turkish threat to (5 Nov 1914), 219; Turkish threats renewed (end Nov 1914), 220, 222; danger to if Russia defeated, 233; Turkish attack towards (Feb 1915), 279; Asquith believes troops for Dardanelles force could be found in, 286; Kitchener says Australian and New Zealand troops no longer needed for defence of, 291-3; Churchill wants troops for Dardanelles assembled in, 300; troops being held ready in, 304;

Egypt—*continued*
Churchill on Britain's position in, 333; Hamilton leaves for Lemnos from, 392; Kitchener raises spectre of Muslim rising in, 423; Churchill wants troops from to reinforce Gallipoli offensive, 522; Kitchener sees danger to if Gallipoli evacuated (Oct 1915), 549; Kitchener sees danger to, if Gallipoli *not* evacuated (Dec 1915), 602; Churchill wants troops at used elsewhere (Jan-May 1916), 686, 692, 772; Churchill wants African troops trained in (May 1916), 772-3; MAPS, 235, 838

Ekersund (Norwegian fiord): possible British base, 21; MAP, 19

Elbe, River (Germany): British plan for raid up, 20; Churchill wants to control approaches of, 37, 52; Churchill fears submarines will sail from, 72; Dutch neutrality a barrier to control of, 98; Churchill's suggestion to send old battleships up (24 Oct 1914), 140; Churchill wishes to blockade German bases at mouth of, 180; MAPS, 19, 53

Elles, Hugh Jamieson: summons Churchill to St Omer (Jan 1916), 679n

Elliot, Sir Francis Edmund Hugh: reports Greeks not afraid of attack by Turkey, 205-6; reports Greek king in favour of joining the Allies, 316; passes on Churchill's appeal for Greek naval participation at Dardanelles, 316; reports Greek king's refusal to accept a pro-allied policy, 329; reports Greek reaction to Dardanelles bombardment, 335, 336; reports renewed Greek interest in giving military support at Gallipoli, 412

Elliot, Maxine: Churchill visits (7 Dec 1915), 600

Ellis, Charles Edward: Lloyd George describes as 'a first class 2nd rate man', 623

Emden (Germany): German fleet secure at, 140; Churchill wants British landing at, 244, 246; MAP, 842

Emden (German light cruiser): sinking merchant ships in Indian Ocean, 137,

Emden—continued
139, 143–4; the Russian light cruiser *Askold* among the ships searching for, 327n

Emmott, 1st Baron (Alfred Emmott): reports Churchill's Cabinet proposal of 26 Aug 1914, 57; strongly opposes Churchill being made Colonial Secretary, 460

Empty Spaces, The (Sarah Churchill): 120n

Enchantress (Admiralty yacht): Fisher joins Churchill on, 145

Enfield Lock (Middlesex): Churchill speaks at (18 Sept 1915), 534

Enos (Turkey): Birdwood wants troops landed between head of Gulf of Xeros and, 392; Churchill proposes despatch of Russian troops from Black Sea via Archangel to (May 1915), 428; Churchill wants as possible British base against Bulgaria (Oct 1915), 544; British military landing at proposed (Oct 1915), 553; MAPS, 545, 840

Enos–Midia line (Turkey): Churchill proposes inviting Bulgarians to advance to, 302, 307, 315; MAP, 840–1

Enver Pasha: Churchill attracted to (1909), 188; Churchill meets in London (1910), 189; his pro-German policy strengthened, 193; Churchill's personal appeals to, 194, 195–6; said to welcome increasing German influence, 198; his dominance over Turkish navy resented by Djemal, 206; refuses German request to close Dardanelles, 207; impressed by German power, 212; argues merits of neutrality and intervention, 213; Churchill hopes, will abandon German cause when British force Dardanelles, 249; said to want 'a fight to the bitter end', 395; appoints Liman von Sanders to command Turkish Fifth Army at Dardanelles (March 1915), 400n; admits (Jan 1916) that Turkey was on verge of defeat in March 1915, 693

Ephesus (Turkey): F. E. Smith favours landing at, 237; MAPS, 838, 842

Epirus (Albania): 230

Epoca: 116n

Erzerum (Turkey): Djemal Pasha records fears of Russian attack on, 212; battle of (1877), 317; MAP, 839

Esbjerg (Denmark): possible British base: 20, 21; MAP, 19

Esher, 2nd Viscount (Reginald Baliol Brett): informs Churchill of impact of his Guildhall remarks, 63; George V describes Churchill's 'monstrous' behaviour to, 87; Stamfordham informs of disagreement between Churchill and George V, 88; and Fisher's return to Admiralty, 154–5; reports Kitchener's words to Churchill about Dardanelles 'You get through! I will find the men', 288; Hankey tells of his scepticism of success at the Dardanelles without 'a biggish army' at hand, 331; describes attack on Dardanelles as 'the finest stroke of the war' (early March 1915), 345; informs Stamfordham of criticism of Churchill's visit to France (6–10 May 1915), 425; and Churchill's proposed visit to the Gallipoli Peninsula (mid-July 1915), 514; J. A. Spender writes to, about Churchill's resignation speech (Nov 1915), 569; at St Omer with Churchill (Dec 1915), 589–90; critical of Churchill accepting command of a Brigade, 608–9, 616; and Churchill's appeal for Fisher's return to the Admiralty (March 1916), 729

Essen (Germany): Churchill plans air raid against, 175; Churchill wants military advance from Dutch coast towards, 245; MAP, 53

Euphrates, River (Turkey): British control mouth of (Dec 1914), 222–3; proposed extension of British control over whole valley of, 509

Europe: Churchill describes Italy as the 'harlot' of, 426n

Evening News: 552n

Ewing, Sir James Alfred: in charge of Room 40 at Admiralty, 179

Exmouth (British battleship): to sail to Dardanelles (12 May 1915), 422, 423

Falaba (British steamship): torpedoed (28 March 1915), 463*n*

Falkland Islands, battle of: preparations for, 182, 262; von Spee defeated at, 183; Churchill elated by, 184; a personal triumph for Fisher, 185; releases British ships for service elsewhere, 250; Churchill sends Bonar Law documents concerning, 455; Churchill recounts victory of, 620

Fao (Turkey): Government of India land military force at (7 Nov 1914), 221; MAP, 839

Far East: British squadron reinforced, 8; British interests in, 42

Fayolle, Marie Emile: visited by Churchill on the western front, 598

Feilding, Geoffrey Percy Thynne: 573

Ferdinand, King of Bulgaria: reported to be upset by prospect of British victory at the Dardanelles (March 1915), 335; pro-German, 348

Fergusson, Charles: praises the improvement in Churchill's battalion, 646; Churchill obtains leave to return to England from, 759–60

Fermanagh (Irish county): boundary dispute of, 4

Festubert (France): battle at (9 May 1915), 523; MAP, 575

Fighting Line, The (Winston S. Churchill): penny pamphlet (published 13 July 1916), 776

First Fleet (Grand Fleet): at Spithead (19 July 1914), 3; sails through Dover Strait into North Sea (29 July 1914), 9; Jellicoe becomes Commander-in-Chief of (2 Aug 1914), 26; Churchill visits at Loch Ewe (17 Sept 1914), 81, 85

First Hundred Thousand, The (Ian Hay): 630*n*

Fisher, Cecil: 49

Fisher, John Arbuthnot, First Baron: arrives at Admiralty (30 July 1914), 13; favours Jellicoe to command First Fleet, 14; enthuses to Balfour about Churchill's courage, 16; gives Churchill advice and encouragement, 16–17;

Fisher, John Arbuthnot—*continued* and formation of Royal Naval Division, 49, 51; praises Churchill's military forecast of 1911, 64; critical of Churchill's 'Dunkirk Circus' and Admiralty 'sycophants', 137; Haldane advises Churchill to bring back to Admiralty, 144; Churchill's admiration for, 145; his return as First Sea Lord, 147–56, 157, 159; Kitchener suggests as First Lord, 166; at War Council (25 Nov 1914), 176; Asquith describes face of, 176*n*; receives copy of intercepted German naval telegrams, 179; wants vigorous coastal offensive towards Ostend, 180; urges importance of offensive naval action to War Council (1 Dec 1914), 181; and Battle of the Falkland Islands, 182–4; as First Sea Lord, 185–7; and plans for bombardment at Dardanelles, 215, 216, 220; wants Greece to attack Gallipoli, 221; Churchill urges need for Baltic offensive on (22 Dec 1914), 225; Hankey proposal for an attack on Turkey circulated to, 229; Churchill informs of plan for North Sea offensive (3 Jan 1915), 234; enthusiastic for attack on Dardanelles (3 Jan 1915), 234–6, and (4 Jan 1915), 237; threatens to resign (4 Jan 1915), 238–40; tells War Council of navy's readiness for a North Sea offensive (7 Jan 1915), 242; enthusiastic for massive troop landings in Holland (9 Jan 1915), 245; believes capture of Constantinople possible if Greek troops act in concert with British naval attack, 247; his part in the planning of the naval attack at the Dardanelles, 253–7, 266, 275; wants British troops landed in Holland (18 Jan 1915), 258; his growing unease about Dardanelles operation, 259–60, 262–5, 268–70; at War Council (28 Jan 1915), 270–3; wants greater French naval participation at Dardanelles, 276; approves Richmond's appeal for troops at Dardanelles (15 Feb 1915), 287;

Fisher, John Arbuthnot—*continued*
favours annexation of Lemnos, 299–300, 322; stresses need for victory at Dardanelles before arrival of Austrian submarines, 323; sceptical of victory at the Dardanelles (4 March 1915), 326; critical of Keyes' appointment as Chief of Staff at Dardanelles, 326; on need to prevent Germany building a fleet after the war, 334; approves (11 March 1915) pressing forward with the naval attack at the Dardanelles, 336–7; his reaction to reports of German submarines passing through Rumania and Bulgaria on way to Turkey, 338; and the problem of mines at the Dardanelles, 345; wants military co-operation, greater activity and greater speed at the Dardanelles (15 March 1915), 346; insists that the 'decisive theatre' remains in the North Sea and the Baltic (16 March 1915), 347–8; orders further battleships to the Dardanelles after the naval setback of 18 March 1915, 354; at War Council (19 March 1915), 355; learns of Turkish ammunition deficiencies, 357–8; learns of secret negotiations with Turkey, 358–9; wants greater French participation at Dardanelles, and British destroyers sent back to home waters (20 March 1915), 360; unwilling (23 March 1915) to agree to Churchill's proposal to insist upon an immediate renewed naval attack at Dardanelles, 364–70; worried about German ammunition on way to Turkey (end-March 1915), 371; discusses with Churchill (25 March 1915) plan for a British offensive in the North Sea, 373; and the danger of a German invasion of Holland, 375, 378–9; unwilling to send further reinforcements to de Robeck (2 April 1915), 382, 383; complains to Jellicoe about the Dardanelles (4 April 1915), 384–5; complains to Churchill about the Dardanelles (5 April 1915), 385–6; answers criticisms of 2nd, 3rd and 4th

Fisher, John Arbuthnot—*continued*
Sea Lords about the Dardanelles, 388; with Churchill, urges Kitchener to despatch 15-inch howitzer to Dardanelles (8 April 1915), 392; his growing opposition to further reinforcements for de Robeck (11–12 April 1915), 393–4; approves (20 April 1915) despatch of *Goliath* to Dardanelles, 397; Richmond describes as 'useless', 399; writes to Jellicoe (22 April 1915) on prospects of victory at the Dardanelles, 400; Churchill seeks to encourage (3 May 1915) about outcome of the Gallipoli battle, 411–12; declines to encourage rumours of his disagreements with Churchill, 413–14; opposed to further independent naval action at the Dardanelles (11 May 1915), 418–20; Churchill withdraws *Queen Elizabeth* from Dardanelles in attempt to placate (12 May 1915), 422–3; protests to Asquith about the Dardanelles (13 May 1915), 424; his criticism of the Dardanelles effective in preventing Churchill from allowing de Robeck to take any further naval initiative, 425–9; tells War Council (14 May 1915) he was against Dardanelles 'from the beginning', 431; Churchill protests to Asquith about (14 May 1915), 434; Churchill seeks compromise with, about Dardanelles reinforcements (14 May 1915), 435; his resignation (15 May 1915), 437–8; Churchill's appeal to (15 May 1915), 439–40; his refusal to remain as First Sea Lord, 441–4; his attempts to win Conservative support (15 May 1915), 444; Churchill informs his brother of the resignation of (18 May 1915), 451; sends Asquith six conditions under which he will 'guarantee the successful termination of the war' (19 May 1915), 452–3; informs Bonar Law (19 May 1915) of Churchill's offer of 'a seat in the Cabinet', 456; continues to refuse to serve under Balfour (22 May 1915), 467; leaves for Scotland (22

Fisher, John Arbuthnot—*continued*
May 1915), 467; 'does not return' (23 May 1915), 468; and the crisis of May 1915, 474–5, 483–4; appointed by Balfour (July 1915) as Chairman of the Board of Inventions and Research, 506–8; Churchill criticizes former lack of guidance and support given by (15 Nov 1915), 566–7; Churchill's resignation speech described as unfair to, 569; Garvin seeks to act as a mediator between Churchill and (Dec 1915), 621; Garvin wants alliance between Lloyd George, Churchill Carson and, 622; active in London as centre of an anti-Asquith movement (Jan–Feb 1916), 699–705, 708–13; and Churchill's demand for his return to the Admiralty, chapter 23, 716–36; Churchill asks his wife to keep in touch with, 739; no political advantage for Churchill in an alliance with (May 1916), 761; Churchill writes to 'destiny has not done with you yet' (10 May 1916), 762; Churchill writes to 'You must not be downhearted' (31 May 1916), 776; and Asquith's promised publication of Dardanelles documents (June 1916), 778–9, 783; and the preparation of evidence for the Dardanelles Commission (July–Aug 1916), 802–8; Churchill writes to about the premature use of the tank on the Somme (Sept 1916), 810

Fitzgerald, John Hamilton Brinsley: Sir J. French's emissary in London (May 1915), 430

FitzGerald, Oswald Arthur Gerald: 232, 313, 394, 410

Fiume (Austria–Hungary): Kitchener rules out landing at, 244

Flannery, Sir John Fortescue: criticizes Churchill's eighth wartime visit to France (12 May 1915), 424

Fleming, Valentine: sends Churchill description of western front (Nov 1914), 227–8; dines with Churchill at St Omer (2 Dec 1915), 593

Flushing (Holland): 374

Flying boats: Churchill purchases from the United States (Nov 1914), 66

Formidable (British battleship): torpedoed off Devon coast, 184–5; loss of impairs British naval margin, 268

Fosters, Messrs (of Lincoln): and the origin of the tank, 536–7

Foudre (French seaplane carrier): 257

Foule, Mathilde Désirée: a refugee from France, 648n

Four And A Half Years (Dr C. Addison): quoted, 797

Fox, Robert: recalls Churchill's attitude to discipline, 638; and to delousing, 640; and to artillery retaliation against the German trenches, 671

France: Churchill proposes alliance with in 1911, 1; and the crisis of July 1914, 2–3, 6–10, 12; the threat to her troopships, 17; Kitchener fears a German attack on, 21–2; and Britain's obligation to, 23–4; British naval co-operation with, 26, 29, 30, 31; Sir John French unwilling to co-operate further with army of, 59; Churchill's first wartime visit to (10 Sept 1914), 72–3; Churchill's second wartime visit to (16 Sept 1914), 80; Churchill's third wartime visit to (22 Sept 1914), 88, 89; Churchill's fourth wartime visit to (26 Sept 1914), 92; Churchill en route to, 103; Churchill's fifth wartime visit to (6 Dec 1914), 163; navy of has control of Mediterranean, 178; and war with Turkey, 216, 230; Churchill's sixth wartime visit to (29 Jan 1915), 277; Lloyd George does not wish to see in control of Palestine, 343; Churchill's seventh wartime visit to (16 March 1915), 348; Hankey recalls the need to defeat Turkey in order to prevent a collapse of morale in, 350; Churchill's eighth wartime visit to (5–10 May 1915), 414, 416–17, 418, 424–5; Churchill emphasizes weakness of (June 1915), 498; Kitchener's fears of a collapse of military morale in (Aug 1915), 523; Churchill leaves for

France—*continued*
service at the front in (Nov 1915), 571

Frankfurt (Germany): 146

Frankland, Thomas Hugh Colville: killed at Gallipoli landing, 404*n*

Franz Ferdinand, Archduke: assassinated (28 June 1914), 2, 4*n*, 188

Fraser, Lovat: wants Churchill to return to London from the trenches (Dec 1915), 618

French, Sir John Denton Pinkstone: reaches Amiens (14 Aug 1914), 47; reports fall of Namur, 54–5; learns of reinforcements, 57; quarrels with Kitchener, 59–62; sends Churchill account of battle of Marne, 71–2; Churchill visits at his HQ (16–17 Sept 1914), 80–1; naval guns proposed for, 90–1; Clementine Churchill worried by her husband's repeated visits to, 92; his reported orders to fire on German white flags, 94; 7th Division not to go to, 102; Churchill wishes to consult, 103; and defence of Antwerp, 109–10, 124; encourages Churchill after Antwerp, 133; Churchill explains plans for naval activity along German-held Channel coast to, 136; Churchill reports on invasion dispute with Kitchener to, 139; sends Oxfordshire Hussars into action, 160; takes Jack Churchill on to his HQ Staff, 161; dispute with Churchill about Royal Naval Air Service, 162; dispute with Churchill over armoured cars, 163; Churchill keeps informed of British Government policy, 164; Churchill's proposed visit to (Dec 1914), 164–7; his visit to London (20 Dec 1914), 167–8; Churchill tries to soothe, 169; favours sending troops to help Montenegro, 237; Churchill wants reinforcements for coastal offensive sent to (7 Jan 1915), 240–1; denies that German trench line cannot be broken, 243–4; Churchill explains his northern plans to, 246–7; at War Council (13 Jan 1915), 251, 252; Churchill writes to

French, Sir John—*continued*
after Dogger Bank action, 262; Churchill's visit to, at request of War Council (29 Jan 1915), 277; reported willing to send troops to help Serbia, 278; doubts whether British troops could fight well in Serbia, 281; Asquith believes Dardanelles troops can come from other forces than those of, 286; caught up in quarrel between Churchill and Kitchener over use of armoured cars on western front, 289–91; and the German threat to Holland (end-March 1915), 374; reluctant to send 15-inch howitzer to the Dardanelles, 391; Churchill's visit to (9 May 1915) criticized in the House of Commons, 424–5; angered by Asquith's claim that he had sufficient ammunition, 430; George V believes Churchill is intriguing with to remove Kitchener, 454; asks Churchill to visit him (Aug 1915), 530; Churchill suggests as Commander of the British forces against Turkey (Oct 1915), 543; asked to send troops to Gallipoli (Oct 1915), 554; and Churchill's arrival on the western front (Nov 1915), 572–4; Churchill stays at St Omer as guest of (1–18 Dec 1915), 588; and Churchill's proposed promotion to Brigadier-General, 596, 610–11, 612; soon likely to be dismissed (5 Dec 1915), 598; discusses Churchill's future military staff, 599; his own uncertain future, 601; decides to give Churchill command of a Brigade (9 Dec 1915), 605–6; removed from command of the British Expeditionary Force (Dec 1915), 609–617; Churchill sees 'a good deal of' (Aug 1916), 798; alleged to be part of a Lloyd George–Churchill–F. E. Smith intrigue against Sir Douglas Haig (Oct 1916), 811

Friedrichshafen (Germany): British air raid on (21 Nov 1914), 172–6, 721, 764; MAP, 173

Frimley (Surrey): internment camp for enemy aliens, 143

Fulton, Robert: recalls musical interlude on the western front, 659

Furse, William Thomas: commands Ninth Division (Jan 1916), 628, 635, 637, 646–7; visits Churchill's forward trenches (2 Feb 1916), 659; Churchill lunches with (6 Feb 1916), 661; wants 9th Division to take the initiative, 666; in favour of Churchill commanding a Brigade, 676; urges Churchill to take his place in Parliament as a critic of Asquith's war policies, 738–9, 743, 746; orders Churchill to return from Parliament to the trenches (April 1916), 758; urges Churchill to join Lloyd George and to break the 'futile Govt' (May 1916), 760

Gaba Tepe (Gallipoli Peninsula): 382; Hamilton decides on military landing at, 393; military landings to the north of, at Ari Burnu (25 April 1915), 402–4, 407, 408, 413; Churchill advocates (13 May 1915) semi-permanent landing stages at, 428; German submarine reported (21 May 1915) on way to attack British battleships at, 463; Triumph torpedoed off (25 May 1915), 471; MAP, 403

Galicia (Austria-Hungary): Russian defeat in, 431

Gallipoli (Turkey): Liman von Sanders sets up his headquarters in, 400n; MAPS, 235, 840

Gallipoli Peninsula: Admiral Limpus suggests (26 April 1914) 'cutting off and starving', 198; Churchill recalls belief in immediate seizure of (Nov 1914), 200–1, 231; Churchill instructs War Office to examine possibility of seizure of, 202–3; Greek troops considered essential for attack on, 204; Churchill contemplates use of Russian troops against, 205; Greeks believe they have sufficient forces to capture, 209; Churchill believes attack on, to be best means of defending Egypt, 220; Fisher wants Greeks to attack, 221; Asquith reports Churchill wants to

Gallipoli Peninsula—continued organize 'a heroic adventure' against, 223; Fisher wants 'Greeks to go for', 235; Kitchener favours attack on, 237, 244; and need for landing of troops at, 260; Churchill recalls his opposition to troop landings at, 274; Richmond describes 'inferior Turkish troops at' (9 Feb 1915), 279; possibility of troops designated for Salonika being sent to (15 Feb 1915), 288–9; Kitchener believes Australian and New Zealand troops 'sufficient at first' for attack on, 293; discussions at the Committee of Imperial Defence (28 Feb 1907) about possibility of an attack on, 294; Turkish communications too vulnerable to submarine attack, 295; War Council (19 Feb 1915) discusses political effects of occupation of, 296; Kitchener on probable Turkish evacuation of, 307; Churchill welcomes possibility of Greek military participation in attack on, 316; and territorial future of, 321–2; Churchill states that with naval action alone, Turks can be forced to evacuate, 325; Greek participation in attack on vetoed by Russia, 328–9; Sir H. Jackson urges (11 March 1915) need for military action on, in conjunction with naval attack, 336; Kitchener worried (13 March 1915) about Turkish military strength on, 341; Fisher wants troops despatched to 'both extremities' of (15 March 1915), 346; Churchill hopes to cut off, by ships at both sides of Bulair Isthmus, 368; de Robeck insists must be occupied by army before any naval attack could succeed, 376; Kitchener supervises plans for military landing on, 381; finally emerges as most favoured landing place, 392–3; military landings on (25 April 1915), 402–20. Churchill advocates (13 May 1915), linking Imbros with anti-submarine nets to, 428; Lloyd George sceptical (14 May 1915) of a British victory at, 432; War Council (14 May

Gallipoli Peninsula—*continued*
1915) discusses possible evacuation of, 432–3; Fisher intends transporting Hamilton's army to Haifa from, 452; Churchill suggests a submarine net 'around the top of', 471; Churchill memorandum (1 June 1915) on danger of prolonged fighting on, 486–7; Churchill's belief in the possibility of a decisive victory on, 489; British proposal for eventual Russian occupation of, 509; Churchill's proposed visit to (mid-July 1915), 510–14; and the renewed attack on (6–10 Aug 1915), 518–22; and the renewed attack on (21–28 Aug 1915), 524; Churchill's confidence in eventual victory at, 534, 546; Churchill sees use for tank on (23 Sept 1915), 538; Dardanelles Committee discusses possible evacuation of (11 Oct 1915), 549–51; Monro advocates evacuation of (31 Oct 1915), 562–3; Cabinet decides to evacuate (23 Nov 1915), 581; Churchill infuriated by idea of evacuation of (Dec 1915), 589; Churchill reflects (Dec 1915) on failure at, 597–8; Cabinet disagreement over evacuation of, 601–2; Churchill believes 'the tale has yet to be told to its conclusion' (15 Dec 1915), 610; evacuation of Helles (Jan 1916), 685–6; Asquith's proposed publication of documents concerning, 778; MAPS, 353, 403, 519, 840

Gardiner, Alfred George: publishes defence of Churchill's actions at Antwerp, 128; pre-war criticisms of Churchill, 132

Garvin, James Louis: an opponent of Churchill, 38; seeks commission for his son, 49; defends Churchill's actions at Antwerp, 127; Churchill describes his feelings after Antwerp to, 133; publishes defence of Churchill's wartime Admiralty administration (23 May 1915), 468–9; Churchill writes to about effect of his Dundee speech, 491; to dine with Lady Randolph Churchill (Nov 1915), 583; Churchill urges his

Garvin, James Louis—*continued*
wife to keep in touch with (Nov 1915), 587; Lady Randolph Churchill dines with (Nov 1915), 594; encouraged by Churchill to keep in touch with C. P. Scott (Dec 1915), 596, 605; Churchill sends survey of war situation to (8 Dec 1915), 604–5; sends Churchill a description of Lloyd George's position (20 Dec 1915), 618–19; Churchill talks to in London (end Dec 1915), 621; sees Lloyd George, Churchill, Carson and Fisher as a 'fighting quartette' (end Dec 1915), 621–2; Churchill asks his wife to keep in touch with (Jan 1916), 688; Fisher's attempt to return to the Admiralty supported by (Jan–Feb 1916), 700, 702–4, 708, 709, 731, 733, 736; and Churchill's criticisms of Asquith's war policies, 739, 741; and Churchill's return to London, 747, 749, 759; advises Fisher in preparation of evidence for the Dardanelles Commission (Sept 1916), 808

Garvin, Roland Gerard: commissioned, 49

Gas: Churchill advocates use of on Gallipoli Peninsula, 470

Gaulois (French battleship): badly damaged at the Dardanelles (18 March 1915), 353; refloated (20 March 1915), 360: MAP, 353

George V, King: at naval review (July 1914), 3; learns Asquith's view of European crisis, 4; Churchill informs, about naval measures, 10; and replacement of Callaghan by Jellicoe, 14–15; Asquith reports on Marine expedition to Ostend to, 56; does not like Churchill's 'rats in a hole' remark, 86–8; Asquith reports on Churchill's Antwerp visit to, 112–13; Asquith reports on fall of Antwerp to, 122, 131; and the replacement of Prince Louis as First Lord by Fisher, 148–54, 440, 441; Asquith reports on Turkish policy to, 211, 215, 219; Churchill informs, of Dogger Bank action, 261; Churchill

George V, King—*continued*
informs, of plan of attack on Dardanelles, 280–1; reviews Royal Naval Division at Blandford, 305–6; Churchill refuses to be influenced by wartime abstinence of, 384; informed (8 April 1915) of encouraging prospects at the Dardanelles, 391; Fisher ordered to return to his post in the name of (15 May 1915), 438; Fisher intimates to Bonar Law (15 May 1915) that he has had an audience with, i.e. resigned, 444; Asquith informs, of his belief that Fisher's mind 'is somewhat unhinged' (19 May 1915), 453; glad to 'get rid of Churchill' from Admiralty, 454; Churchill received in audience by (27 May 1915), 472; Asquith informs (7 June 1915), of decision to reinforce Hamilton's army at the Dardanelles, 494; Asquith informs (1 July 1915), of Cabinet discussion on Bulgaria, 506; and Churchill's proposed mission to the Gallipoli Peninsula (July 1915), 512; and the political crisis of December 1916, 820, 822

George Louis Victor Henry Sergius of Battenberg, Prince: 152–3

Gerard, James W.: and the release of Fisher's daughter from internment in Germany, 146*n*

German East Africa: War Council (10 March 1915) discusses territorial future of, 333

Germany: Churchill seeks naval agreement with, 1–2; and willingness to defend Austria against Russian attack, 6; British warning to, 7; and movement of British Fleet to North Sea, 9; intentions towards Belgium, 9–10; attitude to Austria, 21; declares war on Russia, 25; British ultimatum to, 30–1; Japan declares war on, 43; army of, advances through Belgium, 54; High Command disturbed by rumours of British troops at Ostend, 56; and Turkish policy (before 1914), 189; Churchill envisages Rumanian–Greek–Bulgarian–Serb attack on (22 Sept

Germany—*continued*
1914), 210; checks Russian advance at Tannenberg (26–30 Aug 1914), 224; Churchill resurrects plans for naval offensive against, 225, 228, 236; fear of Russia making a negotiated peace with, 260, 321; ready to strike at Serbia, 273, 278; Kitchener on the need to establish goodwill with, once the war is over, 333; War Council (10 March 1915) discusses war aims towards, 334; sends reinforcements to Turkey via Rumania (end March 1915), 371; said to be about to invade Holland (end March 1915), 373–5; Clementine Churchill insists that Churchill is one of the few Cabinet Ministers to possess 'the power, the imagination, the deadliness' to fight, 459; attacks Rumania (1 Sept 1916), 797

Gerrard, Eugene Louis: commands aircraft squadron in France, 67, 69; plans air raid on Zeppelin sheds inside Germany, 88–9

Ghent (Belgium): problem of refugees from, 97–8; difficulty of defending Antwerp from, 99; Belgian army said to be about to withdraw to, 106; British forces to be organized at, 118; French Marine Fusiliers not to proceed beyond, 121; Rawlinson to meet Belgians at, 122; MAP, 99

Gibb, Andrew Dewar: records 'mutinous spirit' at news of Churchill's command of 6th Royal Scots Fusiliers (Jan 1916), 630; and Churchill's first day as battalion commander, 631–2; persuades Churchill to give a correct infantry order, 632; critical of Churchill's attitude to discipline, 638; records Churchill's attack upon lice, 639; and Churchill's battalion route march, 642; and Churchill's attitude to the battalion Medical Officers, 655*n*; describes first week in trenches in battalion war diary, 656–7; records Churchill's 'dissertation on the laying of sandbags', 674; and Churchill's

Gibb, Andrew Dewar—*continued*
final days with the 6th Royal Scots
Fusiliers (May 1916), 760
Gibbon, Edward: 318
Gibraltar: Churchill offers French Admiralty facilities at, 31; Sir P. Scott
travels on *Queen Elizabeth* as far as, 253;
Admiral de Robeck at, 266
Gillespie, Mrs: protests to Churchill
about the 'scandal' of wounded men
being sent back to the trenches (June
1916), 776
Ginnell, Laurence: cries out in the House
of Commons 'What about the Dardan-
elles?' (9 May 1916), 762
Giornale d'Italia: war correspondent of, at
Antwerp, 115; Churchill's interview
with, on the minorities question, 202
Girouard, Sir Edouard Percy Cranwill:
sent by Kitchener to Antwerp, 103
Gladstone, William Ewart: and Turkish
atrocities, 188
Glasgow (British light cruiser): off South
America, 156–60, 182
Gloucester (British light cruiser): attempts
to thwart escape of *Goeben*, 41
Glyn, Ralph George Campbell: 516
Gneisenau (German cruiser); 156, 158,
182; sunk at battle of Falkland Islands,
183
Godalming (Surrey): and Hoe Farm,
493
Goeben (German battle cruiser): about to
leave Austrian port of Pola (30 July
1914), 17–18; refused coal at Brindisi
and Taranto, 26; followed by British
ships, 28; bombards Philippeville, 29;
Cabinet refuses Churchill's request to
fight before outbreak of war, 30;
Churchill anxious to learn fate of, 36;
escapes British search, 40–2; escape of
a cause for criticism of Churchill, 143,
159, 170, 177, 184; reaches Constantinople (10 Aug 1914), 193; sold to
Turks, 194–5; renamed *Jawuz Sultan
Selim*, 194n; Britain insists on German
crew leaving, 196; action against
Russia feared (26 Aug 1914), 198; expected to be ready to put to sea (2

Goeben—*continued*
Sept 1914), 199; Troubridge instructed (8 Sept 1914) to sink, 206;
'flagrant breach of neutrality' by,
207–8; Carden instructed (21 Sept
1914) to sink, 209; Turkish Government warned about (28 Oct 1914),
214; bombards Russian Black Sea
ports (29 Oct 1914), 215; defeat of
envisaged, 249, 252; Fisher willing to
offer two million pounds for (March
1915), 359; known to be in dilapidated
condition (Aug 1915), 525
Goliath (British battleship): needed at
Dardanelles, 397; sunk at Dardanelles
(12 May 1915), 425
Good Hope (British cruiser): sunk at battle
off Coronel (1 Nov 1914), 157–8, 182
Gordon, General Charles George (1833–
85): 327n
Gordon, Edward Ian Drumearn: to
command amalgamated 6/7 Royal
Scots Fusiliers, 758–9
Gosford, 4th Earl of (Archibald Brabazon Sparrow Acheson): shocked to
learn Churchill not yet a Brigadier
(Feb 1916), 676
Goulding, Sir Edward Alfred: urges
Churchill not to resign from Cabinet
(Oct 1915), 560; Churchill asks his
wife to keep in touch with (Jan 1916),
688; acts as an intermediary between
Churchill and Fisher (Feb 1916), 709;
Churchill seeks advice of (March
1916), 745; Northcliffe informs of his
hostile attitude to Churchill (April
1916), 751; Fisher and Garvin discuss
Dardanelles Commission evidence at
home of (Sept 1916), 808
Grand Fleet, *see* First Fleet
Granet, Edward John: suggests British
air raid on Friedrichshafen, 172
Grant Duff, Evelyn Mountstuart: wants
Britain to apologize for alleged violation of Swiss neutrality by naval
aviators, 174–5
Great Contemporaries (Winston S. Churchill): quoted, on sending of Fleet to
North Sea, 9; on Asquith's letters to

Great Contemporaries—continued
  Venetia Stanley, 21n; on Asquith's behaviour in the political crisis of May 1915, 479; on Balfour during the political crisis of December 1916, 822
Greece: naval rivalry with Turkey, 191; possible British ally against Turkey, 198, 210; possibility of action against Austria, 200; provision of troops to fight Turkey from, 201; Churchill sees 'brilliant but fleeting opportunity' for (31 Aug 1914), 202; troops from considered essential in Gallipoli landings, 203–4; Churchill wants pro-British policy towards, 208; Asquith expects (31 Oct 1914), to join Allies shortly, 216, 219; Fisher wants as Allies' military arm against Gallipoli, 221; lack of troops from, ends British discussions for seizing Gallipoli, 223; Lloyd George wants as ally against Austria, 229; importance of in British plans for the defeat of Turkey, 230, 235, 244, 249; little disposed to help Serbia, 273; Churchill believes could be persuaded to join Allies, 274; Austrian aim to overawe, 277; possibility of troops of to help Serbia, 281–2; Balfour on inducements to, 305; Churchill appeals for immediate naval help from (1 March 1915), 316; Kitchener wants Gallipoli Peninsula handed over to after the war, 321; Churchill wants military support from (4 March 1915), 325–6; Russians refuse to allow as an ally against Turkey, 328–9; Churchill angered by loss of assistance from, 335, 336; Fisher wants Britain to seize the Fleet of, 338; Churchill seeks in vain to overcome Russian veto on help from, 344–5; forced to buy wheat from the United States because of Turkish closure of the Straits, 350; will not get Smyrna after the war unless they join the Allies (April 1915), 383; and effect of the Gallipoli landings on, 412; and the Austrian attack on Serbia (Oct 1915), 549; MAPS, 235, 545, 838, 842
Greene, Conyngham: 42

Greene, Sir William Graham: 16; informs Foreign Office that Admiralty have ordered hostilities to begin against Turkey (31 Oct 1914), 216; learns from Foreign Office that Britain and Turkey are at war (5 Nov 1914), 219; opposed to appointment of Graeme Thomson as Director of Transports (Dec 1914), 298; advises Churchill to moderate criticisms of Kitchener in his Dardanelles evidence (Sept 1916), 807
Greenhill-Gardyne, Alan David: takes Churchill around front-line trenches (12 Feb 1916), 665
Grenadier Guards: Churchill serves with 2nd Battalion of on the western front (Nov–Dec 1915), 573–89, 605–8; Churchill expects to serve as a company officer with, 613
Grenfell, Francis: killed in action, 228n
Grenfell, Riversdale: killed in action, 228
Gretton, John: writes encouragingly to Churchill, 33
Grey, Sir Edward: and Churchill's proposed meeting with Tirpitz, 1–2; and the European crisis of July 1914, 3–4, 6–7, 18; attitude to France on eve of war, 24; at 10 Downing Street on 1 Aug 1914, 25; and military mobilization, 26; speech in House of Commons (3 Aug 1914), 27; and the *Goeben*, 29; policy towards Japan, 42–4; learns of Heligoland Bight action, 59; opposes bombing of military objectives in German towns, 91–2; mentioned, 95; and the defence of Antwerp, 96–108, 112, 116, 119, 121, 130; Asquith finds 'fussy & jumpy' in Cabinet (23 Oct 1914), 139–40; Churchill reports 'Fisher is already a Court Favourite' to, 153; and alleged violation of Swiss neutrality by naval aviators (21 Nov 1914), 173–6; at War Council (25 Nov 1915), 176; Asquith describes face of, 176n; sometimes told of intercepted German naval telegrams, 179; and pre-war Turkish policy, 189–90; and seizure of Turkish battleships, 191–2;

Grey, Sir Edward—*continued*

approves Churchill's appeal to Enver, 194–5; and German sailors on *Goeben* and *Breslau*, 197–8; sceptical of Buxton mission to Balkans, 201; asks Russians about possibility of joint allied action against Turkey, 205; Churchill clashes over Turkish policy with, 207–11; Buxton urges pro-Bulgarian policy on, 213; warns Turkish Government to observe neutrality (28 Oct 1914), 214; and coming of war with Turkey (29 Oct–5 Nov 1914), 215–221; Hankey's proposal for an attack on Turkey circulated to, 229; receives Russian appeal for demonstration against Turks, 232; difficulties of finding Balkan allies, 235; at War Council (7 Jan 1915), 242; favours Zeebrugge operation, 251; wants British naval action in Adriatic, 252, 255; and British command of naval forces at Dardanelles, 256–7, 266–7; believes victory at Dardanelles will determine attitude of all Balkan powers, 272; wants British troops sent to Salonika, 274; and means of shaking Turkish morale, 276; gives Churchill his opinion of Dardanelles operation, 277; gives lunch to Delcassé, 278; circulates War Council with Balkan telegrams, 280; sees secret telegram from Dardanelles, 286; at War Council (16 Feb 1915), 288; believes success at Dardanelles 'worth taking some risk' for, 293; says Christians at Constantinople will 'have to take their chance', 296; in dispute with Churchill over use of Lemnos, 298–300; emphasizes moral effect of gunfire on Turks, 303; supports Kitchener's view that troops are not needed to force the Dardanelles, 310; receives Churchill's list of conditions for the surrender of Turkey, 315; passes on to Greece Churchill's appeal for naval assistance at Dardanelles, 316; approached by Churchill about Turkish post-war settlement, 320; and the future of Constantinople, 320–1; op-

Grey, Sir Edward—*continued*

poses leaflet warfare, 322; pressed by Churchill about help from Greece, 325–6; pressed by Churchill to encourage Italian participation in the war, 327; asked by Churchill to hasten Russian military co-operation against the Turks, 328; warned by Churchill 'you must be bold and violent', 328–9; Asquith describes (7 March 1915), as 'tired out and hysterical', 330; his views on the post-war territorial settlement, 333–5; on 'possibility of bribery' of Balkan officials, 354; favours establishment of independent Arab States, 355; Churchill favours Balfour as Foreign Secretary during absence of, 361; Churchill protests to, about German ammunition for Turkey being allowed through Rumania, 371–2; and the threat of a German invasion of Holland, 374; receives news of dissension among Young Turks in Constantinople, 395; Churchill advises against responding to Greek offer of assistance (30 April 1915), 412; ill (May 1915), 414; Churchill and Lloyd George alleged (10 June 1915) to be seeking removal of, 454; Churchill seeks support from (19 May 1915), 456; remains Foreign Secretary, 469; ill (end-June 1915), 505; and Churchill's proposed visit to Gallipoli (mid-July 1915), 512, 513; critical of Sir Ian Hamilton, 522; critical of Carson's suggested peace terms with Turkey (19 Aug 1915), 523; opposes conscription (Aug 1915), 527; agrees (Sept 1915) to winter campaign at Gallipoli, 539; advocates evacuation of Gallipoli Peninsula (11 Oct 1915), 549; in favour of beginning hostilities against Bulgaria (14 Oct 1915), 553; writes to Churchill after his resignation (Nov 1915), 570; Mrs Churchill describes as 'terribly aged and worn-looking' (April 1916), 756; Lloyd George and Churchill critical of Balkan diplomacy of (Sept 1916), 797; allows Churchill to use the

Grey, Sir Edward—*continued*
Foreign Office printer for his Dardanelles evidence (Sept 1916), 806; Churchill critical of his evidence to the Dardanelles Commission (Oct 1916), 814

Grey, Spenser Douglas Adair: commands aircraft squadron in France, 67; leads bombing raid to Cologne (22 Sept 1914), 89; leads second raid (9 Oct 1914), 123–4, 136; and the possibility of Churchill commanding the forces in East Africa (Nov 1915), 565–6

Grigg, Edward William Macleay: Churchill in dugout with (21–22 Nov 1915), 579–80; Churchill lunching with (26 Nov 1915), 584; Churchill in front line with (28–30 Nov 1915), 588–9; Churchill spends evening with (12 Dec 1915), 607; Churchill writes to (6 Jan 1916), 680

Grigg, Mrs (Elizabeth Deas Thomson): 588

Grosvenor, Lord Hugh William: killed in action, 228

Guépratte, Emile-Paul-Aimable: the senior French officer at the Dardanelles, 351–3

Guest, Frederick Edward: sends Churchill account of battle of Marne, 71; tells Churchill of Ypres battle, 160; acts as link between Churchill and Sir J. French, 161–2, 167; Churchill tells of his desire for an army command, 180; dines at Admiralty House, 238; Churchill consults with Kitchener about his going to Dardanelles, 290; one of Sir J. French's emissaries in London (May 1915), 430; urges Churchill to leave the Government (July, Oct 1915), 551–2

Guildhall (London): Asquith, Bonar Law and Churchill speak at (4 Sept 1914), 62–3

Gulflight (American steamship): torpedoed (1 May 1915), 463n

Gwynn, Stephen Lucius: on Dardanelles Commission, 789

Gwynne, Howell Arthur: sends Churchill plan to destroy Zeppelins, 33; critical of Churchill's actions at Antwerp, 125–7; his criticisms rejected by other newspapers, 128; Press Bureau unwilling to censor his criticisms, 129; Asquith describes as a 'lunatic', 144; British loan to Turkey explained to, 191; advises Asquith (22 April 1915) to remove Churchill from Admiralty, 398–9; informed by Callwell of the May crisis (22 May 1915), 458–9; informed by Callwell of the conscription crisis (July 1915), 527–8; informed by Callwell why Asquith decided not to publish the Dardanelles documents (June 1916), 785; believes he has uncovered an intrigue against Sir Douglas Haig (Oct 1916), 811

Hadji-Mischef, Pantcho: Grey protests to, 372

Haifa (Turkey): Churchill suggests as point of attack, 220; Fisher suggests feint at, 234; Hankey critical that there was no feint at during Dardanelles attack, 345; Richmond wants landing of 80,000 British troops at, to replace Gallipoli landings, 389; Fisher intends to transport Hamilton's army from Gallipoli to, 452; MAPS, 235, 838

Haig, Sir Douglas: Churchill suggests as Chief of the Imperial General Staff (Oct 1915), 544; succeeds Sir John French as commander of the British Expeditionary Force (Dec 1915), 612–26, 618, 619; agrees to let Sir Archibald Sinclair join Churchill's battalion Staff (Jan 1916), 629; Churchill meets, on the road to St Omer (19 Jan 1916), 643; his HQ twenty-eight miles from the front line, 650; has no plans to give Churchill command of a Brigade (Feb 1916), 668; and F. E. Smith's arrest while visiting Churchill on the western front (Jan 1916), 696–7; and Churchill's appeal for Fisher's return to the Admiralty (March 1916), 729; does not

Haig, Sir Douglas—*continued*
   object to Churchill taking up his
   Parliamentary duties again (April
   1916), 757, 759; and Churchill's criticisms of the Somme offensive, 792;
   alleged intrigue against (Oct 1916),
   811–12
Hakewill Smith, Edmund: recalls widespread 'horror' at Churchill's impending command of the 6th Royal Scots
   Fusiliers, 629; and conditions in Ypres
   Salient (Nov 1915), 631; and Churchill's first day in command, 632; and
   Churchill's bomb-throwing, 634; and
   Churchill's excursions into no-man's-
   land, 658; and Churchill's painting
   efforts while on the western front,
   658–9; and Churchill's advocacy of a
   'trench digger', 672; and various incidents of F. E. Smith's visit to Churchill on the western front (29–30 Jan
   1916), 694–7; and Haig's advice to
   Churchill about returning to Parliament (April 1916), 759
Haking, Richard Cyril Byrne: summons
   Churchill from the front line (26 Nov
   1915), 584–5; Churchill might serve
   under, 606
Haldane, 1st Viscount (Richard Burdon
   Haldane): at 10 Downing Street (1
   Aug 1914), 25; and military mobilization, 26; sends Churchill congratulations on Heligoland Bight action, 59;
   enthusiastic about Churchill's military
   predictions, 64; praises Churchill on
   return from Antwerp, 121; urges
   Churchill not to resign from Admiralty, 133; Asquith describes as
   'fussy & jumpy' in Cabinet (23 Oct
   1914), 139; at War Council (7 Jan
   1915), 242; congratulates Churchill on
   Dogger Bank action, 261–2; at War
   Council (28 Jan 1915), 272; belief (28
   Feb 1907) that Gallipoli landing would
   be 'highly dangerous', 294; at War
   Council (24 Feb 1915), 301; approves
   giving Russia a privileged position at
   the Dardanelles in any post-war settlement, 321; reports to Churchill on

Haldane, 1st Viscount—*continued*
   Asquith's praise of his 'untiring
   energy', 330; favours post-war restrictions of armaments, 334; warns
   War Council (19 March 1915) against
   a punitive peace, 355; at War Council
   (14 May 1915), 433; at Violet Asquith's wedding (30 Nov 1915), 595;
   Garvin believes would join a Lloyd
   George–Churchill–Carson–Fisher alliance (Dec 1915), 622; intervenes
   with Churchill to prevent sacking of
   George Lambert, 775n; approves
   Churchill's *Sunday Pictorial* article on
   the coming of war (July 1916), 790
Hall, William Reginald: takes Churchill
   and Fisher message about Turkish
   ammunition deficiencies (19 March
   1915), 357–8; tells Churchill and
   Fisher about course of secret negotiations with Turkey, 358–9; passes on to
   Lord Reading a message from Sir
   Frederick Hamilton that both Fisher
   and Churchill should leave Admiralty
   (17 May 1915), 457, 458
Hamilton, Sir Frederick Tower: 47, 84;
   not on Admiralty War Group, 185;
   expresses doubts about the Dardanelles, 388; and the crisis of May 1915,
   441–2, 444, 448, 449; Fisher proposes
   dismissal of, from Admiralty Board,
   453; believes that both Fisher and
   Churchill should leave the Admiralty
   (17 May 1915), 457; a pioneer of
   the use of shields by infantrymen,
   591n
Hamilton, Sir Ian Standish Monteith:
   praises Churchill's military forecast of
   1911, 64; appointed to command
   Mediterranean Expeditionary Force,
   325; Churchill seeks to hasten departure of, to Dardanelles, 338–9;
   Churchill wants him to attack Turks
   on arrival, 340; leaves London, 341–2,
   343; on way to Dardanelles, 346–7;
   watches naval battle at the Dardanelles (18 March 1915), 352–4; War
   Office cannot help in devising plan to
   land on Gallipoli Peninsula, 355; re-

Hamilton, Sir Ian—*continued*
ports (19 March 1915) on need for a
'deliberate and progressive military
operation' at Dardanelles, 357; wishes
to move troops from Mudros to Egypt
(20 March 1915), 360; wishes to delay
naval attack until arrival of 29th
Division, 263, 264; considers de
Robeck 'a very sound pusher', 371;
encourages de Robeck (30 March
1915) to renew the naval attack, 372;
defends himself against accusation that
he had persuaded de Robeck not to
renew the naval attack, 373; unwilling
to send small parties of men ashore to
cover naval action at the Narrows,
376; de Robeck waits for return of,
from Egypt (end-March 1915), 377;
Fisher wonders whether he has sufficient troops to take Gallipoli Peninsula, 379; and preparations for a
combined attack, 382–3; returns to
Lemnos from Egypt, 392; decides (10
April 1915) on points of attack at
Gallipoli Peninsula, 393; completes
(20 April 1915) plans for Gallipoli
landing five days later, 397; asks
Rupert Brooke to join his Staff, 401;
rejects Birdwood's request to withdraw
from Anzac position on first day of
Gallipoli landings (25 April 1915),
407; Churchill's concern (26 April
1915) for the reinforcement of, 409–10;
believes he can reach his objectives
when attack is renewed, 411, 413;
launches new offensive at Helles (6
May 1915), 414; telegraphs to Kitchener 'the result has been failure' (9
May 1915), 415; to be asked what
force he needs 'to ensure success', 433;
Churchill sends telegram of encouragement to (11 May 1915), 437; opposes
use of gas on Gallipoli Peninsula, 470n;
his army to be reinforced (7 June
1915), 494; opposes landing at Bulair,
495; sends Churchill account of Gallipoli prospects (18 June 1915), 499–
500; informed by Churchill that he is
to receive reinforcements (7 July 1915),

Hamilton, Sir Ian—*continued*
508–9; and Churchill's proposed visit
to the Gallipoli Peninsula (mid-July
1915), 510; Churchill seeks to encourage to ask for more ammunition,
515; and the renewed attack on the
Gallipoli Peninsula (6–10 Aug 1915),
516–17, 518–22; and further attacks
(21–28 Aug 1915), 524; reinforcements to (Aug 1915), 525, 526, 546;
his recall from Gallipoli (Oct 1915),
553–4; and the Government's promised publication of Gallipoli documents (June 1916), 779–81, 783
Hamilton, Duchess of (Nina Mary
Benita Poore): and Fisher's preparation of evidence for the Dardanelles
Commission (Aug 1916), 803
Hammersley, Frederick: 'apathetic', 520;
to be replaced, 522
Hampshire (British cruiser): tracking
down *Emden* in Bay of Bengal (Sept
1914), 139; sinks, with Kitchener on
board (June 1915), 780
Hanbury-Williams, Sir John: reports
Turkish troops threatening Russia in
Caucasus (30 Dec 1914), 231–2
Hankey, Maurice Pascal Alers: opens
'War Book' (29 July 1914), 11; describes popular lack of enthusiasm for
war, 23; and defence of Antwerp, 124;
at War Council (25 Nov 1914) as
Secretary, 176, 220; at War Council
(1 Dec 1914), 180–1; suggests British
military action elsewhere than on
western front, 229–31, 234, 237; at
War Council (7 Jan 1915), 242;
explains to War Council importance of
victory at Dardanelles (8 Jan 1915),
244; at War Council (13 Jan 1915),
252; Fisher pours out criticisms of
Churchill to (19 Jan 1915), 259; Fisher
passes protest to Asquith through, 268;
at War Council (18 Jan 1915), 271;
tells Asquith Dardanelles attack needs
support of 'a fairly strong military
force' (13 Feb 1915), 286; approves
Richmond's appeal for use of army at
Dardanelles (14 Feb 1915), 287; com-

Hankey, Maurice Pascal Alers—*continued*
pares conditions for attack on Gallipoli of 1907 with new conditions of
1915, 294–5; wants troop action concentrated at Dardanelles, 301; at War
Council supports Churchill's plea for
use of troops at the Dardanelles (26
Feb 1915), 309; on impact of Dardanelles bombardments on the Near East
(1 March 1915), 316; his memorandum 'After the Dardanelles. The Next
Step' (1 March 1915), 318–19; records Lloyd George's criticisms of
Grey's Balkan diplomacy, 328; sceptical (9 March 1915) of naval success
at Dardanelles without 'a biggish
army' at hand, 331; reports Churchill's keenness that Sir Ian Hamilton
should attack Turks as soon as he
reaches the Dardanelles, 340; and the
problem of minesweeping at the Dardanelles, 345; highly critical of conduct
of operations at the Dardanelles (15
March 1915); recalls (1 Sept 1916)
economic arguments in favour of an
attack at the Dardanelles in March
1915, 349–50; finds Churchill 'very
depressed' about Dardanelles, 377;
suggests measures needed to challenge
a possible German invasion of Holland, 377–8; recalls (Aug 1916) positive effects of the naval attack of 18
March 1915, 379–80; warns (6 April
1915) of difficulty of landing troops on
the Gallipoli Peninsula, 386; reported
'very anxious about the Dardanelles'
(7 April 1915), 387–8; seeks to create
effective opposition against the Dardanelles, 389; secretary to Committee
to examine British territorial needs in
Turkey, 391; reports (19 April 1915)
that Churchill 'extremely optimistic'
about Dardanelles, 396; learns that
Fisher (20 April) is 'more depressed
than ever' about Dardanelles, 397;
and the Gallipoli landings (25 April
1915), 411; helps Fisher to draw up
reasons against a renewed naval
attack at the Dardanelles (11 May

Hankey, Maurice Pascal Alers—*continued*
1915), 419–20; advises Fisher on need
'to bring Churchill to his bearings' (12
May 1915), 421; encourages Fisher to
protest to Asquith (13 May 1915), 426;
Fisher protests about Churchill to (14
May 1915), 429; at War Council (14
May 1915), 431; angered by the
'bickering & intrigue' between Fisher
and Churchill, 434; believes 'Lord
Fisher madder than ever' (19 May
1915), 453, 805; on Churchill's offer to
Fisher of 'any terms he liked' (19 May
1915), 456; reports (20 May 1915) 'a
consensus of opinion' that both
Churchill and Fisher should leave the
Admiralty, 457; believes Masterton-
Smith 'still hankers after Churchill'
(21 May 1915), 468; Churchill writes
(2 June 1915) about the 'lost opportunities of the war' to, 488; not present
at first meeting of Dardanelles Committee (7 June 1915), 494; chosen by
Kitchener to accompany Churchill to
Gallipoli, 512; goes to Dardanelles by
himself, 515; at Suvla Bay (8 Aug
1915), 518, 521; reports (30 Aug 1915)
on hopes for success at Anzac, 525; and
the origin of the tank, 535, 810;
Churchill wants as Secretary to a
special committee to decide future of
Gallipoli (Oct 1915), 547; and the
ministerial attacks on Kitchener (Oct
1915), 556–7; suggests sending
Churchill on mission to Russia (22
Oct 1915), 560; reports Cabinet
unanimous that Kitchener should
leave War Office (1 Nov 1915), 562;
and speculation on Churchill's future
career (Nov 1915), 563; and effect of
Churchill's departure from the Cabinet, 581, 605; Fisher writes to about
anti-Asquith feeling (Jan 1916), 699–
701, 704; and Churchill's appeal for
Fisher's return to the Admiralty
(March 1916), 729, 731, 734; and the
proposed publication of Dardanelles
documents (June 1916), 778, 783–4;
and Churchill's criticisms (Aug 1916)

Hankey, Maurice Pascal Alers—*continued* of the Somme offensive, 792; and Churchill's evidence to the Dardanelles Commission, 802, 814

Harcourt, Lewis: wants to annex German East Africa as a centre for Indian emigrants, 333; wants acquisition of Turkish port of Marmarice, 334; suggests giving the Holy Places of Palestine as a mandate to the United States, 373; believes Fisher 'has triumphed' (18 May 1915), 452; Emmott implores Asquith not to replace as Colonial Secretary by Churchill, 460; seeks Duchy of Lancaster patronage, 484; hopes Churchill will not resign (Nov 1915), 560; a possible Viceroy of India (1916), 683

Hardinge of Penshurst, 1st Baron (Charles Hardinge): complains that Royal Navy is not doing enough to track down the *Emden*, 139; orders action against Turkey at head of Persian Gulf, 221; his successor as Viceroy of India discussed, 245–6; hopeful about attack on Dardanelles, 324; informed of territorial plans for the partition of Turkey, 334; on advantage to India of a British victory at the Dardanelles, 349

'Harlot of Europe', the: Churchill describes Italy as, 426n

Harmsworth, Harold Alfred Vyvian St George: died of wounds received in action in France (12 Feb 1918), 814n

Harmsworth, Leicester: votes against the Government in the Nigeria debate (Nov 1916), 815n

Harmsworth, Vere Sidney: killed in action in France (13 Nov 1916), 814n

Harper, (?)William: in armoured car skirmish near Cassel, 69

Hawke (British cruiser): torpedoed (15 Oct 1914), 184

Hawtrey, Ralph George: recalls a pre-1914 conversation between Churchill and Lloyd George, 475

Hay, Ian, *see* Beith, John Hay

Hazebrouck (France): 339; Churchill attends lectures at, 641, 642; Churchill entertains his officers at, 647; Churchill meets Lloyd George and Bonar Law at, 696–7; MAP, 631

Hearn, Gordon Risley: discusses trench-works with Churchill, 671

Heligoland (German island): possible British base, 19, 21; Sir Arthur Wilson plans attacks on, 153; MAP, 19

Heligoland Bight: Churchill plans means of reporting German movement in (9 Aug 1914), 38; British naval success in, 58, 62, 84, 88; Churchill wants to blockade 'day and night' (21 Dec 1914), 181; Churchill sees blockade of as preliminary to a Baltic offensive (29 Dec 1914), 226

Henderson, Arthur: becomes President of the Board of Education (May 1915), 470; and the War Policy Committee of the Cabinet (Aug 1915), 527; and the emergence of Lloyd George as Prime Minister (Dec 1916), 822

Henderson, Brodie Haldane: defeated in East Hertfordshire by-election (10 March 1916), 733

Henderson, Wilfred: commands a Brigade of the Royal Naval Division, 51

Hendon (Middlesex): air base at, 66, 240

Henley, Sylvia Laura: and the political crisis of May 1915, 479; Churchill first meets E. L. Spiers at home of, 597

Henri IV (French battleship): sent to Dardanelles to replace the *Bouvet*, 354

Hermes (British seaplane carrier): torpedoed (31 Oct 1914), 159

Hertslet, Sir Cecil: at Antwerp, 111

Herzog, Emile Salomon Wilhelm (André Maurois): and Churchill's delousing committee, 640; possibly the 'vy attentive and spruce' officer who foraged for mutton for Churchill, 655

Hesperian (British steamship): torpedoed (4 Sept 1915), 463n

Hetherington, Thomas Gerard: and the origin of the tank, 536, 538

Hill 60 (Gallipoli Peninsula): 524; MAP, 519

History: Churchill tells Sir John French 'we are on the stage of', 168; Churchill believes that the 'care and vigilance' of British Admirals will be found praiseworthy by, 285; and the Gallipoli landings, 410–508; Churchill on the harsh judgement of, 439, 517; Churchill on Britain's part on the stage of, 534; Churchill believes has no equal in the failures of 1915–16, 604; Sir John French steps 'swiftly' from the stage of, 616; Churchill believes the 'conception' of Gallipoli will be vindicated by, 636; Churchill's reliance upon the judgement of, 826

Hobhouse, Charles Edward Henry: reports (10 June 1915) on alleged intrigues of the previous month, 454, 477

Hoe Farm (Hascombe, near Godalming, Surrey): 493–4, 501–3, 512, 647

Hoffman, Hermann-Arthur: on Swiss opinion following alleged violation of Swiss neutrality by British aviators, 174

Hogge, James Myles: critical of provisions for Royal Naval Division, 169

Hogue (British cruiser): torpedoed (22 Sept 1914), 85; loss of a cause of criticism, 143, 184–5, 532

Holderness, Sir Thomas William: 391

Holland, Arthur Edward Aveling (Tom): at Churchill's battalion sports day (16 Jan 1916), 641; lectures on the battle of Loos (17 Jan 1916), 641; Churchill lunches with (23 Jan 1916), 646; dines with Churchill's battalion (23 Jan 1916), 647; visits Churchill's forward trenches (2 Feb 1916), 659; Churchill dines with at Nieppe (10 Feb 1916), 664; tells Clementine Churchill he hopes her husband may soon command a Brigade, 674; calls on Churchill at Soyer Farm (25 Feb 1916), 676

Holland: independence of, 1; Antwerp dependent upon goodwill of, 96–8; Royal Naval Division internees in, 125, 131, 170; Churchill wants as

Holland—continued
allied power, 244, 247, 252; Fisher wants 750,000 men landed in, 258; Churchill asserts Britain's 'proper line of strategy' is action through, 324; Fisher reminds Churchill of his plan for action in, 348; fears of a German invasion of (end-March 1915), 373–5, 377–9, 385; Churchill believes (Dec 1915) Britain should have landed troops in at beginning of war, 600

Home Rule (for Ireland): a certainty in July 1914, 3; Ulster to be excluded from, 6; Churchill alienates Conservatives by support of, 32; Churchill involved in dispute with Conservatives over (8–14 Sept 1914), 77–80; and Churchill's relations with the Conservatives in the political crisis of May 1915, 476

Home Rule (for the Jews): proposed in Palestine by Herbert Samuel, 343

Home Rule (for Poland): Sazonov dismissed by the Tsar for advocating, 280n

Hood, Horace Lambert Alexander: arranges Austrian Ambassador's departure from England, 45; accompanies Churchill to Dunkirk, 73; accompanies Churchill to Loch Ewe, 82; accompanies Churchill to Antwerp, 105, 107; in charge of naval operations against German-held Belgian coast, 135–6; mentioned, 153

Hood Battalion (Royal Naval Division): Clementine Churchill intervenes to provide proper medical facilities for, 306

Hook of Holland: 374

Hope, Herbert Willes Webley: sifts intercepted German naval messages, 179

Hopwood, Sir Francis John Stephens: Churchill outlines plans for defence of Antwerp to, 100; given garbled story of Churchill's mission to Antwerp, 119–20; Prince Louis talks of resignation to, at time of Antwerp, 145; Fisher tells of 'd—d fools' surrounding Churchill, 146; not a member of

Hopwood, Sir Francis—*continued*
Admiralty War Group, 186; advises Fisher to send Asquith his memorandum of dissent about the Dardanelles (12 May 1915), 421; Fisher seeks support of, 434; and the crisis of May 1915, 441; a possible Viceroy of India (1916), 683; and Churchill's advocacy of Fisher's return to the Admiralty (March 1916), 708–9

'Hornets': Churchill rebuked for describing Royal Naval Air Service pilots as, 765

Hoskins, Arthur Reginald: Churchill describes as 'a good sort of General', 644

Hospice, the (Ploegsteert, Belgium): Churchill's battalion headquarters, 648, 650, 652, 655–6, 662, 663, 674–5; F. E. Smith dines at, 694; F. E. Smith arrested at (30–31 Jan 1916), 695; MAP, 649

Hotel du Commerce (St Omer, France): F. E. Smith kept under arrest at (Jan 1916), 695

House of Commons: questions about defence preparations avoided in (Aug 1914), 11; Churchill defends his naval policy to (11 Nov 1914), 169–71; criticisms of Freidrichshafen air raid in, 173–4; adjourns (27 Nov 1914), 177; Bonar Law's criticisms of Admiralty use of merchant shipping, 282–4; Churchill warns against too much criticism of naval losses (15 Feb 1915), 285; Churchill's visits to France criticized in (12 May 1915), 424–5; Churchill's speeches in (15 Nov 1915), 566–8, (7 March 1916), 716–22, (8 March 1916), 728, (9 May 1916), 761–2, (17 May 1916), 763–9, (23 May 1916), 770–4, (31 May 1916), 775, (24 July 1916), 793–7, (16 Aug 1916), 799–800, (22 Aug 1916), 801–2

Houston, Robert Paterson: sends Clementine Churchill a ring, 40

Howard, Geoffrey William Algernon: 438

Howe, 4th Earl (Richard George Penn Curzon): commands a battalion in the Royal Naval Division, 49

Hozier, Lady Blanche (Lady Blanche Ogilvy): 781

Hozier, Nellie: and Churchill's departure for the trenches (Nov 1915), 571, 583–4; marries Bertram Romilly (Dec 1915), 595; *henceforth see* Romilly, Nellie

Hozier, William Ogilvy: at the Dardanelles, 548, 686–7

Hulderman, Bernhard: 5

Hulke, Frederick Backhouse: critical of the sending of recruits to Antwerp, 126–7

Humphreys, Henry: at the Dardanelles (Sept 1915), 542

Hungarian wheat: Lloyd George's plan to cut Germany off from, 243

Hunter, Sir Charles Roderick: critical of Churchill's imminent command of a Brigade (Dec 1915), 608, 613–14

Hunter-Weston, Aylmer: Churchill suggests as possible commander of Dardanelles troops, 301

Hurstmonceux Castle (Sussex): Churchill paints at (Aug 1916), 798–9

Hurt, Reginald: recalls two encounters with Churchill on the western front, 673–4

Imbros: Churchill proposes (13 May 1915) anti-submarine indicator nets to link Gallipoli Peninsula with, 428

Implacable (British battleship): ordered by Fisher to go to the Dardanelles, 343; on way to Dardanelles, 354, 358; at Gallipoli landings, 404; to leave Dardanelles, 422

Inchcape, 1st Baron (James Lyle Mackay): Fisher describes a resignation threat to, 155

Indefatigable (British battle cruiser): instructed to shadow *Goeben*, 28, 30; to go to Malta, 250; Fisher wants in home waters, 260, 269

India: transportation of troops from, 9, 37, 206; number of Muslims in, 189n; fear of Turkish threat to Muslims of, 195; Government of, lands force at head of Persian Gulf (7 Nov 1914), 221; Fisher wants troops from, to be

India—*continued*
landed in Turkey, 234; F. E. Smith wants troops from, to be landed in Turkey, 238; action against Turks on Suez Canal by troops from (Feb 1915), 279; probable effect of a British success at the Dardanelles on, 324; Montagu's fear of Churchill becoming Viceroy of, 330; will want some territorial compensation in return for her military efforts, 355; Asquith can find no support for Venetia Stanley's suggestion of sending Churchill as Viceroy to, 362; Kitchener said to want Viceroyalty of, 602; Churchill wants greater use of troops from (May 1916), 772–3, 794

India Office: Churchill alleges 'apathy and obstruction of' (July 1916), 794

Indian Ocean: Japan undertakes convoy duties in, 44n; German light cruiser *Emden* sinks merchant shipping in, 137

Indomitable (British battle cruiser): instructed to shadow *Goeben*, 28, 30; Admiral Kerr told to hoist his flag on, 204; ordered to join Admiral Carden at Dardanelles, 209

Inflexible (British battle cruiser): and battle of Falkland Islands, 182–4; to go to Dardanelles, 249n; Fisher wants in home waters, 250, 260, 269; a flagship of Rear-Admiral de Robeck, 266; being sent to Malta for alterations, 332; strikes a mine at the Dardanelles (18 March 1915), 352, 397n; disabled, 354; good progress made in repairs to, 360; thirty-three men killed on, 361n; Fisher wants, in North Sea in view of reported German threat to Holland, 375, 379; MAP (18 March 1915), 353

Inverness (Scotland): Churchill motors to Loch Ewe from (17 Sept 1914), 81

Invincible (British battle cruiser): and battle of Falkland Islands, 182–4

Ireland: and the European crisis of July 1914, 3–4; and the renewed Home Rule crisis (Sept 1914), 77–80; *Audacious* sunk off northern coast of (Oct 1914), 141

Iron Cross: reported to be offered as reward for Churchill's capture, 120

Iron Duke (British battleship): reaches North Sea, 13; Churchill receives pistols from armoury of, 82; Fisher praises senior officers of, 146

Irresistible (British battleship): to go to Dardanelles, 249n; at Dardanelles, 331; disabled in the naval battle (18 March 1915), 352, 397n; sinks, 353; most of her crew rescued, 361n, 371; Fisher upset by loss of, 379; MAP, 353

Isaiah: his description of battle, 71

Islington, 1st Baron (John Poynder Dickson-Poynder): a possible Viceroy of India (1916), 683

Ismid (Turkey): 326

Italy: and the war crisis (July 1914), 3; remains neutral (Aug 1914), 26, 30, 40, 42; and invasion of Libya (1911), 189; effect of possible territorial gains on neutrality of, 202, 243; Grey fears she might 'come out on the wrong side' (6 Sept 1914), 205; Asquith expects she might soon join Allies (31 Oct 1914), 216, 219; not willing to make a decision before the spring of 1915, 244; Asquith stresses importance of intervention of (27 Dec 1914), 225; Lloyd George suggests military arrangements be made against Turkey with, 229; slow evolution of Britain's alliance with, 252–3, 255, 316, 323, 327; forced to buy wheat from the United States because of Turkish closure of the Straits, 350; Cabinet discuss (23 March 1915) how to obtain immediate intervention of, 366; fears of effect on of a setback at the Dardanelles, 389, 394–5; Churchill in Paris for negotiations with (5–8 May 1915), 414; insists upon a British naval force in the Adriatic, 418; Fisher deprecates alliance with, 426; adherence to the Allies imminent (14 May 1915), 436–7; alliance expected within ten days (16 May 1915), 443

'Jack Johnsons' ('Coal Boxes'): Churchill sees exploding near Soissons, 81; seen by Jack Churchill at Gallipoli, 416

Jackson, Sir Henry Bradwardine: King suggests as possible First Sea Lord, 150; studies effect of bombardment of outer forts of the Dardanelles, 219; discusses with Churchill and Fisher best method of forcing Dardanelles, 220; in favour of systematic bombardment of Dardanelles, 238; member of Admiralty War Group, 250; and planning of naval attack at Dardanelles, 253, 255-7; argues need for a 'strong military force' to assist navy at Dardanelles (15 Feb 1915), 287; favours annexation of Lemnos, 324; his plan for attacking Bosphorus forts being sent to Admiral Carden, 327; urges (11 March 1915) immediate military support for the navy in Dardanelles attack, 336; advises annexation of Alexandretta, 349; supports Fisher's refusal to order de Robeck to make a second naval attack without military assistance, 365-7; on Committee to consider British territorial needs in Turkey, 391; with Churchill in Paris during Anglo-Italian negotiations (5-8 May 1915), 414; favoured by Admiralty officials as possible First Sea Lord, 457, 458; Churchill advises as First Sea Lord (21 May 1915), 466; succeeds Fisher as First Sea Lord, and concurs in submarine reinforcements to Dardanelles, 485; examines merits of western and Gallipoli fronts (Oct 1915), 548n; proposes bombardment of Bulgarian port (Oct 1915), 553; and Churchill's appeal for Fisher's return to the Admiralty in place of (March 1916), 724, 726-8

Jade River: Churchill wishes to block German bases at mouth of, 180

Jaffa (Turkey): Churchill proposes French naval command at, 267

Japan: Churchill eager to bring in as an ally, 42-4; naval help sent to Indian Ocean, 139; Churchill and Fisher seek

Japan—continued
naval assistance of, against von Spee, 157-8; navy of has effective command of Pacific, 178; Churchill wants naval force sent to Mediterranean by, 202; possibility of transit of Russian troops for Gallipoli Peninsula through, 205; Churchill wants rifles from, to arm 150,000 Russians (Oct 1915), 561

Jeffreys, George Darell: Churchill trains in Grenadier Guards' Battalion of (Nov-Dec 1915), 574-6, 578, 580; offers to make Churchill his second-in-command, 605; and Churchill's impending promotion to command a Brigade, 608; 'austere', 621

Jellicoe, Sir John Rushworth: becomes Commander-in-Chief of the First Fleet, 14, 16, 26, 39; Clementine Churchill's advice on, 15; Churchill informs of fall of Namur, 55-6; Fisher's prediction that he would become Commander-in-Chief in 1914, 64; provides Churchill with pistols, 82; wants to suppress news of sinking of *Audacious*, 141-2; Gwynne urges Asquith to put in Churchill's place as First Lord, 144; 'a splendid man of business', 145; Fisher urges Churchill to trust implicitly, 146; Fisher declares *'shoot the pessimists'* to, 154; Kitchener does not interfere with, 166; Asquith describes face of, 176n; ordered to send two battle cruisers to South America, 182; learns why it is not wise 'to terrorize Admirals for losing ships', 185; Fisher describes Admiralty War Group to, 186; ships to be used at Dardanelles of no value to, 220, 233; Churchill explains importance of North Sea offensive to (4 Jan 1915), 236 (11 Jan 1915), 247; Fisher protests about Dardanelles to (19 Jan 1915), 259, and (21 Jan 1915), 260; and Dogger Bank action, 261; Churchill declares his fleet unaffected by Dardanelles operation, 264; his protest to Fisher about diversion of ships to

Jellicoe, Sir John Rushworth—*continued*
Dardanelles, 269; Fisher expresses
doubts about Commodore Keyes to,
326; Churchill informs of object of
capture of Constantinople, 331; Fisher
complains about Dardanelles to (2
April 1915), 382, and again (4 April
1915), 384–5; Fisher informs of Kitchener's belief in success at the Dardanelles, 392; Fisher advises to protest
against aeroplanes going to Dardanelles, 397; Churchill praises Fisher's
patronage of, 442; instructed to prepare for a decisive naval battle (17
May 1915), 449; Fisher informs (22
May 1915) that 'Balfour is really more
to blame than Winston' about Dardanelles, 467; Churchill describes 'separation' from Fisher to, 483–4; and
Fisher's attempt to return to the Admiralty (Feb 1916), 701, 724, 729, 730,
731, 733; Churchill critical of his
actions at Jutland (June 1916),
777n
Jellicoe, Lady (Florence Gwendoline
Cayzer): 385n
Jerrold, Douglas: 50n
Jerusalem: Lloyd George does not wish
to see under French control, 343; MAP,
838
Joffre, Joseph Jacques Césaire: Sir John
French told to co-operate with, 60–1;
Sir J. French approves his strategy at
battle of Marne, 72; requests British
troops for Dunkirk garrison, 73, 74;
asked to provide help for defence of
Antwerp, 102; Kitchener and Grey
hold largely responsible for fall of
Antwerp, 124–5; appeals to British for
help in defence of Channel Ports (16
Oct 1914), 135; British seek support of,
for advance eastwards along Belgian
coast, 164; Kitchener asserts German
threat to, 304; and the danger of a
German invasion of Holland (end-
March 1915), 374; Kitchener wants to
urge early offensive upon (20 Aug
1915), 523; persuades Kitchener to
launch a British offensive on the

Joffre, Joseph Jacques Césaire—*continued*
western front in Sept 1915, 526–7;
asked to take over some of the British
line (Oct 1915), 554
Jowett, Benjamin: quoted, 438
Joynson-Hicks, William: urges Government to set up an Air Service (May
1916), 763; criticizes Churchill's use of
the word 'hornets', 765
Judas Iscariot: Clementine Churchill
sees Lloyd George as direct descendant
of, 623
Julius Caesar (Shakespeare): quoted, 736
Jutland, battle of: Churchill describes as
'a tremendous risk', 262; Churchill
drafts communiqué after, 777; Churchill criticizes Asquith for making no
reference to, 793

Karachi (British India): troops transported to France from, 37
Karlsrühe (German light cruiser):
believed in hiding in Caribbean, 264
Kattegat: Churchill plans sending Fleet
through, 52; MAPS, 19, 52
Kavalla (Greece): Fisher wants to ensure
Bulgarian support by encouragement
of aquisition of, 338, 382; Churchill
proposes as possible British base for
attack on Bulgaria, 544; MAPS, 545,
838
Kaye, Mary Forbes: Hamilton dictates
Gallipoli 'diary' to, 779
Keith-Falconer, Adrian: describes depar-
ture of Oxfordshire Hussars for France,
73
Kellaway, Frederick George: seeks to
uncover disagreement between Fisher
and Churchill, 413
Kelly, John Donald: and escape of
Goeben, 41
Kelly, William Archibald Howard:
Churchill praises audacity of, 41
Kemal, Mustafa: protests against too
pro-German a policy for Turkey
(1914), 212; commands Turks on Sari
Bair (Aug 1915), 520
Kemp, Laurence: Signal Officer at
Churchill's battalion headquarters,

Kemp, Laurence—*continued*
658; wounded (16 Feb 1916), 668; kisses nose-piece of shell that wounded him, 670

Kemmel (Belgium): Churchill visits Jack Seely near, 592; MAPS, 575, 631, 649

Kent (British cruiser): off South America, 182

Kephez Bay (Dardanelles): minefield, 369, 370, 377, 390; Fisher refuses to allow de Robeck to make an attack on (May 1915), 418–21, 428; Churchill claims new naval vessels capable of passing minefield at (Aug 1915), 525; the sweeping of mines in an 'incalculable factor' in the Dardanelles operation, 813; MAP, 353

Kerr, Mark Edward Frederic: discusses Greek co-operation in Gallipoli landings, 204, 208–9

Keyes, Roger John Brownlow: commands submarine flotilla, 36; welcomed by Clementine Churchill after Heligoland Bight action, 59; accompanies Churchill to Loch Ewe, 82; frustrated by Navy's passive rôle, 84; warns Churchill about 'live-bait squadron', 85; Fisher critical of, 326, 385; 'spoiling to have at it again' at Dardanelles (21 March 1915), 363; recognizes need for delay in renewing the naval attack, 365; believes that Hamilton influenced de Robeck not to renew naval attack, 373; opposed to further delay at Dardanelles (10 April 1915), 392; reported 'in the best of spirits' (11 April 1915), 393; goes ashore at Y beach (26 April 1915), 407; supports renewed naval attack on the Narrows (9 May 1915), 417; recalls General Monro's attitude to the fighting at Gallipoli, 563n

Khartoum: destruction of Mahdi's tomb at (1898), 327n

Kiel (Germany): British naval squadron at, 2; MAPS, 19, 53, 842

Kiel Canal (Germany): Admiralty plan to seize, 20; Churchill plans attack on,

Kiel Canal (Germany)—*continued*
38, 52; Germans safe behind lock-gates of, 140; Churchill resurrects plan to occupy (Dec 1914), 225–6, 246; Churchill wants it removed from German control once the war is over, 334; MAPS, 19, 53

Kilid Bahr (Gallipoli Peninsula): torpedo tubes at, 218; means of shaking morale of Turkish defenders at, 276; forts damaged at, 328; Kitchener worried about Turkish strength on plateau above, 341; Churchill anticipates need to occupy before ships could force the Narrows, 347; British ships ready to attempt the advance to (18 March 1915), 351; army preparing to attack, 368, 391, 393; hopes of eventual capture of, 429; Churchill wants army to advance to, 487, 494; MAPS, 353, 403

King's Royal Rifle Corps: possibility of Churchill commanding a battalion in (Dec 1915), 615

Kinsky, Charles: one of Churchill's Austrian friends, 45

Kitchener, 1st Earl (Horatio Herbert Kitchener): discusses European crisis with Churchill (28 July 1914), 9–10; further discussion with Churchill (29 July 1914), 11–12; lunches at Admiralty (31 July 1914), 21; intercepted at Dover (4 Aug 1914), 28; at Council of War (5 Aug 1914), 33; discussion with Churchill about Expeditionary Force, 34, 35; finds job for Duke of Marlborough, 36; Churchill thought to be edging over into his domain, 50; wants Royal Naval Division as eventual part of one of his new armies, 51; and fall of Namur, 53–5; approves sending Marine Brigade to Ostend, 56; reported not yet in favour of conscription (26 Aug 1914), 57; Clementine Churchill informs of Heligoland Bight action, 58–9; in dispute with Sir John French, 59–62, 162; asks Churchill to be responsible for aerial defence of Britain (3 Sept 1914), 65,

Kitchener, 1st Earl—*continued*

764; Asquith considers 'absolutely no use' in drafting reassuring Press communiqués, 71; decides to send Yeomanry regiment to Dunkirk, 73, 74; asks Churchill to visit Sir John French in France, 80–1; Churchill proposes use of naval guns to, 91; approves Churchill's fourth visit to France (26 Sept 1914), 92; and the defence of Antwerp, 96–8, 101, 103–10, 112–16, 118–19, 121–2, 124, 130, 131, 134; asks Churchill for naval action against German-held Belgian coast (Oct 1914), 135; fears imminent German invasion (Oct 1914), 137–8, 139; favours keeping loss of *Audacious* secret, 142; quarrel with Lloyd George over Welsh troops, 143; Fisher makes demands of, 155; sympathetic to Churchill after naval defeat off Coronel, 158; his quarrel with Sir John French soothed by Churchill (6 Dec 1914), 163; opposes Churchill's proposed sixth wartime visit to France (mid-Dec 1914), 164–7; his relations with Churchill, 168; his rôle at Antwerp explained to Parliament by Asquith, 169; Churchill suggests training of seventeen-year-old soldiers, 171; at War Council (25 Nov 1914), 176; Asquith describes face of, 176*n*; opposes taking initiative against Turkey (17 Aug 1914), 195; discusses Turkish situation with Churchill (31 Aug 1914), 202; Callwell reports on possibility of Gallipoli landing to (3 Sept 1914), 203; believes 'Turkey should be punished' (23 Sept 1914), 210–11; and coming of war with Turkey, 219, 221; says no troops can be spared to help Serbia (Dec 1914), 224; circulates report of Russian military weakness (end-Dec 1914), 225; Hankey's proposal for an attack on Turkey circulated to, 229; Russians appeal for demonstration against Turks, 232–3; says troops not available for attack on Turkey, 235, 238;

Kitchener, 1st Earl—*continued*

opposes scheme to advance along Belgian coast (Jan 1915), 241; says he can spare troops for landing on German island of Borkum (Jan 1915), 242; warns of German offensive on western front (8 Jan 1915), 243; Churchill sends Dardanelles plans to (12 Jan 1915), 250; and planning of Dardanelles attack, 256, 257, 260; and capture of Alexandretta, 267–8; and Turkish threat to Egypt, 270; believes naval attack on Dardanelles 'vitally important', 271–2; wants British cavalry sent to Serbia, 273–4; wants Churchill to inform Sir J. French that attack on Zeebrugge is to be abandoned, 275; and Dardanelles operation, 277; Churchill critical of, 278; wants best British troops to go to aid of Serbia, 281; believes British troops at Salonika will weaken Turkish morale at Dardanelles, 282; learns of setback at Dardanelles (10 Feb 1915), 286; agrees (16 Feb 1915) to send 29th Division for action at the Dardanelles, 288; quarrels with Churchill about armoured cars on the western front, 289–91; declares (19 Feb 1915) 29th Division not to go to Dardanelles, 291–3; on far-reaching effects of the occupation of Gallipoli Peninsula, 296; Churchill wants military commitment from (20 Feb 1915), 300; opposes sending 29th Division to Dardanelles (24 Feb 1915), 301–2, 304; asserts Anzac troops good enough for 'a cruise in the Sea of Marmora', 303; reiterates his belief that no troops are needed at Dardanelles (26 Feb 1915), 307–10; his influence and stature, 312–13; halts preparation of troop transports for Dardanelles, 313–14; obtains further delay in sending British troops to the Dardanelles (3 March 1915), 322; Churchill presses for a speedy concentration of troops at the Dardanelles (4 March 1915), 324–5; Churchill describes (1899) his

Kitchener, 1st Earl—*continued*
'wicked act' in destroying the Mahdi's tomb, 327*n*; Asquith's praise of (7 March 1915), 330; tells War Council (10 March 1915) that 29th Division *can* go to the Dardanelles 332; declares that Palestine 'would be of no value' to Britain, 333; wants Germany to pay 'an indemnity' when war is over, 334; and Sir Ian Hamilton's departure for the Dardanelles, 338–41; would rather annex Alexandretta than control Palestine, 344; Churchill appeals to, for immediate assembly of troops at Mudros (14 March 1915), 346–7; memorandum on the strategic advantages of the defeat of Turkey (16 March 1915), 349; Sir Ian Hamilton describes naval attack at Dardanelles to (18 March 1915), 353–4; tells War Council (19 March 1915) that War Office does not have enough information to have a Gallipoli landing, 355; Hamilton reports to (19 March 1915) on need for 'a deliberate and progressive military operation' at the Dardanelles, 357; reported 'not dissatisfied' with course of events at Dardanelles (22 March 1915), 360; supports Churchill's desire for a renewed naval attack at the Dardanelles, 366; willing to hasten return of troops from Egypt to the Gallipoli Peninsula, 368; still hopes for a victory by ships alone at the Dardanelles (end March 1915), 372; makes preparations for land operations on the Gallipoli Peninsula, 373, 377, 381, 386–7; and the threat of a German invasion of Holland, 374; in dispute with Churchill over munitions supplies (6–7 April 1915), 386–7; Churchill appeals to, to allow 15-inch howitzer to go from France to the Dardanelles, 391–2; deprecates (11 April 1915) delaying military attack on Gallipoli Peninsula, 395; Churchill's unsent letter to (26 April 1915) about Gallipoli reinforcements, 409–10; learns of failure of renewed

Kitchener, 1st Earl—*continued*
offensive at Helles (6–9 May 1915), 415; angry at decision to withdraw *Queen Elizabeth* from Dardanelles (12 May 1915), 423; explains importance of Dardanelles expedition to Sir G. Riddell (13 May 1915), 427; orders ammunition to go from France to Gallipoli, 431; fears a 'rising in the Moslem world' if Gallipoli abandoned, 432; Churchill reports to Asquith on 'unreasonable' mood of (14 May 1915), 434; George V believes Sir J. French and Churchill are intriguing to remove, 454; *Daily Mail* demands dismissal of (May 1915), 466; informs Churchill 'all seems cheerful' at Dardanelles (22 May 1915), 467; Churchill's last ministerial visitor at the Admiralty (25 May 1915), 469; remains Secretary of State for War, 469; Churchill presses to send gas helmets and canisters to Dardanelles, 470; Churchill reports 'vy friendly to the Dardanelles' (26 May 1915), 471; and the political crisis of May 1915, 474, 479; and the possibility of a Bulair landing, 495; Churchill presses to send more troops to Dardanelles (15 June 1915), 496–7; clashes with Churchill over Turkish ammunition (21 June 1915), 502; says war with Turkey will end once Gallipoli Peninsula captured, 508; agrees to send reinforcements to Gallipoli (5 July 1915), 508; suggests (mid-July 1915) that Churchill visit the Gallipoli Peninsula, 510; wants Hankey to accompany Churchill to Gallipoli Peninsula, 512–14; refuses to approve Churchill's telegram to Hankey about ammunition for Gallipoli, 515; and the Gallipoli offensives (August 1915), 522, 523, 524, 525, 526; and the Calais Conference (6–7 July 1915), 526–7; and conscription (Aug 1915), 527–9; Lloyd George, Churchill and Curzon critical of (Sept 1915), 531; and the future of the Gallipoli

Kitchener, 1st Earl—*continued*
offensive (Sept 1915), 539; Churchill advocates removal of, from War Office (4 Oct 1915), 543; Churchill believes is too busy to study future of Gallipoli (6 Oct 1915); opposes evacuation of Gallipoli (11 Oct 1915), 549; proposes a joint Anglo-Russian attack on Bulgaria (14 Oct 1915), 553; Churchill accuses of neglecting Dardanelles reinforcements, 554; concerted Ministerial attack on (Oct 1915), 556–60, 562; leaves London on Cabinet mission to Dardanelles (Nov 1915), 563; Lady Randolph sends Churchill news of (21 Nov 1915), 582; his precipitate return to London (30 Nov 1915), 589, 595, 601–3, 605; Churchill believes the hour of his exposure 'draws nearer', 608; Churchill sees himself as having to 'procure the dismissal' of, 611; argues against sending troops from Salonika to Dardanelles (Dec 1915), 617; 'purblind', 686; 'overlays the War Office', 691; Churchill seeks release from military duties from (March 1916), 730; Fisher wants Churchill to attack War Office administration of (March 1916), 732, 734; Mrs Churchill describes as 'thinner and sadder' (April 1916), 756; and the proposed publication of Dardanelles documents (June 1916), 779; drowned at sea (5 June 1916), 780; 'he was not going to answer', 780–1; 'the glory had departed', 783; Asquith acts as Secretary of State for War in succession to (6 June– 7 July 1916), 793; his rôle at the time of the Dardanelles the subject of a bitter dispute (Nov 1916), 817–19

Knox, Alfred William Fortescue: reports to War Office about Russian military situation, 224–5

Königen Luise (German minelayer): sunk, 38

Königsberg (German light cruiser): tracked down, 184*n*

Krithia (Gallipoli Peninsula): allied forces fail to capture, 415; MAPS, 403, 519

Kroell, T: 441

Kronprinz Wilhelm (German armoured cruiser): believed to be at large, 264

Kuchuk Chekmeje (Turkey): 249, 326; MAP, 841

Kühlmann, Richard von: his rumoured appointment as German Minister to Holland, 378

Kuleli-Burgas (Turkey): 249; Churchill suggests British military action against (Oct 1915), 544; MAPS, 545, 840

Kungsbacka fiord (Sweden): possible British base, 19, 21; MAP, 19

Kurna (Turkey): Turkish garrison surrenders (7 Dec 1914), 222; MAP, 839

Kut-el-Amara (Turkey): British victory at (Sept 1915), 590

Labour Party: and Conservative policy towards Ireland, 78

La Crèche (France): Churchill's battalion billeted in (24–26 Jan 1916), 647; MAP, 631

Laeso Channel (Denmark): possible British base, 19, 21; MAP, 19

La Fère-en-Tardenois (France): Sir John French's HQ visited by Churchill (16 Sept 1914), 80; MAP, 54

La Gorgue (France): 573, 574, 588; MAP, 575

Lambert, Cecil Foley: not on Admiralty War Group, 184–5; discusses possibility of Gallipoli landings with War Office representatives (1 Sept 1914), 203; expresses doubts about the Dardanelles, 388; opposes Fisher's resignation (16 May 1915), 444; Fisher proposes dismissal of from Admiralty Board (19 May 1915), 453

Lambert, George: not on Admiralty War Group, 186; brings Churchill's message of 'any terms he liked' to Fisher (19 May 1915), 456; and Fisher's attempt to return to the Admiralty (Jan–March 1916), 699– 701, 704, 714, 723; offers to support

Lambert, George—*continued*
Churchill in the House of Commons (May 1916), 774–5

Land Ship Committee (of the Admiralty): and the origin of the tank, 536–7

Lansdowne, 5th Marquess of (Lord Henry Charles Keith Petty-Fitzmaurice): his second son killed in action, 228; present at War Council (10 March 1915), 332–5; becomes Minister without Portfolio (May 1915), 470; at Dardanelles Committee (12 June 1915), 494; agrees on need to send reinforcements to Dardanelles (5 July 1915), 508; agrees (Sept 1915) to winter campaign at Gallipoli, 539; favours conscription (Oct 1915), 556; Churchill encourages not to resign from Cabinet (Nov 1915), 587; opposes Gallipoli evacuation, 601, 617; and the renewed conscription crisis (April 1916), 750

La Panne (Belgium): 599; MAP, 575

Lapeyrère, A. E. H. G. M. Boué de: 18

Larken, Frank: and British action at Alexandretta (18–22 Dec 1914), 222, 233n; his report circulated to the Cabinet (8 Feb 1915), 279

Larmor, Sir Joseph: learns Bonar Law's hostile opinion of Churchill's actions at Antwerp, 132

Latakia (Turkey): Churchill proposes French naval command at, 267

Laurence Farm (east of Ploegsteert, Belgium): Churchill's advanced battalion headquarters (27 Jan–2 May 1916), 652–4, 657–60, 665–73, 676–8, 692, 693, 702, 741, 754, 756, 759; MAP, 649

Laventie (France): Churchill in the front line near (Nov–Dec 1915), 577, 606, 608; MAP, 575

Lavery, Lady (Hazel Martyn): and Churchill's early painting experiments, 503, 582

Lavery, Sir John; 503, 582

Law, Andrew Bonar: approached about possible Coalition on eve of war, 12–

Law, Andrew Bonar—*continued*
13, 22; at Other Club meeting (6 Aug 1914), 35; seeks place for nephews in Royal Naval Division, 48; speaks at Guildhall, 62; praises Churchill's remarks at Guildhall, 63; critical of Churchill's actions at Antwerp, 132, 169; critical of Admiralty's use of merchant shipping, 282–4; present at War Council (10 March 1915), 332–5; Asquith describes as 'of fifth rate quality' (21 March 1915), 361; Sir J. French puts his grievances to (May 1915), 430; and the crisis of 15–17 May 1915, 444–7; Churchill's first appeal to (19 May 1915), 455–6; Churchill's second appeal to (20 May 1915), 461–3; unable to support Churchill's desire to remain at the Admiralty, 464–5; becomes Colonial Secretary, 470; and Conservative suspicions of Churchill in May 1915, 476; Churchill proposes Bulair landing to, 494; Churchill sees as a potential ally, 495; seeks Duchy of Lancaster patronage, 504; opposes Churchill's proposed visit to the Gallipoli Peninsula (mid-July 1915), 513; critical of Sir Ian Hamilton, 522; believes further attacks at Gallipoli will be 'a useless sacrifice' (19 Aug 1915), 523; agrees (Sept 1915) to winter campaign at Gallipoli, 539; pessimistic about the future at Gallipoli (Sept 1915), 539; wants act of war against Bulgaria (Oct 1915), 553; believes Gallipoli positions 'untenable' (5 Nov 1915), 563; member of the Cabinet War Committee (Nov 1915), 563; favours Churchill as commander of the British Forces in East Africa (Nov 1915), 565; speaks sympathetically after Churchill's resignation speech (15 Nov 1915), 568–9; Lady Randolph Churchill invites to dine, 582; Lady Randolph Churchill plans to dine with again, 594; demands immediate Gallipoli evacuation (Nov 1915), 601; his star 'much in the ascendant' (Dec 1915), 617; Churchill

Law, Andrew Bonar—*continued*
refers to, as a possible Prime Minister in succession to Asquith (Dec 1915), 622; Churchill urges his wife to keep in touch with (Jan 1916), 688; his 'growing prestige' (Jan 1916), 689, 691, 692; and the arrest of F. E. Smith while visiting Churchill on the western front (Jan 1916), 695–7; and Fisher's attempt to return to the Admiralty (Jan–Feb 1916), 700–1, 725; Churchill continues to urge his wife to keep in touch with (April 1916), 750; Churchill believes Bonar Law has 'his supreme chance now' (April 1916), 751; opposes Churchill in the House of Commons (17 May 1916), 768, 769–70; his sneers echoed by a lesser man, 774; announces Government intention to publish Dardanelles documents (1 June 1916), 778, 786; Churchill protests to Aitken about 'personal' criticisms of (Aug 1916), 800; Carson's Unionist War Committee critical of, 815; and the fall of Asquith (Oct–Dec 1916), 816–17, 819–23

League of Retired Officers' Cats: Clementine Churchill fears the formation of, 15

Le Havre (France): Sir John French urges defence of, 54–5; British aviators cross to, on way to Belfort, 172; MAP, 54

Leipzig (German light cruiser): 156–7

Le Matin: and the Marconi affair (1912), 623n

Lemnos: wanted as British base for Dardanelles operations, 281; War Council agrees to send 29th Division to, 288; dispute between Churchill and Grey over use of, 298–300; British troops being assembled at, 304; War Office do not want French division at, 314; Fisher wants Britain to annex, after the war, 322; Sir Henry Jackson favours annexation of, 324; Churchill tires to hasten Sir Ian Hamilton's departure for, 338, 342; Hamilton leaves Egypt for, 392; Commander Samson's armoured cars reach, 396; MAPS, 838, 840

Leslie, Leonie Blanche: one of her sons killed in action, 140

Leslie, Norman Jerome Beauchamp: killed in action, 140–1, 228

Leveson, Arthur Cavenagh: and British plans against Germany, 20

Liberal Party: and the coming of war, 9, 20, 23; and Home Rule, 77; and criticisms of Antwerp expedition, 169–70; rumours circulate in, of Churchill's intrigue with Repington to publicize the shell shortage of May 1915, 460; doubts about Churchill's loyalty and judgement in, 477–8; and the growing pressure for conscription (June 1915), 492

Liberal War Committee: 735, 746

Libya: Italian invasion of (1911), 189

Lice: Churchill's discourse on, 639; the attempt to eliminate, 640

Liége (Belgium): importance of German capture of, to British military thinking about Dardanelles, 295

Liérre (Belgium): Churchill motors to Marine HQ at, 115; Rawlinson joins Churchill on road to, 118; MAP, 99

Life of Lord Kitchener (Sir George Arthur): 817n

Lille (France): German armoured cars reported near, 68; Marine Brigade units at, 73; Marine Brigade moves to, 92, 93; French army decides to launch offensive in region of, 105; MAPS, 75, 99, 575, 649

Limpus, Arthur Henry: trains Turkish navy (1912–14), 188, 190; puts to sea (July 1914) to escort *Sultan Osman I* through Dardanelles, 191; on German influence at Constantinople (Aug 1914), 198, 206; Churchill brings mission of, to an end, 207; Churchill accepts Grey's veto on appointment of, to command at Dardanelles, 209; on Turkish naval officer's fears, 212; and installation of torpedo tubes at Kilid Bahr, 218; advises annexation of Lemnos (19 Feb 1915), 300n; writes to Churchill (7 June 1915) 'you are yet young & will be needed again', 482

Limoges (France): 648n

Lipsett, Louis James: and trench 'raids', 636–7; advises Churchill against precipitant return to London (March 1916), 745–6

Listening for the Drums (Sir Ian Hamilton): quoted, on Kitchener's death, 780–1

Littlejohns, Astle Scott: with armoured train at Antwerp, 100, 109

Liverpool: Churchill's speech at (21 Sept 1914), 84, 86

Llewellyn Smith, Sir Hubert: 391

Lloyd George, David: and the European crisis (July 1914), 3, 12; reports Bank of England attitude to the war, 23; Churchill seeks to influence (1 Aug 1914), 23–4; supports need for British intervention (3 Aug 1914), 27; recalls Churchill's mood on outbreak of war, 31; at Other Club meeting (6 Aug 1914), 35; Clementine Churchill uses Blenheim Palace notepaper in writing to, 36; Churchill seeks reassurance from, 55; his views on conscription reported (26 Aug 1914), 57; present at emergency meeting of Ministers (31 Aug 1914), 60; mentioned, 94–5; praises Churchill on return from Antwerp, 121; criticisms of Churchill's actions at Antwerp sent to, 127; speaks critically to Frances Stevenson of Churchill's actions at Antwerp 132; opposes keeping loss of *Audacious* secret, 142; quarrel with Kitchener over Welsh troops, 143; reports Churchill's desire for 'a flashy success', 159; attends War Council (25 Nov 1914), 176; wishes to unite Balkan states against Austria, 200; supports Buxton mission to Balkans, 201; believes bombardment of Dardanelles forts (3 Nov 1914) alerted Turks, 218; searches for alternate war zone to western front (1 Jan 1915), 228–9; Hankey's proposal for an attack on Turkey circulated to, 229; opposes further attacks on western front (Jan 1915), 241; appeals at War Council for attack on Austria (8 Jan 1915), 243; against Zeebrugge

Lloyd George, David—*continued*
attack, 251; 'liked idea' of attack on Dardanelles, 252; wants British force to join Bulgars in attack on Adrianople, 273; believes help to Serbia a paramount British interest, 274, 277; at War Council (16 Feb 1915), 288; tells War Council (19 Feb 1915) troops should be sent to the east, 293; wants British troops in Mesopotamia to go to Dardanelles, 301; asks about Army's rôle if Navy fails at the Dardanelles, 302; Churchill urges need for 115,000 troops at Dardanelles on, 306; appeals at War Council for despatch of 100,000 men to the east 'following close on the fall of the Dardanelles' (26 Feb 1915), 309; Churchill believes has 'more true insight & courage than anyone else' (26 Feb 1915), 311; opposed to Churchill's suggestion of hiring the Turks as mercenaries after the Turkish surrender, 323; wants Grey to take a Balkan initiative, 328; said to favour the imprisonment of men who would not engage in wartime work, 330; on Russian keenness for Constantinople, 332; prepared to give Alexandretta to France to avoid a quarrel, 333; favours Home Rule for the Jews in a British-controlled Palestine, 343; his hopes for an allied Balkan Federation, 349; at the War Council (19 March 1915), 354; opposes a punitive peace which would prevent Germany acting as a counterweight to Russia, 356; rebuts stories of an intrigue against Asquith, 361–2; Margot Asquith warns of Balfour's hostility, 372; quarrels with Churchill (5 April 1915), 383–4; Sir J. French puts his grievances to (May 1915), 430; sceptical (14 May 1915) of outcome of Gallipoli campaign, 432, 433; and Fisher's resignation (15 May 1915), 438–9, 443; his harsh words about Churchill and the war reported by Frances Stevenson (15 May 1915), 440; Bonar Law visits

Lloyd George, David—*continued*

at the Treasury (17 May 1915), 445; argues in favour of a Coalition (17 May 1915), 446, 447; suggests (17 May 1915) Churchill as Colonial Secretary, 448; Churchill does not believe suitable as Secretary of State for War (17 May 1915) 449; reports to Frances Stevenson Asquith's cynical observations about Churchill (18 May 1915), 451; alleged (10 June 1915) by Charles Hobhouse to be part of a plot to remove Kitchener and Grey, 454; Churchill seeks support from (18 May 1915) 456; his four-month opposition to Churchill's naval estimates (1913–14), 462; becomes Minister of Munitions, 470; and the political crisis of May 1915, 475–6; Churchill describes political activities of (12 June 1915), 495; wants Bulgaria as an ally (end June 1915), 505–6; urges need to send sufficient ammunition to Dardanelles (5 July 1915), 508; wants the French to send men and munitions to Dardanelles (Aug 1915), 526; examined by War Policy Committee of the Cabinet (16 Aug 1915), 527, 529; discusses conduct of war with Churchill (14 Sept 1915), 530–1; raises questions of withdrawing from Gallipoli (23 Sept 1915), 538–9; agrees (24 Sept 1915) to winter campaign at Gallipoli, 539; believed by Churchill to have 'forced on a coalition' in May 1915, 541; Churchill proposes as Secretary of State for War (4 Oct 1915), 543–4; and the possibility of Bulgaria as an ally, 544–5; Churchill wants decision about future of Gallipoli to be suggested by (Oct 1915), 547; pleads for British military help for Serbia (11 Oct 1915), 549–50; reported 'sick with Churchill' (11 Oct 1915), 551; opposes any further attack at Gallipoli (14 Oct 1915), 554; highly critical of Kitchener, 556–8; 'fatal' to make him Secretary of State for War (Nov 1915), 560; a member of the Cabinet War

Lloyd George, David—*continued*

Committee (Nov 1915), 563; writes to Churchill after his resignation (Nov 1915), 570; seems to Churchill like a mandarin 'of some remote province of China' (Nov 1915), 587; demands Gallipoli evacuation (Nov 1915), 601; Churchill foresees 'a system à la L.G.' (8 Dec 1915), 605; Garvin describes political position of (20 Dec 1915), 618; Churchill talks to, in London (end-Dec 1915), 621; Garvin wants alliance between Churchill, Fisher, Carson and, 622; Mrs Churchill describes as 'the direct descendant of Judas Iscariot', 623; Churchill believes 'we can work together if occasion arises', 627; and the conscription crisis (Dec 1915), 679; Churchill and his wife disagree over (Jan 1916), 680, 681, 682–3, 691, 698; his political position (Jan 1916), 685, 689; Mrs Churchill lunches with (24 Jan 1916), 690–1; to visit Churchill in France, 692, 693, 694; present after the arrest of F. E. Smith on the western front (31 Jan 1916), 695–7; opens Mrs Churchill's Ponders End canteen (3 Feb 1916), 698–9; Fisher compares Churchill's 'courage' with, 701; his growing discontent with Asquith's leadership (Jan–Feb 1916), 703–5; 722, 723; his attitude to Churchill's appeal for Fisher's return to the Admiralty (March 1916), 725; Churchill urges both his wife and F. E. Smith to keep in touch with (April 1916), 750–1; Churchill writes 'the moment for you to act has come' (10 April 1916), 752; Churchill urges C. P. Scott to see (10 April 1916), 753; critical of Asquith and Balfour (13 April 1916), 755; C. P. Scott sees as a leader of 'a real opposition' to Asquith (16 April 1916), 756–7; has no need of Churchill's support (April 1916), 759, 761; succeeds Kitchener at the War Office (July 1916), 781, 785, 793; Churchill hopes to succeed at

Lloyd George, David—*continued*
Ministry of Munitions, 782–3; proposes secret committee of House of Commons to inquire into Dardanelles operation, 786–7; believed to be behind criticisms of the Somme offensive, 792; Churchill addresses his criticisms of the War Office to (24 July 1916), 794–8; Churchill gets help from in preparing evidence for the Dardanelles Commission (Aug 1916), 805; and the 'tank' 809–11; alleged to be part of an intrigue against Sir Douglas Haig (Oct 1916), 811; and the fall of Asquith (Oct–Dec 1916), 816, 817, 819–21; becomes Prime Minister (6 Dec 1916), 822; his changing attitude towards Churchill, 825

Loch Ewe (Scotland): Churchill visits Grand Fleet at (17 Sept 1914), 81–2

Locker-Lampson, Oliver Stillingfleet: 531

London: Churchill responsible for aerial defence of, 66; Fisher fears 'terrible massacre' in, 239; Churchill outlines air defence plans for (7 Jan 1915), 240

London (British battleship): ordered by Fisher to the Dardanelles (19 March 1915), 354, 358; to leave Dardanelles (12 May 1915), 422

London Support Farm (Ploegsteert, Belgium): 27th Brigade headquarters, 650; Churchill temporarily in command at, 661–2; MAP, 649

London Opera House: Churchill speaks at (11 Sept 1914), 75–7, 80

Long, Walter Hume: writes encouragingly to Churchill (Aug 1914), 32; critical of Churchill's actions at Antwerp, 127, 180; Churchill sends defence of his naval policy to, 159; becomes President of the Local Government Board (May 1915), 470; and Churchill's Irish policies, 476; favours conscription (Oct 1915), 556; Churchill criticizes his support for the Special Register Bill (Aug 1916), 799; Colonial Secretary (Dec 1916), 822; vetoes Churchill's inclusion in Lloyd George's Cabinet (7 Dec 1916), 823

Loos (France), battle of (September 1915): 539; Churchill compares losses at with Dardanelles, 540–1; heavy losses of the 6th Royal Scots Fusiliers at, 628, 631, 633, 637; Churchill attends lecture on, 641; the line at Ploegsteert compared with, 648, 652; Churchill learns more of, from General Tudor (Feb 1916), 662; Churchill urges Parliament not to have a repetition of (May 1916), 774; MAP, 575

Lord Nelson (British battleship): to go to Dardanelles, 249n, 266; at Dardanelles but needing repair, 379; Churchill rejects Fisher's attempt to impose restrictions on de Robeck's use of, 388; Fisher recalls that despatch of, to Dardanelles was his own idea, 394; bombards Chanak, 412; MAP (18 March 1915), 353

Lord Warden Hotel (Dover, Kent): 676

Louis Francis Albert Victor Nicholas of Battenberg, Prince: 153

Louis, Prince, *see* Battenberg, Prince Louis Alexander of

Lowther, Claude: Churchill paints at home of (Aug 1916), 798

Lowther, James William: 681

Loxley, Arthur Noel: seeks to avert triple tragedy, 185

Lumley and Lumley: Churchill's solicitors, 511

Lusitania (British passenger liner): torpedoed (7 May 1915), 463n

Lutyens, Edwin Landseer: 493

Lutzen (Saxony) battle of (1813): 171

Luxembourg: German invasion of, 26

Lyceum Club (London): talk by G. Calza Bedolo to, 115

Lyttelton, Sir Neville: signs study of joint military and naval attack on Dardanelles (19 Dec 1906), 294n

McCracken, Frederick William Nicholas: Churchill's battalion inspected by (7 May 1916), 760

McDavid, Jock: recalls nature of the 6th Royal Scots Fusiliers reserve area,

McDavid, Jock—*continued*
630–1; recalls the impression Churchill formed on reaching his battalion, 633; recalls Churchill's approach to those under his command, 635; recalls Churchill's attitude to discipline, 637–8; and Churchill's delousing efforts, 640; and Churchill's 'pep talk' to his officers when reaching the trenches, 651–2; and Churchill's first excursion into no-man's-land, 657–8; wounded (3 Feb 1916), 659–60; calls on Mrs Churchill in London (7 Feb 1916), 663; Mrs Churchill dines with (14 Feb 1916), 669; in hospital, 670; recalls Churchill's concern for a trench-crossing vehicle, 672–3

Macedonia: 213, 382

MacCallum Scott, Alexander: and Churchill's preparation of evidence for the Dardanelles Commission (Aug 1916), 805

McKee, Mrs Thomas: appeals to Churchill on behalf of her husband (May 1916), 777

McKenna, Mrs (Pamela Jekyll): Fisher expresses criticisms of Churchill to, 137; Fisher expresses criticisms of Prince Louis to, 148; Mrs Churchill lunches with, 693

McKenna, Reginald: present at emergency meeting of Ministers (31 Aug 1914), 60; receives criticisms of Churchill's actions at Antwerp, 127; his naval estimates opposed by Churchill (1909), 179; Asquith's praise of, 330; at War Council (10 March 1915), 333; reports to Asquith on alleged intrigue by Lloyd George and others, 362–3, 477; Fisher regards as an ally, 429, 434; Fisher appeals to (16 May 1915), 441–2; unenthusiastic about Fisher's resignation, 443; helps Hankey to get Fisher away to Scotland (22 May 1915), 467; becomes Chancellor of the Exchequer, 469; seen as an ally for Asquith against a Lloyd George–Curzon–Churchill plot (Oct 1915), 557; a member of the Cabinet

McKenna, Reginald—*continued*
War Committee (Nov 1915), 563; seems to Churchill like a mandarin 'of some remote province of China, (Nov 1915), 587; against Conscription (Dec 1915), 622–3; a possible Viceroy of India (1916), 683; 'enthroned' by Lloyd George at the Treasury, 691; Mrs Churchill reports on 'tepid counter-jumping calculation' of, 693; 'a most noxious creature', 694; and the belief in a Churchill intrigue with Sir John French, 702; and Churchill's appeal for Fisher's return to the Admiralty (March 1916), 732–3

Maclay, Ebenezer: killed in action in France (1918), 283n

Maclay, Sir Joseph Paton: 283

Maclay, William Strang: died of wounds at Gallipoli (1915), 283n

Maclean, Allan: reports German naval victory off Coronel, 158

Macnamara, Thomas James: Fisher insists on dismissal of, 452

Macready, Cecil Frederick Nevil: and the arrest of F. E. Smith while visiting Churchill on the western front (Jan 1916), 696

Madras (India): German light cruiser *Emden* bombards oil tanks at, 137n, 139

Maestricht Appendix (Holland): Churchill expects his aviators will fly across, 175

Magdeburg (German light cruiser): runs aground in Gulf of Finland, 179

Mahdi, the: destruction of his tomb (1898), 327n

Mahon, Bryan Thomas: and the Suvla Bay landings (Aug 1915), 522; commands British troops at Salonika (Oct 1915), 558n

Maidos (Gallipoli Peninsula): British seaplanes to attack, 369; Hamilton decides to land across the Peninsula from, 393; set on fire by British shells (April 1915), 412; Churchill wants renewed attack towards (Sept 1915), 540; MAPS, 403, 519

Mainz (German light cruiser): sunk in Heligoland Bight action (28 Aug 1914), 59

Maison 1875 (Ploegsteert, Belgium): company billets at, 650; shelled, 660: MAP, 649

Majestic (British battleship): to go to Dardanelles, 249n; at Dardanelles, 331, 361n; sunk (27 May 1915), 472; MAP (18 March 1915), 353

Mallet, Louis du Pan: takes Churchill's message to Enver, 195; informs Churchill of movement of German sailors, 197; sends Cunliffe-Owen's report to London (27 Aug 1914), 199; Churchill protests about attitude to Turkey of, 207–8, 210; instructed to protest against German influence in Constantinople, 211; believes war with Turkey could still be avoided (31 Oct 1914), 216

Malta: Churchill meets Kitchener at (1912), 12; Admiral Milne instructed to remain near, 26; Churchill gives French Admiralty facilities at, 31; Mallet wants Limpus to be sent to, 207; Churchill wants troop transports assembled at, 220; *Indefatigable* to go to, 250; Dardanelles fleet to be fitted with mine-bumpers at, 254, 256, 428; Asquith believes troops for Dardanelles could be found at, 286; Royal Naval Division to collect medical supplies at, 306; anti-mine nets sent to Dardanelles from, 390; four British battleships to leave Dardanelles for, 422; Churchill proposes (16 May 1915) sending as many ships as possible from the Dardanelles to, 443; Churchill wants Gallipoli Peninsula troop reinforcements assembled at (June 1915), 497

Malta Conference (1912): Churchill impressed by Kitchener at, 12

Manchester Guardian: praises Churchill for troop transportation, 37; for frankness, 38; for his London Opera House speech (11 Sept 1914), 76; for his Liverpool speech (21 Sept 1914), 84–5; its editor hears Churchill and Lloyd

Manchester Guardian—continued
George criticize further offensives on the western front (Sept 1915), 541; welcomed by Churchill as an ally (Dec 1915), 596; supports Churchill's appeal for Fisher's return to the Admiralty (March 1916), 722, 732; said to be the only paper to report Churchill's parliamentary speeches (Nov 1916), 816

Marconi affair (1912): Lloyd George's 'failure' in, 495; Churchill's belief that Lloyd George owed him a debt as a result of, 623n, 751

Marine Brigade: to form part of Royal Naval Division, 47, 51; sent by Churchill to Ostend, 56; sent by Churchill to Dunkirk, 73; bus drivers enlist in, 74

Marix, Reginald Lennox George: at Dunkirk air base, 68; on bombing raid from Antwerp to Cologne (22 Sept 1914), 89; on raid from Antwerp to Düsseldorf (9 Oct 1914), 123, 136

Markham, Sir Arthur Basil: supports Churchill's criticisms of Asquith (March 1916), 711, 713; a member of the Liberal War Committee, 735n; urges Churchill's return from the trenches to Parliament (April 1916), 749–50

Marlborough, 1st Duke of, *see* Churchill, John

Marlborough, 9th Duke of (Charles Richard John Spencer-Churchill): reconciliation with Churchill, 35–6; Colonel-in-Chief, Oxfordshire Hussars, 73; acts as War Office messenger, 339; and the crisis of May 1915, 468, 476; informs Churchill of Admiralty complacency (Feb 1916), 702

Marlborough, 10th Duke of, *see* Blandford, Marquis of

Marlowe, Thomas: 126

Marmara, Sea of: *Goeben* in, 193; Limpus suggest sending torpedo craft into, 198; Churchill recalls importance of sending a fleet into, at earliest possible moment, 200; Churchill instructs War Office to draw up plans making it

Marmara, Sea of—*continued*
possible for fleet to enter, 202; plan for a joint Anglo-Greek fleet to enter, 204–5; British plan to enter, 248, 257; Kitchener believes Anzac troops 'good enough' for a cruise in, 303; Balfour believes ships alone will secure allied command of, 308; Turkey's principal arsenals on shore of, vulnerable to naval bombardment, 319; Admiral Carden's instructions (5 March 1915) in the event of his entering, 326–7; Admiral de Robeck reluctant to enter (25 March 1915), 369; Churchill believes arrival of ships in, will cut off Turkish army on Gallipoli Peninsula, 370; de Robeck's plans to penetrate, 391, 393; Jack Churchill envisages British ships within two weeks of Gallipoli landings, 408; Churchill wants further naval effort to penetrate (Aug 1915), 525; MAP, 840–1

Marmarice (Turkey): Lewis Harcourt suggests annexation of, 334; MAP, 838

Marne, Battle of (Sept 1914): 71–2, 104, 213

Marseilles (France): 37, 205, 206, 522

Marsh, Edward Howard: finds recruits for Royal Naval Division, 49; his relations with Churchill, 95; rebukes Robinson for criticism of Churchill in *The Times*, 153n; sends Grey a correction of Churchill's minute, 175; asks Grey to approve Buxton mission to Balkans, 201; will translate a Latin phrase for Churchill, 299; informs Violet Asquith of Rupert Brooke's illness, 401; and Brooke's death, 402; allowed to go with Churchill to Duchy of Lancaster, 485; and Churchill's early painting experiments, 502; and Churchill's departure for the front (Nov 1915), 571; 'much excited' at Churchill being with the Guards, 583; Churchill writes to from St Omer (Dec 1915), 595, 610; accompanies Churchill to Africa (1908), 661n; and Churchill's appeal for Fisher's return to the Admiralty (March 1916), 722;

Marsh, Edward Howard—*continued*
and the publication of the Dardanelles documents (June 1916), 784

Matapan, Cape (Greece): *Goeben* reaches, 41

Mary, Queen: 454

Massingham, Henry William: reports on alleged anti-Asquith intrigue, 361–2, 477

Masterman, Charles Frederick Gurney: receives critical report of Churchill's actions at Antwerp, 127; anti-Turk, 211

Masterton-Smith, James Edward: his relations with Churchill, 95; and Fisher's refusal to allow de Robeck to attack the Kephez minefield, 422; and the crisis of May 1915, 436, 437–8, 448, 456, 468; Churchill uses as an intermediary with Balfour, 485, 498, 507, 515, 516, 517; and Admiralty papers, 511; and use of Monitors at the Dardanelles (Sept 1915), 542; and Churchill's defence of his naval air policy (Oct 1915), 561; and Churchill's departure for the front (Nov 1915), 571; and Mrs Churchill's telephone conversation with her husband at St Omer (Dec 1915), 605; and the publication of Dardanelles documents (June 1916), 784

Maurice Victor Donald of Battenberg, Prince: died of wounds received in action, 149, 152

Maurois, André, *see* Herzog, Emile Salomon Wilhelm

Maxse, Ernest George Berkeley: reports speculation that Holland is about to be attacked by Germany (26 March 1915), 373–4

Maxwell, Sir John Grenfell: prepares to resist Turks along Suez Canal (Jan 1915), 270; reports on desertion of large numbers of Turkish troops (Feb 1915), 279

May, Sir William Henry: member of Dardanelles Commission, 789

Mears, Edward Grimwood: Churchill writes to about his Dardanelles policy (19 Oct 1916), 812–13

Mecca (Turkey): Kitchener wants transferred from Turkish to British control, 355

Medea (Dutch merchant vessel): sunk by the Germans, 378

Mehmed Reshad Effendi, Sultan Mehmed V: subservient to Young Turks, 189; Kitchener believes he will abandon Constantinople on hearing of allied naval success at the Dardanelles, 303, 309; said to be 'anxious' about continuation of the war, 396

Mehmed Said Halim: cannot counteract Enver's pro-German policy, 197; reported aware of dangers of a pro-German policy, 198

Memories (Lord Fisher): quoted on Fisher's attempt to leave the War Council (28 Jan 1915), 271

Memories of a Turkish Statesman (Djemal Pasha): quoted, 212

Mensdorff-Pouilly-Dietrichstein, Albert: Churchill arranges his departure from England, 45–6

Mercer Nairne, Lord Charles George Francis: killed in action, 228n

Merris (France): headquarters of the Ninth (Scottish) Division, 628; MAP, 631

Merville (France): Churchill sees 'hideous spectacle' of wounded men at (May 1915), 416; Churchill summoned to, from the front line (Nov 1915), 584; 2nd Battalion Grenadier Guards in reserve at (Dec 1915), 588; MAP, 575

Mesopotamia: Lloyd George believes expedition to 'merely a side issue', 301; probable effect of British success at the Dardanelles on, 324; Fisher wants to annex Alexandretta as an outlet for oil supplies from, 333; Kitchener wants British annexation of, to keep Russia away from, 349; Grey favours setting up of an independent Arab State in, 355; Harcourt proposes as 'an outlet for Indian immigration', 373; Churchill upset by military setbacks in (Dec 1915), 590; Fisher forecasts disaster in (March 1916), 736; MAP, 839

Messina (Italy): *Goeben* streams towards, 26; *Goeben* leaves, 28; *Goeben* returns to, 40, 42; MAP, 29

Meteren (France): Churchill joins the 6th Royal Scots Fusiliers in reserve near, 630; MAP, 631

Methuen, Ethel Christian: Asquith attends wedding of, 438n

Methuen, 3rd Baron (Paul Sanford Methuen): 438n

Metz: 146

Meux, Sir Hedworth: George V suggests as possible First Sea Lord (Oct 1914), 150; his maiden speech an attack on Churchill (March 1916), 723–5, 729

Midia (Turkey): MAP, 841

Mile End: by-election at (25 Jan 1916), 714

Military Medal: Churchill critical of 'niggardly' distribution of (July 1916), 795

Military Operations Gallipoli (Aspinall-Oglander): 522n

Military Service Bill: Sir John Simon's group opposes, 713n; introduced in House of Commons (3 May 1916), 758; Ireland excluded from, 761

Millerand, Alexandre: 261

Milne, Sir Archibald Berkeley: instructions to, 18, 26, 28, 29, 30; fails to concert action with French admiral, 40; his actions approved, 41; Churchill critical of, 42; ordered to establish blockade of Dardanelles (11 Aug 1914), 194

Milner, 1st Baron (Alfred Milner): Churchill urged to join forces with (Dec 1915), 591; appeals for compulsory military service (April 1916), 755–6; unwilling to be reconciled with Churchill (May 1916), 761; and Kitchener's death (June 1916), 781; joins Lloyd George's War Cabinet (Dec 1916), 822

Minerva (British light cruiser): ordered to Akaba, 216; bombards Akaba, 217, 219

Misu, Nicolae: Grey protests to, 372

Mitchell, Cyril John Francis: at Antwerp, 117

Moated Grange Trench (near Neuve Chapelle): 580; MAP, 577

Mobilization, of the British Fleet: Churchill orders test of, 3, 6–7; Cabinet refuses to sanction, 23; Asquith approves, 25

Monarch (British battleship): collision with *Conqueror* (27 Dec 1914) impairs British naval margin, 268

Mond, Sir Alfred Moritz: supports Churchill's criticisms of Asquith (March 1916), 711, 713; a member of the Liberal War Committee, 735*n*; votes against the Government in the Nigeria debate (Nov 1916), 815*n*

Monmouth (British cruiser): off South America, 156; sunk at battle off Coronel (1 Nov 1914), 157–8, 182

Monro, Sir Charles Carmichael: replaces Sir Ian Hamilton at Gallipoli (28 Oct 1915), 554; advocates evacuation of Gallipoli (31 Oct 1915), 563

Mons (Belgium): British troops at, 53; retreat from, 69–70, 104; MAP, 54

Montagu, Edwin Samuel: his dislike of Churchill reported, 329–30; worried about Balfour's influence over Lloyd George and Churchill, 361; Asquith describes 'superstitious mind' of, 362; present at quarrel between Lloyd George and Churchill, 383; engaged to marry Venetia Stanley, 446; writes to Mrs Churchill 'have no misgivings as to the future' (26 May 1915), 472; Churchill seeks three rooms from, 485; suggested as deputy to Asquith at War Office (Nov 1915), 560; 'imperious', 626; gives Mrs Churchill his impression of the Cabinet (Jan 1916), 689

Montagu, Mrs (*for earlier references, see* Stanley, Venetia): Mrs Churchill dines with, 583; entertains Asquith (Dec 1915), 626

Montenegro: possibility of action against Austria, 200–2, 229; Sir J. French favours sending British troops in support of, 237; MAPS, 235, 545, 842

Montevideo (Uruguay): British ships concentrate near, 182

Montgomery, Robert Arthur: and conscription (Aug 1915), 528

Moolenacker (France): Churchill's battalion billeted at, 630; Churchill reaches (5 Jan 1916), 631; a more relaxed atmosphere at, 641; Churchill leaves (24 Jan 1916), 646; MAP, 631

Moore, Archibald Gordon Henry Wilson: 192

Moore, Arthur: reports on 'terrible defeat' of British forces at Mons, 69–70

Morgenthau, Henry, 322, 327

Morley of Blackburn, 1st Viscount (John Morley): resigns from Cabinet (Aug 1914), 27; appeals for compulsory military service (April 1916), 755

Morning Post: Churchill often denounced in, 33; dislikes Churchill's reference to German Fleet as 'rats in a hole', 84; critical of Churchill's actions at Antwerp, 125–9, 180; critical of Churchill's conduct of Admiralty business, 144; publishes report (25 March 1915) of reinforcements on way to Turkey, 371; attacks Fisher (Feb 1916), 705; critical of Churchill's Admiralty administration (Feb 1916), 706; its editor believes he has uncovered an intrigue against Sir Douglas Haig (Sept 1916), 811; opposed to Churchill's inclusion in Lloyd George's Cabinet (Dec 1916), 822–3

Morocco: British recognition of French paramountcy in (1904), 333*n*

Mount of Olives (Turkey): Lloyd George does not wish to see under French control, 343

Mudania (Turkey): 501; MAP, 841

Mudros Bay (Lemnos): an ideal shelter for allied ships, 281, 346; problem of British control of, 298–9; Hamilton wishes to move troops to Egypt from, 360; technical discussions on the Gallipoli landing begin at (11 April 1915), 393; Churchill advises Balfour (26 May 1915) to keep the Dardanelles fleet in the safety of, 471; Sir Charles

Mudros Bay (Lemnos)—*continued*
Monro reaches (Oct 1915), 554; MAP, 840
Mundy, Godfrey Harry Brydges: rebuked for delay in despatch of ships, 183
Munitions, Ministry of: Lloyd George appointed to (May 1915), 470; Churchill hopes to succeed Lloyd George at (Dec 1915), 622; Churchill learns of Lloyd George's willingness to give him a department of (Dec 1915), 622; Churchill sees as 'the easiest opening for me' (April 1916), 751; Churchill compares difficulties in establishment of, with those of an Air Ministry (May 1916), 768; Churchill hopes to succeed Lloyd George at (June 1916), 781–3; Dr Addison succeeds Lloyd George at (Dec 1916), 822
Munstead House (Godalming, Surrey): McKenna sulks at his father-in-law's home at (Dec 1915), 623
Murray, Alexander William Charles Oliphant: Churchill asks his wife to keep in touch with (Jan 1916), 689
Murray, Harriet (Mrs Jock McDavid): 669n
Murray, Sir James Wolfe: at War Council (25 Nov 1914), 176; at War Council Sub-Committee (28 Jan 1915), 273
Muslims: Britain rules more than are ruled by any other power, 189; fears of Turkish pressure on, 195; Kitchener much concerned with problems of, 308n; Churchill instructs that objects venerated by in Constantinople should 'be treated with the utmost respect', 327; Grey wants establishment of an independent State for, 355; Kitchener raises spectre of rising of, in Egypt, 423; Kitchener fears rising of, if Gallipoli abandoned, 432
My African Journey (Winston S. Churchill): 661n

Nalder, John Fielding: in armoured car skirmish near Cassel (Sept 1914), 69

Namur (Belgium): defended by Belgians, 53; captured by Germans, 54–5; importance of fall of to military thinking about Dardanelles, 295; MAP, 54
Napier, Henry Dundas: proposes British attack on Bulgaria (Oct 1915), 553
Napier, Henry Edward: killed at Gallipoli landings (25 April 1915), 409
Napier-Clavering, Francis Donald: recalls Churchill's interest in trench fortifications, 671–2; and Churchill's search for a trench-crossing vehicle, 672–3; his work at Laurence Farm, 676
Napoleon Bonaparte: Churchill warned not to emulate, 129; sends Villeneuve to sea, 145; his boy-soldiers cited by Churchill, 171; his failure to crush nations cited by Haldane, 355–6; his strategy of 1805 praised by Balfour, 389; Churchill returns bust of, to Northcliffe, 782
Nation, the: 361, 477
National Liberal Club (London): Churchill plans (Feb 1916) to unveil portrait at, 707; Churchill gives up plans to unveil portrait at, 708
National Review: 579n
Naval Estimates: crisis of January 1914, 87
Naval Memoirs of Sir Roger Keyes, The: quoted, 563n
Neeld, Mrs (Beatrix Fisher): interned by the Germans, but released, 146
Neeld, Reginald Rundell: interned by the Germans, but released, 146
Nelson, Horatio: sent to Mediterranean, 16; his height referred to by Lord Fisher, 145
Nethe, River (Belgium): Royal Marines defend, 114–16
Neuve Chapelle (France): Churchill trains with the Guards in the trenches near, 574, 605; Churchill visits front-line trenches at, 624; Thomas McKee wounded in throat at battle of, 777; MAPS, 575, 577
Newcastle upon Tyne (Northumberland): Asquith's speech at (20 April 1915), 430

Newfoundland: troops cross Atlantic from, 37

Newton, Henry: his factory at Hazebrouck, 696–7

New York Herald: 538n

New Zealand: refuses to send troops to Europe without British naval escort, 89–90; ratio of troops to inhabitants, 794n

Nice (France): Fisher claims he is about to depart for (12 May 1915), 421

Nicholas Nicolaevitch, Grand Duke: Churchill proposes Anglo-Russian co-operation in Baltic to, 52, 84; his appeal for British help to reduce Turkish pressure in Caucasus, 231–3, 260; regrets Russia cannot take naval initiative in Black Sea, 266; says Russian action against Constantinople dependent upon British ships entering the sea of Marmara, 315; his instructions to the Russian Black Sea Fleet, 344; Churchill appeals to in vain to remove Russian veto on Greek participation at the Dardanelles (March 1915), 345; Churchill wants British troops to be sent to help (May 1916), 772

Nicolson, Sir Arthur: urged to prevent further irritation of Swiss opinion, 175; 'we were before the unknown', 192; learns that Admiralty have ordered hostilities against Turkey, 216; warns Tewfik Pasha about further British hostilities, 217; informs Admiralty that Britain and Turkey are at war, 219

Nicholson, 1st Baron (William Gustavus): on Dardanelles Commission, 789

Nieppe (France): Headquarters of the 9th (Scottish) Division, 661, 664; MAPS, 631, 649

Nieuport (Belgium): Joffre wants British naval action against German positions near (16 Oct 1914), 135

Nigeria: Churchill wants use of troops from 'for war or for labour' (July 1916), 794; Asquith challenged over disposal of German property in (Oct 1916), 815

Nikolaev (Russia): bombarded (29 Oct 1914), 215

1914 (Viscount French of Ypres): quoted on allegations in *The Times* (14 May 1915) of shell shortage at battle of Aubers Ridge, 430

Nish (Serbia): proposed allied advance to, 302

Nordenfelt: obsolete machine gun, destroyed, 326

Northcliffe, 1st Baron (Alfred Charles William Harmsworth): Churchill protests about 'Amiens' despatch to, 70; his papers critical of Churchill's actions at Antwerp, 126, 131; alleged to be trying to replace Asquith by Lloyd George (March 1915), 362; Churchill describes as supporting Lloyd George against Asquith (June 1915), 495; Callwell fears he will discover the facts about conscription (Aug 1915), 528; and discontent with Asquith's Coalition (Oct 1915), 552, 556, 557; on Lord Esher's strange status in France, 589n; attacked by Simon (Nov 1915), 593; and the Marconi affair (1912), 623n; and growing anti-Asquith feeling (Jan–Feb 1916), 699–700, 703, 704; refuses to support Churchill's attacks on Asquith (March 1916), 737; Garvin urges Churchill to write articles for, 747–8; refuses to consider publishing articles by Churchill (April 1916), 751; quarrel with Churchill (June 1916), 781–2; Haig defends Somme offensive to, 792; his *Daily Mail* describes Churchill as a 'megalomaniac' (Oct 1916), 811–12

North Sea: true war station for the First Fleet, 8; Fleet sails secretly to, 9, 12; not defenceless, 31; British blockade of, 46; British naval victory in, essential prelude to Baltic operations, 84; Asquith advises laying of mines in, 93; Churchill resurrects plan for naval offensive across, 225, 234, 235; ships sent to Dardanelles not needed in, 233; Churchill wants to cut off German access to, 241; Fisher wants Britain to

North Sea—*continued*
concentrate its naval strength and action in, 259, 263–4; and Dogger Bank action, 261–2; *Daily Mail* said to have revealed secret information about naval movements in, 270; Fisher insists (16 March 1915) that it is 'the decisive theatre', 347; Fisher wants *Inflexible* and *Queen Elizabeth* in, following reported German threat to Holland, 375; Fisher insists is the place 'where we can beat the Germans', 426; German High Sea Fleet thought to be about to sail into (17 May 1915), 448; the prospect of a decisive naval battle in (17–18 May 1915), 449–50; MAPS, 19, 842

Notre Dame de Lorette (France): Churchill visits trenches at (Dec 1915), 625; MAP, 575

Number of People, A (Sir Edward Marsh): quoted, on Churchill's early painting experiments, 502

Nürnberg (German light cruiser): 156, 158

Observer, the: reconciled to Churchill on outbreak of war, 38, 127; defends Churchill's actions at Antwerp, 128; publishes defence of Churchill's wartime Admiralty administration (23 May 1915), 468–9; supports Churchill, 596, 702

Ocean (British battleship): to go to Dardanelles, 249n, 265; at Dardanelles, 331; strikes a mine (18 March 1915), 352, 397n; sinks, 353, 354; most of her crew rescued, 361n, 371; Fisher upset by loss of, 379; MAP (18 March 1915), 353

O'Connor, Thomas Power: declares Churchill's resignation a 'national tragedy' (Nov 1915), 569

Ode on the Coronation of Edward VII (Sir W. Watson): 146n

Odessa (Russia): bombarded (29 Oct 1914), 215; MAP, 842

Oldenburg (Germany): Churchill wants invasion of (4 Jan 1915), 236

Oliver, Henry Francis: prepares battleship statistics, 8; accompanies Churchill to Dunkirk, 73; accompanies Churchill to Loch Ewe, 82; enthusiastic about air raids on German Zeppelin sheds, 89; at Antwerp, 101, 107, 120; becomes Chief of Staff at the Admiralty, 153; and battle off Coronel, 157; receives copies of intercepted German naval telegrams, 179; member of Admiralty War Group, 185–6, 250; can find no plans for bombardment of Dardanelles (31 Oct 1914), 216; impressed by effect of German guns on the Antwerp forts, 220; wants troop transports kept in Egypt as preparation for attack on Dardanelles, 221; Churchill informs (3 Jan 1915) of plan for a North Sea offensive, 234; shows Churchill's plan to Richmond (4 Jan 1915), 136; supports naval attack at Dardanelles, 238; and planning of Dardanelles attack, 253, 255, 258, 265; and Dogger Bank action, 261; gives War Council a survey of Dardanelles plan of attack (28 Jan 1915), 275; wants Royal Naval Division sent to Dardanelles, 279; and the loading of ships for the Dardanelles, 298; and the appointment of a Governor of Lemnos, 299; Sir H. Jackson urges need for military participation at Dardanelles on, 336; wants de Robeck to make a second attempt to force the Narrows by ships alone, 366; and Fisher's opposition to the Dardanelles, 394; Richmond declares his advice 'not taken', 399; and rumours of twelve German submarines converging on Dardanelles, 400; and withdrawal of *Queen Elizabeth* from Dardanelles, 422; and the crisis of May 1915, 448; Fisher proposes abolition of his post of Chief of Staff, 453; Churchill advises about Dardanelles Commission evidence (Oct 1916), 813–14

Ollivant, Alfred Henry: and offensive against Germany, 20; used by Churchill

Ollivant, Alfred Henry—*continued*
  to influence Lloyd George, 23–4; in
  command of sending Marine and
  Yeomanry force to Dunkirk, 73, 74;
  and the origin of the 'tank', 534
Olympic (passenger liner): sinking of
  Audacious witnessed by passengers on,
  141
Omdurman, battle of (1898): Churchill
  and Hugh Dawnay at, 81; Churchill
  has met most of the Staff of the IInd
  Corps at, 646
O'Neill, Arthur Edward Bruce: killed in
  action, 228
Orde, Sir John: superseded by Nelson,
  16
Orpen, William: paints Churchill's portrait (1916), 792–3
Ostend (Belgium): Churchill sends
  Marine Brigade to, 56, 74, 114; possibility of transfer of Russian troops to,
  58; Royal Naval Air Service air base
  at, 88; reported bombed by German
  airship, 91; Belgian appeal for troops
  at, 98; difficulty of defending Antwerp
  from, 99; Belgians talk of moving
  Government to, 101, 103, 106; Belgians decide not to move to, 112;
  General Rawlinson at, 113; guns for
  Antwerp fail to arrive at, 116; British
  forces disembarking at (6 Oct 1914),
  116; British forces unable to get
  beyond (8 Oct 1914), 122; Spenser-
  Grey and Marix escape to (9 Oct
  1914), 124; British troops from Antwerp escape to, 131; Germans occupy,
  135; 'damnable' if Germans remain in,
  136; fears of German submarine base
  at, 139, 162; Churchill eager for a
  coastal attack towards, 168, 180
Other Club, The: first wartime meeting
  of (6 Aug 1914), 35
Otranto (British merchant cruiser): off
  South America, 156–8, 182
Ottley, Sir Charles Langdale: sent to
  Constantinople (1913), 190; sees
  (1906) no reason to despair of success
  of a joint naval and military attack at
  the Dardanelles, 294

Owler, Stewart: at siege of Antwerp,
  122n
Oxfordshire Hussars: Jack Churchill
  about to leave for France with (Sept
  1914), 58; cross to France, 73; part of
  Churchill's 'Dunkirk Circus', 137;
  under fire near Ypres (Nov 1914),
  160–1; Churchill offered command of
  a battalion of (June 1915), 495; possibility of Churchill serving in France
  with (Sept 1915), 530, and (Nov
  1915), 564; a command in, not seen as
  offering Churchill much scope for his
  energies (Nov 1915), 566; Churchill
  decides to join in France (Nov 1915),
  570–1; Churchill visits headquarters of
  in France (18 Nov 1915), 572; Clementine Churchill wishes her husband
  would stay with, 609
Oxfordshire Hussars in the Great War, The
  (Adrian Keith-Falconer): quoted, 73

Pacific Ocean: Japanese activities in, 42;
  von Spee crosses, 156, 160; Japanese
  navy has effective command of, 178
Pakenham, William Christopher: on
  Churchill's work at the Admiralty,
  482
Paget, Sir Arthur Henry Fitzroy: reports
  from Bulgaria on impact of Dardanelles bombardment, 348; said to be
  working to reconcile Serbs and Bulgars, 396
Painting as a Pastime (Winston S. Churchill): 503n
Paissy (France): Churchill observes shells
  bursting in (16 Sept 1914), 81
Palestine (Turkey): Turkish army moving towards Egypt through, 220;
  Lloyd George favours annexation, of,
  333; Asquith reports on Cabinet views
  about the future of, 343–4; MAP, 838
Palestine Exploration Fund: Kitchener
  attached to (1874), 9n, 308n
Pall Mall Gazette: 38n, 711n; defends
  Churchill's actions at Antwerp, 127;
  Fisher sends Bonar Law a cutting
  from, 444
Panderma (Turkey): 501; MAP, 841

Paris, Archibald: commands Marine Brigade at Dunkirk (Sept 1914), 73; instructions to, 93; at Antwerp (Oct 1914), 109, 115, 116, 118, 121–2; discusses Antwerp with King Albert, 125; wants to land at Smyrna rather than on Gallipoli Peninsula (April 1915), 392; Churchill sends message for Royal Naval Division to (18 May 1915), 451

Paris (France): Sir John French announces intention to retire behind (31 Aug 1914), 59; Kitchener and French meet in, 60–1; British Expeditionary Force in retreat towards, 62; Germans driven away from, 71, 213; Churchill participates in Anglo-Franco-Italian negotiations in (May 1915), 414; Churchill's plan to meet his wife in (Dec 1915), 620

Parnell, William Alastair Damer: in trench raid (Dec 1915), 607

Parsons, Mrs (Viola Tree): 90

Pease, Joseph Albert: records Churchill's remarks in Cabinet (29 July 1914), 10; (26 Aug 1914), 57; (2 Sept 1914), 204; receives critical report of Churchill's actions at Antwerp, 127; on Cabinet decision about Turkey (30 Oct 1914), 215

Pegasus (British light cruiser): sunk off Zanzibar, 184, 187

Peirse, Sir Richard H.: instructed to harass Turkish troop movements, 222

Penang harbour (Straits Settlements): *Emden* sinks Russian and French warships in, 137n

Pepys, Sir Samuel: 348

Perfect, Katherine Elizabeth: 24

Persia: Russians hard pressed by Turks in north of, 232; Britain wants Russia to curb its southward pressure in, 320; Fisher wants to annex Alexandretta in order to secure an outlet for oil supplies from, 333; continued German and Turkish influence in, 349; Turks active in, 686; MAP, 839

Persia (British liner): torpedoed, 688n

Persian Gulf: possibility of anti-Turkish action in, 198, 199, 200; Government of India lands military force at head of, 221; MAP, 839

Petrograd (Russia): MAP, 842

Phaeton (British light cruiser): takes Sir Ian Hamilton to Dardanelles, 342; at the Dardanelles, 352, 353

Philadelphia Public Ledger: publishes photograph of the sinking *Audacious* (14 Nov 1914), 142

Philippeville (Algeria): bombarded by *Goeben*, 29; MAP, 29

Phillips, James Faulkner: 803

Pickford, Sir William: a member of the Dardanelles Commission, 789, 809

Plevna, siege of (1877): 243, 317

Ploegsteert (Belgium): Churchill's battalion allocated to (Jan 1916), 635; Churchill visits, 645; Churchill's battalion in front line trenches at (Jan–May 1916), chapter 21, 648–78; Churchill returns to (13 March 1916), 737; Churchill leaves (19 April 1916); Churchill ordered to return to (27 April 1916), 758; Churchill and his battalion leave (3 May 1916), 759; German air superiority above, 763; MAPS, 575, 631, 649

Plymouth (Devon): *Invincible* and *Inflexible* undergo urgent repairs at, 183

Pola (Austrian port on the Adriatic): German battle cruiser *Goeben* about to leave, 17; MAPS, 29, 842

'Pola': chosen as code name for the Dardanelles attack, 253

Politicians and the War (Lord Beaverbrook): Asquith letter critical of Churchill quoted in, 90; Churchill's annotations on the proof of, concerning Conservative participation at the War Council (10 March 1915), 335n; Churchill's annotation on the proof of concerning his wartime visits to France, 425n; on Churchill's mood of 18 May 1915, 455; Churchill's comment on publication of a letter of his in, 463n; on Churchill's departure for the front in Nov 1915, 571; on

Politicians and the War—continued
Churchill and the political crisis of
December 1916, 819, 821–2

Pomerania (Germany): Fisher designs
cruisers for invasion of coast of, 272

Ponders End (Middlesex): Mrs Churchill's YMCA canteen at, 669; Lloyd
George opens canteen at (3 Feb 1916),
698–9

Ponsonby, Arthur Augustus William
Harry: warns Churchill about war
atmosphere, 21

Port Arthur (Russian territory on the
coast of China; Japanese after 1905):
Russian Fleet caught unawares at
(1904), 13; possibility of Japan allowing transit of Russian troops for Gallipoli through, 205; Churchill compares
siege of, in Russo-Japanese war (1904–
5) with operations on the Gallipoli
Peninsula, 427–8

Portland (Dorset): Fleet ordered not to
leave, 6–7; Fleet ordered to leave, 9

Port Said (Egypt): 206

Portugal: Alliance of 1386 with England,
7n

Postmaster-General: Churchill suggests
as suitable post for Sir Max Aitken
(Dec 1916), 821

Prentis, Osmond James: commands
Wolverine off Smyrna, 217n

Press, the: agrees to voluntary censorship
(27 July 1914), 8; seeks fuller information of military developments,
70–1; not informed of Churchill's visit
to France (10 Sept 1914), 72; critical
of Churchill's visits to France, 90;
critical of Churchill's actions at Antwerp, 125–6, 129, 132–3, 137; critical of
Government prosecution of the war,
139; attacks on Prince Louis for his
German birth, 148; Churchill wants to
escape attacks of, 164; Churchill
praises in Parliament (27 Nov 1914),
178; War Council discusses alleged indiscretions of (28 Jan 1915), 270–1;
Churchill upset by criticisms of, 285;
Churchill's Constituency Chairman
unwilling to be influenced by criticisms

Press, the—*continued*
in (May 1915), 460–1; Churchill criticizes (5 June 1915) the 'irresponsible'
attack of, 489–90; Churchill on
'malice' of (7 July 1915), 509; critical
of Churchill's description of the Dardanelles as 'a legitimate gamble' (Nov
1915), 569; and Churchill's appeal for
Fisher's return to the Admiralty
(March 1916), 725; and Churchill's
recall from the trenches, 758; 'amazingly vicious' (June 1916), 783;
Churchill's conflict with (Nov–Dec
1916), 816, 822–3, 826

Press Bureau: alters 'Amiens' despatch
of *The Times*, 70; Churchill's communiqué issued through, 71; unwilling
to suppress Press criticisms of Churchill's actions at Antwerp, 129; Foreign
Office issue statement to about Turkey
(31 Oct 1914), 217

Prince George (British battleship): to go to
Dardanelles, 249n; at Dardanelles,
331; MAP (18 March 1915), 353

Prince of Wales (British Battleship):
ordered by Fisher to the Dardanelles
(19 March 1915), 354, 358; to leave
Dardanelles (12 May 1915), 422

Princes Islands (Turkey): 344

Pringle, William Mather Rutherford:
believes Churchill involved in the
Repington disclosures of 14 May 1915,
460, 702

Prinz Eitel Freidrich (German armoured
cruiser): believed to be at large, 264

Privy Council: Prince Louis wishes to be
a member of, 149; Asquith agrees to
appoint Prince Louis to, 152

Public Record Act (1967): opens British
Government records after thirty years,
200n

Queen (British battleship): ordered by
Fisher to go to the Dardanelles, 343;
on way to Dardanelles, 354, 358; to
leave Dardanelles, 422

Queen Elizabeth (British battleship): to go
to the Dardanelles, 250, 251, 253, 254,
256, 260, 268, 269; at the Dardanelles,

Queen Elizabeth—continued
300, 331; in the naval attack (18 March 1915), 352; ammunition available for fire across the Gallipoli Peninsula, 358; conference of naval and military commanders held on board (22 March 1915), 363; de Robeck proposes to bombard Chanak by indirect fire across Peninsula from, 369, 382; Fisher wants in North Sea, in view of reported German threat to Holland, 375, 379; will return to home waters, Churchill tells Jellicoe, as soon as attack on Dardanelles successful, 385; Churchill rejects Fisher's attempt to impose restrictions on de Robeck's use of, 388; conference of naval and military commanders held on board (10 April 1915), 392; at Gallipoli landings (25 April 1915), 405–6, 407, 409; naval conference held on board (9 May 1915), 417; Churchill agrees with Fisher's request (12 May 1915) to recall from Dardanelles, 422–3, 433; Kitchener protests about withdrawal of to War Council (14 May 1915), 431, 434, 806; withdrawn, 474; MAP (18 March 1915), 353

Quilter, John Arnold Cuthbert: at Blandford review (25 Feb 1915), 306

Radoslavov, Vasil: and the Bulgarian reaction to the bombardment of the Dardanelles, 335, 348

Ragusa (Austria-Hungary): Kitchener opposes landing at, 244

Rawlinson, Sir Henry Seymour: Churchill meets in France (16 Sept 1914), 81; appointed to command British forces at Antwerp, 113; on way to Antwerp (5 Oct 1914), 114, 115; his forces still disembarking (6 Oct 1914), 116, 117; reaches Antwerp (afternoon of 6 Oct 1914), 118; leaves Antwerp (evening of 6 Oct 1914), 120; to join with Belgians at Ghent, 122; sees value of armoured cars, 163; receives details of an alleged intrigue against Sir Douglas Haig, 811

Randolph Payne & Sons (wine merchants): Churchill's £500 debt to, 511

Rats: Mrs Churchill thinks she would mind them 'more than the bullets', 593; Churchill points out useful rôle of, on western front, 625

'Rats in a hole': Churchill reference to German Fleet (21 Sept 1914), 84

Reading, 1st Baron (Rufus Daniel Isaacs): 457, 458, 691; and the Marconi affair, 623n, 751; opposed to Churchill's precipitate return from the trenches to Parliament (April 1916), 756; and Churchill's desire to succeed Lloyd George at the Ministry of Munitions (June 1916), 783; and 'gossip' about Government reconstruction (Aug 1916), 797

Redmond, John Edward: 572

Red Sea: Turkish gunboats to be intercepted in, 215; *Minerva* sails to Akaba from, 216; British cruisers in, 264

Reed, Hamilton Lyster: at Suvla Bay (Aug 1915), 518, 520

Reliance (British repair ship): Fisher wants returned to home waters from the Dardanelles, 378

Repington, Charles à Court: Churchill defends his Antwerp actions to, 131; alleges shell shortage in France responsible for the failure to seize Aubers Ridge, 430, 431; the effect of his allegations, 445; Churchill believed by some to have intrigued with, 460; Callwell fears he will find out the facts about conscription (Aug 1915), 528

Reshadieh (Turkish battleship): launched (Sept 1913), 190; taken over by Royal Navy, 192; renamed *Erin*, 192n; Churchill offers recompense for, 195–6; Turkish sailors from reach Constantinople, 197

Revenge (British battleship): to bombard German-held Channel coast, 136

Reynolds Weekly Newspaper: 711n

Rhine, River: Churchill's plan to crush fortresses on, 72; Dutch neutrality a barrier to blockade of, 98; Churchill on German desire to control mouth of, 378

Rhodes: 334; MAP, 838

Ribblesdale, 4th Baron (Thomas Lister): and Gallipoli, 582

Richmond, Herbert William: does not believe Churchill is sane, 50–1; writes of Churchill's 'lunatic hands', 110; finds Churchill 'in low spirits' (24 Oct 1914), 140; discusses possibility of Gallipoli landing with War Office representatives (1 Sept 1914), 203; believes Churchill's plan for a North Sea offensive *quite mad*, 236; favours demonstration against Turkey, 257; determined to undermine Churchill's North Sea plans, 258; describes Fisher as 'old & worn out & nervous', 260; wants Royal Naval Division sent to Dardanelles to 'finish off their training properly', 279; opposes attack on Dardanelles unless army is sent to act with navy, 286–7; is told of secret negotiations of 1915 with Turkey, 359n; wants to abandon the Dardanelles and land 80,000 British troops at Haifa, 389; believes Fisher 'useless' and Churchill 'ignorant' (22 April 1915), 399

Richmond (Surrey): 269

Riddell, Sir George Allardice: at Other Club meeting (6 Aug 1914), 35; Churchill explains (22 April 1915) why Dardanelles attack must go on, 397; Churchill explains (29 April 1915) the importance of the fall of Constantinople to, 411; Kitchener explains (13 May 1915) the importance of the Dardanelles expedition to, 427; finds Churchill 'very worn out and harassed' (20 May 1915), 457; records Lloyd George's discontent with Asquith (Jan–Feb 1916), 703–5; and Lloyd George's attitude to Churchill's appeal for Fisher's return to the Admiralty (March 1916), 725; and Lloyd George's criticisms of Asquith and Balfour (April 1916), 755

Riez Bailleul (France): Churchill in reserve billets at (Nov 1915), 586, 588; MAP, 575

Rimington, Michael Frederic: anxious to work in conjunction with armoured cars, 291

Rio de Janeiro: von Spee expected on trade route of, 182

Ritchie, Archibald Buchanan: 'impressed' by the shell damage to Churchill's billets, 660

Ritchie, Sir George: resents the 'unjust outcry' against Churchill (May 1915), 461; Churchill seeks opinion of (March 1916), 745; advises Churchill against criticizing Asquith's war policies, 747

Ritz Hotel (London): Fisher wishes he had become manager of, 441

Ritz Hotel (Paris): Churchill stays incognito at, 414, 425

River Clyde (British collier): run aground at Gallipoli landing (25 April 1915), 404, 405–6, 408–9, 410

River War, The (Winston S. Churchill): severe censures on Kitchener in, 327n

Robertson, Sir George Scott: speaks in Churchill's defence in House of Commons (16 Dec 1915), 614

Robertson, Sir William Robert: Fisher wants in command of attack on Turkey, 234; describes Gallipoli landings as 'the stiffest operation anyone cd undertake', 387; Churchill thinks, will replace Sir J. French as Commander-in-Chief of British forces in France (Dec 1915), 598; and criticisms of the Somme offensive, 792; *Daily Mail* warns Churchill not to intrigue against (Oct 1916), 811–12

Robinson, Charles Napier: reports in *The Times* (22 May 1915) on relief in Admiralty at Churchill's departure, 467

Robinson, Geoffrey: on Cabinet mood of 1 Aug 1914, 24; dines at Admiralty House (4 Aug 1914), 30–1; rebuked by Marsh for criticism of Churchill in *The Times*, 153n; singles out Churchill for criticism (*The Times*, 18 May 1915), 450; Northcliffe informs of Lord Esher's strange status in France, 589n; and Fisher's attempt to return to the

Robinson, Geoffrey—*continued*
Admiralty (Jan–Feb 1916), 700; instructed by Northcliffe not to support Churchill's attack on Asquith (March 1916), 737; Northcliffe defends Somme strategy to, 792

Robley, Christopher Harrington: joins Royal Naval Division, 48, 504

Robley, John Pitcairn: joins Royal Naval Division, 48, 504

Roch, Walter Francis: a member of the Dardanelles Commission, 789; votes against the Government in the Nigeria debate (Nov 1916), 815n

Rolls-Royce cars: armoured for use in France, 163n

Romilly, Bertram Henry Samuel: marries Nellie Hozier (Dec 1915), 595

Romilly, Nellie (*for earlier references, see* Hozier, Nellie): sends Churchill an American schoolboy howler (Feb 1916), 702

Rosoman, Robert Reynolds: said to be 'frightfully keen to see the fun' at the Dardanelles (18 March 1915), 352

Rothermere, 1st Baron (Harold Sidney Harmsworth): and the future of Asquith's Coalition Government (Oct 1915), 552; Churchill urges his wife to keep in touch with (Nov 1915), 587; tells Churchill he has 'emerged unscathed from Gallipoli' (Jan 1916), 688; tries to mediate between Churchill and Northcliffe (March 1916), 748, and (June 1916), 782; Churchill writes articles for (July 1916), 790; gives Churchill portrait by Orpen, 793; writes friendly article about Churchill in *Sunday Pictorial* (12 Nov 1916), 814–15

Rotterdam (Holland): Fisher wants massive British troop landings at (Jan 1915), 245; rumours of a planned British naval landing at, 400

Rouge Croix (France); 584; MAP, 577

Royal Automobile Club (London): Churchill and F. E. Smith at the Turkish baths of (5 Dec 1916), 821

Royal Commission on Fuel and Engines: Fisher appointed Chairman of (1912), 13

Royal Commission on War Inventions (1919): and the origin of the tank, 537

Royal Marine Brigade: and land operations, 11; sent by Churchill to Ostend (26 Aug 1914), 56; sent by Churchill to Dunkirk (Sept 1914), 67; move from Dunkirk to Lille, 92–3; forced to return to Dunkirk, 103; Churchill suggests sending to Antwerp, 105; ordered to proceed to Antwerp, 106, 107; expected at Antwerp, 108; reach Antwerp, 110, 112; Kitchener plans to replace at Antwerp by 7th Division, 113; in action at Antwerp (Oct 1914), 114, 116, 117, 118, 124; use of, at Antwerp, criticized, 126; use of, at Antwerp, defended, 128; on way to Dardanelles, 300; small party of land safely at entrance to Dardanelles, and successfully accomplish mission (1 March 1915), 318; main body of at Lemnos (3 March 1915), 322

Royal Naval Air Service: and the needs of war, 11; units sent to Belgium, 56; air base established at Dunkirk, 65; Churchill circulates memorandum on the wartime development of (June 1915), 486; Churchill defends his policy for (Oct 1915), 561; and the possibility of an East African wing (Nov 1915), 566; 'maltreated', 690; Churchill critical of Balfour's policy for (March 1916), 735; Churchill's anger at criticism of his policy towards (May 1916), 765

Royal Naval College, Greenwich: Bayly appointed President of, 185

Royal Naval Division: established (Aug 1914), 47–8; recruiting for, 49; Churchill's instructions for, 50; criticisms of, 51; not ready to go to Calais, 52; Churchill proposes sending to Antwerp, 107; Churchill awaits arrival of, at Antwerp, 111; Kitchener plans to replace by 7th Division, 113; difficulties in reaching Antwerp, 115; at

Royal Naval Division—*continued*
Antwerp (Oct 1914), 116, 118, 120; given order to withdraw from Antwerp, 122; losses at Antwerp, 125; use of, at Antwerp, criticized, 126; Churchill speech to, on return from Antwerp, 129–30; criticism of its provisions answered by Churchill in Parliament (11 Nov 1914), 169–70; Oliver and Richmond give reason for sending to Dardanelles (Feb 1915), 279; Churchill and Kitchener quarrel over Sir John French's use of (Feb 1915), 289–91; being sent to Dardanelles, 292, 301, 304; reviewed by George V at Blandford (25 Feb 1915), 305–6; on way to Dardanelles, 316, 322; General Paris suggests landing at Smyrna rather than on Gallipoli Peninsula, 392; on the Gallipoli Peninsula, 413, 415; Churchill sends message of encouragement to (18 May 1915), 451; heavy losses of (4–6 June 1915), 496; their 'bold, martial appearance' described by Hamilton (18 June 1915), 500; continual losses of, 504; Churchill angered by rumours of abolition of (Feb 1916), 707

Royal Naval Division, The (D. Jerrold): Churchill's introduction to, 50n

Royal Scots Fusiliers, 6th Battalion: Churchill commands, in reserve (Chapter 20), 628–47; at Ploegsteert (Chapter 21), 648–78, 679, 684; Churchill invites Sir John Simon to do his training with, 685

Rumania: possibility of action against Austria, 200–2, 210; British financial help for, 204; Buxton reports (21 Oct 1914) on hesitations of, 213; Asquith doubts hesitations can be much prolonged (31 Oct 1914), 216, 219; not ready to join Allies (Dec 1914), 224; Asquith stresses importance of intervention of (27 Dec 1914), 225; Lloyd George wants as ally against Austria (1 Jan 1915), 229; importance of, in British plans to defeat Turkey, 230, 235, 243, 244, 249; little disposed to

Rumania—*continued*
help Serbia, 273; Austrian aim to overawe, 277; possibility of troops of, to help Serbia, 281–2; possibility of joining the Allies and facilitating allied advance up Danube, 302, 308; Balfour on inducements to, 305; German submarines said to be on their way to Turkey via, 338; importance to the Allies of support from, 349; German reinforcements for Turkey pass through, 371–2; Churchill fears German armies will overawe (Aug 1915), 524; and the Austrian attack on Serbia (Oct 1915), 549; German–Austrian–Bulgarian attack on (1 Sept 1916), 797; MAPS, 235, 545, 842

Rumpler biplanes (German): at the Dardanelles, 499n

Runciman, Walter: Churchill advocates as First Lord, 112, 113; Asquith's veiled praise for, 330; seen as ally for Asquith against an alleged Lloyd George–Curzon–Churchill plot (Oct 1915), 557; against conscription (Dec 1915), 622

Russia: Churchill proposes alliance with, 1; the crisis of July 1914, 2–3, 6, 21; Germany declares war on, 25; Churchill proposes joint action in Baltic with, 52–3; British Marines rumoured to be troops from, 56; Churchill plans for troops from, 58; naval strength growing, 178; fears Austrian naval attack on Black Sea ports, 193; Enver approaches for territorial guarantees, 196; naval and military action against Bosphorus proposed, 199; Churchill believes 'unconquerable' (31 Aug 1914), 201; asked about possibility of joint allied action against Turkey, 205; effect of closure of Dardanelles on, 213; worsening military situation, 224–5; Churchill plans North Sea–Baltic offensive to bring military help to, 226, 228; Hankey favours active participation of in war against Turkey, 230; appeals to Britain for a demonstration against Turks, 231–3; action

Russia—*continued*

by Royal Navy to relieve pressure on, 248; Churchill's message of encouragement to, 253; fear of a negotiated peace between Germany and, 260; cannot spare troops for action in the Balkans, 280; estimate 50,000 troops needed to capture Constantinople, 292; military weakness of, 307; will not attack Constantinople until British ships enter the Sea of Marmara, 315; Haldane fears will accept German peace offers, 321; refuses to accept Greek participation in attack on Constantinople, 328–9; and British War Council's discussion (10 March 1915) of post-war settlement, 332, 334; refuses Churchill's appeal to abandon veto on Greek help at the Dardanelles, 344–5; economic difficulties as a result of the sealing off of the Black Sea, 350; Hankey recalls (Aug 1916) moral effect of naval attack at Dardanelles on, 380; Asquith tells House of Commons (14 March 1917) of beneficial effect of Dardanelles operation on, 480; Churchill emphasizes weakness of (June 1915), 498; Hankey suggests sending Churchill on mission to (Oct 1915), 560–1; Churchill wants 150,000 troops from, to participate in Anglo-French attack on Turkey (Oct 1915), 561; MAPS, 53, 235, 545, 839, 842

St Andrew's Hall (Glasgow): 643, 681

St Gilles (Belgium): British troops take trains to Ostend from, 131

St Helena: 265

St Nazaire (France): British Admirals urge defence of, 55; MAP, 54

St Omer (France): Sir John French's Headquarters (Oct 1914–Dec 1915), 133, 163, 339; Churchill at (18–19 Nov 1915), 572–4; Churchill Sir J. French's guest at (1–18 Dec 1915), 589–95, 596–605, 606; Churchill remains at (19–23 Dec 1915), 609–21; Churchill returns to (27 Dec 1915–5

St Omer (France)—*continued*

Jan 1916), 622–8, 630; Churchill visits (19 Jan 1916), 643; Churchill summoned to (3 Jan 1916), 679; Lloyd George, Bonar Law and Churchill drive to, 697; MAPS, 575, 649

St Pol (France): 414; MAP, 575

Saint-Seine, Jean Charles Just Benigne, Comte de: proposes Anglo-French Naval co-operation, 18–19; keen on action at the Dardanelles, 257–8

Salonika (Greece): possibility of British action at discussed, 228, 237, 244, 252–3, 260, 274, 277, 278; War Council decide to send troops to (9 Feb 1915), 281–2, 295; Greek Government turn down offer of British troops at (15 Feb 1915), 287–8; Churchill revives possibility of allied landing at, 302, 307; Fisher wants to offer to Bulgaria in return for Bulgarian support against Turkey, 338, 382; Lloyd George wants troops sent from Gallipoli to (Sept 1915), 538; Churchill proposes action based on (5 Oct 1915), 544; Lloyd George wants British troops sent urgently to (11 Oct 1915), 550; Anglo-French force lands at (5 Oct 1915), 558n; Jack Churchill said to be at (Nov 1915), 582; Churchill foresees disaster at (Dec 1915), 590, 800; Churchill wants evacuation of (Dec 1915), 598, 603, 605; Asquith tries to persuade Kitchener to visit, 602; and possibility of sending troops to Gallipoli from (Dec 1915), 617; Churchill on need to use troops at elsewhere (1916), 686, 692, 772; Churchill's continued belief in need for evacuation of (March 1916), 708; MAPS, 29, 545, 842

Samson, Charles Rumney: establishes air base at Dunkirk, 65; acts in co-ordination with armoured cars, 67; reports on skirmish beyond Cassel, 68; the effect of his raids, 69; commands 'Dunkirk Circus', 74; records Churchill's views on aerial strategy (22 Sept 1914), 88; at Lille, 93; forced to return

Samson, Charles Rumney—*continued*
to Dunkirk, 103; his squadron of twelve aeroplanes to go to Dardanelles (March 1915), 316; Fisher wants in home waters rather than at Dardanelles, 379; reaches Lemnos, 396–7

Samson, Felix Rumney: in armoured car skirmish near Cassel, 69

Samuel, Herbert Louis: and the defence of Antwerp (Oct 1914), 100, 119–20; favours British control of Palestine and Home Rule for the Jews there (March 1915), 343–4; present at quarrel between Lloyd George and Churchill (April 1915), 383

Sarajevo (Bosnia): Franz Ferdinand assassinated at, 2, 118

Saracen (British destroyer): 339

Sarell, Philip Charles: on effect of British armoured car raids, 69; on effect of Churchill's visit to Dunkirk (10 Sept 1914), 72

Sari Bair (Gallipoli Peninsula): Sir Ian Hamilton's army fails to reach summit of (25–26 April 1915), 407; Hamilton confident that his forces will reach in May 1915, 411; the second failure to capture (6–11 Aug 1915), 518–21; Turks retain control of (21–28 Aug 1915), 524; Churchill wants renewed attack on (Sept 1915), 540; MAPS, 403, 519

Saros, Gulf of (Turkey), *see* Xeros, Gulf of

Sarrail, General: commands French troops at Salonika (Oct 1915), 558n

Sassoon Dock (Bombay): Churchill dislocates shoulder at (1896), 635n

Sato, Kozo: commands Japanese squadron in Mediterranean (1917), 44n

Sazonov, Sergei Dmitrievich: 280; Grey's assurances to about Constantinople (14 Jan 1915), 320; sends Grey report (22 April 1915) of Turkish shortage of ammunition, 400

Scharnhorst (German cruiser): 156, 158, 182; sunk at battle of Falkland Islands, 183

Scheldt, River: and Antwerp's access to the sea, 96–8; Admiral Oliver disables ships at anchor in, 101; Belgian army withdrawn across, 118; British troops withdraw across, 130; Churchill on German desire to control mouth of, 378

Schleswig-Holstein (Germany): Churchill resurrects plan for invasion of (in Dec 1914), 225–6, (again on 4 Jan 1915), 236–7, (again on 11 Jan 1915), 246; Fisher wants an attack on (16 March 1915), 347; MAP, 842

Scimitar Hill (Gallipoli Peninsula): 524; MAP, 519

Scorpion (British torpedo-boat destroyer): off Smyrna, 217, 219

Scotland: Fisher announces his immediate departure for (15 May 1915), 438, 439; Hankey, McKenna and Crease act in concert to get Fisher away to (22 May 1915), 467

Scots, the: Churchill writes 'I am a vy gt admirer of that race. A wife, a constituency & now a regiment attest the sincerity of my choice' (3 Jan 1916), 629

Scott, Charles Prestwich: reports on hostility of Lloyd George and Churchill to further offensives on the western front (Sept 1915), 541; Churchill urges his wife to keep in touch with (Nov 1915), 587; sends Churchill encouragement (Dec 1915), 596; Churchill urges Garvin to keep in touch with, 605; Fisher's attempt to return to the Admiralty supported by (Jan–Feb 1916), 700–1, 704; and Churchill's demand for Fisher's return (March 1916), 708, 709, 711–12, 713, 722–3, 730–1, 732–3; and Churchill's criticisms of Asquith's war policies, 739, 741–2, 744, 753; hears Lloyd George's criticisms of Asquith and Balfour, 755; his plans for a 'real opposition' led by Lloyd George, Churchill and Carson (April 1916), 756–7; Churchill's political hopes centre on, 759; Churchill has long

Scott, Charles Prestwich—*continued*
discussion with (20 Nov 1916), 816

Scott, Sir Percy Moreton: proposes use of naval guns in France, 90–1; and use of *Queen Elizabeth* at Dardanelles, 250–3

Scutari (Turkey): 326; MAPS, 838, 841

Sedd-el-Bahr (Gallipoli Peninsula): heavy guns of largely destroyed (3 Nov 1914), 218; damage not repaired, 219; British sailors make brief landing at (4 March 1915), 326; military landing at (25 April 1915), 405–6, 407–8; *Goliath* torpedoed off (12 May 1915), 425; Churchill advocates (13 May 1915) semi-permanent landing stages at, 428; MAPS, 353, 403

Seely, John Edward Bernard: at Other Club meeting (6 Aug 1914), 35; Churchill sends reflections to, 83; joins Churchill at Antwerp, 107, 117; Churchill describes Duchy of Lancaster work to, 484; Churchill describes political situation to (12 June 1915), 495; Churchill expresses his frustration to (20 Sept 1915), 538; Churchill visits near Kemmel (2 Dec 1915), 592; presents prizes at Churchill's sports day (16 Jan 1916), 641; Churchill attends lecture with (20 Jan 1916), 643; tells Churchill of conscription debate in London, 685; Churchill writes to about politics and the Dardanelles Commission (31 July 1916), 791; Churchill writes to about Asquith's weakening position (13 Aug 1916), 798, and about the course of the war, 799

Selborne, 2nd Earl of (William Waldegrave Palmer): Churchill sends defence of his naval policy to, 159; becomes President of the Board of Agriculture and Fisheries (May 1915), 470; believes Constantinople, if captured, could be given to Germany in exchange for Belgium, 487–8; and the War Policy Committee of the Cabinet (Aug 1915), 527, 529; agrees (Sept

Selborne, 2nd Earl of—*continued*
1915) to winter campaign at Gallipoli, 539; favours conscription (Oct 1915), 556; opposes Gallipoli evacuation, 601, 617

Senegal: French troops from, at Gallipoli, 413, 415

Serbia: and Austrian hostility, 2; the Austrian ultimatum of 23 July 1914, 4–6; consequences of possible invasion of, 7; possibility of action against Austria, 200–2, 210; British financial help for, 204; hostile to Greece, 221; recaptures Belgrade from Austria (14 Dec 1914), 224; Lloyd George wants British military assistance sent to (1 Jan 1914), 228–9; Hankey suggest territorial inducements for, 230; danger to, if Russia defeated, 233; Fisher wants attack on Austria by, as part of grand design, 235; War Council discusses aid to (28 Jan 1915), 273–4; danger of Austrian attack on, 277–8; danger of Bulgarian attack on, 280, 281–2; Asquith believes best way to help is 'to strike a big blow at the Dardanelles', 293; Churchill wants Dardanelles army of 115,000 to be able to go to the aid of, 307; Hankey wants British naval attack up Danube as means of protecting, 318; Hankey recalls (Aug 1916) effect of naval attack at Dardanelles on, 380; Churchill fears German armies will crush (Aug 1915), 524; attack on believed imminent (Sept–Oct 1915), 538, 544; invaded by Austria (Oct 1915), 549; Churchill reflects (Dec 1915) on policy of, 597; MAPS, 235, 545, 842

Sevastopol (Russia): bombarded (29 Oct 1914), 215

Sheerness (Kent): Churchill welcomes Heligoland Bight victors at, 59; provisions sent to Dunkirk air base from, 67; 15-inch howitzers being built at, 392

Sheridan, Clare Consuelo: her husband killed at Loos (Sept 1915), 595

Sheridan, William Frederick: killed at Loos (Sept 1915), 595

Shipbuilder's Yarn, A (Tennyson D'Eyncourt): quoted, 537

Shipka Pass (Balkan mountains): Turks defeated by the Russians at (1877), 243n

Shuttleworth, 1st Baron (Ughtred James Kay-Shuttleworth): 484–5

Siberia (Russia): Churchill sees use on western front of troops from, 58

Sierra Leone: *Kent* ordered to South America from, 182

Sign Post Lane (near Neuve Chapelle, France): 580; MAP, 577

Silesia (Germany): possible Russian invasion of, if Britain attacks Austria, 243

Simon, Sir John Allsebrook: decides not to resign from Cabinet (Aug 1914), 27; Asquith's praise for (March 1915), 330; becomes Home Secretary, 469; attacks Northcliffe (Nov 1915), 593; and the conscription crisis (Dec 1915), 622; resigns (Jan 1916), 679, 685; and Churchill's criticisms of Asquith (March 1916), 713

Sinai Peninsula: surveyed by Kitchener (1883), 9n; Turks believed to be laying mines off (31 Oct 1914), 217; British ships keep watch for movement of Turkish troops to, 222; crossed by Turkish forces (Feb 1915), 279; MAP, 838

Sinclair, Sir Archibald Henry: dines at Admiralty House (5 Jan 1915), 238; Churchill sees cavalry position near Kemmel with (2 Dec 1915), 593; Churchill wants as his ADC (Dec 1915), 599, 615, 619, 620; Churchill meets at Boulogne, 625; Churchill's second-in-command (Jan–May 1916), 628, 629, 631, 634, 644, 652, 653, 657, 659, 660, 662, 663, 664, 665, 667, 668, 673, 675, 677, 678, 684, 739, 740–1, 742, 756; squadron commander in 2nd Life Guards (July 1916), 791

Sinclair, Mrs (Mabel Sands): 740n

Sinclair, Clarence Granville: 740n

Singapore: dockyard mutiny at suppressed, 44n, 184

Sivas (Turkey): Djemal Pasha records fears of Allied advance on, 212

Sippe, Sidney Vincent: in air raid on Friedrichshafen, 172

Skagerrak: Churchill's plan for sending British Fleet through (Aug 1914), 52; MAPS, 19, 53

Skobelev, Mikhail Dimitrievich: at siege of Plevna (1877), 243

Slade, Sir Edmond John Warre: advises Churchill on naval action against Turkey (31 Oct 1914), 215–16

Slatin, Sir Rudolf Carl: one of Churchill's Austrian friends, 45

Smith, Frederick Edwin: godfather to Churchill's son, 4n; supports Coalition on eve of war, 12; on Conservative support for Liberal policy, 22–3; at Admiralty (1 Aug 1914), 24–5; at Other Club meeting (6 Aug 1914), 35; writes on Churchill in *Contemporary Personalities*, 58; adds paragraph to 'Amiens' despatch of *The Times*, 70; speaks at London Opera House (11 Sept 1914), 75; Churchill anxious to see, 164; with Churchill at Constantinople (1910), 189; favours military landing at Smyrna or Ephesus, 237, 238; Churchill appeals for his help against Tory hostility (March 1915), 330; describes progress at the Dardanelles (15 March 1915) as 'too good to be true', 344; Fisher protests at Churchill talking to, 426; at Admiralty House with Churchill (18 May 1915), 455; becomes Solicitor-General, 470; Margot Asquith alleges as part of a Lloyd George–Curzon–Churchill plot (Oct 1915), 557; Churchill writes to, from St Omer (18 Dec 1915), 615–16; sends Churchill an account of Cabinet discussions, about the evacuation of Gallipoli Peninsula, 617; and the Marconi affair (1912), 523n; writes to Churchill about conscription crisis (11 Jan 1916), 684, 685; sends Chur-

Smith, Frederick Edwin—*continued*
chill news of Cabinet discussions (18 Jan 1916), 688; his visit to Churchill on the western front (30 Jan 1916), 691, 692, 693, 694–7; believes Asquith 'firmer in the saddle than ever' (25 Feb 1916), 708; and Churchill's advocacy of Fisher's return to the Admiralty (March 1916), 709, 736; and Churchill's desire to lead an opposition to Asquith (March–May 1916), 745; Churchill urges to keep in touch with Lloyd George on his behalf (April 1916), 750–1; Churchill writes to, about Verdun, 754; Churchill circulates memorandum to the Cabinet through (Aug 1916), 791–2; and Churchill's preparation of evidence for the Dardanelles Commission (Sept 1916), 806, 807–8; alleged to be part of a Lloyd George–Churchill–French intrigue against Sir Douglas Haig (Oct 1916), 811; and the emergence of Lloyd George as Prime Minister (Dec 1916), 821–2

Smith-Dorrien, Sir Horace Lockwood: appointed to command British forces in East Africa, the command Churchill wanted, 590, 602

Smuts, Jan Christian: 565, 590n

Smyrna (Turkey): Admiral Limpus suggests (26 Aug 1914) possibility of landing near, 198; possibility of feints at, 201; Turkish yacht blown up in harbour of (1 Nov 1914), 217, 219; Kitchener deprecates demonstration at, 232–3; F. E. Smith favours landing at, 237, 238; British naval blockade of, 321; seen as possible area of post-war Greek control, 344, 383; General Paris wants military landing at, as opposed to on Gallipoli Peninsula, 392; MAPS, 838, 842

Sofia (Bulgaria): German sailors pass through, 197; Mustafa Kemal at, 212; British reported not to want support in, 214; German financial activity in, 317; Churchill willing to go on special mission to, 512; Churchill sees as pos-

Sofia (Bulgaria)—*continued*
sible British military objective (Oct 1915), 544; MAP, 545

Soissons (France): Churchill observes fire of French artillery near (16 Sept 1914), 81; MAP, 54

Somme, battle of the (June 1916): 774; Churchill fears repetition of (Aug 1916), 791–2; Churchill critical of Asquith's control of the War Office at the time of, 793–4

Sophie, Queen of Greece: 221

Souchon, Wilhelm: receives secret instructions from Berlin, 193; feared about to take *Goeben* and *Breslau* into Black Sea, 197; becomes Commander-in-Chief of Turkish navy, 206, 208, 209; urged by the Kaiser to hold out at the Dardanelles as long as possible, 357

South Africa, Union of: bad news from, 140; ratio of troops to inhabitants, 794n

Southampton (Hampshire): British aviators set off from, for raid on Friedrichshafen, 172

Soyer Farm (Ploegsteert, Belgium): company billets at, 650; Churchill establishes battalion headquarters at (10 Feb 1916), 663, 664; Churchill leaves (18 Feb 1916), 675; Churchill returns to (20 Feb 1916), 676; MAP, 649

Special Register Bill: Churchill critical of, in House of Commons (16 Aug 1916), 799–800

Spencer: Churchill in Paris under pseudonym of, 414

Spencer, Lord: sends Nelson to Mediterranean, 16

Spender, John Alfred: Churchill seeks to influence in favour of a clear decision about Gallipoli (Oct 1915), 555; on Churchill's resignation speech (Nov 1915), 569

Spiers, Edward Louis: Churchill befriends (Dec 1915), 597–605, 610–11, 620, 622; Churchill visits French front line with, 624–5; Churchill unable to

Spiers, Edward Louis—*continued*
    have on his battalion Staff, 628–9;
    Churchill writes to, about his evi-
    dence to the Dardanelles Commission
    (Oct 1916), 814
Spion Kop, battle of (24 Jan 1900):
    268; Suvla Bay battle compared with,
    520
Spithead (Hampshire): naval review off,
    3
Stamfordham, 1st Baron (Arthur John
    Bigge): at Other Club meeting (6 Aug
    1914), 35; reports on George V's
    critical attitude to Churchill's 'rats in
    a hole' remark, 87; reports on further
    disagreement between George V and
    Churchill, 88; misinformed of Chur-
    chill's Antwerp mission, 119–20; be-
    lieves Churchill 'quite off his head',
    120; on replacement of Prince Louis
    as First Lord by Fisher, 148, 150–1;
    asks Fisher when Falkland Island des-
    patches will be published, 184; his
    son-in-law killed in action, 228;
    George V describes as 'absolutely
    trustworthy', 281; comments on Chur-
    chill's wartime visits to France, 425;
    reports on Asquith's belief that Fisher's
    mind 'is somewhat unhinged' (19
    May 1915), 453; reports on Liberal
    Ministers'   hostility   to   sending
    Churchill to Colonial Office, 454; and
    Churchill's proposed mission to the
    Gallipoli Peninsula (July 1915), 512
Stanley, Beatrice Venetia: letters from
    Asquith to, 21–2, 23, 24, 29, 60, 71, 72,
    74, 90, 95, 101–2, 106, 112, 113, 117,
    120–1, 122, 124, 130, 137, 138, 139,
    141, 142, 143, 144, 147, 149, 151, 152,
    158, 166, 167, 173, 176n, 195, 196,
    204, 205, 216, 219 223 224, 225, 228,
    237, 242, 253, 255, 272, 278, 280, 286,
    290, 300, 303, 306, 310, 316, 325, 332,
    343–4, 360, 361, 362, 363, 366, 387–8,
    410, 426n, 446, 447, 459, 466, 477, 480,
    775n; Churchill refers to letters which
    she received from Asquith, 21n, 90;
    tells Asquith to advise Churchill to
    end his visits to France, 166; often

Stanley, Beatrice Venetia—*continued*
    told by Asquith of intercepted German
    naval telegrams, whose existence was
    not known even to the Cabinet, 179;
    told secret code-name for attack on
    Borkum, 242; letter from Edwin
    Montagu to, 472; *for further references,*
    see Mrs Montagu
Stanley of Alderley, 4th Baron (Edward
    Lyulph Stanley): 626
Star: publishes defence of Churchill's
    actions at Antwerp, 128; praises
    Churchill's Dundee speech of 5 June
    1915, 491
Station Hotel (Hazebrouck, France):
    Churchill entertains his officers at, 647
Steel-Maitland, Arthur Herbert Drum-
    mond Ramsay: Churchill expresses
    his frustration to (Sept 1915), 538;
    breakfasts with Guy Dawnay, 539
Steenwerck (France): 9th (Scottish)
    Division artillery headquarters at,
    677; MAP, 631
Stevens, Henry Marquis: in charge of
    Churchill's transport at Antwerp,
    108–9
Stevenson, Frances Louise: Lloyd George
    speaks critically of Churchill to, 132,
    159; records quarrel between Lloyd
    George and Churchill, 383–4; records
    Lloyd George's comments (15 May
    1915) on Churchill and the war, 440;
    Lloyd George reports Asquith's cynical
    observations about Churchill to (18
    May 1915), 451; reports bitter ex-
    change between Churchill and Lloyd
    George (19 May 1915), 456; reports
    on strength of anti-Churchill feeling
    (24 May 1915), 468; records Lloyd
    George's distrust of Churchill (Sept
    1915), 531; reports Lloyd George 'sick
    with Churchill' (Oct 1915), 551; on
    Churchill's resignation (Nov 1915),
    569;   and   the   opening   of   Mrs
    Churchill's canteen at Ponders End
    (3 Feb 1916), 689–9; comments on
    Churchill's desire for a vigorous
    opposition to Asquith (April 1916),
    757

Stokes Trench Mortar: Churchill impressed by, 540

Stonewall Jackson (British monitor): to go to Dardanelles (12 May 1915), 423; at the Dardanelles (Nov 1915), 687

Stopford, Sir Frederick William: at Suvla Bay (Aug 1915), 518, 520, 522

Strand Magazine: Churchill describes (1921) his early painting experiments in, 502–3

Sturdee, Frederick Charles Doveton: mentioned, 46, 52; suggested by George V as suitable for the Admiralty Board, 150; replaced by Oliver as Chief of Staff (Oct 1914), 153; commands British ships at battle of Falkland Islands, 183; Fisher wants Dardanelles forced by, 235; Churchill writes of as Fisher's possible successor as First Sea Lord, 270

Suandere River (Gallipoli Peninsula): 382, 390; MAP, 353

Submarines, British: enter Baltic, 53

Submarines, German: fail to disrupt movement of Expeditionary Forces, 37; fail to interfere with Marine expedition to Ostend, 56

Sudan: Churchill wants use of native labour from 'for war or for labour' (July 1916), 794

Sudan Campaign (1897–9): Churchill critical of Kitchener's conduct of, 12; Churchill with Hugh Dawnay during, 81; Kitchener's plans for unchallenged, 312

Sueter, Murray Fraser: Churchill sends instructions on anti-aircraft defence to, 66, 67; accompanies Churchill to Dunkirk (10 Sept 1914), 72; at Admiralty aircraft conference (16 Sept 1914), 80; and Churchill's wish for more aeroplanes at Dardanelles (13 May 1915), 428; and the origin of the tank, 534, 536

Suez Canal: defence of, 9; Turks believed to be in a position to attack, 220; Admiral Peirse transfers flag to, 222; British cruisers in, 264; Turks thirty

Suez Canal—*continued*
miles from (Jan 1915), 270; attacked by Turks (Feb 1915), 279, 281, 317; Turks retreat from, 291, 396; Russian light cruiser *Askold* joins defence of, 327n; Churchill proposes (16 May 1915) sending as many ships as possible from Dardanelles to, 443; Churchill advises Balfour (26 May 1915) to keep Dardanelles fleet in the safety of, 471; MAP, 235

Suffren (French battleship): at Dardanelles, 331; MAP, 353

Supreme Command, The (Lord Hankey): quoted on War Council (13 Jan 1915), 252; quoted on Churchill's 'stout attitude' at War Council (14 May 1915), 433

Sultan Osman I (Turkish battleship): built in England (1913–14), 191; boarded by British sailors (1 Aug 1914), 192; renamed *Agincourt*, 192n; Churchill offers recompense for, 195–6; sailors from reach Constantinople, 197

Sunday Pictorial: 552n; Churchill writes four articles for, 790–1, 816; friendly article about Churchill in (12 Nov 1916), 814–15; Churchill defends his Antwerp policy in (26 Nov 1916), 817

Suvla Bay (Gallipoli Peninsula): landing at (Aug 1915), 518–21; Lloyd George wants troops sent to Salonika from (Sept 1915), 538; Churchill opposes evacuation (Sept 1915), 539; Churchill wants renewed offensive at (Nov 1915), 603; MAPS, 403, 519

Swiftsure (British battleship): to go to Dardanelles, 249n, 265, 305; MAP, 353

Swine: Churchill describes certain Conservatives as, 164; F. E. Smith describes the Americans as, 688; Churchill describes his former colleagues as, 693

Swinton, Ernest Dunlop: and the origin of the tank, 535–6, 537n

Switzerland: alleged breach of neutrality of, by British naval aviators (21 Nov 1914), 173–6

Sydney (Australian light cruiser): sinks the *Emden*, 137n

Sykes, Sir Mark: explains need for a swift blow against Turkey, 317–18; on Committee to examine British territorial needs in Turkey, 391

Sylt (German Island): possible British base, 19, 21; Churchill drafts plans for invasion of, 181; MAP, 19

'Sylt': War Council agrees to use as code name for attack on Borkum, 242, 246

Syria (Turkish province): possibility of action against Turkey in, 199; possibility of feints on coast of, 200; Churchill suggests as alternative point of attack, 220; Admiral Peirse instructed to keep watch on ports of, 222; British sailors land on coast of (18–22 Dec 1914), 222–3, 279; Lloyd George wants British action against, 228–9; Kitchener sees no value in action against (2 Jan 1915), 233; French see territorial opportunities in, 266; seen as possible area of post-war French control, 344; Grey favours setting up of an independent Arab state in, 355; Balfour wants Turkish army in, destroyed before making Gallipoli landings, 389; MAP, 838–9

Talaat, Mehmed; Churchill meets, 189; angered by seizure of Turkish ships, 193; reported probably aware of dangers of a pro-German policy, 198; argues merits of neutrality and intervention, 213; negotiates with British emissaries (March 1915), 358–9; said to be advising a negotiated peace, 395

Talbot, Milo George: discusses Gallipoli landing at Admiralty (1 Sept 1914), 203

Talbot cars: armoured for use in France, 163n

Tank: origin of, 534–8, 810–11; use of on the Somme (1916), 809–10

Tannenberg: Russian advance halted at (26–30 Aug 1914), 224; MAP, 842

Taranto (Italy): Goeben refused coal at, 26; MAP, 29

'Taube': German aeroplane, at the Dardanelles, 499

Tautz, Messrs: 579

Teacher, Norman McDonald: Brigade Major, 27th Brigade (1916), 647

Tenedos: British aeroplanes based on, 253, 383; MAP, 840

Tennant, Harold John: 452, 613, 691, 763, 774

Tennyson-d'Eyncourt, Eustace Henry William: and origin of the tank, 536–7, 705–6, 810

Terschelling (Holland): 374

Tewfik, Ahmed Pasha: opens negotiations for second Turkish battleship, 190–1; protests at seizure of Sultan Osman, 192; warned about further British hostilities against Turkey, 217

Thames estuary: and Admiralty plans against Zeppelin attack, 8; German aeroplane flies up (25 Dec 1914), 239

Thameshaven: Balfour surprised that Germans have not bombed naval oil depot at, 182

Thomson, Graeme: discusses possibility of Gallipoli landing with War Office representatives (1 Sept 1914), 203; and loading of troop transports for the Dardanelles, 297–8, 313–14

Thoughts and Adventures (Winston S. Churchill): 503n; quoted, on Churchill's first day with the Grenadier Guards (20 Nov 1915), 574–6; on Churchill's near escape from death (26 Nov 1915), 585

Thourout (Belgium): Marine reconnaissance to, 56; MAP, 75

Thrace: 230, 303, 544, 549; MAPS, 545, 842

Thread in the Tapestry, A (Sarah Churchill): 120n

Thursby, Cecil Fiennes: 422

Tigris, River (Turkey): British control mouth of (Dec 1914), 222–3; proposed extension of British control over whole valley of, 509

Tilbury (Essex): boat sails to Antwerp from, 100

Timbuctoo: 264

Times, The: approves Fleet concentration, 7; praises Churchill (4 Aug

Times, The—continued
1914), 31; praises Churchill's formation of Royal Naval Division, 50; praises Asquith's speech at Guildhall, 62; reports British retreat from Mons, 69–70; publishes letter critical of Churchill's actions at Antwerp, 126; Churchill defends actions in private letter to military correspondent of, 131; and release of Fisher's daughter from internment in Germany, 146*n*; critical of Churchill's farewell letter to Prince Louis, 153; Marsh rebukes Robinson for criticism of Churchill's letter, 153*n*; approves Fisher's return to Admiralty, 154; Churchill's views on the minorities' question published in (Sept 1914), 202; Churchill obituary of Valentine Fleming in (25 May 1917), 227*n*; said to have disclosed whereabouts of secret base of British Battle Cruiser Squadron, 271; Churchill obituary of Rupert Brooke in (26 April 1915), 401–2; alleges (14 May 1915) serious shell shortage in France, 430; the effect of these allegations, 445; singles out Churchill for criticism (18 May 1915), 450; advocates Fisher to replace Churchill as First Lord, 452; Naval Correspondent of reports relief in Admiralty at Churchill's departure, 467; and the Marconi affair (1912), 623*n*; and 'excitement in Washington' at death of U.S. subjects (Jan 1916), 688*n*; and Enver's reflections on the Dardanelles (Jan 1916), 693*n*; and Churchill's criticisms of Asquith (March 1916), 737, 747–8; Churchill's criticisms of Somme offensive meet with no response in, 792; on the public 'relief and satisfaction' that Churchill is to be excluded from Lloyd George's Government (Dec 1916), 822–3

Tirnovo (Bulgaria): 544; MAP, 545

Tokyo (Japan), 42

Toulon (France): 31

Tournai (France): Marine Brigade units at, 73

Townsend, Ernest: paints Churchill's portrait (autumn 1915), 708*n*

Trépont, Felix: and the 'Dunkirk Circus', 93

Trieste (Austria-Hungary): Kitchener rules out landing at, 244

Tritton, William Ashbee: and the origin of the tank, 537

Triumph (British battleship): to go to Dardanelles, 249*n*, 265; at the Dardanelles, 412; sunk (25 May 1915), 472; MAP (18 March 1915), 353

Trotter, Gerald Frederick: 740, 758

Troubridge, Ernest Charles Thomas: unwilling to challenge *Goeben* and *Breslau* (7 Aug 1914), 40–1; instructions (8 Sept 1914) to sink *Goeben* and *Breslau*, 206

Troy (Turkey): Birdwood suggests an attack across the plain of, 392; MAP, 840

Tsing-tau (German naval base on China coast): 156

Tudor, Henry Hugh: visits Churchill at London Support Farm (7 Feb 1916), 662; takes Churchill to see British artillery bombardment (10 Feb 1916), 663–4; Churchill dines with at the Hospice (12 Feb 1916), 665; arranges artillery bombardment of German trenches (14 Feb 1916), 666–7; and an artillery mishap (26 Feb 1916), 677

Tudor, Frederick Charles: not on Admiralty War Group, 185–6; expresses doubts about the Dardanelles operation, 388; opposes Fisher's resignation (16 May 1915), 444; Fisher proposes dismissal of, from Admiralty Board (19 May 1915), 453

Turkey: and arrival of *Goeben* and *Breslau* off Constantinople, 40; British policy towards (before 1914), 188–90; effect of British seizure of battleships on, 193; Grey's offer to respect territorial integrity of, 195; Churchill expects (31 Aug 1914) imminent act of war by, 202; and coming of war with Britain, 203–19; and threat to British in Egypt, 220; British troops land at

Turkey—*continued*

one extremity of (7 Nov 1914), 221; British sailors land on Syrian coast of (18–22 Dec 1914), 22; Asquith reports Churchill 'set on' (5 Dec 1914), 223; Lloyd George suggests attack on (1 Jan 1915), 229; British schemes to create Balkan alliance against, 230; prospects for the defeat of, 249; Sir H. Jackson doubts that attack by ships alone can secure defeat of, 287; Churchill's outline (28 Feb 1915) of conditions for the surrender of, 315; discussion of territorial changes in, 320–2; Churchill says war against should be regarded 'merely as an interlude', 324; Fisher wants (12 March 1915) to give Bulgaria both Salonika and Kavalla—Greek towns— in return for an immediate attack on, 338; Carson's proposed peace terms with (19 Aug 1915), 523; Churchill's war plans against (5 Oct 1915), 544; Churchill argues in favour of use of poison gas against (20 Oct 1915), 554–5; its nearness to defeat in March 1915 mentioned by Enver (Jan 1916), 693; MAPS, 29, 353, 403, 519, 545, 838, 840–1, 842

Twenty-ninth Division: Kitchener proposes sending to Salonika (9 Feb 1915), 281–2; Kitchener agrees to send direct to the Dardanelles (16 Feb 1915), 288–9; Kitchener unwilling to send to the Dardanelles (19 Feb 1915), 291–3; Kitchener 'prepared to send . . . to the east' (19 Feb 1915), 295; Churchill makes transport arrangements for (20 Feb 1915), 297–8; Churchill wants in eastern Mediterranean (24 Feb 1915), 301; Kitchener argues it cannot be spared (24 Feb 1915), 302; decision about destination of postponed (24 Feb 1915), 304; Churchill appeals for (26 Feb 1915), 307–10; not to go to the Dardanelles (26 Feb 1915), 310–11, 312; Churchill learns (27 Feb 1915) that Kitchener has suspended

Twenty-ninth Division—*continued*

transport for, 313–14; Kitchener says it *can* go to Dardanelles (10 March 1915), 332; Sir John French wants in France as 'he did not think there would be much fighting at the Dardanelles' (12 March 1915), 339; Churchill wants military action at Dardanelles before arrival of (12 March 1915), 340; military action at Dardanelles not to take place until arrival of (22 March 1915), 363; at the Gallipoli landings (25 April 1915), 402, 408; in the fighting at Cape Helles (6 May 1915), 415; at Gallipoli, 433; without rest for two months, 504

Tyne, River: Turkish sailors reach (July 1914), 191

Tyrone (Irish county): boundary dispute of, 4

Tyrrell, Sir William George: and the European crisis of July 1914, 6–7; and defence of Antwerp, 103–4; discusses capture of Constantinople with Fisher, 247

Tyrwhitt, Mrs (Angela Corbally): 59

Tyrwhitt, Reginald Yorke: his reception after Heligoland Bight action, 59; accompanies Churchill to Loch Ewe, 82; frustrated by Navy's passive rôle, 84

Ulm: Napoleon defeats Austrians at (1805), 389n

Ulster: proposed boundaries of, 3; Provincial Government imminent in, 5; Churchill seeks to deter rebellion (March 1914), 32; Churchill's action towards contrasted with his actions at Antwerp (Oct 1914), 128

United States of America: Churchill orders flying boats from, 66; and Irish Home Rule, 77, 79; Italy and Greece forced to draw their grain supplies from, 350

United States Steel Corporation: Churchill owns $10,000 stock in, 511n

Unionist War Committee: and the conscription crisis (April 1916), 751–2;

Unionist War Committee—*continued*
not yet strong enough to challenge Asquith (May 1916), 762, 775; leads challenge against Asquith in Parliament (8 Nov 1916), 815
Urfah (Turkey): 344; MAP, 839

Valparaiso (Chile): news of British naval defeat off Coronel reaches, 158
Van (Turkey): captured by Russians, 499; MAP, 839
Vardar River (Greece): 546
Varna (Bulgaria): Kitchener favours Russian attack on (Oct 1915), 553; MAP, 842
Venerable (British battleship): to sail to Dardanelles (12 May 1915), 422, 423
Vengeance (British battleship): to go to Dardanelles, 249n; at Dardanelles, 300, 331, 394; MAP (18 March 1915), 353
Venizelos, Eleutherios: declares not afraid of Turkish attack, 206; his offer of support for Britain overruled, 221; offers Lemnos to Britain as a base, 281; his acceptance of British troops at Salonika overruled, 287; offers Greek help for Dardanelles attack, 315, 322; Churchill asks Grey to press for military action from, 325–6; his pro-allied policy rejected by King Constantine, 329; 'his hands tied' (June 1915), 504
Verdun, battle of (Feb–July 1916): 754, 755, 772, 774, 793, 799
Vesey, Ivo Lucius Beresford: wishes Churchill good luck in his opposition to Asquith (April 1916), 757–8
Viceroyalty of India: Churchill said to covet, 245; Downing Street discussion of appointment to (1916), 683
Vickers: and arms for Antwerp, 100; and building of Turkish dockyard facilities, 190–1
Villarey, Carlo Rey de: 436
Villeneuve, Pierre Charles Jean Baptists Silvestre: sent to sea by Napoleon, 145

Villiers, Sir Francis Hyde: receives report of bombs dropped accidentally, 89; reports Dutch pressure on Belgium, 96; request to Grey about British help for Belgian refugees, 97; and defence of Antwerp, 100, 103–6
Vimy Ridge: Churchill visits trenches on (Dec 1915), 624; MAP, 575
Vladivostock (Russia): possibility of transfer of Russian troops to Gallipoli from, 205; Hankey suggests sending Churchill on mission to (Oct 1915), 561, 611n
von Sanders, Liman: heads German Mission to Turkey, 197n; appointed to command Turkish Fifth Army at the Dardanelles, 400
von Spee, Count Maximilian: commands German Far Eastern Squadron, 156–7, 159–60; defeats British squadron off Coronel (1 Nov 1914), 158; himself defeated at battle of Falkland Islands (8 Dec 1914), 182–4, 481; his defeat 'a risk', 262; Churchill recounts (Dec 1915) victory over, 620
von Tirpitz, Alfred: Churchill wants to meet (May 1914), 1–2
von Wangenheim, Hans Freiherr: signs secret treaty with Turkey (2 Aug 1914), 193; dominant at Constantinople, 197
Vynckier, Jules-Jean: Churchill attends Mass in chapel of, 655; his house shelled, 663

Wake, Hereward: and offensive plans against Germany, 21
Walmer Castle (Kent): 167, 231, 245–6, 300, 329–30, 343, 361, 478, 665–6, 707; MAP, 575
Walshe, Henry Ernest: an unpopular Brigadier-General, 630; leaves Churchill to his own discretion, 634; realizes Churchill's difficulties, 637; Churchill hopes to impress, 641; impressed 'in spite of himself', 642; at London Support Farm, 650; on leave, 661–2; relieved of command, 739; his rebuke to Churchill for 'undue leniency' in punishment, 740

Walton Heath (Surrey): Lloyd George and Churchill 'mutually' alarm each other at (Aug 1916), 797

War Council: meets (25 Nov 1914), 176–7, 220, 221; meets (1 Dec 1914), 180–2; Churchill wants daily meetings of, 231; discusses alternative war zones (5 Jan 1915), 237; Churchill explains air defence and North Sea plans at (7 Jan 1915), 240–2; alternate war zones discussed at (8 Jan 1915), 243–5 and (13 Jan 1915), 251–3; and British co-operation with France, 257; Fisher wants his protest against Dardanelles circulated to, 265; attracted by idea that Dardanelles operation could if unsuccessful be broken off, 267; its approval for Dardanelles operation needed, 268; Fisher announces he will not attend, 269; Fisher ordered to attend, 270; discusses Press indiscretions, 270–1; decides upon Dardanelles operation (28 Jan 1915), 271–2; favours British military aid to Serbia, 273–4; Dardanelles operations outlined to (28 Jan 1915), 275; Balkan telegrams circulated to (6–7 Feb 1915), 280; meets (9 Feb 1915), 281–2; meets (19 Feb 1915), 291–6; meets (24 Feb 1915), 301–4; meets (26 Feb 1915), 307–10; Churchill's unsent protest to, 311; Churchill helps add to self-deception of, 311; Churchill describes Kitchener's authority at, 312–13; meets (3 March 1915), 321–4; meets (10 March 1915), 331–5; Churchill rejects Fisher's proposal for a meeting of, 346; meets (19 March 1915), 354–6; not summoned to discuss advisability of a military landing on the Gallipoli Peninsula, 381; informal meeting of three members of (6 April 1915), 386; meets (14 May 1915), 431; discusses possible evacuation of Gallipoli Peninsula, 432–3; Fisher asked by Lloyd George to withhold his resignation until next meeting of, 439; Fisher insists on dismissal of Sir

War Council—continued
Arthur Wilson from, 452; Sir Arthur Wilson reported 'dumb' at, 459; Churchill to remain a member of, 468, 472; becomes known officially as the 'Dardanelles Committee' (q.v.)

War Diary (Lord Riddell): quoted on Other Club meeting (6 Aug 1914), 35; Churchill's explanation (22 April 1915) of why the Dardanelles must go on, 397–8; Churchill's explanation (29 April 1915) of importance of capture of Constantinople, 411; on Churchill's belief 'I am finished' (20 May 1915), 457; on Lloyd George's growing discontent with Asquith's leadership (Jan 1916), 703–4, 705; on Churchill's appeal for Fisher's return to the Admiralty (March 1916), 725; on Lloyd George's criticisms of Asquith and Balfour (April 1916), 755

Wargrave (Berkshire): 808

Warleigh, Percival Henry: ordered to Akaba, 216; bombards Akaba, 217

War Memoirs (D. Lloyd George): quoted, on the coming of war, 23; on Fisher's resignation (15 May 1915), 438–9; on Bonar Law's insistence upon a Coalition (17 May 1915), 445–6; on Bonar Law's hostility to Churchill (Dec 1916), 822

War Office: Admiralty conference with (27 July 1914), 8; Churchill submits plans to, 20; co-operates with Admiralty, 21; relations with Admiralty, 36; transfers aerial responsibility to Admiralty (3 Sept 1914), 65; responds to Joffre's request for British troops to go to Dunkirk, 73; and use of naval guns in France, 90; declares country unable to resist German invasion, 139; Lloyd George in despair over 'stupidity' of, 143; difficulty of co-operation with Admiralty, 226; and the loading of ships for the Dardanelles, 297–8; does not have enough information to plan a Gallipoli landing, 355; Asquith suggested as Kitchener's replacement at (Nov 1915), 560;

War Office—*continued*
Churchill sees Bonar Law or Lloyd George as Kitchener's successor at (Dec 1915), 622; Churchill's Parliamentary criticisms of (23 May 1916), 771–4; Churchill critical of Asquith taking charge of (6 June–7 July 1916), 793; Churchill addresses his criticisms of, to Lloyd George (24 July 1916), 794–8

War Policy Committee (of the Cabinet): 527–9

Warrender, Sir George John Scott: Clementine Churchill's advice on, 15

Warspite (British battleship): nearly ready to go to Dardanelles, 360

Waterloo, battle of (1815): Churchill believes 'glories of' revived in 1914, 141

Waterlow, H. C.: protests to Churchill against misuse of military manpower (June 1916), 776

Watson, Sir William: 146n

Watt, Harry Anderson: asks question in Parliament about provisions for Royal Naval Division, 170

Wattenberg (Germany): 777

Weber, Erich: orders closure of Dardanelles (27 Sept 1914), 213

Wedgwood, Josiah Clement: commands armoured car squadron in France, 68, 168; his armoured car squadron to go to Dardanelles, 316; reaches Lemnos, 396–7; sends Churchill an account of the Gallipoli landings, 408–9; wounded in the renewed offensive at Helles (9 May 1915), 415; writes of his 'indignation' at Churchill's removal from Admiralty, 483; seeks to defend Churchill's Admiralty administration, 531

Wellington, 1st Duke of (Arthur Wellesley): his Peninsula campaign (1808–14) compared with the Gallipoli campaign, 318

Wemyss, Rosslyn Erskine: commands 12th cruiser squadron, 37, 85; his appointment to govern Lemnos challenged by Grey, 298–9; in charge of

Wemyss, Rosslyn Erskine—*continued*
all transport operations at Lemnos, 348; de Robeck reports on his 'disastrous day' (18 March 1915), 357; opposed to further delay at Dardanelles (10 April 1915), 392; reported 'working very hard' (11 April 1915), 393; advocates renewed naval attack at Dardanelles (Nov 1915), 601–2

Weser, River: Churchill wishes to block German bases at mouth of, 180

Westminster, 2nd Duke of (Hugh Arthur Grosvenor): accompanies Churchill to France (16 Sept 1914), 80; his brother killed in action, 228; and the origin of the tank, 536

Westminster Gazette: 555, 569

The Wharf, Sutton Courtenay (Berkshire): Churchill's discussion with Asquith at (16 May 1915), 444–5; the Churchills frequent visitors to, 478

Whittall, Edwin: negotiating with the Turks, 359

Wilhelm (German Kaiser): 5n, 7; offers *Goeben* and *Breslau* to Turkey, 40; his sister married to King Constantine of Greece, 221; urges German admiral to hold out at Dardanelles for as long as possible, 357; his birthday in 1916, 653

Wilhelmshaven (Germany): German fleet secure at, 140; Churchill wants attack on, 246; Churchill refers to enormous German expenditure on naval facilities at, 283; MAP, 842

Wilson, Sir Arthur Knyvet: Haldane advises Churchill to bring back to Admiralty, 144; returns to Admiralty (Oct 1914), 147, 149, 153, 154; Prince Louis suggests as possible First Sea Lord, 150; receives copies of intercepted German naval telegrams, 179; member of Admiralty War Group, 185–6, 250; criticized by Richmond for supporting Churchill's North Sea plans, 136–7; at War Council (7 Jan 1915), 242; and Dogger Bank action, 261; and the naval setback at the

Wilson, Sir Arthur Knyvet—*continued*
Dardanelles (18 March 1915), 354;
supports Fisher's refusal to order
de Robeck to make a second naval
attack without military assistance,
365–7; and Fisher's opposition to
the Dardanelles, 394; Churchill
suggests to Fisher as his temporary
replacement (16 May 1915), 443;
willing to succeed Fisher as First
Sea Lord, 444; and the prospect
of a decisive naval battle in the
North Sea (17–18 May 1915), 449–50;
Fisher proposes departure of from
Admiralty and War Council, 452;
refuses to serve as First Sea Lord
except under Churchill, 457–8; his
abilities derided, 458, 459; Churchill
believes he can discharge his Admiralty duties effectively with the help
of, 462, 463; Churchill fails to persuade to serve as First Sea Lord under
Balfour, 465–6

Wilson, Henry Hughes: on coming of
war, 23–4; demonstration to Committee of Imperial Defence (1911),
28; comments on rumours of naval
offensives in the Baltic and against
Holland, 400; finds Churchill 'ill
and unhealthy' (7 May 1915), 414;
against despatch of further troops to
Gallipoli, 430; reflects on the lesson
of 'Squiffs lie about ammunition',
431; at St Omer with Churchill
(Nov–Dec 1915), 589–91, 592, 606;
hopes Milner, Carson and Lloyd
George have Asquith 'by the throat'
(April 1916), 755

Wilson, Woodrow: intervenes to release
Fisher's daughter from internment,
146n; interrupts honeymoon on learning of death of U.S. citizens, 688n

Wimborne, 2nd Baron (Ivor Churchill
Guest): lends Churchill his house,
493; sees no immediate political
future for Churchill (Feb 1916), 706,
707; at a bridge evening with Asquith,
708; Churchill tries to find Admiralty
job for (Aug 1914), 775n

Winston Churchill As I Knew Him (Violet
Bonham Carter): quoted on relations
between Churchill and Fisher, 262–3;
Churchill's excitement on learning of
offer of Greek military support at the
Dardanelles (1 March 1915), 315–16;
on Churchill's departure for the
trenches (Nov 1915), 571; on Churchill's advocacy of Fisher's return to
the Admiralty (March 1916), 709,
713, 718, 731–2, 733; on Churchill's
thoughts about the Dardanelles Commission (Aug 1916), 798

Winston Churchill in War and Peace (A.
MacCallum Scott): 805

Winston Spencer Churchill (A. MacCallum
Scott): 805n

With Winston Churchill At the Front
(Andrew Dewar Gibb): quoted, on
Churchill's command of the 6th Royal
Scots Fusiliers, 630, 631–2, 638, 639,
642, 655n, 674, 760

Wolseley cars: armoured for use in
France, 163n

Wolverine (British torpedo-boat destroyer): off Smyrna, 217, 219

Woolwich Arsenal: siege mortars being
made at, 72; Balfour surprised
that Germans have not bombed,
182

World Crisis, The (Winston S. Churchill):
quoted—on Kiel Regatta (June 1914),
2; on the Irish crisis (July 1914), 304;
on a conversation with Albert Ballin
(24 July 1914), 5; on transfer of Fleet
to North Sea, 9; on Fisher's delight
at Fleet reaching North Sea, 13; on
Grey's attitude (3 Aug 1914), 27;
on Kitchener and fall of Namur, 54;
on search for reassurance from Lloyd
George, 55; on Churchill's visit to
Sir John French's headquarters (16
Sept 1914), 80–1; on Fisher's capacity
to return as First Lord, 147; on Callwell's report (3 Sept 1914) on possibility of seizing Gallipoli Peninsula,
203; on a conversation with Kitchener
(2 Jan 1915), 232; on Dogger Bank
action (23–24 Jan 1915), 261; on

World Crisis, The—continued
Asquith's decision to drop Zeebrugge and continue with Dardanelles (28 Jan 1915), 270; on Churchill's decision not to resign when his desire for a renewed naval attack at Dardanelles overruled (23 March 1915), 367; on 'the hideous spectacle' of wounded men during a battle (9 May 1915), 416–17; on Kitchener's anger at learning that the *Queen Elizabeth* is to be withdrawn from Dardanelles (12 May 1915), 423; on effect of Fisher's protest to War Council (14 May 1915) that he was against Dardanelles 'from the beginning', 431; on moment of learning of Fisher's resignation (15 May 1915), 437; on visit to Asquith at The Wharf, Sutton Courtenay (16 May 1915), 444–5; on appeal to Balfour to intercede with the Conservatives (17 May 1915), 445; on Asquith's refusal to let Churchill explain Fisher's resignation to the House of Commons (17 May 1915), 447; on Churchill suggesting Balfour as his possible successor as First Lord, 448; on the events of 17 May 1915, 449; 'my hour had passed', 451; on Kitchener's farewell visit to him at Admiralty (25 May 1915), 469; Churchill's criticisms of General Monro at Gallipoli, 563*n*; on Churchill's criticisms of Jellicoe's conduct at Jutland, 777*n*; on a discussion between Lloyd George and Churchill on the German threat to Rumania (Aug 1916), 797; on the emergence of Lloyd George as Prime Minister (Dec 1916), 820

Würzburg (Germany): Churchill meets Enver Pasha at, 188

Xeros, Gulf of (Turkey): 327, 369, 389, 392, 514; MAP, 840

Yarmouth (British light cruiser): tracking down *Emden* in Bay of Bengal (Sept 1914), 139

Yashiro, Rokurō: Churchill's welcoming telegram to, 43; Churchill and Fisher seek aid from, 157–8

York: miners from, in Royal Naval Division, 500

Young Turks: Churchill attracted by, 188; 'fools' to support Germany, 189; Churchill appears to abandon his sympathy for, 356; Curzon prepared to allow retention of Constantinople by, in return for peace (Oct 1915), 550

YMCA: provide cheap meals for munitions workers, 533

Ypres (Belgium): Marine Brigade units at, 73; front line established east of, 129, 136–7, 213; slaughter in salient of, 139; further heavy casualties at, 160; front stabilized at (Nov 1914), 224; Lloyd George fears destruction of morale by continuation of fighting at, 229; Churchill refers to 'the profitless slaughter pit of' (Aug 1915), 516; Churchill compares artillery danger on Gallipoli with (Oct 1915), 546; losses of the 2nd Battalion Grenadier Guards at (Oct 1914), 576; 6th Battalion Royal Scots Fusiliers at (Nov 1915), 631, 633; Churchill hears cannonade at (14 Feb 1916), 668; MAPS, 75, 575

Yser, River (Belgium): battle on, 129, 137; front line at, 287

Zeebrugge (Belgium): German threat to, 103; fears of development of German submarine base at, 162, 180; Churchill advocates capture of (Jan 1915), 241–2, 245, 246, 251, 265; Fisher opposes diversion of ships to, 263–4; Fisher describes attack on as 'unjustifiable' as a purely naval operation, 268, 269; decision to abandon plans for any attack on, 270, 271, 275, 480; to be bombarded in the event of a German invasion of Holland (end-March 1915), 374; MAPS, 99, 842

Zeppelin: Admiralty plans against attack from, 8; H. A. Gwynne's plan to destroy, 33; Dunkirk base established to counteract, 65; aerial defences of

Zeppelin—*continued*
London against, 66; fear of, against
Grand Fleet, 82; sheds at Düsseldorf
and Cologne raided (22 Sept 1914),
88–9, 91; second raid against sheds
(9 Oct 1914), 122–3; reported effect
of raid, 146; Sir J. French wishes to
decide timing of attacks on, 162;
raid on sheds at Friedrichshafen, 172–
6; drops bomb on Dover, 238–9;
Churchill describes plans to combat,

Zeppelin—*continued*
240; Churchill alleged to be responsible for neglect of defences against,
706; Churchill decides to defend his
former policies towards, 708; Fisher
advises Churchill on speech references
to (March 1916), 711; Churchill
advocates a more active policy in
dealing with, 720–1, 735; Churchill
defends his policy towards, 764–7
Zuyder Zee (Holland): 374